TENTH EDITION

Elements of Argument

A Text and Reader

Annette T. Rottenberg

Donna Haisty Winchell

Clemson University

Bedford/St. Martin's
Boston • New York

For Bedford/St. Martin's

Executive Editor: John E. Sullivan III
Production Editor: Kerri A. Cardone
Senior Production Supervisor: Jennifer Peterson
Senior Marketing Manager: Molly Parke
Editorial Assistant: Alyssa Demirjian
Copyeditor: Helen van Loon
Indexer: Steve Csipke
Permissions Manager: Kalina K. Ingham
Senior Art Director: Anna Palchik
Text Design: Glenna Collett
Cover Design: Donna Lee Dennison
Cover Photo: Courtesy of Veer
Composition: Achorn International, Inc.
Printing and Binding: RR Donnelley and Sons

President: Joan E. Feinberg
Editorial Director: Denise B. Wydra
Editor in Chief: Karen S. Henry
Director of Marketing: Karen R. Soeltz
Director of Production: Susan W. Brown
Associate Director, Editorial Production: Elise S. Kaiser
Managing Editor: Elizabeth M. Schaaf

Library of Congress Control Number: 2011927764

Manufactured in the United States of America.

6 5 4 3 2 1
f e d c b a

For information, write: Bedford/St. Martin's, 75 Arlington Street, Boston, MA 02116
(617-399-4000)

ISBN-13: 978–0–312–64699–8

Acknowledgments

Preface

Purpose

Where do our students — some of our youngest voters and our future leaders — get their take on current events? Where do they get their news? Probably not from sitting down and watching network broadcasts or listening to the radio like their parents and grandparents did. Probably not from reading a newspaper regularly either. More likely they get it from a computer or a cell phone, which means they get it in bits and pieces, and on the run. Where do they read or hear arguments? Again, probably in short digital bursts. Their idea of debate may come from the most recent presidential debates. More likely, it comes from comments made online in response to YouTube videos or Facebook postings. They may get today's political news from Jon Stewart or Glenn Beck, from the cover of *Time* or *Newsweek*, or from skits on *Saturday Night Live*. Their most consistent source of headlines may be cnn.com, fox.com, or Twitter.

In order to get our students to really think about argument, we have to get them to slow down and practice the art of critical reading — and listening. We have to get them to analyze sustained argumentative discourse, and we have to give them a vocabulary to be able to talk about it. The vocabulary we use in *Elements of Argument* is primarily that of Stephen Toulmin, whose model of argument is based on three principal elements: claim, support, and warrant. These three elements answer the questions "What are you trying to prove?" "What have you got to go on?" and "How did you get from evidence to claim?" These questions are precisely the ones that students must ask and answer in analyzing arguments.

We also have to get our students to write sustained argumentative discourse. They have to learn to apply their knowledge of claim, support, and warrant. They have to understand that successful arguments require a blend of *logos*, *pathos*, and *ethos*. Logic is not always enough; it must usually be used in conjunction with legitimate appeal to emotion, and it must come from a trusted speaker or writer. In addition to grounding our text in Toulmin's model of argumentation, we also introduce students to the basics of Aristotle's classical theories of rhetoric and to Carl Rogers's theories of nonconfrontational communication. We stress the significance of audience as a practical matter. In the rhetorical or audience-centered approach to argument, to which we subscribe in this text, success is defined as acceptance of the claim by an audience. Arguers in the real world recognize intuitively that their primary goal is not to demonstrate the purity of their logic, but to win the adherence of their audiences.

To do so, students must read critically and reflect on what others have to say. The Internet has redefined what research means to our students. A large part of the challenge now is not to find sources but to eliminate the thousands of questionable ones. Faced with the temptation to cut and paste instead of read and understand, students need more help than ever with accurate and fair use of sources. We provide that help in the context of an increasingly digital world.

Organization

Part One of *Elements of Argument* introduces Aristotelian, Rogerian, and Toulmin approaches to argumentation, then critical reading and analytical writing. It is rich in readings that support these approaches.

Part Two devotes one chapter apiece to definition and to the chief elements of argument — claim, support, and warrant. The examples are drawn from both print and online sources — essays, articles, speeches, blogs, cartoons, and advertisements. Chapter 8 teaches students to identify and avoid errors in logic, and Chapter 9 deals with the power of word choice in arguing effectively. Each chapter in this section includes examples, readings, discussion questions, and writing suggestions, as well as a selection of readings for analysis and a debate that shows contrasting perspectives on the same controversial issue.

Part Three takes up the process of researching, writing, and presenting arguments. Chapter 10 focuses on planning and research. Chapter 11 covers writing and documentation and provides two sample research papers, one employing the Modern Language Association (MLA) documentation system and the other employing the American Psychological Association (APA) documentation style. Chapter 13 provides guidelines for presenting arguments orally.

Part Four, "Multiple Viewpoints," presents arguers in action. Each of the eight chapters in this part includes six to eight readings on a single controversial issue, presenting that issue from a range of perspectives. The topics are ones now in the news and on engaged citizens' minds: body image, academic integrity, sex and violence in popular culture, freedom of speech, and medical ethics.

Part Five, "Classic Arguments," has been restored in this edition, and it includes such class-tested arguments as Swift's "A Modest Proposal" and Orwell's "Politics and the English Language."

New to This Edition

As is the case with each edition of *Elements of Argument*, we have updated readings throughout to keep information current and subjects interesting. In this tenth edition, over half of the readings are new. Three new Debates examine derogatory use of the word "retard," the environmental costs of recycling plastic, and the social responsibility of business. Three of the Multiple Viewpoints topics are also new; they explore how social networking affects human interactions, the ethics of food production, and how biases shape the news.

We are pleased to offer students more support in researching and documenting research than we have in any previous edition. The research paper in MLA style, on competitive foods and obesity, is new to this edition, and in Chapters 10 and 11 students will be able to follow its author through the research process as she responds to an assignment, and researches, writes, and revises her paper, providing a real-world model of the research process. Chapters 1 through 9 now end with a "Research Readiness" exercise that prepares students for investigating and documenting an independent research topic, helping them practice skills such as narrowing down a list of possible digital sources or writing a summary. Additional sentence templates in Chapter 3 help students understand the effective use of summary and response in argument. And *Elements of Argument* is also more visual than ever before. A fresh new design provides a reinvigorated look and improves navigation in the text, and over 60 new photographs provide visual examples and opportunities for analysis. We are particularly proud of our new blog *Argument Update*. Here, we will add weekly comments and examine world events using the theories and terminology introduced in the text. See *Bits* entry on page x for more information.

An electronic edition of *Elements of Argument* is available at about half the price of the print book. See coursemart.com for details.

You Get More Digital Choices for *Elements of Argument*

Elements of Argument doesn't stop with a book. Online, you'll find both free and affordable premium resources to help students get even more out of the book and your course. You'll also find convenient instructor resources, such as downloadable sample syllabi, classroom activities, and even a nationwide community of teachers. To learn more about or order any of the products below, contact your Bedford/St. Martin's sales representative, e-mail sales support (sales_support@bfwpub.com), or visit the Web site at bedfordstmartins.com.

Companion Web site for *Elements of Argument*
bedfordstmartins.com/rottenberg

Send students to free and open resources, choose flexible premium resources to supplement your print text, or upgrade to an expanding collection of innovative digital content.

Free and open resources for *Elements of Argument* provide students with easy-to-access reference materials, visual tutorials, and support for working with sources.

- Appendix on Writing about Literature
- *TopLinks* with reliable online sources
- *Research and Documentation Online* by Diana Hacker
- *Bedford Bibliographer*: a tool for collecting source information and making a bibliography in MLA, APA, and *Chicago* styles

VideoCentral is a growing collection of videos for the writing class that captures real-world, academic, and student writers talking about how and why they write. *VideoCentral* can be packaged with *Elements of Argument* at a significant discount. An activation code is required. To order *VideoCentral* packaged with the print book, use ISBN 978–1–4576–0452–5.

Re:Writing Plus gathers all of Bedford/St. Martin's premium digital content for composition into one online collection. It includes hundreds of model documents, the first ever peer review game, and *VideoCentral*. *Re:Writing Plus* can be purchased separately or packaged with the print book at a significant discount. An activation code is required. To order *Re:Writing Plus* packaged with the print book, use ISBN 978–1–4576–0451–5.

i-series on CD-ROM

Add more value to your text by choosing one of the following CD-ROMs, free when packaged with *Elements of Argument*. This popular series presents multimedia tutorials in a flexible format — because there are things you can't do in a book. To learn more about package options or any of the products below, contact your Bedford/St. Martin's sales representative or visit bedfordstmartins.com.

ix visual exercises helps students put into practice key rhetorical and visual concepts. To order *ix visual* exercises packaged with the print book, use ISBN 978–1–4576–0435–5.

i-claim: visualizing argument offers a new way to see argument — with 6 tutorials, an illustrated glossary, and over 70 multimedia arguments. To order *i-claim: visualizing argument* packaged with the print book, use ISBN 978–1–4576–0433–1.

Instructor resources

You have a lot to do in your course. Bedford/St. Martin's wants to make it easy for you to find the support you need — and to get it quickly.

Resources for Teaching Elements of Argument 10e is available in PDF that can be downloaded from bedfordstmartins.com/rottenberg. In addition to chapter overviews and teaching tips, the instructor's manual includes sample syllabi and suggestions for classroom activities.

Teaching Central (bedfordstmartins.com/teachingcentral) offers the entire list of Bedford/St. Martin's print and online professional resources in one place. You'll find landmark reference works, sourcebooks on pedagogical issues, award-winning collections, and practical advice for the classroom — all free for instructors.

Bits (bedfordbits.com) collects creative ideas for teaching a range of composition topics in an easily searchable blog. A community of teachers — leading scholars, authors, and editors — discuss revision, research, grammar and style, technology, peer review, and much more. Take, use, adapt, and pass the ideas around. Then, come back to the site to comment or share your own suggestion.

Content cartridges for the most common course management systems — Blackboard, WebCT, Angel, and Desire2Learn — allow you to easily download digital materials for your course. To find the cartridges available with *Elements of Argument*, visit bedfordstmartins.com/rottenberg.

Teaching Argument in the Composition Course, by Timothy Barnett is also available. It offers a range of perspectives, from Aristotle to the present day, on argument and on teaching argument. The twenty-eight readings — many of them classic works in the field — present essential insights and practical information. For ordering information, contact your local sales representative or e-mail us at sales_support@bfwpub.com.

Also Available

A briefer edition, *The Structure of Argument*, Seventh Edition, is available for instructors who prefer a shorter text with fewer readings. It includes Chapters 1 through 12, excluding the Multiple Viewpoints and Classic Arguments. See bedfordstmartins.com for details.

Acknowledgments

This book has profited by the critiques and suggestions of instructors who responded to a questionnaire: Susan Achziger, Community College of Aurora; Marty Ambrose, Edison State College; Laurel Barlow, Weber State University; Jacqueline M. Beamen, Camden County College; Kathy T. Dechter, Columbia Basin College; William Feldman, California Polytechnic State University; Hedda A. Fish, San Diego State University; Amber Folland, Clark College; G. Scott Groce, Black Hills State University; Wayne Harrison, Oregon State University; Elizabeth Johnston, Monroe Community College; Edwina K. Jordan, Illinois Central College; Tim Layton, St. Louis Community College at Florissant Valley; Ann McCage, Scottsdale Community College; Maureen McDonnell, Eastern Connecticut State University; Stephen Moore, Arizona Western College; Carl Peterson, University of Alabama; Nancy E. Raftery, Camden County College; J. Karen Ray, Washburn University; Christopher J. Scalia, University of Virginia's College at Wise; Guy Shebat, Youngstown State; Kimberly M. Shepherd, Washtenaw Community College; Craig L. Shurtleff, Illinois Central College; Amy Jo Swing, Lake Superior College; Karen R. Tolchin, Florida Gulf Coast University; Mircea Tomus, Kirkwood Community College; Robert Williams, Grossmont College; Michael W. Young, La Roche College; and Will Zhang, Des Moines Area Community College.

We are also grateful to those who gave us in-depth feedback: Robert Alexander, Point Park University; Julianne Altenbernd, Cypress College; Lexey A. Bartlett, Fort Hays State University; Nona Ellen Brown, University of Utah; Liona Tannesen Burnham, Northern Virginia Community College; Joseph Couch, Montgomery College; Genesis Downey, Owens Community College; Margaret Ehlen, Ivy Tech Community College; Susan Hudson Fox, California State University, East Bay; James B. Goode, Bluegrass Community & Technical College; Sean Hoade, University of Alabama; Nancy C. Jensen, University of

Utah; Jay Jordan, University of Utah; Sean Elliot Martin, Duquesne University; Erin O'Keefe, Emporia State University; Melanie Richards, Inver Hills Community College; Deborah Richey, Owens Community College; Shannon M. Smith, Owens Community College; James R. Sodon, St. Louis Community College-Florissant Valley; George Trail, University of Houston; Verne Underwood, Rogue Community College; and Thomas E. Winski, Emporia State University.

We also thank those reviewers who chose to remain anonymous.

We are grateful to those at Bedford/St. Martin's who have helped in numerous ways large and small: Joan Feinberg, Denise Wydra, Karen Henry, Steve Scipione, Shannon Walsh, Alyssa Demirjian, Kalina Ingham, Martha Friedman, Linda Zielke, Connie Gardner, Sue Brown, Elizabeth Schaaf, Elise Kaiser, Kerri Cardone, Helen van Loon, Anna Palchik, and, most especially, John Sullivan.

Brief Contents

Contents

18 Are Limits on Freedom of Speech Ever Justified?   671

19 How Far Will We Go to Change Our Body Image? 697

20 In The World Of Medicine, Who Decides What Is Ethical? 724

PART FIVE
Classic Arguments   755

PART 1

Understanding Argument

CHAPTER 1

Approaches to Argument

Because of the First Amendment, Americans have the freedom to speak — and they do, sometimes loudly, sometimes offensively, sometimes movingly. Give a nation with America's diversity freedom of speech, and its people will use it, and they will often disagree. But that, after all, is the point of the First Amendment: Americans can express disagreement without fear of reprisal.

Public education has been a part of America since its beginning because in a country where the citizens choose their leaders, an educated citizenry is in the best interest of all except those who would silence dissenting voices. For centuries, from a time long before thirteen colonies became a country, young men — and eventually young women — have been trained to let their voices be heard. They have been taught the art of rhetoric. You have probably grown up letting your voice be heard, some of you more than others. This course is designed to teach you to be more proficient in expressing your ideas about controversial issues, to argue more effectively in speech, but more so in writing.

Of course, not all arguments end in clear victories for one side or another. Nor should they. In a democratic society of competing interests and values, a compromise between two or more extreme points of view may be the only viable solution to a vexing problem. Although formal debates under the auspices of a debating society, such as those that take place on many college campuses, usually end in winners and losers, real-life problems — both public and private — are often resolved through negotiation. Courtroom battles may result in compromise, and the law itself allows for exemptions and extenuating circumstances.

Most of the argumentative writing in this book will deal with matters of public controversy, an area traditionally associated with the study of argument. As the word *public* suggests, these matters concern us as members of a community. In the arguments you will read, human beings are engaged in explaining and defending their own actions and beliefs and opposing or compromising with those of others. They do this for at least two reasons: (1) to justify what they do and think, both to themselves and to their audiences, and (2) in the process to solve problems and make decisions. In the arguments you will write in this course, you will be doing the same.

A distinction is sometimes made between argument and persuasion. Argument, according to most authorities, gives primary importance to logical appeals. Providing abundant evidence and making logical connections, however, may not be enough to win agreement from an audience. A writer or speaker must take into account an audience's emotional response to the subject matter and the way in which it is presented. Also, success in convincing an audience is almost always inseparable from the audience's belief in the writer's trustworthiness. In this book, we use the term *argument* to represent forms of discourse that attempt to persuade readers or listeners to accept a claim, whether acceptance is based on logical or emotional appeals or, as is usually the case, on both.

In this chapter we will discuss the approaches to argument proposed by the Greek philosopher Aristotle, the American psychologist Carl Rogers, and the British philosopher Stephen Toulmin.

Aristotelian Rhetoric

Aristotle, who wrote a treatise on argument that has influenced its study and practice for well over two thousand years, defined rhetoric as all available means of persuasion. He used the term *logos* to refer to logical appeals and the term *pathos* to refer to emotional appeals. He believed that, in an ideal world, logic alone would be enough to persuade. He acknowledged, however, that in the less-than-ideal real world, effective arguments depend not only on *logos* and *pathos*, but also on the writer's or speaker's credibility, which he called *ethos*. In fact, he considered *ethos* to be the most important element in the arguer's ability to persuade the audience to accept a claim.

Aristotle named intelligence, character, and goodwill as the attributes that produce credibility. Today we might describe these qualities somewhat differently, but the criteria for judging a writer's credibility remain essentially the same. First, writers must convince the audience that they are knowledgeable and as well informed as possible about the subject. Second, they must persuade their audience that they are not only truthful in the presentation of evidence but also morally upright and dependable. Third, they must show that, as arguers with good intentions, they have considered the interests and needs of others as well as their own.

As an example in which the credibility of the arguer is at stake, consider a wealthy Sierra Club member who lives on ten acres of a magnificent oceanside estate and who appears before a community planning board to argue against future development of the area. The board, acting in the interests of all the citizens of the community, will ask themselves: Has the arguer proved that his informa-

Aristotle (384–322 BCE) had ideas about argument that are important and useful to this day.

tion about environmental impact is complete and accurate? Has he demonstrated that he sincerely desires to preserve the wilderness, not merely his own privacy and space? And has he made clear that he has considered the needs and desires of those who might want to live in a housing development by the ocean? If the answers to all of these questions are yes, then the board will hear the arguer with respect, and the arguer will have begun to establish his credibility.

A reputation for intelligence, character, and goodwill is not often earned overnight. And it can be lost more quickly than it is gained. Once writers or speakers have betrayed an audience's belief in their character or judgment, they may find it difficult to persuade an audience to accept subsequent claims, no matter how sound the data and reasoning are.

For Aristotle, *logos, ethos,* and *pathos* constituted the elements of argument. With this triad, he laid the foundation for classical or traditional rhetoric and for all rhetorical theories to follow.

In Aristotle's day, one of the chief goals of rhetorical training was to learn to argue successfully in a court of law on judicial matters or in another public forum on political ones. The primary goal of rhetoric itself was to win — either to win a court case concerning what had happened in the past or to win approval for a political proposal about what should happen in the future.

Beyond what Aristotle teaches us about credibility, how does ancient rhetoric translate to our digital world? It gives us a vocabulary and also gives us a systematic way of thinking about a rhetorical situation. A writer or speaker is always preparing a text *about* something (the subject) and *for* someone (the audience). Since the texts produced in this course will be written, we will use the term *writer* instead of *speaker* in discussing rhetorical situations, although in Aristotle's world, the texts would have been primarily oral.

Rhetoric is largely a study of relationships. The relationship between writer and audience is the rhetorical relationship. That between writer and subject is the referential.[1]

Writers — but more commonly speakers — in Aristotle's world of the fourth century BCE were very limited in audience and in subject matter. As far as the rhetorical relationship is concerned, inventions like the printing press, and later the telegraph, gave the writer access to a wider and wider range of audiences; the computer in general and the Internet in particular have increased exponentially the audiences a writer can reach. The audiences available to a writer are now almost endless, not bound in size or in geographic location.

On a developmental level, individuals used to learn to write for increasingly distant audiences, starting in childhood with writing primarily for a parent or for one teacher, with an occasional letter to someone well known to them. Only later did they sometimes write to people they didn't know personally and to larger groups and, in a few cases, go on to publish their writing. Now elementary students, for good or ill, converse online with others a world away and completely unknown to them on a personal level. The Internet provides everyone a voice on almost any subject.

The amount of information available at the click of a mouse has also exploded with the advent of the Internet. That means that the relationship between writer and subject — the referential relationship — has also changed with the times. Research used to mean going to the library to work with hard copies of texts or using a set of encyclopedias and a small number of reference books available at home. Now a world of information is accessible in a matter of seconds, literally.

If the latest news is as close as your remote control, it is also as close as your computer mouse or even your cell phone. Aristotle gave us a vocabulary for talking about communication (such as the syllogism, treated on p. 26, and logic,

---

[1] These two terms come from James Moffett, *Teaching the Universe of Discourse* (Boston: Houghton Mifflin, 1968), p. 18. He illustrates the two with a grid crossing rhetorical and referential.

In Aristotle's time, the audience was simply those people in front of the speaker. Today, with electronic media, unless the presentation is live, as in this photograph, the audience may be broader and unknown.

treated in Chapter 8), and changes in culture and in technology have led us to redefine that vocabulary for a world vastly different from his.

In the proscribed world of ancient Greece, it was relatively easy to predict what an audience would know about a subject of discourse. There was more of a shared world view than has existed in more recent times. In ancient Greece, rigid rules dictated the organization of a speech, and the examples were drawn from well-known narratives, true or fictional. Today it is much more difficult for a writer to place himself or herself in someone else's position and try to see from that person's point of view.

It is in addressing this relationship between audience and subject that rhetorical theories differ the most in their approach, as we will discuss.

Don't Mourn *Brown v. Board of Education*

JUAN WILLIAMS

L et us now praise the *Brown* decision. Let us now bury the *Brown* decision. With yesterday's Supreme Court ruling ending the use of voluntary schemes to create racial balance among students, it is time to acknowledge that *Brown*'s time has passed. It is worthy of a send-off with fanfare for setting off the civil rights movement and inspiring social progress for women, gays, and the poor. But the decision in *Brown v. Board of Education* that focused on outlawing segregated schools as unconstitutional is now out of step with American political and social realities.

Desegregation does not speak to dropout rates that hover near 50 percent for black and Hispanic high school students. It does not equip society to address the so-called achievement gap between black and white students that mocks *Brown*'s promise of equal educational opportunity.

And the fact is, during the last 20 years, with *Brown* in full force, America's public schools have been growing more segregated — even as the nation has become more racially diverse. In 2001, the National Center for Education Statistics reported that the average white student attends a school that is 80 percent white, while 70 percent of black students attend schools where nearly two-thirds of students are black and Hispanic.

By the early '90s, support in the federal courts for the central work of *Brown* — racial integration of public schools — began to rapidly expire. In a series of cases in Atlanta, Oklahoma City, and Kansas City, Mo., frustrated parents, black and white, appealed to federal judges to stop shifting children from school to school like pieces on a game board. The parents wanted better neighborhood schools and a better education for their children, no matter the racial make-up of the school. In their rulings ending court mandates for school integration, the judges, too, spoke of the futility of using schoolchildren to address social ills caused by adults holding fast to patterns of residential segregation by both class and race.

The focus of efforts to improve elementary and secondary schools shifted to magnet schools, to allowing parents the choice to move their children out of fail-

5

Juan Williams is a former senior correspondent for National Public Radio and a political analyst for Fox News Channel. His books include *Enough: The Phony Leaders, Dead-End Movements, and Culture of Failure That Are Undermining Black America* (2006) and *Thurgood Marshall: American Revolutionary* (1998). The article was published June 29, 2007, on nytimes.com.

The effects of the *Brown* decision are still being dealt with today.

ing schools and, most recently, to vouchers and charter schools. The federal No Child Left Behind plan has many critics, but there's no denying that it is an effective tool for forcing teachers' unions and school administrators to take responsibility for educating poor and minority students.

It was an idealistic Supreme Court that in 1954 approved of *Brown* as a race-conscious policy needed to repair the damage of school segregation and protect every child's 14th-Amendment right to equal treatment under law. In 1971, Chief Justice Warren Burger, writing for a unanimous court still embracing *Brown*, said local school officials could make racial integration a priority even if it did not improve educational outcomes because it helped "to prepare students to live in a pluralistic society."

But today a high court with a conservative majority concludes that any policy based on race — no matter how well intentioned — is a violation of every child's 14th-Amendment right to be treated as an individual without regard to race. We've come full circle.

In 1990, after months of interviews with Justice Thurgood Marshall, who had been the lead lawyer for the N.A.A.C.P. Legal Defense Fund on the *Brown* case, I sat in his Supreme Court chambers with a final question. Almost 40 years later, was he satisfied with the outcome of the decision? Outside the courthouse, the failing Washington school system was hypersegregated, with more than 90 percent of its students black and Latino. Schools in the surrounding suburbs, meanwhile, were mostly white and producing some of the top students in the nation.

Had Mr. Marshall, the lawyer, made a mistake by insisting on racial integration instead of improvement in the quality of schools for black children?

10

His response was that seating black children next to white children in school had never been the point. It had been necessary only because all-white school boards were generously financing schools for white children while leaving black students in overcrowded, decrepit buildings with hand-me-down books and underpaid teachers. He had wanted black children to have the right to attend white schools as a point of leverage over the biased spending patterns of the segregationists who ran schools — both in the 17 states where racially separate schools were required by law and in other states where they were a matter of culture.

If black children had the right to be in schools with white children, Justice Marshall reasoned, then school board officials would have no choice but to equalize spending to protect the interests of their white children.

Racial malice is no longer the primary motive in shaping inferior schools for minority children. Many failing big city schools today are operated by black superintendents and mostly black school boards.

And today the argument that school reform should provide equal opportunity for children, or prepare them to live in a pluralistic society, is spent. The winning argument is that better schools are needed for all children — black, white, brown and every other hue — in order to foster a competitive workforce in a global economy.

Dealing with racism and the bitter fruit of slavery and "separate but equal"   15
legal segregation was at the heart of the court's brave decision 53 years ago. With *Brown* officially relegated to the past, the challenge for brave leaders now is to deliver on the promise of a good education for every child.

Analysis

Viewed from an Aristotelian perspective, Juan Williams uses all three types of appeal: *logos, pathos,* and *ethos.* Williams assumes from the beginning that his audience will be familiar with the 1954 case *Brown v. Board of Education* because it is a significant part of American history. He balances the opening of his essay by equally praising the *Brown* decision and welcoming its demise: It is time for *Brown* to go, but its end should be viewed with respect. He anticipates the negative emotional response that some might have to the end of what many saw and still see as a major step toward racial equality by praising it as "worthy of a send-off with fanfare for setting off the civil rights movement and inspiring social progress for women, gays and the poor." He is appealing to the emotions of his audience and is also presenting himself as an ethical man by acknowledging both the good and the bad of the decision. The thesis that he is trying to support is stated at the end of the second paragraph: "But the decision in *Brown v. Board of Education* that focused on outlawing segregated schools as unconstitutional is now out of step with American political and social realities."

Consider the logical support that Williams offers for this thesis. In paragraph 3, he summarizes the problems with desegregation and then in paragraphs 4–7 looks back in more detail at how the ruling has failed America's children over the last twenty years. In spite of all the promise Americans saw in the ruling, the reality, according to Williams, "mocks *Brown*'s promise of equal educational opportunity." He uses statistics in two places, giving his source in one case but not in the other. He gives less specific information about parents' response, but by that point in the essay, he has established himself as a reasonable man who is fair in his presentation of his case. In an emotional appeal at the end of paragraph 5, he skillfully expresses the futility that parents were feeling and that the judges also expressed in justifying their ruling: "the futility of using schoolchildren to address social ills caused by adults holding fast to patterns of residential segregation by both class and race."

Williams gives his readers no reason to question his logic when, in the second half of the essay, he argues that we have come full circle. We have gone from a "race-conscious policy needed to repair the damage of school segregation and protect every child's 14th-Amendment right to equal treatment under the law" to a Supreme Court decision "that any policy based on race — no matter how well intentioned — is a violation of every child's 14th-Amendment right to be treated as an individual without regard to race."

Some readers will know Juan Williams as a correspondent for National Public Radio and/or as a political analyst for Fox News and may have a preconceived notion of his *ethos*, or character. Those who come to the essay with some knowledge of its author will most likely know that Williams is African American. In the second half of his essay, he contributes significantly to the image of himself as an authority on the subject of racial desegregation when he says that he interviewed Justice Thurgood Marshall over a series of months and had the chance to sit in Marshall's Supreme Court chambers and ask him whether he was satisfied with the outcome of the *Brown* decision. Here is *pathos* as Williams reports Marshall's response. He is appealing to his audience's values when he explains that Marshall, as the lead lawyer for the NAACP Legal Defense Fund on the case, was not concerned primarily with gaining black children the right to sit next to white ones, but with forcing whites to equalize spending for both. Most readers today want to see children treated fairly, and some will be angered that it took such lengths to gain even some progress toward that goal.

Williams's plea at the end of the essay is for a good education for every child. Few in his audience could argue with that goal.

Rogerian Argument

Carl Rogers was a twentieth-century humanistic psychologist who translated his ideas about therapy into communication theory. As a therapist, he believed that the experience of two people meeting and speaking honestly to each other would have a healing effect. In later years he became convinced that the same principles of nondirective, nonconfrontational therapy that emphasized attentive listening could work not only for couples and small groups, but also for large groups, even nations, to create more harmonious relationships.

Carl Rogers (1902–1987), second from right, leads a panel in 1966.

Such nonconfrontational communication between individuals or among groups is hampered, Rogers believed, by the fact that there is no longer anything approaching a shared world view. He wrote:

> From time immemorial, the tribe or the community or the nation or the culture has agreed upon what constitutes the real world. To be sure, different tribes and different cultures might have held sharply different world views, but at least there was a large, relatively unified group which felt assured in its knowledge of the world and the universe, and knew that this perception was *true*.[2]

Those like Copernicus and Galileo who saw reality differently were often condemned or even killed. Rogers wrote, "Although society has often come around eventually to agree with its dissidents . . . there is no doubt that this insistence upon a known and certain universe has been part of the cement that holds a culture together" (103).

That cement is now missing, to the world's peril. Because of the "ease and rapidity of worldwide communication" that Rogers described as early as 1980, there were already as many realities as there were people:

> The only reality I can possibly know is the world as *I* perceive and experience it at this moment. The only reality you can possibly know is the

---

[2] "Do We Need 'a' Reality?" *A Way of Being* (New York: Houghton Mifflin 1980), pp. 102–03.

world as *you* perceive and experience it at this moment. And the only
certainty is that those perceived realities are different. (102)

In the Rogerian approach to argumentation, effective communication requires
both understanding another's reality and respecting it.

Rogers explained his theories of communication in an essay entitled "Communication: Its Blocking and Its Facilitation," which was originally presented as
a speech in 1951.[3] An emotionally maladjusted person suffers from the inability to
communicate effectively with others and with himself. In Rogers's experience,
one of the most potent means of improving such a patient's relationships and
communication with others sounds simple: Just listen with understanding. It is
not that simple, however, because of a very human tendency to listen judgmentally. We tend to respond to an opinion by stating an opinion. Maxine Hairston
was a leader in applying Rogers's theories to composition, and in 1976 she explained how the human rush to judgment hampers communication:

> Value judgments tend to freeze people into the status quo and make them
> commit themselves to a stand, and almost inevitably once a person takes
> a position on an issue, even one as trivial as the merits of a movie or of
> daylight-saving time, the possibility of his listening to a dissenting point
> of view with an open mind diminishes. Instead of wanting to hear both
> sides, he goes on the defensive and becomes more concerned about justifying his own opinion than understanding someone else's point of view.[4]

According to Rogers, "Real communication occurs, and this evaluative tendency
is avoided, when we listen with understanding. What does this mean? It means
to see the expressed idea and attitude from the other person's point of view, to
sense how it feels to him, to achieve his frame of reference in regard to the thing
he is talking about (331–32)."

The tendency to evaluate is most intense when feelings and emotions are
most deeply involved, "so the stronger our feelings, the more likely it is that there
will be no mutual element in the communication. There will be just two ideas,
two feelings, two judgments, missing each other in psychological space" (331).

Rogers's approach to communication is based on this idea of mutual elements or common ground. A writer or speaker and an audience who have very
different opinions on a highly charged emotional issue need a common ground
on which to meet if any communication is going to take place. In the midst
of all of their differences, they have to find a starting point on which they
agree. In 1977 Hairston summed up five steps for using Rogerian argumentation
that incorporate the two essentials of the approach — being able to summarize

[3] "Communication: Its Blocking and Its Facilitation," reprinted in Carl Rogers, *On Becoming
a Person* (Boston: Houghton Mifflin, 1961), pp. 329–37.

[4] "Carl Rogers's Alternative to Traditional Rhetoric," *College Composition and Communication*,
December, 1976, p. 374.

The Rogerian approach tries to bridge the gap between positions held by each party.

another's position with understanding and clarity and to locate common ground between two different positions:

1. Give a brief, objective statement of the issue under discussion.

2. Summarize in impartial language what you perceive the case for the opposition to be; the summary should demonstrate that you understand their interests and concerns and should avoid any hint of hostility.

3. Make an objective statement of your own side of the issue, listing your concerns and interests, but avoiding loaded language or any hint of moral superiority.

4. Outline what common ground or mutual concerns you and the other person or group seem to share; if you see irreconcilable interests, specify what they are.

5. Outline the solution you propose, pointing out what both sides may gain from it. (375–76)

PRACTICE

Read the following article by Joe Sharkey and then Chris Kapper's blog posting in response to it. What steps in the process described by Hairston do you find in Kapper's response to Sharkey?

Airport Screeners Could See X-rated X-rays

JOE SHARKEY

I am looking at a copy of an ad that ran in the back of comic books in the 1950s and early 1960s.

"X-Ray Specs! See Thru Clothing!" blares the copy, which is illustrated with a cartoon of a drooling geek wearing the amazing toy goggles and leering at a shapely woman.

Now, any kid with half a brain knew that X-Ray Specs were a novelty gag that didn't really work. But time marches on and technology makes the impossible possible. Stand by, air travelers, because the Homeland Security Department is preparing to install and test high-tech machines at airport checkpoints that will, as the comic-book ads promised, "See Thru Clothing!"

Get ready for electronic portals known as backscatters, expected to be tested at a handful of airports this year, that use X-ray imaging technology to allow a screener to scan a body. And yes, the body image is detailed. Let's not be coy here, ladies and gentlemen:

"Well, you'll see basically everything," said Bill Scannell, a privacy advo- 5 cate and technology consultant. "It shows nipples. It shows the clear outline of genitals."

The Homeland Security Department's justification for the electronic strip searches has a certain logic. In field test after field test, it found that federal airport screeners using metal-detecting magnetometers did a miserable job identifying weapons concealed in carry-on bags or on the bodies of undercover agents.

In a clumsy response late last year, the department instituted intrusive pat-downs at checkpoints after two planes in Russia blew up from nonmetallic explosives that had apparently been smuggled into the aircraft by female Chechen terrorists. But it reduced the pat-downs after passengers erupted in outrage at the groping last December.

"The use of these more thorough examination procedures has been protested by passengers and interest groups, and have already been refined" by the Transportation Security Administration, Richard Skinner, the acting inspector general of the Homeland Security Department, told a Senate committee in January. Skinner

---

Joe Sharkey is a columnist writing frequently about business travel for the *New York Times*, where the article appeared on May 24, 2005.

said then that the TSA was ramping up tests of new technologies like backscatter imaging.

Last month, Michael Chertoff, the Homeland Security secretary, told a Senate subcommittee that "technology is really what we ultimately have to use in order to get to the next level" in security.

The technology is available, he said. "It's a question of the decision to deploy   10
it and to try to balance that with legitimate privacy concerns," he added. "We haven't put it out yet because people are still hand-wringing about it."

Steve Elson isn't exactly hand-wringing. Let's just say he is mighty skeptical. A former Federal Aviation Administration investigator, Elson led the agency's red team of undercover agents who poked around airports looking for — and finding — holes in security.

"Backscatting has been around for years," he said. "They started talking about this stuff back during the protests when they were grabbing women. Under the right circumstances, the technology has some efficacy and can work. That is, provided we're willing to pay the price in a further loss of personal privacy."

He isn't. "I have a beautiful 29-year-old daughter and a beautiful wife, and I don't want some screeners to be looking at them through their clothes, plain and simple," he said.

Like many security experts, Elson argues for a sensible balance between risk management and risk reduction. On numerous occasions since the 2001 terrorist attacks, he has led reporters on test runs at airports, showing how easy it is to penetrate security throughout the airport.

Thwarting body-scanning technology would be simple, he argues. Because of   15
concerns about radiation, body scanners are designed not to penetrate the skin. All that's needed is someone heavily overweight to go through the system, he said. I won't quote him directly on the details; suffice it to say he posits that a weapon or explosives pack could be tucked into flabby body folds that won't be penetrated by the scanner.

Homeland Security has not identified the airports that will test backscatters. More than a dozen have been selected to test various new technologies.

One maker of backscatters is Rapiscan Security Products, a unit of OSI Systems. "Since the Russian plane tragedy, which is suspected due to suicide bombers, the interest has heightened for these needs, especially for the body scanner," Deepak Chopra, the chief executive of OSI Systems, recently told analysts.

Scannell, the privacy advocate, scorns that reasoning as alarmist nonsense. He does see one virtue, though, for some airport screeners if backscatting technology becomes the norm.

"They'll be paid to go to a peep show," he said. "They won't even need to bring any change."

Freedom to Live Trumps All!

CHRIS KAPPER

I have read many different comments to this story.

The opinions against the technology seem to boil down to this:

1. It is offensive to be viewed naked.
2. Being viewed naked is an affront to personal freedom.
3. This is a slippery slope and once allowed here it will be allowed everywhere until there are virtually no personal freedoms left.

The opinions for the technology seem to boil down to this:

1. Who cares if one is viewed naked?
2. It is better to be seen naked and alive than be dead.
3. This will make the airplanes safer.
4. This is a less obtrusive way to search passengers.

I have to agree — for the most part — with the latter. Here is why:

1. In the demonstration I saw, the screeners could not see the people — all they could see were the images. Therefore, they never saw a person walk up, through, and then leave. The point is that if their own mother walked through, they would have no idea since you can't tell who it is.
2. Nobody else can see your image other than the security operator. That includes other passengers and employees of the airports.
3. This is much less obtrusive than removing shoes, clothing, and emptying out all of your pockets — in front of everyone.
4. The fundamental liberty is the right to life. One's right to live trumps others' rights.
5. It is not only the liberty of the passengers and crew that must be considered here. It is their lives as well as the lives of all the people on the ground as that airplane flies over. Additionally, it is the nation's and even the world's economy and peace that must be considered. Remember what 9/11 did to the economy and the peace in the world?
6. Air travel is not a required means of travel. You can use other public transportation. You can travel by car or even by boat. Air travel is a convenience — and a choice. When you buy your ticket, you agree to be bound by their rules and policies.

Chris Kapper posted this response to Joe Sharkey's article, "Airport Screeners Could See X-rated X-rays," on CNET's TalkBack, on May 27, 2005.

7. For the person who quoted Benjamin Franklin — "They who would give up an essential liberty for temporary security, deserve neither liberty or security." IMHO, this technology does not cause you to give up any ESSENTIAL liberty and there is nothing TEMPORARY about DEATH!

Rogerian argument places more emphasis on the relationship between audience and subject than other rhetorical theories. It emphasizes the audience's view of the subject. In order to understand another's ideas with the clarity and lack of a judgmental attitude that Rogers proposed requires taking on, temporarily, that other's point of view — walking a mile in his shoes — and seeing the subject with his eyes.

Classical oratory did not require that level of identification with an opponent's perspective, as is suggested by the very fact that classical oratory assumed an *opponent*. A speaker composing a speech in the classical or Aristotelian tradition could make certain assumptions about the world in which his audience lived and therefore about his audience's knowledge of his subject. He would certainly try to anticipate his audience's logical and emotional response to the subject. In fact, an expected part of a classical oration was the refutation of opposing positions, but the purpose was to prove others wrong, not to be conciliatory. He would not acknowledge the strengths of his opponent's argument to the extent of compromising his own. The product of his endeavors was a formal speech, not an analysis of a rhetorical situation.

Therein lies another primary difference between Rogerian rhetoric and all other rhetorical theories. An essay can be written using the Rogerian approach to argumentation, and its thesis or claim will be one reconciling opposing positions — at least as far as that is possible with the sorts of emotionally charged subjects that call for a nonconfrontational approach in the first place. The approach is more useful, however, in analyzing a rhetorical situation than in producing formal prose.

Consider the example of management and striking union members. The situation can quickly degenerate into shouting matches and violence with little progress toward resolution. The union can make demands, which the management turns down, and the shouting matches begin again. Rogers would advocate the seemingly simple method of the two sides listening to each other with understanding. Management has to be able to explain the union's position in a way that the union members feel is fair before it can present its own. And then the reverse. This approach is time consuming, but it can keep the discussion from dissolving into anger and impasse. Rogers even suggests that arguing spouses should have to sum up each other's position *in a manner acceptable to the other spouse* before responding to it.

A text using the Rogerian approach merely to record the steps of the process can be rather formulaic. Done well, it can provide an excellent example of analytical writing. Therefore, we will discuss writing based on the Rogerian model primarily in Chapter 3, Analytical Writing. Another use is as a response to an earlier text, as was the case with Kapper's response to Sharkey's essay earlier in this chapter, so you will also see references to Rogers in Chapter 2, Critical Reading.

SAMPLE ESSAY WITH ANALYSIS   Rogerian

Racial Profiling at the Airport: Discrimination We're Afraid to Be Against

MICHAEL KINSLEY

When thugs menace someone because he looks Arabic, that's racism. When airport security officials single out Arabic-looking men for a more intrusive inspection, that's something else. What is the difference? The difference is that the airport security folks have a rational reason for what they do. An Arab-looking man heading toward a plane is statistically more likely to be a terrorist. That likelihood is infinitesimal, but the whole airport rigmarole is based on infinitesimal chances. If trying to catch terrorists this way makes sense at all, then Willie-Sutton logic says you should pay more attention to people who look like Arabs than to people who don't. This is true even if you are free of all ethnic prejudices. It's not racism.

But that doesn't make it OK. Much of the discrimination that is outlawed in this country — correctly outlawed, we (almost) all agree — could be justified, often sincerely, by reasons other than racial prejudice. Without the civil rights laws, employers with nothing personal against blacks might well decide that hiring whites is more cost-efficient than judging each jobseeker on his or her individual merits. Universities could base their admissions policies on the valid assumption that whites, on average, are better-prepared for college. Even though this white advantage is the result of past and present racism, these decisions themselves might be rational and not racially motivated.

All decisions about whom to hire, whom to admit, whose suitcase to ransack as he's rushing to catch a plane are based on generalizations from observable characteristics to unobservable ones. But even statistically valid generalizations are wrong in particular instances. (Many blacks are better prepared for college than

Michael Kinsley is a political journalist and commentator who has written for the *Los Angeles Times* and the *Wall Street Journal*; has been an editor of the *New Republic*, *Harper's*, and the *Washington Monthly*; and founded the online journal *Slate*, where this essay was posted on September 28, 2001. He is a columnist for the *Washington Post* and is perhaps best known for having been cohost of CNN's *Crossfire* for six years.

many whites. Virtually every Arab hassled at an airport is not a terrorist.) Because even rational discrimination has victims, and because certain generalizations are especially poisonous, America has decided that these generalizations (about race, gender, religion, and so on) are morally wrong. They are wrong even if they are statistically valid, and even if not acting on them imposes a real cost.

Until recently, the term "racial profiling" referred to the police practice of pulling over black male drivers disproportionately, on the statistically valid but morally offensive assumption that black male drivers are more likely to be involved in crime. Now the term has become virtually a synonym for racial discrimination. But if "racial profiling" means anything specific at all, it means rational discrimination: racial discrimination with a non-racist rationale. The question is: When is that OK?

The tempting answer is never: Racial discrimination is wrong no matter what   5
the rationale. Period. But today we're at war with a terror network that just killed 6,000 innocents and has anonymous agents in our country planning more slaughter. Are we really supposed to ignore the one identifiable fact we know about them? That may be asking too much.

And there is another complication in the purist view: affirmative action. You can believe (as I do) that affirmative action is often a justifiable form of discrimination, but you cannot sensibly believe that it isn't discrimination at all. Racial profiling and affirmative action are analytically the same thing. When the cops stop black drivers or companies make extra efforts to hire black employees, they are both giving certain individuals special treatment based on racial generalizations. The only difference is that in one case the special treatment is something bad and in the other it's something good. Yet defenders of affirmative action tend to deplore racial profiling and vice versa.

The truth is that racial profiling and affirmative action are both dangerous medicines that are sometimes appropriate. So when is "sometimes"? It seems obvious to me, though not to many others, that discrimination in favor of historically oppressed groups is less offensive than discrimination against them. Other than that, the considerations are practical. How much is at stake in forbidding a particular act of discrimination? How much is at stake in allowing it?

A generalization from stereotypes may be statistically rational, but is it necessary? When you're storming a plane looking for the person who has planted a bomb somewhere, there isn't time to avoid valid generalizations and treat each person as an individual. At less urgent moments, like airport check-in, the need to use ethnic identity as a shortcut is less obvious. And then there are those passengers in Minneapolis last week who insisted that three Arab men (who had cleared security) be removed from the plane. These people were making a cost, benefit, and probability analysis so skewed that it amounts to simple racism. (And Northwest Airlines' acquiescence was shameful.)

So what about singling out Arabs at airport security checkpoints? I am skeptical of the value of these check-in rituals in general, which leads me to suspect that the imposition on a minority is not worth it. But assuming these procedures do work, it's hard to argue that helping to avoid another Sept. 11 is not worth the imposition, which is pretty small: inconvenience and embarrassment, as opposed to losing a job or getting lynched.

A colleague says that people singled out at airport security should be consoled   10
with frequent flier miles. They're already getting an even better consolation: the huge increase in public sensitivity to anti-Muslim and anti-Arab prejudice, which President Bush — to his enormous credit — has made such a focal point of his response to Sept. 11. And many victims of racial profiling at the airport may not need any consolation. After all, they don't want to be hijacked and blown up either.

Analysis

In this essay from September 2001, Kinsley seems to be having an argument with himself. He is, in that two conflicting positions are battling for acceptance in his mind. Each represents a position held by countless others for whom he speaks. This is in keeping with Rogers's belief that conflict can be resolved if those on each side can fairly summarize the position of the other side before summarizing their own. Kinsley is not trying to win an argument but rather to look objectively at the subject from different perspectives. His goal is to decide when each of two ways of looking at the situation is appropriate.

Notice how skillfully Kinsley balances different perspectives. He quickly dismisses as racism the situation where thugs threaten someone who looks Arabic. However, it is perfectly logical, he argues, when Arab-looking men are singled out at airports for additional screening because they are statistically more likely to be terrorists. That, he states bluntly, is not racism.

The other side chimes in: It may not be racism, but it is not okay. Decisions about such things as hiring and college admissions can be rational and not racially motivated. However, as Kinsley writes, "Because even rational discrimination has victims, and because certain generalizations are especially poisonous, America has decided that these generalizations (about race, gender, religion, and so on) are morally wrong. They are wrong even if they are statistically valid, and even if not acting on them imposes a real cost." Racial profiling equals rational discrimination — "racial discrimination with a non-racist rationale." The question that Kinsley raises at the end of paragraph 4 is, "When is that OK?"

Notice how Kinsley once again balances two perspectives: "Racial profiling is wrong no matter what the rationale," but given the events of 9/11, it may be asking too much to ignore "the one identifiable fact we know about [the terrorists]." He uses the term *purist* to describe those who think discrimination is always wrong. That would suggest, though, that racial discrimination is wrong even when it favors the group or individual being discriminated against, as with affirmative action. Kinsley most clearly reveals his own personal perspective when he slips into use of the first person singular in discussing affirmative action.

Kinsley calls both racial profiling and affirmative action "dangerous medicines that are sometimes appropriate." What determines when "sometimes" is appropriate is what is at stake. If airport security measures really work, the safety is worth the small imposition on a minority. If they don't, it is not.

Where is the common ground that is a key component of Rogers's communications theory? What everyone wants — with the exception of terrorists — is safety on the world's commercial flights. Those singled out for additional security screening may not need any other consolation than the fact that they are less likely to be blown up.

The Toulmin Model

Although Aristotle and Rogers, centuries and worlds apart, have both made significant contributions to rhetorical theory, we made the decision to organize this text around an argumentative model that we believe is more helpful in reading and writing arguments in a systematic manner: the Toulmin Model. The late Stephen Toulmin provided the vocabulary about argumentation that gives this book its structure.[5]

Toulmin's model, proposed in 1958 in *The Uses of Argument*, was designed to analyze courtroom arguments. Only after his model had been introduced to rhetoricians by Wayne Brockriede and Douglas Ehninger did he discuss its rhetorical implications in *Introduction to Reasoning* (1979). Of the six key terms in Toulmin's model, we draw heavily on three: claim, support, and warrant.

Stephen Toulmin (1922–2009) developed the model of argumentation that structures this book.

[5] *The Uses of Argument* (Cambridge: Cambridge University Press, 1958).

The Terms of Toulmin Argument

The Claim

The claim (also called a proposition) answers the question "What are you try-ing to prove?" It will generally appear as the thesis statement of your essay, although in some arguments, it may not be stated directly. There are three prin-cipal kinds of claim (discussed more fully in Chapter 5): claims of fact, of value, and of policy. *Claims of fact* assert that a condition has existed, exists, or will exist and are based on facts or data that the audience will accept as being objectively verifiable.

- The diagnosis of autism is now far more common than it was twenty years ago.

- Fast foods are contributing significantly to today's epidemic of child-hood obesity.

- Global warming will affect the coastlines of all continents.

All these claims must be supported by data. Although the last example is an inference or an educated guess about the future, a reader will probably find the prediction credible if the data seem authoritative.

Claims of value attempt to prove that some things are more or less desirable than others. They express approval or disapproval of standards of taste and mo-rality. Advertisements and reviews of cultural events are one common source of value claims, but such claims emerge whenever people argue about what is good or bad, beautiful or ugly.

- Mel Gibson's *Apocalypto* is marred by its excessive violence.

- Abortion is wrong under any circumstances.

- The right to privacy is more important than the need to increase secu-rity at airports.

Claims of policy assert that specific policies should be instituted as solutions to problems. The expression *should, must,* or *ought to* usually appears in the statement.

- The electoral college should be replaced by popular vote as the means of electing a president.

- Attempts at making air travel more secure must not put in jeopardy the passengers' right to privacy.

- Backscatter x-raying ought to be implemented at every American air-port as soon as possible as a means of detecting concealed weapons.

Policy claims call for analysis of both fact and value.

PRACTICE

1. Classify each of the following as a claim of fact, value, or policy.

   a. Solar power could supply 20 percent of the energy needs now satisfied by fossil and nuclear power.

   b. Violence on television produces violent behavior in children who watch more than four hours a day.

   c. Both intelligent design and evolutionary theory should be taught in the public schools.

   d. Some forms of cancer are caused by viruses.

   e. Dogs are smarter than cats.

   f. The money that our government spends on the space program would be better spent solving domestic problems like unemployment and homelessness.

   g. Wherever the number of illegal aliens increases, the crime rate also increases.

   h. Movie sequels are generally inferior to their originals.

   i. Tom Hanks is a more versatile actor than Tom Cruise.

   j. Adopted children who are of a different race than their adoptive parents should be raised with an understanding of the culture of their biological parents.

   k. Average yearly temperatures in North America are already being affected by global warming.

   l. Human activity is the primary cause of global warming.

2. Which claims listed above would be most difficult to support?

3. What type or types of evidence would it take to build a convincing case for each claim?

The Support

Support consists of the materials used by the arguer to convince an audience that his or her claim is sound. These materials include evidence and motivational appeals. The *evidence* or data consist of facts, statistics, and testimony from experts. The *motivational appeals* are the ones that the arguer makes to the values and attitudes of the audience to win support for the claim. The word *motivational* points out that these appeals are the reasons that move an audience to accept a belief or adopt a course of action. (See Chapter 6 for a detailed discussion of support.)

The Warrant

Certain assumptions underlie all the claims we make. In the Toulmin model, the term *warrant* is used for such an assumption, a belief or principle that is taken for granted. It may be stated or unstated. If the arguer believes that the audience shares the assumption, it may be unnecessary to express it. But if the audience seems doubtful or hostile, the arguer may decide to state the assumption to emphasize its importance or argue for its validity. The warrant, stated or not, allows the reader to make the same connection between the support and the claim that the author does. In other words, you have to accept the warrant in order to accept the author's claim based on the evidence provided.

This is how the warrant works. Before he posted on the blog about the proposed x-raying of airline passengers, Kapper had read earlier postings discussing the issue. He considered the arguments he had heard in favor of and against the x-ray technique and actually went so far as to summarize them in his posting. The conclusion he reached, which became the claim of his piece of writing, was that he agrees for the most part with those who argue in favor of the new screening technique. In outline form, a portion of his argument looks like this:

Claim: Backscatter screening should be implemented in America's airports.

Support: Backscatter screening will make planes safer.

Warrant: Any screening technique that will make planes safer should be implemented.

The following example demonstrates how a different kind of warrant, based on values, can also lead an audience to accept a claim.

Claim: Backscatter screening should be implemented in America's airports.

Support: Being seen naked by a security screener is better than dying.

Warrant: Being safe is worth a small loss of privacy.

The warrant — or underlying assumption — behind increased security is that safety is more important than privacy.

Writer's Guide: Learning the Key Terms

Claim — the proposition that the author is trying to prove. The claim may appear as the thesis statement of an essay but may be implied rather than stated directly.

• *Claims of fact* assert that a condition has existed, exists, or will exist and are based on facts or data that the audience will accept as being objectively verifiable.

• *Claims of value* attempt to prove that some things are more or less desirable than others; they express approval or disapproval of standards of taste and morality.

• *Claims of policy* assert that specific plans or courses of action should be instituted as solutions to problems.

Support — the materials used by the arguer to convince an audience that his or her claim is sound; those materials include evidence and motivational appeals.

Warrant — an inference or assumption; a belief or principle that is taken for granted in an argument.

Kapper's title shows how strongly he feels about this warrant: "Freedom to Live Trumps All!"

Let us suppose that the reader agrees with the supporting statement, that being seen naked by a security screener is better than dying. But to accept the claim, the reader must also agree with the principle expressed in the warrant, that being safe is worth a small loss of privacy. He or she can then agree that backscatter screening should be implemented. Notice that this warrant, like all warrants, certifies that the relationship between the support and the claim is sound.

One more important characteristic of the warrant deserves mention. In many cases, the warrant is a more general statement of belief than the claim. It can, therefore, support many claims, not only the one in a particular argument. For example, the warrant you have just read — being safe is worth a small loss of privacy — is a broad assumption or belief that we take for granted and that can underlie claims about many other practices in American society. (For more on warrants, see Chapter 7.)

Toulmin and the Syllogism

You will see some similarities between Toulmin's three-part structure of claim, support, and warrant and the classical deductive syllogism articulated by Aristotle. In fact, a comparison of the two may help in understanding the warrant.

The syllogism is useful for laying out the basic elements of an argument, and lends itself more readily to simple arguments. It is a formula that consists of three elements: (1) the major premise, (2) the minor premise, and (3) the conclusion, which follows logically from the two statements. The following syllogism summarizes a familiar argument.

Major Premise: Advertising of things harmful to our health should be legally banned.

Minor Premise: Cigarettes are harmful to our health.

Conclusion: Therefore, advertising of cigarettes should be legally banned.

Cast in the form of a Toulmin outline, the argument looks like this:

Claim: Advertising of cigarettes should be legally banned.

Support (Evidence):   Cigarettes are harmful to our health.

Warrant: Advertising of things harmful to our health should be legally banned.

Or in diagram form:

Support ———————————————→ *Claim*
Cigarettes are harmful   Advertising of cigarettes
to our health.   should be legally banned.

Warrant
Advertising of things harmful to our
health should be legally banned.

In both the syllogism and the Toulmin model the principal elements of the argument are expressed in three statements. You can see that the claim in the Toulmin model is the conclusion in the syllogism — that is, the proposition that you are trying to prove. The evidence (support) in the Toulmin model corresponds to the minor premise in the syllogism. And the warrant in the Toulmin model resembles the major premise of the syllogism.

In the Toulmin model, the use of the term *warrant* indicates that the validity of the proposition must be established to *guarantee* the claim or make the crossing from support to claim. It makes clear that the arguer must ask *why* such advertising must be banned.

While the syllogism is essentially static, with all three parts logically locked into place, the Toulmin model suggests that an argument is a *movement* from support to claim by way of the warrant, which acts as a bridge. Toulmin introduced the concept of warrant by asking, "How do you get there?" (His first two questions, introducing the claim and support, were "What are you trying to prove?" and "What have you got to go on?")

In addition to the three basic elements, the Toulmin model offers supplementary elements of argument. The *qualifier,* in the form of words like "probably" or "more likely," shows that the claim is not absolute. The *backing* offers support for the validity of the warrant. The *reservation* suggests that the validity of the warrant may be limited. These additional elements, which refine and expand the argument itself, reflect the real flexibility and complexity of the argumentative process.

PRACTICE

1. Report on an argument you have heard or read recently. Identify the parts of that argument — claim, support, warrant — as they are defined in this chapter. What were the strengths and weaknesses of the argument?

2. Choose one of the more controversial claims from the list on page 23. Explain why it is controversial. Would it be difficult to support? Impossible? Are the warrants unacceptable to many people? If there has been a change in recent years in public acceptance of the claim, offer what you think may be an explanation for the change.

No matter what the subject, there are certain basic steps that a writer can take to ensure that not only the proposition, or claim, but the whole argument is worthy of credence. You are not yet an expert in many of the subjects you will deal with in assignments, although you are knowledgeable about many other things, including your cultural and social activities. But there are several ways in which you can develop confidence in your discussion of topics derived from academic disciplines, such as political science, psychology, economics, sociology, and art. The following steps that every writer of argumentative texts should follow will be the basis for Chapters 4–9.

Steps for Writing Argumentative Texts

Defining Key Terms (CHAPTER 4)

Many of the controversial questions you will read or write about are primarily arguments of definition. Such terms as *abortion*, *pornography*, *racism*, *poverty*, *freedom of speech*, and *terrorism* must be defined before useful solutions to the problems they represent can be formulated. Even if the primary purpose of your essay is not definition, you can successfully communicate with an audience only if that audience understands how you are using key terms. That is true whether you are using the Rogerian approach or a more traditional approach. With the Rogerian method you may have to stipulate a definition that both sides can accept if you are to achieve successful communication about strongly held beliefs.

Choosing an Appropriate Claim (CHAPTER 5)

It must be clear to the individual or group that constitutes your audience what change in thought or what action you hope to achieve by presenting your case.

If you are seeking a change in your reader's thinking on a subject, you will have a much greater chance of accomplishing your goal if you consider the audience's current thinking on the subject and are realistic about the extent to which you might hope to change that thinking. The Rogerian approach emphasizes this need to assess fairly your audience's position in order to accommodate that position in writing your claim. If there is something you want your audience to do, that action must be realistically within the power of that audience.

Choosing and Documenting Appropriate Sources (CHAPTER 6)

You must present evidence of careful research, demonstrating that you have been conscientious in finding the best authorities, giving credit, and attempting to arrive at the truth.

Analyzing Assumptions (CHAPTER 7)

You must consider the warrant or assumption on which your argument is based. A warrant need not be expressed if it is so widely accepted that you can assume any reasonable audience will not need proof of its validity. You must be prepared to defend any other warrant. In Rogerian argument, more than in other rhetorical approaches, you must understand both your assumptions and your audience's in order to reconcile the two and establish common ground.

Analyzing Logical Errors (CHAPTER 8)

Understanding the ways in which inductive and deductive reasoning processes work can help you to determine the truth and validity of your arguments, as well as other arguments, and to identify and correct faulty reasoning.

Editing for Appropriate Language (CHAPTER 9)

Another important resource is the careful use of language, not only to define terms and express personal style but also to reflect clarity of thought, to avoid the clichés and outworn slogans that frequently substitute for fresh ideas, and to avoid word choices that would make your audience unwilling to consider your ideas.

Now let's turn to an example of argumentative writing and an analysis based on the Toulmin model.

The Hard Truth of Immigration

ROBERT J. SAMUELSON

Immigration is crawling its way back onto the national agenda — and not just as a footnote to keeping terrorists out. Earlier this year, Congress enacted a law intended to prevent illegal aliens from getting state drivers' licenses, the volunteer "minutemen" who recently patrolled the porous Arizona border with Mexico attracted huge attention, and members of Congress from both parties are now crafting proposals to deal with illegal immigration. All this is good. But unless we're brutally candid with ourselves, it won't amount to much. Being brutally candid means recognizing that the huge and largely uncontrolled inflow of unskilled Latino workers into the United States is increasingly sabotaging the assimilation process.

Americans rightly glorify our heritage of absorbing immigrants. Over time, they move into the economic, political, and social mainstream; over time, they become American rather than whatever they were — even though immigrants themselves constantly refashion the American identity. But no society has a boundless capacity to accept newcomers, especially when many are poor and unskilled. There are now an estimated 34 million immigrants in the United States, about a third of them illegal. About 35 percent lack health insurance and 26 percent receive some sort of federal benefit, reports Steven Camarota of the Center for Immigration Studies. To make immigration succeed, we need (paradoxically) to control immigration.

Although this is common sense, it's common sense that fits uneasily inside our adversarial political culture. You're supposed to be either pro-immigrant or anti-immigrant — it's hard to be pro-immigrant and pro tougher immigration restrictions. But that's the sensible position, as any examination of immigration trends suggests.

Consider a new study of Mexican immigrants by Harvard economists George Borjas and Lawrence Katz. Mexicans are now the single largest group of U.S. immigrants, 30 percent of the total in 2000. Indeed, the present Mexican immigration "is historically unprecedented, being both numerically and proportionately larger than any other immigrant influx in the past century," note Borjas and Katz. In 1920, for example, the two largest immigrant groups — Germans and Italians — totaled only 24 percent of the immigrant population.

Some Mexican-Americans have made spectacular gains, but the overall picture is dispiriting. Among men, about one in 20 U.S. workers is now a Mexican   5

Robert J. Samuelson, a contributing editor at *Newsweek*, has written a column for the *Washington Post* since 1977. This essay appeared in the June 13, 2005, issue of *Newsweek*.

immigrant; in 1970, that was less than one in 100. The vast majority of Mexican workers lacked a high-school diploma in 2000 (63 percent for men, 57 percent for women). Only a tiny share had college degrees (3 percent for men, 5 percent for women). By contrast, only 7 percent of native-born U.S. workers were high-school dropouts and 28 percent were college graduates in 2000. Mexican workers are inevitably crammed into low-wage jobs: food workers, janitors, gardeners, laborers, farm workers. In 2000, their average wages were 41 percent lower than average U.S. wages for men and 33 percent lower for women.

What's particularly disturbing about the Borjas-Katz study is that children of Mexican immigrants don't advance quickly. In 2000, Americans of Mexican ancestry still had lower levels of educational achievement and wages than most native-born workers. Among men, the wage gap was 27 percent; about 21 percent were high-school dropouts and only 11 percent were college graduates. Borjas and Katz can't explain the lags. "What's the role of culture vs. lousy [U.S.] schools?" asks Katz. "It's hard to say." Borjas doubts that the cause is discrimination. Low skills seem to explain most of the gap, he says. Indeed, after correcting for education and age, most of the wage gap disappears. Otherwise, says Borjas, "I don't know."

But some things we do know — or can infer. For today's Mexican immigrants (legal or illegal), the closest competitors are tomorrow's Mexican immigrants (legal or illegal). The more who arrive, the harder it will be for existing low-skilled workers to advance. Despite the recession, immigration did not much slow after 2000, says Camarota. Not surprisingly, a study by the Pew Hispanic Center found that inflation-adjusted weekly earnings for all Hispanics (foreign and American-born) dropped by 2.2 percent in 2003 and 2.6 percent in 2004. "Latinos are the only major group of workers whose wages have fallen for two consecutive years," said the study. Similarly, the more poor immigrants, the harder it will be for schools to improve the skills of their children. The schools will be overwhelmed; the same goes for social services.

We could do a better job of stopping illegal immigration on our southern border and of policing employers who hire illegal immigrants. At the same time, we could provide legal status to illegal immigrants already here. We could also make more sensible decisions about legal immigrants — favoring the skilled over the un-skilled. But the necessary steps are much tougher than most politicians have so far embraced, and their timidity reflects a lack of candor about the seriousness of the problem. The stakes are simple: will immigration continue to foster national pride and strength or will it cause more and more weakness and anger?

Analysis

Immigration is still on the national agenda, as it was when Samuelson wrote this essay in 2005. At that time, Congress was drafting legislation to deal with problems associated with immigration.

To analyze the piece using the Toulmin model, you must think in terms of claim, support, and warrant. At the end of the first paragraph, Samuelson makes this statement: "Being brutally candid means recognizing that the huge and largely uncontrolled inflow of unskilled Latino workers into the United States is increasingly sabotaging the assimilation process." This is a factual statement that his readers must accept in order to accept his claim, but the claim itself is a claim of policy — a statement of what needs to be done about immigration. That statement comes at the end of paragraph 2: "To make immigration succeed, we need (paradoxically) to control immigration." He rewords his claim in the next paragraph when he points out that the sensible position is to be both pro-immigrant and pro-tougher immigration restrictions. His goal in the essay, then, is to support this assertion.

Support consists of evidence and appeals to needs and values. Samuelson is appealing to his readers' American values when he starts his second paragraph by noting that America's "heritage of absorbing immigrants" is something to be proud of. He goes on, though, to counter that with the point that "no society has a boundless capacity to accept newcomers, especially when many are poor and unskilled." He offers statistical evidence regarding the numbers of immigrants America is trying to absorb and the percentage of the immigrant population that are Mexicans. Here he draws on Harvard economists George Borjas and Lawrence Katz for his information.

Samuelson also provides statistical evidence that Mexican immigrants are poorly educated and thus relegated to low-wage jobs — and their children are not progressing very rapidly. When it comes to earnings, Hispanics are losing ground. The more poor immigrants, the more overwhelmed the schools and social services.

The warrant of an essay is what a reader must believe in order to accept that the support offered justifies the claim. What is our understanding of the way the world works that makes us accept, based on the support Samuelson provides, that in order to make immigration succeed, we must control it? Think in terms of a broad statement that might serve as the major premise of a syllogism. In this case, such a statement might be "To be successful, a program needs restrictions controlling it."

Samuelson suggests what could be done to improve the situation, such as making our southern border more secure, favoring skilled over unskilled workers for legal entry, providing legal status to immigrants already here, and enforcing laws about hiring illegal immigrants. In his closing sentence, he again appeals to his readers' values: "The stakes are simple: Will immigration continue to foster national pride and strength or will it cause more and more weakness and anger?"

Assignments for Understanding the Structure of Argument

READING AND DISCUSSION QUESTIONS

1. Consider at what point news stations cross the line between reporting the news and analyzing the news. Think of some examples from recent news stories that illustrate the argumentative nature of today's news coverage.

2. Do you believe that presidential debates are good examples of argumentation? Explain.

3. What are some of the controversial issues in the field of your major or a major that you are considering? Analyze one or more of them using Toulmin's terms: claim, support, and warrant.

4. When you write essays and reports for your classes, how do you establish your credibility? On the other hand, how do students lose their credibility with the instructors who read their work?

WRITING SUGGESTIONS

5. Write an essay in which you support your opinion about whether backscatter screening should be implemented at America's airports.

6. Write an essay in which you discuss how technological advances have changed an audience's ability to evaluate a speaker's *ethos*.

7. Write an essay in which you discuss how both Aristotelian and Rogerian argument are useful in contemporary politics.

8. Write an essay in which you identify some of the issues about which it is most difficult to achieve common ground, and explain why.

Research Readiness: Using Databases

What is the first step you take when you need to do some research?

If your response is to go to Google, the answer is yes and no. In your daily life, if you need to look up some factual information, you can find it quickly on Google or another similar search engine. For most assignments for your classes, the answer is no.

For one thing, remember that Google finds *any* reference to your search term and doesn't discriminate based on quality. Anyone can post on the Internet, so there is no control over accuracy. You will also be inundated with far more sources than you could ever look at.

If you had checked Google for information about Aristotle when this book went to press, you would have found these numbers:

"Aristotle" — 39,600,000 results

"Aristotle" and "argument" — 2,940,000 results

"Aristotle's argument" — 688,000 results

"Aristotle" and "rhetoric" — 195,000 results

"Aristotle's rhetoric" — 120,000 results

Wikipedia will be near the top of the list for many subjects, but don't plan to use Wikipedia as a source for college work. It lacks the authority your professors will expect.

Where, then, do you start? Prowling the shelves of the library? Don't rule out electronic sources. Instead, find out what databases your school has access to and which of those databases are most appropriate for your research.

For example, a good general database for academic subjects is Expanded Academic ASAP. There, a search for information about Aristotle yields these results:

"Aristotle" — subject search 1869 results
                keyword search 3370 results

"Aristotle" and "argument" — 79 results

"Aristotle's argument" — 79 results

"Aristotle" and "rhetoric" — 15 results

"Aristotle's rhetoric" — 15 results

As you can see, by the end of this search, you are reaching a manageable number of sources to explore. Even with 79 results, a quick look at the titles will eliminate some and let you know which ones are worth investigating.

The numbers refer to articles in academic journals, generally the ones most widely accepted by college faculty. Available in separate listings are citations for 615 magazines, 4 books, and 445 newspaper articles.

You will learn more about finding sources in Chapter 10, but as a starting point, do the following.

ASSIGNMENT

1. Every library will have access to different databases for student use. Find a list of the databases available to you and do a search for articles about how Carl Rogers's theories about therapy relate to argument. You will have to try different combinations of terms to find the best information. Write down what you discover about sources available to you.

2. What are two specialized databases that might be a starting point for information related to your major or a major that you might choose?

CHAPTER 2

Critical Reading

A full response to any argument means more than understanding the message. It also means evaluating, deciding whether the message is successful, and then determining *how* it succeeds or fails in persuading us. In making these judgments about the arguments of others, we learn how to deliver our own. We try to avoid what we perceive to be flaws in another's arguments, and we adapt the strategies that produce clear, honest, forceful arguments.

Critical reading is essential for mastery of most college subjects, but its importance for reading and writing about argument, where meaning is often complex and multilayered, cannot be overestimated. The ability to read arguments critically is essential to advanced academic work—even in science and math—since it requires the debate of multifaceted issues rather than the memorization of facts. Just as important, learning to read arguments critically helps you develop the ability to *write* effective arguments, a process valued at the university, in the professional world, and in public life.

Prereading

In the last chapter, you read an essay by Juan Williams entitled "Don't Mourn *Brown v. Board of Education*." You probably were familiar with the court case Williams was writing about. If not, you could discover from the context that he was referring to a famous case that made its way to the Supreme Court in 1954, making school segregation unconstitutional in the United States. You will frequently confront texts dealing with subjects unfamiliar to you, and you should have a plan of action for prereading them; that is, for getting an overview of a piece before you read. Here are a few strategies, illustrated by references to "Don't Mourn *Brown v. Board of Education*":

1. Pay attention to the title, as it may state the purpose of the argument in specific terms. Williams's title immediately announces the "death" of *Brown v. Board of Education*. It also establishes that that death should not be mourned. The reference is clearly to a legal case. If it were one that you were not familiar with, you could either stop and look it up or read on and hope to learn about it as you read. The title captures the reader's desire to read on and find out what happened to alter this famous ruling.

2. Work hard to understand the kind of text you are reading. Was it published recently? Is it a response to another text, or perhaps to an event? Certainly if it is argumentative writing, it is at least a response to a perceived problem. Was there something specific that led an author to write about this subject in this way at this particular time? What background about the subject are you familiar with?

> A quick look at the first few sentences of Williams's article establishes that he is writing in response to a ruling by the Supreme Court the day before that has "killed" the *Brown* decision by "ending the use of voluntary schemes to create racial balance among students."

> A note at the bottom of the first page of each article in this textbook gives the article's date and tells you both when and where the article was published. Otherwise, most titles can be looked up on *Google* or another search engine to get a date and place of publication. Often you can find the whole article online.

> The *Brown v. Board of Education* decision was issued in 1954; Williams's article was published in 2007. The immediate context in which he was writing was a decision by the Supreme Court that had in some way significantly altered the historic ruling.

3. As a rule, the more information you know about an author, the easier and more productive your reading will be. You should learn to read in a way that allows you to discover not just meaning in the text itself but information about the author's point of view, background, motives, and ideology. Such understanding comes from close analysis of a text but also from background reading on the author and/or the subject and discussion with your classmates and instructors on the material.

If you read the analysis that accompanied the article in Chapter 1, you know that Juan Williams is a political commentator for the Fox News Channel and was then a senior correspondent for National Public Radio. These credentials establish him as a respected political journalist, even if the television network for which he works is well known to have a conservative bias. (On the other hand, some accuse NPR of having a liberal bias but not evenly so on all issues.)

The fact that Williams has written a book on Thurgood Marshall, the lead attorney in the *Brown* case and later a Supreme Court justice, would suggest that he is quite knowledgeable on the subject and that he might approach it with sympathy for the side of the plaintiffs, six African American children from Kansas. The fact that Williams is African American may or may not be relevant.

4. Imagine the context in which the author was writing and the target audience. Was it a specific or general audience? Does the text come from a journal that publishes primarily conservative or liberal writers? What values and ideals are shared by the author and the audience most likely to agree with the argument? How might these values help make sense of the context? What sort of audience might be most strongly opposed to the argument and why?

> The racial animosity that existed in the American South 1954 is almost inconceivable to young adults in the early twenty-first century who grew up in racially and culturally diverse schools. Williams, writing for the general audience of the *New York Times* in 2007, would be writing to many who could remember quite well a time of segregated buses, water fountains, restrooms, and restaurants, in addition to schools. The mention of the death of *Brown v. Board of Education* would still strike a nerve with that generation. A title that suggested *not* mourning the death of a ruling that was a landmark in the history of the civil rights movement was risky, so he has to address a potentially hostile response in the opening sentences.

> Young readers would respond to the subject as a historical reference rather than as a personal memory. However, in some cases, they would be approaching it from the perspective of students attending schools still marred by racial tension.

Research Skill: Examining Author, Subject, and Context

Williams's essay is a good example of the value of pre-reading. It is also a good place to start thinking about some of the earliest stages of research. Some background knowledge is essential to understanding the full significance of Williams's argument. If you wanted to refresh your memory of the *Brown* decision, you might go back to a textbook you studied in the past or to class notes, but you are far more likely to go to *Google* or a similar search engine.

Wonderful as our search engines can be—and as much time as they save—us they are not at all discriminating. They are a quick way to get factual information, but when it comes to opinions, you have to do the discriminating yourself.

—If you search Williams's title, for example, the first entry tells you place and date of publication.

—If you search *Brown v. Board of Education*, the first entry is likely to be Wikipedia.

We all know that Wikipedia is an online encyclopedia but also that the authors of its articles are not necessarily experts on their subjects. Often there is even a note that indicates that sources need authentication or that more information is needed. Wikipedia can be useful to get a general idea about a subject but should be used with caution. More authoritative would be an online encyclopedia by a reputable company like Britannica.

Watch closely the URLs for any online sources that you find. As you know, *.com* represents commercial site, *.gov* represents a government site, and *.edu* represents, for the most part, a college or university site. Don't be fooled by an .edu site that also has a tilde (~) followed by a username, though, because that indicates that you are on an individual's site and not the institution's. That individual could be an expert, but he or she may also be a student just like you who is not a specialist in the area.

Organizational sites, those that end in *.org*, must also be used with care. One of the first sites a search engine will list for the *Brown* decision is brownboard .org, which was founded in honor of the plaintiffs and attorneys in the case but may for that reason have a particular bias. A site called nationalcenter.org is a national public policy research institute that could also have its biases that would have to be investigated, but in this case it proves to be a handy source for a copy of the decision rendered by the Supreme Court in 1954.

If you search for Juan Williams, you will find Wikipedia again, then sites for the places that Williams is employed, where you can most likely get good factual information about him and his career. With later entries, you start to

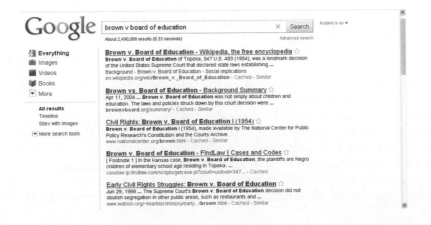

find writing done by Williams himself, such as an article in the online version of the *Wall Street Journal,* another reputable source.

Whenever you move into *.com* sources, keep in mind that you have moved into the commercial realm and must be alert to whatever interests the company or group may have in the way information is presented.

PRACTICE

Apply the Prereading Strategies to the following essay.

Let's Have No More Monkey Trials

CHARLES KRAUTHAMMER

The half-century campaign to eradicate any vestige of religion from public life has run its course. The backlash from a nation fed up with the A.C.L.U. kicking crèches out of municipal Christmas displays has created a new balance. State-supported universities may subsidize the activities of student religious groups. Monuments inscribed with the Ten Commandments are permitted on government grounds. The Federal Government is engaged in a major antipoverty initiative that gives money to churches. Religion is back out of the closet.

But nothing could do more to undermine this most salutary restoration than the new and gratuitous attempts to invade science, and most particularly evolution, with religion. Have we learned nothing? In Kansas, conservative school-board members are attempting to rewrite statewide standards for teaching evolution to make sure that creationism's modern stepchild, intelligent design,

---

Charles Krauthammer, winner of the 1987 Pulitzer Prize for distinguished commentary, writes a nationally syndicated column for the *Washington* Post Writers Group. He also writes for the *Weekly Standard* and the *New Republic*. This piece appeared in Time on August 1, 2005.

infiltrates the curriculum. Similar anti-Darwinian mandates are already in place in Ohio and are being fought over in 20 states. And then, as if to second the evangelical push for this tarted-up version of creationism, out of the blue appears a declaration from Christoph Cardinal Schönborn of Vienna, a man very close to the Pope, asserting that the supposed acceptance of evolution by John Paul II is mistaken. In fact, he says, the Roman Catholic Church rejects "neo-Darwinism" with the declaration that an "unguided evolutionary process—one that falls outside the bounds of divine providence—simply cannot exist."

Cannot? On what scientific evidence? Evolution is one of the most powerful and elegant theories in all of human science and the bedrock of all modern biology. Schönborn's proclamation that it cannot exist unguided—that it is driven by an intelligent designer pushing and pulling and planning and shaping the process along the way—is a perfectly legitimate statement of faith. If he and the Evangelicals just stopped there and asked that intelligent design be included in a religion curriculum, I would support them. The scandal is to teach this as science—to pretend, as does Schönborn, that his statement of faith is a defense of science. "The Catholic Church," he says, "will again defend human reason" against "scientific theories that try to explain away the appearance of design as the result of 'chance and necessity,'" which "are not scientific at all." Well, if you believe that science is reason and that reason begins with recognizing the existence of an immanent providence, then this is science. But, of course, it is not. This is faith disguised as science. Science begins not with first principles but with observation and experimentation.

In this slippery slide from "reason" to science, Schönborn is a direct descendant of the early 17th century Dutch clergyman and astronomer David Fabricius, who could not accept Johannes Kepler's discovery of elliptical planetary orbits. Why? Because the circle is so pure and perfect that reason must reject anything less. "With your ellipse," Fabricius wrote Kepler, "you abolish the circularity and uniformity of the motions, which appears to me increasingly absurd the more profoundly I think about it." No matter that, using Tycho Brahe's most exhaustive astronomical observations in history, Kepler had empirically demonstrated that the planets orbit elliptically.

This conflict between faith and science had mercifully abated over the past four centuries as each grew to permit the other its own independent sphere. What we are witnessing now is a frontier violation by the forces of religion. This new attack claims that because there are gaps in evolution, they therefore must be filled by a divine intelligent designer.

5

How many times do we have to rerun the Scopes "monkey trial"? There are gaps in science everywhere. Are we to fill them all with divinity? There were gaps in Newton's universe. They were ultimately filled by Einstein's revisions. There are gaps in Einstein's universe, great chasms between it and quantum theory. Perhaps they are filled by God. Perhaps not. But it is certainly not science to merely declare it so.

To teach faith as science is to undermine the very idea of science, which is the acquisition of new knowledge through hypothesis, experimentation, and evidence. To teach it as science is to encourage the supercilious caricature of America as a nation in the thrall of religious authority. To teach it as science is to discredit the welcome recent advances in permitting the public expression of religion. Faith can and should be proclaimed from every mountaintop and city square. But it has no place in science class. To impose it on the teaching of evolution is not just to invite ridicule but to earn it.

Comprehension

The first step in the critical reading process is comprehension—understanding what an author is trying to prove. Comprehending academic arguments can be difficult because they are often complex and often challenge accepted notions. Academic writing also sometimes assumes that readers already have a great deal of knowledge about a subject and therefore can require further research for comprehension.

Readers sometimes fail to comprehend a text they disagree with or that is new to them, especially in dealing with essays or books making controversial, value-laden arguments. Some research even shows that readers will sometimes remember only those parts of texts that match their points of view.[1] The study of argument does not require you to accept points of view you find morally or otherwise reprehensible, but to engage with these views, no matter how strange or repugnant they might seem, on your own terms.

Reading arguments critically requires you to at least temporarily suspend notions of absolute "right" and "wrong" and to intellectually inhabit gray areas that do not allow for simple "yes" and "no" answers. Of course, even in these areas, significant decisions about such things as ethics, values, politics, and the law must be made, and in studying argument you shouldn't fall into the trap of simple relativism: the idea that all answers to a given problem are equally correct at all times. We must make decisions about arguments with the understanding that reasonable people can disagree on the validity of ideas. Read others' arguments carefully and consider how their ideas can contribute to or complicate your own. Remember Carl Rogers's approach and look for common ground between your beliefs and those of the author. Also recognize that what appears to be a final solution will always be open to further negotiation as new participants, new historical circumstances, and new ideologies become involved in the debate.

To comprehend difficult texts you should understand that reading and writing are linked processes, and use writing to help your reading. This can mean writing comments in the margins of the book or essay itself or in a separate notebook; highlighting passages in the text that seem particularly important; or freewriting about the author's essential ideas after you finish reading. For complex arguments, write down the methods the author uses to make the argument:

[1]See, for example, Patrick J. Slattery, "The Argumentative, Multiple-Source Paper: College Students Reading, Thinking, and Writing about Multiple Points of View," *Journal of Teaching Writing* 10, Fall/Winter 1991, pp. 181–99.

- Did the text use historical evidence or rely on experts?
- Were emotional appeals made to try to convince readers, or did the text rely on scientific or logical forms of evidence?
- Did the author use analogies or comparisons to help readers understand the argument?
- Was some combination of these or other strategies used? Writing down the author's methods for argumentation can make even the most complex arguments understandable.

Strategies for Comprehending Arguments

1. Skim the article or book for the main idea and overall structure. At this stage, avoid concentrating on details.

    a. Make a skeleton outline of the text in your mind or on paper. From this outline and the text itself, consider the relationship between the beginning, middle, and end of the argument. How has the author divided these sections? Are there subheadings in the body of the text? If you are reading a book, how are the chapters broken up? What appears to be the logic of the author's organization?

    b. From your overview, what is the central claim or argument of the essay? What is the main argument against the author's central claim and how would the author respond to it?

2. Remember that the claim is usually in one of the first two or three paragraphs (if it is an essay) or in the first chapter (if it is a book). The beginning of an argument can have other purposes, however; it may describe the position that the author will oppose or provide background for the whole argument.

3. Pay attention to topic sentences. The topic sentence is usually but not always the first sentence of a paragraph. It is the general statement that controls the details and examples in the paragraph.

4. Don't overlook language signposts, especially transitional words and phrases that tell you whether the writer will change direction or offer support for a previous point—words and phrases like *but, however, nevertheless, yet, moreover, for example, at first glance, more important, the first reason,* and so on.

5. When it comes to vocabulary, you can either guess the meaning of an unfamiliar word from the context and go on or look it up immediately. The first method makes for more rapid reading and is sometimes recommended by teachers, but guessing can be risky. Keep a good dictionary handy. If a word you don't understand seems crucial to meaning, look it up before going on.

6. If you use a highlighter to mark main points, use it sparingly. Marking passages in color is meant to direct you to the major ideas and reduce the necessity for rereading the whole passage when you review. Look over the marked passages and do a five-minute freewrite to sum up the central parts of the argument.

7. Once you are done reading, think again about the original context the text was written in: Why did the author write it and for whom? Why might an editor have published it in a book or journal, and why did your instructor assign it?

SAMPLE ANNOTATED ESSAY

Sex and the Cinema

EDWARD JAY EPSTEIN

Contrast with early days

In the early days of Hollywood, nudity—or the illusion of it—was considered such an asset that director Cecil B. DeMille famously made bathing scenes an obligatory ingredient of his biblical epics. Nowadays, nudity is a decided liability when it comes to the commercial success of the movie. In 2004, none

Examples of Top 25 movies with no sex

of the six major studios' top 25 grossing films, led by *Spider-Man 2*, *Shrek 2*, *Harry Potter and the Prisoner of Azkaban*, and *The Incredibles*, contained any sexually oriented nudity; only one had a restrictive R rating—Warner Bros.' *Troy*—and that was mainly due to the film's gory violence, not its sexual content.

Claim

The absence of sex — at least graphic sex — is key to the success of Hollywood's moneymaking movies. Directors may consider a sex scene artistically integral to their movie, but studios, which almost always have the right to exercise the final cut, also have to consider three factors.

Three factors to consider
I-The rating system

First, there is the rating system. For a film to play in movie theaters belonging to the National Association of Theater Owners—which includes all the multiplexes in America—it first needs to obtain a rating from a board organized by the Motion Picture Association of America—the trade association of the six major studios. All the expenses for rating movies are paid to the MPAA by the studio out of a percentage deducted from box-office receipts. As it presently works, a movie that contains sexually oriented nudity gets either an NC-17 or an R rating, depending

Topic sentence: NC-17
= box-office failure

on how graphically sex is depicted. The NC-17 rating, which forbids theaters from admitting children under the age of 18, is the equivalent of a death sentence as far as the studios are concerned. In fact,

---

Edward Jay Epstein is an investigative reporter who has written over a dozen books, most recently *The Hollywood Economist: The Hidden Financial Reality Behind the Movies* (2010). This essay appeared on August 15, 2005, in *Slate*, a daily online magazine affiliated with the *Washington Post*.

Claudette Colbert in *The Sign of the Cross* (1932), directed by Cecil B. DeMille

Old movies with sex that wouldn't be made today

since the financial disaster of Paul Verhoeven's NC-17 *Showgirls* in 1995, no studio has attempted a wide release of a NC-17 film. As one Paramount executive suggested, because of their sexually related nudity, movies such as Louis Malle's *Pretty Baby*, Bernardo Bertolucci's *Last Tango in Paris*, and Stanley Kubrick's *A Clockwork Orange* would not even be considered by a major studio today. So far this year there has been only one limited release of an NC-17 film by a studio: the documentary *Inside Deep Throat*, which yielded Universal less from the box-office—$330,000—than it cost to wrangle media stars and others to free screenings and dinners to promote it.

If a movie contains less explicit nudity, it earns an R rating, which merely prohibits youth unaccompanied by an adult. Even though this option means that some number of multiplex employees—who might otherwise be selling popcorn—are required to check the identity documents of the teenage audience, theaters accept R rated films, especially when, as was the case with *Troy*, the R is for the sort of graphic violence that is also the principal attrac-

Topic sentence: R-rated movies may get a wide showing, but the rating complicates marketing them.

II-The Wal-Mart consideration

New DVDs = more customers, who buy other products

Wal-Mart's "decency policy" forces studios to avoid sexual content

tion. <u>But even if an R doesn't prevent studios from staging a wide opening of a movie at the multiplexes, it complicates the movie's all-important marketing drive.</u> For one thing, if a film receives an R rating, many television stations and cable networks, particularly teenage-oriented ones, are not allowed to accept TV ads for the movies. In addition, an R rating—especially for sexual content—will preclude any of the fast-food chains, beverage companies, or toy manufacturers that act as the studios' merchandise tie-in partners from backing the movie with tens of millions of dollars in free advertising. As a result, it becomes much more expensive to alert and herd audiences to R rated films.

Second, there is the Wal-Mart consideration. In 2004, the six studios took in $20.9 billion from home-video sales, according to the studios' own internal numbers. Wal-Mart, including its Sam's Club stores, accounted for over one-quarter of those sales, which means that Wal-Mart wrote more than $5 billion in checks to the studios in 2004. Such enormous buying power comes dangerously close to constituting what the Justice Department calls a monopoly—control of a market by a single buyer—and it allows the giant retailer to effectively dictate the terms of trade. Internet mythology aside, Wal-Mart doesn't use its clout to advance any political agenda or social engineering objective, according to a studio executive involved in the process; it is "strictly business." Wal-Mart uses DVDs, especially the weekly released hits, to lure in customers who, while they pass through the store, may buy more profitable items, such as toys, clothing, or electronics.

Wal-Mart's main concern with the content of the DVDs is that they not offend important customers—especially mothers—by containing material that may be inappropriate for children. It guards against this risk with a "decency policy" that consigns DVDs containing sexually related nudity to "adult sections" of the store, which greatly reduces their sales. (Wal-Mart is less concerned with vulgar behavior and language.) These guidelines, in turn, put studios under tremendous pressure to sanitize their films of sexual content. The Wal-Mart buyer would merely have to order for their stores the

5

"in-flight entertainment" version of DVDs, from which studios expunge nudity and other sexually explicit scenes for airline passengers (censorship that almost all directors quietly accept). <u>In light of such leverage, studios have to weigh the Wal-Mart factor with great care.</u>

Finally, <u>movies with nudity are a problem for the studios' other main moneymaker: television.</u> As became abundantly clear in the controversy surrounding Janet Jackson's wardrobe malfunction at Superbowl XXXVIII, broadcast television is a government-regulated enterprise. When the government grants a free license to a station to broadcast over the public airwaves, it does so under the condition that it conform to the rules enforced by the Federal Communications Commission. Among those rules is the standard of "public decency," which among other things specifically prohibits salacious nudity—which is why CBS had to pay a fine for Ms. Jackson's brief exposure. Because the FCC regulates broadcast television (though not cable television), television stations run similar risks—and embarrassments—if they show movies that include even partial nudity. So, before a studio can license such a movie to a broadcast network, it first has to cut out all the nudity and other scenes that run afoul of the decency standard. Aside from the expense involved, it requires the hassle of obtaining the director's permission, which is contractually required by the Directors Guild of America. The same is true in studio sales to foreign television companies, which have their own government censorship. <u>Since graphic sex in movies is a triple liability, the studios can be expected to increasingly find that the artistic gain that comes from including it does not compensate for the financial pain and greenlight fewer and fewer movies that present this problem.</u> We may live in an anything-goes age, but if a studio wants to make money, it has to limit how much of "anything"— at least anything sexually explicit—it shows on the big screen. As one studio executive with an MBA lamented, "We may have to leave sex to the independents."

Sidebar annotations:

Topic sentence: Studios have to take the Wal-Mart factor seriously

III Nudity: a problem for television

Movies on TV must meet standards of "public decency"

Conclusion restates claim

PRACTICE

1. Choose from your school paper or another newspaper an editorial of at least two paragraphs on a controversial subject that interests you. The title will probably reveal the subject. Annotate the editorial as you read, using the Writer's Guide as a set of guidelines and the annotations on "Sex and the Cinema" as a model. Then read the article again. You should discover that annotating the article caused you to read more carefully, more critically, with greater comprehension and a more focused response.

2. Summarize the claim of the editorial in one sentence. Has the author proved his or her point?

3. Annotate Krauthammer's "Let's Have No More Monkey Trials," pages 39–41, keeping all of your marginal notes in the left margin.

Writer's Guide: Annotating a Text

One purpose of annotating a text is to comprehend it more fully. Another is to prepare to write about it.

1. If you use a highlighter as you read a text, use it sparingly. Highlighting too much of a text is not very useful when it comes time to review what you have marked. You might consider a more targeted approach to highlighting, focusing only on thesis statement and topic sentences in an essay, for example, or on conclusions in a report.

2. More useful than highlighting is making marginal notes, perhaps underlining the portion of the text that each note refers to. However, with underlining, as with highlighting, increased quantity equals decreased usefulness. Some of the most useful marginal notes will be those that summarize key ideas in your own words. Such paraphrases force you to understand the text well enough to reword its ideas, and reading the marginal notes is a quick way to review the text when you do not have time to reread all of it.

3. It will be useful to make notes both on what a piece of writing says and how it says it. Notations about how a piece is written can focus on structural devices such as topic sentences, transitional words or phrases, and the repetition of ideas or sentence structure but also on rhetorical concerns such as identifying the claim, support, and warrant; the tone; and the types of appeal.

4. As you annotate a text, you may also want to make note of questions you still have after having read the text. These questions may be the basis for class discussion.

5. You may also find it useful to note similarities that you see between the text you are reading and others you have read or between the text and your own experience.

Research Skill: Summarizing

One skill required by the Rogerian approach to communication is the ability to summarize another's ideas fairly and objectively, just as in more confrontational forms of argumentation a writer or speaker cannot build a successful case on a misunderstanding or misinterpretation of an opponent's position. At least, such a case will not hold up under careful scrutiny. The ability to summarize is also a basic research skill used in writing research papers, as discussed in Chapter 10. Summarizing is the cornerstone on which all other critical reading and writing tasks are built.

When summarizing long or difficult texts, try some of the following strategies to help you comprehend the essential points of the text.

1. Reread the introduction and conclusion after you have read the text once or twice. These two sections should complement each other and offer clues to the most significant issues of the text. An introduction or conclusion is often more than one paragraph; therefore, it is important that you read the first and last few paragraphs of a text to understand what the author is trying to impress upon the reader. If you are summarizing a book, look especially at the preface, the first and last chapters, and any reviewers' comments. These sections won't tell you everything you need to know to summarize an entire book, but they will help you decide which points matter.

2. For a difficult text, you may want to list all the subheadings (if they are used) or the topic sentence of each paragraph. These significant guideposts will map the piece as a whole: What do they tell you about the central ideas and the main argument the author is making? After reviewing the subheads or topic sentences, can you reread the text and engage more easily with its finer points? For a book, you can do the same thing with chapter headings to break down the essential ideas. Remember that when you summarize, you must put another's words into your own (and cite the original text as well), so do not simply let a list of the subheadings or chapter titles stand as your summary. They likely won't make sense when put together in paragraph form, but they will provide you with valuable ideas regarding the central points of the text.

3. Remember that summarizing requires attention to overall meanings and not to specific details. Therefore, avoid including many specific examples or concrete details from the text you are summarizing and try to let your reader know what these examples and details add up to. Some of the specificity and excitement of the original text will be lost, but when summarizing, the goal is to let the reader know the essential meaning of the original text in a clear, straightforward way. Of course, if you need to respond, as part of your argument, to specifics in the essay, you should do so, but you will most likely do so in the form of a paraphrase or a direct quotation.

There are two types of summaries, rhetorical and referential. The two share some characteristics. Both types should

- Be objective instead of expressing opinions.
- Identify the author and the work.
- Use present tense.
- Summarize the main points of the whole work or passage, not just part of it.

A *rhetorical* summary summarizes the text in terms of rhetorical choices the author made. An example:

> In "Let's Have No More Monkey Trials," Charles Krauthammer celebrates the end of the separation of religion from public life at the local, state, and federal levels but argues that the progress made will be undermined by those trying to replace the teaching of evolution with the teaching of intelligent design, a new form of creationism. He notes that Christoph Cardinal Schönborn of Vienna . . .

The other type of summary, a *referential* summary, focuses on ideas rather than on the author's actions and decisions.

> According to Charles Krauthammer in his article "Let's Have No More Monkey Trials," a fifty-year trend toward removing religion from public life is now being reversed. This positive movement, however, is threatened by those who are trying to replace the teaching of evolution with the teaching of intelligent design, a new form of creationism. Christoph Cardinal Schönborn of Vienna has asserted that . . .

PRACTICE

Complete either the rhetorical summary or the referential summary of Krauthammer's essay.

When you try to comprehend an argument, try to imagine other readers' response to it. A writer needs to be able to represent fairly others' views rather than ignoring, demeaning, or misrepresenting them. Carl Rogers taught us to sum up objectively someone else's point of view and to look for common ground in order to make communication about emotionally charged subjects possible. Sometimes you will read an argument, and whether you agree with it or not, you will know that others with strongly held beliefs on the other side of the issue will not even give it a hearing. It may totally ignore their position or represent it unfairly, which blocks communication and makes compromise impossible. There is a tendency to write for those who already agree with us, but they are not the ones who need convincing. At times the best you can do falls short of the ideal solution, but getting the audience to hear your position may be as much as you can hope for.

Evaluation

The second step in the critical reading of arguments involves evaluation—careful judgment of the extent to which the author has succeeded in making a point—which can be difficult because some readers who do not thoroughly engage with an author's point of view may immediately label an argument they disagree with as "wrong," and some readers believe they are incapable of evaluating the work of a published, "expert" author because they do not feel expert enough to make such judgments.

Critically evaluating an argument means not simply reading a text and agreeing or disagreeing with it, but doing serious analytical work that addresses multiple viewpoints before deciding on the effectiveness of an argument.

The following essay supports a claim of value in which, as the title suggests, the author claims that competitive sports are destructive. In arguments about values, the author may or may not suggest a solution to the problem caused by the belief or behavior. If so, the solution will be implicit—that is, unexpressed or undeveloped—as is the case here, and the emphasis will remain on support for the claim.

Notice the difference between the annotations a student made in response to the following essay and those another student made earlier in response to "Sex and the Cinema" (p. 43). In the earlier example, the student was making marginal notes primarily on the ideas presented in the essay. Here the annotations focus on how successfully Kohn argues his case.

Strategies for Evaluating Arguments

1. As you read the argument, don't be timid about asking questions of the text. No author is infallible, and some are not always clear. Disagree with the author if you feel confident of the support for your view, but first read the whole argument to see if your questions have been answered. If not, this may be a signal to read the article again. Be cautious about concluding that the author hasn't proved his or her point.

2. Reading an assigned work is usually a solitary activity, but what follows a reading should be shared. Talk about the material with classmates or others who have read it, especially those who have responded to the text differently than you did. Consider their points of view. You probably know that discussion of a book or a movie strengthens both your memory of details and your understanding of the whole. And defending or modifying your evaluation will mean going back to the text and finding clues that you may have overlooked. Not least, it can be fun to discuss even something you didn't enjoy.

3. Consider the strengths of the argument and examine the useful methods of argumentation, the points that are successfully made (and those which help the reader to better understand the argument), and what makes sense about the author's argument.

4. Consider the weaknesses of the argument and locate instances of faulty reasoning, unsupported statements, and the limitations of the author's assumptions about the world (the warrants that underlie the argument).

5. Consider how effective the title of the reading is and whether it accurately sums up a critical point of the essay. Come up with an alternative title that would suit the reading better, and be prepared to defend this alternative title.

6. Evaluate the organizational structure of the essay. The author should lead you from idea to idea in a logical progression, and each section should relate to the ones before and after it and to the central argument in significant ways. Determine whether the writer could have organized things more clearly, logically, or efficiently.

7. Look at how the author follows through on the main claim, or thesis, of the argument. The author should stick with this thesis and not waver throughout the text. If the thesis does waver, there could be a reason for the shift in the argument, or perhaps the author is being inconsistent. The conclusion should drive home the central argument.

8. Evaluate the vocabulary and style the author uses. Is it too simple or too complicated? The vocabulary and sentence structure the author uses could relate to the audience the author was initially writing for.

SAMPLE ANNOTATED ESSAY

No-Win Situations

ALFIE KOHN

I learned my first game at a birthday party. You remember it: X players scramble for X-minus-one chairs each time the music stops. In every round a child is eliminated until at the end only one is left triumphantly seated while everyone else is standing on the sidelines, excluded from play, unhappy . . . losers.

Good example.

Good use of sarcasm.

This is how we learn to have a good time in America.

Competition

This establishes his expertise on the subject.

Several years ago I wrote a book called *No Contest*, which, based on the findings of several hundred studies, argued that competition undermines self-esteem, poisons relationships, and holds us back from doing our best. I was mostly interested in the win/lose arrangement that defines our workplaces and classrooms, but I found myself nagged by the

---

This article by Alfie Kohn, author of *No Contest:* The *Case Against Competition* (1986) and *The Homework Myth: Why Our Kids Get Too Much of a Bad Thing* (2006), appeared in *Women's Sports and Fitness Magazine* (July–August 1990).

The comparison is flawed because those who compete during the week are mostly spectators on weekends.

following question: If competition is so destructive and counterproductive during the week, why do we take for granted that it suddenly becomes benign and even desirable on the weekend?

This is a particularly unsettling line of inquiry for athletes or parents. Most of us, after all, assume that competitive sports teach all sorts of useful lessons and, indeed, that games by definition must produce a winner and a loser. But I've come to believe that recreation at its best does not require people to try to triumph over others. Quite to the contrary.

Is recreation the same as sports?

An appropriate authority to use.

Terry Orlick, a sports psychologist at the University of Ottawa, took a look at musical chairs and proposed that we keep the basic format of removing chairs but change the goal; the point becomes to fit everyone on a diminishing number of seats. At the end, a group of giggling children tries to figure out how to squish onto a single chair. Everybody plays to the end; everybody has a good time.

5

Not much fun as spectator sports. Our most popular sports draw huge crowds.

Aristotelian versus Rogerian?

This suggests that football, baseball, and basketball offer no advantages. Many would disagree.

At one extreme is cooperative activity. At the other is "war minus the shooting." Competition seems to be a happy medium.

We may be able to do without them, but should we have to?

It might not be the same if it were adults.

Orlick and others have devised or collected hundreds of such games for children and adults alike. The underlying theory is simple: All games involve achieving a goal despite the presence of an obstacle, but nowhere is it written that the obstacle has to be someone else. The idea can be for each person on the field to make a specified contribution to the goal, or for all the players to reach a certain score, or for everyone to work with her partners against a time limit.

Note the significance of an "opponent" becoming a "partner." The entire dynamic of the game shifts, and one's attitude toward the other players changes with it. Even the friendliest game of tennis can't help but be affected by the game's inherent structure, which demands that each person try to hit the ball where the other can't get to it. You may not be a malicious person, but to play tennis means that you try to make the other person fail.

I've become convinced that not a single one of the advantages attributed to sports actually requires competition. Running, climbing, biking, swimming, aerobics—all offer a fine workout without any need to try to outdo someone else. Some people point to the camaraderie that results from teamwork, but that's precisely the benefit of cooperative activity, whose very essence is that *everyone* on the field is working together for a common goal. By contrast, the distinguishing feature of team competition is that a given player works with and is encouraged to feel warmly toward only half of those present. Worse, a we-versus-they dynamic is set up, which George Orwell once called "war minus the shooting."

The dependence on sports to provide a sense of accomplishment or to test one's wits is similarly misplaced. One can aim instead at an objective standard (How far did I throw? How many miles did we cover?) or attempt to do better than last week. Such individual and group striving—like cooperative games—provides satisfaction and challenge without competition.

If large numbers of people insist that we can't do without win/lose activities, the first question to ask is whether they've ever tasted the alternative. When Orlick taught a group of children noncompetitive games, two-thirds of the boys and all of the girls preferred them to the kind that require opponents.

10

If our culture's idea of fun requires beating someone else, it may just be because we don't know any other way.

It may also be because we overlook the psychological costs of competition. Most people lose in most competitive encounters, and it's obvious why that causes self-doubt. But even winning doesn't build character. It just lets us gloat temporarily. Studies have shown that feelings of self-worth become dependent on external sources of evaluation as a result of competition. Your value is defined by what you've done and who you've beaten. The whole affair soon becomes a vicious circle: The more you compete, the more you *need* to compete to feel good about yourself. It's like drinking salt water when you're thirsty. This process is bad enough for us; it's a disaster for our children.

While this is going on, competition is having an equally toxic effect on our relationships. By definition, not everyone can win a contest. That means that each child inevitably comes to regard others as obstacles to his or her own success. Competition leads children to envy winners, to dismiss losers (there's no nastier epithet in our language than "loser!"), and to be suspicious of just about everyone. Competition makes it difficult to regard others as potential friends or collaborators; even if you're not my rival today, you could be tomorrow.

This is not to say that competitors will always detest one another. But trying to outdo someone is not conducive to trust—indeed it would be irrational to trust a person who gains from your failure. At best, competition leads one to look at others through narrowed eyes; at worst, it invites outright aggression.

Changing the Structure of Sports

But no matter how many bad feelings erupt during competition, we have a marvelous talent for blaming the individuals rather than focusing on the structure of the game itself, a structure that makes my success depend on your failure. Cheating may just represent the logical conclusion of this arrangement rather than an aberration. And sportsmanship is nothing more than an artificial way to try to limit the damage of competition. If we weren't set against each other on the court or the track, we wouldn't

It's a bit excessive to rule out completely the possibility that sports do build character.

It's not clear if he has been talking about just children or everyone.

He hasn't supported this idea.

If he has support for this, he should provide it.

need to keep urging people to be good sports; they might well be working *with* each other in the first place.

As radical or surprising as it may sound, the problem isn't just that we compete the wrong way or that we push winning on our children too early. The problem is competition itself. What we need to be teaching our daughters and sons is that it's possible to have a good time—a better time—without turning the playing field into a battlefield.

15

This seems a bit extreme.

"No-Win Situations." Copyright © 1990 by Alfie Kohn. Reprinted from *Women's Sports & Fitness* with the author's permission. For more on this topic, please see www.alfiekohn.org <http://www.alfiekohn.org> or Alfie Kohn's book *No Contest: The Case Against Competition.*

Analysis

The pattern of organization in this essay is primarily a *defense of the main idea*—that competitive sports are psychologically unhealthy. But because the author knows that competitive sports are hugely popular, not only in the United States but in many other parts of the world, he must also try to *refute the opposing view*—that competition is rewarding and enjoyable. In doing so, Kohn fails to make clear distinctions between competitive sports for children, who may find it difficult to accept defeat, and for adults, who understand the consequences of any competitive game and are psychologically equipped to deal with them. Readers may therefore share Kohn's misgivings about competition for children but doubt that his criteria apply equally to adults.

The *claim,* expressed as the *thesis statement* of the essay, appears at the end of paragraph 4: "recreation at its best does not require people to try to triumph over others. Quite to the contrary." The three-paragraph introduction recounts a relevant personal experience as well as the reasons that prompted Kohn to write his essay. Because we are all interested in stories, the recital of a personal experience is a popular device for introducing almost any subject.

The rest of the essay, until the last two paragraphs, is devoted to summarizing the benefits of cooperative play and the disadvantages of competitive sport. The emphasis is overwhelmingly on the disadvantages as stated in the third paragraph: "competition undermines self-esteem, poisons relationships, and holds us back from doing our best." This is the *warrant,* the assumption that underlies the claim. In fact, here Kohn is referring to a larger study that he wrote about competition in workplaces and classrooms. We must accept this broad generalization, which applies to many human activities, before we can agree that the claim about competition in sports is valid.

Kohn relies for support on examples from common experience and on the work of Terry Orlick, a sports psychologist. The examples from experience are ones that most of us will recognize. Here we are in a position to judge for ourselves, without the mediation of an expert, whether the influence of competition in sports is as hurtful as Kohn insists. Orlick's research suggests a solution—adaptations of familiar games that will provide enjoyment but avoid competition. On the other hand, the results from studies by one psychologist whose work we aren't able to verify and the mention of "studies" in paragraph 3 without further attribution are probably not enough to answer all the arguments in favor of competition. Critics may also ask if Kohn has offered support for one of his contentions—that competition "holds us back from doing our best" (para. 3). (Support for this may appear in one of Kohn's books.)

The last two paragraphs sum up his argument that "the problem is competition itself" (para. 15)—the structure of the game rather than the people who play. Notice that the conclusion does not merely repeat the main idea. It also offers a new idea about good sportsmanship that confirms his conclusion.

The language is clear and direct. Kohn's article, which appeared in a women's sports magazine, is meant for the educated general reader, not the expert. This is also the audience for whom most student papers are written. But the written essay need not be unduly formal. Kohn uses contractions and the personal pronouns *I* and *you* to establish a conversational context. One of the particular strengths of his style is the skillful use of transitional expressions, words like *this* and *also* and clauses like *This is not to say that* and *Note the significance of* to make connections between paragraphs and new ideas.

The tone is temperate despite the author's strong feelings about the subject. Other authors, supporting the same argument, have used language that borders on the abusive about coaches and trainers of children's games. But a less inflammatory voice is far more effective with an audience that may be neutral or antagonistic.

You will find it helpful to look back over the essay to see how the examples we've cited and others work to fulfill the writer's purpose.

PRACTICE

Using the annotations on Epstein's "Sex and the Cinema" and Kohn's "No-Win Situations" as models, annotate the following essay.

The Gay Option

STEPHANIE FAIRYINGTON

I came out to my mother in a letter. I was 28. "I was born this way," I wrote, following with the most shattering high note of self-loathing I can think of: "If there were a straight pill," I lamented, "I'd swallow it faster than you can say the word *gay*."

I didn't mean either of these things. I said them because I knew they would elicit pity and absolve my mother of the belief that her parenting was to blame for my same-sex attractions. It worked. Five years later, my mother continues to talk about my lesbianism as if it were a genetic defect like Down syndrome—a parallel she's actually drawn—because clearly, in her mind, no one would choose such a detestable and challenging state of being.

This is not a message I'm proud to have sent. Contrary to how I actually feel about my sexuality, it suggests that I'm drowning in a sea of self-disgust, desperately grasping for a heterosexual lifeboat to sail my way out of it. But would my mother have been as sympathetic and tolerant if she thought I had a choice in the matter? Would conservative allies support us if they believed we could help it?

If the answer is no, and I believe it is, what does it say about our self-worth and status in society if we, as gay people, must practice a politics of pity to secure our place in the world? It says, for one, that we don't have a place at the table. It says that we are tolerated, but not accepted. It says, ultimately, that it's time to change our rhetoric.

Until homosexuality is cast and understood as a valid choice, rather than a biological affliction, we will never rise above our current status. We will remain Mother Nature's mistake, tolerable (to some) because our condition is her fault, not ours.

By choice, I don't mean that one can choose one's sexual propensities any more than one can choose one's personality. What I mean is that it's a choice to act on every desire we have, and that acting on our same-sex attractions is just as valid as pursuing a passion for the Christian faith or Judaism or any other spiritual, intellectual, emotional, or physical craving that does not infringe on the rights of others. And it should be respected as such.

As a firm Kinsey 6—with 6 being the gayest ranking on sexologist Alfred Kinsey's 1-to-6 scale of sexual orientation—I understand the resistance to putting *choice* and *homosexuality* in the same sentence. My same-sex attractions were awakened in me at such a young age that they felt as much a part of me as my limbs. In the late 1990s, when I was coming out, had someone told me that I had

5

Stephanie Fairyington is a research editor for Hachette Filipacchi Media US and a freelance journalist who writes about gender issues. A version of this article appeared in the Winter 2010 issue of *Dissent* as "Choice as Strategy: Homosexuality and the Politics of Pity"; the excerpt here appeared in the *Utne Reader*, May–June 2010.

chosen my deepest, most tender and passionate affections, it would have been like telling me that I had chosen the arms and legs I have.

But I have plenty of desires, like throwing my fists in the faces of conservative Republicans, which for one reason or another, I don't act on; my desire for women is not one of them. Biology is not destiny, and I am the architect of my own life, as is everyone. My point is not to challenge or even enter the debate about whether or not some combination of nature and nurture contributes to the formation of an inclination toward one's own sex. My point is that most inquiries into the origins of homosexuality are suspect, and their service to us is limited, if not perilous.

A politics of *choice* would be one that regards same-sex desire enough to announce it as a conscious decision rather than a predetermined abnormality. No matter how bumpy the ride or long the journey, *choice* as a political strategy is the only ride out of Freaksville.

Forty years ago, gay activists had a similar view, taking their cues from radi-   10 cal lesbian feminists who believed that heterosexuality and homosexuality were products of culture, not nature. "In the absence of oppression and social control," writes historian John D'Emilio, gay liberationists believed that "sexuality would be polymorphous"—fluid, in other words. Back then they talked about "sexual preference," which implies choice, as opposed to "sexual orientation," which does not.

It wasn't until the 1970s that the mental health establishment and its gay allies put forth the view that homosexuality is a permanent psychological condition and debunked the notion that it was a mental illness in need of a cure. Then came the 1980s and 1990s and a slew of shoddy and inconclusive scientific research on the biological origins of gayness, reinforcing the belief that sexuality is predestined. Both psychological and medical discourses formed today's dominant paradigm, which insists that sexuality is inborn and immutable.

The LGBT activists who have helped construct this sexual framework are neither lazy nor naive in their thinking, as D'Emilio points out in his essay "Born Gay?," a crisp case against the politics of biological determinism. As a political strategy, it has helped reap enormous benefits, from antidiscrimination legislation to adoption rights in some states and civil unions in others. The reasons this model of sexuality is politically expedient and effective are threefold.

First, if sexuality is understood as predestined and therefore fixed, it poses less of a challenge to the hetero monolith than does a shifting spectrum of desire. It protects straight people, in other words, from the threat of homosexuality. Second, by presenting homosexuality as a biological fact as firm and absolute as race or sex, gay activists have formed an identity the law can recognize and can follow in the footsteps of civil rights legislation. Third, it's conceptually easier to understand sexuality as a permanent trait rather than the complex, ever-morphing mess that it often is.

But for all the success this politics has had, in the end, it's not only shortsighted but rife with limitations—and dangers. As lesbian activist Joan Nestle told me, it's not good politics to cling to the "born gay" edict because "the use of biological 'abnormalities' was used by the Nazis when they measured the nostril thickness of imprisoned Jews to prove they were an inferior race; and when colonizers measured the brains of Africans to make a case for their enslavement; and when doctors at the turn of the century used the argument that the light weight of women's brains proved their inferiority to men. I do not want to enter into this sad history of biological dehumanization as the basis for gay rights."

All the studies that gay sympathizers and activists invoke to justify our right   15
to same-sex love cast homosexuality as a loud hiccup at the dinner table of normality. As such, we're put on par with other undesirable deviations from nature's norm, taunting eugenics with the keys to eliminating us. This is the ugly underbelly of our biology-centered claims to human rights.

The typical conservative assault on homosexuality casts it as a sinful choice that can be unchosen through a commitment to God and reparative therapy. And the left usually slams into this simplistic polemic by taking up the opposite stance: Homosexuality is not a choice, and because we can't help it, it's not sinful.

By affirming that homosexual practice and identity *are* a choice, we can attach an addendum—it's a good choice—and open the possibility of a more nuanced argument, one that dismantles the logic of the very premise that whom we choose to love marks us as sinful and immoral and interrogates the assumption that heterosexuality is somehow better for the individual and society as a whole.

In my conservative Republican family, signs already point to a kind of readiness to engage homosexuality as a legitimate decision. Recently, I called my mother in California to throw out my "born-gay-pity-me" garbage. She didn't swallow my pill of choice with ease, but managed to cough up an exasperated, "Well, whatever makes you happy." That's one down and a nation to go.

Critical Listening

Of course, not all public arguments are written. Today the art of listening has become an indispensable tool for learning about the world we live in. We watch the news on television and occasionally hear it on the radio. We may be more likely to learn the latest via a video clip on our computer or BlackBerry than to read it in a newspaper.

Most relevant to the kinds of written arguments you will read and write about in this course are television and radio shows that examine social and political problems. The most intelligent and responsible programs usually consist of a panel of experts—politicians, journalists, scholars—led by a neutral moderator (or one who at least allows guests to express their views). Some of these programs are decades old; others are more recent—*Meet the Press, Face the Nation, Hardball with Chris Matthews, The McLaughlin Group, PBS NewsHour*. An outstanding radio show, *Talk of the Nation* on National Public Radio, invites listeners, who are generally informed and articulate, to call in and ask questions of, or comment on remarks made by, experts on the topic of the day.

Several enormously popular radio talk shows are hosted by people with strong, sometimes extreme ideological positions. They may use offensive language and insult their listeners in a crude form of theater. Among the most influential shows are those of Don Imus and Howard Stern. In addition, elections and political crises bring speeches and debates on radio and television by representatives of a variety of views. Some are long and formal, written texts that are simply read aloud, but others are short and impromptu.

Whatever the merits or shortcomings of individual programs, significant general differences exist between arguments on radio and television and arguments in the print media. These differences include the degree of organization and development and the risk of personal attacks.

First (excluding for the moment the long, prepared speeches), contributions to a panel discussion must be delivered in fragments, usually no longer than a single paragraph, weakened by time constraints, interruptions, overlapping speech, memory gaps, and real or feigned displays of derision, impatience, and disbelief by critical panelists. Even on the best programs, the result is a lack of both coherence—or connections between ideas—and solid evidence that requires development. Too often we are treated to conclusions with little indication of how they were arrived at.

The following brief passage appeared in a newspaper review of "Resolved: The flat tax is better than the income tax," a debate on *Firing Line* by an impressive array of experts. It illustrates some of the difficulties that accompany programs attempting to capture the truth of a complicated issue on television or radio.

> "It is absolutely true," says a proponent. "It is factually untrue," counters an opponent. "It's factually correct," responds a proponent. "I did my math right," says a proponent. "You didn't do your math right," says an opponent. At one point in a discussion of interest income, one of the experts says, "Oh, excuse me, I think I got it backward."

No wonder the television critic called the exchange "disjointed and at times perplexing."[2] And these are polished productions compared to the vast majority of the millions of *YouTube* videos available online.

In the sensational talk shows the participants rely on personal experience and vivid anecdotes, which may not be sufficiently typical to prove anything.

Second, listeners and viewers of all spoken arguments are in danger of evaluating them according to criteria that are largely absent from evaluation of written texts. It is true that writers may adopt a persona or a literary disguise, which the tone of the essay will reflect. But many readers will not be able to identify it or recognize their own response to it. Listeners and viewers, however, can hardly avoid being affected by characteristics that are clearly definable: a speaker's voice, delivery, bodily mannerisms, dress, and physical appearance. In addition, listeners may be adversely influenced by clumsy speech containing more slang, colloquialisms, and grammar and usage errors than written texts that have had the benefit of revision.

[2]Walter Goodman, "The Joys of the Flat Tax, Excluding the Equations," *New York Times*, December 21, 1995, sec. C, p. 14.

But if listeners allow consideration of physical attributes to influence their judgment of what the speaker is trying to prove, they are guilty of an ad hominem fallacy—that is, an evaluation of the speaker rather than the argument. This is true whether the evaluation is favorable or unfavorable. (See p. 311 for a discussion of this fallacy.)

Talk shows may indeed be disjointed and perplexing, but millions of us find them both instructive and entertaining. Over time we are exposed to an astonishing variety of opinions from every corner of American life, and we also acquire information from experts who might not otherwise be available to us. Then there is the appeal of hearing the voices, seeing the faces of people engaged in earnest, sometimes passionate, discourse—a short, unrehearsed drama in which we also play a part as active listeners in a far-flung audience.

Strategies for Critical Listening

Listening is hearing with attention, a natural and immensely important human activity, which, unfortunately, many people don't do very well. The good news is that listening is a skill that can be learned and, unlike some other skills, practiced every day without big investments of money and effort.

Here are some of the characteristics of critical listening most appropriate to understanding and responding to arguments.

1. Above all, listening to arguments requires concentration. If you are distracted, you cannot go back as you do with the written word to clarify a point or recover a connection. Devices such as flow sheets and outlines can be useful aids to concentration. In following a debate, for example, judges and other listeners often use flow sheets — distant cousins of baseball scorecards — to record the major points on each side and their rebuttals. For roundtable discussions or debates you can make your own simple flow chart to fill out as you listen, with columns for claims, different kinds of support, and warrants. Leave spaces in the margin for your questions and comments about the soundness of the proof. An outline is more useful for longer presentations, such as lectures. As you listen, try to avoid being distracted by facts alone. Look for the overall pattern of the speech.

2. Listeners often concentrate on the wrong things in the spoken argument. We have already noted the distractions of appearance and delivery. Research shows that listeners are likely to give greater attention to the dramatic elements of speeches than to the logical ones. But you can enjoy the sound, the appearance, and the drama of a spoken argument without allowing these elements to overwhelm what is essential to the development of a claim.

3. Good listeners try not to allow their prejudices to prevent careful evaluation of the argument. This doesn't mean accepting everything or even most of what you hear. It means trying to avoid premature judgments about what is actually said. This precaution is especially relevant when the speakers and their views are well known and the listener has already formed an opinion about them, favorable or unfavorable.

Reading a Visual Argument

> Man has been communicating by pictures longer than he has been using
> words. With the development of photography in this century we are using
> pictures as a means of communication to such an extent that in some
> areas they overshadow verbal language.[3]

Paul Wendt wrote these words long before the digital age. Now we can snap
pictures with our cell phones and send them to the other side of the world.
Most elementary school children know how to use *Google* or another search
engine to find pictures of almost anything imaginable, and by middle school
they know how to go to *YouTube* to see thousands of amateur videos or to submit their own.

Wendt was writing, however, about the persuasive power of pictures, or
pictures as argument. The nation saw the power of the visual in the 2008 presidential campaign when questions for the candidates came for the first time in
the form of video clips submitted via *YouTube*—and campaigns may never be
the same. Questions were not merely read by a moderator or asked by a panel
of journalists. They didn't come in the form of disembodied voices over a telephone line. They came from real people who were visible on the screen to the
candidates and to the whole country. Two women looked straight into the camera and asked the candidates if they would let them get married to each other.
A snowman asked about global warming and what it would mean to his son's
future. A young man asked what they could do to protect his "baby" and held
up an assault rifle. The visual images did not replace the verbal language, but
complemented it. They were an integral part of the argument.

You've probably seen similarly powerful still images in photographic journalism: soldiers in battle, destruction by weather disasters, beautiful natural
landscapes, inhumane living conditions, the great mushroom cloud of early
atomic explosions. These photographs and thousands of others encapsulate arguments of fact, value, and policy. We often don't need to read their captions to
understand what they tell us: *The tornado devastated the town. The Grand Canyon
is our most stupendous national monument. We must not allow human beings to live
like this.*

An exception would be a pair of pictures that gained wide circulation in the
aftermath of Hurricane Katrina in 2005. They seemed innocuous enough when
seen without commentary, except to show the extent of the flooding. One shows
a young black man wading through the chest-deep floodwaters carrying a black
garbage bag. Another shows a young white man also wading through chest-
deep water, wearing a backpack and accompanied by a young white woman
wearing a backpack and dragging a bag. The text accompanying the pictures,

---

[3]Paul Wendt, "The Language of Pictures," in S. I. Hayakawa, ed., *The Use and Misuse of Language* (Greenwich, CT: Fawcett, 1962), p. 175.

"Looting" and "finding"

however, shows the bias of those who described the pictures. Next to the picture of the black youth are these words: "A young man walks through chest deep water after looting a grocery store in New Orleans on Tuesday, August 30, 2005." Notice the difference in the words accompanying the other picture: "Two residents wade through chest deep flood water after finding bread and soda from a local grocery store after Hurricane Katrina came through the area in New Orleans, Louisiana." The wording produced such a response that *Yahoo!* offered this statement:

> News photos are an especially popular section of Yahoo! News. In part, this is because we present thousands of news photos from some of the leading news services, including The Associated Press, Reuters, and Agence France Press. To make this volume of photos available in a timely manner, we present the photos and their captions as written, edited and distributed by the news services with no additional editing at Yahoo! News.
>
> In recent days, a number of readers of Yahoo! News have commented on differences in the language in two Hurricane Katrina-related photo captions (from two news services). Since the controversy began, the supplier of one of the photos has asked all its clients to remove the photo from their databases. Yahoo! News has complied with the AFP request. . . . Yahoo! News regrets that these photos and captions, viewed together, may have suggested a racial bias on our part. We remain committed to bringing our readers the full collection of photos as transmitted by our wire service partners.[4]

Other images provided additional glimpses into the aftermath of Katrina. The photograph of Milvertha Hendricks was striking enough that David Dante Troutt, Charles Ogletree, and Derrick Bell used a color version of it for the cover photo of their book, *After the Storm: Black Intellectuals Explore the Meaning of Hurricane Katrina* (2007).

PRACTICE

1. Look closely at the photograph of a flag-draped woman taken following Hurricane Katrina (Fig. 1). Who is pictured? What sort of expression does she have on her face? Then consider why the elderly woman might have a blanket that looks like an American flag draped over her. What do you know about the rescue of Katrina victims that might be relevant to how you "read" the picture as an argument? Under the circumstances, how might the flag blanket be seen as symbolic? What claim might you infer from the picture?

2. Now compare the picture to the next photo, "At the Time of the Louisville Flood," taken in 1937 by Margaret Bourke-White (Fig. 2). Do you see any similarity in the message being conveyed by each? Explain.

3. Finally, look at the third picture (Fig. 3) and decide if you feel it conveys a similar or a very different message.

---

[4]The Yahoo! News statement can be found at http://news.yahoo.com/page/photostatement.

Figure 1   Eric Gay, "Milvertha Hendricks, 84, waiting in the rain outside the New Orleans Convention Center on September 1, 2005"

Figure 2   Margaret Bourke-White, "At the Time of the Louisville Flood" (1937)

Figure 3   Bruce Chambers, "Edgar Hollingsworth rescued from his home after Hurricane Katrina" (2005)

Edgar Hollingsworth, the seventy-four-year-old man shown being rescued in the third picture, snapped by Bruce Chambers of the *Orange County Register*, survived the hurricane but was found near death in his home fourteen days after the storm. He died four days later in the hospital.

The reactions this third picture has elicited provide an excellent illustration of varied responses to the same visual image. Not every viewer will "read" a picture in the same way. Not every viewer will see it as support for the same argument. These are some of the responses that the picture of Hollingsworth's rescue has produced:

- A typical headline accompanying the photo called the discovery of Hollingsworth a "miracle rescue." According to a report from Post-Gazette.com, "The rescue was a bright spot on a day in which the owners of a nursing home were charged in the deaths of dozens of patients killed by hurricane floodwaters, the death toll in Louisiana jumped to 423 and the New Orleans mayor warned that the city is broke."[5] And according to Keith Sharon of the *Orange County Register*, "The rescue pumped up the spirits of [California] Task Force 5, which has been mostly marking the locations of dead bodies for the last week."[6]

- *USA Today* termed the photo "iconic."[7] Marcia Prouse, director of photography at the *Orange County Register*, had a similar view: "This man's story needs to be told. He's an important symbol of the hurricane. . . . It's anybody's father or grandfather."[8]

- Chambers's picture (p. 66) has become known through the Internet as the *Katrina Pietá*. The *Pietá* alluded to is Michelangelo's famous sculpture of Mary holding the body of Christ after his crucifixion. The way that the National Guardsman is holding Hollingsworth is reminiscent of Mary's pose, and the link to the loving mother of Jesus leads to a positive interpretation of the scene.

- For some, the sight of two white aid workers and one Hispanic one aiding a black man provides a sharp contrast to other images that stress the racial tension that grew out of Katrina's aftermath.

- Others were enraged by rules that could have kept the rescue team from entering Hollingsworth's home to rescue him. Keith Sharon wrote, "In the past few days, the Federal Emergency Management Agency has ordered searchers not to break into homes. They are supposed to look in through a window and knock on the door. If no one cries out for help, they are supposed to move on. If they see a body,

[5]See http://www.post-gazette.com/pg/05257/570999.stm.
[6]See http://www.ocregister.com/blog/rescue/.
[7]See http://www.usatoday.com/news/nation/2005-11-10-hollingsworth-katrina_x.htm.
[8]See http://www.editorandpublisher.com/eandp/news/article_display.jsp?vnu_content_id= 1001137369.

they are supposed to log the address and move on." The rescue team went against orders in breaking down the door to reach Hollingsworth. Sharon added that earlier "they had been frustrated when FEMA delayed their deployment for four days, housing them in the Hyatt Regency in Dallas."[9] The Sharon quotes are referenced on DailyKOS.com, under the title "American Shame: The Edgar Hollingsworth Story."[10]

Just as readers bring to an argument their biases and their own personal store of experiences, so do viewers bring the same to a visual argument.

Photographs, of course, function everywhere as instruments of persuasion. Animal-rights groups show pictures of brutally mistreated dogs and cats; children's rights advocates publish pictures of sick and starving children in desolate refugee camps. On a very different scale, alluring photographs from advertisers—travel agencies, restaurants, sporting goods manufacturers, clothiers, jewelers, movie studios—promise to fulfill our dreams of pleasure.

But photographs are not the only visual images we respond to. We are also susceptible to other kinds of illustrations and to signs and symbols which over the years have acquired connotations, or suggestive significance. The flag or bald eagle, the shamrock, the crown, the cross, the hammer and sickle, and the swastika can all rouse strong feelings for or against the ideas they represent. These symbols may be defined as abbreviated claims of value. They summarize the moral, religious, and political principles by which groups of people live and often die. In commercial advertisements we recognize symbols that aren't likely to enlist our deepest loyalties but, nevertheless, have impact on our daily lives: the apple with a bite in it, the golden arches, the Prudential rock, the Nike swoosh, and a thousand others.

In fact, a closer look at commercial and political advertising, which is heavily dependent on visual argument and is something we are all familiar with, provides a useful introduction to this complex subject. We know that advertisements, with or without pictures, are short arguments, often lacking fully developed support, whose claims of policy urge us to take an action: Buy this product or service; vote for this candidate or issue. The claim may not be directly expressed, but it will be clearly implicit. In print, on television, or on the Internet, the visual representation of objects, carefully chosen to appeal to a particular audience, can be as important as, if not more important than, any verbal text.

In a political advertisement we often see a picture of the candidate surrounded by a smiling family. The visual image is by now a cliché, suggesting traditional values—love and security, the importance of home and children. Even if we know little or nothing about his or her platform, we are expected to make a sympathetic connection with the candidate.

---

[9]Keith Sharon, "Survivor Rescued 16 Days after the Hurricane," *Orange County Register*, September 14, 2005.
[10]See www.dailykos.com/story/2005/9/14/12516/3649.

In a commercial advertisement the image may be a picture of a real or fictitious person to whom we will react favorably. Consider the picture on a jar of spaghetti sauce. As a famous designer remarked, "When you think about it, sauce is mostly sauce. It's the label that makes the difference."[11]And what, according to the designer, does the cheerful face of Paul Newman on jars of his spaghetti sauce suggest to the prospective buyer? "Paul Newman. Paul Newman. Paul Newman. Blue eyes. All the money goes to charity. It's humanitarian, funny, and sexy. Selling this is like falling off a log." Not a word about the quality of the sauce.

Even colleges, which are also selling a product, must think of appropriate images to attract their prospective customers—students. Today the fact that more women than men are enrolled in college has caused some schools to rethink their images. One college official explained:

> We're having our recruiting literature redesigned, and we've been thinking about what's a feminine look and what's a masculine look. We have a picture of a library with a lot of stained glass, and people said that was kind of a feminine cover. Now we're using a picture of the quadrangle.[12]

In addition to the emblem itself, the designer pays careful attention to a number of other elements in the ad: colors, light and shadow, foreground and background, relative sizes of pictures and text, and placement of objects on the page or screen. Each of these contributes to the total effect, although we may be unaware of how the effect has been achieved. (In the ad that follows, you will be able to examine some of the psychological and aesthetic devices at work.)

When there is no verbal text, visual images are less subject to analysis and interpretation. For one thing, if we are familiar with the objects in the picture, we see the whole image at once, and it registers immediately. The verbal message is linear and takes far longer to be absorbed. Pictures, therefore, appear to need less translation. Advertisers and other arguers depend on this characteristic to provide quick and friendly acceptance of their claims, although the image may, in fact, be deceptive.

This expectation of easy understanding poses a danger with another visual ally of the arguer—the graph or chart. Graphics give us factual information at a glance. In addition to the relative ease with which they can be read, they are "at their best . . . instruments for reasoning about quantitative information. . . . Of all methods for analyzing and communicating statistical information, well-designed data graphics are usually the simplest and at the same time the most powerful."[13]

---

[11]Tibor Kalman, "Message: Sweet-Talking Spaghetti Sauce," *New York Times Magazine*, December 13, 1998, p. 81.

[12]*New York Times*, December 6, 1998, p. 38.

[13]Edward R. Tufte, *The Visual Display of Quantitative Information* (Cheshire, CT: Graphics Press, 1983), introduction.

Nevertheless, they may mislead the quick reader. Graphics can lie. "The lies are told about the major issues of public policy—the government budget, medical care, prices, and fuel economy standards, for example. The lies are systematic and quite predictable, nearly always exaggerating the rate of recent change."[14]

Visual images, then, for all their apparent immediacy and directness, need to be read with at least the same attention we give to the verbal message if we are to understand the arguments they represent.

Consider these questions as you analyze images:

1. What does the arguer want me to do or believe? How important is the visual image in persuading me to comply?

2. Has the visual image been accompanied by sufficient text to answer questions I may have about the claim?

3. Are the visual elements more prominent than the text? If so, why?

4. Is the visual image representative of a large group, or is it an exception that cannot support the claim?

5. Does the arrangement of elements in the message tell me what the arguer considers most important? If so, what is the significance of this choice?

6. Can the validity of this chart or graph be verified?

7. Does the visual image lead me to entertain unrealistic expectations? (Can using this shampoo make hair look like that shining cascade on the television screen? Does the picture of the candidate for governor, shown answering questions in a classroom of eager, smiling youngsters, mean that he has a viable plan for educational reform?)

Sample Analysis of an Advertisement

We have pointed out that a commercial advertisement is a short argument that makes an obvious policy claim, which may or may not be explicit: *You should buy this product.* Depending on the medium—television, print, radio, or Internet—an ad may convey its message through language, picture, or sound.

Here is how one analyst of advertising sums up the goals of the advertiser: (1) attract attention, (2) arouse interest, (3) stimulate desire, (4) create conviction, and (5) get action.[15] Needless to say, not every ad successfully fulfills all these objectives. If you examine the ad reproduced on page 71, you can see how the advertiser brings language and visual image together in an attempt to support the claim.

[14]Tufte, *The Visual Display*, p. 76.
[15]J. V. Lund, *Newspaper Advertising* (New York: Prentice-Hall, 1947), p. 83.

The image in the ad appeals to our common knowledge as Americans. We have probably all heard the story of how George Washington, as a boy, chopped down a cherry tree. The clothes that the young boy in the ad is wearing—particularly the tricorner hat—along with the architecture, suggest a colonial setting. The hatchet hidden behind the boy's back combined with the exclamation

"Oops!" calls to mind the specific story about Washington. Upon hearing the story, you may have envisioned a much smaller tree and less substantial damage, but it is critical to the ad's effect that in this rendering of the story of our first president's youth, the tree has fallen on someone's house, possibly the Washingtons'. The ad appears to have been reproduced on parchment, another detail that helps to place the incident historically, and each corner is subtly decorated with a cherry.

What has made the cherry tree story a classic for teaching morals is what the young Washington is said to have done after he chopped down the tree. All of us are familiar with the words "I can not tell a lie," Washington's response when questioned about what he had done. It was a fitting reply for a man who would later be chosen to lead the new nation. The largest text on the page—and the text most likely therefore to catch the attention of a reader casually flipping through *Newsweek*—is a play on this famous quote that changes *I* to *we*. The identification with Washington and his famous words is particularly critical for a company whose name may not be a household word. The designers of the ad, having captured the attention of the reader with the image and the quote, go on in the smaller text to build on the foundation they have established.

Like most ads, this one is a claim of policy asking the audience to buy a product. In this case the product is Encompass Insurance. One of the frustrations of dealing with an insurance company is that not every possible type of loss is covered by the standard policy. Unfortunately, the homeowner often does not find this out until the damage has already been done. The ad is designed to sell the company's *Elite* policy, which "covers many of life's unexpected perils," unlike most insurance companies, which "only cover things that are specifically listed in your policy." The text continues, "It covers pretty much everything that befalls your household, even if something like 'damage caused by child chopping down cherry tree' isn't specifically listed." Two examples of the sorts of damage that the company might cover are Worker's Compensation for an employee in your household and the recovery of lost computer data.

The support for the claim is not specific. The writer carefully avoided absolute statements, using instead such qualifiers as *many, pretty much*, and *most everything*. The last two are colloquial expressions that are designed to suggest that those who work for Encompass are simple folks with whom the average reader could identify. And if you want any more specifics about what the policy actually says—after all, the legal document that is an insurance policy can hardly use such qualifiers—you can call toll-free or visit the company's Web site.

The underlying warrant is that it is better to buy an insurance policy that covers you against damages that are not specifically listed on the policy than one that does not. A person in the market for insurance would certainly want to read the fine print and know the cost of the insurance compared to that offered by other companies before accepting the warrant and thus the claim.

The colloquial language and even the name of the policy—The Encompass Universal Security Policy—Elite—are designed to appeal to the reader's need to feel secure. The word choice also adds a subtle humor, from the cartoonlike "Oops!" to the final echo of the Pledge of Allegiance: "Liberty, Justice, and Really Good Insurance."

Assignments for Critical Reading

READING AND DISCUSSION QUESTIONS

1. Listen to a recording of Martin Luther King Jr.'s "I Have a Dream" and discuss how the language of the speech adds power to the ideas.

2. Watch (and *listen to*) one of the afternoon television talk shows in which guests discuss a controversial social problem. (The *TV Guide*, daily newspapers, and online listings often list the subject. Past topics include when parents abduct their children, when children kill children, and when surgery changes patients' lives.) Analyze the discussion, considering the major claims, the most important evidence, and the declared or hidden warrants. How much did the oral format contribute to success or failure of the arguments?

3. Watch one episode of either the *Daily Show with Jon Stewart* or the *Colbert Report* and discuss how the show, successfully or not, tries to use humor to make serious points about political and/or social issues.

4. Steven Johnson, author of *The Ghost Map* (2006), writes, "It has become a cliché to say that we now live in a society where image is valued over substance, where our desires are continually stoked by the illusory fuel of marketing messages." Do you believe that we live in the society Johnson describes? Explain.

5. Locate an advertisement that you find visually and verbally interesting. Using as a model the analysis of the ad for Encompass Insurance (p. 71), what sorts of observations can you make about your ad? Exchange ads with a classmate and discuss whether the two of you respond in the same way to each ad.

6. Find two articles on opposing sides of a controversial issue such as abortion, gay marriage, or off-shore drilling. Determine what common ground the two authors share. Then share paired articles with classmates and discuss other examples of common ground.

WRITING SUGGESTIONS

7. Write an essay analyzing "Sex and the Cinema" (p. 43). You may choose to support an evaluative claim that analyzes how effective the essay is or one that objectively analyzes how the essay is written.

8. Write an essay evaluating "The Gay Option" (p. 57).

9. Do you agree with Alfie Kohn in "No-Win Situations" (p. 51) that games and sports should not be so competitive? Write an essay explaining why or why not.

10. Choose an editorial from your school newspaper or a local newspaper and write an evaluation of it.

11. Watch one of the television talk shows that features experts on social and political issues, such as the *The O'Reilly Factor, Hannity and Colmes,* or *The McLaughlin Group.* Write a review, telling how much you learned about the subject(s) of discussion. Be specific about the features of the show that were either helpful or not helpful to your understanding.

12. Choose an advertisement, taking into consideration both the visual and the verbal. Turn your observation into the thesis of an essay explaining the ad's argument.

13. Find a picture that you believe makes a political statement and write an analysis, making clear what you believe that statement is.

14. Find two pictures that present either complementary or conflicting arguments. Write an essay explaining the arguments.

15. Write an essay explaining what visual images represent your school and why.

Research Readiness: Skimming and Summarizing

What if you find good sources of information about your research subject, but there is just too much to read and take notes on?

One possibility, of course, is that your subject is too broad, something that you may need to discuss with your instructor. Even if your topic is appropriate for the length of paper you have been assigned, you may find texts that are too long to read in their entirety, and you may want to skim them to find material relevant to your topic. That is a legitimate research technique as long as you do not distort ideas by taking them out of context.

If you are not careful, you can spend too much time taking notes that you will not use. Unless the wording of an idea is particularly striking or significant, you can often summarize an author's ideas while taking notes. It should be very clear in your notes which information is in the author's exact words and which is paraphrase or summary.

In this chapter you have practiced summarizing. Now practice skimming to find relevant information by doing one or more of the following. Do not use any direct quotations (a skill you will learn more about in the next chapter).

ASSIGNMENT

1. Read Barbara Spellman's "Could Reality Shows Become Reality Experiments?" (p. 114). Write a paragraph explaining why Spellman suggests that some reality television shows would be considered unethical if they were run as experiments in psychology.

2. Write a paragraph summarizing Newman P. Birk and Genevieve B. Birk's thoughts in "Selection, Slanting, and Charged Language" (p. 347) about the variety of ways that language is selected and slanted and why word choice is so important.

3. Write a paragraph based on Jacob Neusner's "The Speech The Graduates Didn't Hear" (p. 374) that explains Neusner's position on how well — or poorly — college prepares students for the outside world.

4. Explain in a paragraph or two what Martin Luther King Jr. meant in his speech, "I Have A Dream" (p. 492).

CHAPTER 3

Analytical Writing

Anytime the press cover a major speech, whether by the president, the chairman of the Federal Reserve, or the accused party in the most recent sex scandal, their next step is an analysis of every detail of the speaker's words and manner. People not only like to listen to arguments but they also like to argue about them. Political pundit Bill O'Reilly even has an analyst come in regularly to critique the body language of political and media headliners.

An understanding of the elements of argument provides you not only with the ability to write your own arguments but also with the vocabulary to write about those of others. When you write an essay about an argument that you have read, listened to, or seen, you have two major options. You may choose to make a factual, nonjudgmental statement about the argument, or you may choose to evaluate it.

Writing the Claim

If you examined the most recent McDonald's commercial and wrote an essay explaining what tactics were used to try to persuade consumers to eat at McDonald's or to try McDonald's newest sandwich, you would be supporting a *factual claim*, or a claim of fact. On the other hand, if you evaluated the ad's effectiveness in attracting adult consumers, you would be supporting an *evaluative claim*, or a claim of value. It's the difference between *explaining* Geico's use of a talking gecko in its ads and *praising* that marketing decision. What this means, of course, is that what you write about a commercial or any other type of argument that you see or read will itself have a claim of fact or a claim of value as its thesis.

What about a *claim of policy*, the third type of claim introduced in Chapter 1? In analyzing an argument, it would be rare to have a thesis that expressed what should or should not be done. Claims of policy are future oriented. They do not look back and express what should have been done in the past, but instead look forward to what should be done in the future. You might write an essay about what McDonald's should do in its future ads, but you would not really be writing an analysis.

Think how claims of fact and claims of value might serve as thesis statements for essays *about* written arguments. Charles Adams's essay "Lincoln's Logic" is a criticism of Abraham Lincoln's Gettysburg Address and thus supports a claim of value:

> Lincoln's address did not fit the world of his day. It reflected his logic, which was based on a number of errors and falsehoods.

An objective analysis of the speech, based on a claim of fact, might explain the oration in the context of its time or Lincoln's use of poetic language.

Consider how your thesis would look different if you were making a *statement* about a document instead of making a *judgment*:

Claims of Fact: The Declaration of Independence bases its claim on two kinds of support: factual evidence and appeals to the values of its audience.

As a logical pattern of argument, the Declaration of Independence is largely deductive.

Claims of Value: Jefferson's clear, elegant, formal prose remains a masterpiece of English prose and persuades us that we are reading an important document.

The document's impact is lessened for modern readers because several significant terms are not defined.

What type of thesis does Roger Kaplan support in the following analysis?

Enabling Ignorance

ROGER KAPLAN

Barack Obama's version of the "No Child Left Behind Act" (NCLB) easily made it through Congress this year. Originally passed at the instigation of George W. Bush in 2002, NCLB shows what happens when "expertise" and political huckstering replace common sense and experience. Fortunately, Diane Ravitch has

---

Roger Kaplan was a high school English teacher in New York City and is now a writer in Washington, D.C. He is a contributor to the *American Spectator*, where this article appeared in September 2010.

published a new book showing why the ideas driving NCLB promote the weak-nesses in American public schools without doing anything for their strengths. *The Death and Life of the Great American School System* stands as a cautionary tale on the delusion that something as complex as education can be reformed with quick fixes and federal dollars.

The declining quality of instruction in American public schools became a pe-rennial political issue in 1983 when the Reagan administration issued its "Nation at Risk" report, which called attention to the declining standards and the steady erosion of meaningful, content-rich curricula in many if not most districts.

Ravitch, a Columbia PhD who had earned widespread admiration as a criti-cal historian of American public education, became a prolific leader of the reform movement. She insisted that without attention to the substance of what is taught in schools — the curriculum — change under any name is mere cosmetics.

Ravitch shows that, just when it thought it had reached its goals with the pas-sage of NCLB, the reform movement was subverted by the throw-money-at-it artists in the political and policy-making classes, encouraged by all manner of snake-oil salesmen who saw the get-rich opportunities of school reform (and, for the pinheads, of writing about reform without understanding the public schools' complex social conditions). Instead of restoring guts to education, NCLB, in effect, gutted instruction. At the center of the racket: "testing."

Tests have inherent pedagogical functions beyond their usefulness in assess-ing students' learning. But in the NCLB scheme, testing became the link to every-thing — most ruinously, federal money. Districts and schools raised test scores or lost money and eventually were shut down. By corollary, principals and teachers got merit pay, or pending that, strongly favorable evaluations, according to their kids' test performance. Never had corruption been introduced so brazenly into American schools.

Since the easiest actors to blame for failure in this shoddy program were the teachers, they and their unions were turned into the culprits of America's edu-cational shortcomings. Neither the administrators, who usually knew nothing about anything; nor the politicians, like New York City's Mayor Bloomberg, who were thinking only in terms of administrative efficiency; nor the chancellors, like New York's Joel Klein or Washington, D.C.'s Michelle Rhee, who were think-ing only in terms of meaningless test numbers: none could conceive of anything more intelligent than to tell teachers they were not doing their jobs properly. This resonated with one of the stupider slogans of the NCLB era, which was that "the kids" deserved "excellent teachers." What were they supposed to have — mediocre teachers?

On the other hand, NCLB diminished accountability at the leadership level. While embroiled in disputes with the teachers' union on how to introduce merit pay — a dubious idea — into the school system, it became evident that Ms. Rhee either did not understand or chose to fudge her own budget numbers, and this in a relatively small school system (by big-city standards). Nor has anyone in the D.C. school system ever explained how one of the two or three richest districts in the country, if you count the amount of money nominally available per pupil, is one of the most run-down and under-achieving.

5

"Not my job" is the usual response of employees of the education industry, most of whom are not teachers, when confronted with their own failure. Teachers, who tend to be sweet souls even if prone to *kvetching*, are not finger-pointers by nature, and they take responsibility for what goes on in their classrooms. But what they often tell you is that they are required (by stuffed shirts who are never in classrooms) to concentrate on teaching kids "how to learn."

You cannot, however, teach kids "how to learn" if you do not give them *learning* — facts, substance: what the education writer E. D. Hirsch Jr. calls a content-rich curriculum. History, complete with dates, events, and heroes; math, complete with formulae, equations, and systems of computation; foreign languages, complete with vocabulary drills and verb declensions; music, complete with scales and sheet music; physical education, complete with fitness drills and sports rules — all this has been replaced by "learning to learn" and math-problem and reading-comprehension "strategies." And Hirsch, whose devastating critiques of these trends are supported not only by common sense but by hard science (and by visible results), is viewed as a marginal crank by an education establishment that blocks any real reform by invoking "kids first" slogans the same way the Communists used to invoke the "working class."

Teachers know content must come first, but are advised to stop wasting time   10
transmitting knowledge when they should be showing kids how to think for themselves and ace a test. When a teacher observes that you cannot think for yourself if you have nothing to think about, the principal, superintendent, school counselor, or Department of Education specialist responds that this represents an example of "teacher-centered" learning, sort of like being called a Trotskyist in Stalin's Moscow,[1] and insists students working in small groups can educate themselves.

Undermining teachers' authority in the classroom erodes the democratic and egalitarian premises of public education, since it undercuts the opportunity schools are supposed to provide.

Arguably Ravitch should have explored this theme more deeply, by examining the specific flaw that renders the educational establishment incapable of defending the public service role of public schools. The establishment includes the teachers' unions, whose disputes with district leaderships all too often look like shadow boxing. That unions invariably support liberal Democratic candidates at every election strengthens the sense that they are committed to a status quo amounting to a kind of plantation system for poor and disadvantaged children. Nobody can object to a labor union trying to get better pay and benefits for its members, just as no one should object to criticizing a union for undermining its own industry's economic viability or public credibility.

Of course, one should never ask an author to write the book she did not set out to write, but *The Death and Life of the Great American School System* leaves the

---

[1]Leon Trotsky (1879–1940) was a leader of the Russian Revolution of 1917. He opposed the rise of Joseph Stalin (1879–1953), longtime dictator of the Soviet Union, whose brutal policies led to the extermination of millions of Russians. [EDS. note]

impression that the kind of teachers' union Ravitch pines after has its source in her one, untypical indulgence in historical romanticism, which in turn grows out of the author's admiration for the late Albert Shanker and his successors at the American Federation of Teachers, Sandy Feldman and Randi Weingarten. These are exceptional figures in American education and in American labor history. Too many education union leaders talk the talk of serious reform, then walk the walk of the failed and failing policies Ravitch criticizes so eloquently.

Ravitch passionately lays out the argument that public school teachers are, or should be, missionaries of social advancement and opportunity. They fulfill their role by imbuing children and adolescents with love of learning — a corny idea, maybe, but not a cynical one. They do this not by teaching them "how to learn," but by giving them real knowledge. Teachers must be counselors, pastors, coaches, and community leaders, but knowing and loving what they teach comes first.

The simplicity of this idea is deceptive. Of course, the layman thinks, a teacher   15
has to know his stuff and love it. But the reform movement, as it was hijacked in the '90s and implemented in the '00s under the guise of NCLB, does not know this. By its lights, an excellent teacher is one who raises scores on tests designed to assess not knowledge learned but "skills" in fill-the-bubble exercises that require the same level of talent as choosing lottery numbers. It is only partly whimsical to observe that state-sponsored lotteries became widespread in our nation around the same time as public schools became driven by bubble-tests rather than curricular content.

It is small consolation to observe that the cynicism and corruption introduced by NCLB's testing requirements — which include lowering the bar on tests and laundering their results — reflect a larger rot in American society. It is unfortunate the teachers' unions have not denounced this trend, but they cannot if they trade professional integrity for the American mania for "getting yours." However, pursuing this question would take us beyond the scope that Ravitch wants to cover in *The Death and Life of the Great American School System.*

One of Ravitch's most sensible and profound prescriptions is to know our own history. It comes as no surprise to see how little American history the "experts" know or care for, even as they happily go about burning billions in tax dollars to inflict further damage on our public schools.

Schools are not businesses but civic and neighborhood institutions, and pedagogy is not a how-to-succeed program, but the hard, incremental, frustrating, and exhilarating work of turning savages into civilized citizens. It is not rocket science, but it is a vocation.

The teachers represented by the UFT, the New York teachers' union, know this. So does the author of *The Death and Life of the Great American School System.*

In Kaplan's essay and in the earlier examples based on the Gettysburg Address and the Declaration of Independence, we were looking at one document at a time and thus at a single argument. At times you will want to compare two (or more) arguments, synthesizing their ideas. Again, there are two basic types of thesis that you might choose to support, those that *objectively analyze* the points of comparison or contrast between the two and those that *evaluate* the two in relationship to each other. If you wrote claims about how the two pieces compare, they might look like these:

Claims of Fact: Where Jefferson based his argument primarily on logical appeal, Lincoln depended primarily on emotional appeal.

Because Lincoln's purpose was to dedicate a cemetery, he left implicit most of his references to the political situation that was on the minds of his listeners. Because Jefferson knew he was justifying rebellion for King George III but also for the future, he spelled out explicitly why the colonies were breaking with England.

Claims of Value: Lincoln's address is a period piece that recalls a dark chapter in American history, but Jefferson's Declaration has had a much greater impact as an inspiration for other reform movements worldwide.

Different as the two historical documents are, both the Gettysburg Address and the Declaration of Independence were effective in achieving their respective purposes.

Planning the Structure

When your purpose in writing about an argument is to support a factual claim, you will most likely use a very simple and direct form of organization called *defending the main idea*. In all forms of organization, you need to defend your main idea, or claim, with support; in this case, the support will come from the argument or arguments you are writing about.

At times, your claim may set up the organization of your essay, as was the case with the first example about the Declaration of Independence:

The Declaration of Independence bases its claim on two kinds of support: factual evidence and appeals to the values of its audience.

The body of an essay with this thesis would most likely have two main divisions, one about factual evidence, providing examples, and the other about appeals to values, also providing examples. The other thesis about the Declaration of Independence does not suggest such an obvious structure. An essay based on that thesis would need to explain how the Declaration is an example of deductive reasoning, most likely by first establishing what generalization the document is based on and then what specifics Jefferson uses to prove that the colonists' situation fits that generalization.

Remember that when you compare or contrast two arguments, there will be two basic patterns to choose from for structuring the essay. One, often called *point-by-point* comparison, discusses each point about Subject A and Subject B together before moving on to the second point, where again both subjects are discussed:

I. Introduction
II. Context
    A. Jefferson
    B. Lincoln
III. Implicitness/explicitness
    A. Jefferson
    B. Lincoln
IV. Language
    A. Jefferson
    B. Lincoln
V. Conclusion

The second, often called *parallel order* comparison, focuses in roughly half the essay on Subject A and then in the other half on Subject B. The points made in each half should be parallel and should be presented in the same order:

I. Introduction
II. Jefferson
    A. Context
    B. Implicitness/explicitness of references to politics
    C. Language
III. Lincoln
    A. Context
    B. Implicitness/explicitness of references to politics
    C. Language
IV. Conclusion

Using Sentence Forms to Construct an Argument

When you present an argument that responds to an essay or that uses research, it is important to clearly explain how the previous writer approached the topic, and then explain how your view differs. There's no point in quoting or paraphrasing an author and ending with "and I agree." Indeed, academic writing means explaining current thinking on a topic and showing how it is different from what you believe. Sometimes the points of difference are large, sometimes small. But in writing for college, it is crucial that you explain your own understanding of a situation *and* that you express your own point of view.

It is easier to think about how you might summarize the argument of others and present your own if you have a model from which to work. This kind of model is called a *sentence form*, and it can help you to organize the presentation of others' views and your own responses to them. Here are some basic sentence forms for this kind of work.

PRESENTING ANOTHER'S VIEW

In _____, X claims that _____.

X's conclusion is that _____.

On the topic of _____, X attempts to make the case that
_____.

These sentence forms are useful for presenting a brief summary of another's views on an issue. Note that the final sentence form implies that the writer has failed to make a convincing argument. (You would then go on to explain X's failure.)

PRESENTING ANOTHER'S VIEW USING DIRECT QUOTATIONS

In _____, X writes, "_____."

After discussing the topic of _____, X's conclusion is that
"_____."

X attempts to make the case that "_____."

Quotations are a powerful way to present another's views when the language is particularly striking, clear, and succinct. (For more on using quotations, including a list of alternatives to the verb "writes," see the Writer's Guide: "Incorporating Quotations into Your Text" on p. 88.) These templates help you to employ a key skill in making an argument: showing the work others have done on the issue. The next step is to introduce your own voice.

PRESENTING ANOTHER'S VIEW AND RESPONDING TO IT

She claims _____. It is actually true that _____.

In his essay _____, X writes that _____.
However, _____.

In her essay, X implies _____. However, careful consideration shows that _____.

The formula for this kind of template introduces what the author has to say and then has you take your turn with your own view of the matter.

As this suggests, writing in college means taking part in an ongoing conversation. You need to be respectful of what others say and write, and you need to account for their positions accurately. You'll want to be sure to clearly summarize the author's presentation. We have more to say about summary shortly, but, briefly put, in writing arguments, you must show the author's point before you explain how your ideas differ. You'll need to be able to sum up in a neutral, fair way what the writer says. Then, when you respond, you can agree on some points, but you'll need to focus on the points of disagreement.

Where you agree with some of what a writer says, but not all of it, you must distinguish between the parts you think are correct and those parts that are not. Sentence forms for this kind of response include the following.

AGREEING IN PART

Although most of what X writes about _____ is true, it is not true that _____.

X is correct that _____. But because of _____ it is actually true that _____.

X argues that _____. While it is true that _____ and _____ are valid points, _____ is not. Instead, _____.

These sentence templates ask you to identify those parts of the argument that are valid. Keep in mind that it is rare to disagree totally with every view expressed in an essay. A careful arguer will separate out what is correct and what is not. The writer can then focus energy on showing why these parts are not correct.

At times you'll need to correct a distortion or misstatement of fact. Statistics, for instance, can be and often are manipulated to present the arguer's viewpoint in the best light. You may wish to propose an alternative interpretation or set the statistics in a different context, one more accurate and favorable to your own point of view. Of course, you'll want to be certain that you do not distort statistics. (For more on the importance of using statistics fairly, see the full discussion on pp. 212–13.) Here's a sentence form for correcting factual information in an argument.

CORRECTING A FACTUAL MISTAKE

While X claims _____, it is actually true that _____.

Although X states _____, a careful examination of _____ and _____ indicate that _____.

These templates allow you to identify a mistaken claim of fact in an argument and present evidence opposing it.

More often, rather than correcting clear mistakes of fact, you'll need to refine the argument of a writer. You may find that much of the argument makes sense to you, but that the writer does not sufficiently anticipate important objections. In those cases, a sentence form such as one of the following can help you refine the argument to make a stronger conclusion.

REFINING ANOTHER'S ARGUMENT

Although it is true, as X shows, that _____, the actual result is closer to _____ because _____.

While X claims _____ and _____, he fails to consider the important point _____. Therefore, a more accurate conclusion is _____.

Such sentence forms allow you to clarify and amplify an argument.

At times you'll need to distinguish between the views of two different writers and then weigh in with your own assessment of the situation. When two authors write on the same topic, they will most likely share similar views on some of the points. They will, however, disagree on other points. Similarly, you may find that you agree with some of what each writer has to say, but disagree with some other parts. Your job is to identify the points of contrast between the two authors and then explain how your own position differs from one or both. In those cases, you may find the following sentence forms helpful.

EXPLAINING CONTRASTING VIEWS AND ADDING YOUR POSITION

X says _____. Y says _____. However, _____.

On the topic of _____, X claims that _____.
In contrast, Y argues that _____. However, _____.

A careful writer makes sure the reader understands fine distinctions. The forms above help make those distinctions clear.

While sentence forms may be rather simple — perhaps even simplistic — good writers use them all the time. Once you have tried them out a few times, you'll begin to use them automatically, perhaps without even realizing it. They are powerful tools for incorporating others' views into your own work and then helping you to make careful distinctions about various parts of arguments.

Providing Support

In writing about any argument, you will need to understand the argument and to make it clear to your readers that you do. You cannot write a clear explanation or a fair evaluation if you do not have a clear understanding of your subject.

You will need to look closely at the piece to recall what specific words or ideas led you to the thesis statement that you have chosen to support.

Your support for your thesis will come from the text or texts you are writing about in the form of summary, paraphrase, or quotations. The ability to summarize, paraphrase, and quote material from your source is necessary in writing about arguments, but it is also essential in writing your own arguments, especially those that require research.

Summarizing

A summary involves shortening the original passage as well as putting it into your own words. It gives the gist of the passage, including the important points, while leaving out details. What makes summarizing difficult is that it requires you to capture often long and complex texts in just a few lines or a short paragraph. To summarize well, you need to imagine yourself as the author of the piece you are summarizing and be true to the ideas the author is expressing, even when those ideas conflict with your point of view. You must then move smoothly from being a careful reader to being a writer who, in your own words, recreates another's thoughts.

We summarize for many reasons: to let our boss know the basics of what we have been doing or to tell a friend why she should or should not see a movie. In your classes you are often asked to summarize articles or books, and even when this is not an explicit part of an assignment, the ability to summarize is usually expected. That is, when you are instructed to analyze an essay or to compare and contrast two novels, central to this work is the ability to carefully comprehend and recreate authors' ideas. See pages 48–50 in Chapter 2 for a more detailed treatment of summarizing.

Paraphrasing

Paraphrasing involves restating the content of an original source in your own words. It differs from summarizing in that a paraphrase is roughly the same length as the passage it paraphrases instead of a condensation of a longer passage. You will use paraphrasing when you want to capture the idea but there is nothing about the wording that makes repeating it necessary. You may also use it when the idea can be made clearer by rephrasing it or when the style is markedly different from your own. Here is an example drawn from a student paper:

> Randolph Warren, a victim of the thalidomide disaster himself and founder and executive director of the Thalidomide Victims Association of Canada, reports that it is estimated 10,000 to 12,000 deformed babies were born to mothers who took thalidomide. (40)

There is no single sentence on page 40 of the Warren article that both provides the estimate of number of affected babies and identifies Warren as one of them. Both the ideas were important, but neither of them was worded in such a unique way that a direct quote was needed. Therefore, a paraphrase was the logical choice. In this case, the writer correctly documents the paraphrase using Modern Language Association (MLA) style.

Quoting

You may want to quote passages or phrases from your sources if they express an idea in words more effective than your own. In reading a source, you may come across a statement that provides succinct, irrefutable evidence for an issue you wish to support. If the author of this statement is a professional in his or her field, someone with a great deal of authority on the subject, it would be appropriate to quote that author. A student research paper in Chapter 11 is Angela Mathers' about women in combat. Suppose, during the course of Angela's research for her paper, she found several sources that agree that women in the military who are denied combat experience are, as a result, essentially being denied a chance at promotion to the highest ranks. Others argue that such considerations should not be a deciding factor in assigning women to combat. To represent the latter of these two positions, Angela chose to use a quotation from an authority in the field, using APA style:

> Elaine Donnelly, president of the Center for Military Readiness, says, "Equal opportunity is important, but the armed forces exist to defend the country. If there is a conflict between career opportunities and military necessity, the needs of the military must come first" (as qtd. in "Women in the Military," 2000).

It is especially important in argumentative writing to establish a source's authority on the subject under discussion. The most common way of doing this is to use that person's name and position of authority to introduce the quotation, as in the previous example. It is correct in both MLA and APA styles to provide the author's name in parentheses at the end of the quoted material, but that type of documentation precludes lending to the quote the weight of its having come from an authority. It is likely that those readers not in the military — and even some who are — will not know who Donnelly is just by seeing her name in parentheses. Your writing will always have more power if you establish the authority of each author from whose work you quote, paraphrase, or summarize. To establish authority, you may refer to the person's position, institutional affiliation, publications, or some other similar "claim to fame."

Another example, also using APA style:

> According to the late Ulysses S. Seal III (1982), founder of the Conservation Breeding Specialist Group and of a "computer dating service" for mateless animals, "None of these [zoo] budgets is allocated specifically for species preservation. Zoos have been established primarily as recreational institutions and are only secondarily programs in conservation, education, and research" (p. 74).

Notice that once the name of the author being cited has been mentioned in the writer's own text, it does not have to be repeated in the parentheses.

Writer's Guide: Incorporating Quotations into Your Text

There are three primary means of linking a supporting quotation to your own text. Remember that in each case, the full citation for the source will be listed alphabetically by the author's name in the list of works cited at the end of the paper, or by title if no author is given. The number in parentheses is the page of that source on which the quotation appears. The details of what appears in parentheses will be covered later in the discussion of APA (American Psychological Association) and MLA (Modern Language Association) documentation styles.

• You may choose to make a brief quotation a grammatical part of your own sentence. In that case, you do not separate the quotation from your sentence with a comma, unless there is another reason for the comma, and you do not capitalize the first word of the quotation, unless there is another reason for doing so. In this sort of situation, there may be times when you have to change the tense of a verb, in brackets, to make the quotation fit smoothly into your text or when you need to make other small changes, always in brackets.

Examples:

APA style

James Rachels (1976), University Professor of Philosophy at the University of Alabama at Birmingham and author of several books on moral philosophy, explains that animals' right to liberty derives from "a more basic right not to have one's interests needlessly harmed" (p. 210).

MLA style

James Rachels, University Professor of Philosophy at the University of Alabama at Birmingham and author of several books on moral philosophy, explains that animals' right to liberty derives from "a more basic right not to have one's interests needlessly harmed" (210).

• You may use a traditional speech tag such as "he says" or "she writes." This is the most common way of introducing a quotation. Be sure to put a comma after the tag and to begin the quotation with a capital letter. At the end of the quotation, close the quotation, add the page number and any other necessary information in parentheses, and then add the period.

Examples:

APA style

James Rachels (1976), University Professor of Philosophy at the University of Alabama at Birmingham and author of several books on moral philosophy, writes, "The right to liberty — the right to be free of external constraints on one's actions — may then be seen as derived from a more basic right not to have one's interests needlessly harmed" (p. 210).

MLA style

James Rachels, University Professor of Philosophy at the University of Alabama at Birmingham and author of several books on moral philosophy, writes, "The right to liberty — the right to be free of external constraints on one's actions — may then be seen as derived from a more basic right not to have one's interests needlessly harmed" (210).

Students are sometimes at a loss as to what sorts of verbs to use in these tag statements. Try using different terms from this list or others like them. Remember that in writing about a printed or electronic text, it is customary to write in present tense unless there is a compelling reason to use past tense.

argues	continues	implores	replies
asks	counters	insists	responds
asserts	declares	proclaims	states
concludes	explains	questions	suggests

- You may vary the way you introduce quotations by at times using a colon to separate the quotation from a *complete sentence* that introduces it.

Examples:

APA style

For example, the Zurich Zoo's Dr. Heini Hediger (1985) protests that it is absurd to attribute human qualities to animals at all, but he nevertheless resorts to a human analogy: "Wild animals in the zoo rather resemble estate owners. Far from desiring to escape and regain their freedom, they are only bent on defending the space they inhabit and keeping it safe from invasion" (p. 9).

MLA style

The late Ulysses S. Seal III, founder of the Conservation Breeding Specialist Group and of a "computer dating service" for mateless animals, acknowledges the subordinate position species preservation plays in budgeting decisions: "Zoos have been established primarily as recreational institutions and are only secondarily developing programs in conservation, education, and research" (74).

PRACTICE

Write a summary of Alan Dershowitz's "Is There a Torturous Road to Justice?" (p. 110) using either the rhetorical method, which explains what the author is doing in the piece, or using the referential method, which focuses instead on the ideas. Be sure to remain objective. Include at least one direct quotation in your summary. Identify the author and the title in your first sentence and provide in parentheses the page number for the quotation(s).

Documenting Your Sources

Chapter 11 will provide additional information about documenting sources, but you should start now documenting your use of others' work, even when the only sources you use are essays from this textbook. The single most important thing to remember is why you need to inform your reader about your use of sources. Once it is clear from your writing that an idea or some language came from a source and thus is not your own original thought or language, full documentation provides the reader with a means of identifying and, if necessary, locating your source. If you do not indicate your source, your reader will naturally assume that the ideas and the language are yours. It is careless to forget to give credit to your sources. It is dishonest to intentionally take credit for what is not your own intellectual property. Note, though, that the convention is for authors of magazine articles not to provide page numbers for their sources in the way that you will be expected to do.

The following Writer's Guide provides the general guidelines for documenting your use of sources.

Writer's Guide: Documenting Use of Summary, Paraphrase, and Quotation

1. One of the most common mistakes that student writers make is to think that material needs to be documented only if they use another author's words. In fact, you must give credit for *any ideas* you get from others, not only for wording you get from them.

2. You must identify the author and the location of ideas that you summarize. A *summary* is the condensing of a longer passage into a shorter one, using your own words. You will use summary often in your academic writing when you want to report briefly on an idea covered at greater length in your source.

3. You must identify the author and the location of ideas that you paraphrase. A *paraphrase* is a rewording of another author's idea into your own words. A paraphrased passage is roughly the same length as the original.

4. You must identify the author and the location of language that you quote. A *quotation* is the copying of the exact wording of your source and is placed in quotation marks. Remember that *exact* means just that. You cannot change anything inside quotation marks, with these exceptions: (a) If there is a portion of the quotation that is not relevant to the point that you are making and *that can be omitted without distorting the author's meaning*, you may indicate an omission of a portion of the quotation with an ellipsis (. . .). If there is a sentence break within the portion you are omitting, add a fourth period to the ellipsis to so indicate. (b) If you need to make a very slight change in the quote to make the quote

fit grammatically into your own text or to avoid confusion and if the change does not distort the author's meaning, you may make that slight change and place the changed portion in square brackets ([ ]). This method is used primarily to change the tense of a quoted passage to match that of your text or to identify a person identified in the quotation only by a pronoun.

5. Both the MLA and the APA systems make use of in-text or parenthetical documentation. That means that while a complete bibliographical listing for each work summarized, paraphrased, or quoted in your text is included in a Works Cited or References list at the end of your paper, each is also identified exactly at the point in the text where you use the source. If you are using the MLA system of documentation, the system most commonly used in the humanities, immediately following the sentence in which you use material from a source, you need to add in parentheses the author's name and the page number on which the material you are using appeared in the original source. However, since the credibility of your sources is critical in argumentative writing, it is even better to name the source in your own sentence and to identify the position or experience that makes that person a reliable source for the subject being discussed. In that case, you do not need to repeat the author's name in the parentheses. In fact, any time the author's name is clear from the context, you do not need to repeat it in the parentheses.

Acceptable: The mall has been called "a common experience for the majority of American youth" (Kowinski 3).

Better: According to William Severini Kowinski, author of *The Malling of America*, "The mall is a common experience for the majority of American youth" (3).

In the APA system, the system most commonly use in the social sciences, in-text or parenthetical documentation is handled a bit differently because the citation includes the year of publication. The most basic forms are these:

The mall has been called "a common experience for the majority of American youth" (Kowinski, 1985, p. 3).

Kowinski (1985) writes, "The mall is a common experience for the majority of American youth" (p. 3).

6. Remember that these examples show only the most basic forms for documenting your sources. Some works will have more than one author. Sometimes you will be using more than one work by the same author. Usually Web sites do not have page numbers. Long quotations need to be handled differently from short ones. For all questions about documenting your use of sources not covered here, see Chapter 11.

Note: If you are writing about an essay in this book, you have a slightly more complicated situation than if you were looking at the essay in its original place of publication. Unless your instructor indicates otherwise, use the page numbers on which the essay appears in this textbook when summarizing, paraphrasing, or quoting from it instead of going back to the page numbers of the original. Also, unless your instructor indicates otherwise, use this model for listing in your Works Cited page an essay reprinted here:

Quindlen, Anna. "A New Look, an Old Battle." *Newsweek* April 9, 2001: 72–73. Rpt. in *Elements of Argument: A Text and Reader*. Donna Haisty Winchell and Annette T. Rottenberg. 10th ed. Boston: Bedford/St. Martin's, 2011. 333–35.

Avoiding Plagiarism

Plagiarism is the use of someone else's words or ideas without adequate acknowledgment — that is, presenting such words or ideas as your own. Putting something into your own words is not in itself a defense against plagiarism; the source of the ideas must be identified as well. Giving credit to the sources you use serves three important purposes: (1) it reflects your own honesty and seriousness as a researcher; (2) it enables the reader to find the source of the reference and read further, sometimes to verify that the source has been correctly used; and (3) it adds the authority of experts to your argument. Plagiarism is nothing less than cheating, and it is an offense that deserves serious punishment. You can avoid accidentally slipping into plagiarism if you are careful in researching and writing your papers.

Taking care to document sources is an obvious way to avoid plagiarism. You should also be careful in taking notes and, when writing your paper, indicating where your ideas end and someone else's begin. When taking notes, make sure either to quote word for word or to paraphrase — one or the other, not both. If you quote, enclose any language that you borrow from other sources in quotation marks. That way, when you look back at your notes days or weeks later, you won't mistakenly assume that the language is your own. If you know that you aren't going to use a particular writer's exact words, then take the time to summarize that person's ideas right away. That will save you time and trouble later.

When using someone else's ideas in your paper, always let the reader know where that person's ideas begin and end. Here is an example from a student paper that uses APA style:

> When zoo animals do mate successfully, the offspring is often weakened by inbreeding. According to geneticists, this is because a population of 150 breeder animals is necessary in order to "assure the more or less permanent survival of a species in captivity" (Ehrlich & Ehrlich, 1981, p. 211).

The phrase "according to geneticists" indicates that the material to follow comes from another source, cited parenthetically at the end of the borrowed material. If the student had not included the phrase "according to geneticists," it might look as if she only borrowed the passage in quotation marks, and not the information that precedes that passage.

Examining Some Models

Now that you have read about writing an analytical essay, it will help to see some examples. The first pair of essays are an argument about reality television and an analysis of it. The analysis gives you a model of the type of analytical writing that is the focus of this chapter. This particular analytical essay supports a claim of fact.

You'll note that parenthetical documentation is missing from the analysis essay. Normally when the author's name is clear from the context, as it is in this case, all you need to put in the parentheses is the page number. Because the source is an online magazine, there are no page numbers.

SAMPLE ESSAY AND ANALYTICAL RESPONSE   Claim of Fact

Reality Check

ERIC JAFFE

See: the world of reality television. The cast members bear little resemblance to your usual television actors (but they also seem quite unlike you and me). In exotic settings and high-stakes competitions, strangers are stranded and banded together, elevated to star status as long as they are willing to do and say things we could never imagine. Video editors whirl through raw footage, past the mundane, in search of incidental lusts or brawls. Promises are bound and broken in a single breath. Triumph is declared over enemies who, moments before, were friends who, days before, were strangers. True love may or may not be found, depending on whether the check is real.

Such is the world that has advertisers flocking, Juilliard graduates panhandling, and psychologists wondering whether life could ever come to imitate this peculiar art.

Eric Jaffe has written on behavioral science issues for the *Los Angeles Times*, *Smithsonian*, *Slate*, *Science News*, and the A[ssociation for] P[sychological] S[cience] *Observer*. This article appeared in the *Observer* in March 2005. Jaffe writes the Headcase blog for *Psychology Today*.

Reality television has been criticized for humiliating its cast members.

Reality television has been vilified as the lowest form of entertainment, a threat to intelligence, and catering to (and rising from) the most prurient of human instincts. As such, the shows would seem to offer a bounty of possible examinations from a behavioral perspective. But until recently, the effects of reality television remained sparsely explored. Bryant Paul, Indiana University, offers two explanations for the dearth of literature. First, reality TV is perpetually changing, making it difficult for researchers to collect and analyze data that remain relevant. The other reason is that some researchers do not think it will last. "It's been around three to five years, which is a blink in the bigger scheme," Paul said. "The novelty is wearing off."

If that is the case, losing popularity has never been so popular. Fifty-one million people tuned in to the first-season finale of *Survivor* in August 2000.[1] In January 2003, reality shows accounted for 85 percent of the most valuable TV advertising space in the United States, according to the Cable News Network. Competing plans for entire reality networks — Reality 24-7 and Fox Reality Channel — are in the works. The craze has even reached the classroom. James Hay, University of Illinois at Urbana-Champagne, recently began teaching a course called The Reality TV Syndrome. "I'm often asked, 'Why would you want to teach in higher education the lowest form of television?'" Hay said. "But it's an important matter in everyday life."

And not all researchers believe the fad is fading. "I don't see any signs that it's going away any time soon," said Brad Waite, Central Connecticut State University, who presented reality television research at the American Psychological Society's 16th Annual Convention. "Something so ubiquitous must have an effect on behavior."

5

Passion for Peeping

Flip back to that first *Survivor* finale. As a frame of reference, 51 million viewers is more than watched the 1983 *M*A*S*H* special — the top Nielson-rated show of all time. (Nielson officially ranks shows by time-share and household percentage, however, so *M*A*S*H* still holds the top spot, and *Survivor* doesn't even crack the top 100.) By watching in such high numbers, viewers told network executives to dump their high-priced writers and lovely actors in favor of identifiable people in familiar conflicts. All we really wanted to see was the same thing we saw in the mirror every morning — ourselves. Only different.

According to Waite, a writers' strike loomed in Hollywood around this time. The airwaves were ripe for inexpensive replacements. After *Survivor*, previously impossible profits became, well, a reality.

"It is not difficult to imagine the difference in cost between a whole series where one person wins $1 million and producing a series of *Friends*, where each cast member earns that much each episode," said James Wiltz, Ohio State University. "One big hit in this genre is worth many attempts."

Network executives thought the same thing. The new strain of television soon spread throughout the viewing community, plagiarizing and mutating into myriad subgenres. But as the number of shows grew, so did the media criticism. A month before the *Survivor* finale, *Time* said we had a passion for peeping and that we enjoyed the suffering, mean-spiritedness, and humiliation endured by others. The *New Statesman* blamed not only reality viewers but also participants for the culture of voyeurism. Nearly a year later, a *Newsweek* headline read: "Another reality show, another IQ point disappears."

It was all the negative publicity that motivated Robin Nabi to conduct some   10 of the earliest research on why people watch. "The press suggested we'd reached an all-time low in taste," said Nabi, a communications professor at University of California, Santa Barbara who takes a social-psychological approach to research. "It's frustrating to see these claims not based on any data. I wanted to know if the claims were reflected in the general public."

Why We Watch

The roots of reality television appear in the 1950s show *Queen for a Day*, in which women in dire circumstances competed for the studio audience's sympathy to win fur coats and appliances. Prior to the end of the twentieth century, most reality television research centered on the show *Cops* which follows law enforcement officers on their daily beats. But unlike newer reality shows, people on *Cops* were not removed from their natural setting, and the research mostly addressed the show's violence. *The Real World*, a pioneer of modern reality TV, has aired since 1992, but for years there were too few shows like it to merit a study.

Researching after the turn of the millennium, it did not take Nabi long to debunk some of the criticism. In her *Media Psychology* report, "Reality-Based Television Programming and the Psychology of Its Appeal,"[2] Nabi found the notion of reality watchers as voyeurs questionable at best.

"The idea of voyeurism didn't bear itself out in the data. Viewers wanted to watch other people, but not to see something the characters didn't want them to see," Nabi said, noting that voyeuristic pleasure is undermined when the subject knows he or she is being watched. Besides, said Nabi, viewers are well aware that illicit activity is certain to be censored even if it occurs.

A year later, Ohio State University psychologist Steven Reiss confirmed the absence of voyeurism, though what he found instead was debatably worse. He and collaborator James Wiltz based their research on Reiss's sensitivity theory, which says that most complex human motives can be reduced to 16 basic desires. Each time a desire is realized, a related joy is experienced. Though the motives are universal, they are individually prioritized to reflect our unique comportments, our personal Desire Profiles. Reiss has used these profiles to accurately predict spirituality, underachievement, teamwork — even organ donation.

According to Reiss, media events repeatedly allow people to experience the   15
16 desires and joys. Drawing on the uses and gratification theory — which suggests that people select media to fulfill certain needs — as well as the sensitivity theory, Reiss predicted that reality viewers would display a collective Desire Profile. Finding any difference from the normal profile would have been intriguing. What he and Wiltz found about the basic needs of reality viewers proved that truth is sometimes scarier than fiction.

Reiss's data showed that the largest significant motive for watching reality television was social status, which leads to the joy of self-importance. Only slightly less strong was the need for vengeance, which leads to vindication. "Some people may watch reality TV partially because they enjoy feeling superior to the people being portrayed," Reiss said. "People with a strong need for vengeance have the potential to enjoy watching people being humiliated."

In a content analysis of the five most popular reality shows and the five top scripted dramas and comedies, Waite and collaborator Sara Booker confirmed that reality shows might reflect a desire for viewing humiliation. Using show raters to code character behaviors, they found that reality shows rated higher in humiliation than scripted dramas. (This even after data from "The Swan" — a reality show on which a homely woman receives a makeover, only to then compete in a beauty pageant — was omitted.)

Humilitainment

Waite and Booker call this phenomenon "humilitainment," the tendency for viewers to be attracted to spectacular mortification. Since their study, similarly indecorous shows have popped up like pockmarks on the genre. *Temptation Island* placed dating couples on opposite ends of an island resort and introduced tempters and temptresses whose main purpose, it seems, was to initiate philandering while wearing as little clothing as possible. Some titles alone are enough to evoke disgust: *I Want a Famous Face, Trading Spouses: Meet Your New Mommy, The Virgin*, and the ever-popular font of humiliation: *Who's Your Daddy?*

Humilitainment has a more graceful and precise cousin — the German word *schadenfreude*, which translates to the pleasure one receives at the suffering of others. Colin Wayne Leach and Russell Spears studied schadenfreude as it related to an even more real type of reality contest — World Cup soccer matches. Looking at soccer fans' reactions to their team's losses and rival team's victories, Leach and Spears found that schadenfreude was the result of threatened inferiority. In the wake of losing a competition, schadenfreude is "a covert form of prejudice that is used in the maintenance of self-worth," the authors wrote in the *Journal of Personality and Social Psychology.*

If reality viewers are in fact tuning in to feel better at another person's expense, Waite predicts a maladaptive future for heavy watchers. "They expect it's OK to humiliate and to be humiliated by others, instead of thinking there's something wrong with this behavior," Waite said. "The world they're living in is different from others." In this world according to Waite, the borders separating on-screen from off-screen blend indistinguishably. It is this seamless convergence of fiction and reality that psychologists fear could have a severe behavioral impact.

20

Real People, Real Problems

Each semester, Bryant Paul demonstrates the power of media to his psychology students. He asks how many of them have been to New York. Half raise their hands. He then asks how many of them perceive New York as a dangerous place. The students draw no connection to the previous response, and nearly all the hands are raised.

The theory Paul sets into action is not a new one. It has been around since the late 1960s, when media psychologist George Gerbner stated that exposure to cultural imagery can shape a viewer's concept of reality. Simply put, the more TV a person watches, the more that person believes in the world of TV. Using his "cultivation theory," Gerbner showed that heavy news viewers believed they resided in a "meaner" world, to the point where they might even approve stricter violence interventions.

"In general, one of the negative things about television is that it gives a distorted image of what the rest of the world is like," said APS Fellow and Charter Member Craig A. Anderson, Iowa State University, who focuses mostly on violent media but sees some overlap with reality shows. "TV changes the perception of what is normative."

Mary Beth Oliver, a communications professor at Pennsylvania State University who researches the psychological effects of media on viewers, also wondered what happens when this mean world is a real world.

"I thought the perceived reality would have a strong impact on viewers' social-reality judgments," said Oliver, who studied *Cops* long before the reality boom. Her analysis of crime shows found that African Americans and Latinos were overwhelmingly cast as criminals and whites as police officers. In addition, police were using aggression frequently, particularly if the criminals were minorities.

25

"Reality television requires viewers to disengage from the suffering of other people or to derive enjoyment from it," Oliver said.

To test how greatly these shows were actually influencing worldviews, Oliver asked regular watchers to estimate the prevalence of crime in the real world.

Startlingly, reality crime watchers gave increased crime estimates, particularly for the amount of black crimes. Yet Oliver's most unsettling realization came from a phone call she received from an officer in charge of training at a Roanoke, Virginia, police department. The man had read her research and was very nervous, because every trainee who wanted to sign up for the force was addicted to these reality crime shows.

"He told me it wasn't just for the enjoyment," Oliver recalled. "That's what they thought policing would really be like."

The blurry line between fiction and reality should come as less of a surprise considering that the godmother of reality television, Mary-Ellis Bunim, was an executive producer for the soap opera *As the World Turns* before creating *The Real World* with partner Jonathan Murray. Bunim's obituary in the December 26, 2004, *New York Times Magazine* said her idea was to "craft soap-opera storylines with actual people."

Fulfilling this idea requires a luxury unavailable to normal reality — heavy   30
editing. *The Apprentice* and *Survivor* each shoot for almost a month and a half, turning 1,000 hours of life into about 15 hours of programming. *The Real World*, reality's longest shoot, tapes for five months before producing two dozen episodes. Many researchers, including Paul, find this manipulation problematic.

"Reality TV is just as real as anything else on TV — it's not," Paul said. "They can create any impression they want. One-eighth of an hour one time a week is all viewers get to construct an opinion about a character."

Douglas Gentile, director of research at the National Institute on Media and the Family and psychology professor at Iowa State University, agreed that reality TV's presentation has a large influence on viewers. "One of the things we know from media violence research is that the more realistic the presentation is, the media violence effect seems to be stronger," Gentile said. "Reality TV is claiming it's real, even though there's a striking lack of resemblance to what's really happening in the world. But the average viewers, who aren't as savvy to know how the shows are being produced, are being told that what they're seeing is true."

In addition to how the shows are marketed, rumors linger that cast members exaggerate their behavior and that producers instigate conflict. According to Booker, the character Toni from *Paradise Hotel* admitted letting her rage get the best of her on camera. The villainy of Omarosa from *The Apprentice* seems nothing more than shrewd self-promotion — she still frequents gossip-columns a year after the show's end. Gentile has a clinical term for the insults and antics that come so naturally to reality characters: relational aggression.

"A lot of reality television is very relationally aggressive," he said, describing the term as *I'm having a party and you're not invited*. "Not only do the characters interact unpleasantly to each other, they also spread rumors. This is a classic example of relational aggression — trying to gang up, enhancing one's own status by bringing others down."

Anderson has seen some evidence that relational aggression does not always   35
stop with words. "Relational aggression frequently escalates into physical aggres-

sion," he said. "Many assaults occur between acquaintances, when name-calling escalates beyond saying nasty things."

Waite fears such consistent, ignominious behavior will lead to a modified re-creation of Gerbner's "mean world."

"Is the world of the heavy viewer of modern reality TV a 'mean world' but in a different sense?" he asked. "Is this 'mean world' one in which embarrassment, disrespect, and degradation are common? This to me is one of the most interesting reasons why we study this type of programming."

Improving Reality

If reality television does persist, psychologists may in time grow to understand more about its allure. Waite and Gentile both said that video game users have been recently hooked up to functional Magnetic Resonance Imaging machines; whether for marketing or empirical purposes, reality viewers might not be far behind. Until then, Waite speculates that younger generations are simply accustomed to being on screen. Digital cameras now come standard with most cell phones, and Web cams televise daily adventures, from the quotidian to the erotic, around the clock. "Expectations of privacy have been eroded," Waite said. "Public disclosure, even of formerly private behaviors and feelings, are the expectation."

This intimacy entitlement might explain why 37 million people tuned in after the "Survivor" finale to watch the reunion. Miles away from the island of Pulau Tiga, plain-clothed cast members discussed their feelings and opinions on the experience. To Reiss, this suggests that these once-regular people now hovered somewhere between the celebrity and pedestrian echelons.

"If you pay attention to ordinary people then you're saying ordinary people are 40 important," he said. "People can watch reality TV shows and see ordinary people like themselves become famous, win cash prizes, and move up in their status."

Paul disagrees that a desire to be famous attracts viewers — after all, he says, these people can be famous for you. Rather, the fact that these people were not groomed for celebrity in the traditional sense, that friends of friends invariably went to camp with someone on one of the shows, is the great draw. "The closer someone is to you, the easier it is to empathize," Paul said, "and really good empathy equals really good television."

Nabi stumbled onto this possibility when she found almost as much variety among preference for reality subgenres as she did preference between reality and fiction. In some cases, the very quality that defined one show's enjoyment was anathema to another's — suspense was a draw for reality talent shows, but for a reality crime show it was a major detractor, perhaps because the viewer wondered if the criminal remained at large. To Nabi, this could mean that watching real people, whatever the circumstance, is the real attraction.

"Watching real people on TV is fascinating, just like watching people in the airport is fascinating," she said. "Viewers are interested in people — not pain."

This leads her to think that some of the negativity directed toward reality TV may be unjustified, but it does not solve the riddle of why viewing real people is such an attraction. "Something deeper is happening here that we haven't gotten to."

For the time being, Nabi sees a positive side to viewer malleability and the scientific evidence supporting it. "It is possible that the way producers put their programs together may be influenced by the academic research," she said. In fact, she has already seen an improvement in the way some reality shows depict real events. Previously, "Extreme Makeover" was criticized for making plastic surgery seem beneficial, rapid, and risk-free. In its current season, however, Nabi said the show more clearly depicts the multiple, intensive steps involved in surgical procedures.

An altruistic show even lurks on the horizon — "The Scholar," in which 10 ex-   45
ceptional and financially needy high school seniors from around the country will compete for a full scholarship. "Imagine this concept," wrote Booker at the end of her second study, "using reality television to actually improve reality." Given the genre's impact on behavior, that might not be too unrealistic.

The Reiss Profile

In their 2004 report "Why People Watch Reality TV," published in *Media Psychology*, lead authors Steven Reiss and James Wiltz used the Reiss Profile to explain why certain people watched reality television. Validated by responses from over 10,000 people, the Reiss Profile measures how basic motives result in a particular joy. Reality viewers were found to have significantly higher motives for status and vengeance.

MOTIVE	JOY
ACCEPTANCE: Desire for approval	**SELF-CONFIDENCE**
CURIOSITY: Desire for knowledge	**WONDERMENT**
EATING: Desire for food	**SATIATION**
FAMILY: Desire to raise own children	**LOVE**
HONOR: Desire to obey a traditional moral code	**LOYALTY**
IDEALISM: Desire to improve society (including altruism, justice)	**COMPASSION**
INDEPENDENCE: Desire for autonomy	**FREEDOM**
ORDER: Desire to organize (including desire for ritual)	**STABILITY**
PHYSICAL EXERCISE: Desire to exercise muscles	**VITALITY**
ROMANCE: Desire for sex (including courting)	**LUST**
POWER: Desire to influence (including leadership)	**EFFICACY**
SAVING: Desire to collect	**OWNERSHIP**

SOCIAL CONTACT: Desire for peer companionship   **FUN**
(and desire to play)

STATUS: Desire for prestige   **SELF-IMPORTANCE**
(including desire for attention)

TRANQUILITY: Desire for inner peace   **SAFE, RELAXED**
(prudence, safety)

VENGEANCE: Desire to get even (including desire to win)   **VINDICATION**

REFERENCES AND NOTES

Reiss, S., & Wiltz, J. (2004). Why people watch reality TV. *Media Psychology, 6*, 363–378.

1. Nielsen Media Research. (2000). *Report on television.*
2. Nabi, R. L., Biely, E. N., Morgan, S. J., Stitt, C. R. (2003). Reality-based television programming and the psychology of its appeal. 2003. *Media Psychology, 5*, 303–330.

STUDENT ANALYTICAL RESPONSE   Claim of Fact

Psychoanalyzing Reality TV

DEION MOORE

In his article "Reality Check," which appeared on the Association for Psychological Science Web site in March of 2005, behavioral science writer Eric Jaffe looks at the phenomenon that is reality television from the psychologist's perspective. He weaves together the history of reality television, the history of research on reality television, and the various possible answers to the question why we watch it.

Jaffe traces the evolution — or devolution — of reality television to its roots in the 1950s show *Queen for a Day*, which featured ordinary women in competition for prizes, and to *Cops*, which filmed police officers on the job. The real boom began with the first season of *Survivor*, when a writers' strike left the networks looking for cheap replacements for their breadwinners — and they realized how profitable reality shows could be. Jaffe explains how this "new strain of television soon spread throughout the viewing community, plagiarizing and mutating into myriad subgenres." He writes of how "indecorous shows have popped up like pockmarks on the genre." He points to *Temptation Island*, which "placed dating couples on opposite ends of an island resort and introduced tempters and temptresses whose main purpose, it seems, was to initiate philandering while wearing

At the time he wrote this analysis, Deion Moore was a student at Clemson University.

as little clothing as possible," and other shows whose "titles alone are enough to evoke disgust: *I Want a Famous Face, Trading Spouses: Meet Your New Mommy, The Virgin*, and the ever-popular font of humiliation: *Who's Your Daddy?*"

Until this recent proliferation of reality shows, there were not enough on which to do any substantial research. Besides, some psychologists believe they are not worth the trouble anyway since reality television won't be around for long. Jaffe quotes Bryant Paul of Indiana University, who explains, "It's been around three to five years, which is a blink in the bigger scheme. . . . The novelty is wearing off."

Jaffe points out, though, that an increase in the number of studies being done on reality television shows suggests otherwise, as does their continued popularity. He traces some of the research studies that since 2000 have served to debunk common misconceptions about why people tune in and have offered other explanations.

Robin Nabi at the University of California, Santa Barbara, was one of the first   5
to insist on some data to back up all of the negative press the shows were getting. One common criticism has been that watching reality shows is voyeuristic. Nabi's data, however, do not support this hypothesis about why we watch. She writes, "The idea of voyeurism didn't bear itself out in the data. Viewers wanted to watch other people, but not to see something the characters didn't want them to see." There is not much pleasure in voyeurism anyway if the subjects know they are being watched.

Jaffe next introduces the research of Ohio State University psychologist Steven Reiss, who supports Nabi's conclusion that viewers are not primarily voyeurs. He and his collaborator James Wiltz analyzed viewers' motives in terms of the desires the shows fulfilled for them. The two most common motives they discovered were desire for social status and need for vengeance. The first indicates that viewers want to feel superior to the people they are watching, and the second that they "have the potential to enjoy watching people being humiliated." Brad Waite of Central Connecticut State University and his colleague Sara Booker have called this second desire "humilitainment." They go so far as to predict "a maladaptive future for heavy watchers" who enjoy seeing others being mortified. Mary Beth Oliver, a communications professor at Penn State, agrees with their concern: "Reality television requires viewers to disengage from the suffering of other people or to derive enjoyment from it." The amount of relational aggression exhibited is also a concern.

Jaffe also touches on other less ominous reasons viewers tune in: They like to believe that what they are seeing is real, in spite of the heavy editing that goes on behind the scenes (although this also is alarming if their perception of the real world becomes distorted). They like to see people like themselves become famous and win prizes. They like to see people like themselves, but different. He ties the strands of his argument together in the end by quoting Nabi: "It is possible that the way producers put their programs together may be influenced by the academic research." That is, if reality shows are around long enough.

SAMPLE ESSAY AND ANALYTICAL RESPONSE   Claim of Value

The next pair of essays are another article about reality television and an analysis of it, this time one supporting a claim of value, or an evaluative claim. Again the source is an online source, so there are no page numbers.

The Meaning of Reality (TV)

NOAM SHPANCER

Channel surfing requires "no commitment or concentration."

I don't watch much TV. When I do, I mostly channel surf. Channel surfing, like ocean wave noise, soothes because it requires no commitment or concentration. It provides a relief from the commitments and concentrations that mark the work day.

Channel surfing has other advantages. While I can't tell you the plot line of any particular show, I know something about the TV landscape as a whole; the color palette; the thematic preoccupations.

I have noticed, for example, that those "reality" shows that pack the TV schedule come in two main formats. One involves people who compete for some prize while showing off a skill

Noam Shpancer is a clinical psychologist and professor of psychology at Otterbein College in Westerville, Ohio. He is also a clinician with the Center for Cognitive and Behavioral Psychology in Columbus, Ohio, where he specializes in the treatment of anxiety disorders. He has written a novel called *The Good Psychologist* (2010). His essay appeared on psychologytoday.com on August 10, 2010.

or dealing with a novel situation. The other depicts people who are just followed around, having the minutiae of their lives aired out in public.

The contestants, I find, also fall into two groups. One is made of "performers" — aspiring artists and actors desperate for a stage and assorted odd characters instructed to act up, carnival sideshow-style; those dominate the judgment and novelty shows.

The second, more interesting group is the so-called regular people — housewives, families, high school buddies — who possess no unique skill, no thespian claims, no glaring oddities. These are just asked to be themselves rather than compete or perform.

Psychological research, of course, has been "staging reality shows" for years. Placing people in novel situations and asking them to deal, carrying out fly-on-the-wall naturalistic observations of daily life, and judging people's skill levels are staple psychology research designs. And anyone involved in this field knows their inherent fascination. Look at the grainy videos of Zimbardo's prison experiment, Milgram's obedience studies, Mischel's marshmallow kids; watch the infants attempting to negotiate Ainsworth's "strange situation" and you'll see compelling human drama.[1]

One difference is that in research, the participants do not become stars, public icons, role models, or fodder for water cooler conversations; they usually remain unknown by design, to protect them, and the research. The star of research is not "self," but "truth." In reality shows, "self" is the star while "truth" is inconsequential; the subjects do become known, by design. In fact, getting known is the participants' prime motive.

And that's the other reason these shows are watched: they reflect the cultural dictum that being on TV elevates you, marks you as special and important.

This TV-Special Merit link has a long history, of course. Historically, however, the causal arrow led from Merit to TV. First, you acquired some special value, talent, or achievement in the world; then, by virtue of that accomplishment, you were elevated, via TV, onto the public pedestal. Being on TV rewarded achievement. This causal structure is natural and organic. When things are in proper

5

---

[1]In 1971, Philip Zimbardo, a psychology professor at Stanford University, led researchers in conducting an experiment in which students were randomly assigned roles as prisoners or prison guards in a mock prison. Both "prisoners" and "guards" took their roles to such extremes that the experiment was halted after only six days. In 1961, psychologist Stanley Milgram at Yale tested the willingness of student subjects to inflict electric shocks on other student subjects. No shocks were really administered, but far more subjects than predicted inflicted up to the maximum voltage even when they believed they were inflicting severe pain. In the 1960s, Walter Mischel at Stanford tested the concept of delayed gratification on four-year-olds by giving each a marshmallow and seeing if they could wait twenty minutes before eating it in order to get a second one. Canadian psychologist Mary Ainsworth studied infants' emotional attachment by filming their reactions as a parent and a stranger went in and out of their presence.

order, quality rises to the top. The fastest swimmer gets to climb the medal stand. Appreciating this logic is part of our nature.

But our nature is complex, and reality TV reflects another aspect of that archi-   10 tecture. After all, laboring in the world to gain special skill or achievement is hard and time consuming. It's a burden. And part of our nature is to seek relief from burden. People are always looking for easier, quicker ways to get the good stuff. And you don't have to be super clever to imagine that the TV-Special Merit connection may work both ways; that instead of laboring to become special and thus get on TV, you can get on TV first, and have that make you special.

This latter route, which is currently gaining in America, represents a cunning, even rational, short-term strategy, akin to that used by the ambitious "helicopter mother" who does her daughter's homework in secret, to boost the daughter's chances of getting into Harvard. The mother knows that just as super ability causes admission to Harvard, so does being at Harvard make you appear super able, with all the attendant benefits.

But in the long run, this strategy is risky, because it results in one of two bad outcomes: either the audience realizes the ruse and abandons the show, having wasted precious time and energy for naught (the girl fails at Harvard and flunks out, but not before thwarting the dreams of another, truly deserving applicant); or the audience buys the ruse and takes the mediocrity on offer as truly special, thus narrowing its own horizon (the girl's half-baked ideas are taken as gospel by a culture mesmerized by her Harvard credentials).

You can see variations of the same principle at work throughout the culture. For example, competence naturally breeds self esteem. However, educators and psychologists in the 80s and early 90s, particularly in California, responded to research results showing the competence-self esteem link by concluding that self esteem can cause competence. A whole movement flourished trying to teach children self esteem, in the hope that they would become successful as a result. This of course ended in a waste of time and money, and a betrayal of children. Putting someone on the medal stand is unlikely to turn her into a good swimmer.

The same dynamic can be seen underlying America's troubled relations with food. The work of our biological architect, natural selection, made good things sweet. Our cultural food architects have realized they could exploit the sweet-is-good natural link and make people buy a lot of really bad stuff by just making it sweet. So we are now consuming a lot of bad sweet stuff. And by the time the ruse is discovered, we already weigh 350 pounds and our hearts have exploded.

Which of course makes us ideal contestants for the next big reality show,   15 where the winner of all the challenges gets a heart transplant surgery while the losers are cast away to die.

Live, on TV, it's *Survivor: Mt. Sinai!*

The Meaning of Shpancer (Really)

ASHLEY WILSON

Noam Shpancer opens his essay "The Meaning of Reality (TV)" with the image of him relaxing in front of the TV after a hard day at work, remote in hand, no commitments, no need to concentrate. As he points out, though, he has learned enough from watching the channels flash by to gain some fairly good insights into the nature of reality television. Unfortunately, the essay peaks in the middle with some thought-provoking ideas but comes to a confusing and disappointing conclusion.

Shpancer begins with a simple but workable classification scheme for reality shows: They are about either "people who compete for some prize while showing off a skill or dealing with a novel situation" or "people who are just followed around, having the minutiae of their lives aired out in public." These people themselves, the contestants, also fall into two categories, those who perform and those who simply go about being themselves. Unfortunately, Shpancer offers no examples to support his classification, and he drops this idea to move on to the next.

One of the most important points that Shpancer makes relates reality shows to psychological research. There is certainly validity to his point that psychologists have been conducting their own "reality shows" for years: "Placing people in novel situations and asking them to deal, carrying out fly-on-the-wall naturalistic observations of daily life, and judging people's skill levels are staple psychology research designs." He mentions specific psychological studies that are "compelling human drama" and mentions the scientists' last names, but assumes his audience will know their work. That may be enough for some readers of psychologytoday.com, but others are not given enough information to accept his assertion that they are compelling.

The most original and thought-provoking idea that Shpancer offers is what he refers to as the TV–Special Merit link. That is, the reality shows "reflect the cultural dictum that being on television elevates you, marks you as special and important." The equation generally works the other way: if you proved that you had special value, "you were elevated, via TV, onto the public pedestal." Logic would dictate that hard work helps one win recognition, but reality shows are a way to avoid the hard work but get the recognition anyway. The analogy that Shpancer provides is the "helicopter" mother who helps her daughter get into Harvard by doing her homework for her. A certain level of recognition comes to the daughter by virtue

---

At the time she wrote this analysis, Ashley Wilson was a student at Clemson University.

of being at Harvard, and she may actually get by on her Harvard credentials — or she may flunk out. By analogy, the reality show's audience may accept mediocrity, or they may give up on the show.

Shpancer points out that the same logic led teachers in the 1980s and 1990s to try to guide students to competence by elevating their self-esteem, but the experiment was a failure: "Putting someone on the medal stand is unlikely to turn her into a good swimmer."

The essay loses its coherence, however, when Shpancer next tries to link his theory to "America's troubled relations with food" and ends by envisioning a new reality show with 350-pound contestants "where the winner of all the challenges gets a heart transplant surgery while the losers are cast away to die." Dr. Shpancer must have gotten hungry as he sat there in his recliner channel surfing, or maybe TV requires a little more concentration than he thought.

SAMPLE ESSAY WITH ANALYSIS   Rogerian Argument

In Chapter 1 we discussed how Carl Rogers's theory of communication can serve as a useful approach to resolving a conflict. It can also be a useful approach to analyzing, in writing, the two sides of an argument. The following essay is not a response to another piece of writing but to conflicting ideas.

The first step to resolving a conflict, of course, is to recognize that there is a conflict. The next step is to analyze *both sides* in the conflict. Before you begin, refer back to Maxine Hairston's guidelines for Rogerian argument from "Carl Rogers's Alternative to Traditional Rhetoric" on page 14.

Experienced writers may not adhere strictly to these guidelines, as is the case in the following essay, but as you read, notice where Whitehead includes the steps in a Rogerian analysis of an argument.

Parents Need Help: Restricting Access to Video Games
BARBARA DAFOE WHITEHEAD

A century ago, Jane Addams and other progressive reformers in Chicago responded to the dangers of the industrial age by creating laws and institutions that would protect children from the unwholesome lures of the city streets. Her work is rightly honored. A similar, and equally important, struggle is being waged in Illinois today. On the surface, it's about the sale of video games to kids. It's also

Barbara Dafoe Whitehead is the author of *The Divorce Culture: Rethinking Our Commitments to Marriage and Family* (1998) and *Why There Are No Good Men Left: The Romantic Plight of the New Single Woman* (2003). The column appeared in *Commonweal* on January 28, 2005.

a debate about a deeper question: To what degree does the responsibility for teaching good values to children fall solely on parents? Should some of that responsibility be shared by the state?

Those who make and sell video games say parents alone should bear the responsibility. On the other side is Illinois Governor Rod Blagojevich. He's trying to outlaw the sale of excessively violent or sexually explicit video games to children under eighteen. In his effort to restrict such sales he's making the argument that raising children is a shared responsibility: "Parenting is hard work and the state has a compelling interest in helping parents raise their children to be upstanding men and women."

The governor firmly believes that parents have the primary responsibility for teaching their children right from wrong. He believes just as firmly that parents should not have their efforts subverted by the avalanche of "amusements" that tell kids it is fun to blow people up. "Too many of the video games marketed to our children teach them all of the wrong lessons and all of the wrong values," Blagojevich writes in a "letter to Illinois parents" posted on the state's informational Web site (www.safegamesIllinois.com). "These games use violence, rage, and sexual aggression as play. That is not acceptable. When kids play, they should play like children, not like gangland assassins."

The governor's reference to gangland assassins is not an overstatement. One video game, the top-selling, industry-award-winning Grand Theft Auto: San Andreas, features gang warfare and the killing of prostitutes. Another, released on the forty-first anniversary of the Kennedy assassination, gets players to step into the shoes of Lee Harvey Oswald and to aim at the president's head as his motorcade rolls by. "Content descriptors" for video games also suggest how lurid the violence can be. These games include depictions of "blood and gore (mutilation of body parts)," "intense violence (human injury or death)," and "sexual violence (depictions of rape and other sexual acts)."

No sooner had Blagojevich unveiled his proposal than he faced powerful organized opposition from the entertainment industry. The Illinois Retail Merchants Association, the National Association of Theater Owners, the Entertainment Software Rating Board, and the Motion Picture Association of America took strong exception to the legislation. Imposing a curb on the free market is not the way to protect kids, these critics argued. Instead, parents should screen what their kids are buying and playing. As one lobbyist put it: "Retailers can't be held accountable for lack of oversight by parents."

This is a distortion of the governor's position, and of the problem. No one denies that parents have the primary responsibility for monitoring their kids. Blagojevich points out, though, that the sophisticated technology of video games makes that very hard to do. Consequently, it's up to the state to step in on the side of parents and children to help them cope.

The industry argument would be plausible if it were still 1955. Back then, it was easier for parents to exercise strict oversight. The big, boxy home entertainment technologies of that era — radio, television, and record players — produced images and sounds that parents could see and hear. They came with OFF buttons for parents to push and plugs for parents to pull. All that has changed. The new entertainment technologies include a dizzying and ever-multiplying array of small, portable, individual, kid-friendly devices that defy close parental supervision. It was easy for parents to check on a half-hour TV show. It's much harder to review a video game. The games feature successive levels of difficulty; players must qualify at a lower level before earning the right to move to a higher level. So it takes time and practice before acquiring the skill to progress to the highest level of the game — which may also be its highest level of violence. To ensure that a video game isn't excessively violent, a parent would have to be looking over a child's shoulder until the highest level of play was finally revealed. This could take days.

Moreover, it isn't as if parents and the video-game industry meet each other on a level playing field. This is a multibillion-dollar industry that spends all its time and money devising ever more ingenious ways to market to kids over the heads of their parents and to deliberately undermine the ability of parents to regulate what their children are seeing. And in a tactic called "age compression," the marketers target their appeals to ever-younger kids. Like the youth sex revolution, the youth marketing revolution has migrated down the age scale. Even four-year-olds know what is cool.

To be sure, the industry's Entertainment Software Rating Board has voluntarily established its own ratings system. The trouble is: It isn't enforced. A study by the Federal Trade Commission found that early teens were able to buy games rated M (Mature 17+) 69 percent of the time.

It is telling that the makers and sellers of video games have responded so quickly and vigorously to Governor Blagojevich's very modest proposal. Clearly the corporate sector finds it in its interest to prompt kids to engage in fantasy rape, beheadings, and mass murder. And why should we expect otherwise? Its interest is the bottom line. Violence sells. But isn't it in the compelling interest of the community to curb such violent play?

10

Analysis

In her first paragraph, Whitehead makes clear what is at issue: the sale of video games to children. The larger question is whether parents are solely responsible for values education or whether the state should share some of the burden. In the second paragraph, she establishes the two sides in the controversy: those who make and sell video games and then governor of Illinois, Rod Blagojevich, who wanted to outlaw the sale of extremely violent or sexually explicit video games to those under the age of eighteen. Rogerian guidelines indicate that usually the next step is to present the side that the writer does not agree with, but this time, after a quick reference to the producers and marketers of the games, she focuses on Blagojevich's position. She then turns to the industry's position. Whitehead concedes under what circumstances the industry's claims might be valid: if we were still living in 1955. The closest the two sides come to common ground is Whitehead's acknowledging that the Entertainment Software Rating Board has voluntarily created a rating system for games. Unfortunately, it is not enforced. By the end, she still sees Blagojevich's proposal as very modest and his opponents' as driven by the bottom line. Her thesis comes in the form of a question at the end of the piece and hints at a shared concern for the good of the community: "But isn't it in the compelling interest of the community to curb such violent play?"

READINGS FOR ANALYSIS

The two essays below are an argument written by Alan Dershowitz shortly after the terrorist attacks of September 11, 2001, and an evaluation of it written by Seth Finkelstein approximately three months later. Notice what Finkelstein says about Dershowitz's article but also how each author organizes his essay.

Is There a Torturous Road to Justice?

ALAN M. DERSHOWITZ

The FBI's frustration over its inability to get material witnesses to talk has raised a disturbing question rarely debated in this country: When, if ever, is it justified to resort to unconventional techniques such as truth serum, moderate physical pressure, and outright torture?

The constitutional answer to this question may surprise people who are not familiar with the current U.S. Supreme Court interpretation of the 5th Amendment privilege against self-incrimination: Any interrogation technique, including the use of truth serum or even torture, is not prohibited. All that is prohibited is the introduction into evidence of the fruits of such techniques in a criminal trial against the person on whom the techniques were used. But the evidence could be used against that suspect in a non-criminal case — such as a deportation hearing — or against someone else.

If a suspect is given "use immunity" — a judicial decree announcing in advance that nothing the defendant says (or its fruits) can be used against him in a criminal case — he can be compelled to answer all proper questions. The issue then becomes what sorts of pressures can constitutionally be used to implement that compulsion. We know that he can be imprisoned until he talks. But what if

Alan M. Dershowitz is the Felix Frankfurter Professor of Law at Harvard Law School and a civil liberties attorney who defends the indigent as well as the famous. One of his many works of fiction and nonfiction is *The Case for Moral Clarity: Israel, Hamas, and Gaza* (2009). His article appeared in *Commentary* on November 8, 2001.

Are there circumstances under which we should allow torture?

imprisonment is insufficient to compel him to do what he has a legal obligation to do? Can other techniques of compulsion be attempted?

Let's start with truth serum. What right would be violated if an immunized suspect who refused to comply with his legal obligation to answer questions truthfully were compelled to submit to an injection that made him do so?

Not his privilege against self-incrimination, since he has no such privilege now that he has been given immunity.

What about his right of bodily integrity? The involuntariness of the injection itself does not pose a constitutional barrier. No less a civil libertarian than Justice William J. Brennan rendered a decision that permitted an allegedly drunken driver to be involuntarily injected to remove blood for alcohol testing. Certainly there can be no constitutional distinction between an injection that removes a liquid and one that injects a liquid.

What about the nature of the substance injected? If it is relatively benign and creates no significant health risk, the only issue would be that it compels the recipient to do something he doesn't want to do. But he has a legal obligation to do precisely what the serum compels him to do: answer all questions truthfully.

What if the truth serum doesn't work? Could the judge issue a "torture warrant," authorizing the FBI to employ specified forms of non-lethal physical pressure to compel the immunized suspect to talk?

Here we run into another provision of the Constitution — the due process clause, which may include a general "shock the conscience" test. And torture in general certainly shocks the conscience of most civilized nations.

But what if it were limited to the rare "ticking bomb" case — the situation in which a captured terrorist who knows of an imminent large-scale threat refuses to disclose it?

5

10

Would torturing one guilty terrorist to prevent the deaths of a thousand innocent civilians shock the conscience of all decent people?

To prove that it would not, consider a situation in which a kidnapped child
had been buried in a box with two hours of oxygen. The kidnapper refuses to disclose its location. Should we not consider torture in that situation?

All of that said, the argument for allowing torture as an approved technique,
even in a narrowly specified range of cases, is very troubling.

We know from experience that law enforcement personnel who are given limited authority to torture will expand its use. The cases that have generated the current debate over torture illustrate this problem. And, concerning the arrests made
following the September 11 attacks, there is no reason to believe that the detainees
know about specific future terrorist targets. Yet there have been calls to torture
these detainees.

I have no doubt that if an actual ticking bomb situation were to arise, our law   15
enforcement authorities would torture. The real debate is whether such torture
should take place outside of our legal system or within it. The answer to this seems
clear: If we are to have torture, it should be authorized by the law.

Judges should have to issue a "torture warrant" in each case. Thus we would
not be winking an eye of quiet approval at torture while publicly condemning it.

Democracy requires accountability and transparency, especially when extraordinary steps are taken. Most important, it requires compliance with the rule of
law. And such compliance is impossible when an extraordinary technique, such as
torture, operates outside of the law.

Alan Dershowitz's Tortuous Torturous Argument

SETH FINKELSTEIN

It's torture. Literally. That is, whether or not the United States government
should use torture as a method of interrogation for suspected terrorists is now a
subject of debate.

Surprisingly, long-time civil-libertarian Alan Dershowitz has been writing
unexpectedly in favor of the legal basis for torture. On November 8, 2001, in a
commentary for [the] *Los Angeles Times* "Is There a Torturous Road to Justice?" he
discusses a proposal for a "torture warrant."

Much of the reaction to Alan Dershowitz's advocacy has blurred over a subtle
point. Given that torture is such an incendiary subject, he's been accused of advocating torture itself ("Dershowitz: Make Torture an Option" reads a headline on
cbsnews.com). However, a careful reading of his commentary makes it clear that
he isn't putting forth an argument in favor of torture *per se*. Rather, he postulates

Seth Finkelstein is a computer programmer who has worked extensively doing anticensorware
research. He is the winner of an Electronic Frontier Foundation Pioneer Award. This article was
posted to the Ethical Spectacle Web site in February 2002.

it will occur ("*I have no doubt that if an actual ticking bomb situation were to arise, our law enforcement authorities would torture.*"). His point is then almost tangential from that perspective, a professorial concern with the due process of torture! To wit:

> *The real debate is whether such torture should take place outside of our legal system or within it. The answer to this seems clear: If we are to have torture, it should be authorized by the law.*

In this piece, I will not take up the arguments against torture. That's been done far better elsewhere, by other civil-libertarians such as Harvey Silverglate, or Amnesty International. Rather, I stand in awe of Dershowitz's focus on legal authorization of torture as the *"real debate."* All the moral and practical questions are swept away by his assumption of inevitability. We are left only to consider how to deal with what, if any, judicial procedures should surround torture.

He goes on to assert: 5

> *Democracy requires accountability and transparency, especially when extraordinary steps are taken. Most important, it requires compliance with the rule of law. And such compliance is impossible when an extraordinary technique, such as torture, operates outside of the law.*

While this sounds stirring, on reflection, the meaning of the call for "accountability and transparency" is not at all clear to me. If torture is illegal, then by definition it's operating outside the law. So if a torture warrant is created, obviously torture *with warrant* would be within the law. But there seems to be a tail-wagging-the-dog situation here. Torture doesn't comply with the rule of law because it's against the law. If the law is changed so that torture is permitted (*with warrant*), then it's only become compliant with the rule of law because that rule has been changed to accept it.

What is the *purpose* of the torture warrant? Is it an anti-hypocrisy measure, to force us, as a society, to confront what we are doing? To have a public record of the event, that the defense attorney can use in a trial? To allow the torture to be supervised, with proper medical monitoring, to guard against it becoming life-threatening? To officially provide for doctors to treat the torturee during and after the ordeal?

Perhaps the idea is the simple belief that we can have legal torture, which is bad, but illegal torture would be worse. However, the obvious rebuttal is that we would end up having both legal and illegal torture, feeding off each other. Dershowitz even explicitly takes this into account ("*We know from experience that law enforcement personnel who are given limited authority to torture will expand its use.*").

So, in the face [of] this expansion of authority to torture, what is gained by making it "accountable"? The anti-hypocrisy basis seems to be Dershowitz's rationale, as he justified the above by saying:

> *Judges should have to issue a "torture warrant" in each case. Thus we would not be winking an eye of quiet approval at torture while publicly condemning it.*

Overall, Dershowitz's reasoning seems shockingly convoluted. We end up resolving the conflict between torture and the rule of law by changing the rule of law to accommodate torture. Then an admitted following expansion in torture 10 (both from legal and illegal sources) is brushed aside with the argument that the legal torture would somehow possess accountability and transparency (accountable for what? transparent how?). Suppose Dershowitz is correct that there will be illegal torture under desperate circumstances, and without issuing a torture warrant, as a society we will be "winking an eye" to it. Is he really arguing that it's better to have more torture (due to the admitted effects of the tendency [to] "expand its use"), but at least some of the torture will then be *authorized* torture? That is, judicial process is regarded as so sacred that it's worth **torturing more people** in order to preserve it in the merest formal sense? That's both tortuous and torturous.

READING AND DISCUSSION QUESTIONS

1. What does Dershowitz mean when he says that no interrogation techniques are prohibited? What is?
2. What techniques of compulsion does Dershowitz discuss?
3. What are his main points about torture?
4. What about Dershowitz's argument does Finkelstein find so objectionable?
5. Do you agree with Dershowitz's argument? Why, or why not?

WRITING SUGGESTIONS

6. Dershowitz's article appeared approximately two months after the terrorist attacks of September 11, 2001. Were his ideas logical, considering the circumstances? Explain in an essay.
7. Write an essay explaining under what circumstances you might be willing to accept that torture is appropriate.
8. What are Finkelstein's main criticisms of Dershowitz?

Could Reality Shows Become Reality Experiments?

BARBARA A. SPELLMAN

The first question is, why *don't* reality game shows have to get Institutional Review Board approval? The answer: They are not research. According to the Code of Federal Regulations, research studies are "systematic investigations designed to develop or contribute to generalizable knowledge."

Barbara Spellman is a professor of psychology at the University of Virginia and founder of the Association for Psychological Science Committee on Human Subject Protection. This article was published in the APS *Observer* in March 2005.

But certainly many reality shows touch on issues that could make great questions for behavioral researchers. So, if you were an experimenter with an unlimited budget, could you get IRB approval to run one of these reality shows as "research" and then publish your results in a leading psychology journal? For the most part, probably not. Here's why.

The Reality Review

IRBs are charged with ensuring that research is conducted ethically, and one of the core values of ethical research is respect for the autonomy of the research participants. Participants must be told everything that might "reasonably be expected to influence willingness to participate." That includes the goals of the research, what they will be doing, whether there are any risks or benefits of the study (both physical and psychological), and whether and how much they will be paid. The participants need to know that participation in the research is voluntary and that they can withdraw at any time without penalty.

Usually, this information is communicated with a consent form that the participant reads and signs before engaging in the study. However, sometimes studies can be run in which participants are not given all of this information up front — either something is left out or there is actual deception. Such deception must be necessary and justified and any potential harmful consequences of the deception must be ameliorable.

In addition, IRBs must consider the research question and carefully weigh the potential risks and benefits of the study. To take an extreme example: An experiment with a new drug that might lead to permanent brain damage might be allowable if the new drug were a cure for patients in terminal stages of cancer, but not if it were a cure for ingrown toenails.

So, suppose you proposed one of the shows below to your IRB. You are willing to give the participants a consent form. Would the shows fly?

Two programs would probably get through mostly intact. The first is *American Idol*, in which ambitious young pop singers perform in front of a panel and are judged instantly and often harshly about their abilities.

In the consent form you would tell the participants that they would be singing in front of judges that might judge them harshly — and that they might be made fun of in front of lots of people. As long as no deception was involved — for example, as long as Simon Cowell (the most obnoxious judge) didn't criticize the good people and let the bad ones slide — there is no problem with the study. Informed participants could make the decision that it was worth it for their careers to receive feedback — even harsh feedback — on their singing. In many ways, what happens on *Idol* is not much different from what happens to any new singers trying to break into the field — it just happens more quickly and more publicly.

The problem with *Idol*, though, is: What exactly would the research question be?

Something like *Who's Your Daddy?* might also make the cut, because the research potential is good; however, the lying, deception, and sleaziness would probably have to be eliminated. On this show, a woman who was adopted as a young girl must choose her real father from a dozen older men, all of whom claim to be her biological dad (one actually is). If she gets it right she gets $100,000. If she guesses wrong, the imposter who has fooled her gets the money.

The idea of the research — can people identify relatives — is interesting and possibly valuable. The argument against such research is that it could be traumatic for the participant. That is true, but the participant is over 18 and therefore (we assume) legally eligible to find out who her father is through other channels. The IRB would want to make sure the process is done in the least traumatic way possible and that psychological services are available, should they be necessary. The elements of lying would have to be eliminated. In addition, the IRB might want to cut the prize money from $100,000 to something smaller. Such a large amount might entice someone to do something against his or her best psychological interest.

This show, which was quickly cancelled, had an element of sleaze (so I'm told) in that it was always older men trying to dupe younger women. One could imagine, however, a non-deceptive study in which siblings separated at an early age tried to identify each other. Eliminating the lying, deception, sleaze, and big prize might get the show past the IRB; however, it probably wouldn't get the show past the network executives (who would worry that the eviscerated show would not have enough "juice" for the reality audience).

Too Much Psychological Risk

At the other extreme, there are two programs that could probably never make it through an IRB. The first is *Trading Spouses: Meet Your New Mommy*, in which wives swap homes for a short period of time and experience life in the new home with the other wife's partner, children, and pets.

The subtle problem with *Trading Spouses* is that there is no way to get true consent for or from any minors involved. Typically, consent has to be given by the parent — who is assumed to have the best interest of the child at heart. Also, typically, researchers get minors' "assent" — their agreement (behavioral or written, depending on age) to be in the study. An IRB would worry about real psychological risks to the children and that the children could not truly understand the potential dangers. With the lure of TV fame for the parents perhaps blinding their acknowledgment of potential risks to their children, there is no way that the parent's agreement on behalf of the minor would be seen as "objective."

On *The Swan*, women who believe themselves unattractive are offered complete, often full-body makeovers after a thorough "analysis" of their appearance by the show's plastic surgeons, dentists, etc. After the makeover, they enter a beauty contest with other made-over participants. An IRB would find here that the risks are far too great in proportion to the benefits for these activities to be allowed as research. There are not only physical risks in all of the medical procedures, but there are also great unknown psychological risks — not only for the surgery but also for the majority of participants who lose the after-makeover beauty contest. Those risks would not be perceived as outweighing the potential benefits (to either the individual or society).

15

Too Much Deception?

Sometimes deception is so great that there is no way to imagine that people would have agreed to be in the study had they known at the outset what the study was really about or would involve. For example, in *Joe Millionaire*, dozens of women compete for the hand of a supposed millionaire. When it turns out at the end that he's a minimum wage worker, they must decide whether to stay with him. This show exhibits the classic illegal action of "bait and switch" — entice someone to do something in order to receive a desirable good, then switch to a less desirable good. The very first rule of ethical research is: If it ain't legal then it ain't ethical.

Too Much Physical Risk?

It is hard to see how an IRB would approve of shows with real physical risks, such as *Fear Factor*, in which contestants compete for a cash prize by doing things their competitors might not do, such as eating ground-up rats, jumping off buildings, or laying in a coffin filled with worms. Is there any research question aside from how much physical/psychological pain will people endure for fame and/or money? As mentioned above, IRBs scrutinize excessive payments for research participation watching for potential coercion.

On *Survivor,* a dozen people are left on an island (or other exotic place). They are placed into teams and must compete against each other for food and other provisions. At the end of each show, one person (from the losing team) is voted off the island by his teammates, so backstabbing is prevalent. This scenario is a more interesting case than *Fear Factor* because there are some real possible research questions and because the physical dangers are not as immediate. With an appropriate consent form detailing the potential physical and psychological risks, strong assurances that one could quit the study without repercussion, and a re-worked payment scale, some version of *Survivor* might actually pass.

READING AND DISCUSSION QUESTIONS

1. What is an IRB, and what connection is Spellman trying to make between IRBs and reality shows?
2. How does Spellman answer the question that is her essay's title?
3. Why are examples essential to the success of her essay?
4. Why are researchers required to submit experiments to IRBs even when there is no physical threat?

WRITING SUGGESTIONS

5. Write an essay in which you discuss how some reality shows are like experiments in human behavior. Be sure to give specific examples.
6. Choose one reality show or one type of reality show and write an essay explaining why you think it is so popular.
7. Write an essay explaining what you think is wrong with reality shows. You can focus on one example or several.

A Movie, a Word, and My Family's Battle

PATRICIA E. BAUER

Margaret and I were lingering in front of the multiplex one evening last summer, a mom and her adult daughter laughing about the movie we'd just seen, when a gaggle of cute pre-teen girls sauntered past.

The one in the lead jerked a thumb in our direction and made a goofy face to her friend. "Look. Retard," we heard her say, and Margaret wilted. Her chin trembled. One by one, the other girls turned to look, nudging one another and whispering. The last girl spun all the way around as she slowly walked by, eyes fixed on my daughter.

In her size 6 jeans and Old Navy shirt, Margaret hadn't done anything to attract that unwanted attention. But then, my blond, blue-eyed daughter lives every day behind a face that can be a lightning rod for such talk. The beautiful face I've loved for 24 years displays some of the characteristic signs of Down syndrome, a chromosomal anomaly associated with varying degrees of cognitive impairment.

Last week lightning struck again, not just for Margaret, but for millions of Americans with intellectual disabilities. Ben Stiller's highly anticipated *Tropic Thunder* hit screens across the country. The film packs a powerful combination of explosions, irreverence, crudity, and political incorrectness. It also features many iterations of the word "retard."

With the film's release, the public has plunged headlong into an overheated   5
argument about the borders between comedy and hate speech, political correctness and oversensitivity. I know, because posts that I put on my blog, drawing attention to the movie's marketing and discussion of a character with an intellectual disability, have set off a firestorm in Hollywood and the disability community. Protesters picketed *Tropic Thunder*'s premiere last week, while the film's high-profile stars defended it as a parody aimed at the movie industry.

The film features Stiller, Robert Downey Jr., and Jack Black as unsavory actors who are thrust into a real conflict while filming a war movie. Stiller's character is an actor who previously sought Oscar glory by portraying Simple Jack, a man with an intellectual disability, a bowl haircut reminiscent of state institutions, and few relatable qualities. Cue the retard jokes.

The original marketing campaign, featured on a Web site that was taken down in response to complaints, included an image of Stiller as Simple Jack bearing the

---

Patricia E. Bauer, a former *Washington Post* reporter, edits patriciaebauer.com, a Web site of news and commentary on issues related to disability.

memorable tagline, "Once upon a time . . . There was a retard." Another marketed scene depicts Downey uttering the line that will undoubtedly launch a thousand T-shirts: "Never go full retard."

For years I've tried to figure out how to handle moments like these, when the word "retard" crash-lands at our feet, either aimed directly at Margaret or tossed around as an all-purpose weapon. It has become a routine epithet, used to describe something or someone stupid or worthless or pathetic. For my daughter and my family, it's more like a grenade, and we're the collateral damage. "It's not a good word," Margaret says. "It's mean, it's insulting, and it hurts people's feelings."

As the word has seemingly become increasingly pervasive in recent years, I've tried gently to let others know that it heaps scorn on people who are already stigmatized and may not be in a position to defend themselves. The responses I've gotten? *Gosh, everybody says it. It's just a joke.* Or: *I didn't mean it like that.* Or: *Lighten up. It doesn't mean anything.* People reacted as if I'd offended them when I told tell them that they were insulting my daughter and others like her; they would never insult such people, they said.

Discouraged, I started letting it pass, gritting my teeth, wishing it would go 10 away. Not everyone uses it, and sometimes I wonder whether I'm overreacting. But I hear it at every turn. A clerk in a store apologizes for being "such a retard" when she can't find an item for me. Ouch. Kids at the mall call one another "you big retard." Ouch. A friend tells a long, involved story at my dinner table about her recent fender bender, with a punchline about "some retard" who parked behind her. Ouch. Ouch. Ouch.

With each of these incidents, I hear what others perhaps don't hear. This word, derived from a clinical term used to describe people like my daughter, carries a cultural subtext so huge that we don't even notice it. By using it, we threaten years of progress toward a society that accepts and values all its citizens, including the 14.3 million with cognitive disabilities.

When I was young, kids like my daughter were kept at home or, worse, sent to institutions by the hundreds of thousands. They had no legally guaranteed right to an education.

A man my age who grew up in a small town in Georgia told me about a boy with Down syndrome who lived down the street. The boy wasn't allowed to go to school and was kept behind a board fence in the backyard; neighborhood kids used to climb a tree to spy on him. The man wept as he recalled the view from an overhanging branch.

Over the past 35 years, the legal landscape has been transformed. In 1975, the Individuals with Disabilities Education Act granted children with disabilities the right to a public education, and the federal government pledged to pay a substantial portion of local special-education costs. The Americans with Disabilities Act of 1990 prohibited discrimination against the disabled. A group of people who'd been invisible emerged to work toward taking their rightful place in society.

We've come a long way, but we still have far to go. There are still 38,000 15 people with intellectual and developmental disabilities housed in institutions nationwide. The federal government hasn't kept its promise to fund special education, and millions of children across the country remain poorly served or not served at all.

Meanwhile, adults with intellectual disabilities are on waiting lists for independent living services all over the country; one recent report estimated more than 100,000 in Texas alone. These adults are largely unemployed and frequently live in poverty. Experts estimate that fewer than 20 percent of those of working age are employed, even though research shows that they are reliable and effective workers when given support and matched with appropriate jobs.

Without a coherent federal policy for providing community services and support, millions of families across the country are left to take care of their loved ones on their own. Parents have little assurance that their adult children will be cared for after they die. At last count, 715,000 people were residing with caregivers age 60 and older. As life expectancies increase, that number grows.

On top of all this is the problem of negative public attitudes. Recent research conducted by the University of Massachusetts found that, if given a choice, more than half of young people wouldn't spend time with a student with an intellectual disability. More than half of parents didn't want such students at their children's school. Almost half of the young people surveyed wouldn't sit next to a student like Margaret on a school bus.

I find these facts and statistics terrifying. My husband and I have spent much of the past two decades doing all we can to shield Margaret from the effects of what I've just described. With a lot of hard work on her part, and with the active support of family and friends, she's faring far better than doctors predicted when she was born. She's a high school graduate, works part-time at a Mediterranean restaurant, takes care of her own apartment, and volunteers at her local hospital and senior center. She's a regular at the gym. She has a lively social network, a cell-phone, an e-mail address. That's not to say that her life is rosy all the time, but it seems to be working.

I'd like to hold on to the hope that Margaret's journey reflects our steady national progress toward respecting and valuing all our citizens. But I'm stopped cold by the thought of a major studio constructing an ad campaign and film that prominently feature the word "retard" without a thought to the consequences.   20

According to the nonprofit Arc of the United States, people with developmental disabilities are 4 to 10 times more likely to be victims of violence than those without. There are always people looking to pick on other people. With the introduction of "Never go full retard" into the lexicon, I can't help thinking that those people have been handed both a weapon and a target.

DreamWorks and the actors in *Tropic Thunder* have already said that this is not their problem. They say that the movie targets Hollywood and seeks to criticize past exploitation of people with disabilities in stereotype-filled blockbusters such as *Rain Man* and *Forrest Gump*.

Such criticism is surely present, and it's not wide of the mark. The film is rated "R" for a reason. It's art, even if crude and distasteful, and it's entitled to this country's broad protections for freedom of speech and expression.

Yet *Tropic Thunder* provides another example of the unthinking acceptance of language that promotes oppression. Anticipating public scrutiny, the studio was careful to build nuance and subtlety into the film's racial humor. A white actor who uses blackface to portray a black character is countered at every turn by a black actor critiquing his actions. But there's no on-screen presence countering the Simple Jack portrayal, nor did the filmmakers consult people with intellectual disabilities or their families about the script.

It seems that the studio never considered that its portrayal of people with disabilities would touch a nerve farther below the skin than it would want to go. Again we hear: I didn't mean it like *that,* and lighten up. It doesn't mean anything.   25

For millions of Americans like Margaret and me, it does.

The Case Against Banning the Word "Retard"

CHRISTOPHER M. FAIRMAN

Does the word "retard" have less than three weeks to live? Long before Rahm Emanuel, Sarah Palin, and Rush Limbaugh made the word fodder for political controversy and late-night punch lines, a movement was underway to eliminate it from everyday conversation. Saying, irrefutably, that the word and its variations are hurtful to many, the Special Olympics is leading a campaign to end its use and is promoting a national awareness day on March 3. Nearly 60,000 people have signed on to the following promise on www.r-word.org: "I pledge and support the elimination of the derogatory use of the r-word from everyday speech and promote the acceptance and inclusion of people with intellectual disabilities."

I sympathize with the effort, but I won't be making that pledge. It's not that I've come to praise the word "retard"; I just don't think we should bury it. If the history of offensive terms in America shows anything, it is that words themselves are not the culprit; the meaning we attach to them is, and such meanings change dramatically over time and across communities. The term "mentally retarded" was itself introduced by the medical establishment in the 20th century to supplant other terms that had been deemed offensive. Similarly, the words "gay" and "queer" and even the N-word can be insulting, friendly, identifying, or academic in different contexts.

Christopher M. Fairman is a professor at the Moritz College of Law at Ohio State University. He is the author of a book subtitled *Word Taboo and Protecting Our First Amendment Liberties* (2009). This article appeared in the *Washington Post* on February 14, 2010.

The varied and evolving uses of such words ultimately render self-censorship campaigns unnecessary. And restricting speech of any kind comes with a potential price — needlessly institutionalized taboos, government censorship, or abridged freedom of expression — that we should be wary of paying.

The latest battle over the R-word kicked into high gear with a Jan. 26 *Wall Street Journal* report that last summer White House Chief of Staff Rahm Emanuel blasted liberal activists unhappy with the pace of health-care reform, deriding their strategies as "[expletive] retarded." Palin, the mother of a special-needs child, quickly took to Facebook to demand Emanuel's firing, likening the offensiveness of the R-word to that of the N-word. Limbaugh seized the low ground, saying he found nothing wrong with "calling a bunch of people who are retards, retards," and Palin rushed to his defense, saying Limbaugh had used the word satirically. Comedy Central's Stephen Colbert took her up on it, calling Palin an "[expletive] retard" and adding, with a smile: "You see? It's satire!" 5

Emanuel apologized and promised to take the Word.org pledge, but as March 3 nears, the word may already be an endangered species. Forty-eight states have voted to remove the term "mental retardation" from government agencies and state codes, and legislation is pending in Congress to strike it from any federal statutes that still use it, such as the Individuals With Disabilities Education Act. The largest advocacy group for the intellectually disabled, the Association for Retarded Citizens, is now simply the Arc. Similarly, the American Association of Mental Retardation is now the American Association on Intellectual and Developmental Disabilities. The Centers for Disease Control and Prevention now use "intellectual disability" in place of "mental retardation." The diagnostic manuals used by medical professionals also embrace "intellectual disability" as the official label. Behind the changes is the belief that "retardation" doesn't communicate dignity and respect.

The irony is that the use of "mental retardation" and its variants was originally an attempt to convey greater dignity and respect than previous labels had. While the verb "retard" — meaning to delay or hinder — has roots in the 15th century, its use in reference to mental development didn't occur until the late 19th and early 20th centuries, when medical texts began to describe children with "retarded mental development," "retarded children" and "mentally retarded patients." By the 1960s, "mental retardation" became the preferred medical term, gradually replacing previous diagnostic standards such as "idiot," "imbecile," and "moron" — terms that had come to carry pejorative connotations.

As I was growing up in the 1970s, my father worked for the Texas Department of Mental Health and Mental Retardation, one of the now-renamed state agencies. The term "retardation" was common in my home and life, but it was sterile and clinical. It is only in the past generation that the medical term turned into the slang "retard" and gained power as an insult. The shift is even apparent in popular movies. There was little public controversy when Matt Dillon tried to woo Cameron Diaz in the 1998 hit comedy *There's Something About Mary* by confessing his passion: "I work with retards." (Diaz's character, Mary, had a mentally disabled brother.) But 10 years later, in the comedy *Tropic Thunder*, Robert Downey Jr.'s use of the phrase "full retard" led to picketing and calls for a boycott.

What happened to make the word a target for extinction?

All cultures have taboos. Western culture, particularly in the United States, has several taboos surrounding sexuality, grounded largely in a subconscious fear of the parade of horribles — adultery, unwanted pregnancy, incest, venereal disease — that might befall us because of some sexual behaviors. Sometimes the taboo extends to even uttering the words that describe certain behaviors. You can see word taboo at work in the way Emanuel's blunder was reported: "[expletive] retarded." It's still okay to print the R-word. The F-word? Forget it.

For years, I've been researching taboo language and its interaction with the law, and I have written a law review article and recently a book, both titled with the unprintable four letter F-word. The resilience of word taboos, the multiple usages and meanings of a single word, the rise of self-censorship, and the risks of institutionalized taboo and ultimately censorship are all core issues surrounding the F-word, and they help explain what is happening — and may happen still — with the R-word.

Mental disorders also carry cultural taboos. For centuries, mental illness and disability were poorly understood; as recently as the 1800s, they were thought to be the work of devils and demons. Because the origins of mental illness were a mystery, fears that such conditions could be contagious led to isolation through institutionalization. Shame was often attached to individuals and their families, and the result was stigma.

Fortunately, we've come a long way from those days. It's precisely the new enlightenment and openness about mental disabilities that allow Palin to launch the controversy over "retard." But at a subconscious level, the underlying taboo may explain why we constantly seek new terms for this type of disability, new ways to avoid the old stigmas. Invariably, negative connotations materialize around whatever new word is used; "idiot" becomes an insult and gives way to "retardation," which in turn suffers the same fate, leading to "intellectual disability." This illustrates one of the recurring follies of speech restriction: While there may be another word to use, a negative connotation eventually is found. Offense — both given and taken — is inevitable.

Whatever future offensiveness may emerge, though, are we not better off by purging today's insulting language and making our discourse a little kinder? That is the argument of self-censorship advocates such as Palin, who draws parallels between the use of the R-word and the N-word — the most powerful and insulting of all racial epithets. In some respects, the comparison seems overblown. The N-word invokes some of the foulest chapters in our nation's history; "retard," however harsh, pales in comparison. But there still may be some guidance to be gleaned.

While the N-word endures as an insult, it is so stigmatized that its use is no longer tolerated in public discourse. This is a positive step for us all, of course, but its containment does not come without costs. As Harvard law professor Randall Kennedy described in his 2002 book on the subject, stigmatizing the word has elicited new problems, including an overeagerness to detect insult where none is intended and the use of excessively harsh punishment against those who use the word wrongly.

I've coined a term for overzealous or extreme responses to insulting words: "word fetish." Those under the influence of word fetish aren't content to refrain from using a certain word; they are set on eradicating any use by others. A classic example was the plight of David Howard, a white employee in the D.C. mayor's office in 1999. Howard told staff members that because of budget cuts, he would have to be "niggardly" with available funds. Wrongly believing "niggardly" was a variation of the N-word, black subordinates lobbied for his resignation. Howard ultimately resigned after public protests, though he was soon reinstated. If the campaign against "retard" is successful, an identical risk of word fetish exists. (Imagine that Emanuel had spoken of "retarding the opposition" — would that be unacceptable?)

Like virtually every word in our language, the N-word has multiple uses. While its use as an insult has decreased, there has been a resurgence of the word as a term of identification, even affection, among some African Americans. But should certain groups of people, to the exclusion of others, be allowed to reclaim certain words? If "retard" or "retarded" were similarly restricted, could intellectually disabled individuals appropriate the term for self-identification, essentially reclaiming its original use or developing a new one?

Over time, word fetish can evolve into censorship among private organizations and ultimately direct government control of language and institutionalized word taboo. During the 1980s and 1990s, for example, many colleges and universities sought to reduce discrimination by developing speech codes, often targeting racial hate speech such as the N-word. Even with the most combustible insults, however, there must be some accommodation to their continued use; freedom of expression surely embraces unpopular, even insulting, speech. Luckily, speech codes that have been challenged in court have generally lost because they violated the First Amendment.

The risk of direct government censorship of the word "retard" is real. The New Zealand chapter of the Special Olympics is already calling on the country's Broadcasting Standards Authority (equivalent to our Federal Communications Commission) to deem the word "retard" unacceptable for broadcast. This plea is based upon a single incident involving New Zealand television personality Paul Henry, who described the runner-up in the *Britain's Got Talent* competition, Susan Boyle, as retarded. It is not difficult to imagine calls for a similar broadcast ban emerging here.

The current public awareness campaign surrounding the use of the word "gay" 20 offers better lessons and parallels for the R-word debate. Advocacy groups contend that the phrase "that's so gay" fosters homophobia and that anti-gay language is directly related to violence and harassment against homosexuals. At the same time, there is recognition that much anti-gay language is uttered carelessly and isn't necessarily intended as hurtful — as is probably the case with uses of "retard." The Ad Council and the Gay, Lesbian, and Straight Education Network have developed a Web site, ThinkB4YouSpeak.com, that, much like R-Word.org, encourages the public to sign a pledge to cease using the phrase. (The slogan: "Saying that's so gay is so yesterday.")

By increasing sensitivity and awareness, the campaign hopes to encourage people to think about the possible consequences of their word choices. Such reflection would presumably lead individuals to censor themselves once they understand that others can be hurt by their language.

Inherent in this idea is the realization that words have multiple meanings and that those meanings depend on the context and circumstances surrounding any particular statement. For example, "gay" is a term of identification for homosexuals, but it also can be used as an all-purpose put-down: "That's so gay." Those using it as an insult don't intend to say "that's so homosexual," nor do they necessarily make the conscious leap that homosexuality is bad. (Indeed, the success of the ThinkB4YouSpeak.com campaign depends on this distinction.)

Similarly, the R-word has multiple usages. When Emanuel calls fellow Democrats "retarded" for jeopardizing a legislative plan, the term is a stand-in for "stupid" or "misguided" or "dumb" — it obviously does not mean that they meet the IQ diagnostic standard for intellectual disability. It is quite another thing to look at a person with Down syndrome and call him or her a "retard." So, if there are readily identifiable alternate meanings, what is the reason for censorship?

Differing usages also give rise to reclaiming — when words that have an offensive meaning are deliberately given a new spin. The putative slur is captured, repurposed and owned by the target of insult. We see this when an African American uses the N-word as a term of identification for his friends, or when the word "queer" is reclaimed for TV shows such as *Queer Eye for the Straight Guy* and *Queer as Folk*, and for queer studies and queer theory in university courses. Reclaiming the word "retard" is an option that should involve no risk to freedom of expression.

If interest groups want to pour resources into cleaning up unintentional insults, more power to them; we surely would benefit from greater kindness to one another. But we must not let "retard" go without a requiem. If the goal is to protect intellectually disabled individuals from put-downs and prejudice, it won't succeed. New words of insult will replace old ones. 25

Words are ideas, and we should be reluctant to surrender any of them. Freedom of expression has come at a dear price, and it is not worth abridging, even so we can get along a little better. That's one F-word we really can't do without.

DISCUSSION QUESTIONS

1. Is it acceptable, in your opinion, to use the word "retard"? What if you are just among your friends?

2. In what contexts is Bauer opposed to the use of the word "retard"? Is her position justified? Explain your answer.

3. What claims does Bauer make about the harm that results from the use of "retard"?

4. What emotional appeals does Bauer make in her argument? How persuasive do you find them?

5. What is Fairman's position on the use of the word "retard"?

6. In paragraph 2 of Fairman's piece he cites a pledge from www.r-word.org. In that pledge, what does "derogatory use" mean? Why is that important?

7. Why won't Fairman be making the pledge?

8. Is Fairman making a claim of fact, value, or policy? Explain.

9. Who makes a more compelling case, Bauer or Fairman? Why?

Assignments for Analytical Writing

READING AND DISCUSSION QUESTIONS

1. Choose an editorial from your campus or local newspaper and evaluate it. How successful an argument does it make?

2. Which of the three analyses of reality television presented here provides the strongest argument? Defend your choice.

3. Do you agree with Ravitch's view of education as presented by Roger Kaplan?

4. Barbara Dafoe Whitehead argues that parents need help from the state in controlling their children's leisure activities. Charles Krauthammer (p. 39) argues that parents should not interfere with the way the state says that science should be taught in public schools. Who provides a more convincing argument?

WRITING SUGGESTIONS

5. Choose an editorial from your campus or local newspaper and write an objective analysis of it. Your thesis statement will be a claim of fact.

6. Locate two editorials or two articles that take different stands on the same controversial issue. Write an analysis in which you objectively compare the two as examples of argumentation.

7. Locate two editorials or two articles that take different stands on the same controversial issue. Write an essay in which you argue which of the two is a more effective argument and why.

8. Write an analysis of Eric Jaffe's "Reality Check" (p. 93) that supports a claim of value.

Research Readiness: Incorporating Quotations

What is the best way to include in your own writing what others have to say?

The Writer's Guide on page 88 illustrates three ways of incorporating direct quotations into your own text. The ability to work quotations smoothly into your writing gives it a sophistication that it otherwise would lack. One of the signs of an immature use of sources is having "floating quotations." That means that the writer moves from his or her own text into a direct quote with no specific connection having been made. Another is back-to-back quotations — two direct quotations with none of your own text in between.

Remember that you use quotations to support your ideas, not to replace them. And use them sparingly. Use summary or paraphrase when possible to incorporate another's ideas. Save direct quotations for those times when the wording is particularly important or striking.

ASSIGNMENT

Read each of the following passages. Then for each, write one or two sentences incorporating a quotation. Also incorporate in your sentence(s) the author's name and the title of the work. Choose a different way of incorporating the quote each time so that all three ways are represented: (1) as a grammatical part of your own sentence, (2) with a speech tag such as "he says" or "she writes," and (3) with a complete sentence and a colon.

Put the page number in parentheses and punctuate correctly according to MLA style.

PASSAGE 1

1. From page 158 of "Gay Marriage Shows Why We Need to Separate Church and State," by Howard Moody. So what is marriage? It depends on whom you ask, in what era, in what culture. Like all words or institutions, human definitions, whether religious or secular, change with time and history. When our beloved Constitution was written, blacks, Native Americans, and, to some extent, women were quasihuman beings with no rights or privileges, but today they are recognized as persons with full citizenship rights. The definition of marriage has been changing over the centuries in this nation, and it will change yet again as homosexuals are seen as ordinary human beings.

PASSAGE 2

2. From page 333 of "A New Look, an Old Battle" by Anna Quindlen. The catalytic issue is research on stem cells. These are versatile building blocks that may be coaxed into becoming any other type of cell type; they could therefore hold the key to endless mysteries of human biology, as well as someday help provide a cure for ailments as diverse as diabetes, Parkinson's, spinal-cord degeneration, and Alzheimer's. By some estimates, more than 100 million Americans have diseases that scientists suspect

could be affected by research on stem cells. Scientists hope that the astonishing potential of this research will persuade the federal government to help fund it and allow the National Institutes of Health to help oversee it. This is not political, researchers insist. It is about science, not abortion.

PASSAGE 3

3. From page 163 of "Will It Be Marriage or Civil Union?" by Jo Ann Citron. But let there be no mistake: Whatever happens in Massachusetts is absolutely critical to how the gay marriage question will be answered in the rest of the United States. What happens here is even more important than what happened in Vermont. Here's why. The next marriage case with a reasonable likelihood of success is working its way through the courts in New Jersey, a state with a history of progressive court decisions. New Jersey will be looking very carefully at the way Vermont and Massachusetts have addressed the marriage question. If the Massachusetts SJC [Supreme Judicial Court] ratifies its decision and mandates the issuance of marriage licenses, New Jersey will look at its predecessor states and see two alternative models, marriage and civil union. New Jersey will choose one or the other. But the SJC could fail to confirm its marriage decision and approve instead some form of civil union. Coupled with the Vermont ruling, this will create a critical mass in favor of civil union, an outcome that will make it far more likely that New Jersey will opt for civil union over marriage. After that, the rest of the states will almost certainly fall into line with civil unions, and that will spell the end of gay marriage, probably forever.

PART 2

Analyzing the Elements

4

Definition

The Purposes of Definition

Before we examine the other elements of argument, we need to consider definition, a component you may have to deal with early in writing an essay.

Arguments often revolve around definitions of crucial terms. For example, how does one define *democracy*? Does a democracy guarantee freedom of the press, freedom of worship, freedom of assembly, and freedom of movement? In the United States, we would argue that such freedoms are essential to any definition of *democracy*. But countries in which these freedoms are nonexistent also represent themselves as democracies or governments of the people. In the words of Senator Daniel P. Moynihan, "For years now the most brutal totalitarian regimes have called themselves 'people's' or 'democratic' republics." Rulers in such governments are aware that defining their regimes as democratic may win the approval of people who would otherwise condemn them. In his formidable attack on totalitarianism in *1984*, George Orwell coined the slogans "War Is Peace" and "Slavery Is Freedom," phrases that represent the corrupt use of definition to distort reality.

But even where there is no intention to deceive, the snares of definition are difficult to avoid. How do you define *abortion*? Is it "termination of pregnancy"? Or is it "murder of an unborn child"? During a celebrated trial in 1975 of a physician who performed an abortion and was accused of manslaughter, the prosecution often used the word *baby* to refer to the fetus, but the defense referred to "the products of conception." These definitions of *fetus* reflected the differing judgments of those on opposite sides. Not only do judgments create definitions; definitions influence judgments.

Definitions can indeed change the nature of an event or a "fact." How many farms are there in the state of New York? The answer to the question depends on the definition of *farm*. In 1979 the *New York Times* reported:

> Because of a change in the official definition of the word "farm," New York lost 20 percent of its farms on January 1, with numbers dropping from 56,000 to 45,000. . . .
>
> Before the change, a farm was defined as "any place from which $250 or more of agricultural products is sold" yearly or "any place of 10 acres or more from which $50 or more of agricultural products is sold" yearly. Now a farm is "any place from which $1,000 or more of agricultural products is sold" in a year.[1]

A change in the definition of *poverty* can have similar results. An article in the *New York Times*, whose headline reads, "A Revised Definition of Poverty May Raise Number of U.S. Poor," makes this clear:

> The official definition of *poverty* used by the Federal Government for three decades is based simply on cash income before taxes. But in a report to be issued on Wednesday, a panel of experts convened by the [National] Academy of Sciences three years ago at the behest of Congress says the Government should move toward a concept of poverty based on disposable income, the amount left after a family pays taxes and essential expenses.[2]

The differences are wholly a matter of definition. But such differences can have serious consequences for those being defined, most of all in the disposition of billions of federal dollars in aid of various kinds. In 1992 the Census Bureau classified 14.5 percent of Americans as poor. Under the new guidelines, at least 15 or 16 percent would be poor, and, under some measures recommended by a government panel, 18 percent would be so defined.

In fact, local and federal courts almost every day redefine traditional concepts that can have a direct impact on our everyday lives. The definition of *family*, for example, has undergone significant changes that acknowledge the existence of new relationships. In January 1990 the New Jersey Supreme Court ruled that a family may be defined as "one or more persons occupying a dwelling unit as a single nonprofit housekeeping unit, who are living together as a stable and permanent living unit, being a traditional family unit or the *functional equivalent* thereof" (italics for emphasis added). This meant that ten Glassboro State College students, unrelated by blood, could continue to occupy a single-family house despite the objection of the borough of Glassboro.[3] Even the legal definition of *maternity* has shifted. Who is the mother — the woman who contributes the egg or the woman (the surrogate) who bears the child? Several states, acknowledging the changes brought by medical technology, now recognize a difference between the birth mother and the legal mother.

---

[1]*New York Times*, March 4, 1979, sec. 1, p. 40.
[2]*New York Times*, April 10, 1995, sec. A, p. 1.
[3]*New York Times*, February 1, 1990, sec. B, p. 5.

Does this couple live on a farm? It depends on how you define the term.

Defining the Terms in Your Argument

In some of your arguments you will introduce terms that require definition. We've pointed out that a definition of *poverty* is crucial to any debate on the existence of poverty in the United States. The same may be true in a debate about the legality of euthanasia, or mercy killing. Are the arguers referring to passive euthanasia (the withdrawal of life-support systems) or to active euthanasia (the direct administration of drugs to hasten death)? It is not uncommon, in fact, for arguments about controversial questions to turn into arguments about the definition of terms.

An argument can end almost before it begins if writer and reader cannot agree on definitions of key terms. While clear definitions do not guarantee agreement, they do ensure that all parties understand the nature of the argument.

In the Rogerian approach to argumentation, negotiating a definition that all parties can accept is the starting point to resolving conflict.

Defining Vague and Ambiguous Terms

You will need to define other terms in addition to those in your claim. If you use words and phrases that have two or more meanings, they may appear vague and ambiguous to your reader. In arguments of value and policy abstract terms such as *freedom of speech, justice,* and *equality* require clarification. Despite their abstract nature, however, they are among the most important in the language because they represent the ideals that shape our laws. When conflicts arise, the courts must define these terms to establish the legality of certain practices. Is the Ku Klux Klan permitted to make disparaging public statements about ethnic and racial groups? That depends on the court's definition of *free speech.* Can execution for some crimes be considered cruel and unusual punishment? That, too, depends on the court's definition of *cruel and unusual punishment.*

Consider the definition of *race,* around which so much of American history has revolved, often with tragic consequences. Until recently, the only categories listed in the census were white, black, Asian-Pacific, and Native American, "with the Hispanic population straddling them all." But rapidly increasing intermarriage and ethnic identity caused a number of political and ethnic groups to demand changes in the classifications of the Census Bureau. Some Arab Americans, for example, prefer to be counted as "Middle Eastern" rather than white. Children of black-white unions are defined as black 60 percent of the time, while children of Asian-white unions are described as Asian 42 percent of the time. Research is now being conducted to discover how people feel about the terms being used to define them. As one anthropologist pointed out, "Socially and politically assigned attributes have a lot to do with access to economic resources."[4]

"Socially and politically assigned attributes" can also be the basis for judging others. The definition of *success,* for example, varies among social groups as well as among individuals within the group. One scientist has postulated five signs by which to measure success: wealth (including health), security (confidence in retaining the wealth), reputation, performance, and contentment.[5] Consider whether all of these are necessary to your own definition of *success.* If not, which may be omitted? Do you think others should be added? Notice that one of the signs — reputation — is defined by the community; another — contentment — can be measured only by the individual. The assessment of performance probably owes something to both the group and the individual.

Christopher Atkins, an actor, gave an interviewer an example of an externalized definition of success — that is, a definition based on the standards imposed by other people:

[4]*Wall Street Journal,* September 9, 1995, sec. B, p. 1.
[5]Gwynn Nettler, *Social Concerns* (New York: McGraw-Hill, 1976), pp. 196–97.

Success to me is judged through the eyes of others. I mean, if you're walking around saying, "I own a green Porsche," you might meet somebody who says, "Hey, that's no big deal. I own a green Porsche and a house." So all of a sudden, you don't feel so successful. Really, it's in the eyes of others.[6]

So difficult is the formulation of a universally accepted measure for success that some scholars regard the concept as meaningless. Nevertheless, we continue to use the word as if it represented a definable concept because the idea of success, however defined, is important for the identity and development of the individual and the group. It is clear, however, that when crossing subcultural boundaries, even within a small group, we need to be aware of differences in the use of the word. If contentment — that is, the satisfaction of achieving a small personal goal — is enough, then a person making a minimal salary but doing work that he or she loves may be a success. But you should not expect all your readers to agree that these criteria are enough to define *success*.

PRACTICE

1. Use one or more cases to illustrate how, in a court of law, guilt or innocence can hinge on a matter of definition.

2. Choose two terms that are sometimes confused and define them to make their differences clear. Some examples are *active euthanasia* and *passive euthanasia*, *psychologist* and *psychiatrist*, *manslaughter* and *murder*, *envy* and *jealousy*, *sympathy* and *pity*, and *liberal* and *radical*.

3. Many recent controversial movements and causes are identified by terms that have come to mean different things to different people. Define the following terms, considering any positive or negative connotations of each. Also consider whether there is a term with a similar meaning that has more positive or more negative connotations.

   a. abortion
   b. war on terror
   c. affirmative action
   d. assisted suicide
   e. undocumented workers

Methods for Defining Terms

Reading a dictionary definition is the simplest and most obvious way to learn the basic definition of a term. An unabridged dictionary is the best source because

---

[6]*New York Times*, August 6, 1982, sec. 3, p. 8.

it usually gives examples of the way a word can be used in a sentence; that is, it furnishes the proper context.

In many cases, the dictionary definition alone is not sufficient. It may be too broad or too narrow for your purpose. Suppose, in an argument about pornography, you wanted to define the word *obscene*. *Webster's New International Dictionary* (third edition, unabridged) gives the definition of *obscene* as "offensive to taste; foul; loathsome; disgusting." But these synonyms do not tell you what qualities make an object or an event or an action "foul," "loathsome," and "disgusting." In 1973 the Supreme Court, attempting to narrow the definition of *obscenity*, ruled that obscenity was to be determined by the community in accordance with local standards. One person's obscenity, as numerous cases have demonstrated, may be another person's art. The celebrated trials in the early twentieth century about the distribution of novels regarded as pornographic — D. H. Lawrence's *Lady Chatterley's Lover* and James Joyce's *Ulysses* — emphasized the problems of defining obscenity.

Another dictionary definition may strike you as too narrow. *Patriotism,* for example, is defined in one dictionary as "love and loyal or zealous support of one's country, especially in all matters involving other countries." Some readers may want to include an unwillingness to support government policies they consider wrong.

These limitations are the reason that opening an essay with a dictionary definition is often not a very effective strategy, although it is a strategy often used by beginning writers. In order to initiate the effective discussion of a key term, you should be able to define it in your own words.

Stipulation

In stipulating the meaning of a term, the writer asks the reader to accept a definition that may be different from the conventional one. He or she does this to limit or control the argument. A term like *national security* can be defined by a nation's leaders in such a way as to sanction persecution of citizens and reckless military adventures. Likewise, a term such as *liberation* can be appropriated by terrorist groups whose activities often lead to oppression rather than liberation.

Even the word *violence,* which the dictionary defines as "physical force used so as to injure or damage" and whose meaning seems so clear and uncompromising, can be manipulated to produce a definition different from the one normally understood by most people. Some pacifists refer to conditions in which "people are deprived of choices in a systematic way" as "institutionalized quiet violence." Even where no physical force is employed, this lack of choice in schools, in the workplace, in the black ghettos is defined as violence.[7]

---

[7]Newton Garver, "What Violence Is," in James Rachels, ed., *Moral Choices* (New York: Harper and Row, 1971), pp. 248–49.

A reader and an audience cannot agree on a solution to a problem if they cannot even agree on what they are talking about. Carl Rogers's advice applies here: Listen to how your audience defines a key term. Make clear how you define it. And then work from there toward a definition that you can stipulate as the agreed-upon definition that you will use as you move toward resolution.

In *Through the Looking-Glass* Alice asked Humpty Dumpty "whether you can make words mean so many different things."

> "When *I* use a word," Humpty Dumpty said scornfully, "it means just what I choose it to mean — neither more nor less."[8]

A writer, however, is not free to invent definitions that no one will recognize or that create rather than solve problems between writer and reader.

Negation

To avoid confusion it is sometimes helpful to tell the reader what a term is *not*. In discussing euthanasia, a writer might say, "By euthanasia I do not mean active intervention to hasten the death of the patient."

A negative definition may be more extensive, depending on the complexity of the term and the writer's ingenuity. The former Communist party member Whittaker Chambers, in a foreword to a book on the spy trial of Alger Hiss, defined *communism* this way:

> First, let me try to say what Communism is not. It is not simply a vicious plot hatched by wicked men in a subcellar. It is not just the writings of Marx and Lenin, dialectical materialism, the Politburo, the labor theory of value, the theory of the general strike, the Red Army secret police, labor camps, underground conspiracy, the dictatorship of the proletariat, the technique of the coup d'état. It is not even those chanting, bannered millions that stream periodically, like disorganized armies, through the heart of the world's capitals: Moscow, New York, Tokyo, Paris, Rome. These are expressions, but they are not what Communism is about.[9]

This, of course, is only part of the definition. Any writer beginning a definition in the negative must go on to define what the term *is*.

Examples

One of the most effective ways of defining terms in an argument is to use examples. Both real and hypothetical examples can bring life to abstract and

---

[8]Lewis Carroll, *Alice in Wonderland and Through the Looking-Glass* (New York: Grosset and Dunlap, 1948), p. 238.

[9]*Witness* (New York: Random House, 1952), p. 8.

ambiguous terms. The writer in the following passage defines *preferred categories* (classes of people who are meant to benefit from affirmative action policies) by invoking specific cases:

> The absence of definitions points up one of the problems with preferred categories. . . . These preferred categories take no account of family wealth or educational advantages. A black whose father is a judge or physician deserves preferential treatment over any nonminority applicant. The latter might have fought his way out of the grinding poverty of Appalachia, or might be the first member of an Italian American or a Polish American family to complete high school. But no matter.[10]

Extended Definition

When we speak of an extended definition, we usually refer not only to length but also to the variety of methods for developing the definition. Let's take the word *materialism*. A dictionary entry offers the following sentence fragments as definitions: "1. the doctrine that comfort, pleasure, and wealth are the only or highest goals or values. 2. the tendency to be more concerned with material than the spiritual goals or values." But the term *materialism* has acquired so many additional meanings, especially emotional ones, that an extended definition serves a useful purpose in clarifying the many different ideas surrounding our understanding of the term.

Below is a much longer definition of *materialism*, which appears at the beginning of an essay entitled "People and Things: Reflections on Materialism."[11]

> There are two contemporary usages of the term *materialism*, and it is important to distinguish between them. On the one hand we can talk about *instrumental materialism*, or the use of material objects to make life longer, safer, more enjoyable. By instrumental, we mean that objects act as essential means for discovering and furthering personal values and goals of life, so that the objects are instruments used to realize and further those goals. There is little negative connotation attached to this meaning of the word, since one would think that it is perfectly sensible to use things for such purposes. While it is true that the United States is the epitome of materialism in this sense, it is also true that most people in every society aspire to reach our level of instrumental materialism.
>
> On the other hand the term has a more negative connotation, which might be conveyed by the phrase *terminal materialism*. This is the sense critics use when they apply the term to Americans. What they mean is that we not only use our material resources as instruments to make life more manageable, but that we reduce our ultimate goals to the possession of things. They believe that we don't just use our cars to get from place

---

[10]Anthony Lombardo, "Quotas Work Both Ways," *U.S. Catholic*, February 1974, p. 39.
[11]Mihaly Csikszentmihalyi and Eugene Rochberg-Halton, "People and Things: Reflections on Materialism," *University of Chicago Magazine*, Spring 1978, pp. 7–8.

to place, but that we consider the ownership of expensive cars one of the central values in life. Terminal materialism means that the object is valued only because it indicates an end in itself, a possession. In instrumental materialism there is a sense of directionality, in which a person's goals may be furthered through the interactions with the object. A book, for example, can reveal new possibilities or widen a person's view of the world, or an old photograph can be cherished because it embodies a relationship. But in terminal materialism, there is no sense of reciprocal interaction in the relation between the object and the end. The end is valued as final, not as itself a means to further ends. And quite often it is only the status label or image associated with the object that is valued, rather than the actual object.

In the essay from which this passage is taken, the authors distinguish between two kinds of materialism and provide an extended explanation, using contrast and examples as methods of development. They are aware that the common perception of materialism — the love of things for their own sake — is a negative one. But this view, according to the authors, doesn't fully account for the attitudes of many Americans toward the things they own. There is, in fact, another more positive meaning that the authors call *instrumental materialism*. You will recognize that the authors are *stipulating* a meaning with which their readers might not be familiar. In their essay they distinguish between *terminal materialism*, in which "the object is valued only because it indicates an end in itself," and *instrumental materialism*, "the use of material objects to make life longer, safer, more enjoyable." Since *instrumental materialism* is the less familiar definition, the essay provides a great number of examples that show how people of three different generations value photographs, furniture, musical instruments, plants, and other objects for their memories and personal associations rather than as proof of the owners' ability to acquire the objects or win the approval of others.

The Definition Essay

The argumentative essay can take the form of an extended definition. An example of such an essay is the one from which we've just quoted, as well as the essays at the end of this chapter. The definition essay is appropriate when the idea under consideration is so controversial or so heavy with historical connotations that even a paragraph or two cannot make clear exactly what the arguer wants his or her readers to understand. For example, if you were preparing a definition of *patriotism*, you would probably use a number of methods to develop your definition: personal narrative, examples, stipulation, comparison and contrast, and cause-and-effect analysis.

Writer's Guide: Writing a Definition Essay

The following important steps should be taken when you write an essay of definition.

1. Choose a term that needs definition because it is controversial or ambiguous, or because you want to offer a personal definition that differs from the accepted interpretation. Explain why an extended definition is necessary. Or choose an experience that lends itself to treatment in an extended definition. One student defined *culture shock* as she had experienced it while studying abroad in Hawaii among students of a different ethnic background.

2. Decide on the thesis — the point of view you wish to develop about the term you are defining. If you want to define *heroism*, for example, you may choose to develop the idea that this quality depends on motivation and awareness of danger rather than on the specific act performed by the hero.

3. Distinguish wherever possible between the term you are defining and other terms with which it might be confused. If you are defining *love*, can you make a clear distinction between the different kinds of emotional attachments contained in the word?

4. Try to think of several methods of developing the definition — using examples, comparison and contrast, analogy, cause-and-effect analysis. However, you may discover that one method alone — say, use of examples — will suffice to narrow and refine your definition.

5. Arrange your supporting material in an order that gives emphasis to the most important ideas.

SAMPLE ANNOTATED ESSAY

The Definition of Terrorism

BRIAN WHITAKER

Decide for yourself whether to believe this, but according to a new report there were only 16 cases of international terrorism in the Middle East last year.

That is the lowest number for any region in the world apart from North America (where there were none at

This article was published May 7, 2001, in *Guardian Unlimited*, the daily online version of the British newspaper the *Guardian*. Whitaker is an editor on Comment Is Free, the *Guardian's* Web expansion.

all). Europe had 30 cases — almost twice as many as the Middle East — and Latin America came top with 193.

Statistics on terrorism from before 9/11

The figures come from the U.S. State Department's annual review of global terrorism, which has just been published on the Internet. Worldwide, the report says confidently, "there were 423 international terrorist attacks in 2000, an increase of 8% from the 392 attacks recorded during 1999."

Problems with attempts to define terrorism

No doubt a lot of painstaking effort went into counting them, but the statistics are fundamentally meaningless because, as the report points out, "no one definition of terrorism has gained universal acceptance."

That is an understatement. While most people agree 5
that terrorism exists, few can agree on what it is. A recent book discussing attempts by the UN and other international bodies to define terrorism runs to three volumes and 1,866 pages without reaching any firm conclusion.

U.S. State Department's definition

Using the definition preferred by the state department, terrorism is: "Premeditated, politically motivated violence perpetrated against noncombatant* targets by subnational groups or clandestine agents, usually intended to influence an audience." (The asterisk is important, as we shall see later.)

Definition of "international" terrorism

"International" terrorism — the subject of the American report — is defined as "terrorism involving citizens or the territory of more than one country."

Main point of agreement is motivation

The key point about terrorism, on which almost everyone agrees, is that it's politically motivated. This is what distinguishes it from, say, murder or football hooliganism. But this also causes a problem for those who compile statistics because the motive is not always clear — especially if no one has claimed responsibility.

Example of incidents with no known motivation

So the American report states — correctly — that there were no confirmed terrorist incidents in Saudi Arabia last year. There were, nevertheless, three unexplained bombings and one shooting incident, all directed against foreigners.

Another part of the definition

Another essential ingredient (you might think) is 10
that terrorism is calculated to terrorize the public or a particular section of it. The American definition does not mention spreading terror at all, because that would exclude attacks against property. It is, after all, impossible to frighten an inanimate object.

Among last year's attacks, 152 were directed against a pipeline in Colombia which is owned by multinational oil companies. Such attacks are of concern to the United States and so a definition is required which allows them to be counted.

Questions about which examples meet the criteria

For those who accept that terrorism is about terrorizing people, other questions arise. Does it include threats, as well as actual violence? A few years ago, for example, the Islamic Army in Yemen warned foreigners to leave the country if they valued their lives but did not actually carry out its threat.

More recently, a group of Israeli peace activists were arrested for driving around in a loudspeaker van, announcing a curfew of the kind that is imposed on Palestinians. Terrifying for any Israelis who believed it, but was it terrorism?

Another characteristic

Another characteristic of terrorism, according to some people, is that targets must be random — the intention being to make everyone fear they might be the next victim. Some of the Hamas suicide bombings appear to follow this principle but when attacks are aimed at predictable targets (such as the military) they are less likely to terrorize the public at large.

What terrorism is not

Definitions usually try to distinguish between terrorism and warfare. In general this means that attacks on soldiers are warfare and those against civilians are terrorism, but the dividing lines quickly become blurred.   15

The state department regards attacks against "noncombatant* targets" as terrorism. But follow the asterisk to the small print and you find that "noncombatants" includes both civilians and military personnel who are unarmed or off duty at the time. Several examples are given, such as the 1986 disco bombing in Berlin, which killed two servicemen.

Examples

The most lethal bombing in the Middle East last year was the suicide attack on USS *Cole* in Aden harbor which killed 17 American sailors and injured 39 more.

Unanswered questions

As the ship was armed and its crew on duty at the time, why is this classified as terrorism? Look again at the small print, which adds: "We also consider as acts of terrorism attacks on military installations or on armed military personnel when a state of military hostilities does not exist at the site, such as bombings against U.S. bases."

A similar question arises with Palestinian attacks on quasi-military targets such as Israeli settlements. Many settlers are armed (with weapons supplied by the army) and the settlements themselves — though they contain civilians — might be considered military targets because they are there to consolidate a military occupation.

If, under the state department rules, Palestinian mortar attacks on settlements count as terrorism, it would be reasonable to expect Israeli rocket attacks on Palestinian communities to be treated in the same way — but they are not. In the American definition, terrorism can never be inflicted by a state.

Limitations of American definition

Israeli treatment of the Palestinians is classified as a human rights issue (for which the Israelis get a rap over the knuckles) in a separate state department report.

Denying that states can commit terrorism is generally useful, because it gets the U.S. and its allies off the hook in a variety of situations. The disadvantage is that it might also get hostile states off the hook — which is why there has to be a list of states that are said to "sponsor" terrorism while not actually committing it themselves.

Interestingly, the American definition of terrorism is a reversal of the word's original meaning, given in the Oxford English Dictionary as "government by intimidation." Today it usually refers to intimidation of governments.

The term's original meaning

Its history

The first recorded use of "terrorism" and "terrorist" was in 1795, relating to the Reign of Terror instituted by the French government. Of course, the Jacobins, who led the government at the time, were also revolutionaries and gradually "terrorism" came to be applied to violent revolutionary activity in general. But the use of "terrorist" in an anti-government sense is not recorded until 1866 (referring to Ireland) and 1883 (referring to Russia).

The difficulty of making laws against terrorism

In the absence of an agreed meaning, making laws against terrorism is especially difficult. The latest British anti-terrorism law gets round the problem by listing 21 international terrorist organizations by name. Membership of these is illegal in the UK.

There are six Islamic groups, four anti-Israel groups, eight separatist groups, and three opposition groups. The list includes Hizbullah, which though armed, is a legal political party in Lebanon, with elected members of parliament.

Among the separatist groups, the Kurdistan Workers Party — active in Turkey — is banned, but not the KDP or PUK, which are Kurdish organizations active in Iraq. Among opposition groups, the Iranian People's Muja-hedeen is banned, but not its Iraqi equivalent, the INC, which happens to be financed by the United States.

Issuing such a list does at least highlight the anom-alies and inconsistencies behind anti-terrorism laws. It also points toward a simpler — and perhaps more honest — definition: terrorism is violence committed by those we disapprove of.

This author's stipulated definition

Analysis

In the United States, terrorism has received unprecedented attention since the tragic events of September 11, 2001. You may have been surprised to learn that Whitaker's essay was written in May of that year, before planes crashing into the World Trade Center, the Pentagon, and a field in Pennsylvania forever gave the term new meaning for Americans. Just as the problem of terrorism has not yet been solved, however, the problem of defining terrorism remains unsolved as well. It is still true that "no one definition of terrorism has gained universal acceptance."

The essay starts on an unusual note: "Decide for yourself whether to believe this," referring to the low number of cases of international terrorism reported in the Middle East for 2000. That statement suggests that readers should approach the numbers with skepticism. Although the specific numbers cited in the essay are at first attributed only to "a new report," Whitaker goes on to indicate that his statistical support comes from the U.S. State Department. He acknowledges that "a lot of painstaking effort" went into counting the instances of terrorism, but goes on to declare the numbers "fundamentally meaningless" because of the lack of an agreed-upon definition of the term.

In paragraphs 6 and 7, Whitaker provides the State Department's definitions of terrorism and international terrorism. He then goes on to use a combination of types of support to back up his claim, as is common in writing an extended definition. In paragraphs 8, 10, and 14, he introduces three characteristics of terrorism — that it is politically motivated, that it "is calculated to terrorize the public or a particular section of it," and that its targets must be random. Throughout the body of the essay, he includes examples to illustrate his key points. In paragraph 15, Whitaker employs another technique used often in ex-tended definition: He tells what terrorism is not.

The last third of the essay deals in part with unanswered questions and the limitations of the State Department's definition, illustrating the complications involved in defining terrorism and in passing laws against it.

Only at the end does Whitaker stipulate his own definition of terrorism. He is not providing a technical definition or one that he believes will gain universal acceptance. What he offers is his honest assessment of what Americans really perceive terrorism to be: "violence committed by those we disapprove of."

READINGS FOR ANALYSIS

When Is a Cross a Cross?

STANLEY FISH

Also, when is a menorah a menorah, and when is a crèche a crèche, and when are the Ten Commandments directives given to the Jews by God on Mt. Sinai? These questions, which might seem peculiar in the real world, are perfectly ordinary in the wild and wacky world of Establishment Clause[1] jurisprudence, where in one case (*Lynch v. Donnelly*, 1984) the Supreme Court declared, with a straight judicial face, that a display featuring the baby Jesus, Mary, Joseph, and the wise men conveyed a secular, not a religious message.

In the latest chapter of this odd project of saving religion by emptying it of its content, Justice Anthony Kennedy, writing for a plurality in *Salazar v. Buono*, ordered a district court to reconsider a ruling that Congress had impermissibly promoted religion by devising a plan designed to prevent the removal of a cross standing in the Mojave National Preserve. The cross had originally been erected in 1934 by the Veterans of Foreign Wars to commemorate American soldiers who had died in World War I. In 2002, Frank Buono, a retired Park Service employee, filed suit alleging a violation of the Establishment Clause and "sought an injunction requiring the government to remove the cross."

In litigation unfolding in at least four stages, the District Court and the Appellate Court of the Ninth Circuit determined that "a reasonable observer would perceive a cross on federal land as governmental endorsement of religion." In response, Congress took several actions, including designating the cross and the

---

[1]The part of the First Amendment that states, "Congress shall make no law respecting an establishment of religion." — EDS.

Stanley Fish is a professor of humanities and law at Florida International University and dean emeritus of the College of Liberal Arts and Sciences at the University of Illinois at Chicago. His most recent book is *Save the World on Your Own Time* (2008), about higher education. This article appeared on the *New York Times* online commentary site, the Opinionator, on May 3, 2010.

adjoining land a national memorial and transferring ownership of the land in question to the V.F.W. in exchange for land located elsewhere in the preserve. Turning again to the courts, Buono asked for an injunction against the transfer; the District Court granted it, concluding that "the transfer was an attempt by the Government to keep the cross atop Sunrise Rock and so was invalid."

The issue was Congress's motive. The effect of what it had done was obvious: the cross now stood on private land, which meant, at least theoretically, that there was no longer an Establishment Clause violation because a private party, not the government, was speaking. But the question remained: did the transfer "cure" the violation or did it, as Justice John Paul Stevens contended in dissent, extend and re-perform it?

Now the fun and crazy stuff begins. Kennedy denies that the "emplacement"   5
of the cross was accompanied by any intention "to promote a Christian message." It was "intended simply to honor our Nation's fallen soldiers." (At oral argument Peter Eliasberg, an ACLU lawyer, observed, "There is never a cross on a tombstone of a Jew.") Therefore, Kennedy reasoned, Congress had no "illicit" intention either; it merely sought a way to "accommodate" (a term of art in Establishment Clause jurisprudence) a "symbol often used to honor and respect those whose heroic acts, noble contributions and patient striving help secure an honored place in history for this Nation and its people."

Notice what this paroxysm of patriotism had done: it has taken the Christianity out of the cross and turned it into an all-purpose means of marking secular achievements. (According to this reasoning the cross should mark the winning of championships in professional sports.) It is one of the ironies of the sequence of cases dealing with religious symbols on public land that those who argue for their lawful presence must first deny them the significance that provokes the desire to put them there in the first place.

It has become a formula: If you want to secure a role for religious symbols in the public sphere, you must de-religionize them, either by claiming for them a non-religious meaning as Kennedy does here, or, in the case of multiple symbols in a park or in front of a courthouse, by declaring that the fact of many of them means that no one of them is to be taken seriously; they don't stand for anything sectarian; they stand for diversity. So you save the symbols by leeching the life out of them. The operation is successful, but the patient is dead.

The game being played here by Kennedy (and many justices before him) is "let's pretend." Let's pretend that a cross that, as Kennedy acknowledges, "has been a gathering place for Easter services since it was first put in place," does not breathe Christianity. Let's pretend that Congress, which in addition to engineering a land-swap for the purpose of keeping the cross in place attached a reversionary clause requiring that the "memorial" (no cross is mentioned) be kept as it is, did not have in mind the preservation of a religious symbol. Let's pretend that after all these machinations a "reasonable observer" who knew all the facts would not see the government's hand, but would only see the hands of private parties. (This is what I call the "look, ma, no hands" argument.) Let's pretend that there will be many who, if the cross were removed, would think that the government had conveyed "disrespect for those the cross was seen as honoring." (Stevens points out that Kennedy just made that one up without the support of "any legislative history or findings.")

The trouble with pretending is that it involves a strain; keeping the pretense going is hard, and the truth being occluded often peeks through, as it does when Kennedy protests that the Establishment Clause "does not require eradication of all religious symbols in the public realm" and adds that "the Constitution does not oblige government to avoid any public acknowledgment of religion's role in society."

But I thought that the cross was not, at least in this instance, a religious symbol and that the issue was not government acknowledging religion, but government honoring its dead. At moments like this, the mask slips and the plurality's real concern — "to foster the display of the cross" (Stevens) — is revealed for all (who had no doubt already spied it beneath the subterfuge) to see. The Christian and conservative Web sites that welcomed the decision as a blow for Christianity and against liberalism knew what they were looking at. 10

My distaste for Kennedy's opinion has nothing to do with its result. In general, and for the record, I have no problem with the state accommodating religious symbols and I am not bothered by the thought of a cross standing in a remote part of the Mojave desert even if the land it stands on is owned by the government. I do have a problem with reasoning that is patently dishonest and protests too much about its own motives and the motives of those it defends. But that is what the religion clause drives you to when in one of its clauses — the free exercise clause — it singles out religion for special positive treatment, and in the other clause — the Establishment Clause — it places a warning label (watch out for this stuff; it's trouble) on religion. It's no wonder that the justices who try to deal with this schizophrenia tie themselves in knots and produce opinions that are as unedifying as they are disingenuous.

READING AND DISCUSSION QUESTIONS

1. What is the Establishment Clause?
2. Why does Fish say that the Supreme Court delivered its findings on *Lynch v. Donnelly*, 1984, "with a straight judicial face" (paragraph 1)?
3. How did Congress try to avoid taking down the cross?
4. What are some of the ways that defenders of the cross have tried to deny its Christian symbolism? What is the irony of these arguments?
5. Explain what Fish means when he says, "The operation is successful, but the patient is dead" (paragraph 7).
6. Why does Fish call the government's handling of religious symbols "schizophrenia"?

WRITING SUGGESTIONS

7. Do you think it is possible to reconcile the two clauses to which Fish refers at the end of the essay: the free exercise clause and the Establishment Clause? Explain.

8. Write a Rogerian analysis of the conflict between those who think it is all right to place religious symbols on public land and those who do not.

9. Explain your observations of how public school students feel about the presence or absence of religious symbols — and of prayer — in school.

Faux Friendship

WILLIAM DERESIEWICZ

We live in an age when friendship has become both all and nothing at all. Already the characteristically modern relationship, it has in recent decades become the universal one: the form of connection in terms of which all others are understood, against which they are all measured, into which they have all dissolved. Romantic partners refer to each other as boyfriends and girlfriends. Spouses boast they are best friends. Parents urge their young children and beg their teenage ones to think of them as friends. Teachers, clergy, and even bosses seek to mitigate and legitimate their authority by asking those they oversee to regard them as friends. As the anthropologist Robert Brain has put it, we're friends with everyone now.

Yet what, in our brave new mediated world, is friendship becoming? The Facebook phenomenon, so sudden and forceful a distortion of social space, needs little elaboration. (If we have 768 "friends," in what sense do we have any?) Yet Facebook and MySpace and Twitter — and whatever we're stampeding for next — are just the latest stages of a long attenuation. They have accelerated the fragmentation of consciousness, but they didn't initiate it. They have reified the idea of universal friendship, but they didn't invent it. In retrospect, it seems inevitable that once we decided to become friends with everyone, we would forget how to be friends with anyone. We may pride ourselves today on our aptitude for friendship, but it's not clear that we still even know what it means.

How did we come to this pass? The idea of friendship in ancient times could not have been more different. Far from being ordinary and universal, friendship, for the ancients, was rare, precious, and hard-won. In a world ordered by relations of kin and kingdom, friendship's elective affinities were exceptional, even subversive. David loved Jonathan despite the enmity of Saul; Achilles' bond with

Essayist and critic William Deresiewicz is the author of *A Jane Austen Education: How Six Novels Taught Me about Love, Friendship, and the Things that Really Matter* (2011). This excerpt is from the December 6, 2009, *Chronicle Review* section of *The Chronicle of Higher Education*.

Patroclus outweighed his loyalty to the Greek cause. Friendship was a high calling, demanding extraordinary qualities of character, rooted in virtue and dedicated to the pursuit of goodness and truth.

The rise of Christianity put the classical ideal in eclipse — Christian thought discouraged intense personal bonds, for the heart should be turned to God. The classical notion of friendship, however, was revived by the Renaissance. Truth and virtue, again, above all: "Those who venture to criticize us perform a remarkable act of friendship," wrote Montaigne, "for to undertake to wound and offend a man for his own good is to have a healthy love for him."

Classical friendship, now called romantic friendship, persisted through the 18th and 19th centuries, giving us the great friendships of Goethe and Schiller, Byron and Shelley, Emerson and Thoreau. Wordsworth addressed his magnum opus to his "dear Friend" Coleridge. Meanwhile, the growth of commercial society was shifting the grounds of personal life toward the conditions essential for the emergence of modern friendship. Capitalism, said David Hume and Adam Smith, by making economic relations impersonal, allowed for private relationships based on nothing other than affection and affinity.

5

We don't know the people who make the things we buy and don't need to know the people who sell them. The ones we do know — neighbors, parishioners, people we knew in school, parents of our children's friends — have no bearing on our economic life. We are nothing to one another but what we choose to become, and we can unbecome it whenever we want.

Add to this the growth of democracy, an ideology of universal equality and interinvolvement. We are citizens now, not subjects, bound together directly rather than through allegiance to a monarch. But what is to bind us emotionally,

From the tomb of Niankhkhnum and Khnumhotep, Egypt, c. 2450 BCE

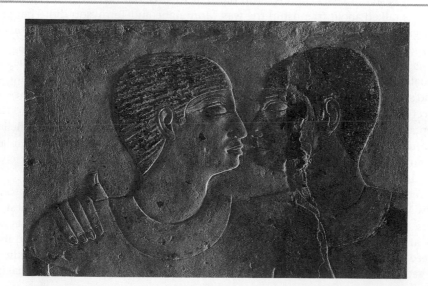

make us something more than an aggregate of political monads? One answer was nationalism, but another grew out of the 18th-century notion of social sympathy: friendship or, at least, friendliness.

It is no accident that *fraternity* made a third with *liberty* and *equality* as the watchwords of the French Revolution. Wordsworth in Britain and Whitman in America made visions of universal friendship central to their democratic vistas. For Mary Wollstonecraft, the mother of feminism, *friendship* was to be the key term of a new domestic democracy.

Now we can see why friendship has become the characteristically modern relationship. Modernity believes in equality, and friendships are egalitarian. Modernity believes in individualism. Friendships serve no public purpose and exist independent of all other bonds. Modernity believes in choice. Friendships, unlike blood ties, are elective. Modernity believes in self-expression. Friends, because we choose them, give us back an image of ourselves. Modernity believes in freedom. We can be friends with whomever we want, however we want, for as long as we want.

Social changes play into the question as well. As industrialization uprooted people from extended families and traditional communities and packed them into urban centers, friendship emerged to salve the anonymity and rootlessness of modern life. The process is virtually instinctive now: You graduate from college, move to New York or L.A., and assemble the gang that takes you through your 20s. Only it's not just your 20s anymore. We have yet to find a satisfactory name for that period of life, now typically a decade but often a great deal longer, between the end of adolescence and the making of definitive life choices. The one thing we know is that friendship is absolutely central to it. 10

Inevitably, the classical ideal has faded. The image of the one true friend, a soul mate rare to find but dearly beloved, has disappeared from our culture. We have our better or lesser friends, even our best friends, but no one in a very long time has talked about friendship the way Montaigne and Tennyson did. That glib neologism *bff* bespeaks an ironic awareness of the mobility of our connections: *Best friends forever* may not be on speaking terms by this time next month.

As for the moral content of classical friendship, its commitment to virtue and mutual improvement, that too has been lost. We have ceased to believe that a friend's highest purpose is to summon us to the good by offering moral advice and correction. We practice, instead, the nonjudgmental friendship of unconditional acceptance and support — "therapeutic" friendship, in sociologist Robert N. Bellah's scornful term. A friend fulfills her duty, we suppose, by taking our side — validating our feelings, supporting our decisions, helping us to feel good about ourselves. We're busy people; we want our friendships fun and friction-free.

Yet even as friendship became universal and the classical ideal lost its force, a new kind of idealism arose, a new repository for some of friendship's deepest needs: the group friendship or friendship circle. Companies of superior spirits go back at least as far as Pythagoras, but the culture of group friendship reached its apogee in the 1960s. Two of the counterculture's most salient and ideologically charged social forms were the commune — a community of friends in self-imagined retreat from a heartlessly corporatized society — and the rock 'n' roll "band," its name evoking Robin Hood's band of Merry Men, its great exemplar the Beatles.

Communes, bands, and other '60s friendship groups were celebrated as joyous, creative places of eternal youth. To go through life within one was the era's Utopian dream; it is no wonder the Beatles' breakup was received as a generational tragedy. It is also no wonder that '60s group friendship began to generate its own nostalgia as the baby boomers began to hit their 30s. *The Big Chill,* in 1983, depicted boomers attempting to recapture the magic of a late-'60s friendship circle. ("In a cold world," the movie's tagline reads, "you need your friends to keep you warm.") The TV series *Thirtysomething* certified group friendship as the new adult norm.

It was only in the 1990s that a new generation, remaining single well into adulthood, found its own images of group friendship in *Seinfeld, Sex and the City,* and, of course, *Friends.* By that point, however, the notion of friendship as a redoubt of moral resistance, a shelter from normative pressures and incubator of social ideals, had disappeared. Your friends didn't shield you from the mainstream, they were the mainstream.

And so we return to Facebook. With the social-networking sites of the new century — Friendster and MySpace were launched in 2003, Facebook in 2004 — the

15

Have social networking sites changed how we define "friend"?

friendship circle has expanded to engulf the whole of the social world, and in so doing has destroyed both its own nature and that of individual friendship itself. Facebook's very premise is that it makes our friendship circles visible. There they are, my friends, all in the same place. Except, of course, they're not in the same place, or, rather, they're not my friends. They're simulacra of my friends, little dehydrated packets of images and information, no more my friends than a set of baseball cards is the New York Mets.

I remember realizing a few years ago that most of the members of what I thought of as my "circle" didn't actually know one another. One I'd met in graduate school, another at a job, one in Boston, another in Brooklyn, one lived in Minneapolis now, another in Israel, so that I was ultimately able to enumerate some 14 people, none of whom had ever met any of the others. To imagine that they added up to a circle, an embracing and encircling structure, was a belief, I realized, that violated the laws of feeling as well as those of geometry.

Facebook, however, seduces us into exactly that illusion, inviting us to believe that by assembling a list, we have conjured a group. Visual juxtaposition creates the mirage of emotional proximity. "It's like they're all having a conversation," a woman I know once said about her Facebook page, full of comments from friends and friends of friends. "Except they're not."

Friendship is devolving, in other words, from a relationship to a feeling — from something people share to something we all hug privately to ourselves in the loneliness of our electronic caves. The same path was long ago trodden by community. As face-to-face community disappeared, we held on to what we had lost — the closeness, the rootedness — by clinging to the word. Now we speak of the Jewish "community" and the medical "community" and the "community" of readers, even though none of them actually is one. What we have instead is, if we're lucky, a "sense" of community — the feeling without the structure; a private emotion, not a collective experience.

Until a few years ago, you could share your thoughts with only one friend at   20 a time (on the phone, say), or maybe with a small group in person. And when you did, you were talking to specific people, and you tailored what you said, and how you said it, to who they were — their interests, their personalities, most of all, your degree of mutual intimacy. Now we're broadcasting our stream of consciousness to all 500 friends at once. We haven't just stopped talking to our friends as individuals, at such moments; we have stopped thinking of them as individuals.

It's amazing how fast things have changed. Not only don't we have Wordsworth and Coleridge anymore, we don't even have Jerry and George. Today, Ross and Chandler would be writing on each other's walls. If Carrie and the girls did manage to find the time for lunch, they'd be too busy checking their BlackBerrys to have a real conversation. *Sex* and *Friends* went off the air just six years ago, and already we live in a different world.

The new group friendship, already vitiated itself, is also cannibalizing our individual friendships as the boundaries between the two blur. The most disturbing thing about Facebook is the extent to which people are willing — are eager — to conduct their private lives in public: "hola cutie-pie! i'm in town on wednesday.

lunch?" "Julie, I'm so glad we're back in touch, xoxo." "Sorry for not calling, am going through a tough time right now."

Perhaps I need to surrender the idea that the value of friendship lies precisely in the space of privacy it creates: not the secrets that two people exchange so much as the unique and inviolate world they build up between them, the spider web of shared discovery they spin out, slowly and carefully, together.

But surely Facebook has its benefits. Long-lost friends can reconnect, far-flung ones can stay in touch. I wonder, though. Having recently moved across the country, I thought Facebook would help me feel connected to the friends I'd left behind. I find the opposite is true. Reading about the mundane details of their lives, a steady stream of trivia and ephemera, leaves me feeling both empty and unpleasantly full, as if I had just binged on junk food, and precisely because it reminds me of the real sustenance, the real knowledge, we exchange by e-mail or phone or face-to-face.

As for getting back in touch with old friends — yes, when they're people you   25
really love, it's a miracle. But most of the time, they're not. They're someone you knew for a summer in camp, or a midlevel friend from high school. They don't matter to you as individuals anymore; they matter because they made up the texture of your experience at a certain moment in your life. Tear them out of that texture — read about their brats, look at pictures of their vacation — and they mean nothing. Tear out enough of them and you ruin the texture itself, replace a matrix of feeling and memory, the deep subsoil of experience, with a spurious sense of familiarity.

Paul Gauguin, *Two Tahiti Women*, 1892.

In order to know people, you have to listen to their stories. E-mail, with its rapid-fire etiquette, already trimmed the letter to a certain acceptable maximum, perhaps 1,000 words. Now, with Facebook, the box is shrinking even more, leaving maybe a third of that as the conventional limit for a message, far less for a comment. (And we all know the deal on Twitter.) Posting information is like pornography, a slick, impersonal exhibition. Exchanging stories is like making love. It is mutual. It is intimate. It takes patience, devotion, sensitivity, subtlety, skill — and it teaches those qualities, too.

They call them social-networking sites for a reason. Networking once meant something specific: climbing the jungle gym of professional contacts in order to advance your career. The truth is that Hume and Smith were not completely right. Commercial society did not eliminate the self-interested aspects of making friends, it just changed the way we went about it. Now, in the age of the entrepreneurial self, even our closest relationships are being pressed onto this template.

A recent book on the sociology of modern science describes a networking event at a West Coast university: "There do not seem to be any singletons — disconsolately lurking at the margins — nor do dyads appear, except fleetingly." No solitude, no friendship, no space for refusal — the exact contemporary paradigm. At the same time, the author assures us, "face time" is valued in this "community" as a "high-bandwidth interaction," offering "unusual capacity for interruption, repair, feedback, and learning."

Actual human contact, rendered "unusual" and weighed by the values of a systems engineer. We have given our hearts to machines, and now we are turning into machines. The face of friendship in the new century.

READING AND DISCUSSION QUESTIONS

1. What are some of the points that Deresiewicz makes about the history of friendship?
2. Explain this quote by David Hume and Adam Smith: "Capitalism . . . by making economic relations impersonal, allowed for private relationships based on nothing other than affection and affinity" (paragraph 5).
3. Why has friendship become the characteristically modern relationship, according to Deresiewicz?
4. How has the duty of a friend changed from what Deresiewicz calls "classical friendship"?
5. How did friendship change in the 1960s? In the 1990s?
6. How has Facebook changed the nature of friendship?

WRITING SUGGESTIONS

7. Discuss the pros and cons of Facebook.
8. Explain whether or not you agree with Deresiewicz about how Facebook has changed the nature of friendship and why.

9. What are the potential dangers of Facebook or other social networking sites?

10. Has being active on Facebook or another social networking site changed your face-to-face relationships with friends? How?

Stop Calling Quake Victims Looters

GUY-URIEL CHARLES

To define someone as a looter is not simply to describe him, or her, through an act, it is to make a moral judgment. It is to characterize the person as lawless and criminal. It connotes someone who is without self-restraint; an animal; wanton and depraved.

It is a description that is void of empathy for someone who is consciously or subconsciously viewed as "the other." Tragically, it fits into the stereotype that many have about people of African descent, be they African Americans or Haitian Americans.

The news media have to stop describing starving Haitians who are simply trying to survive the earthquake and aftershocks that took their homes, their loved ones, and all their possessions by this highly derogatory term.

It's a lesson they should have learned covering the devastation wrought by Hurricane Katrina. I remember the news accounts then that described black residents of New Orleans as "looters," but used benign words to describe white residents engaged in the same action: "taking things."

Academics have found repeated instances of this in media content analyses after disasters. One example, widely disseminated on the Web post-Katrina, juxtaposed an Associated Press photo that showed a young black man wading through chest-high water "after looting a grocery store" (said the caption), with an AFP/Getty photo of a white woman in the same position, although the caption this time described her "finding" food "from a local grocery store."

It is time to put this practice to rest.

Put yourself in the position of the average Haitian in Port-au-Prince. One minute you were going about your business, the next minute the earth shook and literally your world crumbled all around you. But you were one of the lucky ones, you survived the earthquake. Injured? Yes. But alive.

Your first thought is to cry out for your family, especially your kids. But most of your family is buried under a rubble pile somewhere. You had four children but only one survived the earthquake. You have spent the last few days, along with your fellow survivors, digging through the rubble trying to find them.

5

Guy-Uriel Charles is a law professor at Duke Law School and founder of Duke's Center on Law, Race, and Politics. He is Haitian American. The article appeared on CNN.com January 21, 2010.

This photo was taken on January 18, 2010, in Port-au-Prince, Haiti, in the aftermath of a devastating earthquake.

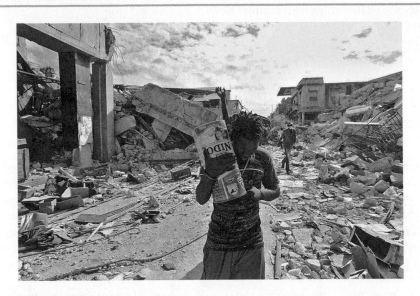

It is now a week after the earthquake, and you have eaten little or nothing. You are hungry and thirsty, and while you hear rumors of aid coming, you have not seen any evidence of it.

You have not heard from the president and indeed you've heard rumors that   10
his wife is dead. Perhaps he left the country; you would too, if you could. There is no police presence at all. No governmental authority to provide support. There are no markets.

The only money you have are the few gourdes (Haitian dollars) that you have in your pockets. The rest of your money is in the safe place you always kept it — but it is now buried with your food. The banks are not open. There is no one to borrow from; they are all in the same boat as you. There are no functioning institutions.

You have family in the United States and they are desperately trying to get you some help. They have contacted all of the big aid agencies, but those agencies have issues of their own. Some have lost staff members. They are doing the best they can, but they have no idea that you exist and you have no way of finding them. The roads are impassable, and they can't get clearance from whoever is in charge of the airport to land their planes, which bring much needed supplies.

They're afraid to go anywhere without security because they've heard that the people are becoming restless. Indeed, though you do not know this, the U.S. military is also worried that citizens will get violent and start stealing. The United Nations is waiting for more troops, and the doctors have stopped treating patients because of those same fears: violence, looting.

Under normal circumstances you would not think of taking food without paying for it. You are what other Haitians would call "bien eleve" not "mal eleve." By that they mean you were well-raised, with manners and dignity.

Haitians put a strong premium on dignity. To take something for which you   15
have not paid does not only offend your sense of legality but also your sense of
personhood. It is undignified. But not only are you starving, so is your only surviving child. You would prefer to pay, but whom? What would you pay with?
You'd prefer to wait, but for whom? How long can you afford to wait?

You feel that your desperate state is evidence that you have been abandoned
by your family, your country, the international community, and Bondié (God).
(The Creole word for God literally means "good God.")

So you take. You take just enough for a couple of days and a couple of family
members. You take and you run to feed those for whom the only measure of fortune is survival in Haiti, post-earthquake. You take and you run.

Are you a looter? Try as we might to prevent it, the answer to that question is
inevitably racialized. We cannot separate the word looting from its racial implications or the supposed crime of looting from its racial origins. In the throes of the
civil rights movement in the United States, many states made looting a crime.
Almost all of these states were southern states that had a history of criminalizing
behavior that they associated more with African Americans than with whites.

Even so, the criminal law, for all of its shortcomings, is often more sophisticated than we are. It recognizes that context matters. It has been developed with
concepts — such as necessity and justification — to identify the circumstances under
which a person who would normally be held culpable can be held either less culpable or not at all culpable. Taking food is different than taking a television.

It is past time for our news media to develop similar sophistication. It is time   20
to stop characterizing black people trying to survive in dire circumstances as looters. Are they takers? Yes. Are they looters? Let's wait for a criminal conviction first.

READING AND DISCUSSION QUESTIONS

1. What is Charles's claim in the article?

2. How is what happened in Haiti after the earthquake similar to what happened in
   New Orleans after Hurricane Katrina?

3. What support does Charles offer for his contention that the answer to the question
   of whether or not a person is considered a looter "is inevitably racialized" (paragraph 18)?

4. Why is "looter" not an appropriate term to use to describe those in Haiti who took
   food and other goods without paying?

5. What does Charles mean when he says that criminal law "is often more sophisticated than we are" (paragraph 19)?

WRITING SUGGESTIONS

6. How would you evaluate the news coverage of the earthquake in Haiti? How do
   you think it compares with news coverage of other natural disasters?

7. Do you agree with Charles that news coverage of such disasters is "racialized"?
   Why, or why not?

DEBATE   Is the Definition of Marriage Changing?

Gay Marriage Shows Why We Need to Separate Church and State

HOWARD MOODY

If members of the church that I served for more than three decades were told I would be writing an article in defense of marriage, they wouldn't believe it. My reputation was that when people came to me for counsel about getting married, I tried to talk them out of it. More about that later.

We are now in the midst of a national debate on the nature of marriage, and it promises to be as emotional and polemical as the issues of abortion and homosexuality have been over the past century. What all these debates have in common is that they involved both the laws of the state and the theology of the church. The purpose of this writing is to suggest that the gay-marriage debate is less about the legitimacy of the loving relationship of a same-sex couple than about the relationship of church and state and how they define marriage.

In Western civilization, the faith and beliefs of Christendom played a major role in shaping the laws regarding social relations and moral behavior. Having been nurtured in the Christian faith from childhood and having served a lifetime as an ordained Baptist minister, I feel obligated first to address the religious controversy concerning the nature of marriage. If we look at the history of religious institutions regarding marriage we will find not much unanimity but amazing diversity — it is really a mixed bag. Those who base their position on "tradition" or "what the Bible says" will find anything but clarity. It depends on which "tradition" in what age reading from whose holy scriptures.

In the early tradition of the Jewish people, there were multiple wives and not all of them equal. Remember the story of Abraham's wives, Sara and Hagar. Sara couldn't get pregnant, so Hagar presented Abraham with a son. When Sara got angry with Hagar, she forced Abraham to send Hagar and her son Ishmael into the wilderness. In case Christians feel superior about their "tradition" of marriage, I would remind them that their scriptural basis is not as clear about marriage as we might hope. We have Saint Paul's conflicting and condescending words about the institution: "It's better not to marry." Karl Barth called this passage the Magna Carta of the single person. (Maybe we should have taken Saint Paul's advice more seriously. It might have prevented an earlier generation of parents from harassing, cajoling, and prodding our young until they were married.) In certain religious branches, the church doesn't recognize the licensed legality of marriage but requires that persons meet certain religious qualifications before the marriage is recognized by the church. For members of the Roman Catholic Church, a "legal

---

Reverend Howard Moody is minister emeritus of Judson Memorial Church in New York City. This article was published in July 2004 in the *Nation*.

divorce" and the right to remarry may not be recognized unless the first marriage has been declared null and void by a decree of the church. It is clear that there is no single religious view of marriage and that history has witnessed some monumental changes in the way "husband and wife" are seen in the relationship of marriage.

In my faith-based understanding, if freedom of choice means anything to individuals (male or female), it means they have several options. They can be single and celibate without being thought of as strange or psychologically unbalanced. They can be single and sexually active without being labeled loose or immoral. Women can be single with child without being thought of as unfit or inadequate. If these choices had been real options, the divorce rate may never have reached nearly 50 percent.

The other, equally significant choice for people to make is that of lifetime commitment to each other and to seal that desire in the vows of a wedding ceremony. That understanding of marriage came out of my community of faith. In my years of ministry I ran a tight ship in regard to the performance of weddings. It wasn't because I didn't believe in marriage (I've been married for sixty years and have two wonderful offspring) but rather my unease about the way marriage was used to force people to marry so they wouldn't be "living in sin."

The failure of the institution can be seen in divorce statistics. I wanted people to know how challenging the promise of those vows was and not to feel this was something they had to do. My first question in premarital counseling was, "Why do you want to get married and spoil a beautiful friendship?" That question often elicited a thoughtful and emotional answer. Though I was miserly in the number of weddings I performed, I always made exceptions when there were couples who had difficulty finding clergy who would officiate. Their difficulty was because they weren't of the same religion, or they had made marital mistakes, or what they couldn't believe. Most of them were "ecclesiastical outlaws," barred from certain sacraments in the church of their choice.

The church I served had a number of gay and lesbian couples who had been together for many years, but none of them had asked for public weddings or blessings on their relationship. (There was one commitment ceremony for a gay couple at the end of my tenure.) It was as though they didn't need a piece of paper or a ritual to symbolize their lifelong commitment. They knew if they wanted a religious ceremony, their ministers would officiate and our religious community would joyfully witness.

It was my hope that since the institution of marriage had been used to exclude and demean members of the homosexual community, our church, which was open and affirming, would create with gays and lesbians a new kind of ceremony. It would be an occasion that symbolized, between two people of the same gender, a covenant of intimacy of two people to journey together, breaking new ground in human relationships — an alternative to marriage as we have known it.

However, I can understand why homosexuals want "to be married" in the old-fashioned "heterosexual way." After all, most gays and lesbians were born of married parents, raised in a family of siblings; many were nourished in churches and synagogues, taught about a living God before Whom all Her creatures were equally loved. Why wouldn't they conceive their loving relationships in terms of marriage and family and desire that they be confirmed and understood as such? It follows that if these gays and lesbians see their relationship as faith-based, they would want a religious ceremony that seals their intentions to become lifelong partners, lovers and friends, that they would want to be "married."

Even though most religious denominations deny this ceremony to homosexual couples, more and more clergy are, silently and publicly, officiating at religious rituals in which gays and lesbians declare their vows before God and a faith community. One Catholic priest who defied his church's ban said: "We can bless a dog, we can bless a boat, but we can't say a prayer over two people who love each other. You don't have to call it marriage, you can call it a deep and abiding friendship, but you can bless it."

We have the right to engage in "religious disobedience" to the regulations of the judicatory that granted us the privilege to officiate at wedding ceremonies, and suffer the consequences. However, when it comes to civil law, it is my contention that the church and its clergy are on much shakier ground in defying the law.

In order to fully understand the conflict that has arisen in this debate over the nature of marriage, it is important to understand the difference between the religious definition of marriage and the state's secular and civil definition. The government's interest is in a legal definition of marriage — a social and voluntary contract between a man and woman in order to protect money, property, and children. Marriage is a civil union without benefit of clergy or religious definition. The state is not interested in why two people are "tying the knot," whether it's to gain money, secure a dynasty, or raise children. It may be hard for those of us who have a religious or romantic view of marriage to realize that loveless marriages are not that rare. Before the Pill, pregnancy was a frequent motive for getting married. The state doesn't care what the commitment of two people is, whether it's for life or as long as both of you love, whether it's sexually monogamous or an open marriage. There is nothing spiritual, mystical, or romantic about the state's license to marry — it's a legal contract.

Thus, George W. Bush is right when he says that "marriage is a sacred institution" when speaking as a Christian, as a member of his Methodist church. But as president of the United States and leader of all Americans, believers and unbelievers, he is wrong. What will surface in this debate as litigation and court decisions multiply is the history of the conflict between the church and the state in defining the nature of marriage. That history will become significant as we move toward a decision on who may be married.

After Christianity became the state religion of the Roman empire in A.D. 325, 15 the church maintained absolute control over the regulation of marriage for some 1,000 years. Beginning in the sixteenth century, English kings (especially Henry VIII, who found the inability to get rid of a wife extremely oppressive) and other monarchs in Europe began to wrest control from the church over marital regulations. Ever since, kings, presidents, and rulers of all kinds have seen how important the control of marriage is to the regulation of social order. In this nation, the government has always been in charge of marriage.

That is why it was not a San Francisco mayor licensing same-sex couples that really threatened the president's religious understanding of marriage but rather the Supreme Judicial Court of Massachusetts, declaring marriage between same-sex couples a constitutional right, that demanded a call for constitutional amendment. I didn't understand how important that was until I read an op-ed piece in the *Boston Globe* by Peter Gomes, professor of Christian morals and the minister of Memorial Church at Harvard University, that reminds us of a seminal piece of our history:

> The Dutch made civil marriage the law of the land in 1590, and the first marriage in New England, that of Edward Winslow to the widow Susannah White, was performed on May 12, 1621, in Plymouth by Governor William Bradford, in exercise of his office as magistrate.
>
> There would be no clergyman in Plymouth until the arrival of the Reverend Ralph Smith in 1629, but even then marriage would continue to be a civil affair, as these first Puritans opposed the English custom of clerical marriage as unscriptural. Not until 1692, when Plymouth Colony was merged into that of Massachusetts Bay, were the clergy authorized by the new province to solemnize marriages. To this day in the Commonwealth the clergy, including those of the archdiocese, solemnize marriage legally as agents of the Commonwealth and by its civil authority. Chapter 207 of the General Laws of Massachusetts tells us who may perform such ceremonies.

Now even though it is the civil authority of the state that defines the rights and responsibilities of marriage and therefore who can be married, the state is no more infallible than the church in its judgments. It wasn't until the mid-twentieth century that the Supreme Court declared antimiscegenation laws unconstitutional. Even after that decision, many mainline churches, where I started my ministry, unofficially discouraged interracial marriages, and many of my colleagues were forbidden to perform such weddings.

The civil law view of marriage has as much historical diversity as the church's own experience because, in part, the church continued to influence the civil law. Although it was the Bible that made "the husband the head of his wife," it was common law that "turned the married pair legally into one person — the husband," as Nancy Cott documents in her book *Public Vows: A History of Marriage and the Nation* (an indispensable resource for anyone seeking to understand the changing nature of marriage in the nation's history). She suggests that "the legal doctrine of marital unity was called coverture . . . [which] meant that the wife could not use legal avenues such as suits or contracts, own assets, or execute legal documents without her husband's collaboration." This view of the wife would not hold water in any court in the land today.

As a matter of fact, even in the religious understanding of President Bush and his followers, allowing same-sex couples the right to marry seems a logical conclusion. If marriage is "the most fundamental institution of civilization" and a major contributor to the social order in our society, why would anyone want to shut out homosexuals from the "glorious attributes" of this "sacred institution"? Obviously, the only reason one can discern is that the opponents believe that gay and lesbian people are not worthy of the benefits and spiritual blessings of "marriage."

At the heart of the controversy raging over same-sex marriage is the religious   20
and constitutional principle of the separation of church and state. All of us can
probably agree that there was never a solid wall of separation, riddled as it is
with breaches. The evidence of that is seen in the ambiguity of tax-free religious
institutions, "in God we trust" printed on our money and "under God" in the
Pledge of Allegiance to our country. All of us clergy, who are granted permission
by the state to officiate at legal marriage ceremonies, have already compromised
the "solid wall" by signing the license issued by the state. I would like to believe
that my authority to perform religious ceremonies does not come from the state
but derives from the vows of ordination and my commitment to God. I refuse to
repeat the words, "by the authority invested in me by the State of New York, I pronounce you husband and wife," but by signing the license, I've become the state's
"handmaiden."

It seems fitting therefore that we religious folk should now seek to sharpen
the difference between ecclesiastical law and civil law as we beseech the state to
clarify who can be married by civil law. Further evidence that the issue of church
and state is part of the gay-marriage controversy is that two Unitarian ministers
have been arrested for solemnizing unions between same-sex couples when no
state licenses were involved. Ecclesiastical law may punish those clergy who disobey marital regulations, but the state has no right to invade church practices and
criminalize clergy under civil law. There should have been a noisy outcry from all
churches, synagogues, and mosques at the government's outrageous contravention
of the sacred principle of the "free exercise of religion."

I come from a long line of Protestants who believe in a "free church in a
free state." In the issue before this nation, the civil law is the determinant of the
regulation of marriage, regardless of our religious views, and the Supreme Court
will finally decide what the principle of equality means in our Constitution in the
third century of our life together as a people. It is likely that the Commonwealth
of Massachusetts will probably lead the nation on this matter, as the State of New
York led to the Supreme Court decision to allow women reproductive freedom.

So what is marriage? It depends on whom you ask, in what era, in what culture. Like all words or institutions, human definitions, whether religious or secular,
change with time and history. When our beloved Constitution was written, blacks,
Native Americans, and, to some extent, women were quasi-human beings with no
rights or privileges, but today they are recognized as persons with full citizenship
rights. The definition of marriage has been changing over the centuries in this
nation, and it will change yet again as homosexuals are seen as ordinary human
beings.

In time, and I believe that time is now, we Americans will see that all the fears
foisted on us by religious zealots were not real. Heterosexual marriage will still
flourish with its statistical failures. The only difference will be that some homosexual couples will join them and probably account for about the same number
of failed relationships. And we will discover that it did not matter whether the
couples were joined in a religious ceremony or a secular and civil occasion for the
statement of their intention.

Will It Be Marriage or Civil Union?

JO ANN CITRON

This fall, while the right was still staggering from the U.S. Supreme Court's decision in *Lawrence v. Texas*,[1] Massachusetts dealt conservatives another body blow when its highest court legalized same-sex marriage. In a 4–3 ruling authored by Chief Justice Margaret Marshall, the Supreme Judicial Court (SJC) held that denying marriage to homosexuals violates the Massachusetts Declaration of Rights, the state constitution. To remedy the violation, the court changed the common-law definition of civil marriage to eliminate its opposite-sex requirement and to compel the issuance of marriage licenses to qualified persons of the same sex. Civil marriage in Massachusetts now means "the voluntary union of two persons as spouses, to the exclusion of all others." The legislature, which was directed to "take such action as it may deem appropriate in light of this opinion," has been running for cover ever since.[2]

A friend recently asked me how important the Massachusetts decision is in the struggle to achieve marriage equality in the United States. I was struck, first of all, by the terms of the question because "marriage equality" is not the same as "marriage." The issue all along has been whether gays will get marriage or some equivalent formality that will make them equal to their heterosexual counterparts. There are those who say that civil union is marriage equality. It's what Vermont said and what many Massachusetts legislators are saying in their desperate search for an escape route from the SJC ruling. It's also what William Eskridge claimed in his 2002 book, *Equality Practice: Civil Union and the Future of Gay Rights*, where he argues that, while there is no principled basis for withholding marriage from gays and lesbians, the gay community should bow to the political will of the majority and move slowly, accepting the equality of civil union now and pressing for marriage later when it becomes more palatable to the majority. Eskridge views *Baker v. State*, the Vermont civil union decision, as the equivalent of *Brown v. Board of Education*, the 1954 landmark civil rights decision that opened the way to racial integration in this country. Marriage activist Evan Wolfson, on the other hand, views *Baker* as the gay rights version of *Plessy v. Ferguson*, the railway carriage case that authorized "separate but equal" status for disfavored minorities.

[1] A 2003 case in which the Supreme Court declared unconstitutional a law that prohibited sexual intercourse between same-sex couples. — EDS.

[2] *Goodridge v. Department of Public Health.*

A former English professor at Bates College, Jo Ann Citron is now an attorney practicing in Boston, specializing in divorce and the ending of domestic partnerships. She has published widely on both literature and law and is currently working on a book, *The Gay Divorcée: How Same-Sex Couples Break Up*. This article was published in the *Gay and Lesbian Review Worldwide* in March–April 2004.

This essay is being written during the 180-day waiting period following the issuance of the decision, a period of either genuine confusion or deliberate obfuscation, depending on the degree of cynicism with which you view the political process. It might be useful at this point to summarize what the court said and how the legislature has responded. The court began by reminding everyone that the Massachusetts marriage statute is a licensing law. Because marriage has always been understood to mean the union of a man and a woman, the statute cannot be construed to authorize issuing a license to two people of the same sex. But to bar gay couples from all the benefits, protections, and obligations that accompany marriage violates the Massachusetts constitution, which means that the current marriage licensing law is unconstitutional. The remedy the court fashioned was to change the common law definition of civil marriage to eliminate its opposite-sex requirement, thereby removing the bar that excludes gay couples from obtaining marriage licenses.

Rather than declare that cities and towns must immediately begin to issue marriage licenses to gays, which would have created chaos, the court granted the legislature 180 days to revise state statutes so as to bring them into line with its ruling and to clean up a complicated domestic relations regulatory scheme that refers to husbands and wives. The court reminded the legislature that it retains "broad discretion to regulate marriage." This means that the Legislature can continue to impose certain restrictions upon persons who wish to marry. The legislature may refuse to authorize granting a marriage license to persons under a certain age, or to siblings, or to a parent and child. It may require a blood test or a birth certificate, or that applicants turn around three times and face north, or anything else that would be constitutional. But, as I read the decision, the legislature may not refuse to grant a license to otherwise qualified gay couples.

The SJC was perfectly clear in stating that the remedy for the constitutional   5
violation was the reformulation of the definition of civil marriage. Yet many legislators, together with the current attorney general, want to take a different view of the matter. They have seized upon the "protections, benefits, and obligations" language in the opinion in the hope that, by providing the benefits that marriage yields in our society, they can avoid providing marriage itself. The legislature has asked the SJC to render an advisory opinion about a civil union bill, and the SJC has invited interested parties to submit briefs. Meanwhile, the Massachusetts constitutional convention is scheduled to meet on February 11, 2004, to vote on a Defense of Marriage Act or DOMA that, in its present form, would not only prevent gay marriage but would also outlaw domestic partner benefits. If the legislature passes the DOMA in a second convention, the measure would appear on the ballot in November of 2006 and voters could, by a simple majority, amend the state constitution to make gay marriage, civil union, and domestic partnerships illegal. The political reality is that such a DOMA will probably not garner the necessary votes either in the legislature or among voters; however, a simple DOMA limiting itself to marriage is more likely to succeed, especially in the face of the SJC decision, which presents the right with what it would call a "clear and present danger." This means that gay marriage could become legal in Massachusetts on May 18, 2004,

via the SJC decision and illegal in Massachusetts on November 14, 2006, via a voter referendum. No one knows what will happen to gay couples who marry in the interim. Let the courts sort through that one!

Massachusetts has a good track record when it comes to gay families: It permits second-parent adoption; it allows two women to appear as "parent" on a child's birth certificate; it protects the relationship between a child and her non-biological parent. At the very least, *Goodridge* is going to yield "marriage equality" in some form of civil union. The problem, of course, is that there is no such thing as "marriage equality" for anyone who files federal income tax returns, bequeaths an estate, or travels outside of Massachusetts. When it comes to federal benefits or the tax-free transfer of marital property or the ability to have another state recognize your Massachusetts relationship, marriage is the only status that will do. This is why some are downplaying the SJC decision, pointing out that even if people are able to marry in Massachusetts, their status will not be recognized by the federal government or by any other state with a DOMA. In that respect, marriage is indeed no different from civil union. In fact, it might even be worse for a while. We're beginning to see judges in some states accept the validity of a Vermont civil union. Even in states with a DOMA, it will be possible to find a judge who would give full faith and credit to a civil union because most DOMA laws have nothing to say about civil unions. Not so with marriage. For the time being, a Massachusetts marriage will be even less portable than a Vermont civil union.

But let there be no mistake: Whatever happens in Massachusetts is absolutely critical to how the gay marriage question will be answered in the rest of the United States. What happens here is even more important than what happened in Vermont. Here's why. The next marriage case with a reasonable likelihood of success is working its way through the courts in New Jersey, a state with a history of progressive court decisions. New Jersey will be looking very carefully at the way Vermont and Massachusetts have addressed the marriage question. If the Massachusetts SJC ratifies its decision and mandates the issuance of marriage licenses, New Jersey will look at its predecessor states and see two alternative models, marriage and civil union. New Jersey will choose one or the other. But the SJC could fail to confirm its marriage decision and approve instead some form of civil union. Coupled with the Vermont ruling, this will create a critical mass in favor of civil union, an outcome that will make it far more likely that New Jersey will opt for civil union over marriage. After that, the rest of the states will almost certainly fall into line with civil unions, and that will spell the end of gay marriage, probably forever.

Ironically, it may also mean the end of marriage in its present form, the one that the right is working so hard to preserve. Conservatives Andrew Sullivan and David Brooks have argued that the best way to protect marriage would be to open it to anyone who wants to vow fidelity and is willing to forego an easy exit from a supposedly permanent relationship. Marriage is, after all, a conservative institution, and persons who enter it with the blessing of the state may not leave it without the state's permission. Already, as a result of the marriage cases and their surrounding discourse, the very term "marriage" is being qualified. We now speak of "civil marriage" to distinguish it from the religious ceremonies that are but one of its aspects. Insofar as material benefits are concerned, marriage is a civil institution. Those material benefits can attach just as easily to any civil institution the state cares to identify. This is, after all, the point of wanting to offer gays something called "union" rather than something called "marriage." Nothing but prejudice prevents state and federal governments from offering to partners in a civil union the identical benefits, protections, and obligations that the state now offers to spouses.

William Eskridge is wrong in thinking that civil union is a step on the path towards marriage. Civil union and marriage are not sequential; they are alternatives to one another. There is no reason to think that the country will permit civil union now and confer marriage later. In fact, the reality is likely to be quite the reverse. Because of equal protection considerations, the civil union alternative will have to be available to straights as well as gays. And if my analysis is correct, it will become more widely available to everyone in the coming years. At the moment, there is little incentive for marriage-eligible couples to elect a civil union. But this will change.

It is not difficult to imagine a tacit compromise in which the right is allowed   10
to maintain its stranglehold on marriage in exchange for allowing the material benefits now associated with it to break free and accompany civil union. This is another reason why the Massachusetts decision in favor of marriage is strategically important. As long as even a single state has legalized marriage, civil union becomes more attractive to the right. And the gay community can leverage those few gay marriage licenses into a demand that marriage benefits attach to civil unions.

In my view, this would be a good outcome. I say this as someone who views marriage as a regressive institution that has never been good to women, that insidiously creates insiders and outsiders, and, most importantly, that violates the separation of church and state at the heart of our form of government. The state should not be in the business of attaching material benefits to a religious institution. The right to social security death benefits, the right to favorable tax treatment, the right to take your formalized relationship with you when you travel, should be detached from marriage altogether and should be awarded according to some other equitable system. To the extent that this becomes so, there will eventually be no material difference between the old form of marriage and the new form of civil unions. Traditional marriage will endure as a religious institution. Already there are hundreds of clergy willing to perform marriage ceremonies for gay congregants and thousands of gay couples who have participated in these ceremonies whose benefits are wholly spiritual. Over time, civil union and civil marriage will ultimately come to mean much the same thing. Whether the SJC ratifies its original position or abandons it, *Goodridge* brings us closer to a consensus around civil union. It is time for the gay community to turn its attention to winning for civil union all the rights, benefits, protections, and obligations of marriage. That is the truly revolutionary project.

DISCUSSION QUESTIONS

1. Why is definition a critical element in Moody's argument? Why is it a critical element in Citron's? Do the two of them agree on a definition of marriage?

2. In the Rogerian approach to argumentation, what steps would Moody and Citron take to reconcile their differences?

3. What is Moody's attitude toward same-sex marriage? Why, in his opinion, do more serious problems arise when it comes to the laws of the state than the theology of the church?

4. Why does Moody believe that President Bush was wrong in saying, as president, that "marriage is a sacred institution"? Were you surprised by Moody's explanation of the history of marriage in the United States?

5. When Citron published her essay, the nation was awaiting Massachusetts's decision on the legality of same-sex marriages. What was her biggest fear about the future of the legal standing of same-sex relationships?

6. Analyze Citron's analogy between decisions regarding same-sex unions and two Supreme Court decisions regarding racial integration, *Plessy v. Ferguson* and *Brown v. Board of Education*.

7. What is the author's claim in each of the two essays?

Assignments for Understanding Definition

READING AND DISCUSSION QUESTIONS

1. Contrast the claims made by Jo Ann Citron in "Will It Be Marriage or Civil Union?" and Howard Moody in "Gay Marriage Shows Why We Need to Separate Church and State."

2. Who has the power to stipulate how a term is defined? The government? The media? Society in a broader sense? Where have you seen examples of each in the readings in this chapter?

WRITING SUGGESTIONS

3. Narrate an experience you have had in which you felt you were either aided or hindered by the fact that you were defined as a member of a specific group. It could be a group such as those defined by gender, race, religious affiliation, or membership on a team or in a club.

4. Would adoption at the state level of a policy prohibiting classifying people by race, color, ethnicity, or national origin be beneficial or pernicious for the individual and for society? In other words, what is good or bad about classifying people?

5. Find a subject in which definition is critical to how statistics are interpreted and which can be argued successfully in a 750- to 1,000-word paper. Your essay should provide proof for a claim.

WRITING ASSIGNMENTS

6. Write about an important or widely used term whose meaning has changed since you first learned it. Such terms often come from the slang of particular groups: drug users, rock music fans, musicians, athletes, computer programmers, or software developers.

7. Write an essay in which you explain how governments sometimes hide the full truth behind euphemisms and other careful word choices.

Research Readiness: Using Encyclopedias

Where can you look for more information about terms whose meanings are controversial?

When there is disagreement about the definition of a term, you may need more than a dictionary definition to clarify the points on which the disagreement is based. Often an encyclopedia will give you a much fuller discussion of the complexities of defining terms that defy simple, clear-cut definitions. The more specialized the encyclopedia, the more useful the information, unless it uses so much jargon that it is useful only to specialists.

For example, "abortion" is defined in the *Encyclopedia Britannica Online* like this:

> **Abortion** — the expulsion of a fetus from the uterus before it has reached the stage of viability (in human beings, usually about the 20th week of gestation). An abortion may occur spontaneously, in which case it is also called a miscarriage, or it may be brought on purposefully, in which case it is often called an induced abortion.

A specialized encyclopedia may provide more detailed information because it may discuss different positions in the debate for or against abortion. What follows is only a portion of an article from the *Encyclopedia of Philosophy*, which also includes a list of works cited that leads to other possible sources:

> The claims to which partisans on both sides of the "abortion" issue appeal seem, if one is not thinking of the abortion issue, close to self-evident, or they appear to be easily defensible. The case against abortion (Beckwith 1993) rests on the proposition that there is a very strong presumption that ending another human life is seriously wrong. Almost everyone who is not thinking about the abortion issue would agree. There are good arguments for the view that fetuses are both living and human. ("Fetus" is generally used in the philosophical literature on abortion to refer to a human organism from the time of conception to the time of birth.) Thus, it is easy for those opposed to abortion to think that only the morally depraved or the seriously confused could disagree with them.
>
> Standard pro-choice views appeal either to the proposition that women have the right to make decisions concerning their own bodies or to the proposition that fetuses are not yet persons. Both of these propositions seem either

to be platitudes or to be straightforwardly defensible. Thus, it is easy for pro-choicers to believe that only religious fanatics or dogmatic conservatives could disagree. This explains, at least in part, why the abortion issue has created so much controversy. The philosophical debate regarding abortion has been concerned largely with subjecting these apparently obvious claims to the analytical scrutiny philosophers ought to give to them.

Consider first the standard argument against abortion. One frequent objection to the claim that fetuses are both human and alive is that we do not know when life begins. The reply to this objection is . . . .

You may find that your library has a database like Gale Virtual Reference Library that lets you search a number of different encyclopedias at the same time. Just the first six entries from the list generated by that database lead to a range of different encyclopedias to investigate:

1. Abortion: I. Medical Perspectives. Allan Rosenfield, Sara Iden, and Anne Drapkin Lyerly. *Encyclopedia of Bioethics.* Ed. Stephen G. Post. Vol. 1. 3rd ed. New York: Macmillan Reference USA, 2004. p. 1–7.

2. Abortion. Menachem Elon. *Encyclopaedia Judaica.* Ed. Michael Berenbaum and Fred Skolnik. Vol. 1. 2nd ed. Detroit: Macmillan Reference USA, 2007. p. 270–273.

3. Abortion. Don Marquis. *Encyclopedia of Philosophy.* Ed. Donald M. Borchert. Vol. 1. 2nd ed. Detroit: Macmillan Reference USA, 2006. p. 8–10.

4. Abortion. *National Survey of State Laws.* Ed. Richard A. Leiter. 6th ed. Detroit: Gale, 2008. p. 339–371.

5. Abortion. *West's Encyclopedia of American Law.* Ed. Shirelle Phelps and Jeffrey Lehman. Vol. 1. 2nd ed. Detroit: Gale, 2005. p. 13–26.

6. Abortion. Mark R. Wicclair and Gabriella Gosman. *Encyclopedia of Science, Technology, and Ethics.* Ed. Carl Mitcham. Vol. 1. Detroit: Macmillan Reference USA, 2005. p. 1–6.

ASSIGNMENT

1. Find out what your library has to offer when it comes to encyclopedias. A librarian may be able to give you a list. Some may be in print and others online. If there is not a list, you can search under "encyclopedia" in the catalog and scan the list for relevant titles.

2. Now choose one of the controversial subjects listed below and investigate what you can learn about it from three different encyclopedias. Do not use more than one general encyclopedia. Cut, paste, and print; photocopy; or take notes on the three and be prepared to discuss what you found. One question you should consider is how useful each would be to a researcher.

Just war
Euthanasia
Same-sex marriage
Sexual harassment

CHAPTER 5

Claims

What are you trying to prove? Claims, or propositions, represent answers to this question. Although they are the conclusions you have reached about your subject, they often appear as thesis statements when you write about that subject. Claims can be classified as *claims of fact, claims of value,* and *claims of policy.*

Claims of Fact

Claims of fact assert that a condition has existed, exists, or will exist and that their support consists of factual information — information such as statistics, examples, and testimony that most responsible observers assume can be verified.

Many facts are not matters for argument: Our own senses can confirm them, and other observers will agree about them. We can agree that a certain number of students were in the classroom at a particular time, that the sun sets in the west, and that a new traffic light has been installed at the intersection of Park and Main.

We can also agree about information that most of us can rarely confirm for ourselves — information in reference books, such as atlases, almanacs, and telephone directories; data from scientific resources about the physical world; and happenings reported in the media. We can agree on the reliability of such information if we trust the observers who report it.

However, the factual map is constantly being redrawn by new data in such fields as history and science that cause us to reevaluate our conclusions. For example, the discovery of the Dead Sea Scrolls in 1947 revealed that some books of the Bible — Isaiah, for one — were far older than we had thought. Recent research has proven that cervical cancer is caused by a virus and that a vaccination given early enough can possibly prevent it. DNA evidence has cleared individuals who served years in prison for crimes they did not commit.

In your conversations you probably generate claims of fact every day, some of which can be verified without much effort, others of which are more difficult to substantiate.

> **Claim:** Most of the students in this class come from towns within fifty miles of Boston.

To prove this the arguer would need only to ask the students in the class where they come from.

> **Claim:** More students entering this fall had AP credit for one or more courses than in any past year.

To prove this claim, the arguer would have to have access to entering students' records from the time Advanced Placement was first accepted to the present.

> **Claim:** The Braves will win the pennant this year.

This claim is different from the others because it is an opinion about what will happen in the future. But it can be verified (in the future) and is therefore classified as a claim of fact.

More complex factual claims about political and scientific matters remain controversial because proof on which all or most observers will agree is difficult or impossible to obtain.

> **Claim:** Bilingual programs have a lower success rate than English-only programs in preparing students for higher education.

> **Claim:** The only life in the universe exists on this planet.

Not all claims are so neatly stated or make such unambiguous assertions. Because we recognize that there are exceptions to most generalizations, we often qualify our claims with words such as *generally, usually, probably,* and *as a rule.* It would not be true to state flatly, for example, "College graduates earn more than high school graduates." This statement is generally true, but we know that some high school graduates who are electricians or city bus drivers or sanitation workers earn more than college graduates who are schoolteachers or nurses or social workers. In making such a claim, therefore, the writer should qualify it with a word that limits the claim.

We have defined a fact as a statement that can be verified. An inference is "a statement about the unknown on the basis of the known."[1] The difference between facts and inferences is important to you as the writer of an argument because an inference is an *interpretation,* or an opinion reached after informed evaluation of evidence.

---

[1]S. I. Hayakawa, *Language in Thought and Action* (New York: Harcourt, Brace, Jovanovich, 1978), p. 35.

You have probably come across a statement such as the following in a newspaper or magazine: "Excessive television viewing has caused the steady decline in the reading ability of children and teenagers." Presented this way, the statement is clearly intended to be read as a factual claim that has been or can be proved. But it is an inference. The facts, which can be and have been verified, are (1) the reading ability of children and teenagers has declined and (2) the average child views television for six or more hours a day. (Whether this amount of time is "excessive" is also an opinion.) The cause-and-effect relation between the two facts is an interpretation of the investigator, who has examined both the reading scores and the amount of time spent in front of the television set and *inferred* that one is the cause of the other. The causes of the decline in reading scores are probably more complex than the original statement indicates. Since we can seldom or never create laboratory conditions for testing the influence of television separate from other influences in the family and the community, any statement about the connection between reading scores and television viewing can only be a guess.

By definition, no inference can ever do more than suggest probabilities. Of course, some inferences are much more reliable than others and afford a high degree of probability. Almost all claims in science are based on inferences, interpretations of data on which most scientists agree. Paleontologists find a few ancient bones from which they make inferences about an animal that might have been alive millions of years ago. We can never be absolutely certain that the reconstruction of the dinosaur in the museum is an exact copy of the animal it is supposed to represent, but the probability is fairly high because no other interpretation works so well to explain all the observable data — the existence of the bones in a particular place, their age, their relation to other fossils, and their resemblance to the bones of existing animals with which the paleontologist is familiar.

Inferences are profoundly important, and most arguments could not proceed very far without them. But an inference is not a fact. The writer of an argument must make it clear when he or she offers an inference, an interpretation, or an opinion that it is not a fact.

SAMPLE ESSAY   Claim of Fact

Picking Sides for the News

ROBERT J. SAMUELSON

We in the news business think we're impartial seekers of truth, but most Americans think otherwise. They view us as sloppy, biased, and self-serving.

Robert J. Samuelson, a contributing editor of *Newsweek*, has written a column for the *Washington Post* since 1977. This article appeared in *Newsweek* on June 28, 2004.

In 1985, 56 percent of the public felt news organizations usually got their facts straight, says the Pew Research Center. By 2002 that was 35 percent. In 1985 the public thought the media "moral" by 54 to 13 percent; by 2003 opinion was split 40 to 38 percent. Americans think the "media make news rather than just report it," says Pew's Andrew Kohut. The obsession with "scandal in high places" is seen as building audiences rather than advancing the public interest.

Still, the latest Pew survey confirms — with lots of numbers — something disturbing that we all sense: People are increasingly picking their media on the basis of partisanship. If you're Republican and conservative, you listen to talk radio and watch the Fox News Channel. If you're liberal and Democratic, you listen to National Public Radio and watch "NewsHour with Jim Lehrer." It's like picking restaurants: Chinese for some, Italian for others. And everyone can punch up partisan blogs — the fast food of the news business. What's disturbing is that, like restaurants, the news media may increasingly cater to their customers' (partisan) tastes. News slowly becomes more selective and slanted.

Rush Limbaugh has 14.5 million weekly listeners. By Pew, 77 percent are conservative, 16 percent moderate, and 7 percent liberal. Or take Fox's 1.3 million prime-time viewers: 52 percent are conservative, 30 percent moderate, and 13 percent liberal. By contrast, 36 percent of Americans are conservative, 38 percent moderate, and 18 percent liberal. The liberals' media favorites are slightly less lopsided. "NewsHour's" audience is 22 percent conservative, 44 percent moderate, and 27 percent liberal. NPR's audience is 31 percent conservative, 33 percent moderate, and 30 percent liberal. Of course, many news outlets still have broad audiences. Daily newspapers are collectively close to national averages; so is CNN.

But the partisan drift may grow because distrust is spreading. In 1988 Pew found that 58 percent of the public thought there was "no bias" in election coverage. Now that's 38 percent: 22 percent find a Democratic bias, 17 percent a Republican. Almost all major media have suffered confidence declines. Among Republicans, only 12 percent say they believe "all or most" of *Newsweek*; for Democrats the figure is twice that, 26 percent. In 1985 the overall figure was higher (31 percent), with little partisan gap. *Newsweek's* numbers typify mainstream media. Only 14 percent of Republicans believe "all or most" of the *New York Times*, versus 31 percent of Democrats.

What's going on? Why should we care?   5

Up to a point, conservative talk radio and Fox represent a desirable backlash against the perceived "liberal bias" of network news and mainstream media. I've worked in the mainstream press for 35 years. Editors and reporters reflexively deny a liberal bias, even though many ordinary people find it and mainstream newsrooms are politically skewed. Here are the latest Pew figures: 7 percent of national reporters and editors are conservative (a fifth the national rate), and 34 percent are liberal (almost twice the national rate). Most reporters I know believe fiercely in being fair and objective. Still, the debate over "what's news and significant?" is warped. Talk radio and Fox add other views.

But the sorting of audiences by politics also poses dangers — for the media and the country. We journalists think we define news, and from day to day, we do. Over the longer run, that's less true. All news organizations must satisfy their audiences. If they don't, they go out of business. "Media bias is product differentiation," says James T. Hamilton of Duke, whose book *All the News That's Fit to Sell* shows how economic forces powerfully shape news judgments. If liberals and conservatives migrate to rival media camps, both camps may ultimately submit to the same narrow logic: like-minded editors and reporters increasingly feed like-minded customers stories that reinforce their world view.

Economic interests and editorial biases will converge. The *New York Times* is now a national paper; 49 percent of its daily circulation is outside the New York area, up from 38 percent five years ago. There's home delivery in 275 markets, up from 171 five years ago. But if the *Times* sells largely to upscale readers (average household income is $90,381, almost twice the national average) with vaguely liberal views, it risks becoming hostage to their sensibilities. No less does Fox risk becoming hostage to its base.

The worthy, if unattainable, ideals of fairness and objectivity will silently erode. Many forces push that way: new technologies (cable, the Internet); the blending of news and entertainment; the breakdown between "hard news" and interpretation; intense competition; changing news habits of the young. The damage will not just be to good journalism. Tom Rosenstiel of the Project for Excellence in Journalism notes that respected national media develop common facts and language that helps hold society together and solve common problems. It will be a sad day when we trust only the media that voice our views.

Claims of Value

Unlike claims of fact, which state that something is true and can be validated by reference to the data, claims of value **make a judgment**. They express approval or disapproval. They attempt to prove that some action, belief, or condition is right or wrong, good or bad, beautiful or ugly, worthwhile or undesirable.

Claim: Democracy is superior to any other form of government.

Claim: Killing animals for sport is wrong.

Claim: The Sam Rayburn Building in Washington is an aesthetic failure.

Some claims of value are simply expressions of taste, likes and dislikes, or preferences and prejudices. The Latin proverb *"De gustibus non est disputandum"* means that we cannot dispute taste. If you love the musical *Billy Elliot*, there is no way for anyone to prove you wrong.

Many claims of value, however, can be defended or attacked on the basis of standards that measure the worth of an action, a belief, or an object. As far as possible, our personal likes and dislikes should be supported by reference to these standards. Value judgments occur in any area of human experience, but whatever the area, the analysis will be the same. We ask the arguer who is defending a claim of value: *What are the standards or criteria for deciding that this action, this belief, or this object is good or bad, beautiful or ugly, desirable or undesirable? Does the thing you are defending fulfill these criteria?*

There are two general areas in which people often disagree about matters of value: aesthetics and morality.

Aesthetics is the study of beauty and the fine arts. Controversies over works of art — the aesthetic value of books, paintings, sculpture, architecture, dance, drama, and movies — rage fiercely among experts and laypeople alike. They may disagree on the standards for judging or, even if they agree about standards, may disagree about how successfully the art object under discussion has met these standards. The Rogerian approach to conflict resolution can be particularly useful in resolving disagreements over the standards for judging. Agreeing on those standards is the first step toward resolving the conflict and is a necessary step before seeking agreement on how well the standards have been met.

Consider a discussion about popular music. Hearing someone praise the singing of Manu Chao, a hugely popular European singer now playing to American crowds, you might ask why he is highly regarded. You expect Chao's fans to say more than "I like him" or "He's great." You expect them to give reasons to support their claims. They might show you a short review from a respected newspaper that says, "Mr. Chao's gift is simplicity. His music owes a considerable amount to Bob Marley . . . but Mr. Chao has a nasal, regular-guy voice, and instead of the Wailers' brooding, bass-heavy undertow, Mr. Chao's band delivers a lighter bounce. His tunes have the singing directness of nursery rhymes."[2] Chao's fans accept these criteria for judging a singer's appeal.

You may not agree that simplicity, directness, and a regular-guy voice are the most important qualities in a popular singer. But the establishment of standards itself offers material for a discussion or an argument. You may argue about the relevance of the criteria, or you may agree with the criteria but argue about the success of the singer in meeting them. Perhaps you prefer complexity to simplicity. Or even if you choose simplicity, you may not think that Chao has exhibited this quality to good effect.

It is probably not surprising then, that, despite wide differences in taste, professional critics more often than not agree on criteria and whether an art object has met the criteria. For example, almost all movie critics agree that *Citizen Kane* and *Gone with the Wind* are superior films. They also agree that *Plan 9 from Outer Space,* a horror film, is terrible.

Value claims about morality express judgments about the rightness or wrongness of conduct or belief. Here disagreements are as wide and deep as in the arts — and more significant. The first two examples on page 174 reveal how controversial such claims can be. Although you and your reader may share many values — among them a belief in democracy, a respect for learning, and a desire for peace — you may also disagree, even profoundly, about other values. The subject of divorce, for example, despite its prevalence in our society, can produce a conflict between people who have differing moral standards. Some people

---

[2]Jon Pareles, *New York Times,* July 10, 2001, p. B1.

may insist on adherence to absolute standards, arguing that the values they hold are based on immutable religious precepts derived from God and biblical scripture. Since marriage is sacred, divorce is always wrong, they say, whether or not the conditions of society change. Other people may argue that values are relative, based on the changing needs of societies in different places and at different times. Since marriage is an institution created by human beings at a particular time in history to serve particular social needs, they may say, it can also be dissolved when other social needs arise. The same conflicts between moral values might occur in discussions of abortion or suicide.

Nevertheless, even where people agree about standards for measuring behavior, a majority preference is not enough to confer moral value. If in a certain neighborhood a majority of heterosexual men decide to harass a few gay men and lesbians, that consensus does not make their action right. In formulating value claims, you should be prepared to ask and answer questions about the way in which your value claims and those of others have been arrived at. Lionel Ruby, an American philosopher, sums it up in these words: "The law of rationality tells us that we ought to justify our beliefs by evidence and reasons, instead of asserting them dogmatically."[3]

Of course, you will not always be able to persuade those with whom you argue that your values are superior to theirs and that they should therefore change their attitudes. What you can and should do, however, as Lionel Ruby advises, is give *good reasons* that you think one thing is better than another. If as a child you asked why it was wrong to take your brother's toys, you might have been told by an exasperated parent, "Because I say so." Some adults still give such answers in defending their judgments, but such answers are not arguments and do nothing to win the agreement of others.

SAMPLE ESSAY   Claim of Value

Crash

ROGER EBERT

Crash tells interlocking stories of whites, blacks, Latinos, Koreans, Iranians, cops and criminals, the rich and the poor, the powerful and powerless, all defined in one way or another by racism. All are victims of it, and all are guilty of it. Sometimes, yes, they rise above it, although it is never that simple. Their negative

---

Roger Ebert has been the film critic of the *Chicago Sun-Times* since 1967 and is the author of more than fifteen books about film. He appeared for years on a televised show about movies. He won the Pulitzer Prize for criticism in 1975, and his reviews are now syndicated in more than two hundred newspapers in the United States, Canada, England, Japan, and Greece.

[3]*The Art of Making Sense* (New York: Lippincott, 1968), p. 271.

impulses may be instinctive, their positive impulses may be dangerous, and who knows what the other person is thinking?

The result is a movie of intense fascination; we understand quickly enough who the characters are and what their lives are like, but we have no idea how they will behave because so much depends on accident. Most movies enact rituals; we know the form and watch for variations. *Crash* is a movie with free will, and anything can happen. Because we care about the characters, the movie is uncanny in its ability to rope us in and get us involved.

Crash was directed by Paul Haggis, whose screenplay for *Million Dollar Baby* led to Academy Awards. It connects stories based on coincidence, serendipity, and luck, as the lives of the characters crash against one another like pinballs. The movie presumes that most people feel prejudice and resentment against members of other groups, and observes the consequences of those feelings.

One thing that happens, again and again, is that people's assumptions prevent them from seeing the actual person standing before them. An Iranian (Shaun Toub) is thought to be an Arab, although Iranians are Persian. Both the Iranian and the white wife of the district attorney (Sandra Bullock) believe a Mexican-American locksmith (Michael Pena) is a gang member and a crook, but he is a family man.

A black cop (Don Cheadle) is having an affair with his Latina partner (Jennifer Esposito), but never gets it straight which country she's from. A cop (Matt Dillon) thinks a light-skinned black woman (Thandie Newton) is white. When a white producer tells a black TV director (Terrence Dashon Howard) that a black character "doesn't sound black enough," it never occurs to him that the director doesn't "sound black," either. For that matter, neither do two young black men (Larenz Tate and Ludacris), who dress and act like college students but have a surprise for us.

You see how it goes. Along the way, these people say exactly what they are thinking, without the filters of political correctness. The district attorney's wife is so frightened by a street encounter that she has the locks changed, then assumes the locksmith will be back with his "homies" to attack them. The white cop can't get medical care for his dying father, and accuses a black woman at his HMO with taking advantage of preferential racial treatment. The Iranian can't understand what the locksmith is trying to tell him, freaks out, and buys a gun to protect himself. The gun dealer and the Iranian get into a shouting match.

I make this sound almost like episodic TV, but Haggis writes with such directness and such a good ear for everyday speech that the characters seem real and plausible after only a few words. His cast is uniformly strong; the actors sidestep clichés and make their characters particular.

For me, the strongest performance is by Matt Dillon, as the racist cop in anguish over his father. He makes an unnecessary traffic stop when he thinks he sees the black TV director and his light-skinned wife doing something they really shouldn't be doing at the same time they're driving. True enough, but he wouldn't have stopped a black couple or a white couple. He humiliates the woman with an invasive body search, while her husband is forced to stand by powerless, because the cops have the guns — Dillon, and also an unseasoned rookie (Ryan Phillippe), who hates what he's seeing but has to back up his partner.

5

That traffic stop shows Dillon's cop as vile and hateful. But later we see him trying to care for his sick father, and we understand why he explodes at the HMO worker (whose race is only an excuse for his anger). He victimizes others by exercising his power and is impotent when it comes to helping his father. Then the plot turns ironically on itself, and both of the cops find themselves, in very different ways, saving the lives of the very same TV director and his wife. Is this just manipulative storytelling? It didn't feel that way to me because it serves a deeper purpose than mere irony: Haggis is telling parables, in which the characters learn the lessons they have earned by their behavior.

Other cross-cutting Los Angeles stories come to mind, especially Lawrence   10
Kasdan's more optimistic *Grand Canyon* and Robert Altman's more humanistic *Short Cuts*. But *Crash* finds a way of its own. It shows the way we all leap to conclusions based on race — yes, all of us, of all races, and however fair-minded we may try to be — and we pay a price for that. If there is hope in the story, it comes because as the characters crash into one another, they learn things, mostly about themselves. Almost all of them are still alive at the end and are better people because of what has happened to them. Not happier, not calmer, not even wiser, but better. Then there are those few who kill or get killed; racism has tragedy built in.

Not many films have the possibility of making their audiences better people. I don't expect *Crash* to work any miracles, but I believe anyone seeing it is likely to be moved to have a little more sympathy for people not like themselves. The movie contains hurt, coldness, and cruelty, but is it without hope? Not at all. Stand back and consider. All of these people, superficially so different, share the city and learn that they share similar fears and hopes. Until several hundred years ago, most people everywhere on earth never saw anybody who didn't look like them. They were not racist because, as far as they knew, there was only one race. You may have to look hard to see it, but *Crash* is a film about progress.

———————

Claims of Policy

Claims of policy argue that certain conditions should exist. As the name suggests, they advocate adoption of policies or courses of action because problems have arisen that call for solution. Almost always *should* or *ought to* or *must* is expressed or implied in the claim.

Claim: Voluntary prayer should be permitted in public schools.

Claim: A dress code should be introduced for all public high schools.

Claim: A law should permit sixteen-year-olds and parents to "divorce" each other in cases of extreme incompatibility.

Claim: Mandatory jail terms should be imposed for drunk driving violations.

In defending such claims of policy you may find that you must first convince your audience that a problem exists. This will require that, as part of your longer argument, you make a factual claim, offering data to prove that present conditions are unsatisfactory. You may also find it necessary to refer to the values that support your claim. Then you will be ready to introduce your policy, to persuade your audience that the solution you propose will solve the problem. If you approach the problem from a Rogerian perspective, you will also point out what both conflicting sides could gain from it.

Consider this policy claim: "The time required for an undergraduate degree should be extended to five years." Immediate agreement with this policy among student readers would certainly not be universal. Some students would not recognize a problem. They would say, "The college curriculum we have now is fine. There's no need for a change. Besides, we don't want to spend more time in school." First, then, the arguer would have to persuade a skeptical audience that there is a problem — that four years of college is no longer enough because the stock of knowledge in almost all fields of study continues to increase. The arguer would provide data to show that students today have many more choices in history, literature, and science than students had in those fields a generation ago and would also emphasize the value of greater knowledge and more schooling compared to the value of other goods the audience cherishes, such as earlier independence. Finally, the arguer would offer a plan for implementing the policy. The plan would have to consider initial psychological resistance, revision of the curriculum, costs of more instruction, and costs of lost production in the workforce. Most important, this policy would point out the benefits for both individuals and society if it were adopted.

In this example, we assumed that the reader would disagree that a problem existed. In many cases, however, the reader may agree that there is a problem but disagree with the arguer about the way to solve it. Most of us, no doubt, agree that we want to reduce or eliminate the following problems: misbehavior and vandalism in schools, drunk driving, crime on the streets, child abuse, pornography, pollution. But how should we go about solving those problems? What public policy will give us well-behaved, diligent students who never destroy school property? Safe streets where no one is ever robbed or assaulted? Loving homes where no child is ever mistreated? Some members of society would choose to introduce rules or laws that punish infractions so severely that wrongdoers would be unwilling or unable to repeat their offenses. Other members of society would prefer policies that attempt to rehabilitate or reeducate offenders through training, therapy, counseling, and new opportunities.

A major mistake that one group can make is to ignore that other opinions even exist. You can only support the notion that your proposed solution is better if you can acknowledge that you are aware of and understand another's perspective. Rogerian analysis is one way of attempting to reconcile such differences of opinion. If one of the disagreeing parties has to state the other's position fairly before offering an opinion, it can be the first step toward a solution both can accept. The resulting claim may not advocate what either side considers the perfect solution, but it may keep the conversation going.

As you ponder what action or change in thought you are proposing as your claim of policy — what should or should not be done — you have to keep your audience in mind. Given their level of emotional involvement with the issue, what proposal might they be willing to consider? A vegetarian may argue that everyone should be a vegetarian but is much more likely to get a hearing if the argument is that every meat eater should learn about the health benefits of vegetarianism before rejecting it. A college student might argue that all general education requirements should be abolished but might be wiser to start with a less ambitious claim: High school and college math and science curricula should be coordinated so that the freshman year of college is not merely a repetition of the senior year in high school. You must also consider what, realistically, your audience can do about the situation. It is one thing to tell a group of parents that school resource officers should be better trained in interacting with students with disabilities. A more realistic solution would be to encourage the parents to write about this issue to the director of the state police training academy. At other times the most you might hope to accomplish is to get your readers to consider the situation from your perspective. Keep this question in mind as you arrive at your claim of policy: What do I want my readers to do or think?

SAMPLE ANNOTATED ESSAY   **Claim of Policy**

College Life Versus My Moral Code

ELISHA DOV HACK

Background that reveals his respect for Yale and his connection to it through his brother

How residency rules have changed

Many people envy my status as a freshman at Yale College. My classmates and I made it through some fierce competition, and we are excited to have been accepted to one of the best academic and extra-curricular programs in American higher education. I have an older brother who attended Yale, and I've heard from him what life at Yale is like.

He spent all his college years living at home because our parents are New Haven residents, and Yale's rules then did not require him to live in the dorms. But Yale's new regulations demand that I spend my freshman and sophomore years living in the college dormitories.

Elisha Dov Hack was a member of the Yale College freshman class of 1997. This article appeared on September 9, 1997, in the *New York Times*. The case brought by Hack and four other Jewish students remained in court until all but Hack had graduated. Hack went on to marry before his 2003 graduation in engineering sciences.

Establishes the problem

I, two other freshmen, and two sophomores have refused to do this because life in the dorms, even on the floors Yale calls "single sex," is contrary to the fundamental principles we have been taught as long as we can remember — the principles of Judaism lived according to the Torah and 3,000-year-old rabbinic teachings. Unless Yale waives its residence requirement, we may have no choice but to sue the university to protect our religious way of life.

Examples of affronts to his religious beliefs

Bingham Hall, on the Yale quadrangle known as the Old Campus, is one of the dorms for incoming students. When I entered it two weeks ago during an orientation tour, I literally saw the handwriting on the wall. A sign titled "Safe Sex" told me where to pick up condoms on campus. Another sign touted 100 ways to make love without having sex, like "take a nap together" and "take a steamy shower together."

Another example of accepted dorm standards

That, I am told, is real life in the dorms. The "freshper-   5
son" issue of the *Yale Daily News* sent to entering students contained a "Yale lexicon" defining *sexile* as "banishment from your dorm room because your roommate is having more fun than you." If you live in the dorms, you're expected to be part of the crowd, to accept these standards as the framework for your life.

Can we stand up to classmates whose sexual morality differs from ours? We've had years of rigorous religious teaching, and we've watched and learned from our parents. We can hold our own in the intellectual debate that flows naturally from exchanges during and after class.

Challenges whether Yale should make it difficult for students to maintain their morals outside of class

But I'm upset and hurt by this requirement that I live in the dorms. Why is Yale — an institution that professes to be so tolerant and open-minded — making it particularly hard for students like us to maintain our moral standards through difficult college years?

Tries to achieve middle ground by acknowledging that morality has changed but argues that exceptions to the policy are already made

We are not trying to impose our moral standards on our classmates or on Yale. Our parents tell us that things were very different in college dormitories in their day and that in most colleges in the 1950s students who allowed guests of the opposite sex into their dorm rooms were subject to expulsion. We acknowledge that today's morality is not that of the 50s. We are asking only that Yale give us the same permission to live off campus that it gives any lower classman who is married or at least twenty-one years old.

Yale is proud of the fact that it has no "parietal rules" and that sexual morality is a student's own business. Maybe this is what Dean Richard H. Brodhead meant when he said that "Yale's residential colleges carry . . . a moral meaning." That moral meaning is, basically, "Anything goes." This morality is Yale's own residential religion, which it is proselytizing by force of its regulations.

Attacks the opposition by defining immorality as Yale's religion

We cannot, in good conscience, live in a place where women are permitted to stay overnight in men's rooms, and where visiting men can traipse through the common halls on the women's floors — in various stages of undress — in the middle of the night. The dormitories on Yale's Old Campus have floors designated by gender, but there is easy access through open stairwells from one floor to the next.

Floors designated by gender are not the solution

The moral message Yale's residences convey today is not one that our religion accepts. Nor is it a moral environment in which the five of us can spend our nights, or a moral surrounding that we can call home.   10

The source of conflict

Yale sent me a glossy brochure when it welcomed me as an entering student. It said, "Yale retains a deep respect for its early history and for the continuity that its history provides — a continuity based on constant reflection and reappraisal." Yale ought to reflect on and reappraise a policy that compels us to compromise our religious principles.

Uses Yale's own advertising against it

Claim of Policy: A university that espouses a willingness to reflect and reappraise should not compel Hack and the other Jewish students to compromise their principles.

Analysis

Notice that Hack's article originally appeared in the *New York Times*. Most would agree that it is unusual to see a piece written by a college freshman in such a prestigious publication, but the fact that he was accepted at Yale immediately establishes him as a member of an academically elite group, as Hack points out in his second sentence. He meets the possible objection that he does not yet know enough about what life at Yale is like by pointing out that his older brother went there. The crucial difference is that the university's rules have been changed in the interim. Where his older brother lived at home, Hack is required by university policy to live on campus his first two years. Therein lies the problem.

Hack most directly states his objection to Yale's residency requirement in his third paragraph — that life in the dorms "is contrary to the fundamental principles [he and four other Jewish students] have been taught as long as [they] can remember — "the principles of Judaism lived according to the Torah and 3,000-year-old rabbinic teachings." He also captures the intensity of his feelings on the subject by stating that he and the four other students who are in the same position "may have no choice but to sue the university to protect [their] religious way of life."

Hack supports his assertion that life in a Yale dormitory would pose a threat to his moral standards by citing examples of posters on dorm walls that advise safe sex and newspaper articles that joke about premarital sex. Hack feels that his religious training has prepared him to defend his moral principles, but he asks why an institution considered so tolerant cannot also be tolerant of those who want to maintain their conservative practices and beliefs: "Why is Yale — an institution that professes to be so tolerant and open-minded — making it particularly hard for students like us to maintain our moral standards through difficult college years?"

Hack heads off a possible objection to his argument by explaining that he and the other Jewish students are not trying to impose their moral standards on others. They simply don't want to have others' standards imposed on them. Some would argue that an assignment to a dorm that has floors designated by gender should be accommodation enough, but even those have open stairwells between floors. If exceptions are made for students who are married or who are twenty-one, why can an exception not be made for those who object to dorm life for religious reasons?

A characteristic of good arguers is that they know well their opponents' position. Hack acknowledges that he even knows well the language Yale uses in "selling" itself to new students. He quotes the brochure that Yale sent him: "Yale retains a deep respect for its early history and for the continuity that its history provides — a continuity based on constant reflection and reappraisal." His request and claim is that Yale should reappraise a position that compels him to compromise his religious principles.

What happened to the lawsuit to which Hack refers? It was tied up in court until 2001, when all of the students involved except Hack had graduated. The students lost the legal battle at all levels, primarily because their case depended on their proving that having to live in a residence hall constituted discrimination based on religion. The university successfully argued that the residence requirement was not discriminatory. Hack graduated from Yale in 2003. All five students chose to live in apartments during their first two years while paying full housing fees for dorm rooms they never occupied.

PRACTICE

Use the claim of policy on page 179: "The time required for an undergraduate degree should be extended to five years." Apply to it Hairston's five steps for Rogerian argumentation (p. 11). Support whichever side of the issue you agree with.

Supersize Your Child?

RICHARD HAYES

In the late 1950s, soon after Watson and Crick had discovered DNA's structure, scientists began predicting that someday we'd be able to genetically engineer our children. We'd design them to be healthy, smart, and attractive, with life spans of 200 years, photographic memories, enhanced lung capacity for athletic endurance, and more. Our children would pass these modifications to their own children and add new ones as well. Humanity would take control of its own evolution and kick it into overdrive.

Few people took these speculations very seriously. Could this sort of genetic engineering really be done? Even if it could, would anyone really want to do it? If they did, wouldn't society step in and set limits? In any event, wouldn't it be decades before we'd have to worry about this?

Now it's 2004, and those decades have passed. The era of genetically modified humans is close upon us. Almost every day we read of new breakthroughs: cloning, artificial chromosomes and now high-tech sex selection. Scientists create genetically modified animals on an assembly-line basis. Biotech entrepreneurs discuss the potential market for genetically modified children at investors' conferences. For the most part, society has not stepped in and set limits.

Last year *Science* magazine reported that a variant of the human 5-HTT gene reduces the risk of depression following stressful experiences. Depression can be a devastating condition. Would it be wrong if a couple planning to start a family used in vitro fertilization procedures to have the 5-HTT gene variant inserted into the embryos of their prospective children? Taken as an isolated instance, many people would be hard-pressed to say that it was.

In 1993, University of California at San Francisco biochemist Dr. Cynthia Kenyon discovered a variant of the DAF-2 gene that doubles the two-week life span of nematode worms. The university filed for patents based on knowledge of the metabolic pathway regulated by the human version of the DAF-2 gene. In 1999, Kenyon and others founded Elixir Pharmaceuticals, a biotech firm. In early 2003, Elixir licensed the university's patent rights to Kenyon's discoveries and secured $17 million in private financing. In an earlier interview with *ABC News*, Kenyon said she saw no reason humans might not be able to achieve 200-year life spans.

5

Richard Hayes is the executive director of the Center for Genetics and Society, a California-based nonprofit organization working for the responsible governance of genetic technologies. This piece was published on the TomPaine.com Web site in February 2004.

"Post-human" Nature

Last June at Yale University, the World Transhumanist Association held its first national conference. The Transhumanists have chapters in more than 20 countries and advocate the breeding of "genetically enriched" forms of "post-human" beings. Other advocates of the new techno-eugenics, such as Princeton University professor Lee Silver, predict that by the end of this century, "All aspects of the economy, the media, the entertainment industry, and the knowledge industry [will be] controlled by members of the GenRich class . . . Naturals [will] work as low-paid service providers or as laborers . . . ."

What happens then? Here's Dr. Richard Lynn, emeritus professor at the University of Ulster, who, like Silver, supports human genetic modification: "What is called for here is not genocide, the killing off of the population of incompetent cultures. But we do need to think realistically in terms of the 'phasing out' of such peoples. . . . Evolutionary progress means the extinction of the less competent."

Notice that I've gone, in just four steps, from reducing susceptibility to depression, to extending the human life span, to the creation of a genetic elite, to proposals that genetically inferior people be "phased out."

When first presented with this scenario, people typically respond in one of two ways. Some say, "It's impossible." Others say, "It's inevitable." Notice what these otherwise diametrically different responses have in common: Both counsel passivity. If the "post-human future" is impossible, there's no need to try to prevent it. If it's inevitable, such efforts would be in vain.

Will it actually be possible to genetically engineer our children? Most scientists who have studied this question conclude that although the techniques need to be refined, there's no reason to believe it can't be done. Meanwhile, research on stem cells, cloning, artificial chromosomes, and more continues to refine those techniques. 10

Many people believe that to suggest that manipulating genes can affect behavioral and cognitive traits in humans is to indulge discredited ideologies of "genetic determinism." It's true that the crude sociobiology of the 1970s has been discredited, as have simplistic notions that there exist "I.Q. genes" or "gay genes" that determine one's intelligence or sexual orientation. But to say that genes have no influence over traits is equally simplistic. Some genes have minimal influence, others have greater influence. Some have influence in the presence of certain environmental factors but no influence otherwise. Few genes determine anything; most confer propensities.

Deepening Inequality

Suppose scientists found a gene giving male children a 15 percent greater chance of growing one inch taller than they would have grown without that gene, all else equal. If fertility clinics offered to engineer embryos to include this gene, would there be customers? Yes. Couples would say, "In this competitive world, I want to do anything I can that might give my child an edge."

Will genetic changes be part of human reproduction in future years?

Once we allow children to be designed through embryo modification, where would we stop? If it's acceptable to modify one gene, why not two? If two, why not 20? Or 200? There are some 30,000 genes in the human genome. Each contributes, in smaller or larger proportions, to some propensity. Where would we stop? On what grounds?

Some suggest we allow embryo modification for certified medical conditions and prohibit it for cosmetic or enhancement purposes. It's unlikely that this would succeed. Prozac, Viagra, and Botox were all developed for medical purposes but in the blink of an eye became hugely profitable cosmetic and enhancement consumer products.

Will the use of genetic engineering to redesign our children exacerbate in-   15
equality? Amazingly, the neo-eugenic advocates don't deny that it will. As good libertarians, they celebrate free markets and social Darwinism, and counsel us to accept a rising tide of genetically enhanced inequality as the inevitable result of human ingenuity and desire.

But couldn't this be prevented? Wouldn't society step in? Several years ago, a team of health policy academics examined a range of proposals, including systems of national health insurance making eugenic engineering available to all, or preferentially to the poor, or by lottery. Despite their best efforts, they couldn't identify any realistic set of policies that would prevent the new eugenic technologies, once allowed at all, from generating unprecedented inequality.

And consider the international implications. What happens when some country announces an aggressive program of eugenic engineering explicitly intended to create a new, superior, omni-competent breed of human? What does the rest of the world do then?

We need to take a deep breath and realize what is going on here. The birth of the first genetically modified child would be a watershed moment in human history. It would set off a chain of events that would feed back upon themselves in ways impossible to control.

Unnatural Selection

Everything we experience, everything we know, everything we do is experienced, known and done by a species — homo sapiens — which evolved through natural selection over hundreds of thousands of years. We differ as individuals, but we are a single human species with a shared biology so fundamental to what we are that we are not even conscious of it, or of the manifold ways it unites us. What happens if we begin changing that fundamental shared biology?

Three hundred years ago the scientific and political leaders of that era took as   20
a self-evident fact the division of humanity into "superior" and "inferior" types, designed by Providence respectively as masters and slaves. Human beings were bred, bought and sold, like cattle or dogs. After three hundred years of struggle and bloodshed we are on the verge — barely — of putting this awful legacy behind us.

Or maybe not. If left uncontrolled, the new human genetic technologies could set us on a trajectory leading to a new Dark Age in which people are once again regarded as little better than cattle or dogs. Here is "bioethicist" Gregory Pence, who has testified in support of human cloning before the U.S. Congress and elsewhere:

> [M]any people love their retrievers and their sunny dispositions around children and adults. Could people be chosen in the same way? Would it be so terrible to allow parents to at least aim for a certain type, in the same way that great breeders . . . try to match a breed of dog to the needs of a family?

The common initial responses to the prospect of the new techno-eugenics — "It's impossible," and "It's inevitable" — are incorrect and unhelpful. The response we need to affirm is at once more realistic and more challenging: The techno-eugenic future certainly is possible, and is certainly not inevitable.

Road to Regulation

In 1997, the Council of Europe negotiated an important international agreement, the Convention on Biomedicine and Human Rights. Thus far, it has been signed by more than two-thirds of the council's 45 member countries. The convention draws the lines on human genetic modification in just the right ways. It allows medical research, including stem cell research, to continue, and does not restrict abortion rights, but it bans genetic modifications that would open the door to high-tech eugenic engineering. Many countries in Asia, Africa, and Latin America have likewise begun to address these issues through legislation.

These efforts are encouraging, but we have a long way to go before such policies are implemented, as they must be, worldwide. In some countries, notably the United States, the politics of the new genetic technologies have become polarized to the point of gridlock. The religious right insists on total bans on nearly all human embryo research, while bio-research interests and the biotech industry insist on nearly total freedom from any meaningful social oversight and accountability.

In other countries, and at the international level, the challenge of a new high-tech, free market eugenics, while worrisome, can seem remote in comparison with the real existing challenges of warfare, hunger, and disease.   25

What is to be done? More than anything, we need to realize the unprecedented nature of the challenges that the new human genetic technologies present. We need to distinguish benign applications of these technologies from pernicious ones, and support the former while opposing the latter. Concerned organizations and individuals need to engage these challenges and make their voices heard worldwide. National and international leaders in politics, the sciences and the arts need to declare that humanity is not going to let itself be split asunder by human genetic technology. The United Nations and other international bodies need to give these issues the highest attention. The hour is late. There is no greater challenge before us.

READING AND DISCUSSION QUESTIONS

1. Hayes alerts us that he is using the organization of his essay to help make his point. Explain where and how he does that. How does he appeal to his readers' need to feel secure? Why might his readers feel their sense of security being threatened?

2. Is Hayes supporting a claim of fact, value, or policy? Where does he state that claim most directly?

3. What types of support does Hayes offer to back up his opinion? How convincing do you find his support to be?

4. Can you identify the warrant underlying Hayes's argument? In order to accept his claim, what assumption of his must you agree with? Does he state his warrant explicitly anywhere in the essay?

WRITING SUGGESTIONS

5. Write an essay in which you either support or argue against Hayes's claim.

6. Write an essay in which you explain your own position on who should set limits on genetic engineering.

7. Choose an invention or scientific development that people once said was impossible and explain how those skeptics were proved wrong.

8. Choose an invention or scientific development and explain how it is now used, for good or ill, for purposes it was never intended to serve.

Saw Good at Tying Things in Knots

WESLEY MORRIS

All anybody should want from a horror movie is the steady tightening in the pit of your stomach. While the new sado-masochistic gross-out flick *Saw* often resembles the ghastliest editions yet of *Fear Factor* and *Survivor* and features some of the grodiest direction this side of *Project Greenlight*, it does manage at times to knead your tummy like dough, using real suspense for a rolling pin.

Most of it is generated from wondering whether the movie will deliver on the promise of one of its posters, which shows a foot severed from its leg. It's the kind of terror that really has nothing to do with the plot, which, by the time it's been fully carried out, is as twisted as your stomach.

A doctor (Cary Elwes) and a bratty young photographer (Leigh Whannell, the movie's writer) wake up on either side of the sort of big, grimy bathroom you see only in bad horror movies and good music videos. Each man's leg is chained to a pipe, and neither has any idea how he got there or what that male body is doing lying dead between them in its undies. There's a gun in one hand, a tape recorder in the other, and a pool of blood around the head.

After beginning the dopey dialogue (mostly from Elwes, who brings a dinner-theater zest to his predicament), both men discover personal notes that indicate what they have to do: One has to kill the other to survive. And while you wait for Joe Rogan or Jeff Probst to supervise the mayhem, the two men start following the series of clues, which have been left on cassette tapes and elsewhere by a sicko watching on a surveillance camera. The contestants (what else are they?) turn up a pair of hacksaws and immediately start using them in vain on their chains. Silly rabbits, hacksaws are for ankles.

By this point, the movie has likely won your dread. So rather than commence with the cutting, *Saw* takes a break, in order for the doctor to treat the photographer to the hunch he has about who might be behind this stunt. It's in these flashbacks that screenwriter Whannell and director James Wan are exposed as being under the dubious influence of every movie in the modern psychopath-movie liquor cabinet — and *The Usual Suspects*, too.

5

Wesley Morris is a film critic at the *Boston Globe* and formerly wrote film reviews and essays for the *San Francisco Examiner* and the *San Francisco Sun-Chronicle*. This review appeared on October 24, 2004, in the *Boston Globe*.

Someone has been rounding up people who've been "wasting their lives" and subjecting them to horrific tortures to prove how much they want to live. While the victims demonstrate this, the editing and photography go predictably nuts, running around them and deliriously speeding up their futile escapes. One man tried to crawl through a nest of barbed wire to freedom. Another was slathered in a flammable jelly and asked to crawl across a floor strewn with glass to decipher a code that would free him. He had to do this holding a candle. (He failed.) The sole "winner" was a woman who had to fish a key from a living man's stomach or her head would explode. Frankly, that looks comparatively easy.

Two detectives on the case — Ken Leung and a never nuttier Danny Glover — fingered the good doctor as the culprit. He was innocent of those crimes but guilty of a lesser one that makes a decent alibi. But the movie persists in dredging up more implausible mysteries and domestic drama, namely through some terribly handled scenes between the doctor and his soon-to-be-jeopardized family.

Eventually, it grows frustrating to watch the movie's puzzle assemble itself — even once it does, there are pieces still missing. Why, for instance, does Glover's freaky character love news clippings as much as the average serial killer? And are we really to believe the major curveball in the final scene?

Not really. But as long as *Saw* stays in that big, nasty bathroom, all we need to believe is the knot in our stomachs.

READING AND DISCUSSION QUESTIONS

1. Morris establishes immediately "[a]ll anybody should want from a horror movie." What is it that all viewers should want?

2. The reference in the first paragraph to the way the movie makes a viewer's stomach feel may not seem significant at first glance, but how does Morris follow through on this idea of a "gut-level" response to horror?

3. How does Morris manage to praise the movie in the first paragraph in spite of referring to it as a "sado-masochistic gross-out flick" with "grody" direction?

4. What other weakness does Morris see in the film?

5. What is Morris's ultimate judgment regarding the film? On what criteria does he base that judgment?

6. How effective is the support that Morris offers for his assessment?

WRITING SUGGESTIONS

7. Write an essay in which you explain your own criteria for evaluating horror films. Or choose another genre (romantic comedy, drama, or mocumentary, for example) and write evaluating criteria for it.

8. If you have seen *Saw*, write an essay explaining whether or not you agree with Morris's assessment of the film.

9. Write your own review of a recent movie, being sure to establish the criteria for evaluation on which you base your review. See Ebert's review of *Crash* earlier in this chapter for another example of a movie review.

Take This Internship and Shove It

ANYA KAMENETZ

My younger sister has just arrived in New Orleans for the summer after her freshman year at Yale. She will be consuming daily snowballs, the local icy treat, to ward off the heat, volunteering to help clean up neighborhoods damaged by Hurricane Katrina and working part time, for pay, at both a literary festival and a local restaurant. Meanwhile, most of her friends from college are headed for the new standard summer experience: the unpaid internship.

Instead of starting out in the mailroom for a pittance, this generation reports for business upstairs without pay. A national survey by Vault, a career information Web site, found that 84 percent of college students in April planned to complete at least one internship before graduating. Also according to Vault, about half of all internships are unpaid.

I was an unpaid intern at a newspaper from March 2002, my senior year, until a few months after graduation. I took it for granted, as most students do, that working without pay was the best possible preparation for success; parents usually agree to subsidize their offspring's internships on this basis. But what if we're wrong?

What if the growth of unpaid internships is bad for the labor market and for individual careers?

Let's look at the risks to the lowly intern. First there are opportunity costs. 5
Lost wages and living expenses are significant considerations for the two-thirds of students who need loans to get through college. Since many internships are done for credit and some even cost money for the privilege of placement overseas or on Capitol Hill, those students who must borrow to pay tuition are going further into debt for internships.

Second, though their duties range from the menial to quasi-professional, unpaid internships are not jobs, only simulations. And fake jobs are not the best preparation for real jobs.

Long hours on your feet waiting tables may not be particularly edifying, but they teach you that work is a routine of obligation, relieved by external reward, where you contribute value to a larger enterprise. Newspapers and business magazines are full of articles expressing exasperation about how the Millennial-generation employee supposedly expects work to be exciting immediately, wears flip-flops to the office, and has no taste for dues-paying. However true this stereotype may be, the spread of the artificially fun internship might very well be adding fuel to it.

Anya Kamenetz, a columnist for *The Village Voice,* is the author of *Generation Debt: How Our Future Was Sold Out for Student Loans, Credit Cards, Bad Jobs, No Benefits, and Tax Cuts for Rich Geezers — and How to Fight Back* (published in 2006 and reissued, with an additional chapter, in 2007).

Duties for an unpaid intern can range from menial to quasi-professional.

By the same token, internships promote over-identification with employers: I make sacrifices to work free, therefore I must love my work. A sociologist at the University of Washington, Gina Neff, who has studied the coping strategies of interns in communications industries, calls the phenomenon "performative passion." Perhaps this emotion helps explain why educated workers in this country are less and less likely to organize, even as full-time jobs with benefits go the way of the Pinto.

Although it's not being offered this year, the A.F.L.-C.I.O.'s Union Summer Internship program, which provides a small stipend, has shaped thousands of college-educated career organizers. And yet interestingly, the percentage of young workers who hold an actual union card is less than 5 percent, compared with an overall national private-sector union rate of 12.5 percent. How are twentysomethings ever going to win back health benefits and pension plans when they learn to be grateful to work for nothing?

So an internship doesn't teach you everything you need to know about coping   10 in today's working world. What effect does it have on the economy as a whole?

The Bureau of Labor Statistics does not identify interns or track the economic impact of unpaid internships. But we can do a quick-and-dirty calculation: according to *Princeton Review*'s "Internship Bible," there were 100,000 internship positions in 2005. Let's assume that out of those, 50,000 unpaid interns are employed full time for 12 weeks each summer at an average minimum wage of $5.15 an hour. That's a nearly $124 million yearly contribution to the welfare of corporate America.

In this way, unpaid interns are like illegal immigrants. They create an oversupply of people willing to work for low wages, or in the case of interns, literally nothing. Moreover, a recent survey by Britain's National Union of Journalists found that an influx of unpaid graduates kept wages down and patched up the gaps left by job cuts.

There may be more subtle effects as well. In an information economy, productivity is based on the best people finding the jobs best suited for their talents, and interns interfere with this cultural capitalism. They fly in the face of meritocracy — you must be rich enough to work without pay to get your foot in the door. And they enhance the power of social connections over ability to match people with desirable careers. A 2004 study of business graduates at a large mid-Atlantic university found that the completion of an internship helped people find jobs faster but didn't increase their confidence that those jobs were a good fit.

With all this said, the intern track is not coming to an end any time soon. More and more colleges are requiring some form of internship for graduation. Still, if you must do an internship, research shows you will get more out of it if you find a paid one.

A 1998 survey of nearly 700 employers by the Institute on Education and the   15
Economy at Columbia University's Teachers College found: "Compared to unpaid internships, paid placements are strongest on all measures of internship quality. The quality measures are also higher for those firms who intend to hire their interns." This shouldn't be too surprising — getting hired and getting paid are what work, in the real world, is all about.

READING AND DISCUSSION QUESTIONS

1. What complaint does Kamenetz have against internships?
2. What two problems does Kamenetz see with unpaid internships?
3. What are the risks to the "lowly intern"?
4. Why is it, according to Kamenetz, better to wait tables than to have an unpaid internship at a prestigious firm? Do you agree?
5. Why does Kamenetz compare unpaid interns to illegal immigrants? Is it a valid comparison?
6. How do interns interfere with "cultural capitalism"?
7. Does your school require internships? If so, where would you like to intern and why? If not, do you plan to have an internship anyway?
8. Where does Kamenetz most clearly state her claim? What type of claim is it?

WRITING SUGGESTIONS

9. Write an essay in which you explain whether or not you agree with Kamanetz's argument against unpaid internships.
10. Write an essay in which you explain how effective Kamenetz is in defending her position.
11. Write an essay in which you argue why you think an internship is valuable for every student.
12. Write an essay in which you argue that internships should not be required at your school.
13. Write an essay in which you explain what you can do while in college to best prepare you for the career you plan to pursue or one that you might pursue. Be specific. Don't depend on the obvious, like "study hard."

DEBATE   What Is the Social Responsibility of Business?

Putting Customers Ahead of Investors

JOHN MACKEY

In 1970 Milton Friedman wrote that "there is one and only one social responsibility of business — to use its resources and engage in activities designed to increase its profits so long as it stays within the rules of the game, which is to say, engages in open and free competition without deception or fraud." That's the orthodox view among free market economists: that the only social responsibility a law-abiding business has is to maximize profits for the shareholders.

I strongly disagree. I'm a businessman and a free market libertarian, but I believe that the enlightened corporation should try to create value for all of its constituencies. From an investor's perspective, the purpose of the business is to maximize profits. But that's not the purpose for other stakeholders — for customers, employees, suppliers, and the community. Each of those groups will define the purpose of the business in terms of its own needs and desires, and each perspective is valid and legitimate.

My argument should not be mistaken for a hostility to profit. I believe I know something about creating shareholder value. When I co-founded Whole Foods Market 27 years ago, we began with $45,000 in capital; we only had $250,000 in sales our first year. During the last 12 months we had sales of more than $4.6 billion, net profits of more than $160 million, and a market capitalization over $8 billion.

But we have not achieved our tremendous increase in shareholder value by making shareholder value the primary purpose of our business. In my marriage, my wife's happiness is an end in itself, not merely a means to my own happiness; love leads me to put my wife's happiness first, but in doing so I also make myself happier. Similarly, the most successful businesses put the customer first, ahead of the investors. In the profit-centered business, customer happiness is merely a means to an end: maximizing profits. In the customer-centered business, customer happiness is an end in itself, and will be pursued with greater interest, passion, and empathy than the profit-centered business is capable of.

Not that we're only concerned with customers. At Whole Foods, we measure our success by how much value we can create for all six of our most important stakeholders: customers, team members (employees), investors, vendors, communities, and the environment. . . .

5

John Mackey was the cofounder in 1980 of Whole Foods Market and is now its CEO. He supports free market economics and the movement for organic food. His article and T. J. Rodgers's, which follows, were part of a debate on the social responsibility of business that appeared in the October 2005 issue of *Reason* magazine.

There is, of course, no magical formula to calculate how much value each stakeholder should receive from the company. It is a dynamic process that evolves with the competitive marketplace. No stakeholder remains satisfied for long. It is the function of company leadership to develop solutions that continually work for the common good.

Many thinking people will readily accept my arguments that caring about customers and employees is good business. But they might draw the line at believing a company has any responsibility to its community and environment. To donate time and capital to philanthropy, they will argue, is to steal from the investors. After all, the corporation's assets legally belong to the investors, don't they? Management has a fiduciary responsibility to maximize shareholder value; therefore, any activities that don't maximize shareholder value are violations of this duty. If you feel altruism towards other people, you should exercise that altruism with your own money, not with the assets of a corporation that doesn't belong to you.

This position sounds reasonable. A company's assets do belong to the investors, and its management does have a duty to manage those assets responsibly. In my view, the argument is not wrong so much as it is too narrow.

First, there can be little doubt that a certain amount of corporate philanthropy is simply good business and works for the long-term benefit of the investors. For example: In addition to the many thousands of small donations each Whole Foods store makes each year, we also hold five 5% Days throughout the year. On those days, we donate 5 percent of a store's total sales to a nonprofit organization. While our stores select worthwhile organizations to support, they also tend to focus on groups that have large membership lists, which are contacted and encouraged to shop our store that day to support the organization. This usually brings hundreds of new or lapsed customers into our stores, many of whom then become regular shoppers. So a 5% Day not only allows us to support worthwhile causes, but is an excellent marketing strategy that has benefited Whole Foods investors immensely.

That said, I believe such programs would be completely justifiable even if they   10
produced no profits and no P.R. This is because I believe the entrepreneurs, not the current investors in a company's stock, have the right and responsibility to define the purpose of the company. It is the entrepreneurs who create a company, who bring all the factors of production together and coordinate it into viable business. It is the entrepreneurs who set the company strategy and who negotiate the terms of trade with all of the voluntarily cooperating stakeholders — including the investors. At Whole Foods we "hired" our original investors. They didn't hire us.

We first announced that we would donate 5 percent of the company's net profits to philanthropy when we drafted our mission statement, back in 1985. Our policy has therefore been in place for over 20 years, and it predates our IPO [Initial Public Offering] by seven years. All seven of the private investors at the time we created the policy voted for it when they served on our board of directors. When we took in venture capital money back in 1989, none of the venture firms objected to the policy. In addition, in almost 14 years as a publicly traded company, almost no investors have ever raised objections to the policy. How can Whole Foods' philanthropy be "theft" from the current investors if the original owners of the company unanimously approved the policy and all subsequent investors made their investments after the policy was in effect and well publicized?

The shareholders of a public company own their stock voluntarily. If they don't agree with the philosophy of the business, they can always sell their investment, just as the customers and employees can exit their relationships with the company if they don't like the terms of trade. If that is unacceptable to them, they always have the legal right to submit a resolution at our annual shareholders meeting to change the company's philanthropic philosophy. A number of our company policies have been changed over the years through successful shareholder resolutions.

Another objection to the Whole Foods philosophy is where to draw the line. If donating 5 percent of profits is good, wouldn't 10 percent be even better? Why not donate 100 percent of our profits to the betterment of society? But the fact that Whole Foods has responsibilities to our community doesn't mean that we don't have any responsibilities to our investors. It's a question of finding the appropriate balance and trying to create value for all of our stakeholders. Is 5 percent the "right amount" to donate to the community? I don't think there is a right answer to this question, except that I believe 0 percent is too little. It is an arbitrary percentage that the co-founders of the company decided was a reasonable amount and which was approved by the owners of the company at the time we made the decision. Corporate philanthropy is a good thing, but it requires the legitimacy of investor approval. In my experience, most investors understand that it can be beneficial to both the corporation and to the larger society.

That doesn't answer the question of why we give money to the community stakeholder. For that, you should turn to one of the fathers of free-market economics, Adam Smith. *The Wealth of Nations* was a tremendous achievement, but economists would be well served to read Smith's other great book, *The Theory of Moral Sentiments*. There he explains that human nature isn't just about self-interest. It also includes sympathy, empathy, friendship, love, and the desire for social approval. As motives for human behavior, these are at least as important as self-interest. For many people, they are more important.

When we are small children we are egocentric, concerned only about our own   15
needs and desires. As we mature, most people grow beyond this egocentrism and begin to care about others — their families, friends, communities, and countries. Our capacity to love can expand even further: to loving people from different races, religions, and countries — potentially to unlimited love for all people and even for other sentient creatures. This is our potential as human beings, to take joy in the flourishing of people everywhere. Whole Foods gives money to our communities because we care about them and feel a responsibility to help them flourish as well as possible.

The business model that Whole Foods has embraced could represent a new form of capitalism, one that more consciously works for the common good instead of depending solely on the "invisible hand" to generate positive results for society. The "brand" of capitalism is in terrible shape throughout the world, and corporations are widely seen as selfish, greedy, and uncaring. This is both unfortunate and unnecessary, and could be changed if businesses and economists widely adopted the business model that I have outlined here.

To extend our love and care beyond our narrow self-interest is antithetical to neither our human nature nor our financial success. Rather, it leads to the further fulfillment of both. Why do we not encourage this in our theories of business and economics? Why do we restrict our theories to such a pessimistic and crabby view of human nature? What are we afraid of?

Put Profits First

T. J. RODGERS

John Mackey's article attacking corporate profit maximization could not have been written by "a free market libertarian," as claimed. Indeed, if the examples he cites had not identified him as the author, one could easily assume the piece was written by Ralph Nader. A more accurate title for his article is "How Business and Profit Making Fit into My Overarching Philosophy of Altruism."

Mackey spouts nonsense about how his company hired his original investors, not vice versa. If Whole Foods ever falls on persistent hard times — perhaps when the Luddites are no longer able to hold back the genetic food revolution using junk science and fear — he will quickly find out who has hired whom, as his investors fire him.

Mackey does make one point that is consistent with, but not supportive of, free market capitalism. He knows that shareholders own his stock voluntarily. If they don't like the policies of his company, they can always vote to change those policies with a shareholder resolution or simply sell the stock and buy that of another company more aligned with their objectives. Thus, he informs his shareholders of his objectives and lets them make a choice on which stock to buy. So far, so good.

It is also simply good business for a company to cater to its customers, train and retain its employees, build long-term positive relationships with its suppliers, and become a good citizen in its community, including performing some philanthropic activity. When Milton Friedman says a company should stay "within the rules of the game" and operate "without deception or fraud," he means it should deal with all its various constituencies properly in order to maximize long-term shareholder value. He does not mean that a company should put every last nickel on the bottom line every quarter, regardless of the long-term consequences.

My company, Cypress Semiconductor, has won the trophy for the Second Harvest Food Bank competition for the most food donated per employee in Silicon Valley for the last 13 consecutive years (1 million pounds of food in 2004). The contest creates competition among our divisions, leading to employee involvement,

Thurman John Rodgers is the founder and CEO of Cypress Semiconductor. He is a strong advocate of laissez-faire capitalism.

company food drives, internal social events with admissions "paid for" by food donations, and so forth. It is a big employee morale builder, a way to attract new employees, good P.R. for the company, and a significant benefit to the community — all of which makes Cypress a better place to work and invest in. Indeed, Mackey's own proud example of Whole Foods' community involvement programs also made a profit.

But Mackey's subordination of his profession as a businessman to altruistic ideals shows up as he attempts to negate the empirically demonstrated social benefit of "self-interest" by defining it narrowly as "increasing short-term profits." Why is it that when Whole Foods gives money to a worthy cause, it serves a high moral objective, while a company that provides a good return to small investors — who simply put their money into their own retirement funds or a children's college fund — is somehow selfish? It's the philosophy that is objectionable here, not the specific actions. If Mackey wants to run a hybrid business/charity whose mission is fully disclosed to his shareholders — and if those shareholder-owners want to support that mission — so be it. But I balk at the proposition that a company's "stakeholders" (a term often used by collectivists to justify unreasonable demands) should be allowed to control the property of the shareholders. It seems Mackey's philosophy is more accurately described by Karl Marx: "From each according to his ability" (the shareholders surrender money and assets); "to each according to his needs" (the charities, social interest groups, and environmentalists get what they want). That's not free market capitalism.

Then there is the arrogant proposition that if other corporations would simply emulate the higher corporate life form defined by Whole Foods, the world would be better off. After all, Mackey says corporations are viewed as "selfish, greedy, and uncaring." I, for one, consider free market capitalism to be a high calling, even without the infusion of altruism practiced by Whole Foods.

If one goes beyond the sensationalistic journalism surrounding the Enron-like debacles, one discovers that only about 10 to 20 public corporations have been justifiably accused of serious wrongdoing. That's about 0.1 percent of America's 17,500 public companies. What's the failure rate of the publications that demean business? (Consider the *New York Times* scandal involving manufactured stories.) What's the percentage of U.S. presidents who have been forced or almost forced from office? (It's 10 times higher than the failure rate of corporations.) What percentage of our congressmen have spent time in jail? The fact is that despite some well-publicized failures, most corporations are run with the highest ethical standards — and the public knows it. Public opinion polls demonstrate that fact by routinely ranking businessmen above journalists and politicians in esteem.

I am proud of what the semiconductor industry does — relentlessly cutting the cost of a transistor from $3 in 1960 to three-millionths of a dollar today. Mackey would be keeping his business records with hordes of accountants on paper ledgers if our industry didn't exist. He would have to charge his poorest customers more for their food, pay his valued employees less, and cut his philanthropy programs if the semiconductor industry had not focused so relentlessly on increasing its profits, cutting his costs in the process. Of course, if the U.S. semiconductor industry had been less cost-competitive due to its own philanthropy, the food industry simply would have bought cheaper computers made from Japanese and Korean silicon chips (which happened anyway). Layoffs in the nonunion semiconductor industry were actually good news to Whole Foods' unionized grocery store clerks. Where was Mackey's sense of altruism when unemployed semiconductor workers needed it? Of course, that rhetorical question is foolish, since he did exactly the right thing by ruthlessly reducing his recordkeeping costs so as to maximize his profits.

I am proud to be a free market capitalist. And I resent the fact that Mackey's   10
philosophy demeans me as an egocentric child because I have refused on moral grounds to embrace the philosophies of collectivism and altruism that have caused so much human misery, however tempting the sales pitch for them sounds.

DISCUSSION QUESTIONS

1. What does Mackey think the social responsibility of business should be? How does this differ from Milton Friedman's belief?

2. How does Whole Foods "create value for all of its constituencies"?

3. Why is Rodgers so vehemently opposed to Mackey's philosophy of the social responsibility of business?

4. How does Rodgers feel that his company aids society, not just its investors?

5. Which of the two do you feel presents a more convincing argument? Why?

Assignments for Understanding Claims

READING AND DISCUSSION QUESTIONS

1. Locate a movie review online or in hard copy that has a clear claim and is based on clear evaluative criteria. Choose a review that is an essay, not just a single paragraph. Bring it to class and share it with your class or group. By looking at a range of different reviews, come to some conclusions about the sort of criteria used in making judgment calls about movies and what sort of claims provide good thesis statements for reviews. What are some other characteristics that all or most good movie reviews share?

2. Consider one or more of your school's policies that you would like to see changed. In your opinion, what exactly is wrong with the policy as it currently exists? What exactly would you recommend be done to improve the situation?

3. Samuelson, in "Picking Sides for the News" (p. 172), argues that different news sources slant their news toward different audiences. Do you agree with his argument? Why, or why not? What examples can you provide in support of your opinion?

WRITING ASSIGNMENTS

4. Choose a controversial issue in the field in which you are majoring or one in which you might major. Practice differentiating among the three types of claims by writing a claim of fact, a claim of value, and a claim of policy on that issue.

5. Choose one of the three claims you wrote for assignment four above and write an essay supporting it.

6. Write an essay arguing that your school should or should not require internships. If your school has a school newspaper, you may choose to write a letter to the editor instead of an essay.

Research Readiness: Acknowledging Reliable Authorities

How can you let your readers know that your sources are reliable?

If you are conscientious in your research and documentation of sources, you need to be sure that your efforts pay off by communicating to your audience relevant information that will strengthen your argument. Not only do you need to know that you are drawing information from reliable authorities, but also your readers need to know that. Below are some quotations and the names of those who are quoted. Do some research and find out what gives the person quoted the authority to speak knowledgeably on the subject of the quotation. Then work the information you found into a lead-in to the quotation, as in the model.

EXAMPLE:

"We are promoting human rights by building homes for people who don't have them." — Jimmy Carter

"We are promoting human rights by building homes for people who don't have them," explains former president Jimmy Carter, who has been involved with Habitat for Humanity International since 1984 and who, with his wife, leads its Jimmy and Rosalynn Carter Work Project one week each year.

1. "[Operation Iraqi Children] is a beautiful way to begin a relationship with the future leaders of Iraq, Afghanistan and other war-torn nations. They have been forgotten for so long. Now there is a chance for them." — Gary Sinise

2. "Innovation has nothing to do with how many R&D dollars you have. When Apple came up with the Mac, IBM was spending at least 100 times more on R&D. It's not about money. It's about the people you have, how you're led, and how much you get it." — Steve Jobs

3. "If gun laws in fact worked, the sponsors of this type of legislation should have no difficulties drawing upon long lists of crime rates reduced by such legislation. That they cannot do so after a century and a half of trying — that they must sweep under the rug the southern attempts at gun control in the 1870–1910 period, the northeastern attempts in the 1920–1939 period, the attempts at both Federal and State levels in 1965–1976 — establishes the repeated, complete and inevitable failure of gun laws to control serious crime." — Orrin G. Hatch

4. "If we want our children to possess the traits of character we most admire, we need to teach them what those traits are and why they deserve both admiration and

allegiance. Children must learn to identify the forms and content of those traits."
— William J. Bennett

5. "The three major brain sciences, brain imaging, pharmacology, and genetics, can work together hand and glove, and when needed hand and glove and foot, to illuminate a mysterious disorder like depression." — J. Raymond DePaulo, Jr.

6. Of a plan by a Florida church to burn Qurans on the anniversary of 9/11 in 2010: "It is precisely the kind of action the Taliban uses and could cause significant problems. Not just here, but everywhere in the world we are engaged with the Islamic community." — General David Petraeus

CHAPTER 6

Support

Types of Support: Evidence and Appeals to Needs and Values

All the claims you make — whether of fact, of value, or of policy — must be supported. Sometimes you will use your own experience as support for a claim. At other times you may conduct interviews, field research, lab experiments, or surveys to obtain support for your position. For the majority of your assignments, you will most likely turn primarily to print and electronic sources.

Support for a claim represents the answer to the question "What have you got to go on?"[1] There are two basic kinds of support in an argument: evidence and appeals to needs and values. When you provide evidence, you use facts, including examples and statistics, and opinions, or interpretations of facts — both your own and those of experts. Another tactic is to appeal to readers' needs (that is, requirements for physical and psychological survival and well-being) and values (or standards for right and wrong, good and bad).

This chapter presents the different types of evidence and appeals you can use to support your claim and examines the criteria by which you can evaluate the soundness of that support.

[1] Stephen Toulmin, *The Uses of Argument* (Cambridge: Cambridge University Press, 1958), p. 98.

Evidence

Factual Evidence

In Chapter 5, we defined facts as statements possessing a high degree of public acceptance. Some facts can be verified by experience alone. Eating too much will make us sick; we can get from Hopkinton to Boston in a half hour by car; in the Northern Hemisphere it is colder in December than in July. The experience of any individual is limited in both time and space, so we must accept as fact thousands of assertions about the world that we ourselves can never verify. Thus we accept the report that human beings landed on the moon in 1969 because we trust those who can verify it. (Country people in Morocco, however, received the news with disbelief because they had no reason to trust the reporters of the event. They insisted on trusting their senses instead. One man said, "I can see the moon very clearly. If a man were walking around up there, wouldn't I be able to see him?")

Factual evidence appears most frequently as examples and statistics, which are a numerical form of examples.

Examples

Examples are the most familiar kind of factual evidence. In addition to providing support for the truth of a generalization, examples can enliven otherwise dense or monotonous prose.

In the following paragraph the writer supports the claim in the topic sentence by offering a series of specific examples.

> Americans expect the next century to bring some striking political and social changes, but people are discerning. Two-thirds believe gay marriages probably will be legal and over half think that fathers will spend as much time and energy with their kids as mothers. Half of the public also predicts that Social Security will probably die; that view is particularly prevalent among younger Americans. But a majority doubts that cigarette smoking will be illegal or that all racial and gender discrimination will disappear.[2]

Hypothetical examples, which create imaginary situations for the audience and encourage them to visualize what might happen under certain circumstances, can also be effective. The following paragraph illustrates the use of hypothetical examples. (The author is describing megaschools, high schools with more than two thousand students.)

> And in schools that big there is inevitably a critical mass of kids who are neither jocks nor artists nor even nerds, kids who are nothing at all,

---

[2]Elizabeth Crowley, "Putting Faith in Technology for Year 3000," *Wall Street Journal*, September 15, 2000, sec. A, p. 10.

nonentities in their own lives. . . . The creditable ballplayer who might have made the team in a smaller school is edged out by better athletes. The artist who might have had work hung in a smaller school is supplanted by abler talents. And the disaffected and depressed boy who might have found a niche, or a friend, or a teacher who noticed, falls between the cracks. Sometimes he quietly drops out. Sometimes he quietly passes through. And sometimes he comes to school with a gun.[3]

All claims about vague or abstract terms would be boring or unintelligible without examples to illuminate them. For example, if you claim that a movie contains "unusual sound effects," you will certainly have to describe some of the effects to convince the reader that your generalization can be trusted.

Statistics

Statistics express information in numbers. In the following example statistics have been used to express raw data in numerical form.

A study released by the Center for Media and Public Affairs in June 1999 states that though television shows a lot of violence, it rarely shows its outcome. "We found that despite the high volume of televised violence, viewers rarely see it causing adverse effects," states the report. The report found serious acts of violence — murder, rape, kidnapping, and assault with a deadly weapon — occurred once every four minutes on the major TV networks. However, it notes that "no physical harm was shown three quarters (75 percent) of the time violence occurred on broadcast series and over two-thirds (68 percent) of the time it occurred on cable programs. A mere 7 percent of violent acts on broadcast shows and 4 percent on cable resulted in fatalities."

The CMPA report notes that in its study, "serious violence was more likely to have tangible consequences, but a majority of even these more brutal acts had no direct harmful results. Fifty-nine percent of acts of serious violence on broadcast series and 54 percent on cable lacked negative consequences." Only in rare instances, about 10 percent, did violence result in some type of mental distress for the victim or another character. "Thus, fully 90 percent of violent acts on broadcast and 87 percent on cable proved psychologically painless," says the report.[4]

Statistics are more effective in comparisons that indicate whether a quantity is relatively large or small and sometimes even whether a reader should interpret the result as gratifying or disappointing. For example, if a novice gambler were told that for every dollar wagered in a state lottery, 50 percent goes back to the players as prizes, would the gambler be able to conclude that the percentage is

---

[3]Anna Quindlen, "The Problem of the Megaschool," *Newsweek*, March 26, 2001, p. 68.
[4]Ron Kaufman, "Filling Their Minds with Death: TV Violence and Children," *TurnOffYourTV.com*, 2004. August 1, 2010. http://turnoffyourtv.com/healtheducation/violencechildren/violencechildren.html.

high or low? Would he be able to choose between playing the state lottery and playing a casino game? Unless he had more information, probably not. But if he were informed that in casino games, the return to the players is over 90 percent and in slot machines and racetracks the return is around 80 percent, the comparison would enable him to evaluate the meaning of the 50 percent return in the state lottery and even to make a decision about where to gamble his money.[5]

Comparative statistics are also useful for measurements over time. For instance, the following statistics show what comparisons based on BMI or body mass index reveal about how Miss America contestants have changed over the years.

> Miss America contestants have become increasing thinner over the past 75 years. In the 1920s, contestants had BMIs in the normal range of 20–25. Since then, pageant winners' body weights have decreased steadily to a level about 12 percent below levels from the mid-1900s. Since 1970, nearly all of the winners have had BMIs below the healthy range, with some as low as 16.9, a BMI that would meet part of the diagnostic criteria for anorexia nervosa.[6]

Diagrams, tables, charts, and graphs can make clear the relations among many sets of numbers. Such charts and diagrams allow readers to grasp the information more easily than if it were presented in paragraph form.

The graphs that constitute Figures 1 and 2 on pages 206 and 207 summarize the information produced by polls about cancer care and cancer costs. The pie charts on page 208 (Figures 3 and 4) clarify coverage of Africa by two popular newsmagazines.

Opinions: Interpretations of the Facts

Opinions or interpretations about facts are the inferences discussed in Chapter 5. They are an indispensable source of support for your claims.

Opinions or interpretations of facts generally take four forms: (1) They may suggest the cause for a condition or a causal connection between two sets of data; (2) they may offer predictions about the future; (3) they may suggest solutions to a problem; (4) they may refer to the opinion of experts.

Causal Connection

A more common term than *causal connections* is *cause-effect relationships*. Here Phyllis Rose analyzes some opinions about what causes anorexia.

---

[5] Curt Suphee, "Lotto Baloney," *Harper's,* July 1983, p. 201.

[6] S. Rubenstein and B. Caballero, "Is Miss America an Undernourished Role Model?" *JAMA* (2000), p. 1569. Qtd. in Jillian Croll, "Body Image and Adolescents," *Guidelines for Adolescent Nutrition Services*, J. Stang and M. Story, eds. (2005). June 9, 2007. http://www.epi.umn.edu/let/pubs/adol_book.shtm.

FIGURE 1
Ratings of Health-Care System for Cancer Care
Note: Don't know and refused responses not shown.
Source: USA Today/Kaiser Family Foundation/Harvard School of Public Health, *National Survey of Households Affected by Cancer* (conducted Aug. 1–Sept. 14, 2006); Employee Benefit Research Institute, *Health Confidence Survey* (conducted June 30–Aug. 6, 2005).

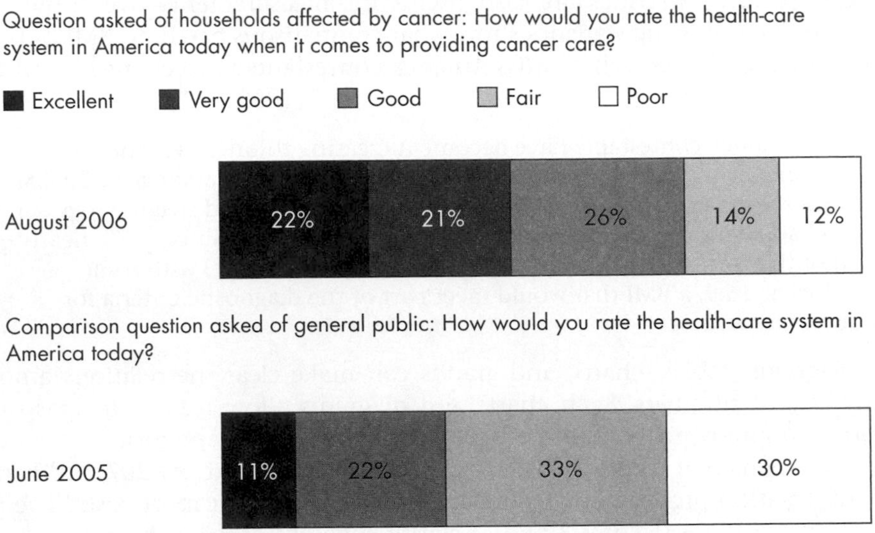

Question asked of households affected by cancer: How would you rate the health-care system in America today when it comes to providing cancer care?

■ Excellent   ■ Very good   ■ Good   ■ Fair   □ Poor

August 2006 | 22% | 21% | 26% | 14% | 12% |

Comparison question asked of general public: How would you rate the health-care system in America today?

June 2005 | 11% | 22% | 33% | 30% |

Anorexia nervosa is a serious, sometimes fatal, disease characterized by self-starvation. It is found largely among young women. Physicians, psychologists, and social scientists have speculated about the causes, which remain unclear. A leading researcher in the field, Hilde Bruch, believes that food refusal expresses a desire to postpone sexual development. Another authority, Joan Blumberg, believes that one cause may be biological, a nervous dysfunction of the hypothalamus. Still others infer that the causes are cultural, a response to the admiration of the thin female body.[7]

Predictions

In the fall and winter of 1989 to 1990 extraordinary events shook Eastern Europe, toppling Communist regimes and raising more popular forms of government. Politicians and scholars offered predictions about future changes in the region. One expert, Zbigniew Brzezinski, former national security adviser under President Carter, concluded that the changes for the Soviet Union might be destructive.

[7] Phyllis Rose, "Hunger Artists," *Harper's,* July 1988, p. 82.

FIGURE 2

Financial Burden of Cancer Care by Insurance Status, Income, and Age

Source: USA Today/Kaiser Family Foundation/Harvard School of Public Health, *National Survey of Households Affected by Cancer* (conducted Aug. 1–Sept. 14, 2006).

Percent saying the cost of cancer care is a *major* burden on their family . . .

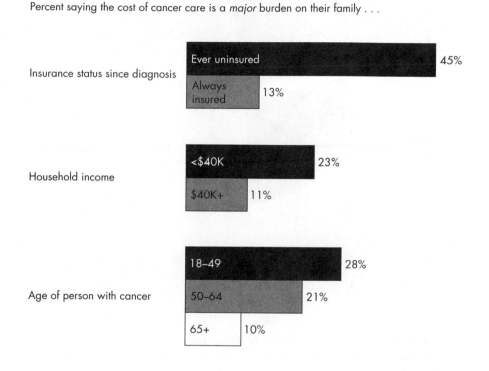

It would be a mistake to see the recent decisions as marking a break-through for democracy. Much more likely is a prolonged period of democ-ratizing chaos. One will see the rise in the Soviet Union of increasingly irreconcilable conflicts between varying national political and social aspirations, all united by a shared hatred for the existing Communist nomenklatura. One is also likely to see a flashback of a nationalist type among the Great Russians, fearful of the prospective breakup of the exist-ing Great Russian Empire.[8]

Solutions to Problems

How shall we solve the problems caused by young people in our cities "who commit crimes and create the staggering statistics in teenage pregnancies and the high abortion rate"? The minister emeritus of the Abyssinian Baptist Church in New York City proposes establishment of a national youth academy with

[8]*New York Times*, February 9, 1990, sec. A, p. 13.

FIGURE 3
Percentages of Five Story Topics about Africa in *Newsweek*, August 1989 to August 1991

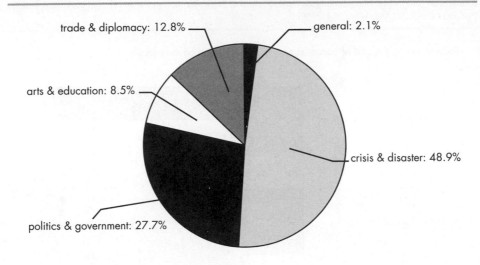

trade & diplomacy: 12.8%

general: 2.1%

arts & education: 8.5%

crisis & disaster: 48.9%

politics & government: 27.7%

FIGURE 4
Percentages of Five Story Topics about Africa in *Time*, August 1989 to August 1991
Source: Jerry Domatob, "Coverage of Africa in American Popular Magazines," *Issue: A Journal of Opinion*, 22 (Winter-Spring 1994): 25.

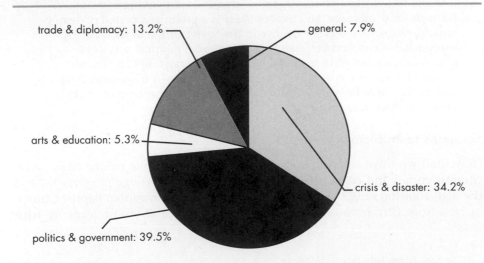

trade & diplomacy: 13.2%

general: 7.9%

arts & education: 5.3%

crisis & disaster: 34.2%

politics & government: 39.5%

fifty campuses on inactive military bases. "It is a 'parenting' institution. . . . It is not a penal institution, not a prep school, not a Job Corps Center, not a Civilian Conservation Camp, but it borrows from them." Although such an institution has not been tried before, the author of the proposal thinks that it would represent an effort "to provide for the academic, moral, and social development of young people, to cause them to become responsible and productive citizens."[9]

Expert Opinion

For many of the subjects you discuss and write about, you will find it necessary to accept and use the opinions of experts. Based on their reading of the facts, experts express opinions on a variety of controversial subjects: whether capital punishment is a deterrent to crime; whether legalization of marijuana will lead to an increase in its use; whether children, if left untaught, will grow up honest and cooperative; whether sex education courses will result in less sexual activity and fewer illegitimate births. The interpretations of the data are often profoundly important because they influence social policy and affect our lives directly and indirectly.

For the problems mentioned above, the opinions of people recognized as authorities are more reliable than those of people who have neither thought about nor done research on the subject. But opinions may also be offered by student writers in areas in which they are knowledgeable. If you were asked, for example, to defend or refute the statement that work has advantages for teenagers, you could call on your own experience and that of your friends to support your claim. You can also draw on your experience to write convincingly about your special interests.

One opinion, however, is not as good as another. The value of any opinion depends on the quality of the evidence and the trustworthiness of the person offering it.

PRACTICE

1. Choose either Figure 1, "Ratings of Health-Care System for Cancer Care" (p. 206), or Figure 2, "Financial Burden of Cancer Care by Insurance Status, Income, and Age" (p. 207). Consider the facts presented in the graph you chose. What is one conclusion you can draw based on those facts? Summarize that conclusion in one sentence and make it the topic sentence for a paragraph. Then use facts from the graph as specific support to complete the paragraph.

2. Do the same with Figure 3 and Figure 4 (p. 208), the pie charts about Africa, but this time consider both charts.

[9]Samuel D. Proctor, "To the Rescue: A National Youth Academy," *New York Times,* September 16, 1989, sec. A, p. 27.

3. Write two possible topic sentences supporting conclusions you were able to draw from the information in Figure 1, one a statement of fact and the other a statement of opinion. Do the same with Figure 2.

Research Skill: Evaluation of Evidence

Before you begin to write, you must determine whether the facts and opinions you have chosen to support your claim are sound. Can they convince your readers? A distinction between the evaluation of facts and the evaluation of opinions is somewhat artificial because many facts are verified by expert opinion, but for our analysis we discuss them separately.

Evaluation of Factual Evidence

As you evaluate factual evidence, you should keep in mind the following questions:

1. Is the evidence up to date? The importance of up-to-date information depends on the subject. If you are defending the claim that suicide is immoral, you will not need to examine new data. For many of the subjects you write about, recent research and scholarship will be important, even decisive, in proving the soundness of your data. "New" does not always mean "best," but in fields where research is ongoing — education, psychology, technology, medicine, and all the natural and physical sciences — you should be sensitive to the dates of the research.

In writing a paper a few years ago warning about the health hazards of air pollution, you would have used data referring only to outdoor pollution produced by automobile and factory emissions. But writing about air pollution today, you would have to take into account new data about indoor pollution, which has become a serious problem as a result of attempts to conserve energy. Because research studies in indoor pollution are continually being updated, recent evidence will probably be more accurate than past research.

2. Is the evidence sufficient? The amount of evidence you need depends on the complexity of the subject and the length of your paper. Given the relative brevity of most of your assignments, you will need to be selective. For the claim that indoor pollution is a serious problem, one example would obviously not be enough. For a 750- to 1,000-word paper, three or four examples would probably be sufficient. The choice of examples should reflect different aspects of the problem: in this case, different sources of indoor pollution — gas stoves, fireplaces, kerosene heaters, insulation — and the consequences for health.

Indoor pollution is a fairly limited subject for which the evidence is clear. But more complex problems require more evidence. A common fault in argument is generalization based on insufficient evidence. In a 1,000-word paper you could not adequately treat the causes of conflict in the Middle East; you could not develop workable proposals for health-care reform; you could not predict the development of education in the next century. In choosing a subject for a brief paper, determine whether you can produce sufficient evidence to convince a reader who may not agree with you. If not, the subject may be too large for a brief paper.

3. Is the evidence relevant? All the evidence should, of course, contribute to the development of your argument. Sometimes the arguer loses sight of the subject and introduces examples that are wide of the claim. In defending a national health-care plan, one student offered examples of the success of health maintenance organizations, but such organizations, although subsidized by the federal government, were not the structure favored by sponsors of the plan. The examples were interesting but irrelevant.

Also keep in mind that not all readers will agree on what is relevant. Is the unsavory private life of a politician relevant to his or her performance in office? If you want to prove that a politician is unfit to serve because of his or her private activities, you may first have to convince some members of the audience that private activities are relevant to public service.

4. Are the examples representative? This question emphasizes your responsibility to choose examples that are typical of all the examples you do not use. Suppose you offered Vermont's experience to support your claim that same-sex marriage should be legal. Is the experience of Vermont typical of what is happening or may happen in other states? Or is Vermont, a small, mostly rural New England state, different enough from other states to make the example unrepresentative?

5. Are the examples consistent with the experience of the audience? The members of your audience use their own experiences to judge the soundness of your evidence. If your examples are unfamiliar or extreme, they will probably reject your conclusion. Consider the following excerpt from Jacob Neusner's hypothetical commencement speech, "The Speech the Graduates Didn't Hear" (pp. 374–75), which is meant to represent a faculty member's response to student apathy.

> For years we have created an altogether forgiving world, in which whatever slight effort you gave was all that was demanded. When you did not keep appointments, we made new ones. When your work came in beyond the deadline, we pretended not to care.
> Worse still, when you were boring, we acted as if you were saying something important. When you were garrulous and talked to hear yourself talk, we listened as if it mattered. When you tossed on our desks writing upon which you had not labored, we read it and even responded, as though you earned a response. When you were dull, we pretended you were smart. When you were predictable, unimaginative, and routine, we listened as if to new and wonderful things. When you demanded free lunch we served it.

If most members of the audience find that such a description doesn't reflect their own attitudes or those of their friends, they will probably question the validity of the claim.

Evaluation of Statistics

The questions you must ask about examples also apply to statistics. Are they recent? Are they sufficient? Are they relevant? Are they typical? Are they consistent with the experience of the audience? But there are additional questions directed specifically to evaluation of statistics.

1. Do the statistics come from trustworthy sources? Perhaps you have read newspaper accounts of very old people, some reported to be as old as 135, living in the Caucasus or the Andes, nourished by yogurt and hard work. But these statistics are hearsay; no birth records or other official documents exist to verify them. Now two anthropologists have concluded that the numbers were part of a rural mythology and that the ages of the people were actually within the normal range for human populations elsewhere.[10]

Hearsay statistics should be treated with the same skepticism accorded to gossip or rumor. Sampling a population to gather statistical information is a sophisticated science; you should ask whether the reporter of the statistics is qualified and likely to be free of bias. Among the generally reliable sources are polling organizations such as Gallup, Roper, and Louis Harris and agencies of the U.S. government such as the Census Bureau and the Bureau of Labor Statistics. Other qualified sources are well-known research foundations, university centers, and insurance companies that prepare actuarial tables. Statistics from underdeveloped countries are less reliable for obvious reasons: lack of funds, lack of trained statisticians, lack of communication and transportation facilities to carry out accurate censuses.

2. Are the terms clearly defined? In an example in Chapter 4, the reference to poverty (p. 132) made clear that any statistics would be meaningless unless we knew exactly how *poverty* was defined by the user. *Unemployment* is another term for which statistics will be difficult to read if the definition varies from one user to another. For example, are seasonal workers employed or unemployed during the off-season? Are part-time workers employed? (In Russia they are unemployed.) Are workers on government projects employed? (During the 1930s they were considered employed by the Germans and unemployed by the Americans.) The more abstract or controversial the term, the greater the necessity for clear definition.

3. Are the comparisons between comparable things? Folk wisdom warns us that we cannot compare apples and oranges. Population statistics for the world's

---

[10]Richard B. Mazess and Sylvia H. Forman, "Longevity and Age Exaggeration in Vilcabamba, Ecuador," *Journal of Gerontology* (1979), pp. 94–98.

largest city, for example, should indicate the units being compared. Greater London is defined in one way, greater New York in another, and greater Tokyo in still another. The population numbers will mean little unless you can be sure that the same geographical units are being compared.

4. Has any significant information been omitted? *The Plain Truth,* a magazine published by the World-Wide Church of God, advertises itself as follows:

> *The Plain Truth* has now topped 5,000,000 copies per issue. It is now the fastest-growing magazine in the world and one of the widest circulated mass-circulation magazines on earth. Our circulation is now greater than *Newsweek.* New subscribers are coming in at the rate of around 40,000 per week.

What the magazine neglects to mention is that it is *free.* There is no subscription fee, and the magazine is widely distributed in drugstores, supermarkets, and airports. *Newsweek* is sold on newsstands and by subscription. The comparison therefore omits significant information.

Evaluation of Opinions

When you evaluate the reliability of opinions in subjects with which you are not familiar, you will be dealing almost exclusively with opinions of experts. Most of the following questions are directed to an evaluation of authoritative sources. But you can also ask these questions of students or of others with opinions based on their own experience and research. Keep them in mind when doing research on the Internet.

1. Is the source of the opinion qualified to give an opinion on the subject? The discussion of credibility in Chapter 1 (pp. 4–7) pointed out that certain achievements by the interpreter of the data — publications, acceptance by colleagues — can tell us something about his or her competence. Although these standards are by no means foolproof (people of outstanding reputations have been known to falsify their data), nevertheless they offer assurance that the source is generally trustworthy. The answers to questions you must ask are not hard to find: Is the source qualified by education? Is the source associated with a reputable institution — a university or a research organization? Is the source credited with having made contributions to the field — books, articles, research studies? Suppose that in writing a paper on organ transplants you came across an article by Peter Medawar. He is identified as follows:

> Sir Peter Medawar, British zoologist, winner of the 1960 Nobel Prize in Physiology or Medicine, for proving that the rejection by the body of foreign organs can be overcome; president of the Royal Society; head of the National Institute for Medical Research in London; a world leader in immunology.

These credentials would suggest to almost any reader that Medawar is a reliable source for information about organ transplants.

If the source is not so clearly identified, you should treat the data with caution. Such advice is especially relevant when you are dealing with popular works about such subjects as miracle diets, formulas for instant wealth, and sightings of monsters and UFOs. Do not use such data until you can verify them from other, more authoritative sources.

In addition, you should question the identity of any source listed as "spokesperson" or "reliable source" or "an unidentified authority." The mass media are especially fond of this type of attribution. Sometimes the sources are people in public life who plant stories anonymously or off the record for purposes they prefer to keep hidden.

Even when the identification is clear and genuine, you should ask if the credentials are relevant to the field in which the authority claims expertise. So specialized are areas of scientific study today that scientists in one field may not be competent to make judgments in another. William Shockley is a distinguished engineer, a Nobel Prize winner for his contribution to the invention of the electronic transistor. But when he made the claim, based on his own research, that blacks are genetically inferior to whites, geneticists accused Shockley of venturing into a field where he was unqualified to make judgments. Similarly, advertisers invite stars from the entertainment world to express opinions about products with which they are probably less familiar than members of their audience. All citizens have the right to express their views, but this does not mean that all views are equally credible or worthy of attention.

2. Is the source biased for or against his or her interpretation? Even authorities who satisfy the criteria for expertise may be guilty of bias. Bias arises as a result of economic reward, religious affiliation, political loyalty, and other interests. The expert may not be aware of the bias; even an expert can fall into the trap of ignoring evidence that contradicts his or her own intellectual preferences. A British psychologist has said:

> The search for meaning in data is bound to involve all of us in distortion to greater or lesser degree. . . . Transgression consists not so much in a clear break with professional ethics, as in an unusually high-handed, extreme or self-deceptive attempt to promote one particular view of reality at the expense of all others.[11]

Before accepting the interpretation of an expert, you should ask: Is there some reason why I should suspect the motives of this particular source?

Consider, for example, an advertisement claiming that sweetened breakfast cereals are nutritious. The advertisement, placed by the manufacturer of the cereal, provides impeccable references from scientific sources to support its claims. But since you are aware of the economic interest of the company in promoting sales, you may wonder if they have reproduced only facts that favor their claims. Are there other facts that might prove the opposite? As a careful

[11]Liam Hudson, *The Cult of the Fact* (New York: Harper and Row, 1972), p. 125.

researcher you would certainly want to look further for data about the advantages and disadvantages of sugar in our diets.

It is harder to determine bias in the research done by scientists and university faculty even when the research is funded by companies interested in a favorable review of their products. If you discover that a respected biologist who advocates the use of sugar in baby food receives a consultant's fee from a sugar company, should you conclude that the research is slanted and that the scientist has ignored contrary evidence? Not necessarily. The truth may be that the scientist arrived at conclusions about the use of sugar legitimately through experiments that no other scientist would question. But it would probably occur to you that a critical reader might ask about the connection between the results of the research and the payment by a company that profits from the research. In this case you would be wise to read further to find confirmation or rejection of the claim by other scientists.

The most difficult evaluations concern ideological bias. Early in our lives we learn to discount the special interest that makes a small child brag, "My mother (or father) is the greatest!" Later we become aware that the claims of people who are avowed Democrats or Republicans or supply-side economists or Yankee fans or zealous San Franciscans or joggers must be examined somewhat more carefully than those of people who have no special commitment to a cause or a place or an activity. This is not to say that all partisan claims lack support. They may, in fact, be based on the best available support. But whenever special interest is apparent, there is always the danger that an argument will reflect this bias.

3. Has the source bolstered the claim with sufficient and appropriate evidence? An author might claim, "Statistics show that watching violence on television leads to violent behavior in children." But if the author gave no further information — neither statistics nor proof that a cause-effect relation exists between televised violence and violence in children, the critical reader would ask, "What are the numbers? Who compiled them?"

Even those who are reputed to be experts in the subjects they discuss must do more than simply allege that a claim is valid or that the data exist. They must provide facts to support their interpretations.

When Experts Disagree

Authoritative sources can disagree. Such disagreement is probably most common in the social sciences. They are called the "soft" sciences precisely because a consensus about conclusions in these areas is more difficult to arrive at than in the natural and physical sciences. Consider the controversy over what determines the best interests of the child where both biological and foster parents are engaged in trying to secure custody. Experts are deeply divided on this issue. Dr. Daniel J. Cohen, a child psychologist and director of the Yale Child Study Center, argues that the psychological needs of the child should take precedence. If the child has a stable and loving relationship with foster parents, that is where

Experts disagree on some questions, such as the reason why dinosaurs became extinct.

he should stay. But Bruce Bozer and Bernadine Dohrn of the Children and Family Justice Center at Northwestern University Law School insist that "such a solution may be overly simplistic." The child may suffer in later life when he learns that he has been prevented from returning to biological parents "who fought to get him back."[12]

But even in the natural and physical sciences, where the results of observation and experiment are more conclusive, we encounter heated differences of opinion. A popular argument concerns the extinction of the dinosaurs. Was it the effect of an asteroid striking the earth? Or widespread volcanic activity? Or a cooling of the planet? All these theories have their champions among the experts.

Environmental concerns also produce lively disagreements. Scientists have lined up on both sides of a debate about the importance of protecting the tropical rain forest as a source of biological, especially mammalian, diversity. Dr. Edward O. Wilson, a Harvard biologist, whose books have made us familiar with the term *biodiversity,* says, "The great majority of organisms appears to reach maximum diversity in the rain forest. There is no question that the rain forests are the world's headquarters of diversity." But in the journal *Science* another biologist, Dr. Michael Mares, a professor of zoology at the University of Oklahoma, argues that "if one could choose only a single South American habitat in which to preserve the greatest mammalian diversity, it would be the dry lands. . . . The dry lands are very likely far more highly threatened than the largely inaccessible rain forests."[13] A debate of more immediate relevance concerns possible dangers in genetically modified foods, as distinguished from foods modified by traditional breeding practices. Dr. Louis Pribyl, a U.S. Food and Drug

[12]*New York Times,* September 4, 1994, sec. E, p. 3.
[13]*New York Times,* April 7, 1992, sec. C, p. 4.

Administration microbiologist, has accused the agency of claiming "that there are no unintended effects that raise the FDA's level of concern. But . . . there are no data to back up this contention." On the other hand, Dr. James Marjanski, the FDA's biotechnology coordinator, maintains that "as long as developers of these foods follow agency guidelines, genetically engineered foods are as safe as any on the market."[14]

How can you choose between authorities who disagree? If you have applied the tests discussed so far and discovered that one source is less qualified by training and experience or makes claims with little support or appears to be biased in favor of one interpretation, you will have no difficulty in rejecting that person's opinion. If conflicting sources prove to be equally reliable in all respects, then continue reading other authorities to determine whether a greater number of experts support one opinion rather than another. Although numbers alone, even of experts, don't guarantee the truth, nonexperts have little choice but to accept the authority of the greater number until evidence to the contrary is forthcoming. Finally, if you are unable to decide between competing sources of evidence, you may conclude that the argument must remain unsettled. Such an admission is not a failure; after all, such questions are considered controversial because even the experts cannot agree, and such questions are often the most interesting to consider and argue about.

Appeals to Needs and Values

Good factual evidence is usually enough to convince an audience that your factual claim is sound. Using examples, statistics, and expert opinion, you can prove, for example, that women do not earn as much as men for the same work. But even good evidence may not be enough to convince your audience that unequal pay is wrong or that something should be done about it. In making value and policy claims, an appeal to the needs and values of your audience is absolutely essential to the success of your argument. If you want to persuade the audience to change their minds or adopt a course of action — in this case, to demand legislation guaranteeing equal pay for equal work — you will have to show that assent to your claim will bring about what they want and care deeply about.

If the audience concludes that the things you care about are very different from what they care about, if they cannot identify with your goals and principles, they may treat your argument with indifference, even hostility, and finally reject it. But you can hope that decent and reasonable people will share many of the needs and values that underlie your claims. Finding these shared needs and values is what Carl Rogers was advocating when he said that the way to improved communication is to try to express your audience's position fairly and to look for common ground between their position and yours.

[14]*New York Times,* December 1, 1999, sec. A, p. 15.

Appeals to Needs

The most familiar classification of needs was developed by the psychologist Abraham H. Maslow in 1954.[15] These needs, said Maslow, motivate human thought and action. In satisfying our needs, we attain both long- and short-term goals. Because Maslow believed that some needs are more important than others, he arranged them in hierarchical order from the most urgent biological needs to the psychological needs that are related to our roles as members of a society.

PHYSIOLOGICAL NEEDS Basic bodily requirements: food and drink; health; sex

SAFETY NEEDS Security; freedom from harm; order and stability

BELONGINGNESS AND LOVE NEEDS Love within a family and among friends; roots within a group or a community

ESTEEM NEEDS Material success; achievement; power, status, and recognition by others

SELF-ACTUALIZATION NEEDS Fulfillment in realizing one's potential

For most of your arguments you won't have to address the audience's basic physiological needs for nourishment or shelter. The desire for health, however, now receives extraordinary attention. Appeals to buy health foods, vitamin supplements, drugs, exercise and diet courses, and health books are all around us. Many of the claims are supported by little or no evidence, but readers are so eager to satisfy the need for good health that they often overlook the lack of facts or authoritative opinion. The desire for physical well-being, however, is not so simple as it seems; it is strongly related to our need for self-esteem and love.

Appeals to our needs to feel safe from harm, to be assured of order and stability in our lives are also common. Insurance companies, politicians who promise to rid our streets of crime, and companies that offer security services all appeal to this profound and nearly universal need. (We say "nearly" because some people are apparently attracted to risk and danger.) At this writing those who monitor terrorist activity are attempting both to arouse fear for our safety and to suggest ways of reducing the dangers that make us fearful.

The last three needs in Maslow's hierarchy are the ones you will find most challenging to appeal to in your arguments. It is clear that these needs arise out of human relationships and participation in society. Advertisers make much use of appeals to these needs.

BELONGINGNESS AND LOVE NEEDS

"Whether you are young or old, the need for companionship is universal." (ad for dating service)

"Share the Fun of High School with Your Little Girl!" (ad for a Barbie doll)

---

[15] *Motivation and Personality* (New York: Harper and Row, 1954), pp. 80–92.

ESTEEM NEEDS

"Enrich your home with the distinction of an Oxford library."

"Apply your expertise to more challenges and more opportunities. Here are outstanding opportunities for challenge, achievement, and growth." (Perkin-Elmer Co.)

SELF-ACTUALIZATION NEEDS

"Be all that you can be." (former U.S. Army slogan)

"Are you demanding enough? Somewhere beyond the cortex is a small voice whose mere whisper can silence an army of arguments. It goes by many names: integrity, excellence, standards. And it stands alone in final judgment as to whether we have demanded enough of ourselves and, by that example, have inspired the best in those around us." (*New York Times*)

Of course, it is not only advertisers who use these appeals. We hear them from family and friends, from teachers, from employers, from editorials and letters to the editor, from people in public life.

Appeals to Values

Needs give rise to values. If we feel the need to belong to a group, we learn to value commitment, sacrifice, and sharing. And we then respond to arguments that promise to protect our values. It is hardly surprising that values, the principles by which we judge what is good or bad, beautiful or ugly, worthwhile or undesirable, should exercise a profound influence on our behavior. Virtually all claims, even those that seem to be purely factual, contain expressed or unexpressed judgments.

For our study of argument, we will speak of groups or systems of values because any single value is usually related to others. People and institutions are often defined by such systems of values. We can distinguish, for example, between those who think of themselves as traditional and those who think of themselves as modern by listing their differing values. One writer contrasts such values in this way:

> Among the values of traditionalism are merit, accomplishment, competition, and success; self-restraint, self-discipline, and the postponement of gratification; the stability of the family; and a belief in certain moral universals. The modernist ethos scorns the pursuit of success; is egalitarian and redistributionist in emphasis; tolerates or encourages sensual gratification; values self-expression as against self-restraint; accepts alternative or deviant forms of the family; and emphasizes ethical relativism.[16]

[16]Joseph Adelson, "What Happened to the Schools," *Commentary,* March 1981, p. 37.

Systems of values are neither so rigid nor so distinct from one another as this list suggests. Some people who are traditional in their advocacy of competition and success may also accept the modernist values of self-expression and alternative family structures. Values, like needs, are arranged in a hierarchy; that is, some are clearly more important than others to the people who hold them. Moreover, the arrangement may shift over time or as a result of new experiences. In 1962, for example, two speech teachers prepared a list of what they called "Relatively Unchanging Values Shared by Most Americans."[17] Included were "puritan and pioneer standards of morality" and "perennial optimism about the future." More than forty-five years later, an appeal to these values might fall on a number of deaf ears.

You should also be aware of not only changes over time but also different or competing value systems that reflect a multitude of subcultures in the United States. Differences in age, sex, race, ethnic background, social environment, religion, even in the personalities and characters of its members define the groups we belong to. Such terms as *honor, loyalty, justice, patriotism, duty, responsibility, equality, freedom,* and *courage* will be interpreted very differently by different groups.

All of us belong to more than one group, and the values of the several groups may be in conflict. If one group to which you belong — say, peers of your own age and class — is generally uninterested in and even scornful of religion, you may nevertheless hold to the values of your family and continue to place a high value on religious belief.

How can a knowledge of your readers' values enable you to make a more effective appeal? Suppose you want to argue in favor of a sex education program in the middle school you attended. The program you support would not only give students information about contraception and venereal disease but also teach them about the pleasures of sex, the importance of small families, and alternatives to heterosexuality. If the readers of your argument are your classmates or your peers, you can be fairly sure that their agreement will be easier to obtain than that of their parents, especially if their parents think of themselves as conservative. Your peers are more likely to value experimentation, tolerance of alternative sexual practices, freedom, and novelty. Their parents are more likely to value restraint, conformity to conventional sexual practices, obedience to family rules, and foresight in planning for the future.

Knowing that your peers share your values and your goals will mean that you need not spell out the values supporting your claim; they are understood by your readers. Convincing their parents, however, who think that freedom, tolerance, and experimentation have been abused by their children, will be a far more challenging task. In one written piece you have little chance of changing

[17] Edward Steele and W. Charles Redding, "The American Value System: Premises for Persuasion," *Western Speech,* 26 (Spring 1962), pp. 83–91.

their values, a result that might be achieved only over a longer period of time. So you might first attempt to reduce their hostility by suggesting that, even if a community-wide program were adopted, students would need parental permission to enroll. This might convince some parents that you share their values regarding parental authority and primacy of the family. Second, you might look for other values to which the parents subscribe and to which you can make an appeal. Do they prize maturity, self-reliance, responsibility in their children? If so, you could attempt to prove, with authoritative evidence, that the sex education program would promote these qualities in students who took the course.

But familiarity with the value systems of prospective readers may also lead you to conclude that winning assent to your argument will be impossible. It would probably be fruitless to attempt to persuade a group of lifelong pacifists to endorse the use of nuclear weapons. The beliefs, attitudes, and habits that support their value systems are too fundamental to yield to one or two attempts at persuasion.

Evaluation of Appeals to Needs and Values

If your argument is based on an appeal to the needs and values of your audience, the following questions will help you evaluate the soundness of your appeal.

1. **Have the values been clearly defined?** If you are appealing to the patriotism of your readers, can you be sure that they agree with your definition? Does patriotism mean "Our country, right or wrong!" or does it mean dissent, even violent dissent, if you think your country is wrong? Because value terms are abstractions, you must make their meaning explicit by placing them in context and providing examples.

2. **Are the needs and values to which you appeal prominent in the reader's hierarchy at the time you are writing?** An affluent community, fearful of further erosion of quiet and open countryside, might resist an appeal to allow establishment of a high-technology firm, even though the firm would bring increased prosperity to the area.

3. **Is the evidence in your argument clearly related to the needs and values to which you appeal?** Remember that the reader must see some connection between your evidence and his or her goals. Suppose you were writing an argument to persuade a group of people to vote in an upcoming election. You could provide evidence to prove that only 20 percent of the town voted in the last election. But this evidence would not motivate your audience to vote unless you could provide other evidence to show that their needs were not being served by such a low turnout.

Writer's Guide: Using Effective Support

1. In deciding how much support you need for your claim, it is always a good idea to assume that you are addressing an audience that may be at least slightly hostile to that claim. Those who already agree with you do not need convincing.

2. Keep a mental, if not a written, list of the different types of support you use in an essay. Few essays will use all of the different types of support, but being aware of all the possibilities will prevent you from forgetting to draw on one or more types of support that may advance your argument.

3. In that checklist of types of support, don't forget that there are two main categories: evidence and appeals to needs and values. Appeals to needs and values will generally need the reinforcement that comes from more objective forms of evidence, but the two in combination can often provide the strongest case for your claim. Aristotle explained that in an ideal world, arguers could depend on logic alone, but we live in a world that is far from ideal.

4. Use the following questions about the evaluation of evidence as a checklist to analyze the support you use in your argumentative essays:

Factual evidence:

- Is the evidence up to date?
- Is the evidence sufficient?
- Is the evidence relevant?
- Are the examples representative?
- Are the examples consistent with the experience of the audience?

Statistics:

- Do the statistics come from trustworthy sources?
- Are the terms clearly defined?
- Are the comparisons between comparable things?
- Has any significant information been omitted?

Opinion:

- Is the source of the opinion qualified to give an opinion on the subject?
- Is the source biased for or against his or her interpretation?
- Has the source bolstered the claim with sufficient and appropriate evidence?

5. Also check your essays against the list of questions regarding appeals to needs and values:

- Have the values been clearly defined?
- Are the needs and values to which you appeal prominent in the reader's hierarchy at the time you are writing?
- Is the evidence in your argument clearly related to the needs and values to which you appeal?

PRACTICE

1. Locate two advertisements from magazines or newspapers that appeal to needs or values or both. Be prepared to explain what needs and/or values the ads appeal to.

2. Share your ads with your classmates so that everyone can get an idea of the range of how ads appeal to needs and values.

3. Choose one of the ads your class compiled and write a paragraph analyzing its appeal to needs and/or values.

4. Write an essay in which you compare two ads for the same product or same type of product in terms of the types of appeal that they use.

SAMPLE ANNOTATED ESSAY

American Dream Is Elusive for New Generation
LOUIS UCHITELLE

Begins an extended example

After breakfast, his parents left for their jobs, and Scott Nicholson, alone in the house in this comfortable suburb west of Boston, went to his laptop in the living room. He had placed it on a small table that his mother had used for a vase of flowers until her unemployed son found himself reluctantly stuck at home.

The reference to his award appeals to those who value academic excellence.

The daily routine seldom varied. Mr. Nicholson, twenty-four, a graduate of Colgate University, winner of a dean's award for academic excellence, spent his mornings searching corporate Web sites for suitable job openings. When he found one, he mailed off a résumé and cover letter — four or five a week, week after week.

His refusal to accept this job goes against the values of those who believe any job is better than none.

Over the last five months, only one job materialized. After several interviews, the Hanover Insurance Group in nearby Worcester offered to hire him as an associate claims adjuster, at $40,000 a year. But even before the formal offer, Mr. Nicholson had decided not to take the job.

Rather than waste early years in dead-end work, he reasoned, he would hold out for a corporate position that would draw on his college training and put him, as he sees it, on the bottom rungs of a career ladder.

Louis Uchitelle worked as a reporter, a foreign correspondent, and the editor of the business news department at the Associated Press before joining the *New York Times* — the source of this article on July 6, 2010 — in 1980. He has taught journalism at Columbia University and is author of *The Disposable American: Layoffs and Their Consequences* (2006).

Scott Nicholson searches for a job while living in his parents' home.

"The conversation I'm going to have with my parents   5
now that I've turned down this job is more of a concern
to me than turning down the job," he said.

Generational conflict about values

He was braced for the conversation with his father in
particular. While Scott Nicholson viewed the Hanover
job as likely to stunt his career, David Nicholson, fifty-
seven, accustomed to better times and easier mobility,
viewed it as an opportunity. Once in the door, the father
has insisted to his son, opportunities will present themselves — as they did in the father's rise over thirty-five
years to general manager of a manufacturing company.

"You maneuvered and you did not worry what the
maneuvering would lead to," the father said. "You knew
it would lead to something good."

Complicating the generational divide, Scott's grandfather, William S. Nicholson, a World War II veteran and
a retired stockbroker, has watched what he described
as America's once mighty economic engine losing its
pre-eminence in a global economy. The grandfather has

Appeal to need for security

encouraged his unemployed grandson to go abroad — to
"Go West," so to speak.

"I view what is happening to Scott with dismay," said
the grandfather, who has concluded, in part from reading

Conflicts with U.S. value system — the belief that U.S. does everything better than anyone else

the *Economist*, that Europe has surpassed America in offering opportunity for an ambitious young man. "We hate to think that Scott will have to leave," the grandfather said, "but he will."

The grandfather's injunction startled the grandson. But as the weeks pass, Scott Nicholson, handsome as a Marine officer in a recruiting poster, has gradually realized that his career will not roll out in the Greater Boston area — or anywhere in America — with the easy inevitability that his father and grandfather recall, and that Scott thought would be his lot, too, when he finished college in 2008.

"I don't think I fully understood the severity of the situation I had graduated into," he said, speaking in effect for an age group — the so-called millennials, eighteen to twenty-nine — whose unemployment rate of nearly 14 percent approaches the levels of that group in the Great Depression. And then he veered into the optimism that, polls show, is persistently, perhaps perversely, characteristic of millennials today. "I am absolutely certain that my job hunt will eventually pay off," he said.

For young adults, the prospects in the workplace, even for the college-educated, have rarely been so bleak. Apart from the 14 percent who are unemployed and seeking work, as Scott Nicholson is, 23 percent are not even seeking a job, according to data from the Bureau of Labor Statistics. The total, 37 percent, is the highest in more than three decades and a rate reminiscent of the 1930s.

The college-educated among these young adults are better off. But nearly 17 percent are either unemployed or not seeking work, a record level (although some are in graduate school). The unemployment rate for college-educated young adults, 5.5 percent, is nearly double what it was on the eve of the Great Recession, in 2007, and the highest level — by almost two percentage points — since the bureau started to keep records in 1994 for those with at least four years of college.

Yet surveys show that the majority of the nation's millennials remain confident, as Scott Nicholson is, that they will have satisfactory careers. They have a lot going for them.

"They are better educated than previous generations and they were raised by baby boomers who lavished a lot of attention on their children," said Andrew Kohut, the Pew Research Center's director. That helps to explain their persistent optimism, even as they struggle to succeed.

Another appeal to need for security and esteem — it's threatening for this generation to be compared to the same age group during the Depression.

Statistical support

More statistical support

Appeal to esteem needs

10

15

So far, Scott Nicholson is a stranger to the triumphal stories that his father and grandfather tell of their working lives. They said it was connections more than perseverance that got them started — the father in 1976 when a friend who had just opened a factory hired him, and the grandfather in 1946 through an Army buddy whose father-in-law owned a brokerage firm in nearby Worcester and needed another stock broker.

From these accidental starts, careers unfolded and lasted. David Nicholson, now the general manager of a company that makes tools, is still in manufacturing. William Nicholson spent the next 48 years, until his retirement, as a stockbroker. "Scott has got to find somebody who knows someone," the grandfather said, "someone who can get him to the head of the line."

While Scott has tried to make that happen, he has come under pressure from his parents to compromise: to take, if not the Hanover job, then one like it. "I am beginning to realize that refusal is going to have repercussions," he said. "My parents are subtly pointing out that beyond room and board, they are also paying other expenses for me, like my cellphone charges and the premiums on a life insurance policy."

Scott Nicholson also has connections, of course, but no one in his network of family and friends has been able to steer him into marketing or finance or management training or any career-oriented opening at a big corporation, his goal. The jobs are simply not there.

The Millennials' Inheritance

The Great Depression damaged the self-confidence of the young, and that is beginning to happen now, according to pollsters, sociologists and economists. Young men in particular lost a sense of direction, Glen H. Elder Jr., a sociologist at the University of North Carolina, found in his study, *Children of the Great Depression*. In some cases they were forced into work they did not want — the issue for Scott Nicholson.

Military service in World War II, along with the G.I. Bill and a booming economy, restored well-being; by the 1970s, when Mr. Elder did his retrospective study, the hardships of the Depression were more a memory than an open sore. "They came out of the war with purpose in their lives, and by age forty most of them were doing well," he said, speaking of his study in a recent interview.

20

Appeal to the need for security

The outlook this time is not so clear. Starved for jobs at adequate pay, the millennials tend to seek refuge in college and in the military and to put off marriage and child-bearing. Those who are working often stay with the jobs they have rather than jump to better paying but less secure ones, as young people seeking advancement normally do. And they are increasingly willing to forgo raises or to settle for small ones.

Expert opinion

"They are definitely more risk-averse," said Lisa B. Kahn, an economist at the Yale School of Management, "and more likely to fall behind."

Statistical support

In a recent study, she found that those who graduated from college during the severe early '80s recession earned up to 30 percent less in their first three years than new graduates who landed their first jobs in a strong economy. Even fifteen years later, their annual pay was 8 to 10 percent less.

Many hard-pressed millennials are falling back on their 25 parents, as Scott Nicholson has. While he has no college debt (his grandparents paid all his tuition and board) many others do, and that helps force them back home.

In 2008, the first year of the recession, the percentage of the population living in households in which at least two generations were present rose nearly a percentage point, to 16 percent, according to the Pew Research Center. The high point, 24.7 percent, came in 1940, as the Depression ended, and the low point, 12 percent, in 1980.

Striving for Independence

Appeal to self-actualization need

"Going it alone," "earning enough to be self-supporting" — these are awkward concepts for Scott Nicholson and his friends. Of the twenty college classmates with whom he keeps up, twelve are working, but only half are in jobs they "really like." Three are entering law school this fall after frustrating experiences in the work force, "and five are looking for work just as I am," he said.

Like most of his classmates, Scott tries to get by on a shoestring and manages to earn enough in odd jobs to pay some expenses.

Examples

The jobs are catch as catch can. He and a friend recently put up a white wooden fence for a neighbor, embedding the posts in cement, a day's work that brought Scott $125. He mows lawns and gardens for half a dozen clients in Grafton, some of them family friends. And he is an active volunteer firefighter.

"As frustrated as I get now, and I never intended to   30
live at home, I'm in a good situation in a lot of ways,"
Scott said. "I have very little overhead and no debt, and it
is because I have no debt that I have any sort of flexibility
to look for work. Otherwise, I would have to have a job,
some kind of full-time job."

That millennials as a group are optimistic is partly
because many are, as Mr. Kohut put it, the children of
doting baby boomers — among them David Nicholson
and his wife, Susan, fifty-six, an executive at a company
that owns movie theaters.

The Nicholsons, whose combined annual income is
north of $175,000, have lavished attention on their three
sons. Currently that attention is directed mainly at sustaining the self-confidence of their middle son.

*Appeal to need for belonging-
ness, love, and self-esteem*

"No one on either side of the family has ever gone
through this," Mrs. Nicholson said, "and I guess I'm impatient. I know he is educated and has a great work ethic
and wants to start contributing, and I don't know what
to do."

Example

Her oldest, David Jr., twenty-six, did land a good job.
Graduating from Middlebury College in 2006, he joined
a Boston insurance company, specializing in reinsurance,
nearly three years ago, before the recession.

"I'm fortunate to be at a company where there is some   35
security," he said, adding that he supports Scott in his determination to hold out for the right job. "Once you start
working, you get caught up in the work and you have
bills to pay, and you lose sight of what you really want,"
the brother said.

He is earning $75,000 — a sum beyond Scott's reach
today, but not his expectations. "I worked hard through
high school to get myself into the college I did," Scott
said, "and then I worked hard through college to graduate with the grades and degree that I did to position
myself for a solid job." (He majored in political science
and minored in history.)

It was in pursuit of a solid job that Scott applied to
Hanover International's management training program.
Turned down for that, he was called back to interview for
the lesser position in the claims department.

"I'm sitting with the manager, and he asked me how
I had gotten interested in insurance. I mentioned Dave's
job in reinsurance, and the manager's response was, 'Oh,
that is about fifteen steps above the position you are

Appeal to the need for self-esteem and self-actualization

interviewing for,'" Scott said, his eyes widening and his voice emotional.

Scott acknowledges that he is competitive with his brothers, particularly David, more than they are with him. The youngest, Bradley, twenty-two, has a year to go at the University of Vermont. His parents and grandparents pay his way, just as they did for his brothers in their college years.

In the Old Days

Going to college wasn't an issue for grandfather Nicholson, or so he says. With World War II approaching, he entered the Army not long after finishing high school and, in the fighting in Italy, a battlefield commission raised him overnight from enlisted man to first lieutenant. That was

Appeal to values

"the equivalent of a college education," as he now puts it, in an age when college on a stockbroker's resumé "counted for something, but not a lot."

He spent most of his career in a rising market, putting customers into stocks that paid good dividends and growing wealthy on real estate investments made years ago, when Grafton was still semi-rural. The brokerage firm that employed him changed hands more than once, but he continued to work out of the same office in Worcester.

Extended example

When his son David graduated from Babson College in 1976, manufacturing in America was in an early phase of its long decline, and Worcester was still a center for the production of sandpaper, emery stones, and other abrasives.

He joined one of those companies — owned by the family of his friend — and he has stayed in manufacturing, particularly at companies that make hand tools. Early on, he and his wife bought the home in which they raised their sons, a white colonial dating from the early 1800s, like many houses on North Street, where the grandparents also live, a few doors away.

David Nicholson's longest stretch was at the Stanley Works, and when he left, seeking promotion, a friend at the Endeavor Tool Company hired him as that company's general manager, his present job.

In better times, Scott's father might have given his son work at Endeavor, but the father is laying off workers, and a job in manufacturing, in Scott's eyes, would be a defeat.

40

45

"If you talk to twenty people," Scott said, "you'll find only one in manufacturing and everyone else in finance or something else."

The Plan

Scott Nicholson almost sidestepped the recession. His plan was to become a Marine Corps second lieutenant. He had spent the summer after his freshman year in "platoon leader" training. Last fall he passed the physical for officer training and was told to report on January 16.

If all had gone well, he would have emerged in ten weeks as a second lieutenant, committed to a four-year enlistment. "I could have made a career out of the Marines," Scott said, "and if I had come out in four years, I would have been incredibly prepared for the workplace."

It was not to be. In early January, a Marine Corps doctor noticed that he had suffered from childhood asthma. He was washed out. "They finally told me I could reapply if I wanted to," Scott said. "But the sheen was gone."

So he struggles to get a foothold in the civilian work force. His brother in Boston lost his roommate, and early last month Scott moved into the empty bedroom, with his parents paying Scott's share of the $2,000-a-month rent until the lease expires on August 31.

And if Scott does not have a job by then? "I'll do something temporary; I won't go back home," Scott said. "I'll be a bartender or get work through a temp agency. I hope I don't find myself in that position."

Concludes his extended example that begins the essay

50

SAMPLE ESSAY WITH ANALYSIS

At times, assignments may ask you to analyze or evaluate the evidence and appeals to needs and values offered in support of a claim. At other times, you will have to discover your own support for use in an argument that you are writing. After the following essay about sport utility vehicles and its reading and discussion questions, you will first find an example of an essay of the type you might write if you were asked to evaluate an author's use of support. It is followed by a student essay that illustrates effective use of support.

The True Costs of SUVs

HAL R. VARIAN

Traffic fatalities in the United States fell steadily from 54,600 in 1972 to 34,900 in 1992. But then they started to rise again, and by 2002 there were 38,300 traffic deaths a year.

Our performance compared with other countries has also deteriorated. America's ranking has fallen from first to ninth over the last thirty years, with Australia, Britain, and Canada all having better records.

A big part of the difference between the United States and other countries seems to be the prevalence of sport utility vehicles and pickups on American highways. Sales of light trucks — SUVs, pickups, and minivans — were about a fifth of total automobile sales thirty years ago. Now they account for more than half.

But aren't large vehicles supposed to be safer than small cars? Yes, they are safer for their occupants in collisions, but their design makes them all the more dangerous for anyone they hit.

Michelle White, an economist at the University of California, San Diego, estimates that for each fatality that light-truck drivers avoid for themselves and their passengers, they cause four fatalities involving car occupants, pedestrians, bicyclists, and motorcyclists. "Safety gains for those driving light trucks," Ms. White said, "come at an extremely high cost to others."   5

Being larger than ordinary vehicles, SUVs and light trucks cause more damage to upper bodies and heads in collisions. Furthermore, their bumpers do not always align with automobile bumpers, and their body structure is stiffer, transferring more force to other vehicles during impact.

A few weeks ago, the auto industry announced a voluntary plan to deal with some of these design problems. They intend to make side-impact airbags standard to help protect heads and upper bodies better in collisions, and they intend to standardize bumper heights.

These will no doubt be helpful improvements, but do they go far enough?

Recently Ms. White examined the econometrics of traffic accidents in an attempt to measure the benefits and costs of changing the number of light trucks on the road. . . .

Ms. White notes that changing average vehicle size could, in principle, increase or decrease the cost of accidents.   10

Suppose the cost of a small vehicle–large vehicle collision is $50, the cost of a small vehicle–small vehicle collision is $45, and the cost of a large vehicle–large vehicle collision is $40.

A professor emeritus in the School of Information Management and Systems at the University of California at Berkeley, Hal R. Varian has written economics textbooks as well as columns for the *New York Times*. He is currently chief economist at *Google*. This piece appeared in the *Times* as the "Economic Scene" article on December 18, 2003.

The results of an accident in New York involving a sport utility vehicle and a smaller car. Traffic fatalities are on the rise, apparently linked to the increase of SUVs.

G. Paul Burnett/*New York Times*

If all vehicles are small, and there are ten accidents a year, the total cost of the accidents is $450. But if 10 percent of the small vehicles are replaced by large ones, the average cost of collisions becomes $458.50, since more collisions will be between large and small vehicles. On the other hand, if 60 percent of the vehicles on the road are large, the average cost of a collision is only $456, since more collisions are between large vehicles.

Think about a safety-conscious soccer mom choosing a vehicle. If there are mostly small cars in her town, she can reduce the risk to her and her family in the event of a collision by buying an SUV.

The unfortunate side effect is that the large SUV would cause significant damage to smaller cars if she was involved in an accident.

The laudable private incentive to choose a safe vehicle could, perversely, reduce overall safety.

15

In addition, Ms. White finds that people involved in single-vehicle crashes are more likely to be killed or seriously injured if they are in SUVs or light trucks rather than cars. This may be a result of the increased likelihood of rollovers.

On the other hand, suppose everybody in town drives an SUV. Then the soccer mom will definitely want to purchase one for herself, since it would both increase her family's safety and reduce the overall costs of collisions.

In this case, private incentives and social incentives are aligned.

The dynamics involved is the same as that of an arms race: If other families buy bigger vehicles, then you will want to as well, if only in self-defense.

To see where we are in this arms race, Ms. White examined crash data main-   20
tained by the National Highway Safety Administration. . . .

Using this data, Ms. White was able to estimate how the probability of fatalities or serious injury varied with the types of vehicles involved in collisions.

For example, in a two-car accident, the probability of a fatality in the car is 38 percent less than in a car–light truck accident. However, in car–light truck accidents, the probability of fatalities in the light truck is 55 percent less than it would be in a truck–truck accident.

If a light truck hits a pedestrian or a cyclist, the probability of fatalities is about 82 percent greater than if a car is involved.

Ms. White then asked what the impact would be of replacing a million light trucks with cars. She considered two models for driver behavior. In the first, she assumed that the former drivers of light trucks would have the same number of accidents as they did when driving trucks. In the second, she assumed that the former drivers of light trucks would have the same accident probabilities as other car drivers.

Using conventional methods for value-of-life calculations, she finds that each   25
light-truck owner who switches to a car saves about $447 in total expected costs of accidents.

Ms. White examines various policies that might persuade drivers to adopt such changes, including changes in liability rules, traffic rules, and insurance rules.

Unfortunately, each of these policies has its problems, so there are no easy solutions.

One interesting way to reduce the arms race problem would be to link automobile liability insurance to gasoline taxes. This means drivers whose cars use more gasoline and those who drive a lot would pay more for their insurance — not unreasonable, since, on average, they impose more costs in accidents.

Aaron Edlin, a professor of economics and law at the University of California, Berkeley, has argued that such "pay at the pump" insurance premiums would have many other benefits (www.bepress.com/aaronedlin/contribution5/). So this type of payment scheme is worth considering for a variety of reasons.

READING AND DISCUSSION QUESTIONS

1. For the purposes of his article, how is Varian defining *light truck*?

2. What relationship does he see between light trucks and the number of traffic fatalities?

3. What type of support does Varian use in the three opening paragraphs? Does he use that type of support anywhere else in the essay?

4. What other types of support does Varian make use of in his essay? What types of support do you find most effective in making his argument? What types do you find least effective?

5. What claim is Varian supporting in the essay?

6. How does Varian document his sources? How does he try to establish that his sources are reliable?

The True Confusion About SUV Costs

BETHANY ROYCE

Hal R. Varian entitled his December 18, 2003, *New York Times* piece on sport utility vehicles "The True Costs of SUVs." A more accurate title might have been "The Confusing Costs of SUVs." While Varian turns to the right type of support for his subject — statistics — his use of that support is more confusing than enlightening.

Varian made a wise choice in appealing to his readers' need to feel safe and secure. His statistics are most appealing when he points out that for twenty years the number of traffic fatalities in our country went down and that parents can feel secure knowing that they can make their children safer by buying light trucks (SUVs, pickups, or minivans) instead of cars. In each case, however, there is a negative side. The number of fatalities started rising again between 1992 and 2002, in part because of the increase in the number of sales of light trucks during that time. And Varian tells us that in making their families safer by buying light trucks, they are increasing the risk of doing more harm to others should they be involved in accidents.

For the rest of his support, Varian draws primarily on research done by Michelle White, whom he identifies only as "an economist at the University of California, San Diego" (231). She may have done excellent work, but the way that Varian explains it is confusing and unconvincing. White tries to predict how the cost of accidents would change depending on the size of the vehicles involved. Instead of using realistic cost estimates, however, she arbitrarily assigns the cost of $50 to a small vehicle–large vehicle collision, the cost of $45 to a small vehicle–small vehicle collision, and the cost of $40 to a large vehicle–large vehicle collision. Varian summarizes what this hypothetical scenario reveals:

> If all vehicles are small, and there are ten accidents a year, the total cost of the accidents is $450. But if 10 percent of the small vehicles are replaced by large ones, the average cost of collisions becomes $458.50, since more collisions will be between large and small vehicles. On the other hand, if 60 percent of the vehicles on the road are large, the average cost of a collision is only $456, since more collisions are between large vehicles. (232)

Average Americans are left wondering what all of this means to them. The hypothetical situation cannot be easily applied to any individual driver and certainly not to any specific accident. How should a reader evaluate the information in attempting to make the decision regarding what size vehicle to buy? The driver who just paid $3000 in car repairs is going to find any of the numbers Varian cites attractive.

Bethany Royce teaches business courses and introductory economics at a two-year college in Florida and writes a consumer advice column for a local newspaper.

There are a lot of "ifs" in Varian's argument. If you live in a town with lots of SUVs, it is safer to drive one yourself. If you live in a town where there are few SUVs, you should drive a car so that you would not be as likely to hurt someone else in a wreck. If you have a single-vehicle accident in an SUV, you are more likely to be killed. If you hit a pedestrian while driving one, you are more likely to kill that person.

There are also few clear conclusions to be drawn from the support that Varian offers. After Ms. White examines "various policies that might persuade drivers to adopt such changes, including changes in liability rules, traffic rules, and insurance rates," the unfortunate conclusion is that "each of these policies has its problems, so there are no easy solutions" [233]. The only solution that Varian advances as "worth considering" is one by a colleague of his at the University of California, Berkeley, that would link a vehicle owner's liability insurance to gas taxes [233]. Overall the article succeeds more in revealing the complexities involved in the increased use of SUVs than in clarifying any of those complexities.

5

SAMPLE STUDENT ESSAY

Safer? Tastier? More Nutritious?
The Dubious Merits of Organic Foods

KRISTEN WEINACKER

Organic foods are attractive to some consumers because of the principles behind them and the farming techniques used to produce them. There is a special respect for organic farmers who strive to maintain the ecological balance and harmony that exist among living things. As these farmers work in partnership with nature, some consumers too feel a certain attachment to the earth (Wolf 1–2). They feel happier knowing that these foods are produced without chemical fertilizers, pesticides, and additives to extend their shelf life (Pickerell; Agricultural Extension Service 5). They feel that they have returned to nature by eating organic foods that are advertised as being healthy for maintaining a vigorous lifestyle. Unfortunately, research has not provided statistical evidence that organic foods are more nutritious than conventionally grown ones.

The debate over the nutritional benefits has raged for decades. Defenders of the nutritional value of organic foods have employed excellent marketing and sales strategies. First, they freely share the philosophy behind their farming and follow up with detailed descriptions of their management techniques. Second, organic farmers skillfully appeal to our common sense. It seems reasonable to believe that organic foods are more nutritious since they are grown without chemical

---

At the time she wrote this essay, Kristen Weinacker was an undergraduate at Clemson University.

fertilizers and pesticides. Third, since the soil in which these crops are grown is so rich and healthy, it seems plausible that these crops have absorbed and developed better nutrients. As Lynda Brown asserts in her book *Living Organic*, "Organic farmers believe that growing crops organically provides the best possible way to produce healthy food" (26). Brown provides beautifully illustrated and enlarged microscopic photographs to show the more developed structure of organic foods compared to conventional products to convince the consumer to believe that organic foods are more nutritious (27). Fourth, many consumers view the higher price tags on organic foods and assume that they must be more nutritious. Generalizations permeate the whole world of organic foods. These marketing strategies persuade the consumer that organic foods are healthier than conventional foods without providing any factual comparisons.

In their book *Is Our Food Safe?* Warren Leon and Caroline Smith Dewaal compare organic and conventionally produced foods. They strongly suggest that consumers buy organic foods to help the environment (68). They believe that organic foods are healthier than conventional ones. However, statistics supporting this belief are not provided. The authors even warn consumers that they need to read product labels because some organic foods may be as unhealthy as conventional ones (68–69). An interesting poll involving 1,041 adults was conducted by ABC News asking, "Why do people buy organic?" Analyst Daniel Merkle concluded that 45 percent of the American public *believes* that organic products are more nutritious than conventionally grown ones. Also, 57 percent of the population maintains that organic farming is beneficial for the environment. According to the pollsters, the primary reason why people bought organic foods is the belief that they are healthier because they have less pesticide residue. However, there has never been any link established between the nutritional value of organic foods and the residue found on them. Clever marketing strategies have made the need for concrete data really not of prime importance for the consumer to join the bandwagon promoting organic foods.

This pervasive belief among the American public that organic foods are probably healthier than conventionally grown foods was reiterated in my telephone interview with Mr. Joseph Williamson, an agricultural county extension agent working with Clemson University. When asked if organically grown foods are more nutritious than those grown conventionally, he replied that they probably were for two reasons. First, organic crops tend to grow more slowly. Therefore, the nutrients have more time to build up in the plants. Second, organic plants are usually grown locally. The fruits and vegetables are allowed to stay on the plants for a longer period of time. They ripen more than those picked green and transported across miles. He contends that these conditions promote a better nutrient buildup. Unfortunately, the extension agent acknowledges that statistical evidence is not available to support the claim that organic products are more nutritious.

An article entitled "Effects of Agricultural Methods in Nutritional Quality: A Comparison of Organic with Conventional Crops" reports on conclusions drawn by Dr. Virginia Worthington, a certified nutrition specialist. Worthington examines why it is so difficult to ascertain if organic foods are more nutritious. First, "the difference in terms of health effects is not large enough to be readily apparent." There is no concrete evidence that people are healthier eating organic foods

5

or, conversely, that people become more ill eating conventionally grown produce. Second, Dr. Worthington notes that variables such as sunlight, temperature, and amount of rain are so inconsistent that the nutrients in crops vary yearly. Third, she points out that the nutrient value of products can be changed by the way products are stored and shipped. After reviewing at least thirty studies dealing with the question if organic foods are more nutritious than conventionally grown ones, Dr. Worthington concludes that there is too little data available to substantiate the claim of higher nutritional value in organic foods. She also believes that it is an impossible task to make a direct connection between organic foods and the health of those people who consume them.

After being asked for thirty years about organic foods by her readers and associates, Joan Dye Gussow, writer for *Eating Well* magazine, firmly concludes that there is "little hard proof that organically grown produce is reliably more nutritious." Reviewing seventy years' worth of studies on the subject, Gussow has no doubt that organic foods should be healthier because of the way they are produced and cultivated. Gussow brings up an interesting point about chemical and pesticide residue. She believes that the fact that organic foods have been found to have fewer residues does not make them automatically more nutritious and healthier for the consumer. As scientific technologies advance, Gussow predicts that research will someday discover statistical data that will prove that organic foods have a higher nutritional value compared to conventionally grown ones.

In order to provide the public with more information about the nature of organic foods, the well-known and highly regarded magazine *Consumer Reports* decided to take a closer look at organic foods in their January 1998 magazine, in an article entitled "Organic Foods: Safer? Tastier? More nutritious?" By conducting comparison tests, their researchers discovered that organic foods have less pesticide residue, and that their flavors are just about the same as conventionally grown foods. These scientists came to the conclusion that the "variability within a given crop is greater than the variability between one cropping system and another." *Consumer Reports* contacted Professor Willie Lockeretz from the Tufts University School of Nutrition Science and Policy. He told researchers that "the growing system you use probably does affect nutrition. . . . But it does it in ways so complex you might be studying the problem forever." Keeping in mind these comments made by Dr. Lockeretz, *Consumer Reports* believes it would be an impossible task to compare the nutritional values of organic and conventional foods. Therefore, researchers at *Consumer Reports* decided not to carry out that part of their comparison testing.

Although statistical evidence is not available at this time to support the claim that organic foods are more nutritious than conventionally grown ones, there is a very strong feeling shared by a majority of the general public that they are. We are called back to nature as we observe the love that organic farmers have for the soil and their desire to work in partnership with nature. We are easily lured to the attractive displays of organic foods in the grocery stores. However, we must keep in mind the successful marketing techniques that have been used to convince us that organic foods are more nutritious than conventionally grown ones. Although common sense tells us that organic foods should be more nutritious, research has not provided us with any statistical data to prove this claim.

WORKS CITED

Agricultural Extension Service. *Organic Vegetable Gardening.* The University of Tennessee. PB 1391.

Brown, Lynda. *Organic Living.* New York: Dorling Kindersley Publishing, Inc., 2000.

Gussow, Joan Dye. "Is Organic Food More Nutritious?" *Eating Well* (May/June 1997). 27 March 2003. <http://www.prnac.net/rodmap-nutrition.html>.

"Effect of Agricultural Methods on Nutritional Quality: A Comparison of Organic with Conventional Crops." *Alternative Therapies* 4 (1998): 58–69. 18 Feb. 2003. <http://www.purefood.org/healthier101101.cfm>.

Leon, Warren, and Caroline Smith DeWaal. *Is Our Food Safe?* New York: Three Rivers Press, 2002.

Merkle, Daniel. "Why Do People Buy Organic?" ABCNews.com. 3 Feb. 2000. 27 March 2003.

"Organic Foods: Safer? Tastier? More Nutritious?" *Consumer Reports.* Jan. 1998. 24 Feb. 2003. <http://www.consumerreports.org/main/detailsv2.jsp?content%3%ecnt_id+18959&f>.

Pickrell, John. "Federal Government Launches Organic Standards." *Science News* 162.17 (Nov. 2002). <http://www.sciencenews.org/20021102/food.asp._17_March 2003>.

Williamson, Joseph. Telephone interview. 28 Feb. 2003.

Wolf, Ray, ed. *Organic Farming: Yesterday's and Tomorrow's Agriculture.* Philadelphia: Rodale Press, 1977.

READINGS FOR ANALYSIS

Connecting the Dots . . . to Terrorism

BERNARD GOLDBERG

Most of the time television is nothing more than a diversion — proof, as the old quip goes, that we would rather do anything than talk to each other. We'd also rather watch a bad sitcom than read a good book. Bad sitcoms get millions of viewers; good books get thousands. In an "entertainment culture," even the news is entertainment. Certainly too much local news has been pure fluff for some time now, with their Ken and Barbie anchors who have nothing intelligent to say but look great while they're saying it. And because network news is losing viewers every year, executives and producers are trying to figure out ways to hold on to the ones they still have. They think cosmetics will work, so they change the anchor desk or they change the graphics. They get the anchor to stand instead of sit. They feature more "news you can use." They put Chandra Levy[18] on all over

---

[18]*Chandra Levy*: A government intern whose disappearance was widely covered in the press in 2001. — EDS.

Bernard Goldberg was a reporter and producer for CBS for more than thirty years. He has won ten Emmy awards and was once rated by *TV Guide* as one of the ten most interesting people on television. This chapter is from his 2002 book *Bias: A CBS Insider Exposes How the Media Distort the News,* written after he left the network.

the place, hoping they can concoct a ratings cocktail by mixing one part missing intern with ten parts sex scandal.

And then something genuinely big and really important happens that shakes us to our core, and all those producers who couldn't get enough of Chandra are through with her. Only in the fickle world of television news can someone who has disappeared without a trace disappear a second time.

And it's when that history-making story comes along that Americans — no matter what their politics, religion, age, race, or sex — turn to television, not just for information, but also for comfort and for peace of mind. It doesn't happen often, but when it does, television becomes a lot more than just a diversion.

It happened when John Kennedy was assassinated. We all turned to Walter Cronkite and Huntley and Brinkley, not just for facts, but also for reassurance — that despite the terrible tragedy, America was going to be okay.

It happened when *Challenger* blew up. And it happened again on September 11, 2001, when a band of religious lunatics declared war on the United States of America to punish us for not wanting to dwell in the fourteenth century, where they currently reside, and, of course, to show the world that their intense hatred of Israel — *and of Israel's friends* — knows no bounds. On September 11, they not only killed as many innocent Americans as they could in the most dramatic way they knew how, but, as the *Wall Street Journal* put it, they also "wiped out any remaining illusions that America is safe from mass organized violence."

On that day we all turned to television. We turned to Dan Rather and Peter Jennings and Tom Brokaw and the others. And they did a fine job, as they often do when covering tragedy. They showed empathy. They were fair and accurate, and the information they passed along to us wasn't filtered through the usual liberal political and social sensibilities. They gave us the news on that day the way they should give us the news *all the time*, whether the story is about race or feminism or taxes or gay rights or anything else. *For a change, they gave it to us straight.*

On the night of September 11, 2001, Peter Jennings made a point about how, in times of danger and tragedy, television serves the function that campfires used to serve in the old days when Americans migrated westward in covered wagons. Back then, they would sit around the campfire and get the news from other travelers about what they should look out for down the road. "Some people pulled the wagons around," Peter said, "and discussed what was going on and tried to understand it." But the campfire was more than just a meeting place where families could pick up important information. The campfire also provided a sense of community, a sense that *we're all in this together*. That's what television was on September 11.

As I listened to Peter tell that story, I thought about another American tragedy that shocked us six years earlier, when Timothy McVeigh — another true believer who cared nothing about killing innocent Americans — blew up the federal building in Oklahoma City. I thought about how it took some of the media elites only a few days before they started to play one of their favorite games — connect the dots. What they found back then — or more accurately, what they convinced themselves they found — was a line stretching from Oklahoma City to the Republican Party to conservatives in general and finally to Rush Limbaugh.

5

Dan Rather said, "Even after Oklahoma City, you can turn on your radio in any city and still dial up hate talk: extremist, racist, and violent from the hosts and those who call in."

Time senior writer Richard Lacayo put it this way: "In a nation that has enter-   10
tained and appalled itself for years with hot talk on radio and the campaign trail, the inflamed rhetoric of the '90s is suddenly an unindicted coconspirator in the blast."

Nina Easton wrote in the *Los Angeles Times*, "The Oklahoma City attack on federal workers and their children also alters the once-easy dynamic between char-ismatic talk show host and adoring audience. Hosts who routinely espouse the same antigovernment themes as the militia movement now must walk a fine line between inspiring their audience — and inciting the most radical among them."

On *Face the Nation*, Bob Schieffer asked this question: "Mr. Panetta, there's been a lot of antigovernment rhetoric, it comes over talk radio, it comes from vari-ous quarters. Do you think that that somehow has led these people to commit this act, do they feed on that kind of rhetoric, and what impact do you think it had?"

Carl Rowan, the late columnist, was quoted in a *Washington Post* story saying that, "Unless Gingrich and Dole[19] and the Republicans say 'Am I inflaming a bunch of nuts?' you know we're going to have some more events. I am absolutely certain the harsher rhetoric of the Gingriches and the Doles . . . creates a climate of violence in America."

And David Broder had this to say in the *Washington Post*: "The bombing shows how dangerous it really is to inflame twisted minds with statements that suggest political opponents are enemies. For two years, Rush Limbaugh described this na-tion as 'America held hostage' to the policies of the liberal Democrats, as if the duly elected president and Congress were equivalent to the regime in Tehran. I think there will be less tolerance and fewer cheers for that kind of rhetoric."

The message was clear: Conservative talk radio and conservative politicians   15
created an antigovernment atmosphere in America that spawned Timothy McVeigh and therefore were at least partially to blame for his terrorism. It's true, of course, that the atmosphere in which we live contributes to everything that happens in our culture. Calling people "kikes" or "niggers" makes it easier to see them as less than human and to treat them as something less than human. But to point fingers at talk radio for somehow encouraging Timothy McVeigh strikes me as a stretch at best; more likely it's just another opportunity for liberal journalists to blame con-servatives for one more evil. And if this kind of connecting the dots is fair game, then should we also accuse Americans who spoke out loudly and forcefully against the war in Vietnam — including many journalists — of contributing to the 1972 bombing of the Pentagon and to other sometimes deadly terrorism, perpetuated by fanatics on the Left? According to the media elites' rulebook, when liberals rant it's called free speech; when conservatives rant it's called incitement to terrorism.

[19]*Gingrich and Dole*: Newt Gingrich (b. 1943) was Speaker of the House of Representatives from 1995 to 1999. Robert Dole (b. 1923) was a Senate majority leader and served in the Senate from 1968 to 1996. — EDS.

As I watched the coverage of the attacks on the Pentagon and the World Trade Center, I wondered why I hadn't seen more stories on television news, long before these zealots flew their hijacked planes into American buildings, about the culture of anti-American hate that permeates so much of the Middle East — stories that might help explain how little Arab children can grow up to become fanatical suicide bombers.

If the media found it so important to discuss the malignant atmosphere created by "hot" conservative talk radio, then why didn't they find it important to delve into this malignant atmosphere that seems to have bred such maniacal killers? Why would journalists, so interested in connecting the dots when they thought they led to Rush Limbaugh, be so uninterested in connecting the dots when there might actually be dots to connect — *from hateful, widely held popular attitudes in much of the Arab world straight to the cockpits of those hijacked jetliners?*

One of the networks put an American Muslim woman on the news who said that no one blamed Christianity when McVeigh killed all those people. Why blame Islam now? The reporter interviewing this woman let her have her say, never bothering to point out that Timothy McVeigh didn't kill all those people in the name of Christianity. Suicide airplane hijackers, on the other hand, are people who actually believe their murderous acts will earn them a one-way ticket to Paradise.

Was what happened on September 11 a subversion of Islam, as pundits and journalists on network and cable TV told us over and over again? Or was it the result of an *honest* reading of the Koran? It's true, of course, that if taken too literally by uncritical minds, just about any holy book can lead to bad things. Still, why are there no Christian suicide bombers, or Jewish suicide bombers, or Hindu suicide bombers, or Buddhist suicide bombers, but no apparent shortage of Muslim suicide bombers? If Islam is "a religion of peace" as so many people from President Bush on down were telling us (and, for what it's worth, I'm prepared to believe that it is), then what exactly is it in the Koran that so appeals to these Islamic fanatics? Don't look for that answer on the network news. A *Lexis-Nexis* search going back to 1991 linking the words "Koran" and "terrorist" produced absolutely nothing that told us what the Koran actually says which *might* encourage a Muslim, no matter how misguided, to commit acts of terrorism.

I understand that even to ask questions about a possible connection between   20
Islam and violence is to tread into politically incorrect terrain. But it seems to me that the media need to go there anyway. And any network that can put thousands of stories on the air about sex and murder should be able to give us a few on the atmosphere that breeds religious zealotry. It might have helped us see what was coming on September 11.

In fact, I learned much more about the atmosphere that breeds suicide bombers from one short article in *Commentary* magazine than I have from watching twenty years of network television news. In its September 2001 issue (which came out before the attack on America), there was an article by Fiamma Nirenstein, an Italian journalist based in Israel, entitled "How Suicide Bombers Are Made." In it, she tells about a "river of hatred" that runs through not just the most radical of Arab nations but also much of what we like to think of as the "moderate" Arab world.

She tells us about a series of articles that ran in the leading government-sponsored newspaper in Egypt, *Al Ahram*, about how Jews supposedly use the blood of Christians to make matzah for Passover.

She tells us about a hit song in Cairo, Damascus, and the West Bank with the catchy title "I Hate Israel."

Why didn't I know this? A computer check soon answered my question. On television, only CNN reported the "I Hate Israel" story. On radio, NPR did a piece. So did the *Christian Science Monitor* and the *Chicago Tribune*. The *Los Angeles Times* ran a short wire service story that said "'I Hate Israel' . . . made an overnight singing sensation of a working-class crooner."

Can you imagine if the big hit song in Israel was "I Hate Palestine" or "I Hate   25
Arabs"? The *New York Times* would have put the story on page one and then run an editorial just to make sure we all got the message — that the song is indecent and contributes to an atmosphere of hate. And since the *Times* sets the agenda for the networks, Dan Rather, Tom Brokaw, and Peter Jennings would have all fallen into line and run big stories on their evening newscasts, too, saying the exact same thing. A week later, Mike Wallace would have landed in Tel Aviv looking absolutely mortified that those Jews would do such a thing.

And that's part of the problem. Despite the liberalism of the media, there is a subtle form of racism at work here. As Fiamma Nirenstein writes, "The Arabs, it is implicitly suggested, are a backward people, not to be held to civilized standards of the West." Of the Israelis, however, the American media expect much more. That is why a song called "I Hate Israel" becomes a big hit, and yet is not a news story. And it is why a series of stories in a government-sponsored newspaper — in a supposedly moderate country — about Jews killing Christians for their blood holds almost no interest for American journalists.

It's true that not long after the twin towers of the World Trade Center came tumbling down, the networks showed us pictures of Palestinians in East Jerusalem honking their horns, firing their guns into the air, and generally having a good old time celebrating the death of so many Americans in New York and Washington. They cheered "God is great" while they handed out candy, which is a tradition in the Arab world when something good happens.

It's not that there's been a total news blackout of anti-American hate in the Middle East — *Nightline* has done some good, intelligent work in this area — it's just that we need more than pictures of happy Palestinians reveling in the death of thousands of Americans. And we need more than what has become a staple of Middle East television news coverage: young children throwing stones at Israeli soldiers — the perfect made-for-television David and Goliath story. What we need are stories that connect the dots, not just back to Afghanistan and its backward and repressive Taliban government, but also between the fanatics in New York and Washington and a cultural environment in the Arab world where even "moderates" hand out candy to celebrate the massacre of Americans.

But here the media — apparently feeling squeamish about stories that put the "underdogs" in a bad light — keep us virtually in the dark. And it's not just little tidbits like "I Hate Israel" and articles about Jews taking Christian blood that I — and almost all Americans — knew nothing about. Here's a quick rundown of what goes on in much of the Middle East as reported by Ms. Nirenstein in *Commentary* — news that is virtually ignored on the big American TV networks:

> In Egypt and Jordan, news sources have repeatedly warned that Israel has distributed drug-laced chewing gum and candy, intended (it is said) to kill children and make women sexually corrupt. . . .
>
> [Palestinian television] recently asserted that, far from being extermination camps, Chelmo, Dachau, and Auschwitz were in fact mere "places of disinfection."
>
> On April 13 — observed in Israel as Holocaust Remembrance Day — the official Palestinian newspaper *Al-Hayat al-Jadida* featured a column . . . entitled "The Fable of the Holocaust."
>
> A columnist in Egypt's government-sponsored Al-Akhbar thus expressed his "thanks to Hitler, of blessed memory, who on behalf of the Palestinians took revenge in advance on the most vile criminals on the face of the earth. Still, we do have a complaint against [Hitler], for his revenge on them was not enough."

In addition to these examples, Ms. Nirenstein cites a textbook for Syrian tenth 30
graders which teaches them that "the logic of justice obligates the application of the single verdict [on the Jews] from which there is no escape: namely, that their criminal intentions be turned against them and that they be exterminated." And she notes that in June 2001, two weeks after the fatal collapse of a Jewish wedding hall in Jerusalem, Palestinian television broadcast a sermon by a Muslim imam praying that "this oppressive Knesset [Israel's parliament] will [similarly] collapse over the heads of the Jews."

I did not know any of that because it's simply not the kind of news that we normally get from the Middle East — certainly not from network evening newscasts or from *Dateline, 20/20,* or *48 Hours,* three news magazine programs that are usually too busy peddling the trivial and sensational to bother with more significant stories. And besides, that kind of news makes liberal journalists uneasy. After all, these are the same people who bend over backwards to find "moral equivalence" between Palestinian terrorists who blow up discos in Tel Aviv filled with teenagers, on the one hand, and Israeli commandos who *preemptively* kill terrorist ringleaders *before* they send their suicide bombers into Israel on a mission to kill Jews, on the other.

On September 11, right after the networks showed us the pictures of Palestinians celebrating American deaths, they also showed us Yasser Arafat expressing his condolences and giving blood for the American victims. This, in its way, represented a kind of moral equivalence: while some Palestinians celebrate, the news anchors were suggesting, their leader does not; he is somber and, we're led to believe, absolutely shocked. But we could have done with a little less moral equivalence on the part of the press and a little more tough journalism. Someone should have asked the leader of the Palestinian people if he understood that the cultures that he and other "moderate" Arab leaders preside over "carefully nurture and inculcate resentments and hatreds against America and the non-Arab world," as a *Wall Street Journal* editorial put it. And if that's asking too much of a field reporter covering a seemingly shaken and distraught Arafat in the wake of September 11, then an anchor back in New York should have wondered out loud about that very connection.

But to have asked such a question might have been viewed as anti-Arab (and therefore pro-Israeli), and reporters and anchors would rather be stoned by an angry mob in Ramallah than be seen in that light. So we didn't learn that day if Chairman Arafat quite understood his role in the celebration he so deplored. Nor did we get an explanation on the news about why there were not thousands of other Arabs in the streets — on the West Bank or in Jerusalem or in the "moderate" Arab countries — expressing their *condolences*. Was it because they are afraid to show support for American victims of terrorism? Or was it because they, like the Palestinians we saw with great big smiles, didn't feel that bad about what happened?

If the networks can give us months and months of Chandra and JonBenét and Lorena Bobbitt and Joey Buttafuoco,[20] then they can give us more than they do about the river of hatred that breeds suicide bombers.

But this is where journalists — given their liberal tendency to empathize with,   35
and sometimes even root for, the "underdog" — run into a big problem: if they start to connect those ideological and religious dots, they may not like what they find.

American journalists who covered the civil rights struggle recognized the pathology of racism and rightly made no allowance for it. They understood that in order for evil to flourish in places throughout the South, all it took was a few fundamentally bad people — while everybody else sat around making believe it wasn't happening, either because they were afraid or because they just didn't want to get involved.

The Middle East, of course, is a place with a long and troubled history. But it should be obvious that a place that turns "I Hate Israel" into a hit, that runs stories in its most important newspaper about Jews killing Christians for their blood, that faults Hitler *only because he did not kill more Jews*, and that celebrates the murder of thousands of innocent Americans is a place populated by many nasty people. Perhaps it has many good people, too, who just don't want to get involved. The point is, a story about all of this is at least as important as a story about Anne Heche and her sex life, even if sex does better in the ratings than disturbing news about raw, ignorant hatred in the world of Islam.

None of this is an argument that the media are intentionally pro-Arab. Rather, like the U.S. State Department, they are pro "moral equivalence." If they connect the dots with stories on the news about hit songs called "I Hate Israel" and all the rest, the Arab world will accuse the "Jewish-controlled" American media of being sympathetic to "Israeli oppression." If journalists — who were so willing to connect the dots when there was a belief that they led to Rush Limbaugh — connected *these* dots, they might find that there are a lot fewer moderates in those moderate places than they keep telling us about.

So they look the other way, which, as Ms. Nirenstein tells us, is not that easy. One has to turn "a determinedly blind eye to this river of hatred . . . [and] to be persuaded that, after all, 'everybody' in the Middle East really wants the same thing."

Obviously, there are legitimate issues about which there are differing view-   40
points in the Middle East: Should Israel blow up the houses that belong to the

---

[20]JonBenét and Lorena Bobbitt and Joey Buttafuoco: JonBenét Ramsey was a six-year-old beauty pageant contestant found murdered in the basement of her home in Boulder, Colorado, the day after Christmas 1996, whose case has never been solved. Lorena Bobbit cut off her husband's penis in 1993 allegedly because of long-term abuse. Joey Buttafuoco's under-aged lover, Amy Fisher, shot his wife in the face in 1992. — EDS.

families of terrorists? Should Israel allow the construction of new settlements on the West Bank? These are two that come quickly to mind.

But moral equivalence and the quest for evenhanded journalism should not stop the media from telling us more — much more in my view — about the kind of backwardness and hatred that is alive and well, *not just in places like Kabul and Baghdad*, but in "moderate" cities and villages all over the Arab world. Even if it means going against their liberal sensibilities and reporting that sometimes even the underdog can be evil.

READING AND DISCUSSION QUESTIONS

1. How does Goldberg support his claim that television draws Americans together in times of crisis?
2. How does he believe the news is different during times of crisis from how it usually is?
3. Explain the title that Goldberg chose for this piece. What does he claim the "media elites" have "connected the dots" to find?
4. What does Goldberg believe the news media are *not* telling Americans? What sort of support does he offer for that part of his argument?
5. What type or types of support that Goldberg uses do you find most effective? Why?

WRITING SUGGESTIONS

6. Analyze the types of support that Goldberg makes use of in his essay.
7. Evaluate the effectiveness of the major types of support that he uses in his essay.
8. Attack or defend the claim that Goldberg is advancing in his essay.
9. What is your personal opinion of the media coverage of the tragedies of September 11?
10. Do you believe that your education has exposed you to recent history as well as the more distant past? Explain.

Abolish the SAT

CHARLES MURRAY

For most high school students who want to attend an elite college, the SAT is more than a test. It is one of life's landmarks. Waiting for the scores — one for verbal, one for math, and now one for writing, with a possible 800 on each — is painfully suspenseful. The exact scores are commonly remembered forever after.

Charles Murray is the W. H. Brady Scholar at the American Enterprise Institute. This article appeared in the July/August 2007 issue of the institute's journal, *The American*.

So it has been for half a century. But events of recent years have challenged the SAT's position. In 2001, Richard Atkinson, president of the University of California, proposed dropping the SAT as a requirement for admission. More and more prestigious small colleges, such as Middlebury and Bennington, are making the SAT optional. The charge that the SAT is slanted in favor of privileged children — "a wealth test," as Harvard law professor Lani Guinier calls it — has been ubiquitous. I have watched the attacks on the SAT with dismay. Back in 1961, the test helped get me into Harvard from a small Iowa town by giving me a way to show that I could compete with applicants from Exeter and Andover. Ever since, I have seen the SAT as the friend of the little guy, just as James Bryant Conant, president of Harvard, said it would be when he urged the SAT upon the nation in the 1940s.

Conant's cause was as unambiguously liberal in the 1940s as income redistribution is today. Then, America's elite colleges drew most of their students from a small set of elite secondary schools, concentrated in the northeastern United States, to which America's wealthy sent their children. The mission of the SAT was to identify intellectual talent regardless of race, color, creed, money, or geography, and give that talent a chance to blossom. Students from small towns and from poor neighborhoods in big cities were supposed to benefit — as I thought I did, and as many readers of *The American* think they did.

But data trump gratitude. The evidence has become overwhelming that the SAT no longer serves a democratizing purpose. Worse, events have conspired to make the SAT a negative force in American life. And so I find myself arguing that the SAT should be ended. Not just deemphasized, but no longer administered. Nothing important would be lost by so doing. Much would be gained.

To clarify my terms: Here, "SAT" will always refer to the verbal and mathematics tests that you have in mind when you recall your own SAT scores. They, along with the writing test added in 2005, are now officially known as "reasoning tests" or SAT I (labels I will ignore). The College Board also administers one-hour achievement tests in English literature, United States history, world history, biology, chemistry, physics, two levels of math, Chinese, French, German, Hebrew, Italian, Japanese, Korean, Latin, and Spanish. These are now called "subject tests" or SAT II (more labels I will ignore).

I do not discuss the College Board's advanced placement (AP) tests that can enable students to get college credit because they cannot serve as a substitute for either the SAT or the achievement tests. Not all schools offer AP courses, and the AP's five-point scoring system conveys limited information.

Start with the proposition that nothing important would be lost by dropping the SAT. The surprising empirical reality is that the SAT is redundant if students are required to take achievement tests.

In theory, the SAT and the achievement tests measure different things. In the College Board's own words from its Web site, "The SAT measures students' verbal reasoning, critical reading, and skills," while the achievement tests "show colleges their mastery of specific subjects." In practice, SAT and achievement test scores are so highly correlated that SAT scores tell the admissions office little that it does not learn from the achievement test scores alone.

5

The pivotal analysis was published in 2001 by the University of California (UC), which requires all applicants to take both the SAT and achievement tests (three of them at the time the data were gathered: reading, mathematics, and a third of the student's choosing). Using a database of 77,893 students who applied to UC from 1996 to 1999, Saul Geiser and Roger Studley analyzed the relationship among high school grades, SAT scores, achievement test scores, and freshman grades in college. Here is what they found:

Achievement tests did slightly better than the SAT in predicting freshman   10
grades. High school grade point average, SAT scores, and achievement test scores were entered into a statistical equation to predict the grade point that applicants achieved during their freshman year in college. The researchers found that achievement tests and high school grade point each had about the same independent role — that is, each factor was, by itself, an equally accurate predictor of how a student will do as a college freshman.

But the SAT's independent role in predicting freshman grade point turned out to be so small that knowing the SAT score added next to nothing to an admissions officer's ability to forecast how an applicant will do in college — the reason to give the test in the first place. In technical terms, adding the SAT to the other two elements added just one-tenth of a percentage point to the percentage of variance in freshman grades explained by high school grade point and the achievement tests.

But what about the students we're most concerned about — those with high ability who have attended poor schools? The California Department of Education rates the state's high schools based on the results from its standardized testing program for grades K–12. For schools in the bottom quintile of the ratings — hard as I found it to believe — the achievement tests did slightly *better* than the SAT in predicting how the test-takers would perform as college freshmen.

What about students from families with low incomes? Children of parents with poor education? Here's another stunner: After controlling for parental income and education, the independent role of the SAT in predicting freshman grade point disappeared altogether. The effectiveness of high school grade point and of achievement tests to predict freshman grade point was undiminished.

All freshman grades are not created equal, so the UC study took the obvious differences into account. It broke down its results by college campus (an A at Berkeley might not mean the same thing as an A at Santa Cruz) and by freshman major (an A in a humanities course might not mean the same thing as an A in a physical science course). The results were unaffected. Again, the SAT was unnecessary; it added nothing to the forecasts provided by high school grades and achievement tests.

Thorough as the Geiser and Studley presentation was, almost any social science   15
conclusion can be challenged through different data or a different set of analyses. The College Board, which makes many millions of dollars every year from the SAT, had every incentive and ample resources to refute the UC results. But it could not.

In 2002, the College Board published its analysis, "The Utility of the SAT I and SAT II for Admissions Decisions in California and the Nation." The College Board's study disentangled some statistical issues that the UC study had not and used a different metric to express predictive validity, but its bottom line was effectively identical. Once high school grade point and achievement test scores are known, the incremental value of knowing the SAT score is trivially small.

Still reluctant to give up on the SAT, I wondered whether the College Board had been unwilling to make the best defense. Perhaps the SAT had made an important independent contribution to predicting college performance in earlier years, but by the time research was conducted in the last half of the 1990s, the test had already been ruined by political correctness. To see where this hypothesis comes from, a little history is required.

Originally, the point of the SAT — whose initials, after all, stood for Scholastic Aptitude Test — was to measure *aptitude*, defined by the dictionary as "inherent ability," rather than to measure academic achievement. But in the aftermath of the 1960s, the concept of aptitude became troublesome. The temper of the times meant that long-observed ethnic and class differences in mental test scores had to be interpreted as the fault of the tests that produced them. Like all other mental tests, the SAT persistently showed such differences; therefore, the SAT had to be a bad test, culturally biased in favor of upper-middle-class white kids.

The psychometricians at the College Board could provide ample data to refute the cultural bias charge, but the College Board was run by people who were eager to demonstrate their own progressive credentials. They ran from the concept of aptitude as the Florentines fled the plague. In the 1980s, the College Board tried to make a semantic case for a difference between scholastic aptitude and intelligence. This was unsuccessful for the good reason that, operationally, there isn't any difference. In 1993, the College Board abandoned aptitude altogether and changed the name of the SAT to "Scholastic Assessment Test." In 1994, it introduced major substantive changes to the SAT that were explicitly intended to link the test more closely to the curriculum.

Did the pre-1994 SAT measure something importantly different from what the post-1994 SAT had measured? Don't bother asking the College Board. The data for answering that question would require the College Board to reveal just how well the original and revised SATs measure the general mental factor g, the stuff of intelligence/aptitude, and the College Board does not want to acknowledge that the SAT measures g at all or, for that matter, that g even exists.

Seen from an outsider's perspective, the changes in 1993–1994 do not look particularly important. Twenty-five antonym items in the SAT Verbal were replaced with reading-comprehension items, on grounds that the antonym items could be compromised by students who memorized vocabulary lists. The math test saw some changes in the answer format. But samples of the new items appear to be plausible measures of g and not obviously inferior to the items they replaced.

Despite the College Board's rhetoric about revamping the SAT to reflect curriculum, the changes in the test in 1993–1994 probably did not have much effect on the SAT's power to measure g — in the jargon, its g-loading. (I would not make the same statement about today's SAT, which has eliminated the highly g-loaded analogy items and added a writing component that carries with it a multitude of scoring problems.)

20

If I am wrong, and the pre-1994 SAT measured g much better than the SAT used for the UC study, then I hope some disaffected College Board psychometrician leaks that news immediately. I will thereupon join a crusade to restore the old SAT. But given the available information, I think it is probable that even analyses conducted prior to the revisions in the test would not have shown a major independent role for the SAT after taking high school transcript and achievement test scores into account. To put it another way, those of us who thought that the SAT was our salvation were probably wrong. Even coming from mediocre high schools, our scores on achievement tests would have conveyed about the same picture to college admissions committees as our scores on the SAT conveyed.

I know how counterintuitive this sounds (I am presenting a conclusion I resisted as long as I could). But the truth about any achievement test, from an AP exam down to a weekly pop quiz, is that the smartest kids tend to get the highest scores. All mental tests are g-loaded to some degree. What was not realized until the UC study was just how high that correlation was for the SAT and the achievement tests.

Before, studies of the relationship had been based on self-selected samples of students who chose to take achievement tests along with the SAT, and there was good reason to think those students were unrepresentative. But by requiring all applicants to take both the SAT and achievement tests, the University of California got rid of this problem — and the correlations were still very high.   25

After the College Board did all of its statistical corrections in its 2002 study and applied them to test-takers from California, it found, for example, that the correlation between the SAT Verbal and the Literature Achievement test was a very high 0.83 (a correlation of 1.0 represents a perfect direct relationship). The correlation between the SAT Math and the Math IC achievement test was 0.86. So I conclude that bright students who do not go to first-rate high schools will do fine without the SAT. Consider these scenarios:

Start with motivated, high-ability students who go to truly bad schools, meaning the worst schools in the inner cities. The bright students' achievement test scores are likely to be depressed by the schools' dreadfulness, but even scores that are just fair will get the attention of an admissions office if the transcript shows Ask and the recommendations are enthusiastic. The nation's top colleges desperately want to increase their enrollment of inner-city blacks and Hispanics, and are willing to make large allowances for bad schooling to do so.

Next, turn to the much larger number of high-ability students who are in schools that are not awful, but mediocre — the typical urban or small-town public school. The curriculum includes all the standard college-prep courses with standard textbooks. A few of the teachers are terrific, but most are no more than ordinary.

The high-ability students in such schools who are playing the game, studying hard, have no problem at all if the SAT is eliminated. They have nearly straight As on their transcripts, which most college admissions offices treat as the most important single source of information. Their letters of recommendation are afire with zeal on their behalf. These students also do well on the achievement tests. A hard-working, high-ability physics student is likely to absorb enough physics from the textbook to do well on the physics achievement test despite a so-so teacher.

In addition, high-ability kids who play the game have usually been reading voraciously — and in the process picked up a great deal of knowledge about history, literature, and culture on their own. This information has been gathered inefficiently, but high-ability students absorb knowledge like a sponge, no matter what schools they attend.

Now consider high-ability students in mediocre schools who do *not* play the classroom game. They are bored with their classes and sometimes get Bs and the occasional C, but they have active minds and are looking for ways to occupy themselves. They spend all their time on the debate team or writing for the high school newspaper, or in the drama department. By the end of high school, they have a long list of accomplishments studding their applications. One way or the other, by the end of high school, students in this category are very likely to have done things that will catch the attention of an admissions officer. And again, their achievement test scores are high. These students are at least as intellectually curious as those who play the game. Their Bs do not mean they didn't absorb the substance of the coursework, and they too have typically encountered and retained large amounts of information outside school.

That leaves the worst case: high-ability students who are alienated by school and perhaps by life. They don't study, don't go out for the debate team, don't read on their own, don't even watch the Discovery Channel. It is possible for them nonetheless to achieve a high score on an individually administered IQ test, despite being hostile and uninterested. Arthur Jensen relates the time he was testing a sullen subject in a juvenile detention facility and came to the vocabulary item "apocryphal." The boy answered, "How the hell should I know? I think the whole Bible is [bunk]." In an individually administered IQ test, the examiner could score his answer as correct, but that same alienated boy is unlikely to get a high score on the SAT because no one, no matter how smart, gets a high score on the SAT without concentrating and trying hard over the course of three stressful hours. So keeping the SAT will not help most students in this category. They won't try hard, and their SAT scores will be mediocre despite their ability.

That leaves an extremely odd set of high-ability students who will be harmed by dropping the SAT — so alienated that they do nothing to express their ability in school, so completely walled off from independent learning that they do poorly on the achievement tests, and yet able to buckle down on the SAT and get a good score. I am not sure that getting a good score under such circumstances is even possible on the SAT Math — too many of the questions presuppose hard work in algebra class — but perhaps it could be done on the SAT Verbal.

In any case, we are now talking about a very few students, and even for them it is not clear whether dropping the SAT introduces an injustice. Should such a student be given a slot that could have been filled by a less-talented student who is eager to give a competitive college his best effort? Being forced to go to an unselective college instead could well be the better outcome for all concerned.

There is good reason to think that a world in which achievement tests have replaced the SAT is not going to be a world in which motivated high-ability students from bad or mediocre schools have less opportunity to get into the college where they belong. It may be a marginally worse world for a small number of

30

unmotivated high-ability students who want to attend selective colleges, but that outcome is not necessarily undesirable.

But why get rid of the SAT? If it works just about as well as the achievement tests in predicting college success, what's the harm in keeping it?   35

The short answer is that the image of the SAT has done a 180-degree turn. No longer seen as a compensating resource for the unprivileged, it has become a corrosive symbol of privilege. "Back when kids just got a good night's sleep and took the SAT, it was a leveler that helped you find the diamond in the rough," Lawrence University's dean of admissions told the *New York Times* recently. "Now that most of the great scores are affluent kids with lots of preparation, it just increases the gap between the haves and the have-nots."

If you're rich, the critics say, you can raise your children in an environment where they will naturally acquire the information the SAT tests. If you're rich, you can enroll your children in Kaplan, or Princeton Review, or even get private tutors to coach your kids in the tricks of test-taking, and thereby increase their SAT scores by a couple of hundred points. If you're rich, you can shop around for a diagnostician who will classify your child as learning-disabled and therefore eligible to take the SAT without time limits. Combine these edges, and it comes down to this: If you're rich, you can buy your kids a high SAT score.

Almost every parent with whom I discuss the SAT believes these charges. In fact, the claims range from simply false, in the case of cultural bias, to not-nearly-as-true-as-you-think, in the case of the others. Take coaching as an example, since it seems to be so universally accepted by parents and has been studied so extensively.

From 1981 to 1990, three separate analyses of all the prior studies were published in peer-reviewed journals. They found a coaching effect of 9 to 25 points on the SAT Verbal and of 15 to 25 points on the SAT Math. In 2004, Derek Briggs, using the National Education Longitudinal Study of 1988, found effects of 3 to 20 points for the SAT Verbal and 10 to 28 points for the SAT Math. Donald Powers and Donald Rock, using a nationally representative sample of students who took the SAT after its revisions in the mid-1990s, found an average coaching effect of 6 to 12 points on the SAT Verbal and 13 to 18 points on the SAT Math. Many studies tell nearly identical stories. On average, coaching raises scores by no more than a few dozen points, enough to sway college admissions in exceedingly few cases.

I am not reporting a scholarly literature with a two-sided debate. No study published in a peer-reviewed journal shows average gains approaching the fabled   40
100-point and 200-point jumps you hear about in anecdotes. While preparing this article, I asked Kaplan and Princeton Review for such evidence. Kaplan replied that it chooses not to release data for proprietary reasons. Princeton Review did not respond at all.

But the coaching business is booming, with affluent parents being the best customers. If the payoff is really so small, why has the market judged coaching to be so successful?

Most obviously, parents who pay for expensive coaching courses ignore the role of self-selection: the students who seem to profit from a coaching course tend to be those who, if the course had not been available, would have worked hard on their own to prepare for the test.

Then parents confuse the effects of coaching with the effect of the basic preparation that students can do on their own. No student should walk into the SAT cold. It makes sense for students to practice some sample items, easily available from school guidance offices and online, and to review their algebra textbook if it has been a few years since they have taken algebra. But once a few hours have been spent on these routine steps, most of the juice has been squeezed out of preparation for the SAT. Combine self-selection artifacts with the role of basic preparation, and you have the reason that independent studies using control groups show such small average gains from formal coaching.

It makes no difference, however, that the charges about coaching are wrong, just as it makes no difference that the whole idea that rich parents can buy their children high SAT scores is wrong. One part of the indictment is true, and that one part overrides everything else: the children of the affluent and well educated really do get most of the top scores. For example, who gets the coveted scores of 700 and higher, putting them in the top half-dozen percentiles of SAT test-takers? Extrapolating from the 2006 data on means and standard deviations reported by the College Board, about half of the 700+ scores went to students from families making more than $100,000 per year. But the truly consequential statistics are these: Approximately 90 percent of the students with 700+ scores had at least one parent with a college degree. Over half had a parent with a graduate degree.

In that glaring relationship of high test scores to advanced parental education, 45 which in turn means high parental IQ, lies the reason that the College Board, politically correct even unto self-destruction, cannot bring itself to declare the truth: The test isn't the problem. The children of the well educated and affluent get most of the top scores because they constitute most of the smartest kids. They are smart because their parents are smart. The parents have passed their smartness along through parenting practices that are largely independent of education and affluence, and through genes that are completely independent of them.

The cognitive stratification of American society — for that's what we're talking about — was not a problem 100 years ago. Many affluent people were smart in 1907, but there were not enough jobs in which high intellectual ability brought high incomes or status to affect more than a fraction of really smart people, and most of the really smart people were prevented from getting those jobs anyway by economic and social circumstances (consider that in 1907 roughly half the adults with high intelligence were housewives).

From 1907 to 2007, the correlation between intellectual ability and socioeconomic status (SES) increased dramatically. The socioeconomic elite and the cognitive elite are increasingly one. If you want the details about how this process worked and how it is transforming America's class structure, I refer you to *The Bell Curve* (1994), the book I wrote with the late Richard Herrnstein. For now, here's the point: Imagine that, miraculously, every child in the country were to receive education of equal quality. Imagine that a completely fair and accurate measure of intellectual ability were to be developed. In that utopia, a fair admissions process based on intellectual ability would fill the incoming classes of the elite colleges predominantly with children of upper-middle-class parents.

In other words, such a perfect system would produce an outcome very much like the one we see now. Harvard offers an easy way to summarize the revolution that accelerated after World War II. As late as 1952, the mean SAT Verbal score of the incoming freshman class was just 583. By 1960, the mean had jumped to 678. In eight years, Harvard transformed itself from a college with a moderately talented student body to a place where the average freshman was intellectually in the top fraction of 1 percent of the national population. But this change did not mean that Harvard became more socioeconomically diverse. On the contrary, it became more homogeneous. In the old days, Harvard had admitted a substantial number of Boston students from modest backgrounds who commuted to classes, and also a substantial number of rich students with average intelligence. In the new era, when Harvard's students were much more rigorously screened for intellectual ability, the numbers of students from the very top and bottom of the socioeconomic ladder were reduced, and the proportion coming from upper-middle-class backgrounds increased.

The other high-ranking schools have similar stories to tell. In a sample of 11 of the most prestigious colleges studied by William Bowen and his colleagues between the mid-1970s and the mid-1990s, the proportion of students in the top SES quartile rose from about a third to a half of all students, while the share in the bottom quartile remained constant at one-tenth. And these were schools such as Princeton and Yale that get first chance to admit the scarce and sought-after candidates of high ability from poor backgrounds.

When, in 2003, Anthony Carnevale and Stephen Rose expanded the definition of top-tier colleges to include 146 schools, fully 74 percent of the students came from families in the top SES quartile, while only 3 percent came from the bottom quartile. Ethnic diversity has increased during the last half century, but not socioeconomic diversity.

Because upper-middle-class families produce most of the smartest kids, there is no way to reform the system (short of disregarding intellectual ability altogether) to prevent their children from coming out on top. We can only make sure that high-ability students from disadvantaged backgrounds realize that the nation's best colleges yearn for their applications and that their chance of breaking out of their disadvantaged situations has never been better — in short, that the system is not rigged. Now, the widespread belief is that the system is rigged, and the SAT is a major reason for that belief. The most immediate effect of getting rid of the SAT is to remove an extremely large and bright red herring. But there are more good effects.

Getting rid of the SAT will destroy the coaching industry as we know it. Coaching for the SAT is seen as the teaching of tricks and strategies — a species of cheating — not as supplementary education. The retooled coaching industry will focus on the achievement tests, but insofar as the offerings consist of cram courses for tests in topics such as U.S. history or chemistry, its taint will be reduced.

A low-income student shut out of opportunity for an SAT coaching school has the sense of being shut out of mysteries. Being shut out of a cram course is less daunting. Students know that they can study for a history or chemistry exam on their own. A coaching industry that teaches content along with test-taking techniques will have the additional advantage of being much better pedagogically — at least the students who take the coaching courses will be spending some of their time learning history or chemistry.

The substitution of achievement tests for the SAT will put a spotlight on the quality of the local high school's curriculum. If achievement test scores are getting all of the parents' attention in the college admissions process, the courses that prepare for those achievement tests will get more of their attention as well, and the pressure for those courses to improve will increase.

The final benefit of getting rid of the SAT is the hardest to describe but is probably the most important. By getting rid of the SAT, we would be getting rid of a totem for members of the cognitive elite.   55

People forget achievement test scores. They do not forget cognitive test scores. The only cognitive test score that millions of people know about themselves is the SAT score. If the score is high, it is seen as proof that one is smart. If the score is not high, it is evidence of intellectual mediocrity or worse. Furthermore, it is evidence that cannot be explained away as a bad grade can be explained away. All who enter an SAT testing hall feel judged by their scores.

Worse yet, there are few other kinds of scores to counterbalance the SAT. Of the many talents and virtues that people possess, we have good measures for quantifying few besides athletic and intellectual ability. Falling short in athletic ability can be painful, especially for boys, but the domain of sports is confined. Intellectual ability has no such limits, and the implications of the SAT score spill far too widely. The 17-year-old who is at the 40th percentile on the SAT has no other score that lets him say to himself, "Yes, but I'm at the 99th percentile in working with my hands," or "Yes, but I'm at the 99th percentile for courage in the face of adversity."

Conversely, it seems to make no difference that high intellectual ability is a gift for which its recipients should be humbly grateful. Far too many students see a high score on the SAT as an expression of their own merit, not an achievement underwritten by the dumb luck of birth.

Hence the final reason for getting rid of the SAT: knowing those scores is too dispiriting for those who do poorly and too inspiriting for those who do well. In an age when intellectual talent is increasingly concentrated among young people who are also privileged economically and socially, the last thing we need are numbers that give these very, very lucky kids a sense of entitlement.

How are we to get rid of the SAT when it is such an established American institution and will be ferociously defended by the College Board and a large test-preparation industry?   60

Actually, it could happen quite easily. Admissions officers at elite schools are already familiar with the statistical story I have presented. They know that dropping the SAT would not hinder their selection decisions. Many of them continue to accept the SAT out of inertia — as long as the student has taken the test anyway, it costs nothing to add the scores to the student's folder.

In that context, the arguments for *not* accepting the SAT can easily find a receptive audience, especially since the SAT is already under such severe criticism for the wrong reasons. Nor is it necessary to convince everyone to take action at the same time. A few high-profile colleges could have a domino effect. Suppose, for example, that this fall Harvard and Stanford were jointly to announce that SAT scores will no longer be accepted. Instead, all applicants to Harvard and Stanford will be required to take four of the College Board's achievement tests, including a math test and excluding any test for a language used at home. If just those two schools took such a step, many other schools would follow suit immediately, and the rest within a few years.

It could happen, and it should happen. There is poignance in calling for an end to a test conceived for such a noble purpose. But the SAT score, intended as a signal flare for those on the bottom, has become a badge flaunted by those on top. We pay a steep educational and cultural price for a test that no one really needs.

READING AND DISCUSSION QUESTIONS

1. What does Murray mean when he says that "data trump gratitude"?
2. What is his claim?
3. What types of support does Murray use? How convincing are they?
4. According to Murray, how is intellectual ability related to socioeconomic status?
5. What is Murray's specific suggestion as to what should be done about the SAT?

WRITING SUGGESTIONS

6. Based on your experience and that of people you know and on your reading, write an essay in which you either agree or disagree with Murray's suggestions.
7. Write an essay analyzing Murray's use of support in the essay.

Marriage-Plus

THEODORA OOMS

The public has been concerned about "family breakdown" for a long time, but it was not until the passage of welfare reform in 1996 that the federal government decided to get into the business of promoting marriage. Although it was little noticed at the time, three of the four purposes of the welfare legislation refer directly or indirectly to marriage and family formation. The law exhorts states to promote "job preparation, work, and marriage," to "prevent and reduce the incidence of out-of-wedlock pregnancies," and to "encourage the formation and maintenance of two-parent families."

Theodora Ooms is a senior consultant to the National Healthy Marriage Resource Center in Fairfax, Virginia. Her article is an annotated version of one that originally appeared in a special issue of *The American Prospect* on "The Politics of the American Family," April 8, 2002.

The Bush administration, as it contemplates this year's extension of welfare legislation, plans to make marriage even more central. The administration's re-authorization proposal, announced February 27, includes $300 million for demonstration grants to focus on promoting healthy marriages and reducing out-of-wedlock births.[21] Meanwhile, Oklahoma Governor Frank Keating has launched a $10 million, multisector marriage initiative, and other smaller-scale government-sponsored initiatives have been enacted in Arizona, Florida, Louisiana, Michigan, and Utah. The federal government is primarily concerned with reducing out-of-wedlock births, which it views as a principal cause of welfare dependency and a host of other social problems. By contrast, state marriage initiatives are most concerned about the effects of high divorce rates and father absence on children.[22]

This new emphasis on marriage as a panacea for social problems is troubling to many liberals. For one thing, it risks being dismissive of children who happen to find themselves in single-parent families. It also can be seen as disparaging single mothers and ignoring the fact that many women have left abusive marriages for good reasons.

That said, it's hard to dismiss an overwhelming consensus of social-science research findings that children tend to be better off, financially and emotionally, when their parents are married to each other. Around 50 percent of all first marriages are expected to end in divorce, and 60 percent of all divorces involve children. One-third of all births are out of wedlock, nearly 40 percent of children do not live with their biological fathers, and too many nonresident fathers neither support nor see their children on a regular basis.

Children living with single mothers are five times as likely to be poor as those in two-parent families. Growing up in a single-parent family also roughly doubles the risk that a child will drop out of school, have difficulty finding a job, or become a teen parent. About half of these effects appear to be attributable to the reduced income available to single parents, but the other half is due to non-economic factors.[23] It's not just the presence of two adults in the home that helps children, as some argue. Children living with cohabiting partners and in stepfamilies generally do less well than those living with both married biological parents.[24]

Marriage also brings benefits to husbands and wives. Married adults are more productive on the job, earn more, save more, have better physical and mental health, and live longer, according to an extensive review of research, conducted

5

[21]See *Working Toward Independence: The President's Plan to Strengthen Welfare Reform*, February 2002. http://www.whitehouse.gov/news/releases/2002/02/welfare-reform-announcement-book.pdf.

[22]Theodora Ooms, "The Role of the Federal Government in Strengthening Marriage," in *Virginia Journal of Social Policy and the Law*, Fall 2001. Available at www.clasp.org.

[23]Sara McLanahan and Julien Teitler, "The Consequences of Father Absence," in *Parenting and Child Development in "Non-Traditional" Families*, ed. Michael E. Lamb (Mahwah, NJ: Lawrence Erlbaum, 1998). Also see Sara McLanahan and Gary Sanderfur, *Growing Up with a Single Parent: What Hurts, What Helps* (Cambridge, MA: Harvard UP, 1994).

[24]See McLanahan and Teitler; Susan L. Brown, "Child Well-Being in Cohabiting Unions" and Wendy D. Manning, "The Implications of Cohabitation for Children's Well-Being," in *Just Living Together: Implications of Cohabitation for Children, Families, and Social Policy*, eds. Alan Booth and Ann C. Crouter (Mahwah, NJ: Lawrence Erlbaum, 2002).

by scholar Linda Waite. Although Waite admits that these findings partly reflect the selection of better-adjusted people into marriage, she finds that when people marry, they act in more health promoting and productive ways.[25]

Conservatives are prone to exaggerate these research findings and underplay the importance of economics. If married people are more likely (other things being equal) to produce thriving children, other things are not, in fact, equal. It's not just the case that single mothers find themselves poor because they are unmarried; they find themselves unmarried because they are poor. Successful marriages are more difficult when husbands and wives are poorly educated, lack access to jobs that pay decently, and cannot afford decent child care. Economic hardship and other problems associated with poverty can wreak havoc on couples' relationships.

The controversy mostly isn't about research, however, but about values.[26] Most people regard decisions to marry, divorce, and bear children as intensely private. Any policy proposals that hint at coercing people to marry, reinforcing Victorian conceptions of gender roles, or limiting the right to end bad marriages are viewed as counter to American values of individual autonomy and privacy. Some worry about the existence of hidden agendas that threaten to put women back into the kitchen, ignore domestic violence, and eliminate public assistance for low-income families. Others fear that holding out marriage as the ideal blames single parents, many of whom do a terrific job under difficult circumstances. Use of the term "illegitimate" is especially offensive because it stigmatizes children (and, in fact, is legally inaccurate, as children born outside of marriage now have virtually the same legal rights as those born within marriage).[27] And some worry that the pro-marriage agenda discriminates against ethnic and sexual minorities and their children, particularly gays and lesbians.

There are also more pragmatic concerns. Skeptics of the pro-marriage agenda observe that the decline in marriage is worldwide, a result of overwhelming social and economic forces that cannot be reversed. In their view, attempts to change family formation behavior are largely futile; we should instead just accept and help support the increasing diversity of family forms. For others, the concern is less about the value of promoting marriage and more about whether government, rather than individuals, communities, or faith institutions, should lead the charge.

Finally, marriage per se is too simplistic a solution to the complex problems of the poor. Marrying a low-income, unmarried mother to her child's father will not magically raise the family out of poverty when the parents often have no skills, no jobs, terrible housing, and may be struggling with depression, substance abuse, or domestic violence. Advocates also worry that funds spent on untested marriage-promotion activities will be taken away from programs that provide desperately needed services for single parents, such as child care.

10

---

[25] Linda J. Waite and Maggie Gallagher, *The Case for Marriage: Why Married People Are Happier, Healthier, and Better Off Financially* (New York: Doubleday, 2000).

[26] Theodora Ooms, *Toward More Perfect Unions: Putting Marriage on the Public Agenda* (Washington, DC: Family Impact Seminar, 1998). Available from tooms@clasp.org.

[27] Ruth-Arlene W. Howe, "Legal Rights and Obligations: An Uneven Evolution," in *Young Unwed Fathers: Changing Roles and Emerging Policies*, eds. Robert I. Lerman and Theodora Ooms (Philadelphia: Temple UP, 1993), pp. 141–69.

In response to some of these concerns — as well as research showing that serious parental conflict harms children — some marriage advocates respond that marriage per se should not be the goal but rather voluntary, "healthy" marriages.[28] They also agree that protections should be built into programs to guard against domestic violence. But this only raises doubts about how "healthy" will be defined, and by whom, and whether we even know how to help people create better relationships.

There also are some plainly foolish ideas in the marriage movement. West Virginia currently gives married families an extra $100 a month in welfare payments as a "marriage incentive." Robert Rector of the Heritage Foundation has proposed giving a $4,000 government bounty to welfare recipients who marry before they have a child and stay married for two years.[29] Charles Murray wants to end public assistance altogether and has proposed eliminating all aid to *unmarried* mothers under 21 in one state to test the idea. This proposal is especially egregious and surely would harm children of single mothers.[30]

Progressives and others thus are placed in a quandary. They don't want to oppose marriage — which most Americans still value highly — but are skeptical of many pro-marriage initiatives. Given that healthy marriage is plainly good for children, however, one can envision a reasonable agenda — one that would gain broad support — that we might call marriage-plus. This approach puts the well-being of children first by helping more of them grow up in married, healthy, two-parent families. However, for many children, the reality is that marriage is not a feasible or even a desirable option for their parents. Thus, a secondary goal is to help these parents — whether unmarried, separated, divorced, or remarried — cooperate better in raising their children. These are not alternative strategies. Children need us to do both.

A marriage-plus agenda does not promote marriage just for marriage's sake. It acknowledges that married and unmarried parents, mothers and fathers, may need both economic resources and non-economic supports to increase the likelihood of stable, healthy marriages and better co-parenting relationships. In addition, a marriage-plus agenda focuses more on the front end — making marriage better to be in — rather than the back end — making marriage more difficult to get out of.

Here are some elements of this agenda.   15

Strengthen "fragile families" at the birth of a child. For many poor families, relationship-education programs may be helpful but not enough. A new national study finds that at the time of their child's birth, one-half of unmarried parents (so-called "fragile families") are living together, and another third are romantically

---

[28]See, for example, Robin Toner, "Welfare Chief Is Hoping to Promote Marriage," *New York Times*, February 19, 2002, sec. A, p. 1.

[29]Robert Rector, *A Plan to Reduce Illegitimacy*, memorandum handed out at a meeting on Capitol Hill in early 2001.

[30]Charles Murray, "Family Formation," in *The New World of Welfare*, eds. Rebecca M. Blank and Ron Haskins (Washington, DC: Brookings Institution Press, 2001), pp. 137–68.

attached but not cohabiting.[31] The majorities of these parents are committed to each other and to their child and have high hopes of eventual marriage and a future together — although these hopes too often are not realized. We should reach out to young parents to help them achieve their desire to remain together as a family. A helpful package of services to offer these young families might include a combination of "soft" services — relationship-skills and marriage-education workshops, financial-management classes, and peer-support groups — and "hard" services, such as job training and placement, housing, medical coverage, and substance-abuse treatment, if necessary. At present, all we do is get the father to admit paternity and hound him for child support.

Reduce economic stress by reducing poverty. Poverty and unemployment can stress couples' relationships to their breaking point. Results of a welfare-to-work demonstration program in Minnesota suggest that enhancing the income of the working poor can indirectly promote marriage. The Minnesota Family Investment Program (MFIP), which subsidized the earnings of employed welfare families, found that marriage rates increased for both single-parent long-term recipients and two-parent families. Married two-parent families were significantly more likely to remain married. MFIP also reduced the reported incidence of domestic abuse.[32]

Provide better-paying jobs and job assistance for the poor. The inability of low-skilled, unemployed men to provide income to their families is a major reason for their failure to marry the mothers of their children. Better employment opportunities help low-income fathers, and men in general, to become responsible fathers and, perhaps, more attractive and economically stable marriage partners.[33] There is also growing support for making changes in the child-support system to ensure that more support paid by fathers goes to the children (rather than being used to recoup government program costs).[34]

Invest more in proven programs that reduce out-of-wedlock childbearing. Teen pregnancy and birth rates have fallen by over 20 percent since the early 1990s, and there is now strong evidence that a number of prevention programs are effective. A related strategy is enforcement of child support. States that have tough, effective

[31] Sara McLanahan et al., *The Fragile Families and Child Wellbeing Study Baseline Report*, August 2001, http://crcw.princeton.edu/fragilefamilies/nationalreport.pdf; and Sara McLanahan, Irwin Garfinkel, and Ronald B. Mincy, "Fragile Families, Welfare Reform, and Marriage," *Welfare Reform and Beyond Policy Brief*, No. 10, November 2001. http://www.brookings.edu/dybdocroot/wrb/publications/pb/pb10.htm. For additional papers from the Fragile Families study, see http://crcw.princeton.edu/fragilefamilies/index.htm.

[32] Virginia Knox, Cynthia Miller, and Lisa A. Gennetian, *Reforming Welfare and Rewarding Work: A Summary of the Final Report on the Minnesota Family Investment Program* (New York: Manpower Demonstration Research Corporation, September, 2000).

[33] See Chapter 4, "The Fading Inner-City Family," in William Julius Wilson, *When Work Disappears: The World of the New Urban Poor* (New York: Alfred A. Knopf, 1996), pp. 87–110; Kathy Edin, "Few Good Men: Why Poor Mothers Don't Marry or Remarry," *The American Prospect*, January 3, 2000.

[34] See Vicki Turetsky, Testimony Given to the Social Security and Family Policy Subcommittee of the U.S. Senate Finance Committee, October 11, 2001; and Vick Turetsky, *What If All the Money Came Home?* (Washington, DC: Center for Law and Social Policy, June, 2000). Both available online at www.clasp.org.

child support systems have been found to have lower nonmarital birth rates, presumably because men are beginning to understand there are serious costs associated with fathering a child.[35]

Institute workplace policies to reduce work/family conflict and stress on couples.   20
Stress in the workplace spills over into the home. Persistent overtime, frequent travel, and inflexible leave policies place great strain on couples at all income levels. Employers are increasingly demanding nonstandard work schedules. A recent study found that married couples with children who work night and rotating shifts are at higher risk of separation and divorce.[36] The absence of affordable and reliable child care forces many parents who would prefer a normal workday to working split shifts solely to make sure that a parent is home with the children.

Reduce tax penalties and other disincentives to marriage. There has always been strong support for reducing marriage tax penalties for many two-earner families. This is a complicated task because the majority of married couples, in fact, receive tax bonuses rather than penalties.[37] A positive step was taken in 2001 to reduce significantly the marriage penalty affecting low-income working families in the Earned Income Tax Credit program. While there is uncertainty about the extent to which these tax-related marriage penalties affect marital behavior, there is broad general agreement that government has a responsibility to "first do no harm" when it comes to marriage.

Similarly, there is near unanimous agreement that government should not make it harder for eligible two-parent families to receive welfare benefits and assistance. In the past, the old welfare program, Aid to Families with Dependent Children, was much criticized for offering incentives to break up families. At least 33 states already have removed the stricter eligibility rules placed on two-parent families,[38] and the president's welfare reauthorization proposal encourages the other states to do the same. In addition, it proposes to end the higher work participation rate for two-parent families, a federal rule that has been criticized widely by the states. Another needed reform would forgive accumulated child-support debt owed by noncustodial fathers if they marry the mothers of their children. (Currently, such debt is owed to the state if the mothers and children are receiving welfare benefits.)[39]

Educate those who want to marry and stay married about how to have healthy relationships and good marriages. A vast industry is devoted to helping couples plan a successful wedding day — wedding planners, 500-page bridal guides, specialty

[35] Robert D. Plotnick, Inhoe Ku, Irwin Garfinkel, and Sara S. McLanahan, *The Impact of Child Support Enforcement Policy on Nonmarital Childbearing.* Paper presented at the Association for Public Policy Analysis and Management, Year 2000 Research Conference in Seattle, WA.

[36] Harriet B. Presser, "Nonstandard Work Schedules and Marital Instability," *Journal of Marriage and the Family* (February 2000).

[37] Congressional Budget Office, *For Better or For Worse: Marriage and the Federal Income Tax* (Washington, DC: Congress of the United States, Congressional Budget Office, June 1997).

[38] Gene Falk and Jill Tauber, *Welfare Reform: TANF Provisions Related to Marriage and Two-Parent Families* (Washington, DC: Congressional Research Service, Library of Congress, October 30, 2001).

[39] Paul Roberts, *An Ounce of Prevention and a Pound of Cure: Developing State Policy on the Payment of Child Support Arrears by Low Income Parents.* (Washington, DC: Center for Law and Social Policy, May 2001). Available online at www.clasp.org.

caterers, the list goes on. But where do young people go to learn about how to sustain good, lifelong marriages? In fact, we now know a lot about what makes contemporary marriages work. With the transformation of gender roles, there now are fewer fixed rules for couples to follow, meaning they have to negotiate daily about who does what and when. In the absence of the legal and social constraints that used to keep marriages together, there's now a premium on developing effective relationship skills. Building on three decades of research, there are a small but rapidly growing number of programs (both religious and secular) that help people from high school through adulthood understand the benefits of marriage for children and for themselves, develop realistic expectations for healthy relationships, understand the meaning of commitment, and learn the skills and attitudes needed to make marriage succeed.[40] Other programs help married couples survive the inevitable ups and downs that occur in most marriages, and remarried couples with the additional challenges of step-parenting. Oklahoma, Utah, and Michigan have begun using government funds to make these relationship- and marriage-education programs accessible to low-income couples. The Greater Grand Rapids Community Marriage Policy initiative is urging area businesses to include marriage education as an Employee Assistance Program benefit, arguing that it's more cost-effective to prevent marital distress than incur the costs of counseling and lost productivity involved when employees' marriages break up.[41]

A marriage-plus agenda that includes activities such as these is not just the responsibility of government. Some of the strategies proposed here are being implemented by private and religious groups, some by governments, and some by partnerships between these sectors. The approach adopted in Oklahoma, Greater Grand Rapids, and Chattanooga, for example, mobilizes the resources of many sectors of the community — government, education, legal, faith, business, and media — in a comprehensive effort to create a more marriage-supportive culture and to provide new services to promote, support, and strengthen couples and marriage and reduce out-of-wedlock childbearing and divorce. This "saturation model" seems particularly promising because it takes into account the many factors that influence individuals' decisions to marry, to divorce, or to remain unmarried. We should proceed cautiously, trying out and evaluating new ideas before applying them widely.

Ironically, in the midst of this furor about government's role in marriage, it's worth noting that the federal government recently has begun to shirk a basic responsibility: counting the numbers of marriages and divorces in the United States. Since budget cuts in 1995, the government has been unable to report on marriage and divorce rates in the states or for the nation as a whole.[42] And, for the first time

25

[40]See Scott Stanley, "Making a Case for Premarital Education," in *Family Relations* (July 2001). Also see *Directory of Couples and Marriage Education Programs* at www.smartmarriages.com.

[41]Personal communication with Mark Eastburg, Ph.D., director of Pine Rest Family Institute, Grand Rapids, Michigan. See Web site for the Greater Grand Rapids Community Marriage Initiative, www.ggrcmarriagepolicy.org.

[42]Stephanie Ventura, "Vital Statistics from the National Center for Health Statistics," in *Data Needs for Measuring Family and Fertility Change after Welfare Reform*, ed. Douglas Besharov (College Park, MD: Maryland School of Public Affairs, Welfare Reform Academy).

in the history of the Census, Americans were not asked to give their marital status in the 2000 survey. What kind of pro-marriage message from the government is that?

If liberals and conservatives are serious about strengthening families for the sake of helping children, liberals ought to acknowledge that noncoercive and egalitarian approaches to bolstering marriage are sound policy. Conservatives, meanwhile, should admit that much of what it takes to make marriage work for the benefit of spouses and children is not just moral but economic.

READING AND DISCUSSION QUESTIONS

1. What does Ooms mean when she says in the first paragraph that in 1996 "the federal government decided to get into the business of promoting marriage"?

2. How does Ooms support her belief that children are better off in a two-parent home?

3. What type of support does she use in the sixth paragraph to argue that "[m]arriage also brings benefits to husbands and wives"?

4. What are some of the problems that arise when government gets involved in promoting marriage?

5. What claim is Ooms supporting? How effective is she in supporting that claim? Are some types of support that she uses more effective than others, in your opinion?

WRITING SUGGESTIONS

6. Write an essay in which you oppose or support Ooms's marriage-plus plan.

7. Analyze the primary types of support that Ooms uses. If you wish, you may go a step further and evaluate the effectiveness of her support.

DEBATE   Is Assuming the Role of Citizen Journalist Worth the Risk?

Praise for Student's Footage of Virginia Tech Mass Killing

LILY YULIANTI

On a CNN *Larry King Live* special report of the student massacre at Virginia Tech that saw thirty-three people killed, King praised Jamal Albarghouti, the Palestinian graduate student who took the eyewitness footage of the immediate aftermath on his cellphone.

At roughly 10 a.m. Albarghouti was at the Blacksburg, Virginia, campus to meet with his graduate adviser. He sensed that something terrible had just happened on

---

Lily Yulianti is a journalist and writer from Indonesia who works in Tokyo as an Indonesian language specialist and broadcaster for Radio Tokyo. As a citizen journalist herself, she posted this article on Korea's massive online outlet for citizen journalists, OhmyNews, on April 17, 2007.

campus, explaining, "Everyone [was] running and screaming. The situation was so frightening. I ran to a safe place and then decided to record the situation using my cellphone."

He then sent his video to CNN's *I-Report*, a citizen-reporter video blog site, which repeatedly used it to accompany its other reporting of the incident. This has been without doubt the worst mass shooting tragedy in U.S. history, and Albarghouti was the one to capture the incident for the world.

His footage, some of it shaky, set the scene inside the campus: an empty road outside a nearby building being approached by three police officers, then sounds of gunshots registering almost simultaneously, the last sounding like a bomb blast.

In the CNN interview with Larry King, Albarghouti explained how the scene   5
reminded him of his homeland of Palestine. King and another CNN news anchor tried to get at why Albarghouti decided not to dash for safety with other students and staffers but chose to stand fast and record the incident. "Weren't you scared? What sort of cellphone did you use? Did you think you were really safe at that time?"

His response was to demonstrate the value of a citizen reporter in providing an on-the-spot report of a history-making, traumatic event, in having the gadget at the ready to take the footage, and in having the presence of mind and the passion to play his historical role. He was not the only eyewitness but also stood his ground as a resourceful citizen reporter, taking the initiative to record the scene.

We can understand how CNN's professional journalists and a famous TV personality like Larry King could be so taken with Albarghouti's "journalism skill." Tempted to discount the capability of ordinary citizens in their chosen field of journalism, there are many well-trained professional journalists, proud of their skill and experience, who become intrigued whenever an unsung citizen reporter performs such a heroic act of historical reportage.

Apart from the unevenness of the footage he provided, Albarghouti showed that being confident in the use of his cellphone and uploading the resulting footage could be taken as matters of course. Above all, he provided King a clear and firm account of the situation, exactly in the manner of a professional TV journalist making a live report. What added special depth and human interest to this live report was his being reminded of the grievous situation in his own country when hearing the gunshots on campus. "I am quite familiar with the sound of gunshots, because they remind me of the situation in the West Bank and Gaza. But when I saw it was happening here, in a peaceful place like this, it was hard to believe."

Such was the personal background of a citizen-reporter that made Larry King say later, "What an irony . . .".

Again, Albarghouti and his cellphone video have shown the power of the or-   10
dinary citizen to capture a news event. Granted that the efforts of ordinary people as citizen journalists are a matter for debate, the traditional media still make a reflexively negative comparison between citizen journalism and that provided by their professionals. Interestingly, when presented with a citizen who sent an exclusive report to the mainstream media, as Albarghouti did to CNN's *I-Report*, they insist on wondering, in grudging amazement, "What made you record the event? How did you record it?"

Of course, the mainstream media should first of all be thankful, because there is a live video record from the site. The role of Albarghouti was not only that of eyewitness but also of a citizen reporter who in fact provided a high-quality report for CNN.

In raising questions like these, professionals in the media show a tendency to overlook the existence of many ordinary citizens out there who embrace the idea of participatory journalism, people who have shifted from being passive media consumers to active citizen reporters, believing they can create a better society if they get involved in conveying the news. They make videos, they write on various issues, and they raise their voices. As for the mainstream media, they have begun to open their doors to citizen reporters, seeing that their well-trained professionals cannot always respond quickly enough to reach the location of an epochal event.

Disaster Photos: Newsworthy or Irresponsible?

MARK MEMMOTT WITH ALAN LEVIN AND GREG LIVADAS

Photos taken by survivors of the London bombings[43] and Tuesday's plane crash in Toronto are prompting concerns by safety investigators and journalism scholars.

At issue: Whether as camera phones and digital cameras multiply, so do the odds that victims will put themselves and others at risk by pausing to snap pictures.

Questions are also being raised about whether the media may be encouraging risky behavior by broadcasting the images.

On the other side of the debate, such photos may aid investigators.

Within a few hours of the London attacks [on] July 7, photos taken by survivors with camera phones were ricocheting around the world on the Internet and on television.   5

Four photos taken Tuesday by Air France Flight 358 passenger Eddie Ho were broadcast later on several outlets, including ABC's *Good Morning America*, CNN, and NBC's *Today*. One was snapped inside the jet moments after it skidded to a halt in Toronto. It shows passengers heading to an exit. The others were taken outside the jet and show passengers fleeing the crippled fuselage.

---

[43] On two different dates in July 2005, London's bus and subway system was the target of a synchronized cluster of bombs. On July 7, fifty-two people were killed and 770 injured. On July 21, four devices were planted on three subways and one bus, as in the previous incident, but this time all failed to go off.

Mark Memmott worked for *USA Today* from 1984 to 2009 as a reporter and editor, and he has been a blogger for NPR since 2009. Alan Levin is a reporter for *USA Today* and Greg Livadas is a former reporter for the *Rochester Democrat and Chronicle* in New York. This article was published on August 4, 2005 on *USAToday.com*.

All three hundred nine people aboard survived.

Ho, nineteen, a South African attending college in Canada, said Thursday in a telephone interview with *USA Today* that his digital camera was in his pocket during the flight. He is an "airline enthusiast" who often takes pictures while flying. Ho sold the photos to two syndicates, which are now reselling them to the media.

Ho said he doesn't think he delayed his exit or anyone else's. "I was running and taking pictures," he said. "I just kept pressing the button." He said he would not have tried to retrieve his camera if it had been in a bag.

Still, a top accident investigation official in the USA strongly advises passengers not to do such things.   10

Mark Rosenker, acting chairman of the National Transportation Safety Board, said, "Your business is to get off the airplane. Your business is to help anybody who needs help." Taking photos is "irresponsible," he said.

Helen Muir, aerospace psychology professor at Cranfield University in Great Britain, said in most crashes "You only have two minutes from the first spark to conditions not being survivable in the cabin." Pausing even for a second "is just what we don't want people to do." But, Muir said, the pictures could be "very valuable to accident investigators." They contain clues to the jet's condition after the crash.

More such photos are inevitable. There are digital cameras in about half of U.S. households and camera phones in about 40 percent, the market research firm IDC estimates. About 92 million camera phones have been sold in the USA, IDC says.

Kelly McBride, who lectures about media ethics at the Poynter Institute for professional journalists, said the media have a responsibility "to refuse to publish photos taken (by amateurs) when someone was obviously risking his life or the lives of others."

McBride said journalists must "talk to the person about the circumstances under   15
which he took the photos and share that information with the public."

Ben Sherwood, executive producer at *Good Morning America*, said there was no reason to think Ho had caused any problems at the scene. "From what we could tell" from the photos, Sherwood said, "one was taken (in the jet) during what appeared to be an orderly evacuation. The others were taken from outside, looking back."

Sherwood said *Good Morning America* "welcomes contributions from people who find themselves in the middle of news stories [but] would never encourage anyone to take an unnecessary risk."

Jonathan Klein, president of CNN/US, said his network "urges folks, on the air, not to take foolish risks." He doubts many survivors are thinking about the media when they pull out their cameras.

"They're taking (pictures) in order to satisfy that primordial urge to record one's history," Klein said.

Mark Glaser, a columnist at the USC Annenberg School of Journalism's *Online   20
Journalism Review*, said, "Over time, people will recognize when it's the right time to use your camera in an emergency."

Unfortunately, he said, "it may take someone dying" because they stopped to take a picture before that "cultural norm" is reached.

DISCUSSION QUESTIONS

1. What, if any, events can you recall that had better or more complete coverage because of the presence of citizen journalists?

2. The South Korean online newspaper to which Yulianti submitted her article, OhmyNews, draws 80 percent of its content from reporters who are not professional journalists. What sort of assumptions would you make about the quality of the reporting you would find in it?

3. What did Larry King mean when he said that Albarghouti's situation was ironic?

4. What is your opinion about what Albarghouti did during the massacre at Virginia Tech?

5. What is your opinion about what Ho did during the evacuation of Air France Flight 358?

6. In general, do you believe that Yulianti or Memmott builds a more compelling case?

Assignments for Providing Support

READING AND DISCUSSION QUESTIONS

1. Consider what types of evidence you find most convincing in an argument. Is the best type of evidence dependent on the topic and the context? Explain.

2. Look for examples in the media of the misuse of evidence. Explain why the evidence is misleading.

3. Use examples to explain which news shows depend on factual evidence and which depend largely on opinion. Do both have a useful role to play in our society? Explain.

4. In the aftermath of the massacre at Virginia Tech, at least one state tried to pass a law allowing registered owners to carry their weapons on school and college campuses. What needs of the people were those who proposed the law appealing to? How could the opponents have used similar types of appeal to argue their case?

5. Consider presidential debates you have seen or other televised coverage of candidates during the months leading up to an election. What are some specific examples of how the candidates try to appeal to the voters' needs and values?

6. Bernard Goldberg argues in his essay, "Connecting the Dots . . . to Terrorism," that the average American citizen is usually ignorant of much of the reality of what goes on in the Arab world. When Americans take a stand on issues such as U.S. involvement in Iraq, to what extent do you believe they are basing that stand on solid supporting evidence?

WRITING ASSIGNMENTS

7. Using Bethany Royce's "The True Confusion about SUV Costs" as a model, write an essay evaluating the use of support in one of the Readings for Analysis.

8. Write an essay explaining the types of support used in one of the Readings for Analysis or comparing the use of support in two of them.

9. Write an essay explaining which of the two authors in the debate over citizen journalists you believe presents a more convincing argument, Lily Yulianti or Mark Memmott.

10. Analyze different television commercials for the same product or similar products. Write an essay supporting a conclusion you are able to draw about the types of appeal used in the commercials.

11. Write a letter about a problem on your campus to the person who is in a position to correct the problem. Provide convincing evidence that a problem exists and, in suggesting a solution to the problem, keep in mind the needs and values of your audience as well as those of others on campus.

Research Readiness: Using Books for Support

When should you turn to books for support, and how do you find them?

When you are writing about controversial issues, you will want to find the most up-to-date sources that you can. You don't want to write in support of a change that has already taken place. You don't want to miss significant developments in the situation you are writing about. If your audience knows more about the latest news regarding your subject than you do, you can look foolish or at least ill-prepared.

It is a fact of the publishing world that it takes considerable time for a new book to reach the shelves of libraries and bookstores, sometimes as much as a year from the time a manuscript is completed. That means that for the most recent news on developing stories and current issues, you may need to turn to magazines, newspapers, and well-maintained and reliable electronic sources.

There may be times, though, when a book will be just the source you need for some material you want to include in your paper. That doesn't mean that you will need to read books in their entirety in researching your topic, but it does mean that you should search out books on your topic and scan the table of contents and index for information on the specific part of the topic that you are writing about. If you find that the whole book seems relevant to your topic, your topic probably needs to be narrowed down. If you find a chapter or smaller segment of a book that is useful, you will cite the author of the book in your documentation if the whole book is by the same author. If the book is a collection of chapters or articles by different authors, you will cite the part you use by the author of that part. Make that distinction clear as you take notes.

Why would a book be useful in researching a current issue? Some problems, of course, have been around for a long time, and there has been ample time for books on them to be published. Also, you may want to research the history of a problem situation or solutions that have been tried in the past. You may also just need some background information on the subject.

Don't rule out books as sources just because they may not be as convenient as searching for sources online. Use either your library's card catalog or online catalog to search for your subject. Try searching by title and also by keyword. A quick search for books on autism, for example, produces 291 sources when searched by keyword and forty-nine when searched by title. Online, you will then usually have the option of limiting those results in various ways — by year, for example, or by linking your keyword with other words that rule out sources not relevant to your search. Doing an advanced search linking the keyword *autism* with *vaccines*, for example, narrows the possibilities to six.

You will also find bound periodicals listed in the card or online catalog, so if you need to find issues of a magazine or journal that are not on the shelf with current issues, you can look in the card catalog or online catalog under the title to find its location in the library.

ASSIGNMENT

1. Do your own search for books (not bound periodicals) on one of these topics.
   - The link between autism and vaccines
   - The link between cell phones and cancer
   - The movement to drop the SAT as a requirement for college admissions
   - The environmental impact of plastic water bottles

2. Create a Works Cited page for three sources that seem to be useful for information on the subject. Remember that on your Works Cited page you will list the whole book if it is the work of a single author.

   Kirby, David. *Evidence of Harm: Mercury in Vaccines and the Autism Epidemic: A Medical Controversy.* New York: St. Martin's Griffin, 2005.

   (Indicate in parenthetical documentation exactly what page you used.)

   The Vaccine Court established to compensate victims in cases of vaccine-related injury or death awards payments from an account funded by taxpayers, not the companies that produce the vaccines, and has a statute of limitations of three years (Kirby 2).

3. In a book that consists of chapters or articles by different authors, cite only the chapter or article that you are using. In that case, include in your Works Cited the page numbers for the whole chapter or article, even if you are not using every page.

   Miller, Kelli. "Hope Renewed." *Recovering Autistic Children.* Eds. Stephen M. Edelson and Bernard Rimland. San Diego: Autism Research Institute, 2003. 245–50.

4. If you need further help with the format for these citations, see Chapter 10.

CHAPTER **7**

Warrants

What Are Warrants?

We now come to the third element in the structure of the argument — the warrant. Claim and support, the other major elements we have discussed, are more familiar in ordinary discourse, but there is nothing mysterious or unusual about the warrant. All our claims, both formal and informal, are grounded in warrants or assumptions that the audience must share with us if our claims are to prove to be acceptable.

The following exercise provides a good starting point for this chapter. Do the assigned task by yourself or in a small group.

PRACTICE

A series of environmental catastrophic events has virtually wiped out human life on Earth. The only known survivors in your vicinity are the eleven listed below. There are resources to sustain only seven. Choose seven of the following people to survive. List them in the order in which you would choose them and be prepared to explain the reasons for your selection: that is, why you chose these particular persons and why you placed them in this certain order.

- Dr. D. — thirty-seven, Ph.D. in history, college professor, in good health (jogs daily), hobby is botany, enjoys politics, married with one child (Bobby).
- Mrs. D. — thirty-eight, rather obese, diabetic, M.A. in psychology, counselor in a mental health clinic, married to Dr. D., has one child.
- Bobby D. — ten, mentally retarded with IQ of 70, healthy and strong for his age.
- Mrs. G. — twenty-three, ninth-grade education, cocktail waitress, worked as a prostitute, married at age sixteen, divorced at age eighteen, one son (Joseph).
- Joseph G. — three months old, healthy.
- Mary E. — eighteen, trade school education, wears glasses, artistic.

- Mr. N. — twenty-five, starting last year of medical school, music as a hobby, physical fitness buff.
- Mrs. C. — twenty-eight, daughter of a minister, college graduate, electronics engineer, single now after a brief marriage, member of Zero Population Growth.
- Mr. B. — fifty-one, B.S. in mechanics, married with four children, enjoys outdoors, much experience in construction, quite handy.
- Father Frans — thirty-seven, Catholic priest, active in civil rights, former college athlete, farming background, often criticized for liberal views.
- Dr. L. — sixty-six, doctor in general practice, two heart attacks in the past five years, loves literature and quotes extensively.

There may have been a great deal of disagreement over which survivors to select. If so, the reason for that disagreement was that in making their choices, different members of your group or of your class as a whole were operating under different assumptions or basing their decisions on different warrants. Some of you may have chosen not to let Mrs. G. survive because she seemed to have nothing particularly vital to offer to the survival of the group as a whole. Others of you may have felt that she should be allowed to survive along with her child, the infant in the group. Some of you, whether you acknowledge it or not, may have opposed letting Mrs. G. survive because she was once a prostitute. Think about the warrant that would underlie the claim that Mrs. G. should not be one of the seven allowed to survive. What assumption — what generalized principle — would a person who made that claim be accepting about women who were once prostitutes? What assumption would underlie the claim that she should be allowed to survive? What assumption would underlie the claim that Bobby D. should be allowed to live (or die)?

Obviously this is an exercise with no right answer. What it can teach us, however, is to consider the assumptions on which our beliefs are based. There are reasons you might have chosen certain individuals to survive that could be stated as general principles: Those who are in the best physical condition should be allowed to survive. Those with the most useful skills should be allowed to survive. Those who are mentally deficient should not be allowed to survive. Those who are most likely to reproduce should be allowed to survive.

Fortunately, this is merely an intellectual exercise. Whenever you take a stand in a real-life situation, though, you do so on the basis of certain general principles that guide your choices. Those general principles that you feel most strongly about exist as part of your intellectual and moral being because of what you have experienced in your life thus far. They have been shaped by your observations, your personal experience, and your participation in a culture. But because these observations, experiences, and cultural associations will vary, the audience may not always agree with the warrants or assumptions of the writer. The success of Rogerian argument depends on identifying at least one assumption, or warrant, that opposing sides share. The success of any argument depends on at least understanding your own warrants and those of your audience.

What does this have to do with your writing? Any time you support an argumentative claim, you have to analyze the assumptions behind the argument and consider whether the members of your audience share the same assumptions. Some warrants are so widely accepted that you do not need to state them or to offer any proof of their validity. If you argue that every new dorm on campus should have a sprinkler system, you probably do not even need to state your warrant. If you did, it would be something like this: Measures that would increase the likelihood that dorm residents would survive a fire should be implemented in all dorms.

What about claims that are more controversial? Why is it so difficult for those who oppose abortion, for example, to communicate with those who favor it and vice versa? Anyone who believes that abortion is the murder of an unborn child is basing that argument on the warrant that a fetus is a child from conception. Many on the other side of the debate do not accept that warrant and thus do not accept the claim. Obviously disagreements on such emotionally charged issues are very difficult to resolve because the underlying warrants are based on firmly held beliefs that are difficult to change. It is always better to be aware of your opponent's warrants, however, than to simply dismiss them as irrelevant.

The British philosopher Stephen Toulmin, who developed the concept of warrants, dismissed more traditional forms of logical reasoning in favor of a more audience-based, courtroom-derived approach to argumentation. He refers to warrants as "general, hypothetical statements, which can act as bridges" and "entitle one to draw conclusions or make claims."[1] The word *bridges* to denote the action of the warrant is crucial. One dictionary defines warrant as a "guarantee or justification." We use the word *warrant* to emphasize that in an argument it guarantees a connecting link — a bridge — between the claim and the support. This means that even if a reader agrees that the support is sound, the support cannot prove the validity of the claim unless the reader also agrees with the underlying warrant. Recall the sample argument outlined in Chapter 1 (p. 25):

Claim: Backscatter screening should be implemented in America's airports.

Support: Backscatter screening will make planes safer.

Warrant: Any screening technique that will make planes safer should be implemented.

Notice that the reader must agree with the assumption that safety is worth undergoing any screening technique, even one that some would consider an invasion of privacy. Simply providing evidence that a certain technique will make planes safer is not enough to convince all readers that backscatter screening should be implemented in America's airports.

The following dialogue offers another example of the relationship between the warrant and the other elements of the argument.

[1] Stephen Toulmin, *The Uses of Argument* (Cambridge: Cambridge University Press, 1958), p. 98.

"I don't think that Larry can do the job. He's pretty dumb."
"Really? I thought he was smart. What makes you say he's dumb?"
"Did you know that he's illiterate — can't read above third-grade level? In my book that makes him dumb."

If we put this into outline form, the warrant or assumption in the argument becomes clear.

Claim: Larry is pretty dumb.

Support: He can't read above third-grade level.

Warrant: Anybody who can't read above third-grade level must be dumb.

We can also represent the argument in diagram form, which shows the warrant as a bridge between the claim and the support.

Support ――――――――――――――――――――――――→ *Claim*

Warrant
(Expressed or Unexpressed)

The argument above can then be written like this:

Support ―――――――――――――――――――→ *Claim*
Larry can't read above   He's pretty dumb.
third-grade level.

Warrant
Anybody who can't read above third-grade
level must be pretty dumb.

Is this warrant valid? We cannot answer this question until we consider the *backing*. Every warrant or assumption rests on something else that gives it authority; this is what we call backing. Backing or authority for the warrant in this example would consist of research data that prove a relationship between stupidity and low reading ability. This particular warrant, we would discover, lacks backing because we know that the failure to learn to read well may be due to a number of things unrelated to intelligence. So if the warrant is unprovable, the claim — that Larry is dumb — is also unprovable, even if the evidence is true. In this case, then, the evidence does not guarantee the soundness of the claim.

Now consider this example of a somewhat more complicated warrant: The beautiful and unspoiled Eastern Shore of Maryland is being discovered by thousands of tourists, vacationers, and developers who will, according to the residents, change the landscape and the way of life, which is now based largely on fishing and farming. In a few years the Eastern Shore may become a noisy, crowded string of resorts. Mrs. Walkup, the Kent County commissioner, says,

Catering to the wealthy puts property back on the tax rolls, but it's going to make the Eastern Shore look like the rest of the country. Everything that made our way of life so special is being eroded. We are a fragile area. The Eastern Shore is still special, but it is feeling pressure from all directions. Lots of people don't seem to appreciate the fact that God made us to need a little peace and quiet now and then.[2]

In simplified form the argument of those opposed to development would be outlined this way:

Claim: Development will bring undesirable changes to the present way of life on the Eastern Shore, a life of farming and fishing, peace and quiet.

Support: Developers will build express highways, condominiums, casinos, and nightclubs.

Warrant: A pastoral life of fishing and farming is superior to the way of life brought by expensive, fast-paced modern development.

Notice that the warrant is a broad generalization that can apply to a number of different situations, while the claim is about a specific place and time. It should be added that in other arguments the warrant may not be stated in such general terms. However, even in arguments in which the warrant makes a more specific reference to the claim, the reader can infer an extension of the warrant to other similar arguments. In the backscatter screening example outlined on page 271, the warrant mentions a specific screening technique. But it is clear that such warrants can be generalized to apply to other arguments in which we accept a claim based on an appeal to our very human need to feel secure.

To be convinced of the validity of Mrs. Walkup's claim, you must first find that the support is true, that the developers plan to introduce drastic changes that will destroy the pastoral life of the Eastern Shore. You may, however, believe that the support is not entirely sound, that the development will be much more modest than residents fear, and that the Eastern Shore will not be seriously altered. Next, you may want to see more justification for the warrant. Is pastoral life superior to the life that will result from large-scale development? Perhaps you have always thought that a life of fishing and farming means poverty and limited opportunities for the majority of the residents. Although the superiority of a way of life is largely a matter of taste and therefore difficult to prove, Mrs. Walkup may need to produce backing for her belief that the present way of life is more desirable than one based on developing the area for new residents and summer visitors. If you find either the support or the warrant unconvincing, you cannot accept the claim.

Remember that a claim is often modified by one or more qualifiers, which limit the claim. Mrs. Walkup might have said, "Development will *probably* destroy *some aspects of* the present way of life on the Eastern Shore." Warrants can also be modified or limited by *reservations*, which remind the reader that there are conditions under which the warrants will not be relevant. Mrs. Walkup

[2]Michael Wright, "The Changing Chesapeake," *New York Times Magazine*, July 10, 1983, p. 27.

might have added, "unless increased prosperity and exposure to the outside world brought by development improve some aspects of our lives." This is the sort of reservation that could be the means of reconciling two different points of view in Rogerian argument.

A diagram of Mrs. Walkup's argument shows the additional elements:

Support ⎯⎯⎯⎯⎯⎯⎯⎯⎯⎯⎯⎯⎯⎯⎯⎯⎯⎯→ *Claim*
The developers will build highways, condos, casinos, nightclubs.

Development will bring undesirable changes to life on the Eastern Shore.

Warrant
A way of life devoted to farming and fishing is superior to a way of life brought by development.

Qualifier
Development will *most likely* bring undesirable changes.

Backing
We have experienced crowds, traffic, noise, rich strangers, and high-rises, and they destroy peace and quiet.

Reservation
But increased development might improve some aspects of our lives.

Claim and support (or lack of support) are relatively easy to uncover in most arguments. One thing that makes the warrant different is that it is often unexpressed and therefore unexamined by both writer and reader because they take it for granted. In the argument about Larry's intelligence, the warrant was stated. But in the argument about development on the Eastern Shore, Mrs. Walkup did not state her warrant directly, although her meaning is perfectly clear. She probably felt that it was not necessary to be more explicit because her readers would understand and supply the warrant.

We can make the discovery of warrants even clearer by examining another argument, in this case a policy claim. We've looked at a factual claim (that Larry is dumb) and a value claim (that Eastern Shore development is undesirable). Now we examine a policy claim that rests on one expressed and one unexpressed warrant. Policy claims are usually more complicated than other claims because the statement of policy is preceded by an array of facts and values. In addition, such claims may represent chains of reasoning in which one argument is dependent on another. These complicated arguments may be difficult or impossible to summarize in a simple diagram, but careful reading, asking the same kinds of questions that the author may have asked about the claim, can help you to find the warrant or chain of warrants that must be accepted before evidence and claim can be linked.

In a familiar argument that appeared a few years ago,[3] the author argues for a radical reform in college sports — the elimination of subprofessional, intermural team sports, as practiced above all in football and basketball. The claim is clear, and evidence for the professional character of college sports not hard to find: the large salaries paid to coaches, the generous perquisites offered to players, the recruitment policies that ignore academic standing, the virtually full-time commitment of the players, the lucrative television contracts. But can this evidence support the author's claim that such sports do not belong on college campuses? Advocates of these sports may ask, "Why not?" In the conclusion of the article the author states one warrant or assumption underlying his claim.

> Even if the money to pay college athletes could be found, though, a larger question must be answered — namely, why should a system of professional athletics be affiliated with universities at all? For the truth is that the requirements of athletics and academics operate at cross purposes, and the attempt to play both games at once serves only to reduce the level of performance of each.

In other words, the author assumes that the goals of an academic education on the one hand and the goals of big-time college sports on the other hand are incompatible. In the article he develops the ways in which each enterprise harms the other.

But the argument clearly rests on another warrant that is not expressed because the author takes for granted that his readers will supply it: The academic goals of the university are primary and should take precedence over all other collegiate activities. This is an argument based on an authority warrant, the authority of those who define the goals of the university — scholars, public officials, university administrators, and others. (Types of warrants are discussed in the following section.)

This warrant makes clear that the evidence of the professional nature of college sports cited above supports the claim that they should be eliminated. If quasiprofessional college sports are harmful to the primary educational function of the college or university, then they must go. In the author's words, "The two are separate enterprises, to be judged by separate criteria. . . . For college

[3]D. G. Myers, "Why College Sports?" *Commentary*, December 1990, pp. 49–51.

sports, the university is not an educational institution at all; it is merely a locus, a means of coordinating the different aspects of the sporting enterprise."

This argument may be summarized in outline form as follows:

Claim: Intermural college team sports should be abolished.

Support: College sports have become subprofessional.

Warrant: The goals of an academic education and big-time college sports are incompatible.

Backing
For the
Warrant: Academic education is the primary goal of the college and must take precedence over athletic activity.

PRACTICE

Read the following argument by Robert A. Sirico. Then summarize the argument in a paragraph. Next, explain what the claim is, what types of support are used, and what the warrant is. Is the warrant one that you agree with? Explain.

An Unjust Sacrifice
ROBERT A. SIRICO

An appeals court in London has made a Solomonic ruling, deciding that eight-week-old twins joined at the pelvis must be separated. In effect, one twin, known as Mary, is to be sacrificed to save the other, known as Jodie, in an operation the babies' parents oppose.

The judges invoked a utilitarian rationale, justified on the basis of medical testimony. The specialists agreed that there is an 80 to 90 percent chance that the strong and alert Jodie could not survive more than a few months if she continued to support the weak heart and lungs of Mary, whose brain is underdeveloped.

This is a heartbreaking case, and the decision of the court was not arrived at lightly. But even the best of intentions, on the part of the state or the parents, is no substitute for sound moral reasoning. Utilitarian considerations like Mary's quality of life are not the issue. Nor should doctors' expert testimony, which is subject to error, be considered decisive.

Here, as in the case of abortion, one simple principle applies: There is no justification for deliberately destroying innocent life. In this case, the court has turned its back on a tenet that the West has stood by: Life, no matter how limited, should be protected.

While this case is so far unique, there are guidelines that must be followed. No human being, for instance, can be coerced into donating an organ — even if the individual donating the organ is unlikely to be harmed and the individual receiving the organ could be saved. In principle, no person should ever be forced to volunteer his own body to save another's life, even if that individual is a newborn baby.

Robert A. Sirico, a Roman Catholic priest, is president of the Acton Institute for the Study of Religion and Liberty in Grand Rapids, Michigan. This article appeared in the September 28, 2000, *New York Times*.

To understand the gravity of the court's error, consider the parents' point of view. They are from Gozo, an island in Malta. After being told of their daughters' condition, while the twins were in utero, they went to Manchester, England, seeking out the best possible medical care. Yet, after the birth on August 8, the parents were told that they needed to separate the twins, which would be fatal for Mary.

They protested, telling the court: "We cannot begin to accept or contemplate that one of our children should die to enable the other one to survive. That is not God's will. Everyone has a right to life, so why should we kill one of our daughters to enable the other one to survive?"

And yet, a court in a country in which they sought refuge has overruled their wishes. This is a clear evil: coercion against the parents and coercion against their child, justified in the name of a speculative medical calculus.

The parents' phrase "God's will" is easily caricatured, as if they believed divine revelation were guiding them to ignore science. In fact, they believe in the merit of science, or they would not have gone to Britain for help in the first place.

But utilitarian rationality has overtaken their case. The lawyer appointed by the court to represent Jodie insisted that Mary's was "a futile life." That is a dangerous statement — sending us down a slippery slope where lives can be measured for their supposed value and discarded if deemed not useful enough.

Some might argue that in thinking about the twins, we should apply the philosophical principle known as "double effect," which, in some circumstances, permits the loss of a life when it is an unintended consequence of saving another. But in this case, ending Mary's life would be a deliberate decision, not an unintended effect.

Can we ever take one life in favor of another? No, not even in this case, however fateful the consequences.

Arguers will often neglect to state their warrants for one of two reasons: First, like Mrs. Walkup, they may believe that the warrant is obvious and need not be expressed; second, they may want to conceal the warrant in the hope that the reader will overlook its weakness.

What kinds of warrants are so obvious that they need not be expressed? Here are a few that will probably sound familiar:

Mothers love their children.

The more expensive the product, the more satisfactory it will be.

A good harvest will result in lower prices for produce.

First come, first served.

These statements seem to embody beliefs that most of us would share and that might be unnecessary to make explicit in an argument. The last statement, for example, is taken as axiomatic, an article of faith that we seldom question in ordinary circumstances. Suppose you hear someone make the claim, "I deserve to get the last ticket to the concert." If you ask why he is entitled to a ticket that you also would like to have, he may answer in support of his claim, "Because I was here first." No doubt you accept his claim without further argument because you understand and agree with the warrant that is not expressed: "If you arrive first, you deserve to be served before those who come later." Your acceptance of the warrant probably also takes into account the unexpressed backing that is based on a belief in justice: "It is only fair that those who sacrifice time and comfort to be first in line should be rewarded for their trouble."

In this case it may not be necessary to expose the warrant and examine it. Indeed, as Stephen Toulmin tells us, "If we demanded the credentials of all warrants at sight and never let one pass unchallenged, argument could scarcely begin."[4]

But even those warrants that seem to express universal truths invite analysis if we can think of claims for which these warrants might not, after all, be relevant. "First in line," for example, may justify the claim of a person who wants a concert ticket, but it cannot in itself justify the claim of someone who wants a vital medication that is in short supply. Moreover, offering a rebuttal to a long-held but unexamined warrant can often produce an interesting and original argument. If someone exclaims, "All this buying of gifts! I think people have forgotten that Christmas celebrates the birth of Christ," she need not express the assumption — that the buying of gifts violates what ought to be a religious celebration. It goes unstated by the speaker because it has been uttered so often that she knows the hearer will supply it. But one writer, in an essay titled "God's Gift: A Commercial Christmas," argued that, contrary to popular belief, the purchase of gifts, which means the expenditure of time, money, and thought on others rather than oneself, is not a violation but an affirmation of the Christmas spirit.[5]

The second reason for refusal to state the warrant lies in the arguer's intention to disarm or deceive the reader, although the arguer may not be aware of this. For instance, failure to state the warrant is common in advertising and politics, where the desire to sell a product or an idea may outweigh the responsibility to argue explicitly. The following advertisement is famous not only for what it says but for what it does not say:

> In 1918 Leona Currie scandalized a New Jersey beach with a bathing suit cut above her knees. And to irk the establishment even more, she smoked a cigarette. Leona Currie was promptly arrested.
>
> Oh, how Leona would smile if she could see you today.
>
> You've come a long way, baby. *Virginia Slims*. The taste for today's woman.

What is the unstated warrant? The manufacturer of Virginia Slims hopes we will agree that being permitted to smoke cigarettes is a significant sign of female lib-

---

[4] *The Uses of Argument* (Cambridge: Cambridge University Press, 1958), p. 106.
[5] Robert A. Sirico, *Wall Street Journal*, December 21, 1993, sec. A, p. 12.

eration. But many readers would insist that proving "You've come a long way, baby" requires more evidence than women's freedom to smoke (or wear short bathing suits). The shaky warrant weakens the claim.

Politicians, too, conceal warrants that may not survive close scrutiny. In the 1983 mayoral election in Chicago, one candidate revealed that his opponent had undergone psychiatric treatment. He did not have to state the warrant supporting his claim. He knew that many in his audience would assume that anyone who had undergone psychiatric treatment was unfit to hold public office. This same assumption contributed to the withdrawal of a vice-presidential candidate from the 1972 campaign.

Types of Warrants

Arguments may be classified according to the types of warrants offered as proof. Because warrants represent the reasoning process by which we establish the relationship between support and claim, analysis of the major types of warrants enables us to see the whole argument as a sum of its parts.

Warrants may be organized into three categories: *authoritative, substantive,* and *motivational.*[6] The *authoritative warrant* is based on the credibility or trustworthiness of the source. If we assume that the source of the data is authoritative, then we find that the support justifies the claim. A *substantive warrant* is based on beliefs about reliability of factual evidence. In the example on page 272 the speaker assumes, although mistakenly, that the relationship between low reading level and stupidity is a verifiable datum, one that can be proved by objective research. A *motivational warrant*, on the other hand, is based on the needs and values of the audience. For example, the warrant about backscatter screening reflects a concern for safety, a value that would cause a reader who held it to agree that more rigid screening techniques are a good idea.

Each type of warrant requires a different set of questions for testing its soundness. The following list of questions will help you to decide whether a particular warrant is valid and can justify a particular claim.

1. *Authoritative* (based on the credibility of the sources)

   Is the authority sufficiently respected to make a credible claim?

   Do other equally reputable authorities agree with the authority cited?

   Are there equally reputable authorities who disagree?

2. *Substantive* (based on beliefs about the reliability of factual evidence)

   Are sufficient examples given to convince us that a general statement is justified? That is, are the examples given representative of the whole community?

[6]D. Ehninger and W. Brockriede, *Decision by Debate* (New York: Dodd, Mead, 1953).

If you have argued that one event or condition can bring about another (a cause-and-effect argument), does the cause given seem to account entirely for the effect? Are other possible causes equally important as explanations for the effect?

If you have used comparisons, are the similarities between the two situations greater than the differences?

If you have used analogies, does the analogy explain or merely describe? Are there sufficient similarities between the two elements to make the analogy appropriate?

3. *Motivational* (based on the values of the arguer and the audience)

Are the values ones that the audience will regard as important?

Are the values relevant to the claim?

SAMPLE ANNOTATED ESSAY

The Case for Torture

MICHAEL LEVIN

Introduction: statement of opposing view

It is generally assumed that torture is impermissible, a throwback to a more brutal age. Enlightened societies reject it outright, and regimes suspected of using it risk the wrath of the United States.

Claim of policy: rebuttal of opposing view

I believe this attitude is unwise. There are situations in which torture is not merely permissible but morally mandatory. Moreover, these situations are moving from the realm of imagination to fact.

Support: hypothetical example to test the reader's belief

Suppose a terrorist has hidden an atomic bomb on Manhattan Island which will detonate at noon on July 4 unless . . . (here follow the usual demands for money and release of his friends from jail). Suppose, further, that he is caught at 10 A.M. of the fateful day, but — preferring death to failure — won't disclose where the bomb is. What do we do? If we follow due process — wait for his lawyer, arraign him — millions of people will die. If the only way to save those lives is to subject the terrorist to the most excruciating possible pain, what grounds can

Michael Levin is a professor of philosophy at the City University of New York. This essay is reprinted from the June 7, 1982, issue of *Newsweek*.

there be for not doing so? I suggest there are none. In any case, I ask you to face the question with an open mind.

Torturing the terrorist is unconstitutional? Probably. But millions of lives surely outweigh constitutionality. Torture is barbaric? Mass murder is far more barbaric. Indeed, letting millions of innocents die in deference to one who flaunts his guilt is moral cowardice, an unwillingness to dirty one's hands. If *you* caught the terrorist, could you sleep nights knowing that millions died because you couldn't bring yourself to apply the electrodes?

Once you concede that torture is justified in extreme cases, you have admitted that the decision to use torture is a matter of balancing innocent lives against the means needed to save them. You must now face more realistic cases involving more modest numbers. Someone plants a bomb on a jumbo jet. He alone can disarm it, and his demands cannot be met (or if they can, we refuse to set a precedent by yielding to his threats). Surely we can, we must, do anything to the extortionist to save the passengers. How can we tell three hundred, or one hundred, or ten people who never asked to be put in danger, "I'm sorry, you'll have to die in agony, we just couldn't bring ourselves to . . ."

Here are the results of an informal poll about a third, hypothetical, case. Suppose a terrorist group kidnapped a newborn baby from a hospital. I asked four mothers if they would approve of torturing kidnappers if that were necessary to get their own newborns back. All said yes, the most "liberal" adding that she would administer it herself.

I am not advocating torture as punishment. Punishment is addressed to deeds irrevocably past. Rather, I am advocating torture as an acceptable measure for preventing future evils. So understood, it is far less objectionable than many extant punishments. Opponents of the death penalty, for example, are forever insisting that executing a murderer will not bring back his victim (as if the purpose of capital punishment were supposed to be resurrection, not deterrence or retribution). But torture, in the cases described, is intended not to bring anyone back but to keep innocents from being dispatched. The most powerful argument against using torture as a punishment or to secure confessions is that such

5

Support: hypothetical example

Support: informal poll

Defense of the claim
a) Not punishment but protection of the innocent

practices disregard the rights of the individual. Well, if the individual is all that important — and he is — it is correspondingly important to protect the rights of individuals threatened by terrorists. If life is so valuable that it must never be taken, the lives of the innocents must be saved even at the price of hurting the one who endangers them.

b) Precedents for torture

Better precedents for torture are assassination and preemptive attack. No Allied leader would have flinched at assassinating Hitler, had that been possible. (The Allies did assassinate Heydrich.) Americans would be angered to learn that Roosevelt could have had Hitler killed in 1943 — thereby shortening the war and saving millions of lives — but refused on moral grounds. Similarly, if nation A learns that nation B is about to launch an unprovoked attack, A has a right to save itself by destroying B's military capability first. In the same way, if the police can by torture save those who would otherwise die at the hands of kidnappers or terrorists, they must.

c) Denial that terrorists have rights

There is an important difference between terrorists and their victims that should mute talk of the terrorists' "rights." The terrorist's victims are at risk unintentionally, not having asked to be endangered. But the terrorist knowingly initiated his actions. Unlike his victims, he volunteered for the risks of his deed. By threatening to kill for profit or idealism, he renounces civilized standards, and he can have no complaint if civilization tries to thwart him by whatever means necessary.

Just as torture is justified only to save lives (not extort   10
confessions or recantations), it is justifiably administered only to those *known* to hold innocent lives in their hands. Ah, but how can the authorities ever be sure they have the right malefactor? Isn't there a danger of error and abuse? Won't We turn into Them?

d) Easy identification of terrorists

Questions like these are disingenuous in a world in which terrorists proclaim themselves and perform for television. The name of their game is public recognition. After all, you can't very well intimidate a government into releasing your freedom fighters unless you announce that it is your group that has seized its embassy. "Clear guilt" is difficult to define, but when 40 million people see a group of masked gunmen seize an airplane on the evening news, there is not much question about who the perpetrators are. There will be hard cases where the situation is murkier. Nonetheless, a line demarcating the legitimate use of torture can be drawn. Torture only the obviously guilty, and only for the sake of saving innocents, and the line between Us and Them will remain clear.

Conclusion warrant: "Paralysis in the face of evil is the greater danger."

There is little danger that the Western democracies will lose their way if they choose to inflict pain as one way of preserving order. Paralysis in the face of evil is the greater danger. Some day soon a terrorist will threaten tens of thousands of lives, and torture will be the only way to save them. We had better start thinking about this.

Analysis

Levin's controversial essay attacks a popular assumption that most people have never thought to question — that torture is impermissible under any circumstances. Levin argues that in extreme cases torture is morally justified to bring about a greater good than the rights of the individual who is tortured.

Against the initial resistance that most readers may feel, Levin makes a strong case. Its strength lies in the backing he provides for the warrant that torture is sometimes necessary. This backing consists in the use of two effective argumentative strategies. One is the anticipation of objections. Unprecedented? No. Unconstitutional? No. Barbaric? No. Second, and more important, are the hypothetical examples that compel readers to rethink their positions and possibly arrive at agreement with the author. Levin chooses extreme examples — kidnapping of a newborn child, planting a bomb on a jumbo jet, detonating an atomic bomb in Manhattan — that draw a line between clear and murky cases and make agreement easier. And he bolsters his moral position by insisting that torture is not to be used as punishment or revenge but only to save innocent lives.

To support such an unpopular assumption the writer must convey the impression that he is a reasonable man, and this Levin attempts to do by a searching definition of terms, the careful organization and development of his argument, including references to the opinions of other people, and the expression of compassion for innocent lives.

Another strength of the article is its readability — the use of contractions, informal questions, conversational locutions. This easy, familiar style is disarming; the reader doesn't feel threatened by heavy admonitions from a writer who affects a superior, moral attitude.

Writer's Guide: Recognizing Warrants

1. Locate in your essay the one sentence that best states your claim, or if there is no single sentence that does so, try to express your claim in a single sentence.

2. If you have not already done so, think about for what audience you are writing. How is that audience likely to respond to your claim? The most important question to ask about your audience regarding warrants is this one: What assumption or assumptions must my audience make to be able to accept my claim? The answer to that question will be the warrant or warrants on which your essay is based.

3. The support you offer will make it easier for your audience to accept your claim. Remember that the warrant is the link between claim and support. It may help to use the formula used in this chapter to think systematically through your argument. Ask yourself what the claim is, what support you are offering, and what warrant connects the two. Do that for each major supporting statement that you make.

4. You may not need to state your warrant directly if it is a universally accepted truth that most reasonable readers would agree with it. You should be able to do so, however, in order to check your own logic.

5. If you are asking the members of your audience to accept a warrant that they are not likely to accept, you must offer backing for that warrant or consider restating your claim in a way that does not ask them to agree to an assumption that they will not be willing to agree with.

READINGS FOR ANALYSIS

We're All Celebrities in Post-Privacy Age

ERIC AUCHARD

Move over, Paris Hilton. We all have celebrity issues in an age when anyone can create an online profile, post confessional videos on YouTube, or make snarky online comments about other people.

The latest generation of Web sites — which attract tens of millions of users daily to share words, photos, and videos about themselves and their friends — make a virtue of openness at the expense of traditional notions of privacy.

Eric Auchard is a columnist for Reuters, covering technology investment. This article appeared online on June 21, 2007.

"My grandparents would have had a different attitude about privacy," says Jeff Jarvis, a former critic for *TV Guide* turned top blogger and columnist for the *Guardian* in London.

"There is a different calculus now," he says.

Sites like Facebook, Photobucket, and Flickr are enjoying surging popularity for allowing people to control their online identities in ways that make the danger of revealing too much information a constant worry — and all part of the game.

"Within the Web realm there is no private self," argues David Weinberger, author of a newly published book, *Everything Is Miscellaneous: The Power of the New Digital Disorder.*

"The closest you can mean is that you are with a small group behind some password-protected mechanism," he says.

The danger of such exposure is that it could affect careers when students seek jobs in the real world or private citizens seek public office.

George W. Bush and Bill Clinton might never have been elected president had sites like Google Inc.'s YouTube or News Corp.'s MySpace, the world's biggest online meeting places, existed to record the events of their younger years.

But while policy makers ponder how to bolster online anonymity, social network users are more concerned about deciding what to reveal about themselves next.

Control, Community Trump Privacy

Most users of the new self-publishing tools report finding a stronger sense of community among friends, family, and random Web site visitors who share their interests.

Facebook, a site started by a Harvard University undergraduate as a way for students to get to know one another, has exploded in popularity among professional users in Britain and the United States since the site took steps to open up to people of all ages over the past year. It now claims 25 million active users, who like the control Facebook gives them over who they let into their network of online acquaintances.

"What Facebook does is it allows me to control my identity and my society — my group of friends," Jarvis says. "You can call it privacy or you can call it publicness. I am controlling both sides of that equation, together — that's the secret."

Highlighting his own change of thinking on the subject of privacy, Jarvis revealed last year in a blog post, entitled "My cheatin' heart," that he was suffering from a medical condition that slowed work on his widely read media criticism blog, *BuzzMachine* (http://www.buzzmachine.com/). Supportive comments, and advice about potential treatments, poured in.

"Revealing a little bit of yourself is the only way to make connections to other people and that is how the Internet works," Jarvis says. "I couldn't have gotten that benefit unless I revealed the condition."

Caterina Fake, co-founder of popular photo sharing site Flickr, said recently that the defining moment for her start-up was when it decided all photos on the site would be public. Previously, photo sites had assumed users' photos should be private, unless deliberately published for public consumption.

Mena Trott, who, with her husband, Ben, developed Movable Type, a software system for publishing blogs, says "control" is a better word than "privacy" for defining oneself in different situations on the Web.

"We think blogging is sharing the stuff you care about with the people you care about," Trott says. "It comes down to control. They may or may not use it. But people want control."

Trott's company, Six Apart, makes publishing tools used by everyone from Hollywood gossip reporters to moms who seek to document their everyday lives, in private or semi-public mode.

"The Internet is often accused of leading to uncivil behavior," Jarvis says.   20
"Identity will lead to civility because we are being watched. It's like living in a small town again."

READING AND DISCUSSION QUESTIONS

1. What experience, if any, have you had with the sort of sites to which Auchard refers: for example, Facebook, Photobucket, and Flickr?
2. What are the pros and cons of posting to such social networking sites?
3. The heading halfway through the article reads, "Control, Community Trump Privacy." Explain what Auchard means by that.
4. What is Auchard's claim?
5. What types of support does he use?
6. What is his warrant?
7. Explain whether or not you accept his warrant.

WRITING SUGGESTIONS

8. Attack or defend this statement made by Auchard: "The danger of such exposure [on the Web] is that it could affect careers when students seek jobs in the real world or private citizens seek public office."
9. Write an essay in which you explain whether or not you believe that it is possible to achieve, on the Web, a balance between publicness and privacy.
10. What are the dangers of exposing personal information on the Internet?
11. Explain why you believe that sites like Facebook and MySpace are so popular.

What's Wrong with Price Gouging?

JEFF JACOBY

There wasn't much [Massachusetts Attorney General] Martha Coakley could do about the massive pipe break that left dozens of Greater Boston towns without clean drinking water over the weekend. So she kept herself busy instead lecturing vendors not to increase the price of the bottled water that tens of thousands of consumers were suddenly in a frenzy to buy.

"We have begun hearing anecdotal reports of the possible price gouging of store-bought water," Coakley announced Sunday. "Businesses and individuals cannot and should not take advantage of this public emergency to unfairly charge consumers . . . for water." Inspectors were being dispatched, "spot-checks" were being conducted, and "if we discover that businesses are engaging in price gouging," she warned, "we will take appropriate legal action."

Governor Deval Patrick got into the act, too. He ordered the state's Division of Standards to "closely monitor bottled water prices" in the area affected by the water emergency. "There is never an excuse for taking advantage of consumers," he intoned, "especially not during times like this."

It never fails. No sooner does some calamity trigger an urgent need for basic resources than self-righteous voices are raised to denounce the amazingly efficient system that stimulates suppliers to speed those resources to the people who need them. That system is the free market's price mechanism — the fluctuation of prices because of changes in supply and demand.

When the demand for bottled water goes through the roof — which is an-   5
other way of saying that bottled water has become (relatively) scarce — the price of water quickly rises in response. That price spike may be annoying, but it's not nearly as annoying as being unable to find water for sale at any price. Rising prices help keep limited quantities from vanishing today, while increasing the odds of fresh supplies arriving tomorrow.

It is easy to demonize vendors who charge what the market will bear following a catastrophe. "After storm come the vultures" *USA Today* memorably headlined a story about the price hikes that followed Hurricane Charley in Florida in 2004. Coakley hasn't called anybody a vulture, at least not yet, but her office has dedicated a telephone hotline and is encouraging the public to drop a dime on "price gougers."

Before you drop that dime, though, consider who really serves the public interest — the merchant who boosts his price during a crisis, or the merchant who refuses to?

A thought experiment: A massive pipe ruptures, tap water grows undrinkable, and consumers rush to buy bottled water from the only two vendors who sell it.

Jeff Jacoby is a columnist for the *Boston Globe*, where this essay and the response that follows appeared on May 4, 2010.

In an emergency should merchants be allowed to charge high prices for water?

Vendor A, not wanting to annoy the governor and attorney general, leaves the price of his water unchanged at 69 cents a bottle. Vendor B, who is more interested in doing business than truckling to politicians, more than quadruples his price to $2.99.

You don't need an economics textbook to know what happens next.

Customers descend on Vendor A in droves, loading up on his 69-cent water.   10
Within hours his entire stock has been cleaned out, and subsequent customers are turned away empty-handed. At Vendor B's, on the other hand, sales of water are slower and there is a lot of grumbling about the high price. But even late-arriving customers are able to buy the water they need — and almost no one buys more than he truly *needs*.

When demand intensifies, prices rise. And as prices rise, suppliers work harder to meet demand. The same *Globe* story that reported yesterday on Coakley's "price-gouging" statement reported as well on the lengths to which bottlers and retailers were going to get more water into customers' hands.

"Suppliers worked overtime, pumping up production at regional bottling facilities and coordinating deliveries," reporter Erin Ailworth noted. Polar Beverages in Worcester, for example, "had emptied out its plant in the city last night and trucked in loads of water from its New York facility."

Letting prices rise freely isn't the only possible response to a sudden shortage. Government rationing is an option, and so are price controls — assuming you don't object to the inevitable corruption, long lines, and black market. Better by far to let prices rise and fall freely. That isn't "gouging," but plain good sense — and the best method yet devised for allocating goods and services among free men and women.

Response to Jacoby

BACKBAYALLTHEWAY

Your editorial urges the audience toward a horrendous logical fallacy. Using Micro101 you claim that a rise in prices should increase supply (true). You then use anecdotal evidence from Polar Beverages to claim that supply has increased (true). Early in your piece, however, you claim that increasing prices help increase supplies and keep water on the shelves. If we are to assume that government price controls have been relatively effective, there appears to be adequate financial incentive to increase water supply without price increases to consumers. This is especially true when considering that wholesale prices (bottlers to retailers) are probably the most heavily monitored and regulated. In the short run, larger payments to Poland Springs aren't going to increase supply beyond the maximum capacity that exists now.

In regards to allocation, your hypothesis is predicated on the idea that all individuals have a similar valuation of bottled water and that water is allocated based on need. Water, in general, is allocated based on ability to pay. If prices were to sky-rocket . . . who would be more likely to drink water straight out of the tap, a family in central Boston or a family in Newton?

To people who have never been exposed to low income areas, the possibility of taking a health risk to save money may seem completely foreign. To those families living paycheck to paycheck, the time/energy needed to boil water or the money needed to buy water can be a true economic hardship.

We all know that this water is *probably* safe to drink, but let's all lay our J.D. degrees on the table and really appreciate the families who have to consider if "probably" is worth the possibility of saving money and getting sick.

READING AND DISCUSSION QUESTIONS

1. Summarize Jacoby's argument as you understand it.
2. How does raising the cost of bottled water in this case compare with similar price gouging when there is a crisis of greater magnitude, affecting more people for a longer period of time? Does Jacoby's argument seem applicable to those cases?
3. How convincing did you find Jacoby's argument to be?
4. What is his warrant? Is it an assumption you can agree with?
5. Do you agree with BackBayalltheWay that Jacoby's argument is a "horrendous logical fallacy"? See the explanations of common fallacies on p. 308.
6. Whose argument do you find more acceptable, Jacoby's or BackBayalltheWay's? Why?

WRITING SUGGESTIONS

7. Write an evaluative essay analyzing Jacoby's essay.
8. Write an essay either agreeing with or arguing against Jacoby's thesis.

9. Write an essay explaining under what circumstances you feel the government —
   local, state, or federal — should step in and impose strict controls on the price of
   essential goods. (You will need to define what you mean by the term "essential
   goods.")

10. Write an essay explaining which of the two arguments about price gouging you
    think presents a better argument and why.

DEBATE   Is Recycling Plastic Good Stewardship or Bad Business?

Why Let Stewardship Get in the Way of a Quick Buck?
JOHN TROTTI

Send recycled plastic to China . . . four days later it's back as air pollution.
— UCLA PROFESSOR

It's time for us to take an honest look at recycling in the United States, focusing
attention on just what it is we're trying to accomplish in the light of environmental stewardship as well as societal needs. Allow me to air some thoughts here,
so you can decide whether this is a worthwhile subject for scrutiny.

It's becoming more and more apparent that many recycled materials have no
viable markets here — often, it is said, because of environmental concerns regarding their processing. And so instead of staying within our borders and under our
control, they are shipped abroad beyond the reach of our environmental regulations and/or permissible practices (WTE for instance[7]); thus their potential environmental impact is not mitigated but merely shifted overseas.

For example, discarded plastics are processed and then sold for around $0.21
per pound abroad, where routinely they are burned for their energy value in
combustors of dubious pollution prevention capability. Not surprisingly, there's
the small matter of air pollution borne on the north temperate zone's prevailing
west-to-east winds, in some cases coming to roost in its place of origin . . . a fitting
climax, all things considered.

This in itself would seem to be reason enough to question the wisdom of the
proposition, but wait . . . there's more.

---

[7] WTE stands for "Waste to Energy," and generally involves burning waste material to generate
electricity. Unregulated burning can provide toxic emissions. — EDS.

John Trotti is the editor of *MSW* [municipal solid waste] *Management* magazine. His article appeared in that publication in September 2008.

It takes about 12 barrels of oil to make one ton of polyethylene, which at to- 5
day's going rate amounts to something in the neighborhood of $115 each . . . so
let's do some math.

We take a commodity — oh, you don't like the word? — OK, a recycled material with a value on the local market of $1,380 and sell it abroad for $0.21 per
pound ($420 per ton). Does this sound a bit strange? Don't worry . . . it gets
stranger still.

After the discarded water- and pop bottles [on which advance disposal fees
were deposited at point-of-purchase] have been collected, sorted, compacted,
baled, and containerized at the ratepayers' expense, the freight is now moved by
surface transport to one of several seaports, where longshoremen stage and load it
aboard cargo vessels for shipment across the bounding main to customers whose
major challenge lies in how long it will take to off-load the recycled material and
commoditize it through the simple expedient of burning it for its caloric value.

Am I hallucinating this? Does the idea of giving up $960 worth of a valuable
commodity — one whose strategic significance ranks right up there with the proliferation of weapons of mass destruction — make sense somewhere or somehow?
Well, if you are so steeped in your belief that burning fuel for American energy
is bad, then shipping it to an economic competitor who intends to put it to the
torch with no pretense of environmental concern beyond a little rhetoric, makes
excellent sense.

Is this what you and I had in mind when we supported the rising tide of environmentalism back in the 1980s and '90s, or were we mistaken in viewing the
hierarchy as a means of forwarding and rewarding stewardship? I don't think so,
but let's look at where a decade-and-a-half has gotten us in terms of true stewardship. On the positive side of the ledger, we are diverting a far higher percentage of
our wastes away from our landfills, and we have seen a growing acceptance to the
use of recycled materials in a variety of products. So, too, have we seen an increase
in the public participation in recycling activities and the apparent success of recycling mandated targets. But are these the real measures of stewardship?

I don't know how much faith you and I should place in diversion figures from 10
around the nation, but supposing they're accurate, how germane are they if we've
relinquished the ability to participate responsibly in their return to the world of
commerce? To me that's the real issue, and I'm not sure those responsible for the
supposed success of recycling really want to know the answer.

DISCUSSION QUESTIONS

1. According to Trotti, what has happened to the "rising tide of environmentalism"
   that existed in the 1980s and 1990s?
2. What are his concerns about the way plastics are being disposed of?
3. Analyze his support. How convincing do you find it to be?
4. How convincing do you find his argument as a whole to be?
5. What is his warrant? Do you agree with it?

Argument for Recycling Is Strong

SHARON KNEISS

Recycling is an important and timely topic and a key contributor to a cleaner environment. We were disappointed to see that *MSW Management's* recent editorial oversimplified and overlooked many of the important gains that the US recycling industry has made in recent decades. Worse, the editorial may have left readers with a grossly inaccurate view of an industry with solid growth potential. The future of plastics recycling is actually quite bright. Here are the facts:

- The market for recycled plastic materials is strong.
- In order to increase recycling, we must work to increase collection opportunities.
- The export market is strong for recyclables based on pure economics.
- Seventy percent of plastics manufactured in the United States are made from natural gas.

Let's start with markets for recycled materials. In many cases, demand for recycled plastics has outpaced our ability to supply them. For almost fifteen years, there have been strong domestic markets to purchase recycled plastics, but the recycling industry has not been able to run at full capacity with limited quantities of collected materials. Today it is clearly the lack of supply of post-consumer plastics that keeps our markets from reaching their full potential.

With the current prices of recycled resins strong but still competitive with the prices of virgin resins, existing domestic markets could easily absorb an increase in supply — if we are able to boost the collection of post-consumer recycled materials. This is why the plastics industry is working aggressively to increase access to away-from-home recycling opportunities, boost municipal recycling of plastic bottles and non-bottle containers, and increase awareness through consumer education.

Despite strong domestic markets, about 50 percent of recovered PET and 20 percent of recovered HDPE is exported to China. Why? Simple economics — empty cargo ships headed back to China and a low wage rate make it difficult for domestic recyclers (particularly those on the West coast) to compete for the material. The important thing is that the materials are being purchased at a fair market price and recycled into useful new products.

But the most deeply concerning point in *MSW Management's* editorial is the suggestion that post-consumer plastics are exported to avoid the environmental impacts of recycling. The processes of cleaning, melting, and filtering post-consumer plastics are generally associated with very low levels of energy, minimal emissions, and tiny amounts of solid waste from labels, dirt, and other non-

5

Sharon Kneiss is vice president of the products divisions of the American Chemistry Council. Her response to Trotti appeared in the November–December 2008 edition of *MSW Management*.

recoverable components. In fact, the American Chemistry Council, Association of Postconsumer Plastics Recyclers, National Association for PET Container Resources, and the PET Resin Association are currently collaborating to generate life cycle inventory data to quantify these important environmental indicators for the plastics recycling industry. These data will be made publicly available as soon as they are complete.

The editorial also made a significant (but sadly common) mistake regarding energy used to produce plastics in the United States. Your column claims that "it takes about 12 barrels of oil to make one ton of polyethylene." Rather, it's barrels of oil equivalents — and the actual number is 10.2 barrels of oil equivalents. In the United States, 80 percent of polyethylene (and 70 percent of plastics overall) is made from domestic natural gas.

Finally, there is the issue of energy recovery, or waste-to-energy (WTE). We believe that *MSW Management*'s contention that plastics are sold abroad and "put to the torch" bears reconsidering because common sense suggests that in today's market it is unlikely that someone would pay a premium for recovered resins just to burn them. While these materials do have value as an energy source, that value is enhanced when recovered plastics are manufactured into useful and efficient new products.

The bottom line is that over the last two decades, plastics recycling has grown by leaps and bounds. Unlike the mixed streams that went straight into asphalt for pennies a pound, today's recovered plastics are sorted, cleaned, and processed to perform at levels competitive with virgin resins. We have versatile technologies, strong markets, and healthy demand both domestically and abroad. But our work is not finished. If the industry has an Achilles heel, it is collection. In our view, recovery is where we should be focusing our collective energies.

America's plastics producers are working to increase away-from-home recycling opportunities; to leverage our investments through creative new partnerships; and to increase the recycling of bottles, bags, rigid plastic containers, and even end-of-life vehicles. And above all, we are working to increase the collection of plastic through greater consumer education and awareness of recycling opportunities. We hope you will join us as we continue this industry's proud history of innovation by removing the remaining barriers to achieving our true recycling potential. Plastic is too valuable a resource to waste.

DISCUSSION QUESTIONS

1. How does Kneiss's view of the future of plastics recycling differ from Trotti's?
2. What does she see as the biggest obstacle to recycling at peak capacity?
3. What are the major flaws that Kneiss sees in Trotti's argument?
4. What suggestions does she have for improving plastics recycling?
5. How convincing is her support?
6. What warrant or warrants underlie her argument?
7. Which argument do you find more convincing, Trotti's or Kneiss's?

Assignments for Analyzing Warrants

READING AND DISCUSSION QUESTIONS

1. Should students be given a direct voice in the hiring of faculty members? On what warrants about education do you base your answer?

2. Discuss the validity of the warrant in this statement from the *Watch Tower* (a publication of the Jehovah's Witnesses) about genital herpes: "The sexually loose are indeed 'receiving in themselves the full recompense, which was their due for their error' (Romans 1:27)."

3. In 2010, a judge in Saudi Arabia had to make the decision whether or not a man could be intentionally paralyzed as punishment for having paralyzed another man in a fight. His victim had requested this punishment. What would the judge's warrant be if he chose to order the punishment? What would it be if he decided not to honor the victim's request?

4. In view of the increasing interest in health in general, and nutrition and exercise in particular, do you think that universities and colleges should impose physical education requirements? If so, what form should they take? If not, why not? What warrant underlies your position?

5. What are some of the assumptions underlying the preference for natural foods and medicines? Can *natural* be clearly defined? Is this preference part of a broader philosophy? Try to evaluate the validity of the assumption.

6. The author of the following passage, Katherine Butler Hathaway, became a hunchback as a result of a childhood illness. Here she writes about the relationship between love and beauty from the point of view of someone who is deformed. Discuss the warrants on which the author bases her conclusions.

   > I could secretly pretend that I had a lover . . . but I could never risk showing that I thought such a thing was possible for me . . . with any man. Because of my repeated encounters with the mirror and my irrepressible tendency to forget what I had seen, I had begun to force myself to believe and to remember, and especially to remember, that I would never be chosen for what I imagined to be the supreme and most intimate of all experience. I thought of sexual love as an honor that was too great and too beautiful for the body in which I was doomed to live.

WRITING ASSIGNMENTS

7. In "An Unjust Sacrifice," Robert A. Sirico presents a case in which he finds no justification for letting one Siamese twin die in order to save the other. His belief in the sanctity of human life appears to be absolute, even when it will most likely lead to the death of both twins. Write an essay in which you give examples of how your value system underlies your political views.

8. Write an essay explaining why you think either John Trotti or Sharon Kneiss make a better argument.

9. Both state and federal governments have been embroiled in controversies concerning the rights of citizens to engage in harmful practices. In Massachusetts, for

example, a mandatory seat-belt law was repealed by voters who considered the law an infringement of their freedom. (It was later reinstated.) Write an essay in which you explain what principles you believe should guide government regulation of dangerous practices.

10. Henry David Thoreau writes, "Unjust laws exist: Shall we be content to obey them, or shall we endeavor to amend them, and obey them until we have succeeded, or shall we transgress them at once?" Write an essay in which you explain under what circumstances you would feel compelled to break the law, or why you feel that you would never do so.

Research Readiness: Identifying Reliable Authorities

How can you tell which online information comes from reliable authorities?

In this chapter we have stressed the need for sufficient and appropriate data and reliable authorities. In Chapter 10 we will discuss, at length, how to research a topic and choose reliable sources for an independent research paper. Anytime you use someone else's words or ideas in your writing or formal speaking you should be aware who that person is; you can start now investigating the reliability of any sources you are thinking of quoting or paraphrasing.

We like to think that if information is in print, it is reliable. Unfortunately, that is not always the case. People with unjust biases and even those who want to sow hatred find their way into print. In general, works that appear in print go through a much more extensive vetting process than what appears online, but there are so-called vanity presses that will publish pretty much anything if the author will pay the cost. There are also all sorts of periodicals that express slanted — and often conflicting — points of view, some of them offensive to many of us. That's what comes of freedom of the press.

When you go online, how can you start to weed through a list of results to find reliable authorities? For one thing, you can learn to "read" the list of results you get from *Google* or other search engines.

ASSIGNMENT

1. Go to Google or another general search engine that you are familiar with. Do a search for either "autism and vaccines" or "cell phones and cancer." (You may have used one of these subjects for an earlier exercise.) Before you click on a link, examine the first ten to fifteen entries in the resulting list. Look at each URL and see what you can learn from it. Also notice any other information that might affect your opinion of the source's reliability or objectivity.

   • Are there sources that you immediately trust as reliable? Which ones, and why?

   • Are there any that you immediately assume will present a biased perspective? Which ones, and why?

   • Are there any that are completely unfamiliar to you? If so, choose two or three and speculate what type of source each might be.

2. Now click on a couple of the sources that you trusted as being reliable. Identify exactly who wrote the document that you have accessed. If you cannot find an author, what does that suggest? If there is an author, search that person's name and see if you find convincing credentials that support the assumption that he or she is qualified to write on the subject at hand.

3. Do the same with at least two sources that you predicted would be biased. Does further investigation support your assumption?

4. Go to at least one of the sources that were unfamiliar to you. Once you look more closely at the source, do you find any evidence of its reliability or lack thereof? Explain.

8

Logic

Throughout the book we have pointed out the weaknesses that cause arguments to break down. In the vast majority of cases these weaknesses represent breakdowns in logic or the reasoning process. We call such weaknesses *fallacies*, a term derived from Latin. Sometimes these false or erroneous arguments are deliberate; in fact, the Latin word *fallere* means "to deceive." But more often these arguments are either carelessly constructed or unintentionally flawed. Thoughtful readers learn to recognize them; thoughtful writers learn to avoid them.

The reasoning process was first given formal expression by Aristotle. In his famous treatises, he described the way we try to discover the truth — observing the world, selecting impressions, making inferences, generalizing. In this process Aristotle identified two forms of reasoning: *induction* and *deduction*. Both forms, he realized, are subject to error. Our observations may be incorrect or insufficient, and our conclusions may be faulty because they have violated the rules governing the relationship between statements. Induction and deduction are not reserved only for formal arguments about important problems; they also represent our everyday thinking about the most ordinary matters. As for the fallacies, they, too, unfortunately, may crop up anywhere, whenever we are careless in our use of the reasoning process.

In this chapter we examine some of the most common fallacies. First, however, a closer look at induction and deduction will make clear what happens when fallacies occur.

Induction

Induction is the form of reasoning in which we come to conclusions about the whole on the basis of observations of particular instances. If you notice that prices on the four items you bought in the campus bookstore are higher than similar items in the bookstore in town, you may come to the conclusion that the campus store is a more expensive place to shop. If you also noticed that most of the instructors you saw on the first day of school were wearing faded jeans and sandals, you might say that your school's teachers are generally informal in their dress. In both cases you have made an *inductive leap*, reasoning from what you have learned about a few examples to what you think is true of a whole class of things.

How safe are you in coming to these conclusions? The reliability of your conclusion depends on the quantity and quality of your observations. Were four items out of the thousands available in the campus store a sufficiently large sample? Would you come to the same conclusion if you chose fifty items? Might another selection have produced a different conclusion? As for the casually dressed instructors, perhaps further investigation would disclose that the teachers wearing jeans were all teaching assistants and that professors usually wore business clothes. Or the difference might lie in the academic discipline; anthropology teachers might turn out to dress less formally than business school teachers.

In these two situations, you could come closer to verifying your conclusions by further observation and experience — that is, by pricing more items at both stores over a longer period of time and by coming into contact with a greater number of teachers during a whole semester. Even without pricing every item in both stores or encountering every instructor on campus, you would be more confident of your generalization as the quality and quantity of your samples increased.

In some cases you can observe all the instances in a particular situation. For example, by acquiring information about the religious beliefs of all the residents of the dormitory, you can arrive at an accurate assessment of the number of Buddhists. But since our ability to make definitive observations about everything is limited, we must also make an inductive leap about categories of things that we ourselves can never encounter in their entirety. For some generalizations, as we have learned about evidence, we rely on the testimony of reliable witnesses who report that they have experienced or observed many more instances of the phenomenon. A television documentary may give us information about unwed teenage mothers in a city neighborhood; four girls are interviewed and followed for several days by the reporter. Are these girls typical of thousands of others? A sociologist on the program assures us that, in fact, they are. She herself has consulted with hundreds of other young mothers and can vouch for the fact that a conclusion about them, based on our observation of the four, will be sound. Obviously, though, our conclusion can only be probable, not certain. The sociologist's sample is large, but can account only for hundreds, not thousands, and there may be unexamined cases that will seriously weaken our conclusions.

In other cases, we may rely on a principle known in science as "the uniformity of nature." We assume that certain conclusions about oak trees in the temperate zone of North America, for example, will also be true for oak trees growing elsewhere under similar climatic conditions. We also use this principle in attempting to explain the causes of behavior in human beings. If we discover that institutionalization of some children from infancy results in severe emotional retardation, we think it safe to conclude that under the same circumstances all children would suffer the same consequences. As in the previous example, we are aware that certainty about every case of institutionalization is impossible. With rare exceptions, the process of induction can offer only probability, not certain truth.

SAMPLE ESSAY   An Inductive Argument

True or False: Schools Fail Immigrants

RICHARD ROTHSTEIN

A common indictment of public schools is that they no longer offer upward mobility to most immigrants. It is said that in the first half of the twentieth century, children learned English, went to college, and joined the middle class but that many of today's immigrants are more likely to drop out, take dead-end jobs, or end up in prison.

Many true accounts reinforce these beliefs. But less noticed are equally valid anecdotes pointing to an opposite claim.

Policy by anecdote is flawed because too often we notice only what confirms our preconceptions. California's recent experience with Mexican immigrants provides ample material for stories about school failure. But on a day to celebrate the American promise, we might also turn to anecdotes of another kind.

Recent college commencements across California featured many immigrants from impoverished families whose first language was Spanish, who came through much-maligned bilingual education programs, learned English, and now head for graduate schools or professions.

At California State University at Fresno, for example, about 700 of 4,000 gradu-   5
ates this spring were Latino, typically the first in their families to attend college. Top-ranked were Pedro Nava and Maria Rocio Magaña, Mexican-born children of farm laborers and cannery workers.

Mr. Nava did not settle in the United States until the third grade. Before that, he lived in migrant labor camps during harvests and in Mexico the rest of the year. His California schooling was in Spanish until the fifth grade, when he was moved to English instruction. Now, with a college degree, he has enrolled in management and teacher training courses.

Ms. Magaña did not place into English classes until the second half of the eleventh grade. Now fluent in both academic and conversational English, she will soon begin a Ph.D. program in anthropology at the University of Chicago.

Their achievements are not unique. Both credit success to their mothers' emphasis on education. Both mothers enrolled in English and high school equivalency courses at the local community college.

Richard Rothstein is a research associate of the Economic Policy Institute, a senior correspondent of the *American Prospect*, and the former national education columnist of the *New York Times*, where this article appeared on July 4, 2001. He is the author of *The Way We Were: Myths and Realities of America's Student Achievement* (1997), *All Else Equal: Are Public and Private Schools Different?* (2003), and *The Charter School Dust-Up* (2005).

Across California, these two-year institutions play an especially important role for immigrants.

Lourdes Andrade just finished her junior year at Brown University, having 10 transferred there after getting associate of arts degrees in history and liberal arts at Oxnard Community College, about forty miles northwest of Los Angeles.

Ms. Andrade arrived here at the age of four and all through elementary school worked with her mother making beds and cleaning bathrooms in hotels. Ms. Andrade, too, attributes her success to her mother's strong academic pressure and also to mentoring she received in a federally financed program to give extra academic support to migrant children.

The program's director, Lorenzo Moraza, also grew up speaking only Spanish. Now a school principal, Mr. Moraza estimates that about 30 percent of the immigrant children he has worked with acquired public school records that led them to college. Those who receive bachelor's degrees are many fewer, but Mr. Moraza says he thinks most drop out of college for economic reasons, not academic ones.

At the Fresno campus, nearly two-thirds of the immigrants and children of immigrants who enter as freshmen eventually graduate. The university operates special support services to help them do so.

You cannot spend time in California without noticing an extensive middle class of Latino schoolteachers, doctors, lawyers, and small-business people. Not all are recent immigrants, but many are. Some attended Catholic schools, but most are products of the public system. Many had bilingual education in the 1970s, 80s, and 90s. California has now banned such instruction, assuming it failed.

There are plenty of anecdotes to support a claim that schools fail immigrant 15 children or an equally persuasive claim that schools serve them well. Getting better statistics should be a priority. Government numbers do not distinguish between students who are immigrants (or whose parents immigrated) from Hispanics with American roots for several generations.

To help interpret California's experience, the best federal data tell only that in 1996, there were 100,000 college students nationwide who were American citizens born in Mexico. This is less than 1 percent of all college students. But uncounted are even larger numbers of those born here to recent migrants.

Even a balanced collection of anecdotes that include successes as well as failures cannot determine whether California schools are less effective than we should expect, and whether wholesale change is needed to move more immigrants to the middle class. But the answer is certainly more complex than the stereotypes of systematic failure that pervade most accounts.

Analysis

An inductive argument proceeds by examining particulars and arriving at a generalization that represents a probable truth. The author of this article arrives at the truth he will defend — that public schools have been more successful than is often acknowledged in moving many immigrants into the middle class — by offering statistical data and a number of stories about immigrants from poor families who have entered graduate school or one of the professions.

Rothstein begins, as many arguers do, with a brief summary of the popular position with which he disagrees. At the end of the third paragraph, he announces that he will provide examples that point to a different conclusion.

The reader should ask three questions of an inductive argument: Is the evidence sufficient? Is it representative? Is it up-to-date? The evidence that Rothstein assembles consists of a series of anecdotes and statistical data about the performance of immigrant students. The success stories of five real persons are impressive, despite limitations imposed by the brevity of the essay, in part because they offer vivid examples of struggle that appeal to our emotions and bring to life an issue with which some of us may not be familiar. But five stories are hardly enough to prove a case; perhaps they are not representative. Rothstein, therefore, adds other data about the rate at which immigrant students graduate and the growing number of Latino professionals and businesspeople.

Although the essay was published in 2001, his numbers are drawn from the 1990s and are thus a bit dated. A look at more recent data would reveal whether his conclusions remain valid.

The reader has some reason to believe that the facts are accurate. At the time this article was published, Rothstein wrote a regular column for a prestigious daily newspaper whose readers would have been quick to find errors in arguments of which they were critical. At the same time, he does not claim that his argument is beyond debate, since the data are incomplete. Even the title suggests that the issue is still unsettled. Modesty in the arguer is always welcome and disposes the reader to view the argument more favorably.

PRACTICE

Read Goldberg's essay "Connecting the Dots . . . to Terrorism" (p. 238). Explain how Goldberg uses inductive reasoning in the essay while not structuring the whole essay around it. What larger purpose does he have in the essay, and how does inductive reasoning help him achieve that purpose?

Deduction

While induction attempts to arrive at the truth, deduction guarantees sound relationships between statements. Unlike the conclusions from induction, which are only probable, the conclusions from deduction are certain. The simplest deductive argument consists of two premises and a conclusion. In outline such an argument looks like this:

Major Premise: All students with 3.5 averages and above for three years are invited to become members of Kappa Gamma Pi, the honor society.

| **Minor Premise:** | George has had a 3.8 average for over three years. |
| **Conclusion:** | Therefore, he will be invited to join Kappa Gamma Pi. |

This deductive conclusion is *valid*, or logically consistent, because it follows necessarily from the premises. No other conclusion is possible. Validity, however, refers only to the form of the argument. The argument itself may not be satisfactory if the premises are not true — if Kappa Gamma Pi has imposed other conditions or if George has only a 3.4 average. The difference between truth and validity is important because it alerts us to the necessity for examining the truth of the premises before we decide that the conclusion is sound.

One way of discovering how the deductive process works is to look at the methods used by Sherlock Holmes, that most famous of literary detectives, in solving his mysteries. His reasoning process follows a familiar pattern. Through the inductive process — that is, observing the particulars of the world — he came to certain conclusions about those particulars. Then he applied deductive reasoning to come to a conclusion about a particular person or event.

On one occasion Holmes observed that a man sitting opposite him on a train had chalk dust on his fingers. From this observation Holmes deduced that the man was a schoolteacher. If his thinking were outlined, it would take the form of the syllogism, the classic form of deductive reasoning:

Major Premise:	All men with chalk dust on their fingers are schoolteachers.
Minor Premise:	This man has chalk dust on his fingers.
Conclusion:	Therefore, this man is a schoolteacher.

One dictionary defines *syllogism* as "a formula of argument consisting of three propositions." The major premise offers a generalization about a large group or class. This generalization has been arrived at through inductive reasoning or observation of particulars. The minor premise makes a statement about a member of that group or class. The third proposition is the conclusion, which links the other two propositions, in much the same way that the warrant links the support and the claim.

If we look back at the syllogism that summarizes Holmes's thinking, we see how it represents the deductive process. The major premise, the first statement, is an inductive generalization, a statement arrived at after observation of a number of men with chalk on their fingers. The minor premise, the second statement, assigns a particular member, the man on the train, to the general class of those who have dust on their fingers.

But although the argument may be logical, it is faulty. The deductive argument is only as strong as its premises. As Lionel Ruby pointed out, Sherlock Holmes was often wrong.[1] Holmes once deduced from the size of a large hat found in the street that the owner was intelligent. He obviously believed that

---

[1] *The Art of Making Sense* (Philadelphia: Lippincott, 1954), ch. 17.

a large head meant a large brain and that a large brain indicated intelligence. Had he lived one hundred years later, new information about the relationship of brain size to intelligence would have enabled him to come to a different and better conclusion.

In this case, we might first object to the major premise, the generalization that all men with chalk dust on their fingers are schoolteachers. Is it true? Perhaps all the men with dusty fingers whom Holmes had so far observed had turned out to be schoolteachers, but was his sample sufficiently large to allow him to conclude that all dust-fingered men, even those with whom he might never have contact, were teachers? Were there no other vocations or situations that might require the use of chalk? In Holmes's day draftsmen or carpenters or tailors might have had fingers just as white as those of schoolteachers. In other words, Holmes may have ascertained that all schoolteachers have chalk dust on their fingers, but he had not determined that *only* schoolteachers could be thus identified. Sometimes it is helpful to draw a Venn diagram, circles representing the various groups in their relation to the whole.

If a large circle (see the figure below) represents all those who have chalk dust on their fingers, we see that several different groups may be contained in this universe. To be safe, Holmes should have deduced that the man on the train *might* have been a schoolteacher; he was not safe in deducing more than that. Obviously, if the inductive generalization or major premise is false, the conclusion of the particular argument is also false or invalid.

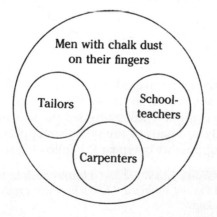

The deductive argument may also go wrong elsewhere. What if the minor premise is untrue? Could Holmes have mistaken the source of the white powder on the man's fingers? Suppose it was not chalk dust but flour or confectioner's sugar or talcum or heroin? Any of these possibilities would weaken or invalidate his conclusion.

Another example, closer to the kinds of arguments you will examine, reveals the flaw in the deductive process.

Major Premise:	All Communists oppose organized religion.
Minor Premise:	Robert Roe opposes organized religion.
Conclusion:	Therefore, Robert Roe is a Communist.

The common name for this fallacy is "guilt by association." The fact that two things share an attribute does not mean that they are the same thing. The following diagram makes clear that Robert Roe and Communists do not necessarily share all attributes. Remembering that Holmes may have misinterpreted the signs of chalk on the traveler's fingers, we may also want to question whether Robert Roe's opposition to organized religion has been misinterpreted.

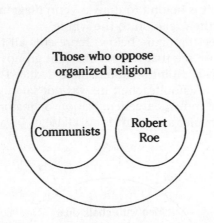

Those who oppose organized religion

Communists

Robert Roe

Some deductive arguments give trouble because one of the premises, usually the major premise, is omitted. As in the warrants we examined in Chapter 7, a failure to evaluate the truth of the unexpressed premise may lead to an invalid conclusion. When only two parts of the syllogism appear, we call the resulting form an *enthymeme*. Suppose we overhear the following snatch of conversation:

"Did you hear about Jean's father? He had a heart attack last week."
"That's too bad. But I'm not surprised. I know he always refused to go for his annual physical checkups."

The second speaker has used an unexpressed major premise, the cause-and-effect warrant "If you have annual physical checkups, you can avoid heart attacks." He does not express it because he assumes that it is unnecessary to do so. The first speaker recognizes the unspoken warrant and may agree with it. Or the first speaker may produce evidence from reputable sources that such a generalization is by no means universally true, in which case the conclusion of the second speaker is suspect.

A knowledge of the deductive process can help guide you toward an evaluation of the soundness of your reasoning in an argument you are constructing. The syllogism is often clearer than an outline in establishing the relations between the different parts of an argument.

Setting down your own or someone else's argument in this form will not necessarily give you the answers to questions about how to support your claim, but it should clearly indicate what your claims are and, above all, what logical connections exist between your statements.

SAMPLE ANNOTATED ESSAY   A Deductive Argument

It's All about Him

DAVID VON DREHLE

The author establishes his knowledge of mass murders, his "claim to authority."

My reporter's odyssey has taken me from the chill dawn outside the Florida prison in which serial killer Ted Bundy met his end, to the charred façade of a Bronx nightclub where Julio Gonzalez incinerated eighty-seven people, to a muddy Colorado hillside overlooking the Columbine High School library, in which Eric Harris and Dylan Klebold wrought their mayhem. Along the way, I've come to believe that we're looking for why in all the wrong places.

I've lost interest in the cracks, chips, holes, and broken places in the lives of men like Cho Seung-Hui, the mass murderer of Virginia Tech. The pain, grievances, and self-pity of mass killers are only symptoms of the real explanation. Those who do these things share one common trait. They are raging narcissists. "I died — like Jesus Christ," Cho said in a video sent to NBC.

His thesis statement (and major premise): mass murderers are narcissists

Psychologists from South Africa to Chicago have begun to recognize that extreme self-centeredness is the forest in these stories, and all the other things — guns, games, lyrics, pornography — are just trees. To list the traits of the narcissist is enough to prove the point: grandiosity, numbness to the needs and pain of others, emotional isolation, resentment, and envy.

The traits of the narcissist

In interviews with Ted Bundy taped a quarter-century ago, journalists Stephen Michaud and Hugh Aynesworth

---

David von Drehle is editor-at-large for *Time* magazine. His most recent book is *Triangle: The Fire That Changed America* (2003). This article appeared in *Time* on April 30, 2007.

captured the essence of homicidal narcissism. Through
hour after tedious hour, a man who killed 30 or more
young women and girls preened for his audience. He
spoke of himself as an actor, of life as a series of roles,
and of other people as props and scenery. His desires
were simple: "control" and "mastery." He took whatever
he wanted, from shoplifted tube socks to human lives,
because nothing mattered beyond his desires. Bundy
said he was always surprised that anyone noticed his
victims had vanished. "I mean, there are so many
people," he explained. The only death he regretted was
his own.

Criminologists distinguish between serial killers like   5
Bundy, whose crimes occur one at a time and who try
hard to avoid capture, and mass killers like Cho. But the
central role of narcissism plainly connects them. Only
a narcissist could decide that his alienation should be
underlined in the blood of strangers. The flamboyant

Other examples of narcissistic
mass murderers

nature of these crimes is like a neon sign pointing to
the truth. Charles Whitman playing God in his Texas
clock tower, James Huberty spraying lead in a California
restaurant, Harris and Klebold in their theatrical trench
coats — they're all stars in the cinema of their self-
absorbed minds.

Freud said narcissists never
grow up. They put their happiness over others' lives.

Freud explained narcissism as a failure to grow up. All
infants are narcissists, he pointed out, but as we grow, we
ought to learn that other people have lives independent
of our own. It's not their job to please us, applaud for us,
or even notice us — let alone die because we're unhappy.

A generation ago, the social critic Christopher Lasch
diagnosed narcissism as the signal disorder of contemporary American culture. The cult of celebrity, the marketing of instant gratification, skepticism toward moral
codes, and the politics of victimhood were signs of a
society regressing toward the infant stage. You don't have
to buy Freud's explanation or Lasch's indictment, however, to see an immediate danger in the way we examine
the lives of mass killers. Earnestly and honestly, detectives and journalists dig up apparent clues and weave
them into a sort of explanation. In the days after Columbine, for example, Harris and Klebold emerged as alien-

Investigators have failed
to recognize narcissism as
the real motivation in mass
murder cases.

ated misfits in the jock culture of their suburban high
school. We learned about their morbid taste in music and
their violent video games. Largely missing, though, was
the proper frame around the picture: the extreme narcis-

Major premise applied to Cho

sism that licensed these boys, in their minds, to murder their teachers and classmates.

Something similar is now going on with Cho, whose florid writings and videos were an almanac of gripes. "I'm so lonely," he moped to a teacher, failing to mention that he often refused to answer even when people said hello. Of course he was lonely.

Outside the context of narcissism, the murderers' actions can seem too logical.

In Holocaust studies, there is a school of thought that says to explain is to forgive. I won't go that far. But we must stop explaining killers on their terms. Minus the clear context of narcissism, the biographical details of these men can begin to look like a plausible chain of cause and effect — especially to other narcissists. And they don't need any more encouragement.

There's a telling moment in Michael Moore's film *Bowling for Columbine*, in which singer Marilyn Manson   10 dismisses the idea that listening to his lyrics contributed to the disintegration of Harris and Klebold. What the Columbine killers needed, Manson suggests, was for someone to listen to them. This is the narcissist's view of narcissism: Everything would be fine if only he received more attention. The real problem can be found in the killer's mirror.

The author reiterates that the killer's problem is not lack of attention but how the killer sees himself.

Analysis

Von Drehle wrote "It's All about Him" shortly after the 2007 massacre at Virginia Tech. Although we cannot know exactly how he arrived at the thesis, we can reasonably assume he went through something of an inductive process on the way to writing this deductive essay. Perhaps he read and watched enough about Cho, the shooter at Virginia Tech, to start to hypothesize about Cho's motivation. His earlier observations of other mass murderers led him to notice similarities among them. Once he arrived at a theory about what they had in common, he had the major premise for a deductive argument that he could test out on other mass murderers. He was able to construct an argument that could be summarized in syllogistic form:

Major Premise: Mass murderers are narcissistic.

Minor Premise: Cho was a mass murderer.

Conclusion: Cho was narcissistic.

In his essay he presents his major premise early and then applies it to other U.S. mass murderers: Ted Bundy, Charles Whitman, James Huberty, Eric Harris, and Dylan Klebold.

If von Drehle's major and minor premises are true, the conclusion, of necessity, must be true. That Cho was a mass murderer is an indisputable fact; thus the minor premise is true. But what of the major premise? If you applied the deduction that mass murderers are narcissistic to mass murderers not mentioned by von Drehle, would the conclusion be the same in each case? In other words, is it true that mass murderers are narcissistic?

Because it would be virtually impossible to apply von Drehle's deduction to all mass murderers, he would have built a more convincing case had he restricted his thesis statement with a word like *most* or *many*. That, however, would have invalidated the deductive logic that tells us that a syllogism's conclusion must be true. As it is, the examples he offers are not enough to convince all readers that his theory of narcissism is valid. Still, he offers a unique look at the motivation of mass murderers and one that makes it impossible for anyone else to be blamed for the crimes that these men and boys have committed. Behind his argument are his many years of journalistic experience and his opening revelation that he has been on the scene during the aftermath of many of the crimes to which he refers.

Common Fallacies

In this necessarily brief review it would be impossible to discuss all the fallacies listed by logicians, but we can examine the ones most likely to be found in the arguments you will read and write. Fallacies are difficult to classify, first, because there are literally dozens of systems for classifying, and second, because under any system there is always a good deal of overlap. Our discussion of the reasoning process, however, tells us where faulty reasoning occurs.

Inductive fallacies, as we know, result from the wrong use of evidence: That is, the arguer leaps to a conclusion on the basis of an insufficient sample, ignoring evidence that might have altered his or her conclusion. Deductive fallacies, on the other hand, result from a failure to follow the logic of a series of statements. Here the arguer neglects to make a clear connection between the parts of his or her argument. One of the commonest strategies is the introduction of an irrelevant issue, one that has little or no direct bearing on the development of the claim and serves only to distract the reader.

It's helpful to remember that, even if you cannot name the particular fallacy, you can learn to recognize it and not only refute it in the arguments of others but avoid it in your own as well.

Hasty Generalization

In Chapter 6 (see pp. 202–68) we discussed the dangers in drawing conclusions on the basis of insufficient evidence. Many of our prejudices are a result of hasty generalization. A prejudice is literally a judgment made before the facts are in. On the basis of experience with two or three members of an ethnic group, for example, we may form the prejudice that all members of the group share the characteristics that we have attributed to the two or three in our experience.

Superstitions are also based in part on hasty generalization. As a result of a very small number of experiences with black cats, broken mirrors, Friday the thirteenth, or spilled salt, some people will assume a cause-and-effect relation between these signs and misfortunes. *Superstition* has been defined as "a notion maintained despite evidence to the contrary." The evidence would certainly show that, contrary to the superstitious belief, in a lifetime hundreds of such "unlucky" signs are not followed by unfortunate events. To generalize about a connection is therefore unjustified.

Faulty Use of Authority

The use of authority — the attempt to bolster claims by citing the opinions of experts — was discussed in Chapter 6. Experts are a valuable source of information on subjects we have no personal experience with or specialized knowledge about. Properly identified, they can provide essential support. The faulty use of authority occurs when individuals are presented as authorities in fields in which they are not. An actor who plays a doctor on television may be hired to advertise the latest sleep medicine but actually has no more expertise with medications than the average consumer. The role that he plays may make him appear to be an authority but does not make him one. No matter how impressive credentials sound, they are largely meaningless unless they establish relevant authority. Both writers and readers need to be especially aware of the testimony of authorities who may disagree with those cited. In circumstances where experts disagree, you are encouraged to undertake a careful evaluation and comparison of credentials.

Post Hoc or Doubtful Cause

The entire Latin term for this fallacy is *post hoc, ergo propter hoc,* meaning, "After this, therefore because of this." The arguer infers that because one event follows another event, the first event must be the cause of the second. But proximity of events or conditions does not guarantee a causal relation. The rooster crows every morning at 5:00 and, seeing the sun rise immediately after, decides that his crowing has caused the sun to rise. A month after A-bomb tests are concluded, tornadoes damage the area where the tests were held, and residents decide that the tests caused the tornadoes. After the school principal suspends daily prayers in the classroom, acts of vandalism increase, and some parents are convinced that failure to conduct prayer is responsible for the rise in vandalism. In each of these cases, the fact that one event follows another does not prove a causal connection. The two events may be coincidental, or the first event may be only one, and an insignificant one, of many causes that have produced the second event. The reader or writer of causal arguments must determine whether another more plausible explanation exists and whether several causes have combined to produce the effect. Perhaps the suspension of prayer was only one of a number of related causes: a decline in disciplinary action, a relaxation of academic standards, a change in school administration, and changes in family structure in the school community.

In a previous section we saw that superstitions are the result not only of hasty generalization but also of the willingness to find a cause-and-effect connection in the juxtaposition of two events. A belief in astrological signs also derives from erroneous inferences about cause and effect. Only a very few of the millions of people who consult the astrology charts every day in newspapers and magazines have submitted the predictions to statistical analysis. A curious reader might try this strategy: Save the columns, usually at the beginning or end of the year, in which astrologers and clairvoyants make predictions for events in the coming year, allegedly based on their reading of the stars and other signs. At the end of the year evaluate the percentage of predictions that were fulfilled. The number will be very small. But even if some of the predictions prove true, there may be other less fanciful explanations for their accuracy.

In defending simple explanations against complex ones, philosophers and scientists often refer to a maxim called *Occam's razor*, a principle formulated by the medieval philosopher and theologian William of Occam. A modern science writer says this principle "urges a preference for the simplest hypothesis that does all we want it to do."[2] In other words, choose the simpler, more credible explanation wherever possible.

We all share the belief that scientific experimentation and research can answer questions about a wide range of natural and social phenomena: evolutionary development, hurricanes, disease, crime, poverty. It is true that repeated experiments in controlled situations can establish what seem to be solid relations suggesting cause and effect. But even scientists prefer to talk not about cause but about an extremely high probability that under controlled conditions one event will follow another.

In the social sciences cause-and-effect relations are especially susceptible to challenge. Human experiences can seldom be subjected to laboratory conditions. In addition, the complexity of the social environment makes it difficult, even impossible, to extract one cause from among the many that influence human behavior.

False Analogy

Many analogies are merely descriptive and offer no proof of the connection between the two things being compared. In recent years a debate has emerged between weight-loss professionals about the wisdom of urging overweight people to lose weight for health reasons. Susan Wooley, director of the eating disorders

---

[2]Martin Gardner, *The Whys of a Philosophical Scrivener* (New York: Quill, 1983), p. 174.

clinic at the University of Cincinnati and a professor of psychiatry, offered the following analogy in defense of her view that dieting is dangerous.

> We know that overweight people have a higher mortality rate than thin people. We also know that black people have a higher mortality rate than white people. Do we subject black people to torturous treatments to bleach their skin? Of course not. We have enough sense to know skin-bleaching will not eliminate sickle-cell anemia. So why do we have blind faith that weight loss will cure the diseases associated with obesity?[3]

But it is clear that the false analogy between black skin and excessive weight does not work. Bleaching one's skin does not eliminate sickle-cell anemia, but there is an abundance of proof that excess weight influences mortality.

Historians are fond of using analogical arguments to demonstrate that particular circumstances prevailing in the past are being reproduced in the present. They therefore feel safe in predicting that the present course of history will follow that of the past. British historian Arnold Toynbee argues by analogy that humans' tenure on earth may be limited.

> On the evidence of the past history of life on this planet, even the extinction of the human race is not entirely unlikely. After all, the reign of man on the Earth, if we are right in thinking that man established his present ascendancy in the middle paleolithic age, is so far only about 100,000 years old, and what is that compared to the 500 million or 900 million years during which life has been in existence on the surface of this planet? In the past, other forms of life have enjoyed reigns which have lasted for almost inconceivably longer periods — and which yet at last have come to an end.[4]

Toynbee finds similarities between the limited reigns of other animal species and the possible disappearance of the human race. For this analogy, however, we need to ask whether the conditions of the past, so far as we know them, at all resemble the conditions under which human existence on earth might be terminated. Is the fact that human beings are also members of the animal kingdom sufficient support for this comparison?

Ad Hominem

The Latin term *ad hominem* means "against the man" and refers to an attack on the person rather than on the argument or the issue. The assumption in such a fallacy is that if the speaker proves to be unacceptable in some way, his or her statements must also be judged unacceptable. Attacking the author of the statement is a strategy of diversion that prevents the reader from giving attention where it is due — to the issue under discussion.

---

[3] *New York Times,* April 12, 1992, sec. C, p. 43.
[4] *Civilization on Trial* (New York: Oxford University Press, 1948), pp. 162–63.

You might hear someone complain, "What can the priest tell us about marriage? He's never been married himself." This ad hominem accusation ignores the validity of the advice the priest might offer. In the same way an overweight patient might reject the advice on diet by an overweight physician. In politics it is not uncommon for antagonists to attack each other for personal characteristics that may not be relevant to the tasks they will be elected to perform. They may be accused of infidelity to their partners, homosexuality, atheism, or a flamboyant social life. Even if certain accusations should be proved true, voters should not ignore the substance of what politicians do and say in their public offices.

This confusion of private life with professional record also exists in literature and the other arts. According to their biographers, the American writers Thomas Wolfe, Robert Frost, and William Saroyan — to name only a few — and numbers of film stars, including Charlie Chaplin, Joan Crawford, and Bing Crosby, made life miserable for those closest to them. Having read about their unpleasant personal characteristics, some people find it hard to separate the artist from his or her creation, although the personality and character of the artist are often irrelevant to the content of the work.

Ad hominem accusations against the person do *not* constitute a fallacy if the characteristics under attack are relevant to the argument. If the politician is irresponsible and dishonest in the conduct of his or her personal life, we may be justified in thinking that the person will also behave irresponsibly and dishonestly in public office.

False Dilemma

As the name tells us, the false dilemma, sometimes called the *black-white fallacy,* poses an either-or situation. The arguer suggests that only two alternatives exist, although there may be other explanations of or solutions to the problem under discussion. The false dilemma reflects the simplification of a complex problem. Sometimes it is offered out of ignorance or laziness, sometimes to divert attention from the real explanation or solution that the arguer rejects for doubtful reasons.

You may encounter the either-or situation in dilemmas about personal choices. "At the University of Georgia," says one writer, "the measure of a man was football. You either played it or worshiped those who did, and there was no middle ground."[5] Clearly this dilemma — playing football or worshiping those who do — ignores other measures of manhood.

Politics and government offer a wealth of examples. In an interview with the *New York Times* in 1975, the Shah of Iran was asked why he could not introduce into his authoritarian regime greater freedom for his subjects. His reply was, "What's wrong with authority? Is anarchy better?" Apparently he considered that only two paths were open to him — authoritarianism or anarchy. Of course, democracy was also an option, which, perhaps fatally, he declined to consider.

---

[5]Phil Gailey, "A Nonsports Fan," *New York Times Magazine,* December 18, 1983, sec. 6, p. 96.

The fallacy of the false dilemma is when an argument presents only two choices.

Slippery Slope

If an arguer predicts that taking a first step will lead inevitably to a second, usually undesirable step, he or she must provide evidence that this will happen. Otherwise, the arguer is guilty of a slippery slope fallacy.

Predictions based on the danger inherent in taking the first step are commonplace:

Legalization of abortion will lead to murder of the old and the physically and mentally handicapped.

The Connecticut law allowing sixteen-year-olds and their parents to divorce each other will mean the death of the family.

If we ban handguns, we will end up banning rifles and other hunting weapons.

Distinguishing between probable and improbable predictions — that is, recognizing the slippery-slope fallacy — poses special problems because only future developments can verify or refute predictions. For example, in 1941 the imposition of military conscription aroused some opponents to predict that the draft was a precursor of fascism in this country. Only after the war, when 10 million draftees were demobilized, did it become clear that the draft had been an insufficient sign for a prediction of fascism. In this case the slippery-slope prediction of fascism might have been avoided if closer attention had been paid to other influences pointing to the strength of democracy.

More recently, the debate about cloning has raised fears of creation of genetic copies of adults. The *New York Times* reported that

> Many lawmakers today warned that if therapeutic cloning went forward, scientists would step onto a slippery slope that would inevitably lead to cloning people.[6]

Most scientists, however, reject this possibility for the foreseeable future.

Slippery-slope predictions are simplistic. They ignore not only the dissimilarities between first and last steps but also the complexity of the developments in any long chain of events.

Begging the Question

If the writer makes a statement that assumes that the very question being argued has already been proved, the writer is guilty of begging the question. In a letter to the editor of a college newspaper protesting the failure of the majority of students to meet the writing requirement because they had failed an exemption test, the writer said, "Not exempting all students who honestly qualify for exemption is an insult." But whether the students are honestly qualified is precisely the question that the exemption test was supposed to resolve. The writer has not proved that the students who failed the writing test were qualified for exemption. She has only made an assertion *as if* she had already proved it.

Circular reasoning is an extreme example of begging the question: "Women should not be permitted to join men's clubs because the clubs are for men only." The question to be resolved first, of course, is whether clubs for men only should continue to exist.

Straw Man

The straw-man fallacy consists of an attack on a view similar to but not the same as the one your opponent holds. It is a familiar diversionary tactic. The name probably derives from an old game in which a straw man was set up to divert attention from the real target that a contestant was supposed to knock down.

---

[6]August 1, 2001, sec. A, p. 11.

A straw-man argument attempts to divert attention away from the real issue.

One of the outstanding examples of the straw-man fallacy occurred in the famous Checkers speech of Senator Richard Nixon. In 1952, during his vice-presidential campaign, Nixon was accused of having appropriated $18,000 in campaign funds for his personal use. At one point in the radio and television speech in which he defended his reputation, he said:

> One other thing I probably should tell you, because if I don't they will probably be saying this about me, too. We did get something, a gift, after the election.
>
> A man down in Texas heard Pat on the radio mention the fact that our two youngsters would like to have a dog, and, believe it or not, the day before we left on this campaign trip we got a message from Union Station in Baltimore saying they had a package for us. We went down to get it. You know what it was?
>
> It was a little cocker spaniel dog, in a crate that he had sent all the way from Texas, black and white, spotted, and our little girl, Tricia, the six-year-old, named it Checkers.

And, you know, the kids, like all kids, loved the dog, and I just want to say this, right now, that regardless of what they say about it, we are going to keep it.[7]

Of course, Nixon knew that the issue was the alleged misappropriation of funds, not the ownership of the dog, which no one had asked him to return.

Two Wrongs Make a Right

The two-wrongs-make-a-right fallacy is another example of the way in which attention may be diverted from the question at issue.

After President Jimmy Carter in March 1977 attacked the human rights record of the Soviet Union, Russian officials responded:

As for the present state of human rights in the United States, it is characterized by the following facts: millions of unemployed, racial discrimination, social inequality of women, infringement of citizens' personal freedom, the growth of crime, and so on.[8]

The Russians made no attempt to deny the failure of *their* human rights record; instead they attacked by pointing out that the Americans are not blameless either.

Non Sequitur

The Latin term *non sequitur,* which means "it does not follow," is another fallacy of irrelevance. An advertisement for a book, *Worlds in Collision,* whose theories about the origin of the earth and evolutionary development have been challenged by almost all reputable scientists, states:

Once rejected as "preposterous"! Critics called it an outrage! It aroused incredible antagonism in scientific and literary circles. Yet half a million copies were sold and for twenty-seven years it remained an outstanding bestseller.

We know, of course, that the popularity of a book does not bestow scientific respectability. The number of sales, therefore, is irrelevant to proof of the book's theoretical soundness — a non sequitur.

Other examples sometimes appear in the comments of political candidates. Donald Trump, the wealthy real-estate developer, in considering a run for president of the United States in 2000, told an interviewer:

My entire life, I've watched politicians bragging about how poor they are, how they came from nothing, how poor their parents and grandparents were. And I said to myself, if they can stay so poor for so many genera-

---

[7]Radio and television address of Senator Nixon from Los Angeles on September 23, 1952.
[8]*New York Times,* March 3, 1977, p. 1.

tions, maybe this isn't the kind of person we want to be electing to higher office. How smart can they be? They're morons. . . . Do you want someone who gets to be president and that's literally the highest paying job he's ever had?[9]

As a brief glance at U.S. history shows, it does not follow that men of small success in the world of commerce are unfit to make sound decisions about matters of state.

Ad Populum

Arguers guilty of the *ad populum* fallacy make an appeal to the prejudices of the people (*populum* in Latin). They assume that their claim can be adequately defended without further support if they emphasize a belief or attitude that the audience shares with them. One common form of ad populum is an appeal to patriotism, which may allow arguers to omit evidence that the audience needs for proper evaluation of the claim. In the following advertisement the makers of Zippo lighters made such an appeal in urging readers to buy their product.

> It's a grand old lighter. Zippo — the grand old lighter that's made right here in the good old U.S.A.
> We truly make an all-American product. The raw materials used in making a Zippo lighter are all right from this great land of ours.
> Zippo windproof lighters are proud to be Americans.

Appeal to Tradition

In making an appeal to tradition, the arguer assumes that what has existed for a long time and has therefore become a tradition should continue to exist *because* it is a tradition. If the arguer avoids telling his or her reader *why* the tradition should be preserved, he or she may be accused of failing to meet the real issue.

The following statement appeared in a letter defending the membership policy of the Century Club, an all-male club established in New York City in 1847 that was under pressure to admit women. The writer was a Presbyterian minister who opposed the admission of women.

> I am totally opposed to a proposal which would radically change the nature of the Century. . . . A club creates an ethos of its own over the years, and I would deeply deplore a step that would inevitably create an entirely different kind of place.
> A club like the Century should surely be unaffected by fashionable whims. . . .[10]

[9]*New York Times,* November 28, 1999, p. 11.
[10]David H. C. Read, letter to the *New York Times,* January 13, 1983, p. 14.

Emotional appeals may be fallacious.

Faulty Emotional Appeals

In some discussions of fallacies, appeals to the emotions of the audience are treated as illegitimate or "counterfeit proofs." All such appeals, however, are *not* illegitimate. As we saw in Chapter 6 on support, appeals to the values and emotions of an audience are an appropriate form of persuasion. You can recognize fallacious emotional appeals if (1) they are irrelevant to the argument or draw attention from the issues being argued or (2) they appear to conceal another purpose. Here we treat two of the most popular appeals — to pity and to fear.

Appeals to pity, compassion, and natural willingness to help the unfortunate are particularly hard to resist. The requests for aid by most charitable organizations — for hungry children, victims of disaster, stray animals — offer examples of legitimate appeals. But these appeals to our sympathetic feelings should not divert us from considering other issues in a particular case. It would be wrong, for example, to allow a multiple murderer to escape punishment because he or she had experienced a wretched childhood. Likewise, if you are asked to contribute to a charitable cause, you should try to learn how many unfortunate people or animals are being helped and what percentage of the contribution will be allocated to maintaining the organization and its officers. In some cases the financial records are closed to public review, and only a small share of the contribution will reach the alleged beneficiaries.

Writer's Guide: Avoiding Logical Fallacies

1. If you are making use of induction, that is, drawing a conclusion based on a number of individual examples, do you have enough examples with variety to justify the conclusion? In other words, will your readers be able to make the inductive leap from examples to the conclusion you are asking them to make?

2. If you are making use of deduction, is your conclusion a logical one based on the premises underlying it? To be sure, write out your argument in the form of a syllogism. Also avoid wording your thesis in absolute terms like *all*, *every*, *everyone*, *everybody*, and *always*.

3. It is relatively easy — and sometimes humorous — to notice other writers' logical fallacies. It is harder to notice your own. Use the list of fallacies in this chapter as a checklist as you read the draft of each of your essays with a critical eye, looking for any breakdown in logic. It may be useful to read your essay aloud to someone because if that listener cannot follow your logic, you may need to clarify your points.

Appeals to fear are likely to be even more effective. But they must be based on evidence that fear is an appropriate response to the issues and that it can move an audience toward a solution to the problem. (Fear can also have the adverse effect of preventing people from taking a necessary action.) Insurance companies, for example, make appeals to our fears of destitution for ourselves and our families as a result of injury, unemployment, sickness, and death. These appeals are justified if the possibilities of such destitution are real and if the insurance will provide relief. It would also be legitimate to arouse fear of the consequences of drunk driving, provided, again, that the descriptions were accurate. On the other hand, it would be wrong to induce fear that fluoridation of public water supplies causes cancer without presenting sound evidence of the probability.

An emotional response by itself is not always the soundest basis for making decisions. Your own experience has probably taught you that in the grip of a strong emotion like love or hate or anger you often overlook good reasons for making different and better choices. Like you, your readers want to be given the opportunity to consider all the available kinds of support for an argument.

PRACTICE

Decide whether the reasoning in the following examples is faulty. Explain your answers.

1. The presiding judge of a revolutionary tribunal, being asked why people are being executed without trial, replies, "Why should we put them on trial when we know that they're guilty?"

2. The government has the right to require the wearing of helmets while operating or riding on a motorcycle because of the high rate of head injuries incurred in motorcycle accidents.

3. Children who watch game shows rather than situation comedies receive higher grades in school. So it must be true that game shows are more educational than situation comedies.

4. The meteorologist predicted the wrong amount of rain for May. Obviously the meteorologist is unreliable.

5. Women ought to be permitted to serve in combat. Why should men be the only ones to face death and danger?

6. If Lady GaGa uses Truvia, it must taste better than Splenda.

7. People will gamble anyway, so why not legalize gambling in this state?

8. Because so much money was spent on public education in the last decade while educational achievement declined, more money to improve education can't be the answer to reversing the decline.

9. He's a columnist for a campus newspaper, so he must be a pretty good writer.

10. We tend to exaggerate the need for Standard English. You don't need much Standard English for most jobs in this country.

11. It's discriminatory to mandate that police officers must conform to a certain height and weight.

12. A doctor can consult books to make a diagnosis, so a medical student should be able to consult books when being tested.

13. Because this soft drink contains so many chemicals, it must be unsafe.

14. Core requirements should be eliminated. After all, students are paying for their education, so they should be able to earn a diploma by choosing the courses they want.

15. We should encourage a return to arranged marriages in this country since marriages based on romantic love haven't been very successful.

16. I know three redheads who have terrible tempers, and since Annabel has red hair, I'll bet she has a terrible temper, too.

17. Supreme Court Justice Byron White was an all-American football player while in college, so how can you say that athletes are dumb?

18. Benjamin H. Sasway, a student at Humboldt State University in California, was indicted for failure to register for possible conscription. Barry Lynn, president of Draft Action, an antidraft group, said, "It is disgraceful that this administration is embarking on an effort to fill the prisons with men of conscience and moral commitment."

19. James A. Harris, former president of the National Education Association: "Twenty-three percent of schoolchildren are failing to graduate and another large segment graduates as functional illiterates. If 23 percent of anything else failed — 23 percent of automobiles didn't run, 23 percent of the buildings fell down, 23 percent of stuffed ham spoiled — we'd look at the producer."

20. A professor at Rutgers University: "The arrest rate for women is rising three times as fast as that of men. Women, inflamed by the doctrines of feminism, are pursuing criminal careers with the same zeal as business and the professions."

21. Physical education should be required because physical activity is healthful.

22. George Meany, former president of the AFL-CIO, in 1968: "To these people who constantly say you have got to listen to these younger people, they have got something to say, I just don't buy that at all. They smoke more pot than we do and if the younger generation are the hundred thousand kids that lay around a field up in Woodstock, New York, I am not going to trust the destiny of the country to that group."

23. That candidate was poor as a child, so he will certainly be sympathetic to the poor if he's elected.

24. When the federal government sent troops into Little Rock, Arkansas, to enforce integration of the public school system, the governor of Arkansas attacked the action, saying that it was as brutal an act of intervention as Russia's sending troops into Hungary to squelch the Hungarians' rebellion. In both cases, the governor said, the rights of a freedom-loving, independent people were being violated.

25. Governor Jones was elected two years ago. Since that time constant examples of corruption and subversion have been unearthed. It is time to get rid of the man responsible for this kind of corrupt government.

26. Are we going to vote a pay increase for our teachers, or are we going to allow our schools to deteriorate into substandard custodial institutions?

27. You see, the priests were right. After we threw those virgins into the volcano, it quit erupting.

28. The people of Rome lost their vitality and desire for freedom when their emperors decided that the way to keep them happy was to provide them with bread and circuses. What can we expect of our own country now that the government gives people free food and there is a constant round of entertainment provided by television?

29. From Mark Clifton, "The Dread Tomato Affliction" (proving that eating tomatoes is dangerous and even deadly): "Ninety-two point four percent of juvenile delinquents have eaten tomatoes. Fifty-seven point one percent of the adult criminals in penitentiaries throughout the United States have eaten tomatoes. Eighty-four percent of all people killed in automobile accidents during the year have eaten tomatoes."

30. From Galileo, *Dialogues Concerning Two New Sciences*: "But can you doubt that air has weight when you have the clear testimony of Aristotle affirming that all elements have weight, including air, and excepting only fire?"

31. Robert Brustein, artistic director of the American Repertory Theatre, commenting on a threat by Congress in 1989 to withhold funding from an offensive art show: "Once we allow lawmakers to become art critics, we take the first step into the world of Ayatollah Khomeini, whose murderous review of *The Satanic Verses* still chills the heart of everyone committed to free expression." (The Ayatollah Khomeini called for the death of the author Salman Rushdie because Rushdie had allegedly committed blasphemy against Islam in his novel.)

READINGS FOR ANALYSIS

On Nation and Race

ADOLF HITLER

There are some truths which are so obvious that for this very reason they are not seen or at least not recognized by ordinary people. They sometimes pass by such truisms as though blind and are most astonished when someone suddenly discovers what everyone really ought to know. Columbus's eggs lie around by the hundreds of thousands, but Columbuses are met with less frequency.

Thus men without exception wander about in the garden of Nature; they imagine that they know practically everything and yet with few exceptions pass blindly by one of the most patent principles of Nature's rule: the inner segregation of the species of all living beings on this earth.

Even the most superficial observation shows that Nature's restricted form of propagation and increase is an almost rigid basic law of all the innumerable forms of expression of her vital urge. Every animal mates only with a member of the same species. The titmouse seeks the titmouse, the finch the finch, the stork the stork, the field mouse the field mouse, the dormouse the dormouse, the wolf the she-wolf, etc.

Only unusual circumstances can change this, primarily the compulsion of captivity or any other cause that makes it impossible to mate within the same species. But then Nature begins to resist this with all possible means, and her most visible protest consists either in refusing further capacity for propagation to bastards or in limiting the fertility of later offspring; in most cases, however, she takes away the power of resistance to disease or hostile attacks.

This is only too natural.

Any crossing of two beings not at exactly the same level produces a medium between the level of the two parents. This means: The offspring will probably stand higher than the racially lower parent, but not as high as the higher one. Consequently, it will later succumb in the struggle against the higher level. Such mating is contrary to the will of Nature for a higher breeding of all life. The precondition for this does not lie in associating superior and inferior, but in the total victory of the former. The stronger must dominate and not blend with the weaker, thus sacrificing his own greatness. Only the born weakling can view this as cruel, but he after all is only a weak and limited man; for if this law did not prevail, any conceivable higher development of organic living beings would be unthinkable.

5

Adolf Hitler (1889–1945) became the Nazi dictator of Germany in the mid-1930s. "On Nation and Race" (editor's title) begins Chapter 11 of *Mein Kampf* (*My Struggle*), vol. 1, published in 1925.

The consequence of this racial purity, universally valid in Nature, is not only the sharp outward delimitation of the various races, but their uniform character in themselves. The fox is always a fox, the goose a goose, the tiger a tiger, etc., and the difference can lie at most in the varying measure of force, strength, intelligence, dexterity, endurance, etc., of the individual specimens. But you will never find a fox who in his inner attitude might, for example, show humanitarian tendencies toward geese, as similarly there is no cat with a friendly inclination toward mice.

Therefore, here, too, the struggle among themselves arises less from inner aversion than from hunger and love. In both cases, Nature looks on calmly, with satisfaction, in fact. In the struggle for daily bread all those who are weak and sickly or less determined succumb, while the struggle of the males for the female grants the right or opportunity to propagate only to the healthiest. And struggle is always a means for improving a species' health and power of resistance and, therefore, a cause of its higher development.

If the process were different, all further and higher development would cease and the opposite would occur. For, since the inferior always predominates numerically over the best, if both had the same possibility of preserving life and propagating, the inferior would multiply so much more rapidly that in the end the best would inevitably be driven into the background, unless a correction of this state of affairs were undertaken. Nature does just this by subjecting the weaker part to such severe living conditions that by them alone the number is limited, and by not permitting the remainder to increase promiscuously, but making a new and ruthless choice according to strength and health.

No more than Nature desires the mating of weaker with stronger individuals,   10
even less does she desire the blending of a higher with a lower race, since, if she did, her whole work of higher breeding, over perhaps hundreds of thousands of years, might be ruined with one blow.

Historical experience offers countless proofs of this. It shows with terrifying clarity that in every mingling of Aryan blood with that of lower peoples the result was the end of the cultured people. North America, whose population consists in by far the largest part of Germanic elements who mixed but little with the lower colored peoples, shows a different humanity and culture from Central and South America, where the predominantly Latin immigrants often mixed with the aborigines on a large scale. By this one example, we can clearly and distinctly recognize the effect of racial mixture. The Germanic inhabitant of the American continent, who has remained racially pure and unmixed, rose to be master of the continent; he will remain the master as long as he does not fall a victim to defilement of the blood.

The result of all racial crossing is therefore in brief always the following:

(a) Lowering of the level of the higher race;

(b) Physical and intellectual regression and hence the beginning of a slowly but surely progressing sickness.

To bring about such a development is, then, nothing else but to sin against   15
the will of the eternal creator.

And as a sin this act is rewarded.

When man attempts to rebel against the iron logic of Nature, he comes into struggle with the principles to which he himself owes his existence as a man. And this attack must lead to his own doom.

Here, of course, we encounter the objection of the modern pacifist, as truly Jewish in its effrontery as it is stupid! "Man's role is to overcome Nature!"

Millions thoughtlessly parrot this Jewish nonsense and end up by really imagining that they themselves represent a kind of conqueror of Nature; though in this they dispose of no other weapon than an idea, and at that such a miserable one, that if it were true no world at all would be conceivable.

But quite aside from the fact that man has never yet conquered Nature in   20
anything, but at most has caught hold of and tried to lift one or another corner of her immense gigantic veil of eternal riddles and secrets, that in reality he invents nothing but only discovers everything, that he does not dominate Nature, but has only risen on the basis of his knowledge of various laws and secrets of Nature to be lord over those other living creatures who lack this knowledge — quite aside from all this, an idea cannot overcome the preconditions for the development and being of humanity, since the idea itself depends only on man. Without human beings there is no human idea in this world; therefore, the idea as such is always conditioned by the presence of human beings and hence of all the laws which created the precondition for their existence.

And not only that! Certain ideas are even tied up with certain men. This applies most of all to those ideas whose content originates, not in an exact scientific truth, but in the world of emotion, or, as it is so beautifully and clearly expressed today, reflects an "inner experience." All these ideas, which have nothing to do with cold logic as such, but represent only pure expressions of feeling, ethical conceptions, etc., are chained to the existence of men, to whose intellectual imagination and creative power they owe their existence. Precisely in this case the preservation of these definite races and men is the precondition for the existence of these ideas. Anyone, for example, who really desired the victory of the pacifistic idea in this world with all his heart would have to fight with all the means at his disposal for the conquest of the world by the Germans; for, if the opposite should occur, the last pacifist would die out with the last German, since the rest of the world has never fallen so deeply as our own people, unfortunately, has for this nonsense so contrary to Nature and reason. Then, if we were serious, whether we liked it or not, we would have to wage wars in order to arrive at pacifism. This and nothing else was what Wilson, the American world savior, intended, or so at least our German visionaries believed — and thereby his purpose was fulfilled.

In actual fact the pacifistic-humane idea is perfectly all right perhaps when the highest type of man has previously conquered and subjected the world to an extent that makes him the sole ruler of this earth. Then this idea lacks the power of producing evil effects in exact proportion as its practical application becomes rare and finally impossible. Therefore, first struggle and then we shall see what can be done. Otherwise mankind has passed the high point of its development and the end is not the domination of any ethical idea but barbarism and consequently chaos. At this point someone or other may laugh, but this planet once moved through the ether for millions of years without human beings and it can do so again some day if men forget that they owe their higher existence, not to the ideas of a few crazy ideologists, but to the knowledge and ruthless application of Nature's stern and rigid laws.

Everything we admire on this earth today — science and art, technology and inventions — is only the creative product of a few peoples and originally perhaps of *one* race. On them depends the existence of this whole culture. If they perish, the beauty of this earth will sink into the grave with them.

However much the soil, for example, can influence men, the result of the influence will always be different depending on the races in question. The low fertility of a living space may spur the one race to the highest achievements; in others it will only be the cause of bitterest poverty and final undernourishment with all its consequences. The inner nature of peoples is always determining for the manner in which outward influences will be effective. What leads the one to starvation trains the other to hard work.

All great cultures of the past perished only because the originally creative race   25
died out from blood poisoning.

The ultimate cause of such a decline was their forgetting that all culture depends on men and conversely; hence that to preserve a certain culture the man who creates it must be preserved. This preservation is bound up with the rigid law of necessity and the right to victory of the best and stronger in this world.

Those who want to live, let them fight, and those who do not want to fight in this world of eternal struggle do not deserve to live.

Even if this were hard — that is how it is! Assuredly, however, by far the harder fate is that which strikes the man who thinks he can overcome Nature, but in the last analysis only mocks her. Distress, misfortune, and diseases are her answer.

The man who misjudges and disregards the racial laws actually forfeits the happiness that seems destined to be his. He thwarts the triumphal march of the best race and hence also the precondition for all human progress, and remains, in consequence, burdened with all the sensibility of man, in the animal realm of helpless misery.

It is idle to argue which race or races were the original representative of human   30
culture and hence the real founders of all that we sum up under the word *humanity*. It is simpler to raise the question with regard to the present, and here an easy, clear answer results. All the human culture, all the results of art, science, and technology that we see before us today, are almost exclusively the creative product of the Aryan. This very fact admits of the not unfounded inference that he alone was the founder of all higher humanity, therefore representing the prototype of all that we understand by the word *man*. He is the Prometheus of mankind from whose bright forehead the divine spark of genius has sprung at all times, forever kindling anew that fire of knowledge which illumined the night of silent mysteries and thus caused man to climb the path to mastery over the other beings of this earth. Exclude him — and perhaps after a few thousand years darkness will again descend on the earth, human culture will pass, and the world turn to a desert.

READING AND DISCUSSION QUESTIONS

1. Find places in the essay where Hitler attempts to emphasize the scientific objectivity of his theories.

2. Are some passages difficult to understand? (See, for example, para. 11.) How do you explain the difficulty?

3. In explaining his ideology, how does Hitler misinterpret the statement that "Every animal mates only with a member of the same species" (para. 3)? How would you characterize this fallacy?

4. Hitler uses the theory of evolution and his interpretation of the "survival of the fittest" to justify his racial philosophy. Find the places in the text where Hitler reveals that he misunderstands the theory in its application to human beings.

5. What false evidence about race does Hitler use in his assessment of the racial experience in North America? Examine carefully the last sentence of paragraph 11: "The Germanic inhabitant of the American continent, who has remained racially pure and unmixed, rose to be master of the continent; he will remain the master as long as he does not fall a victim to defilement of the blood."

6. What criticism of Jews does Hitler offer? How does this criticism help to explain Hitler's pathological hatred of Jews?

7. Hitler believes that pacifism is a violation of "Nature and reason" (para. 21). Would modern scientists agree that the laws of nature require unremitting struggle and conflict between human beings — until the master race conquers?

WRITING SUGGESTIONS

8. Use your responses to the Reading and Discussion Questions as the basis of an essay evaluating Hitler's logic in "On Nation and Race."

9. Do some research in early human history to discover the degree of truth in this statement: "All the human culture, all the results of art, science, and technology that we see before us today, are almost exclusively the creative product of the Aryan" (para. 30). You may want to limit your discussion to one area of human culture.

Teen Sex: The "Holy" vs. Humanistic Approach

LEON F. SELTZER AND DAVID NIOSE

With all the harsh rhetoric of the culture wars, it's easy to forget that secular humanists and conservative Christians share much common ground — even in the sensitive realm of parenting and education. After all, in one way or another, who *doesn't* want their kids to be well-adjusted, honest, and hard-working?

Leon F. Seltzer is a clinical psychologist and author of *Paradoxical Strategies in Psychotherapy* (1986). He coauthored this essay with David Niose, president of the American Humanist Association. It appeared on psychologytoday.com on August 5, 2010.

In some areas, however — such as the teaching of evolution, school prayer, and church-state separation — major ideological differences separate these two camps. And perhaps the most pointed example of this contrast involves premarital sex, particularly as it relates to teens.

The conservative Christian view on teen premarital sex is simple and straight-forward. It's wrong; sinful. And the unyielding nature of this approach explains why such Christians lobby incessantly against public school sex education that goes beyond teaching (preaching?) abstinence, despite all the studies now demonstrating that "abstinence-only" programs serve not to decrease but *increase* the risk of pregnancy and sexually transmitted diseases (STDs).

For example, a September 2009 study in the *Sexuality Research and Social Policy Journal* reported that most abstinence programs fail to delay sexual initiation, while more comprehensive programs show a positive impact, including postponing sexual activity and increasing contraceptive use. Complementing these findings is a January 2007 study published in the *American Journal of Public Health* which concluded that declining teen pregnancy rates in the United States were primarily attributable to improved contraception (and not to abstinence-only education).

As opposed to conservative Christian beliefs about pre-marital sex, the secular   5
humanist view — which is atheistic or, better, non-theistic — doesn't start with "pre-ordained" assumptions about right and wrong but attempts to understand this basic libidinal drive holistically. By seeing sexuality not from the perspective of established religious dogma, but from a bio-socio-cultural vantage point, humanists endeavor to help young people better grasp the complex nature of sexual intimacy. To prompt them to consider the various ramifications — ethical and otherwise — of unrestrainedly letting loose their libido. And to have them question whether giving unmitigated expression to their erotic impulses is finally in their best interests.

These considerations don't necessarily mean waiting until marriage to (relationally, at least) express their sexuality. But hopefully, such self-scrutiny does mean that should they choose to become sexually active, their decision won't be purely emotional, or testosterone-driven; and that it won't, recklessly, put their healthy development or overall well-being at risk either.

Gloria Steinem (an American Humanist Association award winner) has argued — similar to other humanists — for comprehensive sex education, stressing that abstinence-only-until-marriage programs fail to arm teenagers with the essential knowledge required to protect themselves against STDs and pregnancy. And Alice Walker (1997 AHA Humanist of the Year) echoed the view of humanists generally when she stated that sexuality should be acknowledged, affirmed — and even celebrated; and that the practice of punishing young women for enjoying sex is both damaging and counterproductive. Her position calls not for permissiveness as such, but for a healthier understanding of sexuality as a natural phenomenon — not a double-edged "gift" from God, tempting us to stray even as it ensures procreation.

Humanists' respect for our basic nature (sexual or otherwise) leads them to search for solutions consonant with who we actually are — rather than prescribing some artificially decreed, or "unnatural," code of conduct, which can bend us out of shape and eventuate in frustrating feelings of deprivation and unfulfillment. What humanists see as "naturalistic solutions" certainly consider the personal constraints requisite for maintaining a civilized society. But they also affirm that individual and social welfare are complementary, and that personal fulfillment (even while necessitating a certain amount of restraint and self-control) is best achieved through first understanding what is inherent about human nature. Not in a biblical sense, but scientifically. Solutions that result from such an approach are designed to affirm universal values — independent of custom and tradition, time and place.

Much conservative religious dogma approaches sexuality (especially unmarried, teenage sexuality) as inherently objectionable, base and ignoble. Humanists, however, avoid taking such unquestioned, categorical positions. What's ideal to them is that which — in a flexible, non-authoritarian way — complies with The Golden Rule (attempting to honor everyone, and shame no one). This fundamental, overarching ethical tenet — which transcends all historical, religious, and philosophical biases — aspires to integrate the pure with the pragmatic and, above all, "do no harm" to anyone (including one's self).

Moreover, not simply in matters of sexuality but in all areas of ethics and morality, humanism strives to put as few limits on personal freedom and self-expression as possible. At the same time, the positions taken by humanists (see http://www.americanhumanist.org/Who_We_Are/About_Humanism) are ever-mindful of the need to protect society from being trampled upon by rash or rampant hedonism — or anything else that doesn't sufficiently respect the humanity of all of us.   10

Perceiving human sexuality from a viewpoint grounded both in science and nature — as opposed, that is, to some pre-ordained, or "consecrated," fundamentalist Christian viewpoint — humanists search out all relevant information (and seek to verify it) before arriving at a decision. Ethical criteria are definitely part of the equation here — and perhaps the ultimate part at that. But such criteria are still considered in the context of undeniable human realities.

That said, let's look at the facts as they apply to the multiple issues surrounding teen sexuality. One anomalous characteristic of human society (at least in modern western culture) is that, for social reasons, we discourage mating until many years after our children reach the age of fertility. The very notion of an animal's reaching reproductive age but then being forced to wait — at minimum, six to ten years or more — before mating, is rarely, if ever, found elsewhere in nature (except where it's involuntary, due to competitive factors).

This counter-to-nature mating delay can best be understood as tied to the enormous social, economic, and technological changes that have taken place in our modern era. Before then, mating occurred "naturally" — at, or soon after, puberty. Only in modern industrial society do humans find themselves in cultures requiring an unnaturally extended period of sexual dormancy.

Think of it. What could be more antithetical to our nature?! Nonetheless, these facts aren't meant to imply that teen sex should be encouraged simply because that's what's natural. Acknowledging our inborn sexual proclivities hardly constitutes an endorsement of hedonistic romps. But such recognition does represent a good starting point for a productive — and compassionate — discussion of the many intricate issues linked to premarital sex.

We also need to consider, however, that as human animals we've developed   15
technology that has completely transformed our environment. Not only have we constructed highly complex technological societies (with, as already mentioned, economic and social systems that encourage postponing sexual reproduction well into adulthood), we've also developed the remarkable ability to control our reproductive lives through reliable (and easily obtainable) birth control. As a consequence, many of us enjoy unprecedented material comfort and convenience — and, frankly, without the burden of undesired reproductive obligations.

But, alas, our advanced technology and material riches (comparatively speaking, at least) have hardly brought us a utopia. Perhaps because of the dominance of our economic, corporate, and media cultures, our fundamental nature — biological, psychological, and sexual — has in many respects not so much been nurtured as exploited. The same terms that provide unprecedented abundance can also rob us of what we most crave spiritually (or, as some humanists would prefer to put it, non-materially). And they can actually discourage us (and have discouraged us) from living our lives with intelligence and discernment — from acting in what, finally, is in our best interests.

This is nothing short of tragic. For in many ways contemporary society would seem to offer us the best opportunity to achieve personal fulfillment in so many areas of life (including sexual). Yet we seem to inhabit a socio-political environment that often fails to produce a population "adult enough" to seek such fulfillment — let alone achieve it. Attention spans get shorter, instant gratification predominates, intellectual inquiry is often downplayed (or even ridiculed), and meaningful relationships that might have been never really develop. Living in such a society, it's not at all surprising that for a great many individuals a mature understanding of intimacy is sadly lacking. Yet who would deny that being able to wisely mentor our children about how best to deal with their budding sexuality is crucial to good teen parenting?

Returning to the specific theme of this piece, few (if any!) humanist parents would jump for joy at the news that their fifteen-year-old had become sexually active. Their discomfort, however, would not at all relate to seeing their teenage child as having committed a mortal sin. No, their upset would be tied to the threat of their child's being saddled with an unwanted pregnancy — and how this might sabotage the child's future. And they'd certainly worry about their child's emotional readiness to be exploring their sexuality with another at such a tender age. If the relationship soured, would the child be mature enough to handle the fallout? Or might the relationship's "sexual chemistry" prompt the child to impulsively make a commitment oblivious to far more important areas of compatibility? Or, if the child had become indiscriminately sexual, how might that affect their academic performance and later social adjustment; or — more important still — their values and moral development? And what about the risks of an STD? and so on, and so on. . . .

In short, such parents would be examining the situation in a multi-faceted way: developmentally, psycho-socially, and ethically. Without adhering to any traditional faith, caring and responsible parents would yet have much to consider in talking with their child. But they wouldn't begin and end simply by condemning the child because they judged their behavior reprehensible, shameful, or "unholy."

Ironically, though from a different vantage point (and probably with greater   20 tolerance for some teen sexual experimentation), humanist parents would reach pretty much the same conclusion as would their conservative Christian counterparts. That is, both sets of parents would strongly prefer that their child wasn't sexually active. And, of course, that when they did express their sexuality, they did so prudently — and with a more grown-up understanding of what they were getting themselves into. Virtually all parents (whether they're able to articulate it or not) hope that their children will develop the ability to grasp the various ramifications not simply of sexual intimacy but of more general relational intimacy.

The difference, then, between the secular humanist and the conservative Christian viewpoint toward teen sexuality is not so much in the conclusions they arrive at, but in how these conclusions are reached. For secular humanists, matters of shame, divine judgment, or biblical reference do not enter into the deliberative process. Rather, questions of teen sexuality are investigated primarily from scientifically studying nature, with answers derived not from theology but the natural world. Basic human drives are recognized and respected. But in the end, all natural impulses (however strong, tempting, or erotic) are evaluated in the larger context of core individual and societal needs. And intellect — vs. faith — is employed to prepare them, as parents, to provide the best possible guidance for their children.

READING AND DISCUSSION QUESTIONS

1. What Rogerian strategy do Seltzer and Niose use in the first paragraph?
2. Summarize the differences that the authors see between the conservative Christian view of premarital sex and that of the secular humanists.
3. What types of support do Seltzer and Niose make use of in the essay? How effective are they?
4. What do these authors mean when they say that secular humanists advocate a "holistic" approach to understanding human sexuality?
5. Why do the authors feel that a secular humanist approach to sexuality is better for teens than a conservative Christian approach?
6. In what ways does the secular humanist's view of sexuality affirm universal values?
7. How have social, economic, and technological changes in society affected human sexuality?
8. Near the end of the essay, the authors once again try to establish common ground. How?
9. What fallacy does the last sentence illustrate?
10. How convincing do you find Seltzer and Niose's logical support for their position to be?

WRITING SUGGESTIONS

11. Write an essay explaining which points that Seltzer and Niose make in the essay would be acceptable to a conservative Christian audience. In other words, where is there common ground between conservative Christians and secular humanists?

12. Write an essay explaining how realistic you find the authors' suggestions for approaching human sexuality to be.

13. Write an essay expanding on the authors' point that the conservative Christian view of premarital sex is incompatible with the modern world.

Food for Thought (and for Credit)

JENNIFER GROSSMAN

Want to combat the epidemic of obesity? Bring back home economics. Before you choke on your 300-calorie, trans-fat-laden Krispy Kreme, consider: Teaching basic nutrition and food preparation is a far less radical remedy than gastric bypass surgery or fast-food lawsuits. And probably far more effective. Obesity tends to invite such drastic solutions because it is so frustratingly difficult to treat. This intractability, coupled with the sad fact that obese children commonly grow up to be obese adults, argues for a preventative approach. As the new school year begins, we need to equip kids with the skills and practical knowledge to take control of their dietary destinies.

Despite its bad rep as Wife Ed 101, home economics has progressive roots. At the turn of the century it "helped transform domesticity into a vehicle to expand women's political power," according to Sarah Stage in *Rethinking Home Economics: Women and the History of a Profession*. In time, focus shifted from social reform to the practical priorities of sanitation and electrification, and then again to an emphasis on homemaking after World War II — giving ammunition to later critics like Betty Friedan who charged home ec with having helped foster the "feminine mystique."

Banished by feminists, Becky Home-ecky was left to wander backwater school districts. For a while it seemed that mandating male participation might salvage the discipline while satisfying political correctness. By the late 1970s one-third of male high school graduates had some home-ec training, whereas they comprised a mere 3.5 percent of home-ec students in 1962. Since then, "home economics has moved

---

Jennifer Grossman is vice president of the Dole Nutrition Institute, which distributes health information to the public through lectures and publications. Formerly, she was director of Education Policy at the Cato Institute and a speechwriter for President George H. W. Bush. She has written editorials for the *New York Times*, where this column appeared on September 2, 2003; the *Wall Street Journal*; the *Los Angeles Times*; the *New York Post*; the *Weekly Standard*; the *National Review*; and the *Women's Quarterly*.

from the mainstream to the margins of American high school," according to the United States Department of Education, with even female participation — near universal in the 1950s — plummeting by 67 percent.

What has happened since? Ronald McDonald and Colonel Sanders stepped in as the new mascots of American food culture, while the number of meals consumed outside the home has doubled — from a quarter in 1970 to nearly half today. As a result, market economics has increasingly determined ingredients, nutrient content, and portion size. Agricultural surpluses and technological breakthroughs supplied the cheap sweeteners and hydrogenated oils necessary for food to survive indefinitely on store shelves or under fast-food heat lamps.

Unsurprisingly, the caloric density of such foods soared relative to those consumed at home. Good value no longer meant taste, presentation, and proper nutrition — but merely more-for-less. Thus, the serving of McDonald's French fries that contained 200 calories in 1960 contains 610 today. The lure of large was not limited to fast-food, inflating everything from snack foods to cereal boxes.   5

But the hunger for home economics didn't die with its academic exile. Martha Stewart made millions filling the void, vexing home-ec haters like Erica Jong for having "earned her freedom by glorifying the slavery of home." Home and Garden TV, the Food Network, and countless publications thrive on topics once taught by home ec.

All of which begs the question: If the free market has done such a good job of picking up the slack, why bring home ec back? Because much of the D.I.Y. (do-it-yourself) culture is divorced from the exigencies of everyday life. It's more like home rec: catering to pampered chefs with maids to clean up the kitchen.

The new home economics should be both pragmatic and egalitarian. Traditional topics — food and nutrition, family studies, home management — should be retooled for the twenty-first century. Children should be able to decipher headlines about the dangers of dioxin or the benefits of antioxidants. Subjects like home finance might include domestic problem-solving: How would you spend $100 to feed a family of four, including a diabetic, a nursing mother, and infant, for one week?

While this kind of training might most benefit those low-income minority children at highest risk of obesity, all children will be better equipped to make smart choices in the face of the more than $33 billion that food companies spend annually to promote their products. And consumer education is just part of the larger purpose: to teach kids to think, make, fix, and generally fend for themselves.

Some detractors will doubtless smell a plot to turn women back into stitching,   10 stirring Stepford Wives. Others will argue that schools should focus on the basics. But what could be more basic than life, food, home and hearth? A generation has grown up since we swept home ec into the dust heap of history and hung up our brooms. It's time to reevaluate the domestic discipline, and recapture lost skills.

READING AND DISCUSSION QUESTIONS

1. How would the students at the high school you attended have responded to a course such as the one Grossman describes?
2. Do you think that offering such a course would be a good idea? Why, or why not?

3. How convincing is Grossman's argument that there is a need for consumer education? How convincing is her argument that it should be offered in school?

4. Do you find any logical fallacies in her argument? If so, what type of fallacies are they?

WRITING SUGGESTIONS

5. Write a claim of policy essay arguing that the sort of course Grossman describes should be required of high school students.

6. Write an essay refuting what Grossman suggests.

7. Write an essay in which you argue that the majority of teenagers are responsible consumers or that they are not.

DEBATE   Should the Federal Government Fund Embryonic Stem-Cell Research?

A New Look, an Old Battle

ANNA QUINDLEN

Public personification has always been the struggle on both sides of the abortion battle lines. That is why the people outside clinics on Saturday mornings carry signs with photographs of infants rather than of zygotes, why they wear lapel pins fashioned in the image of tiny feet and shout, "Don't kill your baby," rather than, more accurately, "Don't destroy your embryo." Those who support the legal right to an abortion have always been somewhat at a loss in the face of all this. From time to time women have come forward to speak about their decision to have an abortion, but when they are prominent, it seems a bit like grandstanding, and when they are not, it seems a terrible invasion of privacy when privacy is the point in the first place. Easier to marshal the act of presumptive ventriloquism practiced by the opponents, pretending to speak for those unborn unknown to them by circumstance or story.

But the battle of personification will assume a different and more sympathetic visage in the years to come. Perhaps the change in the weather was best illustrated when conservative Senator Strom Thurmond invoked his own daughter to explain a position opposed by the anti-abortion forces. The senator's daughter has diabetes. The actor Michael J. Fox has Parkinson's disease. Christopher Reeve is in a wheelchair because of a spinal-cord injury, Ronald Reagan locked in his own devolving mind by Alzheimer's. In the faces of the publicly and personally beloved lies enormous danger for the life-begins-at-conception lobby.

Anna Quindlen is a Pulitzer Prize–winning journalist and best-selling novelist. This piece appeared in the April 9, 2001, issue of *Newsweek* magazine.

334 CHAPTER 8 • LOGIC

The catalytic issue is research on stem cells. These are versatile building blocks that may be coaxed into becoming any other cell type; they could therefore hold the key to endless mysteries of human biology, as well as someday help provide a cure for ailments as diverse as diabetes, Parkinson's, spinal-cord degeneration, and Alzheimer's. By some estimates, more than 100 million Americans have diseases that scientists suspect could be affected by research on stem cells. Scientists hope that the astonishing potential of this research will persuade the federal government to help fund it and allow the National Institutes of Health to help oversee it. This is not political, researchers insist. It is about science, not abortion.

And they are correct. Stem-cell research is typically done by using frozen embryos left over from in vitro fertilization. If these embryos were placed in the womb, they might eventually implant, become a fetus, then a child. Unused, they are the earliest undifferentiated collection of cells made by the joining of the egg and sperm, no larger than the period at the end of this sentence. One of the oft-used slogans of the anti-abortion movement is "abortion stops a beating heart." There is no heart in this preimplantation embryo, but there are stem cells that, in the hands of scientists, might lead to extraordinary work affecting everything from cancer to heart disease.

All of which leaves the anti-abortion movement trying desperately to hold its hard line, and failing. Judie Brown of the American Life League can refer to these embryos as "the tiniest person," and the National Right to Life organization can publish papers that refer to stem-cell research as the "destruction of life." But ordinary people with family members losing their mobility or their grasp on reality will be able to be more thoughtful and reasonable about the issues involved.

The anti-abortion activists know this, because they have already seen the defections. Some senators have abandoned them to support fetal-tissue research, less promising than stem-cell work but still with significant potential for treating various ailments. Elected officials who had voted against abortion rights found themselves able to support procedures that used tissue from aborted fetuses; perhaps they were men who had fathers with heart disease, who had mothers with arthritis and whose hearts resonated with the possibilities for alleviating pain and prolonging life. Senator Thurmond was one, Senator McCain another. Former senator Connie Mack of Florida recently sent a letter to the president, who must decide the future role of the federal government in this area, describing himself "as a conservative pro-life now former member" of Congress, and adding that there "were those of us identified as such who supported embryonic stem-cell research."

When a recent test of fetal tissue in patients with Parkinson's had disastrous side effects, the National Right to Life Web site ran an almost gloating report: "horrific," "rips to shreds," "media cheerleaders," "defy description." The tone is a reflection of fear. It's the fear that the use of fetal tissue to produce cures for debilitating ailments might somehow launder the process of terminating a pregnancy, a positive result from what many people still see as a negative act. And it's the fear that thinking — really thinking — about the use of the earliest embryo for lifesaving research might bring a certain long-overdue relativism to discussions of abortion across the board.

The majority of Americans have always been able to apply that relativism to these issues. They are more likely to accept early abortions than later ones. They are more tolerant of a single abortion under exigent circumstances than multiple abortions. Some who disapprove of abortion in theory have discovered that they can accept it in fact if a daughter or a girlfriend is pregnant.

And some who believe that life begins at conception may look into the vacant eyes of an adored parent with Alzheimer's or picture a paralyzed child walking again, and take a closer look at what an embryo really is, at what stem-cell research really does, and then consider the true cost of a cure. That is what Senator Thurmond obviously did when he looked at his daughter and broke ranks with the true believers. It may be an oversimplification to say that real live loved ones trump the imagined unborn, that a cluster of undifferentiated cells due to be discarded anyway is a small price to pay for the health and welfare of millions. Or perhaps it is only a simple commonsensical truth.

The Misleading Debate on Stem-Cell Research

MONA CHAREN

Addressing the Democratic National Convention, Ron Reagan told the delegates that in the debate over funding research on embryonic stem cells, we face a choice between "the future and the past; between reason and ignorance; between true compassion and mere ideology." Not satisfied with that contrast, he elaborated that "a few of these folks (who oppose funding this research) are just grinding a political axe, and they should be ashamed of themselves."

It is Reagan who ought to be ashamed. As the mother of a ten-year-old with juvenile diabetes, I yearn more than most for breakthroughs in scientific research. My son takes between four and six shots of insulin daily and must test his blood sugar by pricking his finger the same number of times. This disease affects every major organ system in the body and places him in the high-risk category for more problems than I care to name. When he settles down to sleep at night, I can never be entirely sure that he won't slip into a coma from a sudden low blood sugar. How happily I would take the disease upon myself if I could only spare him! So please don't lecture me about grinding a political axe.

But like millions of others, I am troubled by the idea of embryonic stem-cell research. It crosses a moral line that this society should be loath to cross — even for the best of motives. Taking the stem cells from human embryos kills them. Before turning to the arguments of the pro-research side, permit a word about the pro-life

Mona Charen is a syndicated columnist and a political analyst. From 1984 to 1986, she worked at the White House as a speechwriter for Nancy Reagan and in the Public Affairs Office. This article appeared on townhall.com in August 2004.

position. Too many pro-life activists, it seems to me, have argued this case on the wrong grounds. My inbox is full of missives about the scientific misfires that stem-cell research has led to, as well as breathless announcements that adult stem cells actually hold more promise.

This is neither an honest nor a productive line of argument. The reason pro-lifers oppose embryonic stem-cell research is because they hold life sacred at all stages of development. They ought not to deny this or dress it up in a lab coat to give it greater palatability. The moral case is an honorable one. Leave it at that.

Proponents of embryonic stem-cell research point out that some of the em-bryos currently sitting in freezers in fertility clinics around the world are going to be washed down the drain anyway — which surely kills them, and without any benefit to mankind. This is true. There are several answers to this. The first is that a society that truly honored each human life would take a different approach. Fertility clinics and the couples who use them would understand the moral obligation not to create more embryos than they can reasonably expect to transfer to the mother's uterus. In cases where this was impossible, the embryos could be placed for adoption with other infertile couples (this is already a widespread practice).

Once you begin to pull apart a human embryo and use its parts, you have thoroughly dehumanized it. You have justified taking one life to (speculatively) save another. Despite the rosy future painted by Ron Reagan and others, those of us who follow the field with avid interest have been disappointed by avenues of research that have failed, thus far, to pan out. Still, opponents of stem-cell re-search should not argue that the research is going to be fruitless. No one knows. The problem is that this kind of research is morally problematic. Germany, Italy, Portugal, Luxembourg, and Austria ban it. (The United States does not. We simply withhold federal funding.)

There is something else, as well. While the idea of growing spare parts — say, spinal nerves for a paraplegic — in a Petri dish seems wonderful, it may not be possible to do so from embryonic stem cells. As the *Wall Street Journal* reported on August 12 [2004], scientists have been frustrated by their inability to get stem cells to grow into endoderm (the cells that make up the liver, stomach, and pancreas), whereas they can coax them to become heart and nerve tissue.

"Scientists speculate," the *Journal* explained, "that might be because the em-bryo early on needs blood and nerve tissue to grow, while endoderm-based organs aren't needed until later." If we can use the stem cells of normal human embryos for research, by what logic would we shrink from allowing an embryo to reach a later stage of development in order to study better how endoderm forms?

These are treacherous moral waters we're setting sail in, and those who hesitate ought not to be scorned as ignorant, uncompassionate, or blinkered.

DISCUSSION QUESTIONS

1. Do both of these authors use evidence and appeal to needs and values? Explain. How is your reading of Charen's piece affected by her personal circumstances?

2. In what ways does Charen's choice of words affect her argument?

3. Where does each author most directly state the claim of her piece?

4. Charen makes the statement that embryonic stem-cell research "crosses a moral line that this society should be loath to cross — even for the best of motives" (para. 3). How might Quindlen respond?

5. Which of the two arguments do you find more convincing?

Assignments for Avoiding Flawed Logic

READING AND DISCUSSION QUESTIONS

1. Read through the draft of an essay that you are writing, looking for and correcting any logical fallacies that you find.

2. Compare the argument made to Congress by President Roosevelt on the day after the attack on Pearl Harbor in 1941 and the one made by President Bush after the attacks on the World Trade Center and the Pentagon in 2001.

WRITING ASSIGNMENTS

3. Write an essay explaining the logical fallacies in one of the essays from the Readings for Analysis portion of this chapter.

4. Explain in an essay whether you find Anna Quindlen's or Mona Charen's argument on stem-cell research more convincing, and why.

5. Find the printed text of a major political speech such as a State of the Union Address, a major political convention speech, or an inaugural address and analyze its logic. Does it use an inductive approach, a deductive approach, a combination? What types of support are used? Do you detect any logical fallacies? Write an essay about the speech that supports either a claim of fact or a claim of value.

Research Readiness: Using Up-to-Date Data

Where do I look for the most current data about an evolving issue?

The world of politics is a world of constant change. There is always another election around the corner. Officials grow in public esteem or fall out of favor. Response to natural disasters or environmental threats can make or break a politician's career. Relationships with other countries shift. Laws are passed or vetoed.

The social world changes as well. As individuals, as states, and as a nation, we have had to rethink the definition of marriage. We have had to deal with violence that has grown out of isolation for some of our teens. We see or read about the causes and effects of homelessness.

The world of science is ever evolving. New advances save and improve lives but may raise new ethical questions as well. We have the knowledge to perform transplants, but questions remain as to who gets the small number of organs available.

To write for and about anything less than a static world, you need to have the latest information possible. The challenge is where to find it.

Find the most recent information you can about each of the following and be prepared to discuss how and where you found it.

- The number of American troops in Iraq
- The legality of same-sex marriage
- The use of the SAT for college admissions
- The federal stance on human stem-cell research
- The number of Americans supporting the Tea Party
- The amount of federal funds being spent on space travel
- The status of construction at Ground Zero
- The feasibility of alternative automobile fuels

CHAPTER 9

Language

The Power of Words

Words play such a critical role in argument that they deserve special treatment. An important part of successful writers' equipment is a large and active vocabulary, but no single chapter in a book can give this to you; only reading and study can widen your range of word choices. Even in a brief chapter, however, we can point out how words influence the feelings and attitudes of an audience, both favorably and unfavorably.

One kind of language responsible for shaping attitudes and feelings is *emotive language,* language that expresses and arouses emotions. Understanding it and using it effectively are indispensable to the arguer who wants to move an audience to accept a point of view or undertake an action.

In one of the most memorable speeches in the history of America, President Franklin Delano Roosevelt asked the country both to accept a point of view and to prepare to take action. In his brief speech to Congress he captured some of the grief and the feeling of outrage Americans were experiencing. Except for the most famous phrase in the speech, in which he declares December 7, 1941, a "date which will live in infamy," most of the first portion of the speech establishes the facts. A turning point in the speech comes when he shifts from facts to implications. The speech then builds to its emotional climax in the next-to-last paragraph before he concludes with a declaration of war.

Address to Congress, December 8, 1941

FRANKLIN D. ROOSEVELT

Yesterday, December 7, 1941 — a date which will live in infamy — the United States of America was suddenly and deliberately attacked by naval and air forces of the Empire of Japan.

The United States was at peace with that nation, and, at the solicitation of Japan, was still in conversation with its government and its Emperor looking toward the maintenance of peace in the Pacific.

Indeed, one hour after Japanese air squadrons had commenced bombing in the American island of Oahu, the Japanese Ambassador to the United States and his colleague delivered to our Secretary of State a formal reply to a recent American message. And, while this reply stated that it seemed useless to continue the existing diplomatic negotiations, it contained no threat or hint of war or of armed attack.

It will be recorded that the distance of Hawaii from Japan makes it obvious that the attack was deliberately planned many days or even weeks ago. During the intervening time the Japanese Government has deliberately sought to deceive the United States by false statements and expressions of hope for continued peace.

The attack yesterday on the Hawaiian Islands has caused severe damage to American naval and military forces. I regret to tell you that very many American lives have been lost. In addition, American ships have been reported torpedoed on the high seas between San Francisco and Honolulu.

Yesterday the Japanese Government also launched an attack against Malaya. Last night Japanese forces attacked Hong Kong. Last night Japanese forces attacked Guam. Last night Japanese forces attacked the Philippine Islands. Last night the Japanese attacked Wake Island. And this morning the Japanese attacked Midway Island.

Japan has therefore undertaken a surprise offensive extending throughout the Pacific area. The facts of yesterday and today speak for themselves. The people of the United States have already formed their opinions and well understand the implications to the very life and safety of our nation.

As Commander-in-Chief of the Army and Navy I have directed that all measures be taken for our defense, that always will our whole nation remember the character of the onslaught against us.

No matter how long it may take us to overcome this premeditated invasion, the American people, in their righteous might, will win through to absolute victory.

I believe that I interpret the will of the Congress and of the people when I assert that we will not only defend ourselves to the uttermost but will make it very certain that this form of treachery shall never again endanger us.

Hostilities exist. There is no blinking at the fact that our people, our territory, and our interests are in grave danger.

President Roosevelt addresses Congress on December 8, 1941.

   With confidence in our armed forces, with the unbounding determination of our people, we will gain the inevitable triumph, so help us God.

   I ask that the Congress declare that since the unprovoked and dastardly attack by Japan on Sunday, December 7, 1941, a state of war has existed between the United States and the Japanese Empire.

Long before you thought about writing your first argument, you learned that words had the power to affect you. Endearments and affectionate and flattering nicknames evoked good feelings about the speaker and yourself. Insulting nicknames and slurs produced dislike for the speaker and bad feelings about yourself. Perhaps you were told, "Sticks and stones may break your bones, but words will never hurt you." But even to a small child it is clear that ugly words are as painful as sticks and stones and that the injuries are sometimes more lasting.

Nowhere is the power of words more obvious and more familiar than in advertising, where the success of a product may depend on the feelings that certain words produce in the prospective buyer. Even the names of products may have emotive significance. In recent years a new industry, composed of consultants who supply names for products, has emerged. Although most manufacturers agree that a good name won't save a poor product, they also recognize that the right name can catch the attention of the public and persuade people to buy a product at least once. According to an article in the *Wall Street Journal,* a product name not only should be memorable but also should "remind people of emotional or physical experiences."[1]

PRACTICE

Careful thought and extensive research go into the naming of automobiles, a "big ticket" item for most consumers. What reasoning might have gone into the naming of these models, old and new?

Aspen	Impala	Mustang	Rendezvous
Colorado	Infinity	Nova	Sequoia
Dart	Jaguar	Odyssey	Taurus
Eclipse	Liberty	Quest	Trailblazer
Electra	Malibu	Rainier	Viper
Grand Prix	Matrix	Regal	

What response do the names Mercedes-Benz and Rolls-Royce evoke?

Even scientists recognize the power of words to attract the attention of other scientists and the public to discoveries and theories that might otherwise remain obscure. A good name can even enable the scientist to visualize a new concept. One scientist says that "a good name," such as "quark," "black hole," "big bang," "chaos," or "great attractor," "helps in communicating a theory and can have substantial impact on financing."

It is not hard to see the connection between the use of words in conversation and advertising and the use of emotive language in the more formal arguments you will be writing. Emotive language reveals your approval or disapproval, assigns praise or blame — in other words, makes a judgment about the subject. Keep in mind that unless you are writing purely factual statements, such as scientists write, you will find it hard to avoid expressing judgments. Neutrality does not come easily, even where it may be desirable, as in news stories or reports of historical events. For this reason you need to attend carefully to the statements in your argument, making sure that you have not disguised judgments as statements of fact. In Rogerian argumentation, you need to remain neutral as you summarize your opponent's argument and your own.

Of course, in attempting to prove a claim, you will not be neutral. You will be revealing your judgment about the subject, first in the selection of facts and

[1]*Wall Street Journal,* August 5, 1982, p. 19.

opinions and the emphasis you give to them and second in the selection of words.

Like the choice of facts and opinions, the choice of words can be effective or ineffective in advancing your argument, moral or immoral in the honesty with which you exercise it. The following discussions offer some insights into recognizing and evaluating the use of emotive language in the arguments you read, as well as into using such language in your own arguments where it is appropriate and avoiding it where it is not.

Connotation

The connotations of a word are the meanings we attach to it apart from its explicit definition. Because these added meanings derive from our feelings, connotations are one form of emotive language. For example, the word *rat* denotes or points to a kind of rodent, but the attached meanings of "selfish person," "evil-doer," "betrayer," and "traitor" reflect the feelings that have accumulated around the word.

In Chapter 4 we observed that definitions of controversial terms, such as *poverty* and *unemployment,* may vary so widely that writer and reader cannot always be sure that they are thinking of the same thing. A similar problem arises when a writer assumes that the reader shares his or her emotional response to a word. Emotive meanings originate partly in personal experience. The word *home,* defined merely as "a family's place of residence," may suggest love, warmth, and security to one person; it may suggest friction, violence, and alienation to another. The values of the groups to which we belong also influence meaning. Writers and speakers count on cultural associations when they refer to our country, our flag, and heroes and enemies we have never seen. The arguer must also be aware that some apparently neutral words trigger different responses from different groups — words such as *cult, revolution, police,* and *beauty contest.*

Various reform movements have recognized that words with unfavorable connotations have the power not only to reflect but also to shape our perceptions of things. In 2007, the NAACP went so far as to hold a "funeral for the N — word." The women's liberation movement also insisted on changes that would bring about improved attitudes toward women. The movement condemned the use of *girl* for a female over the age of eighteen and the use in news stories of descriptive adjectives that emphasized the physical appearance of women. And the homosexual community succeeded in reintroducing the word *gay,* a word current centuries ago, as a substitute for words they considered offensive. Now *queer,* a word long regarded as offensive, has been adopted as a substitute for *gay* by a new generation of gays and lesbians, although it is still considered unacceptable by many members of the homosexual community.

Members of certain occupations have invented terms to confer greater respectability on their work. The work does not change, but the workers hope that public perceptions will change if janitors are called custodians, if garbage collectors are called sanitation engineers, if undertakers are called morticians, if people who sell makeup are called cosmetologists. Events considered unpleasant or unmentionable are sometimes disguised by polite terms, called *euphemisms*. During the 1992 to 1993 recession new terms emerged that disguised, or tried to, the grim fact that thousands of people were being dismissed from their jobs: *skill-mix adjustment, workforce-imbalance correction, redundancy elimination, downsizing, indefinite idling,* even a daring *career-change opportunity.* Many people refuse to use the word *died* and choose *passed away* instead. Some psychologists and physicians use the phrase *negative patient care outcome* for what most of us would call *death.* Even when referring to their pets, some people cannot bring themselves to say *put to death* but substitute *put to sleep* or *put down.* In place of a term to describe an act of sexual intercourse, some people use *slept together* or *went to bed together* or *had an affair.*

Polite words are not always so harmless. If a euphemism disguises a shameful event or condition, it is morally irresponsible to use it to mislead the reader into believing that the shameful condition does not exist. In his powerful essay "Politics and the English Language" George Orwell pointed out that politicians and reporters have sometimes used terms like *pacification* or *rectification of frontiers* to conceal acts that result in torture and death for millions of people. An example of such usage was cited by a member of Amnesty International, a group monitoring human rights violations throughout the world. He objected to a news report describing camps in which the Chinese were promoting "reeducation through labor." This term, he wrote, "makes these institutions seem like a cross between Police Athletic League and Civilian Conservation Corps camps." On the contrary, he went on, the reality of "reeducation through labor" was that the victims were confined to "rather unpleasant prison camps." The details he offered about the conditions under which people lived and worked gave substance to his claim.[2]

Perhaps the most striking examples of the way that connotations influence our perceptions of reality occur when people are asked to respond to questions of poll-takers. Sociologists and students of poll-taking know that the phrasing of a question, or the choice of words, can affect the answers and even undermine the validity of the poll. In one case poll-takers first asked a selected group of people if they favored continuing the welfare system. The majority answered no. But when the poll-takers asked if they favored government aid to the poor, the majority answered yes. Although the terms *welfare* and *government aid to the poor* refer to essentially the same forms of government assistance, *welfare* has acquired for many people negative connotations of corruption and shiftless recipients.

In a *New York Times*/CBS poll conducted in January 1998, "a representative sample of Americans were asked which statement came nearer to their opinion: 'Is abortion the same thing as murdering a child, or is abortion not murder because the fetus really isn't a child?'" Thirty-eight percent chose "the fetus really isn't a child." But 58 percent, including a third of those who chose "abortion is

[2]Letter to the *New York Times*, August 30, 1982, p. 25.

the same thing as murdering a child," agreed that abortion "was sometimes the best course in a bad situation." The author of the report suggests an explanation of the fact that a majority of those polled seemed to have chosen "murder" as an acceptable solution to an unwanted pregnancy:

> These replies reveal, at least, a considerable moral confusion.
>
> Or maybe only verbal confusion? Should the question have asked whether abortion came closer, in the respondent's view, to "killing" rather than "murdering" a child? That would leave room for the explanation that Americans, while valuing life, are ultimately not pacifists: killing, they hold, may be justified in certain circumstances (self-defense, warfare, capital punishment).
>
> So one can challenge the wording of the question. Indeed, one can almost always challenge the wording of poll questions. . . . Poll takers themselves acknowledge the difficulty of wording questions and warn against relying too much on any single finding.[3]

This is also true in polls concerning rape, another highly charged subject. Dr. Neil Malamuth, a psychologist at the University of California at Los Angeles, says, "When men are asked if there is any likelihood they would force a woman to have sex against her will if they could get away with it, about half say they would. But if you ask them if they would rape a woman if they knew they could get away with it, only about 15 percent say they would." The men who change their answers aren't aware that "the only difference is in the words used to describe the same act."[4]

The wording of an argument is crucial. Because readers may interpret the words you use on the basis of feelings different from your own, you must support your word choices with definitions and with evidence that allows readers to determine how and why you made them.

Slanting

Slanting, says one dictionary, is "interpreting or presenting in line with a special interest." The term is almost always used in a negative sense. It means that the arguer has selected facts and words with favorable or unfavorable connotations to create the impression that no alternative view exists or can be defended. For some questions it is true that no alternative view is worthy of presentation, and emotionally charged language to defend or attack a position that is clearly right or wrong would be entirely appropriate. We aren't neutral, nor should we be, about the tragic abuse of human rights anywhere in the world or even about infractions of the law such as drunk driving or vandalism, and we should use strong language to express our disapproval of these practices.

---

[3] Peter Steinfels, "Beliefs," *New York Times,* January 24, 1998, sec. A, p. 15.
[4] *New York Times,* August 29, 1989, sec. C, p. 1.

Most of your arguments, however, will concern controversial questions about which people of goodwill can argue on both sides. In such cases, your own judgments should be restrained. Slanting will suggest a prejudice — that is, a judgment made without regard to all the facts. Unfortunately, you may not always be aware of your bias or special interest; you may believe that your position is the only correct one. You may also feel the need to communicate a passionate belief about a serious problem. But if you are interested in persuading a reader to accept your belief and to act on it, you must also ask: If the reader is not sympathetic, how will he or she respond? Will he or she perceive my words as "loaded" — one-sided and prejudicial — and my view as slanted?

R. D. Laing, a Scottish psychiatrist, defined *prayer* in this way: "Someone is gibbering away on his knees, talking to someone who is not there."[5] This description probably reflects a sincerely held belief. Laing also clearly intended it for an audience that already agreed with him. But the phrases "gibbering away" and "someone who is not there" would be offensive to people for whom prayer is sacred.

The following remarks by one writer attacking another appeared in *Salon,* an online magazine:

> Urging the hyperbolic *Salon* columnist David Horowitz to calm down and cite facts instead of spewing insults seems as pointless as asking a dog not to defecate on the sidewalk. In either instance, the result is always and predictably the same: Somebody has to clean up a stinking pile.[6]

An audience, whether friendly or unfriendly, interested in a discussion of the issues, would probably be both embarrassed and repelled by this use of language in a serious argument.

In the mid-1980s an English environmental group, London Greenpeace, began to distribute leaflets accusing the McDonald's restaurants of a wide assortment of crimes. The leaflets said in part:

> McDollars, McGreedy, McCancer, McMurder, McDisease, McProfits, McDeadly, McHunger, McRipoff, McTorture, McWasteful, McGarbage.
>
> This leaflet is asking you to think for a moment about what lies behind McDonald's clean, bright image. It's got a lot to hide. . . .
>
> McDonald's and Burger King are two of the many U.S. corporations using lethal poisons to destroy vast areas of Central American rain forest to create grazing pastures for cattle to be sent back to the States as burgers and pet food. . . .
>
> What they don't make clear is that a diet high in fat, sugar, animal products and salt . . . and low in fiber, vitamins and minerals — which describes an average McDonald's meal — is linked with cancers of the breast and bowel, and heart disease. . . .[7]

[5]"The Obvious," in David Cooper, ed., *The Dialectics of Liberation* (Penguin Books, 1968), p. 17.
[6]July 6, 2000.
[7]*New York Times,* August 6, 1995, sec. E, p. 7. In 1990 McDonald's sued the group for libel. In June 1997, after the longest libel trial in British history, the judge ruled in favor of the plaintiff, awarding McDonald's £60,000. In March 1999 an appeal partially overturned the verdict and reduced the damages awarded to McDonald's by approximately one-third.

Even readers who share the belief that McDonald's is not a reliable source of good nutrition might feel that London Greenpeace has gone too far, and that the name-calling, loaded words, and exaggeration have damaged the credibility of the attackers more than the reputation of McDonald's.

Selection, Slanting, and Charged Language

NEWMAN P. BIRK AND GENEVIEVE B. BIRK

A. The Principle of Selection

Before it is expressed in words, our knowledge, both inside and outside, is influenced by the principle of selection. What we know or observe depends on what we notice; that is, what we select, consciously or unconsciously, as worthy of notice or attention. As we observe, the principle of selection determines which facts we take in.

Suppose, for example, that three people, a lumberjack, an artist, and a tree surgeon, are examining a large tree in the forest. Since the tree itself is a complicated object, the number of particulars or facts about it that one could observe would be very great indeed. Which of these facts a particular observer will notice will be a matter of selection, a selection that is determined by his interests and purposes. A lumberjack might be interested in the best way to cut the tree down, cut it up, and transport it to the lumber mill. His interest would then determine his principle of selection in observing and thinking about the tree. The artist might consider painting a picture of the tree, and his purpose would furnish his principle of selection. The tree surgeon's professional interest in the physical health of the tree might establish a principle of selection for him. If each man were now required to write an exhaustive, detailed report on every thing he observed about the tree, the facts supplied by each would differ, for each would report those facts that his particular principle of selection led him to notice. . . .[1]

The principle of selection then serves as a kind of sieve or screen through which our knowledge passes before it becomes our knowledge. Since we can't notice everything about a complicated object or situation or action or state of our own consciousness, what we do notice is determined by whatever principle of selection is operating for us at the time we gain the knowledge. . . .

[1] Of course, all three observers would probably report a good many facts in common — the height of the tree, for example, and the size of the trunk. The point we wish to make is that each observer would give us a different impression of the tree because of the different principle of selection that guided his observation. [All notes are the authors'.]

This selection first appeared in *Understanding and Using English* (1972). Together, the Birks, specialists in English language and usage, also wrote *A Handbook of Grammar, Rhetoric, Mechanics, and Usage* (1976).

B. The Principle of Slanting

When we put our knowledge into words, a second process of selection, the process of slanting, takes place. Just as there is something, a rather mysterious principle of selection, which chooses for us what we will notice, and what will then become our knowledge, there is also a principle which operates, with or without our awareness, to select certain facts and feelings from our store of knowledge, and to choose the words and emphasis that we shall use to communicate our meaning.[2] Slanting may be defined as the process of selecting (1) knowledge — factual and attitudinal; (2) words; and (3) emphasis, to achieve the intention of the communicator. Slanting is present in some degree in all communication: one may *slant for* (favorable slanting), *slant against* (unfavorable slanting), or *slant both ways* (balanced shifting). . . .

C. Slanting by Use of Emphasis

Slanting by use of the devices of emphasis is unavoidable,[3] for emphasis is simply   5
the giving of stress to subject matter, and so indicating what is important and what is less important. In speech, for example, if we say that Socrates was *a wise old man,* we can give several slightly different meanings, one by stressing *wise,* another by stressing *old,* another by giving equal stress to *wise* and *old,* and still another by giving chief stress to *man.* Each different stress gives a different slant (favorable or unfavorable or balanced) to the statement because it conveys a different attitude toward Socrates or a different judgment of him. Connectives and word order also slant by the emphasis they give: Consider the difference in slanting or emphasis produced by *old but wise, old and wise, wise but old.* In writing, we cannot indicate subtle stresses on words as clearly as in speech, but we can achieve our emphasis and so can slant by the use of more complex patterns of word order, [by choice of connectives, by underlining heavily stressed words, and] by marks of punctuation that indicate short or long pauses and so give light or heavy emphasis. Question marks, quotation marks, and exclamation points can also contribute to slanting.[4] It is impossible either in speech or in writing to put two facts together without giving some slight emphasis or slant. For example, if we have in mind only two facts about a man, his awkwardness and his strength, we subtly slant those facts favorably or unfavorably in whatever way we may choose to join them.

---

[2]Notice that the "principle of selection" is at work as *we take in* knowledge, and that slanting occurs *as we express* our knowledge in words.

[3]When emphasis is present — and we can think of no instance in the use of language in which it is not — it necessarily influences the meaning by playing a part in the favorable, unfavorable, or balanced slant of the communicator. We are likely to emphasize by voice stress, even when we answer *yes* or *no* to simple questions.

[4]Consider the slanting achieved by punctuation in the following sentences: He called the Senator an honest man? *He* called the Senator an honest man? He called the Senator an honest man! He said one more such "honest" senator would corrupt the state.

More Favorable Slanting	Less Favorable Slanting
He is awkward and strong.	He is strong and awkward.
He is awkward but strong.	He is strong but awkward.
Although he is somewhat awkward, he is very strong.	He may be strong, but he's very awkward.

With more facts and in longer passages it is possible to maintain a delicate balance by alternating favorable emphasis and so producing a balanced effect.

All communication, then, is in some degree slanted by the *emphasis* of the communicator.

D. Slanting by Selection of Facts

To illustrate the technique of slanting by selection of facts, we shall examine three passages of informative writing which achieve different effects simply by the selection and emphasis of material. Each passage is made up of true statements or facts about a dog, yet the reader is given three different impressions. The first passage is an example of objective writing or balanced slanting, the second is slanted unfavorably, and the third is slanted favorably.

1. Balanced Presentation

Our dog, Toddy, sold to us as a cocker, produces various reactions in various people. Those who come to the back door she usually growls and barks at (a milkman has said that he is afraid of her); those who come to the front door, she whines at and paws; also she tries to lick people's faces unless we have forestalled her by putting a newspaper in her mouth. (Some of our friends encourage these actions; others discourage them. Mrs. Firmly, one friend, slaps the dog with a newspaper and says, "I know how hard dogs are to train.") Toddy knows and responds to a number of words and phrases, and guests sometimes remark that she is a "very intelligent dog." She has fleas in the summer, and she sheds, at times copiously, the year round. Her blonde hairs are conspicuous when they are on people's clothing or on rugs or furniture. Her color and her large brown eyes frequently produce favorable comment. An expert on cockers would say that her ears are too short and set too high and that she is at least six pounds too heavy.

The passage above is made up of facts, verifiable facts,[5] deliberately selected and emphasized to produce a *balanced* impression. Of course not all the facts about the dog have been given — to supply *all* the facts on any subject, even such a comparatively simple one, would be an almost impossible task. Both favorable

---

[5] *Verifiable* facts are facts that can be checked and agreed upon and proved to be true by people who wish to verify them. That a particular theme received a failing grade is a verifiable fact; one needs merely to see the theme with the grade on it. That the instructor should have failed the theme is not, strictly speaking, a verifiable fact, but a matter of opinion. That women on the average live longer than men is a verifiable fact; that they live better is a matter of opinion, *a value judgment.*

Very different impressions of Toddy will be given depending on how the facts are presented.

and unfavorable facts are used, however, and an effort has been made to alternate favorable and unfavorable details so that neither will receive greater emphasis by position, proportion, or grammatical structure.

2. Facts Slanted Against

That dog put her paws on my white dress as soon as I came in the door, and she made so much noise that it was two minutes before she had quieted down enough for us to talk and hear each other. Then the gas man came and she did a great deal of barking. And her hairs are on the rug and on the furniture. If you wear a dark dress they stick to it like lint. When Mrs. Firmly came in, she actually hit the dog with a newspaper to make it stay down, and she made some remark about training dogs. I wish the Birks would take the hint or get rid of that noisy, shorteared, over-weight "cocker" of theirs.

This unfavorably slanted version is based on the same facts, but now these facts have been selected and given a new emphasis. The speaker, using her selected

10

facts to give her impression of the dog, is quite possibly unaware of her negative slanting.

Now for a favorably slanted version:

3. Facts Slanted For

What a lively and responsible dog! When I walked in the door, there she was with a newspaper in her mouth, whining and standing on her hind legs and wagging her tail all at the same time. And what an intelligent dog. If you suggest going for a walk, she will get her collar from the kitchen and hand it to you, and she brings Mrs. Birk's slippers whenever Mrs. Birk says she is "tired" or mentions slippers. At a command she catches balls, rolls over, "speaks," or stands on her hind feet and twirls around. She sits up and balances a piece of bread on her nose until she is told to take it; then she tosses it up and catches it. If you are eating something, she sits up in front of you and "begs" with those big dark brown eyes set in that light, buff-colored face of hers. When I got up to go and told her I was leaving, she rolled her eyes at me and sat up like a squirrel. She certainly is a lively and intelligent dog.

Speaker 3, like Speaker 2, is selecting from the "facts" summarized in balanced version 1, and is emphasizing his facts to communicate his impression.

All three passages are examples of *reporting* (i.e., consist only of verifiable facts), yet they give three very different impressions of the same dog because of the different ways the speakers slanted the facts. Some people say that figures don't lie, and many people believe that if they have the "facts," they have the "truth." Yet if we carefully examine the ways of thought and language, we see that any knowledge that comes to us through words has been subjected to the double screening of the principle of selection and the slanting of language. . . .

Wise listeners and readers realize that the double screening that is produced by the principle of selection and by slanting takes place even when people honestly try to report the facts as they know them. (Speakers 2 and 3, for instance, probably thought of themselves as simply giving information about a dog and were not deliberately trying to mislead.) Wise listeners and readers know too that deliberate manipulators of language, by mere selection and emphasis, can make their slanted facts appear to support almost any cause.

In arriving at opinions and values we cannot always be sure that the facts that sift into our minds through language are representative and relevant and true. We need to remember that much of our information about politics, governmental activities, business conditions, and foreign affairs comes to us selected and slanted. More than we realize, our opinions on these matters may depend on what newspaper we read or what news commentator we listen to. Worthwhile opinions call for knowledge of reliable facts and reasonable arguments for and against — and such opinions include beliefs about morality and truth and religion as well as about public affairs. Because complex subjects involve knowing and dealing with many facts on both sides, reliable judgments are at best difficult to arrive at. If we want to be fairminded, we must be willing to subject our opinions to continual testing by new knowledge, and must realize that after all they *are* opinions, more

15

or less trustworthy. Their trustworthiness will depend on the representativeness of our facts, on the quality of our reasoning, and on the standard of values that we choose to apply.

We shall not give here a passage illustrating the unscrupulous slanting of facts. Such a passage would also include irrelevant facts and false statements presented as facts, along with various subtle distortions of fact. Yet to the uninformed reader the passage would be indistinguishable from a passage intended to give a fair account. If two passages (2 and 3) of casual and unintentional slanting of facts about a dog can give such contradictory impressions of a simple subject, the reader can imagine what a skilled and designing manipulation of facts and statistics could do to mislead an uninformed reader about a really complex subject. An example of such manipulation might be the account of the United States that Soviet propaganda has supplied to the average Russian. Such propaganda, however, would go beyond the mere slanting of the facts: It would clothe the selected facts in charged words and would make use of the many other devices of slanting that appear in charged language.

E. Slanting by Use of Charged Words

In the passages describing the dog Toddy, we were illustrating the technique of slanting by the selection and emphasis of facts. Though the facts selected had to be expressed in words, the words chosen were as factual as possible, and it was the selection and emphasis of facts and not of words that was mainly responsible for the two distinctly different impressions of the dog. In the passages below we are demonstrating another way of slanting — by the use of charged words. This time the accounts are very similar in the facts they contain; the different impressions of the subject, Corlyn, are produced not by different facts but by the subtle selection of charged words.

The passages were written by a clever student who was told to choose as his subject a person in action, and to write two descriptions, each using the "same facts." The instructions required that one description be slanted positively and the other negatively, so that the first would make the reader favorably inclined toward the person and the action, and the second would make him unfavorably inclined.

Here is the favorably charged description. Read it carefully and form your opinion of the person before you go on to read the second description.

Corlyn

Corlyn paused at the entrance to the room and glanced about. A well-cut black dress draped subtly about her slender form. Her long blonde hair gave her chiseled features the simple frame they required. She smiled an engaging smile as she accepted a cigarette from her escort. As he lit it for her she looked over the flame and into his eyes. Corlyn had that rare talent of making every male feel that he was the only man in the world.

She took his arm and they descended the steps into the room. She walked with an effortless grace and spoke with equal ease. They each took a cup of coffee and joined a group of friends near the fire. The flickering light danced across her face and lent an ethereal quality to her beauty. The good conversation, the crackling logs, and the stimulating coffee gave her a feeling of internal warmth. Her eyes danced with each leap of the flames.

Taken by itself this passage might seem just a description of an attractive girl.   20
The favorable slanting by use of charged words has been done so skillfully that it is inconspicuous. Now we turn to the unfavorably slanted description of the "same" girl in the "same" actions:

Corlyn

Corlyn halted at the entrance to the room and looked around. A plain black dress hung on her thin frame. Her stringy bleached hair accentuated her harsh features. She smiled an inane smile as she took a cigarette from her escort. As he lit it for her she stared over the lighter and into his eyes. Corlyn had a habit of making every male feel that he was the last man on earth.

She grasped his arm and they walked down the steps and into the room. Her pace was fast and ungainly, as was her speed. They each reached for some coffee and broke into a group of acquaintances near the fire. The flickering light played across her face and revealed every flaw. The loud talk, the fire, and the coffee she had gulped down made her feel hot. Her eyes grew more red with each leap of the flames.

When the reader compares these two descriptions, he can see how charged words influence the reader's attitude. One needs to read the two descriptions several times to appreciate all the subtle differences between them. Words, some rather heavily charged, others innocent-looking but lightly charged, work together to carry to the reader a judgment of a person and a situation. If the reader had seen only the first description of Corlyn, he might well have thought that he had formed his "own judgment on the basis of the facts." And the examples just given only begin to suggest the techniques that may be used in heavily charged language. For one thing, the two descriptions of Corlyn contain no really good example of the use of charged abstractions; for another, the writer was obliged by the assignment to use the same set of facts and so could not slant by selecting his material.

F. Slanting and Charged Language

. . . When slanting the facts, or words, or emphasis, or any combination of the three *significantly influences* feelings toward, or judgments about, a subject, the language used is charged language. . . .

Of course communications vary in the amount of charge they carry and in their effect on different people; what is very favorably charged for one person may have little or no charge, or may even be adversely charged, for others. It is sometimes hard to distinguish between charged and uncharged expression. But it is safe to say that whenever we wish to convey any kind of inner knowledge — feelings, attitudes, judgments, values — we are obliged to convey that attitudinal meaning through the medium of charged language; and when we wish to understand the inside knowledge of others, we have to interpret the charged language that they choose, or are obliged to use. Charged language, then, is the natural and necessary medium for the communication of charged or attitudinal meaning. At times we have difficulty in living with it, but we should have even greater difficulty in living without it.

Some of the difficulties in living with charged language are caused by its use in dishonest propaganda, in some editorials, in many political speeches, in most advertising, in certain kinds of effusive salesmanship, and in blatantly insincere, or exaggerated, or sentimental expressions of emotion. Other difficulties are caused by the misunderstandings and misinterpretations that charged language produces. A charged phrase misinterpreted in a love letter; a charged word spoken in haste or in anger; an acrimonious argument about religion or politics or athletics or fraternities; the frustrating uncertainty produced by the effort to understand the complex attitudinal meaning in a poem or play or a short story — these troubles, all growing out of the use of charged language, may give us the feeling that Robert Louis Stevenson expressed when he said, "The battle goes sore against us to the going down of the sun. . . ."

READING AND DISCUSSION QUESTIONS

1. How do the Birks distinguish between the process of selection and the process of slanting?
2. Explain the three types of slanting described by the Birks and illustrate each with examples from your own experience.
3. According to the Birks, why is charged language unavoidable — and ultimately desirable?

WRITING SUGGESTIONS

4. Choose a printed ad and analyze the use of language, applying the Birks' terminology.
5. Choose one or more editorials or letters to the editor and show how word choice reveals a writer's attitude toward a subject.

We find slanting everywhere, not only in advertising and propaganda, where we expect to find it, but in news stories, which should be strictly neutral in their recounting of events, and in textbooks. In the field of history, for example, it is often difficult for scholars to remain impartial about significant events. Like the rest of us, they may approve or disapprove, and their choice of words will reflect their judgments.

The following passage by a distinguished Catholic historian describes the events surrounding the momentous decision by Henry VIII, king of England, to break with the Roman Catholic Church in 1534, in part because of the Pope's refusal to grant him a divorce from the Catholic princess Catherine of Aragon so that he could marry Anne Boleyn.

> The *protracted* delay in receiving an annulment was very *irritating* to the *impulsive* English king. . . . Gradually Henry's former *effusive* loyalty to Rome gave way to a settled conviction of the tyranny of the papal power, and there *rushed* to his mind the recollections of efforts of earlier English rulers to restrict that power. A few *salutary* enactments against the Church might *compel* a favorable decision from the Pope.
>
> Henry seriously opened his campaign against the Roman Church in 1531, when he *frightened* the clergy into paying a fine of over half a million dollars for violating an *obsolete* statute . . . and in the same year he *forced* the clergy to recognize himself as supreme head of the Church. . . .
>
> His *subservient* Parliament then empowered him to stop the payments of annates to the Pope and to appoint bishops in England without recourse to the papacy. *Without waiting longer* for the decision from Rome, he had Cranmer, *one of his own creatures,* whom he had just named Archbishop of Canterbury, declare his marriage null and void. . . .
>
> Yet Henry VIII encountered considerable *opposition* from the *higher clergy,* from the monks, and from many *intellectual leaders.* . . . A *popular uprising* — the Pilgrimage of Grace — was *sternly* suppressed, and such men as the *brilliant* Sir Thomas More and John Fisher, the *aged* and *saintly* bishop of Rochester, were beheaded because they retained their former belief in papal supremacy.[8] [Italics added.]

In the first paragraph the italicized words help make the following points: that Henry was rash, impulsive, and insincere and that he was intent on punishing the church (the word *salutary* means healthful or beneficial and is used sarcastically). In the second paragraph the choice of words stresses Henry's use of force and the cowardly submission of his followers. In the third paragraph the adjectives describing the opposition to Henry's campaign and those who were executed emphasize Henry's cruelty and despotism. Within the limits of this brief passage the author has offered support for his strong indictment of Henry VIII's actions, both in defining the statute as obsolete and in describing the popular opposition. In a longer exposition you would expect to find a more elaborate justification with facts and authoritative opinion from other sources.

The advocate of a position in an argument, unlike the reporter or the historian, must express a judgment, but the preceding examples demonstrate how the arguer should use language to avoid or minimize slanting and to persuade readers that he or she has come to a conclusion after careful analysis. The careful arguer must not conceal his or her judgments by presenting them as if they were statements of fact, but must offer convincing support for his or her choice of words and respect the audience's feelings and attitudes by using temperate language.

Depending on the circumstances, *exaggeration* can be defined, in the words of one writer, as "a form of lying." An essay in *Time* magazine, "Watching Out

[8]Carlton J. H. Hayes, *A Political and Cultural History of Modern Europe,* vol. 1 (New York: Macmillan, 1933), pp. 172–73.

for Loaded Words," points to the danger for the arguer in relying on exaggerated language as an essential part of the argument.

> The trouble with loaded words is they tend to short-circuit thought. While they may describe something, they simultaneously try to seduce the mind into accepting a prefabricated opinion about the something described.[9]

PRACTICE

Locate specific examples of slanted language in the first of these two excerpts from the debate later in the chapter. What effect does the word choice have in the first piece? How does it compare to the word choice in the second passage, on the same topic?

> 1. Grandstanding politicians love to rail against the gun. Inanimate objects are good targets to beat up on. That way, politicians do not have to address the real problems in our society. We pay a price for this craven misdirection, though, in thousands of murders, muggings, rapes, robberies, and burglaries.
>   Yet that is not the greatest danger we face. The Founding Fathers knew that *governments* could turn criminal. That is the principal reason they wanted every man armed: An armed citizenry militates against the development of tyranny. The Founding Fathers did not want every man armed in order to shoot a burglar, although they had nothing against doing so. The Founding Fathers did not want every man armed in order to shoot Bambi or Thumper, although they had nothing against doing so. The Founding Fathers wanted every man armed in order to shoot soldiers or police of tyrannical regimes who suppress the rights of free men. (McGrath 425)

> 2. Americans also have a right to defend their homes, and we need not challenge that. Nor does anyone seriously question that the Constitution protects the right of hunters to own and keep sporting guns for hunting game any more than anyone would challenge the right to own and keep fishing rods and other equipment for fishing — or to own automobiles. To "keep and bear arms" for hunting today is essentially a recreational activity and not an imperative of survival, as it was 200 years ago; "Saturday night specials" and machine guns are not recreational weapons and surely are as much in need of regulation as motor vehicles.
>   Americans should ask themselves a few questions. The Constitution does not mention automobiles or motorboats, but the right to keep and own an automobile is beyond question; equally beyond question is the power of the state to regulate the purchase or the transfer of such vehicle and the right to license the vehicle and the driver with reasonable standards. In some places, even a bicycle must be registered, as must some household dogs. (Burger 419)

[9] *Time*, May 24, 1982, p. 86.

Picturesque Language

Picturesque language consists of words that produce images in the mind of the reader. Students sometimes assume that vivid picture-making language is the exclusive instrument of novelists and poets, but writers of arguments can also avail themselves of such devices to heighten the impact of their messages.

Picturesque language can do more than render a scene. It shares with other kinds of emotive language the power to express and arouse deep feelings. Like a fine painting or photograph, it can draw readers into the picture where they partake of the writer's experience as if they were also present. Such power may be used to delight, to instruct, or to horrify. In 1741 the Puritan preacher Jonathan Edwards delivered his sermon "Sinners in the Hands of an Angry God," in which people were likened to repulsive spiders hanging over the flames of Hell to be dropped into the fire whenever a wrathful God was pleased to release them. The congregation's reaction to Edwards's picture of the everlasting horrors to be suffered in the netherworld included panic, fainting, hysteria, and convulsions. Subsequently Edwards lost his pulpit in Massachusetts, in part as a consequence of his success at provoking such uncontrollable terror among his congregation.

Language as intense and vivid as Edwards's emerges from very strong emotion about a deeply felt cause. In the following paragraph, Lavina Melwani uses picturesque language to call attention to some of the problems faced daily by undocumented workers.

> The rats — bold, tenacious, and totally fearless — are what bothered him the most. Prem, who requested his last name not be used, says the rodents have the run of the old apartment he shares in Baltimore City, Maryland, with five other Nepali men, most of them undocumented. "It is impossible to have beds for six people in two rooms," he says. "So we have small roll-out beds or mattresses on the floor. There are many rats running around the apartment and it's difficult to catch them. We can't complain. The landlord doesn't care. He knows we have to live here and have no choice."[10]

The rules governing the use of picturesque language are the same as those governing other kinds of emotive language. Is the language appropriate? Is it too strong, too colorful for the purpose of the message? Does it result in slanting or distortion? What will its impact be on a hostile or indifferent audience? Will they be angered, repelled? Will they cease to read or listen if the imagery is too disturbing?

[10] "No Roof No Roots No Rights." *Little India*, April 12, 2006, p. 42.

Concrete and Abstract Language

Writers of argument need to be aware of another use of language — the distinction between concrete and abstract. Concrete words point to real objects and real experiences. Abstract words express qualities apart from particular things and events. *Velvety, dark red roses* is concrete; we can see, touch, and smell them. *Beauty* in the eye of the beholder is abstract; we can speak of the quality of beauty without reference to a particular object or event. *Returning money found in the street to the owner, although no one has seen the discovery* is concrete. *Honesty* is abstract. In abstracting we separate a quality shared by a number of objects or events, however different from each other the individual objects or events may be.

Writing that describes or tells a story leans heavily on concrete language. Although arguments also rely on the vividness of concrete language, they use abstract terms far more extensively than other kinds of writing. Using abstractions effectively, especially in arguments of value and policy, is important for two reasons: (1) Abstractions represent the qualities, characteristics, and values that the writer is explaining, defending, or attacking; and (2) they enable the writer to make generalizations about his or her data. Equally important is knowing when to avoid abstractions that obscure the message.

You should not expect abstract terms alone to carry the emotional content of your message. The effect of even the most suggestive words can be enhanced by details, examples, and anecdotes. One mode of expression is not superior to the other; both abstractions and concrete detail work together to produce clear, persuasive argument. This is especially true when the meanings assigned to abstract terms vary from reader to reader.

In establishing claims based on the support of values, for example, you may use such abstract terms as *religion, duty, freedom, peace, progress, justice, equality, democracy,* and *pursuit of happiness.* You can assume that some of these words are associated with the same ideas and emotions for almost all readers; others require further explanation. Suppose you write, "We have made great progress in the last fifty years." One dictionary defines *progress* as "a gradual betterment," another abstraction. How will you define "gradual betterment" for your readers? Can you be sure that they have in mind the same references for progress that you do? If not, misunderstandings are inevitable. You may offer examples: supersonic planes, computers, shopping malls, nuclear energy. Many of your readers will react favorably to the mention of these innovations, which to them represent progress; others, for whom these inventions represent change but not progress, will react unfavorably. You may not be able to convince all of your readers that "we have made great progress," but all of them will now understand what you mean by "progress." And intelligent disagreement is preferable to misunderstanding.

Abstractions tell us what conclusions we have arrived at; details tell us how we got there. But there are dangers in either too many details or too many abstractions. For example, a writer may present only concrete data without telling readers what conclusions are to be drawn from them. Suppose you read the following:

> To Chinese road-users, traffic police are part of the grass . . . and neither they nor the rules they're supposed to enforce are paid the least attention. . . . Ignoring traffic-lights is only one peculiarity of Chinese traffic. It's normal for a pedestrian to walk straight out into a stream of cars without so much as lifting his head; and goodness knows how many Chinese cyclists I've almost killed as they have shot blindly in front of me across busy main roads.[11]

These details would constitute no more than interesting gossip until we read, "It's not so much a sign of ignorance or recklessness . . . but of fatalism." The details of specific behavior have now acquired a significance expressed in the abstraction *fatalism*.

A more common problem, however, in using abstractions is omission of details. Either the writer is not a skilled observer and cannot provide the details, or believes that such details are too small and quiet compared to the grand sounds made by abstract terms. These grand sounds, unfortunately, cannot compensate for the lack of clarity and liveliness. Lacking detailed support, abstract words may be misinterpreted. They may also represent ideas that are so vague as to be meaningless. Sometimes they function illegitimately as short cuts (discussed on pp. 360–65), arousing emotions but unaccompanied by good reasons for their use. The following paragraph exhibits some of these common faults. How would you translate it into clear English?

> We respectively petition, request, and entreat that due and adequate provision be made, this day and the date hereinafter subscribed, for the satisfying of these petitioners' nutritional requirements and for the organizing of such methods of allocation and distribution as may be deemed necessary and proper to assure the reception by and for said petitioners of such quantities of baked cereal products as shall, in the judgment of the aforesaid petitioners, constitute a sufficient supply thereof.[12]

If you had trouble decoding this, it was because there were almost no concrete references — the homely words *baked* and *cereal* leap out of the paragraph like English signposts in a foreign country — and too many long words or words of Latin origin when simple words would do: *requirements* instead of *needs, petition* instead of *ask*. An absence of concrete references and an excess of long Latinate words can have a depressing effect on both writer and reader. The writer may be in danger of losing the thread of the argument, the reader at a loss to discover the message.

The paragraph above, according to James B. Minor, a lawyer who teaches courses in legal drafting, is "how a federal regulation writer would probably write, 'Give us this day our daily bread.'" This brief sentence with its short,

[11] Philip Short, "The Chinese and the Russians," *The Listener,* April 8, 1982, p. 6.
[12] *New York Times,* May 10, 1977, p. 35.

familiar words and its origin in the Lord's Prayer has a deep emotional effect. The paragraph composed by Minor deadens any emotional impact because of its preponderance of abstract terms and its lack of connection with the world of our senses.

Finally, there are the moral implications of using abstractions that conceal a disagreeable reality. Consider this scenario:

> It has long been feared that a President could be making his fateful decision while at a "psychological distance" from the victims of a nuclear barrage; that he would be in a clean, air-conditioned room, surrounded by well-scrubbed aides, all talking in abstract terms about appropriate military responses in an international crisis, and that he might well push to the back of his mind the realization that hundreds of millions of people would be exterminated.
>
> So Roger Fisher, professor of law at Harvard University, offers a simple suggestion to make the stakes more real. He would put the codes needed to fire nuclear weapons in a little capsule, and implant the capsule next to the heart of a volunteer, who would carry a big butcher knife as he accompanied the President everywhere. If the President ever wanted to fire nuclear weapons, he would first have to kill, with his own hands, that human being.
>
> He has to look at someone and realize what death is — what an innocent death is. "It's reality brought home," says Professor Fisher.[13]

The moral lesson is clear: It is much easier to do harm if we convince ourselves that the object of the injury is only an abstraction.

Short Cuts

Short cuts are arguments that depend on readers' responses to words. Short cuts, like other devices we have discussed so far, are a common use of emotive language but are often mistaken for valid argument.

Although they have power to move us, these abbreviated substitutes for argument avoid the hard work necessary to provide facts, expert opinion, and analysis of warrants. Even experts, however, can be guilty of using short cuts, and the writer who consults an authority should be alert to that authority's use of language. Two of the most common uses of short cuts are clichés and slogans.

Clichés

A cliché is an expression or idea grown stale through overuse. Clichés in language are tired expressions that have faded like old photographs; readers no lon-

[13]*New York Times*, September 7, 1982, sec. C, p. 1.

ger see anything when clichés are placed before them. Clichés include phrases like "cradle of civilization," "few and far between," "rude awakening," "follow in the footsteps of," "fly in the ointment."

But more important to recognize and avoid are *clichés of thought*. A cliché of thought may be likened to a formula, which one dictionary defines as "any conventional rule or method for doing something, especially when used, applied, or repeated without thought." Clichés of thought represent ready-made answers to questions, stereotyped solutions to problems, "knee-jerk" reactions. Two writers who call these forms of expression "mass language" describe it this way: "Mass language is language which presents the reader with a response he is expected to make without giving him adequate reason for having this response."[14] These clichés of thought are often expressed in single words or phrases.

Certain cultural attitudes encourage the use of clichés. The liberal American tradition has been governed by hopeful assumptions about our ability to solve problems. A professor of communications says that "we tell our students that for every problem there must be a solution."[15] But real solutions are hard to come by. In our haste to provide them, to prove that we can be decisive, we may be tempted to produce familiar responses that resemble solutions. All reasonable solutions are worthy of consideration, but they must be defined and supported if they are to be used in a thoughtful, well-constructed argument.

Although formulas change with the times, some are unexpectedly hardy and survive long after critics have revealed their weaknesses. Overpopulation is often cited as the cause of poverty, disease, and war. It can be found in the writing of the ancient Greeks 2,500 years ago. "That perspective," says the editor of *Food Monitor,* a journal published by World Hunger Year, Inc., "is so pervasive that most Americans have simply stopped thinking about population and resort to inane clucking of tongues."[16] If the writer offering overpopulation as an explanation for poverty were to look further, he or she would discover that the explanation rested on shaky data. Singapore, the second most densely populated country in the world (18,640 persons per square mile) is also one of the richest ($62,200 per capita income per year). Chad, one of the most sparsely populated (22 persons per square kilometer) is also one of the poorest ($1,900 per capita income per year).[17] Strictly defined, overpopulation may serve to explain some instances of poverty; obviously it cannot serve as a blanket to cover all or even most instances. "By repeating stock phrases," one columnist reminds us, "we lose the ability, finally, to hear what we are saying."

[14]Richard E. Hughes and P. Albert Duhamel, *Rhetoric: Principles and Usage* (Englewood Cliffs, N.J.: Prentice-Hall, 1962), p. 161.

[15]Malcolm O. Sillars, "The New Conservatism and the Teacher of Speech," *Southern Speech Journal* 21 (1956), p. 240.

[16]Letter to the *New York Times,* October 4, 1982, sec. A, p. 18.

[17]www.cia.gov; worldatlas.com.

Slogans

> I have always been rather impressed by those people who wear badges stating where they stand on certain issues. The badges have to be small, and therefore the message has to be small, concise, and without elaboration. So it comes out as "I hate something" or "I love something," or ban this or ban that. There isn't space for argument, and I therefore envy the badge-wearer who is so clear-cut about his or her opinions.[18]

The word *slogan* has a picturesque origin. A slogan was the war cry or rallying cry of a Scottish or Irish clan. From that early use it has come to mean a "catchword or rallying motto distinctly associated with a political party or other group" as well as a "catch phrase used to advertise a product."

Slogans, like clichés, are short, undeveloped arguments. They represent abbreviated responses to often complex questions. As a reader you need to be aware that slogans merely call attention to a problem; they cannot offer persuasive proof for a claim in a dozen words or less. As a writer you should avoid the use of slogans that evoke an emotional response "without giving [the reader] adequate reason for having this response."

Advertising slogans are the most familiar. Some of them are probably better known than nursery rhymes: "Got milk?" "L'Oréal, because I'm worth it," "Nike, just do it." Advertisements may, of course, rely for their effectiveness on more than slogans. They may also give us interesting and valuable information about products, but most advertisements give us slogans that ignore proof — short cuts substituting for argument.

The persuasive appeal of advertising slogans heavily depends on the connotations associated with products. In Chapter 6 (see p. 217, under "Appeals to Needs and Values"), we discussed the way in which advertisements promise to satisfy our needs and protect our values. Wherever evidence is scarce or nonexistent, the advertiser must persuade us through skillful choice of words and phrases (as well as pictures), especially those that produce pleasurable feelings. "Let it inspire you" is the slogan of a popular liqueur. It suggests a desirable state of being but remains suitably vague about the nature of the inspiration. Another familiar slogan — "Noxzema, clean makeup" — also emphasizes a quality that we approve of, but what is "clean" makeup? Since the advertisers are silent, we are left with warm feelings about the word and not much more.

Advertising slogans are persuasive because their witty phrasing and punchy rhythms produce an automatic *yes* response. We react to them as we might react to the lyrics of popular songs, and we treat them far less critically than we treat more straightforward and elaborate arguments. Still, the consequences of failing to analyze the slogans of advertisers are usually not serious. You may be tempted to buy a product because you were fascinated by a brilliant slogan, but if the product doesn't satisfy, you can abandon it without much loss. However,

---

[18]Anthony Smith, "Nuclear Power — Why Not?" *The Listener,* October 22, 1981, p. 463.

Slogans are short, undeveloped arguments.

ignoring ideological slogans coined by political parties or special-interest groups may carry an enormous price, and the results are not so easily undone.

Ideological slogans, like advertising slogans, depend on the power of connotation, the emotional associations aroused by a word or phrase. In the 1960s and 1970s, a period of well-advertised social change, slogans flourished; they appeared by the hundreds of thousands on buttons, T-shirts, and bumper stickers. One of them read, "Student Power!" To some readers of the slogan, distrustful of young people and worried about student unrest on campuses and in the streets, the suggestion was frightening. To others, mostly students, the idea of power, however undefined, was intoxicating. Notice that "Student Power!" is not an argument; it is only a claim. (It might also represent a warrant.) As a claim, for example, it might take this form: Students at this school should have the power to select the faculty. Of course, the arguer would need to provide the kinds of proof that support his or her claim, something the slogan by itself cannot do. Many people, whether they accepted or rejected the claim, supplied the rest of the argument without knowing exactly what the issues were and how a developed argument would proceed. They were accepting or rejecting the slogan largely on the basis of emotional reaction to words.

American political history is, in fact, a repository of slogans. Leaf through a history of the United States and you will come across "Tippecanoe and Tyler, too," "manifest destiny," "fifty-four forty or fight," "make the world safe for democracy," "the silent majority," "the domino theory," "the missile gap," "the window of vulnerability." Each administration tries to capture the attention and allegiance of the public by coining catchy phrases. Roosevelt's New Deal in 1932 was followed by the Square Deal and the New Frontier. Today, slogans must be carefully selected to avoid offending groups that are sensitive to the ways in which words affect their interests. In 1983 Senator John Glenn, announcing his candidacy for president, talked about bringing "old values and new horizons" to the White House. "New horizons" apparently carried positive connotations. His staff, however, worried that "old values" might suggest racism and sexism to minorities and women.

Over a period of time, slogans, like clichés, can acquire a life of their own and, if they are repeated often enough, come to represent an unchanging truth we no longer need to examine. "Dangerously," says the writer quoted above, "policy makers become prisoners of the slogans they popularize."

Following are two examples. The first is part of the second inaugural address of George C. Wallace, governor of Alabama, in 1971. The second is taken from an article in the *Militia News,* the organ of a group that believed the U.S. government was engaged in a "satanic conspiracy" to disarm the American people and then enslave them. Timothy McVeigh, who blew up the Oklahoma City federal building in 1995, was influenced by the group.

> The people of the South and those who think like the South, represent the majority viewpoint within our constitutional democracy, but they are not organized and do not speak with a loud voice. Until the day arrives when the voice of the people of the South and those who think like us is, within the law, thrust into the face of the bureaucrats, only then can the "people's power" express itself legally and ethically and get results. . . . Too long, oh, too long, has the voice of the people been silenced by their own disruptive government — by governmental bribery in quasi- governmental handouts such as H.E.W. and others that exist in America today! An aroused people can save this nation from those evil forces who seek our destruction. The choice is yours. The hour is growing late![19]

> Every gun owner who is the least bit informed knows that those who are behind this conspiracy — who now have their people well placed in political office, in the courts, in the media, and in the schools, are working for the total disarming of the American people and the surrender of our nation and our sovereignty. . . . The time is at hand when men and women must decide whether they are on the side of freedom and justice, the American republic, and Almighty God, or if they are on the side of tyranny and oppression, the New World Order, and Satan.[20]

Whatever power these recommendations might have if their proposals were more clearly formulated, as they stand they are collections of slogans and loaded words. (Even the language falters: Can the voice of the people be "thrust into the face of the bureaucrats"?) We can visualize some of the slogans as brightly colored banners: "Dislodge Big Money!" "Power to the People!" "Save This

[19]Second Inaugural Address as governor of Alabama, January 18, 1971.
[20]Chip Berlet and Matthew N. Lyons, *Right-Wing Populism in America* (New York: Guildford Press, 2000), p. 301.

Nation from Evil Forces!" "The Choice Is Yours!" Do all the groups mentioned share identical interests? If so, what are they? Given the vagueness of the terms, it is not surprising that arguers on opposite sides of the political spectrum — loosely characterized as liberal and conservative — sometimes resort to the same clichés and slogans: the language of populism, or a belief in conspiracies against God-fearing people, in these examples.

Slogans have numerous shortcomings as substitutes for the development of an argument. First, their brevity presents serious disadvantages. Slogans necessarily ignore exceptions or negative instances that might qualify a claim. They usually speak in absolute terms without describing the circumstances in which a principle or idea might not work. Their claims therefore seem shrill and exaggerated. In addition, brevity prevents the sloganeer from revealing how he or she arrived at conclusions.

Second, slogans may conceal unexamined warrants. When Japanese cars were beginning to compete with American cars, the slogan "Made in America by Americans" appeared on the bumpers of thousands of American-made cars. A thoughtful reader would have discovered in this slogan several implied warrants: American cars are better than Japanese cars; the American economy will improve if we buy American; patriotism can be expressed by buying American goods. If the reader were to ask a few probing questions, he or she might find these warrants unconvincing.

Silent warrants that express values hide in other popular and influential slogans. "Pro-life," the slogan of those who oppose abortion, assumes that the fetus is a living being entitled to the same rights as individuals already born. "Pro-choice," the slogan of those who favor abortion, suggests that the freedom of the pregnant woman to choose is the foremost or only consideration. The words *life* and *choice* have been carefully selected to reflect desirable qualities, but the words are only the beginning of the argument.

Third, although slogans may express admirable sentiments, they often fail to tell us how to achieve their objectives. They address us in the imperative mode, ordering us to take an action or refrain from it. But the means of achieving the objectives may be nonexistent or very costly. If sloganeers cannot offer workable means for implementing their goals, they risk alienating the audience.

Sloganeering is one of the recognizable attributes of propaganda. Propaganda for both good and bad purposes is a form of slanting, of selecting language and facts to persuade an audience to take a certain action. Even a good cause may be weakened by an unsatisfactory slogan. The slogans of some organizations devoted to fundraising for people with physical handicaps have come under attack for depicting those with handicaps as helpless. According to one critic, the popular slogan "Jerry's kids" promotes the idea that Jerry Lewis is the sole support of children with muscular dystrophy. Perhaps increased sensitivity to the needs of people with disabilities will produce new words and new slogans. If you assume that your audience is sophisticated and alert, you will probably write your strongest arguments, devoid of clichés and slogans.

SAMPLE ANNOTATED ESSAY

President's Address to the Nation, September 11, 2006

GEORGE W. BUSH

Words like seared, barbarity, and murdered are examples of slanting used appropriately for the author's purpose.

Good evening. Five years ago, this date — September the 11th — was seared into America's memory. Nineteen men attacked us with a barbarity unequaled in our history. They murdered people of all colors, creeds, and nationalities — and made war upon the entire free world. Since that day, America and her allies have taken the offensive in a war unlike any we have fought before. Today, we are safer, but we are not yet safe. On this solemn night, I've asked for some of your time to discuss the nature of the threat still before us, what we are doing to protect our nation, and the building of a more hopeful Middle East that holds the key to peace for America and the world.

It is exaggeration to say that the acts described in this paragraph are distinctly American, but the concrete examples are effective for the author's purpose.

On 9/11, our nation saw the face of evil. Yet on that awful day, we also witnessed something distinctly American: ordinary citizens rising to the occasion, and responding with extraordinary acts of courage. We saw courage in office workers who were trapped on the high floors of burning skyscrapers — and called home so that their last words to their families would be of comfort and love. We saw courage in passengers aboard Flight 93, who recited the 23rd Psalm — and then charged the cockpit. And we saw courage in the Pentagon staff who made it out of the flames and smoke — and ran back in to answer cries for help. On this day, we remember the innocent who lost their lives — and we pay tribute to those who gave their lives so that others might live.

More concrete examples, with the first person I making it clear that Bush has shared moments of grief with the victims' families.

For many of our citizens, the wounds of that morning are still fresh. I've met firefighters and police officers who choke up at the memory of fallen comrades. I've stood with families gathered on a grassy field in Pennsylvania, who take bittersweet pride in loved ones who refused to be victims — and gave America our first victory in the war on terror. I've sat beside young mothers with children who are now five years old — and still long for the

For the second time Bush refers to a more hopeful world.

If the rest of the essay does not provide further explanation, this will be a cliché of thought.

Two of the strongest slanted words here are <u>perverted</u> and, in contrast to the reference to civilized nations, the implication that America's enemies are <u>uncivilized</u>.

On the other hand, to have a <u>calling</u> carries a positive slant, suggesting a religious or at least honorable sense of duty.

The allusion to the Cold War will evoke negative memories for some, depending on their age.

The reference to the war in Iraq as one that America didn't <u>ask for</u> suggests that it was imposed on an unwilling nation.

Suggesting what a loss would mean for America's children is an appeal to emotion.

daddies who will never cradle them in their arms. Out of this suffering, we resolve to honor every man and woman lost. And we seek their lasting memorial in a safer and more hopeful world.

Since the horror of 9/11, we've learned a great deal about the enemy. We have learned that they are evil and kill without mercy — but not without purpose. We have learned that they form a global network of extremists who are driven by a perverted vision of Islam — a totalitarian ideology that hates freedom, rejects tolerance, and despises all dissent. And we have learned that their goal is to build a radical Islamic empire where women are prisoners in their homes, men are beaten for missing prayer meetings, and terrorists have a safe haven to plan and launch attacks on America and other civilized nations. The war against this enemy is more than a military conflict. It is the decisive ideological struggle of the twenty first century, and the calling of our generation.

Our nation is being tested in a way that we have not been since the start of the Cold War. We saw what a handful of our enemies can do with box-cutters and plane tickets. We hear their threats to launch even more terrible attacks on our people. And we know that if they were able to get their hands on weapons of mass destruction, they would use them against us. We face an enemy determined to bring death and suffering into our homes. America did not ask for this war, and every American wishes it were over. So do I. But the war is not over — and it will not be over until either we or the extremists emerge victorious. If we do not defeat these enemies now, we will leave our children to face a Middle East overrun by terrorist states and radical dictators armed with nuclear weapons. We are in a war that will set the course for this new century — and determine the destiny of millions across the world.

For America, 9/11 was more than a tragedy — it changed the way we look at the world. On September the 11th, we resolved that we would go on the offense against our enemies, and we would not distinguish between the terrorists and those who harbor or support them. So we helped drive the Taliban from power in Afghanistan. We put al Qaeda on the run, and killed or captured most of those who planned the 9/11 attacks, including the man believed to be the mastermind, Khalid

5

Sheik Mohammed. He and other suspected terrorists have been questioned by the Central Intelligence Agency, and they provided valuable information that has helped stop attacks in America and across the world. Now these men have been transferred to Guantanamo Bay, so they can be held to account for their actions. Osama bin Laden and other terrorists are still in hiding. Our message to them is clear: No matter how long it takes, America will find you, and we will bring you to justice.

On September the 11th, we learned that America must confront threats before they reach our shores, whether those threats come from terrorist networks or terrorist states. I'm often asked why we're in Iraq when Saddam Hussein was not responsible for the 9/11 attacks. The answer is that the regime of Saddam Hussein was a clear threat. My administration, the Congress, and the United Nations saw the threat — and after 9/11, Saddam's regime posed a risk that the world could not afford to take. The world is safer because Saddam Hussein is no longer in power. And now the challenge is to help the Iraqi people build a democracy that fulfills the dreams of the nearly 12 million Iraqis who came out to vote in free elections last December.

Al Qaeda and other extremists from across the world have come to Iraq to stop the rise of a free society in the heart of the Middle East. They have joined the remnants of Saddam's regime and other armed groups to foment sectarian violence and drive us out. Our enemies in Iraq are tough and they are committed — but so are Iraqi and coalition forces. We're adapting to stay ahead of the enemy, and we are carrying out a clear plan to ensure that a democratic Iraq succeeds.

We're training Iraqi troops so they can defend their nation. We're helping Iraq's unity government grow in strength and serve its people. We will not leave until this work is done. Whatever mistakes have been made in Iraq, the worst mistake would be to think that if we pulled out, the terrorists would leave us alone. They will not leave us alone. They will follow us. The safety of America depends on the outcome of the battle in the streets of Baghdad. Osama bin Laden calls this fight "the Third World War" — and he says that victory for the terrorists in Iraq will mean America's "defeat and disgrace forever." If we yield Iraq to men like bin Laden, our enemies will

---

To be held to account for their actions is a cliché, one that may hide uncomfortable truths, given suspicions aroused about how the U.S. questions prisoners.

Another cliché of thought: a risk that the world could not afford to take.

References to democracy and free elections have positive connotations for most Americans.

The allusion to World War I and World War II by alluding to a Third World War, like the allusion to the Cold War, evokes memories, mostly negative, for older Americans.

Osama bin Laden's reference to America's defeat and disgrace forever is a verbal assault on national pride.

The primary slogan for the war in Iraq: the war on terror.

The enemy is guilty of unspeakable violence. The Iraqi people are steadfast. Our Armed Forces have exhibited skill and resolve, made great sacrifices.

Appeals to Americans' need for security.

Slanted language: the enemy's ideology is hateful.

The use of the adjective legal to modify authority is loaded for those who believe Congress was rushed into passing laws that threaten Americans' right to privacy out of fear.

be emboldened; they will gain a new safe haven; they will use Iraq's resources to fuel their extremist movement. We will not allow this to happen. America will stay in the fight. Iraq will be a free nation, and a strong ally in the war on terror.

We can be confident that our coalition will succeed   10
because the Iraqi people have been steadfast in the face of unspeakable violence. And we can be confident in victory because of the skill and resolve of America's Armed Forces. Every one of our troops is a volunteer, and since the attacks of September the 11th, more than 1.6 million Americans have stepped forward to put on our nation's uniform. In Iraq, Afghanistan, and other fronts in the war on terror, the men and women of our military are making great sacrifices to keep us safe. Some have suffered terrible injuries — and nearly 3,000 have given their lives. America cherishes their memory. We pray for their families. And we will never back down from the work they have begun.

We also honor those who toil day and night to keep our homeland safe, and we are giving them the tools they need to protect our people. We've created the Department of Homeland Security. We have torn down the wall that kept law enforcement and intelligence from sharing information. We've tightened security at our airports and seaports and borders, and we've created new programs to monitor enemy bank records and phone calls. Thanks to the hard work of our law enforcement and intelligence professionals, we have broken up terrorist cells in our midst and saved American lives.

Five years after 9/11, our enemies have not succeeded in launching another attack on our soil, but they've not been idle. Al Qaeda and those inspired by its hateful ideology have carried out terrorist attacks in more than two dozen nations. And just last month, they were foiled in a plot to blow up passenger planes headed for the United States. They remain determined to attack America and kill our citizens — and we are determined to stop them. We'll continue to give the men and women who protect us every resource and legal authority they need to do their jobs.

In the first days after the 9/11 attacks I promised to use every element of national power to fight the terrorists, wherever we find them. One of the strongest weapons

Many abstractions here that are clichés of thought if not supported: <u>power of freedom</u>, <u>clash of civilizations</u>, <u>struggle for civilization</u>, <u>way of life enjoyed by free nations</u>.

in our arsenal is the power of freedom. The terrorists fear freedom as much as they do our firepower. They are thrown into panic at the sight of an old man pulling the election lever, girls enrolling in schools, or families worshiping God in their own traditions. They know that given a choice, people will choose freedom over their extremist ideology. So their answer is to deny people this choice by raging against the forces of freedom and moderation. This struggle has been called a clash of civilizations. In truth, it is a struggle for civilization. We are fighting to maintain the way of life enjoyed by free nations. And we're fighting for the possibility that good and decent people across the Middle East can raise up societies based on freedom and tolerance and personal dignity.

We are now in the early hours of this struggle between tyranny and freedom. Amid the violence, some question whether the people of the Middle East want their freedom, and whether the forces of moderation can prevail. For 60 years, these doubts guided our policies in the Middle East. And then, on a bright September morning, it became clear that the calm we saw in the Middle East was only a mirage. Years of pursuing stability to promote peace had left us with neither. So we changed our policies, and committed America's influence in the world to advancing freedom and democracy as the great alternatives to repression and radicalism.

With our help, the people of the Middle East are now   15
stepping forward to claim their freedom. From Kabul to Baghdad to Beirut, there are brave men and women risking their lives each day for the same freedoms that we enjoy. And they have one question for us: Do we have the confidence to do in the Middle East what our fathers and grandfathers accomplished in Europe and Asia? By standing with democratic leaders and reformers, by giving voice to the hopes of decent men and women, we're offering a path away from radicalism. And we are enlisting the most powerful force for peace and moderation in the Middle East: the desire of millions to be free.

The references to what our <u>fathers and grandfathers</u> did in <u>Europe and Asia</u> is an additional appeal to American pride. Only those who agree with America deserve the label <u>decent</u>.

Across the broader Middle East, the extremists are fighting to prevent such a future. Yet America has confronted evil before, and we have defeated it — sometimes at the cost of thousands of good men in a single battle. When Franklin Roosevelt vowed to defeat two enemies across two oceans, he could not have foreseen D-Day and

Allusions to previous American victories and former presidents who led the nation during World War II and the Cold War.

Iwo Jima — but he would not have been surprised at the outcome. When Harry Truman promised American support for free peoples resisting Soviet aggression, he could not have foreseen the rise of the Berlin Wall — but he would not have been surprised to see it brought down. Throughout our history, America has seen liberty challenged, and every time, we have seen liberty triumph with sacrifice and determination.

At the start of this young century, America looks to the day when the people of the Middle East leave the desert of despotism for the fertile gardens of liberty, and resume their rightful place in a world of peace and prosperity. We look to the day when the nations of that region recognize their greatest resource is not the oil in the ground, but the talent and creativity of their people. We look to the day when moms and dads throughout the Middle East see a future of hope and opportunity for their children. And when that good day comes, the clouds of war will part, the appeal of radicalism will decline, and we will leave our children with a better and safer world.

Desert of despotism and fertile gardens of liberty — picturesque language used for contrast.

On this solemn anniversary, we rededicate ourselves to this cause. Our nation has endured trials, and we face a difficult road ahead. Winning this war will require the determined efforts of a unified country, and we must put aside our differences and work together to meet the test that history has given us. We will defeat our enemies. We will protect our people. And we will lead the twenty first century into a shining age of human liberty.

A specific example that carries emotional impact.

Earlier this year, I traveled to the United States Military Academy. I was there to deliver the commencement address to the first class to arrive at West Point after the attacks of September the 11th. That day I met a proud mom named RoseEllen Dowdell. She was there to watch her son, Patrick, accept his commission in the finest Army the world has ever known. A few weeks earlier, RoseEllen had watched her other son, James, graduate from the Fire Academy in New York City. On both these days, her thoughts turned to someone who was not there to share the moment: her husband, Kevin Dowdell. Kevin was one of the 343 firefighters who rushed to the burning towers of the World Trade Center on September the 11th — and never came home. His sons lost their father that day, but not the passion for service he instilled in them. Here is what RoseEllen says about her boys: "As a mother, I cross my fingers and pray all the time for their safety — but as worried as I am, I'm also proud, and I know their dad would be, too."

A creative play on the two ways that people are <u>brought to their knees.</u>

Our nation is blessed to have young Americans like   20
these — and we will need them. Dangerous enemies have declared their intention to destroy our way of life. They're not the first to try, and their fate will be the same as those who tried before. Nine-Eleven showed us why. The attacks were meant to bring us to our knees, and they did, but not in the way the terrorists intended. Americans united in prayer, came to the aid of neighbors in need, and resolved that our enemies would not have the last word. The spirit of our people is the source of America's strength. And we go forward with trust in that spirit, confidence in our purpose, and faith in a loving God who made us to be free.

Thank you, and may God bless you.

Writer's Guide: Choosing Your Words Carefully

1. Be sure you have avoided language with connotations that might produce a negative reaction in your audience that would weaken your argument.

2. If you have used slanted language, consider whether it will advance your argument instead of weakening it.

3. Use picturesque language where appropriate for your purposes.

4. Replace abstract language with concrete language to be more effective.

5. Edit out any clichés or slogans from your early drafts.

6. Achieve a voice that is appropriate for your subject and audience.

Nobel Prize Acceptance Speech

WILLIAM FAULKNER

I feel that this award was not made to me as a man, but to my work — a life's work in the agony and sweat of the human spirit, not for glory and least of all for profit, but to create out of the materials of the human spirit something which did not exist before. So this award is only mine in trust. It will not be difficult to find a dedication for the money part of it commensurate with the purpose and significance of its origin. But I would like to do the same with the acclaim too, by using this moment as a pinnacle from which I might be listened to by the young men and women already dedicated to the same anguish and travail, among whom is already that one who will some day stand here where I am standing.

Our tragedy today is a general and universal physical fear so long sustained by now that we can even bear it. There are no longer problems of the spirit. There is only the question: When will I be blown up? Because of this, the young man or woman writing today has forgotten the problems of the human heart in conflict with itself which alone can make good writing because only that is worth writing about, worth the agony and the sweat.

He must learn them again. He must teach himself that the basest of all things is to be afraid; and, teaching himself that, forget it forever, leaving no room in his workshop for anything but the old verities and truths of the heart, the old universal truths lacking which any story is ephemeral and doomed — love and honor and pity and pride and compassion and sacrifice. Until he does so, he labors under a curse. He writes not of love but of lust, of defeats in which nobody loses anything of value, of victories without hope and, worst of all, without pity or compassion. His griefs grieve on no universal bones, leaving no scars. He writes not of the heart but of the glands.

Until he relearns these things, he will write as though he stood among and watched the end of man. I decline to accept the end of man. It is easy enough to say that man is immortal simply because he will endure: that when the last ding-dong of doom has clanged and faded from the last worthless rock hanging tideless in the last red and dying evening, that even then there will still be one more sound: that of his puny inexhaustible voice, still talking. I refuse to accept this. I believe that man will not merely endure: He will prevail. He is immortal, not because he alone among creatures has an inexhaustible voice, but because he has

---

William Faulkner was one of the dominant Southern novelists of the early twentieth century. He gave this speech at the Nobel Banquet at City Hall in Stockholm, Sweden, on December 10, 1950, when he accepted the Nobel Prize in Literature for 1949. Some minor revisions, included here, were made when the piece was prepared for publication in *The Faulkner Reader* (Random House, 1954).

a soul, a spirit capable of compassion and sacrifice and endurance. The poet's, the writer's, duty is to write about these things. It is his privilege to help man endure by lifting his heart, by reminding him of the courage and honor and hope and pride and compassion and pity and sacrifice which have been the glory of his past. The poet's voice need not merely be the record of man, it can be one of the props, the pillars to help him endure and prevail.

The Speech the Graduates Didn't Hear

JACOB NEUSNER

We the faculty take no pride in our educational achievements with you. We have prepared you for a world that does not exist, indeed, that cannot exist. You have spent four years supposing that failure leaves no record. You have learned at Brown that when your work goes poorly, the painless solution is to drop out. But starting now, in the world to which you go, failure marks you. Confronting difficulty by quitting leaves you changed. Outside Brown, quitters are no heroes.

With us you could argue about why your errors were not errors, why mediocre work really was excellent, why you could take pride in routine and slipshod presentation. Most of you, after all, can look back on honor grades for most of what you have done. So, here grades can have meant little in distinguishing the excellent from the ordinary. But tomorrow, in the world to which you go, you had best not defend errors but learn from them. You will be ill-advised to demand praise for what does not deserve it, and abuse those who do not give it.

For four years we created an altogether forgiving world, in which whatever slight effort you gave was all that was demanded. When you did not keep appointments, we made new ones. When your work came in beyond the deadline, we pretended not to care.

Worse still, when you were boring, we acted as if you were saying something important. When you were garrulous and talked to hear yourself talk, we listened as if it mattered. When you tossed on our desks writing upon which you had not labored, we read it and even responded, as though you earned a response. When you were dull, we pretended you were smart. When you were predictable, unimaginative, and routine, we listened as if to new and wonderful things. When you demanded free lunch, we served it. And all this why?

Despite your fantasies, it was not even that we wanted to be liked by you. It was that we did not want to be bothered, and the easy way out was pretense: smiles and easy Bs.

5

Formerly a professor at Brown University, Jacob Neusner is Distinguished Service Professor of the History and Theology of Judaism and Senior Fellow of the Institute of Advanced Theology at Bard College. His speech appeared in Brown's *Daily Herald* on June 12, 1983.

It is conventional to quote in addresses such as these. Let me quote someone you've never heard of: Professor Carter A. Daniel, Rutgers University (*Chronicle of Higher Education,* May 7, 1979):

> College has spoiled you by reading papers that don't deserve to be read, listening to comments that don't deserve a hearing, paying attention even to the lazy, ill-informed, and rude. We had to do it, for the sake of education. But nobody will ever do it again. College has deprived you of adequate preparation for the last fifty years. It has failed you by being easy, free, forgiving, attentive, comfortable, interesting, unchallenging fun. Good luck tomorrow.

That is why, on this commencement day, we have nothing in which to take much pride.

Oh, yes, there is one more thing. Try not to act toward your coworkers and bosses as you have acted toward us. I mean, when they give you what you want but have not earned, don't abuse them, insult them, act out with them your parlous relationships with your parents. This too we have tolerated. It was, as I said, not to be liked. Few professors actually care whether or not they are liked by peer-paralyzed adolescents, fools so shallow as to imagine professors care not about education but about popularity. It was, again, to be rid of you. So go, unlearn the lies we taught you. To Life!

READING AND DISCUSSION QUESTIONS

1. Neusner condemns students for various shortcomings. But what is he saying, both directly and indirectly, about teachers? Find places where he reveals his attitude toward them, perhaps inadvertently.

2. Pick out some of the language devices — connectives, parallel structures, sentence variety — that the author uses effectively.

3. Pick out some of the words and phrases — especially adjectives and verbs — used by Neusner to characterize both students and teachers. Do you think these terms are loaded? Explain.

4. Has the author chosen "facts" to slant his article? If so, point out where slanting occurs. If not, point out where the article seems to be truthful.

5. As a student you will probably object to Neusner's accusations. How would you defend your behavior as a student in answer to his specific charges?

WRITING SUGGESTIONS

6. Rewrite Neusner's article with the same "facts" — or others from your experience — using temperate language and a tone of sadness rather than anger.

7. Write a letter to Neusner responding to his attack. Support or attack his argument by providing evidence from your own experience.

8. Write your own short commencement address. Do some things need to be said that commencement speakers seldom or never express?

9. Write an essay using the same kind of strong language as Neusner uses about some aspect of your education of which you disapprove. Or write a letter to a teacher using the same form as "The Speech The Graduates Didn't Hear."

Driving Home Their Point

R. CORT KIRKWOOD

A recent story in the *Press-Enterprise* of Riverside, California, gives the lie to the notion that illegal aliens are just here "to do the jobs Americans won't do" and are largely a law-abiding class of the downtrodden, shifting where they can for work.

In May, the newspaper reported that "activists" warn illegal-alien drivers about sobriety checkpoints so they won't be stopped. That, you see, would mean losing their automobiles, the penalty in some benighted localities for driving without a valid driver's license.

The newspaper opened with the classic anecdotal lede:

> Adrianna Castellon, 16, stood on the sidewalk of a busy Moreno Valley street on a recent school night, yelling at cars rushing past.
> "Checkpoint! Checkpoint ahead!" she screamed. "Turn back while you can!"
> The high school student was among protesters hoping to help illegal immigrants whose vehicles were about to be impounded by police because they were driving without a license.

California, the paper reports, declared 2010 "the 'year of the checkpoint' and plans a record $8 million in checkpoint grants, up from $5 million in 2009." Unsurprisingly, "Latinos" rushed into action faster than Speedy Gonzalez, and not just because an illegal without a license can lose his car for a month.

They allege that police are "profiling" because they set up the checkpoints in   5
mostly "Hispanic" communities. Figures reported in the paper on the number and location of checkpoints prove it:

> A review of Riverside County Sheriff's Department figures shows that in 2009 Inland police in cities with larger percentages of Hispanic residents hosted more checkpoints.
> For example, Temecula, a city of about 105,000 that's 22 percent Hispanic, had five. Riverside, which has 304,000 residents and a 48 percent Hispanic population, did 10. San Bernardino, a 205,000-person city with a 57 percent Hispanic community, had 14. Perris, a city of about 55,000 that's 70 percent Hispanic, had 13. Moreno Valley, where 53 percent of the city's 189,000 residents are Hispanic, held 20 checkpoints — more than any other city in Riverside County. . . .
> In 2009 sheriff's stations in western Riverside County logged 70 vehicle tows in Temecula, 702 in Perris and 1,540 in Moreno Valley, where police impounded the most vehicles. Most belonged to drivers with no license or a suspended license.
> Most Moreno Valley checkpoints have been in the most heavily Hispanic of the city's five voting districts. According to agency records, from 2007 to 2009,

---

R. Cort Kirkwood is a journalist who publishes frequently in *Chronicles: A Magazine of American Culture*, the source of this piece on August 16, 2010, and is the author of *Real Men: Ten Courageous Americans to Know and Admire* (2005).

police hosted a total of 36 checkpoints throughout three city districts where Hispanics are the largest ethnic group.

During the same two-year period police held a total of five checkpoints throughout two districts that are less densely populated and cover the largest area, where whites are the largest racial group.

With that kind of fascism afoot, what's a poor *campesino* to do?

Of course, police denied profiling Mexicans and claimed they "chose the busiest streets and relied on the same four or five spots because they have large areas to park tow trucks and other vehicles," the *Press-Enterprise* reported. So they "began this year spreading checkpoints across the entire city." This hasty admission proved the "Latinos" were right.

The better response would have been to tell the "Latinos" the checkpoints will stand as long as necessary, given this telling statistic, also from the newspaper account: Drivers without licenses account for 40 percent of the nation's hit-and-run crashes. The paper didn't report that statistics show a strong correlation between the number of illegals in a state and the number of unlicensed drivers involved in hit-and-run fatalities. Profiling used to be called good police work.

As reports about illegals go, this one seems ho-hum compared with the usual horror story about an unlicensed Mexican career criminal, hurtling down the street in a Chevy Suburban and killing a child eating ice cream at Baskin-Robbins. Except for one thing: the shift in what Latino "activists" implicitly claim by warning illegals about the checkpoints. In the past, they said illegals needed licenses because they must get to work. Now, licenses don't matter — because illegals must get to work.

And the "Latinos" — Mexicans — don't care who gets killed. Their activism has gone beyond marching in the streets and shouting for open borders. Now it includes public obstruction of justice.

10

DEBATE   Does the Government Have the Right to Regulate Guns?

The Right to Bear Arms

WARREN E. BURGER

Our metropolitan centers, and some suburban communities of America, are setting new records for homicides by handguns. Many of our large centers have up to ten times the murder rate of all of Western Europe. In 1988, there were 9,000 handgun murders in America. Last year, Washington, D.C., alone had more than 400 homicides — setting a new record for our capital.

Warren E. Burger (1907–1995) was chief justice of the United States from 1969 to 1986. This article is from the January 14, 1990, issue of *Parade* magazine.

The Constitution of the United States, in its Second Amendment, guarantees a "right of the people to keep and bear arms." However, the meaning of this clause cannot be understood except by looking to the purpose, the setting, and the objectives of the draftsmen. The first ten amendments — the Bill of Rights — were not drafted at Philadelphia in 1787; that document came two years later than the Constitution. Most of the states already had bills of rights, but the Constitution might not have been ratified in 1788 if the states had not had assurances that a national Bill of Rights would soon be added.

People of that day were apprehensive about the new "monster" national government presented to them, and this helps explain the language and purpose of the Second Amendment. A few lines after the First Amendment's guarantees — against "establishment of religion," "free exercise" of religion, free speech and free press — came a guarantee that grew out of the deep-seated fear of a "national" or "standing" army. The same First Congress that approved the right to keep and bear arms also limited the national army to 840 men; Congress in the Second Amendment then provided:

> A well regulated Militia, being necessary to the security of a free State, the right of the people to keep and bear Arms, shall not be infringed.

In the 1789 debate in Congress on James Madison's proposed Bill of Rights, Elbridge Gerry argued that a state militia was necessary:

> to prevent the establishment of a standing army, the bane of liberty. . . . Whenever governments mean to invade the rights and liberties of the people, they always attempt to destroy the militia in order to raise an army upon their ruins.

We see that the need for a state militia was the predicate of the "right" guaranteed; in short, it was declared "necessary" in order to have a state military force to protect the security of the state. That Second Amendment clause must be read as though the word "because" was the opening word of the guarantee. Today, of course, the "state militia" serves a very different purpose. A huge national defense establishment has taken over the role of the militia of 200 years ago.

Some have exploited these ancient concerns, blurring sporting guns — rifles, shotguns, and even machine pistols — with all firearms, including what are now called "Saturday night specials." There is, of course, a great difference between sporting guns and handguns. Some regulation of handguns has long been accepted as imperative; laws relating to "concealed weapons" are common. That we may be "overregulated" in some areas of life has never held us back from more regulation of automobiles, airplanes, motorboats, and "concealed weapons."

Let's look at the history.

First, many of the 3.5 million people living in the thirteen original Colonies depended on wild game for food, and a good many of them required firearms for their defense from marauding Indians — and later from the French and English. Underlying all these needs was an important concept that each able-bodied man in each of the thirteen independent states had to help or defend his state.

The early opposition to the idea of national or standing armies was maintained under the Articles of Confederation; that confederation had no standing army and wanted none. The state militia — essentially a part-time citizen army, as in Switzerland today — was the only kind of "army" they wanted. From the time of the Declaration of Independence through the victory at Yorktown in 1781, George Washington, as the commander in chief of these volunteer-militia armies, had to depend upon the states to send those volunteers.

When a company of New Jersey militia volunteers reported for duty to Washington at Valley Forge, the men initially declined to take an oath to "the United States," maintaining, "Our country is New Jersey." Massachusetts Bay men, Virginians, and others felt the same way. To the American of the eighteenth century, his state was his country, and his freedom was defended by his militia.

The victory at Yorktown — and the ratification of the Bill of Rights a decade later — did not change people's attitudes about a national army. They had lived for years under the notion that each state would maintain its own military establishment, and the seaboard states had their own navies as well. These people, and their fathers and grandfathers before them, remembered how monarchs had used standing armies to oppress their ancestors in Europe. Americans wanted no part of this. A state militia, like a rifle and powder horn, was as much a part of life as the automobile is today; pistols were largely for officers, aristocrats — and dueling.

Against this background, it was not surprising that the provision concerning firearms emerged in very simple terms with the significant predicate — basing the right on the *necessity* for a "well regulated militia," a state army.

In the two centuries since then — with two world wars and some lesser ones — it has become clear, sadly, that we have no choice but to maintain a standing national army while still maintaining a "militia" by way of the National Guard, which can be swiftly integrated into the national defense forces.

Americans also have a right to defend their homes, and we need not challenge that. Nor does anyone seriously question that the Constitution protects the right of hunters to own and keep sporting guns for hunting game any more than anyone would challenge the right to own and keep fishing rods and other equipment for fishing — or to own automobiles. To "keep and bear arms" for hunting today is essentially a recreational activity and not an imperative of survival, as it was 200 years ago; "Saturday night specials" and machine guns are not recreational weapons and surely are as much in need of regulation as motor vehicles.

Americans should ask themselves a few questions. The Constitution does not mention automobiles or motorboats, but the right to keep and own an automobile is beyond question; equally beyond question is the power of the state to regulate the purchase or the transfer of such vehicle and the right to license the vehicle and the driver with reasonable standards. In some places, even a bicycle must be registered, as must some household dogs.

If we are to stop this mindless homicidal carnage, is it unreasonable:

1. to provide that, to acquire a firearm, an application be made reciting age, residence, employment, and any prior criminal convictions?

2. to require that this application lie on the table for ten days (absent a showing for urgent need) before the license would be issued?

3. that the transfer of a firearm be made essentially as that of a motor vehicle?

4. to have a "ballistic fingerprint" of the firearm made by the manufacturer and filed with the license record so that, if a bullet is found in a victim's body, law enforcement might be helped in finding the culprit?

These are the kinds of questions the American people must answer if we are to preserve the "domestic tranquility" promised in the Constitution.

A God-Given Natural Right

ROGER D. MCGRATH

I do not believe in unilateral disarmament: not for the nation; not for our citizens. Neither did the Founding Fathers. They were students of history, especially of classical antiquity. They knew the history of the Greek city-states and Rome as well as they knew the history of the American colonies. This led them to conclude that an armed citizenry is essential to the preservation of freedom and democracy. Once disarmed, populations either submit meekly to tyrants or fight in vain.

The ancient Greeks knew this. The Greek city-state of Laconia had a population that was five percent Spartan (the warrior aristocracy), one percent *perioeci* (small merchants and craftsmen), and 94 percent *helots* (serfs bound to the soil). It is no mystery how five percent of the population kept 94 percent of the people enslaved. The *helots* were kept disarmed and, if found in possession of a weapon, were put to death.

Meanwhile, most of the Greek city-states were bastions of democracy because they had developed strong middle classes of armed citizens known as *hoplites*. Supplying their own weapons and equipment, the *hoplites* went into battle not out of fear of punishment or in hopes of plunder and booty, as did subject peoples of the Oriental empires, but to defend their liberties and to protect hearth and home. They fought side by side with neighbors, brothers, fathers, sons, uncles, and cousins. They did their utmost to demonstrate courage, side by side with their comrades in arms. If they lost a battle to the armies of an Oriental despot, they stood

---

For fifteen years, Roger McGrath taught courses in the history of the American West, California, and the United States at UCLA and has also taught at California State University, Northridge. His articles have appeared in the *Wall Street Journal, American Guardian, Chronicles,* the *New York Times,* and *Harper's.* He is the author of *Gunfighters, Highwaymen, and Vigilantes* (1984) and coauthor of *Violence in America* (1989). This article appeared in the October 2003 issue of *Chronicles.*

to lose everything — property, freedom, democracy. A defeat for subject peoples usually meant nothing more than a change of rulers.

The ancient Romans also knew this. When Tarquin, the Etruscan king of Rome, issued an order — for the public good, for safety and security — that the Romans be disarmed, they rose in rebellion. Tarquin was driven from the city, and the early Roman Republic was established. For several hundred years, Rome was defended not by a professional army of mercenaries or subject peoples but by armed citizen-soldiers who left the farm from time to time to serve the republic. Once the system broke down, the Roman Republic was transformed into an empire similar to the despotic regimes of the East.

Death and destruction commonly followed disarmament. England did it to the Gaels — the Irish and Scots — and the consequences beggar description. England had been fighting in Ireland for hundreds of years by the time the English got Irish leader Patrick Sarsfield to sign the Treaty of Limerick in 1691. The treaty guaranteed all Irish full civil, religious, and property rights. In return, it required that Sarsfield and more than 20,000 of his soldiers leave Ireland for the Continent.

With the armed defenders of Ireland overseas, England began to abrogate the rights supposedly guaranteed by the treaty. Beginning in 1709, England passed the statutes that collectively became known as the Penal Laws. One of the first of these laws declared that, for public safety, no Irish Catholic could keep and bear arms. Then the Irish Catholic was denied the right to an education, to enter a profession, to hold public office, to engage in trade or commerce, to own a horse of greater value than five pounds, to purchase or lease land, to vote, to attend the worship of his choice, to send his children abroad to receive an education. By the time the last of the Penal Laws was enacted, the Irish, although they were not chattel property, in many ways had fewer rights than black slaves in America. The Irish were kept on a near starvation diet, and their life expectancy was the lowest in the Western world.

Things were not much better in the Highlands of Scotland. England had subdued the Lowlands by the fourteenth century, but the Highlands, the truly Gaelic portion of Scotland, continued to be troublesome well into the eighteenth century. A major rebellion erupted in 1715; another, in 1745. The end for the Highlanders came at the Battle of Culloden in 1746. Following the battle, the English built a series of forts across the Highlands and passed laws for the Highlanders — who were originally Irish, of course — similar to the Penal Laws. England made it a crime for the Highlanders to wear kilts, play bagpipes, and keep and bear arms. A Highlander found with a claymore or any other kind of sword or arm was put to death. The English army, understanding that it is easier to starve a fierce enemy into submission than to fight him, eagerly slaughtered the cattle herds of the Highlands, precipitating a great starvation. Thousands of Highlanders died or fled. The English later engaged in the infamous "clearances" in which thousands more were driven from the land. Without arms, the Highlanders were helpless.

What the English did to the Irish and Scots was not lost on our Founding Fathers or on the colonists in general. More than a quarter of the colonists were Irish

5

or Scottish or Scotch-Irish. When England tried to disarm the American colonists, all under the guise of preserving public order and peace, the colonists reacted violently. While it is rarely taught in schools today, the reason the British army marched to Lexington and Concord was to confiscate the arms caches of the local citizenry.

It is not by accident, then, that the Framers of the Constitution ensured that the government could not infringe on "the right of the people to keep and bear arms." It is important to understand that the Second Amendment grants no right to the people to keep and bear arms. This is a point misunderstood by most Americans today, even by most of those who are interested in keeping their guns.

The Second Amendment, like the First, recognizes a God-given, natural right   10
of the people and guarantees that the government not interfere with the exercise of that right. Note the wording of the amendment. Nowhere does it say, "This Constitution grants the people the right to . . ." Instead, it says "the right of the people . . . shall not be infringed." The right to keep and bear arms, like that of freedom of speech, is known, constitutionally, as an inherent right. By contrast, the Sixth Amendment right to be represented by an attorney in a criminal case is a derivative right — a right that comes from the Constitution.

To understand this is critical to all arguments about guns, or about freedom of speech, or religion, or the press. These freedoms were not given to us by the Founding Fathers. They were recognized by the Founding Fathers as God-given, natural rights that existed long before the establishment of our republic. These rights are not granted to men by a benevolent government but given to man by God. They are not to be destroyed, suppressed, or even compromised. When they are, it is the duty of the citizens to rise in revolt, overthrow the government, and establish a government that will protect these unalienable rights. Sound familiar? It should. This was the philosophy of our Founding Fathers.

The most basic of the natural rights of man is the right to self-preservation, the right to self-defense. No one would deny that we have such a right. In debates at universities and at other public forums, in debates on radio, in debates on television, I have never seen anyone deny that man has a natural right to self-defense. It follows that, if man has a natural right to self-defense, then he has a right to the arms necessary for that self-defense. The right to be armed is a logical and inescapable corollary of the right to self-defense. We cannot have one without the other.

If we do not have the right to the arms necessary for self-defense, then the right of self-defense is purely theoretical — something like having freedom of the press but not being allowed access to a printing press. Can you imagine the National Rifle Association telling the *New York Times* that it has freedom of the press but it may not have printing presses, or that the *Times* can purchase only one printing press per month, or that its writers must undergo background checks by the government, or that it cannot buy ink for the presses in New York City, or that its presses have limits on their speed and capacity, or that its presses must meet certain design requirements? If any of this were suggested, the *Times* would squeal like a stuck pig, and well it should.

Some people, presumably well intentioned, argue that the right to arms (and, thus, the right to self-defense) should be compromised — compromised further than it already has been — in an effort to make society safer. Such a position is ironic on two counts.

First, many of the same people who make gun-restriction arguments, such as the ACLU, would be apoplectic if it were suggested that freedom of speech be curtailed to ensure greater public safety. For example, we could have a two-week waiting period on expressing an opinion after the opinion was duly registered with a government agency. That way, the government could screen the opinion to ensure that it was politically correct.   15

The compromise-your-rights-for-safety argument is also ironic because the thousands of gun laws on the books — municipal, county, state, and federal — have done nothing to stop crime. In fact, they have done the opposite. The laws, for the most part, have disarmed, or made access to guns more difficult for, the law-abiding, peaceable citizen. Criminals do not turn in their guns. Murderers, rapists, and robbers do not obey gun laws. However, they do calculate the risks involved in committing crime. If they can assume that potential victims are unarmed, they are emboldened and are more likely to attack.

John Lott, in *More Guns Less Crime*, an exhaustive county-by-county study of rates of gun ownership and crime, concludes that the counties with the highest rates of gun ownership have the least crime and that those with the lowest rates of gun ownership have the most crime. For years, this has been obvious when looking at cities. Washington, D.C., and New York City, for example, with the most restrictive gun laws in the nation, have, for a generation, been cesspools of crime. Criminals there know that they can count on their victims being unarmed.

I suspect that even deeply disturbed killers, such as the teenage boys in Littleton, Colorado, understood that they could kill with impunity in the disarmed environment of the high school. The presence of a highly trained, armed security guard, with a reputation as an expert marksman, may have deterred them. If not, then the guard might have granted them their suicidal wish before they were able to commit mass murder. One or two key teachers, trained and armed, might also have made a difference. Certainly, gun laws did nothing to stop the killers. The two boys violated more than a dozen different gun laws, including one of the oldest on the books — possession of a sawed-off shotgun. Gun laws promise much and deliver little, because they affect only the law abiding, something like sheep passing resolutions requiring vegetarianism while wolves circle the flock.

I grew up in Los Angeles when gun laws were few and crime was low. Nearly everyone I knew had a 30.06, a couple of .22s, a shotgun, and a revolver or two sitting around their house. We could buy guns mail-order and pick up our ammunition at the local grocery store. A gun was a common companion to the road maps in the glove compartment of the car. Did this cause crime? In 1952, there were 81 murders in Los Angeles. In 1992, forty years and many gun laws later, there were 1,092 murders. If the increase in murder had kept pace with the increase in population, there would have been 142 murders, a 75 percent increase. Instead, murder increased 1,350 percent. Other crimes had similar increases: robbery, 1,540 percent; auto theft, 1,100 percent.

The Los Angeles Police Department used to solve more than 90 percent of the murders committed in the city. Today, the figure is 60 percent. Detectives complain that the caseload is too great to conduct the kind of thorough investigations that were common in the '40s and '50s. It is far worse for lesser crimes. Merchants complain that customers brazenly walk out of their stores without paying for merchandise because they know that the police will not respond (at least in a timely fashion) to a call reporting shoplifting. Cars are stolen so often, some 200 per day, that the LAPD does nothing more than list the vehicle on a "hot sheet" and wish the victim good luck.

In the '50s, if your bicycle were stolen, the police would come out to your house and take a report. Try calling the LAPD today and telling them that your bike has been stolen! The police are simply overwhelmed by the sheer volume of crime and are kept fully occupied by murder, armed robbery, and rape — occupied, that is, by the aftermath of murder, armed robbery, and rape. When police arrive at the scene of a crime, the crime has already taken place — the victim has already been murdered, robbed, or raped.

"Carjacking" has become quite common in Los Angeles, because the carjackers know that California drivers cannot legally carry loaded firearms and will nearly always be unarmed. Occasionally, carjackers make poor choices. Three such carjackers followed my friend's son, Justin, as he drove home in his new car late one night. Little did they know that Justin was a reserve police officer. They did not know that he was well armed and an expert marksman.

When Justin pulled into the family driveway and got out of his car, one of the carjackers jumped out of his own vehicle and yelled at Justin, whose back was turned, "Freeze, motherf — er!" It was exactly what Justin had expected. Justin spun about and emptied the contents of his .45 into the carjacker. The carjacker's partners sped away as fast as their car would take them, leaving their good buddy very dead on my friend's front lawn.

Not long after Justin had sent the carjacker to the great salvage yard in the sky, I read of an off-duty police officer who had a similar encounter. On his way home and wearing plainclothes, he stopped to make a phone call. While he stood talking to his wife on an outdoor public phone, two muggers rushed up to him. One of them brandished a gun and said: "Your wallet!" Instead of pulling out his wallet, the cop drew a gun and sent the mugger to the morgue.

The *Los Angeles Times* noted that the mugger certainly picked on the wrong person. This is the same *Los Angeles Times* that regularly editorializes against an armed citizenry and has never seen a gun law that it did not like. Somehow, the newspaper thinks that disarming peaceable, law-abiding citizens will affect criminal behavior for the better. Disarming peaceable, law-abiding citizens *will* affect criminal behavior — but for the worse. Criminals will be emboldened because their chances of picking on the wrong person will be dramatically reduced. Shouldn't the opposite be the case? Shouldn't every person be the wrong person or, at least, potentially the wrong person?

20

25

Grandstanding politicians love to rail against the gun. Inanimate objects are good targets to beat up on. That way, politicians do not have to address the real problems in our society. We pay a price for this craven misdirection, though, in thousands of murders, muggings, rapes, robberies, and burglaries.

Yet that is not the greatest danger we face. The Founding Fathers knew that *governments* could turn criminal. That is the principal reason they wanted every man armed: An armed citizenry militates against the development of tyranny. The Founding Fathers did not want every man armed in order to shoot a burglar, although they had nothing against doing so. The Founding Fathers did not want every man armed in order to shoot Bambi or Thumper, although they had nothing against doing so. The Founding Fathers wanted every man armed in order to shoot soldiers or police of tyrannical regimes who suppress the rights of free men.

When governments become criminal, they disarm the populace. Then the numbers of deaths reach the tens of thousands, the hundreds of thousands, the millions. Can't happen? Ask the Irish and the Scots, or the Armenians, the Ukrainians, the Jews, the Chinese, the Cambodians.

In the Marine Corps, I was trained never to surrender my weapon. It was good advice then, and it is good advice now. I shall put my faith not in the goodwill of governments but in an armed citizenry — a band of brothers — steeped in the ideology of the Founding Fathers and the spirit of Patrick Henry, who said: "Is life so dear or peace so sweet as to be purchased at the price of slavery and chains? I know not what course others may take, but as for me, give me liberty or give me death."

DISCUSSION QUESTIONS

1. What does Burger understand the intent of the Second Amendment to have been, in context? How has history changed the way it should now be read?

2. What analogy does Burger make between guns and automobiles? Is his point a good one?

3. What questions does Burger believe Americans should be answering if we are to stop what he calls "this mindless homicidal carnage" (para. 16)?

4. Does McGrath make use of history in the same way and for the same purpose as Burger does? Explain.

5. What does McGrath mean when he says, "It is important to understand that the Second Amendment grants no right to the people to keep and bear arms" (para. 9)?

6. What is the warrant underlying Burger's essay? McGrath's?

7. What is McGrath's response to the claim that gun restrictions would make society safer?

8. Do you detect any logical fallacies in either essay?

9. Compare the authors' use of language. Do the authors use slanted or emotive language? Short cuts? Where in McGrath's essay is there a shift in the type of language used, and why?

Assignments for Choosing Fair and Precise Language

READING AND DISCUSSION QUESTIONS

1. Select one or two related bumper stickers visible in your town or city. Examine the hidden warrants on which they are based, and assess their validity.

2. For a slogan found on a bumper sticker or elsewhere, supply the evidence to support the claim in the slogan. Or find evidence that disproves the claim.

3. Examine a few periodicals from fifty or more years ago. Select either an advertising or a political slogan in one of them, and relate it to beliefs or events of the period. Or tell why the slogan is no longer relevant.

4. Discuss the origin of a cliché or slogan. Describe, as far as possible, the backgrounds and motives of its users.

5. Make up your own slogan for a cause that you support. Explain and defend your slogan.

6. Choose a cliché, and find evidence to support or refute it. *Examples:* People were much happier in the past. Mother knows best. Life used to be simpler. Money can't buy happiness.

7. In watching television dramas about law, medicine, or criminal or medical investigation, do you find that the professional language, some of which you may not fully understand, plays a positive or negative role in your enjoyment of the show? Explain your answer.

8. Listen to a radio or television report of a sports event. Do the announcers use a kind of language, especially jargon, that would not be used in print reports? One critic thinks that sports broadcasting has had a "destructive effect . . . on ordinary American English." Is he right or wrong?

9. Whose argument about the right to bear arms do you find more convincing, Burger's or McGrath's? Explain.

WRITING SUGGESTIONS

10. Write an essay analyzing either Neusner's language or Kirkwood's.

11. Choose a popular slogan from advertising or politics. Write an essay explaining how it appeals to needs and values.

12. Write an essay explaining which argument about the right to bear arms you find most convincing, Burger's or McGrath's.

13. Why are short cuts a natural result of ours being a technological age?

14. Analyze a presidential or other debate using some of the terms discussed in this chapter.

15. Locate a copy of President Bush's first speech after the attacks of 9/11 and compare it to Roosevelt's after the bombing of Pearl Harbor.

Research Readiness: Following a Research Trail

How can you investigate a source to determine if it is reliable?

One source that appeared on the results list when students searched "autism and vaccines" on Google for the Research Readiness exercise at the end of Chapter 6 was this one:

> **Vaccines** don't cause *autism*
> Sep 17, 2010 . . . The debate is essentially over and the final word is in: *vaccines* do not cause *autism*. The results of a rigorous study conducted over . . .
> *kottke.org/10/09/vaccines-dont-cause-autism* - Cached

The URL is probably not one that you would recognize. Follow the research trail to decide what you think about the reliability of this source.

A. Clicking on the title of the source leads to the following page. As you look it over, consider your initial response to this question: What can you conclude about who Jason Kottke is and where he got his information about autism and vaccinations?

Kottke.org is a weblog about the liberal arts 2.0 edited by Jason Kottke since March 1998 (archives). You can read about me and kottke.org here. If you've got questions, concerns, or interesting links, send them along.

VACCINES DON'T CAUSE AUTISM

The debate is essentially over and the final word is in: vaccines do not cause autism. The results of a rigorous study conducted over several years were just announced and they confirmed the results of several past studies.

> Basically, the final two groups that were studied consisted of 256 children with ASD [autism spectrum disorders] and 752 matched controls. One very interesting aspect that looks as though it were almost certainly placed into the experimental design based on concerns of anti-vaccine advocates like Sallie Bernard is a group of children who underwent regression. Basically, the study examined whether there was a correlation between ASD and TCV [thimerosal-containing vaccines, i.e. mercury-containing vaccines] exposure. It also examined two subsets of ASD, autistic disorder (AD) and ASD with regression, looking for any indication whether TCVs were associated with any of them. Regression was defined as:
> "the subset of case-children with ASD who reported loss of previously acquired language skills after acquisition."
> Also, when adding up total thimerosal exposure, the investigators also included any thimerosal exposure that might have come prenatally from maternal receipt of flu vaccines during pregnancy, as well as immunoglobulins, tetanus toxoids, and diphtheria-tetanus. In other words, investigators tried to factor in all the various ideas for how TCVs might contribute to autism when designing this study.
> So what did the investigators find? I think you probably know the answer to that question. They found nothing. Nada. Zip. There wasn't even a

hint of a correlation between TCV exposure and either ASD, AD, or ASD with regression:

"There were no findings of increased risk for any of the 3 ASD outcomes. The adjusted odds ratios (95% confidence intervals) for ASD associated with a 2-SD increase in ethylmercury exposure were 1.12 (0.83–1.51) for prenatal exposure, 0.88 (0.62–1.26) for exposure from birth to 1 month, 0.60 (0.36–0.99) for exposure from birth to 7 months, and 0.60 (0.32–0.97) for exposure from birth to 20 months."

The last result is a bit of an anomaly in that it implies that exposure to TCVs from birth to 1 month and birth to 7 months actually protects against ASD. The authors quite rightly comment on this result thusly:

"In the covariate adjusted models, we found that an increase in ethylmercury exposure in 2 of the 4 exposure time periods evaluated was associated with decreased risk of each of the 3 ASD outcomes. We are not aware of a biological mechanism that would lead to this result."

So get your kids (and yourselves) vaccinated and save them & their playmates from this whooping cough bullshit, which is actually killing actual kids and not, you know, magically infecting them with autism. Vaccination is one of the greatest human discoveries ever — yes, Kanye, OF ALL TIME — has saved countless lives, and has made countless more lives significantly better. So: Buck. Up.

By Jason Kottke • Sep 17, 2010 at 11:48 am • autism medicine science vaccines
Source: http://kottke.org/10/09/vaccines-dont-cause-autism

B. Hyperlinks in Kottke's text are indicated in blue. You probably noticed that there is a hyperlink at the top of the page in the description of kottke.org from the words "read about me and kottke.org here." If you went online and clicked on that link, the following page would appear. What impression of Kottke do you start to draw from "The exciting About page"? What sort of ethos is he projecting?

C. You will also see that in the online version of Kottke's article "Vaccines Don't Cause Autism," there was a hyperlink from the words "vaccines do not cause autism" in the first sentence. If you clicked on that link, you would be directed to the article by David H. Gorski from which he drew his information.

Kottke.org is a weblog about the liberal arts 2.0 edited by Jason Kottke since March 1998 (archives). You can read about me and kottke.org here. If you've got questions, concerns, or interesting links, send them along.

THE EXCITING ABOUT PAGE

Hi, my name is Jason Kottke. I currently live in Manhattan with my wife Meg and son Ollie. For fun and income, I build web sites and edit kottke.org. My favorite font right now is Whitney by Hoefler & Frere-Jones. Being generally sober, level-headed, and trustworthy, I'm usually the guy who is chosen to drive. One of my favorite things is that, for a moment after you dip your toe in, you can't tell the difference between really hot water and really cold water.

I believe that when people talk about solving problems with technology, what they're usually talking about is solving problems with design . . . which is to say, the application of psychology in a visual & functional context. I prefer red wine to white, movies to films, jeans to khakis, vanilla to chocolate, Pixar to Dreamworks, the subway to taxis, nonfiction to fiction, and Safari to Firefox. I use a daily face wash in my "T-zone" area. I look like the guy in these photos. I find going to the dentist relaxing. I've lived in WI, IA, MO, MN, CA, NY, NH, and, briefly, France. I don't have a plan.

Need to reach me? Get in touch.

WHAT KOTTKE.ORG MIGHT BE, A LIST:

- The personal site of Jason Kottke. But also his full-time gig.
- A weblog, which is a frequently updated, chronologically ordered collection of hypertext fragments. You'll find the most recent posted stuff on the front page and many ways to get at the older posts on the archive page.
- My wunderkammer. Wunderkammer is a German word meaning, roughly, "cabinet of wonders" or "cabinet of curiousities." Julian Dibbell wrote about weblogs as wunderkammers for the dearly-departed Feed.
- Updated almost daily since March 1998.
- An attempt to track and make sense of "material that connects the insights of science and culture, rather than using one to dismantle the other" (as Steven Johnson puts it).
- Sheer egoism, aesthetic enthusiasm, historical impulse, and even a bit of political purpose. (after George Orwell)
- Small pieces, loosely joined (after David Weinberger's book of the same name).
- Chock full of "wussy PoMo Sedaris-wannabe attitude" (source)
- Speed 3: The Weblog. If I stop writing, the bus will blow up. (source)
- A giant RFC document.
- Not all that it could be.
- Slashdot for the literati (comment via AIM).

Source: http://kottke.org/about/

It's always a good idea to cite the original source of information if you can. There is no reason to cite Kottke instead of citing Gorski himself if you have access to Gorski's original article — especially if you have questions about Kottke's reliability and if he is not an expert who can add insight on the subject at hand. Also going to Gorski's article, which is entitled "The Final Nail in the Mercury-Autism hypothesis?", provides the quoted information in the context of the much longer article in which it originally appeared.

Kottke's whole article, except for the first two sentences and the last three, is a quote from Gorski. Did Kottke accurately and adequately document the fact that his information came from Gorski?

Source: sciencebasedmedicine.org/?p=6775

D. Search the publication in which Gorski's article appeared, *Science-Based Medicine,* and see what you can conclude about its reliability.

E. To be thorough in checking out your sources, if you do not recognize an author you are citing, you should check to see if he or she has a reputation relevant to the subject you are discussing. Gorski's name, where it is listed as author of the article that Kottke cited, is a hyperlink that leads to an interesting page. What is your response, as a researcher, to this page?

PART 3

Researching, Writing, and Presenting Arguments

CHAPTER 10

The Argumentative Paper: Planning and Research

By now you should be fairly adept at picking out claims, support, and warrants (explicit or unstated). The next step is to apply your skills to writing an argument of your own on a subject of your choice or for an assignment on a topic other than those covered in this text. Using what you have learned will enhance your ability to analyze critically the marketing efforts with which we are all bombarded every day. Mastering the writing of arguments also gives you a valuable tool for communicating with other people in school, on the job, and even at home.

In this chapter we move through the various stages involved in preparing to write an argumentative paper: choosing a topic, locating and evaluating sources, and taking notes. We will follow one student, Katie, as she goes through these stages.

Finding an Appropriate Topic

An old British recipe for jugged hare is said to begin, "First, catch your hare." To write an argumentative paper, you first must choose your topic. This is a relatively easy task for someone writing an argument as part of his or her job — a lawyer defending a client, for example, or an advertising executive presenting a campaign. For a student, however, it can be daunting. Which of the many ideas in the world worth debating would make a good subject?

Several guidelines can help you evaluate the possibilities. Perhaps your assignment limits your choices. If you have been asked to write a research paper, you obviously must find a topic on which research is available. If your assignment is more open-ended, you need a topic that is worth the time and effort you expect to invest in it. In either case, your subject should be one that interests you. Don't feel you have to write about what you know — very often finding out what you don't know will turn out to be more satisfying. You should, however, choose a subject that is familiar enough for you to argue about without fearing you're in over your head.

In this chapter we will follow a student, Katie, who has been assigned a research paper for her first-year English class. In preparation for the assignment, the class has viewed the movie *Food, Inc.* This is the assignment that Katie must complete:

The movie *Food, Inc.* raises a multitude of questions about food: the link between the corporate world and our food supply, organic foods, world hunger, alternative fuels, farm workers, childhood obesity. These are just a sampling of the issues raised. For your research essay, choose an argumentative topic related in some way to the issues discussed in the film. Your thesis should be either a claim of value or a claim of policy. Your essay should be 6–8 double-spaced pages and must use at least six sources. There should be some variety in type of sources — books, articles, electronic journals, etc. Use MLA guidelines for documentation.

Invention Strategies

As a starting point, think of conversations you've had in the past few days or weeks that have involved defending a position. Is there some current political issue you're concerned about? Some dispute with friends that would make a valid paper topic? One of the best sources is controversies in the media. Keep your project in mind as you watch TV, read print or online sources, or listen to the radio. You may even run into a potential subject in your course reading assignments or classroom discussions. Fortunately for the would-be writer, nearly every human activity includes its share of disagreement.

As you consider possible topics, write them down. One that looks unlikely at first glance may suggest others or may have more appeal when you come back to it later. Further, simply putting words on paper has a way of stimulating the thought processes involved in writing. Even if your ideas are tentative, the act of converting them into phrases or sentences can often help in developing them.

With the assignment in hand, Katie starts to think about possible topics related to food. She knows that there is also a book called *Food, Inc.*, so she turns to her university library's online catalog and looks it up. She discovers that it is a collection of essays edited by Karl Weber. It looks like a source worth investigating, so she checks it out.

The subtitle of the book is *How Industrial Food Is Making Us Sicker, Fatter, and Poorer — And What We Can Do about It.* That is in keeping with the focus of the film the students saw in class. Katie knows that she doesn't have time to read the whole book for this assignment, but she looks at the preface and table of contents to get ideas about how to find a subject narrow enough to write about. One interesting subject that she has heard about repeatedly on the news and has read about in *Newsweek* is today's epidemic of childhood obesity, and she notices that one chapter in the part of the book that suggests solutions is called "Improving Kids' Nutrition: An Action Tool Kit for Parents." There is also another essay paired with that one and entitled "Childhood Obesity: The Challenge."

Skimming the latter of these two essays immediately gives her some impressive statistics about how bad the problem of childhood obesity is. She knows, though, that childhood obesity is too large a subject and that she has to come up with a thesis about her subject that is either a claim of value or a claim of policy. She has to do more than prove that a problem exists.

In the first of the two essays she runs across a term she is not familiar with: competitive foods. Katie now has the germ of an idea for a topic. She discovers that competitive foods are the "extras" sold to students in addition to or instead of the food served in the cafeteria. She thinks this must certainly be a controversial subject.

Evaluating Possible Topics

Your topic must interest your audience. Who is the audience? For a lawyer it is usually a judge or jury; for a columnist, anyone who reads the newspaper in which his or her column appears. For the student writer, the audience is to some extent hypothetical. You should assume that your paper is directed at readers who are reasonably intelligent and well informed, but who have no specific knowledge of the subject. It may be useful to imagine you are writing for a local or school publication.

Your thesis must be debatable. The purpose of an argument is to defend or refute a thesis, so choose a topic that can be seen from more than one perspective. In evaluating a subject that looks promising, ask yourself: Can a case be made for other views? If not, you have no workable ground for building your own case.

Your thesis must be neither too broad nor too narrow. Consider how long your paper will be, and whether you can do justice to your topic in that amount of space. For example, suppose you want to argue in favor of worldwide nuclear disarmament. Is this a thesis you can support persuasively in a short paper? One way to find out is by listing the potential issues or points about which arguers might disagree. Consider the thesis: "The future of the world is in danger as long as nuclear weapons exist." Obviously this statement is too general. You would have to specify what you mean by the future of the world (the continuation of human life? of all life? of the earth itself?) and exactly how nuclear weapons endanger it before the claim would hold up. You could narrow it down: "Human beings are error-prone; therefore as long as nuclear weapons exist there is the chance that a large number of people will be killed accidentally." Though this statement is more specific and includes an important warrant, it still depends on other unstated warrants: that one human being (or a small group) is in the position to discharge a nuclear weapon capable of killing a large number of people;

that such a weapon could, in fact, be discharged by mistake, given current safety systems. Can you expect to show sufficient evidence for these assumptions in the space available to you?

By now it should be apparent that arguing in favor of nuclear disarmament is too broad an undertaking. A more workable approach might be to defend or refute one of the disarmament proposals under consideration by the U.S. Congress, or to show that nuclear weapons pose some specific danger (such as long-term water pollution) that is sufficient reason to strive for disarmament.

Can a thesis be too narrow? Certainly. If you can prove your point convincingly in a paragraph, or even a page, you need a broader thesis.

At this preliminary stage, don't worry if you don't know exactly how to word your thesis. It's useful to write down a few possible phrasings to be sure your topic is one you can work with, but you need not be precise. The information you unearth as you do research will help you to formulate your ideas. Also, stating a thesis in final terms is premature until you know the organization and tone of your paper. If your topic or assignment does not require research, you may want to move ahead to Chapter 11.

> Katie has narrowed her topic from something related to the movie *Food, Inc.* to childhood obesity to competitive foods in schools. As she continues, she will have to keep asking herself if she can find enough authoritative sources to support her tentative claim — that competitive foods should not be allowed in schools.

Initiating Research

The success of any argument, short or long, depends in large part on the quantity and quality of the support behind it. Research, therefore, can be crucial for any argument outside your own experience. Most papers will benefit from research in the library and elsewhere because development of the claim requires facts, examples, statistics, and informed opinions that are available only from primary and secondary research sources. You should prepare for research by identifying potential resources and learning how they work. Make sure you know how to use the library's catalog and other databases available either in the library or through the campus network. For each database that looks useful, explore how to execute a subject search, how to refine a search, and how to print out or download results. Make sure you know how to find books, relevant reference materials, and journals. Find out whether interlibrary loan is an option and how long it takes. If you plan to use government publications, find out if your library is a depository for federal documents. Identify relevant organizations using the *Encyclopedia of Associations* and visit their Web sites. Finally, discuss your topic with a librarian at the reference desk to make sure you haven't overlooked anything.

Writer's Guide: Keeping Your Research on Track

1. Focus your investigation on building your argument, not merely on collecting information about the topic. Do follow any promising leads that turn up from the sources you consult, but don't be diverted into general reading that has no direct bearing on your thesis.

2. Look for at least two pieces of evidence to support each point you want to make. If you cannot find sufficient evidence, you may need to revise or abandon the point.

3. Use a variety of sources. Seek evidence from different kinds of sources (books, magazines, Web sites, government reports, even personal interviews with experts) and from different fields.

4. Be sure your sources are authoritative. Articles and essays in scholarly journals are more authoritative than articles in college newspapers or in magazines. Authors whose credentials include many publications and years of study at reputable institutions are probably more reliable than newspaper columnists and the so-called man in the street. However, we can judge reliability much more easily if we are dealing with facts and inferences than with values and emotions.

5. Don't let your sources' opinions outweigh your own. Your paper should demonstrate that the thesis and ideas you present are yours, arrived at after careful reflection and supported by research. The thesis need not be original, but your paper should be more than a collection of quotations or a report of the facts and opinions you have been reading.

6. Don't ignore information that opposes the position you plan to support. Your argument is not strengthened by pretending such information does not exist. You may find that you must revise or qualify your position based on what your research reveals. Your readers may be aware of other positions on the issue and may judge you to be unreliable, careless, or dishonest if you do not acknowledge them. It is far better to fairly summarize opposing arguments and refute them than to ignore them.

Mapping Research: A Sample Outline

To explore a range of research activities, let's suppose that you are preparing a research paper, six to ten pages long. You have chosen to defend the following thesis: *Even though thalidomide is infamous for causing birth defects in the 1960s, it has promise as a treatment for cancer and other diseases.* To keep your material under control and give direction to your reading, you would sketch a preliminary outline, which might look like this:

Thalidomide: Changing a Drug's Reputation

    I. Thalidomide's history: a promising drug but a medical nightmare
       A. Explain how drug was developed
       B. Explain the medical disaster it caused
    II. New look at thalidomide: its potential to effectively treat cancer and other diseases
       A. Discuss how it first worked to treat leprosy
       B. Support how it can treat cancer
       C. Support how it can treat other diseases
    III. Conclusion

Now you need to begin the search for the materials that will support your argument. There are two principal ways of gathering the materials — primary research and secondary research. Most writers will not want to limit themselves to one kind of research, but one method may work better than another for a particular project.

> At this point, Katie can sketch only a very rough outline of the shape her essay may take. She knows that her thesis and her outline may have to change as she continues her research.

Competitive Food in Schools

    I. The history of competitive food in schools
       A. Explain what competitive food is
       B. Explain why competitive food is allowed
    II. The dangers of competitive food in schools
       A. Explain the immediate effect on school performance
       B. Explain the long-term health effects
    III. Suggested solutions
    IV. Conclusion

Using Sources: Primary Research

Primary research involves looking for firsthand information. By *firsthand* we mean information taken directly from the original source, including field research (interviews, surveys, personal observations, or experiments). If your topic relates to a local issue involving your school or community, or if it focuses on a story that has never been reported by others, field research may be more valuable than anything available in the library. However, the library can be a source of firsthand information. Memoirs and letters written by witnesses to past events, photographs, contemporary news reports of historical events, or expert testimony presented at congressional hearings are all primary sources that may be available in your library. The Internet, too, can be a source of primary data. A discussion list, newsgroup, or chat room focused on your topic may give you a means to converse with activists and contact experts. Web sites of certain organizations provide documentation of their views, unfiltered by others' opinions. The text of laws, court opinions, bills, debates in Congress, environmental impact statements, and even selected declassified FBI files can be found through government-sponsored Web sites. Other sites present statistical data or the text of historical or political documents.

One of the rewards of primary research is that it often generates new information, which in turn produces new interpretations of familiar conditions. It is a favored method for anthropologists and sociologists, and most physical and natural scientists use observation and experiment at some point as essential tools in their research.

Consider the sample thesis that *even though thalidomide is infamous for causing birth defects in the 1960s, it has promise as a treatment for cancer and other diseases*. It is possible to go to primary sources in addition to or instead of consulting books. For example:

- Interview one or more physicians about current or potential uses of thalidomide.

- Interview someone locally who has had a family member affected by thalidomide.

- Read a first-person account by someone negatively affected by thalidomide use.

- Read a first-person account by someone positively affected by thalidomide use.

- Research newspaper reports from the time period regarding the birth defects caused by thalidomide before its dangers were known.

- Search the Web for reputable sources of information about thalidomide and the uses for which it is currently approved.

The information gleaned from primary research can be used directly to support your claim, or can provide a starting point for secondary research.

Katie and her classmates are not required to use primary sources, but she knows that they have the potential to add significant information to some arguments.

She roughs out a list of possible primary sources:

Interview with parents of school-aged children

Interview with students

Interview with school cafeteria workers/manager

Interview with school/district nutritionist

Printed regulations governing school lunches

Statistics about school nutrition

Statistics about competitive foods

Using Sources: Secondary Research

Secondary research involves locating commentary on and analysis of your topic. In addition to raw evidence found through primary research, secondary sources provide a sense of how others are examining the issues and can provide useful information and analysis. Secondary sources may be written for a popular audience, ranging from news coverage, to popular explanations of research findings, to social analysis, to opinion pieces. Or they may be scholarly publications — experts presenting their research and theories to other researchers. These sources might also come in the form of analytical reports written to untangle possible courses of action, such as a report written by staff members for a congressional committee or an analysis of an issue by a think tank that wants to use the evidence it has gathered to influence public opinion.

Whatever form it may take, be sure when you use a secondary source that you consider the author's purpose and the validity of the material presented to ensure that it is useful evidence for your argument. An opinion piece published in a small-town paper, for example, may be a less impressive source for your argument than an analysis written by a former cabinet member. A description of a scientific discovery published in a magazine will carry less weight as evidence than the article written by the scientists making the discovery presenting their research findings in a scientific journal.

The nature of your topic will determine which route you follow to find good sources. If the topic is current, you may find it more important to use articles than books and might bypass the library catalog altogether. If the topic has to do with social policy or politics, government publications may be particularly useful, though they would be unhelpful for a literary paper. If the topic relates to popular culture, the Internet may provide more information than more traditional publications. Consider what kinds of sources will be most useful as you choose your strategy. If you aren't certain which approaches fit your topic best, consult with a librarian at the reference desk.

Selecting and Searching Databases

You will most likely use one or more *databases* (online catalogs of reference materials) to locate books and articles on your topic. The library catalog is a database of books and other materials owned by the library; other databases may cover articles in popular or specialized journals and may even provide the full text of articles. Some databases may be available only in the library; others may be accessible all over campus. Here are some common features that appear in many databases.

Keyword or Subject Searching. You might have the option of searching a database by *keyword* — using the words that you think are most relevant to your search — or by subject. Typically, a keyword search will search for any occurrence of your search term in titles, notes, or the descriptive headings provided by database catalogers or indexers. The advantage to keyword searching is that you can use terms that come naturally to you to cast your net as widely as possible. The disadvantage is that there may be more than one way to express your topic and you may not capture all the relevant materials unless you use the right keywords.

With *subject searching*, you use search terms from a list of subject headings (sometimes called *descriptors*) established by the creators of the database. To make searching as efficient as possible, they choose one word or phrase to express a subject. Every time a new source is entered into the database, the indexers describe it using words from the list of subject headings: When you use the list to search the database, you retrieve every relevant source. You might find that a database lists these subject headings through a thesaurus feature. The sophisticated researcher will always pay attention to the subject headings or descriptors generally listed at the bottom of a record for clues to terms that might work best and for related terms that might be worth trying.

Searching for More Than One Concept. Most database searches allow you to combine terms using the connectors *and, or,* and *not.* These connectors (also known as *Boolean operators*) group search terms in different ways. If you search for zoos *and* animal rights, for example, the resulting list of sources will include only those that deal with both zoos and animal rights, leaving out any that deal with only one subject and not the other. If you connect terms with *or,* your list will contain sources that deal with either concept: A search for dogs or cats will create a list of sources that cover either animal. *Not* excludes concepts from a search. A search for animal rights *not* furs will search for the concept animal rights and then cut out any sources that deal with furs.

Limiting a Search. Most databases have some options for limiting a search by a number of variables, such as publication date, language, or format. If you find a large number of sources in a database search, you might limit your search to sources published in English in the past three years. If you need a visual aid for a presentation, you might limit a search of the library's catalog to videos, and so on.

Truncating Search Terms with Wild Cards. At times you will search for a word that has many possible endings. A wild card is a symbol that, placed at the end of a word root, allows for any possible ending for a word. For example, *animal** will allow a search for *animal* or *animals.*

Options for Saving Records. You may have the opportunity to print, download, or e-mail to yourself the citations you find in a database. Many databases have a feature for marking just the records you want so you save only those of interest.

Help Screens. Most databases offer some kind of online help that explains how to use the database effectively. If you invest five minutes getting familiar with the basics of a database, it may save you twenty minutes later.

Types of Databases

The Library Catalog. If you want to search for books, videos, or periodical publications, the library catalog is the database to search. Most libraries now have computerized catalogs, but some still have a card catalog. In either case, the type of information provided is the same. Every book in the library has an entry in the catalog that gives its author, title, publisher, date, length, and subject headings and perhaps some notes about its contents. It also gives the call number or location on the shelf and often some indication as to whether it is currently available. You can search the catalog for an author, title, subject, or keyword. Most online catalogs have ways of combining and limiting searches and for printing results. Remember when searching the catalog, though, that entries are created for whole books and not for specific parts of them. If you use too narrow search terms, you may not find a book that has a chapter that includes exactly what you are looking for. Use broad search terms, and check the subject headings for search terms that will work best. Plan to browse the shelves and examine the tables of contents of the books that you find through the catalog to see which, in fact, are most helpful for your topic.

General Periodical Databases. If you want to search for articles, you can find a number of options at your library. Most libraries have a generalized database of periodical articles that may include citations, citations with abstracts (brief summaries), or the entire text of articles. *EBSCOhost, Infotrac, Searchbank, Readers' Guide Abstracts*, and *ProQuest* are all online indexes of this type. Ask a librarian what is available in your library. These are particularly good for finding current information in fairly nonspecialized sources, though they may include some scholarly journals. If you are looking for articles published before the 1980s — say, for news accounts published when the atomic bomb was dropped on Hiroshima — you would most likely need to use a print index such as the *Readers' Guide to Periodical Literature*, which began publication in 1900.

Specialized Databases. In addition to these general databases, you may find you need to delve deeper into a particular subject area. Every academic discipline has some sort of in-depth index to its research, and though the materials they cover tend to be highly specialized, they can provide more substantial support for your claims because they tend to cover sources written by experts in their fields. These resources may be available in electronic or print form:

> *Art Index*
>
> *Biological Abstracts* (the online version is known as *Biosis*)
>
> *Business Periodicals Index*
>
> *ERIC* (focused on education research)
>
> *Index Medicus* (*Medline* or *PubMed* online)
>
> *Modern Language Association International Bibliography* (*MLA Bibliography* online)

Psychological Abstracts (*PsychInfo* or *PsychLit* online)

Sociological Abstracts (*Sociofile* online)

Check with a librarian to find out which specialized databases or indexes that relate to your topic are available in your library.

Database Services. In addition to individual databases, many libraries subscribe to database services that provide access to a number of databases from one search screen. *FirstSearch*, for example, provides access to a variety of subject-specific databases as well as *WorldCat*, a massive database of library catalogs. *LexisNexis* is a collection of databases to over a billion texts, most of them available in full text; it is a strong source for news coverage, legal research, and business information. These may be available to you through the Web anywhere on campus. Again, a visit with a librarian will help you quickly identify what your library has available.

When Katie looks over the list of databases available through her campus library, she finds two general databases that she decides to start with.

The first is Academic OneFile. She does a keyword search for "competitive foods" and gets 76 hits. She has the option to refine this search, so she adds the Boolean operator "AND" plus "school" and narrows the number of hits to 14. She skims these results and sees some titles that look useful. She checks the

Sample Online Catalog Record

You searched for the TITLE — animal rights movement

```
CALL #       Z7164.C45 M38 1994.
AUTHOR       Manzo, Bettina, 1943-
TITLE        The animal rights movement in the United States, 1975-
                 1990 : an annotated bibliography / by Bettina Manzo.
IMPRINT      Metuchen, N.J. : Scarecrow Press, 1994.
PHYS DESCR   xi, 296 p. ; 23 cm.
NOTE         Includes indexes.
CONTENTS     Animal rights movement -- Activists and organizations --
                 Philosophy, ethics, and religion -- Law and legislation
                 -- Factory farming and vegetarianism -- Trapping and
                 fur industry -- Companion animals -- Wildlife --
                 Circuses, zoos, rodeos, dog
SUBJECT      Animal rights movement --United States --Bibliography.
             Animal rights --United States --Bibliography.
             Animal experimentation --United States --Bibliography.
OCLC #       30671149.
ISBN/ISSN    GB95-17241.
```

ones that seem most promising and prints up that narrowed list so that she can try to locate some of the articles later. She chooses the ones labeled "article" instead of ones labeled "report" because the titles of the reports suggest that they are much more technical.

The second general database she tries is EBSCOhost. This time she tries three words linked by the Boolean operator "and": "competitive" AND "food" AND "school." She gets 671 hits. She then tries "competitive food" AND "school" and finds a much more manageable 51. She tries one more refinement: She puts "competitive food" in quotation marks in the search box so that the system will search for those two words together. This produces a manageable 18 citations, so she selects the two that look most promising, chooses the option "add to folder," and then prints up the citations.

Katie decides to look for a specialized database. The one that seems to match her subject best is Food Science and Technology Abstracts. She discovers that this is a specialized EBSCOhost database, so she uses the same procedure that she used earlier, and this time she finds her hits are limited to just 8. She adds two to her folder and prints up the two citations.

When Katie tries to access some of her selected articles by clicking on the title, she finds she would have to pay to access the full text of the articles. She tries pasting the URL into Google, and is able to access the texts free.

Encyclopedias

General and specialized encyclopedias offer quick overviews of topics and easy access to factual information. They also tend to have excellent selective bibliographies, pointing you toward useful sources. You will find a wide variety of encyclopedias in your library's reference collection; you may also have an online encyclopedia, such as *Britannica Online*, available through the Web anywhere on campus. Some specialized encyclopedias include the following:

Encyclopedia of African American History and Culture

Encyclopedia of American Social History

Encyclopedia of Bioethics

Encyclopedia of Educational Research

Encyclopedia of Hispanic Culture in the United States

Encyclopedia of International Relations

Encyclopedia of Philosophy

Encyclopedia of Sociology

Encyclopedia of the United States in the Twentieth Century

Encyclopedia of World Cultures

International Encyclopedia of Communications

McGraw-Hill Encyclopedia of Science and Technology

Political Handbook of the World

Statistical Resources

Often statistics are used as evidence in an argument. If your argument depends on establishing that one category is bigger than another, that the majority of people hold a certain opinion, or that one group is more affected by something than another group, statistics can provide the evidence you need. Of course, as with any other source, you need to be sure that your statistics are as reliable as possible and that you are reporting them responsibly.

It isn't always easy to find things counted the way you want. If you embark on a search for numbers to support your argument, be prepared to spend some time locating and interpreting data. Always read the fine print that explains how and when the data were gathered. Some sources for statistics include these:

U.S. Bureau of the Census. This government agency produces a wealth of statistical data, much of it available on CD-ROM or through the Web at www.census.gov. A handy compilation of their most useful tables is found in the one-volume annual handbook, *Statistical Abstract of the United States*, which also includes statistics from other government sources.

Other Federal Agencies. Numerous federal agencies gather statistical data. Among these are the National Center for Education Statistics, the National Center for Health Statistics, the National Bureau of Labor Statistics, and the Federal Bureau of Investigation, which annually compiles national crime statistics. One handy place to find a wide variety of federal statistics is a Web site called *FedStats* at www.fedstats.gov.

United Nations. Compilations of international data published by the United Nations include the *Demographic Yearbook* and *Statistical Yearbook*. Some statistics are also published by U.N. agencies such as the Food and Health Organization. Some are available from the U.N. Web site at www.un.org.

Opinion Polls. Several companies conduct opinion polls, and some of these are available in libraries. One such compilation is the Gallup Poll series, which summarizes public opinion polling from 1935 to the present. Other poll results are reported by the press. Search a database that covers news publications by using your topic and *polls* as keywords to help you locate some summaries of results.

Government Publications

Beyond statistics, government agencies compile and publish a wealth of information. For topics that concern public welfare, health, education, politics, foreign relations, earth sciences, the environment, or the economy, government documents may provide just the information you need.

The U.S. federal government is the largest publisher in the world. Its publications are distributed free to libraries designated as document depositories across the country. If your library is not a depository, chances are there is a regional depository somewhere nearby. Local, state, and foreign governments are also potential sources of information.

Federal documents distributed to depository libraries are indexed in *The Monthly Catalog of U.S. Government Documents*, available in many libraries as an electronic database. These include congressional documents such as hearings and committee reports, presidential papers, studies conducted by the Education Department or the Centers for Disease Control, and so on. Many government documents are available through the Internet. If you learn about a government publication through the news media, chances are you will be able to obtain a copy at the Web site of the sponsoring agency or congressional body. In fact, government publications are among the most valuable of resources available on the Web because they are rigorously controlled for content. You know you are looking at a U.S. federal government site when you see the domain suffix *.gov* in the URL.

> Katie decides not to look for any more statistics or government documents because there are plenty of statistics in the articles from the book *Food, Inc.*, many of them drawn from federal sources.

Searching the Web

The World Wide Web is an increasingly important resource for researchers. It is particularly helpful if you are looking for information about organizations, current events, political debates, popular culture, or government-sponsored research and activities. It is not an especially good place to look for literary criticism, historical analysis, or scholarly research articles, which are still more likely to be published in traditional ways. Biologists reporting on an important experiment, for example, are more likely to submit an article about it to a prestigious journal in the field than simply post their results on the Web.

Because anyone can publish whatever they like on the Web, searching for good information can be frustrating. Search engines operate by means of automated programs that gather information about sites and match search terms to whatever is out there, regardless of quality. A search engine may locate thousands of Web documents on a topic, but most are of little relevance and dubious quality. The key is to know in advance what information you need and who might have produced it. For example, if your topic has to do with some aspect of free speech and you know that the American Civil Liberties Union is involved in the issue, a trip to the ACLU home page may provide you with a wealth of information, albeit from a particular perspective. If your state's pollution control agency just issued a report on water quality in the area, you may find the report published at their Web site or the e-mail address of someone who could send it to you. The more you know about your topic before you sit down to surf, the more likely you will use your time productively.

If you have a fairly broad topic and no specific clues about where it might be covered, you may want to start your search using a selective guide to good sites. For example, the University of Texas maintains an excellent directory to sites relating to Latin America. Subject guides that selectively list valuable sites can be found at the University of California's *Infomine* at http://infomine.ucr.edu and the *World Wide Web Virtual Library* project at www.vlib.org/Home.html. Reference librarians will also be able to point you to quality sites that relate to your topic.

If you have a fairly specific topic in mind or are looking for a particular organization or document on the Web, a search engine can help you find it. *Google* is one of the best. No matter what search engine you choose, find out how it works, how it ranks results, and how deeply it indexes Web pages. Some search engines will retrieve more results than others simply because of the way the program gathers information from sites. As with databases, there are usually ways to refine a search and improve your results. Many search engines offer an advanced search option that may provide some useful options for refining and limiting a search.

It is important to know what will not be retrieved by a search engine. Because publishing and transmitting texts on the Web is relatively easy, it is becoming more common for libraries to subscribe to databases and electronic journals that are accessed through a Web browser. You may have *Britannica Online* and *LexisNexis* as options on your library's home page. However, the contents of those subscriptions will be available only to your campus community and will not be searched by general Web search engines.

> When Katie turns to the Internet to do some additional searching for relevant material, she uses what she has learned in accessing sources in the databases. She searches for "competitive food" and "school," with "competitive food" in quotation marks in the search box. The search calls up over 15,000 entries, but she notices that the very first one is from the Centers for Disease Control, which she knows to be a reliable source. Within the first 10 she finds listings for articles from the California Department of Education, the federal General Accounting Office, the U.S. Department of Agriculture (USDA), the American Heart Association, and a few other organizations that she will have to investigate. She is pleased that she so easily found a number of authoritative sources. She can tell by the *.gov* at the end of some that they are government sources and that others are organizations (*.org*).
>
> One of the sources was published by healthiergeneration.org. Since she is not familiar with that organization, she calls up its Web site and discovers that it is the Alliance for a Healthier Generation, founded in 2005 by the American Heart Association and Bill Clinton to fight childhood obesity. That is enough information to reassure Katie that it is a reputable site, so she adds it to her list of sources to investigate further. Another listing leads her to FRAC, which proves to be the Food Research and Action Center. Its history indicates that it has an impressive record of fighting for food programs designed to serve the poor and the elderly, including breakfast programs for school children. Again, it seems a source worth pursuing.
>
> She looks up the Web site for the USDA and discovers a list of promising links, including one targeted at childhood obesity and one to a program called the HealthierUS School Challenge.

A quick look at the dates of the articles she is considering indicates that most were published in 2009 or 2010, but she will continue to check dates as she accesses other sources.

Katie feels that she is now ready to take a closer look at the sources she has been finding.

Evaluating Sources

When you begin studying your sources, read first to acquire general familiarity with your subject. Make sure that you are covering both sides of the question — in this case the negative as well as the positive aspects of the use of thalidomide — as well as facts and opinions from a variety of sources. In investigating this subject, you might examine data from doctors, victims of earlier thalidomide use, scientists studying the current uses of thalidomide, the manufacturer of the drug, and recent patients; their varied points of view will contribute to the strength of your claim.

As you read, look for what seem to be the major issues. They will probably be represented in all or most of your sources. Record questions as they occur to you in your reading. What went wrong when thalidomide was used in the 1960s? Why is it again receiving attention? What reasons are there for bringing back such a dangerous drug? Are there advantages that outweigh the dangers? What has changed that might make use of the drug safer today?

Evaluating Print Sources

The sources you find provide useful information that you need for your paper and help you support your claims. One key to supporting claims effectively is to make sure you have the best evidence available. It is tempting when searching a database or the Web to take the first sources that look good, print them or copy them, and not give them another thought until you are sitting down to compose your argument — only to discover that the sources aren't as valuable as they could be. Sources that looked pretty good at the beginning of your research may turn out to be less useful once you have learned more about the topic. And a source that seems interesting at first glance may turn out to be a rehash or digest of a much more valuable source, something you realize only when you sit down and look at it carefully.

To find the right stuff, be a critical thinker from the start of your research process. Scan and evaluate the references you encounter throughout your search. As you examine options in a database, choose sources that use relevant terms in their titles, seem directed to an appropriate audience, and are published in places that will look good in your Works Cited list. For example, a Senate Foreign Relations Committee report will be more impressive as a source than a comparable article in *Good Housekeeping*. An article from the scholarly journal *Foreign Affairs* will carry more clout than an article from *Reader's Digest*, even if they are on the same subject.

Skim and quickly evaluate each source that looks valuable.

- Is it relevant to your topic?
- Does it provide information you haven't found elsewhere?
- Can you learn anything about the author, and does what you learn inspire confidence?

As you begin to learn more about your topic and revise your outline as necessary, you can use sources to help direct your search. If a source mentions an organization, for example, you may use that clue to run a search on the Web for that organization's home page. If a newspaper story refers to a study published in a scientific journal, you may want to seek out that study to see the results of the research firsthand. And if you have a source that includes references to other publications, scan through them, and see which might also prove helpful to you. When you first started your research, chances are you weren't quite sure what you were looking for. Once you are familiar with your topic, you need to concentrate on finding sources that will best support the claims you want to make, and your increasing familiarity with the issue will make it easier to identify the best sources. That may mean a return trip to the library.

Once you have selected some useful sources to support your claims, make a more in-depth evaluation to be sure you have the best evidence available.

- Is it current enough? Have circumstances changed since this text was published?
- Is the author someone I want to call on as an expert witness? Does the author have the experience or credentials to make a solid argument that carries weight with my readers?
- Is it reliable information for my purposes? It may be highly opinionated, but are the basic facts it presents confirmed in other sources? Is the evidence presented in the text convincing?

These questions are not always easy to answer. In some cases, articles will include some information about the author, such as where he or she works. In other cases, no information or even an author's name is given. In that case, it may help to evaluate the publication and its reputation. If you aren't familiar with a publication and don't feel confident making your own judgment, see if it is described in Katz's *Magazines for Libraries*, which evaluates the reputation and quality of periodicals.

Evaluating Web Sources

Web sites pose challenges and offer unique opportunities for researchers, for one reason because they are part of a developing genre of writing. When evaluating a Web site, first examine what kind of site you are reading. Is the Web page selling or advertising goods or services (a business site)? Is it advocating a point of view (an advocacy site) or providing relatively neutral information, such as that found in the yellow pages (an informative or educational site)? Is the Web site addressing the interests of people in a particular organization or with common interests (an information-sharing site)? Is it reporting up-to-the-minute news (a news site) or appealing to some aspect of an individual's life and interests (a personal site)? Useful information for a research paper may be obtained from any of these kinds of Web pages, but it is helpful to know what the main purpose of the site is — and who its primary audience is — when determining how productive it will be for your research.

As you weigh the main purpose of the site, evaluate its original context. Does the site originate in a traditional medium, such as a print journal or an encyclopedia? Is the site part of an online journal, in which case its material had to go through a screening process? Or is the site the product of one individual's or organization's desire to create a Web page, which means the work may not have been screened or evaluated by any outside agency? In that case, the information may still be valuable, but you must be even more careful when evaluating it.

Answering preliminary questions like these helps you before you begin a more specific evaluation of the site's content. To find answers to many of these questions, make a brief overview of the site itself, by looking, for example, at the clues contained in the Web address. That is, *.com* in the address means a business or commercial site; *.edu*, a site sponsored by a university or college; *.k12* is a site associated with a primary or secondary school; *.gov* indicates that the federal government sponsored the site; and *.org* suggests that the site is part of a nonprofit or noncommercial group. Sites originating outside the United States have URLs that end with a two-letter country abbreviation, such as *.uk* for United Kingdom. Although these address clues can reveal a great deal about the origins and purposes of a Web site, remember that personal Web sites may also contain some of these abbreviations. Institutions such as schools and businesses sometimes sponsor individuals' personal Web sites (which are often unscreened by the institution) as well as official institutional sites. One possible key to determining whether a Web site is a personal page, however, is to look for a tilde (~) plus a name or part of a name in the address. Finally, if you are unsure of the sponsoring organization of a page, try erasing all the information in the URL after the first slash (/) and pressing the "Enter" key. Doing so often brings you to the main page of the organization sponsoring the Web site.

Most Web sites include a way to contact the author or sponsoring organization of the site, usually through e-mail. This is often a quick and easy way to get answers to the preliminary questions. If the site contains an address or phone number as part of its contact information, this means the organization or individual is available and probably willing to stand behind the site's content. If you can't find contact information the site may not be suitable to use as a primary resource. The information is not necessarily invalid, but such clues should alert you that information found on that page needs to be verified.

For the next step — that of more closely evaluating the contents of any Web site — Web researchers generally agree on the importance of five criteria: the authority, accuracy, objectivity, currency, and coverage of the site.[1] These criteria are just as important in evaluating traditional print texts, but electronic texts require special care. To understand how these criteria work, let's look at a specific example.

Evaluating a Web Site: One Example

Assume that your observations have led you to conclude that high school students are largely apathetic about government and politics. As a likely future parent, you have decided to research ways of interesting teenagers in the political process. You hypothesize that students who take the whole cyberworld for granted as a part of everyday life might be attracted to an interactive Web site. You do a search on Google using different combinations of keywords, and one site you access looks promising. You want to be sure, however, that the site meets the tests of authority, accuracy, objectivity, currency, and coverage.

The site is Student Voices, designed to teach high school students about government and civic responsibility. Your first job is to evaluate the home page.

The home page design is simple but attractive, and the text is easy to read. There are a number of different features to explore, and the site is typical in that there is no set order for accessing the different links. It is clear from the buttons at the top of the page that the site is used in the context of classes because there are teacher resources as well as student ones.

Clicking on the Student Resources link leads to a useful video called *How to Use the Student Voices Web Site*. This ten-minute video introduces the resources the site offers students. The Teacher Resources page does the same for teachers. Teachers can get a password to the site that allows their students to interact with the material on the site.

The Student Resources page also includes links to a wealth of sources about government, including these:

- Encyclopedia entries on the U.S. president, U.S. senators, the federal government, and state government

- Official government sites, from the White House to the Library of Congress

- Sources that can be used for general research and constitutional research, and for access to voting/elections information

- Major newspapers from across the country and Web sites of the major television networks

---

[1] Wolfgram Memorial Library Web site.

The Student-voices.org home page

The video also explains the different ways that students can use the site interactively. Going back to the home page, you can see its major divisions:

- **Speak Out** is just that — a chance for students to speak out on current political issues. Every few weeks the topic on the home page changes, and the staff of Student Voices presents a brief summary of a "hot" issue such as eminent domain, illegal aliens, or wiretapping. Students can then respond to what they read, read Speak Out on other subjects, or read more on the topic.

- **Polls.** At any given time, there is one question on which students are being polled, plus access to previous polls.

- **What's New.** Clicking on this box takes students to information about what their representatives are voting on at the time.

- **Current News.** The national political news of the day.

The Student-voices.org Student Resources page

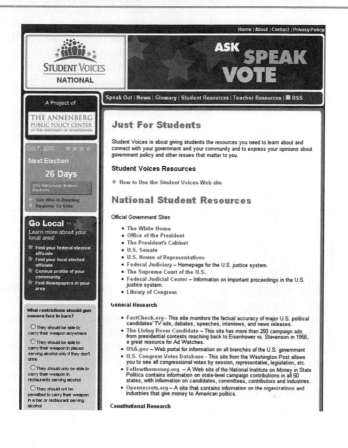

- **Go Local.** These links let the students discover who their local and federal elected representatives are, what their local newspapers are, and what the census reveals about their community.

- **Next Election.** This box is updated every day to reveal how many days until the next election, who is running, and how to register to vote.

The navigation bar also provides a link to a glossary of political terms.

Now that you have an overview of the site, consider whether it meets the criteria for a good source.

Authority. You decide to investigate who is behind this site. At the bottom of the home page is the information that the site is copyrighted by the Annenberg Public Policy Center. A quick check on Google leads you to this center's site, where you discover that the APPC is a part of the University of Pennsylvania. This is the way the center describes its mission:

The Annenberg Public Policy Center of the University of Pennsylvania has been the premier communication policy center in the country since its founding in 1993. By conducting and releasing research, staging conferences and hosting policy discussions, its scholars have addressed the role of communication in politics, adolescent behavior, child development, health care, civics and mental health, among other important arenas. The Center's researchers have drafted materials that helped policy-makers, journalists, scholars, constituent groups and the general public better understand the role that media play in their lives and the life of the nation. The Policy Center maintains offices in Philadelphia and Washington, D.C.

APPC's work has informed the policy debates around campaign finance, children's television, internet privacy, tobacco advertising and the tone of discourse in Washington. Scholars at the Policy Center have offered guidance to journalists covering difficult stories, including terrorist threats, suicide and mental health. The Center's discussions of key public policy issues have brought together industry representatives, advocates, government officials and the scholarly community. Its research has examined what messages work best to reduce the spread of HIV and drug use, how to improve candidate discourse and specific strategies for parents to use to monitor their children's media exposure. APPC has developed materials to help educators and schools do a better job of teaching youth about civic responsibility, democracy and the Constitution.

To further our mission, we are launching this new web site. It is designed to give scholars, the media and the general public expanded access to the work that we began in 1993. We intend to make that complete body of research, including extensive data sets and topline surveys, available as quickly as possible. If there are any questions about materials not yet posted on the site, please contact our Philadelphia office at the number listed at the bottom of this page, or send an email to [the address shown].

The fact that the Annenberg Public Policy Center is part of a reputable university tends to give the information it presents on the site credence. There also is an e-mail address by which to reach someone at Annenberg, which also suggests credibility. The biographies of the staff at Annenberg reveal that they are scholars and journalists with substantial experience in Washington D.C.

Accuracy. Much of the information on the site is factual. The site's affiliation with a major university and its well-qualified staff make a reader inclined to accept that the facts are accurately presented. Since the site is updated daily, news does not get old, as it can with sites that are not well maintained. Those parts of the site that elicit opinion are clearly that — an invitation for students to express their opinions, right or wrong. No one under the age of thirteen is allowed to participate in Speak Out, and those between thirteen and eighteen must have parental permission to participate or to send any personally identifying information. In fact, one other project of the APPC is FactCheck.org, a site that analyzes statements made to the media and points out inaccuracies. There is a link from the home page of Student Voices to FactCheck.org.

Objectivity. Again, it is easier to maintain objectivity when dealing with facts like the outcome of a vote in the Senate or the name of a local representative. Most of the links that provide information about government are linked directly to governmental sites — the House of Representatives, the Library of Congress, and the White House, for example. They are not to sites that present partisan views of the government. The links to broad categories such as U.S. presidents are to MSN's *Encarta*. The links to newspapers are to ones that are well established and well respected, such as the *New York Times* and the *Washington Post*, but they also show a range of possible slants on controversial issues. Included in the list, for example, is the *Christian Science Monitor*.

The factual nature of much of the information on the site increases the odds that the site is objective. The purpose of the whole site is to encourage students to discuss current political issues and to form their own opinions rather than to be presented with set notions as to what the "right" answer is. For those who want to read others' views, the analyses on FactCheck.org could be a starting point.

Currency. The site is updated every day. Although the Speak Out topic remains the same for a few weeks, that schedule allows students time to respond, and the national and state news is updated daily, as are the countdown to the next election and the What's New section.

Coverage. The site covers thoroughly much of the information that students need to learn about the political process on the national, state, and local levels. They can find in one place information that would be much more difficult and time-consuming to locate without its having been brought together in one place. Hypertext works well in such a context because the multiple links put masses of information at the students' fingertips. The Student Resources add great depth to the knowledge available on the home page, where there is also a link to another project of the APPC, Justice Learning, where students can go into more depth about some of the major issues of the day, should they want or need to.

Taking Notes

While everyone has methods of taking notes, here are a few suggestions that should be useful to research writers who need to read materials quickly, comprehend and evaluate the sources, use them as part of a research paper assignment, and manage their time carefully. If you need more detailed help with quoting, paraphrasing, and summarizing, review pages 86–89 in Chapter 3.

When taking notes from a source, summarize instead of quoting long passages. Summarizing as you read saves time. If you feel that a direct quote is more effective than anything you could write and provides crucial support for your argument, copy the material word for word. Leave all punctuation exactly as it appears and insert ellipsis points (". . .") if you delete material. Enclose all quotations in quotation marks and copy complete information about your source, including the author's name, the title of the book or article, the journal name if appropriate, page numbers, and publishing information. If you quote an article that appears in an anthology, record complete information about the book itself.

If you aren't sure whether you will use a piece of information later, don't copy the whole passage. Instead, make a note of its bibliographic information so that you can find it again if you need it. Taking too many notes, however, is preferable to taking too few, a problem that will force you to go back to the source for missing information.

Use the note-taking process as a prewriting activity. Often when you summarize an author's ideas or write down direct quotes, you see or understand the material in new ways. Freewrite about the importance of these quotes, paraphrases, or summaries, or at least about those that seem especially important. If nothing else, take a minute to justify in writing why you chose to record the notes. Doing so will help you clarify and develop your thoughts about your argument.

Taking this prewriting step seriously will help you analyze the ideas you record from outside sources. You will then be better prepared for the more formal (and inevitable) work of summarizing, paraphrasing, and composing involved in thinking critically about your topic and writing a research paper. Maybe most important, such work will help with that moment all writers face when they realize they "know what they want to say but can't find the words to say it." Overcoming such moments does not depend on finding inspiration while writing the final draft of a paper. Instead, successfully working through this common form of writer's block depends more on the amount of prewriting and thoughtful consideration of the notes done early in the research process.

As you take notes, also remember to refer to your outline to ensure that you are acquiring sufficient data to support all the points you intend to raise. Of course, you will be revising your outline during the course of your research as issues are clarified and new ideas emerge, but the outline will serve as a rough guide throughout the writing process. Keeping close track of your outline will also prevent you from recording material that is interesting but not relevant. It may help to label your notes with the heading from the outline to which they are most relevant.

Relying on the knowledge of others is an important part of doing research; expert opinions and eloquent arguments help support your claims when your own expertise is limited. But remember, this is *your* paper. Your ideas and insights into other people's ideas are just as important as the information you uncover at the library or through reputable online sources. When writing an argument, do not simply regurgitate the words and thoughts of others in your essay. Work to achieve a balance between providing solid information from expert sources and offering your own interpretation of the argument and the evidence that supports it. You are entering an ongoing conversation on your topic, not simply recording what others have already said.

Using word-processing software can invigorate the process of note taking and of outlining. Taking notes using a computer gives you more flexibility than using pen and paper alone. For example, you can save your computer-generated notes and your comments on them in numerous places (at home, school, or work, or on a disk); you can cut and paste the text into various documents; you can add to the notes or modify them and still revert to the originals with ease.

You can also link notes to background material on the Web that may be useful once you begin writing drafts of your paper. For example, you could create links to an author's Web page or to any of his or her other works published on the Web. You could create a link to a study or an additional source cited in your notes, or you could link to the work of other researchers who support or argue against the information you recorded.

Because you can record information in any number of ways on your computer, your notes act as tools in the writing process. One of the best ways to start is to open a file for each source; enter the bibliographic information; directly type into the file a series of potentially useful quotations, paraphrases, and summaries; and add your initial ideas about the source. (For each entry, note the correct page references as you go along and indicate clearly whether you are quoting, paraphrasing, or summarizing.) You can then use the capabilities of your computer to aid you in the later stages of the writing process. For example, you can collect all your research notes into one large file in which you group like sources, evaluate whether you have too much information about one issue or one side of an argument, or examine sources that conflict with one another. You can imagine various organizational schemes for your paper based on the central themes and issues of the notes you have taken, and you can more clearly determine which quotes and summaries are essential to your paper and which may not be needed.

When you're ready to begin your first draft, the computer allows you to readily integrate material from your source notes into your research paper by cutting and pasting, thus eliminating the need to retype and reducing the chance of error. You can also combine all the bibliographic materials you have saved in separate files and then use the computer to alphabetize your sources for your final draft.

Although taking notes on the computer does not dramatically change the research process, it does highlight the fact that taking notes, prewriting, drafting a paper, and creating a Works Cited page are integrated activities that should build from one another. When you take notes from a journal, book, or Web site, you develop your note-taking abilities so that they help with the entire writing process.

> Katie has decided to take notes on her sources on her computer. As this book suggests, she will start a new file for each source and compile all of the files into one folder. She does not start taking notes on a source until she looks it over and decides it is one that she will most likely use. At that point, she

puts at the top of the page the part of her outline the information will support. Then she puts in proper form at the top of the page the complete bibliographical information, using the rest of this chapter as a reference, so that when the time comes, she can simply alphabetize her sources and type them up for her Works Cited page.

She reminds herself to write down only what she needs so that she will not take notes that she will not use. She is also careful to put in quotation marks and in exact words any information taken directly from the source. That will remind her later that the notes not in quotation marks are in her own words. She writes down the page number for each idea because she will need that information for her parenthetical documentation. At times she makes notes to herself about why she is including certain information, such as who the author is and why that is important.

This is how a page of Katie's notes looks:

IIB—Long-term health effects

Robert Wood Johnson Foundation. "Childhood Obesity: The Challenge." *Food, Inc.: How Industrial Food Is Making Us Sicker, Fatter and Poorer — And What You Can Do about It*. Ed. Karl Weber. New York: PublicAffairs, 2009. 259–61. Print.

Link to Foundation: http://www.rwjf.org/

Might need to lead in to quotes: The Foundation is "the nation's largest philanthropy devoted exclusively to improving the health and health care of all Americans." 259

In three decades, the obesity rate has quadrupled for those aged 6–11. 259

"If we don't succeed in reversing this epidemic, we are in danger of raising the first generation of American children who will live sicker and die younger than their parents' generation." 259

Because of the difference between calorie intake and the physical activity needed to burn those calories, in ten years an adolescent could gain 58 pounds. 260

50% of children a generation ago walked to school. Now 90% ride. 260

"fewer than four percent of elementary schools provide daily physical education" 260

In some places where obesity is worst, the people can't afford healthy foods, there are convenience stores instead of grocery stores, and it is not safe for children to play outside. 261

Documenting Your Research (MLA SYSTEM)

One of the most effective ways to save yourself time and trouble when you are ready to write your research paper is to document your research as you go along. That way, when the time comes to create your Works Cited page, you will be ready to put the works you used in alphabetical order — or let your computer do it for you — and provide a list of those works at the end of your paper. Some instructors may require a bibliography, or a list of all of the works you consulted (sometimes called simply Works Consulted), but at a minimum you will need a Works Cited page. As that title indicates, the list will be only those works that you quote, paraphrase, or summarize in your paper.

Once you are fairly certain that you will use a certain source, go ahead and put it in proper bibliographic form. That way, if the citation form is complicated, you can look it up or ask your instructor before the last minute. Also, you will realize immediately if you are missing information required by the citation and can record it while the source is still at hand.

Following are examples of the citation forms you are most likely to need as you document your research. In general, for both books and magazines, information should appear in the following order: author, title, and publication information. Each item should be followed by a period. When using as a source an essay that appears in this book, follow the citation model for "Material reprinted from another source," unless your instructor indicates otherwise. Consult the *MLA Handbook for Writers of Research Papers*, Seventh Edition (New York: Modern Language Association of America, 2009) for other documentation models and a list of acceptable shortened forms of publishers.

Print Sources

A BOOK BY A SINGLE AUTHOR

Gubar, Susan. *Racechanges: White Skin, Black Face in American Culture*. New York: Oxford UP, 1997. Print.

TWO OR MORE BOOKS BY THE SAME AUTHOR OR AUTHORS

Gubar, Susan. *Judas: A Biography*. New York: Norton, 2009. Print.

---. *Race Changes: White Skin, Black Face in American Culture*. New York: Oxford UP, 1997. Print.

For the second and subsequent books by the same author, replace the author's name with three hyphens, followed by a period and the title.

AN ANTHOLOGY OR COMPILATION

Dark, Larry, ed. *Prize Stories 1997: The O. Henry Awards*. New York: Anchor, 1997. Print.

The Elements of Citation: Book (MLA)

When you cite a book using MLA style, include the following:

1 Author
2 Title and subtitle
3 City of publication

4 Publisher
5 Date of publication
6 Medium

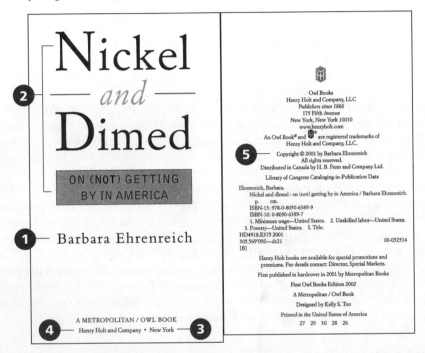

WORKS CITED ENTRY FOR A BOOK IN MLA STYLE

Ehrenreich, Barbara. *Nickel and Dimed: On (Not) Getting by in America.*
New York: Holt, 2001. Print.

A BOOK BY TWO AUTHORS

Alderman, Ellen, and Caroline Kennedy. *The Right to Privacy.* New York: Vintage, 1995.
Print.

NOTE: This form is followed even for two authors with the same last name.

Ehrlich, Paul, and Anne Ehrlich. *Extinction: The Causes and Consequences of the Disappearance of Species.* New York: Random, 1981. Print.

A BOOK BY TWO OR MORE AUTHORS

Heffernan, William A., Mark Johnston, and Frank Hodgins. *Literature: Art and Artifact*. San Diego: Harcourt, 1987. Print.

If there are more than three authors, name only the first and add "et al." (meaning "and others").

A BOOK BY A CORPORATE AUTHOR

Poets & Writers, Inc. *The Writing Business: A Poets & Writers Handbook*. New York: Poets & Writers, 1985. Print.

A WORK IN AN ANTHOLOGY

Head, Bessie. "Woman from America." *Wild Women: Contemporary Short Stories by Women Celebrating Women*. Ed. Sue Thomas. Woodstock: Overlook, 1994. 45-51. Print.

AN INTRODUCTION, PREFACE, FOREWORD, OR AFTERWORD

Callahan, John F. Introduction. *Flying Home and Other Stories*. By Ralph Ellison. Ed. John F. Callahan. New York: Vintage, 1996. 1–9. Print.

MATERIAL REPRINTED FROM ANOTHER SOURCE

Diffie, Whitfield, and Susan Landau. "Privacy: Protections and Threats." *Privacy on the Line: The Politics of Wiretapping and Encryption*. Cambridge, MA: MIT P, 1998. Rpt. in *Elements of Argument: A Text and Reader*. Annette T. Rottenberg and Donna Haisty Winchell. 8th ed. Boston: Bedford/St. Martin's, 2006. 601. Print.

A MULTIVOLUME WORK

Skotheim, Robert Allen, and Michael McGiffert, eds. *Since the Civil War*. Reading: Addison, 1972. Print. Vol. 2 of *American Social Thought: Sources and Interpretations*. 2 vols. 1972.

AN EDITION OTHER THAN THE FIRST

Charters, Ann, ed. *The Story and Its Writer: An Introduction to Short Fiction*. 8th ed. Boston: Bedford/St. Martin's, 2011. Print.

A TRANSLATION

Allende, Isabel. *The House of the Spirits*. Trans. Magda Bogin. New York: Knopf, 1985. Print.

A REPUBLISHED BOOK

Weesner, Theodore. *The Car Thief*. 1972. New York: Vintage-Random, 1987. Print.

NOTE: The only information about original publication you need to provide is the publication date, which appears immediately after the title.

A BOOK IN A SERIES

Eady, Cornelius. *Victims of the Latest Dance Craze*. Chicago: Omnation, 1985. Print.
    Omnation Press Dialogues on Dance Ser. 5.

The series title goes after the publication information and the medium.

AN ARTICLE FROM A DAILY NEWSPAPER

Doctorow, E. L. "Quick Cuts: The Novel Follows Film into a World of Fewer Words."
    New York Times 15 Mar. 1999, sec. B: 1+. Print.

AN ARTICLE FROM A MAGAZINE

Schulhofer, Stephen. "Unwanted Sex." *Atlantic Monthly* Oct. 1998: 55–66. Print.

AN UNSIGNED EDITORIAL

"Medium, Message." Editorial. *Nation* 28 Mar. 1987: 383–84. Print.

ANONYMOUS WORKS

"The March Almanac." *Atlantic Monthly* Mar. 1995: 20. Print.

Citation World Atlas. Maplewood: Hammond, 1999. Print.

AN ARTICLE FROM A JOURNAL WITH SEPARATE PAGINATION FOR EACH ISSUE

Brewer, Derek. "The Battleground of Home: Versions of Fairy Tales." *Encounter*
    54.4 (1980): 52–61. Print.

AN ARTICLE IN A JOURNAL WITH CONTINUOUS PAGINATION THROUGHOUT
THE VOLUME

McCafferty, Janey. "The Shadders Go Away." *New England Review and Bread Loaf
    Quarterly* 9 (1987): 332–42. Print.

MLA style is to include the issue number after the volume number, even though the
volume has continuous pagination throughout the year. In this example, there is no
issue number so only the volume number is included.

A REVIEW

Walker, David. Rev. of *A Wave*, by John Ashbery. *Field* 32 (1985): 63–71. Print.

AN ARTICLE IN A REFERENCE WORK

"Bylina." *The New Princeton Encyclopedia of Poetry and Poetics*. Ed. Alex Preminger
    and T. V. F. Brogan. Princeton: Princeton UP, 1993. Print.

A GOVERNMENT DOCUMENT

United States. National Endowment for the Arts. *2006 Annual Report*. Washington:
    Office of Public Affairs, 2007. Print.

Frequently the Government Printing Office (GPO) is the publisher of federal
government documents.

AN UNPUBLISHED MANUSCRIPT

Leahy, Ellen. "An Investigation of the Computerization of Information Systems
in a Family Planning Program." MS thesis. U of Massachusetts, Amherst, 2010.

A LETTER TO THE EDITOR

Flannery, James W. Letter. *New York Times Book Review* 28 Feb. 1993: 34. Print.

PERSONAL CORRESPONDENCE

Bennett, David. Letter to the author. 3 Mar. 2010. TS.

Include the medium of the correspondence at the end of the entry. Use *TS* for
typescript and *MS* for manuscript (for handwritten letters).

A CARTOON

Henley, Marian. "Maxine." Comic strip. *Valley Advocate* 25 Feb. 2010: 39. Print.

Electronic Sources

A WEB SITE

Heiner, Heidi Anne. *SurLaLune Fairy Tales*. Heidi Anne Heiner, 3 Sept. 2009. Web.
9 Sept. 2010.

Include the name of the author or editor of the Web site, when this information is available; otherwise, begin the entry with the name of the Web site in
italics, followed by a period; the publisher or sponsor of the Web site (usually
found near the copyright information on the site's home page) followed by a
comma and the date of publication or last update. Then add the medium (Web),
a period, and the date you accessed the site.

A PAGE OR ARTICLE WITHIN A WEB SITE

Goodale, Wing, and Tim Divoll. "Birds, Bats and Coastal Wind Farm Development
in Maine: A Literature Review." *BioDiversity Research Institute*. BioDiversity Research Inst., 29 May 2009. Web. 25 Aug. 2010.

A BOOK AVAILABLE ON THE WEB

Kramer, Heinrich, and James Sprenger. *The Malleus Maleficarum*. Trans. Montague
Summers. New York, 1971. MalleusMaleficarum.org. Web. 14 Dec. 2010.

In this case the book had been previously published, and information about its
original publication was included at the site.

AN ARTICLE FROM AN ELECTRONIC JOURNAL

Minow, Mary. "Filters and the Public Library: A Legal and Policy Analysis." *First Monday* 2.12 (1997): n. pag. Web. 28 Nov. 2010.

The Elements of Citation:
Article from a Web site (MLA)

When you cite a brief article from a Web site using MLA style, include the following:

1 Author
2 Title of work
3 Title of Web site
4 Sponsor of site

5 Date of publication or latest update
6 Medium (Web)
7 Date of access

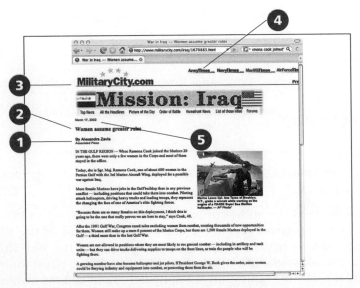

WORKS CITED ENTRY FOR A BRIEF ARTICLE FROM A WEB SITE IN MLA STYLE

```
      1                    2                        3
Zavis, Alexandra. "Women Assume Greater Roles." MilitaryTimes.com.
      4                 5        6        7
Army Times Publishing, 17 Mar. 2003. Web. 23 Aug. 2007.
```

AN ARTICLE FROM A FULL-TEXT DATABASE AVAILABLE THROUGH THE WEB

Warner, Marina. "Pity the Stepmother." *New York Times* 12 May 1991, late ed.: D17. *LexisNexis Universe*. Web. 12 Dec. 2010.

Gura, Mark. "The Gorgeous Mosaic." *School Arts* 93.2 (1993): 26–27. *General Reference Center Gold*. Web. 14 Dec. 2010.

Include the original source information and then add the name of the database in italics, the medium, and your date of access.

The Elements of Citation:
Article from a Database (MLA)

When you cite an article from a database using MLA style, include the following:

1 Author

2 Title of article

3 Title of periodical, volume and issue numbers

4 Date of publication

5 Inclusive pages

6 Name of database

7 Medium (Web)

8 Date of access

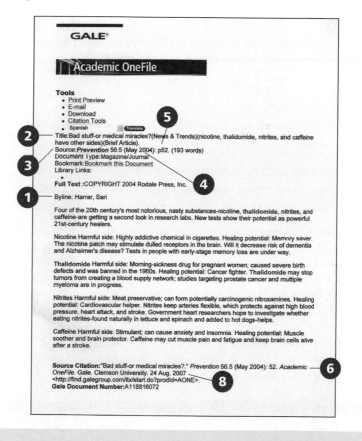

WORKS CITED ENTRY FOR AN ARTICLE FROM A DATABASE IN MLA STYLE

┌── 1 ──┐ ┌─────── 2 ───────────┐ ┌── 3 ──┐ ┌ 4 ┐┌5┐
Harrar, Sari. "Bad Stuff — or Medical Miracles?" *Prevention* 56.5 (2004): 52.

┌──── 6 ────┐ ┌7┐ ┌──8──┐
Academic OneFile. Web. 24 Aug. 2007.

A REPORT FROM A DATABASE

Kassenbaum, Peter. *Cultural Awareness Training Manual and Study Guide*. 1992. ERIC.
Web. 14 Dec. 2010.

Treat educational resources and technical reports found on a database as you
would any other source from a database. Include the name of the database in
italics after the publication information, and then add the medium and your
date of access.

MATERIAL ACCESSED THROUGH A COMPUTER SERVICE

Boynton, Robert S. "The New Intellectuals." Atlantic Monthly Mar. 1995.
America Online. Web. 3 Mar. 2010.

Treat the computer service as the database, then add the medium and your date
of access. Do not include keywords or other information specific to the computer service.

A CD-ROM

Corcoran, Mary B. "Fairy Tale." *Grolier Multimedia Encyclopedia*. Danbury: Grolier,
1995. CD-ROM.

AN ARTICLE FROM A CD-ROM FULL-TEXT DATABASE

"Tribal/DNC Donations." *News from Indian Country* Dec. 1997. CD-ROM.
Ethnic Newswatch. Stamford: SoftLine. 12 Oct. 2007.

Include the original source information and the medium of publication (CD-
ROM), then add the name of the database, the publisher or vendor of the CD-
ROM, and the electronic publication data, if available.

AN ARTICLE FROM AN ELECTRONIC REFERENCE WORK

"Folk Arts." *Britannica*. Encyclopaedia Britannica, 2007. Web. 14 Dec. 2010.

A PERSONAL E-MAIL COMMUNICATION

Franz, Kenneth. "Re: Species Reintroduction." Message to the author. 12 Oct. 2010.
E-mail.

A POSTING TO A DISCUSSION LIST, WEB FORUM, OR NEWSGROUP

Lee, Constance. "Re: Mothers and Stepmothers." *Folklore Discussion List*. Texas A&M
U, 10 Sept. 2007. Web. 24 Oct. 2008.

House, Ron. "Wind Farms: Do They Kill Birds?" *Google Groups: Rec.Animals.Wildlife*.
Google, 7 Sept. 2009. Web. 14 Sept. 2010.

Treat these as short works from a Web site. Include the author of the posting
and the title or subject line of the posting in quotation marks (if there is no
title, use the designation "Online posting" without quotation marks). Then add

the name of the Web site, the sponsor of the site, the date of the posting, the medium, and your date of access.

Other Sources

A LECTURE

Calvino, Italo. "Right and Wrong Political Uses of Literature." Symposium on European Politics. Amherst College, Amherst. 25 Feb. 1976. Lecture.

A FILM

The Voice of the Khalam. Prod. Loretta Pauker. Perf. Leopold Senghor, Okara, Birago Diop, Rubadiri, and Francis Parkes. Contemporary Films/McGraw-Hill, 1971. Film.

Other pertinent information to give in film references, if available, is the writer and director (see model for radio/television program for style).

A TELEVISION OR RADIO PROGRAM

The Shakers: Hands to Work, Hearts to God. Narr. David McCullough. Dir. Ken Burns and Amy Stechler Burns. Writ. Amy Stechler Burns, Wendy Tilghman, and Tom Lewis. PBS. WGBY, Springfield, MA, 28 Dec. 1992. Television.

A VIDEOCASSETTE

Style Wars! Prod. Tony Silver and Henry Chalfont. New Day Films, 1985. Videocassette.

DVD

Harry Potter and the Order of the Phoenix. Prod. David Barron and David Heyman. Warner Bros., 2007. DVD.

A PERFORMANCE

Quilters: A Musical Celebration. By Molly Newman and Barbara Damashek. Dir. Joyce Devlin. Musical dir. Faith Fung. Mt. Holyoke Laboratory Theatre, South Hadley, MA. 26 Apr. 1991. Performance.

AN INTERVIEW

Hines, Gregory. Interview by D. C. Denison. *Boston Globe Magazine* 29 Mar. 1987: 2. Print.

NOTE: An interview conducted by the author of the paper would be documented as follows:

Hines, Gregory. Personal interview. 29 Mar. 1987.

A broadcast interview would be documented as follows:

Hines, Gregory. Interview by Charlie Rose. *Charlie Rose*. PBS. WGBH, Boston, 30 Jan. 2001. Television.

Exercise

We followed Katie as she located some possible sources for her research paper on competitive food in schools. She will examine more than the minimum of six sources required by her assignment, but for this exercise, assume the six that she uses in the final paper are the six listed below. The information from databases is listed as it appeared in the database, with some minor editing, and Katie accessed those sources online. For the date of access, use today's date.

Use the information to write Katie's Works Cited page for her, using MLA documentation.

"Are 'competitive foods' sold at school making our children fat?"
Detail: Larson N; Story M; Health Affairs, 2010 Mar; 29 (3): 430–5 (journal article - research, systematic review) ISSN: 0278-2715 PMID: 20194984 CINAHL AN: 2010589003
Database: CINAHL Plus with Full Text

Title: "The competitive food conundrum: can government regulations improve school food?"
Pub: *Duke Law Journal*
Detail: Ellen J. Fried and Michele Simon. 56.6 (April 2007): p1491(49). (19744 words)
Database: Academic OneFile

Food, Inc.: How Industrial Food Is Making Us Sicker, Fatter and Poorer—And What You Can Do about It
Editor: Karl Weber
Published in New York by PublicAffairs in 2009.
She will use two essays from the book: "Improving Kids' Nutrition: An Action Tool Kit for Parents" by the Center for Science in the Public Interest, pp. 227–57, and "Childhood Obesity: The Challenge" by the Robert Wood Johnson Foundation, pp. 259–61.

Title: *How Competitive Foods in Schools Impact Student Health, School Meal Programs, and Students from Low-Income Families*
Food Research and Action Center, Issue Briefs for Child Nutrition Reauthorization, Number 5. June 2010. 9 pages.

"The Economics of a Healthy School Meal"
Parke Wilde and Mary Kennedy
Choices (an online magazine), 3rd Quarter 2009 | 24(3)

Documenting Your Research (APA SYSTEM)

Following are examples of the bibliographical forms you are most likely to employ if you are using the American Psychological Association (APA) system for documenting sources. If you need the format for a type of publication not listed here, consult the *Publication Manual of the American Psychological Association, Sixth Edition (2010)*.

If you are used to the Modern Language Association (MLA) system for documenting sources, take a moment to notice some of the key differences. In APA style, authors and editors are listed by last name and initials only, and the year comes immediately after the author's or editor's name instead of at or near the end of the entry. Titles in general are not capitalized in the conventional way. The overall structure of each entry, however, will be familiar: author, title, publication information.

Print Sources

A BOOK BY A SINGLE AUTHOR

Briggs, J. (1988). *Fire in the crucible: The alchemy of creative genius*. New York, NY: St. Martin's Press.

MULTIPLE WORKS BY THE SAME AUTHOR IN THE SAME YEAR

Gardner, H. (1982a). *Art, mind, and brain: A cognitive approach to creativity*. New York, NY: Basic Books.

Gardner, H. (1982b). *Developmental psychology: An introduction* (2nd ed.). Boston, MA: Little, Brown.

AN ANTHOLOGY OR COMPILATION

Gioseffi, D. (Ed.). (1988). *Women on war*. New York, NY: Simon & Schuster.

A BOOK BY TWO TO SEVEN AUTHORS OR EDITORS

Atwan, R., & Roberts, J. (Eds.). (1996). *Left, right, and center: Voices from across the political spectrum*. Boston, MA: Bedford Books.

Note: List the names of *all* the authors or editors, with an ampersand before the last one. For eight or more authors, list the first six authors followed by an ellipsis (three dots), and then list the last author's name. In these citations, there is no ampersand before the last author.

A BOOK BY A CORPORATE AUTHOR

International Advertising Association. (1977). *Controversy advertising: How advertisers present points of view on public affairs*. New York, NY: Hastings House.

The Elements of Citation:
Book (APA)

When you cite a book using APA style, include the following:

1 Author

2 Date of publication

3 Title and subtitle

4 City and state of publication

5 Publisher

REFERENCE LIST ENTRY FOR A BOOK IN APA STYLE

Bloom, H. (1994). *The western canon: The books and school of the ages.*

New York, NY: Riverhead Books.

A WORK IN AN ANTHOLOGY

Mukherjee, B. (1988). The colonization of the mind. In D. Gioseffi (Ed.), *Women on war* (pp. 140–142). New York, NY: Simon & Schuster.

AN INTRODUCTION, PREFACE, FOREWORD, OR AFTERWORD

Hemenway, R. (1984). Introduction. In Z. N. Hurston, *Dust tracks on a road* (pp. ix–xxxix). Urbana: University of Illinois Press.

AN EDITION OTHER THAN THE FIRST

Gumpert, G., & Cathcart, R. (Eds.). (1986). *Inter/media: Interpersonal communication in a media world* (3rd ed.). New York, NY: Oxford University Press.

A TRANSLATION

Sartre, J. P. (1962). *Literature and existentialism* (B. Frechtman, Trans.). New York, NY: Citadel Press. (Original work published 1949)

A REPUBLISHED BOOK

James, W. (1969). *The varieties of religious experience: A study in human nature.* London, England: Collier Books. (Original work published 1902)

A BOOK IN A SERIES

Berthrong, D. J. (1976). *The Cheyenne and Arapaho ordeal: Reservation and agency life in the Indian territory, 1875–1907. Vol. 136. The civilization of the American Indian series.* Norman: University of Oklahoma Press.

A MULTIVOLUME WORK

Mussen, P. H. (Ed.). (1983). *Handbook of child psychology* (4th ed., Vols. 1–4). New York, NY: Wiley.

AN ARTICLE FROM A DAILY NEWSPAPER

Hottelet, R. C. (1990, March 15). Germany: Why it can't happen again. *Christian Science Monitor*, p. 19.

AN ARTICLE FROM A PERIODICAL

Gorriti, G. A. (1989, July). How to fight the drug war. *Atlantic Monthly*, 70–76.

AN ARTICLE IN A JOURNAL WITH CONTINUOUS PAGINATION THROUGHOUT THE VOLUME

Cockburn, A. (1989). British justice, Irish victims. *The Nation, 249,* 554–555.

AN ARTICLE FROM A JOURNAL WITH SEPARATE PAGINATION FOR EACH ISSUE

Mukerji, C. (1984). Visual language in science and the exercise of power: The case of cartography in early modern Europe. *Studies in Visual Communication, 10*(3), 30–45.

AN ARTICLE IN A REFERENCE WORK

Frisby, J. P. (1990). Direct perception. In M. W. Eysenck (Ed.), *Blackwell dictionary of cognitive psychology* (pp. 95–100). Oxford, England: Basil Blackwell.

A GOVERNMENT PUBLICATION

United States Dept. of Health, Education, and Welfare. (1973). *Current ethical issues in mental health.* Washington, DC: U.S. Government Printing Office.

AN ABSTRACT

Fritz, M. (1990/1991). A comparison of social interactions using a friendship awareness activity. *Education and Training in Mental Retardation*, 25, 352–359. Abstract retrieved (From *Psychological Abstracts*, 1991, 78, Abstract No. 11474)

When the dates of the original publication and of the abstract differ, give both dates separated by a slash.

AN ANONYMOUS WORK

The status of women: Different but the same. (1992–1993). *Zontian*, 73(3), 5.

A REVIEW

Harris, I. M. (1991). [Review of the book *Rediscovering masculinity: Reason, language, and sexuality*]. *Gender and Society, 5,* 259–261.

Give the author of the review, not the author of the book being reviewed. Use this form for a film review also. If the review has a title, place it before the bracketed material, and treat it like an article title.

A LETTER TO THE EDITOR

Pritchett, J. T., & Kellner, C. H. (1993). Comment on spontaneous seizure activity [Letter to the editor]. *Journal of Nervous and Mental Disease, 181,* 138–139.

PERSONAL CORRESPONDENCE

B. Ehrenreich (personal communication, August 7, 2010).

(B. Ehrenreich, personal communication, August 7, 2010.)

Cite all personal communications to you (such as letters, memos, e-mails, and telephone conversations) in text only, *without* listing them among the references. The phrasing of your sentences will determine which of the two above forms to use.

AN UNPUBLISHED MANUSCRIPT

McIntosh, P. (2008). *White privilege and male privilege: A personal account of coming to see correspondences through work in women's studies*. Working Paper 189. Unpublished manuscript, Wellesley College, Center for Research on Women, Wellesley, MA.

PROCEEDINGS OF A MEETING, PUBLISHED

Guerrero, R. (1972/1973). Possible effects of the periodic abstinence method. In W. A. Uricchio & M. K. Williams (Eds.), *Proceedings of a Research Conference on Natural Family Planning* (pp. 96–105). Washington, DC: Human Life Foundation.

If the date of the symposium or conference is different from the date of publication, give both, separated by a slash. If the proceedings are published annually, treat the reference like a periodical article.

Electronic Sources

AN ARTICLE FROM AN ONLINE PERIODICAL WITH A DOI

Chattopadhyay, P. (2003). Can dissimilarity lead to positive outcomes? The influence of open versus closed minds. *Journal of Organizational Behavior, 24*, 295–312. doi:10.1002/job.118

If the article duplicates the version which appeared in a print periodical, use the same basic primary journal reference. See "An Article from a Periodical." Some online articles have a "digital object identifier" (DOI.) Use the DOI at the end of the entry in place of the URL.

AN ARTICLE FROM AN ONLINE PERIODICAL WITHOUT A DOI

Riordan, V. (2001, January 1). Verbal-performance IQ discrepancies in children attending a child and adolescent psychiatry clinic. *Child and Adolescent Psychiatry On-Line.* Retrieved from http://www.priory.com/psych/iq.htm

If an article does not have a DOI, after the publication information add the exact URL for the article or the URL of the home page of the journal.

A NONPERIODICAL WEB DOCUMENT

Munro, K. (2001, February). *Changing your body image.* Retrieved from http://www.kalimunro.com/article_changing_body_image.html

In general, follow this format: author's name, the date of publication (if no publication date is available, use "n.d."), the title of the document in italics, and the source's URL.

A CHAPTER OR SECTION IN A WEB DOCUMENT

National Council of Welfare, Canada. (1998). Other issues related to poverty lines. In *A new poverty line: Yes, no or maybe?* (chap. 5). Retrieved from http://www.ncwcnbes.net/htmdocument/reportnewpovline/chap5.htm

AN E-MAIL

Do not include personal communications such as e-mails in your list of references. See "Personal Correspondence."

A MESSAGE POSTED TO A NEWSGROUP

Isaacs, K. (2008, January 20). Philosophical roots of psychology [Electronic newsgroup message]. Retrieved from news://sci.psychology.psychotherapy .moderated

Include an online posting in your reference list only if the posting is archived and is retrievable. Otherwise, cite an online posting as a personal communication and do not include it in the list of references. Care should be taken when citing electronic discussions. In general, they are not scholarly sources.

The Elements of Citation:
Article from a Web site (APA)

When you cite an article from a Web site using APA style, include the following:

1 Author

2 Date of publication or most recent update

3 Title of document on Web site

4 Title of section

5 Date of access (only if content is likely to change)

6 URL of document

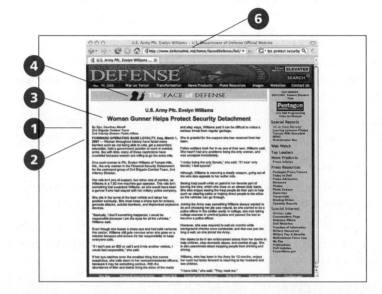

REFERENCE LIST ENTRY FOR A BRIEF ARTICLE FROM A WEB SITE IN APA STYLE

┌─**1**─┐ ┌────**2**────┐ ┌──────────────**3**──────────────┐
Marulli, C. (2007, March 1). Woman gunner helps protect security detachment.

┌─────**4**─────┐ ┌──────**6**──────┐
In *The Face of Defense*. Retrieved from http://www.defenselink.mil/home/

faceofdefense/fod/2007-03/f20070301a.html

AN ARTICLE FROM A DATABASE

Lopez, F. G., Melendez, M. C., Sauer, E. M., Berger, E., & Wyssmann, J. (1998). Internal working models, self-reported problems, and help-seeking attitudes among college students. *Journal of Counseling Psychology, 45*, 79–83. Retrieved from http://www.apa.org/journals/cou

The Elements of Citation:
Article from a Database (APA)

When you cite an article from a database using APA style, include the following:

1 Author

2 Date of publication

3 Title of article

4 Name of periodical

5 Volume and issue numbers

6 Page numbers

7 DOI

8 URL for journal's home page (if no DOI)

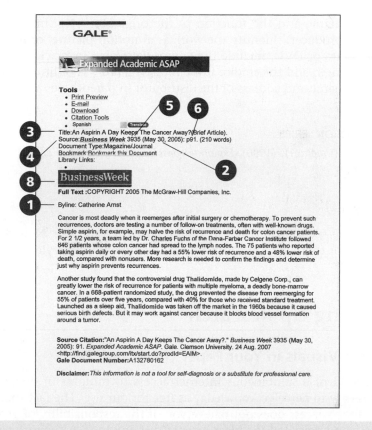

REFERENCE LIST ENTRY FOR AN ARTICLE FROM A DATABASE IN APA STYLE

┌─ **1** ─┐ ┌──── **2** ────┐ ┌────────── **3** ──────────┐ ┌─ **4** ─
Arnst, C. (2005, May 30). An aspirin a day keeps the cancer away? *Business*

──┐┌ **5** ┐┌ **6** ┐ ┌──────── **8** ────────┐
Week 3935, 91. Retrieved from http://businessweek.com/

To cite material retrieved from a database, follow the format appropriate to the work retrieved. If the article has a DOI, include this at the end of the entry. If the article does not have a DOI, include the URL of the periodical's home page at the end of the entry.

Other Sources

A FILM

Wachowski, A., & Wachowski, L. (Writers/Directors). Silver, J. (Producer). (1999). *The matrix* [Motion picture]. United States: Warner Bros.

Include the name and the function of the originator or primary contributor (director or producer). Identify the work as a motion picture, or if you viewed a videocassette or DVD, include the appropriate label in brackets. Include the country of origin and the studio. If the motion picture is of limited circulation, provide the name and address of the distributor in parentheses at the end of the reference.

A TELEVISION SERIES

Jones, R. (Producer). (1990). *Exploring consciousness* [Television series]. Boston, MA: WGBH.

Exercise

Return to the six sources listed in the exercise on page 428. Now do a Works Cited page for those six sources using APA documentation style.

Wrapping Up Research

Including Visuals in Your Paper

In this world of instantaneous Internet access to millions of documents and sites, it is easy to perceive knowledge as free for our use. The fact that information is easy to access does not relieve you of the responsibility of giving credit to those who originated the ideas expressed there. In fact, the ease with which material can be posted to the Internet makes it even more difficult to separate valid information from that which is questionable at best.

Since the Internet is a world of images as well as words, it may give you ideas for livening up your own work with all sorts of visuals. Don't forget, though, that you are obligated to give credit to the source of your visuals along with the ideas and words that you use. A graph or chart may provide just the sort of statistical support that will make a key point in your argument, and it can be easily cut and pasted or scanned into your electronic text, but you must document that graph or chart just as you would text. You should acknowledge the location where you found the visual and as much information as is provided about who produced it. If you use copyrighted graphs or charts in work that you publish either in print or electronic form, you should seek permission for their use. The same is true for photographs and other illustrations, although some books and Web sites offer images that you can use free of charge. You may be surprised to find that something as common as your school's logo is copyrighted and cannot be used on your Web page, for example, without permission.

Keeping Research under Control

How do you know when you have done enough research? If you have kept your outline updated, you have a visual record of your progress. Check this against the guidelines on pages 397. Is each point backed by at least two pieces of support? Do your sources represent a range of authors and of types of data? If a large proportion of your support comes from one book, or if most of your references are to newspaper articles, you probably need to keep working. On the other hand, if your notes cite five different authorities making essentially the same point, you may have collected more data than you need. It can be useful to point out that more than one authority holds a given view and to make notes of examples that are notably different from one another. But it is not necessary to take down all the passages or examples expressing the same idea.

To This Point

Before you leave the library or your primary sources and start writing, check to make sure your research is complete.

1. Does your working outline show any gaps in your argument?
2. Have you found adequate data to support your claim?
3. Have you identified the warrants linking your claim with data and ensured that these warrants too are adequately documented?
4. If you intend to quote or paraphrase sources in your paper, do your notes include exact copies of all statements you may want to use and complete references?
5. Have you answered all the relevant questions that have come up during your research?
6. Do you have enough information about your sources to document your paper?

Compiling an Annotated Bibliography

An annotated bibliography is a list of sources that includes the usual bibliographic information followed by a paragraph describing and evaluating each source. Its purpose is to provide information about each source in a bibliography so that the reader has an overview of the resources related to a given topic.

For each source in an annotated bibliography, the same bibliographic information included in a Works Cited or References list is provided, alphabetized by author. Each reference also has a short paragraph that describes the work, its main focus, and, if appropriate, the methodology used in or the style of the work. An annotation might note special features such as tables or illustrations. Usually an annotation evaluates the source by analyzing its usefulness, reliability, and overall significance for understanding the topic. An annotation might include some information on the credentials of the author or the organization that produced it.

A SAMPLE ANNOTATION USING THE MLA CITATION STYLE

Warner, Marina. "Pity the Stepmother." *New York Times* 12 May 1991, late
    ed.: D17. *LexisNexis Universe*. Web. 12 Dec. 2010.

The author asserts that many fairy tales feature absent or cruel mothers, transformed by romantic editors such as the Grimm brothers into stepmothers because the idea of a wicked mother desecrated an ideal. She argues that figures in fairy tales should be viewed in their historical context and that social conditions often affected the way that motherhood figured in fairy tales. Warner, a novelist and author of books on the images of Joan of Arc and the Virgin Mary, writes persuasively about the social roots of a fairy-tale archetype.

APA style does not call for annotated citations. However, some instructors may require an annotated bibliography, so with either MLA or APA, follow your instructor's guidelines.

CHAPTER 11

The Argumentative Paper: Writing and Documentation

Chapter 10 discusses the planning of an argumentative paper and the process involved in researching topics that require support beyond what the writer knows firsthand. This chapter discusses moving from the planning and researching stage into the actual writing of the paper.

Making a preliminary outline before you conduct any needed research gives direction to your research. If your topic requires no research, a preliminary outline helps you to organize your own thoughts on the subject. Preliminary outlines can change, however, in the process of researching and writing the paper. As you begin drafting the paper, you will need to finalize your decisions about what issues you want to raise.

Once you are satisfied that you have identified all the issues that will appear in your paper, you should begin to determine what kind of organization will be most effective for your argument. Now is the time to organize the results of your thinking into a logical and persuasive form. If you have read about your topic, answered questions, and acquired some evidence, you may already have decided on ways to approach your subject. If not, you should look closely at your outline now, recalling your purposes when you began your investigation, and develop a strategy for using the information you have gathered to achieve those purposes.

Be mindful of the context in which the argument is taking place, and try this procedure for tackling the issues in any controversial problem.

1. Raise the relevant issues and omit those that would distract you from your purpose. Plan to devote more time and space to issues you regard as crucial.

2. Produce the strongest evidence you can to support your factual claims, knowing that the opposing side or critical readers may try to produce conflicting evidence.

3. Defend your value claims by finding support in the fundamental principles with which most people in your audience would agree.

4. Argue with yourself. Try to foresee what kinds of refutation are possible. Try to anticipate and meet the opposing arguments.

5. Consider the context in which your argument will be read and be sensitive to the concerns of your audience.

Organizing the Material

The first point to establish in organizing your material is what type of thesis you plan to present. Is your intention to make readers aware of some problem? To offer a solution to the problem? To defend a position? To refute a position held by others? The way you organize your material will depend to a great extent on your goal. With that goal in mind, look over your outline and reevaluate the relative importance of your issues. Which ones are most convincing? Which are backed up by the strongest support? Which ones relate to facts, and which concern values?

With these points in mind, let us look at various ways of organizing an argumentative paper. It would be foolish to decide in advance how many paragraphs a paper ought to have; however, you can and should choose a general strategy before you begin writing. If your thesis presents an opinion or recommends some course of action, you may choose simply to state your main idea and then defend it. If your thesis argues against an opposing view, you probably will want to mention that view and then refute it. Both these organizations introduce the thesis in the first or second paragraph (called the *thesis paragraph*). You may decide that two or more differing positions have merit and that you want to offer a compromise between or among positions. A fourth possibility is to start establishing that a problem exists and then introduce your thesis as the solution; this method is called *presenting the stock issues*. Although these four approaches sometimes overlap in practice, examining each one individually can help you structure your paper. Let's take a look at each arrangement.

Defending the Main Idea

All forms of organization will require you to defend your main idea, but one way of doing this is simple and direct. Early in the paper state the main idea that you will defend throughout your argument. You can also indicate here the two or three points you intend to develop in support of your claim; or you can raise these later as they come up. Suppose your thesis is that widespread vegetarianism would solve a number of problems. You could phrase it this way: "If the majority of people in this country adopted a vegetarian diet, we would see improvements in the economy, in the health of our people, and in moral sensitivity." You would then develop each of the claims in your list with appropriate data and warrants. Notice that the thesis statement in the first (thesis) paragraph has already outlined your organizational pattern. However, if you find that listing your two or three main ideas in the thesis leads to too much repetition later in the paper, you can introduce each one as it arises in your discussion of the topic. Your thesis would remain more general: "If the majority of people in this country adopted a vegetarian diet, there would be noticeable improvement."

Defending the main idea is effective for factual claims as well as policy claims, in which you urge the adoption of a certain policy and give the reasons for its adoption. It is most appropriate when your thesis is straightforward and can be readily supported by direct statements.

Refuting an Opposing View

Refuting an opposing view means to attack it in order to weaken, invalidate, or make it less credible to a reader. Since all arguments are dialogues or debates — even when the opponent is only imaginary — refutation of another point of view is always implicit in your arguments. As you write, keep in mind the issues that an opponent may raise. You will be looking at your own argument as an unsympathetic reader may look at it, asking yourself the same kinds of critical questions and trying to find its weaknesses in order to correct them. In this way every argument you write becomes a form of refutation.

How do you plan a refutation? Here are some general guidelines.

1. If you want to refute the argument in a specific essay or article, read the argument carefully, noting all the points with which you disagree. This advice may seem obvious, but it cannot be too strongly emphasized. If your refutation does not indicate scrupulous familiarity with your opponent's argument, he or she has the right to say, and often does, "You haven't really read what I wrote. You haven't really answered my argument."

2. If you think that your readers are sympathetic to an opposing view or are not familiar with it, summarize it at the beginning of your paper, providing enough information to give readers an understanding of exactly what you plan to refute. When you summarize, it's important to be respectful of the opposition's views. You don't want to alienate readers who might not agree with you at first.

3. If your argument is long and complex, choose only the most important points to refute. Otherwise the reader who does not have the original argument on hand may find a detailed refutation hard to follow. If the argument is short and relatively simple — a claim supported by only two or three points — you may decide to refute all of them, devoting more space to the most important ones.

4. Attack the principal elements in the argument of your opponent.

   a. Question the evidence. (See pp. 203–15 in the text.) Question whether your opponent has proved that a problem exists.

  b. Attack the warrants or assumptions that underlie the claim. (See pp. 279–80 in the text.)

  c. Attack the logic or reasoning of the opposing view. (Refer to the discussion of fallacious reasoning on pp. 308–19 in the text.)

  d. Attack the proposed solution to a problem, pointing out that it will not work.

5. Be prepared to do more than attack the opposing view. Supply evidence and good reasons in support of your own claim.

   In Chapter 3 we saw a sentence form that can help shape this type of essay:

   In his essay, X writes that _____. However, _____.

A sentence form that might help you write a thesis for this type of essay is this one:

   On the topic of _____, X claims that _____. In contrast, Y argues that _____. However, _____.

See page 82 for additional sentence forms.

Finding the Middle Ground

Although an argument, by definition, assumes a difference of opinion, we know that opposing sides frequently find accommodation somewhere in the middle. As you mount your own argument about a controversial issue, you need not confine yourself to support of any of the differing positions. You may want to acknowledge that there is some justice on all sides and that you understand the difficulty of resolving the issue.

   Consider these guidelines for an argument that offers a compromise between or among competing positions:

1. Early in your essay explain the differing positions. Make clear the major differences separating the two (or more) sides.

2. Point out, whenever possible, that the differing sides already agree to some exceptions to their stated positions. Such evidence may prove that the differences are not so extreme as their advocates insist. Several commentators, writing about the conflict between Democrats and Republicans over President Obama's health-care plan adopted this strategy, suggesting that compromise was possible because the differences were narrower than the public believed.

3. Make clear your own moderation and sympathy, your own willingness to negotiate. An example of this attitude appears in an essay on abortion in which the author infers how Abraham Lincoln might have treated the question of abortion rights.

In this debate I have made my own position clear. It is a pro-life position (though it may not please all pro-lifers), and its model is Lincoln's position on slavery from 1854 until well into the Civil War: tolerate, restrict, discourage. Like Lincoln's, its touchstone is the common good of the nation, not the sovereign self. Like Lincoln's position, it accepts the legality but not the moral legitimacy of the institution that it seeks to contain. It invites argument and negotiation; it is a gambit, not a gauntlet.[1]

4. If you favor one side of the controversy, acknowledge that opposing views deserve to be considered. For example, in another essay on abortion, the author, who supports abortion rights, says,

> Those of us who are pro-choice must come to terms with those thoughtful pro-lifers who believe that in elevating the right to privacy above all other values, the most helpless form of humanity is left unprotected and is, in fact, defined away. They deserve to have their views addressed with sympathy and moral clarity.[2]

5. Provide evidence that accepting a middle ground can offer marked advantages for the whole society. Wherever possible, show that continued polarization can result in violence, injustice, and suffering.

6. In offering a solution that finds a common ground, be as specific as possible, emphasizing the part that you are willing to play in reaching a settlement. In an essay titled "Pro-Life and Pro-Choice? Yes!" the author concludes with this:

> Must those of us who abhor abortion, then, reconcile ourselves to seeing it spread unchecked? By no means. We can refuse to practice it ourselves — or, if we are male, beseech the women who carry our children to let them be born, and promise to support them, and mean it and do it. We can counsel and preach to others; those of us who are religious can pray. . . . What we must not do is ask the state to impose our views on those who disagree.[3]

On a different subject, a debate on pornography, the author, who is opposed to free distribution of obscene material, nevertheless refuses to endorse censorship.

---

[1] George McKenna, "On Abortion: A Lincolnian Position," *Atlantic Monthly,* September 1995, p. 68. (A gauntlet or glove is flung down in order to challenge an opponent to combat; a gambit is the opening move in a chess game, or in the words of one dictionary, "a concession that invites discussion." — EDS.)

[2] Benjamin C. Schwarz, "Judge Ginsburg's Moral Myopia," *New York Times,* July 30, 1993, sec. A, p. 27.

[3] George Church, *Time,* March 6, 1995, p. 108.

I think that, by enlarging the First Amendment to protect, in effect, freedom of expression, rather than freedom of speech and of
the press, the courts made a mistake. The courts have made other
mistakes, but I do not know a better way of defining the interests
of the community than through legislation and through the courts.
So I am willing to put up with things I think are wrong in the hope
that they will be corrected. I know of no alternative that would
always make the right decisions.[4]

Presenting the Stock Issues

Presenting the stock issues, or stating the problem before the solution, is a type
of organization borrowed from traditional debate format. It works for policy
claims when an audience must be convinced that a need exists for changing the
status quo (present conditions) and for introducing plans to solve the problem.
You begin by establishing that a problem exists (need). You then propose a solution (plan), which is your thesis. Finally, you show reasons for adopting the
plan (advantages). These three elements — need, plan, and advantages — are
called the *stock issues*.

For example, suppose you wanted to argue that measures for reducing acid
rain should be introduced at once. You would first have to establish a need for
such measures by defining the problem and providing evidence of damage.
Then you would produce your thesis, a means for improving conditions. Finally
you would suggest the benefits that would follow from implementation of your
plan. Notice that in this organization your thesis paragraph usually appears
toward the middle of your paper, although it may also appear at the beginning.

A sentence form such as the following can guide you in writing an appropriate thesis:

_____ is a problem, but _____ can help resolve it.

For instance, "Childhood obesity is increasing at an alarming rate, but
schools can help by eliminating competitive foods."

Ordering Material for Emphasis

Whichever way you choose to work, you should revise your outline to reflect
the order in which you intend to present your thesis and supporting ideas. Not
only the placement of your thesis paragraph but also the wording and arrangement of your ideas will determine what points in your paper receive the most
emphasis.

Suppose your purpose is to convince the reader that cigarette smoking is a
bad habit. You might decide to concentrate on three unpleasant attributes of

---

[4]Ernest van den Haag, *Smashing Liberal Icons: A Collection of Debates* (Washington, D.C.:
Heritage Foundation, 1981), p. 101.

cigarette smoking: (1) It is unhealthy; (2) it is dirty; (3) it is expensive. Obviously, these are not equally important as possible deterrents. You would no doubt consider the first reason the most compelling, accompanied by evidence to prove the relationship between cigarette smoking and cancer, heart disease, emphysema, and other diseases. This issue, therefore, should be given greater emphasis than the others.

There are several ways to achieve emphasis. One is to make the explicit statement that you consider a certain issue the most important.

> Finally, and *most importantly,* human culture is often able to neutralize or reverse what might otherwise be genetically advantageous consequences of selfish behavior.[5]

This quotation also reveals a second way — placing the material to be emphasized in an emphatic position, either first or last in the paper. The end position, however, is generally more emphatic.

A third way to achieve emphasis is to elaborate on the material to be emphasized, treating it at greater length, offering more data and reasons for it than you give for the other issues.

Making Choices

With a working outline in hand that indicates the order of your thesis and claims, you are almost ready to begin turning your notes into prose. First, however, it is useful to review the limits on your paper to be sure your writing time will be used to the best possible advantage.

Scope

The first limit involves scope. As mentioned earlier, your thesis should introduce a claim that can be adequately supported in the space available to you. If your research has opened up more aspects than you anticipated, you may want to narrow your thesis to one major subtopic. Or you could emphasize only the most persuasive arguments for your position (assuming these are sufficient to make your case) and omit the others. In a brief paper (three or four pages), three issues are probably all you have room to develop. On the other hand, if you suspect your thesis can be proved in one or two pages, look for ways to expand it. What additional issues might be brought in to bolster your argument? Alternatively, is there a larger issue for which your thesis could become a supporting idea?

Style

Other limits on your paper are imposed by the need to make your points in a way that will be persuasive to an audience. The style and tone you choose

---

[5] Peter Singer, *The Expanding Circle* (New York: New American Library, 1982), p. 171.

depend not only on the nature of the subject but also on how you can best convince readers that you are a credible source. *Style* in this context refers to the elements of your prose — simple versus complex sentences, active versus passive verbs, metaphors, analogies, and other literary devices.

It is usually appropriate in a short paper to choose an *expository* style, which emphasizes the elements of your argument rather than your personality. You may want to appeal to your readers' emotions as well as their intellects, but keep in mind that sympathy is most effectively gained when it is supported by believable evidence. If you press your point stridently, your audience is likely to be suspicious rather than receptive. If you sprinkle your prose with jokes or metaphors, you may diminish your credibility by detracting from the substance of your case. Both humor and analogy can be useful tools, but they should be used with discretion.

You can discover some helpful pointers on essay style by reading the editorials in newspapers such as the *New York Times,* the *Washington Post,* or the *Wall Street Journal.* The authors are typically addressing a mixed audience comparable to the hypothetical readers of your own paper. Though their approaches vary, each writer is attempting to portray himself or herself as an objective analyst whose argument deserves careful attention.

Tone

Tone is the approach you take to your topic — solemn or humorous, detached or sympathetic. Style and tone together compose your voice as a writer. Many students assume that every writer has only one voice. In fact, a writer typically adapts his or her voice to the material and the audience. Perhaps the easiest way to appreciate this is to think of two or three works by the same author that are written in different voices. Or compare the speeches of two different characters in the same story, novel, or film. Every writer has individual talents and inclinations that appear in most or all of his or her work. A good writer, however, is able to amplify some stylistic elements and diminish others, as well as to change tone, by choice.

Again, remember your goals. You are trying to convince your audience of something; an argument is, by its nature, directed at people who may not initially agree with its thesis. Therefore, your voice as well as the claims you make must be convincing.

To This Point

The organizing steps that come between preparation and writing are often neglected. Careful planning at this stage, however, can save much time and effort later. As you prepare to start writing, you should be able to answer the following questions:

1. Is the purpose of my paper to persuade readers to accept a potentially controversial idea, to refute someone else's position, to find middle ground, or to propose a solution to a problem?

2. Can or should my solution also incorporate elements of compromise and negotiation?

3. Have I decided on an organization that is likely to accomplish this purpose?

4. Does my outline arrange my thesis and issues in an appropriate order to emphasize the most important issues?

5. Does my outline show an argument whose scope suits the needs of this paper?

6. What questions of style and tone do I need to keep in mind as I write to ensure that my argument will be persuasive?

Writing

Beginning the Paper

Having found a claim you can defend and the voice you will adopt toward your audience, you must now think about how to begin. An introduction to your subject should consist of more than just the first paragraph of your paper. It should invite the reader to give attention to what you have to say. It should also point you in the direction you will take in developing your argument. You may want to begin the actual writing of your paper with the thesis paragraph. It is useful to consider the whole paragraph rather than simply the thesis statement for two reasons. First, not all theses are effectively expressed in a single sentence. Second, the rest of the paragraph will be closely related to your statement of the main idea. You may show why you have chosen this topic or why your audience will benefit from reading your paper. You may introduce your warrant, qualify your claim, and in other ways prepare for the body of your argument. Because readers will perceive the whole paragraph as a unit, it makes sense to approach it that way.

Consider first the kind of argument you intend to present. Does your paper make a factual claim? Does it address values? Does it recommend a policy or action? Is it a rebuttal of some current policy or belief? The answers to those questions will influence the way you introduce the subject.

If your thesis makes a factual claim, you may be able to summarize it in one or two opening sentences. "Whether we like it or not, money is obsolete. The currency of today is not paper or coin, but plastic." Refutations are easy to introduce in a brief statement: "Contrary to popular views on the subject, the institution of marriage is as sound today as it was a generation ago."

A thesis that defends a value is usually best preceded by an explanatory introduction. "Some wars are morally defensible" is a thesis that can be stated as a simple declarative opening sentence. However, readers who disagree may not read any further than the first line. Someone defending this claim is likely to be more persuasive if he or she first gives an example of a situation in which war is or was preferable to peace or presents the thesis less directly.

One way to keep such a thesis from alienating the audience is to phrase it as a question. "Are all wars morally indefensible?" Still better would be to prepare for the question:

> Few if any of us favor war as a solution to international problems. We are too vividly aware of the human suffering imposed by armed conflict, as well as the political and financial turmoil that inevitably result. Yet can we honestly agree that no war is ever morally defensible?

Notice that this paragraph gains appeal from use of the first person *we*. The author implies that he or she shares the readers' feelings but has good reasons for believing those feelings are not sufficient grounds for condemning all wars. Even if readers are skeptical, the conciliatory phrasing of the thesis should encourage them to continue reading.

For any subject that is highly controversial or emotionally charged, especially one that strongly condemns an existing situation or belief, you may sometimes want to express your indignation directly. Of course, you must be sure that your indignation can be justified. The author of the following introduction, a physician and writer, openly admits that he is about to make a case that may offend readers.

> Is there any polite way to introduce today's subject? I'm afraid not. It must be said plainly that the media have done about as sorry and dishonest a job of covering health news as is humanly possible, and that when the media do not fail from bias and mendacity, they fail from ignorance and laziness.[6]

If your thesis advocates a policy or makes a recommendation, it may be a good idea, as in a value claim, to provide a short background. The following paragraph introduces an argument favoring relaxation of controls in high schools.

> "Free the New York City 275,000" read a button worn by many young New Yorkers some years ago. The number was roughly the total of students enrolled in the City's high schools.
>   The condition of un-freedom which is described was not, however, unique to the schools of one city. According to the Carnegie Commission's comprehensive study of American public education, *Crisis in the Classroom*, public schools across the country share a common characteristic, namely, "preoccupation with order and control." The result is that students find themselves the victims of "oppressive and petty rules which give their schools a repressive, almost prison-like atmosphere."[7]

There are also other ways to introduce your subject. One is to begin with an appropriate quotation.

---

[6]Michael Halberstam, "TV's Unhealthy Approach to Health News," *TV Guide*, September 20–26, 1980, p. 24.

[7]Alan Levine and Eve Carey, *The Rights of Students* (New York: Avon Books, 1977), p. 11.

"Reading makes a full man, conversation makes a ready man, and writing makes an exact man." So Francis Bacon told us around 1600. Recently I have been wondering how Bacon's formula might apply to present-day college students.[8]

Or you may begin with an anecdote. In the following introduction to an article about the relation between cancer and mental attitude, the author recounts a personal experience.

Shortly after I moved to California, a new acquaintance sat in my San Francisco living room drinking rose-hip tea and chainsmoking. Like so many residents of the Golden West, Cecil was "into" all things healthy, from jogging to *shiatsu* massage to kelp. Tobacco didn't seem to fit, but he told me confidently that there was no contradiction. "It all has to do with energy," he said. "Unless you have a lot of negative energy about smoking cigarettes, there's no way they can hurt you; you won't get cancer."[9]

Finally, you may introduce yourself as the author of the claim.

I wish to argue an unpopular cause: the cause of the old, free elective system in the academic world, or the untrammeled right of the undergraduate to make his own mistakes.[10]

My subject is the world of Hamlet. I do not of course mean Denmark, except as Denmark is given a body by the play; and I do not mean Elizabethan England, though this is necessarily close behind the scenes. I mean simply the imaginative environment that the play asks us to enter when we read it or go to see it.[11]

You should, however, use such introductions with care. They suggest an authority about the subject that you shouldn't attempt to assume unless you can demonstrate that you are entitled to it. Some instructors do not allow the use of first person in argumentative essays, so check the written guidelines for your assignments or ask your instructor.

Guidelines for Good Writing

In general, the writer of an argument follows the same rules that govern any form of expository writing. Your style should be clear and readable, your organization logical, your ideas connected by transitional phrases and sentences, your paragraphs coherent. The main difference between an argument and expository writing, as noted earlier, is the need to persuade an audience to adopt a belief or take an action. You should assume your readers will be critical rather than

[8] William Aiken, "The Conversation on Campus Today Is, Uh . . . ," *Wall Street Journal,* May 4, 1982, p. 18.

[9] Joel Guerin, "Cancer and the Mind," *Harvard Magazine,* November–December 1978, p. 11.

[10] Howard Mumford Jones, "Undergraduates on Apron Strings," *Atlantic Monthly,* October 1955, p. 45.

[11] Maynard Mack, "The World of Hamlet," *Yale Review,* June 1952, p. 502.

neutral or sympathetic. Therefore, you must be equally critical of your own work. Any apparent gap in reasoning or ambiguity in presentation is likely to weaken the argument.

As you read the essays in this book and elsewhere, you will discover that good style in argumentative writing shares several characteristics:

- Variety in sentence structure: a mixture of both long and short sentences, different sentence beginnings
- Rich but standard vocabulary: avoidance of specialized terms unless they are fully explained, word choice appropriate to a thoughtful argument
- Use of details and examples to illustrate and clarify abstract terms, principles, and generalizations

You should take care to avoid the following:

- Unnecessary repetition: making the same point without new data or interpretation
- Exaggeration or stridency, which can create suspicion of your fairness and powers of observation
- Short paragraphs of one or two sentences, which are common in advertising and newspaper writing to get the reader's attention but are inappropriate in a thoughtful essay

In addition to these stylistic principles, seven general points are worth keeping in mind:

1. Although *you,* like *I,* should be used judiciously, it can be found even in the treatment of weighty subjects. Here is an example from an essay by the distinguished British mathematician and philosopher, Bertrand Russell.

   Suppose you are a scientific pioneer and you make some discovery of great scientific importance and suppose you say to yourself, "I am afraid this discovery will do harm": you know that other people are likely to make the same discovery if they are allowed suitable opportunities for research; you must therefore, if you do not wish the discovery to become public, either discourage your sort of research or control publication by a board of censors.[12]

2. Don't pad. This point should be obvious; the word *pad* suggests the addition of unnecessary material. Many writers find it tempting, however, to enlarge a discussion even when they have little more to say. It is never wise to introduce more words into a paper that has already made its point. If the paper turns out to be shorter than you had hoped, it may mean that you have not sufficiently developed the subject or that the subject was less

[12]"Science and Human Life," in James R. Newman, ed., *What Is Science?* (New York: Simon and Schuster, 1955), p. 12.

substantial than you thought when you selected it. Padding, which is easy to detect in its repetition and sentences empty of content, weakens the writer's credibility.

3. For any absolute generalization — a statement containing words such as *all* or *every* — consider the possibility that there may be at least one example that will weaken the generalization. Such a precaution means that you won't have to backtrack and admit that your generalization is not, after all, universal. A student who was arguing against capital punishment for the reason that all killing was wrong suddenly paused in her presentation and added, "On the other hand, if given the chance, I'd probably have been willing to kill Hitler." This admission meant that she recognized important exceptions to her rule and that she would have to qualify her generalization in some significant way.

4. When offering an explanation, especially one that is complicated or extraordinary, look first for a cause that is easier to accept, one that doesn't strain credibility. For example, years ago a great many people were bemused by reports about the mysterious Bermuda Triangle, which had apparently swallowed up ships and planes since the mid-nineteenth century. The forces at work were variously described as space-time warps, UFOs that transported earthlings to other planets, and sea monsters seeking revenge. But a careful investigation revealed familiar, natural causes. A reasonable person interested in the truth would have searched for more conventional explanations before accepting the bizarre stories of extraterrestrial creatures. He or she would also exercise caution when confronted by conspiracy theories that try to account for controversial political events, such as the assassination of John F. Kennedy.

5. Check carefully for questionable warrants. When necessary, these should be included in your paper to link claims with support. Many an argument has failed because it depended on an unstated warrant with which the reader did not agree. If you were arguing for a physical education requirement at your school, you might make a good case for all the physical and psychological benefits of such a requirement. But you would certainly need to introduce and develop the warrant on which your claim was based — that it is the proper function of a college or university to provide the benefits of a physical education. Many readers would agree that physical education is valuable, but they might question the assumption that an academic institution should introduce a nonintellectual enterprise into the curriculum. At any point where you draw a controversial or tenuous conclusion, be sure your reasoning is clear and logical.

6. Avoid conclusions that are merely summaries. Summaries may be needed in long technical papers, but in brief arguments they create endings that are without force or interest. In the closing paragraph you should find a new idea that emerges naturally from the development of the whole argument.

7. Strive for a paper that is unified, coherent, and emphatic where appropriate. A *unified* paper stays focused on its goal and directs each claim, warrant, and piece of evidence toward that goal. Extraneous information or unsupported claims impair unity. *Coherence* means that all ideas are fully explained and adequately connected by transitions. To ensure coherence, give especially close attention to the beginnings and ends of your paragraphs: Is each new concept introduced in a way that shows it following naturally from the one that preceded it? *Emphasis,* as we have mentioned, is a function partly of structure and partly of language. Your most important claims should be placed where they are certain of receiving the reader's attention: key sentences at the beginning or end of a paragraph, key paragraphs at the beginning or end of your paper. Sentence structure can also be used for emphasis. If you have used several long, complex sentences, you can emphasize a significant point by stating it briefly and simply. You can also create emphasis with verbal flags, such as "The primary issue to consider . . ." or "Finally, we cannot ignore. . . ."

All clear expository prose will exhibit the qualities of unity, coherence, and emphasis. But the success of an argumentative paper is especially dependent on these qualities because the reader may have to follow a line of reasoning that is both complicated and unfamiliar. Moreover, a paper that is unified, coherent, and properly emphatic will be more readable, the first requisite of an effective argument.

The MLA System for Citing Sources

As you write your paper, any time that you make use of the wording or ideas of one of your sources, you must document that use. One of the simplest methods of crediting sources is the Modern Language Association (MLA) in-text system, which is used in the research paper on competitive food in this chapter. In the text of your paper, immediately after any quotation, paraphrase, or idea you need to document, simply insert a parenthetical mention of the author's last name and the page number on which the material appears. You don't need a comma after the author's name or an abbreviation of the word *page* or *p.* For example, the following sentence appears in the sample paper:

> Although there are nutritious competitive options, those do not sell as well as the ones high in sugar, salt, and calories (Hartline-Grafton 2–3).

The parenthetical reference tells the reader that the information in this sentence came from pages of the book or article that appears in the Works Cited at the end of the paper. The complete reference on the Works Cited page provides all of the information readers need to locate the original source:

Hartline-Grafton, Heather. "How Competitive Foods in Schools Impact Student
 Health, School Meal Programs, and Students from Low-Income Families." Issue
 Briefs for Child Nutrition Reauthorization 5. Washington, D.C.: Food Research
 and Action Center, 2010. *EBSCOhost*. Web. 22 Sept. 2010.

If the author's name is mentioned in the same sentence, it is also acceptable to
place only the page numbers in parentheses; it is not necessary to repeat the
author's name. For example,

According to Heather Hartline-Grafton, although there are nutritious competitive options, those do not sell as well as the ones high in sugar, salt, and calories (2–3).

Remember, though, that a major reason for using qualified sources is that they
lend authority to the ideas expressed. The first time an author is mentioned in
the paper, he or she — or they — should be identified by full name and by claim
to authority:

Parke Wilde and Mary Kennedy, both researchers in the Friedman School of Nutrition Science and Policy at Tufts University in Boston, explain some of the complexities in an article entitled "The Economics of a Healthy School Meal."

A last name and page number in parentheses do not carry nearly the same
weight as a full name and credentials. You should save the former for subsequent citations once the author has been fully identified. If more than one
sentence comes from the same source, you do not need to put parentheses
after each sentence. One parenthetical citation at the end of the material from
a source is enough if it is clear from the way you introduce the material where
your ideas end and the source's begin.

According to the Robert Wood Johnson Foundation, a charitable organization
whose goal is to improve the health of all Americans, the rate of obesity for
those between the ages of six and eleven has quadrupled in three decades.
Children are being diagnosed with what used to be considered adult diseases,
like high blood pressure, adult-onset diabetes, and gallstones. The Foundation
reports, "If we don't succeed in reversing this epidemic, we are in danger of
raising the first generation of American children who will live sicker and die
younger than their parents' generation" (259–60).

If you are using more than one work by the same author, you will need
to provide in the parentheses the title or a recognizable shortened form of the
title of the particular work being cited. If the author's name is not mentioned
in the sentence, you should include in parentheses the author's last name, the
title, and the page number, with a comma between the author's name and the
title. If both the author's name and the title of any work being cited are mentioned in the sentence, the parentheses will include only the page number. Had

two works by Hartline-Grafton been listed in the Works Cited, the first example above would have looked like this:

> Although there are nutritious competitive options, those do not sell as well as the ones high in sugar, salt, and calories (Hartline-Grafton, "How Competitive Foods" 2–3).

If there is more than one author, don't forget to give credit to all. Two or three authors are acknowledged by name in the parentheses if not in your own sentence: (Harmon, Livesy, and Jones 23). With four or more authors, use *et al.*, the Latin term for *and others*: (Braithwaite et al. 137).

Some sources do not name an author. To cite a work with an unknown author, give the title, or a recognizable shortened form, in the text of your paper. If the work does not have numbered pages, often the case in Web pages or non-print sources, do not include page numbers. For example,

> In some cases Sephardic Jews, "converted" under duress, practiced Christianity openly and Judaism in secret until recently ("Search for the Buried Past").

Direct quotations should always be introduced or worked into the grammatical structure of your own sentences. If you need help introducing quotations, refer to the Writer's Guide in Chapter 3 (pp. 88–89). Remember, however, that you need to provide parenthetical documentation not only for every direct quotation but also for every paraphrase or summary. Document any words or ideas that are not your own.

As a general rule, you cannot make any changes in a quotation. Two exceptions are clearly marked when they occur. At times you may use brackets to make a slight change that does not change the meaning of the quotation. For example, a pronoun may need to be replaced by a noun in brackets to make its reference clear. Or a verb tense may be changed and bracketed to make the quotation fit more smoothly into your sentence. An ellipsis (. . .) is used when you omit a portion of the quotation that does not change the essential meaning of the quote. You do not need to use ellipses at the beginning or end of a direct quotation. If the omitted portion included the end of one sentence and the beginning of another, there should be a fourth period (. . . .).

If a quotation is more than four typed lines long, it needs to be handled as a block quotation. A block quotation is usually introduced by a sentence followed by a colon. The quotation itself is indented one inch or ten spaces from the left margin. No quotation marks are necessary since the placement on the page informs the reader that it is a quotation. The only quotation marks in a block quotation would be ones copied from the original, as in dialogue. A paragraph break within a block quotation is indented an additional five spaces. The parenthetical citation is the same as with a quotation run into your text, but the period appears before the parenthesis.

With print sources in particular, you will often need to cite one work that is quoted in another or a work from an anthology. For the former, the parenthetical documentation provides name and page number of the source you actually used, preceded by the words "qtd. in":

> The National School Lunch Program has been in existence since 1946 "as a mea-sure of national security, to safeguard the health and well-being of the Nation's children and to encourage the domestic consumption of nutritious agricultural commodities and other food" (qtd. in Center for Science 230).

A work in an anthology is cited parenthetically by the name of the author of the work, not the editor of the anthology: (Simkovich 3).

The list of Works Cited includes all material you have used to write your research paper. This list appears at the end of your paper and always starts on a new page. Center the title Works Cited, double-space between the title and the first entry, and begin your list, which should be arranged alphabetically by author. Each entry should start at the left margin; indent all subsequent lines of the entry five spaces or one-half inch. Number each page, and double-space throughout.

One more point: *Content notes*, which provide additional information not readily worked into a research paper, are also indicated by superscript numbers. Content notes are included on a Notes page before the list of Works Cited.

Revising

The final stage in writing an argumentative paper is revising. The first step is to read through what you have written for mistakes. Next, check your work against the guidelines listed under "Organizing the Material" and "Writing." Have you omitted any of the issues, warrants, or supporting evidence on your outline? Is each paragraph coherent in itself? Do your paragraphs work together to create a coherent paper? All the elements of the argument — the issues raised, the underlying assumptions, and the supporting material — should contribute to the development of the claim in your thesis statement. Any material that is interesting but irrelevant to that claim should be cut. Finally, does your paper reach a clear conclusion that reinforces your thesis?

Be sure, too, that the style and tone of your paper are appropriate for the topic and the audience. Remember that people choose to read an argument be-cause they want the answer to a troubling question or the solution to a recurrent problem. Besides stating your thesis in a way that invites the reader to join you in your investigation, you must retain your audience's interest through a discussion that may be unfamiliar or contrary to their convictions. The outstanding qualities of argumentative prose style, therefore, are clarity and readability.

Style is obviously harder to evaluate in your own writing than organization. Your outline provides a map against which to check the structure of your paper. Clarity and readability, by comparison, are somewhat abstract qualities. Two procedures may be helpful. The first is to read two or three (or more) essays by authors whose style you admire and then turn back to your own writing. Awkward spots in your prose are sometimes easier to see if you get away from it and respond to someone else's perspective than if you simply keep rereading your own writing.

The second method is to read aloud. If you have never tried it, you are likely to be surprised at how valuable this can be. Again, start with someone else's work that you feel is clearly written, and practice until you achieve a smooth rhythmic delivery that satisfies you. And listen to what you are reading. Your objective is to absorb the patterns of English structure that characterize the clearest, most readable prose. Then read your paper aloud, and listen to the construction of your sentences. Are they also clear and readable? Do they say what you want them to say? How would they sound to a reader? According to one theory, you can learn the rhythm and phrasing of a language as you learn the rhythm and phrasing of a melody. And you will often *hear* a mistake or a clumsy construction in your writing that has escaped your eye in proofreading.

Preparing the Manuscript

Print your essay on one side of 8½-by-11-inch white computer paper, double-spacing throughout. Leave margins of 1 to 1½ inches on all sides, and indent each paragraph one-half inch or five spaces. Unless a formal outline is part of the paper, a separate title page is unnecessary. Instead, beginning about one inch from the top of the first page and flush with the left margin, type your name, the instructor's name, the course title, and the date, each on a separate line; then double-space and type the title, capitalizing the first letter of the words of the title except for articles, prepositions, and conjunctions. Double-space and type the body of the paper.

Number all pages at the top right corner, typing your last name before each page number in case pages are mislaid. If an outline is included, number its pages with lowercase roman numerals.

Writer's Guide: Checklist for Argumentative Papers

1. Present a thesis that interests both you and the audience, is debatable, and can be defended in the amount of space available.

2. Back up each statement offered in support of the thesis with enough evidence to give it credibility. Cite data from a variety of sources. Fully document all quotations and direct references to primary or secondary sources.

3. The warrants linking claims to support must be either specified or implicit in your data and line of reasoning. No claim should depend on an unstated warrant with which skeptical readers might disagree.

4. Present the thesis clearly and adequately introduce it in a thesis paragraph, indicating the purpose of the paper.

5. Organize supporting statements and data in a way that builds the argument, emphasizes your main ideas, and justifies the paper's conclusions.

6. Anticipate all possible opposing arguments and either refute or accommodate them.

7. Write in a style and tone appropriate for the topic and the intended audience. Your prose should be clear and readable.

8. Make sure your manuscript is clean, carefully proofed, and typed in an acceptable format.

Use the spell-check and grammar-check functions of your word-processing program, but keep in mind that correctness depends on context. A spell-check program will not flag a real word that is used incorrectly, such as the word *it's* used where the word *its* is needed. Also, a grammar-check function lacks the sophistication to interpret the meaning of a sentence and may flag as incorrect a group of words that is indeed correct while missing actual errors. It is ultimately up to you to proofread the paper carefully for other mistakes. Correct the errors, and reprint the pages in question.

Hedden 1

Kathleen Hedden
Mrs. Swanson
English 102-14
October 29, 2010

Competitive Foods and the Obesity Epidemic

It is difficult these days to watch television or read a newspaper without hearing about the problem of childhood obesity in the United States. Opinions differ as to the best solution for dealing with this problem that threatens the health of a rising generation, but few would deny that it is a problem.

Thomas R. Frieden, head of the Centers for Disease Control and Prevention in Atlanta and thus one of the leading health officials in the country, is among those who have used the term "epidemic" to describe what is happening: "What has changed, in just the course of a generation, is that childhood obesity has become an epidemic," he says. "In the 1960s, 5 percent of children were overweight. Today, nearly 20 percent are" (Frieden, Dietz, and Collins). Concern about obesity is not just concern for how our children — and our future adults — look, but for their present and future health. According to the Robert Wood Johnson Foundation, a charitable organization whose goal is to improve the health of all Americans, the rate of obesity for those between the ages of six and eleven has quadrupled in three decades. Children are being diagnosed with what used to be considered adult diseases, like high blood pressure, adult-onset diabetes, and gallstones. The Foundation reports, "If we don't succeed in reversing this epidemic, we are in danger of raising the first generation of American children who will live sicker and die younger than their parents' generation" (259–60).

The problem of childhood obesity will have to be attacked on several fronts. Parents and other caregivers have to be educated and motivated to control children's diet and physical activity. Because of the number of hours that

Frieden's name and position are used to introduce and lend authority to the quotation.

Article from a journal. Frieden is quoted, but all three authors need to be listed in parentheses. No page numbers because accessed online.

Foundation as author. Since it is mentioned in the text, all that is necessary in parentheses is the page number. The citation covers both paraphrased and quoted material.

Hedden 2

most children spend in school five days a week for a large part of the year, however, the CDC's *Morbidity and Mortality Weekly Report* has stated that "schools are in a unique position to help improve youth dietary behaviors and prevent and reduce obesity" (Centers for Disease Control).

The federal government has long subsidized the nation's school lunch program. The National School Lunch Program has been in existence since 1946 "as a measure of national security, to safeguard the health and well-being of the Nation's children and to encourage the domestic consumption of nutritious agricultural commodities and other food" (qtd. in Center for Science 230).

One problem now is the sale of what are called competitive foods, or those foods and beverages sold in schools but outside of the meal program supported by the federal government. They may be sold through vending machines, snack bars, school stores, or in a la carte lines, but they do not have to meet the nutrition standards that must be met by cafeteria food. They are not supposed to be available in the food service area during lunch, but they sometimes are and in other cases are close by.

Dr. Heather Hartline-Grafton, Senior Nutrition Policy Analyst for the Food Research and Action Center (FRAC), explains how this competitive food contributes to the obesity epidemic:

> Competitive foods are often energy-dense, nutrient-poor items, and their availability at school undermines efforts to promote healthy diets and prevent obesity. Not only do the sales of competitive foods and beverages decrease participation in the school meal programs, but the sales are often subsidized by school meal reimbursements. (1)

Competitive foods are a widespread presence in schools: They are available in 73 percent of elementary schools, 97 percent of middle schools, and 100 percent of high schools, most often in the form of vending machines and a la carte

The organization is the author. No page number because accessed online.

One work quoted in another. The citation is to the work Katie actually used.

Hedden 3

lines. Although there are nutritious competitive options, those do not sell as well as the ones high in sugar, salt, and calories (Hartline-Grafton 2–3).

> Author not mentioned in text, so her name is included with page number in parentheses.

While the U.S. Department of Agriculture has the power to regulate the food served in the school lunch program, it currently has little power to regulate competitive foods. That power depends in part on what foods are defined as foods of minimal nutritional value (FMNVs). Hartline-Grafton explains:

> FMNVs are defined as foods providing less than five percent of recommended intakes for eight key nutrients. Examples include carbonated soda, gum, hard candies, and jelly beans. Other competitive foods, including candy bars, chips, and ice cream, are not considered FMNVs (and therefore not under USDA authority) and may be sold in the cafeteria during meal periods. In short, unlike the federal school lunch and breakfast programs, competitive foods are, for the most part, exempt from federal nutrition standards and regulation. (2)

> Block quotation. Notice that the whole quotation is indented, there are no quotation marks, and the period comes before the parenthesis.

If it is obvious that many competitive foods are a danger to our children's health and well-being and that they are beyond the control of even the USDA's regulations, why are these foods not removed from schools?

One simple answer is because students like them and buy them. Most students are in the habit of eating fast food away from school and see no problem eating it at school. They like the high-fat, high-sugar foods that do not conform to the regulations that school cafeterias must follow.

If students are not willing to monitor their own food intake and the USDA cannot, why do schools continue to allow these foods lacking in nutritional value to be sold? Part of the answer is that some school districts in some states have chosen to regulate the competitive foods sold in the district or to eliminate them entirely. The economics of school meals, however, are much more complicated

Hedden 4

than one might think. Parke Wilde and Mary Kennedy, both researchers in the Friedman School of Nutrition Science and Policy at Tufts University in Boston, explain some of the complexities in an article entitled "The Economics of a Healthy School Meal." Schools are reimbursed a set amount for each lunch subsidized by the federal government. Even when better-off students pay for their lunch, the federal government pays its part. Other students, depending on their parents' income, pay a reduced rate or nothing at all. Even that set formula, however, is affected by competitive foods. Students and their parents are pushing for more nutritious foods than are required by the federal government, and the districts must balance the money lost when students don't eat school lunches with that gained by selling competitive foods. Wilde and Kennedy write,

> Any successful business must understand the economic interactions across its product lines, but these interactions are particularly intense for a school food service. A child who consumes a reimbursable lunch and breakfast will have lower demand for *a la carte* items, while a child who skips a real meal may be hungrier for a snack. This interaction means that school food service decisions about competitive foods strongly affect the federal school meals program, and vice versa.

No page number because an electronic source.

By that logic, if competitive foods were not available, students might opt for the healthier alternative of the school meal.

In September 2010, Congress passed the Healthy, Hunger-Free Kids Act of 2010, a huge step forward in schools' ability to control the foods served at school. The act will "commit an additional $4.5 billion to child-nutrition programs over the next 10 years and implement the most sweeping changes to those programs in decades." In response to the problem of competitive foods, it "directs the U.S. Department of Agriculture to set new nutrition standards for all food served in schools, from lunchrooms to vending machines" (Eisler).

Author not identified in text. No page number because electronic source.

Hedden 5

Ironically, it is not a foregone conclusion that all schools will benefit from this new legislation. They have to adopt the new nutrition standards, which the Institute of Medicine will recommend and the U.S. Department of Agriculture will write. Schools that adopt the new nutrition requirements will get an increase of six cents per meal in their federal reimbursement rate, the first increase since 1973 and one that has long been needed (Eisler). Stipends are also available for those schools that need to upgrade their kitchens to accommodate preparing the more nutritious meals (Wilde and Kennedy).

It seems obvious that all school districts across the country should adopt the new nutritional standards that are being presented to them with the additional incentive of getting more money per meal for school lunches and breakfasts than they currently get. The new standards will remove from schools competitive foods that are particularly unhealthy and replace them with foods that fall under the nutrition guidelines of the new act. Students may not get all of the choices of foods that they would like, but parents, teachers, and school officials — and the students themselves — will know that schools are contributing less to the problem of childhood and adolescent obesity.

Hedden 6

Works Cited

Center for Science in the Public Interest. "Improving Kids'
    Nutrition: An Action Kit for Parents and Citizens."
    Food, Inc.: How Industrial Food Is Making Us Sicker,   A work in an
    Fatter and Poorer — And What You Can Do about It.   anthology
    Ed. Karl Weber. New York: PublicAffairs, 2009. 227–57.
    Print.

Centers for Disease Control and Prevention. "Competitive
    Foods and Beverages Available for Purchase in Second-   A journal article
    ary Schools---Selected Sites, United States, 2006."   accessed online
    MMWR Weekly 29 August 2008: 935–938. *EBSCOhost.*
    Web. 16 Sept. 2010.

Eisler, Peter. "Sweeping School Lunch Bill Clears Senate   A newspaper
    Panel." *usatoday.com.* USA Today, 24 March 2010. Web.   article accessed
    22 Sept. 2010.   online

Frieden, Thomas R., William Dietz, and Janet Collins. "Re-
    ducing Childhood Obesity Through Policy Change:
    Acting Now to Prevent Obesity." *Health Affairs* 29.3   A journal article
    (2010): 357–63. *EBSCOhost.* Web. 15 Sept 2010.   accessed online

Hartline-Grafton, Heather. "How Competitive Foods in
    Schools Impact Student Health, School Meal Programs,   A document ac-
    and Students from Low-Income Families." *Issue Briefs*   cessed online
    for Child Nutrition Reauthorization 5. Washington,
    D.C.: Food Research and Action Center, 2010.
    EBSCOhost. Web. 22 Sept. 2010.

Robert Wood Johnson Foundation. "Childhood Obesity: The
    Challenge." *Food, Inc.: How Industrial Food Is Making*   A work in an
    Us Sicker, Fatter and Poorer — And What You Can Do   anthology
    about It. Ed. Karl Weber. New York: PublicAffairs, 2009.
    259–61. Print.

Wilde, Parke, and Mary Kennedy. "The Economics of a   A journal article
    Healthy School Meal." *Choices* 24.3 (2009): n. pag.   accessed online
    EBSCOhost. Web. 21 Sept. 2010.

The APA System for Citing Sources

Instructors in the social sciences might prefer the citation system of the American Psychological Association (APA), which is used in the paper on women in the military in this chapter. Like the MLA system, the APA system calls for a parenthetical citation in the text of the paper following any quotations from your sources. The APA only recommends that page numbers be included for paraphrases or summaries, but you should provide page numbers for these anyway unless your instructor advises you that they are not necessary. In the text of your paper, immediately after any quotation, paraphrase, or idea you need to document, insert a parenthetical mention of the author's last name and the page number on which the material appears. Unlike the MLA system, the APA system also includes the year of publication in the parenthetical reference, using a comma to separate the items within the citation and using "p." or "pp." before the page number(s). Even if the source has a month of publication, only the year is included in the parenthetical citation. Here is an example:

> As of now, women are restricted from 30 percent of Army assignments and 1 percent of Air Force assignments (Baer, 2003, p. 1A).

The parenthetical reference tells the reader that the information in this sentence comes from page 1A of the 2003 work by Baer that appears on the References page at the end of the paper. The complete publication information that a reader would need to locate Baer's work will appear on the References page:

> Baer, S. (2003, March 3). In Iraq war, women would serve closer to front lines than in past. *The Baltimore Sun*, p. 1A.

If the author's name is mentioned in the same sentence in your text, the year in which the work was published follows it, in parentheses, and the page number only is placed in parentheses at the end of the sentence.

> According to Baer (2003) of the *Baltimore Sun*, as of now, women are restricted from 30 percent of Army assignments and 1 percent of Air Force assignments (p. 1A).

In the APA system, it is appropriate to include only the last name of the author unless you have more than one author with the same name in your list of references, in which case you would include the first initial of the author.

If your list of references includes more than one work written by the same author in the same year, cite the first work as "a" and the second as "b." For example, Baer's second article of 2003 would be cited in your paper like this: (Baer, 2003b).

If a work has two authors, list both in your sentence or in the parentheses, using "and" between them. In these examples from the women in combat paper, there is no page number because the source is a short work from a Web site:

> The fall 2000 suggestion from DACOWITS included a possible recruiting slogan: "A gynecologist on every aircraft carrier!" (Yoest & Yoest, 2001).

> Yoest and Yoest (2001) recall the fall 2000 suggestion from DACOWITS for a possible recruiting slogan: "A gynecologist on every aircraft carrier!"

If there are three to five authors, list them all by last name the first time they are referred to and, after that, by the last name of the first author and the term "et al." (meaning "and others"): (Sommers, Mylroie, Donnelly, & Hill, 2001); (Sommers et al., 2001). Also use the last name of the first author and "et al." when there are more than five authors, which is often the case in the sciences and social sciences.

If no author is given, use the name of the work where you would normally use the author's name, placing the names of short works in quotation marks and italicizing those of book-length works.

When using electronic sources, follow as much as possible the rules for parenthetical documentation of print ones. If no author's name is given, cite by the title of the work. If no date is given, use the abbreviation "n.d." instead. For a long work, if there are no page numbers, as is often the case with electronic sources, give paragraph numbers if the work has numbered paragraphs, or, if the work is divided into sections, the paragraph number within that section:

> Jamison (1999) warned about the moral issues associated with stem cell research, particularly the guilt that some parents felt about letting their children's cells be used (Parental Guilt section, para. 2).

Remember that the purpose of parenthetical documentation is to help a reader locate the information that you are citing.

At times you will need to cite one work that is quoted in another or a work from an anthology. For the former, the parenthetical documentation provides author's name, year of publication, and page number of the source you actually used, preceded by the words "as cited in":

> The female soldier "is, on the average, about five inches shorter than the male soldier, has half the upper body strength, lower aerobic capacity and 37 percent less muscle mass" (as cited in Owens, 1997, Anatomy section, para. 2).

A work in an anthology is cited parenthetically by the name of the author of the work, not the editor of the anthology.

Sample Research Paper (APA Style)

The following paper shows APA citations in the context of an actual text and the format for several different entries on the References page. Angela has used quotations sparingly and has instead made extensive use of summary and paraphrase. Often there is no page number in her parenthetical citations. That is because she was drawing from short online sources in which the paragraphs are not numbered but in which it is easy to find the material she refers to.

The format of the title page illustrates APA guidelines, as does the running head that is on each page.

Notice that Angela's thesis appears as the last sentence in her first paragraph. She carefully documents the restrictions on women that still exist in the U.S. military and argues why those restrictions are appropriate.

Women in Combat 1

The Controversy over Women in Combat

Angela Mathers
English 103-13
Ms. Carter
April 7, 2011

Women in Combat 2

Abstract

Women have served in the U.S. military since World War I. Although many barriers to their complete participation in all phases of military service have been broken, they are still appropriately restricted from direct ground combat assignments. Because women are held to a lower physical standard than men, men in their units cannot trust their ability to perform on the battlefield. One argument in favor of combat assignments for women has been that the lack of combat experience stands in the way of their progressing through the ranks. Such careerism, however, goes against a soldier's sworn duty, and there are ways to advance in the military other than combat service. The social and logistical problems created are an argument against women's serving in close quarters with men. Pregnancy among enlisted women is also inevitable and poses its own medical and logistical problems. Combat assignments for women would be a threat to the effectiveness and readiness of American troops.

Women in Combat 3

The Controversy over Women in Combat

Throughout the history of the military, the role of
women has changed and adapted as the needs of the country have. From Molly Pitcher to Rosie the Riveter, women
have always held a place in making the military what it is
today. Issues have surfaced in the modern military about
the current role of female service members with regard to
combat assignments. Positions on submarines, small destroyers, specialized combat teams, and a handful of other
assignments are restricted to men-only clubs. The factors
determining why women are restricted from these assignments include physical ability, deployability, the cost effectiveness of providing the facilities that women need,
and the effect on the overall readiness of the military.
Women who desire these assignments, and other opponents
of these restrictions, have retorted with reasons that they
should be included, the foremost being women's rights and
their desire to advance up the ranks of the military. However, women are rightly restricted from direct ground combat assignments to ensure the readiness of the military and
the effectiveness of these combat units.

Women were first recruited, and began serving, in the
military during World War I because they were needed to
fill the clerical, technical, and health care jobs that were
left vacant as more men were drafted. All these women,
however, were discharged as soon as the war ended. The
Women's Army Corps (WAC) was founded during World War
II and gave women their own branch of the military. They
served in the same jobs as they did in WWI but with the
addition of non-combatant pilot assignments. Women did
not get their permanent place in the ranks until 1948 when
the Women Armed Services Integration Act was passed
through Congress, allowing them to serve under the conditions that they were not to hold any rank above colonel,
were limited mostly to clerical or health care jobs, and
were not to make up more than 2 percent of the entire
military. They were still limited to their own female only

Margin annotations:

Overview of the controversy

Opposing view

Thesis

A history of women in the military from a source accessed through a subscription service

Women in Combat 4

corps until 1978, when the military was fully integrated and women were allowed to hold any assignment that their male counterparts could except for combat roles. The rules have been relaxed over the years as women have proven themselves in combat support missions, especially in the Persian Gulf War in 1991 ("Women," 2000). They continue to push to be allowed into every job that men hold, and the effect this is having on the military is a fiery issue.

The parenthetical citation shows where paraphrase ends and her ideas begin

According to Baer (2003) of the *Baltimore Sun*, as of now, women are restricted from 30 percent of Army assignments, 38 percent of Marine assignments, and 1 percent of Air Force assignments. From the Navy, women are excluded from the special operations SEAL groups. These exclusions are from Military Occupational Specialities (MOS) "whose primary mission is ground combat" as defined by the Pentagon. They are also excluded from Navy submarines and small battleships that do not have the facilities to accommodate women (p. 1A).

Source and year included in text

Page only in parentheses

There have been many advancements for combat seeking women since the Persian Gulf War. McDonough (2003), writing for the Associated Press, reports that females are now allowed to fly combat missions in fighter jets and bombers for the Air Force and Navy. They can serve in many combat support roles such as combat Military Police companies. They can also be assigned to chemical specialist units that clean up contaminated areas on the battlefield, and to engineering units who build and repair bridges and runways in high risk areas. Women can also pilot the Army's Apache assault helicopters over the battlefield during high risk conditions, and pilot troop carrying helicopters onto the battlefield to deliver troops for a rescue mission during an assault. However, none of these MOSs are in selective special operations units such as Marine Force Recon or Army Airborne Rangers who serve as the "tip of the spear" in ground combat for missions like Operation Enduring Freedom in Afghanistan or Operation Iraqi Freedom.

Author and year in text; no page number because electronic version

Women in Combat 5

The federal government and military have been under
pressure from several sides on the issue of women serving in combat roles in the military. There are those that
believe that all assignments, no matter how demanding
of time, body, talent, and mind should be open to women
as well as men. According to Gerber (2002) of the James   A Web site
MacGregor Burns Academy of Leadership, this is the general
consensus of the Defense Advisory Committee on Women
in the Services (DACOWITS). It was established in 1951 by
General George Marshall but was disbanded when Secretary
of Defense Donald Rumsfeld let its charter run out when it
came up for renewal in 2002. However, its motives could
be called into question as to whether it is rallying for the
good of the military and its purposes or pushing its own
platform that women should be integrated in all parts
just because they believe it is deserved. Former DACOWITS
Chairperson Vickie McCall even told the U.S. Air Force in
Europe News Service, "You have to understand. We don't
report facts, we report perception" (as qtd. in Yoest &   One source
Yoest, 2001). DACOWITS has often teamed up with other   quoted in an-
                                                                     other; source
private women's rights activist groups that believe that the   with two au-
military should be an "equal opportunity employer" along   thors
with all other private and public employers.

        One cause of concern over women's inclusion in com-
bat units has been the rigorous physical standards these
troops must meet in training and in turn on the battlefield.
Many studies have been done to prove or disprove a distinction between men's and women's physical capabilities.
In the quest for evidence, Col. Patrick Toffler, Director of
the United States Military Office of Institutional Research,
reported that it had identified 120 physical differences
(Owens, 1997, p. 40). The female soldier "is, on the aver-   A journal pagi-
age, about five inches shorter than the male soldier, has   nated by issue
half the upper body strength, lower aerobic capacity and
37 percent less muscle mass" (as qtd. in Owens, 1997,
p. 38). Leo (1997) reports in *U.S. News and World Report*   A magazine

Women in Combat 6

that the way that the military accommodates for these differences is called "gender norming" and works by lowering the standards that women have to reach to pass the physical fitness tests. For instance, in the Marines, men are required to climb the length of a rope and females are only required to climb to a point below that marked with a yellow line (p. 14). These standards are mostly for people to enlist in the services; so the bar is significantly raised for those that choose to compete for a MOS in special operations or combat units. Females enrolled in Army Jump School to be paratroopers are still not required to run as far or do as many pushups or sit-ups as their male counterparts. When this double standard is employed in the military, it blurs the distinction as to which soldiers actually have the physical ability to perform on the battlefield.

When there is a question as to the physical abilities of a fellow soldier in a unit, there can be no guarantee that everyone can cover your back as well as you could for them. When there is no trust in a unit, it breaks down. Take, for example, the Marine ideology that no one is left behind on the battlefield. Imagine an officer trying to motivate his troops to jump out of a helicopter in the heat of battle. Some of the soldiers may doubt a female comrade's capability to carry them to safety should they be injured, because she does not have to meet the same physical standards as her male counterparts do. The training is not only meant to prepare the troops for war combat and to show the officers that they meet the physical requirements. It is also a time to begin to build the trust that binds the troop's lives together and prove to each other they have the physical and mental toughness to accomplish the mission and bring each other back safely. How can this trust be established when male soldiers witness some female soldiers being excused from throwing live grenades in practice because they cannot throw the dummy ones far enough to keep from being blown to shreds? "The military should be the real world," said Jeanne Holm, retired two-star General

Women in Combat 7

of the Air Force. "The name of the game is putting together a team that fits and works together. That is the top priority, not social experimentation" (as qtd. in Yoest & Yoest, 2001). The military studies prove that a female body is not equipped to perform the same physical rigors as the male body; therefore, they should not be put in the position where impossible war fighting demands are put on them.

> One source quoted in another

When left out of selective combat positions, there is the possibility that women cannot advance up the ranks because they would not get ample opportunity to prove themselves on the battlefield and gain combat experience. This experience goes a long way because it stands to prove that an officer has the leadership ability to command troops under fire and accomplish the mission. Experience can be gained in many ways, though, since America is not always at war. All officer career fields are necessary to the overall success of the mission, and in order to be promoted every officer must pull his or her weight. Even though the proceedings of the promotion committees are supposed to be kept private, it is no secret that combat experience weighs heavily on promotion picks (Nath, 2002). In a military that is centered on the chain of command, seniority is the most valuable commodity for any member, especially officers. The practice of officers' jockeying for promotions to further their career, stature, and income is called "careerism" (Nath, 2002). This is supposedly prohibited under the Air Force's second core value of "Service Before Self," and similar pledges in the other branches. The argument lies in the conflict between the career ambition of female officers seeking a combat MOS and the needs of a ready military to support the mission.

> No page number given

The truth is, however, that the United States Armed Forces is not an "equal opportunity employer" as many other public and private organizations are. The military is not out to make a profit, or provide a ladder to corporate success. Instead, military officers swear to "support and defend the Constitution of the United States against all

Women in Combat 8

enemies, foreign and domestic; that I will bear the true faith and allegiance to the same" (Oath of Office, 2003). This oath states they are to uphold the best interest of the mission that the Commander in Chief charges them with. Careerism is not an option under this oath because it is only serving the individual's ambition, and not the mission of the military. Elaine Donnelly, President of the Center for Military Readiness, says, "Equal opportunity is important, but the armed forces exist to defend the country. If there is a conflict between career opportunities and military necessity, the needs of the military must come first" (as qtd. in "Women," 2000).

Another concern with females in combat is their deployability, or their availability to be deployed. Because the very nature of combat units is being the "tip of the spear" in battle, they are deployed and away from home much of the year and are used for an indefinite period of time during the war. Donnelly explains that "if you have a pregnancy rate and it's constant, 10 or 15%, you know that out of 500 women on a carrier at least 50 are going to be unavailable before or during the six-month deployment" (Sommers, Mylroie, Donnelly, & Hill, 2001). This pregnancy issue is not just applicable for conception before the deployment, but during deployment, as is evident on Navy aircraft carriers and destroyers that house women. Even though fraternization, defined as "sexual relationships between service members" (Nath, 2002), is illegal, many ships such as the U.S.S. *Lincoln* "report a dozen [pregnancies] a month" (Layton, 2003). In a close quarters environment, where combat units are together every hour of the day, this kind of problem distracts from the mission. Also, sailors on submarines sleep in what they call "hot beds," which are rotating shifts for sleep in the few available beds, and changing this system to accommodate separate quarters for females would not be cost effective. Also, pregnant females aboard aircraft carriers are being taken from their duty, and they must be replaced, which is a

First reference to source with four authors

Different parts of the same sentence cited to different sources

Women in Combat 9

costly endeavor for the military and throws off the working relationship between service members.

When men and women are put in close quarters, it is just human nature that sexual relationships will begin to develop. This fact has been proven all around the military from the pregnancies on board Naval ships all the way up to the Navy's "Tail Hook Convention," where in Las Vegas in 1991, dozens of female officers reported being openly sexually assaulted by male officers, both married and unmarried ("Women," 2000). If there was this kind of distraction within special operation ground combat units, the mission would suffer greatly because fraternization would become a huge issue, for favoritism would ensue. When the mission is not the first thing on these troops' minds, the morale, and most importantly, the trust breaks down.

Another very real barrier to the inclusion of women in these units and on small battleships and submarines is the medical needs of the female body. The fall 2000 suggestion from DACOWITS included as a possible recruiting slogan "A gynecologist on every aircraft carrier! (Yoest & Yoest, 2001). This is a possibility on every base and possibly on huge aircraft carriers, but these needs of women cannot be met in the field hospitals in the deserts of Iraq and Afghanistan where the only goal is to keep soldiers from dying long enough to get them to a base hospital. Another dilemma on forty to fifty person submarines is that if a woman were to get pregnant, as is the proven trend, the vessel would have to make a risky surface to get her off to be cared for and find a replacement for her job on board. DACOWITS also suggested to "ensure an adequate supply of hygiene products during deployment" (Yoest & Yoest, 2001), which is a far cry from reality when Marines who are currently in Iraq already march with a 130-pound rucksack holding their bare living necessities. The military certainly does not have the money to cover these hygiene and medical needs when in high risk areas simply because the resources must go to fulfilling the mission.

Women in Combat 10

As the way we do battle continues to change, so will the roles of males and females; and the military will always have to come up with the best solution to accommodate these differences. As for now, the restrictions that are placed on women's assignments are based in sound reasoning. For the military's purposes, women do not have the physical abilities to fill combat oriented jobs, and the military does not have the resources to make these assignments available to them. The military needs to be aware of and most concerned with the effectiveness and readiness of its troops and figure out the best way to accomplish its mission and preserve America's freedom and sovereignty.

References

Baer, S. (2003, March 3). In Iraq war, women would serve closer to front lines than in past. *The Baltimore Sun*, p. 1A. Retrieved from http://www.baltimoresun.com

Dobbin, M. (2003, March 2). As war looms, women's role in U.S. military expands. *The Modesto Bee*, p. 3A. Retrieved from http://www.modbee.com

Gerber, R. (2002, September 23). Don't send military women to the back of the troop train. *USA Today*. Retrieved from http://www.usatoday.com

Layton, L. (2003, March 15). Navy women finding ways to adapt to a man's world. *The Washington Post*, p. A15. Retrieved from http://www.washingtonpost.com

Leo, J. (1997, August 11). A kinder, gentler army. *U.S. News and World Report, 123*(6), 14.

McDonough, S. (2003, February 10). More U.S. military women edging closer to combat positions in preparation for Iraq war. *The Associated Press*. Retrieved from http://www.ap.org/

Nath, C. (2002). *United States Air Force Leadership Studies*. Washington, DC: Air Education and Training Command, United States Air Force.

Women in Combat 11

Oath of office: U.S. federal and military oath of office. Retrieved from http://www.apfn.org/apfn/oathofoffice.htm

Owens, M. (1997, Spring). Mothers in combat boots: Feminists call for women in the military. *Human Life Review*, 23(2), 35–45.

Sommers, C., Mylroie, L., Donnelly, E., & Hill, M. (2001, October 17). IWF panel: Women facing war. *Independent Women's Forum*. Retrieved from RDS Contemporary Women's Issues.

Warrior women. (2003, February 16). *The New York Times*, sect. 6, p. 23. Retrieved from http://www.nytimes.com

Women in the military. (2000, September 1). *Issues and Controversies*. Retrieved from http://www.2facts.com

Yoest, C., & Yoest, J. (2002, Winter). Booby traps at the Pentagon. *Women's Quarterly*. Retrieved from http://www.bnet.com

CHAPTER 12

Oral Arguments

$\mathbf{A}$ classics scholar points out that the oratorical techniques we use today were "invented in antiquity and have been used to great effect ever since."[1] But history is not our only guide to the principles of public speaking. Much of what we know about the power of persuasive speech is knowledge based on lifelong experience — things we learn in everyday discourse with different kinds of people who respond to different appeals. Early in life you learned that you did not use the same language or the same approach to argue with your mother or your teacher as you used with your sibling or your friend. You learned, or tried to learn, how to convince people to listen to you and to trust you because you were truthful and knew what you were talking about. Although speeches to a larger, less familiar audience will require much more preparation, many of the rules of argument that guided you in your personal encounters can be made to work for you in more public arenas.

You will often be asked to make oral presentations in your college classes. Many jobs, both professional and nonprofessional, will call for speeches to groups of fellow employees or prospective customers, to community groups, and even government officials. Wherever you live, there will be controversies and public meetings about schooling and political candidates, about budgets for libraries and road repairs and pet control. The ability to rise and make your case before an audience is one that you will want to cultivate as a citizen of a democracy. Great oratory is probably no longer the most powerful influence in our society, and computer networks have usurped the role of oral communication in many areas of public life. But whether it's in person or on television there is still a significant role for a live presenter, a real human being to be seen and heard.

Some of your objectives as a writer will also be relevant to you as a speaker: making the appropriate appeal to an audience, establishing your credibility, find-

---

[1] Mary Lefkowitz, "Classic Oratory," *New York Times*, January 24, 1999, sec. W, p. 15.

ing adequate support for your claim. But other elements of argument will be different: language, organization, and the use of visual and other aids.

The Audience

Most speakers who confront a live audience already know something about the members of that audience. They may know why the audience is assembled to hear the particular speaker, their vocations, their level of education, and their familiarity with the subject. They may know whether the audience is friendly, hostile, or neutral to the views that the speaker will express. Analyzing the audience is an essential part of speech preparation. If speakers neglect it, both audience and speaker will suffer. At some time all of us have been trapped as members of an audience, forced to listen to a lecture, a sermon, an appeal for action when it was clear that the speaker had little or no idea what we were interested in or capable of understanding. In such situations the speaker who seems indifferent to the needs of the audience will also suffer because the audience will either cease to listen or reject his claim outright.

In college classes students who make assigned speeches on controversial topics are often encouraged to first survey the class. Questionnaires and interviews can give the speaker important clues to the things he should emphasize or avoid: They will tell him whether he should give both sides of a debatable question, introduce humor, use simpler language, and bring in visual or other aids.

When delivering a speech, it is helpful to know how your audience may react.

But even where such specific information is not immediately available, speakers are well advised to find out as much as they can about the beliefs and attitudes of their audience from other sources. They will then be better equipped to make the kinds of appeals — to reason and to emotion — that the audience is most responsive to.

If you know something about your audience, ask yourself what impression your clothing, gestures and bodily movements, voice, and general demeanor might convey. Make sure, too, that you understand the nature of the occasion — is it too solemn for humor? too formal for personal anecdotes? — and the purpose of the meeting, which can influence your choice of language and the most effective appeal.

Credibility

The evaluation of audience and the presentation of your own credibility are closely related. In other words, what can you do to persuade this particular audience that you are a reliable exponent of the views you are expressing? Credibility, as you learned in Chapter 1, is another name for *ethos* (the Greek word from which the English word *ethics* is derived) and refers to the honesty, moral character, and intellectual competence of the speaker.

Public figures, whose speeches and actions are reported in the media, can acquire (or fail to acquire) reputations for being endowed with those characteristics. And there is little doubt that a reputation for competence and honesty can incline an audience to accept an argument that would be rejected if offered by a speaker who lacks such a reputation. One study, among many that report similar results, has shown that the same speech will be rated highly by an audience that thinks the surgeon general of the United States has delivered it but treated with much less regard if they hear it delivered by a college sophomore.

How, then, do speakers who are unknown to the audience or who boast only modest credentials convince listeners that they are responsible advocates? From the moment the speaker appears before them, members of the audience begin to make an evaluation, based on external signs, such as clothing and mannerisms. But the most significant impression of the speaker's credibility will be based on what the speaker says and how. Does the speaker give evidence of knowing the subject? Of being aware of the needs and values of the audience? Especially if arguing an unpopular claim, does the speaker seem modest and conciliatory?

An unknown speaker is often advised to establish his credentials in the introduction to his speech, to summarize his background and experience as proof of his right to argue the subject he has chosen. A prize-winning and widely reprinted speech by a student begins with these words:

When you look at me, it is easy to see several similarities between us. I have two arms, two legs, a brain, and a heart just like you. These are my hands, and they are just like yours. Like you, I also have wants and desires; I am capable of love and hate. I can laugh and I can cry. Yes, I'm just like you, except for one very important fact — I am an ex-con.[2]

This is a possibly risky beginning — not everybody in the audience will be friendly to an ex-con — but it signifies that the speaker brings some authority to his subject, which is prison reform. It also attests to the speaker's honesty and may rouse sympathy among certain listeners. (To some in the audience, the speaker's allusions to his own humanity will recall another moving defense, the famous speech by Shylock, the Jewish moneylender, in Shakespeare's *The Merchant of Venice*.)

Speakers will often use an admission of modesty as proof of an honest and unassuming character, presenting themselves not as experts but as speakers well aware of their limitations. Such an appeal can generate sympathy in the audience (if they believe the speaker) and a sense of identification with the speaker.

The professor of classics quoted earlier has analyzed the speech of a former senator who defended President Clinton at his impeachment trial. She found that the speaker "made sure his audience understood that he was one of them, a friend, on their level, not above them. He denied he was a great speaker and spoke of his friendship with Mr. Clinton." As the writer points out, this confession brings to mind the speech by Mark Antony in *Julius Caesar*:

I am no orator, as Brutus is,
But (as you know me all) a plain blunt man
That loves my friend; (3.2.226–28)

The similarity of these attempts at credibility, separated by almost four hundred years (to say nothing of the fact that Aristotle wrote about *ethos* 2,500 years ago) tells us a good deal about the enduring influence of *ethos* or character on the speaker's message.

Organization

Look at the student speech on page 490. The organization of this short speech — the usual length of speeches delivered in the classroom — is easily mastered and works for all kinds of claims.

At the end of the first paragraph the speaker states what he will try to prove, that a vegetarian diet contributes to prevention of chronic diseases. In the third paragraph the speaker gives the four points that he will develop in his argument

[2] Richard M. Duesterbeck, "Man's Other Society," in Wil Linkugel, R. R. Allen, and Richard Johannesen, eds., *Contemporary American Speeches* (Belmont, CA: Wadsworth, 1965), p. 264.

for vegetarianism. Following the development of these four topics, the conclusion urges the audience to take action, in this case, to stop eating meat.

This basic method of organizing a short speech has several virtues. First, the claim or thesis statement that appears early in a short speech, if the subject is well chosen, can engage the interest of the audience at once. Second, the list of topics guides the speaker in planning and developing his speech. Moreover, it tells the audience what to listen for as they follow the argument.

A well-planned speech has a clearly defined beginning, middle, and end. The beginning, which offers the introduction, can take a number of forms, depending on the kind of speech and its subject. Above all, the introduction must win the attention of the audience, especially if they have been required to attend, and encourage them to look forward to the rest of the speech. The authors of *Principles of Speech Communication* suggest seven basic attention-getters: (1) referring to the subject or occasion, (2) using a personal reference, (3) asking a rhetorical question, (4) making a startling statement of fact or opinion, (5) using a quotation, (6) telling a humorous anecdote, (7) using an illustration.[3]

The speeches by the ex-con and the vegetarian provide examples of two of the attention-getters cited above — using a personal reference and asking a rhetorical question. In another kind of argument, a claim of fact, the student speaker uses a combination of devices to introduce her claim that culturally deprived children are capable of learning:

> In Charles Schulz's popular cartoon depiction of happiness, one of his definitions has special significance for the American school system. The drawing shows Linus, with his eyes closed in a state of supreme bliss, a broad smile across two-thirds of his face and holding a report card upon which is a big bold "A." The caption reads: "Happiness is finding out you're not so dumb after all." For once, happiness is not defined as a function of material possessions, yet even this happiness is practically unattainable for the "unteachables" of the city slums. Are these children intellectually inferior? Are they unable to learn? Are they not worth the time and the effort to teach? Unfortunately, too many people have answered "yes" to these questions and promptly dismissed the issue.[4]

The middle or body of the speech is, of course, the longest part. It will be devoted to development of the claim that appeared at the beginning. The length of the speech and the complexity of the subject will determine how much support you provide. Some points will be more important than others and should therefore receive more extended treatment. Unless the order is chronological, it makes sense for the speaker to arrange the supporting points in emphatic order, that is, the most important at the end because this may be the one that listeners will remember.

[3] Bruce E. Gronbeck et al., *Principles of Speech Communication*, 13th Brief Ed. (New York: Longman, 1998), pp. 243–47.
[4] Carolyn Kay Geiman, "Are They Really 'Unteachables'?" in Linkugel, Allen, and Johannesen, p. 123.

The conclusion should be brief; some rhetoricians suggest that the ending should constitute 5 percent of the total length of the speech. For speeches that contain several main points with supporting data, you may need to summarize. Or you may return to one of the attention-getters mentioned earlier. One writer recommends this as "the most obvious method" of concluding speeches, "particularly appropriate when the introduction has included a quotation, an interesting anecdote, a reference to an occasion or a place, an appeal to the self-interest of the audience, or a reference to a recent incident."[5]

An example of such an ending appears in a speech given by Bruce Babbitt, Secretary of the Interior, in 1996. Speaking to an audience of scientists and theologians, the secretary defended laws that protected the environment. This is how the speech began:

> A wolf's green eyes, a sacred blue mountain, the words from Genesis, and the answers of children all reveal the religious values manifest in the 1977 Endangered Species Act.

(The children Babbitt refers to had written answers to a question posed at an "eco-expo" fair, "Why Save the Environment?")
And this is the ending of the speech:

> I conclude here tonight by affirming that those religious values remain at the heart of the Endangered Species Act, that they make themselves manifest through the green eyes of the grey wolf, through the call of the whooping crane, through the splash of the Pacific salmon, through the voices of America's children.
>
> We are living between the flood and the rainbow: between the threats to creation on the one side and God's covenant to protect life on the other.
>
> Why should we save endangered species?
>
> Let us answer this question with one voice, the voice of the child at that expo, who scrawled her answer at the very bottom of the sheet:
> "Because we can."[6]

The speaker must also ensure the smooth flow of argument throughout. Coherence, or the orderly connections between ideas, is even more important in speech than in writing because the listener cannot go back to uncover these connections. The audience listens for expressions that serve as guideposts — words, phrases, and sentences to indicate which direction the argument will take. The student speech on vegetarianism uses these words among others: *next, then, finally, here, first of all, whereas, in addition, secondly, in fact, now, in conclusion.* Other expressions can also help the listener to follow the development. Each of the following examples from real speeches makes a bridge from a previous idea

[5] James C. McCroskey, *An Introduction to Rhetorical Communication* (Englewood Cliffs, NJ: Prentice-Hall, 1968), p. 204.

[6] Calvin McLeod Logue and Jean DeHart, eds., *Representative American Speeches, 1995–1996* (New York: Wilson, 1996), p. 70ff.

to a new one: "Valid factual proof, right? No, wrong!" "Consider an illustration of this misinformation." "But there is another way." "Up to this point, I've spoken only of therapy." "And so we face this new challenge." "How do we make this clear?" "Now, why is this so important?"

Language

> It should be observed that each kind of rhetoric has its own appropriate style. That of written prose is not the same as that of spoken oratory.
> — Aristotle

In the end, your speech depends on the language. No matter how accurate your analysis of the audience, how appealing your presentation of self, how deep your grasp of the material, if the language does not clearly and emphatically convey your argument, the speech will probably fail. Fortunately, the effectiveness of language does not depend on long words or complex sentence structure; quite the contrary. Most speeches, especially those given by beginners to small audiences, are distinguished by an oral style that respects the rhythms of ordinary speech and sounds spontaneous.

The vocabulary you choose, like the other elements of spoken discourse we have discussed, is influenced by the kind of audience you confront. A student audience may be entertained or moved to identification with you and your message if you use the slang of your generation; an assembly of elderly church members at a funeral may not be so generous. Use words that both you and your listeners are familiar with, language that convinces the audience you are sharing your knowledge and opinions, neither speaking down to them nor over their heads. As one writer puts it, "You never want to use language that makes the audience appear ignorant or stupid."

Make sure, too, that the words you use will not be considered offensive by some members of your audience. Today we are all sensitive, sometimes hypersensitive, to terms that were once used freely if not wisely. One word, improperly used, can cause some listeners to reject the whole speech.

The short speeches you give will probably not be devoted to elaborating grand abstractions, but it is not only abstract terms that need definition. When you know your subject very well, you forget that others can be ignorant of it. Think whether the subject is one that the particular audience you are addressing is not likely to be familiar with. If this is the case, then explain even the basic terms. In one class a student who had chosen to discuss a subject about which he was extremely knowledgeable, betting on horse races, neglected to define clearly the words *exacta, subfecta, trifecta, parimutuel,* and others, leaving his audience fairly befuddled.

Wherever it is appropriate, use concrete language with details and examples that create images and cause the listener to feel as well as think. One student speaker used strong words to good effect in providing some unappetizing facts about hot dogs: "In fact, the hot dog is so adulterated with chemicals, so contaminated with bacteria, so puffy with gristle, fat, water, and lacking in protein, that it is nutritionally worthless."[7]

Another speech on a far more serious subject offered a personal experience with vivid details. The student speaker was a hemophiliac making a plea for blood donations.

> I remember the three long years when I couldn't even walk because repeated hemorrhages had twisted my ankles and knees to pretzel-like forms. I remember being pulled to school in a wagon while other boys rode their bikes and pushed to my table. I remember sitting in the dark empty classroom by myself during recess while the others went out in the sun to run and play. And I remember the first terrible day at the big high school when I came on crutches and built-up shoes carrying my books in a sack around my neck.[8]

As a rule, the oral style demands simpler sentences. That is because the listener must grasp the grammatical construction without the visual clues of punctuation available on the printed page. Simpler means shorter and more direct. Use subject-verb constructions without a string of phrases or clauses preceding the subject or interrupting the natural flow of the sentence. Use the active voice frequently. In addition to assuring clarity for the audience, such sentences are easier for the speaker to remember and to say. (The sentences in the paragraph above are long, but notice that the sentence elements of subject, verb, and subordinate clause are arranged in the order dictated by natural speech.)

Simpler, however, does not mean less impressive. A speech before any audience may be simply expressed without loss of emotional or intellectual power. One of the most eloquent short speeches ever delivered in this country is the surrender speech in 1877 by Chief Joseph of the Nez Percé Tribe, which clearly demonstrates the power of simple words and sentences.

> I am tired of fighting. Our chiefs are killed. Looking Glass is dead. Toohulsote is dead. The old men are all dead. It is the young men who say no and yes. He who led the young men is dead. It is cold and we have no blankets. The little children are freezing to death. My people, some of them, have run away to the hills and have no blankets, no food. No one knows where they are — perhaps they are freezing to death. I want to have time to look for my children and see how many of them I can find. Maybe I shall find them among the dead. Hear me, my chiefs. I am tired. My heart is sad and sick. From where the sun now stands I will fight no more forever.[9]

---

[7] Donovan Ochs and Anthony Winkler, *A Brief Introduction to Speech* (New York: Harcourt, Brace, Jovanovich, 1979), p. 74.

[8] Ralph Zimmerman, "Mingled Blood," in Linkugel, Allen, and Johannesen, p. 200.

[9] M. Gidley, *Kopet: A Documentary Narrative of Chief Joseph's Last Years* (Chicago: Contemporary Books, 1981), p. 31.

If you are in doubt about the kind of language in which you should express yourself, you might follow Lincoln's advice: "Speak so that the most lowly can understand you, and the rest will have no difficulty."

A popular stylistic device — repetition and balance or parallel structure — can emphasize and enrich parts of your message. Look back to the balanced sentences of the passage from the student speaker on hemophilia, sentences beginning with "I remember." Almost all inspirational speeches, including religious exhortation and political oratory, take advantage of such constructions, whose rhythms evoke an immediate emotional response. It is one of the strengths of Martin Luther King Jr.'s "I Have a Dream" speech. (See p. 492.) Keep in mind that the ideas in parallel structures must be similar and that, for maximum effectiveness, they should be used sparingly in a short speech. Not least, the subject should be weighty enough to carry this imposing construction.

Support

The support for a claim is essentially the same for both spoken and written arguments. Factual evidence, including statistics and expert opinion, as well as appeals to needs and values, is equally important in oral presentations. But time constraints will make a difference. In a speech the amount of support that you provide will be limited to the capacity of listeners to digest and remember information that they cannot review. This means that you must choose subjects that can be supported adequately in the time allotted. The speech by Secretary Babbitt, for example, on saving the environmental protection laws, developed material on animals, national lands, water, his own history, religious tradition, and the history of environmental legislation, to name only the most important. It would have been impossible to defend his proposition in a half-hour speech. Although his subject was far more limited, the author of the argument for vegetarianism could not do full justice to his claim for lack of time. Meat-eaters would find that some of their questions remain unanswered, and even those listeners friendly to the author's claim might ask for more evidence from authoritative sources.

While both speakers and writers use logical, ethical, and emotional appeals in support of their arguments, the forms of presentation can make a significant difference. The reasoning process demanded of listeners must be relatively brief and straightforward, and the supporting evidence readily assimilated. The ethical appeal or credibility of the speaker is affected not only by what is said but by the speaker's appearance, bodily movements, and vocal expressions. And the appeal to the sympathy of the audience can be greatly enhanced by the presence of the speaker. Take the excerpt from the speech of the hemophiliac. The written descriptions of pain and heartbreak are very moving, but place yourself in the audience, looking at the victim and imagining the suffering experienced by the human body standing in front of you. No doubt the effect would be deep and long-lasting, perhaps more memorable even than the written word.

Because the human instrument is so powerful, it must be used with care. You have probably listened to speakers who used gestures and voice inflections that had been dutifully rehearsed but were obviously contrived and worked, unfortunately, to undermine rather than support the speaker's message and credibility. If you are not a gifted actor, avoid gestures, body language, and vocal expressions that are not truly felt.

Some speech theorists treat support or proofs as *nonartistic* and *artistic*. The nonartistic support — factual data, expert opinion, examples — is considered objective and verifiable. Its acceptability should not depend on the character and personality of the speaker. It is plainly different from the artistic proof, which is subjective, based on the values and attitudes of the listener, and therefore more difficult for the speaker to control. This form of support is called artistic because it includes creative strategies within the power of the speaker to manipulate. In earlier parts of this chapter we have discussed the artistic proofs, ways of establishing credibility, and recognizing the values of the audience.

Presentation Aids

Charts, Graphs, Handouts

Some speeches, though not all, will be enhanced by visual and other aids: charts, graphs, maps, models, objects, handouts, recordings, and computerized images. These aids, however, no matter how visually or aurally exciting, should not overwhelm your own oral presentation. The objects are not the stars of the show. They exist to make your spoken argument more persuasive.

Charts and graphs, large enough and clear enough to be seen and understood, can illuminate speeches that contain numbers of any kind, especially statistical comparisons. You can make a simple chart yourself, on paper for use with an easel or on a computer to be projected or to be printed for presentation to an audience. Enlarged illustrations or a model of a complicated machine — say, the space shuttle — would help a speaker to explain its function. You already know that photographs or videos are powerful instruments of persuasion, above all in support of appeals for humanitarian aid, for both people and animals.

Court cases have been won or lost on the basis of diagrams or charts that purport to prove the innocence or guilt of a defendant. Such aids do not always speak for themselves. No matter how clear they are to the designer, they may be misinterpreted or misunderstood by a viewer. Some critics have argued that the jury in the O. J. Simpson case failed to understand the graphs of DNA relationships that experts for the prosecution displayed during the trial. Before you show

Presentation aids such as visuals can enhance your speech.

any diagrams or charts of any complexity to your audience, ask friends if they find them easy to understand.

The use of a handout also requires planning. It's probably unwise to put your speech on hold while the audience reads or studies a handout that requires time and concentration. Confine the subject matter of handouts to material that can be easily grasped as you discuss or explain it.

Audio

Audio aids may also enliven a speech or even be indispensable to its success. One student played a recording of a scene from *Romeo and Juliet*, spoken by a cast of professional actors, to make a point about the relationship between the two lovers. Another student chose to define several types of popular music, including rap, goth, heavy metal, and techno. But he used only words, and the lack of any musical demonstration meant that the distinctions remained unclear.

Video

With sight, sound, and movement, a video can illustrate or reinforce the main points of a speech. A speech warning people not to drink and drive will have a much greater effect if enhanced by a video showing the tragic and often gruesome outcome of car accidents caused by drunk driving. Schools that teach driver's education frequently rely on these bone-chilling videos to show their students that getting behind the wheel is a serious responsibility, not a game. If you want to use video, check to make sure that a computer, Blu-ray, or DVD player and television are available to you. Most schools have an audio-visual department that manages the delivery, setup, and return of all equipment.

Multimedia

Multimedia presentation software programs enable you to combine several different media such as text, charts, sound, and still or moving pictures into one unit. In the business world, multimedia presentations are commonly used in situations where you have a limited amount of time to persuade or teach a fairly large audience. For instance, the promotion director of a leading teen magazine is trying to persuade skeptical executives that a magazine Web site would increase sales and advertising revenue. Since the magazine is sold through newsstand and subscription, some executives question whether the cost of creating and maintaining a Web site outweighs the benefits. Using multimedia presentation software, the promotion director can integrate demographic charts and graphs showing that steadily increasing numbers of teenagers surf the Web, a segment from a television news program reporting that many teens shop online (an attraction for advertisers), and downloaded pages from a competitor's Web site to demonstrate that others are already reaping the benefits of the Internet. People today are increasingly "visual" in their learning styles, and multimedia software may be the most effective aid for an important presentation.

Though effective when done well, technically complicated presentations require large amounts of time and careful planning. First you must ensure that your computer is powerful enough to adeptly handle presentation software. Then you need to familiarize yourself with the program. Most presentation software programs come equipped with helpful tutorials. If the task of creating your own presentation from scratch seems overwhelming, you can use one of the many preformatted presentation templates: You will simply need to customize the content. Robert Stephens, the founder of the Geek Squad, a Minneapolis-based business that provides on-site emergency response to computer problems, gives the following tips for multimedia presentations:

1. In case of equipment failure, always bring two of everything.
2. Back up your presentation on CD-ROM or a Zip drive.
3. Avoid live visits to the Internet. Because connections can fail or be painfully slow, and sites can move or disappear, if you must visit the Internet in

your presentation, download the appropriate pages onto your hard drive ahead of time. It will still look like a live visit.

4. In the end, technology cannot replace creativity. Make sure that you are using multimedia to reinforce not replace your main points.[10]

Make sure that any necessary apparatus will be available at the right time. If you have never used the devices you need for your presentation, practice using them before the speech. Few things are more disconcerting for the speechmaker and the audience than a speaker who is fumbling with his materials, unable to find the right picture or to make a machine work.

Sample Persuasive Speech

The following speech was delivered by C. Renzi Stone to his public speaking class at the University of Oklahoma. Told to prepare a persuasive speech, Stone chose to speak about the health benefits of vegetarianism. Note his attention-grabbing introduction.

---

[10] Robert Stephens as paraphrased in "When Your Presentation Crashes . . . Who You Gonna Call?" by Eric Matson, *Fast Company*, February/March 1997, p. 130.

Live Longer and Healthier: Stop Eating Meat!

C. RENZI STONE

What do Steve Martin, Dustin Hoffman, Albert Einstein, Jerry Garcia, Michael Stipe, Eddie Vedder, Martina Navratilova, Carl Lewis, and twelve million other Americans all have in common? All of these well-known people were or are vegetarians. What do they know that we don't? Consuming a regimen of high-fat, high-protein flesh foods is a sure-fire prescription for disaster, like running diesel fuel through your car's gasoline engine. In the book *Why Do Vegetarians Eat Like That?* David Gabbe asserts that millions of people today are afflicted with chronic diseases that can be directly linked to the consumption of meat. Eating a vegetarian diet can help prevent many of those diseases.

In 1996, twelve million Americans identified themselves as vegetarians. That number is twice as many as in the decade before. According to a recent National Restaurant Association poll found in *Health* magazine, one in five diners say they now go out of their way to choose restaurants that serve at least a few meatless entrees. Obviously, the traditionally American trait of a meat-dominated society has subsided in recent years.

In discussing vegetarianism today, first I will tell how vegetarians are perceived in society. Next, I will introduce several studies validating my claim that a meatless diet is extraordinarily healthy. I will then show how a veggie diet can strengthen the immune system and make the meatless body a shield from unwanted diseases such as cancer and heart disease. Maintaining a strict vegetarian diet can also lead to a longer life. Finally, I will put an image into the audience's mind of a meatless society that relies on vegetables for the main course at breakfast, lunch, and dinner.

Moving to my first point, society generally holds two major misperceptions about vegetarians. First of all, society often perceives vegetarians as a radical group of people with extreme principles. In this view, vegetarians are seen as a monolithic group of people who choose to eat vegetables because they are opposed to the killing of animals for food. The second major misconception is that because vegetarians do not eat meat, they do not get the proper amounts of essential vitamins and minerals often found in meat.

Here is my response to these misconceived notions. First of all, vegetarians are not a homogeneous group of radicals. Whereas many vegetarians in the past did join the movement on the principle that killing animals is wrong, many join the movement today mainly for its health benefits. In addition, there are many different levels of vegetarianism. Some vegetarians eat nothing but vegetables. Others don't eat red meat but do occasionally eat chicken and fish.

Secondly, contrary to popular opinion, vegetarians get more than enough vitamins and minerals in their diet and generally receive healthier nourishment than meat eaters. In fact, in an article for *Health* magazine, Peter Jaret states that vegetarians actually get larger amounts of amino acids due to the elimination of saturated fats which are often found in meat products. Studies show that the health benefits of a veggie lifestyle contribute to increased life expectancy and overall productivity.

Hopefully you now see that society's perceptions of vegetarians are outdated and just plain wrong. You are familiar with many of the problems associated with a meat-based diet, and you have heard many of the benefits of a vegetarian diet. Now try to imagine how you personally can improve your life by becoming a vegetarian.

Can you imagine a world where people retire at age eighty and lead productive lives into their early 100s? Close your eyes and think about celebrating your seventieth wedding anniversary, seeing your great-grandchildren get married, and witnessing one hundred years of world events and technological innovations. David Gabbe's book refers to studies that have shown a vegetarian diet can increase your life expectancy up to fifteen years. A longer life is within your reach, and the diet you eat has a direct impact on your health and how you age.

In conclusion, vegetarianism is a healthy life choice, not a radical cult. By eliminating meat from their diet, vegetarians reap the benefits of a vegetable-based diet that helps prevent disease and increase life expectancy. People, take heed of my advice. There are many more sources of information available for those who want to take a few hours to research the benefits of the veggie lifestyle. If you don't believe my comments, discover the whole truth for yourself.

Twelve million Americans know the health benefits that come with being a   10
vegetarian. Changing your eating habits can be just as easy as making your bed in
the morning. Sure, it takes a few extra minutes and some thought, but your body
will thank you in the long run.

You only live once. Why not make it a long stay?

READING FOR ANALYSIS

I Have a Dream

MARTIN LUTHER KING JR.

F ive score years ago, a great American, in whose symbolic shadow we stand, signed
the Emancipation Proclamation. This momentous decree came as a great beacon
light of hope to millions of Negro slaves who had been seared in the flames of wither-
ing injustice. It came as a joyous daybreak to end the long night of captivity.

But one hundred years later, we must face the tragic fact that the Negro is still
not free. One hundred years later, the life of the Negro is still sadly crippled by
the manacles of segregation and the chains of discrimination. One hundred years
later, the Negro lives on a lonely island of poverty in the midst of a vast ocean of
material prosperity. One hundred years later, the Negro is still languishing in the
corners of American society and finds himself an exile in his own land. So we have
come here today to dramatize an appalling condition.

In a sense we have come to our nation's capital to cash a check. When the
architects of our republic wrote the magnificent words of the Constitution and the
Declaration of Independence, they were signing a promissory note to which every
American was to fall heir. This note was a promise that all men would be guaranteed the unalienable rights of life, liberty, and the pursuit of happiness.

It is obvious today that America has defaulted on this promissory note insofar
as her citizens of color are concerned. Instead of honoring this sacred obligation,
America has given the Negro people a bad check; a check which has come back
marked "insufficient funds." But we refuse to believe that the bank of justice is
bankrupt. We refuse to believe that there are insufficient funds in the great vaults
of opportunity of this nation. So we have come to cash this check — a check that
will give us upon demand the riches of freedom and the security of justice. We
have also come to this hallowed spot to remind America of the fierce urgency of
now. This is no time to engage in the luxury of cooling off or to take the tranquil-

---

In the widely reprinted "I Have a Dream" speech, Martin Luther King Jr. appears as the charis-
matic leader of the civil rights movement. This inspirational address was delivered on August
28, 1963, in Washington, D.C., at a demonstration by two hundred thousand people for civil
rights for African Americans. From *A Testament of Hope* (1986).

izing drugs of gradualism. *Now* is the time to make real the promises of Democracy. *Now* is the time to rise from the dark and desolate valley of segregation to the sunlit path of racial justice. *Now* is the time to open the doors of opportunity to all of God's children. *Now* is the time to lift our nation from the quicksands of racial injustice to the solid rock of brotherhood.

It would be fatal for the nation to overlook the urgency of the moment and to underestimate the determination of the Negro. This sweltering summer of the Negro's legitimate discontent will not pass until there is an invigorating autumn of freedom and equality. Nineteen sixty-three is not an end, but a beginning. Those who hope that the Negro needed to blow off steam and will now be content will have a rude awakening if the nation returns to business as usual. There will be neither rest nor tranquillity in America until the Negro is granted his citizenship rights. The whirlwinds of revolt will continue to shake the foundations of our nation until the bright day of justice emerges.

But there is something that I must say to my people who stand on the warm threshold which leads into the palace of justice. In the process of gaining our rightful place we must not be guilty of wrongful deeds. Let us not seek to satisfy our thirst for freedom by drinking from the cup of bitterness and hatred. We must forever conduct our struggle on the high plane of dignity and discipline. We must not allow our creative protest to degenerate into physical violence. Again and again we must rise to the majestic heights of meeting physical force with soul force. The marvelous new militancy which has engulfed the Negro community must not lead us to a distrust of all white people, for many of our white brothers, as evidenced by their presence here today, have come to realize that their destiny is tied up with our destiny and their freedom is inextricably bound to our freedom. We cannot walk alone.

And as we walk, we must make the pledge that we shall march ahead. We cannot turn back. There are those who are asking the devotees of civil rights, "When will you be satisfied?" We can never be satisfied as long as the Negro is the victim of the unspeakable horrors of police brutality. We can never be satisfied as long as our bodies, heavy with the fatigue of travel, cannot gain lodging in the motels of the highways and the hotels of the cities. We cannot be satisfied as long as the Negro's basic mobility is from a smaller ghetto to a larger one. We can never be satisfied as long as a Negro in Mississippi cannot vote and a Negro in New York believes he has nothing for which to vote. No, no, we are not satisfied, and we will not be satisfied until justice rolls down like waters and righteousness like a mighty stream.

I am not unmindful that some of you have come here out of great trials and tribulations. Some of you have come fresh from narrow jail cells. Some of you have come from areas where your quest for freedom left you battered by the storms of persecution and staggered by the winds of police brutality. You have been the veterans of creative suffering. Continue to work with the faith that unearned suffering is redemptive.

Go back to Mississippi, go back to Alabama, go back to South Carolina, go back to Georgia, go back to Louisiana, go back to the slums and ghettos of our northern cities, knowing that somehow this situation can and will be changed. Let us not wallow in the valley of despair.

I say to you today, my friends, that in spite of the difficulties and frustrations 10 of the moment I still have a dream. It is a dream deeply rooted in the American dream.

I have a dream that one day this nation will rise up and live out the true meaning of its creed: "We hold these truths to be self-evident; that all men are created equal."

I have a dream that one day on the red hills of Georgia the sons of former slaves and the sons of former slaveowners will be able to sit down together at the table of brotherhood.

I have a dream that one day even the state of Mississippi, a desert state sweltering with the heat of injustice and oppression, will be transformed into an oasis of freedom and justice.

I have a dream that my four little children will one day live in a nation where they will not be judged by the color of their skin but by the content of their character.

I have a dream today. 15

I have a dream that one day the state of Alabama, whose governor's lips are presently dripping with the words of interposition and nullification, will be transformed into a situation where little black boys and black girls will be able to join hands with little white boys and white girls and walk together as sisters and brothers.

I have a dream today.

I have a dream that one day every valley shall be exalted, every hill and mountain shall be made low, the rough places will be made plain, and the crooked places will be made straight, and the glory of the Lord shall be revealed, and all flesh shall see it together.

This is our hope. This is the faith with which I return to the South. With this faith we will be able to hew out of the mountain of despair a stone of hope. With this faith we will be able to transform the jangling discords of our nation into a beautiful symphony of brotherhood. With this faith we will be able to work together, to pray together, to struggle together, to go to jail together, to stand up for freedom together, knowing that we will be free one day.

This will be the day when all of God's children will be able to sing with new 20 meaning

My country, 'tis of thee,
Sweet land of liberty,
   Of thee I sing:
Land where my fathers died,
Land of the pilgrims' pride,
From every mountain-side
   Let freedom ring.

And if America is to be a great nation this must become true. So let freedom ring from the prodigious hilltops of New Hampshire. Let freedom ring from the mighty mountains of New York. Let freedom ring from the heightening Alleghenies of Pennsylvania!

Let freedom ring from the snowcapped Rockies of Colorado!

Let freedom ring from the curvaceous peaks of California!

But not only that; let freedom ring from Stone Mountain of Georgia!

Let freedom ring from Lookout Mountain of Tennessee!   25

Let freedom ring from every hill and molehill of Mississippi. From every mountainside, let freedom ring.

When we let freedom ring, when we let it ring from every village and every hamlet, from every state and every city, we will be able to speed up that day when all of God's children, black men and white men, Jews and Gentiles, Protestants and Catholics, will be able to join hands and sing in the words of the old Negro spiritual, "Free at last! free at last! thank God almighty, we are free at last!"

READING AND DISCUSSION QUESTIONS

1. What were the circumstances in which King delivered this speech? Of whom did the audience consist? How might the circumstances and the audience have affected decisions King made in composing the speech? Where in the speech does he most directly refer to his audience?

2. What sort of reputation had King established by the time he gave this speech in 1963? Are there ways in which he establishes his credibility through the speech itself? Explain.

3. How would you describe the organization of the speech?

4. Explain the metaphor of the check. Where else does King make use of metaphorical language?

5. How else does King's use of language lend power to his speech?

6. What allusions do you find in the speech?

WRITING SUGGESTIONS

7. Write an essay analyzing King's speech according to the elements of oral argument discussed in this chapter.

8. Write an essay analyzing King's language as a major source of the effectiveness of this historic speech.

Multiple Viewpoints

The following section contains a variety of viewpoints on eight controversial questions. These questions generate conflict among experts and laypeople alike for two principal reasons. First, even when the facts are not in dispute, they may be interpreted differently by opposing sides. Second, and certainly more difficult to resolve, equally worthwhile values may be in conflict.

Multiple Viewpoints lends itself to classroom debates, both formal and informal. It can also serve as a useful source of informed opinions, which can lead to further research. First, read all the articles in one chapter of a Multiple Viewpoints section. You may wish to begin further research by choosing material to support your claim from two or three articles in the text or by exploring sources on the Web.

Ask the following questions about each controversy:

1. Are there two — or more — different points of view on the subject? Do all sides make clear what they are trying to prove? Summarize their claims.

2. Do all sides share the same goals? If not, how are they different?

3. How important is definition of key terms? Do all sides agree on the definitions? If so, what are they? If not, how do they differ? Does definition become a significant issue in the controversy?

4. How important is evidence in support of the claims? Does the support fulfill the appropriate criteria? If not, what are its weaknesses? Do the authorities have convincing credentials?

5. Do the arguers base any part of their arguments on needs and values that their readers are expected to share? What are they? Do the arguers provide examples of the ways these values function? Is there a conflict of values? If so, which seem more important?

6. What warrants or assumptions underlie the claims? Are they implicit or explicit? Do the arguers examine them for the reader? Are the warrants acceptable? If not, point out their weaknesses.

7. What are the main issues? Is there a genuine debate — that is, does each side try to respond to arguments on the other side?

8. Do the arguers propose solutions to a problem? Are the advantages of their proposals clear? Are there obvious disadvantages?

9. Does each argument follow a clear and orderly organization, one that lends itself to a good outline? If not, what are the weaknesses?

10. Does language play a part in the argument? Are there any examples of misuse of language — slanted or loaded words, clichés, slogans?

11. Do the arguers show an awareness of audience? How would you describe the audience(s) for whom the various arguments are presented?

12. Do you think that one side won the argument? Can you find examples of negotiation and compromise, of attempts to establish a common ground? Explain your answer in detail.

CHAPTER 13

How Are Social Networking Sites Affecting Human Interactions?

It won't be long now until we have our first generation of young adults who can't remember a world without Facebook, just as many young adults today don't remember a time when there wasn't at least one computer in their home. Are Facebook and other similar social networking sites changing their users' lives in significant ways? Are they changing their users' brains in significant ways? If so, are the changes for the better or the worse?

Research suggests that those who turn to social networking sites out of loneliness will remain lonely and that those with offline friendships will find those friendships strengthened by adding an online component to the mix. Some will use the Internet to create whole new selves, but more will simply come to know their old selves better. As one author suggests, "life" online includes friends who exist on the periphery of one's vision but who contribute to the rhythm of one's days. Some will put the most revealing of images out there for the world to see, but will cringe from admitting their mothers as "friends" because that means Mom will see all that they have already been revealing to the rest of the world.

The "self" that a teenager posts after a drinking spree may have repercussions beyond what his mother will think. It may come back to haunt him when he applies for graduate or professional school or for his first job. The world "out there" includes admissions counselors and potential employers as well as the girl that he wanted to impress back in the summer of 2009.

The world for many college students changed in 2004 when Facebook went online. It changed again two years later when Facebook was reinvented to provide a rolling news feed that kept a user up to date on all of the friends to whom she was linked. Scientists weren't far behind in investigating the effects of the resulting hours spent online. In 2006 Baroness Susan Greenfield, a neuroscientist, took part in a debate in the British House of Lords to say that social networking sites were "infantilizing" the brains of children. As the following essays suggest, the debate continues as to whether using social networking sites is rewiring the human brain and if so, whether that is such a bad thing.

Are Social Networks Messing with Your Head?

DAVID DISALVO

BEFORE READING: What sort of observations could you make about the type of people who use social networking sites? Have you noticed any changes in the type(s) of people who do?

Steve is the kind of guy who likes to let everyone know what he is doing in gen-erous detail. His Facebook page is littered with entries such as "Just finished my java mochaccino and about to walk Schnooker" and "Lost recipe for my scrump-tious caramel fudge cake . . . super bummed . . . sigh." He is certain that his online friends want to know exactly what is going on in his life, and what better way to oblige them than with hourly, if not half-hourly, updates?

It is easy to dismiss what Steve and millions of social-network users do every day as the flower of banality, but in truth they are engaged in the largest worldwide experiment in social interaction ever conducted. The Internet has always provided a loose forum for the like-minded to congregate, but social networking contributes considerable structure to the chaos, allowing people to communicate more consis-tently and vigorously than ever before.

In a seminal paper published in 2007, social media researchers Danah Boyd of Microsoft Research New England in Cambridge, Massachusetts, and Nicole B. Ellison of Michigan State University offer a useful three-part definition of social-networking sites: they must provide a forum where users can construct a public or semipublic profile; create a list of other users with whom they share a connection; and view and move around their list of connections and those made by others. Sites that meet these specs include MySpace, LinkedIn, Bebo, Qzone (a massive Chinese site targeted to teens), and the global juggernaut Facebook. Others aimed at an even younger audience also fit, such as Disney's Club Penguin, where kids interact as animated characters in a vibrant online world.

Since its launch at Harvard University in 2004, Facebook has grown in mem-bership to more than 250 million people in 170 countries and territories on every continent — including Antarctica. If Facebook itself were a country, it would be the fourth most populous in the world, just behind the United States. Almost half its users

---

David DiSalvo is a freelance writer whose subjects include science, technology, and culture. He maintains the blog Neuronarrative.com and has had his work published in *Scientific American Mind*, where this piece appeared in January/February 2010.

visit the site every day. Other social-networking sites are also booming. LinkedIn, a site geared for professional networkers, has more than forty million users and adds one member every second. MySpace, the largest social network until Facebook overtook it last year, has 125 million users, and seven million Twitter users broadcast more than eighteen million snippets a day to anyone who will listen. Although adolescents and college students constitute about 40 percent of social-networking users, according to iStrategyLabs in Washington, D.C., the fastest-growing segments on Facebook are Gen Xers nearing age 40 and baby boomers pushing sixty.

Nielsen Online reports that social networking (and associated blogging) is now   5
the fourth most popular online activity, ahead of personal e-mail and behind only search engines, general-interest portals such as MSM, Yahoo, and AOL, and software downloads. Time spent using social-networking sites is growing at three times the rate of overall Internet usage, accounting for almost 10 percent of total time spent online.

As social networks proliferate, they are changing the way people think about the Internet, from a tool used in solitary anonymity to a medium that touches on questions about human nature and identity: who we are, how we feel about ourselves, and how we act toward one another. To better understand this phenomenon, we will investigate the newest thinking about loneliness, self-esteem, narcissism, and addiction and the ways in which social networking might affect the expression of these traits. Old theories about online socializing are falling away, and fresh questions about the psychosocial relevance of social networking are constantly bubbling up.

All the Lonely People

We generally think of loneliness as physical isolation from other people. But that simple definition doesn't begin to capture the condition's pernicious nature: the deep distress people feel when they believe that their social relationships have less meaning than they should. This state can describe those of us wading through a sea of contacts on social-networking sites. Logic would have it that abundant social contacts would be a cure for the blues: the greater the number of contacts, the greater the chance of finding rewarding relationships. The truth of the matter is less straightforward.

Not so long ago the Net was presumed to be an unrelieved social backwater. "Nearly all the initial studies about people who used the Internet for social interaction suggested that they were getting lonelier," says University of Chicago social neuroscientist John Cacioppo, co-author of *Loneliness: Human Nature and the Need for Social Connection*. Those studies were predicated on the notion that people used the Internet to replace face-to-face interactions and that relationships formed online would stay online. "For disabled users who couldn't get around, that [practice] worked well," Cacioppo says, "but for others, it didn't." A person could not even know for sure who was really on the other end of the line. Psychology research focused on this scene with critical eyes, often dismissing online socializing as lonely escapism from the disquiet of real relationships.

Per capita use of Facebook is up 175 percent in the past year, with many users logging on to the site and those of its rivals via mobile devices.

This dire view of social networking began to change as research grew more nuanced. In a 2008 study at California State University, Los Angeles, psychologists Kaveri Subrahmanyam and Gloria Lin interviewed 192 high school students about how they used the Internet for communication, how much time they spent online and which sites they typically frequented. The study participants then completed psychological tests for assessing loneliness and social support. Neither total amount of time spent online nor time spent communicating online correlated with increased loneliness.

These results echoed those of a 2006 study at the University of Sydney by psychologist Andrew Campbell and his colleagues, who found that the amount of time spent interacting online is unrelated to higher levels of anxiety or depression — typical cohorts of loneliness. Besides appearing to be no more socially fearful than other people, heavy online users also thought their time online was psychologically beneficial to them, despite reporting that they believed Internet users overall were lonelier than average.   10

A connection between loneliness and social networking only emerges when the variables are flipped, and researchers study loneliness as a precursor to membership in social networks. To understand why, consider some of the recent insights into the workings of the lonely brain. A 2009 brain-imaging study by Cacioppo and his colleagues showed that the neural mechanisms of lonely and nonlonely people differ according to how they perceive social isolation, the key ingredient of loneliness. While hooked up to a functional MRI machine, the subjects viewed a series of images, some with positive connotations, such as pictures of happy people and

The challenge of pervasive social networking is that it will supplant the richness of real-world relationships with an endless stream of trivial interactions.

money, and others with negative associations, such as scenes of human conflict. As the two groups watched pleasant imagery, the area of the brain that recognizes rewards showed a greater response in nonlonely people than in lonely people. Similarly, the visual cortex of lonely test subjects responded more strongly to unpleasant images of people than to unpleasant images of objects, suggesting the attention of lonely people is especially drawn to human distress. The nonlonely showed no such difference.

These variations in brain activity hint at why a predisposition to loneliness is such a liability for social networkers. "When you're lonely, your brain is in a heightened state of alertness for social threats, even if you're not explicitly looking for them," Cacioppo explains. Insults, snubs, alienation and gossip all elicit much higher levels of stress in the lonely, measurable in part by elevated production of the stress hormone cortisol. The effect is amplified online because social threats are more difficult to anticipate there. A long silence between replies during an online chat can spawn fears that others are locking you out of the conversation and gossiping behind your back. Another source of insecurity is the very currency of social networks: the number of contacts one has. Having a mere handful of contacts when others could fill a stadium with their roster can leave lonely individuals feeling that their desires are moving ever farther out of reach.

It is not surprising, then, that the social networkers who fare the best are the ones who use the technology to support their existing friendships. In a 2007 study of older adults, gerontology doctoral student Shima Sum of the University of Sydney

Social networks may spawn insecurity and anxiety in lonely people, because social threats are hard to read online. But the networks can lessen loneliness if a person's online contacts are also friends in real life.

and her colleagues found that using social networks diminishes loneliness when online social contacts are also offline contacts. When older adults try to use social networks to meet new people, however, they consistently feel lonelier than they did before.

Indeed, face-to-face interaction appears to be the pivotal variable in social-networking effects. In a 2009 study of loneliness and Facebook membership, psychologist Laura Freberg of California Polytechnic State University and her team found that college students who are socially connected in their face-to-face lives bring that persona online and really do derive benefits. The lonely students who used the technology became lonelier.

For try as they might to put on a new set of psychic clothing, lonely people   15 bring their true personalities online, too. A lonely and socially inept person might, for a while, assume the persona of an outgoing and gregarious conversationalist but will have a hard time sustaining the charade. "Loneliness is the deficit between what you want and what you have," Freberg says, "and chronic loneliness makes people act in ways that push others away. Social networking isn't equipped to handle that and can actually make it worse." Social networks might not make people anxious and fearful, but if they feel that way to begin with, others will know soon enough.

Looking in the Mirror

Social networks should, in theory, be a boon for people who need a boost to their self-esteem. They are ready-made venues for testing social skills without the looming embarrassment of failing in the flesh. In a 2008 study of Facebook users, social media researcher Cliff Lampe of Michigan State teased out how advantages can accrue for some online networkers. Lampe's team surveyed 477 Facebook members at the beginning and end of a one-year study period to weigh changes in various measures of psychological well-being. Facebook use correlated strongly with an increase in social capital — tangible social benefits derived from participating in a social network — especially for those with low self-esteem. Social capital boosts self-esteem like high-octane gas boosts a car's performance, conferring better social skills, greater feelings of contentment and increased confidence.

Positive effects were most profound for teens, who seem set to profit over the long term. "Adolescents find ways to make use of these benefits in other parts of their lives," Lampe says, most notably through a greater sense of self-confidence when interacting in person, "so there's a multiplier effect." Communications researcher Patti M. Valkenburg of the University of Amsterdam School of Communications Research in the Netherlands came to the same conclusion in a 2009 study on the social consequences of Internet use for adolescents. Membership in a social-networking site, she found, builds self-esteem by enhancing the development of friendships and the quality of existing relationships.

Adolescents do well on social networks because the context of the Internet helps to stimulate disclosure and self-presentation. Unlike face-to-face communication, social networking allows only limited visual and auditory cues. "Adolescents are less hindered by emotions and physical bothers," Valkenburg says. But not all teens will benefit. Just as for lonely social networkers, adolescents gain when they use the Internet primarily to maintain their existing network. And although using social networks tends to boost self-esteem overall, a predisposition to low self-esteem will intensify the blow from failure whether in person or online.

Perhaps because they are simple to join and make communication so easy, social networks have become havens not only for people with a poor self-image but also for those who seem overly pleased with themselves. Indeed, a recurring criticism of social-networking sites is that they are forums for narcissists demanding the world's attention. Narcissists revel in collecting social contacts — the more the better, no matter how superficial the underlying relationships. And they hijack message boards to ensure that they are the star attraction.

But the same forum that feeds narcissists can also be their undoing. Social psy- 20 chology doctoral student Laura Buffardi of the University of Georgia conducted an experiment to find out what defines online narcissists and how easily others can pick them out. Buffardi and social psychologist W. Keith Campbell ran 130 Facebook users through the Narcissists Personality Inventory (NPI), a research tool that measures narcissism through a questionnaire with a series of choices. Test takers select which of two statements better describes themselves — for example, "I am more capable than other people" versus "there is a lot I can learn from other people." People who score high on the NPI are more likely to cheat and game-play in relationships, monopolize resources, and be excessively materialistic.

What emerged is that online narcissists behave much like offline ones, amassing numerous but shallow relationships and engaging in ceaseless self-promotion. People can generally spot them, too. When untrained strangers viewed a sample of Facebook pages, they were just as good at identifying the narcissists as previous research has found people to be at judging the personality of their friends. The observers pointed to three characteristics that they felt betrayed the narcissists: a large number of contacts, a glamorous appearance, and a staged quality to the main photo.

Narcissists on social-networking sites may not be able to hide from their critics, but a more interesting question might be when their narcissism began: Do they arrive as fully formed egotists drawn to a stage they cannot resist, or are the sites themselves playing a role in creating narcissists? Here the research is inconclusive but intriguing. Some studies suggest that aggregate NPI scores in the U.S. have changed little since 1982; others have found significant upticks in narcissism among some groups of young adults starting in 2002 — which happens to coincide with the birth of social networks. But whether the sites are a breeding ground for narcissists or just a watering hole, it is hard not to think of the spectacular rise of social networking as part and parcel of the culture of entitlement.

Overdoing It

These days people toss around the term "addiction" as casually as they would a Frisbee. But whatever you call an unhealthy attachment, people are spending ever more time on social networks, and some are getting into trouble over it. For context, Nielson Online reports that the seventy million Facebook members in the U.S. spent 233 million hours on the site in April 2009, up from twenty-eight million hours by twenty-three million members the previous April — a 175 percent increase in per capita usage. And according to a study by Nucleus Research in Boston, the most avid users are spending two hours a day on the site while they are at work — helping to cost companies whose employees can access Facebook 1.5 percent of total office productivity.

It is no mystery why social networks have such a pull. Like television, video games and other forms of electronic media, social networks are superb at delivering instant gratification. Judith Donath, director of the Sociable Media Group at the Massachusetts Institute of Technology's Media Lab, says: "Social networking provides a series of mini mental rewards that don't require much effort to receive." These rewards serve as jolts of energy that recharge the compulsion engine, much like the frisson a gambler receives as a new card hits the table. Cumulatively, the effect is potent and hard to resist.

Facebook use can boost self-esteem in adolescents, stimulating disclosure and self-presentation, and giving them a greater sense of self-confidence when interacting in person.

Most people will not imperil their psyches if they spend a little more time on 25 social-networking sites. For them, two hours a day on Facebook may simply mean two hours less in front of the TV. But for people who bring a compulsive personality to the keyboard, those hours can grow rapidly, setting off a cascade of bad consequences at home and work. "Someone with obsessive-compulsive tendencies is predisposed to a range of addictive behaviors," says neuroscientist Gary Small of the University of California, Los Angeles, and author of *iBrain: Surviving the Technological Alteration of the Human Mind.* "Technology has a way of accelerating the compulsive process." In the U.S., the group at risk is pretty big: one in fifty adults has some degree of obsessive-compulsive disorder.

A consistent factor across many of the studies in this realm is that social networking is simply a new forum for bad habits. Social media researcher Scott Caplan of the University of Delaware says, "People who prefer online interaction over face-to-face interaction also score higher on measures of compulsive Internet use and using the Internet to alter their moods." In 2007 Caplan conducted a study of 343 undergraduate students to determine what stoked the fires of compulsive behavior online. He homed in on personality traits that leave people vulnerable, such as loneliness and social anxiety, and online activities that attract people with compulsive tendencies, such as playing video games, watching pornography, and gambling.

Of these variables, social anxiety emerged as the strongest. "Socially anxious individuals who have problems with face-to-face interactions are drawn to the

The Internet is a magnet for people with obsessive-compulsive tendencies. Social networks can deliver the same kind of instant gratification that television and video games do.

unique features of online conversation," Caplan says. In time, they may start using social networking compulsively to regulate their mood, and the self-feeding cycle begins.

Social Networking Tomorrow

Pervasive as it already seems to be, social networking is poised to invade even more areas of our lives. "We're moving into a time when the distinction between being online and offline is going to disappear," Lampe says.

The challenge will be to keep a constant deluge of social connectedness from diluting our real-world relationships by drawing us into trivial interactions. Social networking is what psychologists call a thin-strand technology, lacking many of the essential elements of communication, such as body language and touch. "The power of face-to-face interaction is fundamental to what we are," Cacioppo says.

"We need the richness of it in our lives, and this richness affects our brains." Eventually, he believes, the interaction strands of social networking will grow richer. Cacioppo envisions a time when instead of communicating online in two-dimensional space, we will interact as holograms and preserve more of what makes face-to-face interaction vital.

A dynamic application we are likely to see sooner is cognitive filtering. "The social-network infrastructure is going to be baked into all sorts of different tools, most notably media-sharing services," Boyd says. Cognitive filtering will let users focus on information already vetted by their networks, saving time and aggravation. As you are flipping through movie listings on your smart phone, say, you might first see starred recommendations from your social network and then the other films whose ratings made your cutoff score. The danger is that the technology could limit the perspective of its users and breed insular thinking, turning us into a society of myopic cliques. 30

And that, in microcosm, is why social networking is such an important phenomenon. Beyond dessert recipes, funny pet stories, and tales of what the baby did for the first time this morning, a transformational current is surging. What once seemed a faddish online application is on its way to global ubiquity. Before long, social networking may be part of every communication tool we use — changing how we interact with one another and, in the process, changing us.

Children: Social Networking Sites, A Debate in the House of Lords

SUSAN GREENFIELD

BEFORE READING: How would you answer one of the questions that Baroness Greenfield poses in the following speech: What precisely is the appeal of social networking sites?

The social networking site Facebook turned five years old last week. Arguably, it marks a milestone in a progressive and highly significant change in our culture as tens to hundreds of millions of individuals worldwide, including the very young, are signing up for friendship through a screen. Other noble Lords may follow the noble Lord, Lord Harris, and speak on specific regulatory measures that may be taken to ensure that children come to no physical harm. We hope that personal safety and privacy is soon to be improved in the light of the recommendations made in the report on personal internet security from the Science and Technology Committee and in the *Byron Review Action Plan*. However, as a neuroscientist, I think that there are still two more basic and, if you like, brain-based questions that ultimately need to be addressed. First, why are social networking sites growing? Secondly, what features of the young mind, if any, are being threatened by them? Only when we have insights into these two issues can we devise more general safeguards, rooted not so much in regulation as in education, culture, and society.

I turn to the first question, surely the most telling of all. What precisely is the appeal of social networking sites? First, there is the simple issue of the constraints of modern life, where unsupervised playing outside or going for walks is now perceived as too dangerous. A child confined to the home every evening may find at the keyboard the kind of freedom of interaction and communication that earlier generations took for granted in the three-dimensional world of the street. But even given a choice, screen life can still be more appealing. As Phillip Hodson, fellow of the British Association for Counselling and Psychotherapy, suggests: "Building a Facebook profile is one way that individuals can identify themselves, making them feel important and accepted."

Continuing that train of thought, I recently had a fascinating conversation with a young devotee who proudly claimed to have nine hundred friends. Clearly, there would be no problem here to satisfying that basic human need to belong, to be part

---

Baroness Greenfield is professor of synaptic pharmacology at Lincoln College, Oxford. Her research is focused on the physiology of the brain, particularly as related to Parkinson's disease and Alzheimer's disease, and her books explain the science of the brain and cognition to a lay audience. She is former director of the Royal Institution of Great Britain and was appointed to the British House of Lords by Prime Minister Tony Blair. The debate from which this speech is drawn took place before the House of Lords on February 12, 2009.

of a group, as well as the ability to experience instant feedback and recognition — at least from someone, somewhere, twenty-four hours a day.

At the same time this constant reassurance — that you are listened to, recognized, and important — is coupled with a distancing from the stress of face-to-face, real-life conversation. Real-life conversations are, after all, far more perilous than those in the cyber world. They occur in real time, with no opportunity to think up clever or witty responses, and they require a sensitivity to voice tone, body language, and perhaps even to pheromones, those sneaky molecules that we release and which others smell subconsciously. Moreover, according to the context and, indeed, the person with whom we are conversing, our own delivery will need to adapt. None of these skills are required when chatting on a social networking site.

Although it might seem an extreme analogy, I often wonder whether real conversation in real time may eventually give way to these sanitized and easier screen dialogues, in much the same way as killing, skinning, and butchering an animal to eat has been replaced by the convenience of packages of meat on the supermarket shelf. Perhaps future generations will recoil with similar horror at the messiness, unpredictability, and immediate personal involvement of a three-dimensional, real-time interaction. In the words of one user: "The fact that you can't see or hear other people makes it easier to reveal yourself in a way that you might not be comfortable with. You become less conscious of the individuals involved (including yourself), less inhibited, less embarrassed and less concerned about how you will be evaluated."

It is hard to see how living this way on a daily basis will not result in brains, or rather minds, different from those of previous generations. We know that the human brain is exquisitely sensitive to the outside world. This so-called plasticity has been most famously illustrated by London taxi drivers, who as we know need to remember all the streets of the city, and whose brain scans correspondingly revealed in one study that the part of the brain related to memory is bigger in them than it is in the rest of us.

One of the most exciting concepts in neuroscience is that all experience, every single moment, leaves its mark almost literally on your brain. So you have a unique configuration of brain cell circuits, even if you are a clone — an identical twin. It is this evolving personalization of the brain that we could view as the mind, and it is this "mind" that could therefore be radically changed by prolonged exposure to a new and unprecedented type of ongoing environment, that of the screen.

So, we come to the second basic question: What might now be in jeopardy? First, I would suggest that it is attention span. If the young brain is exposed from the outset to a world of fast action and reaction, of instant new screen images flashing up with the press of a key, such rapid interchange might accustom the brain to operate over such timescales. Perhaps when in the real world such responses are not immediately forthcoming, we will see such behaviors and call them attention deficit disorder. It might be helpful to investigate whether the near total submersion of our culture in screen technologies over the last decade might in some way be linked to the threefold increase over this period in prescriptions for methylphenidate, the drug prescribed for ADHD.

Related to this change might be a second area of potential difference in the young twenty first century mind — a much more marked preference for the here-and-now, where the immediacy of an experience trumps any regard for the consequences. Afer all, whenever you play a computer game, you can always just play it again; everything you do is reversible. The emphasis is on the thrill of the moment, the buzz of rescuing the princess in the game. No care is given for the princess herself, for the content or for any long-term significance, because there is none. This type of activity, a disregard for consequence, can be compared with the thrill of compulsive gambling or compulsive eating. Interestingly, and as an aside, one study has shown that obese people are more reckless in gambling tasks. In turn, the sheer compulsion of reliable and almost immediate reward is being linked to similar chemical systems in the brain that may also play a part in drug addiction. So we should not underestimate the "pleasure" of interacting with a screen when we puzzle over why it seems so appealing to young people; rather, we should be paying attention to whether such activities may indeed result in a more impulsive and solipsistic attitude.

This brings us to a third possible change — in empathy. One teacher of thirty   10 years' standing wrote to me that she had witnessed a change over the time she had been teaching in the ability of her pupils to understand others. She pointed out that previously, reading novels had been a good way of learning about how others feel and think, as distinct from oneself. Unlike the game to rescue the princess, where the goal is to feel rewarded, the aim of reading a book is, after all, to find out more about the princess herself.

Perhaps we should therefore not be surprised that those within the spectrum of autism are particularly comfortable in the cyber world. The Internet has even been linked to sign language, considered as beneficial for autistic people as sign language proved for the deaf. Of course, we do not know whether the current increase in autism is due more to increased awareness and diagnosis of autism, or whether it can — if there is a true increase — be in any way linked to an increased prevalence among people of spending time in screen relationships. Surely it is a point worth considering.

Finally, I draw your Lordships' attention to a fourth issuer: identity. It seems strange that in a society recoiling from the introduction of ID cards, we are at the same time enthusiastically embracing the possible erosion of our identity through social networking sites. One sixteen-year-old intern who worked in my lab last summer summed it up as follows: "I can see that Facebook makes you think about yourself differently when all your private thoughts and feelings can be posted on the Internet for all to see. Are we perhaps losing a sense of where we ourselves finish and the outside world begins?"

With fast-paced, instant screen reactions, perhaps the next generation will define themselves by the responses of others; hence the baffling current preoccupation with posting an almost moment-by-moment, flood-of-consciousness account — I believe it is called Twitter — of your thoughts and activities, however banal.

In summary, I suggest that social networking sites might tap into the basic brain systems for delivering pleasurable experience. However, these experiences are devoid of cohesive narrative and long-term significance.

As a consequence, the mid-21st century mind might almost be infantilized, 15
characterized by short attention spans, sensationalism, inability to empathize and a
shaky sense of identity.

When talking about safeguards, surely we need also to think about safeguarding
the mindset of the next generation so that they may realize their potential as fully-
fledged adult human beings. Of course we cannot turn back the clock, nor would
that be any solution to maximizing the individual's potential in this new century.
However, surely the Government could consider investing in some kind of initiative, the goal of which would be the identification of realistic alternatives — be it
in the classroom, on the screen, in conjunction with the media, or in society as a
whole — for developing a sense of privacy and identity and, above all, a real appreciation of friendship.

As the Internet Rewires Our Brains

KURT CAGLE

BEFORE READING: In what ways does communication via the Internet require different
thought processes than earlier forms of communication? Are they better ways of
thinking or just different?

The Internet, ironically, has been abuzz this week with dire news about how the
social media and the Internet itself is stunting our mental growth, is turning us
into idiot savants, Asperger's[1] and reverting our brains to a more primitive state. The
first such statement came from Lady Greenfield, an Oxford University neurologist,
baroness, and director of the Royal Institution in England, who warned that sites
such as Facebook and Twitter were contributing to the decline of critical skills in
children who used them heavily, claiming that repeated exposure could effectively
rewire the brain.

In a speech earlier to the House of Lords, she told the assembled members of
Parliament that "I often wonder whether real conversation in real time may eventually give way to these sanitized and easier screen dialogues, in much the same
way as killing, skinning, and butchering an animal to eat has been replaced by the
convenience of packages of meat on the supermarket shelf."

Additionally, Lady Greenfield told the Lords a teacher of thirty years had told
her she had noticed a sharp decline in the ability of her pupils to understand others.

---

[1] Asperger's syndrome is characterized by social impairment, among other symptoms. — EDS.

Kurt Cagle, who lives in British Columbia, is an author, developer, and online editor for
O'Reilly Media, an organization dedicated to spreading knowledge of technological innovations through its research, publications, and conferences. His article was posted on oreilly.com
on February 28, 2009.

"It is hard to see how living this way on a daily basis will not result in brains, or rather minds, different from those of previous generations," she said.

She did admit that people with autism spectrum disorders were able to better 5 communicate via such services, but raised the question about whether autism itself is a response to such services.

"Of course, we do not know whether the current increase in autism is due more to increased awareness and diagnosis of autism, or whether it can — if there is a true increase — be in any way linked to an increased prevalence among people of spending time in screen relationships. Surely it is a point worth considering," she added.

Reaction from many in the social media has been swift (the Twitter community in particular spread the link within minutes of the publication of her quotes), and not surprisingly many have rushed to the defense of social media in general and their particular media in particular.

The Medium and the Message

Given both the credentials that Dr. Greenfield has and her significant expertise in the field, it is very likely that some (even all) of her comments have been taken very much out of context by the media. Overall, however, it's worth considering that her fundamental assertions are correct — contemporary children's brains are almost certainly changing in response to social media. The more relevant and important question is whether this is necessarily a bad thing.

First, it's essential to know that the brain rewires itself all the time — every time you learn new information, you are in essence burning a new set of pathways through the neurons in the cerebral cortex — rewiring the brain. Whether the skill is learning calculus or writing a blog, the brain is reshaping itself constantly in response to the intellectual activity going on.

The more telling question is whether such changes to the brain are in fact 10 beneficial or harmful. The introduction of the alphabet and reading brought about major changes in the way that the brain developed, according to Leonard Shlain, author of *The Alphabet vs. the Goddess*. As culture shifted from a largely oral tradition to a written one, Shlain wrote, this shift had a pronounced effect on the ability to reason, creating a world view that was at once more nuanced and symbolic than for those who were preliterate. Yet this came at a cost: the ability to memorize long oral recitations, the key to preserving cultural history, vanished, seemingly overnight. This effect can be seen even today in the extinction of hundreds of languages within the last century that for the most part survived via oral traditions.

Shlain's assertions become somewhat more problematic in the last century, as first radio, then television, then the Internet became the dominant media in use. Radio represented, in his book, the return of the oral tradition, and radio's potential as a mass media hid a more troubling side — radio based speech and music introduces nuances that can't be captured in print, and has the ability to reach a more primal level in our brains, one that can bypass the reasoning part and connect to something that is more emotional, one of the reasons why a speech over the radio can raise so many different emotions compared to reading a transcription.

Shlain argued that the rise of Hitler during the 1930s was made possible partially because Hitler (and Joseph Goebels, Hitler's master of propaganda) used radio to such good effect to stir up emotional support while bypassing the rational part of the brain.

More recently, television has affected a change as well — one in which narratives could generally only be sustained within ten-minute blocks, imagination was suppressed, and the sensitivity to frequently repeated messages could imprint ideas directly into one's head without going through a rationality filter (again, by Shlain's argument, rationality exists as a byproduct of reading). TV created a generation of non-critical thinkers . . . and it is interesting to view the rapid decline of the critical essay as television use rose in the 1960s and on (and moreover, to note that those people who do write and think critically seldom watch television).

Television had a second adverse effect — television is a study in motion, you seldom have more than a second where some animation doesn't happen somewhere on the screen (to the extent that advertisers occasionally show sequences that have no motion for most of the video in order to jar their audience's expectations). However, in real life, you seldom get situations even closely approximating the hyperkinetic whirlpool of TV — for the most part things move very slowly, and there are frequently times of no motion at all. Kids who grow up on television thus often find the real world "boring" because things don't happen at the hyperkinetic pace that they have come to expect, which in turn can manifest itself in behavioral problems and depression.

The Physical Effects of Social Media

So what about social media on the Web? First, keep in mind that unlike previous media, the Internet is not in fact a single medium, but rather is an aggregation of media that can be combined in any number of different ways. This means that any discussion of social media has to be examined in terms of its relevant pieces and the way that they are combined — and that because different Web sites and services tend to stress different mixes of such content, the rules that apply to a blogging site cannot necessarily be carried over to Flickr.

However, there are some common characteristics that have emerged with the Web and social media. One of the first things that happens when you view a Web page is that you perform a very rapid (300–600 millisecond) fast scan that forms an immediate impression of the page, in which the eyes light on elements just fast enough to see their positions, but generally not fast enough to read perhaps a word or two per shift in eye movement. This assessment is perhaps closest to the way that we scan newspapers or magazines, but considerably faster. Indeed, perhaps a more appropriate metaphor is the way that a driver scans a dashboard while keeping his eyes on the road, not so much actually reading but visually checking to insure that nothing is out of place.

This behavior carries over the scanning Web mail, Twitter tags, eBay listings, essentially any kind of array-based content. One consequence of this is that brains wired to best process this may find a stronger tendency to scan blocks of content rather than reading them, useful for picking out context, but at the cost of losing nuance in your reading — and your writing.

Keypad entry has become a second media difference — until the advent of the computer, keyboard competency was limited to writers and secretarial pools. With computers, keyboard entry — effectively speaking with one's fingers — has become ingrained in an entire generation. One offshoot of this is that you see less planning in terms of writing (which carries over to other cerebral tasks), and more of a tendency to just jump in and start producing, revising even as you write. The advantage that derives from this is that there is considerably less effort expended in these short write/edit/revise cycles than there is in the creation of successive drafts, often making for more spontaneous works, but at a cost of loss of cohesiveness when projects extend beyond a certain size or scope.

Much is made of the attention deficit that arises among heavy computer users, an effect which is real, though again it's worth considering it in context. Many actions that occur within Web browsers are becoming more intellectually challenging — the creation of blogs, programming, reviewing and analyzing information — and this requires the consumption of energy by the brain, and an increased "down-time" where the brain can process that information and then accept more. Context switching is a way for the brain to rest, doing less taxing activities momentarily to give the necessary neural pathways the ability to relax and prepare for the next heavy lifting.

However, there's some evidence that this context switching is a deep layer activity, and that the switching is not necessarily done consciously; rather the consciousness makes a semi-aware decision to switch activities based upon subconscious stimulae. Unfortunately, this also carries through to other activities beyond computing, at least for some time after context switching on a computer. People attempt to multitask (which is usually just context switching) even while doing activities that should require full participation.

In July, 2008, *Atlantic* magazine released a very controversial article by Nicholas   20
Carr entitled "Is Google Making Us Stupid?" In it, Carr describes, quite eloquently, the central conundrum facing people who enter into the Internet realm:

> Over the past few years I've had an uncomfortable sense that someone, or something, has been tinkering with my brain, remapping the neural circuitry, reprogramming the memory. My mind isn't going — so far as I can tell — but it's changing. I'm not thinking the way I used to think. I can feel it most strongly when I'm reading. Immersing myself in a book or a lengthy article used to be easy. My mind would get caught up in the narrative or the turns of the argument, and I'd spend hours strolling through long stretches of prose. That's rarely the case anymore. Now my concentration often starts to drift after two or three pages. I get fidgety, lose the thread, begin looking for something else to do. I feel as if I'm always dragging my wayward brain back to the text. The deep reading that used to come naturally has become a struggle.

Deep reading involves "losing oneself" in the words, establishing a world in your head that allows you to escape from the here and now. Some have called it a "fugue state" or "zen state," a mental orientation where the self is subsumed, at least temporarily, in this alternate world. When you transition out of this fugue state, the period can be disorienting, a momentary period where you "wake up" back to full consciousness.

Carr's argument (paraphrased) is that we are losing the ability to enter that fugue state, that the intense concentration for reading is no longer present in people. I find this argument specious. Programmers and writers can easily immerse themselves into that fugue state and write, often for hours at a time, and this concentration is in many respects even more challenging than reading long content.

Yet before condemning the media, consider the physics. On most computers, you are staring into a strong backlit monitor, looking at words made of characters that are comparatively low resolution when compared to print. This means that eyes have to work harder to make out the same information, tire more quickly and hence become averse to staring at longer passages. If a person becomes used to reading media on the computer, they will carry these patterns back to reading books because the behavior becomes intrinsic, even if the reason for the behavior is not.

This scenario makes more sense when watching Kindle readers, who don't deal with the backlit effect because of the e-Ink based screens used. As e-Ink and similar "paper interfaces" become more heavily incorporated into computers and consumer electronics over the next decade, it is likely that one effect of it will be that such trained attention spans will begin to increase again.

From Communities of Place to Communities of Interest

In a similar vein, instant messaging and short burst messaging (such as Twitter or SMS) has come under a cloud of criticism because it supposedly subverts children's language development skills and leads to anti-social behavior. The first contention is, frankly, silly — every generation of kids and teenagers growing up develops a cant or slang that exists primarily to establish their independence from the previous generation. This generation is no different, save that they are one of the first generations to have their own unique communication channel over which to use this slang, a channel that makes it possible for them to communicate remotely.

The consequence of this is that for the first time in history, proximity ceases 25 to be a factor in communication, which in turn means that those kids are able to form friendships and relationships based less upon who is near them and more on who share common interests — a community of interest rather than a community of place. Proximity does play a factor — the strongest friendships usually occur when the friends physically meet, but IM and SMS serve to reinforce those bonds.

Does that make kids anti-social? Actually, I suspect it makes relationships stronger. After moving from Seattle to Victoria, BC, my teenage daughter was despondent about leaving friends that she knew there. However, through social media, she quickly reconnected, making it possible for her to maintain the friendship. Over time, it has attenuated — the girls are developing different interests and life experiences, and as such have less and less in common — but this is true of friendships (and other relationships) in general.

What it does do, however, is place a larger communication divide between those that are online and those that aren't. Lady Greenfield's teacher sees children that are communicating less and less by the channels that she knows about, and therefore sees the emergence of anti-social behavior. Maybe she's just not on the right channel?

The shift from communities of place to communities of interest is going on worldwide, though it is perhaps most apparent in the youngest generation, who are coming of age at a time when much of the foundational work already has been done. Those who would argue for the value of communities of place often use civic involvement as a touchstone — that as people move into cyberspace, they leave many of the issues of their community behind, become apathetic about the world around them.

In my experience, however, the opposite is taking place. Communities of interest can often coincide with communities of place — an interest group forms to solve a particular problem (the introduction of a retail complex in an area that many feel should remain untouched), the group communicates with one another via social media and the occasional SM mediated meetups, and eventually are able to raise enough of a political caucus together to forestall the development or at least force changes. Ten or even twenty years ago, the ability to organize and respond to local political needs were far more primitive, with the results that often the ability of the community of place to respond came only after changes were no longer possible.

Relating this back to both changes in childhood neural development and educa-   30
tion, the "texting" channel is compelling. Friendships formed by proximity can grow if there is commonality of interest, but the obverse isn't true all that often — people thrown together with few common interests will not tend to spontaneously form friendships.

People who grow up together usually also have common interests, but in an era where divorce is rampant, where moving is common due to job relocation or other factors, and where school closings and similar factors force kids to have to rebuild their relationships every three to five years, kids' abilities to relate to one another are often already very poor. Is it little surprise then that social media is increasingly seen by these kids as an alternative to the painful and often humiliating experience of trying to establish friends by direct social interactions?

Educators, especially those from an earlier era, would be well advised to explore these channels more fully. Facebook could be used to communicate with students, tracking running "chats," establishing assignments (and showing results to the students' respective pages), providing rewards and incentives (and the occasional disincentive) in a way that more accurately reflects the worldview of the children. Such a model may seem absurd to many teachers, yet it is a perfectly natural one to those same children, especially as they are far more likely to accept the role of the teacher as a guider and facilitator than they are of the teacher as authoritarian if that teacher can communicate at their level.

The Nuanced Channels of Text

What of the "flattening" effect that such social media purportedly has on communications? Again, some context is needed. Until comparatively recently, text existed solely for asynchronous communication — the author of a book or a magazine article would almost never actually come to where you were and read the entire contents of the work aloud to you or even hand the book to you physically and say "Here is my message or story . . . now respond to it."

Text messaging is synchronous communication using text rather than spoken words, and has effectively never existed before because the mechanism for creating that text is too cumbersome when you can just speak the words to the other people in the discussion. Yet with communities of interest this equation is turned on its head — the visual and aural cues so necessary for spoken communication don't exist, while the speed of text messaging is limited by the speed at which you can type . . . and the current generation types, on average, very, very fast, all the while creating a language that is not all that different from stenographer's notation from sixty years ago.

I am a professional writer and have been working with typewriters and computer keyboards since the mid-1970s. My nearly-sixteen year old daughter has had one typing class when she was in fourth grade. She types faster than I do, with more accuracy. I suspect she is not alone is this. She's gained the speed because it has become a second mode of communication for her, one that she practices every time she IMs her friends or writes her online blog/diaries. 35

Text is, admittedly, far less nuanced as a communication mechanism, and if text by itself was the only carrier of content, I think the arguments about text reducing the subtle clues of oral communication would hold some water. Yet it isn't. As the cost of telephony has dropped and the rise in mobile device numbers has climbed exponentially, voice can be added into the mix (sometimes over the same channels, as most IM services now support some from of VoIP interface) as necessary. With a bit of additional complexity, Webcam video support can be added as well to get even more full spectrum communication.

What this means is that social media communication streams can be as rich as necessary — perhaps not quite to the point of a hologram of the other person hovering above your keyboard, though that day is not far off. What's more, if the additional complexity isn't necessary — and in many cases it actually adds nothing to the message but noise — then it isn't transmitted.

Certainly the brain is adapting to this. The world is becoming increasingly complex, and the ability to filter out the signal from the noise is only becoming more critical rather than less. The childhood brain in particular is being stressed, but those stresses will be a part of their life, and the stresses are in turn shaping the brain to more effectively filter out the irrelevant.

A final thought in an overlong essay — psychologists, especially those that have developed a fairly conservative model of the brain, have pushed the notion of information overload — we are pushing our brains to accept too much information too quickly, and these stresses are affecting all of us. Much of this is due to the fact that for many people over the age of forty, the coping mechanisms of the brain to this stress can only erect a fairly crude barrier. Children, with far more malleable brains, are essentially developing their own mechanisms for handling information management, mechanisms that are still largely hidden to those of us who are older.

The greatest danger that these children face is that well meaning psychologists 40 and educators will label these mechanisms as aberrations, and will try to "correct" them back to a model that no longer really works. We must, we *must*, accept the fact that we are undergoing a decades long transition that is in its own way as profound to the human psyche as the introduction of writing was five thousand years ago, and rather than condemning the new waves of media we should accept that these represent our own future and make the effort to become proficient in them as fully as possible.

Facebook: Watching the Watchers

PATRICK WHITE

BEFORE READING: If you have an account on Facebook or a similar social networking site, are your parents or other adults your "friends"? Why, or why not? If you don't have an account, do you think you would want to "friend" your parents or other adults?

Until seven weeks ago, Shelley van der Spank heard just two words when she asked her two teens about their lives: "Oh, nothing." As in, "What did you learn at school today?" "Oh, nothing." "What are you doing on the computer all day?" "Oh, nothing." "What is this Facebook thing I'm always hearing about?" "Oh, nothing."

Ms. van der Spank eventually figured out that last one for herself. In late April, she signed up for Facebook, added her kids to her friends list, and gained access to a new realm of teen expression she wasn't entirely comfortable with. "I thought some pictures of girls in their bathing suits were a little inappropriate for others to view and told them," Ms. van der Spank says.

But just when she started to think Facebook was an infallible new weapon in the battle to keep tabs on her children, the unexpected happened: The teens began spying on her. "They snoop on my screen, count my friends, view my pictures . . . and offer silly comments," says Ms. van der Spank, who is now resorting to privacy measures normally reserved for teens blocking nosy parents.

Over the past eight months, Facebook has transformed from an online *Animal House*, exclusive to a few million high-school and college kids, to the world's

Patrick White is a Winnipeg-based reporter for the Canadian English language newspaper *Globe and Mail*. His article appeared in the June 12, 2007 edition.

Facebook offers a window into the lives of both children and parents.

seventh-most popular website — a thirty-million-strong social networking portal open to all ages and branches of the family tree. The site now bridges a chasm once rarely crossed between student life and family life by offering a window into the lives of both children and parents. Family dynamics may never be the same.

The students-only world of Facebook began in 2004 as a site for people at Harvard to create a personal profile and search for classmates. By late 2005, any student attending a major American college or high school could sign on and start posting tales of drunken escapades with the photos to prove them in relative privacy.   5

But late last year [2006], Facebook opened up to everyone. Since then, Facebook's total user base has doubled. "It used to be a wide open space," says Fred Stutzman, a University of North Carolina graduate student who's writing his dissertation about Facebook. "Since it opened up, people have been turning on their privacy options. They aren't comfortable any more."

That includes recent converts like Ms. van der Spank. "What I censor is some pictures that I don't want [my kids] to see, but will e-mail my friends for a good laugh — nothing naughty, just not for their eyes," she says.

Jenna Bromberg used to trawl Facebook with all the inhibition of a sorority girl at a spring-break kegger. She exchanged bawdy messages with friends. She broadcasted that she "drinks well with others." She posted boozy party pictures, one showing off her finest beer-bong form. That was until the fourth-year Cornell University student received a troubling message. An all-too-familiar face requested to be Ms. Bromberg's Facebook friend: her mom. "I almost deactivated my entire account right there," Ms. Bromberg says. She was torn, but in the end she couldn't deny her mother. "It's really changed our relationship," she says. "My mother is now looking at pics of me bonging a beer."

Parents have congregated on Facebook to such a degree that in some cases they are now the ones trying to keep their children off the site. Sarah Gallagher, a Vancouver mom, regularly logs on to her profile to chat with friends and seek out former classmates. Yet, her fourteen-year-old daughter is forbidden from joining. Ms. Gallagher has her reasons. She thinks that her daughter's generation is losing the ability to socialize in person. "They don't know how to phone each other and make a date," she says.

But there's another reason. Ms. Gallagher isn't comfortable with her daughter 10 poking around her mother's personal profile. "She's still at the point where she's listening to me," she says of her daughter. "But I don't think I'll have that authority much longer. She's already starting to use the double-standard argument."

Still, Facebook isn't all family dysfunction and tumult. In some cases, the site is actually strengthening family ties. For Ms. van der Spank, Facebook is a source of conversation topics that stirs her teens to insights beyond "Oh, nothing." "I can ask, 'So I saw on Facebook that Amy is not with Joe any more.' The kids open right up and we talk about it, share ideas, laugh. I felt shut out and closed off before Facebook."

Even Ms. Bromberg, the Cornell student, confesses an upside to her mother being on Facebook. "We're closer now, for sure," she says. "She treats me more like a friend than she did before. She sees all my inside jokes. She sees how I treat my friends. If it lets her feel a little better about my lifestyle here, then I'll let her have it."

Brave New World of Digital Intimacy

CLIVE THOMPSON

BEFORE READING: If you use Facebook or a similar social networking site, how would you categorize the people who are your friends on that site? Are there some that you don't really know or barely know? Do you feel as if you are hearing more about their lives than you would like to hear? Explain. If you do not use a social networking site, do you feel left out socially because you don't? Explain.

On September 5, 2006, Mark Zuckerberg changed the way that Facebook worked, and in the process he inspired a revolt.

Zuckerberg, a doe-eyed twenty-four-year-old C.E.O., founded Facebook in his dorm room at Harvard two years earlier, and the site quickly amassed nine million users. By 2006, students were posting heaps of personal details onto their Facebook pages, including lists of their favorite TV shows, whether they were dating (and whom), what music they had in rotation and the various ad hoc "groups" they had joined (like *Sex and the City* Lovers). All day long, they'd post "status" notes explaining their moods — "hating Monday," "skipping class b/c i'm hung over." After each party, they'd stagger home to the dorm and upload pictures of the soused revelry, and spend the morning after commenting on how wasted everybody looked. Facebook became the de facto public commons — the way students found out what everyone around them was like and what he or she was doing.

But Zuckerberg knew Facebook had one major problem: It required a lot of active surfing on the part of its users. Sure, every day your Facebook friends would update their profiles with some new tidbits; it might even be something particularly juicy, like changing their relationship status to "single" when they got dumped. But unless you visited each friend's page every day, it might be days or weeks before you noticed the news, or you might miss it entirely. Browsing Facebook was like constantly poking your head into someone's room to see how she was doing. It took work and forethought. In a sense, this gave Facebook an inherent, built-in level of privacy, simply because if you had 200 friends on the site — a fairly typical number — there weren't enough hours in the day to keep tabs on every friend all the time.

"It was very primitive," Zuckerberg told me when I asked him about it last month. And so he decided to modernize. He developed something he called News Feed, a built-in service that would actively broadcast changes in a user's page to every one of his or her friends. Students would no longer need to spend their time zipping around to examine each friend's page, checking to see if there was any new

---

Clive Thompson is a contributing writer for the *New York Times Magazine, Fast Company*, and *Wired* magazine's Web site, among other places, and a columnist for *Wired* magazine. He writes about science, technology, and culture. This article appeared on NYTimes.com on September 7, 2008.

information. Instead, they would just log into Facebook, and News Feed would appear: a single page that — like a social gazette from the eighteenth century — delivered a long list of up-to-the-minute gossip about their friends, around the clock, all in one place. "A stream of everything that's going on in their lives," as Zuckerberg put it.

When students woke up that September morning and saw News Feed, the first   5
reaction, generally, was one of panic. Just about every little thing you changed on your page was now instantly blasted out to hundreds of friends, including potentially mortifying bits of news — Tim and Lisa broke up; Persaud is no longer friends with Matthew — and drunken photos someone snapped, then uploaded, and tagged with names. Facebook had lost its vestigial bit of privacy. For students, it was now like being at a giant, open party filled with everyone you know, able to eavesdrop on what everyone else was saying, all the time.

"Everyone was freaking out," Ben Parr, then a junior at Northwestern University, told me recently. What particularly enraged Parr was that there wasn't any way to opt out of News Feed, to "go private" and have all your information kept quiet. He created a Facebook group demanding Zuckerberg either scrap News Feed or provide privacy options. "Facebook users really think Facebook is becoming the Big Brother of the Internet, recording every single move," a California student told the *Star-Ledger* of Newark. Another chimed in, "Frankly, I don't need to know or care that Billy broke up with Sally, and Ted has become friends with Steve." By lunchtime of the first day, 10,000 people had joined Parr's group, and by the next day it had 284,000.

Zuckerberg, surprised by the outcry, quickly made two decisions. The first was to add a privacy feature to News Feed, letting users decide what kind of information went out. But the second decision was to leave News Feed otherwise intact. He suspected that once people tried it and got over their shock, they'd like it.

He was right. Within days, the tide reversed. Students began e-mailing Zuckerberg to say that via News Feed they'd learned things they would never have otherwise discovered through random surfing around Facebook. The bits of trivia that News Feed delivered gave them more things to talk about — Why do you hate Kiefer Sutherland? — when they met friends face to face in class or at a party. Trends spread more quickly. When one student joined a group — proclaiming her love of Coldplay or a desire to volunteer for Greenpeace — all her friends instantly knew, and many would sign up themselves. Users' worries about their privacy seemed to vanish within days, boiled away by their excitement at being so much more connected to their friends. (Very few people stopped using Facebook, and most people kept on publishing most of their information through News Feed.) Pundits predicted that News Feed would kill Facebook, but the opposite happened. It catalyzed a massive boom in the site's growth. A few weeks after the News Feed imbroglio, Zuckerberg opened the site to the general public (previously, only students could join), and it grew quickly; today, it has 100 million users.[2]

---

[2] As of October 2010 the site had 500 million users. — EDS.

When I spoke to him, Zuckerberg argued that News Feed is central to Facebook's success. "Facebook has always tried to push the envelope," he said. "And at times that means stretching people and getting them to be comfortable with things they aren't yet comfortable with. A lot of this is just social norms catching up with what technology is capable of."

In essence, Facebook users didn't think they wanted constant, up-to-the-minute   10 updates on what other people are doing. Yet when they experienced this sort of omnipresent knowledge, they found it intriguing and addictive. Why?

Social scientists have a name for this sort of incessant online contact. They call it "ambient awareness." It is, they say, very much like being physically near someone and picking up on his mood through the little things he does — body language, sighs, stray comments — out of the corner of your eye. Facebook is no longer alone in offering this sort of interaction online. In the last year, there has been a boom in tools for "microblogging": posting frequent tiny updates on what you're doing. The phenomenon is quite different from what we normally think of as blogging, because a blog post is usually a written piece, sometimes quite long: a statement of opinion, a story, an analysis. But these new updates are something different. They're far shorter, far more frequent and less carefully considered. One of the most popular new tools is Twitter, a Web site and messaging service that allows its two-million-plus users to broadcast to their friends haiku-length updates — limited to 140 characters, as brief as a mobile-phone text message — on what they're doing. There are other services for reporting where you're traveling (Dopplr) or for quickly tossing online a stream of the pictures, videos or Web sites you're looking at (Tumblr). And there are even tools that give your location. When the new iPhone, with built-in tracking, was introduced in July, one million people began using Loopt, a piece of software that automatically tells all your friends exactly where you are.

For many people — particularly anyone over the age of thirty — the idea of describing your blow-by-blow activities in such detail is absurd. Why would you subject your friends to your daily minutiae? And conversely, how much of their trivia can you absorb? The growth of ambient intimacy can seem like modern narcissism taken to a new, supermetabolic extreme — the ultimate expression of a generation of celebrity-addled youths who believe their every utterance is fascinating and ought to be shared with the world. Twitter, in particular, has been the subject of nearly relentless scorn since it went online. "Who really cares what I am doing, every hour of the day?" wondered Alex Beam, a *Boston Globe* columnist, in an essay about Twitter last month. "Even I don't care."

Indeed, many of the people I interviewed, who are among the most avid users of these "awareness" tools, admit that at first they couldn't figure out why anybody would want to do this. Ben Haley, a thirty-nine-year-old documentation specialist for a software firm who lives in Seattle, told me that when he first heard about Twitter last year from an early-adopter friend who used it, his first reaction was that it seemed silly. But a few of his friends decided to give it a try, and they urged him to sign up, too.

Each day, Haley logged on to his account, and his friends' updates would appear as a long page of one- or two-line notes. He would check and recheck the account several times a day, or even several times an hour. The updates were indeed pretty banal. One friend would post about starting to feel sick; one posted random thoughts like "I really hate it when people clip their nails on the bus"; another Twittered whenever she made a sandwich — and she made a sandwich every day. Each so-called tweet was so brief as to be virtually meaningless.

But as the days went by, something changed. Haley discovered that he was   15
beginning to sense the rhythms of his friends' lives in a way he never had before. When one friend got sick with a virulent fever, he could tell by her Twitter updates when she was getting worse and the instant she finally turned the corner. He could see when friends were heading into hellish days at work or when they'd scored a big success. Even the daily catalog of sandwiches became oddly mesmerizing, a sort of metronomic click that he grew accustomed to seeing pop up in the middle of each day.

This is the paradox of ambient awareness. Each little update — each individual bit of social information — is insignificant on its own, even supremely mundane. But taken together, over time, the little snippets coalesce into a surprisingly sophisticated portrait of your friends' and family members' lives, like thousands of dots making a pointillist painting. This was never before possible, because in the real world, no friend would bother to call you up and detail the sandwiches she was eating. The ambient information becomes like "a type of E.S.P.," as Haley described it to me, an invisible dimension floating over everyday life.

"It's like I can distantly read everyone's mind," Haley went on to say. "I love that. I feel like I'm getting to something raw about my friends. It's like I've got this heads-up display for them." It can also lead to more real-life contact, because when one member of Haley's group decides to go out to a bar or see a band and Twitters about his plans, the others see it, and some decide to drop by — ad hoc, self-organizing socializing. And when they do socialize face to face, it feels oddly as if they've never actually been apart. They don't need to ask, "So, what have you been up to?" because they already know. Instead, they'll begin discussing something that one of the friends Twittered that afternoon, as if picking up a conversation in the middle.

Facebook and Twitter may have pushed things into overdrive, but the idea of using communication tools as a form of "co-presence" has been around for a while. The Japanese sociologist Mizuko Ito first noticed it with mobile phones: lovers who were working in different cities would send text messages back and forth all night — tiny updates like "enjoying a glass of wine now" or "watching TV while lying on the couch." They were doing it partly because talking for hours on mobile phones isn't very comfortable (or affordable). But they also discovered that the little Ping-Ponging messages felt even more intimate than a phone call.

"It's an aggregate phenomenon," Marc Davis, a chief scientist at Yahoo and former professor of information science at the University of California at Berkeley, told me. "No message is the single-most-important message. It's sort of like when you're sitting with someone and you look over and they smile at you. You're sitting here reading the paper, and you're doing your side-by-side thing, and you just sort of let people know you're aware of them." Yet it is also why it can be extremely hard to understand the phenomenon until you've experienced it. Merely looking at a stranger's Twitter or Facebook feed isn't interesting, because it seems like blather. Follow it for a day, though, and it begins to feel like a short story; follow it for a month, and it's a novel.

You could also regard the growing popularity of online awareness as a reaction 20 to social isolation, the modern American disconnectedness that Robert Putnam explored in his book "Bowling Alone." The mobile workforce requires people to travel more frequently for work, leaving friends and family behind, and members of the growing army of the self-employed often spend their days in solitude. Ambient intimacy becomes a way to "feel less alone," as more than one Facebook and Twitter user told me.

When I decided to try out Twitter last year, at first I didn't have anyone to follow. None of my friends were yet using the service. But while doing some Googling one day I stumbled upon the blog of Shannon Seery, a thirty-two-year-old recruiting consultant in Florida, and I noticed that she Twittered. Her Twitter updates were pretty charming — she would often post links to camera-phone pictures of her two children or videos of herself cooking Mexican food, or broadcast her agonized cries when a flight was delayed on a business trip. So on a whim I started "following" her — as easy on Twitter as a click of the mouse — and never took her off my account. (A Twitter account can be "private," so that only invited friends can read one's tweets, or it can be public, so anyone can; Seery's was public.) When I checked in last month, I noticed that she had built up a huge number of online connections: She was now following 677 people on Twitter and another 442 on Facebook. How in God's name, I wondered, could she follow so many people? Who precisely are they? I called Seery to find out.

"I have a rule," she told me. "I either have to know who you are, or I have to know of you." That means she monitors the lives of friends, family, anyone she works with, and she'll also follow interesting people she discovers via her friends' online lives. Like many people who live online, she has wound up following a few strangers — though after a few months they no longer feel like strangers, despite the fact that she has never physically met them.

I asked Seery how she finds the time to follow so many people online. The math seemed daunting. After all, if her one thousand online contacts each post just a couple of notes each a day, that's several thousand little social pings to sift through daily. What would it be like to get thousands of e-mail messages a day? But Seery made a point I heard from many others: awareness tools aren't as cognitively demanding as an e-mail message. E-mail is something you have to stop to open and assess. It's personal; someone is asking for 100 percent of your attention. In contrast, ambient updates are all visible on one single page in a big row, and they're not really directed at you. This makes them skimmable, like newspaper headlines; maybe you'll read them all, maybe you'll skip some. Seery estimated that she needs to spend only a small part of each hour actively reading her Twitter stream.

Yet she has, she said, become far more gregarious online. "What's really funny is that before this 'social media' stuff, I always said that I'm not the type of person who had a ton of friends," she told me. "It's so hard to make plans and have an active social life, having the type of job I have where I travel all the time and have two small kids. But it's easy to tweet all the time, to post pictures of what I'm doing, to keep social relations up." She paused for a second, before continuing: "Things like Twitter have actually given me a much bigger social circle. I know more about more people than ever before."

I realized that this is becoming true of me, too. After following Seery's Twitter 25 stream for a year, I'm more knowledgeable about the details of her life than the lives of my two sisters in Canada, whom I talk to only once every month or so. When I called Seery, I knew that she had been struggling with a three-day migraine headache; I began the conversation by asking her how she was feeling.

Online awareness inevitably leads to a curious question: What sort of relationships are these? What does it mean to have hundreds of "friends" on Facebook? What kind of friends are they, anyway?

In 1998, the anthropologist Robin Dunbar argued that each human has a hardwired upper limit on the number of people he or she can personally know at one time. Dunbar noticed that humans and apes both develop social bonds by engaging in some sort of grooming; apes do it by picking at and smoothing one another's fur, and humans do it with conversation. He theorized that ape and human brains could manage only a finite number of grooming relationships: unless we spend enough time doing social grooming — chitchatting, trading gossip or, for apes, picking lice — we won't really feel that we "know" someone well enough to call him a friend. Dunbar noticed that ape groups tended to top out at fifty-five members. Since human brains were proportionally bigger, Dunbar figured that our maximum number of social connections would be similarly larger: about 150 on average. Sure enough, psychological studies have confirmed that human groupings naturally tail off at around 150 people: the "Dunbar number," as it is known. Are people who use Facebook and Twitter increasing their Dunbar number, because they can so easily keep track of so many more people?

As I interviewed some of the most aggressively social people online — people who follow hundreds or even thousands of others — it became clear that the picture was a little more complex than this question would suggest. Many maintained that their circle of true intimates, their very close friends and family, had not become bigger. Constant online contact had made those ties immeasurably richer, but it hadn't actually increased the number of them; deep relationships are still predicated on face time, and there are only so many hours in the day for that.

But where their sociality had truly exploded was in their "weak ties" — loose acquaintances, people they knew less well. It might be someone they met at a conference, or someone from high school who recently "friended" them on Facebook, or somebody from last year's holiday party. In their pre-Internet lives, these sorts of acquaintances would have quickly faded from their attention. But when one of these far-flung people suddenly posts a personal note to your feed, it is essentially a reminder that they exist. I have noticed this effect myself. In the last few months, dozens of old work colleagues I knew from ten years ago in Toronto have friended me on Facebook, such that I'm now suddenly reading their stray comments and updates and falling into oblique, funny conversations with them. My overall Dunbar number is thus 301: Facebook (254) + Twitter (47), double what it would be without

Some online friendships are deeper than others.

technology. Yet only twenty are family or people I'd consider close friends. The rest are weak ties — maintained via technology.

This rapid growth of weak ties can be a very good thing. Sociologists have long found that "weak ties" greatly expand your ability to solve problems. For example, if you're looking for a job and ask your friends, they won't be much help; they're too similar to you, and thus probably won't have any leads that you don't already have yourself. Remote acquaintances will be much more useful, because they're farther afield, yet still socially intimate enough to want to help you out. Many avid Twitter users — the ones who fire off witty posts hourly and wind up with thousands of intrigued followers — explicitly milk this dynamic for all it's worth, using their large online followings as a way to quickly answer almost any question. Laura Fitton, a social-media consultant who has become a minor celebrity on Twitter — she has more than 5,300 followers — recently discovered to her horror that her accountant had made an error in filing last year's taxes. She went to Twitter, wrote a tiny note explaining her problem, and within ten minutes her online audience had provided leads to lawyers and better accountants. Fritton joked to me that she no longer buys anything worth more than $50 without quickly checking it with her Twitter network.

"I outsource my entire life," she said. "I can solve any problem on Twitter in six minutes." (She also keeps a secondary Twitter account that is private and only for

30

a much smaller circle of close friends and family — "My little secret," she said. It is a strategy many people told me they used: one account for their weak ties, one for their deeper relationships.)

It is also possible, though, that this profusion of weak ties can become a problem. If you're reading daily updates from hundreds of people about whom they're dating and whether they're happy, it might, some critics worry, spread your emotional energy too thin, leaving less for true intimate relationships. Psychologists have long known that people can engage in "parasocial" relationships with fictional characters, like those on TV shows or in books, or with remote celebrities we read about in magazines. Parasocial relationships can use up some of the emotional space in our Dunbar number, crowding out real-life people. Danah Boyd, a fellow at Harvard's Berkman Center for Internet and Society who has studied social media for ten years, published a paper this spring arguing that awareness tools like NewsFeed might be creating a whole new class of relationships that are nearly parasocial — peripheral people in our network whose intimate details we follow closely online, even while they, like Angelina Jolie, are basically unaware we exist.

"The information we subscribe to on a feed is not the same as in a deep social relationship," Boyd told me. She has seen this herself; she has many virtual admirers that have, in essence, a parasocial relationship with her. "I've been very, very sick, lately and I write about it on Twitter and my blog, and I get all these people who are writing to me telling me ways to work around the health-care system, or they're writing saying, 'Hey, I broke my neck!' And I'm like, 'You're being very nice and trying to help me, but though you feel like you know me, you don't.'" Boyd sighed. "They can observe you, but it's not the same as knowing you."

When I spoke to Caterina Fake, a founder of Flickr (a popular photo-sharing site), she suggested an even more subtle danger: that the sheer ease of following her friends' updates online has made her occasionally lazy about actually taking the time to visit them in person. "At one point I realized I had a friend whose child I had seen, via photos on Flickr, grow from birth to one year old," she said. "I thought, I really should go meet her in person. But it was weird; I also felt that Flickr had satisfied that getting-to-know you satisfaction, so I didn't feel the urgency. But then I was like, Oh, that's not sufficient! I should go in person!" She has about four hundred people she follows online but suspects many of those relationships are tissue-fragile. "These technologies allow you to be much more broadly friendly, but you just spread yourself much more thinly over many more people."

What is it like to never lose touch with anyone? One morning this summer at 35 my local cafe, I overheard a young woman complaining to her friend about a recent Facebook drama. Her name is Andrea Ahan, a twenty-seven-year-old restaurant entrepreneur, and she told me that she had discovered that high-school friends were uploading old photos of her to Facebook and tagging them with her name, so they automatically appeared in searches for her.

She was aghast. "I'm like, my God, these pictures are completely hideous!" Ahan complained, while her friend looked on sympathetically and sipped her coffee. "I'm wearing all these totally awful '90s clothes. I look like crap. And I'm like, Why are you people in my life, anyway? I haven't seen you in ten years. I don't know you anymore!" She began furiously detagging the pictures — removing her name, so they wouldn't show up in a search anymore.

Worse, Ahan was also confronting a common plague of Facebook: the recent ex. She had broken up with her boyfriend not long ago, but she hadn't "unfriended" him, because that felt too extreme. But soon he paired up with another young woman, and the new couple began having public conversations on Ahan's ex-boyfriend's page. One day, she noticed with alarm that the new girlfriend was quoting material Ahan had e-mailed privately to her boyfriend; she suspected he had been sharing the e-mail with his new girlfriend. It is the sort of weirdly subtle mind game that becomes possible via Facebook, and it drove Ahan nuts.

"Sometimes I think this stuff is just crazy, and everybody has got to get a life and stop obsessing over everyone's trivia and gossiping," she said.

Yet Ahan knows that she cannot simply walk away from her online life, because the people she knows online won't stop talking about her, or posting unflattering photos. She needs to stay on Facebook just to monitor what's being said about her. This is a common complaint I heard, particularly from people in their twenties who were in college when Facebook appeared and have never lived as adults without online awareness. For them, participation isn't optional. If you don't dive in, other people will define who you are. So you constantly stream your pictures, your thoughts, your relationship status and what you're doing — right now! — if only to ensure the virtual version of you is accurate, or at least the one you want to present to the world.

This is the ultimate effect of the new awareness: It brings back the dynamics   40
of small-town life, where everybody knows your business. Young people at college are the ones to experience this most viscerally, because, with more than 90 percent of their peers using Facebook, it is especially difficult for them to opt out. Zeynep Tufekci, a sociologist at the University of Maryland, Baltimore County, who has closely studied how college-age users are reacting to the world of awareness, told me that athletes used to sneak off to parties illicitly, breaking the no-drinking rule for team members. But then camera phones and Facebook came along, with students posting photos of the drunken carousing during the party; savvy coaches could see which athletes were breaking the rules. First the athletes tried to fight back by waking up early the morning after the party in a hungover daze to detag photos of themselves so they wouldn't be searchable. But that didn't work, because the coaches sometimes viewed the pictures live, as they went online at 2 a.m. So parties simply began banning all camera phones in a last-ditch attempt to preserve privacy.

"It's just like living in a village, where it's actually hard to lie because everybody knows the truth already," Tufekci said. "The current generation is never unconnected. They're never losing touch with their friends. So we're going back to a more normal place, historically. If you look at human history, the idea that you would drift through life, going from new relation to new relation, that's very new. It's just the twentieth century."

Psychologists and sociologists spent years wondering how humanity would adjust to the anonymity of life in the city, the wrenching upheavals of mobile immigrant labor — a world of lonely people ripped from their social ties. We now have precisely the opposite problem. Indeed, our modern awareness tools reverse the original conceit of the Internet. When cyberspace came along in the early '90s, it was celebrated as a place where you could reinvent your identity — become someone new.

"If anything, it's identity-constraining now," Tufekci told me. "You can't play with your identity if your audience is always checking up on you. I had a student who posted that she was downloading some Pearl Jam, and someone wrote on her wall, 'Oh, right, ha-ha — I know you, and you're not into that.'" She laughed. "You know that old cartoon? 'On the Internet, nobody knows you're a dog'? On the Internet today, everybody knows you're a dog! If you don't want people to know you're a dog, you'd better stay away from a keyboard."

Or, as Leisa Reichelt, a consultant in London who writes regularly about ambient tools, put it to me: "Can you imagine a Facebook for children in kindergarten, and they never lose touch with those kids for the rest of their lives? What's that going to do to them?" Young people today are already developing an attitude toward their privacy that is simultaneously vigilant and laissez-faire. They curate their online personas as carefully as possible, knowing that everyone is watching — but they have also learned to shrug and accept the limits of what they can control.

It is easy to become unsettled by privacy-eroding aspects of awareness tools. But   45
there is another — quite different — result of all this incessant updating: a culture of people who know much more about themselves. Many of the avid Twitterers, Flickrers and Facebook users I interviewed described an unexpected side-effect of constant self-disclosure. The act of stopping several times a day to observe what you're feeling or thinking can become, after weeks and weeks, a sort of philosophical act. It's like the Greek dictum to "know thyself," or the therapeutic concept of mindfulness. (Indeed, the question that floats eternally at the top of Twitter's Web site — "What are you doing?" — can come to seem existentially freighted. What are you doing?) Having an audience can make the self-reflection even more acute, since, as my interviewees noted, they're trying to describe their activities in a way that is not only accurate but also interesting to others: the status update as a literary form.

Laura Fitton, the social-media consultant, argues that her constant status updating has made her "a happier person, a calmer person" because the process of, say, describing a horrid morning at work forces her to look at it objectively. "It drags you out of your own head," she added. In an age of awareness, perhaps the person you see most clearly is yourself.

Online Lives, Offline Consequences: Professionalism, Information Ethics, and Professional Students

ISAAC GILMAN

BEFORE READING: How could what college students post online now affect their ability to get into graduate school or professional school in the future or to get a job?

Introduction

The growth of the Internet over the past decade has made many tasks and personal interactions easier and faster. Students who have never experienced higher education without Google take for granted their ability to access information and entertainment at the click of a mouse and to live online lives unimpeded by anything except modem speed. For students enrolled in professional graduate programs (e.g. medicine, law, education), it is inevitable that their online experiences will shape their understanding of what is appropriate and what is ethical — which could have unanticipated professional consequences. To ensure that students' behaviors do not jeopardize their future careers, educators must understand the online activities that present ethical and professional issues and make every effort to educate students about appropriate behavior and interactions in an online environment (Gardner; Workman).

Academic Honesty and Information Ethics

For educators, perhaps the most familiar ethical issue facing students is that of academic honesty. For today's Internet-savvy students, who have become accustomed to cutting and pasting information on the fly with little attention to citations, the opportunity to use "free" online information is often too tempting to refuse. Studies over the past ten to fifteen years have confirmed that the ease of the Internet has exacerbated the misuse of others' intellectual property (Auer and Krupar; Szabo and Underwood 180). In an "open" online environment, there is no accountability for those who may inappropriately provide/use others' work. Thanks to the speed of cut-and-paste, there is also little time for students to even consider whether or not their use is ethical (Bodi 459). Even for students who do stop to consider their actions, one study found that the majority of students "would give in to Internet

Isaac Gilman is the Scholarly Communications and Research Services Librarian and Assistant Professor at Pacific University in Oregon, where he has helped graduate students and the university as a whole understand the ethics of copyright and intellectual property. This article appeared in the January–February 2009 issue of *Interface*, the electronic journal of the Berglund Center for Internet Studies at Pacific University.

plagiarism under the right combination of situational and personal factors" (Szabo and Underwood 196).

As familiar (and frustrated) as educators are with the unethical use of intellectual property, students are even more familiar with faculty lectures condemning the same. Honor codes, lectures on paper mills, and the evils of plagiarism — even the use of plagiarism detection services like Turnitin.com — have largely failed to make a lasting impression on students who do not recognize the seriousness of the issue (Harris 4). For many students, like 380 undergraduates surveyed about downloading copyrighted content, the use/misuse of others' intellectual property is still seen as a "victimless crime" (Siemens and Kopp 118). Indeed, for undergraduate students who believe that anything accessible is free, who do not anticipate publishing a journal article and who may never depend on a scholarly or professional reputation, it can be difficult to convey the significance of academic honesty.

However, for graduate students who may one day contribute to the professional literature, creating ethical habits for the use of others' intellectual property is of the utmost significance. Whether these students go on to become academics or practitioners, their scholarly record and actions will likely contribute to their reputation and career prospects, for better or worse. Works created as students may also persist for years if posted online (as is the case with many theses, dissertations, and other culminating projects), and it is vital that students understand from the beginning of their programs not only how to avoid plagiarism but also how to ethically — and legally — use copyrighted materials.

Social Networking and Professionalism

Though both educators and students are largely familiar with the issues of plagiarism and academic honesty, it is an entirely new issue that poses the greatest threat to students' professionalism — and one which has, on its face, nothing to do with students' academic performance or professional aspirations.

Over the past decade, the social/communication possibilities on the World Wide Web have grown exponentially, with one of the most notable developments being the creation of social networking sites — MySpace, Facebook, et al. As with many technologies, students were early (and fervent) adopters, with Facebook the popular choice of nearly 80–90 percent of United States college students (Educause). Profiles on social networking sites like Facebook allow students to communicate with friends, share photos and videos, and connect with people with similar interests. For students, their online profiles and communities are as personal as their offline friendships and interactions — and, often, are an extension of their offline activities, with Facebook used as a collaborative event planner and photo album.

While social networking sites and the Web connect students to one another, another connection is created that students may not anticipate (or enjoy). With student photos, blogs, comments, and affiliations publicly available online (unless privacy settings are adjusted by the student), the digital world has removed the divide between "personal and professional identities" (Thompson et al. 954). Students' (and employees') professionalism and fitness is no longer judged solely

5

Old but still visible postings on social networking sites may not put job candidates in the best light.

on their academic and on-the-job performance, but on their very public personal personas. Newspapers, blogs, and academic reports from the past five years are filled with stories of schools and employers who have begun accessing social networking profiles looking for any untoward information as a means of evaluation/investigation (Capriccioso; Epstein; Steinbach and Deavers; Vorster; Wilson; Read; Thomas; Bergstrom). New online services are dedicated to digging up digital dirt on prospective employees, with the promising of "automat[ing] candidate research across forty-one social networks" (Spokeo).

The blurring of the line between personal and professional identities is an important issue for any student or employee, but particularly so for those in professional fields wherein public perception of professional competence and appropriate separating from patients, clients, or students are vital. Though there is nothing inherently unethical about the use of social networking sites, publicly sharing unprofessional content (e.g. explicit or inappropriate comments/photos) or excessive personal information may be compromising for professionals. Educators and re-searchers from medical, law, education, and pharmacy schools have all expressed concern that professional students may not understand the consequences of their online activities, or the risk of their personal offline activities being made public online by others (Thompson et al.; Cain; Farnan et al.; Mangan).

Research and anecdotal evidence suggest that professional students either do not share educators' concerns or are not aware that their online lives could have any bearing on their professionalism. In a recent study at the University of Florida, only 37.5 percent (n=362) of medical students and residents had private (view-able only by designated friends) Facebook profiles. The same study found that, in a small sample of students with public profiles (n=10), 70 percent of the students had photographs of themselves with alcohol and 30 percent had pictures or videos that showed "drunkenness, overt sexuality, foul language and patient privacy vio-lations in non-US locations" (Thompson et al. 955–56). Students in the study also belonged to Facebook groups with highly unprofessional names; e.g. "I don't need sex cause grad school f**ks me every day," "Party of Important Male Physicians (PIMP)," "Physicians look for trophy wives in training" (Ferdig et al.). There is also evidence to suggest that current undergraduates (and future professional students) share the same lack of concern and awareness. In a separate study by the same researchers at the University of Florida, researchers analyzed Facebook profiles of three hundred elementary education majors. Of the students with public profiles, 75 percent listed their sexual orientation and 73 percent had personal photo al-bums available (Univ. of Florida). A 2005 study by researchers at Carnegie Mellon University (CMU), determined that less than 1 percent of CMU Facebook users (n=4,450; a mix of students and faculty) had changed their default privacy settings to limit the visibility of their profiles (Gross and Acquisti). An informal online survey by the Pacific *Index*,the student newspaper at Pacific University (Oregon), found that 33 percent of respondents believed they would never get in trouble for photos posted on Facebook, while 17 percent were "not going to worry about what people think of my personal life" ("Do You Post"). Comments made in a thread started by a prospective pharmacy student on an online message board confirm all of these findings:

> mrsengle: "Pharmacists are in such high demand, employers put up with a LOT. As long as you have a license, don't have a DUI or possessions charge, have a degree and a pulse, you shouldn't worry about them check-ing an old myspace [sic] page" ("Grad schools/employers").

YouTube and Beyond

Unprofessional content posted on Facebook is not the only area of online concern   10
for professional educators. Other venues for sharing personal (and/or unprofes-sional) material include blogs and video sharing sites such as YouTube. In one recent case, medical students posted a musical parody they had filmed on YouTube, which featured the students dancing in the anatomy lab, drinking "blood" (chocolate)

from plastic skulls, and lying in body bags. The video was subsequently removed from YouTube at the request of the dean of the medical school (Farnan et al.).

The medical students' YouTube video illustrates an important reason for addressing online professionalism with professional students: There are notable differences between generations regarding what is/is not humorous, acceptable, and appropriate. As one educator has observed, "[w]hat looks like plagiarism, slander, copyright infringement, and embarrassing public behavior is for many students just creative and social entertainment" (Workman). While many students are beginning to understand that their personal behavior is reflective on their professional identities (Young), some still have not made the connection, or even believe that what they are doing — and posting online — has the possibility of offending anyone.

Whether or not students believe that their online activities should have any relevance to their academic and professional lives, it is growing increasingly clear that students' online personalities will be at issue for schools, employers, and other professionals. There has been a call for lawyer's bar applications to include the "cyber equivalent" of a background check (Stellato), and in an unprecedented move, applicants who wished to work in President Barack Obama's administration were required to complete a background check that included the following requests:

- "Please list [. . .] any posts or comments on blogs or other websites you have authored, individually or with others. Please list all aliases or "handles" you have used to communicate on the Internet."

- "If you have ever sent an electronic communication, including but not limited to an email, text message or instant message, that could suggest a conflict of interest or be a possible source of embarrassment to you, your family, or the President-Elect if it were made public, please describe."

- "Please provide the URL address of any websites that feature you in either a personal or professional capacity (e.g., Facebook, MySpace, etc.)." (Obama-Biden Transition)

Conclusion

Professional students must understand the implications of their online activities and the importance of extending professionalism to their online lives. To convey this understanding, there should be comprehensive instruction provided for all professional students that addresses the issues of intellectual property, plagiarism, social networking, blogging, personal Web sites, e-mail etiquette, etc. Individual workshops do already exist (Mangan), but to be the most effective, this instruction should be either integrated into program curriculum or made a required elective, and must be closely tied to the relevant professional association's code of ethics/conduct.

"E-literacy" (incorporating information ethics and online behavior standards) should be treated as a necessary competency for students to achieve, much like any other required knowledge/skills they receive in the course of their programs. Above all else, e-literacy instruction must help students realize that their online actions are not segregated from their professional lives, that their offline lives can easily end up online, and that anything posted on the Internet will persist long after it is removed. The guiding question for professional students should be, "Would it be appropriate for my mother/employer/patient/client to see what I am about to post?" (Keenan). Because if they have a computer and an Internet connection, they probably will.

Currently, the default Facebook setting allows any users in a student's network (not just those designated as "Friends") to view all information in that student's profile. The default setting for posted photo albums is to be visible to *all* Facebook users.

WORKS CITED

Auer, Nicole J., and Ellen M. Krupar. "Mouse Click Plagiarism: The Role of Technology in Plagiarism and the Librarian's Role in Combating It." *Library Trends* 49.3 (2001). Print.

Bergstrom. Ida. "Facebook can ruin your life. And so can MySpace, Bebo . . ." *The Independent*, 10 February 2008. Web. 6 May 2008.

Bodi, Sonia. "Ethics and Information Technology: Some Principles to Guide Students." *The Journal of Academic Librarianship* 24.6 (1998): 459. Print.

Cain, Jeff. "Online Social Networking Issues Within Academia and Pharmacy Education." *American Journal of Pharmaceutical Education* 72.1 (1998). Print.

Capriccioso, R. 2006. "Facebook Face Off." *Inside Higher Ed*, 14 February 2006. Web. 10 January 2009.

"Do you post photos on your Facebook that could possibly get you in trouble?" Poll. *The Pacific Index*, 2008. Web. 6 May 2008.

Educause. 7 things you should know about Facebook II. *Educause Learning Initiative*; 2007. Web. 10 January 2009.

Epstein, D. 2003. "Cleaning Up Their Online Acts." *Inside Higher Ed*, 3 October 2003. Web. 10 January 2009.

Farnan, Jeanne M., John A.M. Paro, Jennifer Higa, Jay Edelson and Vineet M. Arora. "The YouTube Generation: Implications for Medical Professionalism." *Perspectives in Biology and Medicine* 51.4 (2008). Print.

Ferdig, Richard E., Kara Dawson, Erik W. Black, Nicole M. Paradise Black and Lindsay A. Thompson. "Medical students' and residents' use of online social networking tools: Implications for teaching professionalism in medical education." *First Monday* 13.9 (2008). Web. 12 October 2008.

Gardner, Stephanie F. 2006. "Preparing for the Nexters." *American Journal of Pharmaceutical Education* 70(4): Article 87. Print.

"Grad schools/employers and Facebook/Myspace" Online bulletin board. *City-Data.com*, posted 26 July 2007. Web. 6 May 2008.

Gross, Ralph, and Alessandro Acquisti. "Information Revelation and Privacy in Online Social Networks (the Facebook case) [Pre-proceedings version]." *ACM Workshop on Privacy in the Electronic Society* (WPES), 2005. Print.

Harris, Benjamin R. "Credit Where Credit is Due: Considering Ethics, *Ethos*, and Process in Library Instruction on Attribution." Education Libraries 28.1 (2005): 4. Print.

Keenan, T. P. "On the Internet, Things Never Go Away Completely," in *IFIP International Federation for Information Processing*, Vol. 262 (The Future of Identity in the Information Society).

Eds. Simone Fischer-Hubner, Penny Duquenoy, Albin Zuccato and Leonardo Marctucci. Boston: Springer, 2008. Print.

Mangan, Katherine. 2007. "Etiquette for the Bar." *The Chronicle of Higher Education*, 12 January 2007. Web. 5 December 2008.

Obama-Biden Transition Project. "Background Check Questionnaire." 2008. Web. 4 January 2009.

Read, Brock. "A MySpace Photo Costs a Student a Teaching Certificate." *The Chronicle of Higher Education,* 27 April 2007. Print.

Siemens, Jennifer C., and Steven W. Kopp. "Teaching Ethical Copyright Behavior: Assessing the Effects of a University-Sponsored Computing Ethics Program." *NASPA Journal* 43.4 (2006): 118. Print.

Spokeo Inc. Web. 2 November 2008. <http://www.spokeo.com/hr/>

Steinbach, Sheldon, and Lynn Deavers. "The Brave New World of MySpace and Facebook." *Inside Higher Ed*, 3 April 2007. Print.

Stellato, Jesse. "e-Ethics: Professional Responsibility of Law Students on the Internet." *Eagleionline*, 18 October 2007. Web. 5 January 2009.

Szabo, Attila, and Jean Underwood. "Cybercheats: Is Information and Communication Technology Fuelling Academic Dishonesty?" *Active Learning in Higher Education* 5.2 (2004): 180.

Thomas, Owen. "Bank Intern Busted by Facebook." *Your Privacy is an Illusion* (blog), 12 November 2007. Web. 6 May 2008.

Thompson, Lindsay A., Kara Dawson, Richard Ferdig, Erik W. Black, J. Boyer, Jade Coutts and Nicole Paradise Black. "The Intersection of Online Social Networking with Medical Professionalism." *Journal of General Internal Medicine* 23.7 (2008): 954. Web. 6 May 2008.

University of Florida College of Education. "UF Study Looks at Preservice Teachers' Facebook Entries." Web. 4 January 2009. <http://www.heinz.cmu.edu/~acquisti/papers/privacy-facebook-gross-acquisti.pdf>

Vorster, Gareth. "Online social networking sites could have a negative impact on your career progression, new research has found." *Personnel Today*, 4 February 2008. Web. 6 May 2008.

Wilson, Erin. 2008. "Facebook Professionalism and Privacy." Blog. *UNI Journalism*, 6 May 2008. Web. 24 November 2008. Web.

Workman, Thomas A. "The Real Impact of Virtual Worlds." *The Chronicle of Higher Education*, 19 September 2008. Web. 16 October 2008.

Young, Jeffrey R. "Educause Survey Shows Students Watch Their Privacy on Facebook." *The Chronicle of Higher Education*, 12 June 2008. Web. 13 June 2008.

Thinking and Writing about Social Networking Sites

QUESTIONS FOR DISCUSSION AND WRITING

1. Susan Greenfield's speech to the British House of Lords caused a firestorm of response. Why do you think many who heard audio or read a transcript of the speech were outraged?

2. Compare either DiSalvo's or Cagle's view on the effects of social networking to those of Greenfield.

3. What is Patrick White's thesis in "Facebook: Watching the Watchers"? Explain whether you agree or disagree with that thesis and why.

4. Contrast DiSalvo's claim about social networking to that of Thompson.

5. Choose one of the essays in this chapter and explain to what extent your own experience with social networking either supports or contradicts its claim.

6. What should undergraduate students — and even younger students — do now to protect themselves from the type of future problems that Gilman predicts?

7. What is your response to Gilman's statements that admissions officers and potential employers use social networking sites to make decisions about applicants?

8. What are some of the other dangers associated with social networking?

9. What changes in social networking do you foresee?

CHAPTER 14

What Is the Role of Sex and Violence in Popular Culture?

The ongoing controversy about explicit sex and violence in movies, television shows, rap music, and computer and video games does not seem likely to subside soon. Depictions of sex and violence become increasingly graphic and increasingly accessible each year. William F. Baker and George Dessart in their book *Down the Tube* (1998) write, "In its simplest terms, the business of television in this country is the buying and selling of eyeballs." The same might be said of the business of making movies or producing computer and video games and the success of rap music and rap music videos that openly celebrate violence and sexism, all of which reinforce the notion that if sex and violence sell, no shortage of entrepreneurs will be ready to cash in.

Are some forms of popular entertainment necessarily dangerous and immoral? How much are viewers affected by continued exposure to depictions of explicit sex and violence? Researchers have argued the point for years, but today a majority believe that long-term viewing does, in fact, alter the behavior of certain audiences. In recent years, what appear to be copycat crimes have followed the release of particularly violent films. Experts also debate the relative effects of fictional and real-life images: Which are more disturbing and potentially more corrupting — the graphic creations in movies or the daily reports of real-life horrors in the news? And do children recognize the difference?

Not surprisingly, even where agreement exists on the nature of the problem, there is disagreement about solutions. However strongly some critics feel about the dangers of exposure, they argue that the dangers of government censorship may, in the long run, be greater. But if government intervention is rejected, can other solutions — a rating system for television shows and music albums, a V-chip in the TV set allowing parents to block undesirable programs, respect by producers for the so-called family hour, and above all, closer monitoring by parents — guarantee that young people will be insulated from exposure to sex and violence in the media? Most Americans are not optimistic.

Of course, popular culture is not the only source of exposure. Movies, television, music, and games reflect the activities, tastes, fantasies, and prejudices of a larger society. Reducing the amount of sex and violence in the media is certainly easier than reforming a whole society. Still, questions remain: Why are some of the most popular forms of entertainment those with the highest body count and the most grisly depiction of carnage and suffering? To what extent can any reform in popular entertainment successfully address the problems of crime and immorality?

Does Watching Sex on Television Influence Teens' Sexual Activity?

REBECCA L. COLLINS ET AL.

BEFORE READING: How would you answer the question posed in the title of this essay?

The average American teenager watches three hours of television a day. Typical teen fare contains heavy doses of sexual content, ranging from touching, kissing, jokes, and innuendo to conversations about sexual activity and portrayals of intercourse. Sex is often presented as a casual activity without risk or consequences. Conventional wisdom holds that the messages young viewers absorb from television promote sexual activity in this group. Yet, despite the prevalence of this view, there has been little empirical study to date of how watching sex on television influences teenagers' sexual behavior.

Two recent studies led by RAND Health behavioral scientist Rebecca Collins examined the impact of TV sex on teenagers' sexual beliefs and activities. The results supported the view that watching shows with sexual content may influence teen sexual behavior, but also found that some viewing effects can be positive.

- Watching TV shows with sexual content apparently hastens the initiation of teen sexual activity.
- Sexual talk on TV has the same effect on teens as depictions of sex.

This Highlight summarizes RAND Health research reported in the following publications: Collins, Rebecca L., Marc N. Elliott, Sandra H. Berry, David E. Kanouse, Dale Kunkel, Sarah B. Hunter, and Angela Miu, "Watching Sex on Television Predicts Adolescent Initiation of Sexual Behavior," *Pediatrics*, Vol. 114, No. 3, September 2004; Collins, Rebecca L., Marc N. Elliott, Sandra H. Berry, David E. Kanouse, and Sarah B. Hunter, "Entertainment Television as a Healthy Sex Educator: The Impact of Condom-Efficacy Information in an Episode of *Friends*," *Pediatrics*, Vol. 112, No. 5, November 2003.

- Shows with content about contraception and pregnancy can help to educate teens about the risks and consequences of sex — and can also foster beneficial dialogue between teens and parents.

Exposure to TV Sex May Hasten the Initiation of Sexual Activity among Teens

Unplanned pregnancies and sexually transmitted diseases (STDs) are more common among youth who begin sexual activity at earlier ages. Thus, early initiation of intercourse is an important public health issue. It is widely believed that TV plays a role in hastening the initiation of sexual activity in teens. The first RAND study, funded by the National Institute of Child Health and Human Development, examined this issue. Analysts surveyed a national sample of households containing an adolescent from twelve to seventeen years old. A total of 1,762 adolescents were asked about their sexual experiences and also their television-viewing habits and, one year later, were surveyed again.

The researchers measured levels of exposure to three kinds of sexual content on television: (1) sexual behavior, such as kissing, intimate touching, and implied or depicted intercourse, (2) talk about sexual plans or desires or about sex that has occurred, and expert advice, and (3) talk about or behavior showing the risks of or the need for safety in regard to sexual activity: abstinence, waiting to have sex, portrayals mentioning or showing contraceptives, and portrayals related to consequences, such as AIDS, STDs, pregnancy, and abortion.

The results showed that heavy exposure to sexual content on television related   5
strongly to teens' initiation of intercourse or their progression to more advanced sexual activities (such as "making out" or oral sex) apart from intercourse in the following year. Youths who viewed the greatest amounts of sexual content were two times more likely than those who viewed the smallest amount to initiate sexual intercourse during the following year (see figure) or to progress to more-advanced levels of other sexual activity. In effect, youths who watched the most sexual content "acted older": a twelve-year-old at the highest levels of exposure behaved like a fourteen- or fifteen-year-old at the lowest levels.

The study also identified other factors that increased the likelihood that teens would initiate intercourse, including being older, having older friends, getting lower grades, engaging in rule-breaking such as skipping class, and sensation-seeking.

A different set of factors was found to decrease the likelihood of first intercourse. Many of these factors centered on parent characteristics, including having parents who monitored teens' activities, having parents who were more educated or who were clearly disapproving of teens' having sexual relations, and living with both parents. Other factors that reduced the likelihood of having sex included being more religious and feeling less depressed or anxious than other youths. Most of these characteristics were also related to how much sex teens saw on television; however, viewing sexual content on TV was related to advances in sexual behavior even after these other factors were taken into account.

Across all age groups, teens who saw the most sex on television were twice as likely to initiate intercourse within the next year as were those who saw the least.

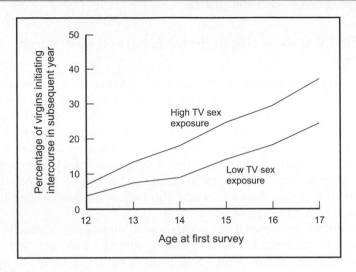

The results also showed that talk about sex on TV had virtually the same effect on teen behavior as depictions of sexual activity. This finding runs counter to the widespread belief that portrayals of action have a more powerful impact than talk.

The study found no strong connection between delays in sexual behavior and TV content that dealt with risks, except among African American youths, indicating that this group may be more strongly affected by portrayals of the negative consequences of sex. However, given the rarity of such programming, the study did not conclude that there is no effect on youth from other ethnic groups. Rather, it concluded that more-effective tests of such material are needed. One way to test such effects is to examine the impact of particular shows or episodes that deal with sexual risk. The second study, following, took this approach.

TV Can Also Inform Teens about Risks and Foster Communication with Parents

Can television play a more positive role in promoting adolescent sexual aware-   10
ness? The other study examined television's potential as a tool for educating teens about sexual risks and safe behavior. Funded by the Kaiser Family Foundation, it examined the effect on teenage viewers of a particular episode of a popular sitcom (*Friends*) that dealt with condom efficacy. During the episode, one of the main characters (Rachel) reveals that she is pregnant, even though she and another character (Ross) used a condom during intercourse. The show gave specific information about condom-efficacy rates, noting that they are successful 95% of the time.

At the time of the episode's first airing (2003), *Friends* was the most popular show on American television. According to the Nielsen Corporation, 1.67 million adolescents between the ages of twelve and seventeen saw this episode. The possibility of condom failure and the resulting consequence of pregnancy were thus vividly communicated to a very large adolescent audience, as was the message that condoms almost always work. Given the size of the audience, the episode's potential to influence large numbers of teens was enormous.

To gauge the episode's impact, RAND used information from its earlier study to identify adolescents who watch *Friends* regularly, and phoned them to ask about the *Friends* condom episode and assess its impact on their perceptions of condom use and failure. The results showed that

- the majority of teens (65 percent) whose viewing of the episode could be confirmed recalled the show's specific information about condom-efficacy rates.

- the majority of teen viewers continued to perceive condoms as somewhat or very effective, as in the earlier survey, though the episode caused about equal amounts of positive and negative change in that perception.

- as a result of watching the episode, many teens (10 percent of viewers) talked with a parent or another adult about the effectiveness of condoms.

- teens' reactions to the episode were changed by viewing or discussing the episode with an adult. These teens were more than twice as likely to recall information about condom efficacy.

The study did not find dramatic changes in teens' sexual knowledge or belief. However, it looked at only a single episode of television, and one that included the somewhat complicated message that condoms almost always work, but sometimes fail, and with huge consequences. The researchers concluded that entertainment shows that include portrayals of sexual risks and consequences can potentially have two beneficial effects on teen sexual awareness: They can teach accurate messages about sexual risks, and they can stimulate a conversation with adults that can reinforce those messages.

Implications

Taken together, the two studies suggest the need to reduce teens' exposure to sexual content on television and to explore greater use of entertainment shows to inform teens about risk. Reducing the amount of sexual talk and behavior on television, or the amount of time that adolescents are exposed to them, could appreciably delay the onset of sexual activity. At the same time, increasing the percentage of portrayals of sexual risk and safety relative to other sexual content might also inhibit early sexual activity, increase knowledge of sexual risks and how to be safe, and stimulate dialogue with parents.

Reducing teens' exposure to portrayals of sex on television poses challenges, however. An alternative approach that has worked with violent content may also work with sexual content: having parents view programs with their children and discuss their own beliefs regarding the behavior depicted. Doing so can reinforce the benefits of accurate risk information and positive messages and may help to limit the negative effects of sexual portrayals that do not contain risk information.   15

Sex and the Internet: Challenging the Myths

NANCY WILLARD

BEFORE READING: What "myths" might Willard be referring to regarding sex and the Internet?

In the past year or so, a vast amount of news coverage has addressed the issue of online sexual predators. The volume and tone of much of that coverage has succeeded in creating a false impression of what actually is going on. The degree of fear mongering is out of proportion to the actual dangers — and is creating significant concern.

Young people, the vast majority of whom generally are making safe choices online (but who also might make a mistake or get into a risky situation), perceive that adults are so fearful about Internet issues, it's unsafe to communicate with them about any online concerns. And yet, it's essential that we adults — "Digital Immigrants" — gain a better understanding of the risks our young "Digital Natives" are facing.

It is necessary to understand that the vast majority of young people who are sexually abused are abused by someone in their own family or community. It is probable that those local abusers now also are using the Internet and other technologies to groom and maintain control over those young people. For example, a teacher in my community was just arrested for sexual abuse of some students — and he was communicating with his victims electronically.

With respect to the concerns presented by online sexual predators, some significant misperceptions must be addressed so we can get to the point of providing accurate guidance to address the real concerns.

MYTH 1. Adult predators abound.

Let's start with the statement "One in five youth have been sexually solicited on-   5
line." (More recently, the statistic has been changed to "one in seven.") When people hear that statement, they assume that the "solicitation" has been made by a dangerous adult predator. That isn't what the studies revealed, however.

The figures above come from two studies, conducted by the Crimes Against Children Research Center: *Online Victimization: A Report on the Nation's Youth* and *Online Victimization of Youth: Five Years Later*. In those studies, teens were asked to report on "any situation where someone on the Internet attempted to get them to talk about sex when they did not want to or asked them unwanted sexual questions

---

Nancy Willard is the executive director of the Center for Safe and Responsible Internet Use and cyberbully.org. She has published two books on cyber threats and cyber bullying. This article appeared in *Education World*, April 4, 2007.

about themselves." Now, you tell me how often that happens in middle and high schools every day.

Sure enough, in the first study, 48 percent of the "sexual solicitors" were thought to be other teens, 20 percent were thought to between eighteen and twenty-five, and 4 percent were thought to be older than twenty-five, the remainder were unknown. In the second study, 43 percent were thought to be other teens, 30 percent were thought to be between 18 and 25, and 9 percent were thought to be over twenty-five. Only 4 percent were [known to be] adults over 25. Of course, the identified age is speculative because many people, teens and adults, lie about their age. More significantly, 75 percent of the young people in the first study and 66 percent in the second study indicated they were not upset or afraid.

Now hidden within that data are incidents that present significant concerns. Questions we must ask include: What behavior was actually measured? How does that behavior relate to predatory grooming by adults? Did the study provide evidence of predation or was the behavior primarily sexual harassment/ propositioning? And most significantly, how can we effectively prepare young people to avoid placing themselves in positions of possible risk online, detect when they are at risk, and respond effectively?

MYTH 2. The child is always the victim.

The following statement is from the FBI document *A Parent's Guide to Internet Safety*. "Understand, even if your child was a willing participant in any form of sexual exploitation, that he/she is not at fault and is the victim. The offender always bears the complete responsibility for his or her actions."

Legally, that is accurate, but it's also necessary to recognize that some teens are   10 engaging in behavior that appears to be intentional and directed at arranging sexual "hook-ups" with others. Take the example of Christina Long, a thirteen-year-old girl who accidentally was killed while having sex with a man she met online. (H. A. Valetk, "Teens and the Internet: Disturbing 'Camgirl' Sites Deserve a Closer Look," Findlaw Legal News and Commentary, January 23, 2003.). Reportedly, Christina was using the Internet to make arrangements to meet men for sex. Her user name was "2hot2handle" and her Web site with provocative pictures was entitled "Sexy me for you to see." Note also, that all the situations reported on *Dateline*'s "To Catch a Predator" involve arrangements for "hook-ups" with an apparently willing teen.

The adults who engage in this activity clearly are taking advantage of the young people and committing a crime. But to develop effective intervention strategies, it is necessary to recognize that, for some teens, engaging with online sexual predators is an intentional activity.

MYTH 3. Online predators deceive teens about their intentions or use personal contact information to track victims and abduct them.

Internet-Initiated Sex Crimes Against Minors: Implications for Prevention Based on Findings from a National Study, another study by the Crimes Against Children Research

Center of actual arrests where teens met in person with an online sexual predator, found that deception about sexual motivations was rare.

The offenders openly sexually solicited the victims. The victims knew they were interacting with men who were interested in them sexually. The victims went willingly with the offender and most met with the offender more than once. After the arrest, half the victims described themselves as in love with, or good friends with, the offender. Unfortunately, they did not ask further about the other half, who presumably met to have sex with men they were not good friends with.

(The victims, by the way, were between the ages of thirteen and fifteen; 75 percent were girls, 25 percent were boys. That does not mean that sixteen-year olds are not meeting with online predators, but if they meet willingly, there is no crime. It is important to note that predators do not appear to be targeting children. Young men who are exploring sexual orientation questions likely are more at risk.)

MYTH 4. We can teach teens about online sexual predators without using the word "sex" or discussing risky sexual encounters.

Two leading Internet safety education programs for middle school students, NetSmartz 15 and i-Safe do not use the word "sex"; do not discuss the sexual intentions of predators; do not address why these sexual relationships are risky. Why? Apparently because middle school students should not know anything about sex. (!)

The common guidance provided to teens about Internet concerns is, "Tell a trusted adult if you come across any information or anyone sends you a message that makes you feel scared or uncomfortable." My question is, if adults are too uncomfortable to talk about risky sex with teens, then how do we expect teens to be comfortable reporting to adults that they have received an unacceptable sexual message or that a person they are communicating with online has engaged them in discussions about sex?

In an earlier article, I discussed the issues related to online stranger literacy. A proactive strategy for addressing the very real concerns of online sexual predation is grounded in effective stranger literacy skills. But teens also must know how to prevent themselves from getting into risky situations, detect when someone unsafe is communicating with them, and respond effectively.

Unfortunately, those teens who intentionally seek out those types of online relationships are not likely to listen to important safety messages. To address that concern, we need to educate the counselors and others who are working with youth at risk — and encourage savvy teens to report to a trusted adult if they know that another teen is making bad choices online.

My new book, *Cyber-Safe Kids, Cyber-Savvy Teens: Helping Young People Learn to Use the Internet Safely and Responsibly*, has just been published. I have a new Web site for the book. The URL is http://cyber-safe-kids.com. On that Web site are free, reproducible booklets — one for parents and one for teens. In addition to guidance about stranger literacy, I provide the following guidance about online sexual predators.

Don't Hook-Up With Online Losers/Online Sexual Predators

Online sexual predators are older people, generally men, who are using the Internet   20
to form relationships with teens that will ultimately result in sexual activity. Online
sexual predators also might try to get teens to send them sexually explicit images.

Recognize Predator Techniques

Online predators use techniques called "grooming" to manipulate and seduce teens.
They look for teens who are vulnerable or who show signs they are interested in,
or have questions about, sex. They are very friendly, offer many compliments, and
might offer gifts or opportunities. They will try to become a teen's best online secret
"friend" and might interfere with a teen's relationships with others. When they have
established trust, they will start to talk about sexual issues. They want teens to think
of them as a "sexual mentor." Some teens are embarrassed to report those interactions because the predator has manipulated them into talking about or engaging
in sexual activities. Teens must understand that predators are master manipulators.

Don't Attract Online Losers

Don't do things online that could attract a predator. Don't post sexually provocative
images, join online groups to discuss sex, share intimate personal information, or
share information that makes you appear vulnerable.

What You Must Know

- Sexual predators are not lovers or mentors. They are abusers and losers.
- Meeting with a sexual predator could result in sexually transmitted disease,
  forced engagement in risky sex, abduction, and even murder.
- Help get rid of online losers. Save all evidence of any contact by a possible
  predator and report it to a trusted adult, the Web site or service, the police,
  and the agency in your country that handles these reports.

Friends don't let friends hook-up with online losers! If you think a friend has become involved with an online predator, encourage your friend to terminate contact
and report it. If your friend is not willing to report it, tell a trusted adult yourself.

Cultural Studies and "Forensic Noir"

THOMAS DOHERTY

BEFORE READING: Why are some of the most popular television shows graphic in their portrayal of the victims of crime? Do you personally like to watch the "forensic" dramas that focus on crime scene investigations and autopsies? Why, or why not?

"Apparently, people will watch forensics seven nights a week," shrugs David Caruso, star of the hit show *CSI: Miami,* a spinoff of the hit show *CSI: Crime Scene Investigation.* Shilling for the series on Fox's *Pat Sajak Weekend* earlier this year, he cited a CBS survey indicating that autopsy-driven entertainment is the hottest trend in American popular culture. Indeed, avid morgue attendants may also tally up the body count on HBO's *Autopsy,* NBC's *Law & Order: Criminal Intent,* Court TV's *Forensic Files,* A&E's *Cold Case Files,* and, in a more mordant vein, HBO's *Six Feet Under.* As the current season gets under way, CBS also gives us the scientific and forensically flavored *Cold Case* and *Navy NCIS.*

All over television, it seems rigor mortis has become de rigueur.

The purest form of the genre has been dubbed "forensic noir," and already its conventions have hardened like a plaster mold on a femur. A phalanx of experts bearing tweezers and baggies mills around yellow police tape and scours the site for bits of evidence. Back at headquarters, men and women in white lab coats collate data and conduct microscopic analysis on blood, drugs, wood, paint, insects, dirt, metal, and anything else known to the periodic table of elements. The recurring close-ups show investigators sniffing the tips of their white-gloved fingers. Could this be dextromethorphan? Blindsided by science, the culprit is nailed, the case closed.

With such tantalizing roadkill littering the media landscape, one might have expected circling scholars to have already descended for a hermeneutical feast. However, forensic noir is not yet one of the dominant intellectual categories of early twenty-first-century scholarship. In fact, even the last meeting of the ultrahip Society for Cinema and Media Studies failed to devote a panel to the topic (although wait till next year), and the genre is still too new a phenomenon to inspire the title of a university-press book (heads up, Ph.D. students).

Still, forensic noir has been anticipated and mapped by another kind of CSI team: 5
Cultural-Studies Intellectuals, a dauntless band of scholars committed to digging

---

Thomas Doherty is a professor of American studies at Brandeis University and author of *Hollywood's Censor: Joseph I. Breen and the Production Code Administration* (2007); *Pre-Code Hollywood: Sex, Immorality, and Insurrection in American Cinema, 1930–1934* (1999); *Projections of War: Hollywood, American Culture, and World War II* (1993); and *Teenagers & Teenpics: The Juvenilization of American Movies in the 1950s* (1988). This article appeared in the October 24, 2003, issue of *The Chronicle of Higher Education.*

into the symbolic meanings of the corporeal body. Their preliminary findings are likely to inform and guide future inquiries into a genre that has single-handedly revitalized both the flat-lined formula of the detective series and the flat ratings of prime-time network television.

Of course, the latest academic foray into criminal territory also partakes of a rich literary and cinematic tradition. From Victor Hugo to Mario Puzo, the sordid denizens of the underworld have been rehabilitated as merely refracted images of mainstream values, figures whose deviant ways illuminate the greater deviance of a soul-destroying culture: the Corleone family as the moral equivalents of the Rockefellers, only with better cuisine. Like the televisual CSI teams, however, the agents of cultural studies take the corpus delicti for their main text. The criminal himself is interesting only insofar as he produces the body.

Any examination of the body-as-text within the groves of academe begins with the high priest of high theory, Michel Foucault, the French philosopher who died in 1984 but who lives on as the animating footnote of the field. In his 1975 study *Discipline and Punish: The Birth of the Prison*, Foucault cast a cold eye on "the power and knowledge relations that invest human bodies and subjugate them by turning them into objects of knowledge." Brandishing the inevitable pun on the "body politic," he inspected bodies docile and tortured, under surveillance and under the knife. Soon humanities scholars who were once enchanted by the sensuous pulchritude of Renaissance nudes or the chiseled features of Hollywood stars embraced an altogether different body of scholarship. Now their patients were not just etherized but embalmed upon a table.

Foucault's timing was dead-on for stateside consumption.

Just as his work was being translated and taught in graduate seminars, a new criminal avatar was stalking the back roads of American culture, pushing aside drug dealers, gang bangers, and rogue CIA agents as the villain of choice for popular entertainment: the serial killer. Unlike the outlaw of the Old West or the gangster of the urban frontier, the serial killer struck at random, committed murder for no financial gain, and racked up a double-digit body count with absolutely no remorse. Yet, as a product of the mobility and anonymity of late twentieth-century life, he was a peculiarly American figure, cruising the two-lane blacktops of the prairie, picking up lone hitchhikers, and befriending truck-stop waitresses. No ordinary murderer, he seemed an almost supernatural creature of the night.

Although popular culture understood the new modus operandi immediately,   10 the flummoxed forces of law enforcement were slower on the uptake. A predator who crossed state lines and murdered for reasons of his own, the serial killer operated under the radar of traditional police practices. The cops turned to the statistics and science of national databanks, criminal profilers, and crime labs with the forensic expertise to link bodies to each other, and the killer to the bodies.

Using Foucault as a desk reference, an eclectic array of scholarship on pornography, horror, homicide, violent spectacle, and the delights of observing the same also looked anew at those bodies dead or alive. Linda Williams's pioneering *Hard Core: Power, Pleasure, and the "Frenzy of the Visible"* (University of California Press, 1989) and Carol J. Clover's *Men, Women, and Chain Saws: Gender in the Modern Horror*

Film (Princeton University Press, 1992) scoped out the scene early; more recent entries include Mark I. Seltzer's *Serial Killers: Death and Life in America's Wound Culture* (Routledge, 1998), Philip L. Simpson's *Psycho Paths: Tracking the Serial Killer Through Contemporary American Film and Fiction* (Southern Illinois University Press, 2000), and Joel Black's *The Reality Effect: Film Culture and the Graphic Imperative* (Routledge, 2002).

By common consent, the famous curtain opener to Foucault's *Discipline and Punish* — an excruciating, play-by-play account of an execution by torture in eighteenth-century France — laid out the preferred method for surgical exegesis. However, it was Williams, a professor of film studies and rhetoric at the University of California at Berkeley, who introduced the elastic term "body genre" into the conversation, detecting an impulse at once voyeuristic and scientific behind cinematic spectatorship. "The desire to see and know more about the human body," she noted, "underlies the very invention of cinema." Although Williams's own lens was focused mainly on gender and pornography, her outlook suggests why the naked exposure of human organs, gushing fluids, and bodily penetration — scenes that comprise what might be called the "money shots" of forensic noir — are so ubiquitous.

This energetic body work is a far better test kit for tracing the tropes of forensic noir than the criticism on what may seem to be the TV fare's parent genre, film noir. Any kinship between the two noirs is only skin-deep. A moody mesh of German expressionism and French existentialism, film noir languishes in a cloud of smoky atmospherics and moral ambiguities, a lush dream world that, for all its dark tone and mean streets, has proved extraordinarily popular, even beloved. To take a classic example: In Robert Siodmak's fluorescent version of Ernest Hemingway's *The Killers* (1946), the investigator is obsessed with the *why* of a mysterious murder, not the how or even the who, when he seeks the motive for a contract hit, and the reason the victim accepted his own execution with such stoic resignation. More a mutant offspring than a direct descendent, forensic noir retains the mystery and murder but rejects the hopeless surrender to the forces of fate that waft through film noir.

Besides, bio-labs and operating rooms require bright lighting, high-tech implements, and smoke-free conditions. Film noir is hard-boiled, resigned, and romantic; forensic noir is air-conditioned, tenacious, and scientific. Film noir is body heat; forensic noir is body stiff. Quoting the film critic André Bazin, Indiana University's James Naremore, in his elegant study *More Than Night: Film Noir and its Contexts* (University of California Press, 1998), reminds us that, for the French critics who first embraced Hollywood's "black" films — a generation woozy on Sartre, unfiltered Gitanes, and postwar angst — Humphrey Bogart was an existential icon because the alcoholic lines visible on his face revealed "the corpse on reprieve within all of us." The icon of forensic noir gets his philosophy from the *Physician's Desk Reference*, cuts into too many charcoal-filled lungs to think smoking is cool, and succumbs to existential angst only when a rookie cop contaminates the crime scene.

Similarly, though rooted in vintage police procedurals such as Jack Webb's just-the-facts-ma'am *Dragnet* (1951–59, 1967–70) and Quinn Martin's *The F.B.I.* (1965–74), and glimpsed in sanitized form in *Quincy* (1976–83), forensic noir can be readily   15 distinguished from its generic ancestors. It is marked by two obsessions: a superstitious faith in better detecting through chemistry and a ghoulish relish in the rituals of medical dissection. Unlike the hero of the classic police shows, the rule-breaking maverick who played hunches and infuriated the by-the-book captain, the forensic cop is a clinical practitioner of the scientific method, at home amid the sinks, slabs, and scalpels of the morgue. The *locus classicus* for the genre is the scene in *The Silence of the Lambs* (1991), when the FBI profiler Jack Crawford and the trainee Clarice Starling spread Vicks VapoRub under their nostrils to examine a decomposed corpse, the victim of a serial killer. On television, the model was *The X Files* (1993–2002), where another pair of FBI agents — he an excitable agent provocateur, she a level-headed pathologist — spent almost a decade probing and being probed by swarms of extraterrestrial species.

In addition to the usual comforts of serial narrative soothingly resolved in a fixed time frame, forensic noir provides a crash course in the genetic ingenuity of real-life crime fighting, a vocation that is increasingly a matter of fibers, microbes, and DNA. Whether at the FBI or on *CSI*, the emblematic clue is no longer the matchbook cover but saliva or semen, a telltale trace that cracks the case once the results come back from the lab. Significantly, though, the boundless faith in forensic experts is confined to matters after the fact: So resourceful during the crime-scene sweep, the new FBI-*CSI* team has little predictive ability. Quite literally, their skill is all postmortem.

However, once the body is bagged and tagged, forensic noir lives up to its name. Corpses on slabs appear as featured players while body parts and bone fragments serve as set design. The trademark gag shows the coroner digging into his work while munching a slice of pizza. The rookie agent chokes; the home audience smirks. In *The Reality Effect,* Black, a professor of comparative literature at the University of Georgia, finds it unsurprising that a mass-mediated audience awash in spectacles of virtual reality should seek a jolt of flesh-and-blood reality in a "return to art's primitive, ritual originals — to 'regress' from a sublimated aesthetic of ideas and contemplation to an aesthetic of cruelty and sensation."

Innovations in special-effects technology have heightened the impact of the anatomy lessons. CGI (computer-generated imagery) and grisly makeup mock-ups can now render the most grotesque eviscerations with stomach-churning verisimilitude. To enhance the mood, the dissections are accompanied by the buzz of a surgical saw cutting through bone and the whoosh of blood splattering onto a face mask. The camera then zooms in for a traveling shot through the corridors of a human orifice — ears, nose, mouth, you get the picture.

The fixation on the body of the victim represents a telling shift away from the former site of detective work, the mind of the murderer. As with university budget lines, the sure payoffs from the hard sciences have channeled investments away from the uncertain returns of the soft sciences. Preferring pathology to psychology, forensic detectives admit that human motives are beyond their ken.

Where once crime dramas confidently dragged out sociologists and psychologists to offer reassuring explanations for criminal deviance — think of the shrink in   20

By permission of Mike Luckovich and Creators Syndicate, Inc.

the coda to Alfred Hitchcock's *Psycho* (1960) — even liberal Hollywood has given up the quest for a Freudian magic bullet to help comprehend the killer. Unable either to prevent crime, or to understand the criminal, the heroes of forensic noir settle for matching up DNA. They seek closure more than justice; catching the killer is a bonus.

Another even darker cultural impulse may also account for the proliferation of forensic noir. "This knowledge and this mastery constitute what might be called the political technology of the body," declared the chief coroner himself in *Discipline and Punish*. The intrusions of a surveillance society find an apt metaphor in violations of the body conducted by curious technicians. In probing, prying, and cutting into the citizen's no-longer-private parts, the state asserts its ultimate power over the individual, a kind of unanswerable last tag.

How much more can viewers stomach? How much further can television test the limits of forensic noir? In London last year, a doctor conducted a public autopsy for the delectation of a crowd of paying spectators. In the United States, a television producer may already be pitching a high-concept show that will combine the current obsession with a more traditional fixation: *Celebrity Autopsy*.

Hollow Claims about Fantasy Violence

RICHARD RHODES

BEFORE READING: As you grow older, does violence in the media appeal to you more — or less? Can you account for your reactions?

The moral entrepreneurs are at it again, pounding the entertainment industry for advertising its Grand Guignolesque[1] confections to children. If exposure to this mock violence contributes to the development of violent behavior, then our political leadership is justified in its indignation at what the Federal Trade Commission has reported about the marketing of violent fare to children. Senators John McCain and Joseph Lieberman have been especially quick to fasten on the FTC report as they make an issue of violent offerings to children.

But is there really a link between entertainment and violent behavior?

The American Medical Association, the American Psychological Association, the American Academy of Pediatrics, and the National Institutes of Mental Health all say yes. They base their claims on social science research that has been sharply criticized and disputed within the social science profession, especially outside the United States. In fact, no direct, causal link between exposure to mock violence in the media and subsequent violent behavior has ever been demonstrated, and the few claims of modest correlation have been contradicted by other findings, sometimes in the same studies.

History alone should call such a link into question. Private violence has been declining in the West since the media-barren late Middle Ages, when homicide rates are estimated to have been ten times what they are in Western nations today. Historians attribute the decline to improving social controls over violence — police forces and common access to courts of law — and to a shift away from brutal physical punishment in child-rearing (a practice that still appears as a common factor in the background of violent criminals today).

The American Medical Association has based its endorsement of the media   5
violence theory in major part on the studies of Brandon Centerwall, a psychiatrist in Seattle. Dr. Centerwall compared the murder rates for whites in three countries from 1945 to 1974 with numbers for television set ownership. Until 1975, television broadcasting was banned in South Africa, and "white homicide rates remained

[1] Grand Guignol, a popular theater founded in Paris in 1897 to present graphic performances of crimes — EDS.

Richard Rhodes is the author of more than two dozen books, including *The Making of the Atomic Bomb* (1986), which won a Pulitzer Prize for nonfiction, and *Why They Kill: The Discoveries of a Maverick Criminologist* (1999). The *New York Times* printed this article on September 17, 2000.

stable" there, Dr. Centerwall found, while corresponding rates in Canada and the United States doubled after television was introduced.

A spectacular finding, but it is meaningless. As Franklin E. Zimring and Gordon Hawkins of the University of California at Berkeley subsequently pointed out, homicide rates in France, Germany, Italy, and Japan either failed to change with increasing television ownership in the same period or actually declined, and American homicide rates have more recently been sharply declining despite a proliferation of popular media outlets — not only movies and television, but also video games and the Internet.

Other social science that supposedly undergirds the theory, too, is marginal and problematic. Laboratory studies that expose children to selected incidents of televised mock violence and then assess changes in the children's behavior have sometimes found more "aggressive" behavior after the exposure — usually verbal, occasionally physical.

But sometimes the control group, shown incidents judged not to be violent, behaves more aggressively afterward than the test group; sometimes comedy produces the more aggressive behavior; and sometimes there's no change. The only obvious conclusion is that sitting and watching television stimulates subsequent physical activity. Any kid could tell you that.

As to those who claim that entertainment promotes violent behavior by desensitizing people to violence, the British scholar Martin Barker offers this critique: "Their claim is that the materials they judge to be harmful can only influence us by trying to make us be the same as them. So horrible things will make us horrible — not horrified. Terrifying things will make us terrifying — not terrified. To see something aggressive makes us feel aggressive — not aggressed against. This idea is so odd, it is hard to know where to begin in challenging it."

Even more influential on national policy has been a twenty-two year study by   10
two University of Michigan psychologists, Leonard D. Eron and L. Rowell Huesmann, of boys exposed to so-called violent media. The Telecommunications Act of 1996, which mandated the television V-chip, allowing parents to screen out unwanted programming, invoked these findings, asserting, "Studies have shown that children exposed to violent video programming at a young age have a higher tendency for violent and aggressive behavior later in life than children not so exposed."

Well, not exactly. Following 875 children in upstate New York from third grade through high school, the psychologists found a correlation between a preference for violent television at age eight and aggressiveness at age eighteen. The correlation — 0.31 — would mean television accounted for about 10 percent of the influences that led to this behavior. But the correlation only turned up in one of three measures of aggression: the assessment of students by their peers. It didn't show up in students' reports about themselves or in psychological testing. And for girls, there was no correlation at all.

Despite the lack of evidence, politicians can't resist blaming the media for violence. They can stake out the moral high ground confident that the First Amendment will protect them from having to actually write legislation that would be likely to alienate the entertainment industry. Some use the issue as a smokescreen to avoid having to confront gun control.

But violence isn't learned from mock violence. There is good evidence — causal evidence, not correlational — that it's learned in personal violent encounters, beginning with the brutalization of children by their parents or their peers.

The money spent on all the social science research I've described was diverted from the National Institute of Mental Health budget by reducing support for the construction of community mental health centers. To this day there is no standardized reporting system for emergency-room findings of physical child abuse. Violence is on the decline in America, but if we want to reduce it even further, protecting children from real violence in their real lives — not the pale shadow of mock violence — is the place to begin.

A Desensitized Society Drenched in Sleaze

JEFF JACOBY

BEFORE READING: What's the difference between the violence depicted in popular movies and described in the lyrics of some rap songs and the violence portrayed in *Macbeth* or a classic Greek play like *Oedipus Rex*?

I was seventeen years old when I first saw an X-rated movie. It was Thanksgiving in Washington, D.C. My college dorm had all but emptied out for the holiday weekend. With no classes, no tests, and nobody around, I decided to scratch an itch that had long been tormenting me.

I used to see these movies advertised in the old *Washington Star,* and — like any seventeen-year-old boy whose sex life is mostly theoretical — I burned with curiosity. I wondered what such films might be like, what awful, thrilling secrets they might expose.

And so that weekend I took myself to see one. Full of anticipation, nervous and embarrassed, I walked to the Casino Royale at 14th Street and New York Avenue. At the top of a long flight of stairs, a cashier sat behind a cage. "Five dollars," he demanded — steep for my budget, especially since a ticket to the movies in the late seventies usually cost $3.50. But I'd come this far and couldn't turn back. I paid, I entered, I watched.

For about twenty minutes. The movie, I still remember, was called *Cry for Cindy,* and what I saw on the screen I'd never seen — I'd never even imagined — before. A man and a woman, oral sex, extreme closeups. The sheer gynecological explicitness

---

Jeff Jacoby is a columnist for the *Boston Globe*, where this essay appeared on June 8, 1995.

of it jolted me. Was *this* the forbidden delight hinted at by those ads? This wasn't arousing, it was repellent. I was shocked. More than that: I was ashamed.

I literally couldn't take it. I bolted the theater and tumbled down the   5
steps. My heart was pounding and my face was burning. I felt dirty. Guilty. I was conscience-stricken.

All that — over a dirty movie.

Well, I was an innocent at seventeen. I was naive and inexperienced, shy with girls, the product of a parochial-school education and a strict upbringing. Explicit sex — in the movies, music, my social life — was foreign to me. Coming from such an environment, who *wouldn't* recoil from *Cry for Cindy* or feel repelled by what it put up on that screen?

But here's the rub: Dirty movies don't have that effect on me anymore. I don't make a practice of seeking out skin flicks or films with explicit nudity, but in the years since I was seventeen, I've certainly seen my share. Today another sex scene is just another sex scene. Not shocking, not appalling, nothing I feel ashamed to look at. Writhing bodies on the screen? Raunchy lyrics in a song? They may entertain me or they may bore me, but one thing they no longer do is make me blush.

I've become jaded. And if a decade and a half of being exposed to this stuff can leave *me* jaded — with my background, my religious schooling, my disciplined origins — what impact does it have on kids and young adults who have never been sheltered from anything? What impact does it have on a generation growing up amid dysfunctional families, broken-down schools, and a culture of values-free secularism?

If sex- and violence-drenched entertainment can desensitize me, it can desen-   10
sitize anyone. It can desensitize a whole society. It can drag us to the point where nothing is revolting. Where nothing makes us blush.

And what happens to an unblushing society? Why, everything. Central Park joggers get raped and beaten into comas. Sixth-graders sleep around. Los Angeles rioters burn down their neighborhood and murder dozens of their neighbors. The Menendez boys blow off their parents' heads. Lorena Bobbitt mutilates her husband in his sleep. "Artists" sell photographs of crucifixes dunked in urine. Prolife fanatics open fire on abortion clinics. Daytime TV fills up with deviants. The U.S. Naval Academy fills up with cheaters. The teen suicide rate goes through the roof.

And we get used to all of it. We don't blush.

The point isn't that moviegoers walk out of Oliver Stone's latest grotesquerie primed to kill. Or that Geto Boys' sociopathic lyrics ("Leavin' out her house, grabbed the bitch by her mouth / Drug her back in, slam her down on the couch. / Whipped out my knife, said, 'If you scream I'm cutting,' / Open her legs and . . .") cause rape. The point is that when blood and mayhem and sleazy sex drench our popular culture, we get accustomed to blood and mayhem and sleazy sex. We grow jaded. Depravity becomes more and more tolerable because less and less scandalizes us.

Of course, the entertainment industry accepts no responsibility for any of this. Time Warner and Hollywood indignantly reject the criticisms heaped on them in recent days. We don't cause society's ills, they say, we only reflect them. "If an artist wants to deal with violence or sexuality or images of darkness and horror," said film director Clive Barker, "those are legitimate subjects for artists."

They are, true. Artists have dealt with violence and sexuality and horror since time immemorial. But debauchery is not art. There is nothing ennobling about a two-hour paean to bloodlust. To suggest that Snoop Doggy Dogg's barbaric gang-rape fantasies somehow follow in the tradition of Sophocles' tragic drama, Chaucer's romantic poetry, or Solzhenitsyn's moral testimony is to suggest that there is no difference between meaning and meaninglessness. 15

For Hollywood and Time Warner, perhaps there no longer is. The question before the house is, what about the rest of us?

Gore for Sale

EVAN GAHR

BEFORE READING: Did you enjoy violent video games when you were younger? Can you explain why they did or did not appeal to you?

Fresh corpses litter the ground. Blood is everywhere. Victims moan and beg for mercy. Others scream for help.

This may sound like a horrific scene from the Littleton, Colorado, shooting. But players of the computer game Postal just call it fun. They assume the role of Postal Dude, who snaps one day and mows down everyone in sight. For added realism, as the Web site of the developer (Running with Scissors) proudly states: "Corpses stay where they fall for the duration of the game — no mysterious disappearing bodies." But they do not fall right away. First "watch your victims run around on fire."

If you have a perverse fascination with violence, it's no longer necessary to skulk around in search of underground entertainments. Just visit your neighborhood electronics store. At the Wiz on Manhattan's Upper East Side, the notorious game Grand Theft Auto is smack in the middle of a display rack behind the cashier. The game's story line: As either a "gansta" or "psycho bitch" you will be "running over innocent pedestrians, shooting cops, and evading the long arm of the law."

In another game, Duke Nukem (manufactured by GT Interactive), sex and violence combine. Determined to expel from Los Angeles the aliens who are kidnapping scantily clad women, Duke Nukem trolls the seedy quarters of the city and shoots anyone who gets in his way. He even kicks his victims' decapitated heads through goalposts to celebrate.

Evan Gahr is a journalist who has worked as the Washington correspondent for *Jewish World Review* and as an adjunct scholar at the Washington-based Center for Equal Opportunity. This article appeared in the *Wall Street Journal* on April 30, 1999.

In Doom, one of the most popular among violent video games and a favorite   5
of one of the Littleton murderers, the player wanders through a maze of rooms,
corridors, and halls killing everything in sight. Survive and you make it to the next
level. For lethal power you can choose among a pistol, shot gun, rocket launcher,
and chainsaw. The aliens and monsters don't go down easily. Bodily fluid spurts all
over the walls; aliens are left to lie in pools of blood, their limbs sometimes dangling
in the air.

The manufacturer of Doom, id Software, advises that you should "prepare for the
most intense mutant-laden, blood-spattered action ever. You don't just play Doom —
you live it." You certainly do.

A more advanced version of Doom, called Quake, is an "ultra-violent gore-
fest," as one online reviewer called it. Players wander through a maze and use every
weapon imaginable to slay aliens. (The nail gun is a big hit.) There's heightened realism because you can view any part of the game from an endless number of angles.
For example, it's possible to bounce a grenade off a wall to hit someone around the
corner. Lucky you.

What is going on here? Well, for one thing entrepreneurship. Violent computer
games are a small but influential part of the $6.2 billion video- and computer-game
market. They have proliferated in recent years and are now deeply embedded in
youth culture. They are played either on play stations (Nintendo or Sony), PCs, or
the Internet, where you battle it out with other players.

With each new release players are promised seemingly endless amounts of blood
and gore. The more people you kill and maim the better. It is an entire subculture
that uses 3D graphics, spectacular sound effects, and other computer-driven bells
and whistles to blur the distinction between reality and fantasy — and to celebrate
criminality. The game titles speak for themselves: Blood, Bedlam, Death Rally, and
Redneck Rampage.

The idea is not just to kill but to kill with glee. Last year, a new joy-stick system   10
promised: "You get better accuracy and control, but what are you going to do with
all the extra bodies? Be the first on your block to make your neighbors say, 'What's
that smell?'" Another manufacturer, Interplay Productions, celebrates "the sheer
ecstasy of crunching bones against their bumper" in its game Carmageddon. "Drive
whatever you want, wherever you want, and over whoever you want. You make the
rules. Your motto. Just kill, baby." And watch the blood spatter on the windshield.

Video-game violence is not new. As Eric Rozenman noted in a recent *Washington
Times* article, one of the earlier games, Death Race, caused quite a commotion in the
mid-1970s: "The game involved an automobile driver running down pedestrians.
The latter expired with unconvincing moans, the skilled motorists recording a tally
of crucifixes."

Even Space Invaders was considered too violent when it was released in the
late 1970s. But the games have become progressively more violent ever since — and
vivid. The most remarkable breakthrough came in 1992, when a first-person shooter
game called Wolfenstein 3-D hit the market.

Previously, players looked at the screen as if from above. With Wolfenstein 3-D,
however, you see the action from the on-screen character's point of view. You be-

come the character. The following year Doom was introduced. A deluge of first-person shooter games followed.

These caught the attention of Senator Joseph Lieberman (Democrat, Connecticut). He and Senator Herb Kohl (Democrat, Wisconsin) held hearings on the games in 1993. Prodded by the senators, the industry adopted a voluntary rating system. Yet the ratings are not even enforced by stores, and incredibly violent games are often rated suitable for kids. More important, parents don't seem to realize what their kids are playing.

Should they be concerned? What message, for example, does Grand Theft Auto send? Jayson Bernstein, spokesman for the manufacturer, American Softworks Corp., says, "It's just a game." Industry spokesmen also defend their products by contending that there are no studies that conclusively link computer games to violence.

Some academics, too, say the games get a bum rap. The real problem is — big surprise here — social injustice. Henry Jenkins, director of Comparative Media Studies at MIT, recently argued that the focus on video-game violence seems to be the most recent strategy of our culture to shift focus away from the obvious root causes of violence: urban conditions, poverty, and the ready availability of guns.

And so on. Luckily, for those who worry about a culture in which these games thrive, a small backlash is evident. In January, the city of Stanton, California, allowed a new arcade to open only after it promised not to use violent or sexually charged games. The Minnesota Legislature is considering banning the sale of violent games to children under eighteen. In Chicago, about fifty people recently demanded that Toys "Я" Us stop selling violent video games and toys. The protesters, from a partnership of several churches, held a mock funeral outside the store. The store ignored them. In the wake of Littleton, how will such protests play?

Like other refuse that litters the cultural landscape, these computer games didn't just magically appear one day. They have flourished in a cultural milieu in which most anything goes. These days, to paraphrase FDR, it sometimes seems that we have nothing left to stigmatize but stigma itself. When parents and community members try to fight such garbage, or even quarantine it, they are derided in certain quarters as intolerant zealots or enemies of the First Amendment.

But if twelve-year-olds wake up one day and discover they no longer have such easy access to Redneck Rampage, free speech will survive. And everyone else might even be a bit safer.

The Internet and Sex Industries:
Partners in Global Sexual Exploitation

DONNA M. HUGHES

BEFORE READING: Why are the Internet and sex industries such natural partners?

Industrialization and Globalization of Sexual Exploitation

The sexual exploitation of women and children and the trafficking of women for purposes of prostitution have existed for all of recorded history, but the escalation and "industrialization" of sexual exploitation are less than a few decades old. The sex industry, as defined in this article, is the collection of legal and illegal, single and multi-party operations that profit from the selling of women and children through trafficking, organized prostitution and/or pornography.[1]

The trafficking of women and girls has reached crisis proportions around the world. Each year, an estimated four million people, mostly women and girls, are trafficked throughout the world, and one million children are trafficked into local and international sex industries [1]. The selling of young women into sexual bondage has become one of the fastest growing international criminal enterprises, earning traffickers an estimated US$6 billion per year [2]. Recently, U.S. Secretary of State Madeline Albright met with fourteen women Foreign Ministers to draft a letter of concern about the increased trafficking of women [3] and First Lady Hilary Clinton has made public condemnations of this growing trade [4], [5].

Sexual exploitation, as defined in this article, refers to all practices by which a person achieves sexual gratification or financial gain through the abuse or exploitation of a woman or child by abrogating her human right to dignity, equality, autonomy, and physical and mental well-being. Around the world today, women and children are increasingly vulnerable to sexual exploitation when they are refugees or migrants and when they are suffering from the effects of poverty, racism, and caste systems. Women and children are compelled into sex industries by varying degrees of violence, ranging from prior victimization and lack of economic alternatives, to deception, debt bondage, and enslavement. Under these conditions, women and children are increasingly becoming commodities to be bought, sold, and consumed by organized crime rings, tourists, military personnel, and men seeking sexual entertainment or non-threatening marriage partners.

---

[1]Although there is sexual exploitation of men in gay pornography and prostitution, this paper will focus exclusively on the sexual exploitation of women and children.

Donna M. Hughes is Professor and Carlson Endowed Chair of the Women's Studies Program at the University of Rhode Island. She has completed research on the trafficking of women and girls for sexual exploitation in the United States, Russia, Ukraine, and Korea. The essay appeared in *Technology and Society Magazine* in Spring 2000.

Much of this article will focus on the United States, as this country is mainly responsible for the industrialization of prostitution and pornography, either in the U.S. or in prostitution centers spawned by demand from U.S. military personnel. The United States is also the main home of the Internet pornography industry. In the United States, the modern sex industry had its origins in the 1950s and 1960s, and has steadily expanded since then. Currently, it is in a steep growth phase, and is meeting with little effective resistance from communities and lawmakers. The growth and industrialization of the sex industry is based on *de jure* legalization through liberalization of laws regulating prostitution and pornography and *de facto* legalization through wide scale tolerance of men's sexual abuse and exploitation of women and children in organized forms.

Technology has given the sex industry new means of exploiting, marketing, and delivering women and children as commodities to male buyers. Usually when a new technology is introduced into a system of exploitation it enables those with power to intensify the harm and expand the exploitation. The growth and expansion of the sex industry is closely intertwined with new technology. In the early years it followed new technological innovations, later it assisted the public adoption of new technology, and recently, the success of technology is dependent on the sex industry. The Internet as a communications medium would exist without the sex industry, but the *Internet industry* would not be growing and expanding at its present rate without the sex industry. According to an exhibitor at the 1998 Adultdex, a trade show for the Internet sex industry, "The whole Internet is being driven by the adult industry. If all this [referring to products at a sex industry trade show] were made illegal tomorrow, the Internet would go back to being a bunch of scientists discussing geek stuff in email" [6].

The Internet industry does not like to admit how much it is being supported by the sex industry, but a few indicators are revealing.

- The sex industry is among the top five groups buying state-of-the-art computer equipment [7].

- Sex industry businesses were the first to buy and use expensive T3 phone lines that transmit compressed, high-resolution images [8].

- One of the largest Internet companies in the world, Digex, whose largest customer is Microsoft Corporation, has a sex industry site as its second largest customer [9].

- One of the Web site designers who works at a large sex industry Web site described his work as a "dream job" because any new technology was available for the asking [10].

- In 1998, US$1billion was spent online on "adult content," 69 percent of the total Internet content sales [11].

The Sex and Internet Industries: Partners in Growth and Development

In 1994, Netscape, with its multimedia capabilities, initiated a new and popular information transmission medium, the World Wide Web. From the beginning, those in the sex industry saw the potential of the Web, and the Internet industry encouraged the sex industry to use the Web. The first Web-based prostitution business, A Personal Touch Services, from Seattle, WA, U.S.A., appeared in late September, 1994 [12]. In late 1994, Brandy's Babes, a Phoenix, AZ, prostitution service also started advertising on the Web. *The Internet Business Journal* described this site as the most significant Internet marketing innovation of 1994 [13].

At the beginning of 1995, there were two hundred businesses on the World Wide Web selling "erotica services" and products [13]. By mid-1995, strip clubs set up advertising Web sites. They featured pornographic photos of strippers and women engaged in types of legal prostitution offered at that club, such as couch dancing, table dancing, shower shows, and dominatrix acts [14]. In August 1995, a search on Yahoo found 391 listings under "Business and Economy: Companies: Sex" for phone sex numbers, adult CD-ROMS, X-rated films, adult computer software, live videoconferencing, prostitution tours, escort services, and mail-order-bride agencies. A year later, in August 1996 there were 1,676 listings, a four fold increase in one year [15].

Mainstream publications from the sex industry quickly moved to the Web. *Playboy* made its debut in 1994. Its content on the Web is designed to appeal to a younger, wealthier audience, the majority of which (75 percent) do not subscribe to the print *Playboy* magazine [16]. In 1996, Playboy magazine's site was the eleventh most visited site on the Web [17]. In 1997, the site generated US$2 million in advertising revenue. Many of *Playboy*'s online advertisers are exclusive to the Web and do not buy advertising in the print publication [16]. In April 1996, when *Penthouse* went online, its Web site recorded the highest number of visits for publication sites on the Web [18].

Organized prostitution tours from the U.S. started appearing on the Web in Spring 1995. International travel and tourism are components of globalization. A type of tourism, engaged in almost exclusively by men, is prostitution tourism, whereby men from wealthy countries in North America, Europe, and Asia travel to well-known sex industry centers in order to buy women and children in prostitution. Alan J. Munn, from New York City, advertised group prostitution tours to the Dominican Republic and Nevada, U.S.A., on the Web in spring 1995. Calling himself PIMPS 'R' US, he offered four days and three night trips to a "wonderful setting" which includes "many female prostitutes." A tour guide on the trip provided "practical information about how to find and deal with prostitutes and how to arrange group orgies." . . . His tour packages also included instruction in html, so the men could use the tour as a tax deduction [19].

Advertisement for prostitution tours to Asian, European, and South American locations soon followed. "Tropical Paradise Vacations" to Central America and the Caribbean were advertised for "single men." An advertisement for Erotic Vacations to Costa Rica quoted a price, which included double occupancy rooms and intra-country flights, booked for two. Men were told that "Your companion [a euphemism for prostitute] will meet you at your hotel . . ." If the tourise choses [sic] a longer tour his "companion" was changed half way through the trip, so the man could buy two women on the longer prostitution tours [20]. In early 1998, Pakistani pimps were

10

advertising on the Web for "Pakistan Dating Services" in The Diamond Market in Lahore [21].

Individual men, upon returning from their prostitution tours and business trips, use Internet newsgroups, such as alt.sex.prostitution, to post information on where to go to buy women and girls in prostitution in hundreds of cities throughout the world. Their writings reveal cruel, racist, misogynist attitudes and treatment of the women and girls they bought on their trips. Numerous accounts by human rights groups have revealed that many women and girls are literally enslaved in the sex industry. The men's writings reveal that they know, accept, and exploit women and girls held in sexual slavery [22]. In writings on this newsgroup, establishments where women and girls are enslaved are recommended for men who perpetrate sadistic sexual violence [23].

Another global enterprise premised on men's search for compliant, non-threatening women is the mail-order bride business. Bride traffickers advertise their forms of sexual exploitation through catalogues on the Internet. For a fee they offer to assist men in finding a "loving and devoted" woman whose "views of relation-ships have not been ruined by unreasonable expectations." The women advertised on the Internet are "known to be pleasers and not competitors. They are feminine, NOT feminist." One of the first mail-order-bride catalogs on the Web, *Asian Bride Magazine*, appeared in mid-1995 [24]. Many of the international "introduction ser-vices," as the agencies often call themselves, specialize in women from certain re-gions of the world: Latin America, Southeast Asia, the former Soviet Union, and even Africa [25].

Internet technology enables Web pages to be quickly and easily updated; so mail-order-bride agents update their selection of women weekly. The Internet reaches a global audience faster and less expensively than any other media. One mail-order-bride agent explained why he preferred operating on the Internet, "So when the World Wide Web came along, I saw that it was a perfect venue for this kind of busi-ness. The paper catalogs were so expensive that the quality was usually very poor; but on the Web you can publish high-resolution full-color photos which can be browsed by everyone in the WORLD" [25].

One of the sources of many mail-order-brides for men in the U.S. is the Phil- 15 ippines. Each year, due to poverty and lack of employment opportunities, 19,000 women leave the Philippines, either as migrant laborers or mail-order-brides. Some mail-order-bride agents operating out of the U.S. include young teenage girls in their catalogues on their Web sites. One agent offering women and girls from the Philip-pines complained that the U.S. government "won't give a visa to a bride under age sixteen." In his catalog of potential brides there were nineteen girls under seventeen years of age; one named Hazel was thirteen; another, Eddy Mae was fourteen [26].

In March 1999, the United States Immigration and Naturalization Service (INS) reported that there were over 200 mail-order-bride agencies operating in the U.S. with the number rapidly increasingly. Each year, 4,000 to 6,000 women, mostly from the Philippines or the new independent states (NIS) of the former Soviet Union, are brought to the U.S. through mail-order-bride agents. The U.S. government is starting to do more investigation of bride agents out of concern that women from the bride trade are vulnerable to exploitation and violence [27].

In late spring 1995, live videoconferencing, a technology that enables live person-to-person video and audio transmission, was introduced to the Internet [28]. By late 1995 the new video technology was delivering strip shows and live sex shows to buyers over the Internet [29]. The electronic merger of pornography and prostitution had arrived. Either by keyboard or telephone the buyers could communicate and direct the sex shows taking place in another state, or even another country or continent. One of the first live videoconferencing sex industry sites was Virtual Dreams, running off the CTSNET server in San Diego, CA. The site advertised itself as follows: "Virtual Dreams uses cutting-edge technology to bring you the most beautiful girls in the world. Using our software and your computer, you can interact real time and one-on-one with the girl of your dreams. Ask her anything you wish. She is waiting to please you!" [30].

Most of the owners of sex industry sites with live-sex shows moved to the Internet from phone-sex operations [10]. One advantage they had was money for the capital investment. For example, the Internet Entertainment Group (IEG), owned by Seth Warshavsky who had a phone sex business, invested US$3 million in computers and communications equipment to start up his Web site.[2] In interviews, online live-sex show promoters claim that men talking to and buying women over the Internet is just a step up in the distanced interactivity of audio prostitution created by phone sex lines. They say they have an advantage in understanding how to create and market long distance sexual exploitation. In creating shows they say they think in terms of action and response, creating "free-floating, computer-facilitated, user-directed fantasy." . . . According to the Internet Entertainment Group, in 1997, the buyers for live strip shows are 90 percent male, 70 percent living in the United States, and 70 percent are between ages eighteen and forty.[3]

The Internet industry thrives on the sex industry and looks to it for innovation. Technicians from the Internet sex industry have developed new techniques to deliver high quality multimedia. In November 1996, Warshavsky of IEG announced a new video transmission technique called push video. This development made it possible to view streaming video without downloading and installing special software.

In 1997, entrepreneurs looking to the Web as a site of future investment were told by mainstream computer industry advisors to use sex industry sites as their guide. "If you haven't visited a pornography Web shop in a while, you should. It will show you the future of online commerce . . . Web pornographers are the most innovative entrepreneurs on the Internet" [31]. In May 1999, New York New Media Association, *The Industry Standard-The Newsmagazine of the Internet Economy* and Sun Microsystems sponsored a seminar entitled "The Frontier of Business and Tech-

20

---

[2] That amount includes twelve SGI servers, twelve Pentium-based video servers, two Oracle servers for credit card processing, two T3 connections and forty-eight PCs for point to point videoconferencing and long distance telephone billing [10].

[3] This data comes from credit card companies [10].

nology: What You Can Learn from the Online Sex Industry." Presenters talked about how "the online sex industry drives innovation," such as credit card transaction technology, methods for streaming multimedia content, and new business models [32].

The sex industry has developed many of the ways of doing business over the Internet. Privacy, security, and fast payment transactions are necessary elements for the sex industry to sell over the Internet. Men are usually secretive about their exploitation of women and children and one of the factors in the success of the online sex industry has been men's ability to download pornography or engage in online prostitution from the privacy of their homes or offices. The pimps of the sex industry also depend on men's impulse buying, so quick financial transactions are crucial for their profits. Sex industry businesses were on the leading edge of online payment schemes with credit cards. At the beginning of 1995, only a few sites were accepting credit card payments by e-mail. In early 1996, Warshavsky's Internet Entertainment Group introduced "ecommerce software," which provided buyers with fast, secure, online credit card transactions [33].

The Internet sex industry is also leading the way in Web database management. Many of the sex industry sites have tens of thousands of images and video clips, which need to be organized in multiple and easily accessible ways. Lapis Labs in Tuscon, Arizona, is an example. As of early 1998, Lapis Labs operated twenty-five sex industry Web sites which contained 150,000 images, 1,000 downloadable Quick Time videos and seven hundred RealVideo live videos, and received 15,000 to 30,000 buyers each day. The owners say, "If it's legal, we have it. There's some material that I personally find repulsive, but not everyone has the same tastes." This site has a sophisticated search engine that enables the buyer to search images and film clips by gender, sexual act, number of people in scene, race, and hair-color attributes that form the bases for popular racist and sexist stereotypes used in the sex industry. In interviews, the co-founder of Lapis Labs refuses to give his name, claiming he likes to be known "as a technology company rather than a sex company" [9].

The close connection between the sex industry and the Internet industry and the lack of regulation of the Internet has allowed many unethical practices to occur. For example, some of the most violent and degrading pornographic Web sites use techniques to keep the viewer trapped on that site. Some pornographic Web sites remove the standard navigation tool bar to make it difficult to leave a site. Others disable the browser commands, such as "back," "exit," or "close," that are needed to get off the Web site. Whenever the viewer clicks on one of these escape commands, another pornographic Web site opens on the screen, leading to an endless number of browser windows opening on the screen, with no way to close them. In some cases, the only way to end the trap is to shut down the computer, without closing applications, or following normal shutdown procedures. A sampling of thirty-five pornographic Web sites found that 34 percent were designed to make it difficult to leave [34]. Internet Service Providers have made no move to stop this type of unethical activity.

Over the past six years, the sex industry and the Internet industry have been linked in their expansion and development. Technology historians point out that the sex industry is often the first to adopt new technology and open up new areas, and eventually, mainstream businesses take over. Unfortunately, the sexual exploitation of women and children continues at the new expanded level and doesn't subside as the technology becomes mainstream and is adopted by mainstream commercial operations.

Sex Industry Revenue on the Internet

Although some portions of the sex industry are legal in some countries, the major-   25
ity of activities of buying and selling women and girls by traffickers, pimps, male buyers, and pornographers are illegal in most countries. Therefore, determining the actual revenue generated by the sex industry is difficult. It can be assumed that most figures refer only to the legal sector of the sex industry, the smallest portion, and don't include the money made illegally through the sale of women in illegal brothels, massage parlors, and the street, or the sale of illegal materials, such as child pornography. Internationally, it is estimated that the sex industry makes at least $20 billion a year [35]. In 1996 Americans spent more than US$9 billion on pornographic videos, peep shows, live sex shows, pornographic cable programs, pornographic magazines, and computer pornography. That amount is more than many other entertainment industries, such as film, music, and theater. To give some further context, US$9 billion, according to War on Want, is enough to provide debt relief for the world's twenty poorest countries [36].

Estimates of the number of sex industry sites and the amount of money being made on the Internet vary. Analysts do agree that a lot of money is being made and the rate of growth is exponential. According to David Schwartz, a phone sex business operator who switched to the online sex business, "The Internet is where the big money is right now" [6]. Sex industry sites on the Internet draw a lot of traffic and are highly profitable; established sex industry sites can expect to make from 50 to 80 percent profits [7].

In 1996, one report estimated that the Web had six hundred commercial pornography sites, which were expected to generate revenues of US$51.5 million [17]. Popular sex industry sites, such as the one run by Danni Ashe, a former stripper, sells pornographic videos, digital images, magazines, and video peep shows. In mid-1996 her site was visited 1.5 million times per day and was expected to bring in US$1.2 million in 1996 [17].

In 1997, an Internet magazine reported that there were ten thousand sex industry sites [37]. A Sacramento firm that handles online credit card transactions said that in 1997, the largest sex industry sites had revenues of US$1 million per month, while the smaller sites took in approximately US$10,000 per month [6], [38]. A midsize site that was accessed 50,000 times per day made approximately US$20,000 each month. According to Forrester Research, an Internet industry analyst, the sex industry made US$137 million on the Web in 1997 [7].

By early 1998, Internet industry analysts estimated that the sex industry revenue from the Internet alone was US$1 billion per year. Forrester Research reported that "We know of at least three sites doing more than US$100 million a year" [39].

ClubLove, one of Internet Entertainment Group's main Web sites, was visited more than seven million times per day in early 1998. At that time the "club" had approximately 600,000 members who paid the US$19.95 subscription fee [40].

In 1999, Datamonitor reported that "adult content" sales on the Internet, which   30 excludes revenues from the sales of merchandise or advertising, was nearly US$1 billion dollars, and comprised 69 percent of the total Internet content sales. Eighty-four percent of the content sales were from U.S.-based Web sites. This market research firm predicted that by 2003 the "adult content" sales would reach US$3.1 billion, half the anticipated revenue of online content sales [11].

Pornography has always been a high profit industry. In the early 1970s in the United States, the pornography industry generated revenues of approximately US$8–10 million per year. The combination of high profit and low enforcement of obscenity laws made this a logical place for organized crime activity. By 1977, the distribution of pornography in the United States was almost entirely controlled by organized crime. In the late 1970s the Federal Bureau of Investigation (FBI) reported that just a few individuals with direct ties to organized crime controlled almost all of the multi-million dollar pornography industry in the United States and its international distribution [41]. By the late nineties the U.S. sex industry was generating US$9 billion per year — a 100,000 percent increase over a twenty-five year period [36].

To what extent organized crime syndicates influence and control Internet technology or the sex industry on the Internet is not known. But organized crime's use of computer and communications technology to control the sex industry was revealed in October 1998, when United States Federal agents intervened in a plot to harm or kill six people who operated escort services in Las Vegas. Two "enforcers," slang for hired torturers or killers, and four members of the Gambino organized crime family were arrested. The crime group pressured a computer technician to hack into local telephone company switches and reroute calls from men seeking to buy women in prostitution to businesses that they controlled [42].

The enormous profits made by the sex industry on the Internet have attracted many budding entrepreneurs, unscrupulous operators, and probably organized crime syndicates. Intense competition has led many operators to attract buyers by supplying new material and more extreme images, such as bondage, torture, bestiality, and child pornography. Real women and children are used to create these images, leading to increased violence and exploitation of women and children as more and more degrading and violent images, videos, and live performances are marketed and sold.

Search Engines, Advertising, and the Sex Industry

Many Internet Service Providers (ISPs) and online services do not like to admit to the extent of the sex industry's importance in Internet commerce, but the large ISPs profit from the sex industry by carrying their sites and online services. Search engines and directories also take in considerable amounts of money from the sex industry as advertising revenue.

. . . Analyses of the searches on Web search engines show what subjects are   35
being sought on the Web. In 1995, a study of the searches on one Web search engine found that 47 percent of the eleven thousand most-repeated searches were for
pornography [43], [44].

Soon after the sex industry began to go online, its leaders recognized the promotional value of search engines. On December 19, 1994, The Shrimp Club, an
organization of men who live or travel in Southeast Asia, set up a Web site to give
men information on events, parties, and products that featured Asian women. As
part of their promotional strategy they ensured that their Web site was listed in Web
search engines. This aggressive marketing garnered them fifteen thousand accesses
to their Web site in the first week [13]. This priming of search engines was a strategy
that all sex industry businesses on the Internet would adopt. As sex industry businesses increasingly moved to the Web, they placed paid advertisements for their
sites with search engines and online services. Eventually, the success of a search
engine depended on accepting advertising from the sex industry, as the case of Snap
Online demonstrates.

In December 1997, partially in response to public complaints of the pervasive-
ness of the sex industry on the Internet and parents' concerns about children viewing sex industry sites or their advertising, CNET announced Snap Online, a Web
directory safe for children. The Snap search engine was advertised as having no
pornographic Web sites in its directory. In the press release, CNET said, "Snap Online does not accept any pornographic advertising, nor does it contain pornographic
listings in its directory of more than 100,000 hand-selected Web sites." Nine months
later, in August 1998, CNET announced that Snap would be including pornographic
Web sites in its directory, and admitted that pornographic sites could be found
through Snap for some time. Anyone searching for pornography on Snap would
automatically be rolled over to the search engines Infoseek and Inktomi, which
index pornography.

Snap's executive producer, Katharine English, defended the decision by saying,
"Our statistics show that 40 percent of our users are looking for this kind of material. This is a user-driven decision." The decision was rationalized by pointing out
that everyone else is doing it, so they had to also. Katharine English said, "If you
search for bestiality, you'll find it there. It's not like we're standing out." The lack
of profitability was due to loss of advertising revenue from the sex industry [45].
Pornographic advertising banners on search engines are the "cash cow," or certain
moneymakers, for the Web search engines and indexes. The owner of a Web site,
search engine, or Web directory is paid each time a viewer clicks on an advertisement on that page. Advertisers pay in the range of 12 cents to US$1 per click. The
Snap Online example demonstrates the reliance of Internet search engines on the
sex industry. Without the sex industry many services on the Web would close.

Globalization and the Commodification of Women and Children

Looking at the growth and profits of the sex industry, it is easy to overlook the
human cost. The profits of the sex industry are based on sexual exploitation, which
first has to be acted out on real women and girls. Sexual exploitation traumatizes

and scars women and girls for life [46]. Research on women in prostitution in San Francisco found that 82 percent had been physically assaulted and 68 percent had been raped while in prostitution. Sixty-eight percent suffered from post-traumatic stress disorder [47]. Similar research on women in prostitution from South Africa, Thailand, Turkey, the United States, and Zambia found that 73 percent had been physically assaulted and 62 percent raped while in prostitution and 67 percent suffered from post-traumatic stress disorder [48].

It is widely assumed that women and girls enjoy being in prostitution and making pornography, while research findings reveal that women and girls are often tricked and coerced into the sex industry. The United Nations estimates that there are 200 million people around the world forced to live as sexual or economic slaves [49]. Few women choose to be in the sex industry. If any choice is involved it is usually the last choice, when no other options are available. Each year hundreds of Ukrainian women are trafficked into the United States. Most of the women believe they will be employed as waitresses or nannies, only to be forced into the sex industry using debt bondage once they arrive. In a survey of 476 Ukrainian women, zero percent responded that a job in the sex industry was an "acceptable job abroad" [50]. In a research study from San Francisco, 88 percent of women in prostitution said they wanted to get out of prostitution, 73 percent said they needed job training, and 67 percent said they needed drug and alcohol treatment [51]. Internationally, 92 percent of women in prostitution report that they wanted to leave prostitution [48]. These findings reveal the harm done to women in the sex industry and their desire not to be in the sex industry.

Intensifying Harm

The expansion of the global sex industry, especially on the Internet, has intensified the harm to the victims, and normalized and globalized the victimization and exploitation. Two components of globalization, rapid development and deployment of information technology and the industrialized commodification of women and children, have become linked to expand and truly internationalize sexual exploitation. The lack of regulation of the Internet and prevailing uncritical views on the sex industry are contributing to the escalation of the global sexual exploitation of women and children through global advertising of prostitution tours and online marketing. The United States is the founder and leader of both of these industries, but their impact is felt profoundly all over the world, especially by women and children.

REFERENCES

1. R. Cook, "Clampdown on child sex tourism," *BBC News*, U.K., Apr. 4, 1998.

2. L. Shelley, Professor, American University, and Director, UN Institute for Transnational Organized Crime Studies, in Parliamentary Hearings, Russian State Duma, Oct. 9–10, 1997, Personal Communication with Kristen Hansen, CEELI attorney in Russia.

3. T. Deen, "Women Foreign Ministers seek end to human trafficking," Inter Press Service, Oct. 5, 1999.

4. "First Lady to fight prostitution," *AP Online*, Nov. 18, 1997.

5. M. Bjorgulfsdottir, "First Lady: End trafficking of women," Associated Press, Oct. 10, 1999.

6. C. Said, "Adultdex Trade Show: Sex sells on the Net," *San Francisco Chronicle*, Nov. 19, 1998.

7. "Surfing for sex," *The Guardian*, May 14, 1998.

8. "X-rated sites pace online industry," *Chicago Sun Times*, June, 24, 1997.

9. "Tucsonan does boffo business in 'adult' sites," *Arizona Daily Star*, Feb. 14, 1998.

10. F. Rose, "Sex sells — Young, ambitious Seth Warshavsky is the Bob Guccione of the 1990s," *Wired*, no. 5, Dec. 12, 1997.

11. E. Moore, "Adult content grabs lion's share of revenue," *Adult Video News Online*, May 26, 1999.

12. A. Bosley, "Escort Agency — A Personal Touch Services," Selling Sex in Cyberspace, *The Internet Business J.*, p. 4, Jan. 1995.

13. M. W. Strangelove, "Internet advertising review — The Internet has hormones," Selling Sex in Cyberspace, *The Internet Business J.*, p. 10, Jan. 1995.

14. Fantasy Show Bar, Summer 1995.

15. Yahoo, http://www.yahoo.com, Aug. 8, 1996.

16. R. Runett, "Hefner highlights Playboy transitions to TV, Web," Connections @ the digital edge, http://www.digitaledge.org/connections98/hefner.html, accessed Oct. 8, 1998.

17. J. Simons, "The Web's dirty secret; Sex sites make lots of money," *U.S. News & World Rep.*, Aug. 19, 1996.

18. Nielsen survey, as cited in *Wired* [Online] no. 5, Dec. 12, 1997.

19. A. J. Munn, "PIMPS 'R' US Goes to the Dominican Republic," *The World Sex Guide* Summer 1995 (updated Aug. 1995), World Wide Web http://www.panix.com/~zz/exDR.html

20. The Travel Connection, "A tropical paradise vacation is waiting for you!" World Wide Web http://www.travelxn.com/fer/fer2.htm (accessed Nov. 18, 1995).

21. S. Adeeb, "On-line prostitution condemned," *Pakistan News Service/Information Times Exclusive*, Feb. 1998.

22. D. M. Hughes, "Sex tours via the Internet," *Agenda: A Journal about Women and Gender* (South Africa), no. 28, pp. 71–76, 1996.

23. D. M. Hughes, *Pimps and Predators on the Internet-Globalizing the Sexual Exploitation of Women and Children.* Coalition Against Trafficking in Women, pp. 13–17, 1999.

24. *Asian Bride Magazine*, Summer 1995.

25. B. W. Toms, 1995, 1996. Santa Barbara International Center. World Wide Web http://www.rain.org/~sbintl/ourstory.html

26. World Class Services, http://www.Filipina.com/filipinas, 7 Nov. 1996.

27. L. H. Sun, "Mail order brides of the '90s are met via Internet and on 'Romance Tours,'" *Washington Post*, Mar. 8, 1999.

28. News Release: "White Pine and Cornell team up to bring real-time desktop videoconferencing to Internet users worldwide," [Online] http://www.wpine.com/press.htm, May 3, 1995.

29. *Wired* [Online], no. 5, Dec. 12, 1997.

30. Virtual Connections, Live Nude Video Teleconferencing, http://www.cts.com/~talon, accessed Oct. 29, 1995.

31. Taylor and Jerome, "Pornography as innovator," *PC Computing*, Feb. 1997.

32. "New York New Media Association Presents an Exclusive Panel," *PR Newswire*, May 26, 1999.

33. F. Rose, "Sex sells — Today's sex industry, tomorrow's mainstream," *Wired*, no. 5, Dec. 12, 1997.

34. The National Institute on Media and the Family, "Violence and sexually explicit Web sites hold surfer's hostage," *PRNewswire*, Sept. 1, 1998.

35. "Giving the customer what he wants . . . ," *The Economist*, Feb. 14, 1998.

36. "The land of the free," *The Guardian*, Nov. 26, 1997.

37. *Inter@ctive Week* survey results, "X-rated sites pace online industry," *Chicago Sun Times*, 24 June 1997.

38. C. Ochs, President, Valley Internet Services.

39. "Some cybersex companies weaving webs of deceit," *Seattle Post-Intelligencer*, Aug. 28, 1998.

40. "Wired for sex — A growing cyberporn empire in Seattle takes a new twist on an old trade," *Seattle Post-Intelligencer*, Apr. 27, 1998.

41. *Final Report of the Attorney General's Commission on Pornography.* Rutledge Hill Press, 1986, p. 293.

42. J. Markoff, "Indictment says mob is going high-tech, six men arrested in alleged Vegas computer scheme," *New York Times*, Oct. 17, 1998.

43. Study by Prof. Harold Thimbleby, Prof. of Computing Research, Middlesex Univ., U.K.

44. S. Connor, "Pornography most popular subject for Internet searches," *The Independent — London*, Sept. 13, 1995.

45. "Snap's G-rated sites adds XXX-rated searches," *Reuters*, Aug. 3, 1998.

46. D. M. Hughes and C. M. Roche, *Making the Harm Visible? The Global Sexual Exploitation of Women and Girls-Speaking Out and Providing Services*, The Coalition Against Trafficking in Women, 1999.

47. M. Farley and H. Barkan, "Prostitution, violence against women, and posttraumatic stress disorder," *Women and Health*, vol. 27, no. 3, pp. 37–49, 1998.

48. M. Farley, I. Barat, M. Kiremire, and U. Sezgin, "Prostitution in five countries: Violence and post-traumatic stress disorder," *Feminism & Psychology*, vol. 8, no. 4, pp. 405–426, 1998.

49. Director General of the United Nations Bureau, Vienna, *Associated Foreign Press*, Nov. 13, 1997.

50. International Organization for Migration, *Information Campaign Against Trafficking in Women from Ukraine, Research Report.* Int. Organization for Migration, July 1998.

51. N. Hotaling, "What happens to women in prostitution in the United States," in *Making the Harm Visible*, D. M. Hughes and C. M. Roche, Eds. The Coalition Against Trafficking in Women, 1999, pp. 239–251.

Thinking and Writing about Sex and Violence in Popular Culture

QUESTIONS FOR DISCUSSION AND WRITING

1. Explain to what extent the RAND studies accurately reflect the effect that watching sex on television has on teenagers, according to your observations of teenagers.

2. The RAND studies focus on televised sex. Are teenagers more influenced by the sex in movies than that on television? Why, or why not? What other influences determine a teen's level of sexual activity?

3. Some schools have organizations that stress abstinence. If you are aware of such organizations, how would you describe the attitude that other students have toward those who advocate abstinence?

4. Doherty makes this statement: "The fixation on the body of the victim represents a telling shift away from the former site of detective work, the mind of the murderer" (para. 19). Do you agree? Explain.

5. How would you explain the popularity of forensic shows such as *CSI: Crime Scene Investigation*?

6. What evidence do you find in these essays that establishes a cause-and-effect relationship between TV violence and actual crimes?

7. Rhodes provides evidence from several studies to prove that TV and movie violence does not influence the behavior of young viewers. How convincing is it?

8. Several authors contend that TV or movie violence is not to blame for the high crime rate among young people. What causes do you suggest?

9. You are probably familiar with some of the games Gahr describes or others like them. Do you agree with the manufacturers that they are harmless? How does Gahr answer objections about violations of "freedom of speech"?

10. Do you agree with Willard that the "child" or teenager is not always the victim when it comes to sex solicited on the Internet? Why, or why not?

CHAPTER 15

What Are the Ethical Costs of Putting Food on Our Tables?

All of us at times think of food as a guilty pleasure. Mostly it is when we give in to the temptation to eat foods that we know are not healthy or that will make it a littler harder to fit into our favorite pair of jeans. A generation or two ago, parents or grandparents who remembered the Great Depression told children to clean their plates and to be grateful to have so much good food while children in other countries had little or none. More recently, parents may feel a twinge of guilt as they buy their kids a Happy Meal for the third time in one week — but at least the kids like the toys.

Today there is increasing awareness that we have more to worry about than how many calories are in our French fries and how much sugar is in our sodas. We have to worry about whole generations of children who because of obesity are confronting what used to be considered adult diseases like coronary artery disease and adult-onset diabetes. We have to worry about our poor who live in "food deserts" far from supermarkets where healthy foods are available. We've been forced to think a bit more about where our food comes from and what life is like for the laborers who help move it from the fields to our tables. We would rather forget that many are illegal immigrants who are treated little better than slaves. We would rather forget, too, pictures we have seen of the way animals live on factory farms.

The realization is dawning upon more of us that our way of farming may not be sustainable, so in addition to worrying about what food is doing to our bodies we must confront what it is doing to our environment. A return to the small farm or a move to organic farming seems desirable, but can either — or both — meet the food needs of the masses?

There are ethical questions about our food and how it is produced that cannot be answered easily. The conversation, however, has begun.

Food Fight

MICHAEL POLLAN

BEFORE READING: What do you think Pollan might mean by the term "food fight" in his title?

It might sound odd to say this about something people deal with at least three times a day, but food in America has been more or less invisible, politically speaking, until very recently. At least until the early 1970s, when a bout of food price inflation and the appearance of books critical of industrial agriculture threatened to propel the subject to the top of the national agenda, Americans have not had to think very hard about where their food comes from, or what it is doing to the planet, their bodies, and their society.

The dream that the age-old "food problem" had been largely solved for most Americans was sustained by the tremendous postwar increases in the productivity of American farmers, made possible by cheap fossil fuel (the key ingredient in both chemical fertilizers and pesticides) and changes in agricultural policies that emphasized boosting yields of commodity crops (corn and soy especially) at any cost.

But although cheap food is good politics, it turns out there are significant costs — to the environment, to public health, to the public purse, even to the culture — and as these became impossible to ignore in recent years, food has come back into view. Beginning in 2001 with the publication of Eric Schlosser's *Fast Food Nation* and, the following year, Marion Nestle's *Food Politics*, the food journalism of the past decade has succeeded in making clear connections between the methods of industrial food production, agricultural policy, foodborne illness, childhood obesity, the decline of the family meal, and, notably, the decline of family income beginning in the 1970s.

Falling wages made fast food both cheap to produce and a welcome, if not indispensable, option for pinched and harried families. The picture of the food economy Schlosser painted resembles an upside-down version of the social compact sometimes referred to as "Fordism": Instead of paying workers well enough to allow them to buy things like cars, as Henry Ford proposed to do, companies like Wal-Mart and McDonald's pay their workers so poorly that they can afford only the cheap, low-quality food these companies sell.

Michael Pollan is an award-winning writer and journalist who focuses, according to his Web site, on "the places where nature and culture intersect: on our plates, in our farms and gardens, and in the built environment." He has written four *New York Times* bestsellers: *Food Rules: An Eater's Manual* (2010); *In Defense of Food: An Eater's Manifesto* (2008); *The Omnivore's Dilemma: A Natural History of Four Meals* (2006); and *The Botany of Desire: A Plant's-Eye View of the World* (2001). He has been a contributing writer to the *New York Times Magazine* since 1987 and in 2010 was named one of *Time*'s 100 most influential people. This article was published in the *New York Review of Books* on September 24, 2010.

Cheap food has become an indispensable pillar of the modern economy. But it is   5
no longer an invisible or uncontested one. One of the most interesting social movements to emerge in the past few years is the "food movement," or perhaps I should
say "movements," since it is unified as yet by little more than the recognition that
industrial food production is in need of reform because its social/environmental/
public health/animal welfare/gastronomic costs are too high.

It's a big, lumpy tent, and sometimes the various factions beneath it work at cross-
purposes. For example, activists working to strengthen federal food safety regulations
have recently run afoul of local-food advocates, who fear that the new regulation will
cripple the revival of small-farm agriculture. But there are indications that these
various voices may be coming together in something that looks more and more like
a coherent movement. Many in the animal welfare movement have come to see that
a smaller-scale, more humane animal agriculture is a goal worth fighting for. Stung
by charges of elitism, activists for sustainable farming are starting to take seriously
hunger and poverty.

Viewed from a middle distance, the food movement coalesces around the recognition that today's food and farming economy is "unsustainable" — that it can't
go on in its current form much longer without courting a breakdown of some kind,
whether it be environmental, economic, or both.

For some in the movement, the more urgent problem is environmental: The food
system consumes more fossil fuel energy than we can count on in the future and
emits more greenhouse gas than we can afford to emit. In the past few years, several
major environmental groups have come to appreciate that a diversified, sustainable
agriculture — which can sequester large amounts of carbon in the soil — holds the
potential not just to mitigate but actually to help solve environmental problems.

But perhaps the food movement's strongest claim on public attention today is
the fact that the American diet of highly processed food laced with added fats and
sugars is responsible for the epidemic of chronic diseases that threatens to bankrupt
the health care system. The health care crisis probably cannot be addressed without
addressing the catastrophe of the American diet, and that diet is the direct (even if
unintended) result of the way that our agriculture and food industries have been
organized.

Michelle Obama's recent foray into food politics suggests that the administration   10
has made these connections. Her new Let's Move campaign to combat childhood
obesity might at first blush seem fairly anodyne, but in announcing the initiative
in February, and in a surprisingly tough speech to the Grocery Manufacturers Association in March, the first lady has shifted the conversation about diet from the
industry's preferred ground of "personal responsibility" to a frank discussion of the
way food is produced and marketed.

"We need you not just to tweak around the edges," she told the assembled food
makers, "but to entirely rethink the products that you're offering, the information
that you provide about these products, and how you market those products to our
children."

So far, at least, Michelle Obama is the food movement's most important ally in
the administration, but there are signs of interest elsewhere. Under Commissioner

Margaret Hamburg, the Food and Drug Administration has cracked down on deceptive food marketing. Attorney General Eric Holder recently avowed the Justice Department's intention to pursue antitrust enforcement in agribusiness. At his side was Secretary of Agriculture Tom Vilsack, who launched a new initiative aimed at promoting local food systems as a way to both rebuild rural economies and improve access to healthy food.

Though Vilsack has so far left mostly undisturbed his department's traditional deference to industrial agriculture, the new tone in Washington and the appointment of a handful of respected reformers has elicited a somewhat defensive, if not panicky, reaction from agribusiness. The American Farm Bureau recently urged its members to go on the offensive against "food activists," and a trade association representing pesticide makers called CropLife America wrote to Michelle Obama suggesting that her organic garden had unfairly maligned chemical agriculture and encouraging her to use "crop protection technologies" — i.e., pesticides.

The first lady's response is not known; however, the president subsequently rewarded CropLife by appointing one of its executives to a high-level trade post. This and other industry-friendly appointments suggest that while the administration may be sympathetic to elements of the food movement's agenda, it isn't about to take on agribusiness, at least not directly, at least until it senses at its back a much larger constituency for reform.

One way to interpret Michelle Obama's deepening involvement in food issues 15
is as an effort to build such a constituency, and in this she may well succeed. It's a mistake to underestimate what a determined first lady can accomplish. Lady Bird Johnson's "highway beautification" campaign also seemed benign, but in the end it helped raise public consciousness about "the environment" (as it would soon come to be known). And while Michelle Obama has explicitly limited her efforts to exhortation ("We can't solve this problem by passing a bunch of laws in Washington," she told the Grocery Manufacturers, no doubt much to their relief), her work is already creating a climate in which just such a "bunch of laws" might flourish: a handful of state legislatures are considering levying new taxes on sugar in soft drinks, proposals considered hopelessly extreme less than a year ago.

The political ground is shifting, and the passage of health care reform may accelerate that movement. If health insurers can no longer keep people with chronic diseases out of their patient pools, it stands to reason that those companies will develop a keener interest in preventing those diseases. They will then discover that they have a large stake in things like soda taxes and in precisely which kinds of calories the farm bill is subsidizing.

It would be a mistake, however, to conclude that the food movement's agenda can be reduced to a set of laws, policies, and regulations, important as these may be. What is attracting so many people to the movement today is a much less conventional kind of politics, one that is about something more than food. The movement is also about community, identity, pleasure, and, most notably, about carving out a new social and economic space removed from the influence of big corporations and government.

One can get a taste of this social space simply by hanging around a farmers market. Farmers markets are thriving, and there is a lot more going on in them than the exchange of money for food. Someone is collecting signatures on a petition. Someone else is playing music. Children are everywhere, sampling fresh produce. Friends and acquaintances stop to chat. Someone buying food here may be acting not just as a consumer but also as a neighbor, a citizen, a parent, a cook.

Though seldom articulated as such, the attempt to redefine, or escape, the traditional role of consumer has become an important aspiration of the food movement. The modern marketplace would have us decide what to buy strictly on the basis of price and self-interest; the food movement proposes that we enlarge our understanding of both terms, suggesting that not just "good value" but also ethical and political values should inform buying decisions, and that we'll get more satisfaction from our eating when they do.

Put another way, the food movement has set out to foster new forms of civil 20 society. But instead of proposing that space as a counterweight to an overbearing state, as is usually the case, the food movement poses it against the dominance of corporations and their tendency to insinuate themselves into any aspect of our lives from which they can profit. As Wendell Berry writes, corporations "will grow, deliver, and cook your food for you and (just like your mother) beg you to eat it. That they do not yet offer to insert it, prechewed, into your mouth is only because they have found no profitable way to do so."

The corporatization of something as basic and intimate as eating is, for many of us today, a good place to draw the line.

Food is invisible no longer and, in light of the mounting costs we've incurred by ignoring it, it is likely to demand much more of our attention in the future. It is only a matter of time before politicians seize on the power of the food issue, which besides being increasingly urgent is also almost primal, in some sense proto-political.

For where do all politics begin if not in the high chair? — at that fateful moment when mother, or father, raises a spoonful of food to the lips of the baby who clamps shut her mouth, shakes her head no, and for the first time awakens to and asserts her sovereign power.

The Rich Get Richer, the Poor Go Hungry

SHARON ASTYK AND AARON NEWTON

BEFORE READING: When you were a child and you left food on your plate, you may have been told that children in other parts of the world were going hungry. Did you ever believe that? Do you believe it now? Why, or why not?

What is the most common cause of hunger in the world? Is it drought? Flood? Locusts? Crop diseases? Nope. Most hunger in the world has absolutely nothing to do with food shortages. Most people who go to bed hungry, both in rich and in poor countries, do so in places where markets are filled with food that they cannot have.

Despite this fact, much of the discourse about reforming our food system has focused on the necessity of raising yields. Though it is true that we might need more food in coming years, it is also true that the world produces more food calories than are needed to sustain its entire population. The problem is unequal access to food, land, and wealth, and any discussion must begin not from fantasies of massive yield increases, but from the truth that the hunger of the poor is in part a choice of the rich.

Inequity and politics, not food shortages, were at the root of almost all famines in the twentieth century. Brazil, for example, exported $20 billion worth of food in 2002, while millions of its people went hungry. During Ethiopian famines in the 1980s, the country also exported food. Many of even the poorest nations can feed themselves — or *could* in a society with fairer allocation of resources.

It can be hard to grasp the degree to which the Western lifestyle is implicated. We don't realize that when we buy imported shrimp or coffee we are often literally taking food from poor people. We don't realize that our economic system is doing harm; in fact, the system conspires to make it nearly impossible to figure out whether what we're doing is destructive or regenerative.

We have been assured that "a rising tide lifts all boats," that it is necessary for us to make rich people richer, because that will, in turn, enrich the poor. The consequences have been disastrous — for the planet and for the people whose food systems have been disrupted, who never had a chance to be lifted by any tide.   5

Journalist Jeremy Seabrook, in his book *The No-Nonsense Guide to World Poverty*, describes First World efforts to eliminate poverty and hunger this way:

> "It is now taken for granted that relief of poverty is the chief objective of all politicians, international institutions, donors and charities. This dedication is revealed most clearly in a determination to preserve [the poor]. Like

Sharon Astyk is a former academic, a writer, and a farmer in upstate New York. She is the author of *Depletion and Abundance: Life on the New Home Front* (2008), and coauthor, with Aaron Newton, of *A Nation of Farmers: Defeating the Food Crisis on American Soil* (2009). Newton is a sustainable systems land planner in North Carolina. This excerpt is from *A Nation of Farmers*.

all great historical monuments, there should be a Society for the Preservation of the Poor; only, since it is written into the very structures of the global economy, no special arrangements are required. There is not the remotest chance that poverty will be abolished, but every chance that the poor themselves might perish."

It is hard for many of us to recognize that the society we live in helps create poverty and insecurity, but it is true. Our economy is based on endless growth. We're told that if the rich get richer, it makes other people less poor. Think about it for a moment — about how crazy that is. Wouldn't it make much more sense to enrich the poor directly, to help them get land and access to resources?

Historically, rural people have been quite poor, but often, despite their poverty, could grow enough food to feed themselves. Over recent decades, however, industrial agriculture and widespread industrialization have moved large chunks of the human population into cities, promising more wealth. But rising food and energy prices (rising because of this move and this urban population's new demands for energy and meat) have left people unable to feed their families.

Multinational food companies have also worked their way into the food budgets of the poor. Faith D'Aluisio and Peter Menzel are the authors of *Hungry Planet*. "Few of the families we met [in the developing world] could afford a week's worth of a processed food item at one time," they report in the *Washington Post*, "so the global food companies make their wares more affordable by offering them in single-serving packets."

Around the world, industrial agriculture has consolidated land ownership into   10
the hands of smaller and smaller populations. Rich nations dumped cheap subsidized grain on poor nations. Local self-sufficiency was destroyed. Now, as the price of food has risen dramatically, those created dependencies on cheap grain, which doesn't exist anymore, mean that millions are in danger of starvation.

Real alleviation of poverty and hunger means reallocating the resources of our world into the hands of people who need them most. This is not only ethically the right thing to do, it is necessary. There is no hope that newly industrializing nations will help us fight climate change if it means a great inequity between their people and those of the United States. Russia, India, and China have all said so explicitly. The only alternative to the death of millions in a game of global chicken is for everyone to accept that the world cannot afford rich people — in any nation.

What is the best strategy of reallocation? One — that is, for those of us who live in nations where there is plenty of land and food so that we don't have to rely on the exports of poor nations — would be to enable the world's farmers to eat what they grow and to have sufficient land to feed themselves and their neighbors.

Most of the world's poorest people are urban slum dwellers (often displaced farmers) or land-poor farmers, agroecologist Peter Rosset notes. Both groups are increasing, in large degree because of economic policies that favor food for export and allow large quantities of land to be held in the hands of the richest.

"The expansion of agricultural production for export, controlled by wealthy elites who own the best lands, continually displaces the poor to ever more marginal areas for farming," Rosset writes in *Food Is Different*. "They are forced . . . to try to eke

out a living on desert margins and in rainforests. As they fall deeper into poverty . . .
they are often accused of contributing to environmental degradation."

In this system, poor people who depend on the land, and who best understand   15
the urgency of preserving it, are forced by necessity to degrade and destroy it — and
they, rather than we, are held responsible. But a large part of the responsibility rests
on the way we eat. This is an important point, because it acknowledges that there
are things that we in wealthy nations can do to enable poorer people to eat better —
or even to eat at all.

One way to do this is simply to grow our own food, to rely not on foods grown
thousands of miles away but on foods grown at local farms and gardens. We also
can concentrate on creating food sovereignty in poor nations. We can cut back on
global food trade, importing primarily high-value, fair-traded dry goods that take
little energy to transport, and place limits on food speculation, which drives up
prices so that multinational corporations can get richer at the expense of the poor.

Most of all, we can recognize that self-sufficiency is as urgent in the rich world as
in the poor. Globalization's demise is coming. The rising costs of transportation and
the trade deficit in the United States make it inevitable that we will increasingly be
looking to meet our basic needs locally.

When we grow our own food, or buy it directly from local farmers, we take
power away from multinationals. We make it harder for them to extract wealth and
the best land of other nations — and if they don't need that land, local farmers may
be able to use it for their own needs.

We also put power in the hands of our neighbors, many of whom are also victims of globalization. There are 49 million people in the United States who can't
consistently afford a basic nutritious diet. It turns out that the things that make us
poor — lack of education, lack of access to land and home, and the industrial economy — are precisely the things that make other people poor. By creating local food
systems, we can enrich our immediate neighbors as we stop impoverishing our distant ones.

The Organic Myth

DIANE BRADY

BEFORE READING: What reasons would some consumers give for not buying organic foods? What difficulties might there be in mass marketing organic foods?

Next time you're in the supermarket, stop and take a look at Stonyfield Farm yogurt. With its contented cow and green fields, the yellow container evokes a bucolic existence, telegraphing what we've come to expect from organic food: pure, pesticide-free, locally produced ingredients grown on a small family farm.

So it may come as a surprise that Stonyfield's organic farm is long gone. Its main facility is a state-of-the-art industrial plant just off the airport strip in Londonderry, New Hampshire, where it handles milk from other farms. And consider this: Sometime soon a portion of the milk used to make that organic yogurt may be taken from a chemical-free cow in New Zealand, powdered, and then shipped to the United States. True, Stonyfield still cleaves to its organic heritage. For Chairman and CEO Gary Hirshberg, though, shipping milk powder nine thousand miles across the planet is the price you pay to conquer the supermarket dairy aisle. "It would be great to get all of our food within a ten-mile radius of our house," he says. "But once you're in organic, you have to source globally."

Hirshberg's dilemma is that of the entire organic food business. Just as mainstream consumers are growing hungry for untainted food that also nourishes their social conscience, it is getting harder and harder to find organic ingredients. There simply aren't enough organic cows in the United States, never mind the organic grain to feed them, to go around. Nor are there sufficient organic strawberries, sugar, or apple pulp — some of the other ingredients that go into the world's best-selling organic yogurt.

Now companies from Wal-Mart to General Mills to Kellogg are wading into the organic game, attracted by fat margins that old-fashioned food purveyors can only dream of. What was once a cottage industry of family farms has become Big Business, with all that that implies, including pressure from Wall Street to scale up and boost profits. Hirshberg himself is under the gun because he has sold an 85 percent stake in Stonyfield to the French food giant Groupe Danone. To retain management control, he has to keep Stonyfield growing at double-digit rates. Yet faced with a supply crunch, he has drastically cut the percentage of organic products in his line. He also has scaled back annual sales growth, from almost 40 percent to 20 percent. "They're all mad at me," he says.

As food companies scramble to find enough organically grown ingredients, they   5
are inevitably forsaking the pastoral ethos that has defined the organic lifestyle. For

---

Diane Brady is senior editor for corporate coverage at *Business Week*. This article was that magazine's cover story on October 16, 2006.

some companies, it means keeping thousands of organic cows on industrial-scale feedlots. For others, the scarcity of organic ingredients means looking as far afield as China, Sierra Leone, and Brazil — places where standards may be hard to enforce, workers' wages and living conditions are a worry, and, say critics, increased farmland sometimes comes at a cost to the environment.

Everyone agrees on the basic definition of organic: food grown without the assistance of man-made chemicals. Four years ago, under pressure from critics fretting that the term "organic" was being misused, the U.S. Agriculture Dept. issued rules. To be certified as organic, companies must eschew most pesticides, hormones, antibiotics, synthetic fertilizers, bioengineering, and radiation. But for purists, the philosophy also requires farmers to treat their people and livestock with respect and, ideally, to sell small batches of what they produce locally so as to avoid burning fossil fuels to transport them. The USDA rules don't fully address these concerns.

Hence the organic paradox: The movement's adherents have succeeded beyond their wildest dreams, but success has imperiled their ideals. It simply isn't clear that organic food production can be replicated on a mass scale. For Hirshberg, who set out to "change the way Kraft, Monsanto, and everybody else does business," the movement is shedding its innocence. "Organic is growing up."

Certainly, life has changed since 1983, when Hirshberg teamed up with a back-to-the-land advocate named Samuel Kaymen to sell small batches of full-fat plain organic yogurt. Kaymen had founded Stonyfield Farm to feed his six kids and, as he puts it, "escape the dominant culture." Hirshberg, then twenty-nine, had been devoted to the environment for years, stung by memories of technicolor dyes streaming downriver from his father's New Hampshire shoe factories. He wrote a book on how to build water-pumping windmills and, between 1979 and 1983, ran the New Alchemy Institute, an alternative-living research center on Cape Cod. He was a believer.

But producing yogurt amid the rudimentary conditions of the original Stonyfield Farm was a recipe for nightmares, not nirvana. Meg, an organic farmer who married Hirshberg in 1986, remembers the farm as cold and crowded, with a road so perilous that suppliers often refused to come up. "I call it the bad old days," she says. Adds her mother, Doris Cadoux, who propped up the business for years: "Every time Gary would come to me for money, Meg would call to say 'Mama, don't do it.'"

Farming without insecticides, fertilizers, and other aids is tough. Laborers often 10 weed the fields by hand. Farmers control pests with everything from sticky flypaper to aphid-munching ladybugs. Manure and soil fertility must be carefully managed. Sick animals may take longer to get well without a quick hit of antibiotics, although they're likely to be healthier in the first place. Moreover, the yield per acre or per animal often goes down, at least initially. Estimates for the decline from switching to organic corn range up to 20 percent.

Organic farmers say they can ultimately exceed the yields of conventional rivals through smarter soil management. But some believe organic farming, if it is to stay true to its principles, would require vastly more land and resources than is currently being used. Asks Alex Avery, a research director at the Hudson Institute think tank: "How much Bambi habitat do you want to plow down?"

Impossible Standard

For a sense of why Big Business and organics often don't mix, it helps to visit Jack and Anne Lazor of Butterworks Farm. The duo have been producing organic yogurt in northeastern Vermont since 1975. Their forty-five milking cows are raised from birth and have names like Peaches and Moonlight. All of the food for the cows — and most of what the Lazors eat, too — comes from the farm, and Anne keeps their charges healthy with a mix of homeopathic medicines and nutritional supplements. Butterworks produces a tiny nine thousand quarts of yogurt a week, and no one can pressure them to make more. Says Jack: "I'd be happiest to sell everything within ten miles of here."

But the Lazors also embody an ideal that's almost impossible for other food producers to fulfill. For one thing, they have enough land to let their modest-sized herd graze for food. Many of the country's nine million-plus dairy cows (of which fewer than 150,000 are organic) are on farms that will never have access to that kind of pasture. After all, a cow can only walk so far when it has to come back to be milked two or three times a day.

Stewards of the Land

When consumers shell out premiums of 50 percent or more to buy organic, they are voting for the Butterworks ethic. They believe humans should be prudent custodians not only of their own health but also of the land and animals that share it. They prefer food produced through fair wages and family farms, not poor workers and agribusiness. They are responding to tales of caged chickens and confined cows that never touch a blade of grass; talk of men losing fertility and girls becoming women at age nine because of extra hormones in food. They read about pesticides seeping into the food supply and genetically modified crops creeping across the landscape.

For Big Food, consumers' love affair with everything organic has seemed like a gift from the gods. Food is generally a commoditized, sluggish business, especially in basic supermarket staples. Sales of organic groceries, on the other hand, have been surging by up to 20 percent in recent years. Organic milk is so profitable — with wholesale prices more than double that of conventional milk — that Lyle "Spud" Edwards of Westfield, Vermont, was able to halve his herd, to twenty-five cows, this summer and still make a living, despite a 15 percent drop in yields since switching to organic four years ago. "There's a lot more paperwork, but it's worth it," says Edwards, who supplies milk to Stonyfield. 15

The food industry got a boost four years ago when the USDA issued its organic standards. The "USDA Organic" label now appears on scores of products, from chicken breasts to breakfast cereal. And you know a tipping point is at hand when Wal-Mart Stores Inc. enters the game. The retailer pledged this year to become a center of affordable "organics for everyone" and has started by doubling its organic offerings at 374 stores nationwide. "Everyone wants a piece of the pie," says George L. Siemon, CEO of Organic Valley, the country's largest organic farm co-operative. "Kraft and Wal-Mart are part of the community now, and we have to get used to it."

The corporate giants have turned a fringe food category into a $14 billion business. They have brought wider distribution and marketing dollars. They have imposed better quality controls on a sector once associated with bug-infested, battered produce rotting in crates at hippie co-ops. Organic products now account for 2.5 percent of all grocery spending (if additive-free "natural" foods are included, the share jumps to about 10 percent). And demand could soar if prices come down.

But success has brought home the problems of trying to feed the masses in an industry where supplies can be volatile. Everyone from Wal-Mart to Costco Wholesale Corp. is feeling the pinch. Earlier this year, Earthbound Farm, a California producer of organic salads, fruit, and vegetables owned by Natural Selection Foods, cut off its sliced-apple product to Costco because supply dried up — even though Earthbound looked as far afield as New Zealand. "The concept of running out of apples is foreign to these people," says Earthbound cofounder Myra Goodman, whose company recalled bagged spinach in the wake of the recent *E. coli* outbreak. "When you're sourcing conventional produce, it's a matter of the best product at the best price."

Inconsistency is a hallmark of organic food. Variations in animal diet, local conditions, and preparation make food taste different from batch to batch. But that's anathema to a modern food giant. Heinz, for one, had a lot of trouble locating herbs and spices for its organic ketchup. "We're a global company that has to deliver consistent standards," says Kristen Clark, a group vice-president for marketing. The volatile supply also forced Heinz to put dried or fresh organic herbs in its organic Classico pasta sauce because it wasn't able to find the more convenient quick-frozen variety. Even Wal-Mart, master of the modern food supply chain, is humbled by the realities of going organic. As spokesperson Gail Lavielle says: "You can't negotiate prices in a market like that."

While Americans may love the idea of natural food, they have come to rely on 20 the perks of agribusiness. Since the widespread use of synthetic pesticides began, around the time of World War II, food producers have reaped remarkable gains. Apples stay red and juicy for weeks. The average harvested acre of farmland yields 200 percent more wheat than it did seventy years ago. Over the past two decades chickens have grown 25 percent bigger in less time and on less food. At the same time, the average cow produces 60 percent more milk, thanks to innovations in breeding, nutrition, and synthetic hormones.

It's also worth remembering how inexpensive food is these days. Americans shell out about 10 percent of their disposable income on food, about half what they spent in the first part of the twentieth century. Producing a budget-priced cornucopia of organic food won't be easy.

Exhibit A: Gary Hirshberg's quest for organic milk. Dairy producers estimate that demand for organic milk is at least twice the current available supply. To quench this thirst, the United States would have to more than double the number of organic cows — those that eat only organic food — to 280,000 over the next five years. That's a challenge, since the number of dairy farms has shrunk to 60,000, from 334,000 in 1980, according to the National Milk Producers Federation. And almost half the milk produced in the United States comes from farms with more than five hundred cows, something organic advocates rarely support.

What to do? If you're Hirshberg, you weigh the pros and cons of importing organic milk powder from New Zealand. Stonyfield already gets strawberries from China, apple puree from Turkey, blueberries from Canada, and bananas from Ecuador. It's the only way to keep the business growing. Besides, Hirshberg argues, supporting a family farmer in Madagascar or reducing chemical use in Costa Rica is just as important as doing the same at home.

Perhaps, but doing so risks a consumer backlash, especially when the organic food is from China. So far there is little evidence that crops from there are tainted or fraudulently labeled. Any food that bears the USDA Organic label has to be accredited by an independent certifier. But tests are few and far between. Moreover, many consumers don't trust food from a country that continues to manufacture DDT and tolerates fakes in other industries. Similar questions are being asked about much of the developing world. Ronnie Cummins, national director of the nonprofit Organic Consumers Association, claims organic farms may contribute to the destruction of the Amazon rain forest, although conventional farming remains the proven culprit.

Imported organics are a constant concern for food companies and supermarkets. It's certainly on Steve Pimentel's mind. "Someone is going to do something wrong," says Costco's assistant general merchandise manager. "We want to make sure it's not us." To avoid nasty surprises, Costco makes sure its own certifiers check that standards are met in China for the organic peanuts and produce it imports. Over at Stonyfield, Hirshberg's sister, Nancy, who is vice-president of natural resources, was so worried about buying strawberries in northeastern China that she ordered a social audit to check worker conditions. "If I didn't have to buy from there," she says, "I wouldn't." 25

For many companies, the preferred option is staying home and adopting the industrial scale of agribusiness. Naturally, giant factory farms make purists recoil. Is an organic label appropriate for eggs produced in sheds housing more than one hundred thousand hens that rarely see the light of day? Can a chicken that's debeaked or allowed minimal access to the outdoors be deemed organic? Would consumers be willing to pay twice as much for organic milk if they thought the cows producing it spent most of their outdoor lives in confined dirt lots?

Ethical Challenges?

Absolutely not, say critics such as Mark Kastel, director of the Organic Integrity Project at the Cornucopia Institute, an advocacy group promoting small family farms. "Organic consumers think they're supporting a different kind of ethic," says Kastel, who last spring released a high-profile report card labeling eleven producers as ethically challenged.

Kastel's report card included Horizon Organic Dairy, the number one organic milk brand in the United States, and Aurora Organic Dairy, which makes private-label products for the likes of Costco and Safeway Inc. Both dairies deny they are ethically challenged. But the two do operate massive corporate farms. Horizon has eight thousand cows in the Idaho desert. There, the animals consume such feed as corn, barley, hay, and soybeans, as well as some grass from pastureland. The company is currently reconfiguring its facility to allow more grazing opportunities. And none of this breaks USDA rules. The agency simply says animals must have "access to pasture." How much is not spelled out. "It doesn't say [livestock] have to be out there, happy and feeding, eighteen hours a day," says Barbara C. Robinson, who oversees the USDA's National Organic Program.

But what gets people like Kastel fuming is the fact that big dairy farms produce tons of pollution in the form of manure and methane, carbon dioxide, and nitrous oxide — gases blamed for warming the planet. Referring to Horizon's Idaho farm, he adds: "This area is in perpetual drought. You need to pump water constantly to grow pasture. That's not organic."

Aurora and Horizon argue their operations are true to the organic spirit and that   30 big farms help bring organic food to the masses. Joe E. Scalzo, president and CEO of Horizon's owner, WhiteWave, which is owned by Dean Foods Co., says: "You need the twelve-cow farms in Vermont — and the four thousand milking cows in Idaho." Adds Clark Driftmier, a spokesman for Aurora, which manages 8,400 dairy cows on two farms in Colorado and Texas: "We're in a contentious period with organics right now."

At the USDA, Robinson is grappling with the same imponderables. In her mind the controversy is more about scale than animal treatment. "The real issue is a fear of large corporations," she says. Robinson expects the USDA to tighten pasture rules in the coming months in hopes of moving closer to the spirit of the organic philosophy. "As programs go," she says, "this is just a toddler. New issues keep coming up."

Few people seem more hemmed in by the contradictions than Gary Hirshberg. Perhaps more than anyone, he has acted as the industry's philosopher king, lobbying governments, proselytizing consumers, helping farmers switch to organic, and giving 10 percent of profits to environmental causes. Yet he sold most of Stonyfield Farm to a $17 billion French corporation.

He did so partly to let his original investors cash out, partly to bring organic food to the masses. But inevitably, as Stonyfield has morphed from local outfit to national brand, some of the original tenets have fallen by the wayside. Once Danone bought a stake, Stonyfield founder Samuel Kaymen moved on. "I never felt comfortable with the scale or dealing with people so far away," he recalls, although he says Hirshberg has so far managed to uphold the company's original principles.

The hard part may be continuing to do so with Danone looking over his shoulder. Hirshberg retains board control but says his "autonomy and independence and employment are contingent on delivering minimum growth and profitability." Danone Chairman and CEO Franck Riboud expresses admiration for the man he considers to be Danone's organic guru, but adds: "Gary respects that I have to answer to shareholders."

The compromises that Hirshberg is willing to make say a lot about where the or-   35 ganic business is headed. "Our kids don't have time for us to sit on our high horses and say we're not going to do this because it's not ecologically perfect," says Hirshberg. "The only way to influence the powerful forces in this industry is to become a powerful force." And he's willing to do that, even if it means playing by a new set of rules.

The Climate Crisis at the End of Our Fork

ANNA LAPPÉ

BEFORE READING: How could what we eat affect global warming?

We could hear audible gasps from the two dozen New York state farmers gathered at the Glynwood Center on a cold December day in 2007 when NASA scientist Cynthia Rosenzweig, one of the world's leading experts on climate change and agriculture, explained the slide glowing on the screen in front of us.

The Glynwood Center, an education nonprofit and farm set on 225 acres in the Hudson Valley, had brought Rosenzweig to speak to area farmers about the possible impact of climate change on the region. Pointing to an arrow swooping south from New York, Rosenzweig said: "If we don't drastically reduce greenhouse gas emissions by 2080, farming in New York could feel like farming in Georgia.

"It was all projections before. It's not projections now — it's observational science," said Rosenzweig. We are already seeing major impacts of climate change on agriculture: droughts leading to crop loss and salinization of soils, flooding causing waterlogged soils, longer growing seasons leading to new and more pest pressures, and erratic weather shifting harvesting seasons, explained Rosenzweig.

When people think about climate change and food, many first think of the aspect of the equation that Rosenzweig focused on that day — the impact of climate change on farming. But when it comes to how the food system impacts global warming, most draw a blank.

Challenged to name the human factors that promote climate change, we typically picture industrial smokestacks or oil-thirsty planes and automobiles, not Pop-Tarts or pork chops. Yet the global system for producing and distributing food accounts for roughly *one-third* of the human-caused global warming effect. According to the United Nation's seminal report, *Livestock's Long Shadow*, the livestock sector alone is responsible for eighteen percent of the world's total global warming effect — more than the emissions produced by every plane, train, and steamer ship on the planet.[1]

Asked what we can do as individuals to help solve the climate change crisis, most of us could recite these eco-mantras from memory: Change our light bulbs! Drive less! Choose energy-efficient appliances! Asked what we can do as a nation, most of

5

Anna Lappé writes and speaks worldwide on sustainability, food politics, globalization, and social change. In 2002, she and her mother, Frances Moore Lappé, published *Hope's Edge: The Next Diet for a Small Planet* (2002), which celebrates movements to address the root causes of hunger and poverty. Her third book, *Eat the Sky* (2010), is about food, farming, and climate change. This essay appeared in *Food, Inc.: How Industrial Food Is Making Us Sicker, Fatter, and Poorer — and What You Can Do about It* (2009).

us would probably mention promoting renewable energy and ending our addiction to fossil fuels. Few among us would mention changing the way we produce our food or the dietary choices we make.

Unfortunately, the dominant storyline about climate change — its biggest drivers and the key solutions — diverts us from understanding how other sectors, particularly the food sector, are critical parts of the *problem*, but even more importantly can be vital strategies for *solutions*.

If the role of our food system in global warming comes as news to you, it's understandable. Many of us have gotten the bulk of our information about global warming from Al Gore's wake-up call *An Inconvenient Truth*, the 2006 Oscar-winning documentary that became the fourth-highest grossing nonfiction film in American history.[2] In addition to the record-breaking doc, Gore's train-the-trainer program, which coaches educators on sharing his slideshow, has further spread his central message about the threat posed by human-made climate change. But Gore's program offers little information about the connection between climate change and the food on your plate.

Mainstream newspapers in the United States haven't done a much better job of covering the topic. Researchers at Johns Hopkins University analyzed climate change coverage in sixteen leading U.S. newspapers from September 2005 through January 2008. Of the 4,582 articles published on climate change during that period, only 2.4 percent addressed the role of the food production system, and most of those only peripherally. In fact, just half of one percent of all climate change articles had "a substantial focus" on food and agriculture.[3] Internationally, the focus hasn't been much different. Until recently, much of the attention from the international climate change community and national coordinating bodies was also mostly focused on polluting industries and the burning of fossil fuels, not on the food sector.

This is finally starting to change. In the second half of 2008, writers from *O: The Oprah Magazine* to the *Los Angeles Times* started to cover the topic, increasing the public's awareness of the food and climate change connection. In September 2008, Dr. Rajendra Pachauri, the Indian economist serving his second term as chair of the United Nations Intergovernmental Panel on Climate Change, made a bold statement about the connection between our diet and global warming. Choosing to eat less meat, or eliminating meat entirely, is one of the most important personal choices we can make to address climate change, said Pachauri.[4] "In terms of immediacy of action and the feasibility of bringing about reductions in a short period of time, it clearly is the most attractive opportunity," said Pachauri. "Give up meat for one day [a week] initially, and decrease it from there."[5]

Why does our food system play such a significant role in the global warming effect? There are many reasons, including the emissions created by industrial farming processes, such as fertilizer production, and the carbon emissions produced by trucks, ships, and planes as they transport foods across nations and around the world. Among the main sources of the food system's impact on climate are land use changes, especially the expansion of palm oil production, and effects caused by contemporary agricultural practices, including the emissions produced by livestock.

10

The Land Use Connection

Let's look at land use first. A full 18 percent of the world's global warming effect is associated with "land use changes," mostly from the food system.[6] The biggest factors are the destruction of vital rainforests through burning and clearing and the elimination of wetlands and peat bogs to expand pasture for cattle, feed crops for livestock, and oil palm plantations, especially in a handful of countries, Brazil and Indonesia chief among them.[7]

What do Quaker Granola Bars and Girl Scout Cookies have to do with the climate crisis?[8] These processed foods — along with other popular products, including cosmetics, soaps, shampoo, even fabric softeners — share a common ingredient, one with enormous climate implications: palm oil.[9] As the taste for processed foods skyrockets, so does the demand for palm oil, production of which has more than doubled in the last decade.[10] Today, palm oil is the most widely traded vegetable oil in the world, with major growth in the world's top two importing countries, India and China.[11]

As oil palm plantations expand on rainforests and peat lands in Southeast Asia, the natural swamp forests that formerly filled those lands are cut down and drained, and the peat-filled soils release carbon dioxide and methane into the atmosphere. (Methane is a key greenhouse gas with twenty-three times the global warming impact of carbon dioxide.) In a recent study, researchers estimate that producing one ton of palm oil can create fifteen to seventy tons of carbon dioxide over a twenty-five year period.[12]

Three of the world's biggest agribusiness companies are major players in the palm oil market, which is concentrated in two countries — Malaysia and Indonesia — where in 2007, 43 percent and 44 percent of the world's total palm oil was produced, respectively.[13] Wilmar, an affiliate of the multinational giant Archer Daniels Midland, is the largest palm oil producer in the world;[14] soy behemoth Bunge is a major importer of palm oil into the United State (although at the moment it doesn't own or operate any of its own facilities);[15] and grain-trading Cargill owns palm plantations throughout Indonesia and Malaysia.[16] These three companies and others producing palm oil claim that guidelines from the Roundtable on Sustainable Palm Oil (RSPO), established in 2004 by industry and international non-profits, ensure sustainable production that minimizes the destruction of forest and peat bogs as well as deleterious effects on the global climate.[17]

However, some environmental and human rights groups argue that loopholes in the Roundtable's regulations still leave too much wiggle room. Says Greenpeace, "The existing standards developed by the RSPO will not prevent forest and peat land destruction, and a number of RSPO members are taking no steps to avoid the worst practices of the palm oil industry."[18]

We also know from new data that palm plantation expansion on peat land is not slowing. According to Dr. Susan Page from the University of Leicester, deforestation rates on peat lands have been increasing for twenty years, with one-quarter of all deforestation in Southeast Asia occurring on peat lands in 2005 alone.[19]

The other side of the land use story is deforestation driven by the increased production of livestock, expanding pasture lands and cropland for feed. In Latin America, for instance, nearly three-quarters of formerly forested land is now occupied by pastures; feed crops for livestock cover much of the remainder.[20] Globally, one-third of the world's arable land is dedicated to feed crop production.[21] Poorly managed pastures lead to overgrazing, compaction, and erosion, which release stored carbon into the atmosphere. With livestock now occupying 26 percent of the planet's ice-free land the impact of this poor land management is significant.[22]

Raising livestock in confinement and feeding them diets of grains and other feedstock — including animal waste by-products — is a relatively recent phenomenon. In the postwar period, intensification of animal production was seen as the path to productivity. As livestock were confined in high stocking densities often far from where their feed was grown, a highly inefficient and environmentally costly system was born.

As a British Government Panel on Sustainable Development said in 1997, "Farming methods in the last half century have changed rapidly as a result of policies which have favored food production at the expense of the conservation of biodiversity and the protection of the landscape."[23] Despite these environmental costs, confined animal feeding operations (CAFOs) spread in the 1960s and 1970s into Europe and Japan and what was then the Soviet Union. Today, CAFOs are becoming increasingly common in East Asia, Latin America, and West Asia.

As the largest U.S.-based multinational meat companies, including Tyson, Cargill, and Smithfield, set their sights overseas, the production of industrial meat globally is growing.[24] In addition, the increasing supply of meat in developing countries flooded with advertising for Western-style eating habits is leading to a potential doubling in demand for industrial livestock production, and therefore feed crops, from 1997–1999 to 2030.[25]

Although the shift from traditional ways of raising livestock to industrial-scale confinement operations is often defended in the name of "efficiency," it's a spurious claim. As a way of producing edible proteins, feedlot livestock production is inherently inefficient. While ruminants such as cattle naturally convert inedible-to-humans grasses into high-grade proteins, under industrial production, grain-fed cattle pass along to humans only a fraction of the protein they consume.[26] Debates about this conversion rate abound. The U.S. Department of Agriculture estimates that it takes seven pounds of grain to produce one pound of beef.[27] However, journalist Paul Roberts, author of *The End of Food*, argues that the true conversion rate is much higher. While feedlot cattle need at least ten pounds of feed to gain one pound of live weight, Roberts states, nearly two-thirds of this weight gain is for inedible parts, such as bones, other organs, and hide. The true conversion ratio, Roberts estimates, is twenty pounds of grain to produce a single pound of beef, 7.3 pounds for pigs, and 3.5 pounds for poultry.[28]

The inefficiency of turning to grain-fed livestock as a major component of the human diet is devastating in itself, especially in a world where nearly one billion people still go hungry. But now we know there is a climate cost as well. The more consolidation in the livestock industry — where small-scale farmers are pushed out

This industrial-scale feedlot in Colorado holds 120,000 cattle.

and replaced by large-scale confinement operations — the more land will be turned over to feed production. This production is dependent on fossil fuel–intensive farming, from synthesizing the human-made nitrogen fertilizer to using fossil fuel–based chemicals on feed crops. Each of these production steps cost in emissions contributing to the escalating greenhouse effect undermining our planet's ecological balance.

The Agriculture Connection

One reason we may have been slow to recognize the impact of the food system on climate change may be a certain "carbon bias." While carbon dioxide is the most abundant human-made greenhouse gas in the atmosphere, making up 77 percent of the total human-caused global warming effect, methane and nitrous oxide contribute nearly all the rest.[29] (Other greenhouse gases are also relevant to the global warming effect, but are currently present in much smaller quantities and have a less significant impact.)[30] Agriculture is responsible for most of the human-made methane and nitrous oxide in the atmosphere, which contribute 13.5 percent of total greenhouse gas emissions, primarily from animal waste mismanagement, fertilizer overuse, the natural effects of ruminant digestion, and to a small degree rice production.[31] (1.5 percent of total emissions come from methane produced during rice cultivation).[32]

Though livestock only contribute nine percent of carbon dioxide emissions, the sector is responsible for 37 percent of methane and 65 percent of nitrous oxide.[33] Here again, recent changes in agricultural practices are a significant factor.

25

For centuries, livestock have been a vital part of sustainable food systems, providing muscle for farm work and meat as a vital protein source. Historically, properly grazed livestock produced numerous benefits to the land: Hooves aerate soil, allowing more oxygen in the ground, which helps plant growth; their hoof action also presses grass seed into the earth, fostering plant growth, too; and, of course, their manure provides natural fertilizer. Indeed, new self-described "carbon farmers" are developing best management practices to manage cattle grazing to reduce compaction and overgrazing and, mimicking traditional grazing patterns, increasing carbon sequestration in the soil.[34]

But modern livestock production has steered away from these traditional practices toward the industrial-style production described above and to highly destructive overgrazing. In sustainable systems tapping nature's wisdom, there is no such thing as waste: Manure is part of a holistic cycle and serves to fertilize the same lands where the animals that produce it live. In CAFOs, there is simply too much waste to cycle back through the system. Instead, waste is stored in manure "lagoons," as they're euphemistically called. Without sufficient oxygenation, this waste emits methane and nitrous oxide gas. As a consequence of industrial livestock production, the United States scores at the top of the world for methane emissions from manure. Swine production is king in terms of methane emissions, responsible for half of the globe's total.[35]

The sheer numbers of livestock exacerbate the problem. In 1965, eight billion livestock animals were alive on the planet at any given moment; ten billion were slaughtered every year. Today, thanks in part to CAFOs that spur faster growth and shorter lifespan, twenty billion livestock animals are alive at any moment, while nearly fifty-five billion are slaughtered annually.[36]

Ruminants, such as cattle, buffalo, sheep, and goats, are among the main agricultural sources of methane. They can't help it; it's in their nature. Ruminants digest through microbial, or enteric, fermentation, which produces methane that is then released by the animals, mainly through belching. While this process enables ruminants to digest fibrous grasses that we humans can't convert into digestible form, it also contributes to livestock's climate change impact. (Enteric fermentation accounts for 25 percent of the total emissions from the livestock sector; land use changes account for another 35.4 percent; manure accounts for 30.5 percent.)[37]

In addition to the ruminants' digestive process, emissions from livestock can be traced back to the production of the crops they consume. Globally, 33 percent of the world's cereal harvest and 90 percent of the world's soy harvest are now being raised for animal feed.[38] Feed crop farmers are heavily dependent on fossil fuels, used to power the on-farm machinery as well as used in the production of the petroleum-based chemicals to protect against pests, stave off weeds, and foster soil fertility on large-scale monoculture fields. In addition, these crops use up immense quantities of fertilizer. In the United States and Canada, half of all synthetic fertilizer is used for feed crops.[39] In the United Kingdom, the total is nearly 70 percent.[40] To produce this fertilizer requires tons of natural gas; on average 1.5 tons of oil equivalents are used up to make one ton of fertilizer.[41] Yet in the United States, only about half of the nitrogen fertilizer applied to corn is even used by the crop.[42] This needless waste is all the more alarming because nitrogen fertilizer contributes roughly three-quarters of the country's nitrous oxide emissions.

Erosion and deterioration of soils on industrial farms is another factor in the food   30 sector's global warming toll. As industrial farms diminish natural soil fertility and disturb soil through tillage, soil carbon is released into the atmosphere.[43] Because industrialized agriculture also relies on huge amounts of water for irrigation, these farms will be more vulnerable as climate change increases drought frequency and intensity and decreases water availability. Globally, 70 percent of the world's available fresh water is being diverted to irrigation-intensive agriculture.[44]

The Waste and Transportation Connection

The sources of food system emissions on which we've focused so far — including land use changes and agricultural production — are responsible for nearly one-third of the total human-made global warming effect. That's already quite a lot, but other sectors include emissions from the food chain, including transportation, waste, and manufacturing.

For example, 3.6 percent of global greenhouse gas emissions come from waste, including landfills, wastewater, and other waste.[45] The food production system contributes its share to this total. After all, where does most of our uneaten food and food ready for harvest that never even makes it to our plates end up? Landfills. Solid waste, including food scraps, produces greenhouse gas emissions from anaerobic decomposition, which produces methane, and from carbon dioxide as a by-product of incineration and waste transportation.[46]

An additional 13.1 percent of the emissions that contribute to the global warming effect come from transportation, toting everything from people to pork chops.[47] The factory farming industry, in particular, demands energy-intensive shipping. CAFOs, for example, transport feed and live animals to feedlots and then to slaughter. Then the meat must be shipped to retail distribution centers and to the stores where it is sold to us consumers.

Americans, in particular, import and export a lot of meat. In 2007, the United States exported 1.4 billion pounds of beef and veal (5.4 percent of our total production of beef)[48] and imported 3.1 billion pounds of the same.[49] One could argue that a lot of that transport is unnecessary from a consumer point of view and damaging from an environmental point of view.

Globally, international trade in meat is rapidly accelerating. As recently as 1995,   35 Brazil was exporting less than half-a-million dollars' worth of beef. A little more than a decade later, the Brazilian Beef Industry and Exporters Association estimates the value of beef exports could reach $5.2 billion and expects revenues of $15 billion from beef exports by 2013.[50]

All of these billions of pounds of meat being shipped around the world add significantly to the carbon emissions from transportation. So do the Chilean grapes shipped to California, the Australian dairy destined for Japan, or the Twinkies toted across the country — all the meat and dairy, drinks, and processed foods shipped worldwide in today's globalized food market.

The Organic Solution

The globalized and industrialized food system has not only negative health consequences — think of all those Twinkies, that factory-farmed meat, and that chemically
raised produce — but a climate change toll as well. But the news is not all bad. Once
we gaze directly at the connection between food, farming, and global warming, we
see plenty of cause for hope.

First, unlike many other climate change conundrums, we already know many
of the steps we can take now to reduce carbon emissions from the food sector. For
instance, we know that compared with industrial farms, small-scale organic and sustainable farms can significantly reduce the sector's emissions. Small-scale sustainable
agriculture relies on people power, not heavy machinery, and depends on working
with biological methods, not human-made chemicals, to increase soil fertility and
handle pests. As a result, small-scale sustainable farms use much fewer fossil fuels
and have been found to emit between one-half and two-thirds less carbon dioxide
for every acre of production.[51]

We also are just beginning to see results from long-term studies showing how organic farms create healthy soil, which has greater capacity to store carbon, creating
those all-important "carbon sinks."[52] By one estimate, converting 10,000 medium
sized farms to organic would store as much carbon in the soil as we would save in
emissions if we took one million cars off the road.[53]

We're closer than ever to global consensus about the direction in which we need   40
to head. In April 2008, a report on agriculture initiated by the World Bank, in partnership with the United Nations and representatives from the private sector, NGOs,
and scientific institutions from around the world, declared that diverse, small-holder
sustainable agriculture can play a vital role in reducing the environmental impacts
of the agriculture sector.

The result of four years of work by hundreds of scientists and reviewers,[54] the
International Assessment of Agricultural Science and Technology for Development
(IAASTD) calls for supporting agroecological systems; enhancing agricultural biodiversity; promoting small-scale farms; and encouraging the sustainable management
of livestock, forest, and fisheries, as well as supporting "biological substitutes for
agrochemicals" and "reducing the dependency of the agricultural sector on fossil
fuels."[55] A civil society statement timed with the report's release declared that the
IAASTD represents the beginning of a "new era of agriculture" and offers "a sobering
account of the failure of industrial farming."[56] Said Greenpeace, the IAASTD report
recommends a "significant departure from the destructive chemical-dependent, one-
size-fits-all model of industrial agriculture."[57]

(Not everyone involved in the process was happy with the final report, which
was signed by fifty-seven governments.[58] Chemical giant and agricultural biotechnology leader Syngenta and Monsanto, for instance, refused to sign on to the final
document. No public statements were given at the time.[59] But in an interview, Syngenta's Martin Clough told me, "When it became pretty evident that the breadth of
technologies were not getting equal airtime, then I think the view was that there was
no point in participating. It's important to represent the technological options and
it's equally important to say that they get fair play. That wasn't happening."[60]

Despite the chemical industry holdouts, there is also consensus that sustainable farming practices create more resilient farms, better able to withstand the weather extremes of drought and flooding already afflicting many regions as a result of climate change. In other words, mitigation is adaptation. Because organic farms, by their design, build healthy soil, organic soils are better able to absorb water, making them more stable during floods, droughts, and extreme weather changes. In one specific example, conventional rice farmers in a region in Japan were nearly wiped out by an unusually cold summer, while organic farmers in the same region still yielded 60 to 80 percent of their typical production levels.[61]

In ongoing studies by the Pennsylvania-based Rodale Institute, organic crops outperformed nonorganic crops in times of drought, yielding 35 to 100 percent more in drought years than conventional crops.[62] Visiting a Wisconsin organic farmer just after the major Midwest flooding of the summer of 2008, I could see the deep ravines in the surrounding corn fields caused by the recent flooding, while I spent the afternoon walking through a visibly unscathed biodiverse organic farm.

Encouraging sustainable agriculture will not only help us reduce emissions and adapt to the future climate chaos, it will have other beneficial ripples: addressing hunger and poverty, improving public health, and preserving biodiversity. In one study comparing organic and conventional agriculture in Europe, Canada, New Zealand, and the United States, researchers found that organic farming increased biodiversity at "every level of the food chain," from birds and mammals, to flora, all the way down to the bacteria in the soil.[63]   45

Finally, we know that shifting toward sustainable production need not mean sacrificing production. In one of the largest studies of sustainable agriculture, covering 286 projects in fifty-seven countries and including 12.6 million farmers, researchers from the University of Essex found a yield increase of 79 percent when farmers shifted to sustainable farming across a wide variety of systems and crop types.[64] Harvests of some crops such as maize, potatoes, and beans increased 100 percent.[65]

Here's the other great plus: We all have to eat, so we can each do our part to encourage the shift to organic, sustainable farming every time we make a choice about our food, from our local market, to our local restaurants, to our local food policies.

I was recently talking with Helene York, director of the Bon Appétit Management Company Foundation, an arm of the Bon Appétit catering company, which serves eighty million meals a year at four hundred venues across the country. York has been at the forefront of educating consumers and chefs about the impacts of our culinary choices on climate change, including leading the charge of the foundation's "Low Carbon Diet," which has dramatically reduced greenhouse gas emissions associated with their food. She summed up the challenge of awakening people to the food and climate change connection this way: "When you're sitting in front of a steaming plate of macaroni and cheese, you're not imagining plumes of greenhouse gases. You're thinking, dinner."

But the truth is those plumes of gases are there nonetheless, in the background of how our dinners are produced, processed, and shipped to our plates. Thankfully, more and more of us eaters and policymakers are considering the climate crisis at the end of our fork and what we can do to support the organic, local, sustainable food production that's better for the planet, more pleasing to the palette, and healthier for people too.

NOTES

1. Henning Steinfeld et al., *Livestock's Long Shadow: Environmental Issues and Options* (Rome: Food and Agriculture Organization of the United Nations, 2006). While livestock is responsible for 18 percent of total emissions, transportation is responsible for a total of 13 percent of the global warming effect.

2. Film stats from Box Office Mojo. Available online at http://www.boxofficemojo.com/movies/?page=main&id=inconvenienttruth.htm.

3. R. A. Neff, I. L. Chan, and K. A. Smith, "Yesterday's Dinner, Tomorrow's Weather, Today's News?: US Newspaper Coverage of Food System Contributions to Climate Change," *Public Health Nutrition* (2008).

4. Rajendra Pachauri, "Global Warming — The Impact of Meat Production and Consumption on Climate Change," paper presented at the Compassion in World Farming, London, September 8, 2008.

5. Ibid.

6. N. H. Stern, *The Economics of Climate Change: The Stern Review* (Cambridge: Cambridge University Press, 2007), 539.

7. Ibid.

8. Ingredients for Quaker Granola Bar available online: https://www.wegmans.com/webapp/wcs/stores/servlet/ProductDisplay?langId=1&storeId=10052&productId=359351&catalogId=10002&krypto=QJrbAudPd0vzXUGByeatog%3D%3D&ddkey=http:ProductDisplay.

9. Marc Gunther, "Eco-Police Find New Target: Orcos," *Money*, August 21, 2008. Available online at http://money.cnn.com/2008/08/21/news/companies/palm_oil.fortune/index.htm?postversion=2008082112.

10. Ibid.

11. USDA FAS, "Indonesia: Palm Oil Production Prospects Continue to Grow," December 31, 2007. Total area for Indonesia palm oil in 2006 is estimated at 6.07 million hectares according to information from the Indonesia Palm Oil Board (IPOB). Available online at http://www.pecad.fas.usda.gov/highlights/2007/12/Indonesia_palmoil/.

12. "New Data Analysis Conclusive About Release of CO_2 When Natural Swamp Forest Is Converted to Oil Palm Plantation," CARBOPEAT Press Release, December 3, 2007. Dr. Sue Page or Dr. Chris Banks (CARBOPEAT Project Office), Department of Geography, University of Leicester, UK.

13. USDA FAS.

14. "Palm Oil Firm Wilmar Harming Indonesia Forests-Group," Reuters, July 3, 2007. Available at http://www.alertnet.org/thenews/newsdesk/SIN344348.htm.

15. Bunge Corporate Web site. Online at http://www.bunge.com/about-bunge/promoting_sustainability.html.

16. See information at Cargill-Malaysia's Web site, http://www.cargill.com.my/, and Cargill-Indonesia, http://www.cargill.com/news/issues/palm_current.htm.

17. See, for instance, Cargill's position statement: http://www.cargill.com/news/issues/palm_roundable.htm#TopOfPage. Bunge: http://www.bunge.com/about-bunge/promoting_sustainbility.html.

18. Greenpeace. See, for instance, http://www.greenpeace.org.uk/forests/faq-palm-oil-forests-and-climate-change.

19. "New Data Analysis . . ." For more information, see "Carbon-Climate-Human Interactions in Tropical Peatlands: Vulnerabilities, Risks & Mitigation Measures."

20. Steinfeld et al., xxi.

21. Ibid., xxi.

22. Ibid.

23. British Government Panel on Sustainable Development, *Third Report*, 1997. Department of the Environment.

24. From company annual reports, Tyson and Smithfield, 2007.

25. Steinfeld et al., 45.

26. For further discussion, see Paul Roberts, *The End of Food* (Boston: Houghton Mifflin, 2008), 293. See also Frances Moore Lappé, *Diet for a Small Planet*, 20th anniversary ed. (New York: Ballantine Books, 1991).

27. Conversion ratios from USDA, from Allen Baker, Feed Situation and Outlook staff, ERS, USDA, Washington, D.C.

28. Roberts, quoting "Legume versus Fertilizer Sources of Nitrogen: Ecological Trade-offs and Human Need," *Agriculture, Ecosystems, and Environment* 102 (2004): 293.

29. World GHG Emissions Flow Chart, World Resources Institute, Washington, D.C. Based on data from 2000. All calculations are based on CO_2 equivalents, using 100-year global warming potentials from the IPCC (1996). Land use change includes both emissions and absorptions. Available online at http://cait.wri.org/figures.php?page=/World-FlowChart.

30. According to the IPCC, greenhouse gases relevant to radiative forcing include the following (parts per million [ppm] and parts per trillion [ppt] are based on 1998 levels): carbon dioxide (CO_2), 365 ppm; methane (CH_4), 1,745 ppb; nitrous oxide (N_2O), 314 ppb; tetrafluoromethane (CF_4), 80 ppt; hexafluoroethane (C_2F_6), 3 ppt; sulfur hexafluoride (SF_6), 4.2 ppt; trifluoromethane (CHF_3), 14 ppt: 1,1,1,2-tetrafluoroethane ($C_2H_2F_4$), 7.5 ppt; 1,1-Difluoroethane ($C_2H_4F_2$), 0.5 ppt.

31. IPPC, *Climate Change 2007: Fourth Assessment Report of the Intergovernmental Panel on Climate Change* (New York: Cambridge University Press, 2007), Graphic 13.5.

32. World GHG Emissions Flow Chart, World Resources Institute.

33. Steinfeld et al., 79. See also, for instance, http://www.fao.org/ag/magazine/0612spl.htm.

34. See, for example, Carbon Farmers of Australia. http://www.carbonfarmersofaustralia.com.au.

35. Steinfeld et al.

36. United Nations FAO, quoting Anthony Weis, *The Global Food Economy: The Battle for the Future of Farming* (London: Zed Books, 2007), 19.

37. J. McMichael et al., "Food, Livestock Production, Energy, Climate Change, and Health," *The Lancet* 370 (2007): 1253–1263.

38. Pachauri.

39. Steinfeld et al.

40. Ibid.

41. CNN, "All About: Food and Fossil Fuels," March 17, 2008, cnn.com. Available online at http://edition.cnn.com/2008/WORLD/asiapcf/03/16/eco.food.miles/; author communication with Professor Jonathan Lynch, University of Pennsylvania.

42. Author communication with Lynch.

43. Stern.

44. See for instance, Niles Eldredge, Life on Earth: An Encyclopedia of Biodiversity, Ecology, and Evolution (Santa Barbara, Calif.: ABC-CLIO, 2002). Online at http://www.landistitute .org/vnews/display.v/ART/2002/08/23/439bd36c9acfl.

45. World GHG Emissions Flow Chart, World Resources Institute.

46. For more detail, see Environmental Protection Agency, "General Information on the Link Between Solid Waste and Greenhouse Gas Emissions." Available online at http://www.epa .gov/climatechange/wycd/waste/generalinfo.html#q1.

47. IPCC. See Figure 1, Chapter 2.

48. Most recent data available from USDA/ERS, U.S. Cattle and Beef Industry, 2002–2007. Available online at http/www.ers.usda.gov/news/BSECoverage.htm.

49. Pounds noted here are measured by commercial carcass weight. U.S. Red Meat and Poultry Forecasts. Source: World Agricultural Supply and Demand Estimates and Supporting Materials. From USDA/ERS. See also http://www.ers.usda.gov/Browse/TradeInternational Markets/.

50. Data from Brazilian Beef Industry and Exporters Association. Cited in "Brazilian Beef Break Records in September," October 3, 2008, The Beef Site. Available online at http:// www.thebeefsite.com/news/24565/brazilian-beef-break-records-in-september.

51. IPCC.

52. http://www.rodaleinstitute.org.

53. See, for instance, studies from the Rodale Institute, found here: http://www.newfarm.org/ depts/NFfield_trials/1003/carbonsequest.shtml.

54. Editorial, "Deserting the Hungry?" Nature 451 (17 January 2008): 223–224 doi:10.1038/ 451223b; published online January 16, 2008. Available at http://www.nature.com/nature/ journal/v451/n7176/full/451223b.html.

55. Executive Summary, 9. IAASTD, "Summary Report," paper presented at the International Assessment of Agricultural Science and Technology for Development, Johannesburg, South Africa, April 2008.

56. "Civil Society Statement from Johannesburg, South Africa: A New Era of Agriculture Begins Today," April 12, 2008. Available online at http://www.agassessment.org/docs/Civil_ Society_Statement_on_IAASTD-28Apr08.pdf.

57. Greenpeace Press Release, "Urgent Changes Needed in Global Farming Practices to Avoid Environmental Destruction," April 15, 2008.

58. Fifty-seven governments approved the Executive Summary of the Synthesis Report. An additional three governments — Australia, Canada, and the United States of America — did not fully approve the Executive Summary of the Synthesis Report, and their reservations are entered in the Annex. From the Executive Summary of IAASTD, "Summary Report."

59. Nature, 223–224.

60. Author interview with Martin Clough, head of biotech R & D and president of Syngenta Biotechnology, Inc., based in North Carolina; and Anne Birch, director with Corporate Affairs, Syngenta, September 9, 2008.

61. Nadia El-Hage Scialabba and Caroline Hattam, "General Concepts and Issues in Organic Agriculture," in Organic Agriculture, Environment and Food Security, ed. Environment and Natural Resources Service Sustainable Development Department (Rome: Food and Agri-

culture Organization of the United Nations, 2002), chapter 1. Available online at http://www.fao.org/docrep/005/y4137e/y4137e01.htm#P0_3.

62. "Organic crops perform up to 100 percent better in drought and flood years," November 7, 2003, Rodale Institute. Online at www.newfarm.org.

63. D. G. Hole et al., "Does Organic Farming Benefit Biodiversity?," Biological Conservation 122 (2005): 113–130, quoting James Randerson, "Organic Farming Boosts Biodiversity," *New Scientist* October 11, 2004. Note: *New Scientist* emphasizes that neither of the two groups of researchers — from the government agency, English Nature, and from the Royal Society for the Protection of Birds — "has a vested interest in organic farming."

64. Jules Pretty, *Agroecological Approaches to Agricultural Development* (Essex: University of Essex, 2006).

65. Ibid.

Cheap Food: Workers Pay the Price

ARTURO RODRIGUEZ, WITH ALEXA DELWICHE AND SHEHERYAR KAOOSJI

BEFORE READING: What are some of the problems that farm workers face even today, in the early twenty-first century? How are those problems linked to the whole food industry in America?

Death in the Fields

Young grapevines thrive in the fierce summer sun of California's Central Valley. But the same early summer heat that helps bring life to the bountiful produce millions of Americans enjoy can also destroy. Unlike the young grapevines, assured of constant irrigation and hydration, farmworker Maria Isabel Vasquez Jimenez had to do without water as she labored in the fields in direct sunlight on a 95-degree day in May 2008.

After almost nine hours of work, Maria became dizzy and collapsed to the ground. Her boyfriend Florentino Bautista ran to her, held her in his arms, and begged for help. The foreman walked over to them and stood over the couple, reassuring Bautista and telling him that "this happens all the time." Remedies devised by the

Arturo Rodriguez has been an activist and organizer for farm workers since his college days and has been the president of the United Farm Workers since the death of Cesar Chavez in 1993. Alexa Delwiche was a researcher for the UFW before leaving to work for the San Francisco Board of Supervisors. Sheheryar Kaoosji is a research analyst for the Change to Win federation, a group of labor unions, including the UFW. This essay appeared in *Food, Inc.: How Industrial Food Is Making Us Sicker, Fatter, and Poorer — And What You Can Do about It* (2009).

foreman and supervisor ranged from applying rubbing alcohol to placing a wet bandanna on Maria's body. Finally, Maria's boyfriend and coworkers were allowed to take her to a clinic, though the foreman told them to lie about where she was working. It took almost two hours to get the young woman to the clinic. Immediately upon her arrival, the clinic called an ambulance for the hospital. By the time she arrived at the hospital, her body temperature was 108.4 degrees.

Maria held on for two days, but her young body could not withstand the stress. Having arrived in the United States from a small village in Oaxaca only months before and having worked in the fields for only three days, seventeen-year-old Maria died, leaving her family and loving boyfriend forever. It's difficult to accept that such an injustice could occur in 2008. But tragic stories like Maria's are all too common in American agriculture.

Statistics tell part of the story. The rate of death due to heat stress for farmworkers is twenty times greater than for the general population.[1] In the past five years, thirty-four farm workers have died due to heat exposure in the United States. Six of those deaths occurred in the summer of 2008 alone.[2] The actual number is likely much higher because many farmworker deaths are not recorded as heat deaths, and some are not recorded at all.

Maria's death is a poignant example of how the pressures for decreased prices   5 in our food system inevitably lead to exploitation of the workers at the lowest end of the economic chain. Food producers and retailers have successfully abdicated responsibility for the well-being of the workforce that makes their profits possible, aided and abetted by a callous and uninvolved government.

Who is to blame for these senseless and preventable deaths? The farm labor contractors who are hired by the growers to provide them with workers? The growers who actually own the crops and employ the contractors? Or the State of California, which is tasked with enforcing labor regulations that mandate shade, drinking water, and rest breaks for farmworkers toiling in the sun-baked fields?

From a moral perspective, there is more than enough blame to go around. But the system of agricultural production our society has created is designed to shield major corporations from any legal responsibility for their actions or inactions. The layers of subcontracting built into American agriculture are designed to shift responsibility downward from the largest firms to the smallest. Charles Shaw wine, sold exclusively at Trader Joe's and nicknamed affectionately by its customers "Two Buck Chuck," is solely produced by Bronco Wine Company, the largest wine-grape grower in the United States.[3] West Coast Grape Farming, a subsidiary of Bronco Wine and owner of the vineyard in which Maria died, hired Merced Farm Labor, an independent farm labor contractor, to provide workers to harvest their grapes. While Maria and her boyfriend were not picking grapes directly for the Charles Shaw label, both Bronco Wine Company and West Coast Grape Farming are owned and operated by the same Franzia family, which singlehandedly supplies more than 360 million bottles of wine to Trader Joe's each year.

If this supply chain seems unnecessarily complicated, well, that's the point. Maria Isabel's employer was neither Trader Joe's, nor Charles Shaw—producer and—

Farmworkers harvest lettuce in California, where temperatures in the field often exceed 100 degrees.

winemaker Bronco Wines, but a farm labor contractor with no discernible assets and no traceable relationship to the product sold. Thus, the retailer and producer are shielded from responsibility. Maria Isabel may die, but Charles Shaw wine is still on sale for $1.99 per bottle. Trader Joe's liberal, consumer-friendly reputation is preserved. And a farm labor contractor in Merced, California, quietly goes out of business. But the system that led to Maria Isabel's death continues without change.

The precariousness of a farmworker's life extends far beyond heat deaths. Fatality and injury rates for farmwork rank second in the nation, second only to coal mining.[4] The U.S. Environmental Protection Agency (EPA) estimates that U.S. agricultural workers experience ten thousand to twenty thousand acute pesticide-related illnesses each year, though they also admit that this is likely a significant underestimate.[5] Drinking water and sanitary conditions — basic rights most American workers take for granted — are denied to farmworkers on a daily basis.

The plight of many farmworkers is made worse by their tenuous legal status as   10
U.S. residents. Guest workers brought in under the government-sponsored H2-A visa

program are routinely cheated out of wages, forced to pay exorbitant fees to recruiters, and virtually held captive by employers who seize their documents. Slavery — not in a metaphorical or symbolic sense, but in the literal meaning of the word — still exists on farms scattered throughout the country. In 2004, the United States Department of Justice investigated 125 cases of slave labor on American farms, involving thousands of workers.[6] Their shaky legal status helps explain farmworkers' vulnerability. Workers hesitate to report labor law violations for fear of losing their jobs or being deported. But workplace fear is just one variable in a systemic problem: the institutionalized acceptance of farmworkers as second-class citizens. The injustices farmworkers experience are by no means accidental.

Most Americans would be horrified to realize that the foods they eat are produced under conditions like these. Their lack of knowledge about these realities is attributable not to public apathy but to deliberate obfuscation by the companies that market foods and unconscionable neglect by the government agencies that should be safeguarding workers. As food production has become increasingly complex, it has become nearly impossible for consumers to gather information on their food purchases. Product labels reveal little information about a food's origin and contents and tell consumers nothing of the plight of those harvesting and processing their food. As a result, farmworkers in America are left to suffer incredible poverty and abuse in an industry characterized by great wealth and enormous profits.

Retailer Power and Its Impact on Farmers

Food production in the United States is a high-technology, modern process. Produce and animal varieties are meticulously bred, designed, and genetically engineered by food scientists, supported by large academic programs at public land-grant universities across the nation and in government agencies like the USDA and FDA. Products are packaged, distributed, and sold throughout the nation and exported worldwide using the same state-of-the-art, just-in-time logistics systems that move other goods throughout the international economy.

But despite the high-tech systems that streamline and control the flow of goods to the nation's dinner tables, a farmworker's job is remarkably similar to the life of Chinese and Japanese immigrants at the turn of the twentieth century, of Mexican migrants in the 1920s, of white Dust Bowl migrants during the Depression, or black and Mexican migrant workers since the 1940s. Crops eaten raw, such as grapes, strawberries, and lettuce, require careful and steady human hands to retain the physical and visual perfection required by the modern consumer. Much of the so-called specialty crops (that is, fruits and vegetables) that the nation consumes are grown in the heat of California's Central and Coachella valleys, where daytime temperatures stay in the triple digits throughout harvesting season.

Strawberry and lettuce workers bend thousands of times a day, picking valuable produce from the rich earth of the central coast of California that John Steinbeck once wrote about. Apple workers fill bags with up to seventy pounds of produce, carrying them up and down ladders across the Yakima Valley of Washington state. The story is retold every generation, with workers toiling for minimum wages to feed the population of the United States.   15

Most people are surprised to learn that the conditions of farm laborers have not been dramatically improved since the days of *Grapes of Wrath*. In fact, the story has gotten worse in recent years. The growers that employ farmworkers have been experiencing a historic squeeze in prices from the retailers that purchase their produce. The retail food sector has been inexorably consolidating for decades, culminating in the dominance of Wal-Mart over the grocery industry, representing between 20 and 40 percent of the sales volume of various food products in the United States. Today, the top five retailers control over 60 percent of the market.[7] Thanks to this consolidation, a relative handful of companies wield enormous power over food supplies — power they use to demand ever-lower prices for the fruits, vegetables, and other commodities they stock. Growers have responded to these pressures, providing picture-perfect produce at deflationary prices, sourcing them from around the world in order to provide year-round supplies to the retailers.

And consumers have reaped the benefits. The average American family now spends less than 10 percent of its income on food, the lowest percent in history.[8] In 1950, this figure was 20 percent. As writer and grower David Mas Masumoto described it in a poem he presented at the 2008 Slow Food Festival, "I remember $2-a-box peaches in 1961 and $2-a-box peaches in 2007."[9]

But everyday low prices for consumers (and increasing profits for the shareholders of the giant retailers) have created serious consequences for growers. Each year, farmers capture less of the consumers' food dollar. For example, in 1982, farmers received 34 percent and 33 percent of what consumers paid for fresh vegetables and fresh fruit, respectively, at retail food stores; by 2004, these farm shares had declined to 19 percent for fresh vegetables and 20 percent for fresh fruit.[10]

One result of this squeeze is that only gigantic agribusinesses can survive in the new farming economy. Massive state-sponsored infrastructure, especially the dam and levee system developed in California over the twentieth century, allowed large California growers to achieve unprecedented scale while successfully gobbling up smaller growers farm by farm. Such scale also benefits top retailers that depend on the considerable quantities supplied by only the largest growers. Medium-sized family growers now depend on selling prime agricultural land to the developers. Organic growers who once hoped to provide a new model of agriculture have been pushed to the periphery by high certification costs and loose standards that allow the largest growers to dominate the mainstream organic market.

But ultimately the effects of retail consolidation have trickled down the production line to workers, causing wages and benefits for workers throughout the food system to stagnate. Today, even a modest wage increase for workers on a farm could threaten a supplier's contract with a retailer. Furthermore, growers and labor contractors often find the easiest way to minimize labor costs is by cutting corners on labor and safety standards. Some labor contractors even admit that "breaking the law is the only way you can make decent money."[11] Of course, there are exceptions, and many decent employers in the industry exist. But the system results in a constant push for lower costs, with no basic standards across the industry. There is no high road — only a low road populated by growers racing one another to reach rock bottom.

Agricultural "Exceptionalism" and the Subsidy Economy

This situation is not sustainable, nor is it accidental. In large measure, it can be traced 20 back to government policies designed to produce the very system that now distorts agricultural production in this country.

The State of California, where almost half of U.S. produce is grown and 40 percent of farm laborers work, provides a vivid illustration of how this process has worked. The policies pursued by California as well as by the federal government have promoted corporate agricultural interests for over a century.[12] By demanding a set of immigration policies that guaranteed cheap labor and made these workers dependent on the government through assistance programs (or on the growers themselves through labor camps), a permanent underclass in the fields was cultivated.[13] This is a policy called "agricultural exceptionalism" — the exemption of agriculture from labor and other laws under the Jeffersonian theory that food production is not only a crucial U.S. industry but also a superior way of life that deserves special preservation and protection. This mindset has dominated U.S. policy in land use, labor law, and direct and indirect farm subsidies for a century.

As a result, although government exists in part to protect the powerless from the powerful, government has done little to benefit the agricultural workers who feed the nation. While most workers won historic labor protections through the Fair Labor Standards Act of 1938 — which set minimum wage requirements, overtime laws, and child labor laws — powerful lobbying by agribusiness succeeded in excluding farmworkers from protection under these laws.[14] The minimum wage now applies to farmworkers in most cases, but overtime provisions still do not. Furthermore, to this day, the age limit for children working in agriculture differs from other businesses. Children under the age of fourteen cannot be employed in any other industry; in agriculture the age limit is twelve. No age restrictions apply to children working on family farms.

Agribusiness also managed to exclude farmworkers from another piece of New Deal legislation, the National Labor Relations Act, which gave workers the right to form unions and bargain collectively. So when the limited rights farmworkers actually enjoy are violated, they are denied the ability to organize themselves to demand fair treatment.

One of the most egregious examples of agricultural exceptionalism has been the government's failure to reduce farmworkers' exposure to pesticides because of the profit loss growers might suffer if pesticides were more tightly regulated. Cleverly, regulation of farmworker exposure to pesticides was placed under the jurisdiction of the EPA, famous for its use of "cost-benefit analysis" when determining whether to place restrictions on the use of chemicals.[15] The phrase sounds innocuous, even reasonable, but, in practice, reliance on cost-benefit analysis means that a hazardous pesticide will not be restricted by the EPA if the economic hardship to the grower is considered to be greater than the hazards to farmworker or consumer health. If pesticide protection for farmworkers were under the jurisdiction of the Occupational Safety and Health Administration (OSHA), cost-benefit analysis would not be required — a simple finding that workers' lives were at risk would suffice to justify regulation.

More than twenty years ago, the EPA concluded that farmworkers were dis- 25 proportionately affected by the use of pesticides. Indeed, a large body of scientific literature has documented this relationship. A study of 146,000 California Hispanic farmworkers concluded that, when compared to the general Hispanic population, farmworkers were more likely to develop certain types of leukemia by 59 percent, stomach cancer by 70 percent, cervical cancer by 63 percent, and uterine cancer by 68 percent.[16] Despite this evidence, the EPA has failed to enact any mitigation procedures to address farmworkers' chronic exposure to pesticides.

Thanks to the importance of agriculture to the California economy, agribusiness has been especially powerful at the state government level. One result has been an amazingly lopsided set of water management policies: only three rivers in California remain undammed, and 80 percent of the water collected is consumed by agriculture.[17] Both small- and large-scale growers purchase vast amounts of imported river water at just a fraction of the true price, their purchases subsidized by state and federal taxpayer dollars. Indeed, in some regions of California, the average urban water user pays seventy-five times the price of a grower. Not only have these subsidies encouraged extremely inefficient water use by agricultural producers, but they have allowed growers and retailers to profit in their ability to produce crops more cheaply than otherwise possible, all at the expense of the taxpayer. Meanwhile, more than 635 miles of rivers and streams in the Central Valley have been classified as unsafe for fishing, swimming, or drinking due to pollution from agricultural runoff.[18] And as drought risk intensifies throughout the state, the bulk of the state's water continues to be dumped, quite literally, into the Central Valley for growers either to use for crops or to resell for profit to urban water districts, desperate for the precious resource.

Immigration Policy as a Tool of Agribusiness

Over the last century, the most important policy perpetuating the existence of an underclass of agricultural workers has been U.S. immigration policy. Today, almost 80 percent of the 2.5 million farm workers in the United States were born outside of the United States.[19] The overwhelming majority of farmworkers are from Mexico. Estimates vary, but at least 50 percent of the workforce is not authorized to work in the United States.[20]

The roots of Mexican migration patterns lie in a series of U.S.-approved guest programs created during the twentieth century specifically to address farm labor needs and in lax enforcement of immigration laws by the federal government during periods in which no guest worker programs were in place.[21]

The most recent wave of labor migration to the United States was spurred by the North American Free Trade Agreement (NAFTA) and other trade liberalizing policies. The entrance of cheap, government-subsidized U.S. corn into the Mexican economy in the wake of NAFTA signaled to Mexican corn producers that there was no future left for them in agriculture. And they were right. Government investment in Mexican agriculture fell by 90 percent.[22] Almost two million subsistence farmers were displaced. Some farmers fled to urban areas in Mexico, while others decided there was nowhere else to go but north of the border.[23]

So NAFTA, after having been branded by both Republicans and Democrats as   30 the solution to combating poverty in Mexico and reducing migrations to the United States, only deepened the problem. Rather than improving the economic situation on both sides of the border as promised, NAFTA helped produce a *decrease* in real wages in Mexico between 1995 and 2009.[24] Annual migration to the United State *increased* from 2.5 million unauthorized immigrants in 1995 to 11 million in 2005.[25] As a result of the effects of NAFTA on food production in southern Mexico, Oaxacans are now the fastest growing population of farmworkers in the United States. Today, one in five families in Mexico depends on remittances from the United States, the total averaging almost $24 billion a year.[26]

Since NAFTA's implementation, the only serious U.S. immigration policy enacted to address the influx of migrants was Operation Gatekeeper (1995), the policy of deterring migration by increasing border enforcement in the border cities of San Diego and El Paso.[27] This policy only shifted migration patterns farther east into more harsh and inhospitable desert. Mexican farmworkers leave their families and risk their lives crossing a dangerous and increasingly militarized border because there are no other options left. To risk is to hope for better.

Tragically, since 1995, deaths along the United States/Mexico border have doubled.[28] In 2005, 472 people died in the desert, with heat exposure and dehydration as the leading causes of death. And when migrants do survive, their best and often only shot at employment in the United States is the lowest-paid, most-dangerous, least-respected occupations of all — including agriculture. In a world of free trade for goods and closed borders for people, those who survive the passage can check their rights at the gate.

Farm Workers Looking Up at the Poverty Line

It's difficult for a family of four living at the official poverty level to get by, making just $21,000 per year.[29] But compare that with a farmworker family's annual wage of roughly $13,000, a sum comparable to one acre's profit for a strawberry field.[30] Farmworkers continue to be among the lowest-paid laborers in the United States, with only dishwashers earning less.[31] The majority of farmworkers live below the poverty line, with real wages hovering around minimum wage.[32] Benefits are even more meager. Less than one-tenth of workers have employer-paid health insurance for non-work related health care, and just 10 percent receive paid holidays or vacation time.[33]

As we've noted, a significant factor accounting for the low wages of farmworkers is the large proportion of unauthorized immigrant workers employed in agriculture. Undocumented workers have few employment options, thus making workers more willing to accept low wages.[34] The use of farm labor contractors (FLCs), hired by growers to provide workers, also helps explain the low wages for farmworkers. FLCs are notorious for paying lower wages in order to compete with the other thousands of contractors desperate for a grower's business. Farm labor contractors provide almost 50 percent of farm labor in California, a number that grows every year both in California and in the rest of the nation.

U.S. policymakers consistently support and facilitate agricultural producers' dependence on low-wage labor. Some may believe that the poor compensation of immigrant workers will be augmented by a safety net of government assistance programs designed to help the working poor. Yet undocumented status and extreme poverty have proven to be insurmountable barriers that prevent many farmworker families from actually accessing much of this assistance.

While the legal status of workers is no impediment when hiring workers for poverty-level wages, the same status excludes these workers from their only opportunities to make ends meet through government assistance. Less than one in five farmworkers use means-tested services such as Temporary Assistance to Needy Families; housing vouchers; Women, Infants, and Children; food stamps; Medicaid; or the National School Lunch Program, citing legal status and cost as significant barriers.[35] And even though each week a percentage of farmworkers' paychecks flows into the Social Security system, most will never see a dime of it. Only two percent of farmworkers report ever receiving any social security benefits.[36] Far from being a drain to the system, those working without authorization actually provide Social Security with an average annual subsidy of nearly $7 billion.[37]

High rates of poverty contribute to shocking health problems among farmworkers. Nearly 80 percent of male farmworkers are overweight.[38] And one in five males have at least two of three risk factors for chronic disease, such as high cholesterol, high blood pressure, or obesity, putting them at heightened risk to suffer from heart disease, stroke, asthma, and diabetes. Many farmworkers have never visited a doctor's office or any other type of medical facility, including an emergency room. And as migrant workers return to Mexico, the costs associated with medical treatment for their high rates of chronic disease will be borne by Mexican society, thus creating a greater strain on the already fragile Mexican economy.

Poverty rates among farmworkers extend into their housing options. Interestingly, in 2005, the three least affordable places to live in the United States, measured by the percentage of income spent on rent or mortgage payments, were areas with high farmworker populations: Salinas, CA; Watsonville, CA; and Petaluma/Santa Rosa, CA.[39] In expensive cities such as these, affordable housing options are in such short supply that workers often are forced to live wherever they can find shelter, from abandoned cars to tin-roofed shanties.

Squalid living conditions in labor camps, reminiscent of those we associate with the 1930s, still exist for farmworkers today. In May 2008, more than one hundred migrant fruit pickers from Washington were found living in tents in a Central Valley cherry orchard in California without access to clean water. They were bathing in drainage ditches.

There have been some model housing programs created in California and Florida, but generally speaking, substandard living conditions are the norm for farmworkers. While some workers live in employer-provided housing, many families instead choose to crowd into rented apartments, sharing space appropriate for a single family with as many as ten to twenty other people. Poor sanitation and proximity to pesticide-laden fields create serious public health risks for farmworker families. But these are the conditions workers must accept when left with no other options.

Government's Malign Neglect

It isn't enough to demand that government should create more laws to protect farmworkers. The ones that do exist aren't enforced. Agricultural land is too vast for government to patrol; there are more than eighty thousand farms in California alone, employing well over half a million workers.[40] CAL-OSHA, the state agency responsible for worker safety enforcement, conducted fewer than three hundred inspections between 2007 and 2008.[41] Penalties are meager, and often violations are never even collected.

California holds the reputation for the most pro-farmworker legislation in the nation, yet the state provides many examples of the inadequacies of government enforcement. California remains the only state to enact any legislation granting farmworkers basic labor rights. The Agricultural Labor Relations Act (ALRA) of 1975 provides agricultural workers with organizing rights and protects workers from workplace retaliation from employers due to union involvement. However, even after unions gained organizing rights, the State of California ignored most of these rights once conservatives had regained the state house in 1983. The growers reasserted their ability to intimidate, and the United Farm Workers' ability to organize workers returned to the pre-law level that year, when the Republican-appointed Agricultural Labor Relations Board determined that even the cold-blooded murder of pro-union farmworker Rene Lopez by a company goon did not amount to an unfair labor practice.

Despite the existence of ALRA, union density rates among farmworkers remain low. Growers were found by the State of California to have intimidated, threatened, and offered bribes to workers at union elections in 2005 and 2006, but there have been no meaningful penalties, only an offer of another chance for workers to try to organize under such conditions.[42]

The failure to enforce heat protection laws provides another example. In 2005, California passed a law to protect workers from death due to heat stroke. The law requires that employers provide fresh water, shade, and additional breaks when the temperature goes above 95 degrees. Yet more farmworkers have died in the three years since the law's enactment than the three years prior.[43] More than one-third of the farms visited by CAL-OSHA in 2007 were out of compliance with the heat regulations.

Pesticide spraying provides yet another example. California leads the nation   45
in pesticide protection for farmworkers, which includes one of only two pesticide
spraying reporting systems in the nation. Even so, pesticide spraying continues at
high rates, and the burden for reporting rests with the workers, keeping reporting
rates low.

The Union Is the Solution

Farmworkers have long known that, though government may try to protect them, ultimately it will not stand with them. Workers without representation have no chance
of even bringing a claim to enforcement agencies without facing threats of firing,
deportation, or worse. The most effective solution for workers has been to organize
and collectively demand improved wages, benefits, and working conditions. Unionized workers have the protections that allow them to speak up when something
goes wrong.

Unfortunately, the policy of excluding agriculture from laws that affect the rest
of the country (especially labor law) lives on. And rather than a remnant of the past,
it may in fact be a harbinger of where the American economy is headed in the
twenty-first century. The abused and exploited second tier of the American labor force
has expanded from agricultural workers to include many food-processing workers
across the nation as well as employees in other sectors dominated by people of color,
such as hospitality, janitorial work, trucking, and security. Millions of these workers
effectively have no rights and no chance of basic protections without organizing
themselves into unions.

The history of the meatpacking industry in the twentieth century is an example
of the effect unions can have on an industry. Long one of the dirtiest, lowest-paying,
most-dangerous urban jobs, as depicted in Upton Sinclair's 1906 novel *The Jungle*,
meatpacking was transformed in the 1930s into a well-paying, respected, and safer
job because the workers organized the Meatpackers' Union. The daily tasks of these
jobs were not transformed by unionization, but the union allowed its members to
improve their working conditions, raise families, buy homes, and even overcome the
racial discrimination that existed in postwar cities such as Chicago and Minneapolis.
At the same time, food safety and quality were boosted by workers with such crucial
rights as whistle-blowing and the ability to affect assembly line speeds, benefiting not
just workers but consumers.

In recent years, the same price pressures from retailers such as Wal-Mart that
have depressed agricultural wages have resulted in meat processing being moved to
rural, nonunion facilities run by such strongly antiunion meat and poultry firms as
Tyson and Smithfield. The result has been declining standards, wages, and quality in
the meatpacking industry. The jobs that once supported the working class in Mid-
western cities have been redesigned to exploit workers from around the world, who
have no ability to complain about or question unsafe and unfair practices. Progress
has turned back, to the detriment of both rural and urban economies, workers, and
consumers. Once again, only big retailers and food processors win.

There is hope for better conditions. Only about 5 percent of U.S. farmworkers   50
are unionized. The unionized workers don't always make much more than other
farmworkers (though some do), but they do get health insurance and even a pension,
which are increasingly rare even for white-collar workers. More important, union
workers have the right to speak up on the job. They have the freedom to advocate for
issues that matter to them without fear of dismissal. They can establish procedures
with their supervisors for days it gets too hot in the fields and workers feel their
health may be at risk. The value of this is remarkable both for the basic conditions
of the workplace and the quality and sustainability of the food produced. And a
farmworker union with higher density would be a powerful ally to the environmental justice movement that is rising across the nation, empowered to address global as
well as kitchen-table issues in the food processing industry.

Cesar Chavez, founder and leader of the United Farm Workers until his death in
1993, focused much of his work on environmental issues such as pesticide use, the
dangers of monoculture, and the benefits of natural production methods, understanding that collective bargaining was a meaningless tool if farmworkers were still being
poisoned in the fields. He recognized that pesticide use is an issue that clearly affects
both workers and consumers.

The safety and well-being of farmworkers, consumers, and the environment have
always been secondary to profits in the eyes of the big agricultural interests. So,
when the government failed to address concerns about the harmful effects of organ-
ophosphates on workers, consumers, and the environment, Chavez and the UFW
used union contracts to regulate pesticides. Union contracts in 1970 achieved what no
U.S. government agency ever had: key provisions restricting the use of the five most
dangerous pesticides.[44]

Unfortunately, the current system for farmworkers to choose a union is broken.
The sad truth is that the federal agencies designed to oversee the food system and
its workforce — the Food and Drug Administration, the U.S. Department of Agriculture, the Department of Labor, and the Environmental Protection Agency — as well
as the State of California's Agricultural Labor Relations Board, have little practical
ability to conduct a fair union election, let alone regulate pesticides, food safety, or
worker safety in the fields.

It is even worse in other states. The agricultural exceptionalism of the 1930s remains dominant, and there is no way for farmworkers to organize in the rest of the
country. Many young farmworkers don't know what a union is, having grown up in
a post-NAFTA North America of economic instability, migration, and constant fear.

Farm Workers and Consumer Power

This litany of problems has a solution. It is to change the balance of power when   55
it comes to our food. Workers have never had the power to balance out the strength
of agribusiness. But consumers have enormous power when they are activated and
informed.

The two UFW-led grape boycotts of the 1960s and 1970s were unprecedented
in their scope, duration, and effectiveness because they combined the power of the

farmworker, on strike in California, and the consumer, refusing to purchase the product across the country. This boycott was able to defeat the power of the retailer and grower because the consumer, the final arbiter of the transaction, took action.

So why has the consumer abdicated this power in more recent years? Have consumers made a Faustian bargain, accepting worker exploitation in exchange for low prices? If so, the actual benefits to consumers are meager. University of California at Davis agricultural economist Philip Martin has computed that farmworker wages and benefits levy a total cost of $22 per year on each American household.[45] Furthermore, he found that to raise average farmworker wages by 40 percent, bringing workers from below the poverty line to above it, would cost the average household only $8 more for produce each year.[46]

Thankfully, consumer awareness in the food system has reached unprecedented levels, and the ability to create change to the food system has made important strides because of consumer preference. The organics continues to grow. Wal-Mart, long criticized for its irresponsible buying practices and cheap products, now carries organics and purchases locally grown produce when possible. Concern over the treatment of animals has led to ballot propositions banning caged animals and has changed the buying practices of major fast-food outlets. The growth explosion of Whole Foods from a niche natural foods store to a $6 billion powerhouse proves that consumers are willing to pay more for quality food.

The principle of sustainability recognizes the interdependence of our food system. And worker dignity, respect, and health and safety are fundamental to a sustainable system. Purchasing organic strawberries doesn't mean much if workers are still dying in fields. This same force that exploits farmworkers also pollutes our environment, impoverishes rural communities, and sickens consumers. Unless the balance of power is shifted away from valuing profits over human life, no one is protected.

Cesar Chavez once noted, "In the old days, miners would carry birds with them to warn against poison gas. Hopefully, the birds would die before the miners. Farmworkers are society's canaries."[47] The integrity of the food system begins with just conditions for workers.

Only the consumer has the power to support farmworkers in their struggle for representation. And only with an empowered workforce will there be an organized, principled counterbalance to the food production sector, defending sustainability, safety, and other standards. When workers are empowered, consumers are protected. Working together to take the following steps, we can make our food system more just, sustainable, and healthy.

What Can You Do?

If you share the concerns we've described in these pages, here are some practical steps you can take to support our efforts to improve the conditions of the workers who provide you with the food that you and your family eat:

- Become educated on farmworker issues. Start by visiting the resource at www .ufw.org.

- Support union and other advocacy campaigns for workers in the food system.
- Demand that retailers provide more transparent information on the working and living conditions of their suppliers' workforce.
- When they're available, always purchase products that guarantee workers' rights and express your support and approval to retailers so they'll be encouraged to stock such products.
- Support comprehensive immigration reform.
- Support policies that assist the working poor, such as increasing the minimum wage, living wage ordinances, and universal health care.
- Buy organic. Even though organic production does not provide workers with any additional wages, benefits, or respect, they are spared the detrimental effects associated with pesticides.

While it's time for consumers to mobilize and participate in reforming the food system, it is equally important for farmworker and food system advocates from every step of the supply chain to come together and engage in a serious dialogue. It is our responsibility as advocates to create opportunities for consumers to use their power in improving the lives of food-system workers. Whether this occurs through the development of a "Socially Just" food certification label, through an extensive consumer awareness campaign, through legislation, or through an entirely new vision, now is the time to organize ourselves, to work together, to implement the type of societal transformation that we envision every morning when we get out of bed, and to renew our struggle for economic and social justice.

NOTES

1. Centers for Disease Control, "Heart-Related Deaths Among Crop Workers: United States, 1992–2006," 57, no. 24 (June 2008). Available online at http://www.cdc.gov/mmwr/preview/mmwrhtml/mm572a1.ht.

2. Garance Burke, "More Farm Deaths in Heat Despite Calif. Crackdown," Associated Press, August 21, 2008. Available online at http://www.usatoday.com/news/nation/2008–08–20–3205167992_x.htm.

3. "California: Strawberries, Vegetables, Water," *Rural Migration News* 14, no. 3 (July 2008). Available online at http://migration.ucdavis.edu/rmn/comments.php?id=1330_0_5_0.

4. William Kandel, "A Profile of Hired Farmworkers, a 2008 Update," Economic Research Report No. ERR-60, USDA, July 2008. Available online at http://www.ers.usda.gov/publications/err60/err60.pdf.

5. U.S. General Accountability Office (GAO), "Pesticides: Improvement Needed to Ensure the Safety of Farm Workers and Their Children," GAO/RCED-00-40, 2000, citing a 1993 U.S. EPA study. Available online at www.gao.gov/archive/2000/rc00040.pdf.

6. Oxfam, "Like Machines in the Fields: Workers Without Rights in American Agriculture," Research Paper, March 2004. Available online at http://www.oxfamamerica.org/newsandpublications/publications/research_reports/art7011.html/OA-Like_Machines_in_the_Fields.pdf.

7. Ibid., citing Linda Calvin et al., *U.S. Fresh Fruit and Vegetable Marketing: Emerging Trade Practices, Trends, and Issues* (Washington, D.C.: Economic Research Service, U.S. Department of Agriculture, January 2001, Agricultural Economic Report No. 795. Available online at http://www.crs.usda.gov/publications/aer795.

8. USDA, "Food CPI, Prices and Expenditures: Food Expenditures by Families and Individuals as a Share of Disposable Personal Income," Economic Research Service, June 17, 2008. Available online at http://www.ers.usda.gov/briefing/CPIFoodandExpenditures/Data/table7.htm.

9. Jane Black, "Slow Food at Full Speed: They Ate It Up." *Washington Post*, September 3, 2008. Available online at http://www.washingtonpost.com/wp-dyn/content/story/2008/09/02/ST2008090202273.html.

10. Hayden Stewart, "How Low Has the Farm Share of Retail Food Prices Really Fallen?" Economic Research Report No. ERR-24, August 2006. Available online at www.ers.usda.gov/Publications/ERR24/.

11. Daniel Rothenberg, *With These Hands: The Hidden World of Migrant Farmworkers Today* (Berkeley: University of California Press, 1998), 97.

12. Philip Martin, "Labor Relations in California Agriculture," In *University of California Institute for Labor and Employment: The State of California Labor*, 2001. Available online at http://repositories.cdlib.org/ile/scl2001/Section7.

13. Ibid.

14. Keith Cunningham-Parmeter, "A Poisoned Field: Farm Workers, Pesticide Exposure, and Tort Recovery in an Era of Regulatory Failure," *New York University Review of Law & Social Change* 28: 431.

15. Ibid.

16. Margaret Reeves, Anne Katten, and Martha Guzman, "Fields of Poison," (Darby, Pa.: Diane Publishing, 2002), citing a study by P. K. Mills and S. Kwong, "Cancer Incidence in the United Farm Workers of America (UFWA) 1987–1997," *American Journal of Industrial Medicine* 40 (2001): 596–603. Available online at http://www.ufw.org/white_papers/report.pdf.

17. Liquid Gold: A California Exhibition. An Exhibit by the Water Resources Center Archives. University of California at Berkeley. Online at http://www.lib_berkeley.edu/WRCA/exhibit.html.

18. The Environmental Justice Water Coalition, "Thirsty for Justice: A People's Blueprint for California Water," 2005. Available online at http://www.cjcw.org/Thirsty%20for%20Justice.pdf.

19. U.S. Department of Labor (DOL), *Findings of the National Agricultural Workers Survey (NAWS) 2001–2002: A Demographic and Employment Profile of United States Farmworkers* (Washington, D.C.: U.S. Department of Labor, March 2005), Research Report No. 9. Available online at http://www.dol.gove/asp/programs/agworker/report_8.pdf.

20. Kandel.

21. Martin.

22. Public Citizen, "Down on the Farm: NAFTA'S Seven-Years War on Farmers and Ranchers in the U.S., Canada and Mexico," June 2001. Available online at http://www.citizen.org/documents/ACFF2.PDF.

23. Ibid.

24. Giselle Henriques and Raj Patel, "Agricultural Trade Liberalization and Mexico," Food First, Policy Brief 7, 2003, available online at http://www.foodfirst.org/pubs/policy/pb7.pdf.

25. Philip Martin, "NAFTA and Mexico-US Migration," 2005. Available online at http://giaonini.ucop.edu/Mex_USMigration.pdf.

26. Tracy Wilkinson, "Less Money Going to Mexico as US Economy Falters," *Los Angeles Times*, October 2, 2008. Available online at http://www.latimes.com/news/printedition/asection/la-fg-mexmoney2-2008oct02,0,2037607.story.

27. Connie de la Vega and Conchita Lozano, 2005, "Advocates Should Use Applicable International Standards to Address Violations of Undocumented Workers' Rights in the United States," *Hastings Race & Poverty Law Journal* 3, 35.

28. General Accountability Office, "Illegal Immigration: Border Crossing Deaths Have Doubled Since 1995; Border Patrol's Efforts to Prevent Deaths Have Not Been Fully Evaluated," GAO-06-770, August 2006. Available online at http://www.gao.gov/new.items/d06770.pdf.

29. Department of Health and Human Services, "Annual Update of the HHS Poverty Guidelines," *Federal Register* 73, no. 15 (January 23, 2008): 3971–3972. Available online at http://aspe.hhs.gov/POVERTY/08fedreg.htm.

30. Kandel.

31. Ibid.

32. DOL.

33. Kandel.

34. Ibid.

35. DOL.

36. Ibid.

37. Eduardo Porter, "Illegal Immigrants Are Bolstering Social Security with Billions," *New York Times*, April 5, 2005. Available online at www.nytimes.com/2005/04/05/business/05immigration.html.

38. Don Villarejo et al., "Suffering in Silence: A Report on the Health of California's Agricultural Workers," California Institute of Rural Studies, Sponsored by California Endowment, 2001. Available online at www.fachc.org/pdf/mig_suffering%20in%20silence.pdf

39. Alina Tugend, "The Least Affordable Place to Live? Try Salinas," *New York Times,* May 7, 2006, real estate section. Available online at www.nytimes.com/2006/05/07/realestate/07california.html.

40. USDA, Census on Agriculture, 2002. Available online at http://www.nass.usda.gov/Census/Pull_Data_Census.jsp.

41. Data were gathered from OSHA's inspection database. Query included all establishments engaged in crop or livestock production from September 1, 2007, and September 1, 2008. Available online at http://www.osha.gov/pls/imis/industry.html. 994 inspections were conducted during the same time period for all crop and livestock establishments (approximately 2.1 million farms or 938 million acres) in the United States during the same time period.

42. *United Farm Workers v. VINCENT B. ZANINOVICH & SONS, A CALIFORNIA CORPORATION*, 34 ALRB No. 3 (2008).

43. Burke.

44. Robert Gordon, "Poisons in the Fields: The United Farm Workers, Pesticides, and Environmental Politics," *The Pacific Historical Review* 68, no. 1 (Feb. 1999): 51–77. Available online at http://links.jstor.org/sici?sici=0030–8684%28199902%2968%3A1%3C51%APITFTU%3E2.0.CO%3B2–8.

45. "How We Eat: 2005," *Rural Migration News* 13, no. 3 (July 2007). Available online at http://migration.ucdavis.edu/rmn/more.php?id=1229_0_5_0.

46. Ibid.

47. Address by Cesar Chavez, President, United Farm Workers of America, AFL-CIO, Pacific Lutheran University, Tacoma, Washington, March 1989. Available online at http://www.ufw.org/_page.php?menu=research&inc=history/10.html.

The Fight Over Food Deserts: Corporate America Smacks Its Way Down

ERIC HOLT-GIMÉNEZ

BEFORE READING: How can you explain the seeming paradox that lower-income individuals suffer from a higher rate of obesity than those of a higher economic level?

This June the City of Chicago approved Walmart's bid to open up dozens of new facilities, beginning with grocery stores in the city's chronically underserved South side. Just a month earlier the company committed $2 billion dollars to fight hunger in the United States. But behind the high profile donations is a decidedly less charitable story repeating itself throughout corporate America.

In large part fueled by Michelle Obama's goal to eliminate food deserts in seven years, Walmart has set the PR machine in motion around its new battle cry: "The Great Grocery Smackdown:"

"If you've always lived near a grocery store or fresh market, here's something you've probably never considered: There are neighborhoods across the United States where it's nearly impossible to find fresh produce. These places are called 'Food Deserts" and Walmart is committed to removing them from our communities.' The Walmart proposal for Chicago has been framed as "the beginning of a major private-sector effort to address the food desert problem on the South side."

Walmart sees Chicago's South side as the key to the rest of the city — in fact as the key to all cities. According to the *Chicago Tribune*, in a recent meeting with Mayor Daley Walmart offered to open grocery stores in food deserts in exchange for access to the other, more desirable locations. "We have very small market share in the large cities within the United States, so we see a big opportunity for us to grow in those urban markets," said Hank Mullany, who runs Walmart stores in the Midwest, Northeast, and mid-Atlantic regions.

Not only will the company bring fresh produce in smaller grocery stores, the employer claims it will bring 12,000 jobs to Chicago.   5

A recent study out of Loyola University in Chicago focusing on the impact of a Walmart that opened on the west side of Chicago in 2006 indicates that the new facility cost the local economy as many jobs as it created. The Loyola University study also examined tax revenues for eighteen months before and after the retailer opened its doors and found no evidence of increased local economic activity.

Eric Holt-Giménez, a food system researcher and agro ecologist, is the executive director of FoodFirst/Institute for Food and Development Policy and the author of the 2009 *Food Rebellions! Crisis and the Hunger for Justice*. The article was posted on the *Huffington Post* on July 14, 2010.

In 2008, Walmart settled 63 cases of wage theft for a total of $352 million. Even when the company does pay the agreed upon wage, workers still come up short. According to Good Jobs First, taxpayers subsidize Walmart stores through numerous forms of public assistance — Medicaid, Food Stamps, public housing — that often allow workers to subsist on the company's low wages. A report by the House Education and Workforce Committee conservatively places these costs deferred by the retail giant at $420,750 per store; the Walmart Foundation's per-store charitable giving is just 11 percent of that amount ($47,222). Now adding to the pot of public funds to be had, Michelle Obama and other well intentioned groups concerned with food deserts may have made these areas much more profitable than they once were. As part of her Let's Move campaign the First Lady has pledged $400 million/year to ensure that all Americans have access to affordable food. In the words of Brahm Ahmadi, founder of People's Grocery in West Oakland,

> "We're seeing a lot of funding being rolled out, but also what we're seeing is the corporate retail industry who literally two to three years ago wouldn't even talk to you about this [food deserts], now almost salivating over the opportunity for the windfalls that will come from free public money, essentially. Even though they could easily finance themselves to open stores in the inner city neighborhoods, why should they when the administration is perfectly happy to give them more money to do it?"

Walmart is not the only major grocery chain salivating at the thought of public subsidies: Tesco, Target, Safeway, and Supervalu have all announced plans to open stores in urban centers.

But hunger and food security stem from poverty that in the United States comes from unemployment and poor wages. The solution to food security in America must come through a revitalized food economy — one that pays workers a living wage, that includes worker and minority owned businesses, and that keeps food dollars in local communities. Walmart does none of that.

Seventeen percent of American jobs are in the food system, and those jobs are among the lowest paid in the country. If food industry leaders are serious about improving food access, they need to start by tackling food insecurity where it starts — with sub-poverty wages. No amount of fresh produce will cure America's food and health gap unless it comes with a commitment to fight its root causes — poverty and inequality. To really fight food deserts, the Obamas should start by supporting living wages for workers and support the food businesses that create true economic development in the communities that need it most.

Thinking and Writing about the Ethics of Food

QUESTIONS FOR DISCUSSION AND WRITING

1. Explain what Pollan means when he writes, "Cheap food has become an indispensable pillar of the modern economy. But it is no longer an invisible or uncontested one" (para. 5).

2. Astyk and Newton argue that "the hunger of the poor is in part a choice of the rich" (para. 2). Explain what they mean by that.

3. If, as Astyk and Newton argue, the cause of hunger is unequal access to food, land, and wealth, how can any individual make a difference? How can any government?

4. Some would argue that going to the lengths that some of the farmers described in Diane Brady's article do to produce organic food defeats the purpose of going organic in the first place. Do you agree? Explain.

5. Brady quotes Mark Kastel, who states, "Organic consumers think they're supporting a different kind of ethic" (para. 27). What is this different kind of ethic that organic consumers support?

6. What problems would Diane Brady see in what Anna Lappé proposes as solutions to the effect that food production is having on the global climate?

7. What are some of the practical reasons that farm workers live and work in such deplorable conditions? What sort of ethical or unethical thinking allows it to happen?

CHAPTER 16

Is Academic Integrity on Our College Campuses under Assault?

Consider the irony captured in the opening of a 2003 essay on academic integrity from the *New York Times*:

> "Academic cheating is a major problem and has negative results on everyone involved."
>
> So goes the first sentence of a recently composed essay on cheating in academia. To get the whole essay, though, you'll need to pay for a membership at DirectEssays.com, an Internet operation that promises access to "over 101,000 high-quality term papers and essays."[1]

Some students may have been guilty of cheating since the first school opened, but no one can deny that the Internet has made it much easier. With dozens of sites offering term papers and essays for a price, the temptation is hard to resist when pressure builds and deadlines loom. It is so much easier to cut and paste others' words and ideas together than to come up with original ones. Add to that the fact that some students have used their cell phones to text answers during exams and have hacked into computers to change their grades and those of their friends. It seems the more we progress technologically the more we regress morally.

There are varying opinions on why students cheat and on what might be done to prevent cheating. Central to most theories, though, is the belief that the academic community in which the students live and write makes a difference as to whether or not they give in to the temptation to buy a term paper or to download an assignment from their roommate's computer and what sort of approach to the issue of academic integrity might compel them to say no. Are students less likely to cheat on a campus that has an honor code? Are they willing to sign an honor code that requires them to turn in any other student observed cheating? And what about the mixed message

[1] Mark Edmundson, "How Teachers Can Stop Cheaters," *New York Times*, September 9, 2003, p. A29.

sent to students on those campuses that require an honor code yet also submit those same students' papers to an online plagiarism detection service?

Term papers and essays are not all that is being downloaded on our college campuses. Students download so much illegal music that universities in some cases are being criticized for allowing the activity to go unchecked. Numbers of students have settled by paying $3,000 rather than be charged with illegal downloads.

The most recent site that caters exclusively to college students is *Playboy U*. Now they can attend parties at Hugh Hefner's Playboy Mansion — online, of course — and can enjoy all that the online universe of *Playboy* has to offer — minus the total nudity. All it takes is an .edu e-mail address, but any faculty or staff caught using the site will be blocked.

Thus the question: Is academic integrity under assault on our college campuses? Is integrity in general under assault?

Expect, but Respect, Original Work by Students

BILL WALSH

BEFORE READING: Was cheating a common occurrence at the high school you attended? What sort of attitude did those who did not cheat have toward those who did?

Poetic justice can be sweet, like when a thief gets something stolen from him or when an antiplagiarism company gets sued for . . . copyright infringement.

Do you remember ever copying phrases, sentences, or even whole passages from the book for some school assignment? Well, today's students do the same thing — with the Internet. Only with literally billions of Web sites out there in cyberspace, it's getting harder for teachers to see (or prove) that a student copied something or used words that were not his own.

Enter a company called Turnitin.com. They tout themselves as a "plagiarism prevention" service. Student assignments are fed into the company's Web site, and a powerful search engine compares each student paper with (according to the company) over twelve billion Web pages, more than 10,000 newspapers, magazines and journals, thousands of books, and in excess of forty million student papers. The teacher and/or student gets the paper back electronically, with portions that seem to have been copied from other sources highlighted. The report presents a "similarity index" and a copy of the original material which it thinks was copied. Turnitin stresses that they do not accuse or punish students for plagiarism — that's up to the

---

Bill Walsh was a columnist for the *Billerica* [Massachusetts] *Minuteman* when this article appeared there on May 24, 2007.

teachers and professors. Turnitin merely points out passages which seem to have a lot in common.

Actually, the service can be used in many ways. Some schools or teachers feed kids' papers into the service to detect plagiarism, and if any is found, the student fails. Other disciplinary action may follow, based on the school's rules and academic honesty policy.

Other schools (including the one where I teach) try to avoid the "gotcha" ap-   5
proach and attempt instead to use Turnitin as a learning tool. It's the student who submits the paper and gets the report back. What follows are timely lessons and examples on proper citation, paraphrasing, and how to quote another source. The student can rewrite and resubmit the paper numerous times, fixing himself any possible plagiarism (conscious or subconscious).

Thousands of colleges, universities, and high schools subscribe to Turnitin, at about 87 cents per student per year. The company's revenue is in the tens of millions of dollars annually. Approximately 100,000 papers are submitted to the company every day. It's a very big — and successful — business.

But there's a problem, and it involves the archiving and use of student papers. Turnitin says that over half of all unoriginal work comes from students copying other kids' papers, and so it's very proud of its growing collection of papers from more than ten million students. Each paper that a student submits is added to millions of papers Turnitin already has in its database, and against which all new papers are compared.

Students claim that the company is using their work without permission as part of its business. Adding each new paper to the company's database, the students claim, is actually infringing on the students' intellectual property, making money from it, and violating the very copyright laws Turnitin is supposed to be protecting. Students do not submit their work voluntarily they claim; they're forced to do so by their schools or teachers.

Some high school students in Virginia found a sympathetic attorney who agreed to handle their case for free. He then advised them to register the copyright of their papers ($45 each) and to explicitly tell both their teacher and Turnitin that the papers were now protected intellectual property and not to be added to Turnitin's database. When the company ignored their request, the students sued for $900,000 ($150,000 per copyright violation). *Time* magazine reports that the case will probably go to court this fall.

For their part, Turnitin has engaged its own attorneys, who have reportedly   10
examined copyright law and contend that the kids have no case.

Computers and the Internet have certainly revolutionized writing in general and research in particular. To get the facts for just this column, for instance, I checked dozens of Web sites, downloaded news stories, and read Turnitin's own promotional literature — right here in my den.

All new technology has its price, and the ease of plagiarism is one of the prices we pay for the wealth of information at our fingertips through the Internet. And while one company has tried to use that same wealth of information and computer technology to catch those who would steal it, they in turn have been accused of violating the very precepts they say they're protecting.

Some lawyers say that the students have an excellent chance of prevailing in their lawsuit.

Sometimes there are no easy answers, no computer-driven solutions to our moral quagmires. Once again those who try to insure honesty and morality run afoul of basic tenets of right and wrong themselves.

You can't steal stuff. That's something students need to learn, but not from the hands of those who expropriate student work to teach them that very important lesson.   15

Battling Term-Paper Cheats

JULIE RAWE

BEFORE READING: Do you believe that faculty should ____mit all of their students' essays to a plagiarism detection site in order to catch any ____dent who might have used sources without giving them credit? Explain why, or w____ ____ot.

Affordabletermpapers.com charges a minimur ____ $9.95 per page for a custom-written essay. Rush jobs cost $24.95 a pa____ ____e site, which dutifully states that its papers should be used for "assistance ____ses only" — uh-huh — guarantees that customers won't run into trouble wit ____iarism or they'll get their money back and a free rewrite. There are hundre____ ____online paper mills like this one, catering to all the stressed-out, disaffected, ____t plain lazy students with Internet access and a credit card or money order. ____st as the Internet has made it easier for kids to cheat, it's also helping high sc____s and colleges ferret out the flimflammers. Every day more than 100,000 pape____re fed into Turnitin.com, a plagiarism-detection site that compares each subm____on with billions of Web pages, tens of thousands of journals and periodicals, a____a growing archive of some forty million student papers. More than seven thousa____educational institutions use the system, including Harvard and Oxford. But whil____urnitin lets faculty level the playing field, many students — even the straight arrows — see its use as a breach of trust.

Amid startling data on the prevalence of cheating — in an undergraduate survey conducted this academic year at a dozen colleges by Rutgers professor Donald Mc-Cabe, 67 percent of the 13,248 respondents admitted to having cheated at least once on a paper or test — some students are getting administrators to rethink their use of gotcha tools. Nova Scotia's Mount St. Vincent University went as far as banning Turnitin after the student-union president complained that it created "a culture of mistrust, a culture of guilt."

Julie Rawe is a senior editor for *Time* magazine, in which this article appeared on May 17, 2007.

Aside from the guilty-until-proved-innocent argument, many students are apoplectic that a for-profit entity — which charges 87 cents per student per year for plagiarism detection — is making money off their homework. As soon as a paper is vetted for cut-and-paste plagiarism, it joins a database against which every new submission will be compared. Thus, argues a recent op-ed in the Texas A&M newspaper, the company should have to pay to use these works, "without which their service would be crippled." Concerns about intellectual-property rights as well as cost led the University of Kansas to announce last fall that it was turning off Turnitin. Faculty protested so vehemently, however, that the school quickly signed up again.

But many teachers are torn when it comes to Turnitin. "How do you reconcile this [service] with a place that's trying to presume honor?" asks Bob Thompson, Duke University's vice provost for undergraduate education. Duke, which recently endured a cheating scandal at its business school, no longer uses Turnitin — in part because it did not like adding to the company's database — and this spring expanded its honor code by obligating students to take action if they observe or hear about cheating. "We will truly lose the battle if we think we're going to fight technology with technology," says Tim Dodd, executive director of the Duke-affiliated Center for Academic Integrity. "Kids will always be two generations ahead of us."

Meanwhile, students at a high school in McLean, Virginia, are trying to bring   5
down Turnitin by suing its parent company, iParadigms, for alleged copyright infringement. To file such a lawsuit, a writer has to pay $45 to register a copyright, be it for a Pulitzer prize–winning novel or a ninth-grader's meanderings on *Animal Farm*, and the penalty per copyright violation can be as much as $150,000. So if the McLean High School students prevail with their copyrighted essays — a trial will probably begin this fall — ambulance-chasing lawyers will start tailing school buses, and Turnitin may have to close up shop.

"We've got to come back to reality," iParadigms CEO John Barrie says of the copyright suit. "These aren't nuclear-missile secrets." Papers are being archived at the same time as testing sites install cell-phone detectors to keep students from text-messaging answers or finding them online. One result of the high-tech cheating wars: paranoia. McCabe says fewer students are filling out his anonymous surveys. "Students started accusing me of getting their IP address," he says.

But given how easy it is to pluck a term paper off the Web, it's hard to argue against using Turnitin to curb academic dishonesty. That's why some schools, including McLean, rely on both honor codes and plagiarism-detection software to keep students on the up-and-up — without seeing these methods as being at odds with each other. The Air Force Academy, which expelled fifteen first-year cadets this month for cheating, takes great pride in its honor code but also checks for plagiarism. Says Joey Smith, twenty-two, chairman of the cadets' honor committee: "It's the whole idea of trust but verify."

Which is why it would be a shame if the McLean Committee for Student Rights succeeds in dismantling Turnitin. Yes, it is important to trust students. But an equally important lesson is that cheating shouldn't be rewarded. What's so terrible about making students think long and hard when an affordable term paper is just a click away?

exams. From the more than six thousand students who responded, I learned several important lessons.

The incidence of cheating was higher than I expected, and many students were quite willing to admit their transgressions. For example, 47 percent of students attending a school with no honor code reported one or more serious incidents of test or exam cheating during the past year, as did 24 percent of students at schools with honor codes. While such comparisons would seem to support the power of honor codes, it was not the code itself that was the most critical factor. Rather, the student culture that existed on campus concerning the question of academic integrity was more important. The existence of a code did not always result in lower levels of cheating. More importantly, the converse was also true: some campuses achieved high levels of integrity without an honor code. While these campuses were doing many of the same things as campuses with codes — e.g., making academic integrity a clear campus priority and placing much of the responsibility for student integrity on the students themselves — they did not use a pledge and they did not mandate unproctored exams. What was important was the culture of academic integrity to which incoming students were exposed.

Many of the students I surveyed were troubled by the failure of their institution,   5
and often its faculty, to address the issue of cheating. Because they believed that weak institutional policies and unobservant or unconcerned faculty were "allowing" others to cheat and, thereby, to gain an unfair advantage, students viewed cheating as a way to level the playing field. This was a particular problem on large campuses and in courses with large enrollments — environments where, arguably, it is harder to establish a strong, positive community culture.

In 1993 (McCabe and Trevino 1996), I surveyed nine medium to large universities that, thirty years earlier, had participated in the landmark study of college cheating conducted by William Bowers (1964). Bowers's project surveyed over five thousand students on ninety-nine campuses across the country and provided considerable insight on how often students were cheating and why. Two outcomes of my 1993 project are particularly noteworthy in comparison to Bowers's results. First, there were substantial increases in self-reported test and exam cheating at these nine schools. For example, 39 percent of students completing the 1963 survey acknowledged one or more incidents of serious test or exam cheating; by 1993, this had grown to 64 percent. Based on student responses to the 1993 survey, however, it was difficult to tell how much of this change represented an actual increase in cheating, and how much was simply a reflection of changing student attitudes about cheating. In 1993, many students simply did not see cheating as a big deal, so it was easier to acknowledge — especially in an anonymous survey.

Second, there was no change in the incidence of serious cheating on written work; 65 percent of students in 1963 acknowledged such behavior, and 66 percent did so in 1993. However, student comments in the 1993 survey suggested that this younger generation of students was more lenient in defining what constitutes plagiarism. Although survey questions were worded to ask students about a specific behavior, without labeling it as cheating, more than a trivial number of students in 1993 said they had not engaged in a particular behavior, while providing an expla-

It Takes a Village: Academic Dishonesty and Educational Opportunity

DONALD L. MCCABE

BEFORE READING: What might McCabe have been suggesting about the link between community and cheating by calling his piece "It Takes a Village"?

For the last fifteen years, I have researched questions of academic integrity. My initial interest in these questions was driven by my own experience as an undergraduate at Princeton University in the mid-1960s. Graduating from a high school where cheating was common, I was particularly intrigued by one item I received among the blizzard of forms and papers Princeton sent me as I prepared to matriculate: information about the Princeton honor code. I was informed that exams would be unproctored; that, on every exam, I would have to affirm that I had not cheated or seen anyone else cheat by signing a pledge (which I can still recite verbatim almost forty years after my graduation); and that all alleged violations of the code would be addressed by a student honor committee. Although somewhat skeptical in light of my high school experience, I headed off to Princeton confident I would do my part to uphold this seventy-year-old tradition. Apparently, the overwhelming majority of my classmates felt the same way. During my four years at Princeton, I never observed, suspected, or heard of anyone cheating, although surely there were at least some minor transgressions of the code.

When I returned to academia after more than twenty years in the corporate world, where I witnessed firsthand the continuous erosion in the ethical values of recent college graduates, I was intrigued by the opportunity to conduct meaningful research on academic integrity. I was particularly curious to see whether campus honor codes were still a viable strategy and to explore the impact they were having on a new generation of students. While I remain a strong advocate of honor codes, my thinking about academic integrity has evolved over the last fifteen years — often in surprising ways.

The problem

In the fall of 1990, I surveyed students at thirty-one of the country's most competitive colleges and universities (McCabe and Trevino 1993). Fourteen institutions had traditional academic honor codes, and seventeen did not, having chosen instead to "control" student dishonesty through such strategies as the careful proctoring of

Donald L. McCabe is professor of management and global business at Rutgers University and founding president of the Center for Academic Integrity. His article appeared in *Liberal Education* in Summer–Fall 2005.

nation of why the instances in which they actually had done so were not cheating. The ethics of cheating is very situational for many students.

Just as technology has enabled new forms of cheating that are becoming popular with students, that same technology has made it easier to reach large numbers of students in surveys. Since 2001, I have been conducting Web-based surveys that make it possible to reach an entire campus population with relative ease. However, many students are concerned that it is easier to identify the source of electronically submitted surveys, so they elect either not to participate or to do so while being cautious about what they say. While it is hard to get people to be honest about their dishonesty in any circumstances, it is even harder to get them to do so when they are concerned about the anonymity of their responses. This is reflected in notably lower rates of self-reported cheating in Web surveys and lower levels of participation (as low as 10–15 percent on average compared to 25–35 percent for written surveys in this project).

A Web survey found that 21 percent of students have cheated on exams. Other surveys find that the percentage of cheaters approaches two-thirds of students.

Nonetheless, in these Web surveys of over forty thousand undergraduates on sixty-eight campuses in the United States and Canada, conducted over the last two academic years, 21 percent of respondents have acknowledged at least one incident of serious test or exam cheating, and 51 percent have acknowledged at least one incident of serious cheating on written work. Although most had engaged in other cheating behaviors as well, four out of every five students who reported they had cheated on a written assignment acknowledged that they had engaged in some form of Internet-related cheating — either cut-and-paste plagiarism from Internet sources or submitting a paper downloaded or purchased from a term-paper mill or Web site. Although the self-reported rates of cheating found in these Web surveys are lower than in earlier surveys, they clearly are still of concern. In addition, the difference may relate more to research methodology than to any real change.

Of concern to whom?

Each campus constituency tends to shift the "blame" for cheating elsewhere. This is   10
a major problem. Many students argue, with some justification, that campus integrity policies are ill-defined, outdated, biased against students, and rarely discussed by faculty. They also fault faculty who look the other way in the face of obvious cheating. They are even more critical of faculty who, taking "the law" into their own hands when they suspect cheating, punish students without affording them their "rights" under the campus integrity policy. Many faculty believe that these campus policies are overly bureaucratic and legalistic and that they often find "guilty" students innocent. Some faculty argue that they are paid to be teachers, not police, and that, if students have not learned the difference between right and wrong by the time they get to college, it's not their job to teach them — especially in a publish-or-perish world. Although the evidence suggests otherwise, many also believe it's too late to change student behavior at this point.

Faculty also complain about administrators who fail to support them in the face of what they perceive as obvious cases of cheating. They complain about administrators who, at least in the minds of some faculty, are more concerned with whether the student is a star athlete, the child of a major donor, or has achieved some other favored status. Of course, many administrators can detail a litany of the ways in which they think faculty shirk their responsibilities in the area of academic integrity. Still others complain that students are only concerned with grades; how they obtain those grades is less important for many.

The most appropriate response to student cheating depends in large part on the goals of the institution. If the primary goal is simply to reduce cheating, then there are a variety of strategies to consider, including increased proctoring, encouraging faculty to use multiple versions of exams and not to recycle old tests and exams, aggressively using plagiarism detection software, and employing stronger sanctions to punish offenders. But while such strategies are likely to reduce cheating, I can't imagine many people would want to learn in such an environment. As educators, we owe our students more than this, especially when cheating may reflect cynicism about what they perceive as eroding moral standards in the academy and in society.

Today's students seem to be less concerned with what administrators and/or faculty consider appropriate behavior and much more concerned with the views and behavior of their peers. Students do expect to hear the president, the provost, a dean, or some other official tell them during orientation how they are about to become academic "adults," adults who respect the learning process and who, among other things, don't cheat. And many students want to hear this message. But it's clear from student comments in my surveys that the real "proof" for students is in the behavior of their peers and the faculty. Regardless of the campus integrity policy, if students see others cheating, and faculty who fail to see it or choose to ignore it, they are likely to conclude that cheating is necessary to remain competitive. Many students ask, "If faculty members aren't concerned about cheating, why should I be?"

It takes a village

I have always been intrigued by the African tribal maxim that it takes a village to raise a child. In a similar sense, I would argue it takes the whole campus community — students, faculty, and administrators — to effectively educate a student. If our only goal is to reduce cheating, there are far simpler strategies we can employ, as I have suggested earlier. But if we have the courage to set our sights higher, and strive to achieve the goals of a liberal education, the challenge is much greater. Among other things, it is a challenge to develop students who accept responsibility for the ethical consequences of their ideas and actions. Our goal should not simply be to reduce cheating; rather, our goal should be to find innovative and creative ways to use academic integrity as a building block in our efforts to develop more responsible students and, ultimately, more responsible citizens. Our campuses must become places where the entire "village" — the community of students, faculty, and administrators — actively works together to achieve this goal. As Ernest Boyer observed almost two decades ago (Boyer 1987, 184), "integrity cannot be divided. If high standards of conduct are expected of students, colleges must have impeccable integrity themselves. Otherwise the lessons of the 'hidden curriculum' will shape the undergraduate experience. Colleges teach values to students by the standards they set for themselves."

In setting standards, faculty have a particularly important role to play; students look to them for guidance in academic matters — not just to their peers. In particular, to help students appropriately orient themselves and develop an appropriate mental framework as they try to make sense of their college experience, faculty must recognize and affirm academic integrity as a core institutional value. Without such guidance, cheating makes sense for many students as they fall back on strategies they used in high school to negotiate heavy work loads and to achieve good grades.

One of the most important ways faculty can help is by clarifying their expectations for appropriate behavior in their courses. Although faculty certainly have the primary responsibility here, they should share this responsibility with students. Not only does such "consultation" result in policies in which students feel a greater degree of ownership and responsibility, but it also helps to convince students they truly are partners in their own education. Nonetheless, faculty do have a unique

15

and primary role to play in the classroom, and it is incumbent upon them not only to minimize opportunities to engage in academic dishonesty (even if only out of fairness to honest students) but also to respond in some way when cheating is suspected. While some may argue over the most appropriate response, it is essential that there be some response. As noted earlier, students suggest that faculty who do nothing about what appears to be obvious cheating simply invite more of the same from an ever-increasing number of students who feel they are being "cheated" by such faculty reluctance.

While faculty can do much to improve the climate of academic integrity in their campus "villages," they should not be expected to shoulder this burden alone. University administrators need to look more carefully at the role they play. The Center for Academic Integrity at Duke has encouraged, and helped, many campuses to examine their academic integrity policies, yet there are still many schools that have not reviewed their policies in decades. Instead of reacting to an increasing number of faculty complaints about Internet plagiarism by simply subscribing to a plagiarism detection service, for example, perhaps these schools should take a more comprehensive look at their integrity policies. While some may decide that plagiarism detection software is an appropriate component of their integrity policy, I trust many more will conclude that it's time to abandon their almost exclusive reliance on deterrence and punishment and to look at the issue of academic dishonesty as an educational opportunity as well.

Over the last fifteen years, I have become convinced that a primary reliance on deterrence is unreasonable and that, if we truly believe in our role as educators, we would do better to view most instances of cheating as educational opportunities. While strong sanctions clearly are appropriate for more serious forms of cheating, it's also clear that most student cheating is far less egregious. What, for example, is an appropriate sanction for a student who cuts and pastes a few sentences from a Web site on the Internet without citation? In some cases, this behavior occurs out of ignorance of the rules of citation or is motivated by a student's failure to properly budget his or her time. In a last minute effort to complete the two papers s/he has due that week, as well as study for a test on Friday, s/he panics. If the student is a first-time "offender," what's the educational value of a strong sanction?

Having decided that sanctions do little more than to permanently mar a student's record, an increasing number of schools are taking a more educational approach to academic dishonesty. They are striving to implement strategies that will help offending students understand the ethical consequences of their behavior. These strategies seem often to be win-win situations. Faculty are more willing to report suspected cheating, or to address it themselves, when they understand that educational rather than punitive sanctions are likely to result. A common choice now is to do nothing or to punish the student privately, which makes it almost impossible to identify repeat offenders. On a growing number of campuses, however, faculty are being encouraged to address issues of cheating directly with students. As long as the student acknowledges the cheating and accepts the faculty member's proposed remedy, the faculty member simply sends a notation to a designated party and never gets involved with what many consider the unnecessary bureaucracy and legalisms of campus judicial systems.

When more faculty take such actions, students who cheat sense they are more likely to be caught, and the overall level of cheating on campus is likely to decline. Administrators, especially student and judicial affairs personnel, can then devote more of their time and resources to proactive strategies. For example, several schools have developed mini-courses that are commonly part of the sanction given to first-time violators of campus integrity policies; others have devoted resources to promoting integrity on campus, rather than investing further in detection and punishment strategies. A common outcome on campuses implementing such strategies is a greater willingness on the part of faculty to report suspected cheating. They view sanctions as more reasonable, designed to change behavior in positive ways, demonstrating to students that inappropriate behavior does have ethical consequences. As students quickly learn that second offenses will be dealt with much more strongly, increased reporting also serves as an effective deterrent to continued cheating.

Of course, the most effective solution to student cheating is likely to vary from campus to campus, depending on the unique campus culture that has developed over the course of a school's history. Indeed, no campus is likely to reach the ideal state where the proactive strategies I have described are sufficient in and of themselves. Rather, some balance of punishment and proactive strategies will be optimal on each campus and, although that optimum will vary from campus to campus, punishment will always have some role. The stakes are high for most college students today, who think their entire future — their chances of gaining admission to professional school, getting job interviews with the best companies recruiting on campus, etc. — depends on a few key grades. It is, therefore, unrealistic to think that none will succumb to the temptation to cheat.

Students, even the most ethical, want to know that offenders will be punished so that other students will be deterred from engaging in similar behaviors. In fact, I am often surprised by the comments many students offer in my surveys calling for stronger punishments for students who engage in serious cheating. While they are willing to look the other way when someone engages in more trivial forms of cheating to manage a heavy workload, for example, they are far less forgiving of students who cheat in more explicit ways on major tests or assignments. The difficult task for every school is to find the appropriate balance between punishment and proactive strategies that deters students who would otherwise cheat when the opportunity arises yet that also works to build a community of trust among students and between students and faculty, a campus community that values ethical behavior and where academic integrity is the norm.

The need to achieve some balance between punishment and proactive strategies was well summarized for me this spring when I made a presentation at the Coast Guard Academy in New London, Connecticut. A second classman who was listening to my emphasis on proactive strategies suggested that, since students see so much cheating in high school and in the larger society, deterrence probably plays an important role in reducing cheating in college. In his own case, he suggested that during his first two years at the academy the biggest factor in his decision not to cheat was fear of the strong sanctions that existed and were often used. But during those two years, he was also exposed to many proactive messages about why integrity matters, especially in an occupation where the lives of so many may depend on doing one's job with integrity. He observed that he has now reached the point where he wouldn't think of cheating — no longer for fear of punishment, but because he understands the importance of integrity. However, for him, and perhaps for many other students, those strong rules helped him learn behaviors that he could later understand and value for more idealistic reasons. No campus may ever reach a truly ideal combination, but deterrence and proactive strategies both should play an important role in any academic integrity policy.

Do something

It is impossible to know whether such proposals will work on every campus. But to those campuses that have doubts about the effectiveness of such strategies, I offer the same advice I give students when they express concern about reporting peers they suspect of cheating because of the fear of reprisal or because they believe sanctions on their campus are too severe. Do something! While I'm sure there are some campuses where the modest suggestions offered here may not work as well as other possible choices, I'm even more convinced that any campus that has not reviewed its integrity policies for some time is derelict in its responsibilities to its students and likely has a degree of discontent among its faculty. Perhaps even more important, it is depriving its students of an important learning opportunity in the true liberal arts tradition.

REFERENCES

Bowers, W. J. 1964. Student dishonesty and its control in college. New York: Bureau of Applied Social Research, Columbia University.

Boyer, E. L. 1987, *College: The undergraduate experience in America*. New York: Harper & Row.

McCabe, D. L., and L. K. Trevino. 1996. What we know about cheating in college: Longitudinal trends and recent developments. *Change* 28, 28–33.

_____. 1993. Academic dishonesty: Honor codes and other contextual influences. *Journal of Higher Education* 64, 522–38.

Bulletproof Assessment, War Stories, and Tactics: Avoiding Cybercheating

SUSAN STONEY AND MARK MCMAHON

BEFORE READING: What are some ways that college faculty might fight against plagiarism?

Cybercheating

The advent of the Internet has brought academics a surfeit of information, broadened their research, and generally improved the accessibility of courses. However, it has also increased the opportunities for students to cheat by various means. Cybercheating has become so prevalent in Australian universities that the Federal Education Minister, Dr. Brendan Nelson, has stated that the higher education industry is at risk (ABC, 2003).

Cybercheating covers a wide range of academic misconduct, from cutting and pasting from the Web, to buying papers from papermills and even eBay. This "Napsterization" of knowledge (Boynton, 2001) is an inevitable outcome of the e-society in which we live. Students are so used to finding anything they want from the Internet, from music and movies to product information, that they automatically turn to this source when asked to produce an assignment, and believe that information on the Internet is free for appropriation as they wish (Stoney & Stoney, 2001). There are myriad statistics on the prevalence of cybercheating in its various forms. In 2002 it was estimated that up to 14 percent of Australian university students were plagiarizing from the Web (Foster, 2002b), and a review of the statistics collected by www.plagiarism.org shows that almost 80 percent of students admit to cheating at least once, with 12 percent of students reporting themselves as serial cheaters. University of California–Berkeley officials believe that cheating has increased an estimated 744 percent from 1993 to 1997 (Overbeck, 2000). This, of course, coincides with the advent of the Internet into common usage in Universities. Interestingly, www.plagiarism.org reports that 90 percent of students believe that cheaters are never caught, or if they are, are not appropriately disciplined. Furthermore, a survey conducted by Aaron and Georgia (1994) cited in (Bricault, 1998), shows that university student affairs officers believe that the problem of cheating has not been addressed adequately.

These statistics show that cybercheating is endemic in universities around the world, and that academics and administrators have to wage a war to both stop and

Susan Stoney is head of the Centre for Learning and Teaching at Edith Cowan University in Perth, Australia, and Mark McMahon is a senior lecturer in Interactive Multimedia there. The paper was presented at the Twenty-first Australian Society for Computers in Learning in Tertiary Education conference in 2004.

prevent such cheating. When students are caught cheating, they can become litigious. A recent case at the University of Kent has highlighted this when a student, who plagiarized in his third year of study and was excluded from his course, is now suing the university for not catching him sooner. The student admits to downloading information from the Internet, but claims that he did not realize there was a problem as it was not detected earlier in his course. The student is demanding a refund of his course fees as he cannot complete the course in which he was enrolled (Sherriff, 2004).

There have also been cases where students failed for plagiarizing have had their marks reinstated. A large Australian university was recently embroiled in such an incident where fifteen students received pass marks when they had previously failed. The incident was referred to the NSW Independent Commission against Corruption, with the university claiming that there had been a misunderstanding of their policy (ABC, 2003).

In such a climate, the issue of plagiarism can rightly be described as a battle-   5
ground, where a war is waged between students and institutions, and played out using all of the means afforded by contemporary digital technologies. In this contemporary scenario, three main strategies dominate. The war can be fought through intelligence, where knowledge afforded by Internet technologies is the primary weapon. This war is also a propaganda war, as policies and litigation compete for supremacy. Finally this paper argues that the best offense is good defense — bulletproof approaches need to be developed to protect against the onslaught of cybercheating.

Fighting with intelligence

Since the cold war, intelligence has been one of the primary tools for war. However, as recent events have shown, decisions made on the basis of intelligence are only as good as the availability, accuracy, and ability to use the intelligence itself.

One of the major intelligence tools for plagiarism in the digital age is the World Wide Web. It is an easy task for the educator to use a Web search engine with a sample of a student's work to identify whether it already exists on the Web. This is probably the most common strategy used by educators to "trap" plagiarized work. However, when the enemy has the same access to the intelligence that you do, you can end up in a war of digital "brinkmanship" with each party trying to outplay the other.

One tool provided to institutions is a Web-based repository of copyright materials that can be used as a benchmark to check students' work. One example of this is Turnitin.com (http://www.turnitin.com/). This self proclaimed "standard in online plagiarism prevention" (Turnitin.com, 2004) contains a database of existing publications from a variety of sources. Each time a subscriber submits an article to check for plagiarism that article is added to the database. Plagiarism.org reports that 30 percent of a large sampling of Berkeley students were caught plagiarizing directly from the Internet when their assignments were run through a Turnitin.com test (http://www.plagiarism.org/).

While an effective digital solution on some levels, the Turnitin approach raises a number of issues. Firstly, its database, while large, is still limited. Secondly, the automatic storage of articles raises its own intellectual property issues, as student work is being "published" to the database, often without their permission (Foster, 2002a). An interesting weakness of this type of software has been highlighted by Dehnart (1999), who ran his own thesis through a plagiarism testing service and was told that it was plagiarized. After an examination of the detailed analysis, he found that the company had found a copy of his thesis online and was comparing the two. The worrying aspect of this is that a busy academic may not examine the detailed analysis to pick up such anomalies, and graduate students, in particular, may be falsely accused of plagiarism.

Another issue, that of whether it is ethically appropriate for students to be force- 10 fully contributing to the value of an external commercial entity, is yet to be resolved.

Such approaches are also only useful where plagiarized content takes the form of written articles. In technology based courses, the work may take the form of a digital graphic, audio, animation, or computer software product. Solutions to iden- tify plagiarism in these newer digital forms are not so well developed.

It is here where the student has the intelligence advantage. Firstly, they have access to the same digital resources as their lecturers, which already levels the battle- field. Secondly, they are usually much more adept at using digital technologies to source information. In being able to source a broader variety of copyright material than the lecturer may be able to access they can often remain undetected. Add to that the now instant availability of services that offer to complete university as- sessments for you, and the problem appears insurmountable. These online "paper mills" offer expertise in many areas and provide written work that is often unique and undetectable by plagiarism software.

War story: When intelligence fails

Although lecturers may be highly skilled in their areas of expertise, they may lack the digital "savvy" to identify cybercheating. One lecturer describes how he got lucky: I was running a unit in 3 Dimensional Modeling and Animation. One of the assign- ments was for students to create a 3D model from a physical toy and create several rendered images of their toy in different settings. On the whole the assignment was completed quite well.

It was only several weeks later when I was browsing one of the 3D Web com- munities that I noticed a forum post by a guy, "Count Zero," who claimed to have produced a toy in 3D was and asking for feedback. I downloaded the files and was amazed to see a 3D scene containing a fully realized toy as well as six rendered images that were instantly recognizable as an assignment submitted by one of my students.

I e-mailed "Count Zero" and found out that he was not my student, but had 15 received a request from someone on a different community asking for help with modeling a toy. He directed me to the original community and thread. When I got there I was stunned to see a post by my student requesting help and submitting scanned photos of his toy. Count Zero, being the community minded 3D artist that he was, had gone to the extent of completing the toy for the student and posting the files to the forum.

I was fuming. The whole time, my student had claimed this was all his own work, didn't provide any reference to the forum, and hadn't even bothered to re-render or modify the work in any way. I went into the files for both my student and Locust and found that they were exactly the same right down to the smallest polygon.

If it wasn't for the fact that I'm a 3D nut and was a regular lurker on the 3D communites I'd never have caught him! (Extract from interview with Seamus.)

Fighting with propaganda

In *Manufacturing Consent*, Noam Chomsky (1988) argued the intrinsicness of propaganda to democracy. When you cannot control people's actions directly, you have to control the way people think. While directed primarily at the media, universities, too, rely on propaganda as their primary tool of control. In the university system, we call it "education" but while we try to phrase our policies in terms of student centered and constructivist principles, the fact remains that universities are large institutions that communicate ideas in value laden ways:

> Universities . . . are not independent institutions. There may be independent people scattered around in them but that is true of the media as well. And it's generally true of corporations. It's true of Fascist states, for that matter. But the institution itself is parasitic. It's dependent on outside sources of support and those sources of support, such as private wealth, big corporations with grants, and the government (which is so closely interlinked with corporate power you can barely distinguish them). (Chomsky, 1997)

A section of one large university's strategic plan includes the notion of "professionalism," which is described as "demonstrating the highest standard of professional behavior in relationships with students, staff, and the community."

While professionalism is a somewhat loose depiction of the university's traditional roles, the equal emphasis placed upon seeking new markets and a view of the student as a customer, makes it difficult to argue against the contention that rather than educating students, universities are now in the business of trading in degrees. This raises concerns with regard to the relationship between universities and students over issues such as plagiarism.

Most universities have policies and procedures that are designed to ensure the   20
student is aware of his or her responsibilities regarding plagiarism. This "propaganda" model seeks to ensure compliance through education. It is a "carrot and stick" approach to communication.

The carrot is offered in the form of activities and assessments that are designed to teach students about the dangers of plagiarism. Forms that these can take include:

- Providing plagiarism information at orientation sessions.

- Providing courses in referencing and study skills.

- Incorporating the "Intelligence Model" by using tools such as "www.turnitin .com" as a means of educating students about what plagiarism is.

- Incorporating the notion of "honor" as part of the university ethos.
  (Boynton, 2001)

The stick comes in the form of procedures designed to regulate over transgressions of the plagiarism policy. Students attach assignment cover sheets to their work that require them to sign off on it being free of plagiarism. Some courses have students agree to terms and conditions before submitting electronic assignments. There are also warnings about penalties defined for transgressions permanently available from the student home page.

But the student is your customer and isn't the customer always right? When concerns over issues such as plagiarism are balanced with competing market driven concerns, propaganda starts to become an increasingly ineffectual weapon. After all, threats and persuasion can only do so much.

War story: Negotiating lies

Although Universities have policies that require staff to make every effort to detect plagiarism, there are many staff who believe that it is simply not worth the effort. The following extract from a staff interview highlights some of these issues:

> My story involves a postgraduate student ("Edwin") who was working on a major paper. He was able to pick his own topic, but it had to revolve around a particular theme.
>
> When the paper was submitted to me, I was immediately suspicious due to the fact that it talked about a study, which was not described in the paper, and the fact that the paper did not hang together. I decided to Google sections of the paper to see whether any of it had been plagiarized.
>
> I found every part of the paper, which had been "mosaiced" together from six Web sites. None of these Web sites were cited in the paper, all the cited references being those from the original papers from which this one had been drawn.
>
> I immediately notified the administration of the plagiarism, and Edwin was advised that he had failed the paper (and the unit), and he was supplied with the evidence. I checked some of the work he had done prior to this, and found that he had used some of this same material in another paper without it being recognized as plagiarism, although he failed this unit as well. Because he had failed these units, he automatically failed his course. He finished up suing the University for breach of contract. In the end the University refunded his fees with interest. He was also allowed back to the University to finish his course. This has left me feeling powerless, and makes me wonder why I would bother to spend time and effort checking to see whether students are doing the right thing. I also feel for the students who do put in the effort as they finish up with an identical degree to the ones who are academically dishonest. (Extract from interview with Amelia.)

Fighting with armor

A study by two faculty members from Harvard University and University of Illinois has 25
shown that it is almost impossible to deter students from plagiarizing through warnings; instead they found that demonstrating to students the efficacy of plagiarizing

detection algorithms had a far greater effect (Braumoeller & Gains, 2001), although they do discuss the intellectual property issues outlined earlier in this paper.

This is the failure of propaganda and intelligence approaches. Their ultimate reliance on counteractive measures or a misplaced faith in the intentions of others weakens their value as tactics. If education fails, then an ineffectual counterstrike is going to do little to alter the course of the war. What this paper proposes is a preemptive measure referred to [as a] bulletproof assessment. By building assessment items that are armored against the possibility of cybercheating, the war itself may be averted. This does not mean that propaganda and intelligence do not have their place; rather they need to be combined with a clear battle strategy to prevent the opportunity of plagiarism in the first place.

Such measures can be built into course outlines before the semester begins. Forms of armor can include:

- Giving the students the resources yourself and requiring them to use only those. Thus students may not be engaging heavily in research but still need to synthesize information in their own ways.

- Getting the students to provide the resources as part of their assessment. Making students provide the original artifacts, such as photocopies of articles, and printouts of Web pages brings the intelligence battle down to a level field. Lecturers can easily crosscheck assignments against the references used.

- Making assignments highly contemporary. There are several approaches here. Students can be required to provide very up-to-date references, which immediately outdates paper mill products, or they can be required to contextualize their responses to an up-to-date medium. An example of this is where students respond to a provided news or journal article using their research as a basis for this response, but requiring them to transform their understandings to critique a specific product.

- Setting a series of developmental steps for the paper. Students then are required to respond to formative feedback; they may need to provide oral reports justifying a position and explaining the terms they have used.

None of these approaches is an instant fix to the problem of cybercheating. Oral reporting can be time consuming, for example, and the affordances of digital technologies in accessing up-to-date information place constraints upon the tactic of contemporizing assignments. To be fully effective, bulletproof assessments require multiple layers of armor and may still involve tactics aligned to intelligence and propaganda. With information being so easily shared through synchronous communication technologies, cyber "copying" between students is endemic in large units of study, where duplicate assignments are hard to distinguish. Using tools such as turnitin.com combined with assessment strategies that ensure submissions are up-to-date, adapted to a specific and unique context, and involve formative verification such as staged submission and oral reporting, many of the current examples of cybercheating can be beaten.

Best of all, bulletproof assessment can make students better learners. Students engage in a process that requires multiple forms of evidence, and a reflection on their performance. A final layer of armor may be the requirement of a metalearning essay where students write an overview of their paper or product, explaining how they went about writing it, describing major obstacles and issues, and outlining what they learned (Harris, 2002). Such self monitoring activities can involve connecting new information to former knowledge, selecting thinking strategies deliberately, and planning, monitoring, and evaluating thinking processes, and are associated with the promotion of student metacognitive skills (Nelson & Narens, 1994).

The war against plagiarism is an on-going one. Digital technologies make it an evolving battle of shifting powers and political intrigue, in which maintaining the edge in knowledge and policy is a continual struggle. The best approach is to combine these with preventative tactics that effectively armor you against the possibility of cybercheating. Bulletproof assessment is the ultimate aim, where the very possibility of plagiarism is limited, and where the inherent limitations of waging the war with propaganda and intelligence are overcome.

30

REFERENCES

Chomsky, N. (1997). What makes mainstream media mainstream. *Z Magazine, October.* [verified 26 Oct. 2004] http://www.chomsky.info/articles/19ff710 —.htm

Chomsky, N. & Herman, E. S. (1988). *Manufacturing Consent.* Pantheon Books.

ABC (2003). *Watchdog to probe uni plagiarism scandal.* Sunday, 3 August. [23 Jun. 2004, verified 26 Oct. 2004] http://www.abc.net.au/newcastle/news/200308/s916119.htm

Boynton, R. (2001). *Is honor up for grabs? Education isn't about surveillance. Washington Post,* 27 May. [verified 26 Oct. 2004] http://www.washingtonpost.com/ac2/wp-dyn/ A80312-2001May26?language=printer

Braumoeller, B. F. & Gains, B. J. (2001). Actions do speak louder than words: Deterring plagiarism with the use of plagiarism detection software. *PS: Political Science and Politics,* 34(4, Dec.), [verified 26 Oct. 2004] http://www.apsanet.org/PS/dec01/braumoeller.cfm

Bricault, D. (1998). *Legal Aspects of Academic Dishonesty: Policies, Perceptions, and Realities.* [2 Jul. 2004, verified 26 Oct. 2004] http://campus.northpark.edu/esl/dishnst.html#legal

Dehnart, A. (1999). The Web's plagiarism police. *Salon Technology.* [4 Jun. 2004, verified 26 Oct. 2004] http://www.salon.com/tech/feature/1999/06/14/plagiarism/

Foster, A. L. (2002a). Plagiarism-detection tool creates legal quandary. *The Chronicle of Higher Education,* 48(36). [verified 26 Oct. 2004] http://chronicle.com/free/v48/i36/36a03701.htm

Foster, A. L. (2002b). Up to 14% of Australian university students may be plagiarising from web, study suggests. *The Chronicle of Higher Education,* 20 November [verified 26 Oct. 2004] http://chronicle.com/free/2002/11/2002112001t.htm

Harris, R. (2002). Anti-plagiarism strategies for research papers. *VirtualSalt.* [verified 26 Oct. 2004] http://www.virtualsalt.com/antiplag.htm

Nelson, T. O. & Narens, L. (1994). The role of metacognition in problem solving. In J. Metcalfe & A. Shiminura (Eds), *Metacognition* (pp. 207–226). Cambridge: MIT Press.

Overbeck, B. K. (2000). *Plagiarism statistics.* [23 Jun. 2004, verified 26 Oct. 2004] http://iml.jou.ufl.edu/projects/Spring2000/Overbeck/stats.html

Plagiarism.org (n.d.). http://www.plagiarism.org/

Seamus. (2004). Interview on plagiarism. By M. McMahon. Perth.

Sherriff, L. (2004). Web-cheat student to sue university. *The Register*, 28 May.

Stoney, M. & Stoney, S. (2001). Copyright law for using the Internet in Teaching and Learning. Paper presented at the *8th International Conference on Information & Literacy*, Spetses, Greece.

Turnitin.com (2004). *Turnitin*. http://www.turnitin.com/

Universities Strike Back in Battle over Illegal Downloads

AMY BRITTAIN

BEFORE READING: Why do you think college students will steal music by downloading it from the Internet when they would not think of stealing a CD from a music store?

In addition to paying hefty tuition and footing the bill for costly textbooks, university students may also need to pay prominent record labels a chunk of change if they choose to illegally download music on the Internet.

The 2006–07 academic year was an aggressive one for the Recording Industry Association of America's crackdown on illegal downloads by college students. RIAA sent three times more copyright violation notices to universities than it did the previous academic year. Hundreds of prelitigation letters offered to settle for about $3,000.

Statistics show that college students illegally obtained two-thirds of their music and accounted for 1.3 billion illegal downloads in 2006 alone — in what the RIAA estimates as millions of dollars in losses directly attributed to college students. Now, Congress is taking action and pressuring universities to tighten network security and ethical standards — even comparing digital piracy to plagiarizing term papers in an effort to change the mind-set of students and administrators. Result: Universities are getting new software, and students are getting the message.

"If you're on a college campus, that's where they're looking," says Kent State University student Dave Bachman, who in April settled for $3,000 with RIAA.

Students now have more options than ever for obtaining music legally with the   5
introduction of free or inexpensive programs that cater to the college crowd. Many universities have seen a reduction in copyright violation notices after promoting such legal programs. One such program, the Ruckus Network, reworked its format

---

When she wrote this essay, Amy Brittain was a student in the Manship School of Mass Communication at Louisiana State University, where she served as in-depth editor for the online edition of LSU's *Daily Reveille*. The essay was published in the online version of the *Christian Science Monitor* (www.csmonitor.com) on June 18, 2007.

in January to provide free, legal music downloads to all US college students with a valid ".edu" e-mail address. Though it won't release hard figures, Ruckus says that since it opened the floodgates to all college students, it has experienced a 60 percent increase in users and now serves "hundreds of thousands."

The accelerating adoption of digital music has contributed to a 13 percent drop in physical music sales in 2006 (and down more than 30 percent from its 1999 peak) and a nearly 75 percent increase in digital sales that same year, according to RIAA year-end charts.

The online music industry has evolved dramatically since Northeastern University student Shawn "Napster" Fanning introduced a peer-to-peer (P2P) file-sharing service in 1999 known as Napster. The RIAA sued soon after, and in 2001 the Ninth Circuit Court of Appeals ruled that Napster could not facilitate the trade of copyrighted music. Napster shut down and partially settled in an agreement to pay copyright holders millions.

Since then, other services have provided free, but illegal, methods for P2P file sharing. In P2P sharing, a user establishes an account, downloads music or video files, and lets other users download his or her files in turn. The problem: Copyrighted music changes hands for free, and record labels don't get the licensing control guaranteed under 1998's Digital Millennium Copyright Act.

Many Napster copycats, including Kazaa, iMesh, BearShare, and Grokster, have settled with record labels for damages. Kazaa — once the premier P2P service, with 4.2 million users — settled in July, agreeing to copyright filters.

LimeWire is the last P2P giant standing, but several major record labels have a   10
joint lawsuit pending to shut it down. According to the NPD Group, an entertainment research firm, LimeWire accounted for 62 percent of P2P downloads in 2006.

The free and easy access to P2P services has long plagued university administrators. Not only do such downloads take up a lot of "bandwidth," costing campuses thousands of dollars, the downloads themselves are more likely to contain viruses and spyware that can infest the university's system. Spyware, which can transmit a user's Web-browsing habits to advertisers, may even be bundled with P2P software — and linger after the P2P program is uninstalled.

In March, US Rep. Ric Keller (R) of Florida introduced a bill to increase funds for antipiracy.

"For every one Justin Timberlake, there are hundreds of sound technicians, back-up singers, and retail workers who are hurt by illegal downloading," Representative Keller said in a phone interview. "It costs our economy billions of dollars, thousands of jobs, and we lose a great deal of tax revenue."

An immunity clause in the Digital Millennium Copyright Act of 1998 protects universities from lawsuits related to illegal file sharing on campus networks.

But that immunity could be reconsidered, Keller says pointedly, "if we find that   15
we continue to have a situation where over half of the college students continue to illegally download and the colleges do nothing about it."

Many universities are enlisting technology to deter piracy. Software programs like Audible Magic installs a campuswide filter to stop the flow of copyrighted material.

Charles Wright, an associate vice president at the University of Utah in Salt Lake City, testified to Congress that RIAA copyright violation notices to his campus declined more than 90 percent since the software was installed two years ago. The University of Florida saved hundreds of thousands of dollars in bandwidth costs after implementing Red Lambda, a program that blocks P2P systems.

While Napster, iTunes, and Rhapsody Music now have subscription-based services for the general public, Ruckus uses an ad-supported model. (A Rensselaer Polytechnic Institute student who uses Ruckus and LimeWire says Ruckus is "not very user friendly" because "there are way too many advertisements on it.")

According to Ruckus spokesman Chris Lawson, schools with Ruckus contracts get extra benefits, such as a local server that reduces bandwidth consumption, and a movie and TV library that students can subscribe to for about $15 per semester. Mr. Lawson says students from nine hundred universities have registered with the service, and some 120 universities have Ruckus contracts.

The music is free to students to download and play, but if a user wants to   20
transfer files to a portable music player, he or she must pay about $20 per semester. Note: Ruckus uses Microsoft Digital Rights Management software; it won't work with Apple computers or iPods.

The Top 10 campuses for illegal file downloads

The Recording Industry Association of America recently released a list of schools it says most frequently violated the Digital Millennium Copyright Act from September 2006 to mid-February 2007. The Top 10:

1. Ohio University (1,287 violations)
2. Purdue University (1,068)
3. University of Nebraska, Lincoln (1,002)
4. University of Tennessee, Knoxville (959)
5. University of South Carolina (914)
6. University of Massachusetts at Amherst (897)
7. Michigan State University (753)
8. Howard University (572)
9. North Carolina State University (550)
10. University of Wisconsin, Madison (513)

Since the list was published in February, the RIAA has noted progress:

- University of South Carolina has had no notices since the list was published.
- Ohio University received only about seven notices in May after it installed network-protection tools.
- Michigan State University has only received fourteen notices.
- Howard University has gotten just three notices.

Thinking and Writing about Academic Integrity

QUESTIONS FOR DISCUSSION AND WRITING

1. Explain whether or not you believe that students should be required to sign a statement on exams indicating that they have neither received nor given help on the test.

2. What is your opinion of honor codes? What if that code includes the statement that the student will report any instances of cheating that he or she observes?

3. Walsh and Rawe express different views about the use of Turnitin.com to detect plagiarism. Which do you agree with, and why?

4. Do you agree with the students who brought a lawsuit against Turnitin.com that the company has no right to add students' essays to its database — and make money from their use — without the students' consent?

5. Explain whether or not you believe that McCabe offers a realistic solution for dealing with plagiarism.

6. Do you agree with McCabe that "it takes a village" to educate a student? Does it "take a village" to provide that student with character education, or is that something that the individual or the individual and his or her family should be responsible for?

7. How closely do McCabe's figures on the frequency of cheating match your observations?

8. Analyze Stoney and McMahon's tactics that universities can use to fight plagiarism.

9. Do any of the authors represented in this chapter present tactics that you believe would be successful in discouraging plagiarism? Can you suggest tactics that you believe would be more effective?

10. Why do you think so many college students are willing to break the law by downloading music illegally?

CHAPTER 17

What Biases Shape the News That We See and Hear?

Rush Limbaugh, Glenn Beck, Sean Hannity, Lou Dobbs, Bill O'Reilly, Ann Coulter. Theirs are the voices of the radical right. Arianna Huffington, Jon Stewart, Rachel Maddow, Lawrence O'Donnell. These are their counterparts on the liberal left. Fox News leans to the right. CNN leans to the left. According to one author represented here, moderates are "a happy medium between the nutjobs." Only a relatively small percentage of Americans see no bias in reporting done by the mainstream media, or what another author calls the "lamestream media."

It's no wonder that tempers flare and blood pressure rises over claims of media bias. There's a fine line between news and commentary. There's also a fine line between news and entertainment. Glenn Beck, for example, has called himself a commentator, an entertainer, and a rodeo clown. He has also identified himself with the late Peter Finch's character Howard Beale from the 1976 film *Network*, who came to be known as the Mad Prophet of the Airwaves and whose catchphrase was "I'm as mad as Hell, and I'm not going to take this anymore!" Bill Press, on the left, named his most recent book *Toxic Talk: How the Radical Right Has Poisoned America's Airwaves* (2010). Bernard Goldberg, on the right, named his *A Slobbering Love Affair: The True (And Pathetic) Story of the Torrid Romance Between Barack Obama and the Mainstream Media* (2009). The one thing that all sides agree on is that the days of objective news reporting are over — a serious concern no matter what one's political persuasion.

Media/Political Bias

ANDREW R. CLINE

BEFORE READING: What bias do you perceive, if any, in the way that the news is presented by the major television networks? If you do not watch televised news, what individual news anchors or talk show hosts have you heard mentioned elsewhere as having obvious conservative or liberal leanings?

There is no such thing as an objective point of view.

No matter how much we may try to ignore it, human communication always takes place in a context, through a medium, and among individuals and groups who are situated historically, politically, economically, and socially. This state of affairs is neither bad nor good. It simply is. Bias is a small word that identifies the collective influences of the entire context of a message. Politicians are certainly biased and overtly so. They belong to parties and espouse policies and ideologies. And while they may think their individual ideologies are simply common sense, they understand that they speak from political positions.

Journalists, too, speak from political positions but usually not overtly so. The journalistic ethics of objectivity and fairness are strong influences on the profession. But journalistic objectivity is not the pristine objectivity of philosophy. Instead, a journalist attempts to be objective by two methods: (1) fairness to those concerned with the news and (2) a professional process of information gathering that seeks fairness, completeness, and accuracy. As we all know, the ethical heights journalists set for themselves are not always reached. But, all in all, like politics, it is an honorable profession practiced, for the most part, by people trying to do the right thing.

The press is often thought of as a unified voice with a distinct bias (right or left depending on the critic). This simplistic thinking fits the needs of ideological struggle, but is hardly useful in coming to a better understanding of what is happening in the world. I believe journalism is an under-theorized practice. In other words, journalists often do what they do without reflecting upon the meaning of the premises and assumptions that support their practice. I say this as a former journalist. I think we may begin to reflect upon journalistic practice by noticing that the press applies a narrative structure to ambiguous events in order to create a coherent and causal sense of events.

For citizens and information consumers (which are one in the same today), it is   5
important to develop the skill of detecting bias. Remember: Bias does not suggest that a message is false or unfair. . . .

Andrew R. Cline teaches journalism at Missouri State University. He maintains his *Rhetorica: Press-Politics Journal* log on the Rhetorica Network in order to explain the persuasive tactics of politics and the press. This explanation of bias is posted on the "Rhetorica Critical Meter" portion of the site.

Critical questions for detecting bias

1. What is the author's/speaker's socio-political position? With what social, political, or professional groups is the speaker identified?
2. Does the speaker have anything to gain personally from delivering the message?
3. Who is paying for the message? Where does the message appear? What is the bias of the medium? Who stands to gain?
4. What sources does the speaker use, and how credible are they? Does the speaker cite statistics? If so, how were the data gathered, who gathered the data, and are the data being presented fully?
5. How does the speaker present arguments? Is the message one-sided, or does it include alternative points of view? Does the speaker fairly present alternative arguments? Does the speaker ignore obviously conflicting arguments?
6. If the message includes alternative points of view, how are those views characterized? Does the speaker use positive words and images to describe his/her point of view and negative words and images to describe other points of view? Does the speaker ascribe positive motivations to his/her point of view and negative motivations to alternative points of view?

Bias in the news media

Is the news media biased toward liberals? Yes. Is the news media biased toward conservatives? Yes. These questions and answers are uninteresting because it is possible to find evidence — anecdotal and otherwise — to "prove" media bias of one stripe or another. Far more interesting and instructive is studying the inherent, or *structural*, biases of journalism as a professional practice — especially as mediated through television. I use the word "bias" here to challenge its current use by partisan critics. A more accepted, and perhaps more accurate, term would be "frame." These are some of the professional frames that structure what journalists can see and how they can present what they see.

1. **Commercial bias**: The news media are money-making businesses. As such, they must deliver a good product to their customers to make a profit. The customers of the news media are advertisers. The most important product the news media delivers to its customers are readers or viewers. Good is defined in numbers and quality of readers or viewers. The news media are biased toward conflict (re: bad news and narrative biases below) because conflict draws readers and viewers. Harmony is boring.
2. **Temporal bias**: The news media are biased toward the immediate. News is what's new and fresh. To be immediate and fresh, the news must be ever-changing even when there is little news to cover.
3. **Visual bias**: Television (and, increasingly, newspapers) is biased toward visual depictions of news. Television is nothing without pictures. Legitimate news

that has no visual angle is likely to get little attention. Much of what is important in politics — policy — cannot be photographed.

4. **Bad news bias**: Good news is boring (and probably does not photograph well, either). This bias makes the world look like a more dangerous place than it really is. Plus, this bias makes politicians look far more crooked than they really are.

5. **Narrative bias**: The news media cover the news in terms of "stories" that must have a beginning, middle, and end — in other words, a plot with antagonists and protagonists. Much of what happens in our world, however, is ambiguous. The news media apply a narrative structure to ambiguous events suggesting that these events are easily understood and have clear cause-and-effect relationships. Good storytelling requires drama, and so this bias often leads journalists to add, or seek out, drama for the sake of drama. Controversy creates drama. Journalists often seek out the opinions of competing experts or officials in order to present conflict between two sides of an issue (sometimes referred to as the authority-disorder bias). Lastly, narrative bias leads many journalists to create, and then hang on to, master narratives — set story lines with set characters who act in set ways. Once a master narrative has been set, it is very difficult to get journalists to see that their narrative is simply one way, and not necessarily the correct or best way, of viewing people and events.

6. **Status quo bias**: The news media believe "the system works." During the "fiasco in Florida,"[1] recall that the news media were compelled to remind us that the Constitution was safe, the process was working, and all would be well. The mainstream news media never question the structure of the political system. The American way is the only way, politically and socially. In fact, the American way is news. The press spends vast amounts of time in unquestioning coverage of the process of political campaigns (but less so on the process of governance). This bias ensures that alternate points of view about how government might run and what government might do are effectively ignored.

7. **Fairness bias**: No, this is not an oxymoron. Ethical journalistic practice demands that reporters and editors be fair. In the news product this bias manifests as a contention between/among political actors (also re: narrative bias above). Whenever one faction or politician does something or says something newsworthy, the press is compelled by this bias to get a reaction from an opposing camp. This creates the illusion that the game of politics is always contentious and never cooperative. This bias can also create situations in which one faction appears to be attacked by the press. For example, politician A announces some positive accomplishment followed by the press seeking a negative comment from politician B. The point is not to disparage politician A but to be fair to politician B. When politician A is a conservative, this practice appears to be liberal bias.

---

[1] The disputed 2000 presidential election included a partial recount of votes in Florida. — EDS.

8. **Expediency bias:** Journalism is a competitive, deadline-driven profession. Reporters compete among themselves for prime space or air time. News organizations compete for market share and reader/viewer attention. And the 24-hour news cycle — driven by the immediacy of television and the internet — creates a situation in which the job of competing never comes to a rest. Add financial pressures to this mix — the general desire of media groups for profit margins that exceed what's "normal" in many other industries — and you create a bias toward information that can be obtained quickly, easily, and inexpensively. Need an expert/official quote (status quo bias) to balance (fairness bias) a story (narrative bias)? Who can you get on the phone fast? Who is always ready with a quote and always willing to speak (i.e. say what you need them to say to balance the story)? Who sent a press release recently? Much of deadline decision making comes down to gathering information that is readily available from sources that are well known.

9. **Glory bias:** Journalists, especially television reporters, often assert themselves into the stories they cover. This happens most often in terms of proximity, i.e. to the locus of unfolding events or within the orbit of powerful political and civic actors. This bias helps journalists establish and maintain a cultural identity as knowledgeable insiders (although many journalists reject the notion that follows from this — that they are players in the game and not merely observers). The glory bias shows itself in particularly obnoxious ways in television journalism. News promos with stirring music and heroic pictures of individual reporters create the aura of omnipresence and omnipotence. I ascribe the use of the satellite phone to this bias. Note how often it's used in situations in which a normal video feed should be no problem to establish, e.g. a report from Tokyo I saw recently on CNN. The jerky pictures and fuzzy sound of the satellite phone create a romantic image of foreign adventure.

Structural Bias as Theory

I have asserted that some critics of the press think of it as speaking with a unified voice with a distinct ideological bias. I have further asserted that this simplistic thinking fits the needs of ideological struggle, but is hardly useful in coming to a better understanding of what is happening in the world. For that better understanding we need a theory.

A theory offers us a model that tells us why things happen as they do. Further, a theory allows us to predict outcomes and behavior. Assertions of ideological bias do neither. While we can expect the press to demonstrate ideological biases in regard to certain issues or other localized phenomena, these and other behaviors are explained and predicted by the structural biases. Since the press sometimes demonstrates a conservative bias, asserting that the press is liberal neither predicts nor explains. Since the press sometimes demonstrates a liberal bias, asserting that the press is conservative neither predicts nor explains.

Test this for yourself. Choose a situation that is current — preferably breaking right now. For each of the structural biases listed above, write down what you would expect the press to do based on that bias. Then, complete the exercise with a concluding statement that takes into account as many of the structural biases as possible. Now, follow the situation for a few days and note how the press behaves. I think you will find that you have successfully predicted press behavior.

News media assumptions about language and discourse

Simply communicating by written or spoken words introduces bias to the message. If, as asserted earlier, there is no such thing as an objective point of view, then there cannot be objective or transparent language, i.e. a one-to-one correspondence between reality and words such that I may accurately represent reality so that you experience it as I do. Language mediates our lived experiences. And our evaluation of those experiences are reflected in our language use. Rhetoric scholar James A. Berlin once said that language is "never innocent." By this he meant that language cannot be neutral; it reflects and structures our ideologies and world views. To speak at all is to speak politically. The practice of journalism, however, accepts a very different view of language that creates serious consequences for the news consumer. Most journalists do their jobs with little or no thought given to language theory, i.e. how language works and how humans use language. Most journalists, consciously or not, accept a theory (metaphor) of language as a transparent conduit along which word-ideas are easily sent to a reader or viewer who then experiences reality as portrayed by the words.

From George Lakoff's *Moral Politics* (U of Chicago P), journalism *falsely* asserts that:

1. **Concepts are literal and nonpartisan**: The standard six-question rubric of journalism (who, what, when, where, why, how) cannot capture the complexity of issues as seen through, and expressed by, the incompatible moral systems of liberals and conservatives.

2. **Language use is neutral**: "Language is associated with a conceptual system. To use the language of a moral or political conceptual system is to use and to reinforce that conceptual system."

3. **News can be reported in neutral terms**: Not if #2 is correct. To choose a discourse is to choose a position. To attempt neutrality confuses the political concepts. Is it an "inheritance tax" or a "death tax"? What could possibly be a neutral term? To use both in the name of balance is confusing because most news articles don't have the space, and most TV treatments don't have the time, to fully explain the terms and why liberals prefer one and conservatives prefer the other. There's no time or space to explain why this language difference matters (beyond political tactics) to the formation, implementation, and evaluation of policy.

4. **Mere use of language cannot put anyone at a disadvantage**: Again, see #2.

5. **All readers and viewers share the same conceptual system**: We share the same English language, i.e. its grammar. We often do not share dialects or the denotations and connotations of concepts, lived experience, and ideologies. The statement "I am a patriotic American" means something entirely different to liberals and conservatives. That difference is more than a matter of connotation. The differences in connotation spring from different moral constructs. What the conservative means by that statement appears immoral to the liberal and vice versa.

These false assumptions by journalists, rather than overt politicking, help create the political bias news consumers often detect in news reporting. A conservative will quite naturally assert a conservative world view by using concepts in ways comfortable to conservatives. The same goes for liberals. It is often pointed out that most news reporters are Democrats or vote for Democrats. Party affiliation, however, tells us nothing about political ideology and the moral concepts that undergird it. There are conservative Democrats and liberal Republicans. Be that as it may, the ethics of journalistic practice strongly urge reporters to adopt the assumptions about language listed above and the structural biases listed above. The ethics of journalistic practice encourage journalists to adopt a (nonexistent) neutral language to mitigate any effects of ideological bias. There simply is no concerted or sustained effort to slant the news for political purposes by mainstream news outlets.

Anti-bias crusading as an elitist practice

Accuracy in Media claims the news media are biased toward liberal politics. Fairness & Accuracy in Media claims the news media are biased toward conservative politics. Supporters of these views see one group as right and the other as wrong. But the reality is not that simple. Yes, AIM and FAIR each point out coverage that appears to bolster their various claims. At times, the media do seem to be biased one way or the other. What these groups don't say, however, is that their mistrust of the media is also a mistrust of the people. Those who complain most about media bias would see themselves as able to identify it and resist it. They get upset about it because they question whether the average American is able to do the same. If the average American can identify it and resist it, then there is little need to get upset about bias. The AIM and FAIR web sites are full of material to help hapless Americans avoid the cognitive ravages of the "evil" conservatives or the "slandering" liberals and their media lackeys. I believe the average American is quite capable of identifying problems with news coverage. In my opinion, crusading against political bias in the news media is an elitist practice.

America's Town Meeting

BILL PRESS

BEFORE READING: The following essay is the conclusion of Bill Press's book *Toxic Talk* (2010). Speculate about how the term *toxic talk* could apply to political discourse.

Finally, a few words about the contribution of talk radio and the importance of getting it right.

One thing for sure: Right-wing or left, talk radio's here to stay. As long as there are traffic jams and debates over issues around the dinner table, listeners will tune in to talk radio: to listen, to learn, to laugh, and to participate. After all, it's the only chance many people have to voice their opinions publicly — and anonymously, if they care to. Nobody really knows if "Vernon from Washington, D.C." is really Vernon from Washington or Mark from Bend, Oregon. Yes, people can — and do — express their political opinions anonymously on the Internet, in blogs, chat rooms, and so forth. But a lot of people don't have the time, or know-how, to express their opinions electronically, and talk radio will always be a more direct and more communal medium.

No doubt, talk radio will continue to grow and expand, adapting to new technologies and new opportunities. The only questions are: Will talk radio continue to be as one-sided as it is today? And will so much of it continue to be so mean and ugly?

As I stated at the outset, I'm a big champion of talk radio, whether talk show hosts come from the left, right, or middle. Indeed, the more I listen to talk radio, and the more hours I spend behind the microphone, talking about the issues and taking calls from listeners, the more I value and appreciate both the power and the promise of the medium.

My experience as a host has taught me two things about talk radio. First, after voting, there's no better way to involve people in the workings of democracy. By offering good, lively talk radio, both on the left and the right, and by giving people the opportunity to weigh in and voice their opinions, we are performing a very valuable public service. There is no better democratic (small "d"!) platform available anywhere, so easily accessible to so many people at the same time.

We also offer an important service by providing people someplace where they can feel at home in an increasingly complex and confusing world. Jack Swanson, program director of KSFO and KGO in San Francisco, and one of the most gifted (and colorful!) radio executives in the country, put it this way: "You know what people want most in the world, besides love? People want to be told. 'You're right.' Whether

5

Bill Press has long been a media commentator and political insider and co-hosted MSNBC's *Buchanan and Press*, CNN's *Crossfire*, and *The Spin Room*. He currently writes a nationally syndicated weekly newspaper column. This essay is the concluding chapter of his most recent book, *Toxic Talk: How the Radical Right Has Poisoned America's Airwaves* (2010).

you're here at conservative KSFO or at liberal KPFA in Berkeley, the core value is the same." Listeners, in other words, know there's one place on the dial where they can find themselves among friends — whether it's friends on the right, or friends on the left. And that place is talk radio. Listening to talk radio by themselves, at home or in the car, they suddenly don't feel so lonely.

But . . . Here's the second lesson, I believe: Talk radio is not really serving the public when it gets so ugly and when it remains so overwhelmingly one-sided.

Talk radio has already had enormous influence over America's political process. Unfortunately, as we hear from listening to most conservative talk show hosts, that influence has mostly been in a negative direction: tearing people apart, exploiting divisive issues, pitting one group against another, and denying honest differences of opinion. That's the perversion of toxic talk, which has seriously damaged the level of political discourse in this country.

As Americans, political debate is not only protected by the Constitution, it is part of our nature. It's in our blood. We learned the value of robust discussion of the issues from our Founding Fathers and Mothers. But at the very heart of that debate lies the premise that unites us as Americans: We all want what's best for this country, we may just differ on how to get there. Unfortunately, that essential premise gets lost on right-wing talk radio. Instead, it's all us versus them. I'm right, you're wrong. Or, worse yet, I know what's right for America — and you're un-American if you think otherwise. There's no room for dissent, no room for honest differences of opinion, no room for thought. And anybody who disagrees with me, from the president of the United States on down, is a pinko, commie, racist, socialist, moron, Nazi, idiot, or worse. That kind of talk radio — as practiced by Rush Limbaugh, Glenn Beck, Sean Hannity, Michael Savage, Mark Levin, Laura Ingraham, Neal Boortz, Lou Dobbs, and others — violates every rule of civil discourse and does a disservice to our democracy. It is fundamentally un-American. And Americans deserve better.

Americans deserve to hear more than a right-wing chorus on the radio, too.   10
We are, after all, a great and diverse nation. And, to reflect that diversity, we need a wide-open sounding board on the radio. The greater the mix of voices, the better talk radio mirrors what America's all about, and the better it is for listeners and for the country. In order to become informed citizens, people need to be exposed to more than just one point of view.

Talk radio's been called "America's front porch." I like to think of it as "America's town meeting." In colonial times, it was easier to keep people informed and achieve consensus — admittedly, in part because so many Americans were excluded from full citizenship. Town fathers just called a meeting to present the facts, debate the issues, and make a decision. Today, it's almost impossible. Our cities are so big, people are so busy, issues are so complex, the electorate is more diverse, and special interests are so powerful that it's hard to convince people to bother to vote, let alone get involved in the political process.

Few people have time for town meetings anymore. And fewer and fewer people take time to read the daily newspaper or watch the evening news. But whether driving to work or puttering around the kitchen, everybody has time to listen to talk radio. It's the easiest and most direct way to engage the voting public today: not only informing them of the issues, but giving them the opportunity to join the national debate.

That's what so great about talk radio. You don't need a master's degree or consulting contract. You don't need to learn how to make your own Web site. You don't have to pay a fee. You don't have to leave the comfort of your own home, office, or car. To participate, all you need is a set of ears. And an opinion — and who doesn't have plenty of those? With one set of ears, one opinion, and one phone call, anybody can join the national conversation on any issue, and be listened to and taken as seriously as any other caller.

With its capacity to empower every listener fully, and empower all of its listeners equally, talk radio can be the most democratic form of communication. But talk radio will never achieve its full potential so long as it's overwhelmingly dominated by right-wing ministers of hate.

We need to fumigate our airwaves of toxic talk by ensuring there are more diverse 15 opinions to be heard on the radio, all around the country. The solution to a problem like Rush Limbaugh and his horde of thin-skinned bullies is twofold. First, we must point out, time and time again, how right-wing radio hosts are misrepresenting the truth and mischaracterizing their enemies. That's the role of progressive talk show hosts. Eternal vigilance is the price of a free and functioning civil society. In order to respond to the wave of lies cascading from right-wing radio, we also must fight fire with fire and build and support a national progressive media and radio network that can stand up to the right-wing money machine.

Our Founding Fathers knew that the best response to bad or wrong-headed ideas are better ones, aired in open debate. Free speech and impassioned but civil argument have always been the American way. But the right-wing stranglehold on radio has threatened our ability to conduct an honest political debate, and its intolerance of opposing arguments has polluted and diminished our politics.

In short, we have let the airwaves — and our political system — be consumed with a poisonous cloud of toxic talk. Now's the time to get active, get involved, build a powerful progressive media machine, and help clean up the air.

Most Americans Just Don't Trust Them

BERNARD GOLDBERG

BEFORE READING: It is often suggested that the mainstream media have a liberal bias. What exactly are the "mainstream media" and how true is the claim that their reporting is biased?

Another nail has just been hammered into the coffin of the so-called mainstream media, an institution I like to call the lamestream media.

A press release accompanying a Gallup poll that has just been released says, "For the fourth straight year, the majority of Americans say they have little or no trust in the mass media to report the news fully, accurately, and fairly. The 57 percent now saying this is a record high by one percentage point."

For years, I have been talking and writing about bias in the mainstream media, liberal media bias to be precise. I have said there is no conspiracy. The network TV anchors don't go to work in the morning, summon their top lieutenants, dim the lights, pull down the shades, give the secret handshake and salute, and then say, "How are we going to nail those conservatives today."

I was a correspondent at CBS News for 28 years and I can assure you that despite what some on the Right may think, it doesn't happen that way. I wish it did, because no one would put up with that kind of blatant bias. The way it really happens is worse.

The problem is groupthink. There simply are too many liberals in America's big, important newsrooms. News executives worship at the altar of diversity, but what has it gotten us? White liberals and black liberals, male liberals and female liberals, Latino liberals, Asian liberals, gay liberals and straight liberals.   5

I have no quarrel with racial, ethnic, and gender diversity. It's not a good thing to have the news filtered only through white men. But what about some intellectual diversity in the newsroom? How about a little diversity of opinion?

No, I don't want those opinions turning up in straight news stories. But just as we need women and minorities in the newsroom in order to get a different *perspective* on the news, we also need conservatives to add their perspective to the dominant liberal news culture in our newsrooms.

Bernard Goldberg is a television news reporter and author who has won ten Emmy awards for his work, first at CBS and more recently on the HBO program *Real Sports*. His first book, *Bias: A CBS Insider Exposes How the Media Distort the News* (2001), became a *New York Times* number one bestseller, and his other four have all made the list as well. The title of his most recent book speaks for itself: *A Slobbering Love Affair: The True (And Pathetic) Story of the Torrid Romance Between Barack Obama and the Mainstream Media* (2009). This article was posted on September 29, 2010, on BernardGoldberg.com.

Which brings us back to that new Gallup poll. "Nearly half of Americans (48%) say the media are too liberal," we are told. "One-third say the media are just about right while 15% say they are too conservative."

And this was my favorite line from Gallup: "Democrats and liberals remain far more likely than other political and ideological groups to trust the media and to perceive no bias."

Gee, I wonder why. Could it be because liberals like the liberal bias they're getting from journalists who keep telling themselves they're *not* biased? Could it be because those supposedly objective journalists are putting out information slanted to the left, which is just fine with those liberals and Democrats whose views also slant to the left?   10

Sorry, my lefty friends, liberal media bias is real. It is not a figment of fevered conservative imaginations. And it's one of the reasons so-called mainstream journalism is dying.

As I say at the end of my book, *A Slobbering Love Affair*, which chronicles the media's embarrassing adoration of Barack Obama during the presidential campaign:

> The grim reaper is knocking on the mainstream media's door, and they remain gloriously oblivious. They have reached a tipping point but refuse to believe it. The corrosion that is eating away at their credibility has been happening slowly. It's like acid rain; one day you look around all the trees are dead. Nobody pays attention until it's too late.
>
> And when they become so irrelevant that no one listens to them anymore, they undoubtedly will lash out at their critics for poisoning the well. They will remain arrogant and clueless and blame the media bashers for damaging their standing with the public. But their demise won't come from the outside. It will be an inside job, the result of one too many self-inflicted wounds.
>
> When that day comes it will be very bad indeed for the mainstream media. Pray, that their demise doesn't also lead to ours.

The numbers in this new Gallup poll ought to make all of us worry, and that includes liberals who are happy with the media. Everyone knows that we can't have a free country without a free press. But neither can we have a free country — not for long anyway — without a *fair* press. And when, as Gallup tells us, "the majority of Americans say they have little or no trust in the mass media to report the news fully, accurately, and fairly" that is very bad news indeed — no matter what your politics.

The Age of Limbaugh: When Politics and Popular Entertainment Collide

JESSE WALKER

BEFORE READING: What examples can you think of where "politics and popular entertainment collide," to quote Walker's subtitle?

Just a few days after he was sworn in as president, Barack Obama asked the opposition to ignore its partisan instincts and help him develop a stimulus package. "You can't just listen to Rush Limbaugh and get things done," he admonished.

It was the beginning of a big year for Limbaugh, a radio host whose influence had seemed to be waning not long before. Allies and critics alike were soon describing him as the "head of the Republican Party," not least when the actual head of the Republican National Committee criticized the famous broadcaster only to quickly cave to rank-and-file pressure and apologize for his remarks. Beloved by the true-believing party base, disdained by center-right compromisers, and detested by the left, Limbaugh has towered over every noisy Washington debate of 2009 and 2010.

Now he is the subject of a breezy biography, Zev Chafets' *Rush Limbaugh: An Army of One*. In Chafets' telling, Limbaugh comes across as a likeable loner with the same combination of confidence and insecurity that has fueled entertainers for eons. The book began as a magazine profile, and it still reads like one, complete with first-person segments about the author's interactions with Limbaugh and the people who know him. Chafets, a journalist and novelist who once worked as a press officer for Israeli Prime Minister Menachem Begin, leans heavily on recent events — over a third of the book is devoted to the latest two years of Limbaugh's life — and he is generally sympathetic, though not entirely uncritical, toward his subject. There is much more here about Limbaugh's impact on politics than his impact on radio, and while Chafets compares Rush to a series of celebrities, from Elvis to Muhammad Ali, he doesn't really explore Limbaugh's status as a pop icon.

Limbaugh isn't really the head of the GOP, but he isn't an ordinary commentator either. Part vaudeville showman and part ward leader, Limbaugh straddles the line between politics and popular culture. He is the most notable example of a political species that emerged only recently: a person whose power derives not from his constituents but from his fans.

This is not the distant fandom that fuels the rise of a Ronald Reagan or an Arnold   5
Schwarzenegger. Such celebrities' fame may allow them to bypass the traditional

---

Jesse Walker is managing editor of *Reason* magazine and author of *Rebels on the Air: An Alternative History of Radio in America* (2004). This review essay is from the August/September 2010 issue of *Reason*.

Rush Limbaugh gives a speech in Michigan.

early stages of a political career — the low-level legwork that lets voters and donors know who a candidate is. But when they enter electoral politics, they still need to establish a conventional political organization.

Nor is Limbaugh's following the type that allowed earlier generations of broadcasters to influence the public debate. It's much more participatory than that.

Limbaugh interacts directly with his audience. He doesn't just speak but listens, and the callers don't just listen but argue. Limbaugh is always in charge of the show, and he manipulates his medium like a master. But the intimacy of radio gives him a relationship with his followers that's considerably different from that enjoyed by ordinary politicians and pundits.

It is effective theater, and because it is effective theater it is also effective politics. Limbaugh is not in the habit of urging his audience to call their congressmen, but when he asked them to do so during the debate over Obama's health care bill, they telephoned in droves. Whenever a public figure criticizes Limbaugh, his listeners will dutifully launch an angry fusillade of calls and emails on their own. And when Republicans swept to historic victories in the congressional elections of 1994, the GOP freshman class knew who to thank, naming Limbaugh an honorary member of their caucus. Obama's admonition — "You can't just listen to Rush Limbaugh and get things done" — unintentionally expressed something important about the show: It asks its audience *not* to "just listen" but to actively involve themselves in both the program (by calling in) and the political process (by backing conservative candidates and causes).

When something like a fan culture appears in politics — when a public figure's supporters feel an intense personal connection to him, and the figure in question takes a showman's delight in trying to fine-tune their reactions — the leader is often accused of being a demagogue. Because intellectuals have traditionally distrusted the mass media, this has been especially true when the leader's pulpit is the television or the radio. But the situation is usually more complicated than that. With Limbaugh, it's *much* more complicated. When callers launch their spiels with the word "dittos," announcing that they agree with what the host just said, they're not simply falling in line behind Limbaugh's opinions; they're offering him feedback. If he directs his listeners' emotions as skillfully as any performing artist, he also gives them a role in driving his show. And he's not just a leader but an entertainer, with a style that owes more to disc jockeys and stand-up comics than to conventional political oratory.

Rush Limbaugh got his start as a Top 40 DJ. Significantly, he got into broadcast- 10 ing because he loved music, not because he loved politics. The most ideological element of his early radio work was that it *wasn't* ideological: He played pop singles, read the news, and performed other tasks for tightly formatted AM stations at a time when more countercultural outlets were mixing their experimental, genre-bending freeform sets with left-leaning grumblings about The Man. Limbaugh would later deride those DJs and their listeners as "long-haired, dope-smoking, maggot-infested, good time rock 'n' roll plastic banana FM types."

At the same time, as Chafets shows, Limbaugh pushed back against the restrictions of his format, a habit that didn't always lead to good relations with station management. When political talk radio took off in the early '90s, it was, in one respect at least, a throwback to the old days of freeform FM: *The host was in charge.* He was free to improvise a long monologue, to take calls, to do risky comedy bits, and even to insert some music into the mix; you didn't know at the beginning of a show where the next few hours would take you. Suddenly there was more creative freedom on the AM band than on FM — a radical reversal from the hippie days.

Fans of the Limbaugh show tune in not just to hear right-wing opinions but for the host's on-air persona (he plays an over-the-top egotist) and the world he constructed around it (his show has its own jargon and catchphrases, a horde of running gags, and a set of customs for the callers). Even the mic technique is distinctive: Limbaugh punctuates his comments with coughs, shuffles his papers noisily at the appropriate junctures, and, in general, gives his show a sound that is as singular as its viewpoint.

His success announced a new era in which politics and popular culture would be blended more thoroughly than ever before: a time when shock jocks are as significant as policy wonks and getting good ratings is as important as getting out the vote. That puts Limbaugh in an interesting relationship not just with his audience but with his targets. Talk radio thrives on populist outrage, so its strongest moments come when it channels public opposition to a controversial policy. Its most uncomfortable moments come when it finds itself playing defense rather than offense. And its most ridiculous moments come when the news cycle is quiet, leaving the host thrashing around to gin up a good controversy for the day. Like the funnyman in a double act, the talk show host always needs a foil.

It should surprise no one, then, that Limbaugh's popularity leaped when Bill Clinton became president, nor that he lost his momentum after he helped engineer the Republican victories of 1994. And it shouldn't be a shock that the transition away from Republican rule has reinvigorated him. Limbaugh, in turn, has been a convenient target for the media-savvy Democratic commander-in-chief, who has good reasons to prefer a Limbaugh-led GOP. (Rush is as unpopular with swing-vote centrists as he is popular among his fans.) It isn't that Limbaugh wants the Democrats to be in power. It's just that his show is strongest when they are.

At the same time, he's a very loyal Republican. He's more likely to dissent from the party line than, say, Sean Hannity, but he is nowhere near as independent as Glenn Beck or Bill O'Reilly. Limbaugh's brand of conservatism is indebted to the three-legged stool associated with his hero, Ronald Reagan: a hawkish foreign policy, business-friendly economics, and social conservatism. But he built on the Reagan legacy in two other ways, each of which played a role in the right's changing fortunes in the late twentieth and early twenty-first centuries.

One was his fealty to the GOP. Limbaugh has never held to Reagan's famous Eleventh Commandment — "Thou shalt not speak ill of a fellow Republican" — but when push comes to shove he will pick partisan loyalty over ideological intransigence. He will criticize the party, but he always ultimately falls in behind it. Thus, while he doesn't usually have guests on his show, in 1992 he broadcast a fawning interview with President George H.W. Bush, who was in a tough (and ultimately unsuccessful) reelection fight against Bill Clinton. At one point Rush claimed — absurdly, given the environmental and anti-discriminatory legislation that Bush had signed, the drug war he had stepped up, and the new powers his administration had taken during the Gulf War — that the chief difference between Bush and Clinton was that Bush believed in limited government. The host knew better, but he also knew what message would sell.

The second development was Limbaugh's loose approach to social issues. The broadcaster is, at least nominally, a social conservative. He is unfriendly to the gay movement (though he has toned that down over the years) and he supports drug prohibition (despite his own run-ins with the law). But he hasn't led a socially conservative life. Besides his well-publicized OxyContin and Viagra busts, he is on his fourth marriage and has a far from puritanical attitude toward cigars, food, and other legal pleasures. He puts much more stress on economic and foreign policy than on public morals, and, to borrow Robert Kaiser's phrase about Ronald Reagan, he shows signs of being a "closet tolerant."

This doesn't add up to a libertarian stance. If it did he'd be more concerned about the effects of the drug war (which *is* opposed, interestingly, by his frequent guest host Walter Williams). Indeed, Limbaugh's tolerance extends to many practices that libertarians oppose, such as the abuses at Abu Ghraib (which prompted the host to exclaim, "You ever heard of emotional release? You ever heard of the need to blow some steam off?"). Whatever this worldview is, it is neither libertarian nor traditionalist. Yet it is increasingly common.

As a portrait of Limbaugh the man, Chafets' book is an enjoyable read. There are occasional errors, but nothing serious; and while I don't always agree with the

author's political opinions, they aren't central to the book. You get the sense sometimes that Chafets got too close to his subject, but even that has an advantage: It
makes it easier to see Limbaugh's life from the subject's point of view.

If something is missing here, it's a sense of Limbaugh's impact on the world be-   20
yond standard politics. Limbaugh's show was an early sign that politics and pop culture had collided, but it was hardly the final one; in his wake, the broadcasting world
has seen right-wing talkers with different styles (Sean Hannity, Glenn Beck), coun-
terprogrammers on the left (Jon Stewart, Rachel Maddow), a sitting politician who
resigned her office because she felt she could be more influential in a Rush-like role
(Sarah Palin), a liberal entertainer who moved from writing anti-Limbaugh books and
hosting his own radio show to getting elected to the U.S. Senate (Al Franken). Meanwhile, the Internet has made the boundary between politics and pop culture even
blurrier, in an environment where the audience is even more active and autonomous
than in talk radio.

For more than two decades, Limbaugh has helped a particular form of conservatism get a hearing. But his greater legacy might be a world where people with
radically different views can change the world using Limbaugh's techniques. The president was wrong: You *can* listen to Rush Limbaugh and get things done, even if your
politics and Limbaugh's are diametrically opposed.

Secrets of Talk Radio

DAN SHELLEY

BEFORE READING: What sorts of news make you angry? Are there times when it is the
reporter or the commentator, not the news, that angers you? Explain.

first got into journalism because I thought I could make a difference.
    I wrote for the school newspaper and did "news" reports on a radio station a
friend and I started at my high school in Springfield, Missouri. I got my first professional job at age twenty, while still in college, at a local radio station's news department. Three years later, I became a news director, and twelve years after that, in
1995, I was recruited to move to Milwaukee to become news director at WTMJ, one
of the largest and most successful news/talk radio stations in America.

As is clear from his essay, Dan Shelley is the former news director at WTMJ in Milwaukee, which
he describes as "one of the largest and most successful news/talk radio stations in America."
He is now a digital media executive in New York. The piece appeared on November 24, 2008,
on milwaukeemagazine.com.

Talk show host Charlie Sykes of WTMJ in Milwaukee.

That was where my real education occurred.

I worked for three years as news director, and then, in 1998, gained the additional title of assistant program director, a role I held until leaving the station in July 2006. From that position, I worked closely with our talk show hosts and became intimately familiar with how they appeal to listeners and shape their vision of the world. Let me tell you some of the lessons I learned.

To begin with, talk show hosts such as Charlie Sykes — one of the best in the   5
business — are popular and powerful because they appeal to a segment of the population that feels disenfranchised and even victimized by the media. These people believe the media are predominantly staffed by and consistently reflect the views of social liberals. This view is by now so long-held and deep-rooted, it has evolved into part of virtually every conservative's DNA.

To succeed, a talk show host must perpetuate the notion that his or her listeners are victims, and the host is the vehicle by which they can become empowered. The host frames virtually every issue in us-versus-them terms. There has to be a bad guy against whom the host will emphatically defend those loyal listeners.

This enemy can be a politician — either a Democratic officeholder or, in rare cases where no Democrat is convenient to blame, it can be a "RINO" (a "Republican In Name Only," who is deemed not conservative enough). It can be the cold, cruel government bureaucracy. More often than not, however, the enemy is the "mainstream media" — local or national, print or broadcast.

Sometimes, it can even be their own station's news director. One year, Charlie targeted me because I had instructed my midday news anchor to report the Wimbledon tennis results, even though the matches wouldn't be telecast until much later in the day. Charlie gave out my phone number and e-mail address on the air. I was flooded with hate mail, nasty messages, and even one death threat from a federal law enforcement agent whom I knew to be a big Charlie fan.

In the talk radio business, this concept, which must be mastered to be successful, is called "differentiating" yourself from the rest of the media. It is a brilliant marketing tactic that has also helped Fox News Channel thrive. "We report, you decide" and "Fair and Balanced" are more than just savvy slogans. They are code words signaling that only Fox will report the news in a way conservatives see as objective and truthful.

Forget any notion, however, that radio talk shows are supposed to be fair, even-   10
handed discussions featuring a diversity of opinions. The Fairness Doctrine, which required this, was repealed twenty years ago. So talk shows can be, and are, all about the host's opinions, analyses, and general worldview. Programmers learned long ago that benign conversations led by hosts who present all sides of an issue don't attract large audiences. That's why Kathleen Dunn was forced out at WTMJ in the early '90s and why Jim and Andee were replaced in the mid-'90s by Dr. Laura. Pointed and provocative are what win.

There is no way to win a disagreement with Charlie Sykes. Calls from listeners who disagree with him don't get on the air if the show's producer, who generally does the screening, fears they might make Charlie look bad. I witnessed several occasions when Senator Russ Feingold, former Mayor John Norquist, Mayor Tom Barrett, or others would call in but wouldn't be allowed on the air.

Opponents are far more likely to get through when the producer is confident Charlie can use the dissenting caller to reinforce his original point. Ask former *Milwaukee Journal Sentinel* Publisher Keith Spore, or former Police Chief Arthur Jones. How can Charlie do that? By belittling the caller's point of view. You can always tell, however, when the antagonist has gotten the better of Charlie. That's when he starts attacking the caller personally.

But the worst fate comes for those who ignore Charlie when he asks on the air why they did or didn't do something, and they never respond. That leaves him free to make his point unabated, day after day. The most frequent victims of this were *Journal Sentinel* Editor Marty Kaiser and Managing Editor George Stanley.

Charlie knew they would rarely call or e-mail to answer his criticism, so he could both criticize decisions they had made and blast them for not having the guts to come on his show and respond. What little credibility they had among Charlie's audience would decline by a thousand cuts. It would have been far better for them to face Charlie head on and take their lumps so he would move on to the next victim — I mean, topic.

One entire group that rarely gets on the air are the elderly callers — unless they   15
have something extraordinary to say. Sadly, that doesn't happen often. The theory is that old-sounding callers help produce old-skewing audiences. The target demo is twenty-five to fifty-four, not sixty-five and older.

Talk radio, after all, is in the entertainment business. But that doesn't mean it has no impact on public policy. Quite the contrary.

The stereotyped liberal view of the talk radio audience is that it's a lot of angry, uneducated white men. In fact, the audience is far more diverse. Many are business-people, doctors, lawyers, academics, clergy, or soccer moms and dads. Talk show fans are not stupid. They will detect an obvious phony. The best hosts sincerely believe everything they say. Their passion is real. Their arguments have been carefully crafted in a manner they know will be meaningful to the audience, and that validates the views these folks were already thinking.

Yet while talk show audiences aren't being led like lemmings to a certain conclusion, they can be carefully prodded into agreement with the Republican views of the day.

Conservative talk show hosts would receive daily talking points e-mails from the Bush White House, the Republican National Committee and, during election years, GOP campaign operations. They're not called talking points, but that's what they are. I know, because I received them, too. During my time at WTMJ, Charlie would generally mine the e-mails, then couch the daily message in his own words. Midday talker Jeff Wagner would be more likely to rely on them verbatim. But neither used them in their entirety, or every single day.

Charlie and Jeff would also check what other conservative talk show hosts around the country were saying. Rush Limbaugh's Web site was checked at least once daily. Atlanta-based nationally syndicated talker Neal Boortz was another popular choice. Select conservative blogs were also perused. 20

A smart talk show host will, from time to time, disagree publicly with a Republican president, the Republican Party, or some conservative doctrine. (President Bush's disastrous choice of Harriet Miers for the Supreme Court was one such example.) But these disagreements are strategically chosen to prove the host is an independent thinker, without appreciably harming the president or party. This is not to suggest that hosts don't genuinely disagree with the conservative line at times. They do, more often than you might think. But they usually keep it to themselves.

One of the things that makes a talk show host good — especially hosts of the caliber of Sykes — is that his or her arguments seem so solid. You fundamentally disagree with the host, yet can't refute the argument because it sounds so airtight. The host has built a strong case with lots of supporting facts.

Generally speaking, though, those facts have been selectively chosen because they support the host's preconceived opinion, or can be interpreted to seem as if they do. In their frustration, some talk show critics accuse hosts of fabricating facts. Wrong. Hosts do gather evidence, but in a way that modifies the old Joe Friday maxim: "Just the facts *that I can use to make my case,* ma'am."

Hint: The more talk show hosts squawk about something — the louder their voice, the greater their emotion, the more effusive their arguments — the more they're worried about the issue. For example, talk show hosts eagerly participated in the 2004 Swift Boating of John Kerry because they really feared he was going to win. This is a common talk show tactic: If you lack compelling arguments in favor of your candidate or point of view, attack the other side. These attacks often rely on two key rhetorical devices, which I call *You Know What Would Happen If* and *The Pre-emptive Strike*.

Using the first strategy, a host will describe something a liberal has said or done   25
that conservatives disagree with, but for which the liberal has not been widely criticized, and then say, "You know what would happen if a conservative had said (or
done) that? He (or she) would have been filleted by the 'liberal media.'" This is particularly effective because it's a two-fer, simultaneously reinforcing the notion that
conservatives are victims and that "liberals" are the enemy.

The second strategy, *The Preemptive Strike*, is used when a host knows that news
reflecting poorly on conservative dogma is about to break or become more widespread. When news of the alleged massacre at Haditha first trickled out in the summer of 2006, not even Iraq War chest-thumper Charlie Sykes would defend the U.S.
Marines accused of killing innocent civilians in the Iraqi village. So he spent lots of
air time criticizing how the "mainstream media" was sure to sensationalize the story
in the coming weeks. Charlie would kill the messengers before any message had even
been delivered.

Good talk show hosts can get their listeners so lathered up that they truly can
change public policy. They can inspire like-minded folks to flood the phone lines
and e-mail inboxes of aldermen, county supervisors, legislators, and federal lawmakers. They can inspire their followers to vote for candidates the hosts prefer. How? By
pounding away on an issue or candidate, hour after hour, day after day. Hosts will ex-
tol the virtues of the favored candidate or, more likely, exploit whatever Achilles heel
the other candidate might have. Influencing elections is more likely to occur at the
local rather than national level, but that still gives talk radio power.

By the way, here's a way to prognosticate elections just by listening to talk
shows: Except in presidential elections, when they will always carry water for the
Republican nominee, conservative hosts won't hurt their credibility by backing candidates they think can't win. So if they're uncharacteristically tepid, or even silent,
about a particular race, that means the Democrat has a good chance of winning. Nor
will hosts spend their credibility on an issue where they know they disagree with
listeners. Charlie, for example, told me just before I left TMJ that Wisconsin's 2006
anti-gay marriage amendment was misguided. But he knew his followers would likely
vote for it in droves. So he declined to speak out directly against it.

This brings us to perhaps the most ironic thing about most talk show hosts.
Though they may savage politicians and others they oppose, they fear criticism or
critiques of any kind. They can dish it out, but they can't take it.

One day during a very bad snowstorm, I walked into the studio during a com-   30
mercial break and suggested to Charlie that he start talking about it rather than
whatever conservative topic he'd been discussing. Charlie assumed, as he usually did
in such situations, that I was being critical of his topic. In reaction, he unplugged his
head phones, stood up, and told me that I might as well take over the show because
he wasn't going to change his topic. I was able to quickly strike a bargain before the
end of the break. He agreed to take a few calls about the storm, but if it didn't strike
a nerve with callers, he could return to his original topic.

The snowstorm was the topic of the rest of his show that day. And afterward,
Charlie came to my office and admitted I'd been right. But we would go through scenarios such as this many times through the years.

Another tense moment arose when the Harley-Davidson 100th anniversary was captivating the community — and our on-air coverage — in 2003, but Charlie wanted to talk about school choice for seemingly the 100,000th time. He literally threw a fit, off the air and on, belittling other hosts, the news department, and station management for devoting resources to Harley's 100th coverage. "The Green House" newsman Phil Cianciola countered that afternoon with a joke about Charlie riding a Harley wearing loafers. Charlie complained to management about Phil and wouldn't speak civilly about him in my presence again.

Hosts are most dangerous when someone they've targeted for criticism tries to return the fire. It is foolish to enter into a dispute with someone who has a 50,000-watt radio transmitter at his or her disposal and feels cornered. Oh, and calling a host names — "right-winger," "fascist," "radio squawker," etc. — merely plays into his or her hands. This allows a host like Sykes to portray himself as a victim of the "left-wing spin machine," and will leave his listeners, who also feel victimized, dying to support him. In essence, the host will mount a Hillary Rodham Clinton "vast right-wing conspiracy" attack in reverse.

A conservative emulating Hillary? Yep. A great talk show host is like a great college debater, capable of arguing either side of any issue in a logical, thorough, and convincing manner. This skill ensures their continuing success regardless of which political party is in power. For example:

- In the talk show world, the line-item veto was the most effective way to control government spending when Ronald Reagan was president; it was a violation of the separation of powers after President Clinton took office.

- Perjury was a heinous crime when Clinton was accused of lying under oath about his extramarital activities. But when Scooter Libby, Vice President Dick Cheney's top aide, was charged with lying under oath, it was the prosecutor who had committed an egregious act by charging Libby with perjury.

- "Activist judges" are the scourge of the earth when they rule it is unconstitutional to deny same-sex couples the rights heterosexuals receive. But judicial activism is needed to stop the husband of a woman in a persistent vegetative state — say Terri Schiavo — from removing her feeding tube to end her suffering.

To amuse myself while listening to a talk show, I would ask myself what the host   35
would say if the situation were reversed. What if alleged D.C. Madam client Senator David Vitter had been a Democrat? Would the reaction of talk show hosts have been so quiet you could hear crickets chirping? Hardly.

Or what if former Representative Mark Foley had been a Democrat? Would his pedophile-like tendencies have been excused as a "prank" or mere "overfriendly e-mails"? Not on the life of your teenage son.

Suppose Al Gore was president and ordered an invasion of Iraq without an exit strategy. Suppose this had led to the deaths of more than 4,000 U.S. troops and actually made that part of the world *less* stable. Would talk show hosts have dismissed criticism of that war as unpatriotic? No chance.

Or imagine that John Kerry had been president during Hurricane Katrina and that his administration's rescue and rebuilding effort had been horribly botched. Would talk show hosts have branded him a great president? Of course not.

It was Katrina, finally, that made me truly see the light. Until then, 10 years into my time at TMJ, while I might have disagreed with some stands the hosts took, I did think there were grounds for their constant criticism of the media. I had convinced myself that the national media had an intrinsic bias that was, at the very least, geographical if not ideological, to which talk radio could provide an alternative.

Then along came the worst natural disaster in U.S. history. Journalists risked   40
their lives to save others as the storm hit the Gulf Coast. Afterward, journalists endured the stench and the filth to chronicle the events for a stunned world. Then they documented the monumental government incompetence for an outraged nation. These journalists became voices for the voiceless victims, pressing government officials to get help to those who needed it.

Yet, while New Orleans residents were still screaming for help from the rooftops of their flooded homes, journalists were targeted by talk show hosts, Charlie and Wagner among them. Not the government, but journalists. Stories detailing the federal government's obvious slowness and inefficiency were part of an "angry left" conspiracy, they said. Talk show hosts who used e-mailed talking points from the conservative spin machine proclaimed the Katrina stories were part of a liberal "media template." The irony would have been laughable if the story wasn't so serious.

I went to Charlie and Jeff and told them my concerns. They waved me off. I went to Program Director Rick Belcher and told him I thought Charlie and Jeff had things terribly wrong. He disagreed. I was distraught. I felt I was actively participating in something so inconsistent with reality that even most conservative talk radio devotees would see this. But in a way, it was merely a more obvious example of how talk radio portrayed reality selectively.

I was a dedicated program manager. I helped the hosts at my station do show prep by finding stories I knew would pique their interest and fire up their constituencies. I met with Charlie Sykes daily, about a half-hour before show time, to help him talk through topics before going on the air. Charlie is one of the smartest people I know, but he performs at his best with that kind of preparation.

I often defended Jeff Wagner from upset moderates and liberals in the community. Jeff's a very good talk show host whose brilliance is overshadowed only by his stubbornness.

I helped our program directors try to find the right role for Mark Reardon, who,   45
in my opinion, was always miscast (he wasn't as right-wing as Sykes or Wagner and his job was switched several times). Ultimately, that miscasting helped his career, because WTMJ laid him off, after which he became a talk show star in St. Louis, a much larger market.

I worked with news and sports hosts, too — Robb Edwards, Jon Belmont, Ken Herrera, Jonathan Green, Len Kasper, Bill Michaels — to help them craft ways to sound human and "real" behind the microphone without violating the separation of church and state that existed between the station's talk and news programming. Sometimes I succeeded. Sometimes I didn't.

And we were successful, consistently ranking No. 1 among persons twelve and older and in the top five in the advertiser-coveted twenty-five to fifty-four demo. Yet I was often angrily asked, once by then-Mayor John Norquist, why we just didn't change our call letters to "WGOP." The complaints were just another sign of our impact.

I left WTMJ with some regret, attracted by an offer to work in the cutting edge field of digital media at one of the nation's largest news and entertainment conglomerates. By then, I had worked more than twenty-six years in radio news and more than twenty-three as a news director. In the constant push for ratings, I had seen and helped foster the transformation of AM radio and the rise of conservative hosts. They have a power that is unlikely to decline.

Their rise was also helped by liberals whose ideology, after all, emphasizes tolerance. Their friendly toleration of talk radio merely gave the hosts more credibility. Yet an attitude of intolerance was probably worse: It made the liberals look hypocritical, giving ammunition to talk show hosts who used it with great skill. 50

But the key reason talk radio succeeds is because its hosts can exploit the fears and perceived victimization of a large swath of conservative-leaning listeners. And they feel victimized because many liberals and moderates have ignored or trivialized their concerns and have stereotyped these Americans as uncaring curmudgeons.

Because of that, there will always be listeners who believe that Charlie Sykes, Jeff Wagner, and their compatriots are the only members of the media who truly care about them.

In response to this story, we received the following e-mail from WTMJ:

> We are surprised and saddened that a former employee, who worked with us for ten years, would choose to attack our talk shows hosts and company in this manner. Neither the station nor our hosts were offered a chance to comment on the claims made by the author. Newsradio 620 WTMJ stands by Charlie Sykes and Jeff Wagner and will continue to give their listeners the opportunity to share and participate in the best local talk programming in Milwaukee.

Steve Wexler
Executive Vice President
Television & Radio Operations
Journal Broadcast Group

Polarized News? The Media's Moderate Bias

JAMES PONIEWOZIK

BEFORE READING: Do you consider yourself a liberal, a conservative, or somewhere in the middle politically? On what grounds? Do you think it is good or bad to be in the middle? Why?

In the argument between the White House and Fox News over whether the cable channel is a conservative mouthpiece, you would think that Fox's viewers would have its back. Not entirely. In an October 29 Pew Research Center survey, TV-news viewers named Fox the most ideological outlet — and 48 percent of Fox's own viewers called it "mostly conservative" (27 percent of Fox fans said it was "neither in particular," while 17 percent said it was "mostly liberal," suggesting that pollsters called G. Gordon Liddy's house more than once).

Now that's not exactly the same as the White House's charge that Fox is essentially a political operation. But it suggests that those "fair and balanced" ads don't fool the people actually watching the stuff. Fox isn't alone, though: the survey showed that far more viewers saw ABC, CBS, CNN, MSNBC and NBC as liberal than saw them as conservative.

All of which underlines the obvious: the news audience, if not news itself, is getting more polarized. But categories like Pew's "liberal," "conservative" and "neither" imply that our society is as simplistic about media bias as we are about politics (when in fact both involve nuanced positions), and they overlook the most significant bias out there: moderate bias.

As anyone following health reform knows, centrism is a political position too. And you see moderate bias — i.e., a preference for centrism — whenever a news outlet assumes that the truth must be "somewhere in the middle." You see it whenever an organization decides that "balance" requires equal weight for an opposing position, however specious: "Some, however, believe global warming is a myth." (Moderate bias would also require me to find a countervailing liberal position and pretend that it is equivalent to global-warming denial. Sorry.)

Often, moderate bias is just the result of caution, but the effect is to bolster centrist political positions — not least by implying that they are not political positions at all but occupy a happy medium between the nutjobs. Meanwhile, conservatives see moderate bias as liberal, and liberals see it as conservative — letting journalists conclude that it's not bias at all.

5

James Poniewozik was the media critic and editor at Salon.com and now writes *Time* magazine's Tuned In column and its online version, which focus on television and other media. This article appeared on Time.com on November 4, 2009.

Moderate bias also grows from a related phenomenon: status-quo bias. Journalists, like anyone, have a built-in bias toward believing that what was true yesterday will be true tomorrow. Establishment news outlets grow cozy and comfortable with other establishments. One reason some journalists insufficiently questioned the run-up to the Iraq war and underestimated the housing bubble was that they listened to their usual, credentialed sources — and the history of the past decade is the history of the experts being wrong.

And especially in the top ranks of journalism, there's class bias. If I wanted to look at potential conflicts of interest in reporters covering bank bailouts, for instance, I'd be less concerned about their party affiliation than whether they're based (like me) in New York City, where the economy lives and dies on finance.

Look at our political debates today. Is it liberal or conservative to oppose multi-billion-dollar payouts for the bankers and insurers who flushed our economy down their gold-plated toilets? Our conception of politics is broken if it cannot account for the fact that Michael Moore and Glenn Beck come to some of the same conclusions while having very different philosophies. Yet pollsters and the media still rely on it, to frame politicians and themselves.

Sure enough, actual politics is proving the left-right spectrum to be inadequate. Three big off-year elections involved major candidates who were independent (New York City mayor and New Jersey governor) or third-party (the congressional election in New York, where the Conservative Party candidate forced out the Republican, who endorsed the Democrat). That's not to say "liberal" and "conservative" are useless, but they're not nearly enough.

Pretty plainly, Fox News is full of conservative opinion hosts, while its news   10
wing has fixated on anti-Obama causes célèbres from ACORN to the tea-party protests. (Equally plainly, the White House is not concerned about fighting the bias of, say, MSNBC hosts who agree with it.) But Sean Hannity's Republicanism, Beck's populism, and Mike Huckabee's Christian conservatism are very different — as are, say, Rachel Maddow's progressivism and Chris Matthews' Democratic insiderdom. American politics has civil libertarians and Wall Street conservatives and social-justice moralist-populists and much more.

And they all, in these unsettled times, have various issues with the centrist establishment — which has its own permutations and camps. All of this promises wild and interesting times for journalists to cover, but they won't be able to do it from the neutral center. Because there isn't one, and there never was.

Thinking and Writing about Media Bias

1. The Fairness Doctrine, introduced in 1949, was repealed in 1987. What is the Fairness Doctrine and why have some in recent years pushed for it to be reinstated?

2. Do you agree with some of the authors here that network news is biased? What evidence would you offer for that claim? Is there a distinction between what is

supposed to be objective reporting and what is commentary? Can you tell the difference? Explain.

3. Recently, protestors have been appearing at funerals of Americans killed in action to protest the government's stance on gays in the military. Is this a legitimate use of freedom of expression? Don't the news media have the right to refuse to cover these events? Explain.

4. Jesse Walker writes about how Rush Limbaugh exists on the borderline between news and entertainment. Think of another example of a news commentator who crosses the line into the entertainment business and write your own profile modeled on Walker's.

5. Choose one of the conservative news commentators and explain why you agree with him or her on one or more key political issues.

6. Choose one of the liberal news commentators and explain why you agree with him or her on one or more key political issues.

7. Do you agree with Cline that it is the nature of the job that leads to bias in the media? Explain.

CHAPTER 18

Are Limits on Freedom of Speech Ever Justified?

The First Amendment to the Constitution of the United States reads, "Congress shall make no laws respecting an establishment of religion, or prohibiting the free expression thereof; or abridging the freedom of speech, or of the press; or the right of the people peaceably to assemble, and to petition the Government for a redress of grievances." (The first ten amendments were ratified on December 15, 1791, and form what is known as the Bill of Rights.) The arguments in this section will consider primarily the issue of "abridging the freedom of speech."

The limits of free speech in the United States are constantly being adjusted as social values change and new cases testing those limits emerge. Several prominent areas of controversy are emphasized in the following selection of essays.

In 1969, the U.S. Supreme Court ruled that neither students nor teachers "shed their constitutional right to freedom of speech or expression at the schoolhouse gate" (*Tinker v. Des Moines Independent School District*). High schools, colleges, and universities are places where the exchange of ideas is generally welcome. The controversy arises over whether or not there are some ideas — some language, some symbols — that are not welcome. The First Amendment has been at the heart of court cases over everything from racist and sexist speech to the words or symbols printed on a T-shirt.

Those same students and teachers step outside the "schoolhouse gate" to confront a world in which many feel even the news is not fit for children, let alone prime-time television or even many movies rated G or PG, which one parent claims now stands for "profanity guaranteed." Rap music enrages those who find its attitude toward women and its call to violence offensive while others defend it as art protected by the First Amendment. The Federal Communications Commission has tightened its enforcement of rules against language or actions that go against the "public interest," but many consumers argue that it has not done enough. One of the authors included here even argues that the very existence of the FCC is unconstitutional.

Tom Toles
First Amendment

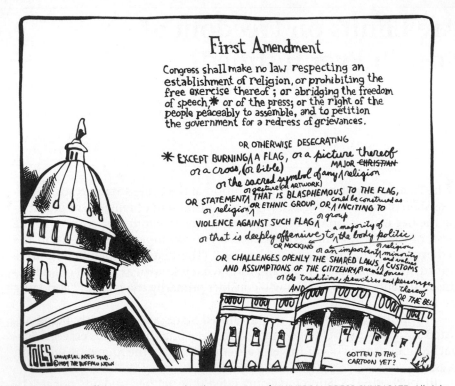

Times of crisis resurrect old concerns about freedom of speech. Do American citizens have the right to speak out against a war in which Americans are fighting and dying? Should they? In some of these selections you will hear a sincere expression of concern that even in our patriotism we must not sacrifice our First Amendment right to freedom of speech.

Student Sues School District for Banning Anti-War T-Shirt

ALANA KEYNES

BEFORE READING: What restrictions, if any, did your high school have on what words, pictures, or symbols could be displayed on students' clothing? How did you feel about that policy? Was it necessary, in your opinion? Why, or why not?

A case addressing students' right to protest the Iraqi war in school has landed in the courts, with the American Civil Liberties Union (ACLU) suing a Michigan school district on behalf of a student sent home for wearing a T-shirt calling President Bush an "International Terrorist."

The suit, filed March 27 at the U.S. Eastern District Court of Michigan, alleges that Dearborn, Michigan, school officials violated the free-speech rights of Bretton Barber, a junior at Dearborn High School, since there was no evidence the T-shirt caused any disruption at school.

"There are strong indications in this case that the reaction of Dearborn High School officials to Barber's T-shirt was prompted by their disagreement with the message," the complaint states. "The only rationale given when Barber pressed for one was that the shirt would promote terrorism, which plainly could not have been a serious contention."

School administrators' claim that the shirt was disruptive is a "ludicrous charge," said Wendy Wagenheim, spokeswoman for the ACLU of Michigan. "They don't want to rock the boat in any way." There have been no instances of students causing problems by fighting with each other or teachers over the message conveyed in the T-shirt, she said. The complaint cites *Castorina v. Madison County School Board* (246 F.2d 536), the 6th Circuit Court of Appeals' decision that school officials could not ban two Kentucky students from wearing T-shirts with a picture of the Confederate flag to school (*ED*, March 12, 2001). Michigan is one of four states governed by the 6th Circuit.

Administrators also did not have a right to send Barber home, according to the complaint, because legal precedent only permits schools to discipline students who are violating a written rule, and the Dearborn district does not have a policy banning political speech. 5

But the 11th Circuit Court of Appeals ruled last month that a Florida school district could suspend students who brought Confederate flags to school, though there was no written policy prohibiting them on campus (*ED*, March 26).

Alana Keynes was on the editorial staff at *Education Daily*, where this article appeared on April 4, 2003.

Wagenheim said she is not concerned that the 11th Circuit ruling will affect the ACLU's case, since federal appellate courts often issue conflicting rulings.

A spokesman from the Dearborn school district refused to comment on the suit. The district's superintendent issued a statement saying "this is now an issue for the courts to decide. The school district has no further remarks at this time."

Students' and teachers' right to express their views about the war has become a major issue in schools nationwide, as administrators continue to grapple with the appropriate limits of free speech in school (*ED*, March 21).

This is the first case the ACLU has taken on students' free-speech rights in response to the Iraqi war, Wagenheim said, but many of its offices nationwide have received calls from students inquiring about their right to demonstrate against the war during school hours.

"Those inquiries are common occurrences at this point," she said.

The "Bong Hits 4 Jesus" Student Speech Case: With Kenneth Starr Seeking High Court Review of the Ninth Circuit Decision, Is Someone Blowing Smoke?

JULIE HILDEN

BEFORE READING: What limitations are there currently on the language used by public school students? What cases can you recall from your own experience or the media that involved censorship of student speech?

Last Monday, September 11, former Independent Counsel Kenneth Starr — now a lawyer at Kirkland & Ellis — asked the Supreme Court to review a March 10 decision by the U.S. Court of Appeals for the Ninth Circuit, in the case of *Frederick v. Morse*. The decision upheld a public high school student's First Amendment right to display a banner off campus. Starr represents the school district on a pro bono basis. . . .

Julie Hilden is both an attorney and a novelist. After graduating from Yale Law School, she worked for several years as a litigation associate for a Washington, D.C., law firm, specializing in First Amendment issues. Since 1999, she has been a columnist for FindLaw, an online source for legal news and commentary where this article appeared on September 18, 2006.

The Facts of the *Frederick* Case

The *Frederick* case grew out of an incident in which Juneau, Alaska, high school senior Joseph Frederick unfurled a banner reading "Bong Hits 4 Jesus" on a public sidewalk. He did so during a privately sponsored rally where townspeople watched the Olympic torch pass by. Students were released from school to attend the rally. The high school's "pep band" and cheerleaders performed there, but the court found that teacher supervision of other students at the rally was "minimal or nonexistent."

Frederick and his friends made sure they unfurled their banner when TV cameras were passing by — but the school's principal, Deborah Morse, who was also attending the rally, went up to Frederick, grabbed the banner, crumpled it up, and suspended him for ten days.

Frederick later sued, invoking the federal civil rights statute that allows plaintiffs to seek money damages for government infringements of their constitutional rights, including First Amendment rights.

In my view, the principal's conduct was appalling. She didn't just tell Frederick   5
to put his sign away, or that it was inappropriate, nor did she warn him that he could be suspended. Rather, she actually went right up to him on a public street and destroyed his banner.

This is the kind of thing that we believe cannot happen in this country. Is it suddenly acceptable simply because the victim is eighteen? What happened to school officials' duty to try to convince students — first, by setting the right example — to solve their differences with reason, not violence? Ironically, if Frederick had ripped up another student's poster on school grounds, he surely would have been suspended for doing so.

In short, the example this principal is setting is a very ugly one. No wonder the Ninth Circuit held — on the separate question of the principal's claim to immunity under the federal civil rights statute — that "it would be clear to a reasonable [principal] that [her] conduct was unlawful in the situation [she] confronted." (As a result, the principal herself may face liability for damages; she is a co-defendant in the case, along with the school board.)

How could this kind of behavior strike Starr, or Kirkland & Ellis, as so worthy of protecting, that it was worth taking this case on for the school district as a pro bono project?

The Legal Standards for Public School Students' Speech

There are three Supreme Court cases setting forth standards for public school students' speech — which were considered by the Ninth Circuit — but only one is relevant here.

One of the cases, *Hazelwood School Dist. v. Kuhlmeier* — addressing school-   10
sponsored speech — doesn't apply because neither Frederick's banner (nor the rally itself) was school-sponsored in the sense that, for instance, a school-funded student newspaper is.

A second case, *Bethel School Dist. No. 3 v. Fraser* — which was relied on by the district court, but distinguished by the Ninth Circuit — doesn't apply because it addresses only vulgar, lewd, obscene, and otherwise "plainly offensive" speech, and because the Ninth Circuit has interpreted that to mean, in essence, obscenity or, at least, speech involving four-letter words or similarly profane language.

Finally, there is *Tinker v. Des Moines Independent Community School Dist.* Its rule is simple: Student speech — other than speech that falls under the precedents noted above — can only be punished or otherwise regulated if it "materially disrupts classwork or involves substantial disorder or invasion of the rights of others." Moreover, to support the punishment or regulation, school districts must cite "evidence that [the punishment] is necessary to avoid material or substantial interference with schoolwork or discipline."

Applying the Legal Standard in the *Frederick* Case

The Juneau School District had an exceptionally weak case under *Tinker*.

In support of its case that Frederick's banner was disruptive, the District claimed that the banner would be read by many at the rally as "advocating or condoning illegal drug use."

Similarly, School Superintendent Peggy Cowan recently told CNN that this case   15
is appropriate for Supreme Court review because it raises "an important question about how the First Amendment applies to pro-drug messages in an educational setting."

But even if this was, to some extent, a pro-drug message, that wasn't all it was. The district itself acknowledged that Frederick could have been not just responding to, but parodying the school's anti-drug message (and parody is strongly protected by the First Amendment). Moreover the "for Jesus" part shouldn't be left out of the analysis; juxtaposing "Bong Hits," the informal "4" for "for," and "Jesus" may also send a message that religion shouldn't be taken so seriously, and a message that Jesus was more laid-back, and would have been more sympathetic to the counterculture, than some authoritarians would admit.

I'm not, of course, claiming that this message was well-thought out. To the contrary, it reads like a spur-of-the-moment lark, a prank. But I do think that it meant something different and more complicated, than just, say, a "Smoke Pot" banner would have. (Frederick himself said the banner was intended to be meaningless and funny, and he just wanted to get it on television. However, as many First Amendment cases have shown, words often have an impact beyond their intended meaning.)

The District also claimed that if the principal had done nothing, the district would have been seen by many as giving its imprimatur to Frederick's pro-drug message. But that claim seems ridiculous: If the District was as avid about spreading its anti-drug message as it claims that it was, no one would believe that it had suddenly changed its policy by merely deciding not to rip up Frederick's poster. If anything, onlookers might believe the District tolerated Frederick's poster out of a healthy respect for the First Amendment, or that the school district simply wasn't worried about its own message being undermined by a poorly-thought-out sophomoric sign.

Why the Ninth Circuit Is Right, and Starr Is Wrong, in This Case

Because this case is such a clear First Amendment violation, and because the Ninth Circuit rightly sided with the student, there's no good reason here for Supreme Court review.

In explaining why review was sought, Eric Hagen, an attorney from Starr's office who also worked on the Supreme Court petition, told a reporter, "It makes it a little harder when teachers and principals in their daily duties might be subject to a damages lawsuit and be held personally liable." But it's only harder for teachers and principals to perform their daily duties when the lines for liability are unclear.   20

As noted above, there are few First Amendment violations clearer than a government employee's crumpling up someone's banner at a privately sponsored rally on a public street. That's censorship with a capital "C." If the Supreme Court does want to make the line between permissible disciplinary action and impermissible First Amendment violation clearer, perhaps it should wait for a subtler, closer case.

Ironically, I think most schoolchildren, if taught a bit about the First Amendment, could easily identify this as an obvious violation. Their teachers and principals ought at least to be able to do the same. . . .

The Case against School Prayer

ANNIE LAURIE GAYLOR

BEFORE READING: Did your school(s) observe a moment of silence or have daily school prayer? Do you believe that such practices violate the policy of separation of church and state? Explain.

> "I pledge allegiance to the flag of the United States of America, and to the republic for which it stands, one nation indivisible, with liberty and justice for all."
> — THE "GODLESS" PLEDGE OF ALLEGIANCE, AS IT WAS RECITED BY GENERATIONS
> OF SCHOOL CHILDREN, BEFORE CONGRESS INSERTED A RELIGIOUS PHRASE,
> "UNDER GOD," IN 1954.

In 1978 Annie Laurie Gaylor was cofounder, with her mother, of the Freedom from Religion Foundation, described on the organization's Web site as "the largest group of atheists and agnostics in North America," founded "to promote freethought and defend the constitutional principle of the separation of state and church." With her husband, Gaylor is copresident of the organization, and she also edits *Freethought Today* and frequently publishes and makes presentations on the separation of church and state. This article is from the organization's Web site.

The original pre-1954 Pledge, without "under God."

The PLEDGE to the FLAG

I PLEDGE ALLEGIANCE
to the FLAG of the
UNITED STATES of AMERICA
and to the REPUBLIC for which
IT STANDS
ONE NATION INDIVISIBLE
with LIBERTY and JUSTICE
for ALL

Keep the Church and State Forever Separate

Should Students Pray in Public Schools? Public schools exist to educate, not to proselytize. Children in public schools are a captive audience. Making prayer an official part of the school day is coercive and invasive. What 5-, 8-, or 10-year-old could view prayers recited as part of class routine as "voluntary"? Religion is private, and schools are public, so it is appropriate that the two should not mix. To introduce religion in our public schools builds walls between children who may not have been aware of religious difference before.

Why Should Schools Be Neutral? Our public schools are for *all* children, whether Catholic, Baptist, Quaker, atheist, Buddhist, Jewish, agnostic. The schools are supported by *all* taxpayers, and therefore should be free of religious observances and coercion. It is the sacred duty of parents and churches to instill religious beliefs, free from government dictation. Institutionalizing prayers in public schools usurps the rights of parents.

School prayer proponents mistake government *neutrality* toward religion as *hostility*. The record shows that religious beliefs have flourished in this country not in spite of but because of the constitutional separation of church and state.

What Happens When Worship Enters Public Schools? When religion has invaded our public school system, it has singled out the lone Jewish student, the class Unitarian or agnostic, the children in the minority. Families who protest state/church violations in our public schools invariably experience persecution. It was commonplace prior to the court decision against school prayer to put non-religious or nonorthodox children in places of detention during bible-reading or prayer recitation. The children of Supreme Court plaintiffs against religion in schools, such as Vashti McCollum, Ed Schempp, and Ishmael Jaffree, were beaten up on the way to and from school, their families subjected to community harassment and death threats for speaking out in defense of a constitutional principle. We know from history how harmful and destructive religion is in our public schools. In those school districts that do not abide by the law, school children continue to be persecuted today.

Can't Students Pray in Public Schools Now? Individual, silent, personal prayer never 5
has and never could be outlawed in public schools. The courts have declared *government-fostered* prayers unconstitutional — those led, required, sanctioned, scheduled, or suggested by officials.

It is dishonest to call any prayer "voluntary" that is encouraged or required by a public official or legislature. By definition, if the government suggests that students pray, whether by penning the prayer, asking them to vote whether to pray, or setting aside time to pray, it is endorsing and promoting that prayer. It is coercive for schools to schedule worship as an official part of the school day, school sports or activities, or to use prayer to formalize graduation ceremonies. Such prayers are more "mandatory" than "voluntary."

What's Wrong with a "Voluntary" Prayer Amendment? Proponents of so-called "voluntary" school prayer amendment (such as the one proposed in 1995) are admitting that our secular Constitution prohibits organized prayers in public schools. Otherwise, why would an amendment to our U.S. Constitution be required? The nation must ask whether politically-motivated Newt Gingrich & Co. are wiser than James Madison, principal author of the Constitution, and the other founders who engineered the World's oldest and most successful constitution!

The radical school prayer amendment would negate the First Amendment's guarantee against government establishment of religion. Most distressing, it would be at the expense of the civil rights of children, America's most vulnerable class. It would attack the heart of the Bill of Rights, which safeguards the rights of the individual from the tyranny of the majority.

What Would the Prayer Amendment Permit? The text of the proposed federal amendment (as of January, 1995) reads:

> *"Nothing in this Constitution shall be construed to prohibit individual or group prayer in public schools or other public institutions. No person shall be required by the United States or by any State to participate in prayer. Neither the United States or any State shall compose the words of any prayer to be said in public schools."*

Since the right to "individual prayer" already exists, the real motive is to instill "group prayer."

No wording in this amendment would prevent the government from *selecting*   10 the prayer, or the particular version of the bible it should be taken from. Nothing restricts prayers to "nondenominational" or "nonsectarian" (not that such a restriction would make it acceptable). Nothing would prevent a school from selecting the Lord's Prayer or other prayers to Jesus, and blasting it over the intercom. For that matter, nothing would prevent the school from sponsoring prayers to Allah or Zoroaster. Nothing would prevent principals, teachers, or clergy from leading the students. Nothing would prevent nonparticipating students from being singled out. The proposal also seeks to institutionalize group prayer in other public settings, presumably public-supported senior centers, courthouses, etc.

School prayer supporters envision organized, vocal, group recitations of prayer, daily classroom displays of belief in a deity or religion, dictated by the majority. Those in the minority would be compelled to conform to a religion or ritual in which they disbelieve, to suffer the humiliation and imposition of submitting to a daily religious exercise against their will, or be singled out by orthodox classmates and teachers as "heretics" or "sinners" for not participating.

Haven't Public Schools Always Had Prayer? At the time the U.S. Supreme Court issued its 1962 and 1963 decrees against school-sponsored prayers and bible-reading, it is estimated religious observances were unknown in about half of the nation's public schools.

Horace Mann, the father of our public school system, championed the elimination of sectarianism from American schools, largely accomplished by the 1840's. Bible reading, prayers, or hymns in public schools were absent from most public schools by the end of the 19th century, after Catholic or minority-religion immigrants objected to Protestant bias in public schools.

Until the 20th century, only Massachusetts required bible-reading in the schools, in a statute passed by the virulently anti-Catholic Know Nothing Party in the 1850's. Only after 1913 did eleven other states make prayers or bible-reading compulsory. A number of other states outlawed such practices by judicial or administrative decree, and half a dozen state supreme courts overruled devotionals in public schools.

As early as the 1850's, the Superintendent of Schools of New York State ordered   15 that prayers could no longer be required as part of public school activities. The Cincinnati Board of Education resolved in 1869 that "religious instruction and the reading of religious books, including the Holy Bible, was prohibited in the common schools of Cincinnati."

Presidents Ulysses S. Grant and Theodore Roosevelt spoke up for what Roosevelt called "absolutely nonsectarian public schools." Roosevelt added that it is "not our business to have the Protestant Bible or the Catholic Vulgate or the Talmud read in these schools."

For nearly half a century, the United States Supreme Court, consistent with this nation's history of secular schools, has ruled against religious indoctrination through schools (*McCollum v. Board of Education*, 1948), prayers and devotionals in public schools (*Engel v. Vitale*, 1962), and prayers and bible-reading (*Abington School District v.*

Schempp, 1963), right up through the 1992 *Weisman* decision against prayers at public school commencements and *Santa Fe v. Doe* (2000) barring student-led prayers at public school events.

How Can Prayer Be Harmful? Contrary to right-wing claims, piety is not synonymous with virtue. People should be judged by their actions, not by what religion they believe in or how publicly or loudly they pray.

Some Americans believe in the power of prayer; others believe nothing fails like prayer. Some citizens say prayer makes them feel better, but others contend that prayer is counterproductive to personal responsibility. Such a diversity of views is constitutionally protected; our secular government simply is not permitted to pick a side in religious debates.

"The hands that help are better far than lips that pray," wrote Robert G. Inger- 20 soll. Who could disagree?

Should Government Become "Prayer Police"? How ironic that those campaigning on an anti-Big Government theme, who contend that government should get out of our private lives, would seek to tell our children who to pray to in our public schools! As many editorials across the country have pointed out, the school prayer debate seems calculated to deflect attention away from the more pressing economic questions facing our nation. As one conservative governor put it: "If we don't deal with the economic issues, we'll need more than prayer to solve our problems."

Can't Moral Decline Be Traced to the Prayer Decisions? Some politicians like to blame everything bad in America upon the absence of school prayer. Get real! Entire generations of Americans have grown up to be law-abiding citizens without ever once reciting a prayer in school! If prayer is the answer, why are our jails and prisons bulging with born-agains! Japan, where no one prays at school, has the lowest crime rate of any developed nation.

Institutionalizing school prayer cannot raise the SAT scores (only more studying and less praying can do that). It is irrational to charge that the complicated sociological problems facing our everchanging population stem from a lack of prayer in schools.

One might just as well credit the lack of prayer with the great advances that have taken place since the 1962 and 1963 decisions on prayer. Look at the leap in civil liberties, equality, environmental awareness, women's rights, science, technology, and medicine! The polio scare is over. Fountains, buses, schools are no longer segregated by law. We've made great strides in medical treatment. We have VCRs and the computer chip. The Cold War has ended! Who would turn the clock back?

What about the Rights of the Majority? Our political system is a democratic republic 25 in which we use majority vote to elect certain officials or pass referenda. But we do not use majority vote to decide what religion, if any, our neighbors must observe! The "majority" is free to worship at home, at tax-exempt churches, on the way to and from school, or privately in school. There are sixteen school-less hours a day when children can pray, not to mention weekends.

Many in the "majority" do not support school prayers. And if the majority religion gets to choose which prayers are said in schools, that would mean a lot of Protestant kids will be reciting Catholic prayers! The Roman Catholic Church is the single largest denomination in our country. Should Protestant minorities be excused so the classroom can pray in unison to the Virgin Mary? In a few school districts, Muslims outnumber other religions. Should Christian minorities march into the hall with their ears covered while the principal prays to Allah over the intercom?

What's Wrong with a Moment of Silence? Given the regimentation of school children, it would make more sense to have a "moment of bedlam" than a "moment of silence"! Obviously, the impetus for "moments of silence or meditation" is to circumvent the rulings against religion in schools. The legislative history of such state laws reveals the religious motives behind the legislation, as in the Alabama law struck down by the U.S. Supreme Court in 1985 calling for a "moment of silence for meditation or prayer."

When a "moment of silence" law was enacted in Arkansas at the suggestion of then-Gov. Bill Clinton, the law mandating this meaningless ritual was later repealed following popular indifference. We know from experience that many teachers and principals would regard a "moment of silence" mandate as a green light to introduce prayers, causing more legal challenges at the expense of taxpayers.

Should Commencements Start with Prayers? In 1992, the Court ruled in *Lee v. Weisman* that prayers at public school commencements are an impermissible establishment of religion: "The lessons of the First Amendment are as urgent in the modern world as the 18th Century when it was written. One timeless lesson is that if citizens are subjected to state-sponsored religious exercises, the State disavows its own duty to guard and respect that sphere of inviolable conscience and belief which is the mark of a free people," wrote Justice Kennedy for the majority. He dismissed as unacceptable the cruel idea that a student should forfeit her own graduation in order to be free from such an establishment of religion.

What About "Student-Initiated" Prayer? This is a ruse proposed by extremist Christian   30
legal groups such as the Rutherford Institute, and the American Center for Law and Justice run by televangelist Pat Robertson. Religious coercion is even worse at the hands of another student, subjecting students to peer pressure, pitting students in the majority against students in the minority, treating them as outsiders with school complicity.

Imposing prayer-by-majority-vote is flagrant and insensitive abuse of school authority. Such schools should be teaching students about the purpose of the Bill of Rights, instead of teaching them to be religious bullies. Some principals or school boards have even made seniors hold open class votes on whether to pray at graduation, leading to hostility and reprisal against those students brave enough to stand up for the First Amendment.

"The notion that a person's constitutional rights may be subject to a majority vote is itself anathema," wrote Judge Albert V. Bryan, Jr. in a 1993 ruling in Virginia, one of several similar district court rulings around the nation banning any prayer, whether student- or clergy-led.

We cannot put liberties protected by our Bill of Rights up to a vote of school children! Should kindergartners be forced to vote about whether to pray before their milk and cookies? Under such reasoning, what would make it wrong for students to vote to segregate schools or otherwise violate the civil liberties of minorities?

Keep the State and Church Forever Separate Our founders wisely adopted a secular, godless constitution, the first to derive its powers from "We, the People" and the consent of the governed, rather than claiming divine authority. They knew from the experience of religious persecution, witchhunts, and religious discrimination in the Thirteen Colonies, and from the bloody history left behind in Europe, that the surest path to tyranny was to entangle church and state. That is why they adopted a secular constitution whose only references to religion are exclusionary, such as that there shall be no religious test for public office (Art. VI). There were no prayers offered at the Constitutional Convention, which shows their intent to separate religion from secular affairs.

Prayers in schools and religion in government are no panacea for social ills — they are an invitation to divisiveness. More people have been killed in the name of religion than for any other cause. As Thomas Paine pointed out, "Persecution is not an original feature in any religion; but it is always the strongly marked feature of all religions established by law."   35

Even Jesus Was against School Prayer "Thou shalt not be as the hypocrites are: for they love to pray standing in the synagogues and in the corners of the streets, that they may be seen of men. . . . But thou, when thou prayest, enter into thy closet, and when thou hast shut thy door, pray to thy Father which is in secret." — *Matt.* 6:5–6.

> "There is no such source and cause of strife, quarrel, fights, malignant opposition, persecution, and war, and all evil in the state, as religion. Let it once enter our civil affairs, our government would soon be destroyed. Let it once enter our common schools, they would be destroyed."
> — Supreme Court of Wisconsin, Weiss v. District Board, March 18, 1890

> "Leave the matter of religion to the family altar, the church, and the private school, supported entirely by private contributions. Keep the church and state forever separate."
> — Ulysses S. Grant, "The President's Speech at Des Moines" (1875)

> "Congress shall make no law respecting an establishment of religion, or prohibiting the free exercise thereof."
> — First Amendment, Bill of Rights, U.S. Constitution

Thomas Jefferson, author of the sweeping Virginia Statute of Religious Freedom, stating that no citizen "shall be compelled to frequent or support any religious worship, place, or ministry whatsoever . . ." and that to "compell a man to furnish contributions of money for the propagation of [religious] opinions which he disbelieves is sinful and tyrannical."

"I contemplate with sovereign reverence that act of the whole American people which declared that their legislature should make no law 'respecting an establishment of religion, or prohibiting the free exercise thereof,' thus building a wall of separation between church and state."

— PRESIDENT THOMAS JEFFERSON, 1802 LETTER TO THE BAPTISTS
OF DANBURY, CONNECTICUT

Supreme Court Cases Opposing Religious Worship in Schools

McCollum v. Board of Education, 333 U.S. 203, 212 (1948).
> Struck down religious instruction in public schools. The case involved school-sponsored religious instruction in which the sole nonreligious student, Jim McCollum, was placed in detention and persecuted by schoolmates in Champaign, Illinois.

Tudor v. Board of Education of Rutherford, 14 N.J. 31 (1953), cert. denied, 348 U.S. 816 (1954).
> Let stand a lower court ruling that the practice of allowing volunteers to distribute Gideon Bibles at public school was unconstitutional.

Engel v. Vitale, 370 U.S. 421 (1962).
> Declared prayers in public school unconstitutional.

Abington Township School District v. Schempp, 374 U.S. 203 (1963).
> Declared unconstitutional devotional bible-reading and recitation of the Lord's Prayer in public schools.

Epperson v. Arkansas, 393 U.S., 97, 104 (1968).
> Struck down state law forbidding schools to teach the science of evolution.

Stone v. Graham, 449 U.S. 39 (1980).
> Declared unconstitutional the posting of the Ten Commandments in classrooms.

Wallace v. Jaffree, 472 U.S. 38, 72 (1985).
> Overturned law requiring daily "period of silence not to exceed one minute . . . for meditation or daily prayer."

Jager v. Douglas County School District, 862 F.2d 824 (11th Cir.), cert. denied, 490 U.S. 1090 (1989).
> Let stand a lower court ruling in Georgia that pre-game invocations at high school football games are unconstitutional.

Lee v. Weisman, 120 L. Ed. 2d 467 (1992).
> Ruled prayers at public school graduations an impermissible establishment of religion.

Berger v. Rensselaer, 982 F.2d 1160 (7th Cir.), cert. denied, 124 L. Ed. 254 (1993).
> Let stand ruling barring access to Gideons to pass out bibles in Indiana schools.

Santa Fe Independent School District v. Doe, 530 U.S. 290 (2000).
> Barred student-led prayers at public school functions.

Why We Need to Abolish the FCC

ROBERT GARMONG

BEFORE READING: The Federal Communications Commission regulates what can be said on the air. Do you believe that the FCC is too restrictive, not restrictive enough, or generally right on target in deciding what should be allowed on the broadcast media?

Since the infamous "wardrobe malfunction" at the Super Bowl, there have been strident demands for a crackdown by a tougher, stricter Federal Communications Commission. The FCC's various commissioners now call for the power to regulate cable TV in addition to broadcast media.

In June, Congress voted to increase the maximum fine the FCC can impose tenfold, from $27,500 to $275,000. Commissioner Michael Copps has vowed that he will not be satisfied until "I see us send one or two . . . cases for license revocation."

In this headlong rush to expand the government's authority over the media, no one has paused to consider whether the government should have such authority in the first place. No one has noticed that the very existence of the FCC is a flagrant violation of the right to free speech.

Central Premise of the United States

Throughout history, the norm was tyranny over the mind. Men were allowed to speak only by government imprimatur, until America's First Amendment established freedom of speech as a central premise of our nation.

The First Amendment declares that "Congress shall pass no law . . . abridging   5
the freedom of speech, or of the press." This language could not be clearer, or more absolute: no matter who disagrees with you or considers your speech offensive, the government may not abridge your right to say it.

Free speech is the protection of the rational mind and its literary, intellectual, and scientific products. It means the absolute right to express one's views, so long as one does not violate the rights of others.

Free speech means no American should fear the fate of Galileo, persecuted for daring to assert scientific truths that contradicted the official Church's doctrines, nor that of Socrates, put to death for offending the state.

Yet the FCC exists to dictate what can be said on-air. Each year since the early days of radio, every broadcast station must apply to the FCC for permission to use the airwaves. In exchange for their licenses, broadcasters must promise to serve the "public interest." Stations that the FCC regards as having failed to do so can be fined, or even shut down, at the FCC's sole discretion.

Robert Garmong teaches philosophy at Dongbai University in China. This article originally appeared in the *San Diego Business Journal* on August 9, 2004.

The putative justification for the FCC's regulation of broadcasters is that the airwaves are public property. But just as the government does not own — and so has no legitimate control over — the presses of the *New York Times*, so it has no business regulating what may be broadcast over airwaves.

The airwaves, which would be useless without the transmission networks cre- 10 ated by radio and TV stations, belong to the individuals and companies that developed them. Broadcasters should not have to plead to the authorities for annual licenses, any more than a homeowner should have to beg for an annual license to use the patch of land he has developed.

No other media in America is subjected to such persecution. If the *New York Times* or Barnes & Noble publishes and distributes content some members of the public disapprove of, the government cannot threaten them with fines or penalties. But let Howard Stern offend a listener, and Clear Channel is hammered with more than a million dollars in fines.

"Indecency" Crackdown

So far, only "indecency" has been targeted by the FCC's crackdown — but politicians on both sides of the aisle have begun whispering demands to censor PBS or the Fox News Channel on the grounds that their alleged biases violate the "public interest."

Both the liberals, with their political correctness, and the conservatives, with their puritanical religious ethic, claim to speak for the "public interest." Can it be long before the two sides begin the battle over which ideas and values Americans are allowed to see and hear on-air?

As the FCC wields its club ever more fiercely, broadcasters are running scared. Clear Channel has canceled its "shock-jock" programs. Skittish station managers have bleeped out words such as "urinate," "damn," and "orgy" from the Rush Limbaugh program. Most ominous, the National Association of Broadcasters convened a "Summit on Responsible Programming" to define industrywide standards of self-censorship.

America was founded on the freedom of speech — on the right and responsibil- 15 ity of the individual to decide what to say, and what to listen to. Yet in the name of protecting ourselves from being offended — and almost without noticing it — we are well on the way to surrendering that crucial right to the control of the omnipotent state.

Freedom of Speech and My Right to Silence at Bath Time

PATTI WALDMEIR

BEFORE READING: What is your opinion of the do-not-call registry designed to keep citizens from receiving calls from telemarketers? Are there two sides to the argument?

It is funny how the U.S. Constitution intrudes into one's daily life in America. Some countries do not even have one; ours dictates the smallest details of mundane life — such as whether I can bathe my children in peace or catch a catnap on a Sunday without an invasion of the telemarketers.

Today a federal appeals court in Oklahoma will address the pressing national question of whether I have a constitutional right to silence at bath time.

The case before the court tests the constitutionality of the federal do-not-call registry, which allows Americans to assert their right to silence by banning commercial telemarketing calls. The registry is wildly popular — the single most popular thing the federal government has done in years. But that does not make it constitutional; and the fate of do-not-call efforts could well foretell the future of do-not-spam.

Either way, it is a question of commercial free speech: advertisers have a right to broadcast their wares, but consumers have a right to refuse to listen. This case will test the role of government in helping consumers block their ears. It could have big implications, not just for junk calls and junk e-mail but also for the future of corporate free speech in America.

Eventually, one of the new generation of do-not-advertise cases will probably   5
end up before the U.S. Supreme Court, but that may take a while. Until then, proponents of a crackdown can brandish powerful quotes from former Supreme Court justices that appear to condemn the invasion of the advertisers: Justice Louis Brandeis said the right to be let alone was "the right most valued by civilized men"; Justice William O. Douglas said it was "the beginning of all freedoms." They were not talking about telemarketing. But their views are a powerful rhetorical tool for those who think a man's home should be more than a spam receptacle.

So what happens when a man's right to preserve the privacy of his castle collides with the free speech rights of advertisers? That is the issue before the 10th circuit court of appeals in Tulsa today: Can the government help consumers place a gag order on telemarketers by enforcing a national do-not-call list? Or does the first amendment to the U.S. Constitution prohibit the registry as a free speech violation?

Patti Waldmeir writes a column about law and society for the *Financial Times* in Shanghai. Before her move to China, she was the U.S. editor for the *Financial Times*, based in Washington, D.C., and then was stationed in London. This article appeared in the *Financial Times* on November 10, 2003.

Judge Edward Nottingham became one of the most despised men in America when he struck down the registry as unconstitutional in September. And the grounds for his ruling made it seem all the more absurd: He objected because the registry would block only commercial calls and not charitable solicitations. Judge Nottingham argued that the government had no right to discriminate between a sales pitch from AT&T and one from the Policemen's Benevolent Association. Ironically, he struck down the registry not because it banned too much speech but because it banned too little.

But although his decision enraged the 50 million American households that had already signed up for the registry, that does not make it wrong. Judge Nottingham insisted the government had failed to show why the registry should apply to one kind of call and not the other. Charitable calls disrupt my nap and bother my bath time just as surely as any other solicitation. In fact, I find charity calls from the police even more upsetting than offers of double-glazing and cheap credit. I do not feel threatened by window salesmen; but when policemen ask me for funds, I feel I have been hit for protection money. Both kinds of call are annoying and upsetting. Should one be allowed and not the other?

There is no satisfactory answer to that question, says Stuart Banner of UCLA law school, who argues that every do-not-advertise effort will encounter first amendment problems. If government enforces a ban against all solicitation, commercial and non-commercial, it may be restricting speech that is essentially political and that enjoys the highest form of first amendment protection. Commercial speech gets less protection; but the government still needs a good reason to hinder it unless it is fraudulent. So there is no way, he argues, to write a do-not-call or do-not-spam rule that does not end up in the courts.

Still, he predicts most such efforts will survive because most judges are prag-   10
matic rather than purist: "Judges don't usually pursue constitutional doctrines to their logical end if doing so would require dashing the hopes of tens of millions of Americans (especially if some of those Americans are judges, as I imagine they are)," he wrote recently in the *Washington Post*. In a world where judges get spam too, do-not-spam efforts probably have a guaranteed future.

As Michael Powell, chairman of the Federal Communications Commission, said when the FCC do-not-call registry was first challenged: "I refuse to believe that the Constitution of the United States shuts down the ability of consumers to protect the sanctity of their homes." He is probably right, which is good news for the sanctity of bath time. But it could be seriously bad news for commercial speech in the United States: Telemarketers have rights too. We all share the same constitution; somehow, it must protect us all.

Dare Call It Treason

ERIC FONER

BEFORE READING: Do you believe that Americans should be able to speak out against a war their country is involved in? Brainstorm what you know about the history of such dissent in the United States.

Few traditions are more American than freedom of speech and the right to dissent. But an equally powerful American tradition has been the effort by government and private "patriots" to suppress free expression in times of crisis. During the fighting in Iraq, former military leaders who criticized planning for the war were denounced for endangering troops in the field and warned to remain silent. A number of scholars, including myself, were branded "Traitor Professors" on a television talk show. If criticism of a war while it is in progress makes one a traitor, that category will have to include Abraham Lincoln, who denounced the Mexican War while serving in Congress in 1847; Mark Twain, who vehemently attacked government policy in the Spanish-American and Philippine wars at the turn of the last century; and Martin Luther King Jr., who eloquently called for an end to the war in Vietnam.

With the exception of World War II, every significant war in American history has inspired vigorous dissent. Many colonists remained loyal to Britain during the American Revolution. Most New Englanders opposed the War of 1812. Numerous Americans considered the Mexican War an effort to extend the territory of slavery. Both North and South were internally divided during the Civil War. World War I and Vietnam produced massive antiwar movements. This is part of our democratic tradition.

Equally persistent, however, have been efforts to suppress wartime dissent. The Alien and Sedition Acts during the "quasi-war" with France in 1798 allowed the president to deport aliens and made it illegal to criticize the government. Both Union and Confederate governments suppressed opposition newspapers and jailed critics. World War I witnessed a massive repression of freedom of speech, with critics of the war, socialists, and labor leaders jailed or deported; those suspected of disloyalty rounded up by private vigilantes; and the speaking of German banned in some places. Universities, including my own, fired professors who opposed American involvement.

Self-proclaimed patriots not only seek to determine the boundaries of acceptable speech about the present but rewrite history to create a more politically useful past. During World War I, the Committee on Public Information, a government

Eric Foner is the DeWitt Clinton Professor of History at Columbia University. He is an elected fellow of the American Academy of Arts and Sciences and the British Academy and has served as president of both the Organization of American Historians and the American Historical Association. Foner has written a number of books about American history, including the 2004 textbook *Give Me Liberty! An American History*.

propaganda agency, published pamphlets demonstrating the "common principles" of Oliver Cromwell, Jean-Jacques Rousseau, and Thomas Jefferson in order to create a historical lineage for the Anglo-French-American military alliance. Today, statements about history that in normal times would seem uncontroversial have been labeled treasonous. Daniel Pipes said in his syndicated newspaper column that I "hate America" because I noted that Japan invoked the idea of preemptive war to justify its attack on Pearl Harbor (a point also made by that well-known anti-American, Arthur Schlesinger Jr.). My comment to a reporter that the United States has frequently embarked on military ventures without being attacked, as in Haiti, the Dominican Republic, and Vietnam, prompted accusations of treason in the media.

In the aftermath of the Civil War, a far greater crisis than the war on Iraq, the   5
Supreme Court in the *Milligan* case invalidated the use of military tribunals to try civilians. The Court proclaimed that the Constitution is not suspended in wartime: "It is a law for rulers and people, equally in war and in peace." Alas, we have not always lived up to this ideal. The history of civil liberties in the United States is not a straight-line trajectory toward ever-greater freedom. It is a complex story in which victories can prove temporary and regression can follow progress.

Our civil liberties are neither self-enforcing nor self-correcting. Historians today view past suppressions of free speech as shameful episodes. But we are now living through another moment when many commentators, both in and out of government, seem to view freedom of expression as at best an inconvenience and at worst unpatriotic. The incessant attacks on dissenters as traitors are intended to create an atmosphere of shock and awe within the United States, so that those tempted to speak their mind become too intimidated to do so.

George W. Bush has claimed that America's enemies wish to destroy our freedoms. If we surrender freedom of speech in the hope that this will bring swifter victory on current and future battlefields, who then will have won the war?

The Imus Fallout: Who Can Say What?

JAMES PONIEWOZIK

BEFORE READING: What restrictions, if any, are there on what language can be used on the radio? Are those restrictions the same as for television? Should they be?

Say this for Don Imus: the man knows how to turn an economical phrase. When the radio shock jock described the Rutgers women's basketball team, on the April 4 *Imus in the Morning*, as "nappy-headed hos," he packed so many layers of offense into the statement that it was like a perfect little diamond of insult. There was a racial element, a gender element, and even a class element (the joke implied that the Scarlet Knights were thuggish and ghetto compared with the Tennessee Lady Vols).

Imus was a famous, rich, old white man picking on a bunch of young, mostly black college women. So it seemed pretty cut-and-dried that his bosses at CBS Radio would suspend his show — half frat party, half political salon for the Beltway elite — for two weeks, and that MSNBC would cancel the TV simulcast. And that Imus would plan to meet with the students he offended. Case closed, justice served, lesson — possibly — learned. Move on.

But a reasonable person could ask, What was the big deal? And I don't mean the lots-of-black-rappers-say-"hos" argument, though we'll get to that. Rather, I mean, what celebrity isn't slurring some group nowadays?

I exaggerate slightly. But our culture has experienced an almost psychotic outburst of -isms in the past year. Michael Richards and "nigger." Isaiah Washington and "faggot." Senator George Allen and "macaca." Mel Gibson and "f__ing Jews."

But we also live in a culture in which racially and sexually edgy material is often — legitimately — considered brilliant comment, even art. Last year's most critically praised comedy, *Borat: Cultural Learnings of America for Make Benefit Glorious Nation of Kazakhstan*, won Sacha Baron Cohen a Golden Globe for playing a Kazakh journalist who calls Alan Keyes a "genuine chocolate face" and asks a gun-shop owner to suggest a good piece for killing a Jew. Quentin Tarantino has made a career borrowing tropes from blaxploitation movies. In the critics-favorite sitcom *The Sarah Silverman Program*, the star sleeps with God, who is African American and who she assumes is "God's black friend." And the current season of *South Park* opened with an episode about a Michael Richards-esque controversy erupting when a character blurts the word *niggers* on *Wheel of Fortune*. (He answers a puzzle — N-GGERS — for which the clue is "People who annoy you"; the correct answer is "naggers.")

5

James Poniewozick worked as the media critic and media section leader for the online magazine Salon.com before he joined *Time* in 1999 as media and television critic. This article was published on April 12, 2007.

This is not to say that *Borat* made Imus do it or to make excuses for Imus. Even in the midst of his apology tour last week, Imus did enough of that for himself, citing his charity work, his support of black Senate candidate Harold Ford Jr., even his booking the black singing group Blind Boys of Alabama on his show. (He didn't mention how, last fall, he groused about persuading the "money grubbing" "Jewish management" to okay the booking.)

But in the middle of his stunning medley of sneer, apology, and rationalization, Imus asked a pretty good question: "This phrase that I use, it originated in the black community. That didn't give me a right to use it, but that's where it originated. Who calls who that and why? We need to know that. I need to know that."

So let's ask.

Imus crossed a line, boorishly, creepily, paleolithically. But where is that line nowadays? In a way, the question is an outgrowth of something healthy in our society: the assumption that there is a diverse audience that is willing to talk about previously taboo social distinctions more openly, frankly, and daringly than before. It used to be assumed that people were free to joke about their own kind (with some license for black comedians to talk about how white people dance). Crossing those lines was the province of the occasional "socially conscious artist," like Dick Gregory or Lenny Bruce, who was explicit about his goals: in Bruce's words, to repeat "'niggerniggernigger' until the word [didn't] mean anything anymore."

Now, however, we live in a mash-up world, where people — especially young   10
people — feel free to borrow one another's cultural signifiers. In a now classic episode of *Chappelle's Show*, comic Dave Chappelle plays a blind, black white supremacist who inadvertently calls a carload of rap-listening white boys "niggers." The kids' reaction: "Did he just call us niggers? Awesome!" The country is, at least, more pop-culturally integrated — one nation under Jessica Alba, J. Lo and Harold & Kumar — and with that comes greater comfort in talking about differences.

But that's a harder attitude for older people — who grew up with more cultural and actual segregation — to accept or to mimic. Part of the problem with Imus' joke was that it was so tone-deaf. "That's some rough girls from Rutgers," he said. "Man, they got tattoos . . . That's some nappy-headed hos there." The joke played badly in every community, raising memories of beauty bias (against darker skin and kinkier hair) that dates back to slavery. Tracy Riley, thirty-seven, of Des Moines, Iowa, who is of mixed race, said the incident was among her four kids' first exposures to overt racism. "Our kids don't see color the way we do," she said. "They don't see it as much. 'You're my friend or not,' but it's not about race."

The line was as damning as anything for what it suggested about Imus' thought process: a sixty-six-year-old white male country-music fan rummaging in his subconscious for something to suggest that some young black women looked scary, and coming up with a reference to African-American hair and a random piece of rap slang. (Maybe because older, male media honchos are more conscious of — and thus fixated on — race than gender, much of the coverage of Imus ignored the sexual part of the slur on a show with a locker-room vibe and a mostly male guest list. If Imus had said "niggas" rather than "hos," would his bosses have waited as long to act?)

So who gets to say "ho," in an age when *Pimp My Ride* is an innocent car show and *It's Hard Out Here for a Pimp* is an Oscar-winning song? As even Essence Carlson, one of the Rutgers students Imus insulted, acknowledged at a press conference, black rap artists labeled young black women as "hos" long before Imus did. And while straight people may not be able to say "faggot," *Queer Eye for the Straight Guy* and *Will & Grace* helped mainstream the nonhostile gay joke for straight people. But all this reappropriation and blurring — distinguishing a good-natured "That's so gay!" from a homophobic one — has created a situation in which, when Richards went off on his Laugh Factory rant, it was possible to wonder if he was playing a character.

The license to borrow terms other people have taken back can worry even edgy comics. A few months ago, I interviewed Silverman, who argued that her material was not racist but about racism (and I agree). But she added something that surprised me, coming from her: "I'm not saying 'I can say nigger because I'm liberal.' There is a certain aspect of that that I'm starting to get grossed out by. 'Oh, we're not racist. We can say it.'"

Comedians work through these danger zones in the presence of other comics. In a comedians' get-together or a TV writers' room, nothing is off-limits: without airing the joke that goes too far, you can never get to the joke that flies in front of an audience. Trouble might come if material meant for that smaller audience went public, as in 1993, when Ted Danson got in trouble after word got out of a Friars Club routine he did in blackface, though his jokes were defended — and reportedly written by — his then girlfriend Whoopi Goldberg.

Today, because of cable and YouTube, because of a media culture that rewards the fastest, least censoring mouth, we are all in the writers' room. (Friars Club roasts are now televised on Comedy Central.) Punditry and gonzo comedy have become less and less distinguishable. (And I'm not talking here about *The Daily Show*, whose host Jon Stewart is, ironically, one of the most conservative defenders of the idea of sober, evenhanded news — see his 2004 tirade against Tucker Carlson.) Got something on your mind? Say it! Don't think about it! If you don't, the next guy in the greenroom will! C'mon, it'll kill!

Right-wing pundit Ann Coulter is probably the best example of this, playing a constant game of "Can you top this?" with herself, as in March, when she told the Conservative Political Action Conference that she would have a comment on Senator John Edwards, "but it turns out that you have to go into rehab if you use the word faggot." Coulter is only the most egregious example — from Bill O'Reilly on Fox to Glenn Beck on CNN, offense is the coin of the cable realm.

The flip side of the instant-attention era is the gotcha era. We may be more inured to shock than ever, but when someone manages to find and cross a line, we're better able to generate, spread, and sustain offense. You get eaten by the same tiger that you train. Imus got special love from the media over the years because his show was such a media hangout. But when the controversy erupted, it snowballed in part because the media love to cover the media.

Every public figure — athlete, pundit, actor — now has two audiences: the one he or she is addressing and the one that will eventually read the blogs or see the viral video. A few have adapted, like Stephen Colbert, whose routine at last year's White House Correspondents' Association dinner was decried by attendees as rude and shrill — but made him a hero to his YouTube audience. Imus, a thirty-plus-year veteran of radio shock, seemed to underestimate the power of the modern umbrage-amplification machine. The day after his remarks, Imus said dismissively on air that people needed to relax about "some idiot comment meant to be amusing." Shockingly, they did not, and by the next day, Imus had tapped an inner wellspring of deepest regret.

As in so many scandals, the first response may have been the most authentic —   20 at least we're inclined to take it that way because the contrition cycle has become so familiar. You blurt. You deny. You apologize. You visit the rehab center or speak with the Official Minority Spokesperson of your choice and go on with your life. Although — or maybe because — it's so easy to get caught today, it's also easier to get forgiven. In 1988 Jimmy (the Greek) Snyder was fired by CBS for saying black athletes were "bred" to be better than whites. In 1996 CBS golf analyst Ben Wright was suspended indefinitely after he was quoted as saying that lesbians had hurt the sport.

To his credit, Imus never played the "I'm sick" card. Perhaps he felt confident because he had been legitimized by his high-profile guests. Imus could have made a remark just as bad years ago and suffered few if any consequences. Scratch that: Imus did make remarks as bad or worse for years. Speaking about Gwen Ifill, the African-American PBS anchor who was then White House correspondent for the *New York Times*, he said, "Isn't the *Times* wonderful? It lets the cleaning lady cover the White House." He called a *Washington Post* writer a "boner-nosed, beanie-wearing Jewboy" and Arabs "towelheads."

Yet politicians and journalists (including *Time* writers) still went on his show to plug their candidacies and books because Imus knew how to sell. "If Don Imus likes a book," says Katie Wainwright, executive director of publicity at publisher Hyperion, "not only does he have the author on, he will talk about it before, during and after, often for weeks afterwards." The price: implicitly telling America that the mostly white male Beltway elite is cool with looking the other way at racism. They compartmentalized the lengthy interviews he did with them from the "bad" parts of the show, though the boundary was always a little porous. And evidently many still do. "Solidarity forever," pledged *Boston Globe* columnist Tom Oliphant in a phone interview with Imus on April 9. Senator John McCain and Rudolph Giuliani said they would return to the show. "I called him a little while ago to talk to him about it personally," Giuliani told the *New York Times*. "And I believe that he understands that he made a very big mistake." (Senator Barack Obama, who appeared on the show once, has said he will not go back; other politicians have hedged.)

In fact, while there might be more media and blogger scrutiny of Imus' future guests, his suspension may have inoculated them — if his radio show survives. The show draws 2 million daily listeners, and it's a more valuable property on radio than it was on TV. (It brings in about $15 million annually for CBS Radio compared with several million for MSNBC.) But the show has already lost advertisers, including American Express, Staples, and Procter & Gamble.

Imus argued repeatedly that his critics should consider the "context" of his larger life, including the formidable work for sick children he does through his Imus Ranch charity. But it's not Imus Ranch he broadcasts from twenty hours a week. You can't totally separate the lives of celebrities from their work — it didn't excuse Gibson that he attacked the Jews in his free time — but finally what determines who can make what jokes is the context of their work: the tone of their acts, the personas they present, the vehicles they create for their work.

That context is not as kind to Imus. He comes out of the shock jock tradition, 25 but all shock jocks are not created equal. If Opie & Anthony or Mancow had made the "nappy-headed" comment, it wouldn't have been a blip because future presidents do not do cable-news interviews with Opie & Anthony and Mancow.

Then there's personality, or at least persona. Compared with Imus, for instance, his rival Howard Stern may be offensive, but he's also self- deprecating, making fun of his own satyrism, looks, and even manly endowment. Imus doesn't take it nearly as well as he dishes it out. His shtick is all cowboy-hatted swagger, and his insults set him up as superior to his targets and the alpha dog to his supplicant guests.

Imus uses jokes to establish his power, in other words. He's hardly the only humorist to do that. But making jokes about difference — race, gender, sexual orientation, the whole list — is ultimately about power. You need to purchase the right to do it through some form of vulnerability, especially if you happen to be a rich, famous white man. But the I-Man — his radio persona, anyway — is not about vulnerability. (The nickname, for Pete's sake: I, Man!) That's creepy enough when he's having a big-name columnist kiss his ring; when he hurled his tinfoil thunderbolts at a team of college kids, it was too much. "Some people have said, 'Well, he says this all the time,'" Rutgers' team captain Carson told *Time*. "But does that justify the remarks he's made about anyone?"

Of course, assessing Imus' show is a subjective judgment, and setting these boundaries is as much an aesthetic call as a moral one. It's arbitrary, nebulous and, yes, unfair. Who doesn't have a list of artists or leaders whose sins they rationalize: Elvis Costello for calling Ray Charles a "blind, ignorant nigger," Eminem for peppering his lyrics with "faggot," Jesse Jackson for "Hymietown," D. W. Griffith for lionizing the Klan, or T. S. Eliot for maligning Jews?

You might say that there's no excuse and that I'm as big a hypocrite as Imus' defenders for suggesting that there is one. Which may be true. That's finally why "Where's the line?" is a misleading question. There are as many lines as there are people. We draw and redraw them by constantly arguing them. This is how we avoid throwing out the brilliance of a Sacha Baron Cohen — who offends us to point out absurdities in our society, not just to make "idiot comments meant to be amusing" — with a shock jock's dirty bathwater. It's a draining, polarizing but necessary process.

Which may be why it was such a catharsis to see the Rutgers players respond 30 to Imus at their press conference in their own words. "I'm a woman, and I'm someone's child," said Kia Vaughn. "I achieve a lot. And unless they've given this name, a 'ho,' a new definition, then that is not what I am." She stood with her teammates, a row of unbowed, confident women. For a few minutes, anyway, they drew a line we could all agree on and formed a line we could all get behind.

Thinking and Writing about the Limits on Freedom of Speech

QUESTIONS FOR DISCUSSION AND WRITING

1. How do you believe the court should decide in the case of the student who wore the anti-war T-shirt?

2. Can you think of circumstances in which creative freedom should bow to social responsibility? Explain.

3. Explain your position on how much control there should be on what is broadcast over the air waves — and who should control it.

4. Although the majority of Americans seem to celebrate the do-not-call registry, Waldmeir explains that there are two sides to the controversy. Write an essay in which you make clear why this is not a clear-cut case of one group being right and the other wrong.

5. Do you believe there should be any restrictions on Americans' right to speak out against a war they believe is wrong? Explain.

6. Don Imus was fired as a result of his remark on the air about the Rutgers women's basketball team. Explain in an essay whether you think his firing was an appropriate response.

7. Many believe that rap music goes too far in its demeaning of women and its championing of violence (an argument that was used often in defending Imus's remark). Defend rap as an artistic expression of a culture or argue that it does indeed go too far.

8. Explain to what extent you agree with Gaylor's arguments against school prayer.

9. The introduction to this chapter quotes a Supreme Court justice who wrote that neither students nor teachers "shed their constitutional right to freedom of speech or expression at the schoolhouse gate." Do the examples in the readings support that statement or argue against it?

CHAPTER 19

How Far Will We Go to Change Our Body Image?

We live in a society where appearance matters. How much it matters is clear from magazines, television shows, movies, and advertisements. It is clear from the number of diets hyped on talk shows and in bookstores. It is clear from the alarming number of young women — and, increasingly, young men — with anorexia and bulimia, from the celebrities that our youth, male and female, choose to idolize and emulate, and from the drastic increase in recent years in the amount of plastic surgery being performed. We exercise, count our carbs, and are acutely aware of the face that stares back at us in the mirror.

Cosmetic surgery has changed countless lives by correcting birth defects and other abnormalities. It does not save lives, although at times cosmetic surgery may be closely linked to corrective surgery, as when a cleft lip is corrected in conjunction with correcting a cleft palate or when plastic surgery repairs the ravages of severe burns once the burns themselves are no longer life threatening. A cleft palate interferes with one's health. A cleft lip is repaired primarily for aesthetic reasons. The scars left on a burn victim may require plastic surgery to help heal the psychological damage left after the body has healed.

Having a nose job or a breast enlargement purely for aesthetic reasons was once the sort of thing only movie stars and the extremely wealthy would have considered. Today many average citizens are enhancing or reshaping their bodies. For some, changing each imperfection becomes an obsession. Women are generally accused of being the most conscious of body image. The steroids that men take, though, improve physique as well as athletic performance — and increase the chances of lasting damage to the body.

The dangers associated with the use of drugs, diets, and plastic surgery to enhance body image are the frequent focus of argumentative speech or writing. The psychological dangers may be as grave as the physical ones. We must question why so many are willing to tamper with their physical appearance and wonder how they feel once the changes are made. To whose model of physical perfection are we aspiring? Is it right, for example, to seek to remove physical signs of ethnicity? Some regard such changes as a betrayal of the race. In changing what makes each of us distinct, are we giving in, as one author included here suggests, to "the tyranny of the normal"? How much are we willing to spend — how much money and how much pain or discomfort — to look good?

From *Body Image and Adolescents*

JILLIAN CROLL

BEFORE READING: What forces shaped your feelings about your size and shape during early adolescence? Did they have a positive or negative effect on the way you perceived your own body?

Body image is the dynamic perception of one's body — how it looks, feels, and moves. It is shaped by perception, emotions, physical sensations, and is not static, but can change in relation to mood, physical experience, and environment. Because adolescents experience significant physical changes in their bodies during puberty, they are likely to experience highly dynamic perceptions of body image. Body image is influenced strongly by self-esteem and self-evaluation, more so than by external evaluation by others. It can, however, be powerfully influenced and affected by cultural messages and societal standards of appearance and attractiveness. Given the overwhelming prevalence of thin and lean female images and strong and lean male images common to all westernized societies, body image concerns have become widespread among adolescents.

- 50–88 percent of adolescent girls feel negatively about their body shape or size.[1,2]

- 49 percent of teenage girls say they know someone with an eating disorder.[1]

- Only 33 percent of girls say they are at the "right weight for their body," while 58 percent want to lose weight. Just 9 percent want to gain weight.[3]

- Females are much more likely than males to think their current size is too large (66 percent vs. 21 percent).[4]

Jillian Croll completed her doctorate in nutrition and epidemiology and master's of public health at the University of Minnesota and a master's in nutrition at the University of Vermont. She teaches in the Department of Food Science and Nutrition at the University of Minnesota. She has authored numerous book chapters and articles on nutritional treatment of eating disorders, body image, sports participation, and adolescent health. The excerpt here is reprinted from *Guidelines for Adolescent Nutrition Services* (2005).

- Over one-third of males think their current size is too small, while only 10 percent of women consider their size too small.[4]

- Strikingly, while only 30 percent of older adolescents surveyed consider their current size acceptable to *them*, 85 percent of females and 95 percent of males considered their current size socially acceptable for *others*.[4]

- 85 percent of young women worry "a lot" about how they look and twice as many males as females say they are satisfied with their appearance.[5]

- A report by the American Association of University Women indicated that for girls, "the way I look" is the most important indicator of self-worth, while for boys, self-worth is based on abilities, rather than looks.[6]

Going through puberty can amplify body image concerns. Puberty for boys brings characteristics typically admired by society — height, speed, broadness, and strength. Puberty for girls brings with it characteristics often perceived as less laudable, as girls generally get rounder and have increased body fat. These changes can serve to further enhance dissatisfaction among girls.[7] Going through puberty later or earlier than peers can have an impact on body image as well as psychological health. Generally, early development for girls and late development for boys present the greatest challenges to healthy body image.[8]

Etiology/Contributing Factors

Media Messages Strong social and cultural forces influence body image in young people. From childhood to adulthood, television, billboards, movies, music videos, video games, computer games, toys, the Internet, and magazines convey images of ideal attractiveness, beauty, shape, size, strength, and weight. Consider these statistics from the TV-Turnoff Network.[9]

- Adolescents watch an average of 28 hours of television per week.

- American youth spend, on average, 900 hours a year in school and an average of 1,023 hours a year watching television.

- The average American consumes 11.8 hours per day of media of all kinds.

- Children view more than 20,000 commercials per year.

- 75 percent of all adolescents spend at least 6 hours a week watching music videos.[10]

Eight million children at 12,000 schools across the country watch television at school each day via Channel One, an in-school broadcast current events program provided (including TV and VCR equipment) free of charge to schools. The program includes ten minutes of broadcast news and current events coverage and two minutes of advertisements for products such as chips, candy, and beauty-aids. These advertisements promote poor body image through their "beauty" ads and provide mixed messages regarding adolescent lifestyle.[11]

In childhood, popular toys such as action figures and dolls have similar body shapes: tall and slender for female figures and tall, slender, and muscular for male figures. The body shapes advertised by these toys, dolls and media sources are not realistic (see Table 1). If Barbie were real, her neck would be too long and thin to support the weight of her head, and her upper body proportions would make it difficult for her to walk upright. If Ken were real, his huge barrel chest and enormously thick neck would nearly preclude him from wearing a shirt.

Magazines targeted at female adolescents are full of images of young, slim, attractive, blemish-free females with small waists, large chests and only ever-so-slightly-rounded hips, while magazines produced for males are full of strong, lean, attractive, blemish-free males, frequently displayed with the aforementioned females in close proximity. Beauty pageants continue to be a popular and avidly watched showcase of ideal societal beauty.

- The average female model is 5'10" and weighs 110 pounds. The average American female is 5'4" and weighs 144 pounds. That makes the average model at least 30 pounds lighter and 6 inches taller than the average female looking at her.

- Over 800 million Barbie dolls have been sold and annual sales amount to more than 1 billion dollars.[12] If Barbie were real, given her proportions, she would barely be able to stand upright.

- Miss America contestants have become increasingly thinner over the past seventy-five years. In the 1920s, contestants had BMIs in the normal range of 20–25. Since then, pageant winners' body weights have decreased steadily to a level about 12 percent below levels from the mid-1900s. Since 1970, nearly all of the winners have had BMIs below the healthy range, with some as low as 16.9, a BMI that would meet part of the diagnostic criteria for anorexia nervosa.[13]

TABLE 1 If Barbie and Ken Were Real				
	If Barbie was a real female	Real female	If Ken was a real male	Real male
Height (ft, in)	7'2"	5'2"	7'8"	6'
Chest (in)	40	35	50	40
Waist (in)	22	28	43	33
Neck Circumference (in)	12	12.2	23.4	15.5
Neck Length (in)	6.2	3.0	6.35	5.5

Source: Statistics from Brownell KD, Napolitano MA. Distorting reality for children: body size proportions of Barbie and Ken dolls. Int J Eat Disord 1995;18(3):295–298.

- Even educational materials have messages regarding body size. Textbook images of girls have gotten more slender every decade since 1900, while images of boys have not changed significantly.[14]

- Adolescent females watching the most media idealizing thin body types, such as soap operas and movies, report the highest body dissatisfaction and those watching music videos report a strong drive for thinness.[15]

- Young women surveyed before and after being shown fashion and beauty magazines have decreased self-image and increased desire to lose weight as compared to young women shown news magazines. Females report they exercise and diet more in response to fashion magazine images.[2,16]

- Drive to attain the ideal standard of attractiveness for males (bigger, bulkier, and more muscular) has been associated with poor self-esteem and depression.[17]

- While most body image research has been done with white youth, research does indicate that African-American adolescents, particularly females, tend to have healthier body images than their white counterparts. However, even among African-American females, as their body shapes and sizes get further from the cultural idealized shape and size, body dissatisfaction increases.[8]

- Asian Americans may have healthier body images than their white, African-American, or Hispanic peers due to cultural norms influencing modesty and are the only group in which boys and girls have similarly high body satisfaction.[8] However, as more acculturation in American society occurs, body satisfaction decreases and body image concerns arise, particularly among males.[8]

Familial Messages Familial concerns and pressures may also contribute to increased body dissatisfaction and body image concerns. Socialization encourages males to strive to become stronger and more developed, while females are to make their bodies more beautiful. Parents tend to become less positive and more critical regarding their children's appearance, eating and physical activity as they move into and through adolescence. Adolescents receive the most criticism regarding their physical appearance and the most efforts to change their appearance.[18] Parental overconcern with children being thin or encouragement to avoid being fat can influence young people to become constant dieters and use unhealthy weight control methods.[16] Health professionals should work with parents to help them encourage their children to be healthy in a manner that supports healthy body image development.

Consequences

While the contributing factors may vary, the outcomes are similar. Overconcern with body image and shape can lead to restrictive dieting and unhealthy weight control methods which may lead to potentially dangerous disordered eating behaviors. Societal reinforcement of body image concern, in the form of a multibillion-dollar diet and weight loss industry, aids in maintenance of body dissatisfaction and the elusive search for the perfect body. Societal promotion of the thin ideal may also lead to prejudicial treatment of overweight individuals or teasing based on weight and shape, especially among youth. Overconcern with body image can have damaging effects.

- In large-scale studies, approximately 30 percent of boys and over 55 percent of girls report using unhealthy weight control methods such as vomiting, laxatives, diet pills, cigarette smoking, and diuretics in an effort to lose weight.[19,20]

- At eight years old, girls believe that weight control is strongly associated with self-worth and view dieting as a means of improving self-worth.[21]

- Poor body image often leads to dieting, which can lead to unhealthy weight control behaviors, disordered eating, and ultimately eating disorders.

- Poor body image is strongly associated with low self-esteem and low self-worth, both of which can severely limit the potential for youth to succeed.

- Teasing related to weight and shape is implicated as contributing to disordered eating.[22]

Screening/Assessment

Given the ubiquitous nature of body image concerns and socio-cultural messages regarding body shape and size, as well as the complexity of the nature of body image, it is prudent to screen all adolescents for body image issues and work to foster a healthy body image among all youth. . . .

REFERENCES

1. EPM Communications. Youth Markets Alert 2000;12:8.

2. Field AE, Cheung L, Wolf AM, Herzog DB, Gortmaker SL, Colditz GA. Exposure to the mass media and weight concerns among girls. Pediatrics 1999;103(3):E36.

3. SmartGirl Speaks. Eating disorder quick poll reports. SmartGirl.org, University of Michigan. http://www.smartgirl.org/. Accessed 07/14/04.

4. Rand CS, Resnick JL, Seldman RS. Assessment of socially acceptable body sizes by university students. Obes Res 1997;5(5):425–429.

5. A cappella: A report on the realities, concerns, expectations, and barriers experienced by adolescent women in Canada. Ottawa: Canadian Teacher's Federation, 1990.

6. How schools shortchange girls: The AAUW report. A study of major findings in education. Washington, DC: American Association of University Women Educational Foundation, 1992.

7. O'Dea JA, Abraham S. Onset of disordered eating attitudes and behaviors in early adolescence: interplay of pubertal status, gender, weight, and age. Adolescence 1999;34 (136): 671–679.

8. Siegel JM, Yancey AK, Aneshensel CS, Schuler R. Body image, perceived pubertal timing, and adolescent mental health. J Adolesc Health 1999;25(2): 155–165.

9. Facts and figures about our TV habits. TV-Turnoff Network. http://www.tvturnoff.org/. Accessed 7/14/04.

10. Television Viewing Study. Teenage Research Unlimited, 1996.

11. Reid LGA, Gedissman A. Required TV program in school encourages poor lifestyle choices. AAP News. November 2000. American Academy of Pediatrics. http://www.aap.org/advocacy/reidll00.htm. Accessed 7/14/04.

12. Billion Dollar Barbie. New York Times Magazine 1994;27:22.

13. Rubinstein S, Caballero B. Is Miss America an undernourished role model? JAMA 2000; 283(12):1569.

14. Davis J, Oswalt R. Societal influences on a thinner body size in children. Percept Mot Skills 1992;74(3 Pt l):697–698.

15. Tiggemann M, Pickering AS. Role of television in adolescent women's body dissatisfaction and drive for thinness. Int J Eat Disord 1996;20(2):199–203.

16. Field AE, Camargo CA, Jr., Taylor CB, Berkey CS, Roberts SB, Colditz GA. Peer, parent, and media influences on the development of weight concerns and frequent dieting among preadolescent and adolescent girls and boys. Pediatrics 2001;107(l):54–60.

17. McCreary DR, Sasse DK. An exploration of the drive for muscularity in adolescent boys and girls. J Am Coll Health 2000;48(6):297–304.

18. Striegel-Moore RH, Kearney-Cooke A. Exploring parents' attitudes and behaviors about their children's physical appearance. Int J Eat Disord 1994;15(4):377–385.

19. Emmons L. Dieting and purging behavior in black and white high school students. J Am Diet Assoc 1992;92(3):306–312.

20. Neumark-Sztaiaer D, Story M, Falkner NH, Behuring T, Resnick MD. Sociodemographic and personal characteristics of adolescents engaged in weight loss and weight/muscle gain behaviors: who is doing what? Prev Med 1999;28(l):4–5.

21. Hill AJ, Pallin V. Dieting awareness and low self-worth: Related issues in 8-year-old girls. Int J Eat Disord 1998;24:405–413.

22. Taylor CB, Sharpe T, Shisslak C, Bryson S, Estes LS, Gray N, McKnight KM, Crago M, Kraemer HC, Killen JD. Factors associated with weight concerns in adolescent girls. Int J Eat Disord 1998;24(1):31–42.

On Pins and Needles Defending Artistic Expression

CAROL ROSE

BEFORE READING: Do you see tattoos as a form of artistic expression? Why or why not?

Stroll down any Massachusetts street on a sunny day and you will see a lot of bare skin adorned with some nifty (and some not-so-nice) tattoos.

Once the emblem of American GIs and Japanese yakuzas, tattoos have become ubiquitous among the under-thirty crowd. It's the rare person who hasn't fallen

Carol Rose is a lawyer and journalist and is executive director of the American Civil Liberties Union of Massachusetts. She posted this article on the On Liberty column of Boston.com on April 8, 2010.

Tattoos have become common among those under thirty.

under the spell of the needle and dye. Even the trend-setting Institute for Contemporary Art in Boston is opening an exhibit next week featuring Mexican tattoo artist Dr. Lakra.

But did you know that tattooing was recently illegal in Massachusetts and many other states? It's true. It took a lawsuit by the ACLU in 2000 to strike down restrictions on tattoo artists in Massachusetts, thus ensuring that this ancient form of self-expression is no longer criminalized in our Commonwealth.

On April 15 at 7 p.m., the ICA will feature a conversation about the case with ACLU attorney Sarah Wunsch, who was co-counsel with Harvey Schwartz in litigating the challenge to the Massachusetts law banning tattooing.

To some people, such legal victories seem only skin deep. But on closer examination, the right to tattoo is part and parcel of our right to artistic expression. 5

The art of "body art" goes back literally thousands of years. Tattooed mummies have been found in all parts of the world, including Egypt, Libya, Asia, and South America. A five thousand year old man, nicknamed "otzi the ice man" by the people who dug him up, reportedly bore fifty-seven tattoos — although they may have simply been scars from arthritis (apparently it can be hard to tell the difference after 5,000 years).

The first tattoo shop in New York was set up in 1846 and came to Boston soon thereafter. Soldiers from both sides in the Civil War revived the ancient tradition of wearing tattoos as a sign of military prowess. Today, surveys show that more than one-third of Americans under age thirty have tattoos, and the numbers are growing.

Despite the historical persistence of tattooing, however, the law on tattooing as free expression isn't a slam-dunk. States have some right to ensure the sanitary operation of tattoo parlors and courts are still sorting out the hard cases, such as whether employers can require employees to cover tattoos. But our nation nonetheless has made progress in defense of tattooing as a fundamental form of artistic expression. Even South Carolina and Oklahoma — two hold-out states — recently passed laws legalizing tattooing as skin art.

Personally, I am content to let Mother Nature etch her motif into my tender hide without additional help from dye and needles. But even I can't resist the fascination with tattooing as an ancient and compelling form of human expression. As the ICA enticement for its upcoming show attests: "From cave walls to touch screens, no surface is off limits to the creativity of artists and designers. What about the most accessible surface of all, our own bodies?"

Do Thin Models Warp Girls' Body Image?

NANCI HELLMICH

BEFORE READING: Examine fashion magazines or search the Internet for images of runway models. What is your impression of the models? Are they too thin?

When Frederique van der Wal, a former Victoria's Secret model, attended designers' shows during New York's Fashion Week this month, she was "shocked" by the waiflike models who paraded down the catwalk. They seemed even skinnier than in previous years.

"This unnatural thinness is a terrible message to send out. The people watching the fashion shows are young, impressionable women," says van der Wal, host of *Cover Shot* on TLC.

Psychologists and eating-disorder experts are worried about the same thing. They say the fashion industry has gone too far in pushing a dangerously thin image that women, and even very young girls, may try to emulate.

Nanci Hellmich is a Life section reporter for *USA Today* and has covered diet and nutrition for the last twenty-five years. This article appeared in *USA Today* on August 25, 2006.

"We know seeing super-thin models can play a role in causing anorexia," says Nada Stotland, professor of psychiatry at Rush Medical College in Chicago and vice president of the American Psychiatric Association. Because many models and actresses are so thin, it makes anorexics think their emaciated bodies are normal, she says. "But these people look scary. They don't look normal."

The widespread concern that model thinness has progressed from willowy to   5
wasted has reached a threshold as evidenced by the recent actions of fashion show organizers.

The Madrid fashion show, which ended Saturday, banned overly thin models, saying it wanted to project beauty and health. Organizers said models had to be within a healthy weight range.

That means a 5-foot-9 woman would need to weigh at least 125 pounds.

Officials in India, Britain, and Milan also have expressed concerns, but some experts say consumers in the USA will have to demand models with fuller figures for it to happen here.

"The promotion of the thin, sexy ideal in our culture has created a situation where the majority of girls and women don't like their bodies," says body-image researcher Sarah Murnen, professor of psychology at Kenyon College in Gambier, Ohio. "And body dissatisfaction can lead girls to participate in very unhealthy behaviors to try to control weight."

Experts call these behaviors disordered eating, a broad term used to describe a   10
range of eating problems, from frequent dieting to anorexia nervosa (which is self-starvation, low weight, and fear of being fat) to bulimia nervosa (the binge-and-purge disorder).

Girls today, even very young ones, are being bombarded with the message that they need to be super-skinny to be sexy, says psychologist Sharon Lamb, co-author of *Packaging Girlhood: Rescuing Our Daughters from Marketers' Schemes.*

It used to be that women would only occasionally see rail-thin models, such as Twiggy, the '60s fashion icon. "But now they see them every day. It's the norm," Lamb says, from ads, catalogs, and magazines to popular TV shows such as *America's Next Top Model* and *Project Runway.* "They are seeing skinny models over and over again."

On top of that, gaunt images of celebrities such as Nicole Richie and Kate Bosworth are plastered on magazine covers, she says.

What worries Lamb most is that these images are filtering down to girls as young as nine and ten. Some really sexy clothes are available in children's size 6X, says Lamb, a psychology professor at Saint Michael's College in Colchester, Vermont. "Girls are being taught very young that thin and sexy is the way they want to be when they grow up, so they'd better start working on that now," she says.

Lamb believes it's fine for girls to want to feel sexy and pretty when they are   15
teenagers, but that shouldn't be their primary focus. "If they are spending all their time choosing the right wardrobe, trying to dance like an MTV backup girl, and applying lip gloss, it robs them of other options."

Some girls don't want to participate in sports because they're afraid they'll bulk up. Some won't try to play an instrument such as a trombone because it doesn't fit their image of what a "girly girl" should do, she says.

It begins in youth

There's no question younger girls are getting this message, says Murnen, who has studied this for fifteen years. "We have done studies of grade-school girls, and even in grade one, girls think the culture is telling them that they should model themselves after celebrities who are svelte, beautiful and sexy."

Some girls can reject that image, but it's a small percentage: 18 percent in Murnen's research. Those girls were shown to have the highest body esteem. Murnen and her colleagues reviewed twenty-one studies that looked at the media's effect on more than 6,000 girls, ages ten and older, and found those who were exposed to the most fashion magazines were more likely to suffer from poor body images.

Societies throughout the ages have had different ideals for female beauty, says Katie Ford, chief executive officer of Ford Models, whose megastar models include Christie Brinkley and Rachel Hunter. "You can look as far back as Greek statues and paintings and see that. It's part of women's fantasy nature," Ford says. "The question is: When does that become destructive?"

She doesn't buy into the idea that fashion models are creating a cult of thinness   20 in the USA. "The biggest problem in America is obesity. Both obesity and anorexia stem from numerous issues, and it would be impossible to attribute either to entertainment, be it film, TV or magazines."

Anatomy of a runway model

This year's fashion shows in New York featured a mix of figure types, some of them a little more womanly and some thin, says Ford, whose agency had about twenty models in shows of top designers, including Ralph Lauren, Bill Blass, Marc Jacobs and Donna Karan. "Our models who did very well this season were not super-skinny. However, there were some on the runway who were very thin."

Cindi Leive, editor in chief of *Glamour* magazine, says some models were teens who hadn't developed their curves yet, which is one reason they appeared so thin. "You do see the occasional model on the runway looking like she should go from the fashion show to the hospital. You hear stories of girls who come to model and are collapsing because they haven't eaten in days. Any responsible model booker will tell you they turn away girls who get too thin."

Runway models have to have a certain look, says Kelly Cutrone, owner of People's Revolution, a company that produces fashion shows around the world. Her company produced sixteen fashion shows in New York, including one for designer Marc Bouwer.

The runway models this year were no thinner than years before, she says. "I didn't see any difference in the girls at all. When they bend over, are you going to see the rib cage? Yes, they are thin naturally."

Women shouldn't be comparing themselves with these girls, she says. "These   25 girls are anomalies of nature. They are freaks of nature. They are not average. They are naturally thin and have incredibly long legs compared to the rest of their body. Their eyes are wide set apart. Their cheekbones are high."

Most runway models are fourteen to nineteen, with an average age of sixteen or seventeen, she says. Some are older. Many are 5-foot-10 or 5-foot-11. They average 120 to 124 pounds. They wear a size 2 or 4. "If we get a girl who is bigger than a 4, she is not going to fit the clothes," Cutrone says. "Clothes look better on thin people. The fabric hangs better."

Stephanie Schur, designer of her own line, Michon Schur, had her first official runway show in New York a few weeks ago. When she was casting models, she looked for women who had "a nice glow, a healthy look."

She encountered a few models who looked unhealthy. "They tend to be extremely pale, have thin hair and don't have that glow."

But many of today's runway models look pretty much alike, Schur says. "They are all pretty girls, but no one really stands out. For runway it's about highlighting the clothes. It's finding the girls that make your clothes look best."

Schur says she doesn't believe many young girls today are going to try to imitate   30
what they see on the fashion runways. She says they are more likely to look to actresses for their ideal body image.

It's not surprising that women want to be slender and beautiful, because as a society "we know more about women who look good than we know about women who do good," says Audrey Brashich, a former teen model and author of *All Made Up: A Girl's Guide to Seeing Through Celebrity Hype and Celebrating Real Beauty*.

For several years, Brashich worked for *Sassy* and *YM* magazines and read thousands of letters from girls and teens who wanted to become a famous model, actress or singer.

And no wonder, she says. "As a culture, we are on a first-name basis with women like Paris Hilton or Nicole Richie," she says. "The most celebrated, recognizable women today are famous primarily for being thin and pretty, while women who are actually changing the world remain comparatively invisible. Most of us have a harder time naming women of other accomplishments." The idolizing of models, stars and other celebrities is not going to change "until pop culture changes the women it celebrates and focuses on."

Women come in all sizes

Glamour's Leive believes the media have a powerful influence on women's body images and a responsibility to represent women of all sizes. "We do not run photos of anybody in the magazine who we believe to be at an unhealthy weight. We frequently feature women of all different sizes. We all know that you can look fabulous in clothes without being a size 2."

Ford believes the trend next year will be to move toward more womanly figures.   35
Model van der Wal agrees and says she's trying to include women of varying figure types in *Cover Shot*. "Women come in lots of different sizes and shapes, and we should encourage and celebrate that."

Cutrone says models will become heavier if that's what consumers demand. "If people decide thin is out, the fashion industry won't have thin models anymore. Have you spent time with fashion people? They are ruthless. They want money.

"And the one thing they know is people want clothes to cover their bodies," Cutrone says. "Unfortunately, most people aren't comfortable with their bodies."

All to Be Tall

JOE KITA

BEFORE READING: Should any restrictions be placed on unnecessary plastic surgery? Where would you draw the line?

Vertically challenged men are paying up to $80,000 to have their legs broken, caged, and then lengthened.

The gain: 3 inches.

The pain: extraordinary.

The cages surround Jim Conran's legs like little scaffolds. Each has eleven metal pins that screw into his broken bones. Every six hours, he must turn these pins ever so slightly in order to tighten wires that pull the bones apart and align them correctly. He has been doing this now for sixty-eight days. And all the time, the pain has been intensifying.

"It's like tuning a violin," he explains. "With each turn of the knobs, the liga-   5
ments and muscles and skin come under more tension. Each day everything gets tighter. It's incredibly painful." So much so that Conran[1] won't allow himself to sleep for longer than three hours. "I'm frightened I'll miss a dose of medication, and the pain will get ahead of me," he says. Recently, he was given morphine, and that's helped somewhat. But he's still confined to a wheelchair and can stagger only short distances around his Manhattan apartment.

Before you start pitying Conran, you should know that he was not in a horrible accident that shattered his legs, nor does he suffer from a birth defect that's finally being corrected. No, he is an otherwise healthy, forty-five-year-old, single attorney who is paying $70,000 for this voluntary procedure. In fact, he's been looking forward to this for much of his life. Despite how it seems, he is living his dream.

You see, Jim Conran is $5'5\frac{3}{4}$ tall. Or rather, he was $5'5\frac{3}{4}$ tall. In the past few months, he has "grown" 1 millimeter per day (about $\frac{1}{25}$") by turning his twenty-two pins ever so precisely. And as he's done so, new bone has been steadily forming in the gaps

---

[1] The name has been changed for privacy. —EDS.

Joe Kita is executive writer for *Men's Health* magazine and author of *Wisdom of Our Fathers* (1999) and *The Father's Guide to the Meaning of Life* (2000). This article appeared in the January/ February 2004 issue of *Men's Health*.

where the segments of tibia and fibula are being pulled apart. When he last checked —
and he checks daily — he was $5'8\frac{1}{4}''$. When he (hopefully) reaches his goal height of
5'9" and this violin tuning ends, he's confident his life will finally be in harmony.

Short. It's a five-letter word that carries four-letter connotations for men below
the national average of 5'9". Unless you're one of them, you don't know how much it
hurts to be called that.

Imagine this scenario. You've been accepted at Harvard, West Point, and Annap-
olis. You're an A student. You've won seven varsity letters, and you nearly qualified for
the Olympics. Yet to get into West Point (your first choice), you must meet a height
requirement of 5'6". You're slightly below that. So the night before your admit-
tance physical, you have your father repeatedly whack you on top of the head with
a textbook in order to raise a bump. Next day, you officially measure in at $5'6\frac{1}{16}''$. You
go on to graduate with honors, serve your country overseas, and eventually end up
as an aide to the president of the United States. And you know, your whole life long,
that you might have missed all of this — by a quarter inch.

"From a very early age, you start getting clear, institutionalized messages that   10
you're less desirable," says George Holdt, the soldier in question, who, like Conran, is
now undergoing limb lengthening. "From the violence you experience in school to
the behavior you encounter throughout your social and professional life, the discrimination is always there."

Today, height requirements in any workplace are largely a thing of the past (the
military's cutoff is now 5'). But it's an example of the frustration that is the legacy
of the diminutive man. And no, it isn't his imagination. Numerous scientific studies
have verified the advantages of height. For example, taller men . . .

. . . Are more likely to be hired. When recruiters in one study from Eastern
Michigan University were asked to choose between two equally qualified candidates
who differed in height, 72 percent chose the taller applicant.

. . . Make more money. Graduating seniors at the University of Pittsburgh who
were 6'2" or taller enjoyed starting salaries $4,000 higher than counterparts 5'5" or
under. Economists at the University of Pennsylvania even estimate that added height
is worth nearly 2 percent in additional income per inch per annum.

. . . Are chosen as leaders. Nancy Etcoff, Ph.D., a professor of psychology at Harvard Medical School, points out in her book *Survival of the Prettiest*, "the easiest way
to predict the winner in a United States election is to bet on the taller man." Of 43
American presidents, only five have been significantly below average height. What's
more, Etcoff cites a study of *Fortune* 500 CEOs that found that more than half were
taller than 6 feet, and just 3 percent were shorter than 5'7".

. . . Make better first impressions. Surveys by Henry Biller, Ph.D., a professor of   15
psychology at the University of Rhode Island and coauthor of *Stature and Stigma*, show
that compared with shorter men, guys of average and above-average height are seen
as "more mature, uninhibited, positive, secure, masculine, active, complete, successful, optimistic, dominant, capable, confident, and outgoing."

While all of this pisses off short guys, what really bothers them is how they're
viewed by women. Walter W. Windisch, Ph.D., is a psychologist in Towson, Mary-

land, who evaluates short men who are considering limb lengthening. "The average patient," he notes, "is twenty-eight years old, male, college educated, professional, of some financial means, the product of parents who expressed concern about height, and, in every case, single."

Indeed, if you read the personals section of your local newspaper or log onto any online dating service, you'll find lots of ads from women listing height preferences. Why are they so particular, especially when they're paying by the letter? Certainly a portion of it stems from the statistics cited earlier — that taller men earn more and enjoy a higher social status. Some of it also comes from Hollywood, where leading ladies routinely look up into the eyes of the tall, dark, and handsome man. It's the romantic ideal. But a good chunk is also based on an almost primitive assessment. Is he a good provider, a worthy protector, a gifted procreator? And on some anthropological level, it's as if she ultimately decides the short man is not. Less than one-half of 1 percent of women marry men who are shorter than they are, according to Etcoff.

"Someone once asked Sigmund Freud, 'What is the goal of life?' and his answer was, 'To love and to work,'" says Windisch. "That's a fairly good summary of what's bugging these guys. They're looking to love and be loved, to work and be valued. It's just that their stature, something totally beyond their control, is keeping them from it."

About 2,500 kilometers east of Moscow, at the western edge of Siberia, is the Ilizarov Scientific Center for Restorative Traumatology and Orthopedics. Located in the Russian city of Kurgan, in the shadow of the Ural Mountains, it was founded in 1971 by Professor Gavriil Abramovich Ilizarov. Decades earlier, faced with treating a large number of World War II veterans with complicated limb fractures, he began experimenting with "circular external fixators" to keep bones aligned and to speed healing. Their use as limb-lengthening tools, however, was discovered by accident. While Ilizarov was on vacation, a nurse adjusted a fixator in the wrong direction. When he returned and examined the patient's X-ray, he noticed new bone forming in the gap. This set the stage for a variety of new applications, including the correction of leg-length deformities, bow legs, anchondroplasia (dwarfism), and, lately, short stature. More than a half century later, the Ilizarov method — as it's come to be known — is still being used in a surprisingly unevolved form throughout the world.

Here's how it works: After taking a series of X-rays to map out the precise dimensions of the bones, the surgeon orders a regional anesthetic and makes two half-inch-long incisions in each leg (usually below the knee). Using a surgical chisel, he then cracks the tibias and fibulas, being careful to disrupt as little of the surrounding tissue as possible. (Note: When a doctor breaks your legs, it's called an "osteotomy.") Next, he attaches the circular aluminum frames. This requires piercing each leg with eleven arrow-sharp carbide pins and pushing them in until they bottom out against bone. The pins are of varying lengths and diameters, with the thicker ones being positioned closer to the breaks for added stability. Once the pins are in position, the surgeon slowly screws them into the hard calcium-and-collagen shell that surrounds the marrow. The rest is comparatively straightforward: Affix the adjustment wires to

20

the pins, sew the two osteotomy incisions shut, treat and bandage the pin wounds. For all that's involved, the entire operation takes just $2\frac{1}{2}$ hours. Patients typically remain in the hospital for two to three days, after which they can take a dozen or so steps.

But this is the easy part. The frames usually stay on for three to six months, during which time the bones are gradually separated. This is called the "distraction phase." All but one of the men we spoke with said that, even with heavy doses of narcotics, such as Vicodin, the resulting pain was just on the edge of bearable.

"It will reduce the toughest man to a crying little girl in a matter of weeks," says Jack Turner, a 39-year-old salesman who "grew" $2\frac{1}{2}$ inches as a result of this surgery.

"It's an act of aggression against your own body," adds Conran.

Just as difficult is the helplessness that results. Patients are dependent on wheelchairs, walkers, and the supportive arms of friends and relatives to get around. Most are bedridden except for periodic doctor visits and daily physical therapy. Work is out of the question. This is true not only during the distraction phase but also for three months or more after the frames come off and the new bone is hardening. "You need somebody to take care of you virtually all the time," says Rick Morgan, another patient. "Sometimes you can't even reach the bathroom."

Although some doctors make lofty promises, most legs won't tolerate being   25
stretched past three inches. It's not the bones that balk but rather the muscles and tendons that surround them. Overall, there's a 25 percent complication rate from this surgery, with the most frequent problem being pin-site infection. That's why patients are given a prescription for oral antibiotics, which they're told to begin taking at the first sign of redness, tenderness, or discolored drainage at the pin entry points. If an infection goes unnoticed, it will spread into the deep leg tissue and then the bone.

A less common but still serious complication is nerve damage. In one study review of 814 limb lengthenings, approximately 10 percent of patients had experienced some form of temporary nerve damage, characterized by chronic pain or impaired motor skills.

But the most catastrophic possibility doesn't present itself until the frames are removed. Even though the doctor will have taken X-rays to gauge structural integrity (the whiter the area, the stronger the bone), there's still a chance that what took months of agonizing pain and tens of thousands of dollars to build will, at the moment of truth, snap. Or the new bone will hold, only to buckle and break weeks later. Either way, doctors call this a refracture; there's a one-in-twelve chance of its happening.

If you're a short man seeking salvation through surgery, you've probably heard of the International Center for Limb Lengthening, in Baltimore. An affiliate of Sinai Hospital, the ICLL was the first facility of its kind in North America and remains the largest — half of all the limb lengthenings for height are performed here. The bulk of its business, however, deals with correcting functional deformities. "I'm very strict when it comes to doing this surgery on otherwise healthy people," says forty-seven-year-old chief surgeon Dror Paley, M.D., himself 6'. "In fact, I try to discourage it. The magnitude of what you have to go through is so large, it's not in the realm of having your nose done or your tummy tucked."

Dr. Paley generally will not operate on men over 5'6" (or women over 5'2"), and he requires that all prospective patients first undergo an intensive, ten-hour psychological exam by Windisch. Only about 10 percent go on to have the operation. "You must be careful," says Dr. Paley. "I've had some real nutcases — people who were willing to sell their houses, steal their wives' money, do unbelievable things for a few extra inches."

Depending on the facility and the specifics of the case, those inches typically 30 run between $50,000 and $80,000. When limb lengthening is done on a healthy person, medical insurance won't pay for it. However, if done to correct a leg-length discrepancy, bow legs, or any other limb deformity, it is usually covered.

Some of those people who can't raise the necessary funds or who don't pass the screening process go elsewhere — like Jack Turner, who ended up in Italy after being "dumped," as he calls it, by Dr. Paley. "The cost turned out to be one-eighth what it was in America," he explains, "and I felt I got better care."

And yet, even though it's been almost three years since Turner had his operation, he says he's still at only 80 percent of his former physical ability. "I don't think anyone can break both legs and come back 100 percent," he says. "For instance, I can't run as fast, and I have pain when the weather is damp."

The long-term effects are unknown. Although some doctors insist that dwarves who were lengthened as much as a foot decades ago show no traces of bone weakening or arthritis, other experts remain skeptical. "There's an enormous risk," says Michael Ain, M.D., a 4'3" orthopedic surgeon at Johns Hopkins Hospital in Baltimore. "Nobody really knows what's going to happen to people getting this surgery."

Neither the American Society for Aesthetic Plastic Surgery nor the American Academy of Orthopedic Surgeons (AAOS) endorses cosmetic limb lengthening. Others condemn it outright. "I'm appalled that our society has become so imbued with self-image that patients are willing to put their necks on the line like this. There are just too many risks," says William Tipton, M.D., director of medical affairs for the AAOS. "And the surgeons who are doing these operations on otherwise healthy people should remember this: *Primum non nocere*. That's Latin for 'First, no injury.'"

One of those surgeons is S. Robert Rozbruch, M.D., director of the Institute for 35 Limb Lengthening and Reconstruction at the Hospital for Special Surgery, in New York City. He counters: "Seeing the profound impact this surgery can have on someone has convinced me that, for a very select group of people, it should be brought out of the closet and done more freely."

Paul Steven Miller, for one, thinks limb lengthening is unnecessary. Miller is an attorney and the commissioner of the U.S. Equal Employment Opportunity Commission. He also happens to be a 4'5" dwarf, who has experienced height discrimination firsthand. "One law firm told me they feared their clients would think they were running a circus freak show if they hired me," he recounts. Nonetheless, Miller says cosmetic limb lengthening is "silly." "I have a hard time believing it really makes a difference in these people's lives."

With predicted advances in limb lengthening, combined with the recent FDA approval of growth-hormone therapy for short children, will Diminutive Man soon take his place next to Cro-Magnon in the Museum of Natural History? Are we entering an era of stature cleansing?

"The way we need to judge this," says David Sandberg, Ph.D., an associate professor of psychiatry at the University of Buffalo's School of Medicine, "is not by what's happening physically to these patients. Rather, what must be demonstrated is that increased height is actually translating into a better quality of life."

And only the patients themselves can assess that. Among the men we spoke with, sentiments are mixed. "It's kind of like the old P. T. Barnum thing," says Turner, "where you pay a quarter to go look at something that isn't very good. But when you come out, you have to basically say it was great. Not getting 3+ inches was disappointing, but on the other hand, I'm much more comfortable being 5'7" than 5'4+". I can only surmise that it's making subtle differences in my life. Overall, I think it's a great way for men with a height issue to increase their rank in the pecking order, but you're not going to suddenly be dating supermodels."

"Before I had this surgery, I was depressed and very self-conscious," says Mark 40 Pace, DO, an osteopath in South Florida who was 4'11". "I was afraid to walk into a roomful of children because they would make fun of me, and I could barely talk to women. I had zero confidence. Now, I'm just under 5'3", and the difference is unbelievable. I'm seeing eye-to-eye with people, and I'm actually dating."

"I've gained about $2\frac{1}{2}$ inches," says Conran, "and it feels great. In fact, I'm reluctant to let the thrill wear off. I'm almost 5'9". Now, I sure don't consider that tall, but it's not short. It's average, and that's all I ever wanted to be. I wanted to be accepted on my own merits without having my height held against me."

"I can't wait to walk down the streets of New York City, visit my old neighborhood, and see things from a slightly different perspective," adds Jose Rodriguez, who recently got his frames removed and is $2\frac{3}{4}$ inches taller. "Those extra inches make you a little more confident, a little more happy, and the day a little brighter."

If you're still skeptical, Rodriguez suggests an experiment. "Take a few books, set them on the floor, and stand on top of them," he says. "You don't think a couple of inches can make a difference, but it's amazing."

Smooth Operations

ALLISON SAMUELS

BEFORE READING: Why do you think few African Americans elected to have cosmetic surgery until quite recently?

Long before Janet Jackson revealed a little too much of her body, Tanisha Rollins was obsessed with having one just like it. After watching the singer strut in a 1993 video, Rollins embarked on a quest for washboard abs. For the next decade she stuck to a rigorous regimen. But her abs pretty much stayed the same. Then a friend skipped all the hard work and got a tummy tuck. "I was just like, 'What magazines have you been reading?!'" says Rollins, twenty-nine, an administrative assistant in Dayton, Ohio. She thought nipping and tucking was only for "rich white people and Michael Jackson," not African American women like her, making $30,000 a year.

Last year Rollins shelled out $5,000 for a tummy tuck of her own, joining the small but growing ranks of African Americans opting for cosmetic surgery. The number of blacks seeking facial or reconstructive surgery more than tripled between 1997 and 2002, reflecting both the growing affluence of African Americans and the subtle easing of some long-held cultural taboos against such procedures. Except for the Jacksons (or perhaps because of them), even black celebrities, whose looks are essential to their livelihood, have been loath to go under the knife. "I was just so worried about looking crazy or looking like Jennifer Grey, who no one recognized after she had her nose job," says one forty-year-old black actress, who decided last year to have her nose and breasts done after being inspired by singer Patti LaBelle. (Though LaBelle, sixty, talks about her nose job, the actress requested anonymity.)

In an age when plastic surgeons advertise their services on the subway, it may come as a surprise that cosmetic surgery is frowned upon in the black community. "People want to look good," says Dr. Karen Low, who is African American and a plastic surgeon in Greensboro, North Carolina, "but they also want to avoid any criticism that might come from the community, which has for years supported larger frames, wider noses, and not-so-perfect features. Changing those things is sometimes seen as an insult to our ancestors and to the culture." Rollins experienced that backlash when she told her family she was having a tummy tuck. Not only did they think it was risky and expensive, they couldn't understand why she wanted to tinker with "God's work." "It's hard telling your mother that you don't want to look like her when you're fifty," Rollins says. "I think my mother resented that and felt hurt, but I had to be honest."

Allison Samuels is a correspondent in *Newsweek*'s Los Angeles bureau, covering sports and entertainment. Earlier she worked as a researcher at Quincy Jones Entertainment and as a reporter for the *Los Angeles Times*. She is on the UCLA Black Studies Department Board of Directors. This article is from the July 5, 2004, issue of *Newsweek*.

There's a lot more at work here than simple vanity. "I think African American women have finally just decided that it's time to love ourselves," says *Essence* magazine beauty editor Miki Taylor. African Americans have become the biggest consumers of beauty products in the United States, spending at least $20 billion a year, as companies like L'Oreal, which opened its Institute for Ethnic Hair and Skin Research in 2003, are well aware. The increase in plastic surgery is in many ways an extension of that trend.

Blacks accounted for nearly 5 percent of the 8.7 million cosmetic-surgery procedures done last year. As the numbers have grown, doctors have had to adapt to their clientele. For starters, black women and white women tend to want to tune up different areas of their bodies. While the nose is Job No. 1 for whites, black women's top request is the tummy tuck. Breast enhancement? More black women want reductions. "Let's be clear that I did it for my health," says rapper-actress Queen Latifah, who went from a double-E bra cup to a D. Facelifts are not as popular as they are among white women, a testament, perhaps, to a long-held belief in the African American community: "Black don't crack."

But black skin does scar, much more easily than white skin, and that has been a big deterrent to African Americans considering elective surgery. Doctors try to be as minimally invasive as possible, using lasers and making smaller incisions, hiding scars in inconspicuous places, and using electron-beam radiation to diminish the appearance of scars. Dermatologist Marcia Glenn, who opened Odyssey Medispa in Marina del Rey, California, with an eye toward African American women like herself, encourages patients to try less-invasive procedures like Botox before choosing surgery.

Like many women who have cosmetic surgery, Patti LaBelle was hoping to cut away at her insecurities in the process. Looking at childhood pictures, "I realized I wasn't a very good-looking girl," says the singer, who was teased mercilessly about her broad nose. "I didn't like the way that made me feel." As middle age sank in, she hoped surgery would make her feel better about herself. Rather than go for a button nose, LaBelle was sensitive about keeping her features looking African American. "Nothing drastic, just enough to make me feel and look as good as I could," she says. "If, in a few years, I want to get some more work done on my chin or my neck, I will."

The Tyranny of the Normal

LESLIE FIEDLER

BEFORE READING: How do you define the term *normal* as it applies to physical appearance? Is the ability to be physically "normal" related to social class?

I am not a doctor or a nurse or a social worker, confronted in my daily rounds with the problem of physical disability; not even a lawyer, philosopher, or theologian trained to deal with its moral and legal implications. I am only a poet, novelist, critic — more at home in the world of words and metaphor than fact, which is to say, an expert, if at all, in reality once removed. Yet despite this, I have been asked on numerous occasions to address groups of health-care professionals about this subject — no doubt because I once published a book called *Freaks: Myths and Images of the Secret Self*. In that book, I was primarily interested in exploring (as the subtitle declares) the fascination of "normals" with the sort of congenital malformations traditionally displayed at Fairs and Sideshows, and especially the way in which such freaks are simultaneously understood as symbols of the absolute Other and the essential Self. Yet in the long and difficult process of putting that study together (it took almost six years of my life and led me into dark places in my own psyche I was reluctant to enter), I stumbled inadvertently into dealing also with the subject of "the care of imperiled newborns."

How difficult and dangerous a topic this was I did not realize, however, until just before my book was due to appear. I was at a party celebrating the imminent event when I mentioned offhand to one of my fellow-celebrants, a young man who turned out to be an M.D., one of the discoveries I had made in the course of my research: that in all probability more "abnormal" babies were being allowed to die (in effect, being killed) in modern hospitals than had been in the Bad Old Days when they were exposed and left to perish by their fathers. And I went on to declare that in my opinion, at least, this was not good; at which point, my interlocutor screamed at me (rather contradictorily, I thought) that what I asserted was simply not true — and that, in any case, it was perfectly all right to do so. Then he hurled his Martini glass at the wall behind me and stalked out of the room.

He did not stay long enough for me to explain that our disagreement was more than merely personal, based on more than the traditional mutual distrust of the scientist and the humanist. Both of our attitudes, I wanted to tell him, had deep primordial roots: sources far below the level of our fully conscious values and the facile

Leslie Fiedler (1917–2003) was best known as a literary critic and theorist. Until his death, he for many years was on the American literature faculty at the State University of New York at Buffalo. His interest in variations on the "normal" was spurred by research and interviews he did for his book *Freaks: Myths and Images of the Secret Self* (1978). This essay is from his book of the same title: *The Tyranny of the Normal* (1996).

rationalizations by which we customarily defend them. It is, therefore, to certain ancient myths and legends that we must turn — and here my literary expertise stands
me in good stead — to understand the roots of our deep ambivalence toward fellow
creatures who are perceived at any given moment as disturbingly deviant, outside
currently acceptable physiological norms. That ambivalence has traditionally impelled us toward two quite different responses to the "monsters" we beget. On the
one hand, we have throughout the course of history killed them — ritually at the beginning, as befits divinely sent omens of disaster, portents of doom. On the other
hand, we have sometimes worshiped them as if they were themselves divine, though
never without overtones of fear and repulsion. In either case, what prompted our
response was a sense of wonder and awe: a feeling that such "unnatural" products
of the natural process by which we continue the species are mysterious, uncanny,
finally "taboo."

Though it may not be immediately evident, the most cursory analysis reveals that
not only have that primitive wonder and awe persisted into our "scientific," secular age, but so also have the two most archaic ways of expressing it. In the first place,
we continue to kill, or at least allow to die, monstrously malformed neonates. We
euphemize the procedure, however, disguise the superstitious horror at its roots, by
calling what we do "the removal of life supports from nonviable *terata*" (*terata* being
Greek for "monster"). Moreover, thanks to advanced medical techniques, we can do
better these days than merely fail to give malformed preemies a fair chance to prove
whether or not they are really "viable." We can detect and destroy before birth,
babies likely to be born deformed; even abort them wholesale when the occasion
arises, as in the infamous case of the Thalidomide babies of the sixties. That was a
particularly unsavory episode (which we in this country were spared), since the phocomelic infants,[1] carried by mothers dosed with an antidote prescribed for morning
sickness, were in the full sense of the word "iatrogenic[2] freaks." And the doctors who
urged their wholesale abortion (aware that less than half of them would prove to be
deformed, but why take chances?) were in many cases the very ones who had actually prescribed the medication.

To be sure, those responsible for such pre-infanticide did not confess — were   5
not even aware, though any poet could have told them — that they were motivated by vestigial primitive fears of abnormality, exacerbated by their guilt at having
caused it. They sought only, they assured themselves and the rest of the world, to
spare years of suffering to the doomed children and their parents; as well as to allevi-
ate the financial burden on those parents and the larger community, which would
have to support them through what promised to be a nonproductive lifetime. We
do, however, have at this point records of the subsequent lives of some of the Thalidomide babies whose parents insisted on sparing them (a wide-ranging study was
made some years later in Canada), which turned out to have been, from their own
point of view, at least, neither notably nonproductive, nor especially miserable. None

---

[1] *Phocomelic infants*: Children born with extremely short limbs. [All notes are the editors'.]
[2] *Iatrogenic*: A condition inadvertently caused by a doctor or by medical treatment.

of them, at any rate, were willing to confess that they would have wished themselves dead.

But such disconcerting facts do not faze apologists for such drastic procedures. Nor does the even more dismaying fact that the most wholehearted, full-scale attempt at teratacide occurred in Hitler's Germany, with the collaboration, by the way, of not a few quite respectable doctors and teratologists, most notably a certain Etienne Wolff of the University of Strasbourg. Not only were dwarfs and other "useless people" sent to Nazi extermination camps and parents adjudged "likely" to beget anomalous children sterilized; but other unfortunate human beings regarded — at that time and in that society — as undesirable deviations from the Norm were also destroyed: Jews and Gypsies first of all, with Blacks, Slavs, and Mediterraneans presumably next in line. It is a development which should make us aware of just how dangerous enforced physiological normality is when the definition of its parameters falls into the hands of politicians and bureaucrats. And into what other hands can we reasonably expect it to fall in any society we know or can imagine in the foreseeable future?

Similarly, even as the responsibility for the ritual slaughter of Freaks was passing from the family to the State, the terrified adoration of Freaks was passing from the realm of worship to that of entertainment and art. To be sure, the adoration of Freaks in the Western world was never a recognized religion but at best an underground Cult. Think, for instance, of the scene in Fellini's *Satyricon*,[3] in which a Hermaphrodite is ritually displayed to a group of awestricken onlookers, who regard him as more than a curiosity, though not quite a god: after all, the two reigning myth-systems of our culture, the Hellenic and the Judaeo-Christian, both disavowed the portrayal of the divine in freakish guise, regarding as barbarous or pagan the presentation of theriomorphic, two-headed, or multilimbed divinities.

Yet there would seem always to have been a hunger in all of us, a need to behold in quasi-religious wonder our mysteriously anomalous brothers and sisters. For a long time, this need was satisfied in Courts for the privileged few, at fairs and sideshows for the general populace, by collecting and exhibiting Giants, Dwarfs, Intersexes, Joined Twins, Fat Ladies, and Living Skeletons. Consequently, even in a world that grew ever more secular and rational, we could still continue to be baffled, horrified, and moved by Freaks, as we were able to be by fewer and fewer other things once considered most sacred and terrifying. Finally though, the Sideshow began to die, even as the rulers of the world learned to be ashamed of their taste for human "curiosities." By then, however, their images had been preserved in works of art, in which their implicit meanings are made manifest.

Walk through the picture galleries of any museum in the western world and you will find side by side with the portraits of Kings and Courtesans depictions of the Freaks they once kept to amuse them, by painters as distinguished as Goya and Velasquez. Nor has the practice died out in more recent times, carried on by artists

---

[3] Fellini's *Satyricon*: Federico Fellini (1920–1993) was an Italian film director known for bizarre and colorful films, including *Satyricon* (1969).

as different as Currier and Ives (who immortalized such stars of P. T. Barnum's side-show as General Tom Thumb) and Pablo Picasso (who once spent more than a year painting over and over in ever shifting perspectives the dwarfs who first appeared in Velasquez's *Las Meninas*). Nor did other popular forms of representation abandon that intriguing subject. Not only have photographers captured on film the freaks of their time, but after a while they were portrayed in fiction as well. No sooner, in fact, had the novel been invented, than it too began to portray the monstrous and malformed as objects of pity and fear and — however secularized — wonder, always wonder. Some authors of the nineteenth century, indeed, seem so freak-haunted that remembering them, we remember first of all the monsters they created. We can scarcely think of Victor Hugo, for instance, without recalling his grotesque Hunch-back of Notre Dame, any more than we can recall Charles Dickens without thinking of his monstrous dwarf, Quilp, or our own Mark Twain without remembering "Those Incredible Twins." And the tradition has been continued by postmodernists like John Barth and Donald Barthelme and Vladimir Nabokov, who, turning their backs on almost all the other trappings of the conventional novel, still reflect its obsession with Freaks.

In the twentieth century, the images of congenital malformations are, as we might expect, chiefly preserved in the artform it invented, the cinema: on the one hand, in Art Films intended for a select audience of connoisseurs, like the surreal fantasies of Fellini and Ingmar Bergman; and on the other, in a series of popular movies from Todd Browning's thirties' masterpiece, *Freaks*, to the more recent *Elephant Man*, in its various versions. Browning's extraordinary film was by no means an immediate success; in fact, it horrified its earliest audience and first critics, who drove it from the screen and its director into early retirement. But it was revived in the sixties and has since continued to be replayed all over the world, particularly in colleges and universities. And this seems especially appropriate, since in the course of filming his fable of the Freaks' revenge on their "normal" exploiters, Browning gathered together the largest collection of showfreaks ever assembled in a single place: an immortal Super-Sideshow, memorializing a popular artform on the verge of disappearing along with certain congenital malformations it once "starred" (but that are now routinely "repaired"), like Siamese Twins.

For this reason, perhaps, we are these days particularly freak-obsessed, as attested also by the recent success of *The Elephant Man* on stage and TV and at the neigh-borhood movie theatre. The central fable of that parabolic tale, in which a Doctor, a Showman, the Press, and the Public contend for the soul of a freak, though the events on which it is based happened in Victorian times, seems especially opposite to our present ambivalent response to human abnormality, reminding us of what we now otherwise find it difficult to confess except in our REM sleep: that those wretched caricatures of our idealized body image, which at first appear to represent the absolutely "Other" (thus reassuring us who come to gape that we are "normal") are really a revelation of what in our deepest psyches we recognize as the Secret Self. After all, not only do we know that each of us is a freak to someone else; but in the depths of our unconscious (where the insecurities of childhood and adolescence never die) we seem forever freaks to ourselves.

Perhaps it is especially important for us to realize that *there are no normals*, at a moment when we are striving desperately to eliminate freaks, to normalize the world. This misguided impulse represents a third, an utterly new response to the mystery of human anomalies — made possible for the first time by modern medical technology and sophisticated laboratory techniques. Oddly enough (and to me terrifyingly), it proved possible for such experimental scientists to produce monsters long before they learned to prevent or cure them. To my mind, therefore, the whole therapeutic enterprise is haunted by the ghosts of those two-headed, three-legged, one-eyed chicks and piglets that the first scientific teratologists of the eighteenth century created and destroyed in their laboratories.

Nonetheless, I do not consider those first experimenters with genetic mutation my enemies, for all their deliberate profanation of a mystery dear to the hearts of the artists with whom I identify. Nor would I be presumptuous, heartless enough to argue — on esthetic or even moral grounds — that congenital malformations under no circumstances be "repaired," or if need be, denied birth, to spare suffering to themselves or others. I am, however, deeply ambivalent on this score for various reasons, some of which I have already made clear, and others of which I will now try to elucidate. I simply do not assume (indeed, the burden of evidence indicates the contrary) that being born a freak is per se an unendurable fate. As I learned reading scores of biographies of such creatures in the course of writing my book about them, the most grotesque among them have managed to live lives neither notably worse nor better than that of most humans. They have managed to support themselves at work which they enjoyed (including displaying themselves to the public); they have loved and been loved, married and begot children — sometimes in their own images, sometimes not.

More often than not, they have survived and coped; sometimes, indeed, with special pride and satisfaction because of their presumed "handicaps," which not a few of them have resisted attempts to "cure." Dwarfs in particular have joined together to fight for their "rights," one of which they consider to be *not* having their size brought up by chemotherapy and endocrine injections to a height we others call "normal," but that they refer to, less honorifically, as "average." And I must say I sympathize with their stand, insofar as the war against "abnormality" implies a dangerous kind of politics, which beginning with a fear of difference, eventuates in a tyranny of the Normal. That tyranny, moreover, is sustained by creating in those outside the Norm shame and self-hatred — particularly if they happen to suffer from those "deformities" (which are still the vast majority) that we cannot prevent or cure.

Reflecting on these matters, I cannot help remembering not only the plight of the Jews and Blacks under Hitler but the situation of the same ethnic groups — more pathetic-comic than tragic, but deplorable all the same — here in supposedly non-totalitarian America merely a generation or two ago. At that point, many Blacks went scurrying off to their corner pharmacy in quest of skin bleaches and hair straighteners; and Jewish women with proud semitic beaks turned to cosmetic surgeons for nose jobs. To be sure, as the example of Barbra Streisand makes clear, we have begun to deliver ourselves from the tyranny of such ethnocentric Norms in the last decades of the twentieth century; so that looking Niggerish or Kike-ish no longer seems as freakish as it once did, and the children of "lesser breeds" no longer eat their hearts out because they do not look like Dick and Jane, the WASP-lets portrayed in their Primers.

But the Cult of Slimness, that aberration of Anglo-Saxon taste (no African or Slav or Mediterranean ever believed in his homeland that "no one can be too rich or too thin") still prevails. And joined with the Cult of Eternal Youth, it has driven a population growing ever older and fatter to absurd excesses of jogging, dieting, and popping amphetamines — or removing with the aid of plastic surgery those stigmata of time and experience once considered worthy of reverence. Nor do things stop there; since the skills of the surgeon are now capable of recreating our bodies in whatever shape whim and fashion may decree as esthetically or sexually desir-able: large breasts and buttocks at one moment, meagre ones at another. But why *not*, after all? If in the not-so-distant future, the grosser physiological abnormalities that have for so long haunted us disappear forever — prevented, repaired, aborted, or permitted to die at birth — those of us allowed to survive by the official enforc-ers of the Norm will be free to become ever more homogeneously, monotonously beautiful; which is to say, supernormal, however that ideal may be defined. And who except some nostalgic poet, in love with difference for its own sake, would yearn for a world where ugliness is still possible? Is it not better to envision and work for one where all humans are at last *really* equal — physiologically as well as socially and politically?

But, alas (and this is what finally gives me pause), it is impossible for all of us to achieve this dubious democratic goal — certainly not in the context of our soci-ety as it is now and promises to remain in the foreseeable future: a place in which supernormality is to be had not for the asking but only for the buying (cosmetic surgery, after all, is not included in Medicare). What seems probable, therefore, as a score of science-fiction novels have already prophesied, is that we are approaching with alarming speed a future in which the rich and privileged will have as one more, ultimate privilege the hope of a surgically, chemically, hormonally induced and pre-served normality — with the promise of immortality by organ transplant just over the horizon. And the poor (who, we are assured on good authority, we always have with us) will be our sole remaining Freaks.

Thinking and Writing about Body Image

QUESTIONS FOR DISCUSSION AND WRITING

1. Charles Cooley once wrote: "Our sense of ourselves . . . is formed by our imagina-tion of the way we appear in the eyes of others. Other people are a looking glass in which we see not merely our own reflection but a judgment about the value of

that reflection." Use your own experience, your research, or a combination of both to agree or disagree.

2. Jot down some of the conclusions about cosmetic surgery that you have reached after having read some or all of the selections in this unit. Use those conclusions to write one example of a claim of fact, one of a claim of value, and one of a claim of policy about cosmetic surgery. Develop one of those claims as the thesis for an essay, using one or more of the readings to support it.

3. Do the research necessary to find out what percentage of those having cosmetic surgery are men, what percentage are women, and what types of surgery are most frequent for each gender. Present the results of your research in an essay based on a claim of fact.

4. Write an essay in which you explain to what extent Croll's observations about body image and adolescents are consistent with your own observations.

5. Explain in an essay to what extent you believe Americans' views of what is attractive are shaped by television, movies, and advertisements.

6. Which of the essays in this unit do you believe makes most effective use of support? Explain.

7. Write an essay in which you explain what point Fiedler is making when he uses the term "the tyranny of the normal" and discuss whether you agree with him or not.

8. Write an essay explaining under what circumstances there need to be legal restrictions on body modification.

9. How would you answer the question that Hellmich asks in her title? Are there other factors at work that warp girls' body image, like the actresses to whom Hellmich refers?

10. Argue for or against the claim that thin models warp girls' body image.

11. Write an essay explaining why you think many girls today have negative body image.

12. Write an essay in which you argue whether or not you think boys are as concerned with body image as girls are.

CHAPTER 20

In the World Of Medicine, Who Decides What Is Ethical?

With virtually every advance in medical science come new questions about medical ethics. "First, do no harm" sounds simple, but it doesn't help a doctor decide which of two patients should receive a donor heart. A donor registry exists, but amid suspicions that donor organs might go to the highest bidder or that those with no insurance might never even make it to the list. In desperation, some potential recipients have even started advertising for directed donations of organs.

It has become necessary to look closely at the definition of life itself — and of death. When are potential donors legally dead so that their organs can be harvested? How long should donors be kept alive artificially waiting for the harvesting? Well-publicized cases have focused national attention on the issue of who has the right to decide to terminate life support.

The ability to freeze and store embryos has been a godsend to many families. Now a decision must be made as to what should be done with leftover frozen embryos, and heated debate continues over what use should be made of embryonic stem cells. Is it ethical to use them at all, even if they show promise in treating conditions such as Parkinson's, diabetes, and spinal cord injuries? Should research into their use be postponed in light of promising new research into the possibility of growing stem cells from other body cells?

Doctors are human beings too, with their own value systems. Does a doctor have the right to refuse to treat a patient because to do so would violate that doctor's own moral code? What if the doctor neglects to inform the patient of all viable options for treatment because some violate the doctor's personal code of ethics?

Complex as the science is that makes possible brave new worlds of medicine, equally complex are the accompanying moral issues.

Need an Organ? It Helps to Be Rich

JOY VICTORY

BEFORE READING: When there is a waiting list for donor organs, how is the decision made as to who will get them? Do you think that our country's system for deciding which patients get donor organs is fair? Explain why or why not.

B rian Shane Regions is dying.
Medications sustain the thirty-four-year-old for now, but a heart transplant is his only hope of a cure for his congestive heart failure — as is the case for the thousands of others who suffer from irreversible heart damage. But Regions lacks health insurance and receives inconsistent care for his condition. He said some of his doctors have casually suggested that he should be on the waiting list for a new heart, but not one has helped him pursue it.

"There's really nothing I can do," said Regions, a freelance photographer in Campti, Louisiana. "I don't have the insurance to do it right now. They are treating the symptoms. I'm managing, but I know I'm slowly getting worse and it's not going to get any better."

It's the harsh reality of the organ transplant field: Patients who are uninsured or unable to pay are sometimes denied lifesaving treatment because hospitals can't afford to foot the bill for the surgery or the extensive recovery. And while inadequate health care is a big problem in general for uninsured Americans, organ transplants raise unique ethical issues, said the authors of a report in the *Journal of the American College of Cardiology*. While the uninsured or poor can't easily receive organs, they do donate them: As many as 25 percent of organs come from the uninsured, according to estimates by the authors of "Health Insurance and Cardiac Transplantation: A Call for Reform." Or, in other words, as the report states: "Individuals donate their hearts, although they themselves would not have been eligible to receive a transplant had they needed one." But whether the organ transplant system is fair or not depends on whom you ask.

Most bioethicists say the organ transplant system should be "equal opportunity" — that anyone who is willing to donate should be eligible for a transplant themselves, regardless of the ability to pay. But some say the health care system is full of similar examples in which either the poor or the rich (but mostly the rich) are at an advantage and transplants are just a small part of a bigger problem.

5

Joy Victory has written about health issues for newspapers and for ABC News. This article appeared on ABC News online on January 20, 2006.

A woman waits for surgery to transplant her kidney to her husband.

The "Wallet Biopsy"

To find matching donor organs, transplant centers rely on the United Network for Organ Sharing, or UNOS, a nonprofit organization that maintains a nationwide patient waiting list. Organs are then typically dispensed to the sickest patients or to those who have been waiting a long time. UNOS maintains the list, but it's left up to 256 organ transplant centers across the United States to decide who *gets* on the list. Each center sets its own criteria, which often include the patient's ability to pay. Laura Siminoff, a bioethicist, called this the "wallet biopsy," during which a person's financial standing comes under scrutiny.

"Every transplant center can do what they want," said Siminoff, who directs the bioethics program at Case Western University and is a board member of the Minority Organ Tissue and Transplant Education Program in Cleveland. "Centers have different practices. And if you're a well-to-do patient, you can shop around to centers. But if you don't have any money, you will go wherever is closest, and their policies are what you are stuck with."

Trying to Help the Poor

Thankfully, not all transplant centers turn away uninsured patients, pointed out Mary Simmerling, a bioethics fellow at the MacLean Center for Clinical Medical Ethics at the University of Chicago. She also runs a regional ethics consortium on organ transplants. "Some [centers] have the luxury of really helping their transplant candidates to pay for the medications," she said, referring to the anti-rejection drugs that must be taken post-transplant and can sometimes cost more than the surgery itself.

The staff at the University of Michigan Transplant Center tries to help uninsured patients find a way to pay, said Dr. Jeffrey Punch, director of the transplant center. For some patients, financial assistance through Medicare or Medicaid can be arranged, although there are income limits. "At our transplant center we have evaluated thousands of patients for liver transplantation, and we virtually never do a transplant without a plan for how it will be paid for," he said. "But we have only very rarely turned down a patient because of lack of insurance. In virtually all circumstances, the patient can arrange coverage of some sort." However, because there is little governance over the transplant centers, it is not known how many people receive care like that at UMich or are turned away because of a lack of money, said Dr. Mark Drazner, a cardiologist at the University of Texas Southwestern Medical Center.

A Lack of Data

To get a clearer picture of the problem, Drazner and the other authors of "Health   10 Insurance and Cardiac Transplantation" set out to compile data on organ transplant recipients and donors to see how many were uninsured. But they didn't find any nationwide data, so they relied primarily upon a database of 420 families of organ donors, known as the National Study of Family Consent to Organ Donation. Siminoff conducted it. In her survey of hundreds of Pennsylvania and Ohio families, 23 percent of organ donors were uninsured. She believes that a national survey would produce a number similar to that. But her database is not enough to make that assertion, Punch said. "The article . . . merely assumes that everyone without health insurance cannot get a transplant. They quote four references to this point, none of which offer empirical evidence to their assertion," Punch said of the paper. Also, he said it is not fair to compare the ability to donate organs with the ability to receive organs. "Donating organs has no risk, damages no party, and causes no problem with any large-scale religious communities. I agree entirely that the uninsured people in our country are a huge public problem, but I disagree that this can be used to indict the practice of organ donation as unfair."

Siminoff feels a bit differently. "From a very clinical point of view, you can ask what is the difference if the donor is dead? Except as a society we don't view dead people as garbage. People have very definite feelings about how dead bodies should be treated and what they represent," she said. "Families [of donors] can be harmed if they felt the person was desecrated or not treated with respect. It could have irreparable damage."

Looking at the Decisions

For patients like Regions, these are nominal concerns. His failing heart, and lack of health care, takes precedent. At the moment, he's not sure what he's going to do. He visits online support groups and works as a photographer when he has the energy. But after researching what it would take to have a transplant, he said that any measure taken to help the uninsured should include the enormous cost of immunosuppressant medications that people have to take for the rest of their lives after a transplant. "The aftermath of the heart transplant, or any transplant, would cost more than the actual surgery itself," Regions said, adding that people who have reasonably good health insurance are still burdened by the cost of medication. Plus, Siminoff noted, even having private health insurance doesn't make this issue go away. "Health insurance comes and goes in this country, and some of the people [who receive transplants] are never able to go back to work full time and [they] lose health insurance," Siminoff said. This sometimes forces people to stop taking the medication, putting them in the same poor health they were in before the transplant, Simmerling, the bioethicist, said.

"We really tend to think of transplants [and the organ transplant list] as different — it's held up as this oasis of fairness and neutrality," Simmerling said. "But when you really start to look at how decisions are made it has a lot to do with socioeconomic status."

No Quick Solutions

While this is probably correct, some said the organ transplant system is no less fair than other areas of medicine or life in general. Put another way: Being poor is not easy.

"The primary source of inequity here is the failure to provide universal insur-   15 ance coverage for all citizens or residents," said Norman Daniels, a professor of population ethics at the Harvard School of Public Health. "Remember, we are the only industrialized country to fail to do that."

Family law professor Timothy Jost agreed. "It is unethical not to provide heart transplants for the poor, but only because it is unethical to deny the poor health care generally," said Jost, at the Washington and Lee University School of Law in Lexington, Virginia.

Drazner and the other study authors do not disagree with this notion. But they hope that the report at least spurs interest in the creation of a national registry that tracks that and other important information about donors and recipients. "It's good to have all the players involved to address the situation and be aware of the financial aspects that need to be considered," he said.

Tom Mayo, a Southern Methodist University bioethicist who helped write the report, said the enormous cost of organ transplants means they can't be excluded from any debate on national health care. At the very least, he hopes the report will raise that concern among policymakers. "How much of a health care budget should go into a transplant budget?" he said. "This opens the door to a much broader debate. This is an area where line drawing has been done and will continue for the indefinite future."

Ethics of Organ Donation

LAWRENCE A. HOWARDS

BEFORE READING: Why is the decision to harvest organs from one patient to try to save the life of another difficult both ethically and medically?

Many of us have signed the backs of our driver's license allowing the harvesting and donation of body organs such as corneas, kidneys, liver, lungs, and heart if we are hopelessly brain injured and on life support.[1] What may then happen to us could range from the gift of life to murder. The problem is deciding the difference between dead and nearly dead.

The difference is important and can be illustrated by a character in the movie *The Princess Bride*. In this movie, a prince has most, but not all life extracted from him. "Is he dead?" a character asks. "No, only nearly dead. We can revive him," is the answer. That perfectly illustrates the problem in organ donation.

It is very hard to define death in a person with a heartbeat and some intact vital functions, supported by a ventilator and intravenous drugs. Defining death was easier when the definition of death was, simply, no heartbeat and no effort to breathe. Three actual case histories not only should make physicians uncomfortable, but also describe how hard it is to make a decision.

- A thirty-two-year-old man is totally unresponsive to pain and makes no effort to breathe on his own following a traffic accident. He is brought to the operating room for removal of his liver and kidneys. The anesthesiologist in charge of keeping his heart beating to preserve the organs before their removal gives an antidote to muscle relaxants that were given when the accident victim was first hospitalized. The dead man begins to breathe and grimaces in pain as the surgeons cut. "Stop!" calls out the anesthesiologist. "This man is still alive!" "Too late," answers a member of the surgical team. "We have already removed his liver."

- An eighteen-year-old man with a massive brain injury is being wheeled to the operating room. On the way, he seems to make some twitching movements. The anesthesiologist points this out to the harvesting team. They tell the anesthesiologist that there is no brain wave activity, and the man will not breathe on his own. The donation continues.

---

[1]Gail Van Norman, M.D. University of Washington, Seattle, WA. Presented at the Midwest Anesthesia Conference, May 1, 1999.

Dr. Lawrence A. Howards was comedical director of the Sinai Samaritan Pain Clinic at Sinai Samaritan Hospital in Milwaukee, Wisconsin, when he wrote this article for the *Milwaukee Journal Sentinel Online*, June 20, 1999.

- A young woman has lapsed into a coma during childbirth from a rare complication. She has been on a ventilator for three days and is totally unresponsive. On the way to the operating room, the anesthesiologist notes that the ventilator has been set to give too much inflation. After correcting this problem, the patient begins to breathe on her own. The transplant team wants to go ahead because everything is set up for an organ transplant. The anesthesiologist refuses to assist in the operation. The surgeons tell him that they will continue without his help. He calls an administrator to stop the procedure. Several days later, the woman is able to sit up in bed and can talk to her husband.

I am certain you find these case histories just as disturbing as I have found them. In an examination of these three patients, the first and third patients were only nearly dead. The second patient was really dead by definition.[2] All fifty states use the same definition of brain death, an isoelectric (flat) EEG, no ventilatory effort, and an absence of reflexes originating in the brain. Reflexes originating in the spinal cord, as in the second example, are not considered a sign of life. In Europe, an isoelectric EEG is considered brain death.

We are bound to protect individuals until the moment of death in order to   5
prevent what could be interpreted as murder. However, there are some special circumstances when live humans may be used for donor organs as in the case of anencephalic newborns.[3] The law considers babies born without brains *non persons*. This allows the legal use of their organs.

The problem with the use of *non persons* is just who fits into this definition. In Nazi Germany, the term *unter menchen*, which basically means the same thing, was applied eventually to cripples, the mentally retarded, the insane, and later, Gypsies and Jews in a slippery slope of unethical behavior. This is not the only slippery slope that we must avoid. As two of the three case histories illustrate, an eagerness to harvest donor organs may result in poorly diagnosed death accidentally, or possibly, deliberately.

In Medieval times, noblemen were buried with a bell they could ring if revived in their caskets. Being buried alive in that medically unenlightened era was a distinct possibility. Today, we use medical tests, some of which are dependent on the perfect functioning of complicated electronic devices. Clearly, this is wrong. Most, but not all, doctors use more than just an EEG showing no brain wave activity because the brain may recover after showing no activity, and a loose connection or malfunctioning transistor can give a false result.

It is now recommended that several things are needed before declaring a person with a beating heart a corpse.

---

[2]*Ad Hoc* Committee of Harvard Medical School, definition of brain death and irreversible coma. JAMA 1968: Vol. 205, pp. 85–90.
[3]Council on Ethical and Judicial Affairs, AMA. JAMA 1995: Vol. 273: pp. 1614–1618.

- No brain wave activity.

- Fully reversed sedation, anesthetics, and muscle relaxants that may mimic a death-like condition by causing reduced brain wave activity and lack of responsiveness or coma.

- No attempt to breathe in the presence of normal blood gases during ventilator support.

- No cranial reflexes.

- Brain stem evoked potentials are absent. (This test is not always available.)

- No blood flow to the brain. (This test is not always available.)

You will notice I did not include coma as criteria, although a person with the above conditions certainly would be in a coma.

The problem with declaring a person dead because [he or she appears] to be in a   10
hopeless coma is a controversial problem, especially in a young person. Miraculous recoveries from coma are well recorded. Further, recent evidence indicates that the victim of coma may be aware of what is going on.

A coma victim may not fit into the definition of death as I have described it. I don't believe these people should be considered organ donors until their coma condition has been diagnosed as hopeless. This is particularly hard to do on a person who is breathing without life support and is a task that should not be undertaken lightly.

Living wills can help caregivers make a decision between life and death. Anyone making the decision between life and death must follow strict guidelines to avoid murder. Organ harvesting teams must practice with scrupulous ethics and avoid "for profit" motivation.

Equally, people should not act unethically and arrange to be paid for their organs while they are alive. The definition of a *non person* must be very clear and not subject to interpretation. Anesthesiologists must always act as a patient advocate before participating in organ harvesting.

Cancer and the Constitution — Choice at Life's End

GEORGE J. ANNAS

BEFORE READING: Do you believe that patients who have exhausted all approved treatments for cancer should be allowed to take experimental drugs? What are the pros and cons?

J. M. Coetzee's violent, anti-apartheid *Age of Iron*, a novel the *Wall Street Journal* termed "a fierce pageant of modern South Africa," is written as a letter by a retired classics professor, Mrs. Curren, to her daughter, who lives in the United States. Mrs. Curren is dying of cancer, and her daughter advises her to come to the United States for treatment. She replies, "I can't afford to die in America. . . . No one can, except Americans."[1] Dying of cancer has been considered a "hard death" for at least a century, unproven and even quack remedies have been common, and price has been a secondary consideration. Efforts sponsored by the federal government to find cures for cancer date from the establishment of the National Cancer Institute (NCI) in 1937. Cancer research was intensified after President Richard Nixon's declaration of a "war on cancer" and passage of the National Cancer Act of 1971.[2] Most recently, calls for more cancer research have followed the announcement by Elizabeth Edwards, wife of presidential candidate John Edwards, that her cancer is no longer considered curable.

Frustration with the methods and slow progress of mainstream medical research has helped fuel a resistance movement that distrusts both conventional medicine and government and that has called for the recognition of a right for terminally ill patients with cancer to have access to any drugs they want to take. Prominent examples include the popularity of Krebiozen in the 1950s and of laetrile in the 1970s. As an NCI spokesperson put it more than twenty years ago, when thousands of people were calling the NCI hotline pleading for access to interleukin-2, "What the callers are saying is, 'Our mother, our brother, our sister is dying at this very moment. We have nothing to lose.'"[2] Today, families search the Internet for clinical trials, and even untested chemicals such as dichloroacetate, that seem to offer them some hope. In addition, basing advocacy on their personal experiences with cancer, many families have focused their frustrations on the Food and Drug Administration (FDA), which they see as a government agency denying them access to treatments they need.

George J. Annas is the William Fairfield Warren Distinguished Professor and chair of the Department of Health Law, Bioethics, and Human Rights at the Boston University School of Public Health as well as a professor in the university's schools of medicine and law. He is cofounder of Global Lawyers and Physicians, a transnational professional association that promotes human rights and health, and is the author of many books on health law and bioethics. The article was published in the *New England Journal of Medicine* on July 26, 2007.

In May 2006 these families won an apparent major victory when the Court of Appeals for the District of Columbia, in the case of *Abigail Alliance v. Von Eschenbach* (hereafter referred to as *Abigail Alliance*),[3] agreed with their argument that patients with cancer have a constitutional right of access to investigational cancer drugs. In reaction, the FDA began the process of rewriting its own regulations to make it easier for terminally ill patients not enrolled in clinical trials to have access to investigational drugs.[4] In November 2006, the full bench of the Court of Appeals vacated the May 2006 opinion, and the case was reheard in March 2007.[5] The decision of the full bench, expected by the fall, will hinge on the answer to a central question: Do terminally ill adult patients with cancer for whom there are no effective treatments have a constitutional right of access to investigational drugs their physicians think might be beneficial?

The Constitutional Controversy

The Abigail Alliance for Better Access to Developmental Drugs (hereafter called the Abigail Alliance) sued the FDA to prevent it from enforcing its policy of prohibiting the sale of drugs that had not been proved safe and effective to competent adult patients who are terminally ill and have no alternative treatment options. The Abigail Alliance is named after Abigail Burroughs, whose squamous-cell carcinoma of the head and neck was diagnosed when she was only nineteen years old. Two years later, in 2001, she died. Before her death she had tried unsuccessfully to obtain investigational drugs on a compassionate use basis from ImClone and AstraZeneca and was accepted for a clinical trial only shortly before her death. Her father founded the Abigail Alliance in her memory.[6]

The district court dismissed the Abigail Alliance lawsuit. The appeals court, in a two-to-one opinion written by Judge Judith Rogers, who was joined by Judge Douglas Ginsburg, reversed the decision. It concluded that competent, terminally ill adult patients have a constitutional "right to access to potentially life-saving post-Phase I investigational new drugs, upon a doctor's advice, even where that medicine carries risks for the patient," and remanded the case to the district court to determine whether the FDA's current policy violated that right.[3]

The Right to Life

The appeals court found that the relevant constitutional right was determined by the due-process clause of the Fifth Amendment: "no person shall be . . . deprived of life, liberty, or property without due process of law." In the court's words, the narrow question presented by *Abigail Alliance* is whether the due-process clause "protects the right of terminally ill patients to make an informed decision that may prolong

EDS. Note: On August 7, 2007, the District of Columbia Circuit Court of Appeals voted 8–2 against the Abigail Alliance, and on January 14, 2008, the Supreme Court declined to take up the issue.

life, specifically by use of potentially life-saving new drugs that the FDA has yet to approve for commercial marketing but that the FDA has determined, after Phase I clinical human trials, are safe enough for further testing on a substantial number of human beings."[3]

The court answered yes, finding that this right has deep legal roots in the right to self-defense, and that "Barring a terminally ill patient from the use of a potentially life-saving treatment impinges on this right of self-preservation."[3] In a footnote, the court restated this proposition: "The fundamental right to take action, even risky action, free from government interference, in order to save one's own life undergirds the court's decision."[3] The court relied primarily on the *Cruzan* case,[7] in which the Supreme Court recognized the right of a competent adult to refuse life-sustaining treatment, including a feeding tube:

> The logical corollary is that an individual must also be free to decide for herself whether to assume any known or unknown risks of taking a medication that might prolong her life. Like the right claimed in *Cruzan*, the right claimed by the [Abigail] Alliance to be free of FDA imposition does not involve treatment by the government or a government subsidy. Rather, much as the guardians of the comatose [sic] patient in *Cruzan* did, the Alliance seeks to have the government step aside by changing its policy so the individual right of self-determination is not violated.[3]

The appeals court concluded that the Supreme Court's 1979 unanimous decision on laetrile,[8] in which the Court concluded that Congress had made no exceptions in the FDA law for terminally ill cancer patients, was not relevant because laetrile had never been studied in a phase 1 trial and because the Court did not address the question of whether terminally ill cancer patients have a constitutional right to take whatever drugs their physicians prescribe.

The Dissent

Judge Thomas Griffith, the dissenting judge, argued that the suggested constitutional right simply does not exist. He noted, for example, that the self-defense cases relied on are examples of "abstract concepts of personal autonomy," and cannot be used to craft new rights. As to the nation's history and traditions, he concluded that the FDA's drug-regulatory efforts have been reasonable responses "to new risks as they are presented."[3] Accepting his argument leaves the majority resting squarely on *Cruzan* and the laetrile case. As to *Cruzan*, the dissent argued that "A tradition of protecting individual *freedom* from life-saving, but forced, medical treatment does not evidence a constitutional tradition of providing affirmative *access* to a potentially harmful, even fatal, commercial good."[3] As to the laetrile case, the judge noted simply that the Court had agreed with the FDA that, "For the terminally ill, as for anyone else, a drug is unsafe if its potential for inflicting death or physical injury is not offset by the possibility of therapeutic benefit."[3,8]

Finally, the dissenting judge argued that if the new constitutional right were 10 accepted, it was too vague to be applied only to terminally ill patients seeking drugs that had been tested in phase 1 trials. Specifically, the judge asked, must the right also apply to patients with "serious medical conditions," to patients who "cannot afford potentially life-saving treatment," or to patients whose physicians believe "marijuana for medicinal purposes . . . is potentially life saving?"[3] In other words, there is no principled reason to restrict the constitutional right the majority created to either terminally ill patients or to post–phase 1 drugs.

Discussion

The facts as illustrated by stories of patients dying of cancer while trying unsuccessfully to enroll in clinical trials are compelling, and our current system of ad hoc exceptions is deeply flawed. The central constitutional issue, however, rests primarily on determining whether this case is or is not like the right-to-refuse-treatment case of Nancy Cruzan, a woman in a permanent vegetative state whose family wanted tube feeding discontinued because they believed that discontinuation was what she would have wanted. I do not think *Abigail Alliance* is like *Cruzan*. Rather, it is substantially identical to cases involving physician-assisted suicide, in which a terminally ill patient claims a constitutional right of access to physician-prescribed drugs to commit suicide.

The Supreme Court has decided, unanimously, that no right to physician-prescribed drugs for suicide exists.[9,10] There is no historical tradition of support for this right. And although the right seems to be narrowly defined, it is unclear to whom it should apply — why only to terminally ill patients? Don't patients in chronic pain have even a stronger interest in suicide? Why is the physician necessary, and why are physician-prescribed drugs the only acceptable method of suicide? None of these questions can be answered by examining the Constitution.[11]

Similarly, in *Abigail Alliance*, the new constitutional right proposed has no tradition in the United States, and it cannot be narrowly applied. For example, why should a constitutional right apply only to people who have a particular medical status? And why should a physician be involved at all? If patients have a right to autonomy, why isn't the requirement of a government-licensed physician's recommendation at least as burdensome as the requirement of the FDA's approval of the investigational drug? And why would the Constitution apply only to investigational drugs for which phase 1 trials have been completed? Why not include access to investigational medical devices, like the artificial heart, or even to Schedule I controlled substances, like marijuana or lysergic acid diethylamide (LSD)? If it is a constitutional right, these should be available too, at least unless the state can demonstrate a "compelling interest" in regulating them.

My prediction is that after rehearing this case en banc, the full Circuit Court will reject the position of the Abigail Alliance for the same reasons that the Supreme Court rejected the "right" of terminally ill patients to have access to physician-prescribed drugs they could use to end their lives.[9,10,11] To decide otherwise would entirely undermine the legitimacy of the FDA. Patients in the United States have always had a right to refuse any medical treatment, but we have never had a right to demand mistreatment, inappropriate treatment, or even investigational or experimental interventions. This will not, however, be the end of the matter. After the physician-assisted–suicide cases, the fight appropriately shifted to the states, although so far only one, Oregon, has provided its physicians with immunity for prescribing life-ending drugs to their competent, terminally ill patients.[12] In the *Abigail Alliance* case, the debate will continue in the forum in which it began — the FDA — and in Congress.

Congress

Congressional action also had its birth with the story of one patient with cancer and   15 was also heavily influenced by another individual patient involved in a controversy over removal of a feeding tube. "Terri's Law" was enacted in Florida in 2003 to try to prevent the removal of a feeding tube from Terri Schiavo; the case was substantially similar to *Cruzan*. Terri's case gained national attention two years later.[13] In the midst of it, in March 2005, the *Wall Street Journal* asserted, in an editorial titled "How About a 'Kianna's Law'?," "If Terri Schiavo deserves emergency federal intervention to save her life, people like Kianna Karnes deserve it even more."[14] At the time, Kianna Karnes was a forty-four-year-old mother of four who was dying of kidney cancer. Her only hope of survival, according to the editorial, was to gain access to one of two experimental drugs in clinical trials, but neither of the two companies running the trials (Bayer and Pfizer) would make the drugs available to her on a compassionate-use basis. This was because, according to the *Wall Street Journal*, the FDA "makes it all but impossible" for the manufacturers "to provide [drugs] to terminal patients on a 'compassionate use' basis."[14]

Almost immediately after the editorial was published, both drug manufacturers contacted Kianna's physicians to discuss releasing the drugs to her. But within two days after publication, she was dead. The *Wall Street Journal* editorialized, "Isn't it a national scandal that cancer sufferers should have to be written about in the *Wall Street Journal* to be offered legal access to emerging therapies once they've run out of other options?"[15] It noted that Mrs. Karnes' father, John Rowe — himself a survivor of leukemia — was working with the Abigail Alliance on a "Kianna's Law." That law, formally titled the "Access, Compassion, Care, and Ethics for Seriously Ill Patients Act" or the "ACCESS Act," was introduced in November 2005 and is an attempt to make it much easier for seriously ill patients to gain access to experimental drugs.[16,17]

The act begins with a series of congressional findings, including that "Seriously ill patients have a right to access available investigational drugs, biological products, and devices." The act permits the sponsor to apply for approval to make an investigational drug, biologic product, or device available on the basis of data from a completed phase 1 trial, "preliminary evidence that the product may be effective against a serious or life-threatening condition or disease," and an assurance that the clinical trial will continue.[17] The patient, who must have exhausted all approved treatments, must provide written informed consent and must also sign "a written waiver of the right to sue the manufacturer or sponsor of the drug, biological product, or device, or the physicians who prescribed the product or the institution where it was administered, for an adverse event caused by the product, which shall be binding in every State and Federal court."[17]

Although Congress is the proper forum to address this issue, this initial attempt has some of the same problems as the *Abigail Alliance* decision: the patients to whom it applies are ambiguously classified, and clinical research seems to be equated with clinical care. Also troubling is that the patients (and would-be subjects) are asked to assume all of the risks of the uncontrolled experiments, and current rules of research — which protect subjects by prohibiting mandatory waivers of rights — are jettisoned, with the requirement of such waivers becoming the price of obtaining the investigational agent from an otherwise reluctant drug company.

FDA Proposal

In direct response to *Abigail Alliance*, the FDA proposed amending its rules to encourage more drug companies to offer their investigational drugs through compassionate-use programs.[4] These programs first came into prominence during the early days of infection with the human immunodeficiency virus (HIV) and AIDS, when there were no effective treatments and AIDS activists insisted that they have early access to investigational drugs because, in the words of their inaccurate slogan, "A Research Trial Is Treatment Too."[18] Because the FDA could not stand the political pressure generated by the activists, the compassionate-use program was developed as a kind of political safety valve to provide enough exceptions to save their basic research rules. In early December 2006, the FDA continued this political-safety-valve approach by issuing new proposed regulations with a title that could have been taken directly from the AIDS Coalition to Unleash Power (ACT-UP): "Expanded Access to Investigational Drugs for Treatment Use."[19]

The FDA's expanded-access proposal applies to "seriously ill patients when there is no comparable or satisfactory alternative therapy to diagnose, monitor, or treat the patient's disease or condition."[4] Manufacturers are required to file an "expanded access submission," and the product must be administered or dispensed by a licensed physician who will be considered an "investigator," with all the reporting requirements that role entails.[3]

Whether or not the proposal is adopted, it will do little to increase access, since the major bottleneck in the compassionate-use program has never been the FDA. The manufacturers have no incentives to make their investigational products available outside clinical trials. This is because direct access to investigational drugs by individuals may make it more difficult to recruit research subjects, and thus to conduct the clinical trials necessary for drug approval, and could also subject the drug manufacturer to liability for serious adverse reactions. Even without a lawsuit, a serious reaction to a drug outside a trial could adversely affect the trial itself.[4,16,20] The drug companies are right to worry that the approaches of the judiciary, Congress, and the FDA will probably make clinical trials more difficult to conduct, because few seriously ill patients who have exhausted conventional treatments would rather be randomly assigned to an investigational drug than have a guarantee that they will receive the investigational drug their physician recommends for them. This could result in significant delays in the approval and overall availability of drugs that demonstrate effectiveness — a result no one favors. Even if patients with cancer are willing buyers, drug manufacturers are not willing sellers.

Physicians and Patients

The cover story for all the proposed changes is patients' choice. But without scientific evidence of the risks and benefits of a drug, choice cannot be informed, and for seriously ill patients, fear of death will predictably overcome fear of unknown risks. This is understandable. As psychiatrist Jay Katz, the leading scholar on informed consent, has noted, when medical science seems impotent to fight nature, "all kinds of senseless interventions are tried in an unconscious effort to cure the incurable magically through a 'wonder drug,' a novel surgical procedure, or a penetrating psychological interpretation."[21] Another *Wall Street Journal* article, entitled "Saying No to Penelope,"[22] illustrates the impossibility of limiting access to unproven cancer drugs to competent adults. The article tells the story of four-year-old Penelope, who is dying from neuroblastoma that has proved resistant to all conventional treatments. Her parents seek "anything [that] has a prayer of saving her." In her father's words, "The chance of anything bringing her back from the abyss now is very low. But the only thing I know for sure is if we don't treat her, she will die." With Penelope hospitalized and in pain, her parents continue "searching Penelope's big brown eyes for clues as to how long she wants to continue to battle for life."

It is suggested that the requirement of a physician's recommendation can safeguard against "magical thinking" and help make informed consent real.[23] But as Katz has noted, although physicians (and, he could have added, drug companies) often justify such last-ditch interventions as simply being responsive to patient needs, the interventions "may turn out to be a projection of their own needs onto patients."[21]

Government and the Market

Another recurrent theme is the belief that government regulation is evil, a central tenet of the laetrile litigation of the 1970s. The court hearing *Abigail Alliance* was correct to note that laetrile never underwent a phase 1 trial, but every indication was that the drug, also known as vitamin B17, was harmless, albeit also ineffective against cancer. Laetrile became a legal cause celebre in 1972, when California physician John A. Richardson was prosecuted for promoting laetrile. Richardson was a member of the John Birch Society, which quickly formed the Committee for Freedom of Choice in Cancer Therapy, with more than 100 committees nationwide.[24] It took another seven years before the FDA prevailed in its case against laetrile before the Supreme Court.[8] The basic arguments against FDA regulation remain the same today: the FDA follows a "paternalistic public policy that prevents individuals from exercising their own judgment about risks and benefits. If the FDA must err, it should be on the side of patients' freedom to choose."[25]

Public Policy

The FDA will prevail again today, not only because there is no constitutional right of access to unapproved drugs but also because even if there were, the state has the same compelling interest in approving drugs as it has in licensing physicians. From a public policy view, the *Abigail Alliance* court, the Congress, and the FDA all seem to be suffering from the "therapeutic illusion" in which research, designed to test a hypothesis for society, is confused with treatment, administered in the best interests of individual patients.[21,26,27] Of course there is a continuum, and it is perfectly understandable that many patients with cancer, told that there is nothing conventional medicine can do for them, will want access to whatever is available in or outside the context of clinical trials. But this is a problem for patients, physicians, the FDA, and drug manufacturers. First, because terminally ill patients can be harmed and exploited, there are better and worse ways to die.[21,26] Second, it is only through research, not "treatment," that cancer may become a chronic illness that is treated with a complex array of drugs, given either together or in a progression.[28,29] The right to choose in medicine is a central right of patients, but the choices can and should be limited to reasonable medical alternatives, which themselves are based on evidence.

This is, I believe, good public policy. But it is also much easier said than done.[30] Death is feared and even dreaded in our culture, and few Americans are able to die at home, at peace, with our loved ones in attendance, without seeking the "latest new treatment." There always seems to be something new to try, and there is almost always anecdotal evidence that it could help. This is one reason that even extremely high prices do not affect demand for cancer drugs, even ones that add little or no survival time.[31,32] When does caring for the patient demand primary attention to palliation rather than to long-shot, high-risk, investigational interventions? Coetzee's Mrs. Curren, who rejected new medical treatment for her cancer and insisted on dying at home, told her physician, whom she saw as "withdrawing" from her after giving her a terminal prognosis — "His allegiance to the living, not the dying" — "I have no illusions about my condition, doctor. It is not [experimental] care I need, just help with the pain."[1]

REFERENCES

1. Coetzee JM. Age of iron. London: Seeker & Warburg, 1990.
2. Patterson JT. The dread disease: cancer and modern American culture. Cambridge, MA: Harvard University Press, 1987.
3. Abigail Alliance v. Von Eschenbach, 445 F.3d 470 (DC Cir 2006). Vacated 469 F.3d 129 (DC Cir 2006).
4. Proposed rules for charging for investigational drugs and expanded access to investigational drugs for treatment use. Rockville, MD: Food and Drug Administration, 2006. (Accessed July 6, 2007, at http://www.fda.gov/cder/regulatory/applications/IND_PR.htm.)
5. Abigail Alliance v. Von Eschenbach, 429 F.3d 129 (DC Cir 2006).
6. Jacobson PD, Parmet WE. A new era of unapproved drugs: the case of Abigail Alliance v. Von Eschenbach. JAMA 2007;297:205–208. [Free Full Text]
7. Cruzan v. Director, Missouri Dept. of Health, 497 U.S. 261 (1990).
8. United States v. Rutherford, 442 U.S. 544 (1979).
9. Washington v. Glucksberg, 521 U.S. 702 (1997).
10. Vacco v. Quill, 521 U.S. 793 (1997).
11. Annas GJ. The bell tolls for a constitutional right to assisted suicide. N Engl J Med 1997;337:1098–1103. [Free Full Text]

12. Gonzales v. Oregon, 546 U.S. 243 (2006).

13. Annas GJ. "I want to live": medicine betrayed by ideology in the political debate over Terri Schiavo. Stetson Law Rev 2005;35:49–80. [Medline]

14. How about a "Kianna's Law"? Wall Street Journal. March 24, 2005:A14.

15. Kianna's legacy. Wall Street Journal. March 29, 2005:Al4.

16. Groopman J. The right to a trial: should dying patients have access to experimental drugs? The New Yorker. December 18, 2006:40–7.

17. ACCESS Act (Access, Compassion, Care, and Ethics for Seriously Ill Patients), S. 1956, 109th Cong (2005).

18. Annas GJ. Faith (healing), hope and charity at the FDA: the politics of AIDS drug trials. Villanova Law Rev 1989;34:771–797. [Medline]

19. FDA proposes rules overhaul to expand availability of experimental drugs: the agency also clarifies permissible charges to patients. Rockville, MD: Food and Drug Administration, December 11, 2006. (Accessed July 6, 2007, at http://www.fda.gov/bbs/topics/NEWS/ 2006/ NEW01520.html.)

20. Prud'homme A. The cell game: Sam Waksal's fast money and false promises — and the fate of ImClone's cancer drug. New York: Harper Business, 2004.

21. Katz J. The silent world of doctor and patient. New Haven, CT: Yale University Press, 1984:151.

22. Anand G. Saying no to Penelope: father seeks experimental cancer drug, but a biotech firm says risk is too high. Wall Street Journal. May 1, 2007:A1.

23. Robertson J. Controversial medical treatment and the right to health care. Hastings Cent Rep 2006;36:15–20. [CrossRef][ISI][Medline]

24. Culbert ML. Vitamin B17: Forbidden weapon against cancer. New Rochelle, NY: Arlington House, 1974.

25. Miller HI. Paternalism costs lives. Wall Street Journal. March 2, 2006:A15.

26. Annas GJ. The changing landscape of human experimentation: Nuremberg, Helsinki, and beyond. Health Matrix J Law Med 1992;2:119–40.

27. Appelbaum PS, Lidz CW. Re-evaluating the therapeutic misconception: response to Miller and Joffe. Kennedy Inst Ethics J 2006;16:367–373. [CrossRef][ISI]

28. Nathan D. The cancer treatment revolution: How smart drugs and other therapies are renewing our hope and changing the face of medicine. New York: John Wiley, 2007.

29. Brugarolas J. Renal-cell carcinoma — molecular pathways and therapies. N Engl J Med 2007;356:185–186. [Free Full Text]

30. Callahan D. False hopes: why America's quest for perfect health is a recipe for failure. New York: Simon and Schuster, 1998.

31. Berenson A. Hope, at $4,200 a dose: Why a cancer drug's cost doesn't hurt demand. New York Times. October 1, 2006:BU1.

32. Anand G. From Wall Street, a warning about cancer drug prices. Wall Street Journal. March 15, 2007:A1.

Pillow Angel Ethics

NANCY GIBBS

BEFORE READING: What are some circumstances in which what is medically possible is not ethical?

What kind of doctors would agree to intentionally shorten and sterilize a disabled six-year-old girl to make it easier for her parents to take care of her? The question has had message boards steaming for days, but the answers are in no way easy.

Dr. Daniel Gunther and Dr. Douglas Diekema, who first revealed the details of "The Ashley Case" in the *Archives of Pediatric and Adolescent Medicine*, think that many of their critics don't understand the nature of this case. Talk to them, and you confront every modern challenge in weighing what medicine can do, versus what it should.

The case: Ashley is a brain-damaged girl whose parents feared that as she got bigger, it would be much harder to care for her; so they set out to keep her small. Through high-dose estrogen treatment over the past two years, her growth plates were closed and her prospective height reduced by about thirteen inches, to 4'5". "Ashley's smaller and lighter size," her parents write on their blog "makes it more possible to include her in the typical family life and activities that provide her with needed comfort, closeness, security, and love: meal time, car trips, touch, snuggles, etc." They stress that the treatment's goal was "to improve our daughter's quality of life and not to convenience her caregivers."

But the treatment went further: doctors removed her uterus to prevent potential discomfort from menstrual cramps or pregnancy in the event of rape; and also her breast tissue, because of a family history of cancer and fibrocystic disease. Not having breasts would also make the harness straps that hold her upright more comfortable. "Ashley has no need for developed breasts since she will not breast feed," her parents argue, "and their presence would only be a source of discomfort to her."

The parents say that the decision to proceed with "The Ashley Treatment" was   5 not a hard one for them, but the same cannot be said for the doctors. "This was something people hadn't thought about being a possibility, much less being done," says Diekema, who chairs the bioethics committee of the American Academy of Pediatrics and was brought in to consult on this case. For the ethics committee of Seattle Children's Hospital, which reviewed the proposed treatment, "it took time to get past the initial response — 'wow, this is bizarre' — and think seriously about the reasons for the parents' request," says Diekema.

Nancy Gibbs was named a senior editor of *Time* magazine in October 1991, chief political writer in 1996, editor at large in 2002, and executive editor in 2010.

First they had to be sure there would be no medical harm: removing breast buds, Gunther says, is a much less invasive procedure than a mastectomy. The hormone treatment was commonly used forty years ago on lanky teenage girls who didn't want to get any taller. "The main risk," Gunther says, "is of thrombosis or blood clot, which is a risk in anybody taking estrogen. It's hard to assess in a young child because no one this young has been treated with estrogen." There were very few reports of thrombosis among the teenage patients, he says, "So I suspect the risk is fairly low. After treatment is finished, I don't see any long-term risk, and we've eliminated the risk of uterine and breast cancer."

The ethics committee essentially did a cost-benefit analysis and concluded that the rewards outweighed the risks. Keeping Ashley smaller and more portable, the doctors argue, has medical as well as emotional benefits: more movement means better circulation, digestion and muscle condition, and fewer sores and infections. "If you're going to be against this," Gunther says, "you have to argue why the benefits are not worth pursuing."

They knew that the treatment would be controversial, though they did not quite foresee the media storm that would erupt when they decided to publish the case and invite their peers to weigh in. "I felt we were doing the right thing for this little girl — but that didn't keep me from feeling a bit of unease," admits Diekema. "And that's as it should be. Humility is important in a case like this."

Gunther also understands why the case has inspired such intense feelings — but notes that "visceral reactions are not an argument for or against." This was not a girl who was ever going to grow up, he says. She was only going to grow bigger. "Some disability advocates have suggested that this course of treatment is an abuse of Ashley's 'rights' and an affront to her 'dignity.' This is a mystery to me. Is there more dignity in having to hoist a full-grown body in harness and chains from bed to bath to wheelchair? Ashley will always have the mind of an infant, and now she will be able to stay where she belongs — in the arms of the family that loves her."

But how far would Drs. Gunther and Diekema take this argument? Would they   10
agree to amputate a child's legs to keep her lighter and more portable? Hormone treatment is nowhere near as risky and disfiguring as amputation, Diekema retorts; it just accelerates a natural process by which the body stops growing. Parents of short children give them growth hormones for social more than medical reasons, he notes. How can it be O.K. to make someone "unnaturally" taller but not smaller? To warnings of a slippery slope, Gunther tilts the logic the other way: "The argument that a beneficial treatment should not be used because it might be misused is itself a slippery slope," he says. "If we did not use therapies available because they could be misused, we'd be practicing very little medicine."

"Adoption" of Frozen Embryos a Loaded Term

JEFFREY P. KAHN

BEFORE READING: Below, Kahn quotes estimates that "over 200,000 embryos are left over from in vitro fertilization (IVF) attempts to help couples have children." What do you think should be done with these "leftover" frozen embryos?

The estimates are striking: over 200,000 embryos are left over from in vitro fertilization (IVF) attempts to help couples have children. The unused embryos are frozen in labs all over the United States, waiting for a decision about what will be done with them.

Unlike other countries, most notably Britain, the United States has no rules about how long human embryos can remain frozen before a decision about their fate must be made. This has led to a growing number of unused frozen embryos, with many suggestions but little consensus about what should happen to them. As it stands, couples can leave the embryos frozen for later use, donate them to other couples, donate them for research uses, or discard them.

In late July, the Bush administration's Department of Health and Human Services announced it was making funds available to "support development and delivery of public awareness campaigns on embryo adoption." The goal is to help couples better understand their options, or to advocate for a particular option — depending on political perspective. What's interesting is the focus on "adoption" of embryos, especially to the exclusion of the other legitimate options available to couples. What does such a funding program mean for how we should think of human embryos, and for the future of reproductive technologies in the wake of stem cell research?

Can embryos be "adopted"?

The use of the term "embryo adoption" puts a particular spin on the difficult issues surrounding what should happen to frozen embryos. It makes the obvious parallel between donating embryos and adopting children. In the process, the funding program implicitly grants embryos particular moral status without argument or discussion.

Up to now, the more general term "embryo donation" has been used to describe both giving embryos to other couples and donating embryos for research purposes, such as stem cell research. Both are legitimate decisions for dealing with frozen   5

Jeffrey P. Kahn is director and holds the Maas Family Endowed Chair in Bioethics at the Center for Bioethics at the University of Minnesota; he is a professor, Department of Medicine, University of Minnesota Medical School. His column "Ethics Matters" is a biweekly feature from the Center for Bioethics and CNN Interactive. This essay appeared on CNN.com on September 17, 2002.

embryos, but the new focus on "adoption" effectively narrows embryo donation to couples who will try to create pregnancies with them — research labs won't "adopt" embryos. This perspective has implications not only for reproductive medicine, but for the abortion debate as well. If embryos created by IVF deserve an emphasis on their adoption, what about those embryos created the "regular" way inside a woman's womb?

Who gets to decide?

There is nothing wrong with government efforts to inform the public about available programs. But reproductive liberty demands that individuals be free to decide whether, when, and how they will reproduce, and it remains to be seen whether the government's plan unjustifiably limits that freedom. In the end, individuals should be free to determine what should happen to the embryos that are created for them, and donating embryos to other couples is only one option.

For the federal government to fund programs to exclusively encourage donation to other couples is to use public money to endorse a particular view about the status of embryos and what should be done with them.

Most important, it is a step away from couples controlling the fate of their embryos, and toward viewing embryos as needing government protection and the help of groups that seek to "place" them with caring families. The way we're heading, it's a short step to lab freezers being called orphanages, and social workers assigned to look after the interests of their frozen charges. Is it cold in here, or is it just me?

Doctors' Beliefs Hinder Patient Care

SABRINA RUBIN ERDELY

BEFORE READING: What are some situations in which a doctor's personal beliefs might interfere with his or her ability to prescribe a certain medication or perform a certain procedure?

Lori Boyer couldn't stop trembling as she sat on the examining table, hugging her hospital gown around her. Her mind was reeling. She'd been raped hours earlier by a man she knew — a man who had assured Boyer, thirty-five, that he only wanted to hang out at his place and talk. Instead, he had thrown her onto his bed and assaulted her. "I'm done with you," he'd tonelessly told her afterward. Boyer

---

Sabrina Rubin Erdely is an award-winning feature writer and investigative journalist based in Philadelphia. Her work has appeared in *Rolling Stone*, *SELF*, *GQ*, *The New Yorker*, *Mother Jones*, *Glamour*, and *Men's Health*, among other national magazines. This article, in its updated form, was posted on MSNBC.com on June 22, 2007.

had grabbed her clothes and dashed for her car in the freezing predawn darkness. Yet she'd had the clarity to drive straight to the nearest emergency room — Good Samaritan Hospital in Lebanon, Pennsylvania — to ask for a rape kit and talk to a sexual assault counselor. Bruised and in pain, she grimaced through the pelvic exam. Now, as Boyer watched Martin Gish, M.D., jot some final notes into her chart, she thought of something the rape counselor had mentioned earlier.

"I'll need the morning-after pill," she told him.

Dr. Gish looked up. He was a trim, middle-aged man with graying hair and, Boyer thought, an aloof manner. "No," Boyer says he replied abruptly. "I can't do that." He turned back to his writing.

Boyer stared in disbelief. *No?* She tried vainly to hold back tears as she reasoned with the doctor: She was midcycle, putting her in danger of getting pregnant. Emergency contraception is most effective within a short time frame, ideally seventy-two hours. If he wasn't willing to write an EC prescription, she'd be glad to see a different doctor. Dr. Gish simply shook his head. "It's against my religion," he said, according to Boyer. (When contacted, the doctor declined to comment for this article.)

Boyer left the emergency room empty-handed. "I was so vulnerable," she says.   5 "I felt victimized all over again. First the rape, and then the doctor making me feel powerless." Later that day, her rape counselor found Boyer a physician who would prescribe her EC. But Boyer remained haunted by the ER doctor's refusal — so profoundly, she hasn't been to see a gynecologist in the two and a half years since. "I haven't gotten the nerve up to go, for fear of being judged again," she says.

Doctors refusing treatment

Even under less dire circumstances than Boyer's, it's not always easy talking to your doctor about sex. Whether you're asking about birth control, STDs, or infertility, these discussions can be tinged with self-consciousness, even embarrassment. Now imagine those same conversations, but supercharged by the anxiety that your doctor might respond with moral condemnation — and actually refuse your requests.

That's exactly what's happening in medical offices and hospitals around the country: Catholic and conservative Christian health care providers are denying women a range of standard, legal medical care. Planned Parenthood M.D.s report patients coming to them because other gynecologists would not dole out birth control prescriptions or abortion referrals. Infertility clinics have turned away lesbians and unmarried women; anesthesiologists and obstetricians are refusing to do sterilizations; Catholic hospitals have delayed ending doomed pregnancies because abortions are only allowed to save the life of the mother. In a survey published this year in the *New England Journal of Medicine*, 63 percent of doctors said it is acceptable to tell patients they have moral objections to treatments, and 18 percent felt no obligation to refer patients elsewhere. And in a recent SELF.com poll, nearly 1 in twenty respondents said their doctors had refused to treat them for moral, ethical, or religious reasons. "It's obscene," says Jamie D. Brooks, a former staff attorney for the National Health Law Program who continues to work on projects with the Los Angeles advocacy group. "Doctors swear an oath to serve their patients. But instead, they are allowing their religious beliefs to compromise patient care. And too often, the victims of this practice are women."

Compared with the highly publicized issue of pharmacists who refuse to dispense birth control and emergency contraception, physician refusals are a little-discussed topic. Patients denied treatment rarely complain — the situation tends to feel so humiliatingly personal. And when patients do make noise, the case is usually resolved quietly. "The whole situation was traumatizing and embarrassing, and I just wanted to put it behind me," Boyer says. She came forward only after a local newspaper reported an almost identical story: In July 2006, retail clerk Tara Harnish visited the same ER after being sexually assaulted by a stranger, was examined by the same Dr. Gish — and when her mother called Dr. Gish's office the next day to get EC for Harnish, she was refused. "Then I knew it wasn't just me, that this was a larger problem and it could happen to anybody," Boyer says.

Harnish, twenty-one, was shocked by the way the doctor treated her. "He seemed more concerned with saving the (potential) pregnancy than he was with my health," she says. "He turned me away when I needed medical help. That's not what a doctor is supposed to do." Harnish was too shaken by her rape to pursue the matter; her mother called Harnish's gynecologist for a prescription. Then she called the newspaper. Despite the attention the story attracted, Dr. Gish continues to work at Good Samaritan Hospital. Spokesman Bill Carpenter will only say that "the issue has been resolved internally, and we're going to move forward."

In many cases, women don't even know a doctor is withholding treatment. 10 Boyer and Harnish, for example, wouldn't have realized they'd been denied care if they'd been among the estimated one in three women who don't know about EC. In the *New England Journal of Medicine* survey, 8 percent of physicians said they felt no obligation to present all options to their patients. "When you see a doctor, you presume you're getting all the information you need to make a decision," notes Jill Morrison, senior counsel for health and reproductive rights at the National Women's Law Center in Washington, D.C. "Especially in a crisis situation, like a rape, you often don't think to question your care. But unfortunately, now we can't even trust doctors to tell us what we need to know."

An ethical dilemma

To many doctors, however, the issue represents a genuine ethical dilemma. "The physician's number-one creed is 'First, do no harm,'" says Sandy Christiansen, M.D., an ob/gyn in Frederick, Maryland, who is active in the Christian Medical and Dental Associations, a 16,000-member group for health care professionals based in Bristol, Tennessee. "I know that life begins at conception, and that each person has inherent value. That includes the life of the unborn." Dr. Christiansen says she will not give abortion referrals, opposes EC, and, while she has prescribed birth control, is reconsidering the morality of that position. "Doctors are people, too," she adds. "We have to be able to leave the hospital and live with ourselves. If you feel in your heart an action would cause harm to somebody — born or unborn — it's legitimate to decline to participate."

The American Medical Association in Chicago, the nation's largest physician group, effectively agrees with her; its policy allows a doctor to decline a procedure if it conflicts with her moral ideology. The law also favors medical professionals. In 1973, following *Roe v. Wade*, Congress passed the so-called Church Amendment, allowing federally funded health care providers to refuse to do abortions. In the years since, forty-six states have adopted their own abortion refusal clauses — or, as proponents call them, conscience clauses — allowing doctors to opt out. Now many states have gone further. Sixteen legislatures have given doctors the right to refuse to perform sterilizations; eight states say doctors don't have to prescribe contraception. "This is about the rights of the individual, about our constitutional right to freedom of religion," says Frank Manion, an attorney with the American Center for Law and Justice, a legal group in Washington, D.C. Founded by minister Pat Robertson, the organization has represented health care providers and lobbied for laws that protect them. "We're not trying to deny anybody access to treatment," Manion adds. "We're saying, 'Don't make your choice my choice.'"

When Elizabeth Dotts walked into her new doctor's office for a gynecologic exam and checkup, she didn't realize she was treading into the front lines of a culture war. "I was just going for my annual visit, nothing out of the ordinary," says the twenty-six-year-old YWCA grant coordinator. Dotts, who was single, had recently moved to Birmingham, Alabama, and was seeing an M.D. recommended by a coworker. The visit was unremarkable until she asked for a refill of her birth control prescription. That's when the doctor informed her that he was Catholic and the pills were against his religion.

"The look he gave me actually made me feel ashamed," Dotts says. "Like I had this wild and crazy sex life. Like he was trying to protect me from myself." Her bewilderment quickly turned to anger — "I thought, 'Wait, what in the world? Where am I?'" — especially when she remembered that her insurance covered only one annual gynecology checkup. Dotts, who'd majored in religion in college, got tough with the doctor.

"I'm glad for you that you're faithful," she told him. "But don't push it on me.   15
I'm here for my treatment, and I expect you to give it to me." Five minutes of verbal sparring later, the doctor relented with a six-month prescription — but only after Dotts told him she had been put on the Pill to relieve menstrual cramping, not to prevent pregnancy. Dotts grabbed the prescription and left, resolving to find herself a new gynecologist. "Before, walking into a doctor's office, I assumed we were on the same side," she says. "I don't make that assumption now. I ask a million questions and advocate for myself."

Bills to protect patients

This tug-of-war between physicians and patients is playing out in state legislatures, where a handful of bills aim to protect women. A Pennsylvania proposal, for example, would compel ER doctors to provide rape victims with information about emergency contraception and to dispense it on request — a law already on the books in California, Massachusetts, New Jersey, New Mexico, New York, Ohio, and Washington. A federal version of the bill is under consideration by a House subcommittee.

But such efforts have been more than matched by those of conscience-clause activists. Since 2005, twenty-seven states introduced bills to widen refusal clauses. Four states are considering granting carte blanche refusal rights — much like the law adopted by Mississippi in 2004, which allows any health care provider to refuse practically anything on moral grounds. "It's written so broadly, there's virtually no protection for patients," says Adam Sonfield, senior public policy associate for the Washington, D.C., office of the Guttmacher Institute, a reproductive-health research group. Sonfield notes that many refusal clauses do not require providers to warn women about restrictions on services or to refer them elsewhere. "You have to balance doctors' rights with their responsibilities to patients, employers, and communities," he adds. "Doctors shouldn't be forced to provide services, but they can't just abandon patients."

In theory, the laws aren't aimed solely at women's health — a bill in New Jersey lists eye doctors and prosthetics technicians as examples of providers who'd be allowed to refuse care based on their beliefs. But Morrison warns women not to be fooled. "I ask you, what belief would keep someone from fitting a patient with a prosthetic limb?" she asks. "What they're really after is limiting access to women's health care. Reproductive health is seen as something other than regular health care" — not a straightforward matter of treating and healing, but something laden with morality — "and if you treat it that way, it becomes something providers can say yes or no to." Men, for the most part, escape such scrutiny: It's pretty hard to imagine someone being made to feel he's going straight to hell for choosing to take Viagra or get a vasectomy. And if women come to fear their doctors' judgments, a new set of problems can develop. "Then you have women who don't communicate with their doctors or avoid getting care," Morrison warns. "Any way you look at it, it's dangerous for women."

Complaint filed, but case closed

The stakes were high for Realtor Cheryl Bray when she visited a physician in Encinitas, California, two and a half years ago. Though she was there for a routine physical, the reason for the exam was anything but routine: Then a single 41-year-old, Bray had decided to adopt a baby in Mexico and needed to prove to authorities there that she was healthy. "I was under a tight deadline," Bray remembers; she had been matched with a birth mother who was less than two months from delivering. Bray had already passed a daunting number of tests — having her taxes certified, multiple background checks, home inspections by a social worker, psychological evaluations. When she showed up at the office of Fred Salley, M.D., a new doctor a friend had recommended, she was looking forward to crossing another task off her list. Instead, ten minutes into the appointment, Dr. Salley asked, "So, your husband is in agreement with your decision to adopt?"

"I'm not married," Bray told him.

"You're not?" He calmly put down his pen. "Then I'm not comfortable continuing this exam."

20

Bray says she tried to reason with Dr. Salley but received only an offer for a referral at some future date. Dr. Salley disputes this, telling SELF that he offered to send Bray to another doctor in his group that day. "My decision to refer Ms. Bray was not because she was unmarried; rather, it was based on my moral belief that a child should have two parental units," he adds. "Such religious beliefs are a fundamental right guaranteed by the Constitution of the United States."

Bray sobbed in her parked car for another forty-five minutes before she could collect herself for the drive home. "I had a lot of pent-up emotions," she remembers. "When you are going through an adoption, you have to prove that you are a fit parent at every stage. I really felt put through the ringer, and the doctor compounded that feeling."

Bray managed to get an appointment with another physician about a month later and was approved for the adoption two weeks before her daughter, Paolina, was born. But she remained furious enough that she filed a complaint against Dr. Salley with the Medical Board of California — and then was shocked when, in April 2006, the board closed the case without taking any action. When she complained to Dr. Salley's employer, a clinic official wrote back that "based on personally held conscience and moral principles" her doctor had been within his rights to refuse her as a patient. "Apparently," she says, "it's OK to discriminate against somebody, as long as it's for religious reasons."

Providers often prevail

It's true that several lawsuits have favored health providers who refuse services based   25
on their principles. In a 2002 wrongful-termination case in Riverside County, California, for example, a born-again Christian nurse was fired for refusing to give out emergency contraception — but she was vindicated when the jury agreed that her rights had been violated, awarding her $19,000 in back pay and $28,000 for emotional distress. And in a recent case in San Diego, an appeals court ruled against thirty-five-year-old Guadalupe Benitez. Hoping to start a family with her lesbian partner, Benitez received fertility treatments for nearly a year at North Coast Women's Care Medical Group in Encinitas. But when drugs and home inseminations failed, two doctors and a nurse all bowed out of doing an intrauterine insemination, saying their religion would not allow it.

Their reasoning is in dispute: Benitez has claimed both doctors told her they objected to her sexual orientation. Carlo Coppo, a lawyer for the doctors, says they refused because she was unmarried. Benitez, who went on to have three children with the help of another clinic, has appealed to the California Supreme Court and is awaiting its decision.

Her attorney, Jennifer C. Pizer of Lambda Legal in Los Angeles, says she's heard from numerous lesbians denied access to fertility treatments. "Reproductive medicine has given human beings choices that didn't exist in previous generations, but the rules about how we exercise those choices should be the same for all groups of people," she argues. Allowing doctors to refer a patient to someone else, she adds, is the equivalent of a restaurant telling a black person, "Go next door. We don't serve your kind here."

In the end, the women in all of the incidents above were able to get the treatment they wanted, even if they had to go elsewhere. So one could see doctor refusals as a mere inconvenience. "In 99.9 percent of these cases, the patients walk away with what they came for, and everyone's satisfied," Manion asserts. "I know there's the horror story of the lonely person in the middle of nowhere who meets one of my clients. But those cases are so rare." Access to reproductive health care, however, is already a challenge in some areas. "Out here, it's a very real issue," says Stacey Anderson of Planned Parenthood of Montana in Helena. "We have some really gigantic counties where if you're refused a service by a primary care physician or a gynecologist, you might have to drive two, three hours to find another."

Moreover, you don't need to be in a rural area to have limited access, points out attorney Brooks; all you need to be is poor. "Lower-income people who are refused health care are trapped," Brooks says. "They can't pay out of pocket for these services. And they may not have transportation to go elsewhere. So they really don't have options."

What's best for the patient

If there's one thing both sides can agree on, it's this: In an emergency, doctors need   30 to put aside personal beliefs to do what's best for the patient. But in a world guided by religious directives, even this can be a slippery proposition.

Ob/gyn Wayne Goldner, M.D., learned this lesson a few years back when a patient named Kathleen Hutchins came to his office in Manchester, New Hampshire. She was only fourteen weeks pregnant, but her water had broken. Dr. Goldner delivered the bad news: Because there wasn't enough amniotic fluid left and it was too early for the fetus to survive on its own, the pregnancy was hopeless. Hutchins would likely miscarry in a matter of weeks. But in the meanwhile, she stood at risk for serious infection, which could lead to infertility or death. Dr. Goldner says his devastated patient chose to get an abortion at local Elliot Hospital. But there was a problem. Elliot had recently merged with nearby Catholic Medical Center — and as a result, the hospital forbade abortions.

"I was told I could not admit her unless there was a risk to her life," Dr. Goldner remembers. "They said, 'Why don't you wait until she has an infection or she gets a fever?' They were asking me to do something other than the standard of care. They wanted me to put her health in jeopardy." He tried admitting Hutchins elsewhere, only to discover that the nearest abortion provider was nearly 80 miles away in Lebanon, New Hampshire — and that she had no car. Ultimately, Dr. Goldner paid a taxi to drive her the hour and a half to the procedure. (The hospital merger has since dissolved, and Elliot is secular once again.)

"Unfortunately, her story is the tip of the iceberg," Dr. Goldner says. Since the early 1990s, hospitals have been steadily consolidating operations to save money; so many secular community hospitals have been bought up that, today, nearly one in five hospital beds is in a religiously owned institution, according to the nonprofit group MergerWatch in New York City.

What is standard of care?

Every Catholic hospital is bound by the ethical directives of the U.S. Conference of Catholic Bishops, which forbid abortion and sterilization (unless they are lifesaving), in vitro fertilization, surrogate motherhood, some prenatal genetic testing, all artificial forms of birth control, and the use of condoms for HIV prevention. Baptist and Seventh Day Adventist hospitals may also restrict abortions. Which means that if your local hospital has been taken over — or if you're ever rushed to the nearest hospital in an emergency — you could be in for a surprise at the services you can't get.

You wouldn't necessarily know a hospital's affiliation upon your arrival. "The   35
name of the hospital may not change after a merger, even if its philosophy has," Morrison notes. "The community is often in the dark that changes have taken place at all." The burden to know falls entirely on the patient, who can either search the Catholic Health Association's directory of member hospitals (at CHAUSA.org) or ask her doctor outright. Either way, says Morrison, "it requires you to be an extremely educated consumer."

Family physician Debra Stulberg, M.D., was completing her residency in 2004 when West Suburban Medical Center in Oak Park, Illinois, was acquired by the large Catholic system Resurrection Health Care. "They assured us that patient care would be unaffected," Dr. Stulberg says. "But then I got to see the reality." The doctor was struck by the hoops women had to jump through to get basic care. "One of my patients was a mother of four who had wanted a tubal ligation at delivery but was turned down," she says. "When I saw her not long afterward, she was pregnant with unwanted twins."

And in emergency scenarios, Dr. Stulberg says, the newly merged hospital did not offer standard-of-care treatments. In one case that made the local paper, a patient came in with an ectopic pregnancy: an embryo had implanted in her fallopian tube. Such an embryo has zero chance of survival and is a serious threat to the mother, as its growth can rupture the tube. The more invasive way to treat an ectopic is to surgically remove the tube. An alternative, generally less risky way is to administer methotrexate, a drug also used for cancer. It dissolves the pregnancy but spares the tube, preserving the women's fertility. "The doctor thought the noninvasive treatment was best," Dr. Stulberg recounts. But Catholic directives specify that even in an ectopic pregnancy, doctors cannot perform "a direct abortion" — which, the on-call ob/gyn reasoned, would nix the drug option. (Surgery, on the other hand, could be considered a lifesaving measure that indirectly kills the embryo, and may be permitted.) The doctor didn't wait to take it up with the hospital's ethical committee; she told the patient to check out and head to another ER. (Citing patient confidentiality, West Suburban declined to comment, confirming only that as a Catholic hospital, it adheres to religious directives "in every instance.")

Turns out, the definition of *emergency* depends on whom you ask. Dr. Christiansen, the pro-life ob/gyn, says she would not object to either method of ending an ectopic pregnancy. "I do feel that the one indication for abortion is to save the mother's life — that's clear in my mind," she says. "But the reality is, the vast majority of abortions are elective. There are very, very few instances where the mother's life is truly in jeopardy." She can recall having seen only one such situation: During Dr. Christiansen's residency, a patient in the second trimester of pregnancy had a detached placenta; the attending physician performed an abortion to save the woman from bleeding to death. "That was a legitimate situation," Dr. Christiansen says. But in general, "it's a pure judgment call. A doctor would have to be in the situation and decide whether it constitutes a life-threatening emergency or not."

Raise your hand if you'd like to be the test case.

Thinking and Writing about Medical Ethics

QUESTIONS FOR DISCUSSION AND WRITING

1. Why do advances in medicine so often bring ethical complications? What examples come to mind?

2. If you were a doctor, are there situations in which your personal beliefs might preclude your prescribing a certain medication or performing a certain procedure? How would you justify this to your patients?

3. Sometimes parents will not allow their children to have certain types of medical care (such as blood transfusions) because of their religious beliefs. Doctors have on occasion gone to court to win the right to go against the parents' wishes. Could you ever support such a move? Why, or why not? Under what circumstances?

4. If the choice were yours, would you be willing to permit the harvesting of a loved one's organs? On what would you base your decision?

5. What factors should enter into the decision as to who should receive donor organs? Should a patient who receives a donor organ be expected to donate his or her organs at death?

6. Do you believe that patients who receive donor organs should meet the living donors who donated them? What are the pros and cons?

7. Summarize the main points in Annas's argument. How convincing is his argument?

8. How convincing did you find Ashley's parents' argument in "Pillow Angel Ethics"?

9. Explain why Kahn's argument in " 'Adoption' of Frozen Embryos a Loaded Term" is based largely on definition. Or do the same for Howards's "Ethics of Organ Donation."

10. Explain why, to you, the use of human embryonic stem cells in research is an ethical problem or not.

11. Speculate as to some ethical dilemmas in the field of medicine that are likely to arise in the future.

12. Explain how both Victory's and Howards's arguments are strengthened by the use of examples. Which other author or authors here use examples as a major type of support?

13. Do you find Victory's argument convincing support for national health care? Explain.

14. Research and report the outcome of the case of *Abigail Alliance v. Von Eschenbach*.

15. Write a defense of your position on human embryonic stem-cell research.

PART 5

Classic Arguments

From Crito

PLATO

Socrates: . . . Ought a man to do what he admits to be right, or ought he to betray the right?

Crito: He ought to do what he thinks right.

Socrates: But if this is true, what is the application? In leaving the prison against the will of the Athenians, do I wrong any? Or rather do I not wrong those whom I ought least to wrong? Do I not desert the principles which are acknowledged by us to be just — what do you say?

Crito: I cannot tell, Socrates; for I do not know.

Socrates: Then consider the matter in this way: — Imagine that I am about to play truant (you may call the proceeding by any name which you like), and the laws of the government come and interrogate me: "Tell us, Socrates," they say: "what are you about? Are you not going by an act of yours to overturn us — the laws, and the whole state, as far as in you lies? Do you imagine that a state can subsist and not be overthrown, in which the decisions of law have no power, but are set aside and trampled upon by individuals?" What will be our answer, Crito, to these and the like words? Any one, and especially a rhetorician, will have a good deal to say on behalf of the law which requires a sentence to be carried out. He will argue that this law should not be set aside; and shall we reply, "Yes, but the state has injured us and given an unjust sentence." Suppose I say that?

Crito: Very good, Socrates.

Socrates: "And was that our agreement with you?" the law would answer; "or were you to abide by the sentence of the state?" And if I were to express my astonishment at their words, the law would probably add: "Answer, Socrates, instead of opening your eyes — you are in the habit of asking and answering questions. Tell us, — What complaint have you to make against us which justifies you in attempting to destroy us and the state? In the first place did we not bring you into existence? Your father married your mother by our aid and begat you. Say whether you have any

5

Plato, who died in 347 B.C., was one of the greatest Greek philosophers. He was a student of the Greek philosopher Socrates, whose teachings he recorded in the form of dialogues between Socrates and his pupils. In this dialogue, Crito visits Socrates — who is in prison, condemned to death for corrupting the youth of Athens — and tries to persuade him to escape. Socrates, however, refuses, basing his decision on his definition of justice and virtue. From Plato's *Crito*, trans. Benjamin Jowett, 3rd ed. (New York: Dial Press, 1982).

objection to urge against those of us who regulate marriage?" None, I should reply. "Or against those of us who after birth regulate the nurture and education of children, in which you also were trained? Were not the laws, which have the charge of education, right in commanding your father to train you in music and gymnastics?" Right, I should reply. "Well then, since you were brought into the world and nurtured and educated by us, can you deny in the first place that you are our child and slave, as your fathers were before you? And if this is true you are not on equal terms with us; nor can you think that you have a right to do to us what we are doing to you. Would you have any right to strike or revile or do any other evil to your father or your master, if you had one, because you have been struck or reviled by him, or received some other evil at his hands? — you would not say this? And because we think right to destroy you, do you think that you have any right to destroy us in return, and your country as far as in you lies? Will you, O professor of true virtue, pretend that you are justified in this? Has a philosopher like you failed to discover that our country is more to be valued and higher and holier far than mother or father or any ancestor, and more to be regarded in the eyes of the gods and of men of understanding? Also to be soothed, and gently and reverently entreated when angry, even more than a father, and either to be persuaded, or if not persuaded, to be obeyed? And when we are punished by her, whether with imprisonment or stripes, the punishment is to be endured in silence, and if she leads us to wounds or death in battle, thither we follow as is right; neither may any one yield or retreat or leave his rank, but whether in battle or in a court of law, or in any other place, he must do what his city and his country order him; or he must change their view of what is just: and if he may do no violence to his father or mother, much less may he do violence to his country." What answer shall we make to this, Crito? Do the laws speak truly, or do they not?

Crito: I think that they do.

Socrates: Then the laws will say, Consider, Socrates, if we are speaking truly that in your present attempt you are going to do us an injury. For, having brought you into the world, and nurtured and educated you, and given you and every other citizen a share in every good which we had to give, we further proclaim to any Athenian by the liberty which we allow him, that if he does not like us when he has become of age and has seen the ways of the city, and made our acquaintance, he may go where he pleases and take his goods with him. None of us laws will forbid him or interfere with him. Any one who does not like us and the city, and who wants to emigrate to a colony or to any other city, may go where he likes, retaining his property. But he who has experience of the manner in which we order justice and administer the state, and still remains, has entered into an implied contract that he will do as we command him. And he who disobeys us is, as we maintain, thrice wrong; first, because in disobeying us he is disobeying his parents; secondly, because we are the authors of his education; thirdly, because he has made an agreement with us that he will duly obey our commands; and he neither obeys them nor convinces us that our commands are unjust; and we do not rudely impose them, but give him the alternative of obeying or convincing us; — that is what we offer, and he does neither.

"These are the sort of accusations to which, as we were saying, you, Socrates, will be exposed if you accomplish your intentions; you, above all other Athenians." Suppose now I ask, why I rather than anybody else? They will justly retort upon me that I above all other men have acknowledged the agreement. "There is clear proof," they will say, "Socrates, that we and the city were not displeasing to you. Of all Athenians you have been the most constant resident in the city, which, as you never leave, you may be supposed to love. For you never went out of the city either to see the games, except once when you went to the Isthmus, or to any other place unless when you were on military service; nor did you travel as other men do. Nor had you any curiosity to know other states or their laws: your affections did not go beyond us and our state; we were your special favorites, and you acquiesced in our government of you; and here in this city you begat your children, which is a proof of your satisfaction. Moreover, you might in the course of the trial, if you had liked, have fixed the penalty at banishment; the state which refuses to let you go now would have let you go then. But you pretended that you preferred death to exile, and that you were not unwilling to die. And now you have forgotten these fine sentiments, and pay no respect to us the laws, of whom you are the destroyer; and are doing what only a miserable slave would do, running away and turning your back upon the compacts and agreements which you made as a citizen. And first of all answer this very question: Are we right in saying that you agreed to be governed according to us in deed, and not in word only? Is that true or not?" How shall we answer, Crito? Must we not assent?

Crito: We cannot help it, Socrates.

Socrates: Then will they not say: "You, Socrates, are breaking the covenants and agreements which you made with us at your leisure, not in any haste or under any compulsion or deception, but after you have had seventy years to think of them, during which time you were at liberty to leave the city, if we were not to your mind, or if our covenants appeared to you to be unfair. You had your choice, and might have gone either to Lacedaemon or Crete, both which states are often praised by you for their good government, or to some other Hellenic or foreign state. Whereas you, above all our Athenians, seemed to be so fond of the state, or, in other words, of us her laws (and who would care about a state which has no laws?), that you never stirred out of her; the halt,

10

the blind, the maimed were not more stationary in her than you were. And now you run away and forsake your agreements. Not so, Socrates, if you will take our advice; do not make yourself ridiculous by escaping out of the city.

"For just consider, if you transgress and err in this sort of way, what good will you do either to yourself or to your friends? That your friends will be driven into exile and deprived of citizenship, or will lose their property, is tolerably certain; and you yourself, if you fly to one of the neighboring cities, as, for example, Thebes or Megara, both of which are well governed, will come to them as an enemy, Socrates, and their government will be against you, and all patriotic citizens will cast an evil eye upon you as a subverter of the laws, and you will confirm in the minds of the judges the justice of their own condemnation of you. For he who is a corrupter of the laws is more than likely to be a corrupter of the young and foolish portion of mankind. Will you then flee from well-ordered citizens and virtuous men? And is existence worth having on these terms? Or will you go to them without shame, and talk to them, Socrates? And what will you say to them? What you say here about virtue and justice and institutions and laws being the best things among men? Would that be decent of you? Surely not. But if you go away from well-governed states to Crito's friends in Thessaly, where there is a great disorder and licence, they will be charmed to hear the tale of your escape from prison, set off with ludicrous particulars of the manner in which you were wrapped in a goatskin or some other disguise, and metamorphosed as the manner is of runaways; but will there be no one to remind you that in your old age you were ashamed to violate the most sacred laws from a miserable desire of a little more life? Perhaps not, if you keep them in a good temper; but if they are out of temper you will hear many degrading things; you will live, but how? — as the flatterer of all men, and the servant of all men; and doing what? — eating and drinking in Thessaly, having gone abroad in order that you may get a dinner. And where will be your fine sentiments about justice and virtue? Say that you wish to live for the sake of your children — you want to bring them up and educate them — will you take them into Thessaly and deprive them of Athenian citizenship? Is this the benefit which you will confer upon them? Or are you under the impression that they will be better cared for and educated here if you are still alive, although absent from them; for your friends will take care of them? Do you fancy that if you are an inhabitant of Thessaly they will take care of them, and if you are an inhabitant of the other world that they will not take care of them? Nay: but if they who call themselves friends are good for anything, they will — to be sure they will.

"Listen, then, Socrates, to us who have brought you up. Think not of life and children first, and of justice afterwards, but of justice first, that you may be justified before the princes of the world below. For neither will you nor any that belong to you be happier or holier or juster in this life, or happier in another, if you do as Crito bids. Now you depart in innocence, a sufferer and not a doer of evil; a victim, not of the laws of men. But if you go forth, returning evil for evil, and injury for injury, breaking the covenants and agreements which you have made with us, and wronging those whom you ought least of all to wrong, that is to say, yourself, your friends, your country, and us, we shall be angry with you while you live, and our brethren, the laws in the world below, will receive you as an enemy; for they will know that you have done your best to destroy us. Listen, then, to us and not to Crito."

This, dear Crito, is the voice which I seem to hear murmuring in my 15 ears, like the sound of the flute in the ears of the mystic; that voice, I say, is humming in my ears, and prevents me from hearing any other. And I know that anything more which you may say will be vain. Yet speak, if you have anything to say.

Crito: I have nothing to say, Socrates.

Socrates: Leave me then, Crito, to fulfill the will of God, and to follow whither he leads.

DISCUSSION QUESTIONS

1. What debt to the law and his country does Socrates acknowledge? Mention the specific reasons for which he owes obedience. Is the analogy of the country to parents a plausible one? Why, or why not?

2. Explain the nature of the implied contract that exists between Socrates and the state. According to the state, how has Socrates forfeited his right to object to punishment?

3. What appeal does that state make to Socrates' sense of justice and virtue?

WRITING SUGGESTIONS

4. Socrates bases his refusal to escape the death penalty on his definition of justice and virtue. Basing your own argument on other criteria, make a claim for the right of Socrates to try to escape his punishment. Would some good be served by his escape?

5. The analogy between one's country and one's parents is illustrated at great length in Socrates' argument. In the light of modern ideas about the relationship between the state and the individual in a democracy, write a refutation of the analogy. Perhaps you can think of a different and more fitting one.

A Modest Proposal

JONATHAN SWIFT

It is a melancholy object to those who walk through this great town[1] or travel in the country, when they see the streets, the roads, and cabin doors, crowded with beggars of the female sex, followed by three, four, or six children, all in rags and importuning every passenger for an alms. These mothers, instead of being able to work for their honest livelihood, are forced to employ all their time in strolling to beg sustenance for their helpless infants, who, as they grow up, either turn thieves for want of work, or leave their dear native country to fight for the Pretender in Spain, or sell themselves to the Barbados.[2]

I think it is agreed by all parties that this prodigious number of children in the arms, or on the backs, or at the heels of their mothers, and frequently of their fathers, is in the present deplorable state of the kingdom a very great additional grievance; and therefore whoever could find out a fair, cheap, and easy method of making these children sound, useful members of the commonwealth would deserve so well of the public as to have his statue set up for a preserver of the nation.

But my intention is very far from being confined to provide only for the children of professed beggars; it is of a much greater extent, and shall take in the whole number of infants at a certain age who are born of parents in effect as little able to support them as those who demand our charity in the streets.

As to my own part, having turned my thoughts for many years upon this important subject, and maturely weighed the several schemes of other projectors,[3] I have always found them grossly mistaken in their computation. It is true, a child just dropped from its dam may be supported by her milk for a solar year, with little other nourishment; at most not above the value of two shillings, which the mother may certainly get, or the value in scraps, by her lawful occupation of begging; and it is exactly at one year that I propose to provide for them in such a manner as instead

---

[1] Dublin. — EDS. [All notes are the editors'.]

[2] The Pretender was James Stuart, who was exiled to Spain. Many Irish men had joined an army attempting to return him to the English throne in 1715. Others had become indentured servants, agreeing to work for a set number of years in Barbados or other British colonies in exchange for their transportation out of Ireland.

[3] Planners.

This essay is acknowledged by almost all critics to be the most powerful example of irony in the English language. (*Irony* means saying one thing but meaning another.) In 1729 Jonathan Swift (1667–1745), prolific satirist and dean of St. Patrick's Cathedral in Dublin, was moved to write in protest against the terrible poverty in which the Irish were living under British rule. Notice that the essay is organized according to one of the patterns outlined in Part Two of this book (see Presenting the Stock Issues, Chapter 11, p. 443). First, Swift establishes the need for a change, then he offers his proposal, and finally, he lists its advantages.

of being a charge upon their parents or the parish, or wanting food and raiment for the rest of their lives, they shall on the contrary contribute to the feeding, and partly to the clothing, of many thousands.

There is likewise another great advantage in my scheme, that it will prevent   5
those voluntary abortions, and that horrid practice of women murdering their bastard children, alas, too frequent among us, sacrificing the poor innocent babes, I doubt, more to avoid the expense than the shame, which would move tears and pity in the most savage and inhuman breast.

The number of souls in this kingdom being usually reckoned one million and a half, of these I calculate there may be about two hundred thousand couples whose wives are breeders; from which number I subtract thirty thousand couples who are able to maintain their own children, although I apprehend there cannot be so many under the present distress of the kingdom; but this being granted, there will remain an hundred and seventy thousand breeders. I again subtract fifty thousand for those women who miscarry, or whose children die by accident or disease within the year. There only remain an hundred and twenty thousand children of poor parents annually born. The question therefore is, how this number shall be reared and provided for, which, as I have already said, under the present situation of affairs, is utterly impossible by all the methods hitherto proposed. For we can neither employ them in handicraft or agriculture; we neither build houses (I mean in the country) nor cultivate land. They can very seldom pick up a livelihood by stealing till they arrive at six years old, except where they are of towardly parts;[4] although I confess they learn the rudiments much earlier, during which time they can however be looked upon only as probationers, as I have been informed by a principal gentleman in the county of Cavan, who protested to me that he never knew above one or two instances under the age of six, even in a part of the kingdom so renowned for the quickest proficiency in that art.

I am assured by our merchants that a boy or a girl before twelve years old is no salable commodity; and even when they come to this age they will not yield above three pounds, or three pounds and a half a crown at most on the Exchange; which cannot turn to account either to the parents or the kingdom, the charge of nutriment and rags having been at least four times that value.

I shall now therefore humbly propose my own thoughts, which I hope will not be liable to the least objection.

I have been assured by a very knowing American of my acquaintance in London, that a young healthy child well nursed is at a year old a most delicious, nourishing, and wholesome food, whether stewed, roasted, baked, or boiled; and I make no doubt that it will equally serve in a fricassee or a ragout.[5]

I do therefore humbly offer it to public consideration that of the hundred and   10
twenty thousand children, already computed, twenty thousand may be reserved for breed, whereof only one fourth part to be males, which is more than we allow to sheep,

[4] Innate talents.
[5] Stew.

black cattle, or swine; and my reason is that these children are seldom the fruits of marriage, a circumstance not much regarded by our savages, therefore one male will be sufficient to serve four females. That the remaining hundred thousand may at a year old be offered in sale to the persons of quality and fortune through the kingdom, always advising the mother to let them suck plentifully in the last month, so as to render them plump and fat for a good table. A child will make two dishes at an entertainment for friends; and when the family dines alone, the fore or hind quarter will make a reasonable dish, and seasoned with a little pepper or salt will be very good boiled on the fourth day, especially in winter.

I have reckoned upon a medium that a child just born will weigh twelve pounds, and in a solar year if tolerably nursed increaseth to twenty-eight pounds.

I grant this food will be somewhat dear, and therefore very proper for landlords, who, as they have already devoured most of the parents, seem to have the best title to the children.

Infant's flesh will be in season throughout the year, but more plentiful in March, and a little before and after. For we are told by a grave author, an eminent French physician,[6] that fish being a prolific diet, there are more children born in Roman Catholic countries about nine months after Lent than at any other season; therefore, reckoning a year after Lent, the markets will be more glutted than usual, because the number of popish infants is at least three to one in this kingdom; and therefore it will have one other collateral advantage, by lessening the number of Papists among us.

I have already computed the charge of nursing a beggar's child (in which list I reckon all cottagers, laborers, and four-fifths of the farmers) to be about two shillings per annum, rags included; and I believe no gentleman would repine to give ten shillings for the carcass of a good fat child, which, as I have said, will make four dishes of excellent nutritive meat, when he hath only some particular friend or his own family to dine with him. Thus the squire will learn to be a good landlord, and grow popular among the tenants; the mother will have eight shillings net profit, and be fit for work till she produces another child.

Those who are more thrifty (as I must confess the times require) may flay the   15
carcass; the skin of which artificially[7] dressed will make admirable gloves for ladies, and summer boots for fine gentlemen.

As to our city of Dublin, shambles[8] may be appointed for this purpose in the most convenient parts of it, and butchers we may be assured will not be wanting; although I rather recommend buying the children alive, and dressing them hot from the knife as we do roasting pigs.

A very worthy person, a true lover of his country, and whose virtues I highly esteem, was lately pleased in discoursing on this matter to offer a refinement upon my scheme. He said that many gentlemen of his kingdom, having of late destroyed

---

[6] A reference to Swift's favorite French writer, François Rabelais (1494?–1553), who was actually a broad satirist known for his coarse humor.

[7] With art or craft.

[8] Butcher shops or slaughterhouses.

their deer, he conceived that the want of venison might be well supplied by the bodies of young lads and maidens, not exceeding fourteen years of age nor under twelve, so great a number of both sexes in every county being now ready to starve for want of work and service; and these to be disposed of by their parents, if alive, or otherwise by their nearest relations. But with due deference to so excellent a friend and so deserving a patriot, I cannot be altogether in his sentiments; for as to the males, my American acquaintance assured me from frequent experience that their flesh was generally tough and lean, like that of our schoolboys, by continual exercise, and their taste disagreeable; and to fatten them would not answer the charge. Then as to the females, it would, I think with humble submission, be a loss to the public, because they soon would become breeders themselves; and besides, it is not improbable that some scrupulous people might be apt to censure such a practice (although indeed very unjustly) as a little bordering upon cruelty; which, I confess, hath always been with me the strongest objection against any project, how well soever intended.

But in order to justify my friend, he confessed that this expedient was put into his head by the famous Psalmanazar,[9] a native of the island Formosa, who came from thence to London above twenty years ago, and in conversation told my friend that in his country when any young person happened to be put to death, the executioner sold the carcass to persons of quality as a prime dainty; and that in his time the body of a plump girl of fifteen, who was crucified for an attempt to poison the emperor, was sold to his Imperial Majesty's prime minister of state, and other great mandarins of the court, in joints from the gibbet, at four hundred crowns. Neither indeed can I deny that if the same use were made of several plump young girls in this town, who without one single groat to their fortunes cannot stir abroad without a chair, and appear at the playhouse and assemblies in foreign fineries which they never will pay for, the kingdom would not be the worse.

Some persons of a desponding spirit are in great concern about that vast number of poor people who are aged, diseased, or maimed, and I have been desired to employ my thoughts what course may be taken to ease the nation of so grievous an encumbrance. But I am not in the least pain upon that matter, because it is very well known that they are every day dying and rotting by cold and famine, and filth and vermin, as fast as can be reasonably expected. And as to the younger laborers, they are now in almost as hopeful a condition. They cannot get work, and consequently pine away for want of nourishment to a degree that if any time they are accidentally hired to common labor, they have not strength to perform it; and thus the country and themselves are happily delivered from the evils to come.

I have too long digressed, and therefore shall return to my subject. I think the   20
advantages by the proposal which I have made are obvious and many, as well as of the highest importance.

---

[9] Georges Psalmanazar was a Frenchman who pretended to be Japanese and wrote an entirely imaginary *Description of the Isle Formosa.* He had become well known in gullible London society.

For first, as I have already observed, it would greatly lessen the number of Papists, with whom we are yearly overrun, being the principal breeders of the nation as well as our most dangerous enemies; and who stay at home on purpose to deliver the kingdom to the Pretender, hoping to take their advantage by the absence of so many good Protestants, who have chosen rather to leave their country than to stay at home and pay tithes against their conscience to an Episcopal curate.

Secondly, the poorer tenants will have something valuable of their own, which by law may be made liable to distress,[10] and help to pay their landlord's rent, their corn and cattle being already seized and money a thing unknown.

Thirdly, whereas the maintenance of an hundred thousand children, from two years old and upwards, cannot be computed at less than ten shillings a piece per annum, the nation's stock will be thereby increased fifty thousand pounds per annum, besides the profit of a new dish introduced to the tables of all gentlemen of fortune in the kingdom who have any refinement in taste. And the money will circulate among ourselves, the goods being entirely of our own growth and manufacture.

Fourthly, the constant breeders, besides the gain of eight shillings sterling per annum by the sale of their children, will be rid of the charge of maintaining them after the first year.

Fifthly, this food would likewise bring great custom to taverns, where the vint- 25 ners will certainly be so prudent as to procure the best receipts for dressing it to perfection, and consequently have their houses frequented by all the fine gentlemen, who justly value themselves upon their knowledge in good eating; and a skillful cook, who understands how to oblige his guests, will contrive to make it as expensive as they please.

Sixthly, this would be a great inducement to marriage, which all wise nations have either encouraged by rewards or enforced by laws and penalties. It would increase the care and tenderness of mothers toward their children, when they were sure of a settlement for life to the poor babes, provided in some sort by the public, to their annual profit instead of expense. We should see an honest emulation among the married women, which of them could bring the fattest child to the market. Men would become as fond of their wives during the time of their pregnancy as they are now of their mares in foal, their cows in calf, or sows when they are ready to farrow; nor offer to beat or kick them (as is too frequent a practice) for fear of a miscarriage.

Many other advantages might be enumerated. For instance, the addition of some thousand carcasses in our exportation of barreled beef, the propagation of swine's flesh, and improvements in the art of making good bacon, so much wanted among us by the great destruction of pigs, too frequent at our tables, which are no way comparable in taste or magnificence to a well-grown, fat, yearling child, which roasted whole will make a considerable figure at a lord mayor's feast or any other public entertainment. But this and many others I omit, being studious of brevity.

Supposing that one thousand families in this city would be constant customers for infants' flesh, besides others who might have it at merry meetings, particularly weddings and christenings, I compute that Dublin would take off annually about

---

[10] Subject to possession by lenders.

twenty thousand carcasses, and the rest of the kingdom (where probably they will be sold somewhat cheaper) the remaining eighty thousand.

I can think of no one objection that will possibly be raised against this proposal, unless it should be urged that the number of people will be thereby much lessened in the kingdom. This I freely own, and it was indeed one principal design in offering it to the world. I desire the reader will observe, that I calculate my remedy for this one individual kingdom of Ireland and for no other that ever was, is, or I think ever can be upon earth. Therefore let no man talk to me of other expedients: of taxing our absentees at five shillings a pound: of using neither clothes nor household furniture except what is of our own growth and manufacture: of utterly rejecting the materials and instruments that promote foreign luxury: of curing the expensiveness of pride, vanity, idleness, and gaming in our women: of introducing a vein of parsimony, prudence, and temperance: of learning to love our country, in the want of which we differ even from Laplanders and the inhabitants of Topinamboo:[11] of quitting our animosities and factions, nor acting any longer like the Jews, who were murdering one another at the very moment their city was taken:[12] of being a little cautious not to sell our country and conscience for nothing: of teaching landlords to have at least one degree of mercy toward their tenants: lastly, of putting a spirit of honesty, industry, and skill into our shopkeepers; who, if a resolution could now be taken to buy only our native goods, would immediately unite to cheat and exact upon us in the price, the measure, and the goodness, nor could ever yet be brought to make one fair proposal of just dealing, though often and earnestly invited to it.

Therefore I repeat, let no man talk to me of these and the like expedients, till he hath at least some glimpse of hope that there will ever be some hearty and sincere attempt to put them in practice.

But as to myself, having been wearied out for many years with offering vain, idle, visionary thoughts, and at length utterly despairing of success, I fortunately fell upon this proposal, which, as it is wholly new, so it hath something solid and real, of no expense and little trouble, full in our own power, and whereby we can incur no danger in disobliging England. For this kind of commodity will not bear exportation, the flesh being of too tender a consistence to admit a long continuance in salt, although perhaps I could name a country which would be glad to eat up our whole nation without it.

After all, I am not so violently bent upon my own opinion as to reject any offer proposed by wise men, which shall be found equally innocent, cheap, easy, and effectual. But before something of that kind shall be advanced in contradiction to my scheme, and offering a better, I desire the author or authors will be pleased maturely to consider two points. First, as things now stand, how they will be able to find food and raiment for an hundred thousand useless mouths and backs. And secondly, there being a round million of creatures in human figure throughout this kingdom, whose sole subsistence put into a common stock would leave them in debt two millions

---

[11] District of Brazil.

[12] During the Roman siege of Jerusalem (A.D. 70), prominent Jews were charged with collaborating with the enemy and put to death.

of pounds sterling, adding those who are beggars by profession to the bulk of farmers, cottagers, and laborers, with their wives and children who are beggars in effect; I desire those politicians who dislike my overture, and may perhaps be so bold to attempt an answer, that they will first ask the parents of these mortals whether they would not at this day think it a great happiness to have been sold for food at a year old in this manner I prescribe, and thereby have avoided such a perpetual scene of misfortunes as they have since gone through by the oppression of landlords, the impossibility of paying rent without money or trade, the want of common sustenance, with neither house nor clothes to cover them from the inclemencies of the weather, and the most inevitable prospect of entailing the like of greater miseries upon their breed forever.

I profess, in the sincerity of my heart, that I have not the least personal interest in endeavoring to promote this necessary work, having no other motive than the public good of my country, by advancing our trade, providing for infants, relieving the poor, and giving some pleasure to the rich. I have no children by which I can propose to get a single penny; the youngest being nine years old, and my wife past childbearing.

DISCUSSION QUESTIONS

1. What implicit assumption about the treatment of the Irish underlies Swift's proposal? Do expressions such as "just dropped from its dam" (para. 4) and "whose wives are breeders" (para. 6) give the reader a clue?

2. In this essay Swift assumes a persona; that is, for the purposes of the proposal he makes, he pretends to be a different person. Describe the characteristics of that person. Point out the places in the essay that reveal them.

3. In several places, however, Swift reveals himself as the outraged witness of English cruelty and indifference. Note the language that seems to reflect his own feelings.

4. Throughout the essay Swift recites lists of facts, many of them in the form of statistics. How do these facts contribute to the persuasiveness of his argument? How do they affect the reader?

5. What social practices and attitudes of both the Irish and the English does Swift condemn?

6. Does Swift offer any solutions for the problems he attacks? How do you know?

7. When this essay first appeared in 1729, some readers took it seriously and accused Swift of monstrous cruelty. Can you think of reasons that these readers failed to recognize the ironic intent?

WRITING SUGGESTIONS

8. Try an ironical essay of your own. Choose a subject that clearly lends itself to such treatment. As Swift did, use logic and restraint in your language.

9. Choose a problem for which you think you have a solution. Defend your solution by using the stock issues as your pattern of organization.

Civil Disobedience

HENRY DAVID THOREAU

I heartily accept the motto, — "That government is best which governs least"; and I should like to see it acted up to more rapidly and systematically. Carried out, it finally amounts to this, which also I believe, — "That government is best which governs not at all"; and when men are prepared for it, that will be the kind of government which they will have. Government is at best but an expedient; but most governments are usually, and all governments are sometimes, inexpedient. The objections which have been brought against a standing army, and they are many and weighty, and deserve to prevail, may also at last be brought against a standing government. The standing army is only an arm of the standing government. The government itself, which is only the mode which the people have chosen to execute their will, is equally liable to be abused and perverted before the people can act through it. Witness the present Mexican war, the work of comparatively a few individuals using the standing government as their tool; for, in the outset, the people would not have consented to this measure.

This American government, — what is it but a tradition, though a recent one, endeavoring to transmit itself unimpaired to posterity, but each instant losing some of its integrity? It has not the vitality and force of a single living man; for a single man can bend it to his will. It is a sort of wooden gun to the people themselves. But it is not the less necessary for this; for the people must have some complicated machinery or other, and hear its din, to satisfy that idea of government which they have. Governments show thus how successfully men can be imposed on, even impose on themselves, for their own advantage. It is excellent, we must all allow. Yet this government never of itself furthered any enterprise, but by the alacrity with which it got out of its way. *It* does not keep the country free. *It* does not settle the West. *It* does not educate. The character inherent in the American people has done all that has been accomplished; and it would have done somewhat more, if the government had not sometimes got in its way. For government is an expedient by which men would fain succeed in letting one another alone; and, as has been said, when it is most expedient, the governed are most let alone by it. Trade and commerce, if they were not made of India-rubber, would never manage to bounce over the obstacles which legislators are continually putting in their way; and, if one were to judge these men wholly by the effects of their actions, and not partly by their intentions,

Henry David Thoreau (1817–1862), philosopher and writer, is best known for *Walden*, an account of his solitary retreat to Walden Pond, near Concord, Massachusetts. Here he remained for more than two years in an effort to "live deliberately, to front only the essential facts of life." "Civil Disobedience" was first given as a lecture in 1848 and published in 1849. It was widely read and influenced both Mahatma Gandhi in the passive-resistance campaign he led against the British in India and Martin Luther King Jr. in the U.S. civil rights movement.

they would deserve to be classed and punished with those mischievous persons who put obstructions on the railroads.

But, to speak practically and as a citizen, unlike those who call themselves no-government men, I ask for, not at once no government, but *at once* a better government. Let every man make known what kind of government would command his respect, and that will be one step toward obtaining it.

After all, the practical reason why, when the power is once in the hands of the people, a majority are permitted, and for a long period continue, to rule, is not because they are most likely to be in the right, nor because this seems fairest to the minority, but because they are physically the strongest. But a government in which the majority rule in all cases cannot be based on justice, even as far as men understand it. Can there not be a government in which majorities do not virtually decide right and wrong, but conscience? — in which majorities decide only those questions to which the rule of expediency is applicable? Must the citizen ever for a moment, or in the least degree, resign his conscience to the legislator? Why has every man a conscience, then? I think that we should be men first, and subjects afterward. It is not desirable to cultivate a respect for the law, so much as for the right. The only obligation which I have a right to assume, is to do at any time what I think right. It is truly enough said, that a corporation has no conscience; but a corporation of conscientious men is a corporation *with* a conscience. Law never made men a whit more just; and, by means of their respect for it, even the well-disposed are daily made the agents of injustice. A common and natural result of an undue respect for law is, that you may see a file of soldiers, colonel, captain, corporal, privates, powder-monkeys, and all, marching in admirable order over hill and dale to the wars, against their wills, aye, against their common sense and consciences, which makes it very steep marching indeed, and produces a palpitation of the heart. They have no doubt that it is a damnable business in which they are concerned; they are all peaceably inclined. Now, what are they? Men at all? or small moveable forts and magazines, at the service of some unscrupulous man in power? Visit the Navy-Yard, and behold a marine, such a man as an American government can make, or such as it can make a man with its black arts, — a mere shadow and reminiscence of humanity, a man laid out alive and standing, and already, as one may say, buried under arms with funeral accompaniments, though it may be, —

> Not a drum was heard, nor a funeral note,
> As his corse to the rampart we hurried;
> Not a soldier discharged his farewell shot
> O'er the grave where our hero we buried.

The mass of men serve the state thus, not as men mainly, but as machines, with   5
their bodies. They are the standing army, and the militia, jailers, constables, posse comitatus, &c. In most cases there is no free exercise whatever of the judgment or of the moral sense; but they put themselves on a level with wood and earth and stones; and wooden men can perhaps be manufactured that will serve the purpose as well. Such command no more respect than men of straw, or a lump of dirt. They have the same sort of worth only as horses and dogs. Yet such as these even are commonly esteemed good citizens. Others, — as most legislators, politicians, lawyers, ministers,

and office-holders, — serve the State chiefly with their heads; and, as they rarely make any moral distinctions, they are as likely to serve the Devil, without *intending* it, as God. A very few, as heroes, patriots, martyrs, reformers in the great sense, and *men*, serve the state with their consciences also, and so necessarily resist it for the most part, and they are commonly treated as enemies by it. A wise man will only be useful as a man, and will not submit to be "clay," and "stop a hole to keep the wind away," but leave that office to his dust at least: —

> I am too high-born to be propertied,
> To be a secondary at control,
> Or useful serving-man and instrument
> To any sovereign state throughout the world.

He who gives himself entirely to his fellow-men appears to them useless and selfish; but he who gives himself partially to them is pronounced a benefactor and philanthropist.

How does it become a man to behave toward this American government today? I answer that he cannot without disgrace be associated with it. I cannot for an instant recognize that political organization as *my* government which is the *slave's* government also.

All men recognize the right of revolution; that is, the right to refuse allegiance to, and to resist, the government, when its tyranny or its inefficiency are great and unendurable. But almost all say that such is not the case now. But such was the case, they think, in the Revolution of '75. If one were to tell me that this was a bad government because it taxed certain foreign commodities brought to its ports, it is most probable that I should not make an ado about it, for I can do without them. All machines have their friction; and possibly this does enough good to counterbalance the evil. At any rate, it is a great evil to make a stir about it. But when the friction comes to have its machine, and oppression and robbery are organized, I say, let us not have such a machine any longer. In other words, when a sixth of the population of a nation which has undertaken to be the refuge of liberty are slaves, and a whole country is unjustly overrun and conquered by a foreign army, and subjected to military law, I think that it is not too soon for honest men to rebel and revolutionize. What makes this duty the more urgent is the fact, that the country so overrun is not our own, but ours is the invading army.

Paley, a common authority with many on moral questions, in his chapter on the "Duty of Submission to Civil Government," resolves all civil obligation into expediency; and he proceeds to say, "that so long as the interest of the whole society requires it, that is, so long as the established government cannot be resisted or changed without public inconveniency, it is the will of God that the established government be obeyed, and no longer. . . . This principle being admitted, the justice of every particular case of resistance is reduced to a computation of the quantity of the danger and grievance on the one side, and of the probability and expense of redressing it on the other." Of this, he says, every man shall judge for himself. But Paley appears never to have contemplated those cases to which the rule of expediency does not apply, in which a people, as well as an individual, must do justice, cost what it may. If I have unjustly wrested a plank from a drowning man, I must restore it to him though I drown myself. This, according to Paley, would be inconvenient. But he that would save his life, in such a case, shall lose it. This people must cease to hold slaves, and to make war on Mexico, though it cost them their existence as a people.

In their practice, nations agree with Paley; but does any one think that Massachusetts does exactly what is right at the present crisis? 10

> A drab of state, a cloth-'o-silver slut,
> To have her train borne up, and her soul trail in the dirt.

Practically speaking, the opponents to a reform in Massachusetts are not a hundred thousand politicians at the South, but a hundred thousand merchants and farmers here, who are more interested in commerce and agriculture than they are in humanity, and are not prepared to do justice to the slave and to Mexico, *cost what it may*. I quarrel not with far-off foes, but with those who, near at home, cooperate with, and do the bidding of, those far away, and without whom the latter would be harmless. We are accustomed to say, that the mass of men are unprepared; but improvement is slow, because the few are not materially wiser or better than the many. It is not so important that many should be as good as you, as that there be some absolute goodness somewhere; for that will leaven the whole lump. There are thousands who are *in opinion* opposed to slavery and to the war, who yet in effect do nothing to put an end to them; who, esteeming themselves children of Washington and Franklin, sit down with their hands in their pockets, and say that they know not what to do, and do nothing; who even postpone the question of freedom to the question of free-trade, and quietly read the prices-current along with the latest advice from Mexico, after dinner, and, it may be, fall asleep over them both. What is the price-current of an honest man and patriot today? They hesitate, and they regret, and sometimes they petition; but they do nothing in earnest and with effect. They will wait, well disposed, for others to remedy the evil, that they may no longer have it to regret. At most, they give only a cheap vote, and a feeble countenance and God-speed, to the right, as it goes by them. There are nine hundred and ninety-nine patrons of virtue to one virtuous man; but it is easier to deal with the real possessor of a thing than with the temporary guardian of it.

All voting is a sort of gaming, like checkers or backgammon, with a slight moral tinge to it, a playing with right and wrong, with moral questions; and betting naturally accompanies it. The character of the voters is not staked. I cast my vote, perchance, as I think right; but I am not vitally concerned that that right should prevail. I am willing to leave it to the majority. Its obligation, therefore, never exceeds that of expediency. Even voting *for the right* is *doing* nothing for it. It is only expressing to men feebly your desire that it should prevail. A wise man will not leave the right to the mercy of chance, nor wish it to prevail through the power of the majority. There is but little virtue in the action of masses of men. When the majority shall at length vote for the abolition of slavery, it will be because they are indifferent to slavery, or because there is but little slavery left to be abolished by their vote. *They* will then be the only slaves. Only *his* vote can hasten the abolition of slavery who asserts his own freedom by his vote.

I hear of a convention to be held at Baltimore, or elsewhere, for the selection of a candidate for the presidency, made up chiefly of editors, and men who are politicians by profession; but I think, what is it to any independent, intelligent, and respectable man what decision they may come to? Shall we not have the advantage of his wisdom and honesty, nevertheless? Can we not count upon some independent votes? Are there not many individuals in the country who do not attend conventions? But no: I find that the respectable man, so called, has immediately drifted from his position, and despairs of his country, when his country has more reason to despair of him. He forthwith adopts one of the candidates thus selected as the only *available* one, thus providing that he is himself *available* for any purposes of the demagogue. His vote is of no more worth than that of any unprincipled foreigner or hireling native, who may have been bought. O for a man who is *a man*, and, as my neighbor says, has a bone in his back which you cannot pass your hand through! Our statistics are at fault: The population has been returned too large. How many *men* are there to a square thousand miles in this country? Hardly one. Does not America offer any inducement for men to settle here? The American has dwindled into an Odd Fellow, — one who may be known by the development of his organ of gregariousness, and a manifest lack of intellect and cheerful self-reliance; whose first and chief concern, on coming into the world, is to see that the Almshouses are in good repair; and, before yet he has lawfully donned the virile garb, to collect a fund for the support of the widows and orphans that may be; who, in short, ventures to live only by the aid of the Mutual Insurance company, which has promised to bury him decently.

It is not a man's duty, as a matter of course, to devote himself to the eradication of any, even the most enormous wrong; he may still properly have other concerns to engage him; but it is his duty, at least, to wash his hands of it, and, if he gives it no thought longer, not to give it practically his support. If I devote myself to other pursuits and contemplations, I must first see, at least, that I do not pursue them sitting upon another man's shoulders. I must get off him first, that he may pursue his contemplations too. See what gross inconsistency is tolerated. I have heard some of my townsmen say, "I should like to have them order me out to help put down an insurrection of the slaves, or to march to Mexico; — see if I would go"; and yet these very men have each, directly by their allegiance, and so indirectly, at least, by their money, furnished a substitute. The soldier is applauded who refuses to serve in an unjust war by those who do not refuse to sustain the unjust government which makes the war; is applauded by those whose own act and authority he disregards and sets at nought; as if the State were penitent to that degree that it hired one to scourge it while it sinned, but not to that degree that it left off sinning for a moment. Thus, under the name of Order and Civil Government, we are all made at last to pay homage to and support our own meanness. After the first blush of sin, comes its indifference; and from immoral it becomes, as it were, *un*moral, and not quite unnecessary to that life which we have made.

The broadest and most prevalent error requires the most disinterested virtue to sustain it. The slight reproach to which the virtue of patriotism is commonly liable, the noble are most likely to incur. Those who, while they disapprove of the character and measures of a government, yield to it their allegiance and support, are undoubtedly its most conscientious supporters, and so frequently the most serious obstacles to reform. Some are petitioning the State to dissolve the Union, to disregard the requisitions of the President. Why do they not dissolve it themselves, — the union between themselves and the State, — and refuse to pay their quota into its treasury? Do not they stand in the same relation to the State, that the State does to the Union? And have not the same reasons prevented the State from resisting the Union which have prevented them from resisting the State?

How can a man be satisfied to entertain an opinion merely, and enjoy *it*? Is there   15 any enjoyment in it, if his opinion is that he is aggrieved? If you are cheated out of a single dollar by your neighbor, you do not rest satisfied with knowing that you are cheated, or with saying that you are cheated, or even with petitioning him to pay you your due; but you take effectual steps at once to obtain the full amount, and see that you are never cheated again. Action from principle, the perception and the performance of right, changes things and relations; it is essentially revolutionary, and does not consist wholly with anything which was. It not only divides states and churches, it divides families; ay, it divides the *individual*, separating the diabolical in him from the divine.

Unjust laws exist: Shall we be content to obey them, or shall we endeavor to amend them, and obey them until we have succeeded, or shall we transgress them at once? Men generally, under such a government as this, think that they ought to wait until they have persuaded the majority to alter them. They think that, if they should resist, the remedy would be worse than the evil. But it is the fault of the government itself that the remedy *is* worse than the evil. *It* makes it worse. Why is it not more apt to anticipate and provide for reform? Why does it not cherish its wise minority? Why does it cry and resist before it is hurt? Why does it not encourage its citizens to be on the alert to point out its faults, and *do* better than it would have them? Why does it always crucify Christ, and excommunicate Copernicus and Luther, and pronounce Washington and Franklin rebels?

One would think, that a deliberate and practical denial of its authority was the only offence never contemplated by government; else, why has it not assigned its definite, its suitable and proportionate penalty? If a man who has no property refuses but once to earn nine shillings for the State, he is put in prison for a period unlimited by any law that I know, and determined only by the discretion of those who placed him there; but if he should steal ninety times nine shillings from the State, he is soon permitted to go at large again.

If the injustice is part of the necessary friction of the machine of government, let it go, let it go: Perchance it will wear smooth, — certainly the machine will wear out. If the injustice has a spring, or a pulley, or a rope, or a crank, exclusively for itself, then perhaps you may consider whether the remedy will not be worse than the evil; but if it is of such a nature that it requires you to be the agent of injustice to another, then, I say, break the law. Let your life be a counter friction to stop the machine. What I have to do is to see, at any rate, that I do not lend myself to the wrong which I condemn.

As for adopting the ways which the State has provided for remedying the evil, I know not of such ways. They take too much time, and a man's life will be gone.

I have other affairs to attend to. I came into this world, not chiefly to make this a good place to live in, but to live in it, be it good or bad. A man has not everything to do, but something; and because he cannot do *everything*, it is not necessary that he should do *something* wrong. It is not my business to be petitioning the Governor or the Legislature any more than it is theirs to petition me; and, if they should not hear my petition, what should I do then? But in this case the State has provided no way: Its very Constitution is the evil. This may seem to be harsh and stubborn and unconciliatory; but it is to treat with the utmost kindness and consideration the only spirit that can appreciate or deserves it. So is all change for the better, like birth and death, which convulse the body.

I do not hesitate to say, that those who call themselves Abolitionists should at 20 once effectually withdraw their support, both in person and property, from the government of Massachusetts, and not wait till they constitute a majority of one, before they suffer the right to prevail through them. I think that it is enough if they have God on their side, without waiting for that other one. Moreover, any man more right than his neighbors, constitutes a majority of one already.

I meet this American government, or its representative, the State government, directly, and face to face, once a year — no more — in the person of its tax-gatherer; this is the only mode in which a man situated as I am necessarily meets it; and it then says distinctly, Recognize me; and the simplest, the most effectual, and, in the present posture of affairs, the indispensablest mode of treating with it on this head, of expressing your little satisfaction with and love for it, is to deny it then. My civil neighbor, the tax-gatherer, is the very man I have to deal with, — for it is, after all, with men and not with parchment that I quarrel, — and he has voluntarily chosen to be an agent of the government. How shall he ever know well what he is and does as an officer of the government, or as a man, until he is obliged to consider whether he shall treat me, his neighbor, for whom he has respect, as a neighbor and well-disposed man, or as a maniac and disturber of the peace, and see if he can get over this obstruction to his neighborliness without a ruder and more impetuous thought or speech corresponding with his action? I know this well, that if one thousand, if one hundred, if ten men whom I could name, — if ten *honest* men only, — aye, if *one* HONEST man, in this State of Massachusetts, *ceasing to hold slaves*, were actually to withdraw from this copartnership, and be locked up in the county jail therefor, it would be the abolition of slavery in America. For it matters not how small the beginning may seem to be: What is once well done is done forever. But we love better to talk about it: That we say is our mission. Reform keeps many scores of newspapers in its service, but not one man. If my esteemed neighbor, the State's ambassador, who will devote his days to the settlement of the question of human rights in the Council Chamber, instead of being threatened with the prisons of Carolina, were to sit down the prisoner of Massachusetts, that State which is so anxious to foist the sin of slavery upon her sister, — though at present she can discover only an act of inhospitality to be the ground of a quarrel with her, — the Legislature would not wholly waive the subject the following winter.

Under a government which imprisons any unjustly, the true place for a just man is also a prison. The proper place today, the only place which Massachusetts has provided for her freer and less desponding spirits, is in her prisons, to be put out and locked out of the State by her own act, as they have already put themselves out by their principles. It is there that the fugitive slave, and the Mexican prisoner on parole, and the Indian come to plead the wrongs of his race, should find them; on that separate, but more free and honorable ground, where the State places those who are not *with* her, but *against* her, — the only house in a slave State in which a free man can abide with honor. If any think that their influence would be lost there, and their voices no longer afflict the ear of the State, that they would not be as an enemy within its walls, they do not know by how much truth is stronger than error, nor how much more eloquently and effectively he can combat injustice who has experienced a little in his own person. Cast your whole vote, not a strip of paper merely, but your whole influence. A minority is powerless while it conforms to the majority; it is not even a minority then; but it is irresistible when it clogs by its whole weight. If the alternative is to keep all just men in prison, or give up war and slavery, the State will not hesitate which to choose. If a thousand men were not to pay their tax-bills this year, that would not be a violent and bloody measure, as it would be to pay them, and enable the State to commit violence and shed innocent blood. This is, in fact, the definition of a peaceable revolution, if any such is possible. If the tax-gatherer, or any other public officer, asks me, as one has done, "But what shall I do?" my answer is, "If you really wish to do any thing, resign your office." When the subject has refused allegiance, and the officer has resigned his office, then the revolution is accomplished. But even suppose blood should flow. Is there not a sort of blood shed when the conscience is wounded? Through this wound a man's real manhood and immortality flow out, and he bleeds to an everlasting death. I see this blood flowing now.

I have contemplated the imprisonment of the offender, rather than the seizure of his goods, — though both will serve the same purpose, — because they who assert the purest right, and consequently are most dangerous to a corrupt State, commonly have not spent much time in accumulating property. To such the State renders comparatively small service, and a slight tax is wont to appear exorbitant, particularly if they are obliged to earn it by special labor with their hands. If there were one who lived wholly without the use of money, the State itself would hesitate to demand it of him. But the rich man, — not to make any invidious comparison, — is always sold to the institution which makes him rich. Absolutely speaking, the more money, the less virtue; for money comes between a man and his objects, and obtains them for him; and it was certainly no great virtue to obtain it. It puts to rest many questions which he would otherwise be taxed to answer; while the only new question which it puts is the hard but superfluous one, how to spend it. Thus his moral ground is taken from under his feet. The opportunities of living are diminished in proportion as what are called the "means" are increased. The best thing a man can do for his culture when he is rich is to endeavor to carry out those schemes which he entertained when he was poor. Christ answered the Herodians according to their condition. "Show me the tribute-money," said he; — and one took a penny out of his pocket; — if you use money which has the image of Cæsar on it, and which he has made current and valuable, that is, *if you are men of the State*, and gladly enjoy the advantages of Cæsar's government, then pay him back some of his own when he demands it; "Render therefore to Cæsar that which is Cæsar's, and to God those things which are God's," — leaving them no wiser than before as to which was which; for they did not wish to know.

When I converse with the freest of my neighbors, I perceive that, whatever they may say about the magnitude and seriousness of the question, and their regard for the public tranquility, the long and the short of the matter is, that they cannot spare the protection of the existing government, and they dread the consequences to their property and families of disobedience to it. For my own part, I should not like to think that I ever rely on the protection of the State. But, if I deny the authority of the State when it presents its tax-bill, it will soon take and waste all my property, and so harass me and my children without end. This is hard. This makes it impossible for a man to live honestly, and at the same time comfortably, in outward respects. It will not be worth the while to accumulate property; that would be sure to go again. You must hire or squat somewhere, and raise but a small crop, and eat that soon. You must live within yourself, and depend upon yourself always tucked up and ready for a start, and not have many affairs. A man may grow rich in Turkey even, if he will be in all respects a good subject of the Turkish government. Confucius said: "If a state is governed by the principles of reason, poverty and misery are subjects of shame; if a state is not governed by the principles of reason, riches and honors are the subjects of shame." No: Until I want the protection of Massachusetts to be extended to me in some distant southern port, where my liberty is endangered, or until I am bent solely on building up an estate at home by peaceful enterprise, I can afford to refuse allegiance to Massachusetts, and her right to my property and life. It costs me less in every sense to incur the penalty of disobedience to the State, than it would to obey. I should feel as if I were worth less in that case.

Some years ago, the State met me in behalf of the Church, and commanded me 25 to pay a certain sum toward the support of a clergyman whose preaching my father attended, but never I myself. "Pay," it said, "or be locked up in the jail." I declined to pay. But, unfortunately, another man saw fit to pay it. I did not see why the schoolmaster should be taxed to support the priest, and not the priest the schoolmaster; for I was not the State's schoolmaster, but I supported myself by voluntary subscription. I did not see why the lyceum should not present its tax-bill, and have the State to back its demand, as well as the Church. However, at the request of the selectmen, I condescended to make some such statement as this in writing: — "Know all men by these presents, that I, Henry Thoreau, do not wish to be regarded as a member of any incorporated society which I have not joined." This I gave to the town clerk; and he has it. The State, having thus learned that I did not wish to be regarded as a member of that church, has never made a like demand on me since; though it said that it must adhere to its original presumption that time. If I had known how to name them, I should then have signed off in detail from all the societies which I never signed on to; but I did not know where to find a complete list.

I have paid no poll-tax for six years. I was put into a jail once on this account, for one night; and, as I stood considering the walls of solid stone, two or three feet thick, the door of wood and iron, a foot thick, and the iron grating which strained the light, I could not help being struck with the foolishness of that institution which treated me as if I were mere flesh and blood and bones, to be locked up. I wondered that it should have concluded at length that this was the best use it could put me to, and had never thought to avail itself of my services in some way. I saw that, if there was a wall of stone between me and my townsmen, there was a still more difficult one to climb or break through, before they could get to be as free as I was. I did not for a moment feel confined, and the walls seemed a great waste of stone and mortar. I felt as if I alone of all my townsmen had paid my tax. They plainly did not know how to treat me, but behaved like persons who are underbred. In every threat and in every compliment there was a blunder; for they thought that my chief desire was to stand the other side of that stone wall. I could not but smile to see how industriously they locked the door on my meditations, which followed them out again without let or hindrance, and *they* were really all that was dangerous. As they could not reach me, they had resolved to punish my body; just as boys, if they cannot come at some person against whom they have a spite, will abuse his dog. I saw that the State was half-witted, and it was timid as a lone woman with her silver spoons, and that it did not know its friends from its foes, and I lost all my remaining respect for it, and pitied it.

Thus the State never intentionally confronts a man's sense, intellectual or moral, but only his body, his senses. It is not armed with superior wit or honesty, but with superior physical strength. I was not born to be forced. I will breathe after my own fashion. Let us see who is the strongest. What force has a multitude? They only can force me who obey a higher law than I. They force me to become like themselves. I do not hear of *men* being *forced* to live this way or that by masses of men. What sort of life were that to live? When I meet a government which says to me, "Your money or your life," why should I be in haste to give it my money? It may be in a great strait, and not know what to do: I cannot help that. It must help itself; do as I do. It is not worth the while to snivel about it. I am not responsible for the successful working of the machinery of society. I am not the son of the engineer. I perceive that, when an acorn and a chestnut fall side by side, the one does not remain inert to make way for the other, but both obey their own laws, and spring and grow and flourish as best they can, till one, perchance, overshadows and destroys the other. If a plant cannot live according to its nature, it dies; and so a man.

The night in prison was novel and interesting enough. The prisoners in their shirt-sleeves were enjoying a chat and the evening air in the doorway, when I entered. But the jailer said, "Come, boys, it is time to lock up"; and so they dispersed, and I heard the sound of their steps returning into the hollow apartments. My roommate was introduced to me by the jailer, as "a first-rate fellow and a clever man." When the door was locked, he showed me where to hang my hat, and how he managed matters there. The rooms were white-washed once a month; and this one, at least, was the whitest, most simply furnished, and probably the neatest apartment in the town. He naturally wanted to know where I came from, and what brought me there; and, when I had told him, I asked him in my turn how he came there, presuming him to be an honest man, of course; and, as the world goes, I believe he was. "Why," said he, "they accuse me of burning a barn; but I never did it." As near as I could discover, he had probably gone to bed in a barn when drunk, and smoked his pipe there; and so a barn was burnt. He had the reputation of being a clever man, had been there some three months waiting for his trial to come on, and would have to wait as much longer; but he was quite domesticated and contented, since he got his board for nothing, and thought that he was well-treated.

He occupied one window, and I the other; and I saw, that if one stayed there long, his principal business would be to look out the window. I had soon read all the tracts that were left there, and examined where former prisoners had broken out, and where a grate had been sawed off, and heard the history of the various occupants of that room; for I found that even here there was a history and a gossip which never circulated beyond the walls of the jail. Probably this is the only house in the town where verses are composed, which are afterward printed in a circular form, but not published. I was shown quite a long list of verses which were composed by some young men who had been detected in an attempt to escape, who avenged themselves by singing them.

I pumped my fellow-prisoner as dry as I could, for fear I should never see him again; but at length he showed me which was my bed, and left me to blow out the lamp. 30

It was like travelling into a far country, such as I had never expected to behold, to lie there for one night. It seemed to me that I never had heard the town-clock strike before, nor the evening sounds of the village; for we slept with the windows open, which were inside the grating. It was to see my native village in the light of the Middle Ages, and our Concord was turned into a Rhine stream, and visions of knights and castles passed before me. They were the voices of old burghers that I heard in the streets. I was an involuntary spectator and auditor of whatever was done and said in the kitchen of the adjacent village-inn, — a wholly new and rare experience to me. It was a closer view of my native town. I was fairly inside of it. I never had seen its institutions before. This is one of its peculiar institutions; for it is a shire town. I began to comprehend what its inhabitants were about.

In the morning, our breakfasts were put through the hole in the door, in small oblong-square tin pans, made to fit, and holding a pint of chocolate, with brown bread, and an iron spoon. When they called for the vessels again, I was green enough to return what bread I had left; but my comrade seized it, and said that I should lay that up for lunch or dinner. Soon after, he was let out to work at haying in a neighboring field, whither he went every day, and would not be back till noon; so he bade me good-day, saying that he doubted if he should see me again.

When I came out of prison, — for some one interfered, and paid that tax, — I did not perceive that great changes had taken place on the common, such as he observed who went in a youth, and emerged a tottering and gray-headed man; and yet a change had to my eyes come over the scene, — the town, and State, and country, — greater than any that mere time could effect. I saw yet more distinctly the State in which I lived. I saw to what extent the people among whom I lived could be trusted as good neighbors and friends; that their friendship was for summer weather only; that they did not greatly propose to do right; that they were a distinct race from me by their prejudices and superstitions, as the Chinamen and Malays are; that, in their sacrifices to humanity, they ran no risks, not even to their property; that, after all, they were not so noble but they treated the thief as he had treated them, and hoped, by a certain outward observance and a few prayers, and by walking in a particular straight though useless path from time to time, to save their souls. This may be to judge my neighbors harshly; for I believe that many of them are not aware that they have such an institution as the jail in their village.

It was formerly the custom in our village, when a poor debtor came out of jail, for his acquaintances to salute him, looking through their fingers, which were crossed to represent the grating of a jail window, "How do ye do?" My neighbors did not thus salute me, but first looked at me, and then at one another, as if I had returned from a long journey. I was put into jail as I was going to the shoemaker's to get a shoe which was mended. When I was let out the next morning, I proceeded to finish my errand, and having put on my mended shoe, joined a huckleberry party, who were impatient to put themselves under my conduct; and in half an hour, — for the horse was soon tackled, — was in the midst of a huckleberry field, on one of our highest hills, two miles off, and then the State was nowhere to be seen.

This is the whole story of "My Prisons."   35

I have never declined paying the highway tax, because I am as desirous of being a good neighbor as I am of being a bad subject; and, as for supporting schools, I am doing my part to educate my fellow-countrymen now. It is for no particular item in the tax-bill that I refuse to pay it. I simply wish to refuse allegiance to the State, to withdraw and stand aloof from it effectually. I do not care to trace the course of my dollar, if I could, till it buys a man, or a musket to shoot one with, — the dollar is innocent, — but I am concerned to trace the effects of my allegiance. In fact, I quietly declare war with the State, after my fashion, though I will still make what use and get what advantage of her I can, as is usual in such cases.

If others pay the tax which is demanded of me, from a sympathy with the State, they do but what they have already done in their own case, or rather they abet injustice to a greater extent than the State requires. If they pay the tax from a mistaken interest in the individual taxed, to save his property or prevent his going to jail, it is because they have not considered wisely how far they let their private feelings interfere with the public good.

This, then, is my position at present. But one cannot be too much on his guard in such a case, lest his action be biased by obstinacy, or an undue regard for the opinions of men. Let him see that he does only what belongs to himself and to the hour.

I think sometimes, Why, this people mean well; they are only ignorant; they would do better if they knew how: why give your neighbors this pain to treat you as they are inclined to? But I think again, this is no reason why I should do as they do, or permit others to suffer much greater pain of a different kind. Again, I sometimes say to myself, When many millions of men, without heat, without ill will, without personal feelings of any kind, demand of you a few shillings only, without the possibility, such is their constitution, of retracing or altering their present demand, and without the possibility, on your side, of appeal to any other millions, why expose yourself to this overwhelming brute force? You do not resist cold and hunger, the winds and the waves, thus obstinately; you quietly submit to a thousand similar necessities. You do not put your head into the fire. But just in proportion as I regard this as not wholly a brute force, partly a human force, and consider that I have relations to those millions as to so many millions of men, and not of mere brute or inanimate things, I see that appeal is possible, first and instantaneously, from them to the Maker of them, and, secondly, from them to themselves. But, if I put my head deliberately into the fire, there is no appeal to fire or to the Maker of fire, and I have only myself to blame. If I could convince myself that I have any right to be satisfied with men as they are, and to treat them according, and not according, in some respects, to my requisitions and expectations of what they and I ought to be, then, like a good Mussulman and fatalist, I should endeavor to be satisfied with things as they are, and say it is the will of God. And, above all, there is this difference between resisting this and a purely brute or natural force, that I can resist this with some effect; but I cannot expect, like Orpheus, to change the nature of the rocks and trees and beasts.

I do not wish to quarrel with any man or nation. I do not wish to split hairs, to   40
make fine distinctions, or set myself up as better than my neighbors. I seek rather, I may say, even an excuse for conforming to the laws of the land. I am but too ready to conform to them. Indeed, I have reason to suspect myself on this head; and each year, as the tax-gatherer comes round, I find myself disposed to review the acts and position of the general and State governments, and the spirit of the people, to discover a pretext for conformity.

> We must affect our country as our parents;
> And if at any time we alienate
> Our love or industry from doing it honor,
> We must respect effects and teach the soul
> Matter of conscience and religion,
> And not desire of rule or benefit.

I believe that the State will soon be able to take all my work of this sort out of my hands, and then I shall be no better a patriot than my fellow-countrymen. Seen from a lower point of view, the Constitution, with all its faults, is very good; the law and the courts are very respectable; even this State and this American government are, in many respects, very admirable and rare things, to be thankful for, such as a great many have described them; but seen from a point of view a little higher, they are what I have described them; seen from a higher still, and the highest, who shall say what they are, or that they are worth looking at or thinking of at all?

However, the government does not concern me much, and I shall bestow the fewest possible thoughts on it. It is not many moments that I live under a government, even in this world. If a man is thought-free, fancy-free, imagination-free, that which *is not* never for a long time appearing *to be* to him, unwise rulers or reformers cannot fatally interrupt him.

I know that most men think differently from myself; but those whose lives are by profession devoted to the study of these or kindred subjects, content me as little as any. Statesmen and legislators, standing so completely within the institution, never distinctly and nakedly behold it. They speak of moving society, but have no resting-place without it. They may be men of a certain experience and discrimination, and have no doubt invented ingenious and even useful systems, for which we sincerely thank them; but all their wit and usefulness lie within certain not very wide limits. They are wont to forget that the world is not governed by policy and expediency. Webster never goes behind government, and so cannot speak with authority about it. His words are wisdom to those legislators who contemplate no essential reform in the existing government; but for thinkers, and those who legislate for all time, he never once glances at the subject. I know of those whose serene and wise speculations on this theme would soon reveal the limits of his mind's range and hospitality. Yet, compared with the cheap professions of most reformers, and the still cheaper wisdom and eloquence of politicians in general, his are almost the only sensible and valuable words, and we thank Heaven for him. Comparatively, he is always strong, original, and, above all, practical. Still his quality is not wisdom, but prudence. The lawyer's truth is not Truth, but consistency, or a consistent expediency. Truth is always in harmony with herself, and is not concerned chiefly to reveal the justice that may consist with wrong-doing. He well deserves to be called, as he has been called, the Defender of the Constitution. There are really no blows to be given by him but defensive ones. He is not a leader, but a follower. His leaders are the men of '87. "I have never made an effort," he says, "and never propose to make an effort; I have never countenanced an effort, and never mean to countenance an effort, to disturb the arrangement as originally made, by which the various States came into the Union." Still thinking of the sanction which the Constitution gives to slavery, he says, "Because it was a part of the original compact, — let it stand." Notwithstanding his special acuteness and ability, he is unable to take a fact out of its merely political relations, and behold it as it lies absolutely to be disposed of by the intellect, — what, for instance, it behooves a man to do here in America today with regard to slavery, but ventures, or is driven, to make some such desperate answer as the following, while professing to speak absolutely, and as a private man, — from which what new and singular code of social duties might be inferred? "The manner," says he, "in which the governments of those States where slavery exists are to regulate it, is for their own consideration, under their responsibility to their constituents, to the general laws of propriety, humanity, and justice, and to God. Associations formed elsewhere, springing from a feeling of humanity, or any other cause, have nothing whatever to do with it. They have never received any encouragement from me, and they never will."[1]

They who know of no purer sources of truth, who have traced up its stream no higher, stand, and wisely stand, by the Bible and the Constitution, and drink at it there with reverence and humility; but they who behold where it comes trickling into this lake or that pool, gird up their loins once more, and continue their pilgrimage toward its fountainhead.

---

[1] These extracts have been inserted since the Lecture was read.

No man with a genius for legislation has appeared in America. They are rare in the history of the world. There are orators, politicians, and eloquent men, by the thousand; but the speaker has not yet opened his mouth to speak, who is capable of settling the much-vexed questions of the day. We love eloquence for its own sake, and not for any truth which it may utter, or any heroism it may inspire. Our legislators have not yet learned the comparative value of free-trade and of freedom, of union, and of rectitude, to a nation. They have no genius or talent for comparatively humble questions of taxation and finance, commerce and manufactures and agriculture. If we were left solely to the wordy wit of legislators in Congress for our guidance, uncorrected by the seasonable experience and the effectual complaints of the people, America would not long retain her rank among the nations. For eighteen hundred years, though perchance I have no right to say it, the New Testament has been written; yet where is the legislator who has wisdom and practical talent enough to avail himself of the light which it sheds on the science of legislation?

The authority of government, even such as I am willing to submit to, — for I will cheerfully obey those who know and can do better than I, and in many things even those who neither know nor can do so well, — is still an impure one: To be strictly just, it must have the sanction and consent of the governed. It can have no pure right over my person and property but what I concede to it. The progress from an absolute to a limited monarchy, from a limited monarchy to a democracy, is a progress toward a true respect for the individual. Even the Chinese philosopher was wise enough to regard the individual as the basis of the empire. Is a democracy, such as we know it, the last improvement possible in government? Is it not possible to take a step further towards recognizing and organizing the rights of man? There will never be a really free and enlightened State, until the State comes to recognize the individual as a higher and independent power, from which all its own power and authority are derived, and treats him accordingly. I please myself with imagining a State at last which can afford to be just to all men, and to treat the individual with respect as a neighbor; which even would not think it inconsistent with its own repose, if a few were to live aloof from it, not meddling with it, nor embraced by it, who fulfilled all the duties of neighbors and fellowmen. A State which bore this kind of fruit, and suffered it to drop off as fast as it ripened, would prepare the way for a still more perfect and glorious State, which also I have imagined, but not yet anywhere seen.

45

DISCUSSION QUESTIONS

1. Summarize briefly Thoreau's reasons for arguing that civil disobedience is sometimes a *duty*.

2. Thoreau, like Martin Luther King Jr. in "Letter from Birmingham Jail" (p. 811), speaks of "unjust laws" (para. 16). Do they agree on the positions that citizens should take in response to these laws? Are Thoreau and King guided by the same principles? In Plato's "Crito" (p. 757), what does Socrates say about obedience to unjust laws?

3. What examples of government policy and action does Thoreau use to prove that civil disobedience is a duty? Explain why they are — or are not — effective.

4. Why do you think Thoreau provides such a detailed account of one day in prison? (Notice that King does not give a description of his confinement.) What observation about the community struck Thoreau when he emerged from jail?

WRITING SUGGESTIONS

5. Argue that civil disobedience to a school policy or action is justified. (Examples might include failure to establish an ethnic studies department, refusal to allow ROTC on campus, refusal to suspend a professor accused of sexual harassment.) Be specific about the injustice of the policy or action and the values that underlie the resistance.

6. Under what circumstances might civil disobedience prove to be dangerous and immoral? Can you think of cases of disobedience when *conscience*, as Thoreau uses the term, did not appear to be the guiding principle? Try to identify what you think is the true motivation for the resistance.

The Crisis

CARRIE CHAPMAN CATT

I have taken for my subject, "The Crisis," because I believe that a crisis has come in our movement which, if recognized and the opportunity seized with vigor, enthusiasm and will, means the final victory of our great cause in the very near future. I am aware that some suffragists do not share this belief; they see no signs nor symptoms today which were not present yesterday; no manifestations in the year 1916 which differ significantly from those in the year 1910. To them, the movement has been a steady, normal growth from the beginning and must so continue until the end. I can only defend my claim with the plea that it is better to *imagine* a crisis where none exists than to fail to recognize one when it comes; for a crisis is a culmination of events which calls for new considerations and new decisions. A failure to answer the call may mean an opportunity lost, a possible victory postponed.

Carrie Chapman Catt (1859–1947) was an outspoken advocate of women's suffrage and the founder of the League of Women Voters. This speech was given in September 1916 in Atlantic City, New Jersey, at a special convention of the National American Woman Suffrage Association, of which she was president. Her powerful speech is one of the one hundred most important speeches in American history. In it she presents the war in Europe taking place at that time as an opportunity to push for women's right to vote. European women had proven to be such effective "war assets" that it would be hard for them to ever be relegated to the inferior positions they had occupied before the war. American women could hardly be satisfied with less.

The object of the life of an organized movement is to secure its aim. Necessarily, it must obey the law of evolution and pass through the stages of agitation and education and finally through the stage of realization. As one has put it: "A new idea floats in the air over the heads of the people and for a long, indefinite period evades their understanding but, by and by, when through familiarity, human vision grows clearer, it is caught out of the clouds and crystalized into law." Such a period comes to every movement and is its crisis. In my judgment, that crucial moment, bidding us to renewed consecration and redoubled activity has come to our cause. I believe our victory hangs within our grasp, inviting us to pluck it out of the clouds and establish it among the good things of the world.

If this be true, the time is past when we should say: "Men and women of America, look upon that wonderful idea up there; see, one day it will come down." Instead, the time has come to shout aloud in every city, village and hamlet, and in tones so clear and jubilant that they will reverberate from every mountain peak and echo from shore to shore: "The Woman's Hour has struck."[1] Suppose suffragists as a whole do not believe a crisis has come and do not extend their hands to grasp the victory, what will happen? Why, we shall all continue to work and our cause will continue to hang, waiting for those who possess a clearer vision and more daring enterprise. On the other hand, suppose we reach out with united earnestness and determination to grasp our victory while it still hangs a bit too high? Has any harm been done? None!

Therefore, fellow suffragists, I invite your attention to the signs which point to a crisis and your consideration of plans for turning the crisis into victory.

First: We are passing through a world crisis. All thinkers of every land tell us so; and that nothing after the great war will be as it was before. Those who profess to know, claim that 100 millions of dollars are being spent on the war every day and that 2 years of war have cost 50 billions of dollars or 10 times more than the total expense of the American Civil War. Our own country has sent 35 millions of dollars abroad for relief expenses.

Were there no other effects to come from the world's war, the transfer of such unthinkably vast sums of money from the usual avenues to those wholly abnormal would give so severe a jolt to organized society that it would vibrate around the world and bring untold changes in its wake.

But three and a half millions of lives have been lost. The number becomes the more impressive when it is remembered that the entire population of the American Colonies was little more than three and one-half millions. These losses have been the lives of men within the age of economic production. They have been taken abruptly from the normal business of the world and every human activity from that of the humblest, unskilled labor to art, science and literature has been weakened by their

5

---

[1] This phrase refers to the frustration of woman's rights activists in the post–Civil War period who were told to defer the demand for woman suffrage because this was "the Negro's hour." [All notes are by Karlyn Kohrs Campbell, the editor of *Man Cannot Speak for Her* (Greenwood, 1989).]

loss. Millions of other men will go to their homes, blind, crippled and incapacitated to do the work they once performed. The stability of human institutions has never before suffered so tremendous a shock. Great men are trying to think out the consequences but one and all proclaim that no imagination can find color or form bold enough to paint the picture of the world after the war. British and Russian, German and Austrian, French and Italian agree that it will lead to social and political revolution throughout the entire world. Whatever comes, they further agree that the war presages a total change in the status of women.

A simple-minded man in West Virginia, when addressed upon the subject of woman suffrage in that state, replied, "We've been so used to keepin' our women down, 'twould seem queer not to." He expressed what greater men feel but do not say. Had the wife of that man spoken in the same clear-thinking fashion, she would have said, "We women have been so used to being kept down that it would seem strange to get up. Nature intended women for doormats." Had she so expressed herself, these two would have put the entire anti-suffrage argument in a nutshell.

In Europe, from the Polar Circle to the Aegean Sea, women have risen as though to answer that argument. Everywhere they have taken the places made vacant by men and in so doing, they have grown in self-respect and in the esteem of their respective nations. In every land, the people have reverted to the primitive division of labor and while the men have gone to war, women have cultivated the fields in order that the army and nation may be fed. No army can succeed and no nation can endure without food; those who supply it are a war power and a peace power.

Women by the thousands have knocked at the doors of munition factories and, in the name of patriotism, have begged for the right to serve their country there. Their services were accepted with hesitation but the experiment once made, won reluctant but universal praise. An official statement recently issued in Great Britain announced that 660,000 women were engaged in making munitions in that country alone. In a recent convention of munition workers, composed of men and women, a resolution was unanimously passed informing the government that they would forego vacations and holidays until the authorities announced that their munition supplies were sufficient for the needs of the war and Great Britain pronounced the act the highest patriotism. Lord Derby addressed such a meeting and said, "When the history of the war is written, I wonder to whom the greatest credit will be given; to the men who went to fight or to the women who are working in a way that many people hardly believed that it was possible for them to work." Lord Sydenham added his tribute. Said he, "It might fairly be claimed that women have helped to save thousands of lives and to change the entire aspect of the war. Wherever intelligence, care and close attention have been needed, women have distinguished themselves." A writer in the *London Times* of July 18, 1916, said: "But, for women, the armies could not have held the field for a month; the national call to arms could not have been made or sustained; the country would have perished of inanition and disorganization. If, indeed, it be true that the people have been one, it is because the genius of women has been lavishly applied to the task of reinforcing and complementing the genius of men. The qualities of steady industry, adaptability, good judgement and

10

concentration of mind which men do not readily associate with women have been conspicuous features."

On fields of battle, in regular and improvised hospitals, women have given tender and skilled care to the wounded and are credited with the restoration of life to many, many thousands. Their heroism and self-sacrifice have been frankly acknowledged by all the governments; but their endurance, their skill, the practicality of their service, seem for the first time, to have been recognized by governments as "war power." So, thinking in war terms, great men have suddenly discovered that women are "war assets." Indeed, Europe is realizing, as it never did before, that women are holding together the civilization for which men are fighting. A great search-light has been thrown upon the business of nation-building and it has been demonstrated in every European land that it is a partnership with equal, but different responsibilities resting upon the two partners.

It is not, however, in direct war work alone that the latent possibilities of women have been made manifest. In all the belligerent lands, women have found their way to high posts of administration where no women would have been trusted two years ago and the testimony is overwhelming that they have filled their posts with entire satisfaction to the authorities. They have dared to stand in pulpits (once too sacred to be touched by the unholy feet of a woman) and there, without protest, have appealed to the Father of All in behalf of their stricken lands. They have come out of the kitchen where there was too little to cook and have found a way to live by driving cabs, motors and streetcars. Many a woman has turned her hungry children over to a neighbor and has gone forth to find food for both mothers and both families of children and has found it in strange places and occupations. Many a drawing-room has been closed and the maid who swept and dusted it is now cleaning streets that the health of the city may be conserved. Many a woman who never before slept in a bed of her own making, or ate food not prepared by paid labor, is now sole mistress of parlor and kitchen.

In all the warring countries, women are postmen [sic], porters, railway conductors, ticket, switch and signal men. Conspicuous advertisements invite women to attend agricultural, milking and motor-car schools. They are employed as police in Great Britain and women detectives have recently been taken on the government staff. In Berlin, there are over 3,000 women streetcar conductors and 3,500 women are employed on the general railways. In every city and country, women are doing work for which they would have been considered incompetent two years ago.

The war will soon end and the armies will return to their native lands. To many a family, the men will never come back. The husband who returns to many a wife, will eat no bread the rest of his life save of her earning.

What, then, will happen after the war? Will the widows left with families to support cheerfully leave their well-paid posts for those commanding lower wages? Not without protest! Will the wives who now must support crippled husbands give up their skilled work and take up the occupations which were open to them before the war? Will they resignedly say: "The woman who has a healthy husband who can earn for her, has a right to tea and raisin cake, but the woman who earns for herself and a husband who has given his all to his country, must be content with butterless bread"? Not without protest! On the contrary, the economic axiom, denied and evaded for centuries, will be blazoned on every factory, counting house and shop: "Equal pay for equal work"; and common justice will slowly, but surely enforce that law. The European woman has risen. She may not realize it yet, but the woman "doormat" in every land has unconsciously become a "doorjamb"! She will have become accustomed to her new dignity by the time the men come home. She will wonder how she ever could have been content lying across the threshold now that she discovers the upright jamb gives so much broader and more normal a vision of things. The men returning may find the new order a bit queer but everything else will be strangely unfamiliar too, and they will soon grow accustomed to all the changes together. The "jamb" will never descend into a "doormat" again.

The male and female anti-suffragists of all lands will puff and blow at the economic change which will come to the women of Europe. They will declare it to be contrary to Nature and to God's plan and that somebody ought to do something about it. Suffragists will accept the change as the inevitable outcome of an unprecedented world's cataclysm over which no human agency had any control and will trust in God to adjust the altered circumstances to the eternal evolution of human society. They will remember that in the long run, all things work together for good, for progress and for human weal.

The economic change is bound to bring political liberty. From every land, there comes the expressed belief that the war will be followed by a mighty, oncoming wave of democracy for it is now well known that the conflict has been one of governments, of kings and Czars, Kaisers and Emperors; not of peoples. The nations involved have nearly all declared that they are fighting to make an end of wars. New and higher ideals of governments and of the rights of the people under them, have grown enormously during the past two years. Another tide of political liberty, similar to that of 1848, but of a thousandfold greater momentum, is rising from battlefield and hospital, from camp and munitions factory, from home and church which, great men of many lands, tell us, is destined to sweep over the world. On the continent, the women say, "It is certain that the vote will come to men and women after the war, perhaps not immediately but soon. In Great Britain, which was the storm centre of the suffrage movement for some years before the war, hundreds of bitter, active opponents have confessed their conversion on account of the war services of women. Already, three great provinces of Canada, Manitoba, Alberta, and Saskatchawan [sic], have given universal suffrage to their women in sheer generous appreciation of their war work. Even Mr. Asquith, world renouned [sic] for his immovable opposition to the Parliamentary suffrage for British women, has given evidence of a change of view.[2] Some months ago, he announced his amazement at the utterly unexpected skill, strength and resource developed by the women and his

---

[2] Herbert Henry Asquith (1852–1928), British prime minister (1908–1916) and leader of the Liberal party until 1925, when he was raised to the peerage; he opposed woman suffrage.

gratitude for their loyalty and devotion. Later, in reply to Mrs. Henry Fawcett, who asked if woman suffrage would be included in a proposed election bill, he said that when the war should end, such a measure would be considered without prejudice carried over from events prior to the war.[3] A public statement issued by Mr. Asquith in August, was couched in such terms as to be interpreted by many as a pledge to include women in the next election bill.

In Great Britain, a sordid appeal which may prove the last straw to break the opposition to woman suffrage, has been added to the enthusiastic appreciation of woman's patriotism and practical service and to the sudden comprehension that motherhood is a national asset which must be protected at any price. A new voters' list is contemplated. A parliamentary election should be held in September but the voters are scattered far and wide. The whole nation is agitated over the questions involved in making a new register. At the same time, there is a constant anxiety over war funds, as is prudent in a nation spending 50 millions of dollars per day. It has been proposed that a large poll tax be assessed upon the voters of the new lists, whereupon a secondary proposal of great force has been offered and that is, that twice as much money would find its way into the public coffers were women added to the voters' list. What nation, with compliments fresh spoken concerning women's patriotism and efficiency, could resist such an appeal?

So it happens that above the roar of cannon, the scream of shrapnel and the whirr of aeroplanes, one who listens may hear the cracking of the fetters which have long bound the European woman to outworn conventions. It has been a frightful price to pay but the fact remains that a womanhood, well started on the way to final emancipation, is destined to step forth from the war. It will be a bewildered, troubled and grief-stricken womanhood with knotty problems of life to solve, but it will be freer to deal with them than women have ever been before.

"The Woman's Hour has struck." It has struck for the women of Europe and for those of all the world. The significance of the changed status of European women has not been lost upon the men and women of our land; our own people are not so unlearned in history, nor so lacking in National pride that they will allow the Republic to lag long behind the Empire, presided over by the descendant of George the Third. If they possess the patriotism and the sense of nationality which should be the inheritance of an American, they will not wait until the war is ended but will boldly lead in the inevitable march of democracy, our own American specialty. Sisters, let me repeat, the Woman's Hour has struck! 20

Second: As the most adamantine rock gives way under the constant dripping of water, so the opposition to woman suffrage in our own country has slowly disintegrated before the increasing strength of our movement. Turn backward the pages of our history! Behold, brave Abbie Kelley rotten-egged because she, a woman, essayed

---

[3] Millicent Garrett Fawcett, the leading figure in the National Union of Women's Suffrage Societies, which began in 1867 and stood apart from the more militant suffrage organizations.

to speak in public.[4] Behold the Polish Ernestine Rose startled that women of free America drew aside their skirts when she proposed that they should control their own property.[5] Recall the saintly Lucretia Mott and the legal-minded Elizabeth Cady Stanton, turned out of the [W]orld's Temperance Convention in London and conspiring together to free their sex from the world's stupid oppressions.[6] Remember the gentle, sweet-voiced Lucy Stone, egged because she publicly claimed that women had brains capable of education.[7] Think upon Dr. Elizabeth Blackwell, snubbed and boycotted by other women because she proposed to study medicine.[8] Behold Dr. Antoinette Brown Blackwell, standing in sweet serenity before an Assembly of howling clergymen, angry that she, a woman dared to attend a Temperance Convention as a delegate. Revere the intrepid Susan B. Anthony mobbed from Buffalo to Albany because she demanded fair play for women. These are they who builded with others the foundation of political liberty for American women.

Those who came after only laid the stones in place. Yet, what a wearisome task even that has been! Think of the wonderful woman who has wandered from village to village, from city to city, for a generation compelling men and women to listen and to reflect by her matchless eloquence. Where in all the world's history has any movement among men produced so invincible an advocate as our own Dr. Anna Howard Shaw? Those whom she has led to the light are Legion. Think, too, of the consecration, the self-denial, the never-failing constancy of that other noble soul set in a frail but unflinching body, — the heroine we know as Alice Stone Blackwell![9] A woman who never forgets, who detects the slightest flaw in the weapons of her adversary, who knows the most vulnerable spot in his armor, president over the *Woman's Journal* and, like a lamp in lighthouse, the rays of her intelligence, far-sightedness

[4] Abigail ("Abby") Kelley [Foster] (1810–1887), abolitionist and woman's rights lecturer, spoke first in 1838 to a mixed audience in Philadelphia's Pennsylvania Hall. A powerful agitator, she was attacked as a Jezebel and faced angry mobs outraged at a woman speaking effectively to mixed audiences against slavery.

[5] An allusion to the 1836 effort to petition the New York Legislature to amend the Married Woman's Property Act.

[6] Lucretia Coffin Mott and other women were not seated as delegates at the World Anti-Slavery Convention in 1840. Cady Stanton was present but not a delegate.

[7] Lucy Stone (1818–1893), the first Massachusetts woman to take [earn] a college degree (Oberlin, 1847). She became a lecturer for the American Anti-Slavery Society, but also spoke on woman's rights prior to the emergence of a movement, fearlessly facing hostile audiences. Defying convention, she kept her own name after her marriage to Henry Blackwell in 1855. She became the leader of the New England wing of the suffrage movement, a founder of the American Woman Suffrage Association and of the *Woman's Journal* (1870), which after 1872 she and her husband, and later her daughter, Alice Stone Blackwell, edited.

[8] Elizabeth Blackwell (1821–1910), the first woman of modern times to graduate in medicine. She received her degree in 1849 from Geneva College, and founded the New York Infirmary for Women and Children in 1857, and the Woman's Medical College of the New York Infirmary in 1868.

[9] Daughter of Lucy Stone and Henry Blackwell (1857–1950). Following graduation from Boston University in 1881, she bore the main burdens of editing the *Woman's Journal*, the country's leading woman's rights newspaper founded by her parents, for the next thirty-five years.

and clear-thinking have enlightened the world concerning our cause. The names of hundreds of other brave souls spring to memory when we pause to review the long struggle.

The hands of many suffrage master-masons have long been stilled; the names of many who laid the stones have been forgotten. That does not matter. The main thing is that the edifice of woman's liberty nears completion. It is strong, indestructible. All honor to the thousands who have helped in the building.

The four Cornerstones of the foundations were laid long years ago. We read upon the first: "We demand for women education, for not a high school or college is open to her"; upon the second, "We demand for women religious liberty for in few churches is she permitted to pray or speak"; upon the third, "We demand for women the right to own property and an opportunity to earn an honest living. Only six, poorly-paid occupations are open to her, and if she is married, the wages she earns are not hers"; upon the fourth, "We demand political freedom and its symbol, the vote."

The stones in the foundation have long been overgrown with the moss and   25
mould of time, and some there are who never knew they were laid. Of late, four capstones at the top have been set to match those in the base, and we read upon the first: "The number of women who are graduated from high schools, colleges and universities is legion"; upon the second, "The Christian Endeavor, that mighty, undenominational church militant, asks the vote for the women and the Methodist Episcopal Church, and many another, joins that appeal"; upon the third, "Billions of dollars worth of property are earned [and] owned by women; more than 8 millions of women are wage-earners. Every occupation is open to them"; upon the fourth: "Women vote in 12 States; they share in the determination of 91 electoral votes."

After the capstones and cornice comes the roof. Across the empty spaces, the roof-tree has been flung and fastened well in place. It is not made of stone but of two *planks* — planks in the platform of the two majority parties, and these are well supported by planks in the platforms of all minority parties.

And we who are the builders of 1916, do we see a crisis? Standing upon these planks which are stretched across the top-most peak of this edifice of woman's liberty, what shall we do? Over our heads, up there in the clouds, but tantalizing [sic] near, hangs the roof of our edifice, — the vote. What is our duty? Shall we spend time in admiring the capstones and cornice? Shall we lament the tragedies which accompanied the laying of the cornerstones? Or, shall we, like the builders of old, chant, "Ho! all hands, all hands, heave to! All hands, heave to!" and while we chant, grasp the overhanging roof and with a long pull, a strong pull and a pull together, fix it in place forevermore?

Is the crisis real or imaginary? If it be real, it calls for action, bold, immediate and decisive.

Let us then take measure of our strength. Our cause has won the endorsement of all political parties. Every candidate for the presidency is a suffragist. It has won the endorsement of most churches; it has won the hearty approval of all great organizations of women. It has won the support of all reform movements; it has won the progressives of every variety. The majority of the press in most States is with us. Great men in every political party, church and movement are with us. The names of the greatest men and women of art, science, literature and philosophy, reform, religion and politics are on our lists.

We have not won the reactionaries of any party, church or society, and we never   30
will. From the beginning of things, there have been Antis. The Antis drove Moses out of Egypt; they crucified Christ who said, "Love thy neighbor as thyself" [Matt. 19:19, 22:39]; they have persecuted Jews in all parts of the world; they poisoned Socrates, the great philosopher; they cruelly persecuted Copernicus[10] and Galileo,[11] the first great scientists; they burned Giordano Bruno at the stake because he believed the world was round;[12] they burned Savonarola who warred upon church corruption;[13] they burned Eufame McIlyane [sic] because she used an anaesthetic;[14] they burned Joan d'Arc for a heretic; they have sent great men and women to Siberia to eat their hearts out in isolation; they burned in effigy William Lloyd Garrison; they egged Abbie Kelley and Lucy Stone and mobbed Susan B. Anthony. Yet, in proportion to the enlightenment of their respective ages, these Antis were persons of intelligence and honest purpose. They were merely deaf to the call of Progress and were enraged because the world insisted upon moving on. Antis male and female there still are and will be to the end of time. Give to them a prayer of forgiveness for they know not what they do; and prepare for the forward march.

We have not won the ignorant and illiterate and we never can. They are too undeveloped mentally to understand that the institutions of today are not those of yesterday nor will be those of tomorrow.

We have not won the forces of evil and we never will. Evil has ever been timorous and suspicious of all change. It is an instinctive act of self-preservation which makes it fear and consequently oppose votes for women. As the Hon. Champ Clark said the other day: "Some good and intelligent people are opposed to woman suffrage; but all the ignorant and evil-minded are against it."[15]

---

[10] Nicholas Copernicus (1473–1543), Polish astronomer, whose great work, the foundation of modern astronomy, was *De revolutionibus orbium coelestium* (1543), dedicated to Pope Paul III.

[11] Galileo Galilei (1564–1642), Italian astronomer, mathematician, and physicist, who constructed the first complete astronomical telescope, and whose investigations confirmed the Copernican theory of the solar system. In 1616 that theory was denounced as dangerous to faith, but in 1632 Galileo published a work which supported it, and was tried in 1633 by the Inquisition and forced to recant all beliefs and writings holding that the earth and other planets revolved about the sun.

[12] Giordano Bruno (1548–1600), Italian philosopher. His major metaphysical works were *De la causa, principio, et uno* (1584) and *De l'infinito, universo et mondi* (1584). Tried for heresy in Venice in 1591 by the Inquisition, he was imprisoned, then burned to death at Rome.

[13] Girolamo Savonarola (1452–1498), Italian religious reformer, prior of San Marco, the Dominican house in Florence. He was excommunicated by Pope Alexander VI for disobedience after he continued to preach against the scandalously corrupt papal court. Under torture he supposedly confessed to being a false prophet and was hanged for schism and heresy.

[14] Euphemia MacCalyean was sentenced to be burned in Scotland on June 15, 1591, for attempting to relieve her pains in giving birth to twins and for other charges related to witchcraft.

[15] James Beauchamp Clark (1850–1921), member U.S. House of Representatives (1893–1895, 1897–1921). He became Democratic leader (1907) and Speaker (1911–1919), and in 1912 was

These three forces are the enemies of our cause.

Before the vote is won, there must and will be a gigantic final conflict between the forces of progress, righteousness and democracy and the forces of ignorance, evil and reaction. That struggle may be postponed, but it cannot be evaded or avoided. There is no question as to which side will be the victor.

Shall we play the coward, then, and leave the hard knocks for our daughters, or   35
shall we throw ourselves into the fray, bare our own shoulders to the blows, and thus bequeath to them a politically liberated womanhood? We have taken note of our gains and of our resources, and they are all we could wish. Before the final struggle, we must take cognizance of our weaknesses. Are we prepared to grasp the victory? Alas, no! Our movement is like a great Niagara with a vast volume of water tumbling over its ledge but turning no wheel. Our organized machinery is set for the propagandistic stage and not for the seizure of victory. Our supporters are spreading the argument for our cause; they feel no sense of responsibility for the realization of our hopes. Our movement lacks cohesion, organization, unity and consequent momentum.

Behind us, in front of us, everywhere about us are suffragists, — millions of them, but inactive and silent. They have been "agitated and educated" and are with us in belief. There are thousands of women who have at one time or another been members of our organization but they have dropped out because, to them the movement seemed negative and pointless. Many have taken up other work whose results were more immediate. Philanthropy, charity, work for corrective laws of various kinds, temperance, relief for working women and numberless similar public services have called them. Others have turned to the pleasanter avenues of clubwork, art or literature.

There are thousands of other women who have never learned of the earlier struggles of our movement. They found doors of opportunity open to them on every side. They found well-paid posts awaiting the qualified woman and they have availed themselves of all these blessings; almost without exception they believe in the vote but they feel neither gratitude to those who opened the doors through which they have entered to economic liberty nor any sense of obligation to open other doors for those who come after.

There are still others who, timorously looking over their shoulders to see if any listeners be near, will tell us they hope we will win and win soon but they are too frightened of Mother Grundy to help.[16] There are others too occupied with the small things of life to help. They say they could find time to vote but not to work for the vote. There are men, too, millions of them, waiting to be called. These men and women are our reserves. They are largely unorganized and untrained soldiers with little responsibility toward our movement. Yet these reserves must be mobilized. The final struggle needs their numbers and the momentum those numbers will bring. Were

the leading Democratic candidate for the presidency until William Jennings Bryan shifted his support to Woodrow Wilson.

[16] Public opinion personified.

never another convert made, there are suffragists enough in this country, if combined, to make so irresistible a driving force that victory might be seized at once.

How can it be done? By a simple change of mental attitude. If we are to seize the victory, that change must take place in this hall, here and now!

The old belief, which has sustained suffragists in many an hour of discourage-   40
ment, "woman suffrage is bound to come," must give way to the new, "The Woman's Hour has struck." The long drawn out struggle, the cruel hostility which, for years was arrayed against our cause, have accustomed suffragists to the idea of indefinite postponement but eventual victory. The slogan of a movements sets its pace. The old one counseled patience; it said, there is plenty of time; it pardoned sloth and half-hearted effort. It set the pace of an educational campaign. The "Woman's Hour has struck" sets the pace of a crusade which will have its way. It says: "Awake, arise, my sisters, let your hearts be filled with joy, — the time of victory is here. Onward March."

If you believe with me that a crisis has come to our movement, — if you believe that the time for final action is now, if you catch the rosy tints of the coming day, what does it mean to you? Does it not give you a thrill of exaltation; does the blood not course more quickly through your veins; does it not bring a new sense of freedom, of joy and of determination? Is it not true that you who wanted a little time ago to lay down the work because you were weary with long service, now, under the compelling influence of a changed mental attitude, are ready to go on until the vote is won. The change is one of spirit! Aye, and the spiritual effect upon you will come to others. Let me borrow an expression from Hon. John Finlay: What our great movement needs now is a "mobilization of spirit", — the jubilant, glad spirit of victory. Then let us sound a bugle call here and now to the women of the Nation: "The Woman's Hour has struck." Let the bugle sound from the suffrage headquarters of every State at the inauguration of a State campaign. Let the call go forth again and again and yet again. Let it be repeated in every article written, in every speech made, in every conversation held. Let the bugle blow again and yet again. The political emancipation of our sex call[s] you, women of America, arise! Are you content that others shall pay the price of your liberty?

Women in schools and counting house, in shops and on the farm, women in the home with babes at their breasts and women engaged in public careers will hear. The veins of American women are not filled with milk and water. They are neither cowards nor slackers. They will come. They only await the bugle call to learn that the final battle is on.

DISCUSSION QUESTIONS

1. What are the signs Catt sees that suggest America's crisis point in the fight for women's suffrage might turn into victory?
2. In what ways has World War I changed the role of women in Europe?
3. What does Catt predict will happen to women's status in Europe once the war is over?
4. Explain Catt's metaphor of woman as doormat or as doorjamb.

5. Explain the metaphor of the construction of a building that Catt uses to describe the suffrage movement.

6. In what ways does Catt appeal to the emotions of those listening to her speech in 1916?

7. What other effective argumentative strategies does Catt use in the speech?

8. How does she use language effectively to strengthen her speech?

WRITING SUGGESTIONS

9. Argue that Catt's speech is a blend of appeal to the reason and to the emotions of her audience.

10. How does she use her analysis of what is happening in Europe to appeal to an American audience?

11. Explain how Catt's speech, given in 1916, still has relevance in the early twentieth century.

Warfare: An Invention — Not a Biological Necessity

MARGARET MEAD

Is war a biological necessity, a sociological inevitability, or just a bad invention? Those who argue for the first view endow man with such pugnacious instincts that some outlet in aggressive behavior is necessary if man is to reach full human stature. It was this point of view which lay back of William James's famous essay, "The Moral Equivalent of War," in which he tried to retain the warlike virtues and channel them in new directions. A similar point of view has lain back of the Soviet Union's attempt to make competition between groups rather than between individuals. A basic, competitive, aggressive, warring human nature is assumed, and those who

Margaret Mead (1901–1978) was the first American anthropologist to study childhood, adolescence, and gender. Her work focused primarily on culture rather than biology or race as the primary factor in determining variations in human behavior and personality. As a graduate student, she conducted field research on adolescence and sexuality in Samoa. Her resulting work, the best-selling *Coming of Age in Samoa* (1928), made her a household name in the United States. She went on to publish forty-four books, including *Growing Up in New Guinea* (1930) and *Sex and Temperament* (1935), and hundreds of articles. Her early research in Samoa has been challenged by Derek Freeman, an anthropologist who characterizes Mead's work as being anti-evolutionary and fundamentally flawed in its portrayal of sexuality in the South Seas. Freeman's accusations, however, have been discredited by many scholars who recognize Mead's important contributions to the field. The following article, in which Mead argues that warfare is a cultural invention and not a biological necessity, was published in *Asia* in 1940.

wish to outlaw war or outlaw competitiveness merely try to find new and less socially destructive ways in which these biologically given aspects of man's nature can
find expression. Then there are those who take the second view: warfare is the inevitable concomitant of the development of the state, the struggle for land and natural resources of class societies springing, not from the nature of man, but from the
nature of history. War is nevertheless inevitable unless we change our social system
and outlaw classes, the struggle for power, and possessions; and in the event of our
success warfare would disappear, as a symptom vanishes when the disease is cured.

One may hold a compromise position between these two extremes; one may
claim that all aggression springs from the frustration of man's biologically determined drives and that, since all forms of culture are frustrating, it is certain each new
generation will be aggressive and the aggression will find its natural and inevitable
expression in race war, class war, nationalistic war, and so on.

All three positions are very popular today among those who think seriously
about the problems of war and its possible prevention, but I wish to urge another
point of view, less defeatist perhaps than the first and third and more accurate than
the second: that is, that warfare, by which I mean recognized conflict between two
groups as groups, in which each group puts an army (even if the army is only fifteen
pygmies) into the field to fight and kill, if possible, some of the members of the army
of the other group — that warfare of this sort is an invention like any other of the
inventions in terms of which we order our lives, such as writing, marriage, cooking
our food instead of eating it raw, trial by jury, or burial of the dead, and so on. Some
of this list anyone will grant are inventions: trial by jury is confined to very limited
portions of the globe; we know that there are tribes that do not bury their dead but
instead expose or cremate them; and we know that only part of the human race has
had the knowledge of writing as its cultural inheritance. But, whenever a way of doing things is found universally, such as the use of fire or the practice of some form of
marriage, we tend to think at once that it is not an invention at all but an attribute
of humanity itself. And yet even such universals as marriage and the use of fire are
inventions like the rest, very basic ones, inventions which were, perhaps, necessary
if human history was to take the turn that it has taken, but nevertheless inventions.
At some point in his social development man was undoubtedly without the institution of marriage or the knowledge of the use of fire.

The case for warfare is much clearer because there are peoples even today who
have no warfare. Of these the Eskimos are perhaps the most conspicuous examples,
but the Lepchas of Sikkim described by Geoffrey Gorer in *Himalayan Village* are as
good. Neither of these peoples understands war, not even defensive warfare. The idea
of warfare is lacking, and this idea is as essential to really carrying on war as an alphabet or a syllabary is to writing. But, whereas the Lepchas are a gentle, unquarrel-
some people, and the advocates of other points of view might argue that they are not
full human beings or that they had never been frustrated and so had no aggression
to expand in warfare, the Eskimo case gives no such possibility of interpretation.
The Eskimos are not a mild and meek people; many of them are turbulent and troublesome. Fights, theft of wives, murder, cannibalism, occur among them — all out-
bursts of passionate men goaded by desire or intolerable circumstance. Here are men

faced with hunger, men faced with loss of their wives, men faced with the threat of extermination by other men, and here are orphan children, growing up miserably with no one to care for them, mocked and neglected by those about them. The personality necessary for war, the circumstances necessary to goad men to desperation are present, but there is no war. When a travelling Eskimo entered a settlement, he might have to fight the strongest man in the settlement to establish his position among them, but this was a test of strength and bravery, not war. The idea of warfare, of one group organizing against another group to maim and wound and kill them was absent. And, without that idea, passions might rage but there was no war.

But, it may be argued, is not this because the Eskimos have such a low and undeveloped form of social organization? They own no land, they move from place to place, camping, it is true, season after season on the same site, but this is not something to fight for as the modern nations of the world fight for land and raw materials. They have no permanent possessions that can be looted, no towns that can be burned. They have no social classes to produce stress and strains within the society which might force it to go to war outside. Does not the absence of war among the Eskimos, while disproving the biological necessity of war, just go to confirm the point that it is the state of development of the society which accounts for war and nothing else?

We find the answer among the pygmy peoples of the Andaman Islands in the Bay of Bengal. The Andamans also represent an exceedingly low level of society; they are a hunting and food-gathering people; they live in tiny hordes without any class stratification; their houses are simpler than the snow houses of the Eskimo. But they knew about warfare. The army might contain only fifteen determined pygmies marching in a straight line, but it was the real thing none the less. Tiny army met tiny army in open battle, blows were exchanged, casualties suffered, and the state of warfare could only be concluded by a peacemaking ceremony.

Similarly, among the Australian aborigines, who built no permanent dwellings but wandered from water hole to water hole over their almost desert country, warfare — and rules of "international law" — were highly developed. The student of social evolution will seek in vain for his obvious causes of war, struggle for lands, struggle for power of one group over another, expansion of population, need to divert the minds of a populace restive under tyranny, or even the ambition of a successful leader to enhance his own prestige. All are absent, but warfare as a practice remained, and men engaged in it and killed one another in the course of a war because killing is what is done in wars.

From instances like these it becomes apparent that an inquiry into the causes of war misses the fundamental point as completely as does an insistence upon the biological necessity of war. If a people have an idea of going to war and the idea that war is the way in which certain situations, defined within their society, are to be handled, they will sometimes go to war. If they are a mild and unaggressive people, like the Pueblo Indians, they may limit themselves to defensive warfare, but they will be forced to think in terms of war because there are peoples near them who have warfare as a pattern, and offensive, raiding, pillaging warfare at that. When the pattern of warfare is known, people like the Pueblo Indians will defend themselves, taking

5

advantage of their natural defenses, the mesa village site, and people like the Lep-chas, having no natural defenses and no idea of warfare, will merely submit to the invader. But the essential point remains the same. There is a way of behaving which is known to a given people and labeled as an appropriate form of behavior; a bold and warlike people like the Sioux or the Maori may label warfare as desirable as well as possible, a mild people like the Pueblo Indians may label warfare as undesir-able, but to the minds of both peoples the possibility of warfare is present. Their thoughts, their hopes, their plans are oriented about this idea — that warfare may be selected as the way to meet some situation.

So simple peoples and civilized peoples, mild peoples and violent, assertive peoples, will all go to war if they have the invention, just as those peoples who have the custom of dueling will have duels and peoples who have the pattern of vendetta will indulge in vendetta. And, conversely, peoples who do not know of dueling will not fight duels, even though their wives are seduced and their daughters ravished; they may on occasion commit murder but they will not fight duels. Cultures which lack the idea of the vendetta will not meet every quarrel in this way. A people can use only the forms it has. So the Balinese have their special way of dealing with a quarrel between two individuals: if the two feel that the causes of quarrel are heavy, they may go and register their quarrel in the temple before the gods, and, making offerings, they may swear never to have anything to do with each other again. . . . But in other societies, although individuals might feel as full of animosity and as unwilling to have any further contact as do the Balinese, they cannot register their quarrel with the gods and go on quietly about their business because registering quarrels with the gods is not an invention of which they know.

Yet, if it be granted that warfare is, after all, an invention, it may nevertheless be   10
an invention that lends itself to certain types of personality, to the exigent needs of autocrats, to the expansionist desires of crowded peoples, to the desire for plunder and rape and loot which is engendered by a dull and frustrating life. What, then, can we say of this congruence between warfare and its uses? If it is a form which fits so well, is not this congruence the essential point? But even here the primitive material causes us to wonder, because there are tribes who go to war merely for glory, having no quarrel with the enemy, suffering from no tyrant within their boundaries, anx-ious neither for land nor loot nor women, but merely anxious to win prestige which within that tribe has been declared obtainable only by war and without which no young man can hope to win his sweetheart's smile of approval. But if, as was the case with the Bush Negroes of Dutch Guiana, it is artistic ability which is necessary to win a girl's approval, the same young man would have to be carving rather than going out on a war party.

In many parts of the world, war is a game in which the individual can win counters — counters which bring him prestige in the eyes of his own sex or of the opposite sex; he plays for these counters as he might, in our society, strive for a tennis championship. Warfare is a frame for such prestige-seeking merely because it calls for the display of certain skills and certain virtues; all of these skills — riding straight, shooting straight, dodging the missiles of the enemy and sending one's own straight to the mark — can be equally well exercised in some other framework and, equally, the virtues endurance, bravery, loyalty, steadfastness — can be displayed in other contexts. The tie-up between proving oneself a man and proving this by a success in organized killing is due to a definition which many societies have made of manliness. And often, even in those societies which counted success in warfare a proof of human worth, strange turns were given to the idea, as when the plains Indians gave their highest awards to the man who touched a live enemy rather than to the man who brought in a scalp — from a dead enemy — because the latter was less risky. Warfare is just an invention known to the majority of human societies by which they permit their young men either to accumulate prestige or avenge their honor or acquire loot or wives or slaves or sago lands or cattle or appease the blood lust of their gods or the restless souls of the recently dead. It is just an invention, older and more widespread than the jury system, but none the less an invention.

But, once we have said this, have we said anything at all? Despite a few stances, dear to the instances of controversialist, of the loss of the useful arts, once an invention is made which proves congruent with human needs or social forms, it tends to persist. Grant that war is an invention, that it is not a biological necessity nor the outcome of certain special types of social forms, still once the invention is made, what are we to do about it? The Indian who had been subsisting on the buffalo for generations because with his primitive weapons he could slaughter only a limited number of buffalo did not return to his primitive weapons when he saw that the white man's more efficient weapons were exterminating the buffalo. A desire for the white man's cloth may mortgage the South Sea Islander to the white man's plantation, but he does not return to making bark cloth, which would have left him free. Once an invention is known and accepted, men do not easily relinquish it. The skilled workers may smash the first steam looms which they feel are to be their undoing, but they accept them in the end, and no movement which has insisted upon the mere abandonment of usable inventions has ever had much success. Warfare is here, as part of our thought; the deeds of warriors are immortalized in the words of our poets, the toys of our children are modeled upon the weapons of the soldier, the frame of reference within which our statesmen and our diplomats work always contains war. If we know that it is not inevitable, that it is due to historical accident that warfare is one of the ways in which we think of behaving, are we given any hope by that? What hope is there of persuading nations to abandon war, nations so thoroughly imbued with the idea that to resort to war is, if not actually desirable and noble, at least inevitable whenever certain defined circumstances arise?

In answer to this question I think we might turn to the history of other social inventions, and inventions which must once have seemed as finally entrenched as warfare. Take the methods of trial which preceded the jury system: ordeal and trial by combat. Unfair, capricious, alien as they are to our feeling today, they were once the only methods open to individuals accused of some offense. The invention of trial by jury gradually replaced these methods until only witches, and finally not even witches, had to resort to the ordeal. And for a long time the jury system seemed the best and finest method of settling legal disputes, but today new inventions, trial before judges only or before commissions, are replacing the jury system. In each case the old method was replaced by a new social invention. The ordeal did not go out because people thought it unjust or wrong; it went out because a method more congruent with the institutions and feelings of the period was invented. And, if we despair over the way in which war seems such an ingrained habit of most of the human race, we can take comfort from the fact that a poor invention will usually give place to a better invention.

For this, two conditions, at least, are necessary. The people must recognize the defects of the old invention, and someone must make a new one. Propaganda against warfare, documentation of its terrible cost in human suffering and social waste, these prepare the ground by teaching people to feel that warfare is a defective social institution. There is further needed a belief that social invention is possible and the invention of new methods which will render warfare as out of date as the tractor is making the plough, or the motor car the horse and buggy. A form of behavior becomes out of date only when something else takes its place, and, in order to invent forms of behavior which will make war obsolete, it is a first requirement to believe that an invention is possible.

DISCUSSION QUESTIONS

1. Mead uses a common organizational strategy — refuting the opposing view. In this essay she refutes several theories about the origin of warfare. Summarize these theories. Where does she state her own thesis?

2. Mead supports her argument with examples and analogies. Are they all equally convincing? How can a reader assess the strengths and weaknesses of her examples?

3. In the last part of her essay Mead acknowledges that war is a "usable invention" (para. 12). How does she answer this apparent weakness in her argument?

4. What solution to the problem of warfare does Mead propose? Do you find any flaws in her proposal? Explain your agreement or disagreement with the plausibility of her solution.

WRITING SUGGESTIONS

5. In an article entitled "Where Have All the Young Men Gone? The Perfect Substitute for War," the author marvels at the significance of a gathering in 1998 of more than a million people to celebrate France's victory in the World Cup, a soccer game. "The vast majority of Europeans," he writes, "have found a way to hate one another without hacking one another to pieces."[1] (In a tragic irony, this article appeared in 1999 during the brutal "ethnic cleansing" of ethnic Albanians in Kosovo and the bombing of Serbia by NATO forces.)

   Argue that sporting events do or do not represent a substitute for war. Develop two or three issues — similarities or differences — that support your claim.

6. Pacifism is defined by *Webster's New International Dictionary* as "opposition to war or the use of military force for any purpose." If you consider yourself to be a paci-

[1] Paul Auster, *New York Times Magazine*, April 4, 1999, p. 144.

fist, write a defense of your belief, using examples and analogies to make your position clear. But if you believe with Bertrand Russell, the British mathematician and philosopher, that "Absolute pacifism, as a method of gaining your ends, is subject to very severe limitations,"[2] defend your point of view, again using examples, as Mead does.

[2] *Dictionary of the Mind* (New York: Philosophical Library, 1952), p. 162.

Politics and the English Language

GEORGE ORWELL

Most people who bother with the matter at all would admit that the English language is in a bad way, but it is generally assumed that we cannot by conscious action do anything about it. Our civilization is decadent and our language — so the argument runs — must inevitably share in the general collapse. It follows that any struggle against the abuse of language is a sentimental archaism, like preferring candles to electric light or hansom cabs to aeroplanes. Underneath this lies the half-conscious belief that language is a natural growth and not an instrument which we shape for our own purposes.

Now, it is clear that the decline of a language must ultimately have political and economic causes: It is not due simply to the bad influence of this or that individual writer. But an effect can become a cause, reinforcing the original cause and producing the same effect in an intensified form, and so on indefinitely. A man may take to drink because he feels himself to be a failure, and then fail all the more completely because he drinks. It is rather the same thing that is happening to the English language. It becomes ugly and inaccurate because our thoughts are foolish, but the slovenliness of our language makes it easier for us to have foolish thoughts. The point is that the process is reversible. Modern English, especially written English, is full of bad habits which spread by imitation and which can be avoided if one is willing to take the necessary trouble. If one gets rid of these habits one can think more clearly, and to think clearly is a necessary first step towards political regeneration: So that the fight against bad English is not frivolous and is not the exclusive concern of professional writers. I will come back to this presently, and I hope that by that time the meaning of what I have said here will have become clearer. Meanwhile, here are five specimens of the English language as it is now habitually written.

This essay, written shortly after World War II, develops George Orwell's claim that careless and dishonest use of language contributes to careless and dishonest thought and political corruption. Political language, he argues, is "largely the defense of the indefensible." But Orwell (1903–1950), novelist, critic, and political satirist — best known for his books *Animal Farm* (1945) and *1984* (1949) — believes that bad language habits can be reversed, and he lists rules for getting rid of some of the most offensive. This essay first appeared in *Horizon* in April 1946.

These five passages have not been picked out because they are especially bad — I could have quoted far worse if I had chosen — but because they illustrate various of the mental vices from which we now suffer. They are a little below the average, but are fairly representative samples. I number them so that I can refer back to them when necessary:

(1) I am not, indeed, sure whether it is not true to say that the Milton who once seemed not unlike a seventeenth-century Shelley had not become out of an experience ever more bitter in each year, more alien *[sic]* to the founder of that Jesuit sect which nothing could induce him to tolerate.
Professor Harold Laski (Essay in *Freedom of Expression*)

(2) Above all, we cannot play ducks and drakes with a native battery of idioms which prescribes such egregious collocations of vocables as the Basic *put up with* for *tolerate* or *put at a loss* for *bewilder*.
Professor Lancelot Hogben (*Interglossa*)

(3) On the one side we have the free personality: By definition it is not neurotic, for it has neither conflict nor dream. Its desires, such as they are, are transparent, for they are just what institutional approval keeps in the forefront of consciousness; another institutional pattern would alter their number and intensity; there is little in them that is natural, irreducible, or culturally dangerous. But *on the other side*, the social bond itself is nothing but the mutual reflection of these self-secure integrities. Recall the definition of love. Is not this the very picture of a small academic? Where is there a place in this hall of mirrors for either personality or fraternity?
Essay on psychology in *Politics* (New York)

(4) All the "best people" from the gentlemen's clubs, and all the frantic fascist captains, united in common hatred of Socialism and bestial horror of the rising tide of the mass revolutionary movement, have turned to acts of provocation, to foul incendiarism, to medieval legends of poisoned wells, to legalize their own destruction of proletarian organizations, and rouse the agitated petty-bourgeoisie to chauvinistic fervor on behalf of the fight against the revolutionary way out of the crisis.

Communist pamphlet

(5) If a new spirit *is* to be infused into this old country, there is one thorny and contentious reform which must be tackled, and that is the humanization and galvanization of the BBC. Timidity here will bespeak cancer and atrophy of the soul. The heart of Britain may be sound and of strong beat, for instance, but the British lion's roar at present is like that of Bottom in Shakespeare's *Midsummer Night's Dream* — as gentle as any sucking dove. A virile new Britain cannot continue indefinitely to be traduced in the eyes or rather ears, of the world by the effete languors of Langham Place, brazenly masquerading as "standard English." When the Voice of Britain is heard at nine o'clock, better far and infinitely less ludicrous to hear aitches honestly dropped than the present priggish, inflated, inhibited, school-ma'amish arch braying of blameless bashful mewing maidens!
Letter in *Tribune*

Each of these passages has faults of its own, but, quite apart from avoidable ugliness, two qualities are common to all of them. The first is staleness of imagery: The other is lack of precision. The writer either has a meaning and cannot express it, or he inadvertently says something else, or he is almost indifferent as to whether his words mean anything or not. The mixture of vagueness and sheer incompetence is the most marked characteristic of modern English prose, and especially of any kind of political writing. As soon as certain topics are raised, the concrete melts into the abstract and no one seems to think of turns of speech that are not hackneyed: Prose consists less and less of *words* chosen for the sake of their meaning, and more and more of *phrases* tacked together like the sections of a prefabricated hen-house. I list below, with notes and examples, various of the tricks by means of which the work of prose-construction is habitually dodged:

Dying metaphors.   A newly invented metaphor assists thought by evoking a visual   5
image, while on the other hand a metaphor which is technically "dead" (e.g., *iron resolution*) has in effect reverted to being an ordinary word and can generally be used without loss of vividness. But in between these two classes there is a huge dump of worn-out metaphors which have lost all evocative power and are merely used because they save people the trouble of inventing phrases for themselves. Examples are: *ring the changes on, take up the cudgels for, toe the line, ride roughshod over, stand shoulder to shoulder with, play into the hands of, no axe to grind, grist to the mill, fishing in troubled waters, rift within the lute, on the order of the day, Achilles' heel, swan song, hotbed.* Many of these are used without knowledge of their meaning (what is a "rift," for instance?), and incompatible metaphors are frequently mixed, a sure sign that the writer is not interested in what he is saying. Some metaphors now current have been twisted out of their original meaning without those who use them even being aware of the fact. For example, *toe the line* is sometimes written *tow the line*. Another example is *the hammer and the anvil*, now always used with the implication that the anvil gets the worst of it. In real life it is always the anvil that breaks the hammer, never the other way about: A writer who stopped to think what he was saying would be aware of this, and would avoid perverting the original phrase.

Operators or verbal false limbs.   These save the trouble of picking out appropriate verbs and nouns, and at the same time pad each sentence with extra syllables which give it an appearance of symmetry. Characteristic phrases are: *render inoperative, militate against, make contact with, be subjected to, give rise to, give grounds for, have the effect of, play a leading part (role) in, make itself felt, take effect, exhibit a tendency to, serve the purpose of*, etc., etc. The keynote is the elimination of simple verbs. Instead of being a single word, such as *break, stop, spoil, mend, kill*, a verb becomes a *phrase*, made up of a noun or adjective tacked on to some general-purpose verb such as *prove, serve, form, play, render*. In addition, the passive voice is wherever possible used in preference to the active, and noun constructions are used instead of gerunds (*by examination of* instead of *by examining*). The range of verbs is further cut down by means of the *-ize* and *de-* formation, and the banal statements are given an appearance of profundity by means of the *not un-* formation. Simple conjunctions and prepositions are replaced by such phrases as *with respect to, having regard to, the fact that, by dint of, in view of, in the interests of, on the hypothesis that;* and the ends of sentences are saved from anticlimax by such resounding commonplaces as *greatly to be desired, cannot be left out of account, a development to be expected in the near future, deserving of serious consideration, brought to a satisfactory conclusion,* and so on and so forth.

Pretentious diction. Words like *phenomenon, element, individual* (as noun), *objective, categorical, effective, virtual, basic, primary, promote, constitute, exhibit, exploit, utilize, eliminate, liquidate,* are used to dress up simple statements and give an air of scientific impartiality to biased judgments. Adjectives like *epoch-making, epic, historic, unforgettable, triumphant, age-old, inevitable, inexorable, veritable,* are used to dignify the sordid processes of international politics, while writing that aims at glorifying war usually takes on an archaic color, its characteristic words being: *realm, throne, chariot, mailed fist, trident, sword, shield, buckler, banner, jackboot, clarion.* Foreign words and expressions such as *cul de sac, ancien régime, deus ex machina, mutatis mutandis, status quo, gleichshaltung, weltanschauung,* are used to give an air of culture and elegance. Except for the useful abbreviations *i.e., e.g.,* and *etc.,* there is no real need for any of the hundreds of foreign phrases now current in English. Bad writers, and especially scientific, political, and sociological writers, are nearly always haunted by the notion that Latin or Greek words are grander than Saxon ones, and unnecessary words like *expedite, ameliorate, predict, extraneous, deracinated, clandestine, subaqueous,* and hundreds of others constantly gain ground from their Anglo-Saxon opposite numbers.[1] The jargon peculiar to Marxist writing (*hyena, hangman, cannibal, petty bourgeois, these gentry, lackey, flunkey, mad dog, White Guard,* etc.) consists largely of words and phrases translated from Russian, German, or French; but the normal way of coining a new word is to use a Latin or Greek root with the appropriate affix and, where necessary, the *-ize* formation. It is often easier to make up words of this kind (*deregionalize, impermissible, extramarital, nonfragmentatory,* and so forth) than to think up the English words that will cover one's meaning. The result, in general, is an increase in slovenliness and vagueness.

Meaningless words. In certain kinds of writing, particularly in art criticism and literary criticism, it is normal to come across long passages which are almost completely lacking in meaning.[2] Words like *romantic, plastic, values, human, dead, sentimental, natural,*

---

[1] An interesting illustration of this is the way in which the English flower names which were in use till very recently are being ousted by Greek ones, *snapdragon* becoming *antirrhinum, forget-me-not* becoming *myosotis,* etc. It is hard to see any practical reason for this change of fashion: It is probably due to an instinctive turning-away from the more homely word and a vague feeling that the Greek word is scientific. [All notes are Orwell's.]

[2] Example: "Comfort's catholicity of perception and image, strangely Whitmanesque in range, almost the exact opposite in aesthetic compulsion, continues to evoke that trembling atmospheric accumulative hinting at a cruel, an inexorably serene timelessness. . . . Wrey Gardiner scores by aiming at simple bull's-eyes with precision. Only they are not so simple, and through this contended sadness runs more than the surface bittersweet of resignation" (*Poetry Quarterly*).

vitality, as used in art criticism, are strictly meaningless in the sense that they not only do not point to any discoverable object, but are hardly ever expected to do so by the reader. When one critic writes, "The outstanding feature of Mr. X's work is its living quality," while another writes, "The immediately striking thing about Mr. X's work is its peculiar deadness," the reader accepts this as a simple difference of opinion. If words like *black* and *white* were involved, instead of the jargon words *dead* and *living*, he would see at once that language was being used in an improper way. Many political words are similarly abused. The word *fascism* has now no meaning except insofar as it signifies "something not desirable." The words *democracy, socialism, freedom, patriotic, realistic, justice*, have each of them several different meanings which cannot be reconciled with one another. In the case of a word like *democracy*, not only is there no agreed definition, but the attempt to make one is resisted from all sides. It is almost universally felt that when we call a country democratic we are praising it: Consequently the defenders of every kind of regime claim that it is a democracy, and fear that they might have to stop using the word if it were tied down to any one meaning. Words of this kind are often used in a consciously dishonest way. That is, the person who uses them has his own private definition, but allows his hearer to think he means something quite different. Statements like *Marshal Pétain was a true patriot, The Soviet Press is the freest in the world, The Catholic Church is opposed to persecution*, arc almost always madc with intcnt to deceive. Other words used in variable meanings, in most cases more or less dishonestly, are: *class, totalitarian, science, progressive, reactionary, bourgeois, equality*.

Now that I have made this catalog of swindles and perversions, let me give another example of the kind of writing that they lead to. This time it must of its nature be an imaginary one. I am going to translate a passage of good English into modern English of the worst sort. Here is a well-known verse from Ecclesiastes:

> I returned and saw under the sun, that the race is not to the swift, nor the battle to the strong, neither yet bread to the wise, nor yet riches to men of understanding, nor yet favor to men of skill; but time and chance happeneth to them all.

Here it is in modern English:

> Objective consideration of contemporary phenomena compels the conclusion that success or failure in competitive activities exhibits no tendency to be commensurate with innate capacity, but that a considerable element of the unpredictable must invariably be taken into account.

This is a parody, but not a very gross one. Exhibit (3), above, for instance, contains several patches of the same kind of English. It will be seen that I have not made a full translation. The beginning and ending of the sentence follow the original meaning fairly closely, but in the middle the concrete illustrations — race, battle, bread — dissolve into the vague phrase "success or failure in competitive activities." This had to be so, because no modern writer of the kind I am discussing — no one capable of using phrases like "objective consideration of contemporary phenomena" — would ever tabulate his thoughts in that precise and detailed way. The

10

whole tendency of modern prose is away from concreteness. Now analyze these two sentences a little more closely. The first contains forty-nine words but only sixty syllables, and all its words are those of everyday life. The second contains thirty-eight words of ninety syllables: Eighteen of its words are from Latin roots, and one from Greek. The first sentence contains six vivid images, and only one phrase ("time and chance") that could be called vague. The second contains not a single fresh, arresting phrase, and in spite of its ninety syllables it gives only a shortened version of the meaning contained in the first. Yet without a doubt it is the second kind of sentence that is gaining ground in modern English. I do not want to exaggerate. This kind of writing is not yet universal, and outcrops of simplicity will occur here and there in the worst-written page. Still, if you or I were told to write a few lines on the uncertainty of human fortunes, we should probably come much nearer to my imaginary sentence than to the one from Ecclesiastes.

As I have tried to show, modern writing at its worst does not consist in picking out words for the sake of their meaning and inventing images in order to make the meaning clearer. It consists in gumming together long strips of words which have already been set in order by someone else, and making the results presentable by sheer humbug. The attraction of this way of writing is that it is easy. It is easier — even quicker once you have the habit — to say *In my opinion it is a not unjustifiable assumption that* than to say *I think*. If you use ready-made phrases, you not only don't have to hunt about for words; you also don't have to bother with the rhythms of your sentences, since these phrases are generally so arranged as to be more or less euphonious. When you are composing in a hurry — when you are dictating to a stenographer, for instance, or making a public speech — it is natural to fall into a pretentious, Latinized style. Tags like *a consideration which we should do well to bear in mind* or *a conclusion to which all of us would readily assent* will save many a sentence from coming down with a bump. By using stale metaphors, similes, and idioms, you save much mental effort, at the cost of leaving your meaning vague, not only for your reader but for yourself. This is the significance of mixed metaphors. The sole aim of a metaphor is to call up a visual image. When these images clash — as in *The Fascist octopus has sung its swan song, the jackboot is thrown into the melting pot* — it can be taken as certain that the writer is not seeing a mental image of the objects he is naming; in other words he is not really thinking. Look again at the examples I gave at the beginning of this essay. Professor Laski (1) uses five negatives in fifty-three words. One of these is superfluous, making nonsense of the whole passage, and in addition there is the slip *alien* for akin, making further nonsense, and several avoidable pieces of clumsiness which increase the general vagueness. Professor Hogben (2) plays ducks and drakes with a battery which is able to write prescriptions, and, while disapproving of the everyday phrase *put up with*, is unwilling to look *egregious* up in the dictionary and see what it means. (3), if one takes an uncharitable attitude towards it, is simply meaningless: Probably one could work out its intended meaning by reading the whole of the article in which it occurs. In (4), the writer knows more or less what he wants to say, but an accumulation of stale phrases chokes him like tea leaves blocking a sink. In (5), words and meaning have almost parted company. People who write in this manner usually have a general emotional meaning —

they dislike one thing and want to express solidarity with another — but they are not interested in the detail of what they are saying. A scrupulous writer, in every sentence that he writes, will ask himself at least four questions, thus: What am I trying to say? What words will express it? What image or idiom will make it clearer? Is this image fresh enough to have an effect? And he will probably ask himself two more: Could I put it more shortly? Have I said anything that is avoidably ugly? But you are not obliged to go to all this trouble. You can shirk it by simply throwing your mind open and letting the ready-made phrases come crowding in. They will construct your sentences for you — even think your thoughts for you, to a certain extent — and at need they will perform the important service of partially concealing your meaning even from yourself. It is at this point that the special connection between politics and the debasement of language becomes clear.

In our time it is broadly true that political writing is bad writing. Where it is not true, it will generally be found that the writer is some kind of rebel, expressing his private opinions and not a "party line." Orthodoxy, of whatever color, seems to demand a lifeless, imitative style. The political dialects to be found in pamphlets, leading articles, manifestos, White Papers, and the speeches of undersecretaries do, of course, vary from party to party, but they are all alike in that one almost never finds in them a fresh, vivid, home-made turn of speech. When one watches some tired hack on the platform mechanically repeating the familiar phrases — *bestial atrocities, iron heel, bloodstained tyranny, free peoples of the world, stand shoulder to shoulder* — one often has a curious feeling that one is not watching a live human being but some kind of dummy; a feeling which suddenly becomes stronger at moments when the light catches the speaker's spectacles and turns them into blank discs which seem to have no eyes behind them. And this is not altogether fanciful. A speaker who uses that kind of phraseology has gone some distance towards turning himself into a machine. The appropriate noises are coming out of his larynx, but his brain is not involved as it would be if he were choosing his words for himself. If the speech he is making is one that he is accustomed to make over and over again, he may be almost unconscious of what he is saying, as one is when one utters the responses in church. And this reduced state of consciousness, if not indispensable, is at any rate favorable to political conformity.

In our time, political speech and writing are largely the defense of the indefensible. Things like the continuance of British rule in India, the Russian purges and deportations, the dropping of the atom bombs on Japan, can indeed be defended, but only by arguments which are too brutal for most people to face, and which do not square with the professed aims of political parties. Thus political language has to consist largely of euphemism, question-begging, and sheer cloudy vagueness. Defenseless villages are bombarded from the air, the inhabitants driven out into the countryside, the cattle machine-gunned, the huts set on fire with incendiary bullets: This is called *pacification*. Millions of peasants are robbed of their farms and sent trudging along the roads with no more than they can carry; this is called *transfer of population* or *rectification of frontiers*. People are imprisoned for years without trial, or shot in the back of the neck, or sent to die of scurvy in Arctic lumber camps: This is called *elimination of unreliable elements*. Such phraseology is needed if one wants to name things without calling up mental pictures of them. Consider for instance some comfortable English professor defending Russian totalitarianism. He cannot say outright, "I believe in killing off your opponents when you can get good results by doing so." Probably, therefore, he will say something like this:

> While freely conceding that the Soviet régime exhibits certain features which the humanitarian may be inclined to deplore, we must, I think, agree that a certain curtailment of the right to political opposition is an unavoidable concomitant of transitional periods, and that the rigors which the Russian people have been called upon to undergo have been amply justified in the sphere of concrete achievement.

The inflated style is itself a kind of euphemism. A mass of Latin words fall upon the facts like soft snow, blurring the outlines and covering up all the details. The great enemy of clear language is insincerity. When there is a gap between one's real and one's declared aims, one turns as it were instinctively to long words and exhausted idioms, like a cuttlefish squirting out ink. In our age there is no such thing as "keeping out of politics." All issues are political issues, and politics itself is a mass of lies, evasions, folly, hatred, and schizophrenia. When the general atmosphere is bad, language must suffer. I should expect to find — this is a guess which I have not sufficient knowledge to verify — that the German, Russian, and Italian languages have all deteriorated in the last ten or fifteen years, as a result of dictatorship.

But if thought corrupts language, language can also corrupt thought. A bad   15 usage can spread by tradition and imitation, even among people who should and do know better. The debased language that I have been discussing is in some ways very convenient. Phrases like *a not unjustifiable assumption, leaves much to be desired, would serve no good purpose, a consideration which we should do well to bear in mind,* are a continuous temptation, a packet of aspirins always at one's elbow. Look back through this essay, and for certain you will find that I have again and again committed the very faults I am protesting against. By this morning's post I have received a pamphlet dealing with conditions in Germany. The author tells me that he "felt impelled" to write it. I open it at random, and here is almost the first sentence that I see: "(The Allies) have an opportunity not only of achieving a radical transformation of Germany's social and political structure in such a way as to avoid a nationalistic reaction in Germany itself, but at the same time of laying the foundations of a cooperative and unified Europe." You see, he "feels impelled" to write — feels, presumably, that he has something new to say — and yet his words, like cavalry horses answering the bugle, group themselves automatically into the familiar dreary pattern. This invasion of one's mind by ready-made phrases (*lay the foundations, achieve a radical transformation*) can only be prevented if one is constantly on guard against them, and every such phrase anesthetizes a portion of one's brain.

I said earlier that the decadence of our language is probably curable. Those who deny this would argue, if they produced an argument at all, that language merely reflects existing social conditions, and that we cannot influence its development by any direct tinkering with words and constructions. So far as the general tone or spirit of a language goes, this may be true, but it is not true in detail. Silly words and expressions have often disappeared, not through any evolutionary process but owing to the conscious action of a minority. Two recent examples were *explore every avenue* and *leave no stone unturned,* which were killed by the jeers of a few journalists. There is a long list of flyblown metaphors which could similarly be got rid of if enough people would interest themselves in the job; and it should also be possible to laugh the *not un-* formation out of existence,[3] to reduce the amount of Latin and Greek in the average sentence, to drive out foreign phrases and strayed scientific words, and, in general, to make pretentiousness unfashionable. But all these are minor points. The defense of the English language implies more than this, and perhaps it is best to start by saying what it does *not* imply.

To begin with it has nothing to do with archaism, with the salvaging of obsolete words and turns of speech, or with the setting up of a "standard English" which must never be departed from. On the contrary, it is especially concerned with the scrapping of every word or idiom which has outworn its usefulness. It has nothing to do with correct grammar and syntax, which are of no importance so long as one makes one's meaning clear, or with the avoidance of Americanisms, or with having what is called a "good prose style." On the other hand it is not concerned with fake simplicity and the attempt to make written English colloquial. Nor does it even imply in every case preferring the Saxon word to the Latin one, though it does imply using the fewest and shortest words that will cover one's meaning. What is above all needed is to let the meaning choose the word, and not the other way about. In prose, the worst thing one can do with words is to surrender to them. When you think of a concrete object, you think wordlessly, and then, if you want to describe the thing you have been visualizing you probably hunt about till you find the exact words that seem to fit. When you think of something abstract you are more inclined to use words from the start, and unless you make a conscious effort to prevent it, the existing dialect will come rushing in and do the job for you, at the expense of blurring or even changing your meaning. Probably it is better to put off using words as long as possible and get one's meaning as clear as one can through pictures or sensations. Afterwards one can choose — not simply *accept* — the phrases that will best cover the meaning, and then switch round and decide what impression one's words are likely to make on another person. This last effort of the mind cuts out all stale or mixed images, all prefabricated phrases, needless repetitions, and humbug and vagueness generally. But one can often be in doubt about the effect of a word or a phrase, and one needs rules that one can rely on when instinct fails. I think the following rules will cover most cases:

(i) Never use a metaphor, simile, or other figure of speech which you are used to seeing in print.

(ii) Never use a long word where a short one will do.

(iii) If it is possible to cut a word out, always cut it out.

---

[3] One can cure oneself of the *not un-* formation by memorizing this sentence: *A not unblack dog was chasing a not unsmall rabbit across a not ungreen field.*

(iv) Never use the passive where you can use the active.

(v) Never use a foreign phrase, a scientific word, or a jargon word if you can think of an everyday English equivalent.

(vi) Break any of these rules sooner than say anything outright barbarous.

These rules sound elementary, and so they are, but they demand a deep change in attitude in anyone who has grown used to writing in the style now fashionable. One could keep all of them and still write bad English, but one could not write the kind of stuff that I quoted in those five specimens at the beginning of this article.

I have not here been considering the literary use of language, but merely language as an instrument for expressing and not for concealing or preventing thought. Stuart Chase and others have come near to claiming that all abstract words are meaningless, and have used this as a pretext for advocating a kind of political quietism. Since you don't know what Fascism is, how can you struggle against Fascism? One need not swallow such absurdities as this, but one ought to recognize that the present political chaos is connected with the decay of language, and that one can probably bring about some improvement by starting at the verbal end. If you simplify your English, you are freed from the worst follies of orthodoxy. You cannot speak any of the necessary dialects, and when you make a stupid remark its stupidity will be obvious, even to yourself. Political language — and with variations this is true of all political parties, from Conservatives to Anarchists — is designed to make lies sound truthful and murder respectable, and to give an appearance of solidity to pure wind. One cannot change this all in a moment, but one can at least change one's own habits, and from time to time one can even, if one jeers loudly enough, send some worn-out and useless phrase — some *jackboot, Achilles' heel, hotbed, melting pot, acid test, veritable inferno,* or other lump of verbal refuse — into the dustbin where it belongs.

DISCUSSION QUESTIONS

1. Orwell disagrees with a common assumption about language. What is it? Where in the essay does he attack this assumption directly?

2. What faults do his five samples of bad language have in common? Select examples of these faults in each passage.

3. What "tricks" (para. 4) for avoiding good prose does Orwell list? Do you think that some are more dangerous or misleading than others? Explain the reasons for your answer.

4. What different reasons does Orwell suggest for the slovenliness of much political writing and speaking? What examples does he give to support these reasons? Are they persuasive?

5. How does Orwell propose that we get rid of our bad language habits? Do you think his recommendations are realistic? Can the teaching of writing in school assist in the remedy?

6. Why does Orwell urge the reader to "look back through this essay" to find "the very faults I am protesting against" (para. 15)? Can you, in fact, find any?

WRITING SUGGESTIONS

7. Choose a speech or an editorial whose meaning seems to be obscured by pretentious diction, meaningless words, euphemism, or "sheer cloudy vagueness." Point out the real meaning of the piece. If you think that its purpose is deceptive, expose the unpleasant truth that the author is concealing. Use Orwell's device, giving concrete meaning to any abstractions. (One source of speeches is a publication called *Vital Speeches of the Day*. Another is the *New York Times*, which often prints in full, or excerpts major portions of, speeches by leading figures in public life.)

8. Orwell's essay appeared before the widespread use of television. Do you think that TV makes it harder for politicians to be dishonest? Choose a particular public event — a war, a street riot, a terrorist activity, a campaign stop — and argue either for or against the claim that televised coverage makes it harder for a politician to engage in "sheer cloudy vagueness." Or does it make no difference at all? Be specific in your use of evidence.

Letter from Birmingham Jail

MARTIN LUTHER KING JR.

A Call for Unity: A Letter from Eight White Clergymen

April 12, 1963

We the undersigned clergymen are among those who, in January, issued "An Appeal for Law and Order and Common Sense," in dealing with racial problems in Alabama. We expressed understanding that honest convictions in racial matters could properly be pursued in the courts, but urged that decisions of those courts should in the meantime be peacefully obeyed.

Since that time there had been some evidence of increased forebearance and a willingness to face facts. Responsible citizens have undertaken to work on various problems which cause racial friction and unrest. In Birmingham, recent public events have given indication that we all have opportunity for a new constructive and realistic approach to racial problems.

Martin Luther King Jr. (1929–1968) was a clergyman, author, distinguished civil rights leader, and winner of the Nobel Prize for peace in 1964 for his contributions to racial harmony and his advocacy of nonviolent response to aggression. He was assassinated in 1968. In "Letter from Birmingham Jail," he appears as a historian and philosopher. He wrote the letter from a jail cell on April 16, 1963, after his arrest for participation in a demonstration for civil rights for African Americans. The letter was a reply to eight Alabama clergymen who, in the first letter reprinted here, had condemned demonstrations in the streets. King's essay is from *A Testament of Hope* (1986).

However, we are now confronted by a series of demonstrations by some of our Negro citizens, directed and led in part by outsiders. We recognize the natural impatience of people who feel that their hopes are slow in being realized. But we are convinced that these demonstrations are unwise and untimely.

We agree rather with certain local Negro leadership which has called for honest and open negotiation of racial issues in our area. And we believe this kind of facing of issues can best be accomplished by citizens of our own metropolitan area, white and Negro, meeting with their knowledge and experience of the local situation. All of us need to face that responsibility and find proper channels for its accomplishment.

Just as we formerly pointed out that "hatred and violence have no sanction in   5 our religious and political traditions," we also point out that such actions as incite to hatred and violence, however technically peaceful those actions may be, have not contributed to the resolution of our local problems. We do not believe that these days of new hope are days when extreme measures are justified in Birmingham.

We commend the community as a whole, and the local news media and law enforcement officials in particular, on the calm manner in which these demonstrations have been handled. We urge the public to continue to show restraint should the demonstrations continue, and the law enforcement officials to remain calm and continue to protect our city from violence.

We further strongly urge our own Negro community to withdraw support from these demonstrations, and to unite locally in working peacefully for a better Birmingham. When rights are consistently denied, a cause should be pressed in the courts and in negotiations among local leaders, and not in the streets. We appeal to both our white and Negro citizenry to observe the principles of law and order and common sense.

(Signed)
C.C.J. Carpenter, D.D., L.L.D., Bishop of Alabama; Joseph A. Durick, D.D., Auxiliary Bishop, Diocese of Mobile-Birmingham; Rabbi Milton L. Grafman, Temple Emanu-El, Birmingham, Alabama; Bishop Paul Hardin, Bishop of the Alabama–West Florida Conference of the Methodist Church; Bishop Nolan B. Harmon, Bishop of the North Alabama Conference of the Methodist Church; George M. Murray, D.D., L.L.D., Bishop Coadjutor, Episcopal Diocese of Alabama; Edward V. Ramage, Moderator, Synod of the Alabama Presbyterian Church in the United States; Earl Stallings, Pastor, First Baptist Church, Birmingham.

King's Reply from Birmingham Jail

My dear Fellow Clergymen,

While confined here in the Birmingham city jail, I came across your recent statement calling our present activities "unwise and untimely." Seldom, if ever, do I pause to answer criticism of my work and ideas. If I sought to answer all of the criticisms that cross my desk, my secretaries would be engaged in little else in the course of the day, and I would have no time for constructive work. But since I feel that you are men of genuine good will and your criticisms are sincerely set forth, I would like to answer your statement in what I hope will be patient and reasonable terms.

I think I should give the reason for my being in Birmingham, since you have been influenced by the argument of "outsiders coming in." I have the honor of serving as president of the Southern Christian Leadership Conference, an organization operating in every southern state, with headquarters in Atlanta, Georgia. We have some eighty-five affiliate organizations all across the South — one being the Alabama Christian Movement for Human Rights. Whenever necessary and possible we share staff, educational, and financial resources with our affiliates. Several months ago our local affiliate here in Birmingham invited us to be on call to engage in a nonviolent direct-action program if such were deemed necessary. We readily consented and when the hour came we lived up to our promises. So I am here, along with several members of my staff, because we were invited here. I am here because I have basic organizational ties here.

Beyond this, I am in Birmingham because injustice is here. Just as the eighth-century prophets left their little villages and carried their "thus saith the Lord" far beyond the boundaries of their hometowns; and just as the Apostle Paul left his little village of Tarsus and carried the gospel of Jesus Christ to practically every hamlet and city of the Graeco-Roman world, I too am compelled to carry the gospel of freedom beyond my particular hometown. Like Paul, I must constantly respond to the Macedonian call for aid.

Moreover, I am cognizant of the interrelatedness of all communities and states. I cannot sit idly by in Atlanta and not be concerned about what happens in Birmingham. Injustice anywhere is a threat to justice everywhere. We are caught in an inescapable network of mutuality, tied in a single garment of destiny. Whatever affects one directly affects all indirectly. Never again can we afford to live with the narrow, provincial "outside agitator" idea. Anyone who lives in the United States can never be considered an outsider anywhere in this country.

You deplore the demonstrations that are presently taking place in Birmingham. 5 But I am sorry that your statement did not express a similar concern for the conditions that brought the demonstrations into being. I am sure that each of you would want to go beyond the superficial social analyst who looks merely at effects, and does not grapple with underlying causes. I would not hesitate to say that it is unfortunate that so-called demonstrations are taking place in Birmingham at this time, but I would say in more emphatic terms that it is even more unfortunate that the white power structure of this city left the Negro community with no other alternative.

In any nonviolent campaign there are four basic steps: (1) collection of the facts to determine whether injustices are alive, (2) negotiation, (3) self-purification, and (4) direct action. We have gone through all of these steps in Birmingham. There can be no gainsaying of the fact that racial injustice engulfs this community.

Birmingham is probably the most thoroughly segregated city in the United States. Its ugly record of police brutality is known in every section of this country. Its unjust treatment of Negroes in the courts is a notorious reality. There have been more unsolved bombings of Negro homes and churches in Birmingham than any city in this nation. These are the hard, brutal, and unbelievable facts. On the basis of these conditions Negro leaders sought to negotiate with the city fathers. But the political leaders consistently refused to engage in good faith negotiation.

Then came the opportunity last September to talk with some of the leaders of the economic community. In these negotiating sessions certain promises were made by the merchants — such as the promise to remove the humiliating racial signs from the stores. On the basis of these promises Reverend Shuttlesworth and the leaders of the Alabama Christian Movement for Human Rights agreed to call a moratorium on any type of demonstrations. As the weeks and months unfolded we realized that we were the victims of a broken promise. The signs remained. Like so many experiences of the past we were confronted with blasted hopes, and the dark shadow of a deep disappointment settled upon us. So we had no alternative except that of preparing for direct action, whereby we would present our very bodies as a means of laying our case before the conscience of the local and national community. We were not unmindful of the difficulties involved. So we decided to go through a process of self-purification. We started having workshops on nonviolence and repeatedly asking ourselves the questions, "Are you able to accept blows without retaliating?" "Are you able to endure the ordeals of jail?" We decided to set our direct-action program around the Easter season, realizing that with the exception of Christmas, this was the largest shopping period of the year. Knowing that a strong economic withdrawal program would be the by-product of direct action, we felt that this was the best time to bring pressure on the merchants for the needed changes. Then it occurred to us that the March election was ahead and so we speedily decided to postpone action until after election day. When we discovered that Mr. Connor was in the run-off, we decided again to postpone action so that the demonstrations could not be used to cloud the issues. At this time we agreed to begin our nonviolent witness the day after the run-off.

This reveals that we did not move irresponsibly into direct actions. We too wanted to see Mr. Connor defeated; so we went through postponement after postponement to aid in this community need. After this we felt that direct action could be delayed no longer.

You may well ask, "Why direct action? Why sit-ins, marches, etc.? Isn't negotia- 10 tion a better path?" You are exactly right in your call for negotiation. Indeed, this is the purpose of direct action. Nonviolent direct action seeks to create such a crisis and establish such creative tension that a community that has constantly refused to negotiate is forced to confront the issue. It seeks so to dramatize the issue that it can no longer be ignored. I just referred to the creation of tension as a part of the work of the nonviolent resister. This may sound rather shocking. But I must confess that I am not afraid of the word tension. I have earnestly worked and preached against violent tension, but there is a type of constructive nonviolent tension that is necessary for growth. Just as Socrates felt that it was necessary to create a tension in the mind so that individuals could rise from the bondage of myths and half-truths to the unfettered realm of creative analysis and objective appraisal, we must see the need of having nonviolent gadflies to create the kind of tension in society that will help men to rise from the dark depths of prejudice and racism to the majestic heights of understanding and brotherhood. So the purpose of the direct action is to create a situation so crisis-packed that it will inevitably open the door to negotiation. We, therefore, concur with you in your call for negotiation. Too long has our beloved Southland been bogged down in the tragic attempt to live in monologue rather than dialogue.

One of the basic points in your statement is that our acts are untimely. Some have asked, "Why didn't you give the new administration time to act?" The only answer that I can give to this inquiry is that the new administration must be prodded about as much as the outgoing one before it acts. We will be sadly mistaken if we feel that the election of Mr. Boutwell will bring the millennium to Birmingham. While Mr. Boutwell is much more articulate and gentle than Mr. Connor, they are both segregationists, dedicated to the task of maintaining the status quo. The hope I see in Mr. Boutwell is that he will be reasonable enough to see the futility of massive resistance to desegregation. But he will not see this without pressure from the devotees of civil rights. My friends, I must say to you that we have not made a single gain in civil rights without determined legal and nonviolent pressure. History is the long and tragic story of the fact that privileged groups seldom give up their privileges voluntarily. Individuals may see the moral light and voluntarily give up their unjust posture; but as Reinhold Niebuhr has reminded us, groups are more immoral than individuals.

We know through painful experience that freedom is never voluntarily given by the oppressor; it must be demanded by the oppressed. Frankly, I have never yet engaged in a direct-action movement that was "well-timed," according to the timetable of those who have not suffered unduly from the disease of segregation. For years now I have heard the words "Wait!" It rings in the ear of every Negro with a piercing familiarity. This "Wait" has almost always meant "Never." It has been a tranquilizing thalidomide, relieving the emotional stress for a moment, only to give birth to an ill-formed infant of frustration. We must come to see with the distinguished jurist of yesterday that "justice too long delayed is justice denied." We have waited for more than 340 years for our constitutional and God-given rights. The nations of Asia and Africa are moving with jetlike speed toward the goal of political independence, and we still creep at horse and buggy pace toward the gaining of a cup of coffee at a lunch counter. I guess it is easy for those who have never felt the stinging darts of segregation to say, "Wait." But when you have seen vicious mobs lynch your mothers and fathers at will and drown your sisters and brothers at whim; when you see hate-filled policemen curse, kick, brutalize, and even kill your black brothers and sisters with impunity; when you see the vast majority of your 20 million Negro brothers smothering in an airtight cage of poverty in the midst of an affluent society; when you suddenly find your tongue twisted and your speech stammering as you seek to explain to your six-year-old daughter why she can't go to the public amusement park that has just been advertised on television, and see tears welling up in her little eyes when she is told that Funtown is closed to colored children, and see the depressing clouds of inferiority begin to form in her little mental sky, and see her begin to distort her little personality by unconsciously developing a bitterness toward white people; when you have to concoct an answer for a five-year-old son asking in agonizing pathos: "Daddy, why do white people treat colored people so mean?"; when you take a cross-country drive and find it necessary to sleep night after night in the uncomfortable corners of your automobile because no motel will accept you; when you are humiliated day in and day out by nagging signs reading "white" and "colored"; when your first name becomes "nigger" and your middle name becomes "boy" (however old you are) and your last name becomes "John," and when your wife and mother are never given the respected title "Mrs."; when you are harried by day and haunted by night by the fact that you are a Negro, living constantly at tiptoe stance never quite knowing what to expect next, and plagued with inner fears and outer resentments; when you are forever fighting a degenerating sense of "nobodiness"; then you will understand why we find it difficult to wait. There comes a time when the cup of endurance runs over, and men are no longer willing to be plunged into an abyss of injustice where they experience the blackness of corroding despair. I hope, sirs, you can understand our legitimate and unavoidable impatience.

You express a great deal of anxiety over our willingness to break laws. This is certainly a legitimate concern. Since we so diligently urge people to obey the Supreme Court's decision of 1954 outlawing segregation in the public schools, it is rather strange and paradoxical to find us consciously breaking laws. One may well ask, "How can you advocate breaking some laws and obeying others?" The answer is found in the fact that there are two types of laws: There are *just* and there are *unjust* laws. I would agree with Saint Augustine that "An unjust law is no law at all."

Now what is the difference between the two? How does one determine when a law is just or unjust? A just law is a man-made code that squares with the moral law or the law of God. An unjust law is a code that is out of harmony with the moral law. To put it in the terms of Saint Thomas Aquinas, an unjust law is a human law that is not rooted in eternal and natural law. Any law that uplifts human personality is just. Any law that degrades human personality is unjust. All segregation statutes are unjust because segregation distorts the soul and damages the personality. It gives the segregator a false sense of superiority, and the segregated a false sense of inferiority. To use the words of Martin Buber, the great Jewish philosopher, segregation substitutes an "I-it" relationship for the "I-thou" relationship, and ends up relegating persons to the status of things. So segregation is not only politically, economically, and sociologically unsound, but it is morally wrong and sinful. Paul Tillich has said that sin is separation. Isn't segregation an existential expression of man's tragic separation, an expression of his awful estrangement, his terrible sinfulness? So I can urge men to disobey segregation ordinances because they are morally wrong.

Let us turn to a more concrete example of just and unjust laws. An unjust law is a code that a majority inflicts on a minority that is not binding on itself. This is difference made legal. On the other hand, a just law is a code that a majority compels a minority to follow that it is willing to follow itself. This is sameness made legal. 15

Let me give another explanation. An unjust law is a code inflicted upon a minority which that minority had no part in enacting or creating because they did not have the unhampered right to vote. Who can say that the legislature of Alabama which set up the segregation laws was democratically elected? Throughout the state of Alabama all types of conniving methods are used to prevent Negroes from becoming registered voters, and there are some counties without a single Negro registered to vote despite the fact that the Negro constitutes a majority of the population. Can any law set up in such a state be considered democratically structured?

These are just a few examples of unjust and just laws. There are some instances when a law is just on its face and unjust in its application. For instance, I was arrested Friday on a charge of parading without a permit. Now there is nothing wrong with an ordinance which requires a permit for a parade, but when the ordinance is used to preserve segregation and to deny citizens the First Amendment privilege of peaceful assembly and peaceful protest, then it becomes unjust.

I hope you can see the distinction I am trying to point out. In no sense do I advocate evading or defying the law as the rabid segregationist would do. This would lead to anarchy. One who breaks an unjust law must do it *openly, lovingly* (not hatefully as the white mothers did in New Orleans when they were seen on television screaming, "nigger, nigger, nigger"), and with a willingness to accept the penalty. I submit that an individual who breaks a law that conscience tells him is unjust, and willingly accepts the penalty by staying in jail to arouse the conscience of the community over its injustice, is in reality expressing the very highest respect for law.

Of course, there is nothing new about this kind of civil disobedience. It was seen sublimely in the refusal of Shadrach, Meshach, and Abednego to obey the laws of Nebuchadnezzar because a higher moral law was involved. It was practiced superbly by the early Christians who were willing to face hungry lions and the excruciating pain of chopping blocks, before submitting to certain unjust laws of the Roman Empire. To a degree academic freedom is a reality today because Socrates practiced civil disobedience.

We can never forget that everything Hitler did in Germany was "legal" and everything the Hungarian freedom fighters did in Hungary was "illegal." It was "illegal" to aid and comfort a Jew in Hitler's Germany. But I am sure that if I had lived in Germany during that time I would have aided and comforted my Jewish brothers even though it was illegal. If I lived in a Communist country today where certain principles dear to the Christian faith are suppressed, I believe I would openly advocate disobeying these antireligious laws. I must make two honest confessions to you, my Christian and Jewish brothers. First, I must confess that over the last few years I have been gravely disappointed with the white moderate. I have almost reached the regrettable conclusion that the Negro's great stumbling block in the stride toward freedom is not the White Citizen's Councilor or the Ku Klux Klanner, but the white moderate who is more devoted to "order" than to justice; who prefers a negative peace which is the absence of tension to a positive peace which is the presence of justice; who constantly says, "I agree with you in the goal you seek, but I can't agree with your methods of direct action"; who paternalistically feels that he can set the timetable for another man's freedom; who lives by the myth of time and who constantly advises the Negro to wait until a "more convenient season." Shallow understanding from people of good will is more frustrating than absolute misunderstanding from people of ill will. Lukewarm acceptance is much more bewildering than outright rejection.

I had hoped that the white moderate would understand that law and order exist for the purpose of establishing justice, and that when they fail to do this they become dangerously structured dams that block the flow of social progress. I had hoped that the white moderate would understand that the present tension of the South is merely a necessary phase of the transition from an obnoxious negative peace, where the Negro passively accepted his unjust plight, to a substance-filled positive peace, where all men will respect the dignity and worth of human personality. Actually, we who engage in nonviolent direct action are not the creators of tension. We merely bring to the surface the hidden tension that is already alive. We bring it out in the open where it can be seen and dealt with. Like a boil that can never be cured as long as it is covered up but must be opened with all its pus-flowing ugliness to the natural medicines of air and light, injustice must likewise be exposed, with all of the tension its exposing creates, to the light of human conscience and the air of national opinion before it can be cured.

In your statement you asserted that our actions, even though peaceful, must be condemned because they precipitate violence. But can this assertion be logically made? Isn't this like condemning the robbed man because his possession of money precipitated the evil act of robbery? Isn't this like condemning Socrates because his unswerving commitment to truth and his philosophical delvings precipitated the misguided popular mind to make him drink the hemlock? Isn't this like condemning Jesus because His unique God-consciousness and never-ceasing devotion to His will precipitated the evil act of crucifixion? We must come to see, as federal courts have consistently affirmed, that it is immoral to urge an individual to withdraw his efforts to gain his basic constitutional rights because the quest precipitates violence. Society must protect the robbed and punish the robber.

I had also hoped that the white moderate would reject the myth of time. I received a letter this morning from a white brother in Texas which said: "All Christians know that the colored people will receive equal rights eventually, but it is possible that you are in too great of a religious hurry. It has taken Christianity almost two thousand years to accomplish what it has. The teachings of Christ take time to come to earth." All that is said here grows out of a tragic misconception of time. It is the strangely irrational notion that there is something in the very flow of time that will inevitably cure all ills. Actually time is neutral. It can be used either destructively or constructively. I am coming to feel that the people of ill will have used time much more effectively than the people of good will. We will have to repent in this generation not merely for the vitriolic words and actions of the bad people, but for the appalling silence of the good people. We must come to see that human progress never rolls in on wheels of inevitability. It comes through the tireless efforts and persistent work of men willing to be co-workers with God, and without this hard work time itself becomes an ally of the forces of social stagnation. We must use time creatively, and forever realize that the time is always ripe to do right. Now is the time to make real the promise of democracy, and transform our pending national elegy into a creative psalm of brotherhood. Now is the time to lift our national policy from the quicksand of racial injustice to the solid rock of human dignity.

You spoke of our activity in Birmingham as extreme. At first I was rather disappointed that fellow clergymen would see my nonviolent efforts as those of the extremist. I started thinking about the fact that I stand in the middle of two opposing forces in the Negro community. One is a force of complacency made up of Negroes who, as a result of long years of oppression, have been so completely drained of self-respect and a sense of "somebodiness" that they have adjusted to segregation, and of a few Negroes in the middle class who, because of a degree of academic and economic security, and because at points they profit by segregation, have unconsciously become insensitive to the problems of the masses. The other force is one of bitterness and hatred, and comes perilously close to advocating violence. It is expressed in the various black nationalist groups that are springing up over the nation, the largest and best known being Elijah Muhammad's Muslim movement. This movement is nourished by the contemporary frustration over the continued existence of racial discrimination. It is made up of people who have lost faith in America, who have absolutely repudiated Christianity, and who have concluded that the white man is an incurable "devil." I have tried to stand between these two forces, saying that we need not follow the "do-nothingism" of the complacent or the hatred and despair of the black nationalist. There is the more excellent way of love and nonviolent protest. I'm grateful to God that, through the Negro church, the dimension of nonviolence entered our struggle. If this philosophy had not emerged, I am convinced that by now many streets of the South would be flowing with floods of blood. And I am further convinced that if our white brothers dismiss us as "rabble-rousers" and "outside agitators" those of us who are working through the channels of nonviolent direct action and refuse to support our nonviolent efforts, millions of Negroes, out of frustration and despair, will seek solace and security in black nationalist ideologies, a development that will lead inevitably to a frightening racial nightmare.

Oppressed people cannot remain oppressed forever. The urge for freedom will 25 eventually come. This is what happened to the American Negro. Something within has reminded him of his birthright of freedom; something without has reminded him that he can gain it. Consciously and unconsciously, he has been swept in by what the Germans call the *Zeitgeist*, and with his black brothers of Africa, and his brown and yellow brothers of Asia, South America, and the Caribbean, he is moving with a sense of cosmic urgency toward the promised land of racial justice. Recognizing this vital urge that has engulfed the Negro community, one should readily understand public demonstrations. The Negro has many pent-up resentments and latent frustrations. He has to get them out. So let him march sometime; let him have his prayer pilgrimages to the city hall; understand why he must have sit-ins and freedom rides. If his repressed emotions do not come out in these nonviolent ways, they will come out in ominous expressions of violence. This is not a threat; it is a fact of history. So I have not said to my people "get rid of your discontent." But I have tried to say that this normal and healthy discontent can be channelized through the creative outlet of nonviolent direct action. Now this approach is being dismissed as extremist. I must admit that I was initially disappointed in being so categorized.

But as I continued to think about the matter I gradually gained a bit of satisfaction from being considered an extremist. Was not Jesus an extremist in love — "Love your enemies, bless them that curse you, pray for them that despitefully use you." Was not Amos an extremist for justice — "Let justice roll down like waters and righteousness like a mighty stream." Was not Paul an extremist for the gospel of Jesus Christ — "I bear in my body the marks of the Lord Jesus." Was not Martin Luther an extremist — "Here I stand; I can do none other so help me God." Was not John Bunyan an extremist — "I will stay in jail to the end of my days before I make a butchery of my conscience." Was not Abraham Lincoln an extremist — "This nation cannot survive half slave and half free." Was not Thomas Jefferson an extremist — "We hold these truths to be self-evident, that all men are created equal." So the question is not whether we will be extremist but what kind of extremist will we be. Will we be extremists for hate or will we be extremists for love? Will we be extremists for the preservation of injustice — or will we be extremists for the cause of justice? In that dramatic scene on Calvary's hill, three men were crucified. We must not forget that all three were crucified for the same crime — the crime of extremism. Two were extremists for immorality, and thusly fell below their environment. The other, Jesus Christ, was an extremist for love, truth, and goodness, and thereby rose above his environment. So, after all, maybe the South, the nation, and the world are in dire need of creative extremists.

I had hoped that the white moderate would see this. Maybe I was too optimistic. Maybe I expected too much. I guess I should have realized that few members of a race that has oppressed another race can understand or appreciate the deep groans and passionate yearnings of those that have been oppressed and still fewer have the vision to see that injustice must be rooted out by strong, persistent, and determined action. I am thankful, however, that some of our white brothers have grasped the meaning of this social revolution and committed themselves to it. They are still all too small in quantity, but they are big in quality. Some like Ralph McGill, Lillian Smith, Harry Golden, and James Dabbs have written about our struggle in eloquent, prophetic, and understanding terms. Others have marched with us down nameless streets of the South. They have languished in filthy roach-infested jails, suffering the abuse and brutality of angry policemen who see them as "dirty nigger-lovers." They, unlike so many of their moderate brothers and sisters, have recognized the urgency of the moment and sensed the need for powerful "action" antidotes to combat the disease of segregation.

Let me rush on to mention my other disappointment. I have been so greatly disappointed with the white church and its leadership. Of course, there are some notable exceptions. I am not unmindful of the fact that each of you has taken some significant stands on this issue. I commend you, Reverend Stallings, for your Christian stance on this past Sunday, in welcoming Negroes to your worship service on a nonsegregated basis. I commend the Catholic leaders of this state for integrating Springhill College several years ago.

But despite these notable exceptions I must honestly reiterate that I have been disappointed with the church. I do not say that as one of the negative critics who can always find something wrong with the church. I say it as a minister of the gospel, who loves the church; who was nurtured in its bosom; who has been sustained by its spiritual blessings, and who will remain true to it as long as the cord of life shall lengthen.

I had the strange feeling when I was suddenly catapulted into the leadership of   30 the bus protest in Montgomery several years ago that we would have the support of the white church. I felt that the white ministers, priests, and rabbis of the South would be some of our strongest allies. Instead, some have been outright opponents, refusing to understand the freedom movement and misrepresenting its leaders; all too many others have been more cautious than courageous and have remained silent behind the anesthetizing security of the stained-glass windows.

In spite of my shattered dreams of the past, I came to Birmingham with the hope that the white religious leadership of this community would see the justice of our cause, and with deep moral concern, serve as the channel through which our just grievances would get to the power structure. I had hoped that each of you would understand. But again I have been disappointed. I have heard numerous religious leaders of the South call upon their worshipers to comply with a desegregation decision because it is the *law,* but I have longed to hear white ministers say, "Follow this decree because integration is morally *right* and the Negro is your brother." In the midst of blatant injustices inflicted upon the Negro, I have watched white churches stand on the sideline and merely mouth pious irrelevancies and sanctimonious trivialities. In the midst of a mighty struggle to rid our nation of racial and economic injustice, I have heard so many ministers say, "Those are social issues with which the gospel has no real concern," and I have watched so many churches commit themselves to a completely otherworldly religion which made a strange distinction between body and soul, the sacred and the secular.

So here we are moving toward the exit of the twentieth century with a religious community largely adjusted to the status quo, standing as a taillight behind other community agencies rather than a headlight leading men to higher levels of justice.

I have traveled the length and breadth of Alabama, Mississippi, and all the other southern states. On sweltering summer days and crisp autumn mornings I have looked at her beautiful churches with their lofty spires pointing heavenward. I have beheld the impressive outlay of her massive religious education buildings. Over and over again I have found myself asking: "What kind of people worship here? Who is their God? Where were their voices when the lips of Governor Barnett dripped with words of interposition and nullification? Where were they when Governor Wallace gave the clarion call for defiance and hatred? Where were their voices of support when tired, bruised, and weary Negro men and women decided to rise from the dark dungeons of complacency to the bright hills of creative protest?"

Yes, these questions are still in my mind. In deep disappointment, I have wept over the laxity of the church. But be assured that my tears have been tears of love. There can be no deep disappointment where there is not deep love. Yes, I love the church; I love her sacred walls. How could I do otherwise? I am in the rather unique position of being the son, the grandson, and the great-grandson of preachers. Yes, I see the church as the body of Christ. But, oh! How we have blemished and scarred that body through social neglect and fear of being nonconformists.

There was a time when the church was very powerful. It was during that pe- 35
riod when the early Christians rejoiced when they were deemed worthy to suffer
for what they believed. In those days the church was not merely a thermometer
that recorded the ideas and principles of popular opinion; it was a thermostat that
transformed the mores of society. Wherever the early Christians entered a town the
power structure got disturbed and immediately sought to convict them for being
"disturbers of the peace" and "outside agitators." But they went on with the conviction that they were "a colony of heaven," and had to obey God rather than man.
They were small in number but big in commitment. They were too God-intoxicated
to be "astronomically intimidated." They brought an end to such ancient evils as
infanticide and gladiatorial contest.

Things are different now. The contemporary church is often a weak, ineffectual
voice with an uncertain sound. It is so often the archsupporter of the status quo.
Far from being disturbed by the presence of the church, the power structure of the
average community is consoled by the church's silent and often vocal sanction of
things as they are.

But the judgment of God is upon the church as never before. If the church of
today does not recapture the sacrificial spirit of the early church, it will lose its authentic ring, forfeit the loyalty of millions, and be dismissed as an irrelevant social
club with no meaning for the twentieth century. I am meeting young people every
day whose disappointment with the church has risen to outright disgust.

Maybe again, I have been too optimistic. Is organized religion too inextricably
bound to the status quo to save our nation and the world? Maybe I must turn my
faith to the inner spiritual church, the church within the church, as the true *ecclesia*
and the hope of the world. But again I am thankful to God that some noble souls
from the ranks of organized religion have broken loose from the paralyzing chains
of conformity and joined us as active partners in the struggle for freedom. They have
left their secure congregations and walked the streets of Albany, Georgia, with us.
They have gone through the highways of the South on tortuous rides for freedom.
Yes, they have gone to jail with us. Some have been kicked out of their churches,
and lost support of their bishops and fellow ministers. But they have gone with the
faith that right defeated is stronger than evil triumphant. These men have been the
leaven in the lump of the race. Their witness has been the spiritual salt that has
preserved the true meaning of the gospel in these troubled times. They have carved
a tunnel of hope through the dark mountain of disappointment.

I hope the church as a whole will meet the challenge of this decisive hour. But
even if the church does not come to the aid of justice, I have no despair about the
future. I have no fear about the outcome of our struggle in Birmingham, even if
our motives are presently misunderstood. We will reach the goal of freedom in Birmingham and all over the nation, because the goal of America is freedom. Abused
and scorned though we may be, our destiny is tied up with the destiny of America.
Before the Pilgrims landed at Plymouth we were here. Before the pen of Jefferson
etched across the pages of history the majestic words of the Declaration of Independence, we were here. For more than two centuries our foreparents labored in this
country without wages; they made cotton king; and they built the homes of their

masters in the midst of brutal injustice and shameful humiliation — and yet out of a bottomless vitality they continued to thrive and develop. If the inexpressible cruelties of slavery could not stop us, the opposition we now face will surely fail. We will win our freedom because the sacred heritage of our nation and the eternal will of God are embodied in our echoing demands.

I must close now. But before closing I am impelled to mention one other point 40 in your statement that troubled me profoundly. You warmly commended the Birmingham police force for keeping "order" and "preventing violence." I don't believe you would have so warmly commended the police force if you had seen its angry violent dogs literally biting six unarmed, nonviolent Negroes. I don't believe you would so quickly commend the policemen if you would observe their ugly and inhuman treatment of Negroes here in the city jail; if you would watch them push and curse old Negro women and young Negro girls; if you would see them slap and kick old Negro men and young boys; if you will observe them, as they did on two occasions, refuse to give us food because we wanted to sing our grace together. I'm sorry that I can't join you in your praise for the police department.

It is true that they have been rather disciplined in their public handling of the demonstrators. In this sense they have been rather publicly "nonviolent." But for what purpose? To preserve the evil system of segregation. Over the last few years I have consistently preached that nonviolence demands that the means we use must be as pure as the ends we seek. So I have tried to make it clear that it is wrong to use immoral means to attain moral ends. But now I must affirm that it is just as wrong, or even more so, to use moral means to preserve immoral ends. Maybe Mr. Connor and his policemen have been rather publicly nonviolent, as Chief Pritchett was in Albany, Georgia, but they have used the moral means of nonviolence to maintain the immoral end of flagrant racial injustice. T. S. Eliot has said that there is no greater treason than to do the right deed for the wrong reason.

I wish you had commended the Negro sit-inners and demonstrators of Birmingham for their sublime courage, their willingness to suffer, and their amazing discipline in the midst of the most inhuman provocation. One day the South will recognize its real heroes. They will be the James Merediths, courageously and with a majestic sense of purpose facing jeering and hostile mobs and the agonizing loneliness that characterizes the life of the pioneer. They will be old, oppressed, battered Negro women, symbolized in a seventy-two-year-old woman of Montgomery, Alabama, who rose up with a sense of dignity and with her people decided not to ride the segregated buses, and responded to one who inquired about her tiredness with ungrammatical profundity: "My feet is tired, but my soul is rested." They will be the young high school and college students, young ministers of the gospel, and a host of their elders courageously and nonviolently sitting-in at lunch counters and willingly going to jail for conscience's sake. One day the South will know that when these disinherited children of God sat down at lunch counters they were in reality standing up for the best in the American dream and the most sacred values in our Judeo-Christian heritage, and thusly, carrying our whole nation back to those great wells of democracy which were dug deep by the Founding Fathers in the formulation of the Constitution and the Declaration of Independence.

Never before have I written a letter this long (or should I say a book?). I'm afraid that it is much too long to take your precious time. I can assure you that it would have been much shorter if I had been writing from a comfortable desk, but what else is there to do when you are alone for days in the dull monotony of a narrow jail cell other than write long letters, think strange thoughts, and pray long prayers?

If I have said anything in this letter that is an overstatement of the truth and is indicative of an unreasonable impatience, I beg you to forgive me. If I have said anything in this letter that is an understatement of the truth and is indicative of my having a patience that makes me patient with anything less than brotherhood, I beg God to forgive me.

I hope this letter finds you strong in the faith. I also hope that circumstances   45
will soon make it possible for me to meet each of you, not as an integrationist or a civil rights leader, but as a fellow clergyman and a Christian brother. Let us all hope that the dark clouds of racial prejudice will soon pass away and the deep fog of mis-understanding will be lifted from our fear-drenched communities and in some not too distant tomorrow the radiant stars of love and brotherhood will shine over our great nation with all of their scintillating beauty.

Yours for the cause of Peace and Brotherhood,
Martin Luther King Jr.

DISCUSSION QUESTIONS

1. King uses figurative language in his letter. Find some particularly vivid passages, and evaluate their effect in the context of this letter.

2. Explain King's distinction between just and unjust laws. Are there dangers in attempting to make such a distinction?

3. What characteristics of mind and behavior does King exhibit in the letter? Select the specific passages that provide proof.

4. Why does King say that "the white moderate" (para. 27) is a greater threat to African American progress than the outspoken racist? Is his explanation convincing?

5. How does King justify his philosophy of nonviolence in the face of continued aggression against Americans who are of African descent?

WRITING SUGGESTIONS

6. Can you think of a law against which defiance would be justified? Explain why the law is unjust and why refusal to obey is morally defensible.

7. In paragraph 12 King lists the grievances of African Americans in this country. King's catalog is similar to the lists in the Declaration of Independence. Can you think of any other group that might compile a list of grievances? If so, choose a group, and draw up such a list making sure that your list is as clear and specific as those you have read.

Acknowledgments

George J. Annas. "Cancer and the Constitution: Choice at Life's End." From *The New England Journal of Medicine: Health, Law, Ethics and Human Rights*, Volume 357: 408-413, July 26, 2007, Number 4. Reprinted by permission.

Sharon Astyk and Aaron Newton. "The Rich Get Richer, The Poor Go Hungry." From *A Nation of Farmers: Defeating the Food Crisis on American Soil*, 2009. Reprinted by permission.

Eric Auchard. "We're All Celebrities in Post-Privacy Age." From Reuters.com, June 21, 2007. All rights reserved. Republication or redistribution of Thomson Reuters content, including by framing or similar means, is expressly prohibited without the written consent of Thomson Reuters. Thomson Reuters and its logo are registered trademarks of the Thomson Reuters group of companies around the world. © Thomson Reuters 2007. Thomson Reuters journalists are subject to an Editorial Handbook which requires fair presentaiton and disclosure of relevant interests.

Patricia E. Bauer. "A Movie, a Word and My Family's Battle" by Patricia E. Bauer from *The Washington Post*, August 17, 2008. Reprinted by permission of the author.

Diane Brady. "The Organic Myth" from *Business Week*, Oct. 16, 2006. Used with permission of Bloomberg Businessweek.com Permissions Copyright © 2011. All rights reserved.

Amy Brittain. "Universities Strike Back in Battle Over Illegal Downloads." From *Christian Science Monitor*, June 18, 2007, by Christian Science Publishing Society. Copyright 2007 Reproduced with permission of Christian Science Monitor in the format Textbook and Other book via Copyright Clearance Center.

Kurt Cagle. "As the Internet Rewires Our Brains" by Kurt Cagle from *O'Reilly Community*, February 28, 2009, http://broadcast.oreilly.com/2009/02/as-the-internet-rewires-our-br.html. Reprinted by permission.

Mona Charen. "The Misleading Debate on Stem Cell Research." From Townhall.com, August 20, 2004. Copyright © 2004 by News America Syndicate. Reprinted by permission of Mona Charen and Creator's Syndicate, Inc.

Jo Ann Citron. "Will it be Marriage or Civil Union?" From *The Gay & Lesbian Review Worldwide*, March/April 2004, v. 11 i2, p. 10(2). Copyright © 2004 Jo Ann Citron. Reprinted by permission of the author and the Gay & Lesbian Review Worldwide.

Andrew R. Cline. "Media/Political Bias," from http://rhetorica.net/ Reprinted by permission of the author.

Jillian Croll. "Body Image and Adolescents." From Stang J, Story M. (Eds), Guidelines for Adolescent Nutrition Services. Copyright © 2005 Center for Leadership, Education, and Training in Maternal and Child Nutrition, Division of Epidemiology and Community Health, School of Public Health, University of Minnesota.

Alan M. Dershowitz. "Is There a Torturous Road to Justice?" From *The Los Angeles Times*, Commentary, November 8, 2001. Reprinted by permission of the author.

David DiSalvo. "Are Social Networks Messing with Your Head?" Reproduced with permission. Copyright © 2010 Scientific American, a division of Nature America, Inc. All rights reserved.

Thomas Doherty. "Cultural Studies and Forensic Noir." From *Chronicle of Higher Education*, October 24, 2003. Copyright © 2003 by Thomas Doherty. Reprinted by permission of the author.

Roger Ebert. "Crash." Taken from the *Roger Ebert* column by Roger Ebert © 2005 The Ebert Company. Dist. By Universal Uclick. Reprinted by permission. All rights reserved.

Edward Jay Epstein. "Sex and the Cinema." From Slate.com, August 15, 2005. Reprinted by permission.

Sabrina Rubin Erdely. "Doctors' Beliefs Hinder Patient Care." June 22, 2007. MSNBC.com (online) (only staff-produced materials may be used) Copyright 2007 by MSNBC Interactive News, LLC. Reproduced with permission of MSNBC Interactive News, LLC in the format Textbook and Other book via Copyright Clearance Center.

Christopher M. Fairman. "The Case Against Banning the Word 'Retard'" by Christopher M. Fairman from *The Washington Post*, February 14, 2010. Reprinted by permission of the author.

Stephanie Fairyington. "Choice As Strategy: Homosexuality and the Politics of Pity," *Dissent* vol 57, no 1 (Winter 2010), pp. 7-10. Reprinted with permission of the University of Pennsylvania Press.

William Faulkner. "Nobel Prize Acceptance Speech." © The Nobel Foundation 1949. Reprinted by permission.

Leslie Fiedler. "Tyranny of the Normal." From *Tyranny of the Normal: Essays on Bioethics, Theology & Myth* by Leslie Fiedler. Reprinted by permission of David R. Godine, Publisher, Inc. Copyright © 1996 by Leslie Fiedler.

Seth Finkelstein. "Alan Dershowitz's Tortuous Torturous Argument." From *Ethical Spectacle*, February 2002. Reprinted by permission of the author.

Stanley Fish. "When Is a Cross a Cross?" From *The New York Times*, May 3, 2010, © 2010 The

Sharon Kneiss. "Argument for Recycling Is Strong" from *MSW Management*, November-December 2008. Reprinted by permission.

Alfie Kohn. "No-Win Situations." Copyright © 1990 by Alfie Kohn. Reprinted from *Women's Sports & Fitness* with the author's permission. For more on this topic, please see www.alfiekohn.org or Kohn's book *No Contest: The Case Against Competition*.

Charles Krauthammer. "Let's Have No More Monkey Trials." From *Time*, August 8, 2005. Reprinted by permission of the author.

Anna Lappé. "The Climate Crisis at the End of Our Fork." From *Food, Inc.*, edited by Karl B. Weber, 2009, The Perseus Books Group. Reprinted by permission

Michael Levin. "The Case for Torture." Originally published in *Newsweek*, June 7, 1982. Copyright © 1982 by Michael Levin. Reprinted by permission of the author.

Roger D. McGrath. "A God Given Natural Right 'Shall Not Be Infringed.'" From *Chronicles*, October 2003. Copyright © 2003. Reprinted by permission of the author.

Howard Moody. "Gay Marriage Shows Why We Need to Separate Church and State." Reprinted with permission from the July 5, 2004 issue of *The Nation*. For subscription information, call 1-800-333-8536. Portions of each week's Nation magazine can be accessed at http://www.thenation.com.

Charles Murray. "Abolish the SAT" from *The American*, July/August, 2007. Reprinted by permission.

Theodora Ooms. "Marriage-Plus." Annotated and excerpted from a special issue of *The American Prospect* on "The Politics of the American Family," April 8, 2002. Copyright © 2002 by the American Prospect. Reprinted by permission of the author.

George Orwell. "Politics and the English Language." Copyright © 1946 by Sonia Brownell Orwell and renewed 1974 by Sonia Orwell. Reprinted from his volume *Shooting An Elephant and Other Essays* by permission of Harcourt, Inc. Reprinted by permission of Bill Hamilton as the Literary Executor of the Estate of the Late Sonia Brownell Orwell and Secker & Warburg Ltd.

Michael Pollan. "Food Fight" by Michael Pollan, from *The Food Movement, Rising*, from *The New York Review of Books*. June 10, 2010. Reprinted by permission of International Creative Management, Inc.

James Poniewozik. "The Imus Fallout: Who Can Say What?" From Time.com, April 12, 2007. Copyright © 2007 TIME INC. Reprinted by permission. TIME is a registered trademark of Time Inc. All rights reserved.

James Poniewozik. "Polarized News? The Media's Moderate Bias" by James Poniewozik from *Time* magazine, November 4, 2009. Copyright © 2009, Time Inc. All rights reserved. Reprinted by permission.

Bill Press. "America's Town Meeting." From *Toxic Talk* by Bill Press, copyright © 2010 by author, and reprinted by permission of Thomas Dunne Books, an imprint of St. Martin's Press, LLC.

Anna Quindlen. "A New Look, an Old Battle." Published in *Newsweek*, April 9, 2001, pp. 72-73. Copyright © 2001 by Anna Quindlen. Reprinted by permission of International Creative Management, Inc.

(Rebecca Collins et al) Rand Health. "Does Watching Sex on Television Influence Teens' Sexual Activity?" From RAND Health Research Highlights. Copyright © 2004 RAND Corporation.

Julie Rawe. "Battling Term-Paper Cheats." From *Time, Inc.*, May 17, 2007. Copyright © 2007 TIME INC. Reprinted by permission. TIME is a registered trademark of Time Inc. All rights reserved.

Richard Rhodes. "Hollow Claims about Fantasy Violence." From *The New York Times*, September 17, 2000, © 2000 The New York Times. All rights reserved. Used by permission and protected by the Copyright Laws of the United States. The printing, copying, redistribution, or retransmission of this Content without express written permission is prohibited.

Arturo Rodriguez. "Cheap Food: Workers Pay the Price" From *Food, Inc.*, edited by Karl B. Weber, 2009, The Perseus Books Group. Reprinted by permission.

Richard Rothstein. "True or False: Schools Fail Immigrants." From The New York Times, July 4, 2001, © 2001 *The New York Times*. All rights reserved. Used by permission and protected by the Copyright Laws of the United States. The printing, copying, redistribution, or retransmission of the Material without express written permission is prohibited.

Allison Samuels. "Smooth Operations: A Taboo falls as cosmetic surgery gains in popularity among African-Americans, stars and average folk, too." From *Newsweek*, July 5, 2004. Copyright © 2004 Newsweek, Inc. All rights reserved. Used by permission and protected by the Copyright Laws of the United States. The printing, copying, redistribution, or retransmission of the Material without express written permission is prohibited.

Robert J. Samuelson. "The Hard Truth of Immigration." From Newsweek.com, June 13, 2005. Copyright © 2005. The Newsweek/Daily Beast Company LLC. All rights reserved. Used by permission and protected by the Copyright Laws of the United States. The printing, copying, redistribution, or retransmission of the Material without express written permission is prohibited.

PHOTO CREDITS

GLOSSARY

Abstract language: language expressing a quality apart from a specific object or event; opposite of *concrete language*

Ad hominem: "against the man"; attacking the arguer rather than the *argument* or issue

Ad populum: "to the people"; playing on the prejudices of the *audience*

Anecdotal evidence: stories or examples used to illustrate a *claim* but that do not prove it with scientific certainty

Appeal to tradition: a proposal that something should continue because it has traditionally existed or been done that way

Argument: a process of reasoning and advancing proof about issues on which conflicting views may be held; also, a statement or statements providing *support* for a *claim*

Aristotelian rhetoric: the approach to oral persuasion espoused by Aristotle (384 BC–322 BC) and used to shape school curricula well into the nineteenth century; a rhetorical theory based on using a combination of logos, ethos, and pathos to move an audience to a change in thought or action

Audience: those who will hear an *argument;* more generally, those to whom a communication is addressed

Authoritative warrant: a *warrant* based on the credibility or trustworthiness of the source

Backing: the assurances on which a *warrant* or assumption is based

Begging the question: making a statement that assumes that the issue being argued has already been decided

Claim: the conclusion of an argument; what the arguer is trying to prove

Claim of fact: a *claim* that asserts something exists, has existed, or will exist, based on data that the *audience* will accept as objectively verifiable

Claim of policy: a *claim* asserting that specific courses of action should be instituted as solutions to problems

Claim of value: a *claim* that asserts some things are more or less desirable than others

Cliché: a worn-out expression or idea, no longer capable of producing a visual image or provoking thought about a subject

Common ground: used in Rogerian argument to refer to any concept that two opposing parties agree on and that can thus be used as a starting point for negotiation

Concrete language: language that describes specific, generally observable, persons, places, or things; in contrast to *abstract language*

Connotation: the overtones that adhere to a word through long usage

Credibility: the audience's belief in the arguer's trustworthiness; see also *ethos*

Data: facts or figures from which a conclusion may be inferred; see *evidence*

Deduction: reasoning by which we establish that a conclusion must be true because the statements on which it is based are true; see also *syllogism*

Definition: an explanation of the meaning of a term, concept, or experience; may be used for clarification, especially of a *claim,* or as a means of developing an *argument*

Definition by negation: defining a thing by saying what it is not

Empirical evidence: *support* verifiable by experience or experiment

Enthymeme: a *syllogism* in which one of the premises is implicit

Ethos: the qualities of character, intelligence, and goodwill in an arguer that contribute to an *audience's* acceptance of the *claim*

Euphemism: a pleasant or flattering expression used in place of one that is less agreeable but possibly more accurate

Evidence: *facts* or opinions that support an issue or *claim;* may consist of *statistics,* reports of personal experience, or views of experts

Extended definition: a *definition* that uses several different methods of development

Fact: something that is believed to have objective reality; a piece of information regarded as verifiable

Factual evidence: *support* consisting of *data* that are considered objectively verifiable by the audience

Fallacy: an error of reasoning based on faulty use of *evidence* or incorrect *inference*

False analogy: assuming without sufficient proof that if objects or processes are similar in some ways, then they are similar in other ways as well

False dilemma: simplifying a complex problem into an either/or dichotomy

Faulty emotional appeals: basing an argument on feelings, especially pity or fear — often to draw attention away from the real issues or conceal another purpose

Faulty use of authority: failing to acknowledge disagreement among experts or otherwise misrepresenting the trustworthiness of sources

Hasty generalization: drawing conclusions from insufficient evidence

Induction: reasoning by which a general statement is reached on the basis of particular examples

Inference: an interpretation of the *facts*

Logos: argument based on reason

Major premise: see *syllogism*

Minor premise: see *syllogism*

MLA: the Modern Language Association, a professional organization for college teachers of English and foreign languages

Motivational appeal: an attempt to reach an *audience* by recognizing their *needs* and *values* and how these contribute to their decision making

Motivational warrant: a type of *warrant* based on the *needs* and *values* of an *audience*

Need: in the hierarchy of Abraham Maslow, whatever is required, whether psychological, or physiological, for the survival and welfare of a human being

Non sequitur: "it does not follow"; using irrelevant proof to buttress a *claim*

Paraphrase: to restate the content of an original source in your own words

Pathos: appeal to the emotions

Persuasion: the use of a combination of logos, ethos, and pathos to move an audience

Picturesque language: words that produce images in the minds of the *audience*

Plagiarism: the use of someone else's words or ideas without adequate acknowledgment

Policy: a course of action recommended or taken to solve a problem or guide decisions

Post hoc: mistakenly inferring that because one event follows another they have a causal relation; from *post hoc ergo propter hoc* ("after this, therefore because of this"); also called "doubtful cause"

Proposition: see *claim*

Qualifier: a restriction placed on the *claim* may not always be true as stated

Quote: to repeat exactly words from a printed, electronic, or spoken source

Referential relationship: the relationship between a writer and his or her subject

Referential summary: a summary that focuses on ideas rather than on the author's actions and decisions

Refutation: an attack on an opposing view to weaken it, invalidate it, or make it less credible

Reservation: a restriction placed on the *warrant* to indicate that unless certain conditions are met, the warrant may not establish a connection between the *support* and the *claim*

Rhetorical relationship: the relationship between writer and audience

Rhetorical summary: a condensation of passage in the writer's own words that stresses the author's decisions as a writer

Rogerian argument: a rhetorical theory based on the counseling techniques of Carl Rogers (1902–1987) that emphasizes a search for common ground that would allow two opposing parties to start negotiations

Slanting: selecting *facts* or words with *connotations* that favor the arguer's bias and discredit alternatives

Slippery slope: predicting without justification that one step in a process will lead unavoidably to a second, generally undesirable step

Slogan: an attention-getting expression used largely in politics or advertising to promote support of a cause or product

Statistics: information expressed in numerical form

Stipulative definition: a *definition* that makes clear that it will explore a particular area of meaning of a term or issue

Straw man: disputing a view similar to, but not the same as, that of the arguer's opponent

Style: choices in words and sentence structure that make a writer's language distinctive

Substantive warrant: a *warrant* based on beliefs about the reliability of *factual evidence*

Summary: a condensation of a passage into a shorter version in the writer's own words

Support: any material that serves to prove an issue or *claim;* in addition to *evidence,* it includes appeals to the *needs* and *values* of the *audience*

Syllogism: a formula of deductive *argument* consisting of three propositions: a major premise, a minor premise, and a conclusion

Thesis: the main idea of an essay

Toulmin model: a conceptual system of argument devised by the philosopher Stephen Toulmin; the terms *claim, support, warrant, backing, qualifier,* and *reservation* are adapted from this system

Two wrongs make a right: diverting attention from the issue by introducing a new point, e.g., by responding to an accusation with a counteraccusation that makes no attempt to refute the first accusation

Values: conceptions or ideas that act as standards for judging what is right or wrong, worthwhile or worthless, beautiful or ugly, good or bad

Warrant: a general principle or assumption that establishes a connection between the *support* and the *claim*

INDEX OF SUBJECTS

INDEX OF AUTHORS
AND TITLES